The 18th Century

1701-1800

Great Events from History

The 18th Century

1701-1800

Volume 1
1701-1774

Editor

John Powell

Oklahoma Baptist University

SALEM PRESS

Pasadena, California   Hackensack, New Jersey

Editor in Chief: Dawn P. Dawson

Editorial Director: Christina J. Moose

Acquisitions Editor: Mark Rehn

Research Supervisor: Jeffry Jensen

Research Assistant Editor: Rebecca Kuzins

Manuscript Editors: Desiree Dreeuws, Andy Perry

Production Editor: Joyce I. Buchea

Design and Layout: James Hutson

Graphics: William Zimmerman

Photo Editor: Cynthia Breslin Beres

Editorial Assistant: Dana Garey

Cover photos (pictured clockwise, from top left): Declaration, 1776 (The Granger Collection, New York); Blanchard's Balloon (The Granger Collection, New York); Whitney's Cotton Gin (The Granger Collection, New York); Istanbul mosque (EPA/Landov); California mission (The Granger Collection, New York); Peking barges (The Granger Collection, New York)

Some of the essays in this work originally appeared in the following Salem Press sets: *Chronology of European History: 15,000 B.C. to 1997* (1997, edited by John Powell; associate editors, E. G. Weltin, José M. Sánchez, Thomas P. Neill, and Edward P. Keleher) and *Great Events from History: North American Series, Revised Edition* (1997, edited by Frank N. Magill). New material has been added.

Library of Congress Cataloging-in-Publication Data

Great events from history. The 18th century, 1701-1800 / editor John Powell.

    p. cm.

Includes bibliographical references and index.

ISBN-10: 1-58765-279-X (set : alk. paper)

ISBN-10: 1-58765-308-7 (v. 1 : alk. paper)

ISBN-10: 1-58765-309-5 (v. 2 : alk. paper)

ISBN-13: 978-1-58765-279-0 (set : alk. paper)

ISBN-13: 978-1-58765-308-7 (v. 1 : alk. paper)

ISBN-13: 978-1-58765-309-4 (v. 2 : alk. paper)

  1. Eighteenth century. I. Title: 18th century, 1701-1800. II. Title: Eighteenth century, 1701-1800. III. Powell, John, 1954- IV. Chronology of European history, 15,000 B.C. to 1997. V. Great events from history, North American series. 1997.

  D286.G74 2006

  909.7—dc22

2006005406

First Printing

PRINTED IN THE UNITED STATES OF AMERICA

CONTENTS

1700's

1710's

1720's

Contents

1750's

1760's

1770's

PUBLISHER'S NOTE

Great Events from History: The Eighteenth Century, 1701-1800, is the fifth installment in the ongoing *Great Events from History* series, which was initiated in 2004 with the two-volume *Great Events from History: The Ancient World, Prehistory-476*, followed by *The Middle Ages, 477-1453* (2 vols., 2005), *The Renaissance & Early Modern Era, 1454-1600* (2 vols., 2005), and *The Seventeenth Century, 1601-1700* (2 vols., 2006). When completed, the series will extend through the nineteenth and twentieth centuries and comprise more than 5,000 essays covering the milestones of world history.

EXPANDED COVERAGE

Like the rest of the series, the current volumes represent both a revision and a significant expansion of the twelve-volume *Great Events from History* (1972-1980), incorporating essays from the *Chronology of European History: 15,000 B.C. to 1997* (3 vols., 1997), *Great Events from History: North American Series, Revised Edition* (4 vols., 1997), and *Great Events from History: Modern European Series* (3 vols., 1973). These volumes form the foundation on which the new and heavily expanded series is built. However, that original foundation now forms only a modest percentage of the whole. Across the new series, more than one-third of the text is completely new. In addition, the new series adds hundreds of illustrations, tables, primary source documents, lists, appendixes, and finding aids in the form of keyword, categorized, personage, and subject indexes.

In the case of *The Eighteenth Century*, the new content constitutes more than two-thirds of the set: To the 105 original essays we have added more than 238 completely new essays—commissioned especially for the new series and appearing here for the first time—for a total of 343 essays. Bibliographies for the old essays have been expanded and updated. All essays are cross-referenced both internally, to one another, and externally, to the companion essays in the two-volume *Great Lives from History: The Eighteenth Century* (simultaneous publication, 2006). A section containing maps of world regions in the eighteenth century, plus new appendixes, numerous sidebars, quotations from primary source documents, lists, maps, and illustrations have been included.

SCOPE OF COVERAGE

The century receives worldwide coverage with a priority for meeting the needs of history students at the high school and undergraduate levels. Events covered include the curriculum-oriented geopolitical events of the era—from the War of the Spanish Succession through the American and French Revolutions, from the collapse of the South Sea Bubble to the rise of Napoleon. Also, however, the essays address key social and cultural developments in daily life: the expansion of the Atlantic slave trade; the "Enlightenment" in Europe; the excavation of Pompeii; the beginnings of the abolitionist movement in North America; the seeds of the woman suffrage movement; and the opening of Japan to foreign influence. Scientific achievements boomed in this post-Newtonian age, so the major advancements in astronomy, chemistry, geology, mathematics, physics, biology, and genetics are thoroughly covered here—as are many of their practical applications. The eighteenth century gave rise to a wealth of inventions that would lay the groundwork for the Industrial Revolution: from Jethro Tull's seed drill to Kay's flying shuttle, Whitney's cotton gin, and Volta's battery. The first Arab printing press emerged during the eighteenth century. Watt's steam engine opened the door to cross-continental railroad transportation. The earliest piloted balloon flights carried human beings across land and sea a century before the Wright brothers' excursion at Kitty Hawk. The practice of medicine began to take modern shape, as Edward Jenner developed a reliable smallpox vaccination (replacing the risky practice of variolation) and early anesthetics made dentistry and surgery more practicable. Neoclassicism flourished in the arts, architecture, and music from Bach to Mozart; theater began to be regarded a profession worthy of permanent institutions such as Covent Garden and La Scala, both of which opened in this era. The emphasis of this collection, therefore, is on those turning points that redirected contemporary affairs and shaped the modern world—not only geopolitically but also in the experience of everyday life from its practical exigencies to its highest achievements.

By category, the contents include events that fall into one or more of the following areas: agriculture (10 essays), anthropology (6), archaeology (2), architecture

(11), art (11), astronomy (8), biology (10), business and labor (2), cartography (2), chemistry (18), civil rights (1), colonization (28), communications (12), cultural and intellectual history (20), dance (2), diplomacy and international relations (37), economics (17), education (11), engineering (3), environment (7), expansion and land acquisition (58), exploration and discovery (10), geography (1), geology (4), government and politics (92), health and medicine (10), historiography (3), inventions (20), laws, acts, and legal history (28), literature (23), manufacturing (15), mathematics (11), music (11), natural disasters (4), organizations and institutions (24), philosophy (23), physics (10), religion and theology (23), science and technology (85), social issues and reform (36), theater (10), trade and commerce (13), transportation (4), wars, uprisings, and civil unrest (105), and women's rights (2).

The scope of this set is equally broad geographically, with essays on events associated with the following countries or regions: Afghanistan (1 essay), Africa (5), Algeria (1), American colonies (40), Argentina (2), Australia (3), Austria (12), Balkans (2), Belize (1), Bolivia (1), Brazil (4), Bulgaria (1), Burma (1), Cambodia (1), Canada (13), Caribbean (7), Central America (1), China (3), Colombia (1), Cuba (2), Denmark (2), Ecuador (2), Egypt (3), El Salvador (1), England (81), Ethiopia (1), Europe (6), France (65), French Guiana (1), Germany (25), Greece (1), Guatemala (1), Haiti (2), Hawaii (1), Honduras (1), Hungary (1), India (6), Indonesia (1), Iran (2), Ireland (8), Italy (14), Jamaica (4), Japan (4), Korea (1), Lebanon (1), Mexico (3), Morocco (1), Netherlands (5), New Zealand (1), Oman (2), Ottoman Empire (8), Pacific Islands (4), Paraguay (2), Peru (2), Philippines (1), Poland (3), Polynesia (1), Portugal (5), Prussia (12), Russia (21), Scotland (16), Serbia (1), South Africa (1), Southeast Asia (7), Spain (13), Sweden (2), Switzerland (4), Syria (2), Thailand (1), Tibet (1), Ukraine (1), United States (48), Uruguay (2), Venezuela (1), Vietnam (2), Virgin Islands (1), Wales (3), West Africa (1), and worldwide (2).

ESSAY LENGTH AND FORMAT

The essays have an average length of 1,600 words (4-8 columns) and adhere to a uniform format. The ready-reference top matter of every essay prominently displays the following information:
- the most precise *date* (or date range) of the event
- the *common name* of the event
- a *summary paragraph* that identifies the event and encapsulates its significance

- where appropriate, any *also known as* name for the event
- the *locale*, or where the event occurred, including both contemporary and (where different) modern place-names
- the *categories*, or the type of event covered, from Art to Government to Military History to Transportation
- *Key Figures*, a list of the major individuals involved in the event, with birth and death dates, a brief descriptor, and regnal dates or terms of office where applicable

The text of each essay is divided into the following sections:
- *Summary of Event*, devoted to a chronological description of the facts of the event
- *Significance*, assessing the event's historical impact
- *Further Reading*, an annotated list of sources for further study
- *See also*, cross-references to other essays within the *Great Events* set, and
- *Related articles*, which lists essays of interest in Salem's companion publication, *Great Lives from History: The Eighteenth Century, 1701-1800* (2 vols., 2006).

SPECIAL FEATURES

A section of historical maps appears in the front matter of both volumes, displaying world regions in the eighteenth century to assist in placing the events' locales. Accompanying many of the essays are maps, quotations from primary source documents, lists, and time lines—as well as approximately 150 illustrations: images of artworks, battles, buildings, people, and other icons of the period.

Because the set is ordered chronologically, a *Keyword List of Contents* appears in the front matter to both volumes and alphabetically lists all essays, permuted by all keywords in the essay's title, to assist in locating events by name.

In addition, several research aids appear as appendixes at the end of Volume 2:
- The *Time Line* lists major events in the eighteenth century; unlike the Chronological List of Entries (see below), the Time Line is a chronological listing of events by subject area and lists not only those events covered in the set but also many other key developments during the period.
- The *Glossary* defines terms and concepts associated with the period.
- The *Bibliography* cites major sources on the period.

- *Electronic Resources* provides URLs and descriptions of Web sites and other online resources devoted to period studies.
- The *Chronological List of Entries* organizes the contents chronologically in one place for ease of reference.

Finally, four indexes round out the set:

- The *Geographical Index* lists essays by region or country.
- The *Category Index* lists essays by type of event (Agriculture, Architecture, Art, and so on).
- The *Personages Index* includes major personages discussed throughout.
- The *Subject Index* includes persons, concepts, terms, battles, works of literature, inventions, organizations, artworks, musical compositions, and many other topics of discussion.

USAGE NOTES

The worldwide scope of *Great Events from History* often results in the inclusion of names and words that must be transliterated from languages that do not use the Roman alphabet, and in some cases, more than one system of transliteration exists. In many cases, transliterated words in this set follow the American Library Association and Library of Congress (ALA-LC) transliteration format for that language. However, if another form of a name or word is judged to be more familiar to the general audience, it is used instead. The Pinyin transliteration is used for Chinese topics, with Wade-Giles variants provided for major names and dynasties; in a few cases, a common name that is not Pinyin has been used. Sanskrit and other South Asian names generally follow the ALA-LC transliteration rules, although again, the more familiar form of a word is used when deemed appropriate for the general reader.

Titles of books and other literature appear, upon first mention in the essay, with their full publication and translation data as known: an indication of the first date of publication or appearance, followed by the English title in translation and its first date of appearance in English; if no translation has been published in English, and if the context of the discussion does not make the meaning of the title obvious, a "literal translation" appears in roman type.

In the listing of Key Figures and in parenthetical material within the text, the editors have used these abbreviations: "r." for "reigned," "b." for "born," "d." for "died," and "fl." for flourished. Where a date range appears appended to a name without one of these designators, the reader may assume it signifies birth and death dates or, if context indicates, a term of office not considered a "reign."

THE CONTRIBUTORS

Salem Press would like to extend its appreciation to all who have been involved in the development and production of this work. Special thanks go to John Powell, Associate Professor of History at Oklahoma Baptist University, who developed the contents list and coverage notes for contributing writers to ensure the set's relevance to the high school and undergraduate curricula. The essays were written and signed by historians, political scientists, and scholars of regional studies as well as independent scholars. Without their expert contributions, a project of this nature would not be possible. A full list of their names and affiliations appears in the front matter of this volume.

Contributors

Richard Adler
University of Michigan—Dearborn

Thomas L. Altherr
Metropolitan State College of Denver

Emily Alward
Henderson, Nevada, District Libraries

Majid Amini
Virginia State University

Earl R. Andresen
University of Texas at Arlington

Anita Baker-Blocker
Independent Scholar

John W. Barker
University of Wisconsin—Madison

David Barratt
Independent Scholar

Robert A. Becker
Louisiana State University

Richard A. Bennett
Southern Polytechnic State University

Alvin K. Benson
Utah Valley State College

Donna Berliner
University of Texas at Dallas

Milton Berman
University of Rochester

Warren M. Billings
Independent Scholar

Pegge A. Bochynski
Salem State College

James J. Bolner
Independent Scholar

Suzanne Riffle Boyce
Independent Scholar

Daniel A. Brown
California State University, Fullerton

Kendall W. Brown
Brigham Young University

Michael A. Buratovich
Spring Arbor University

Joseph P. Byrne
Belmont University

Gary A. Campbell
Michigan Technological University

Byron D. Cannon
University of Utah

Jack Carter
University of New Orleans

Ranes C. Chakravorty
University of Virginia

John G. Clark
Independent Scholar

Michael D. Clark
Independent Scholar

Stephen Cresswell
West Virginia Wesleyan College

Norma Crews
Independent Scholar

Richard A. Crooker
Kutztown University

Edward R. Crowther
Adams State College

David H. Culbert
Independent Scholar

Marsha Daigle-Williamson
Spring Arbor University

Frank Day
Clemson University

M. Casey Diana
University of Illinois at Urbana-Champaign

Paul E. Doutrich
York College of Pennsylvania

T. W. Dreier
Portland State University

Thomas Drucker
University of Wisconsin—Whitewater

Margaret Duggan
South Dakota State University

Robert P. Ellis
Independent Scholar

James W. Endersby
University of Missouri

Robert F. Erickson
Independent Scholar

Thomas L. Erskine
Salisbury University

Elisabeth Faase
Athens Regional Medical Center

Randall Fegley
Pennsylvania State University

James E. Fickle
Memphis State University

Richard D. Fitzgerald
Onondaga Community College

George J. Flynn
SUNY—Plattsburgh

Charles H. Ford
Norfolk State University

John G. Gallaher
Southern Illinois University at Edwardsville

Michael J. Garcia
Arapahoe Community College

Nancy M. Gordon
Independent Scholar

Margaret Bozenna Goscilo
University of Pittsburgh

Kelley Graham
Butler University

Johnpeter Horst Grill
Mississippi State University

James M. Haas
Independent Scholar

Michael Haas
University of Hawaii

Irwin Halfond
McKendree College

Gavin R. G. Hambly
University of Texas at Dallas

C. James Haug
Mississippi State University

Thomas E. Helm
Western Illinois University

Mark C. Herman
Edison College

R. Don Higginbotham
Independent Scholar

Jane F. Hill
Independent Scholar

Kay Hively
Independent Scholar

John R. Holmes
Franciscan University of Steubenville

Ronald W. Howard
Mississippi College

Mary Hurd
East Tennessee State University

Raymond Pierre Hylton
Virginia Union University

Farhad Idris
Frostburg State University

Charles S. Inman
Independent Scholar

Robert Jacobs
Central Washington University

Bruce E. Johansen
University of Nebraska at Omaha

David Kasserman
Independent Scholar

Edward P. Keleher
Purdue University—Calumet

Leigh Husband Kimmel
Independent Scholar

James Knotwell
Wayne State College

Michael Kugler
Northwestern College

Jeri Kurtzleben
University of Northern Iowa

Linda Rochell Lane
Tuskegee University

Eugene Larson
Los Angeles Pierce College

Joseph Edward Lee
Winthrop University

Steven Lehman
John Abbott College

Denyse Lemaire
Rowan University

Thomas Tandy Lewis
St. Cloud State University

Victor Lindsey
East Central University

Roger D. Long
Eastern Michigan University

Anne C. Loveland
Louisiana State University

Eric v.d. Luft
SUNY, Upstate Medical University

David C. Lukowitz
Hamline University

R. C. Lutz
CII

Michael McCaskey
Georgetown University

Sandra C. McClain
James Madison University

Edward J. Maguire
Independent Scholar

Paul T. Mason
Independent Scholar

Laurence W. Mazzeno
Alvernia College

Diane P. Michelfelder
Utah State University

Liesel Ashley Miller
Mississippi State University

Michael J. Mullin
Augustana College

Alice Myers
Simon's Rock College of Bard

John Myers
Simon's Rock College of Bard

Bryan D. Ness
Pacific Union College

Charles H. O'Brien
Western Illinois University

Robert J. Paradowski
Rochester Institute of Technology

Samuel C. Pearson
Independent Scholar

Jan Pendergrass
University of Georgia

Nis Petersen
New Jersey City University

R. Craig Philips
Michigan State University

John R. Phillips
Purdue University—Calumet

Erika E. Pilver
Westfield State College

Marguerite R. Plummer
*Louisiana State University in
    Shreveport*

Clifton W. Potter, Jr.
Lynchburg College

Dorothy T. Potter
Lynchburg College

Victoria Price
Lamar University

Christina Proenza-Coles
Virginia State University

George F. Putnam
Independent Scholar

Steven J. Ramold
Eastern Michigan University

Germaine M. Reed
Independent Scholar

Kevin B. Reid
Henderson Community College

Rosemary M. Canfield Reisman
Charleston Southern University

William L. Richter
Independent Scholar

Edward A. Riedinger
Ohio State University Libraries

Charles W. Rogers
*Southwestern Oklahoma State
    University*

JoAnne M. Rogers
*Southwestern Oklahoma State
    University*

Carl Rollyson
Baruch College, CUNY

John Alan Ross
Eastern Washington University

Robert Ross
Independent Scholar

Irving N. Rothman
University of Houston

Joseph R. Rudolph, Jr.
Towson University

Dorothy C. Salem
Cuyahoga Community College

Virginia L. Salmon
Northeast State Community College

José M. Sánchez
Independent Scholar

Elizabeth D. Schafer
Independent Scholar

William J. Scheick
University of Texas at Austin

Glenn Schiffman
Independent Scholar

Zoë A. Schneider
Georgetown University

Beverly Schneller
Millersville University

Larry Schweikart
University of Dayton

Rose Secrest
Independent Scholar

Martha A. Sherwood
University of Oregon

Anna Sloan
Five Colleges (Mt. Holyoke)

Sonia Sorrell
Pepperdine University

Joseph L. Spradley
Wheaton College

Barbara C. Stanley
East Tennessee State University

Pamela R. Stern
University of Arkansas

Paul Stewart
Southern Connecticut State University

Leslie Stricker
Park University

Fred Strickert
Wartburg College

Taylor Stults
Muskingum College

Charles R. Sullivan
University of Dallas

Robert D. Talbott
University of Northern Iowa

Emily Teipe
Fullerton College

Cassandra Lee Tellier
Capital University

Emory M. Thomas
Independent Scholar

Leslie V. Tischauser
Prairie State College

Evelyn Toft
Fort Hays State University

Paul B. Trescott
Southern Illinois University

Spencer C. Tucker
Virginia Military Institute

Robert D. Ubriaco, Jr.
Illinois Wesleyan University

Paul Varner
Oklahoma Christian University

Mary E. Virginia
Independent Scholar

Deborah D. Wallin
Skagit Valley College—Whidbey

Shawncey Webb
Taylor University

Paul A. Whelan
Independent Scholar

Richard Whitworth
Ball State University

John D. Windhausen
Saint Anselm College

Robert Zaller
Drexel University

KEYWORD LIST OF CONTENTS

LIST OF MAPS, TABLES, AND SIDEBARS

ASIA IN THE EIGHTEENTH CENTURY

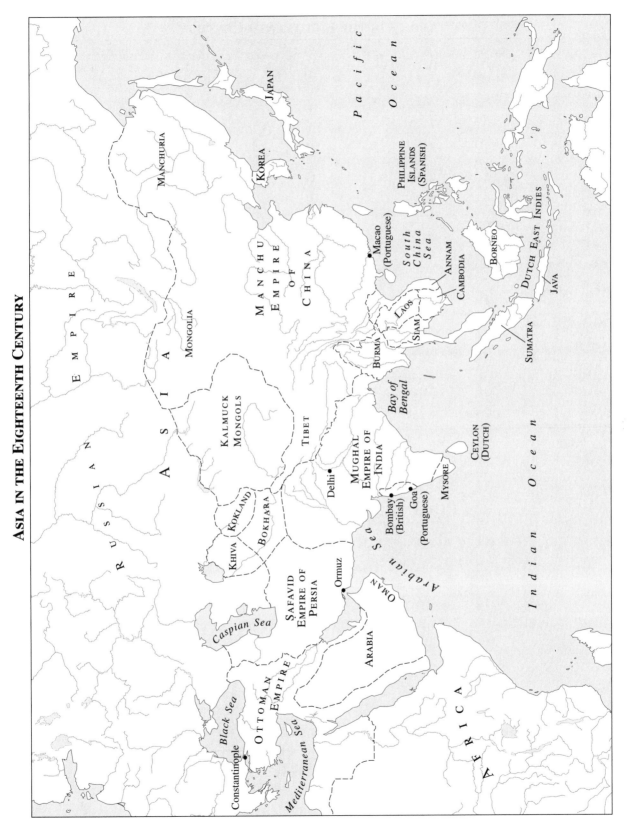

MANCHURIA

JAPAN

KOREA

Pacific

Ocean

MANCHU EMPIRE OF CHINA

PHILIPPINE ISLANDS (SPANISH)

MONGOLIA

Macao (Portuguese)

South China Sea

BORNEO

ANNAM

CAMBODIA

DUTCH EAST INDIES

R U S S I A N   E M P I R E

Laos

SIAM

JAVA

SUMATRA

KALMUCK MONGOLS

TIBET

BURMA

Bay of Bengal

MUGHAL EMPIRE OF INDIA

CEYLON (DUTCH)

Delhi

MYSORE

KOKLAND

BOKHARA

KHIVA

SAFAVID EMPIRE OF PERSIA

Ormuz

Bombay (British)

Goa (Portuguese)

Indian Ocean

Arabian Sea

Caspian Sea

OMAN

ARABIA

A F R I C A

OTTOMAN EMPIRE

Black Sea

Constantinople

Mediterranean Sea

AFRICA IN THE EIGHTEENTH CENTURY

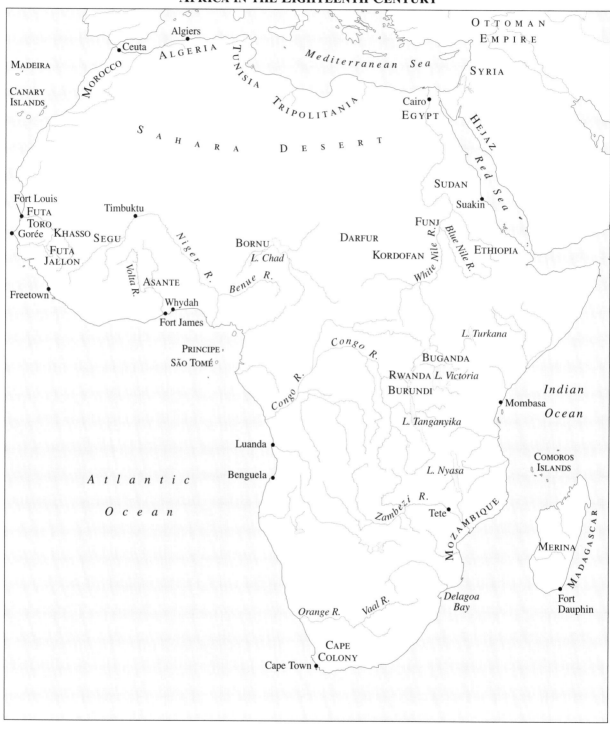

SOUTH AMERICA IN THE EIGHTEENTH CENTURY

Porto Bello

Caracas

DUTCH
GUIANA

Paramaribo
Cayenne

FRENCH
GUIANA

Santa Fé de Bogota

NEW
GRANADA

Quito

Japurá R.

Negro R.

Amazon R.

Manaus

A m a z o n B a s i n

Purus R.

Madeira R.

Lima

A
n
d
e
s

P
E
R
U

M
o
u
n
t
a
i
n
s

Cuzco

Arequipa

La Plata

Santa Cruz

B R A Z I L

Bahia (Salvador)

Paraná R.

Minas Novas

Rio de Janeiro

Asuncion

Porto Alegre

Colonia do
Sacramento

Santiago

Buenos Aires

Montevideo

Negro R.

P
a
t
a
g
o
n
i
a

Patagonia

P a c i f i c   O c e a n

A t l a n t i c

O c e a n

**Malvinas
(Falkland Islands)**

= Portuguese South America

= Spanish South America

NORTH AMERICA, 1775

GREENLAND

Baffin Bay

ALASKA

Kodiak
Island

Alexander
Archipelago

Hudson
Bay

Rupert's
Land

James Bay

Newfoundland

C A N A D A

Q U E B E C

Louisbourg

Q. *Great Lakes*

St. Lawrence R.

Quebec

Nova Scotia

New Hampshire
Massachusetts
Rhode Island
Connecticut
New York
New Jersey
Delaware
Maryland
Virginia

Penn-
sylvania

San Carlos
San Antonio
San Luis Obispo

San
Gabriel

Colorado R.

Rio Grande

LOUISIANA

Ohio R.

North Carolina

South Carolina

San Diego

Santa Fe

El Paso

Mississippi R.

Georgia

Florida

NEW SPAIN

New
Orleans

Pacific

Ocean

Cuba

Belize

C a r i b b e a n   S e a

Atlantic Ocean

Mosquito
Coast

Europe in the Eighteenth Century

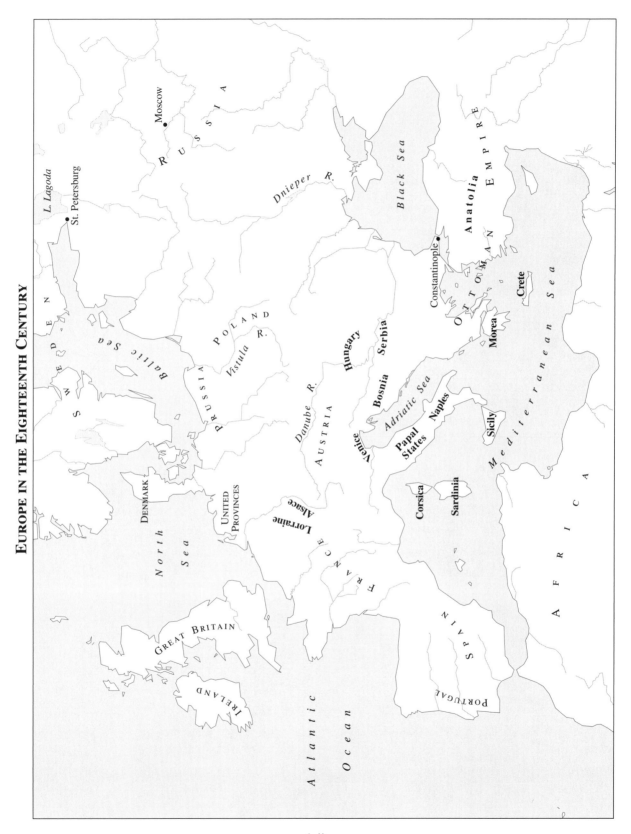

The 18th Century

1701-1800

18th century
EXPANSION OF THE ATLANTIC SLAVE TRADE

Benefiting from the complicity of European nations, the Atlantic slave trade expanded dramatically during the eighteenth century. This development set the stage for the mass transportation of Africans to the Americas, with more than 70 percent of all slaves arriving in the New World after 1700. Although an antislavery movement emerged in the late eighteenth century, economic influences obstructed its effectiveness.

LOCALE: West Africa; New World colonies
CATEGORIES: Trade and commerce; economics; social issues and reform; colonization

KEY FIGURES

John Hawkins (1532-1595), the first Englishman to trade in slaves between West Africa and the West Indies
Charles Pinckney (1757-1824), adviser to George Washington and a powerful political figure who argued that slavery was necessary in the colonies
William Wilberforce (1759-1833), leader of the Society for the Abolition of the Slave Trade

SUMMARY OF EVENT

Portugal, which established the Atlantic slave trade in the mid-fifteenth century and remained its dominant force until the beginning of the eighteenth century, enslaved thousands of Africans for work on sugar plantations in Brazil. Operating on a limited scale initially, the trade increased after Christopher Columbus made his voyage in 1492 and opened the New World to Europeans. Beginning in the 1550's, the Spanish transported Africans into their Central American and South American colonies. The French and the Dutch entered the trade in the 1650's to provide workers for their holdings in the Caribbean.

In 1562, British admiral John Hawkins inaugurated the British slave trade by profitably transporting African captives during a three-year period (through 1565) to Caribbean colonies claimed and ruled by the Spanish. Because of Spain's objections to this encroachment on its territory, England remained on the sidelines for another century. In the mid-1600's the demand for labor in Britain's Caribbean and North American colonies prompted British investors to enter the trade. By the beginning of the eighteenth century, England ruled the slave market, with both British seamen and those from the New England colonies pursuing the lucrative business. Great Britain and other European countries transported approximately three million Africans to the New World during the 1600's. The next century saw that number double. It is estimated that eleven million Africans were enslaved and transported to the Americas and the Caribbean during the entire course of the slave trade.

The leaders of the various nations considered slaves essential to the expansion of their far-flung colonies, which produced profitable and popular commodities such as sugar, coffee, and tobacco. Charles Pinckney, a prominent politician, slaveholder, and close associate of George Washington, summed up his belief in the economic necessity of slavery by calling African slaves raw materials that were essential for planters to cultivate their land. Others involved in the trade justified the practice by arguing that slavery figured in the divine plan. By "rescuing" Africans from savagery and converting them to Christianity, they believed they were doing God's work.

Considering the competitive nature of the trade, an endless series of disputes and clashes took place on the high seas and at various ports when one nation would accuse another of infringing on its territory. By winning the Seven Years' War (1756-1763) they fought against France, the British gained several French colonies in the Caribbean. Earlier, Great Britain faced the brutal First Maroon War in Jamaica when the British attempted to take the colony from Spain in 1730. The *asiento de negros*, established by the Spanish in the 1600's, added to the complications. The *asiento* was essentially a license issued for a fee to supply slaves to a specific colony, but it was not always a guarantee against disputes. Slave uprisings and rebellions in Saint Vincent, Grenada, and Saint Domingue (which became Haiti in 1804) caused additional problems. Africa, too, faced upheavals brought by the slave trade. The unceasing demand for captives led to skirmishes between the coastal Africans who profited from the trade and those who lived in central Africa, the area from which most of the slaves were drawn.

Much has been recorded about the horrific conditions on what is known as the Middle Passage—the lengthy sea journey between Africa's west coast and the Americas. Even though the human "cargo" was extremely valuable, the captives faced poor sanitary conditions, little if any medical attention, and inadequate types and amounts of food. As a result, many died during the first

---

DEALING IN SLAVES

Dutch West India Company employee William Bosman, the company's chief factor, or European agent, at Elmina along the Guinea Coast in West Africa in the late seventeenth and early eighteenth century, documented slave dealing. Slave dealing and trading included the cooperation of local African chiefs, who would receive customs duty in exchange for giving the Europeans the right to buy slaves. The language here clearly evokes the "commodity" status of the African captives.

When these slaves come to Fida [in present-day Dahomey], they are put in Prison all together, and when we treat concerning buying them, they are all brought together in a large Plain; where by our Chirurgeons [surgeons], whose Providence it is, they are thoroughly examined, even to the smallest Member, and that naked too both Men and Women, without the least Distinction or Modesty. Those which are approved as good are set on one side; and the lame or faulty are set by as *Invalides*, which are here called *Mackrons*. . . .

The *Invalides* and the Maimed being thrown out . . . the remainder are numbered, and it is entered who delivered them. In the meanwhile, a burning Iron with the Arms or Name of the Companies, lyes in the Fire; with which ours are marked on the Breast. . . .but we yet take all possible care that they are not burned too hard, especially the Women who are more tender then the Men.

We are seldom long detained in the buying of these Slaves, because their price is established, the Women being . . . cheaper than the Men. . . . When we have agreed with the Owners of the Slaves, they are returned to their Prison.

Source: William Bosman, "A New and Accurate Description of Guinea" (1705), excerpted in *The Horizon History of Africa*, edited by Alvin M. Josephy, Jr. (New York: American Heritage, 1971), p. 335.

---

phase of their bondage. In some instances, the slave traders threw the sick overboard to prevent the spread of disease. One ship's physician described how the deck, where hundreds of slaves were chained, was covered with blood, mucus, and excrement—a scene he found so repugnant that it lay beyond human imagination. After arriving in a foreign port, the dejected and frightened survivors faced humiliating auctions, where prospective buyers judged the survivors as if they were livestock.

Although England captured the market in the 1700's, it would also lead the movement to end slave trading. Initial efforts concentrated on ending the trade, not slavery itself, even though that remained the ultimate goal of the Society for the Abolition of the Slave Trade (formed in 1787). Two years later, William Wilberforce joined the society. He was influenced by John Newton, a former slave trader who had experienced a dramatic conversion that led him into the ministry and into the abolition movement.

After years of urging the British parliament to abolish the trade, Wilberforce finally succeeded: In 1807 both

houses passed a law ending the transportation of slaves from Africa to the Caribbean and North American colonies. This act, which was influenced in part by economic circumstances, caused ripples throughout the European community, and one by one other nations followed suit. In the next few years most European nations abolished slavery as well, and, in 1833, the British parliament halted the practice throughout its global empire. The slave trade continued on a limited scale until Brazil and Cuba were pressured during the 1860's into banning the importation of slaves.

SIGNIFICANCE

The expansion of the slave trade marked a significant point in world history, but the stain it left did not miraculously vanish with its demise beginning in the early nineteenth century. The practice had long-lasting effects on both the slaves and their "masters." The immediate impact was economic. Because the wealth Great Britain and other European nations gained through their colonial ventures relied on slave labor, abolition deprived plantation owners of their most vital resource. As a result, various forms of slavery and slave trading continued not only in the United States, where it was not abolished until 1863, but in other regions as well.

From the outset, African slaves had not been docile in their captivity. Uprisings took place in the 1700's, and the resistance continued into the nineteenth century, with bands of runaway and freed slaves sabotaging plantations. At the same time, the freed slaves who wanted to settle and take advantage of the prosperity they had helped create found themselves outcasts and lived in conditions little different from enslavement. Although slavery had faded into the past, it was replaced by racism—a new form of bondage that was to have lasting consequences.

Africa's role in the slave trade helped to determine the continent's destiny. Through alliance with Great Britain and European countries, the coastal slave traders inadvertently opened up Africa to colonial exploitation. Once the overseas scramble for the continent succeeded, the empire builders no longer transported Africans into bondage but enslaved them on their own land.

—*Robert Ross*

FURTHER READING

Andrews, William L., and Henry Louis Gates, Jr., eds. *Slave Narratives*. New York: Library of America, 2000. This work presents ten slave narratives, first published between 1772 and 1864.

Blackburn, Robin. *The Making of New World Slavery*. New York: Verso, 1997. Blackburn traces the institution of slavery from the ancient world to its reemergence in the mid-fifteenth century through 1800.

Grant, R. G. *The African-American Slave Trade*. Hauppauge, N.Y.: Barron's, 2003. Grant provides an excellent introduction to the history of slavery through a readable, brief text. Includes good illustrations.

Klein, Herbert S. *The Atlantic Slave Trade*. New York: Cambridge University Press, 1999. Klein surveys the economic, social, cultural, and political ramifications of the slave trade.

Monaghan, Tom. *The Slave Trade*. New York: Raintree Steck-Vaughn, 2003. Monaghan surveys the development of the transatlantic slave trade, slave practices in the Americas, and slavery's legacy. Includes extensive illustrations.

Streissguth, Thomas, ed. *Slavery*. San Diego, Calif.: Greenhaven Press, 2001. An anthology containing documents by historical figures and scholars examining the slave trade, with articles on foreign perspectives, life in bondage, the abolition debate, and instances of defiance, rebellion, and escape.

Thomas, Hugh. *The Slave Trade*. New York: Simon & Schuster, 1997. This 900-page volume explores the complete history of the Atlantic slave trade, with details on its beginnings and internationalization, graphic descriptions of the voyages, and an account of the abolition movement. The most complete study available.

Walvin, James. *Black Ivory: A History of British Slavery*. Washington, D.C.: Howard University Press, 1994. Walvin compares slavery in the Americas with slavery in the Caribbean, tracing the development of the trade and its economic roots, the transport of human cargo, and the life of slaves in the colonies.

_____. *Making the Black Atlantic: Britain and the African Diaspora*. London: Cassell, 2000. Walvin stresses Great Britain's crucial role not only in the slave trade but in the abolition movement as well. Points out that slavery laid the economic foundations of the modern world and continues to exert influence on racial attitudes.

SEE ALSO: Sept., 1720: Collapse of the South Sea Bubble; 1730-1739: First Maroon War; Nov. 23, 1733: Slaves Capture St. John's Island; Sept. 9, 1739: Stono Rebellion; Jan. 24, 1744-Aug. 31, 1829: Dagohoy Rebellion in the Philippines; 1760-1776: Caribbean Slave Rebellions; Apr. 14, 1775: Pennsylvania Society for the Abolition of Slavery Is Founded; July 2, 1777-1804: Northeast States Abolish Slavery; 1780-1781: Rebellion of Tupac Amaru II; Apr. 12, 1787: Free African Society Is Founded; Aug. 22, 1791-Jan. 1, 1804: Haitian Independence; Mar. 16, 1792: Denmark Abolishes the Slave Trade; Feb. 12, 1793: First Fugitive Slave Law; July, 1795-Mar., 1796: Second Maroon War.

RELATED ARTICLES in *Great Lives from History: The Eighteenth Century, 1701-1800*: Benjamin Banneker; Joseph Boulogne; Olaudah Equiano; Benjamin Franklin; First Earl of Mansfield; Nanny; Guillaume-Thomas Raynal; Benjamin Rush; Samuel Sewall; Granville Sharp; Toussaint Louverture; George Washington; Phillis Wheatley; William Wilberforce.

c. 1701
OMAN CAPTURES ZANZIBAR

Portugal's decline during the 1600's led to cracks in its control of East Africa. Oman took advantage of Portugal's weakness to seize Zanzibar by 1701, effectively ending Lisbon's rule north of Mozambique.

LOCALE: Zanzibar (now in Tanzania, Kenya, and Somalia)
CATEGORIES: Expansion and land acquisition; wars, uprisings, and civil unrest

KEY FIGURES
Saif I ibn Sulṭān (d. 1711), imam of Oman, r. 1692-1711
Sulṭān bin Saif (d. 1688), imam of Oman, r. 1649-1688
Balᶜarab bin Sulṭān (d. 1692), imam of Oman, r. 1688-1692

SUMMARY OF EVENT
For centuries the richest place in Africa, Zanzibar was the lucrative hub of trade routes between Africa, Arabia, and India, supplying slaves, gold, ivory, spices, tortoiseshell, and mangrove poles in exchange for textiles, metalwork, and glass. From the eighth century onward, lateen-rigged wooden sailing ships, or *dhows*, used trade winds to sail northeast to India and Persia during the spring and summer, then back in the autumn and winter.

The eighteenth century region of Zanzibar included what is now Zanzibar Island, as well as portions of modern Kenya and Somalia, but the island of Zanzibar was its center. Locally known as Unguja, Zanzibar is a limestone island, fifty-three miles north to south and twenty-four miles east to west. It is located in the Indian Ocean some forty miles by boat from Dar es Salaam, the modern capital of Tanzania. Arabs called the eastern African coast and its adjacent islands Zinj el Barr, or "Land of the Blacks." This served as a general designation until the late 1400's, after which the name was used only for Unguja. Historically tied to Zanzibar are Pemba Island, which lies about thirty miles north, and the smaller Mafia Island seventy-five miles south. As Zanzibar is located 6 degrees south of the equator, hot, humid weather moderated by frequent breezes prevails. Heavy rains from March to May and lesser rains in October and November water the region.

Portuguese navigator Vasco da Gama landed in Oman on his way to India in 1498 and visited Zanzibar on his return voyage. At that time, the most important place in East Africa was the Shirazi gold trading center of Kilwa,

built a mile off the coast in the 1200's. The accounts of both fourteenth century Arab traveler Ibn Baṭṭūṭah and sixteenth century Portuguese sailors attest to Kilwa's importance. Lisbon gained control of Zanzibar; soon conquered Kilwa, Pemba, Mombasa, Lamu, and Hormuz; and sacked Muscat. Gold trading was rerouted, and Kilwa declined. However, far from its European base, Portugal's far-flung empire was challenged by Omani Arabs, who had plied the Indian Ocean from the eastern end of the Arabian peninsula for centuries.

Oman's imams, often mistakenly called sultans, ruled from the inland mountain fortress of Rostaq. However, increasing interest in seaborne trade and naval power led them to focus on Muscat, their main port and eventually their capital. In 1649, Imam Sulṭān bin Saif defeated the Portuguese at Muscat and chased them to India. The ships he captured proved superior to his *dhows* in firepower and formed the core of a rebuilt Omani navy. Following his victory, the imam, bolstered by ten thousand soldiers and twenty-eight ships, arrived in Zanzibar to aid the island's exiled Queen Mwana wa Mwana. Sacking Portuguese settlements on Zanzibar and Pemba, he took four hundred prisoners. The Portuguese dead included Viceroy Manoel de Nazereth. Before returning to Oman, Sulṭān bin Saif appointed a member of the El-Harthy family to rule Zanzibar.

Sulṭān bin Saif had come to power in accordance with a nine-hundred-year-old tradition of elections. However, his dying decree handed power to his son, Balᶜarab bin Sulṭān. Thus began Oman's hereditary succession. Sulṭān's descendants, the Yaᶜrubi Dynasty, established a trading empire stretching from Kilwa in east Africa to Gwadar in present-day Pakistan. However, the Portuguese challenge continued. In 1686, Portugal had captured and executed the Sultan of Pate. Delegations from both Pate and the Shirazi of Zanzibar went to Muscat seeking help from Imam Saif I ibn Sulṭān as a fellow Muslim.

Between 1696 and 1698, the Omanis under Saif I ibn Sulṭān expelled the Portuguese from Zanzibar Island, captured Fort Jesus in Mombasa, and stormed the Portuguese fortress on Pate, forcing the Europeans to withdraw south to Mozambique. An exact date of the final demise of Portuguese power in Zanzibar is debatable, but the Omanis were clearly in control of the coast north of Mozambique by 1701, by which time Zanzibar Island had become an Omani stronghold.

The island's defenses were strengthened with the completion of a fort armed with cannon from Sulṭān bin Saif's eighty-gun flagship *Al-Falaq* (the dawn). Built between 1698 and 1701 on the ruins of a Portuguese chapel, this quadrilateral fort dominated the town with high, dark brown walls topped by crenellated battlements and turrets. From here, the Omanis controlled one thousand miles of the mainland coast from Somalia to Mozambique.

The Arab hold on the area was consolidated with the establishment of a trading post, garrison, and prison on Kilwa. Portuguese attempts to recolonize Mombasa in 1699, 1703, and 1710 failed. Queen Mwana wa Mwana returned to Zanzibar from Yemen in 1710. However, her successors were overshadowed by Omani governors. Small and easy to defend, the islands provided ideal bases for the Arabs, who had learned well from their enemies.

While Zanzibar's Arabs continued to pay allegiance to governors appointed by the imam in Muscat, they enjoyed much autonomy. The mainstay of their economy was trade. Arab caravans reached into Africa's interior, a lucrative area for slaves and ivory. Over a period of almost four centuries, between 700,000 and 1.2 million slaves were taken from the mainland. Numbering sixty-five hundred per year by 1834, slaves from as far away as Malawi and Uganda were shipped through Zanzibar to the Middle East and India. Most wealth remained in the hands of Omani landowners and traders, who isolated themselves and seldom intermarried with Africans.

Significance

Political stability did not accompany Oman's wealth and new territories. Although the Portuguese ceased to be any threat after 1730, new difficulties arose. Beginning with an invasion by the Persians during a succession dispute in 1737, Oman cycled between periods of trade-generated prosperity and bitter strife within its ruling class. Taking advantage of this situation, the Arab governor of Mombasa declared his independence in 1741 and established the Mazrui Dynasty, which ruled the Kenyan port city until it was reintegrated into Zanzibar in 1837. Also in 1741, Aḥmad ibn Said defeated the Persians and, returning to an earlier tradition, was elected imam in Oman. Upon his death, hereditary succession continued in the form of a new dynasty, the Busaidi, which has continued in power to the present. However, Arab power in the region had by then been supplanted by European empires.

Omani fortunes appeared to improve in 1820, when Imam Said ibn Sulṭān, also known as Sayyid Said, expelled the Wahabis, rebuilt his navy, and strengthened his empire with British help. Under his guidance, the Swahili Coast's fertile lands were transformed. Around 1818, sailors returned from Indonesia with cloves, a hitherto unknown spice that thrived on East Africa's islands along with more than fifty other spices and fruit. Most Hadimu and many slaves from the mainland were forced to work on plantations, which eventually produced a third of the imam's revenues. Officially transferring his court to Stone Town, Said ignored troubled Oman and devoted his efforts to Zanzibar, from which Islamic and Arab influence spread. Furthering Oman's decline, many Arabs departed for better lives in Africa, where they built the palatial coral-stone homes with ornate carved doors and balconies that still characterize Zanzibar and the Swahili Coast.

—*Randall Fegley*

Further Reading

Alpers, E. A. *Ivory and Slaves in East Central Africa to the Later Nineteenth Century.* London: Heinemann, 1975. A good account of Zanzibar and the east African slave trade.

Hawley, Donald. *Oman and Its Renaissance.* London: Stacey International, 1984. This official reference on Oman includes much on the imams and Zanzibar.

Moorehead, Alan. *The White Nile.* New York: Penguin, 1971. Moorehead's exciting account of European influence in east and northeast Africa begins with a chapter on Zanzibar during the late Omani period.

Segal, Ronald. *Islam's Black Slaves: The Other Black Diaspora.* New York: Farrar, Straus and Giroux, 2001. An analysis of the thousand years of slave trading between Africa, India, and the Middle East, including much on Zanzibar.

Strandes, Justus. *The Portuguese Period in East Africa.* Translated by Jean F. Wallwork. Edited by J. S. Kirkman. Nairobi, Kenya: East African Literature Bureau, 1961. Excellent source on Portugal's African empire.

See also: June 10, 1749: Saʿīd Becomes Ruler of Oman; 1750: Treaty of Madrid; Dec., 1768-Jan. 10, 1773: Bruce Explores Ethiopia; 1775: Spanish-Algerine War; 1779-1803: Frontier Wars in South Africa.

Related articles in *Great Lives from History: The Eighteenth Century, 1701-1800*: James Bruce; Mentewab.

1701
PLUMIER PUBLISHES *L'ART DE TOURNER*

Charles Plumier's L'Art de tourner *provided the basis for advances in manufacturing at the beginning of the eighteenth century. It cataloged every significant development in the history of lathes and prepared the way for further advances in the art of turning wood, that is, making objects from wood using a lathe.*

LOCALE: Lyons, France
CATEGORIES: Science and technology; art; manufacturing

KEY FIGURES

Charles Plumier (1646-1704), French mathematician, biologist, and woodturner
Louis XIV (1638-1715), king of France, r. 1643-1715
Peter the Great (1672-1725), czar of Russia, r. 1682-1725

SUMMARY OF EVENT

Charles Plumier was born in Marseilles, a port in southern France, on April 20, 1646. Little is known of his parents or his childhood, other than that his father was a carpenter and woodturner. When he was sixteen, Plumier entered the Marseilles monastery of the Minims, an order founded by Saint Francis of Paola in 1469. The monks of this order, which had grown to more than four hundred cloisters, practiced extreme asceticism, abstaining from all meat and dairy products while engaging in arduous manual and intellectual work. Plumier dedicated himself to the study of the sciences, particularly physics and mathematics, showing such promise that soon after his arrival at the monastery he was sent to Toulouse to study under Father Emmanuel Maignan, a famous Minim mathematician and turner. Though the two skills seem unrelated today, mathematics lay at the heart of wood turning, both in the construction of the lathes and in the design and execution of the items to be turned.

Saint Francis of Paola had spent many years of his life in France during the reign of Charles VIII, who built two cloisters in France and one in Rome to be used only by French monks. For seven years (from 1643 to 1650), Emmanuel Maigan had been a resident at the Roman monastery, Trinita dei Monti, and had built a wood shop where he had practiced turning. It was there that Maigan sent his young student to further his education. Plumier was inspired by his teacher's accomplishments, and during his free time he used Maigan's tools to make the turnings for the choir stalls in the monastery's church.

Turning and mathematics did not consume all of Plumier's time; while in Rome, he studied botany with Paolo Boccone, an Italian botanist, and Philippe Sergeant and Pierre-Joseph Garidel, two botanists from Provence, the region surrounding Marseilles. Returning to France, he continued studying botany, becoming so well known in the field that he was chosen by Louis XIV to accompany the king's botanist, Joseph Donat Surian, to the French Antilles in 1689. On his return, Plumier wrote his first book, *Description des plantes de l'Amérique* (1693; description of the plants of America). The volume impressed Louis XIV sufficiently that he appointed Plumier royal botanist and sent him back to the Antilles two more times, in 1693 and 1695, to continue cataloging the native flora and evaluating the economic and medicinal properties they might have. By the time of his death, Plumier had published fifteen volumes of plants illustrated with six thousand drawings.

Though Plumier continued to work on the data he had acquired in America, publishing *Nova plantarum americanarum genera* (1703-1704; new genera of American plants) and *Traité des fougères de l'Amérique* (1705; treatise on the ferns of America), increasingly his attention focused on his old hobby of turning. In 1689, the year Plumier first was sent to the New World, France's most celebrated turner, Nicolas Grollier de Servière, had died. His work—both the lathes that he used and the intricate objects that he produced—had attracted national attention; King Louis XIV had visited his shop and marveled at what he saw. After Grollier's death, his son kept the shop intact. Plumier, visiting this shrine to machine precision, was inspired to write a treatise on the state of lathes and turning. He illustrated his book with some of Grollier's art pieces made on the lathe.

Approaching his project with the precision and order of his botanical studies, between 1695 and 1701 Plumier began visiting turners all over Europe, making detailed drawings of every type of lathe he saw. In France, he met M. de Maubois, who was the turner for the king in the Louvre. He studied art pieces made by Faucher Poitevin, like himself born in Marseilles, who was the most celebrated turner at the time. When not searching out contemporary turners, he researched the history of the craft, tracing it back to its mythical origins under the reign of King Solomon.

The culmination of Plumier's research was his treatise *L'Art de tourner* (1701; the art of turning). The text detailed the progress made from antiquity to modern times, describing, explaining, and diagramming every type of lathe. Plumier's book made its way to Russia, where Peter the Great, himself an accomplished turner, had it translated into Russian. It became the standard source in Europe for information on the technical basis for turning as the eighteenth century began its accelerating march into industrial production.

Charles Plumier did not live to see his work gain the wide popularity that it ultimately enjoyed. Pleurisy caused his untimely death in 1704 in Santa Maria, near Cadiz, Spain, where he was preparing for his fourth expedition to America.

SIGNIFICANCE

Charles Plumier was both a scientist and an artisan, whose life illustrated the integration of those endeavors that laid the foundation for the intellectual and industrial revolutions of the eighteenth century's Enlightenment. For him, as for many of his peers, there was no natural boundary between mathematics and its application in turning, no difference in the precise order of numbers and the systematic categorization of the plant world, no difference in the rigorous methodologies that allowed him to see the range of plants that inhabited the Antilles and to comprehend the variety of lathes in use in Europe. His great skill was to assemble the bodies of information that would allow his readers, both in biology and in turning, to see what was known and to use that knowledge as the basis for building a better future. He was a part of the great intellectual excitement of the seventeenth century that provided the systematic foundation for the spectacular advances of the century to follow.

—*Denyse Lemaire and David Kasserman*

FURTHER READING

Bunch, Brian, and Alexander Hellemans. *The History of Science and Technology: A Browser's Guide to the Great Discoveries, Inventions, and the People Who Made Them from the Dawn of Time to Today.* Boston: Houghton Mifflin, 2004. Provides a wealth of information on the history of science, technology, and invention. Readers will appreciate the clarity of the text.

Gribbin, John. *The Scientists: A History of Science Told Through the Lives of Its Greatest Inventors.* New York: Random House, 2004. This book is easy to read and describes the evolution of science in the last five hundred years.

Porter, Roy. *Eighteenth-Century Science.* Vol. 4 in *The Cambridge History of Science.* New York: Cambridge University Press, 2003. Offers a comprehensive survey of the revolution of the sciences during the Enlightenment.

SEE ALSO: 1701: Tull Invents the Seed Drill; 1733: Kay Invents the Flying Shuttle; 1759: Wedgwood Founds a Ceramics Firm; 1764: Invention of the Spinning Jenny; 1779: Crompton Invents the Spinning Mule; Feb. 14, 1788: Meikle Demonstrates His Drum Thresher; 1793: Whitney Invents the Cotton Gin; 1795: Invention of the Flax Spinner.

RELATED ARTICLE in *Great Lives from History: The Eighteenth Century, 1701-1800*: Peter the Great.

1701
TULL INVENTS THE SEED DRILL

Jethro Tull's invention of the seed drill revolutionized farming. The drill replaced the wasteful and labor-intensive broadcast method of seeding and paved the way for subsequent advances in mechanized agricultural machinery.

LOCALE: Howberry, Crowmarsh (near Wallingford), Oxfordshire, England

CATEGORIES: Inventions; agriculture; science and technology

KEY FIGURES

Jethro Tull (1674-1741), English agriculturalist and inventor

John Worlidge (fl. 1669-1698), early designer of a seed drill and the probable source of some of Tull's ideas

Gabriel Plattes (1600-1655), early patent holder for a seed drill that was never made

Taddeo Cavalini (fl. late sixteenth century), early Italian inventor of a seed drill that closely resembled Tull's

Henri-Louis Duhamel du Monceau (1700-1782), French agriculturalist, tree expert, and chemist

John Mills (d. 1784?), Englishman living in France who translated Monceau's work into English

SUMMARY OF EVENT

Seeding methods in early eighteenth century England were essentially those that had been practiced for thousands of years. Broadcasting was widespread. Workers walked over a field, casting seed in sweeping motions as they went. As a result, even with skilled broadcasters, a great deal of grain was wasted, and some parts of the field were sparsely covered while others were overseeded. While broadcasting could be used somewhat effectively with grains, the method was not appropriate for vegetables, which had to be planted in rows. Primitive seed-dropping devices were used with vegetables. Hand-dibbing was also used: One worker walked ahead, using a tube with punches in it to make holes in the ground; another walked behind, depositing the seed in the holes and covering the seed with earth. A later improvement involved a tube attached to a primitive plow, but the flow of seeds still could not be regulated. In the sixteenth century, a setting board was used that allowed seeds to be dispersed three inches deep in the soil and at intervals of three inches.

Although Jethro Tull is acknowledged as the inventor of the seed drill, his was not the first seed drill to be designed. Taddeo Cavalini designed a seed drill in the late sixteenth century that he claimed would use only half the grain and still yield one-third more crop than if broadcasting were used, but there is no evidence that such a machine was ever made. Other inventors, most not farmers themselves, also designed seed drills. Alexander Hamilton, Daniel Ramsay, and Gabriel Plattes obtained patents for their seed drills, but only Plattes left a record of what the machine would have looked like. Later, John Worlidge designed a seed drill, but it was not actually made and used until much later. In fact, though Tull initially claimed that his invention was not dependent on any earlier accounts of seed drills, he later acknowledged that he had seen drafts of John Worlidge's drill. Tull, however, was the first person to construct a seed drill that worked.

A country gentleman of means, Tull was Oxford educated and later was admitted to the bar in 1699, but instead of practicing law, he left London for his father's farm at Howberry, Crowmarsh, where he conducted his agricultural experiments. He was one of several agronomists who worked on what was then called the Norfolk System. Tull did not like the wasteful broadcasting method of sowing seeds, but his workers were tied to the traditional broadcasting technique. Tull wanted his workers to make channels, sow smaller quantities of seed, and

Jethro Tull's seed drill. (Hulton Archive/Getty Images)

then cover the seeds with soil. In his absence, his workers turned to broadcasting, so around 1701, Tull designed and made his seed drill.

The drill, which was later described and illustrated in his *The New Horse Houghing Husbandry: Or, An Essay on the Principles of Tillage and Vegetation* (1731), was horse drawn and consisted of three narrow hoes, which allowed for the seeding of three rows at a time. The hoes had passages behind them that guided the seed from the funnels above to the channels in the ground. The hoes, the framework supporting them, and the shafts resting on the ground were carried by the four wheels of the machine. The large front wheels carried the seed box and the dropper unit that fed the center hoe, and the two smaller rear wheels carried the droppers and seed boxes feeding the other two hoes. The dropper unit consisted of the case at the bottom of the seed box and the notched axle that passed through it. The axle with notches and cavities turned the wheels, took on the grain from the boxes above, and dropped it into the funnels that went behind the hoes. The passage of grain past the notched dropper had a brass cover and an adjustable spring similar to the tongue in an organ. (Tull had earlier taken apart an organ and noticed its rotating cylinder.)

Tull's machine initially had limited success. Tull did succeed in growing wheat on the same field for thirteen successive years without having to let the field lie fallow (that is, allow the field to "rest" between crops to build up depleted soil nutrients). He never had the chance to use the seed drill for the planting of sainfoin, a kind of legume that was Tull's favorite crop. Tull's seed drill was not widely adopted after he demonstrated its viability. The drill had its detractors, and there was considerable controversy about its usefulness.

In 1709, as a result of some pulmonary problems (he was often sick), Tull toured Europe, hoping to recover his health. He observed seeding practices, particularly in France and Germany, and incorporated European approaches into his own thinking. In 1731, his *The New Horse Houghing Husbandry* helped spread his ideas.

Also in 1709, Tull moved from Crowmarsh to Prosperous Farm, at Hungerford, Berkshire, where he continued to work on agricultural machines. In addition to the seed drill, he invented a horse hoe and a four-hoed plough. His was a holistic approach to farming, but few farmers actually adopted all of his ideas, particularly his belief that hoeing the soil made the use of manure unnecessary.

After his death in 1741, the controversy over Tull's ideas abated, but following Henri-Louis Duhamel du Monceau's *Traité de la culture des terres suivant les principes de M. Tull anglais* (1753-1761; *A Practical Treatise of Husbandry*, 1759, 1762), a six-volume "extract" of Tull's ideas, and John Mills's translation of the French book into English, the debate renewed. Despite some critics, this time Tull's ideas, perhaps because of Monceau's book, carried the day. There were, however, still some farmers and many field hands who clung tenaciously to the past and who were suspicious of "new" ideas. Tull had argued that his drill and his agricultural methods were financially advantageous, but he did not have the financial accounts to support his claims. Ultimately, the battle was won on the agricultural fields.

SIGNIFICANCE

Scholars specializing in agricultural machinery claim that all subsequent seeding machines were derivative copies or were heavily influenced by Jethro Tull's designs. His theories were widely promulgated, especially in France, where his works were translated by Monceau. Despite the fact that his seed drill worked, it was not until the nineteenth century that it was manufactured on a large scale. His methods were even more effective after 1830, when the subsoil plow broke up deeper levels of the soil, aerating it, and by 1866 a modification of his seed drill was a common implement on every farm in England. According to G. E. Fussell, a leading historian of farm machinery, Jethro Tull's first seed drill with its internal moving parts was the precursor of complex twentieth century agricultural machines. Though some of his theories are still debated, his invention of the seed drill remains one of the most important agricultural advances of all time.

—*Thomas L. Erskine*

FURTHER READING

Bourde, André. *The Influence of England on the French Agronomes*. Cambridge, England: Cambridge University Press, 1953. Duhamel du Monceau modified Tull's theories about farming and translated them into French. Bourde demonstrates how thoroughly Tull influenced French agriculture.

Fussell, G. E. *The Farmer's Tools: A History of British Farm Implements, Tools, and Machinery Before the Tractor Came, from A.D. 1500-1900*. London: Andrew Melrose, 1952. Discusses the predecessors of Tull's seed drill and provides helpful illustrations.

_____. *Jethro Tull: His Influence on Mechanized Agriculture*. Reading, Berkshire, England: Osprey, 1973. Thorough coverage of Tull's life, his inventions and those of his predecessors, and his standing among agricultural giants.

SEE ALSO: 1705-1712: Newcomen Develops the Steam Engine; Jan. 7, 1714: Mill Patents the Typewriter; 1733: Kay Invents the Flying Shuttle; 1747: Marggraf Extracts Sugar from Beets; 1760's: Beginning of Selective Livestock Breeding; 1764: Invention of the Spinning Jenny; 1765-1769: Watt Develops a More Effective Steam Engine; 1767-1771: Invention of the Water Frame; 1779: Crompton Invents the Spinning Mule; Feb. 14, 1788: Meikle Demonstrates His Drum Thresher; 1790: First Steam Rolling Mill; 1793: Whitney Invents the Cotton Gin; 1795: Invention of the Flax Spinner.

RELATED ARTICLES in *Great Lives from History: The Eighteenth Century, 1701-1800*: Alexander Hamilton; Jethro Tull.

c. 1701-1721
GREAT NORTHERN WAR

The Great Northern War established Russia as the dominant power in the Baltic region and led to Sweden's decline as a great military power in Europe.

ALSO KNOWN AS: Second Northern War
LOCALE: Central and northeastern Europe
CATEGORIES: Wars, uprisings, and civil unrest; expansion and land acquisition

KEY FIGURES

Peter the Great (1672-1725), emperor of Russia, r. 1682-1725

Charles XII (1682-1718) king of Sweden, r. 1697-1718

Augustus II (1670-1733), elector of Saxony, r. 1697-1733, and king of Poland, r. 1697-1704, 1709-1733

Frederick IV (1671-1730), king of Denmark, r. 1699-1730

Johann Reinhold von Patkul (1660-1707), Livonian noble

Stanisław I (1677-1766), king of Poland, r. 1704-1709, 1733-1736

Adam Ludwig Lewenhaupt (1659-1719), Swedish general

Aleksandr Danilovich Menshikov (1673-1729), Russian military commander

Georg Heinrich von Görtz (1668-1719), German politician serving Charles XII

Ivan Stepanovich Mazepa (1639-1709), Cossack military leader

SUMMARY OF EVENT

The Great Northern War—during most of which Russia, Saxony-Poland, and Denmark allied against Sweden—was fought primarily in Saxony, Poland, the Baltic regions, and Russia. It was essentially the continuation of an earlier, inconclusive struggle between Sweden and Russia for control of the eastern Baltic region. This time, however, the struggle was decisive, and Russia emerged victorious to become the dominant power in the Baltic, while Sweden's Charles XII was defeated.

During the early part of the war, the great powers of Western Europe were occupied with their own conflict, the War of the Spanish Succession. After 1713, when that war was in its final stages, Britain and Hanover noticed Russia's aggression, and they attempted to limit Russia's domination of the Baltic Sea. Prussia, meanwhile, took advantage of Sweden's plight and captured Swedish Pomerania. The Ottoman Turks became involved in the conflict as well, granting Charles XII asylum after his defeat at the Battle of Poltava.

In 1699, Czar Peter the Great of Russia had joined Denmark and Saxony-Poland in a secret coalition against Sweden. All three powers had territorial ambitions: King Frederick IV of Denmark wanted Holstein-Gottorp; the ruler of Saxony-Poland, Augustus II, had his eyes on Livonia and Lithuania; and Peter himself dreamed of expanding Russia to the Baltic coast. The idea of this anti-Swedish coalition may have originated with the Livonian nobleman Johann Reinhold von Patkul.

Between January and August, 1700, Saxony-Poland, Denmark, and Russia declared war on Sweden. However, Charles XII, who had come to the Swedish throne at the age of fifteen, was an effective military leader. He quickly defeated Frederick IV, who was forced to sign the Treaty of Travendal on August 8, 1700. The Swedish king then moved against Augustus II, defeating him in Poland. He effectively deposed Augustus as Polish king and replaced him with Stanisław I Leszczyński. Then he defeated Augustus in Saxony as well and forced him formally to renounce the Polish throne in the Treaty of Altranstädt in September, 1706. Patkul was turned over to the Swedes, who executed him. In the wake of these defeats, Russia found itself fighting Sweden alone for three years. Not until after the Battle of Poltava in 1709 did Denmark and Saxony-Poland rejoin the Russians in the war against Sweden.

Charles XII moved against Russia soon after Peter the Great declared war on Sweden in August, 1700. The Swedish king defeated a Russian force that was besieging the Baltic seaport of Narva on November 30, 1700. After the Siege of Narva was broken, Charles XII thought that Russia was no longer a threat, and over the next six years he turned his attention to the defeat of Augustus II. This decision allowed Peter the Great to reorganize his military, build a Baltic navy, and seize Swedish towns in the Baltic region. In the autumn of 1702, he captured Nöteborg, on the mouth of the Neva River, and renamed it Schlüsselburg ("key fortress"). In early 1703, Peter started the construction of St. Petersburg, the future capital of Russia, near Schlüsselburg. While the Swedish king was occupied in Poland and Saxony, Russia was also able to overrun Dorpat and Narva (1705) and Courland (1705-1706).

After the defeat of Saxony in late 1706, Charles XII again turned his attention to Russia and devoted the following year to building up his army for an invasion of that country. Peter the Great had supported Poland's nobles in their struggle against Charles by giving them massive subsidies. He also supported anti-Swedish resistance by Lithuanian nobles. He knew that Sweden would eventually invade Russia. In anticipation of the Swedish invasion, Peter withdrew his forces from the Baltic areas he had captured (except St. Petersburg). He engaged in a scorched-earth policy, devastating border regions that might provision Charles XII's army. He also fortified the Kremlin in Moscow.

In January, 1708, the Swedish king crossed Berezina and moved toward Mogilev on his way to Moscow. By

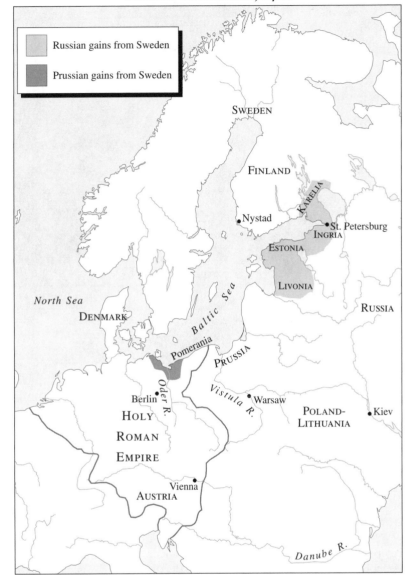

TREATY OF NYSTAD, 1721

- Russian gains from Sweden
- Prussian gains from Sweden

July, Charles had defeated the Russians at Holovzin and reached Mogilev. However, lack of supplies, poor roads, and resistance by the Russians made it difficult to advance any farther into Russian territory. In September, 1708, the Swedish king decided not to take Moscow and instead to invade the more accessible Ukraine in order to solve his supply problems.

Charles expected to obtain additional men and supplies from another Swedish army under the command of general Adam Ludwig Lewenhaupt, but Lewenhaupt was defeated by Peter and his general, Aleksandr Danilo-

The Swedish army carrying the body of Charles XII after the Battle of Frederikshald. (R. S. Peale and J. A. Hill)

vich Menshikov, at the Battle of Lesnaya on September 28, 1708. Although Lewenhaupt did join Charles, he had lost his supplies and much of his artillery, and the aid that Charles expected from Ivan Stepanovich Mazepa, the Cossack leader of the western Ukraine, failed to materialize, because Menshikov attacked Mazepa, who escaped with only two thousand Cossacks to support Charles's cause. At the Battle of Poltava on July 8, 1709, Peter and Menshikov decisively defeated Charles, who was forced to seek asylum with the Turks. His presence in the Ottoman Empire led to a Russian-Turkish war in December, 1710. This war against the Ottomans proved disastrous for Peter, who was defeated at the Battle of the Pruth River in 1711, resulting in the loss of Azov.

Charles XII left the Ottoman Empire under the pseudonym Captain Peter Frisk and arrived in Stralsund on November 11, 1714. Charles arrived in Sweden in early 1715 to find new enemy coalitions arrayed against him, coalitions including Prussia and Hanover. A plan organized by Baron Georg Heinrich von Görtz and accepted by Peter in 1713 called for Prussia to support the duke of Holstein's claim to the Swedish throne. In return, Prussia would be allowed to keep Swedish Pomerania. Charles

XII did not see the end of the war: He was killed in battle in December, 1718, at Frederikshald, Norway. With Charles dead, Peter's armies and his Baltic fleet could move at will against Swedish positions in the eastern Baltic region, including Finland and the Swedish coast. In February, 1720, Sweden signed peace treaties with Hanover and Prussia at Stockholm, and in June, 1720, Denmark and Sweden agreed to the Treaty of Frederiksborg. Hanover obtained Bremen and Verden, Prussia gained Stettin and portions of Pomerania, and Denmark obtained part of Schleswig. Russia and Sweden agreed to the Treaty of Nystad on September 11, 1721, which awarded Estonia, Livonia, Ingria, and Karelia to Russia.

SIGNIFICANCE

The Great Northern War ended Sweden's role as a great European power. It lost its hold on its northeastern German and Baltic territories to Prussia and Russia. Prussia gained much of Swedish Pomerania, paving the way for its massive eastern territorial expansion during the second half of the eighteenth century and its rise to German dominance in the nineteenth century. Meanwhile, as the leading power in Eastern Europe, Russia became much more involved in European affairs, playing a decisive role in major European conflicts in the eighteenth, nineteenth, and twentieth centuries. Russia also gained direct influence over Poland and, because Peter maintained a policy of Russian dynastic intermarriages with nobles in Courland, Wolfenbüttel, Mecklenburg, and Holstein, the country faced future entanglements in German affairs and wars.

Symbolic of Russia's rise as a great European power and its victory over Sweden, Peter in 1721 assumed the title of czar (emperor). There was apprehension among some leading European philosophers and officials of Russia's rise as a great power. The German philosopher Gottfried Wilhelm Leibniz (1646-1716) reacted to the Russian victory at Poltava by suggesting that Peter the Great would become the new "Turk of the North."

—*Johnpeter Horst Grill*

FURTHER READING

Anderson, M. S. *Peter the Great: Profiles in Power*. 2d ed. New York: Longman, 1995. Detailed and balanced short summary of the war in chapter 4.

Bain, Robert Nisbet. *Charles XII and the Collapse of the Swedish Empire, 1682-1719*. Freeport, N.Y.: Books for Libraries Press, 1964. Originally published in 1895, it is still useful for an evaluation of Charles XII as a military leader.

Chance, J. F. *George I and the Northern War*. London: Smith, Elder, 1909. A still-useful work on the diplomatic history of the conflict during its later stages.

Englund, Peter. *The Battle That Shook Europe: Poltava and the Birth of the Russian Empire*. New York: I. B. Tauris, 2003. Excellent use of memoirs and diaries of participants, with special emphasis on the Swedish experience.

Frost, Robert I. *The Northern Wars: War, State, and Society in Northeastern Europe, 1558-1721*. New York: Longman, 2000. The only scholarly study of the long-term conflict in the Baltic region available in English.

Hatton, R. M. *Charles XII of Sweden*. New York: Weybright and Talley, 1968. Essential for understanding the motives and policies of the Swedish king.

Hughes, Lindsey. *Russia in the Age of Peter the Great*. New Haven, Conn.: Yale University Press, 1998. Chapter 2 offers a solid, recent scholarly review of all of Peter's wars between 1696 and 1725.

Rothstein, A. *Peter the Great and Marlborough: Politics and Diplomacy in Converging Wars*. New York: St. Martin's Press, 1986. Valuable for Russian diplomatic relations with Britain during the early stages of the conflict.

Sumner, B. H. *Peter the Great and the Emergence of Russia*. New York: Collier, 1962. The last chapter provides a general evaluation of Peter's legacy on Russian foreign policy after the Treaty of Nystadt.

Wolf, John B. *The Emergence of the Great Powers, 1685-1715*. New York: Harper and Row, 1962. Includes an interesting chapter evaluating the relationship between the Great Northern War and the War of the Spanish Succession.

SEE ALSO: May 27, 1703: Founding of St. Petersburg; June 27, 1709: Battle of Poltava; Nov. 20, 1710-July 21, 1718: Ottoman Wars with Russia, Venice, and Austria; Oct. 21, 1727: Treaty of Kiakhta.

RELATED ARTICLES in *Great Lives from History: The Eighteenth Century, 1701-1800*: Charles XII; Peter the Great.

c. 1701-1750
BACH PIONEERS MODERN MUSIC

Bach pioneered modern music, creating a vast library of compositions for keyboard and stringed instruments and ushering in technical innovations that would influence later generations of musicians and composers.

LOCALE: Germany
CATEGORY: Music

KEY FIGURE
Johann Sebastian Bach (1685-1750), German
    composer and musician

SUMMARY OF EVENT

Johann Sebastian Bach lived and died almost unnoticed, but he has since come to represent a milestone in the history of Western music. Regarded as antiquated even during his lifetime, he was called "Old Bach" or "Papa Bach" by his enormous family, his patrons, his few musical acquaintances, and his ever-critical employers. His innovative genius has proven to be among the greatest in musical history.

Many basic factors in modern music were initiated or actually invented by Bach. Examples include the use of the tempered scale and his introduction of a much-needed new keyboard technique, which has now become standard. Bach composed a great many of the definitive foundation works, not only for keyboard but also for violin and cello. Chronologically, he can be said to mark the end of the prolific and variegated Baroque era, which extended roughly from 1600 to the year of his death, 1750.

In the view of most early music historians, Bach saw himself primarily as a church musician and teacher. He looked upon composing and performing on the organ as nothing more than part of his working routine. According to such historians, no thought of musical immortality or even of enjoying personal acclaim ever entered his mind; he thought of himself as simply a humble servant of God, expressing his faith through his work—music.

Later music critics and historians have argued with this view of Bach, however. They have pointed to his *Coffee* and *Peasant* cantatas, written for the clientele of Zimmermann's Coffee House in Leipzig, and his semi-operatic *Phoebus and Pan*, for the same audience, as evidence of Bach's secular pursuits. These later reviewers hold that a view of Bach as a strictly religious man is incomplete and misleading, since much of his livelihood apparently derived from his composition of secular music.

Whatever Bach's focus, his output was tremendous. Each work was usually performed soon after he wrote it, on the specific occasion for which it was composed. This fact explains the importance and prolificacy of the cantatas, each one a substantial work involving many performers both vocal and instrumental. Solos, duets, recitatives, choruses, and instrumental accompaniments all formed a part of Bach's oeuvre. Almost all were written for church use. To be found among these alone are five complete yearly sets, each set including one piece for each Sunday plus those for special days, for a total of 295 original compositions.

The colossal Mass in B Minor (not a Catholic mass) and the two passions, the *St. Matthew Passion* and the *St. John Passion*, were only 3 of several monumental works, together with 3 oratorios (*Ascension*, *Christmas*, and *Easter*), 6 motets, 1 magnificat, nearly 200 cantatas, 143 chorale preludes for organ, and numerous other works. Bach's position as cantor made it necessary for him to write instrumental music for teaching, as none existed at the time. The rest of his instrumental work, which is not confined to the church, needs a catalog for itself alone. The keyboard music includes such monuments as the *Goldberg Variations* and the two volumes of preludes and fugues making up *The Well-Tempered Clavier*. The partitas, concertos, suites, many miscellaneous works, and about three hundred compositions for solo organ, some of them in substantial multiple forms, swell the list. Evidently, there was much more material than this, but it has been lost. It is known, for instance, that Bach's death left his wife and younger children nearly destitute. Many of his compositions were sold to provide basic necessities.

Begun in 1748—two years before he died, arguably crowning his body of work, and left unfinished—is *The Art of the Fugue*. Every kind of fugue imaginable can be found in this work, all consummate in their mastery. Many of them are built on the letters of his own name, and there is not a measure that does not bear the imprint of that name. Bach left no clear indication as to the medium for performance of the fugues, although the harpsichord seems to be the most satisfactory one. They are sometimes performed on the organ or by a string quartet, as well as being arranged for four hands at the keyboard or even for an orchestra. The work was published in its unfinished state in 1751.

It should be pointed out that Bach was never dry or dull. His credo of composition demanded that every strand of sound have its indispensable part in the whole structure, intellectually and emotionally. This fundamental principle is evident in all his works.

At a time in history when the average life expectancy was thirty years, Bach died at the age of sixty-five, leaving behind Anna Magdalena Bach, the second of his two wives. By these wives, he had a total of either twenty or twenty-one children—sources disagree on the number—of whom ten survived to adulthood. Whether an overflow of his genius or his mastery of teaching was responsible, at least three of his sons, Wilhelm Friedemann Bach, Carl Philipp Emanuel Bach, and Johann Christian Bach, became well-known composers and performers in their own right. Here the resemblance ends. Bach's sons never really understood their father and tended to be patronizing toward him and his music, which they considered old-fashioned. This opinion was shared by their contemporaries as well, and as a result the voice of Johann Sebastian Bach was silenced publicly for about one hundred years.

SIGNIFICANCE

From a historical standpoint, it would be difficult to overstate the influence of Bach on modern music. For example, one spring morning in 1789, a young man in his early thirties visited the celebrated choir school at St. Thomas's Church in Leipzig. The choir started a Bach motet, one of many unpublished works in existence only at this church in the form of the composer's own separate voice parts. Immediately, the visitor jumped up and asked excitedly, "What is that?" He later added, "This is indeed something from which we can learn."

The visitor called for all the voice parts available and, laying them out all around him, managed somehow to piece the music together in his mind while others present drew back respectfully. This respect was well placed, for the man so engrossed in those dusty old voice parts was Wolfgang Amadeus Mozart, and when he left that day he carried with him a small piece of that manuscript as a treasured possession. He also carried much more: striking new insights into musical composition, resulting at last in his own sublime use of complex contrapuntal textures inspired by Bach's trailblazing techniques.

When only eleven years old, Ludwig van Beethoven had recognized the essential value of Bach and had already mastered *The Well-Tempered Clavier*, a set of compositions that intrigued him all his life. Beethoven's late works, especially the quartets, bear the unmistakable Bach trademark. Franz Liszt, Joseph Haydn, Felix Mendelssohn, Robert Schumann, Johannes Brahms, and to a lesser degree Richard Wagner all came under the influence of the great master who failed to recognize his own worth and whose basic contribution to music was so poorly regarded by his contemporaries that almost a century was to pass before the full measure of his genius would begin to enrich the world. In addition to being a musician's musician and a composer's composer, Bach influenced such diverse musical forms as jazz, folk, rock, synthesizer, and other electronic music.

—*Charles S. Inman, updated by Barbara C. Stanley*

FURTHER READING

Forkel, Johann N. *Über J. S. Bachs Leb, Kunst und Kunstwerke*. Translated by C. S. Terry. Reprinted in *The Bach Reader: A Life of Johann Sebastian Bach in Letters and Documents*, edited by Hans T. David and Arthur Mendel. Rev. ed. New York: W. W. Norton, 1966. The only firsthand account of Bach's life and work, with information provided from his sole appreciative son, Carl Philipp Emanuel.

Hindemith, Paul. *J. S. Bach: Heritage and Obligation*. New Haven, Conn.: Yale University Press, 1952. An important evaluation by a leading twentieth century composer.

Kupferberg, Herbert. *Basically Bach: A Three Hundredth Birthday Celebration*. New York: McGraw-Hill, 1985. Written by a well-regarded music critic, this work is an informative, well-researched, but decidedly lighthearted collection of anecdotal information about Bach, his music, and his place in music history.

Marshall, Robert L. *The Music of Johann Sebastian Bach: The Sources, the Style, the Significance*. New York: Schirmer Books, 1989. An essay collection, with subjects ranging from Bach's life to his impact on modern music, by Marshall, author of a definitive two-volume work on Bach.

Schweitzer, Albert. *J. S. Bach*. Rev. ed. Translated by Ernest Newman. London: A. & C. Black, 1952. A highly acclaimed biography written by the famous Bach specialist and organist.

Terry, Charles Sanford. *Bach: A Biography*. 2d ed. London: Oxford University Press, 1933. One of the oldest "modern" biographies of Bach. Terry, one of the best-known musical scholars and translators of his day, provides a scholarly account that explores different aspects of Bach's personality and music. Illustrated with seventy-six photographs of places associated with Bach's life.

Williams, Peter. *The Life of Bach*. New York: Cambridge University Press, 2004. An examination of

Bach the man and the composer. Williams questions whether centuries of acclaim for Bach's music have made it impossible to evaluate the composer's work objectively.

Wolff, Christoph. *Johann Sebastian Bach: The Learned Musician*. New York: W. W. Norton, 2000. Biography by a noted Bach scholar focusing on Bach's performing and composing. Wolff analyzes Bach's innovations in harmony and counterpoint within the context of European musical and social history.

SEE ALSO: c. 1709: Invention of the Piano; Apr. 13, 1742: First Performance of Handel's *Messiah*; Jan., 1762-Nov., 1766: Mozart Tours Europe as a Child Prodigy; Apr. 27, 1784: First Performance of *The Marriage of Figaro*; 1795-1797: Paganini's Early Violin Performances.

RELATED ARTICLES in *Great Lives from History: The Eighteenth Century, 1701-1800*: Johann Sebastian Bach; George Frideric Handel; Joseph Haydn; Wolfgang Amadeus Mozart.

February 4, 1701-February 4, 1703
REVENGE OF THE FORTY-SEVEN RONIN

After the lord of Ako was disgraced and forced to kill himself, his samurai devised a plan for a revenge killing that took two years to carry out. Though they succeeded and were regarded as heroes, the Tokugawa shogunate forced them to commit suicide for defying its authority. Their deed has been celebrated in numerous stories, plays, and films as a model of loyalty and courage in the face of injustice and tyranny.

ALSO KNOWN AS: Ako Incident
LOCALE: Edo (now Tokyo), Japan; Ako, Japan
CATEGORIES: Wars, uprisings, and civil unrest; government and politics

KEY FIGURES
Asano Naganori (1667-1701), lord of the Ako domain, who was ordered to kill himself
Horibe Yasubē (1670-1703), an Ako warrior and leader of the revenge attack against Kira
Kira Yoshinaka (Kira Kozukenosuke; 1641-1702), a shogunate official in charge of state ceremonies, who ordered Asano's suicide
Ōishi Yoshio (Ōishi Kuranosuke; 1659-1703), Asano's chief samurai
Yanagisawa Yoshiyasu (1658-1714), Shogun Tsunayoshi's grand chamberlain and then senior councillor
Tokugawa Tsunayoshi (1646-1709), shogun, r. 1680-1709

SUMMARY OF EVENT
During the rule of Shogun Tokugawa Iemitsu (r. 1623-1651), traditions of court etiquette were instituted at Edo Castle to make this shogunal headquarters into a palace equal in prestige to the Imperial Palace in Kyoto. As part of this refining process, a representative of the Kira family, one of a group of aristocratic houses known as *koke* (lofty families) put in charge of various shogunate ceremonial occasions, was sent to Kyoto to study Imperial Palace etiquette. *Koke* lords had the same status as daimyo, great lords of feudal domains. Kira lords were in charge of supervising ceremonies at Edo Castle during periodic visits to the shogun by envoys from the emperor in Kyoto.

Kira Yoshinaka, also known as Kira Kozukenosuke, began his career as a page at Edo Castle in 1653, at the age of twelve, and spent nearly five decades as an official there, gaining a reputation as an authority on court etiquette. He became so entrenched in his position that he behaved condescendingly toward feudal lords visiting Edo Castle, unless they gave him money or costly gifts. The shogun, Tokugawa Tsunayoshi, ruled as an autocrat, and his chief councillor, Yanagisawa Yoshiyasu, was more a close friend than an adviser. Influential courtiers such as Kira and Yanagisawa concentrated on pleasing the shogun to maintain their own positions.

Though Kira was the supervisor of ceremonies during the visits of Kyoto imperial envoys to Edo Castle, the actual costs were borne by *tozama* daimyo, "outer" feudal lords of domains distant from Edo, generally less favored by the shogun than his court officials, or lords from domains nearer Edo. Outer lords took turns paying for these visits, and when their turn came they also had to participate in the ceremonies.

On February 4, 1701, Asano Naganori, lord of the Ako domain, which was located on the coast of the Inland Sea (now the western end of Hyōgo prefecture), and Date Muneharu, lord of the Yoshida domain on the west coast of the island of Shikoku, were selected to host a Lunar New Year visit of imperial envoys and receive them at Edo Castle. Kira, the authority on etiquette and protocol, was to preside as *kimo-iri*, master of ceremonies. The envoys arrived in Edo on March 11, and a series of welcoming events began, during which Kira appeared to treat Date very kindly, and seemed to slight Asano. Believing that this was because Date had bribed Kira, Asano completely lost patience on March 14 and physically attacked Kira, cutting his forehead and shoulder with his sword.

The shogunate court authorities arrested Asano, because drawing a weapon in Edo Castle was a capital offense. Kira was sent home to recover, but Asano was ordered to commit suicide a few hours later, and he did. His samurai, now masterless and therefore to be called ronin, were summoned late that afternoon to take away Asano's corpse. A hasty funeral was conducted at the Sengaku Temple. On March 17, Asano's Edo estate and personal residence were confiscated, and on March 26, his samurai in Ako were notified that the Asano lands and castle in

A woodcut print depicting a ronin, or masterless samurai. (Library of Congress)

Ako were also being confiscated. That same day, Kira resigned his official post at Edo Castle and went into retirement. The Asano followers in Ako, led by the chief samurai Ōishi Yoshio, also known as Ōishi Kuranosuke, would not hand over the castle immediately. They began a series of meetings and discussions, finally deciding to leave the castle on April 12. Some Asano ronin chose to make the best of things and seek other employment, but Ōishi and many other ronin decided to seek revenge.

The ronin, led by Ōishi, felt that their lord had been provoked by Kira's insolence and had been unjustly forced to kill himself. They thought that his death was rushed and undignified, and that the swift confiscation of Asano properties was motivated by greed on the part of the authorities. Kira's resignation failed to satisfy them, and they wished to kill him, to avenge the wrongs done to their lord and themselves. They knew that Kira was still favored by the shogunate, that killing him would be an unforgivable challenge to its authority, and that they would be severely punished.

Ōishi and his followers decided to wait for a good opportunity to kill Kira anyway, and so decided to pretend that they, like the other ronin, were planning to forget and move on. On April 19, Ōishi relinquished Ako Castle to the authorities and sent requests to the shogunate for the restoration of the Asano holdings to their deceased lord's younger brother, Asano Daigaku, and for the punishment of Kira. Ōishi's followers agreed to lie low and see whether these requests were granted before taking action. They went their separate ways, behaving as if they were parting permanently. On June 25, 1701, Ōishi left Ako and moved to Kyoto, where he pretended to go into retirement. Horibe Yasubē, a warrior dedicated to the Ako cause, operated clandestinely in Edo. This was the beginning of the greatest real-life revenge drama in Japanese history.

On December 12, 1701, Kira retired from his position as a domain lord, and his adopted son was named his successor. There were no indications that he would be punished. Then, on July 18, 1702, the shogunate ordered Daigaku permanently confined in Hiroshima, in the custody of an Asano relative. Since it was clear that the Asano lands would not be restored, the dispossessed ronin began preparations to kill Kira, and by early November they secretly had made their way to Edo.

The Ako warriors planned to attack December 5 but learned there would be a citywide security alert because the shogun was visiting Yanagisawa's mansion that day. They changed the date to December 14, since their lord had died on March 14 of the previous year. Reduced to forty-six warriors, they followed a plan to kill Kira with minimal collateral death and damage, to demonstrate that this was justified revenge, not a vendetta. Led by Ōishi and Horibe Yasubē, the Ako warriors broke in, overcame Kira's guards, killed Kira, and brought his head to the grave of their lord at the Sengoku Temple, before turning themselves in.

SIGNIFICANCE

On February 4, 1703, all forty-six of the Ako warriors were forced to kill themselves and were interred at the Sengaku Temple. Kira's estate was confiscated the same day, and his adopted son was arrested and died in captivity in 1706 at Suwa Castle, in what is now Nagano prefecture. The Ako lands never were restored to the Asano family, but Asano Daigaku was released from his confinement in Hiroshima in 1710, the year after Tsunayoshi died, and was given a small feudal domain.

The earliest story based on the Ako incident, as the "revenge" is also known, appeared in 1705, and the first dramatization was performed several years later, with the characters only thinly disguised. Tsunayoshi's regime remained a hateful memory for many years, and Yanagisawa was portrayed as his evil adviser in many popular stories and dramatizations. In its performance versions, the Ako incident came to be known as Chushingura, and the play is called *Kanadehon Chushingura* (wr. c. 1748; *Chushingura: The Treasury of Loyal Retainers*, 1971). It became a Japanese metaphor for unrelenting resistance to corrupt power, even under the most adverse conditions. There have been more than one hundred dramatizations, and a number of major novels, films, and television versions, of the tale.

—*Michael McCaskey*

FURTHER READING

Allyn, John. *The Forty-Seven Ronin Story*. Tokyo: Tuttle, 1970. A retelling of the story of the Ako incident.

Bito Masahide. "The Ako Incident, 1701-03." *Monumenta Nipponica* 58, no. 2 (Summer, 2003): 149-169. A focused and detailed account of the Ako incident by a Japanese scholar of the Edo period. Translated by Henry D. Smith.

Brandon, James R. *Chushingura: Studies in Kabuki and the Puppet Theatre*. Honolulu: University of Hawaii Press, 1982. An account of the way the Ako incident became a theatrical epic.

Ikegami, Eiko. *The Taming of the Samurai: Honorific Individualism and the Making of Modern Japan*. Cambridge, Mass.: Harvard University Press, 1995. An excellent account of the life of the samurai. The Ako incident is examined in the chapter "The Vendetta of the Forty-Seven Samurai."

Jansen, Marius B. *Warrior Rule in Japan*. New York: Cambridge University Press, 1995. A reliable and detailed scholarly account of the history of the samurai.

Keene, Donald. *Chushingura: The Treasury of Loyal Retainers*. New York: Columbia University Press, 1997. An annotated translation and historical study of the classic 1748 drama.

Ravina, Mark. *Land and Lordship in Early Modern Japan*. Stanford, Calif.: Stanford University Press, 1998. A study of the way in which changing national conditions in the mid-Tokugawa period challenged the traditional roles of domain warlords and their samurai.

Till, Barry. *The Forty-Seven Ronin: A Story of Samurai Loyalty and Courage*. Petaluma, Calif.: Pomegranate, 2005. An introduction to the story of the Ako incident.

Yamamoto, Tsunetomo. *Hagakure: The Book of the Samurai*. New York: Kodansha America, 2000. A classic samurai manual, written around the time of the Ako incident by a loyal Nabeshima domain samurai.

SEE ALSO: June 20, 1703: Chikamatsu Produces *The Love Suicides at Sonezaki*; 1786-1787: Tenmei Famine.
RELATED ARTICLES in *Great Lives from History: The Eighteenth Century, 1701-1800*: Chikamatsu Monzaemon; Hakuin; Honda Toshiaki; Ogyū Sorai; Suzuki Harunobu; Tokugawa Yoshimune.

May 26, 1701-September 7, 1714
WAR OF THE SPANISH SUCCESSION

The death of Spain's King Charles II sparked the first of several eighteenth century wars of succession. The Spanish throne was the nominal source of the conflict, but more at stake was the international balance of power, as every major power in Europe struggled for advantage.

ALSO KNOWN AS: Queen Anne's War (in North America; 1702-1713)

LOCALE: Europe; North America; Mediterranean Sea; Africa; India

CATEGORIES: Wars, uprisings, and civil unrest; diplomacy and international relations; expansion and land acquisition

KEY FIGURES

Philip V (1683-1746), king of Spain, r. 1700-January, 1724, August 31, 1724-1746

Louis XIV (1638-1715), king of France, r. 1643-1715

William III (1650-1702), king of England, Scotland, and Ireland, r. 1689-1702, and stadtholder of the Netherlands, r. 1672-1702

Leopold I (1640-1705), Holy Roman Emperor, r. 1658-1705

Charles III (1685-1740), Austrian archduke, pretender to the Spanish throne, and Holy Roman Emperor as Charles VI, r. 1711-1740

First Duke of Marlborough (John Churchill; 1650-1722), earl of Marlborough, 1689-1702, and English commander in chief of the English and Dutch armies

Eugene of Savoy (1663-1736), imperial general and co-commander of the Grand Alliance armies

Queen Anne (1665-1714), queen of England, Scotland, and Ireland, r. 1702-1714

SUMMARY OF EVENT

Upon the death of the last Spanish Habsburg ruler, Charles II (r. 1665-1700), France's Louis XIV rejected the Second Partition Treaty (1700), which had divided the Spanish Empire between the Austrian Habsburg archduke Charles III and the French Bourbon dauphin Louis (Louis XIV's son). Instead, Louis accepted the last will and testament of Charles II, which designated Philip, duke of Anjou, as heir to the entire Spanish Empire. Philip became Philip V and initiated Bourbon rule of Spain. The Austrian Habsburgs denounced Philip's coronation, because the treaty Louis XIV had rejected designated Charles III as king of Spain.

Louis XIV had conducted an aggressive foreign policy since 1667, including several wars of imperial expansion. With Louis's grandson on the Spanish throne and controlling the Spanish military, the other European powers became worried about increasing French and Bourbon hegemony. It was even conceivable that Philip V could accede to the French throne, resulting in a joint French and Spanish Bourbon empire. In the face of this threat, England and the Netherlands banded together with the Holy Roman Empire to form the Grand Alliance. Bavaria sided with the Bourbons. As the war progressed, Portugal, Savoy, and other German and Italian states joined in the conflict as well. The War of the Spanish Succession thus involved most of the nations of Europe.

Europe's great nations were colonial empires in the early eighteenth century, and the war resulted in battles throughout the world, in areas as widespread as coastal Africa and India, North America (where the conflict was known as Queen Anne's War), and the Caribbean Sea. Continental Europe and its surrounding waters were the major theaters, however. The War of the Spanish Succession produced nine major battles, twenty-seven smaller engagements, twenty-five sieges, and several naval actions.

When the war began, the anti-French alliance had not yet formed, and the Austrians acted alone. Emperor Leopold I ordered Eugene of Savoy to attack Milan, in northern Italy, which he did on May 26, 1701. In July, Eugene again defeated the French at Capri. It was several months later, on September 7, 1701, that the Grand Alliance was formulated by the Austrian Habsburgs, the English, and the Dutch. The alliance treaty stipulated that France and Spain were not to be ruled by a single monarch, that the Habsburgs would support William III and the Protestant succession in England, that the Dutch and English could retain French and Spanish possessions seized in the Caribbean, and that territorial compensation would be made in Italy for the Habsburgs' losses.

The Grand Alliance did not officially declare war on France until May 15, 1702. As new members joined the alliance, they were granted concessions and promised advantages in return for their allegiance. As a result, the aims of the alliance escalated: It had to conquer more territory in order to dole out more territory, for example. The Methuen Treaty (1703) between Portugal and En-

WAR OF THE SPANISH SUCCESSION

North Sea

UNITED PROVINCES

THE EMPIRE

PRINCE BISHOPRIC
OF LIÈGE

ARCHBISHOPRIC
OF COLOGNE

Oudenarde
Mons — Ramillies
Malplaquet
Denain

Frankfurt

Landau

Hochstadt — Blenheim

BAVARIA

LORRAINÈ

Freiburg

AUSTRIA

FRANCHE-COMTÉ

FRANCE

SWISS
CONFEDERATION

REPUBLIC OF VENICE

Venice

SAVOY-
PIEDMONT

Mantua

Parma

GENOA

PAPAL STATES

Battle sites

Mediterranean Sea

in 1702. English naval actions in the Mediterranean produced notable gains in Gibraltar (1704) and Barcelona (1705), which enabled the English to land and support Archduke Charles III in his bid for the Spanish crown. Additionally, the English captured Minorca (1708), but allied losses in Spain at Almanza (1707), Brihuega (1710), and Villaviciosa (1710) allowed Philip V to retain his throne. Tremendous victories by Marlborough at Ramillies (1706) and Oudenarde (1708) in the Spanish Netherlands prevented France from conquering the Netherlands and caused Louis XIV to propose peace negotiations; however, when the Grand Alliance demanded that Louis XIV use French troops to dislodge Philip V from the Spanish throne, the negotiations collapsed and the war continued.

Marlborough and Eugene beat the French in the bloodiest battle of the eighteenth century, the Battle of Malplaquet (1709) in France. Eugene's desire to press on toward Paris was overruled, however. Ironically, by this point the original aims of the Grand Alliance had been accomplished, but the global conflict had taken on such momentum that it was now difficult to stop. In the Caribbean and North American theaters, the English took from the French St. Christopher (St. Kitts; 1702) and Port Royal, Nova Scotia (1710), but they were unsuccessful in attacks on St. Augustine, Florida (1702) and Quebec (1711). In addition to these naval actions, privateers from many nations roamed the Caribbean, and both the French and English involved Native Americans in the struggle in North America, which produced an atrocity that would shock English colonial settlers—the 1704 massacre and abduction of the inhabitants of Deerfield, Massachusetts, by the French allies, the Abenakis.

War exhaustion eventually set in, and a major domestic shift in policy in England led to a series of secret British-French negotiations in 1710, as the English government attempted to secure commercial and territorial advantages while allowing Philip V to retain the throne of Spain. These negotiations received an added impetus in February, 1711, when Holy Roman Emperor Joseph I

gland created a drastic change in the focus of the war when it stipulated that Charles III was to become king of Spain. The death of William III in 1702 made Anne queen and removed Louis XIV's lifelong enemy. William's role as Louis's nemesis, however, was taken on by John Churchill, earl and soon-to-be duke of Marlborough, who had been designated commander in chief of all English and Dutch forces in July, 1701. Marlborough had tremendous success in the Spanish Netherlands against the French in 1703. Marlborough and Prince Eugene, moreover, formed a remarkable partnership and cooperated in several battles. Their most glorious victory was at the Battle of Blenheim (1704), in which they protected Vienna from attack and removed French-Bavarian troops from German territory.

A combined British-Dutch fleet captured a portion of the Spanish silver fleet at Vigo Bay in northwestern Spain

(r. 1705-1711) suddenly died. Charles III became Emperor Charles VI, but his new title undercut the alliance's efforts to install him as Spain's king, since to do so would re-create the empire of Charles V (r. 1519-1556), uniting Spanish and Austrian territories and again unsettling the European balance of power.

France and England put forward the preliminary articles of a peace settlement by October, 1711. Marlborough, a major obstacle to peace since he favored continuing the war, was disgraced and dismissed from office. The Congress of Utrecht (January, 1712-April, 1713) met to hammer out the formal framework of the British-French peace and to coerce England's allies into accepting it. When the allies balked at peace, the English government halted its military actions against the French. Eugene attempted to continue the allied resistance against Louis XIV without British assistance, but he suffered a crushing defeat at Denain, in the Spanish Netherlands, on July 24, 1712.

The Battle of Denain strengthened France's negotiating position at Utrecht, and finally, on April 11, 1713, France, England, the Dutch, and several allies signed a series of bilateral arrangements collectively known as the Treaty of Utrecht. Emperor Charles VI and Eugene continued the struggle against France and Spain, confident that Eugene could win a decisive battle to ensure Charles VI's recognition as king of Spain. Eventually, however, Eugene's lack of success against French arms led him to negotiate the Treaty of Rastatt with the French on March 7, 1714. The final agreement, the Treaty of Baden between the estates of the Holy Roman Empire and France, was signed September 7, 1714, bringing the longest, costliest, and bloodiest of Louis XIV's wars to an end.

SIGNIFICANCE

The War of the Spanish Succession exhausted the resources of several European powers, which therefore declined in its aftermath. It led directly to major shifts in the status quo of European power. The substantial commercial, political, and territorial advantages that Great Britain acquired at Utrecht made it the strongest European power and strengthened its colonial empire. Control of the strategically important territories of Gibraltar and Minorca enhanced the British naval presence in the Mediterranean. Nova Scotia, Newfoundland, Hudson's Bay, and the Caribbean island of St. Christopher were all added to Britain's colonial holdings in North America. St. Christopher in particular improved Britain's commercial standing. The *asiento de negros*—the contract to provide African slaves to Spain's American colonies—was transferred to Britain as well. This contract drew the British into heavy involvement in the Atlantic slave trade. It also offered opportunities for illicit trade with Spanish colonies.

Although the Austrians had continued to fight after the Treaty of Utrecht, dissatisfied with their spoils from the war, they had in fact made major gains: Austria acquired the Spanish Netherlands, Naples, Milan, Tuscan ports, and Sardinia. Prussia also gained territory in western Europe. Its ruler, moreover, gained international recognition of his title. While his predecessor, Frederick I, had been merely king in Prussia, Frederick William I became king of Prussia.

Although the Dutch were awarded a barrier, or buffer zone, of fortresses in the Spanish Netherlands as a defense against possible French aggression, their tremendous expenditures in the war greatly weakened them. Philip V retained the throne of Spain but had to renounce any claim to the French throne; fortunately for the peace of Europe, this renunciation was never put to the test. Loss of substantial territories weakened the Spanish Empire. Loss of colonial possessions coupled with the tremendous financial burden of the war left France near bankruptcy when Louis XIV died in 1715. France would struggle with this burden for most of the eighteenth century, and it would lead eventually to the French Revolution.

—Mark C. Herman

FURTHER READING

Chandler, David. *The Art of Warfare in the Age of Marlborough.* New York: Hippocrene Books, 1976. A noted military historian's treatment of European wars in the late seventeenth and early eighteenth centuries; contains extensive treatment of the War of the Spanish Succession.

Francis, David. *The First Peninsular War, 1703-1713.* New York: St. Martin's Press, 1975. A detailed examination of the battles in the Spanish theater of the war.

Frey, Linda, and Marsha Frey, eds. *The Treaties of the War of the Spanish Succession.* Westport, Conn.: Greenwood Press, 1995. This reference work contains entries on the battles, generals, and rulers involved in the war, as well as the agreements that ended it.

Hattendorf, John B. *England in the War of the Spanish Succession.* New York: Garland, 1987. This work analyzes the conduct of England's war effort and concludes that it amounted to pursuit of a "grand strategy."

Kamen, Henry. *Empire: How Spain Became a World Power, 1492-1763*. New York: HarperCollins, 2003. The importance of the war as a crucial turning point in Spanish history is a strong feature of this survey.

SEE ALSO: May 15, 1702-Apr. 11, 1713: Queen Anne's War; Aug. 13, 1704: Battle of Blenheim; Mar. 23-26, 1708: Defeat of the "Old Pretender"; Sept. 11, 1709: Battle of Malplaquet; Apr. 11, 1713: Treaty of Utrecht; Mar. 7, 1714, and Sept. 7, 1714: Treaties of Rastatt and Baden; 1720: Financial Collapse of the John Law System; Oct. 10, 1733-Oct. 3, 1735: War of the Polish Succession; Dec. 16, 1740-Nov. 7, 1748: War of the Austrian Succession.

RELATED ARTICLES in *Great Lives from History: The Eighteenth Century, 1701-1800*: Queen Anne; Charles VI; Eugene of Savoy; Frederick I; Frederick William I; Louis XV; First Duke of Marlborough; Philip V.

June 12, 1701
ACT OF SETTLEMENT

The Act of Settlement ensured the Protestant succession to the English throne and increased the power of Parliament. As a result of its passage, the Hanover Dynasty was installed as the ruling family of Great Britain in 1714, and the Stuarts were permanently disenfranchised.

LOCALE: England

CATEGORIES: Government and politics; laws, acts, and legal history

KEY FIGURES

Queen Anne (1665-1714), queen of England, Scotland, and Ireland, r. 1702-1714

George I (1660-1727), king of Great Britain and Ireland, r. 1714-1727

James II (1633-1701), king of England, Scotland, and Ireland, r. 1685-1688

Mary of Modena (1658-1718), queen of England, Scotland, and Ireland, r. 1685-1688

Mary II (1662-1694), queen of England, Scotland, and Ireland, r. 1689-1694

Sophia (1630-1714), electress of Hanover, r. 1692-1698, and granddaughter of James I

William III (1650-1702), king of England, Scotland, and Ireland, r. 1689-1702

SUMMARY OF EVENT

The 1701 Act of Settlement anticipated the likelihood that the succession to the English throne as limited by the Bill of Rights of 1689 would fail. Earlier, in 1687 and 1688, in an attempt to procure liberty of conscience for his Christian subjects, the Catholic James II (James VII in Scotland) had issued proclamations that bitterly alienated the Church of England. He had also eluded the Test Act of 1673, which excluded Catholics from all civil and military offices and Parliament by providing them with military commissions, and promoting them to high office. These affronts to Parliament contributed to his overthrow, which was accelerated by the birth of his son in June, 1688. The notion of a Catholic succession led the parliamentary opposition to solicit James's elder daughter Mary and her Dutch Protestant husband, William III of Orange, to accept the British monarchy. On February 13, 1689, Mary and her husband William were jointly offered the throne, and on April 11 she, as James's daughter, became Queen Mary II, and William, her husband, became King William III.

The Bill of Rights concluded the bloodless Glorious Revolution and settled the succession on Mary's children and, in default of issue, on the children of her sister Anne and then on those of William. Yet Mary died childless in 1694, as did William in 1702. Anne ascended the throne, but Queen Anne's only surviving child, the duke of Gloucester, had died in 1700. According to the principle of strict hereditary right, the Crown should have descended to the children of James II by his second marriage to Mary of Modena, a Catholic. This branch of the Stuart Dynasty was Roman Catholic, however, and to the great majority of a nation as fiercely Protestant as the English, a Catholic king was anathema.

The Act of Settlement, passed June 12, 1701, accordingly provided that if the line of succession described twelve years earlier in the Bill of Rights should be exhausted, the Crown was to pass to the aged Sophia, electress of Hanover, the last surviving offspring of Elizabeth, daughter of the Stuart king James I and Frederick V, elector Palatine, or to her Protestant descendants. Sophia was the wife of Ernest Augustus, who in 1692 became the first elector of Hanover. The principle of succession, first enunciated in the Bill of Rights and still enshrined in the British constitution, was reaffirmed, that the sovereign must not be a Roman Catholic or even be married to one. The Act of Settlement, by requiring the king to "take an oath to uphold the Church of England as by law established," also prescribed, as the Bill of Rights had not, that the sovereign must be a communicant of the Church of England, evidence that the Church enjoyed a somewhat stronger position than in 1689.

The act's major provisions, including the provision that the ruler be an Anglican, were not to take effect until the Hanoverian line succeeded to the throne. This occurred when Queen Anne died in 1714. Sophia's son George I succeeded Anne to the throne in 1714, and the house of Hanover, the ruling dynasty of the electorate (later kingdom) of Hanover in Germany, supplied five British monarchs between 1714 and 1837.

Because the Hanoverian kings would be foreigners and rulers also of a sovereign state in Germany, which they might be expected to favor, the Act of Settlement imposed on them certain restrictions calculated to protect England from such conflict of interest. Yet the restrictions were equally a reaction against the practices of the unpopular William III, who was himself a foreigner and stadtholder of Holland. In an effort to control him, Parliament had refused to support his costly anti-French campaigns and compelled him to accept the Bill of Rights in 1689 and the 1694 Triennial Act, which required that a new Parliament should meet at least once every three years.

The Act of Settlement stipulated that the sovereign might not leave the British Isles or wage war in defense of his non-British dominions without the consent of Parliament. No foreigner, even though a naturalized British subject, was to be a privy councillor, or a member of the House of Commons or the House of Lords, or hold any office civil or military, or receive any grant of land from the Crown. These prohibitions, however, did not altogether prevent the Hanoverians George I and George II from troubling British politics. Since females were barred from the Hanoverian throne, the connection was severed on the

---

ACT OF SETTLEMENT

In addition to settling the British line of succession upon the House of Hanover, the 1701 Act of Settlement, in the section excerpted here, placed specific limitations and conditions upon the powers of the Crown that the Hanovers were to inherit.

And whereas it is requisite and necessary that some further provision be made for securing our religion, laws and liberties, from and after the death of His Majesty and the Princess Anne of Denmark, and in default of issue of the body of the said Princess, and of His Majesty respectively; be it enacted by the King's most excellent majesty, by and with the advice and consent of the Lords Spiritual and Temporal, and Commons, in Parliament assembled, and by the authority of the same,

That whosoever shall hereafter come to the possession of this Crown, shall join in communion with the Church of England, as by law established;

That in case the Crown and imperial dignity of this Realm shall hereafter come to any person, not being a native of this Kingdom of England, this nation be not obliged to engage in any war for the defence of any dominions or territories which do not belong to the Crown of England, without the consent of Parliament;

That no person who shall hereafter come to the possession of this Crown, shall go out of the dominions of England, Scotland, or Ireland, without the consent of Parliament;

That from and after the time that the further limitation by this act shall take effect, all matters and things relating to the well governing of this Kingdom, which are properly cognizable in the Privy Council by the laws and customs of this Realm, shall be translated there, and all resolutions taken thereupon shall be signed by such of the Privy Council as shall advise and consent to the same;

That after the said limitation shall take effect as aforesaid, no person born out of the Kingdoms of England, Scotland, or Ireland, or the dominions thereunto belonging (although he be naturalized or made a denizen, except such as are born of English parents) shall be capable to be of the Privy Council, or a member of either House of Parliament, or to enjoy any office or place of trust, either civil or military, or to have any grant of lands, tenements or hereditaments from the Crown, to himself or to any other or others in trust for him;

That no person who has an office or place of profit under the King, or receives a pension from the Crown, shall be capable of serving as a member of the House of Commons;

That after the said limitation shall take effect as aforesaid, judges commissions be made quamdiu se bene gesserint, and their salaries ascertained and established; but upon the address of both Houses of Parliament it may be lawful to remove them;

That no pardon under the Great Seal of England be pleadable to an impeachment by the Commons in Parliament.

Source: "Act of Settlement." English Historical Documents, 1660-1714, edited by Andrew Browning (London: Eyre & Spottiswoode, 1953), pp. 129-134. http://www.jacobite.ca/documents/1701settlement.htm. Accessed November 18, 2005.

accession of Queen Victoria to the throne of Great Britain in 1837.

Several clauses of the Act of Settlement were designed to reduce the sovereign's considerable part in government and increase the role of Parliament. Instead of the large and unwieldy Privy Council, William III consulted a small and informal group of confidential advisers giving collective advice and known as the "cabinet council," a body unknown to the constitution. This practice made it difficult for Parliament to influence royal policy because it could not easily identify for possible future indictment particular advisers responsible for measures it disliked. It also enabled William to ignore leading politicians whose advice he did not want. The act therefore required not only that matters of state were to be transacted in the Privy Council but also that resolutions of that council were to be signed by the person who had advised and approved them.

Parliament's mood soon changed, however, and the clause was repealed in 1705, long before it could take effect. Another clause, excluding from the House of Commons any person "who has an office of place of profit under the king, or receives a pension from the crown," was intended to deprive the king of one of his chief means of influencing the Commons. That clause was substantially modified before 1714, however, so that members of the House of Commons, whenever they accepted an office, had only to resign their seats and stand for reelection.

Judicial independence was assured in effect by giving judges tenure during good behavior; henceforth the king might remove them only on the request of both the House of Commons and the House of Lords. They were, moreover, to receive fixed salaries in lieu of fees. Finally, persons impeached by the House of Commons could no longer plead the royal pardon, which prevented the king from protecting unpopular ministers from the wrath of Parliament.

SIGNIFICANCE

The Act of Settlement determined the course of British royal history through the eighteenth and nineteenth centuries. Despite ongoing threats from Roman Catholic Stuart pretenders, George I was succeeded by his son George II in 1727, by his great-grandson George III in 1760, and by George IV in 1820 and William IV in 1830. In 1837, the British throne passed to a granddaughter of George III, Victoria, while the kingdom of Hanover, which could not be inherited by females, passed to the next male descendant of George III. Victoria married Prince Albert of Saxe-Coburg-Gotha, at which time the

British royal family acquired the surname of Wettin, which it kept until the name was changed to Windsor in 1917.

—James M. Haas, updated by M. Casey Diana

FURTHER READING

Black, Jeremy. *The Hanoverians: The History of a Dynasty*. London: Hambledon and London, 2004. Although this book focuses on the reigns of the five Hanoverian monarchs, chapter 1, "The House of Hanover," includes a brief description of the events leading to the Act of Settlement.

Kemp, Betty. *King and Commons, 1660-1832*. London: Macmillan, 1959. Discusses the power relations between the British monarchy and Parliament and how the Act of Settlement solidified Parliament's position.

Kishlansky, Mark. *A Monarchy Transformed: Britain, 1603-1714*. Vol. 6 in *The Penguin History of Britain*. London: Allen Lane, 1996. Chapter 12, "A European Union, 1689-1702," provides information about the Hanoverian succession.

Ogg, David. *England in the Reigns of James II and William III*. Oxford, England: Clarendon Press, 1955. Scholarly work that argues that the Act of Settlement was a completion of the Bill of Rights, a restraint on the Hanover Dynasty, and instrumental in the creation of parliamentary supremacy.

Redman, Alvin. *The House of Hanover*. Reprint. New York: Funk & Wagnalls, 1969. While this work covers the entire Hanover Dynasty, it provides a section on the importance of the Act of Settlement and a complete bibliography.

Trevor, Meriol. *The Shadow of a Crown: The Life Story of James II of England and James VII of Scotland*. London: Constable, 1988. Biographical account of James's life that includes his alienation of the Church of England, affronts to Parliament, and dismissal from the throne, as well as the ascension of his daughter Mary and son-in-law William III of Orange.

SEE ALSO: Feb., 1706-Apr. 28, 1707: Act of Union Unites England and Scotland; Mar. 23-26, 1708: Defeat of the "Old Pretender"; Dec., 1711: Occasional Conformity Bill; Sept. 6, 1715-Feb. 4, 1716: Jacobite Rising in Scotland; 1721-1742: Development of Great Britain's Office of Prime Minister; Aug. 19, 1745-Sept. 20, 1746: Jacobite Rebellion; July 2-Aug. 1, 1800: Act of Union Forms the United Kingdom.

RELATED ARTICLES in *Great Lives from History: The Eighteenth Century, 1701-1800*: Queen Anne; George I; George II; George III.

July 9, 1701
MARSH BUILDS IRELAND'S FIRST PUBLIC LIBRARY

Marsh's Library, Ireland's first library open to the public, acquired and preserved several extensive collections of books, including the finest private library at that time in England. The library's founding was revolutionary, given its mission of free and open access to all, which included disenfranchised, and uneducated, Dubliners.

LOCALE: Dublin, Ireland
CATEGORIES: Education; cultural and intellectual history

KEY FIGURES

Narcissus Marsh (1638-1713), archbishop who founded Marsh's Library near Dublin's St. Patrick's Cathedral

Edward Stillingfleet (1635-1699), bishop of Worcester, scholar, and book collector

Jonathan Swift (1667-1745), Irish writer, dean of St. Patrick's Cathedral, and a Marsh's Library governor

SUMMARY OF EVENT

Dublin prospered economically during the resplendent eighteenth century Georgian era. New suburbs spread beyond the city's old medieval walls, and new bridges crisscrossed the River Liffy to accommodate the bustling city's expansion. Dublin also gained cultural attention, attracting playwrights such as Willipam Congreve. Jonathan Swift was dean of Dublin's St. Patrick's Cathedral from 1713 to 1745. George Frideric Handel conducted the first public performance of the *Messiah* in Dublin in 1742, and Archbishop Narcissus Marsh opened Ireland's first public library, Marsh's Library, located behind St. Patrick's Cathedral.

Dublin also was a rich and lively city for the Protestant Ascendancy, those of English background who were Protestant. However, for Dublin's Catholic poor and for the majority of the rest of the country, life was mostly one of abject poverty. Ireland had been a colonized country for more than five hundred years. The Battle of the Boyne (1690) saw the Catholic king James II defeated in Ireland by the Protestant king William III, resulting in an era of Protestant preeminence. The Irish parliament (whose members were mostly of the Protestant Ascendancy) passed extremely harsh and discriminatory penal laws that curtailed the Catholic population's ability to own land, forbade them from pursuing professions such

as law and medicine, and outlawed their right to a Catholic education. The majority of Ireland's population became ignorant, poor, and deprived. Indeed, many of Ireland's people had to attend school surreptitiously, hidden behind hedges from the police, or they had to flee to Catholic France.

Shortly after his arrival, the deeply pious Marsh discovered that there was no public library in Dublin. There was a library, but it belonged to Dublin's Trinity College. Only students and staff had access, and if a student wanted a book, he had to find a member of the staff to stay with him while he did his research. Marsh believed a public library would make it easier for students to take full advantage of their education, and easier for Dubliners to educate themselves. For Marsh to establish a public library in Dublin was revolutionary, and he stipulated that all be given free access.

Marsh was born in Wiltshire, England, in 1638. Early in his life, he had been fascinated by science, mathematics, music, Asian languages, and medieval history. Throughout his years, he collected books in Hebrew, Arabic, and Turkish. He was educated in Oxford and sent to Ireland as provost of Trinity College in 1679. From the beginning of his tenure at Trinity, he showed concern for the students and the quality of their education, believing it to be substandard. Soon after arriving in Dublin, Marsh was intent upon opening a public library. Finally, in 1700, he wrote a letter to Dr. Thomas Smith, a friend in England, asking for help in recommending books. Marsh explained that his living quarters at the archbishop's palace lacked a library, and he complained that his own books lay about in disarray in three separate, inconvenient rooms. Approval for the building of the library was granted to Marsh on July 9, 1701. In 1707, the library was formally incorporated by an act of Parliament ("An Act for Settling and Preserving a Public Library For Ever").

Known originally as the Library of Saint Sepulchre, the Marsh Library in its earliest form was stocked primarily with Marsh's own books. The holdings were greatly expanded in 1705 after Marsh purchased the nearly ten-thousand-book collection of Edward Stillingfleet, the bishop of Worcester, who at one time engaged in a major controversy with the philosopher John Locke on the doctrine of the Trinity. Stillingfleet's collection, believed to be the finest private library in England at the time, attests to Stillingfleet's wide-ranging scholarship and knowledge of books.

1700's

25

In 1745, John Stearne (1660-1745), bishop of Clogher, bequeathed his books to the library, including one of the oldest in the collection, Cicero's *Letters to His Friends*, which was printed in 1472. The library also inherited the collection of Elias Bouhéreau, a medical doctor and Huguenot (Protestant) refugee from France in 1695 and the library's first librarian. Also, to this day, the library holds vast numbers of medical, theological, legal, and music manuscripts dating to 1400, as well as rare sixteenth century musical compositions from the Continent. Writer Jonathan Swift was a Marsh Library governor, but he did not contribute any of his books to its collection. Bram Stoker, author of the novel *Dracula*, studied in the library, and James Joyce mentions the Marsh Library in his novel *Ulysses* (1922).

SIGNIFICANCE

The establishment in 1701 of Marsh's Library, the first public library in Ireland, immediately impacted Dubliners, providing a vast intellectual and cultural resource to the disenfranchised and subjugated. It also provided a home for preserving some of the greatest literary treasures of the past, part of Europe's great intellectual and cultural heritage. The interior of the library, with its outstanding dark oak paneling, provided a place where anyone could request a book to read. To a colonized population that was forbidden an education, the library offered possibilities for social and political change.

As of the early twenty-first century, the library contained four major collections of more than twenty-five thousand books on the sixteenth, seventeenth, and eighteenth centuries; more than five thousand books printed in England before 1700; and twelve hundred books printed in England before 1640. The volumes cover law, medicine, travel, mathematics, navigation and exploration, music, science, and classical literature. Many are in Latin, the universal common language of scholars from earlier eras, but many others are in English, French, Italian, and Greek. A separate room in the library houses books and periodicals relating to Irish history.

—*M. Casey Diana*

An interior view of Marsh's Library in Dublin, Ireland's first library open to the public. (Library of Congress)

FURTHER READING

Battles, Matthew. *Library: An Unquiet History.* New York: Norton, 2003. A history of libraries as well as the forces in history that try to destroy information and communication.

Gillespie, Raymond, ed. *Scholar Bishop: The Recollections and Diary of Narcissus Marsh, 1638-1696.* Cork, Ireland: Cork University Press, 2003. A detailed account of the life of Narcissus Marsh, who was both clergyman and scholar. The editor's introduction covers religious and political contexts. Includes Marsh's letters and diary.

Harris, Michael H. *History of Libraries in the Western World.* Metuchen, N.J.: Scarecrow Press, 1995. A general survey of library history, originally published in 1984.

McCarthy, Muriel. *Marsh's Library: All Graduates and Gentlemen.* Dublin: Four Courts Press, 2003. Traces in great detail the history of the Marsh Library and recalls Marsh's life, his determination to build a library for the Irish public, and the library's establishment. Also provides accounts of the building's many famous readers.

McCarthy, Muriel, and Ann Simmons, eds. *The Making of Marsh's Library: Learning, Politics, and Religion in Ireland, 1650-1750.* Dublin: Four Courts Press, 2004. This book contains the scholarly papers presented at the 2001 conference on the making of Marsh's Library to celebrate the tercentenary of the library.

SEE ALSO: 1741: Leadhills Reading Society Promotes Literacy; Apr. 13, 1742: First Performance of Handel's *Messiah*.

RELATED ARTICLES in *Great Lives from History: The Eighteenth Century, 1701-1800:* George Frideric Handel; Jonathan Swift.

1702 or 1706
FIRST ARABIC PRINTING PRESS

Arabic-language printing began at Aleppo in Syria in the first decade of the eighteenth century, although the first printing press in Lebanon had been established in 1610 by Maronite Christians, who produced an edition of the Psalms in Syriac.

LOCALE: Aleppo, Syria
CATEGORIES: Cultural and intellectual history; science and technology; religion and theology

KEY FIGURES

Athanasius Dabbas (1647-1724), Syrian printer
Ibrahim Müteferrika (1674?-1745), Turkish printer
Franciscus Raphelengius (1539-1597), Dutch publisher, printer, and designer of type
Peter Kirsten (1575-1640), Polish printer and designer of type
ʿAbd Allāh Zākhir (1684-1748), Lebanese printer and designer of type
Giambattista Raimondi (1536-1614), Italian founder of the Medici Oriental Press

SUMMARY OF EVENT

The history of Arabic printing began in Germany, Italy, and France, when fifteenth century Arabic-language woodblock printing was replaced by Arabic-language type fonts. These fonts were easily exported to Christian missionaries, through whom they reached the Middle East. In 1595, Franciscus Raphelengius developed an Arabic font that was used through 1895. The prospect of printing in a language that read from right to left with twenty-nine letters, twenty-two of which had four variations in typography, was at first daunting. In 1613, though, Raphelengius published an Arabic grammar to guide printers' efforts to publish accurate texts.

Meanwhile, in Breslau (Wrocław), Peter Kirsten improved upon Raphelengius's type, and in 1608, the type was approved by the Swedish government for Arabic-language printing. Key to the success of European printing in Arabic was the Medici Oriental Press, established by Giambattista Raimondi, whose edition of the Gospels was imported into Lebanon in 1588. At the demise of the Medici press, François Savary de Breve's type succeeded the Raphelengius-Kirsten type and influenced missionaries' press work in Lebanon and Syria, as well as in France, Spain, and Romania.

Arabic printing in the eighteenth century targeted two groups: missionaries, who needed portable religious texts and scriptures, and philologists, who wanted to collect and study Arabic texts and needed modern type for their scholarship. In 1786-1787, Catherine the Great of Russia made an Arabic Qurʾān available for her newly conquered Turkish subjects after the Treaty of Kuchuk Kainarji (1774). The text was based on a translation of the Qurʾān from Latin into Arabic that was first printed in Venice in 1694. It was not until 1878 that G. S. Sablukov would publish the first Arabic-to-Arabic translation of the Qurʾān.

The rise of printing in Syria, Lebanon, and the Ottoman Empire as a whole was a political phenomenon as much as it was a cultural one. According to differing sources, the head of the Byzantine Orthodox Church, Athanasius Dabbas, started the first printing press in Aleppo in either 1702 or 1706. His decision to found an Arabic press was partly a reaction to the importation of texts in other languages by both of the major Christian communities in Syria (Orthodox and Catholic). The output of the Aleppo press was small, at just eight texts in five years, and the origins of the type used and of the printing press itself are uncertain.

The Aleppo press, despite its small output, set an important precedent. From 1733 until his death in 1748, ʿAbd Allāh Zākhir operated a press from the monastery of St. John the Baptist in a Lebanese hill town, As-Suwayr, for the Jesuit missionaries. Zākhir designed his own type based on imported books. Like his predecessor Dabbas, with whom he had differences in matters of Orthodox faith, Zākhir published eight titles in press runs of roughly eight hundred. Zākhir's press issued a total of sixty-nine Arabic titles, including a widely used edition of the Psalter that was first printed in 1735 and remained in print until the business's cessation in 1899.

A key figure in Arabic printing history, Ibrahim Müteferrika, was captured from Hungary in 1692, became a translator in Turkey, and opened a printing press

27

in his home in 1727. He introduced movable type to Turkey, and he likely printed his books on paper imported from Poland. Between 1729 and 1742, he issued seventeen titles in Istanbul with the support of the government. His business was patronized by Seit Mehmet, who, like his father, was open to European influences, especially to works in French. Under Seit Mehmet Paşa (r. 1718-1730), Müteferrika printed a variety of secular works, including histories, a multivolume dictionary, geographies, navigational works, and maps.

Müteferrika knew Latin, French, Hungarian, German, and English, which enabled him to translate many practical and theoretical works, imported from private collections as well as early libraries, and to print them in reasonably priced editions for a variety of readers. Müteferrika's press was a key component of the Tulip Age of the Ottoman Empire, which was characterized by Turkey's return as a center of learning and the arts. The 1727 royal proclamation, in effect licensing Müteferrika to print, listed ten reasons that printing benefited the empire. Chief among the benefits listed were that printed books lasted longer than scribal copies, were cheap and potentially plentiful, and would aid in the spread of Islam and in the preservation of the Ottoman Empire.

Napoleon Bonaparte brought an Arabic press to Cairo in 1798 to print political literature. Nearly immediately upon entrance into Egypt, the printer Marc Aurel and the philologist Joseph Marcel began Arabic language printing at their press, Imprimerie Orientale et Française. By January, 1799, the press had a staff of eighteen printers and three proofreaders, and its books were available in five languages, including Turkish. The building that housed the press was destroyed in 1800, when the citizens of Cairo revolted against Napoleon. When the French left Egypt in 1801, they removed their printing equipment. Indeed, two contemporary studies of the Egyptian government composed in 1785 and 1801 discuss the role of scribes in the preparation of government records and reports, making no mention of printing or of printed books.

SIGNIFICANCE

Arabic-language printing mirrored religious, political, and cultural tensions present in the Middle East between 1702 and 1801. Islam forbade Arabic-language printing and the printing of religious texts, while Christian Catholics and eventually American Protestant missionaries (after 1820) relied on Arabic-language texts and book printing. While Turkish leaders embraced the French version of Western culture and the printing press of the

Transylvanian convert Müteferrika as part of the Enlightenment, the Syrians drove out the mainly French Jesuits, and the Egyptians destroyed Napoleon's printing shop. Culturally, the printing press represented the educational changes that would soon occur, leading to increased literacy, the first newspapers and magazines in Arabic, and the desire for books of all types, creating a reading public that slowly formed and spread across the Arab world.

—Beverly Schneller

FURTHER READING

Ahmad, Maqsoud. "The Arabic Printing Press in Turkey and the Arab East." *Islamic Culture: An English Quarterly* 61, no. 1 (January, 1987): 79-86. Provides an overview of the development of the Arabic printing press beginning in 1514 in Fano, Italy, under Pope Leo X and ending with the state of Egyptian printing in 1868.

Antonius, George. *The Arab Awakening: The Story of the Arab National Movement*. New York: G. P. Putnam, 1946. Provides useful background on the history of the Arab world and culture from the fifteenth to the nineteenth centuries.

Atiyeh, George N., ed. *The Book in the Islamic World: The Written Word and Communication in the Middle East*. Albany: State University of New York Press, 1995. Examines the role of the book in the sociocultural world of the Middle East; includes Christopher N. Murphy's translation of the 1727 document by Seit Mahmet Paşa allowing Müteferrika to begin printing in Arabic type.

Ayalon, Ami. *Reading Palestine Printing and Literacy, 1900-1948*. Austin: University of Texas Press, 2004. Addresses the links between education and consumership of books; includes historical background.

Cahn, Michael. "The Printing Press as an Agent in the History of Linguistic Ideas." *Proceedings of the Conference of the German Association of University Teachers of English* 15 (1993): 47-58. Discusses, using historical examples, how printing presses act as a source of change when a language first appears in print.

Hanebuut-Benz, Eva, et al. *Middle Eastern Languages and the Print Revolution: A Cross-Cultural Encounter*. Westhofen, Germany: Verlag-Skulima, 2002. An important collection of essays printed in English and German with many illustrations of woodblock and movable type printing. The key essays are Geoffrey Roper's "Early Arabic Printing in Europe," Dagmar Glass and Roper's "Arabic Book Printing and Newspaper Printing in the Arab World," and Harmut Bobzin's "From Venice to Cairo: On the History of Arabic Editions of the Koran."

Hanna, Nelly. *In Praise of Books.* Syracuse, N.Y.: Syracuse University Press, 2003. Chapter 4 is a study of book ownership, readership, and printing in Egypt from the seventeenth through the eighteenth century.

Hitti, Philip K. *History of Syria: Including Lebanon and Palestine.* 2d ed. London: Macmillan, 1957.

_____. *Lebanon in History from the Earliest Times to the Present.* London: Macmillan, 1957. These two works are comprehensive histories of Syria and Lebanon, providing useful historical and cultural details about the early Christian periods.

Shaw, Stanford P. *Empire of the Gazis: The Rise and Decline of the Ottoman Empire, 1280-1808.* Vol. 1 in *History of the Ottoman Empire and Modern Turkey.* New York: Cambridge University Press, 1976. Useful summary of the Tulip Age, Turkey's place in the Enlightenment, and the career of Ibrahim Müteferrika.

Shaw, Stanford P., trans. *Ottoman Egypt in the Age of the French Revolution, by Huseyn Effendi.* Cambridge, Mass.: Harvard University Press, 1964.

_____. *Ottoman Egypt in the Eighteenth Century: The "Nizamname-I Nisir" of Cezzar Ahmed Pasha.* Cambridge, Mass.: Harvard University Press, 1962. English translations of two contemporary accounts of the Egyptian government and its role as a source of wealth for the Ottoman Empire. Discusses the roles of the scribes in government document production.

SEE ALSO: 1718-1730: Tulip Age; 1748-1755: Construction of Istanbul's Nur-u Osmaniye Complex; Oct., 1768-Jan. 9, 1792: Ottoman Wars with Russia; July 21, 1774: Treaty of Kuchuk Kainarji; Apr. 12, 1798-Sept. 2, 1801: Napoleon's Egyptian Campaign; July 19, 1799: Discovery of the Rosetta Stone.

RELATED ARTICLES in *Great Lives from History: The Eighteenth Century, 1701-1800*: Ahmed III; Catherine the Great; Mustafa III.

May 15, 1702-April 11, 1713
QUEEN ANNE'S WAR

The death of Charles II brought about the War of the Spanish Succession, a struggle for power between the major nations of Europe, which inevitably spread to their colonial territories. In the portion of the war fought in the Americas, known separately as Queen Anne's War, Great Britain gained territory and commercial concessions and consolidated its status as the world's most powerful empire.

ALSO KNOWN AS: War of the Spanish Succession (in Europe; 1701-1714)
LOCALE: British, French, and Spanish North America
CATEGORIES: Wars, uprisings, and civil unrest; expansion and land acquisition

KEY FIGURES
Queen Anne (1665-1714), queen of England, Scotland, and Ireland, r. 1702-1714
Hovenden Walker (d. 1728), English naval commander
John Hill (d. 1735), British military commander
First Duke of Marlborough (John Churchill; 1650-1722), commander in chief of the British and Dutch armies
Joseph Dudley (1647-1720), governor of Massachusetts
James Moore (1640-1706), governor of Carolina

Francis Nicholson (1655-1728), military leader and governor of several English colonies
First Viscount Bolingbroke (Henry St. John; 1678-1751), English secretary of state
Samuel Vetch (1668-1732), English merchant, military commander, and colonial governor

SUMMARY OF EVENT
By the seventeenth century, colonial rivalries had involved European powers in global conflicts. The first, the Nine Years' War (1689-1697), primarily a British-French conflict, was known as King William's War in North America, where all captured territory was restored by the Treaty of Ryswick in 1697. Warfare was renewed in the War of the Spanish Succession (1701-1714), whose North American phase was known as Queen Anne's War.

The origins of Queen Anne's War involved the question of who would succeed the sickly, childless Charles II as ruler of the vast Spanish Empire. Attempts to partition the empire between Louis XIV's son and Emperor Leopold I's son came to naught when Louis XIV accepted Charles II's will, which left the Spanish Empire to Philip of Anjou, Louis XIV's grandson. Provocative actions by Louis XIV and the new Spanish king, Philip V, coupled

29

with the fear that one person might eventually rule France and Spain, led William III, ruler of England and the Netherlands, to organize the Grand Alliance of England, the Netherlands, and the emperor. The object of the alliance was to prevent the union of France and Spain and to gain commercial and territorial benefits. On May 15, 1702, the Grand Alliance formally declared war against France and Spain. English and allied troops under the command of John Churchill, first duke of Marlborough, won significant victories on the Continent, while the English navy captured Gibraltar in 1704 and established a presence in the Mediterranean.

In North America, fighting between English colonists and their Native American allies on one side, and the French, the Spanish, and their Native American allies on the other, occurred in Canada, New England, the southern border of Carolina, Florida, and the Caribbean, where privateers operated. New York escaped attack by the French because the latter feared disturbing the neutrality of the Iroquois.

The English fleet seized the French West Indian island of St. Christopher (St. Kitts) in July, 1702, but an attack on Guadeloupe was unsuccessful in 1703. James Moore, governor of Carolina, led a raid of five hundred militia and three hundred Yamasees on St. Augustine, Florida, in October, 1702. Although they sacked the town, they were unsuccessful in capturing the fort. The following year, Moore led fifty militia and one thousand Native Americans in an attack on Spanish missions west of St. Augustine, destroying thirteen missions and carrying off thirteen hundred Native Americans to be used as slaves. Actions such as these led to a joint French-Spanish retaliatory attack on Charleston in August, 1706. This assault failed, and the following year, the Carolinians raided Pensacola, Florida. Repeated requests by the Carolinians to the English government for military assistance and the construction of forts went unanswered.

In New England, members of the Abenaki tribe, urged on and sometimes led by the French, attacked isolated settlements. The worst of these episodes was the February, 1704, attack on Deerfield, Massachusetts, which resulted in the death of fifty and the capture of more than one hundred residents. Some of the captured residents were later killed, others were ransomed, and the remainder settled in Canada. Massachusetts's governor, Joseph Dudley, made a secret peace overture to the French governor of Quebec, Philippe de Rigaud, Marquis de Vaudreuil. This attempt failed, as the French insisted that New York and the other northern colonies be brought into the plan and that the English relinquish their right to fish off the coast of Newfoundland, an area that the French and English regarded as valuable for training sailors.

One colonial objective was to eject the French from North America, and colonists expected English assistance to accomplish that end. One target of colonial aggression was Port Royal in Acadia (Nova Scotia). Several raids against the town had failed. After 1709, the English increased their military involvement in North America. Samuel Vetch, a merchant and soldier, had devised a plan to attack Quebec. Supported by the governors of New York and Massachusetts, Vetch journeyed to England and received cabinet support for a joint British-colonial attack on Canada in 1709. New York, Massachusetts, Connecticut, Rhode Island, and New Hampshire provided fifteen hundred men, who were to march on Montreal from Albany. One thousand others were to join English forces for an assault on Quebec and Port Royal by sea.

Preparations were made in England and North America, but favorable developments in European peace negotiations led the English to assign their forces to occupy Spain in anticipation of a peace treaty. When Louis XIV did not consent to the peace terms, the English determined that additional pressure on France in Europe was required and canceled their plans for Canada. Upon learning of the change in English plans, the colonial governors decided to postpone the assault until the following year.

Vetch and Colonel Francis Nicholson, a former colonial governor, commanded a successful raid on Port Royal (renamed Annapolis Royal) in September and October, 1710, which involved colonial forces and five hundred English troops. Buoyed by success, Nicholson and four Mohawks met with the new Tory ministry in London to plan an attack on Canada. The ministers saw French Canada as a threat to English colonies and trade, and were eager to offset Marlborough's popularity with an American victory. The first Viscount Bolingbroke, one of the secretaries of state, was the strongest proponent of action. He took the lead in planning the Walker expedition (1711), the first significant action against Canada launched from England.

An army commanded by Nicholson was to march from Albany to Montreal, and Admiral Sir Hovenden Walker's sixty ships were to land General John Hill's five thousand troops to attack Quebec. Because of navigational errors, the fleet foundered on rocks in the St. Lawrence River, losing about nine hundred men. The remnant of the fleet returned to England. News of the expedition's failure reached London in October, 1711, after secret preliminary peace articles had been signed by England and France. Nicholson was ordered to halt his overland march.

This expedition had been launched despite the fact that the English ministry had initiated secret peace negotiations with France in late 1710 and by October, 1711, had established a general framework for peace. In December, 1711, Marlborough was dismissed, and the Congress of Utrecht (1712, 1713) convened to force England's allies to accept the British-French terms and put them into the formal treaty. In May and June, 1712, the English and French agreed to a suspension of arms in Europe, which was extended to North America in September, 1712.

SIGNIFICANCE

The war was ended by the Treaty of Utrecht, signed on April 11, 1713. Among its major provisions were the recognition of Philip V as Spanish king. Philip in turn renounced any claim to the French throne. England won significant advantages through the grant of the *asiento de negros*, a contract to supply Spanish colonies with slaves, and by its acquisition of Gibraltar from Spain. However, England's greatest acquisitions came in North America, where France relinquished Hudson Bay, Acadia, and Newfoundland. France retained Cape Breton Island and the right to catch and dry fish on Newfoundland's coast. St. Christopher in the Caribbean was acquired by the English. These advantages secured for England commercial and territorial benefits that weakened the American colonial empires of France and Spain.

Casualties among the American colonists were about four hundred. The English lost approximately nine hundred in the Walker expedition and hundreds more in the failed raid on Guadeloupe. Native American losses were high, and the peace settlement recognized the Iroquois as English subjects and allowed English merchants to trade with western Native Americans. Intercolonial cooperation had improved, but cooperation between the colonists and England was not good. British-French and British-Spanish rivalries resumed in subsequent conflicts for control of North America.

—Mark C. Herman

FURTHER READING

Arnade, Charles W. *The Siege of St. Augustine in 1702*. Gainesville: University of Florida Press, 1959. This short monograph provides background information and an account of the colonial attack.

Crane, Werner W. *The Southern Frontier, 1670-1732*. Reprint. Ann Arbor: University of Michigan Press, 1956. Provides a detailed narrative of action along the southern border of the English colonies in the era of the war.

Eccles, William J. *France in America*. New York: Harper & Row, 1972. Discusses the war from the French colonial perspective.

Graham, Gerald S., ed. *The Walker Expedition to Quebec, 1711*. Toronto: Champlain Society, 1953. Reprint. New York: Greenwood Press, 1969. The introduction examines the expedition and analyzes the relevant primary sources.

Hattendorf, John B. *England in the War of the Spanish Succession: A Study of the English View and Conduct of Grand Strategy, 1702-1712*. New York: Garland, 1987. The only major work to date to examine the formation and implementation of English strategy in the war. Analyzes the place of the Walker expedition in the conduct of the war.

Lenman, Bruce. *Britain's Colonial Wars, 1688-1783*. New York: Longman, 2001. A history of British imperialism and expansion in the eighteenth century; discusses the connection of these policies to Britain's colonial wars.

Parkman, Francis. *A Half-Century of Conflict*. 1892. Reprint. New York: Collier Books, 1962. This classic account needs to be read in conjunction with other sources to correct a strong colonial bias.

Schama, Simon. *The Wars of the British, 1603-1776*. Vol. 2 in *A History of Britain*. New York: Hyperion, 2001. This volume, a companion to a BBC television program, recounts the wars Britain engaged in during the seventeenth and eighteenth centuries, conflicts that Schama claims were "eminently predictable, improbable, and avoidable."

SEE ALSO: May 26, 1701-Sept. 7, 1714: War of the Spanish Succession; Aug. 13, 1704: Battle of Blenheim; Mar. 23-26, 1708: Defeat of the "Old Pretender"; Sept. 11, 1709: Battle of Malplaquet; Sept. 22, 1711-Mar. 23, 1713: Tuscarora War; Apr. 11, 1713: Treaty of Utrecht; Mar. 7, 1714, and Sept. 7, 1714: Treaties of Rastatt and Baden; Summer, 1714-1741: Fox Wars; Sept. 6, 1715-Feb. 4, 1716: Jacobite Rising in Scotland.

RELATED ARTICLES in *Great Lives from History: The Eighteenth Century, 1701-1800*: Queen Anne; First Viscount Bolingbroke; First Duke of Marlborough.

July 24, 1702-October 1, 1704
CAMISARD RISINGS IN THE CÉVENNES

The risings of the Camisards—Protestant peasants in the Cévennes region of southern France—renewed the religious unrest between Catholics and Protestants that had plagued France during the Reformation. This rebellion challenged the absolute authority of the French king and the alliance of church and state.

LOCALE: Cévennes, Languedoc, France
CATEGORIES: Wars, uprisings, and civil unrest; religion and theology; government and politics

KEY FIGURES
Jean Cavalier (1681-1740), leader of the Camisards
Roland Laporte (1675-1704), leader of the Camisards
Duc de Villars (Claude-Louis-Hector de Villars; 1653-1734), marshal of France and later marshal general of France, 1733
François de Langlade de Chayla (d. 1702), French abbot and inspector of missions in the Cévennes
Victor-Maurice de Broglie (comte de Broglie; 1646-1727), French military commander and later marshal of France, 1724
Marquis de Montrevel (Nicolas Auguste de La Baume; 1645-1716), marshal of France
Louis XIV (1638-1715), king of France, r. 1643-1715

SUMMARY OF EVENT
As a result of persecution of the Huguenots (French Protestants) at the end of the reign of Louis XIV, the Protestant peasants of the Cévennes rose up against the Crown in an effort to preserve their way of life. In 1685, Louis XIV had revoked the Edict of Nantes, by which his grandfather Henry IV had granted freedom of religion to Protestants. Louis's reasons for revoking the edict were both personal and political. Along with Madame de Maintenon, his former mistress and then wife, Louis XIV had become extremely pious at the end of his life and wished to atone for his sins. Cleansing France of the heretics who had rejected the Catholic faith was one way to accomplish this end. He also believed that his power as an absolute monarch would be strengthened by unifying the country under one religion. In addition, the campaign to convert the Protestants provided an additional source of revenue to the Crown, which was then burdened with enormous debts as a result of the king's extravagant lifestyle and continuous wars. In order to convince the Protestants to accept Catholicism, special militia taxes (*taxes de milices*) doubling or tripling their property taxes were

levied against them, and soldiers were billeted in their homes.

In his zeal to eradicate the practice of the Protestant faith from France, Louis XIV had approved a policy, referred to as Dragonades, for converting Protestants by using various forms of persecution. In addition to being heavily taxed and forced to house the worst of royal troops in their homes, Protestants were forbidden to hold religious services, and those who did were severely punished. Many who refused to accept Catholicism were imprisoned, deported, or executed. These persecutions were especially severe in the Cévennes region, long a stronghold of religious heresy dating back to the Cathars in the Middle Ages.

The Protestants of the Cévennes were given to prophesying publicly and to being taken by fits of shaking and sobbing as they were filled with the Spirit. These public demonstrations, coupled with resistance to conversion,

A skirmish in the Camisard risings. (R. S. Peale and J. A. Hill)

resulted in a retaliatory persecution of almost fanatical proportions by François de Langlade de Chayla, abbot and inspector of missions of the Cévennes. Protestants, especially ministers, were imprisoned or sent to the galleys. Faced with such dangers, many fled from France. Abbot de Chayla caught them, if possible, and imprisoned them in his house at Pont-de-Montvert, where he made a final attempt to convert them by using torture.

On the night of July 24, 1702, a group of Cévennois peasants, who had for seventeen years resisted royal demands nonviolently, finally took up arms. They attacked the house of Abbot de Chayla, liberating their comrades and killing the abbot. Thus began the War of the Camisards. Wearing shirts or smocks (from which the name "Camisards" is derived), the rebel peasants raided Catholic villages, burned churches, prevented new converts from attending mass, and terrorized and killed those opposed to their cause.

The government sent troops to quell the insurgents. Using guerrilla tactics, the rebels under the leadership of Roland Laporte and Jean Cavalier successfully stood against the royal forces despite being severely outnumbered. Cavalier repeatedly engaged the royal troops, who were led first by Victor-Maurice de Broglie, the comte de Broglie, and then (from February 14, 1703) by the Marquis de Montrevel. On February 10, 1703, Cavalier routed the king's troops at Vagnas. He was defeated at Tour de Billot on April 30 but escaped capture and replenished his forces. Almost a year later, on April 16, 1704, he met Marshal de Montrevel's forces at the bridge of Nages. With only one thousand men to fight against five thousand, Cavalier was defeated but retreated successfully with two-thirds of his men. Laporte, with an army that eventually numbered one thousand, terrorized the region from Nîmes to Alais. Both Cavalier and Laporte were possessed of a natural expertise for leading men into battle. Their forces were disciplined and eager to fight under their leadership.

The rebellion caused serious problems for Louis XIV. France was simultaneously engaged in the War of the Spanish Succession and needed all of its troops on that front. The king had committed two generals and thirty

CÉVENNES REGION, FRANCE

thousand troops to suppressing the peasant rebellion in the Cévennes, without success. He thus sent the duke de Villars to the Cévennes with orders to pacify the region.

Villars arrived in Nîmes on April 21, 1704. He quickly surmised that the aid the Camisards received from the local Protestants, even if they had not joined the rebel forces, contributed greatly to their success. Therefore, he devised a plan to isolate the Camisards. He created fear in the peasants by stating that he would shoot, hang, or break on the wheel those who remained in rebellion. However, to those who surrendered within eight days he offered royal amnesty and the opportunity to leave France with their families and goods, if they wished. He also appealed to the provincial upper classes to demonstrate their loyalty to the king and managed to instill a sense of security in those recently converted to Catholicism.

Having thus taken steps to eliminate the sympathetic noncombatants as a factor, Villars planned a strong military maneuver against the Camisards themselves. Utilizing mixed regiments of cavalry and infantry, he sent twenty-five thousand troops into the mountains of the

Cévennes, where the Camisards were hiding. Cut off from their supplies, they were soon forced by hunger to leave their mountain hideouts. Royal troops then engaged them on open terrain. Villars personally presented letters of pardon to rebels who surrendered.

On May 11, 1704, Cavalier entered into negotiations with Marshal Villars at Pont d'Avne, near Alais. Assuring his followers that the Holy Spirit had directed him to negotiate with Marshal Villars, Cavalier convinced them to cease fighting. Cavalier then requested pardon from Louis XIV and asked that his followers be permitted to leave France. Cavalier received a commission as colonel, presented to him by Villars, and a pension of twelve hundred livres. In addition, he was to command a Camisard regiment that would serve in Spain. On June 21, 1704, Cavalier left the Cévennes with one hundred Camisards. At Paris, he was given an audience by Louis XIV and presented an explanation of the Camisard uprising to the king.

Although he also entered into negotiations with Villars, Laporte refused to cease fighting unless he had definite assurance that the privileges granted in the Edict of Nantes would be restored. He was shot and killed on August 14, 1704. With the submission of Cavalier and the death of Laporte, the rebellion in the Cévennes came to an end. On October 1, 1704, Villars officially informed Louis XIV that the Cévennes had been pacified.

SIGNIFICANCE

Many Protestants of the Cévennes emigrated to England either during or after the Camisard risings. In 1706, one group of ex-Camisards led by Elie Marion arrived in London. They formed a vocal and demonstrative religious sect that preached its faith publicly. Believing themselves to be filled with the Holy Spirit, they prophesied and went into states of ecstasy, shaking, dancing, shouting, and speaking in strange languages. These "French Prophets," as many inhabitants of London called them, often met with scorn and suffered some official repression. They did, however, influence a sect of Quakers, who adopted some of their doctrines and rituals of worship. Under the leadership of James and Ann (Lee) Wardley, they shook, shouted, and danced, earning for themselves the name Shakers. Members of this sect later settled in the United States.

The rebellion of the Camisards in the Cévennes represents another important chapter in the history of Languedoc. This southern region of France had already been the scene of a great religious conflict, the Albigensian Crusade of 1209-1213. In that crusade, Philippe

Auguste had sent an army to eradicate the heretical sect known as Cathars. There are several similarities between these two conflicts. Philippe Auguste's reasons for attacking the Cathars, like those of Louis XIV, were both religious and political, while the Cathars like the Camisards were motivated by religious fervor alone. Both the Cathars and the Camisards refused to submit and renounce their religion in spite of persecution. Jean Cavalier stated that the rebels under his command viewed themselves as the descendants of the Albigensians and believed it was their destiny to fight against superstition and persecution.

The rising of the Camisards in the Cévennes foreshadowed the eventual rejection of the alliance between Church and state in France. The Camisards believed in their right to freedom of conscience and considered themselves loyal Frenchmen. Their rebellion was a direct assault on the absolute power of the king. King and state were no longer identical in the minds of the French peasants—a crucial change in ideology from the Renaissance. The French Revolution, which would bring the fall of the monarchy and religious freedom, would have been unthinkable without this split in the French imagination between loyalty to the nation and loyalty to the Crown.

—Shawncey Webb

FURTHER READING

Briggs, Robin. *Early Modern France, 1560-1715*. London: Oxford University Press, 1998. Discusses absolutism in France, Henry IV, the Edict of Nantes, Louis XIV, and the revocation of the edict.

Frey, Linda, and Marsha Frey, eds. *The Treaties of the War of the Spanish Succession: An Historical and Critical Dictionary*. Westport, Conn.: Greenwood Press, 1995. Dictionary giving quick access to information on specific items.

Lewis, Warren Hamilton. *The Splendid Century: Life in the France of Louis XIV*. Garden City, N.Y.: Doubleday Anchor Books, 1957. Information on all aspects of the reign of Louis XIV, especially the galleys and persecution of Huguenots.

Potter, David E., ed. *France in the Later Middle Ages, 1200-1500*. London: Oxford University Press, 2003. Good treatment of religious conflict, especially the Cathars, and the Albigensian Crusades.

SEE ALSO: May 26, 1701-Sept. 7, 1714: War of the Spanish Succession; Sept. 11, 1709: Battle of Malplaquet; Sept. 8, 1713: Papal Bull *Unigenitus*; May, 1727-1733: Jansenist "Convulsionnaires" Gather at

Saint-Médard; Aug. 19, 1745-Sept. 20, 1746: Jacobite Rebellion; Apr. 27-May, 1775: Flour War; May 5, 1789: Louis XVI Calls the Estates-General; June 20, 1789: Oath of the Tennis Court; July 14, 1789: Fall of the Bastille; Apr. 20, 1792-Oct., 1797: Early Wars of

the French Revolution; Jan. 21, 1793: Execution of Louis XVI.

RELATED ARTICLES in *Great Lives from History: The Eighteenth Century, 1701-1800*: Georges Danton; Louis XV; Louis XVI; Robespierre.

1703-1711
HUNGARIAN REVOLT AGAINST HABSBURG RULE

While the Habsburgs battled the Bourbons to gain greater power in Europe, the peasants of Hungary staged a rebellion against their Habsburg king, seeking Hungarian independence from the Habsburg Holy Roman Empire. The failure of the rebellions confirmed the strength of the Habsburg Empire and the predominance of the Hungarian nobility.

ALSO KNOWN AS: Kuruc rebellion

LOCALE: Hungary

CATEGORIES: Wars, uprisings, and civil unrest; government and politics; social issues and reform

KEY FIGURES

János Vak Bottyán (1643?-1709), Hungarian rebel leader

Joseph I (1678-1711), Habsburg Holy Roman Emperor, r. 1705-1711

Sándor Károlyi (1669-1743), Hungarian rebel general

Leopold Kollonitsch (1631-1707), archbishop-primate of Hungary

Leopold I (1640-1705), king of Hungary, r. 1655-1705, and Holy Roman Emperor, r. 1658-1705

Louis XIV (1638-1715), king of France, r. 1643-1715

Ferenc II Rákóczi (1676-1735), the symbol of anti-Habsburg feeling in Hungary

SUMMARY OF EVENT

February of 1699 saw the death of the heir apparent to Charles II, the Habsburg ruler of Spain. Leopold I, the king of Hungary, then proclaimed his family successor to the Habsburgs. Yet Louis XIV, the powerful king of France, opposed Leopold's declaration, provoking the War of the Spanish Succession in 1701. In June of 1703, with Leopold I's position in doubt, Ferenc II Rákóczi joined a Hungarian peasant army that was formed to fight for the country's independence.

The immediate cause of the Hungarian revolt was the Habsburg decision to double taxes and to conscript soldiers, a policy instigated by Leopold Kollonitsch, the archbishop-primate of Hungary. Kollonitsch was also

part of the effort to convert the non-Catholic majority of Hungarians to Catholicism. Although many of Hungary's magnates were Catholic and benefited from the Habsburg monarchy's patronage, many more Hungarian lords lived on lands far away from the center of power and resented their limited rights under a foreign ruling line.

Ferenc II, the grandson of György II Rákóczi (a prince of Transylvania honored for his anti-Habsburg record), initially had tried to negotiate an alliance with Louis XIV, but when that effort failed, he capitalized on the intensifying movement in Hungary to reject any kind of foreign domination. By early 1705, Rákóczi had taken control of nearly all of Hungary, solidifying his power base on his own estates and spreading out in southern Austria. By contrast, Leopold I ruled only the border regions on the west and certain Saxon districts. Yet he held on, bolstered by the defeat of Louis XIV's allies at the Battle of Hochstadt (August 13, 1704). Indeed, Leopold was still too powerful for Rákóczi to defeat in a head-on conflict. Even more threatening to Rákóczi was the string of Habsburg military successes in other parts of Europe, which permitted Habsburg emperor Joseph I to concentrate his plan of attack on Hungary.

Without a straightforward military solution, Rákóczi's actions became muddled. In the fall of 1707, he offered the Hungarian throne to the Bavarian elector, at the same time diverting his attention to Poland, where he had a slim chance of becoming king. With the aid of the latter maneuver, Rákóczi hoped to enlist the support of Peter the Great's Russia. Such complex manipulations took time, involving simultaneous diplomatic initiatives in several European courts. In fact, Rákóczi was not able to arrange a meeting with the czar until May 12, 1711, by which time much had changed in Hungary and in Europe.

In Hungary, Rákóczi had to contend with tensions between the lords and the peasants. A great many landowners and nobility favored the war of independence. As the nobility took over the peasant army, the Hungarian masses became disenchanted and then weary of war. They resented this aristocratic usurpation of what had been a grassroots effort to free the country, which meant to them not only expelling occupying powers but also eliminating the feudal system which kept them beholden to a master class. Rákóczi had promised freedom to the peasant soldiers and their descendants, but then he reversed himself and bowed to aristocratic pressure. In 1708, when he returned to his initial promise and succeeded in getting a law passed that freed serfs in arms and their children, the delay had already demoralized his peasant followers.

In addition, economic conditions steadily worsened throughout the period of rebellion. Although Rákóczi promised to rehabilitate areas devastated by war, in practice his officials devoted much of their time to collecting the heavy taxes needed for military campaigns. Indeed, the level of taxation was higher than that of the most onerous periods of Habsburg rule in Hungary. Putting more money in circulation merely debased the value of the currency, and the peasants suffered while the revenues for war petered out.

This degradation of the country, begun in 1704, continued for seven years, throughout which Rákóczi's support dwindled. The independence movement, however, was periodically buoyed by military victories. János Vak Bottyán, a brilliant soldier, conquered and held much territory. Whatever his shortcomings as a political or diplomatic strategist, Rákóczi remained an inspiring figure, a towering personality whom his closest followers held in awe. Although the legislature elected Rákóczi "commanding prince," and he continued to dominate this governing body, he was never elected king. Even when the legislature disqualified the Habsburgs from claiming the Hungarian throne, elements of the nobility had it in mind to invite a foreigner to become king rather than Rákóczi.

Finally, with the cost of the war reaching an intolerable level, not even the fierce desire to have a native-born ruler could stop efforts to sue for peace. Rákóczi's forces were isolated, with only France sending some aid, and Joseph I successfully reconquered parts of Hungary and resettled them with Serbs and others who would not owe allegiance to Rákóczi. At the same time, Rákóczi found he could not rely on his own nobles, who refused to carry their share of the tax burden or to honor his pledges to the non-Catholic peasants that they would be free to worship as they chose. After 1708, Habsburg armies steadily gained ground against Rákóczi's once-invincible forces.

On April 30, 1711, while Rákóczi was abroad, his remaining supporters, led by General Sándor Károlyi, negotiated a treaty that upheld the prerogatives of the nobility and affirmed Habsburg rule under Joseph I. Not a word was mentioned of peasants' rights. Nothing had changed in the lives of the serfs. The nobility received a general amnesty, so that no aristocrat was punished for challenging Habsburg rule. As long as a lord swore a loyalty oath within three years, he would recover or retain his estates. Rákóczi preferred exile to accepting such ignominious terms. Joseph I agreed to abide by an earlier treaty (1687) that established certain Hungarian constitutional and religious rights, but in fact none of the rebels' aims were achieved and they received no guarantees of reform.

SIGNIFICANCE

Lasting nearly eight years, Ferenc II Rákóczi's rebellion was the longest insurrection in the history of the Habsburg monarchy. The Habsburgs had to invest much of their fortune and more than 100,000 men in the effort to subdue Rákóczi's forces. They had no choice, however, as reestablishment of the monarchy's grip on Hungary was essential to its survival in other parts of Europe—notably along the Habsburgs' German and Italian borders. Thus, although it ultimately failed, the rebellion demonstrated that European peasantry could constitute a force to be reckoned with. It thus foreshadowed the anti-bourgeois revolutions of the nineteenth century (1848) to a greater extent than it did the successful eighteenth century bourgeois revolutions against the aristocracy in France and the Americas.

—*Carl Rollyson*

FURTHER READING

Evans, R. J. W. *The Making of the Habsburg Monarchy, 1550-1700: An Interpretation*. 3d ed. New York: Oxford University Press, 1991. Chapter 7, "Hungary: Limited Rejection," provides a comprehensive overview of Habsburg domination of Hungary, comparing Rákóczi with his predecessors and his successors in the effort to win the country's independence.

Ignotus, Paul. *Hungary*. New York: Praeger, 1972. Chapter 1, "The Foundation of European Hungary," concentrates on Rákóczi's "emotional and sensitive personality" and his feeling of family pride, as well as his identification with the destitute and the oppressed, whether they were nobles or peasants.

Ingrao, Charles. *The Habsburg Monarchy, 1618-1815*. New York: Cambridge University Press, 1994. Described as the "first accessible and comprehensive history of the early modern Habsburg monarchy."

Chapter 4, "Facing West: The Second Habsburg Empire (1700-1740)," provides a precise analytical account of the revolt in the context of the Habsburgs' competition with the other great European powers.

Lendvai, Paul. *The Hungarians: A Thousand Years of Victory in Defeat.* Translated by Ann Major. Princeton, N.J.: Princeton University Press, 2003. This overview of Hungarian history includes chapter 14, "Ferenc Rákóczi's Fight for Freedom from Habsburgs," an account of Rákóczi's uprising.

Slottman, William B. *Ference Rákóczi and the Great Powers.* Boulder, Colo.: East European Monographs, 1997. The late Slottman, a professor at the University of California, Berkeley, specialized in the history of the Habsburgs. This biography of Rákóczi, recounting his efforts to win Hungarian independence, was adapted from Slottman's doctoral dissertation.

Sugar, Peter F., Peter Hanak, and Tibor Frank, eds. *A History of Hungary.* Bloomington: Indiana University Press, 1990. Chapter 8, "The Later Ottoman Period and Royal Hungary, 1606-1711," has a clear overview of the events leading up to and following the revolt against the Habsburgs. Includes maps and bibliography.

SEE ALSO: May 26, 1701-Sept. 7, 1714: War of the Spanish Succession; Nov. 20, 1710-July 21, 1718: Ottoman Wars with Russia, Venice, and Austria; Mar. 7, 1714, and Sept. 7, 1714: Treaties of Rastatt and Baden; Oct. 20, 1740: Maria Theresa Succeeds to the Austrian Throne; Dec. 16, 1740-Nov. 7, 1748: War of the Austrian Succession; 1775-1790: Joseph II's Reforms.

RELATED ARTICLES in *Great Lives from History: The Eighteenth Century, 1701-1800*: Charles VI; Joseph II; Maria Theresa.

May 27, 1703
FOUNDING OF ST. PETERSBURG

Czar Peter the Great created the city of St. Petersburg on the nortwestern frontier of Russia to be a window to the West, a Western-style, modern capital far from the eastward-looking traditions of Moscow.

LOCALE: St. Petersburg, Russia
CATEGORY: Government and politics

KEY FIGURES

Peter the Great (1672-1725), czar of Russia, r. 1682-1725

Aleksandr Danilovich Menshikov (1673-1729), Russian general who built the first fortress of St. Petersburg

Alexis Petrovich (1690-1718), Peter's son and member of the opposition faction

SUMMARY OF EVENT

For centuries, since the Mongol conquest, Russia had been largely cut off from Western Europe and had become predominantly Asian in its culture. Although the monarch's title of "czar" came from the Latin "caesar," the Russian government was fundamentally an Oriental despotism based upon the czar's priestly role in the Russian Orthodox Church. Czar Peter the Great, however, was different from his predecessors. He was a tall, robust man (growing to six foot, seven inches, an extraordinary

height for a man of his time) with a very active mind. Dissatisfied with the stifling atmosphere of intrigue in the Kremlin, he spent much of his time in boisterous activities with the foreigners in Moscow's German Quarter. There, he encountered all manner of Western ideas and skills and grew steadily convinced that Russia was already backward and was falling further and further behind the nations of Western Europe. Peter believed that Russia's only hope lay in adopting the cultural patterns that had made the Western nations strong.

At the same time, he knew that he could never accomplish his vision amid the traditionalist factions of Moscow, who would fight any sort of change as sacrilege against Russia's Orthodox heritage. He felt that his only hope lay in building a new city, where he could surround his court and nobility with the proper environment to foster the attitudes he wanted to inculcate. He wanted a city with the sort of architecture he had seen during his 1697-1698 Grand Embassy, in which he had toured Europe with a company of like-minded advisers.

For his new city, Czar Peter chose a stretch of land, newly captured in the Great Northern War, located on the Gulf of Finland, not far from Lake Lagoda, where the Neva River branches into an intricate delta and estuary. So confident was he of his victory that he did not wait for the formal peace treaty ceding the land to Russia from

Peter the Great at the founding of St. Petersburg. (Francis R. Niglutsch)

Sweden but sent a contingent of soldiers under General Aleksandr Danilovich Menshikov to construct a fortress on one of the islands, where its guns could bar the passage of enemy ships. The foundation of this fortress, the Peter and Paul Fortress, was laid on May 27, 1703 (May 16 by the Old Style calendar). The Peter and Paul Fortress was to form the nucleus for Peter's new city, to which he gave the Dutch-sounding name of Sankht-Peter-Burkh, which would soon be Russified to St. Petersburg by its reluctant inhabitants.

Peter himself laid out the plans for his new city, drawing a grid of straight lines and right angles along the Neva River. This design stood in sharp contrast to the traditional pattern of Russian cities, which radiated out in concentric circles from a central fortress, or kremlin. The latter pattern can still be seen in modern Moscow, with its Boulevard, Garden, and Outer Ring Roads connected by long radials that all converge upon the Kremlin and Red Square in the city's heart.

While traditional Russian structures were built in wood, Peter mandated that his new city would be built in stone. He wanted to ensure that his city would not burn down in the fires such as those that frequently swept Moscow and other traditional cities. To that end, he mandated that every carriage coming to the city must carry with it at least one building stone. However, because of the lay of the land along the Neva estuary, St. Petersburg proved particularly susceptible to flooding, particularly when prevailing westerly winds forced water from the Gulf of Finland to back up into the Neva River.

To build the broad avenues and stately palaces in the Western style Peter envisioned, he imported thousands of state and royal serfs from estates all over Russia. It is estimated that more than thirty thousand people perished in the process, and it is sometimes said that St. Petersburg was built as much upon the bones of the serfs as of the stone of Peter the Great's vision.

By 1712, St. Petersburg had grown enough that Peter felt confident in naming it his new imperial capital, relegating tradition-bound Moscow to the role of second city. Peter mandated that his nobles build mansions in his new city and dwell in them for a set portion of each year. There they had to shave their long beards and set aside their Asiatic traditional robes in favor of Western coats and breeches. In a break from the long tradition of seclusion of women in the *terem*, Peter ordered that women must appear at St. Petersburg's social functions. Instead of spending their time in needlework and pious prayers, Russian noblewomen would now hold salons in the French style, discussing intellectual matters, art, and literature.

However, these changes did not come without resistance from traditionalist factions. Peter's own son, Czarevich (crown prince, literally "son of the czar") Alexis Petrovich, became involved with a group of priests and noblemen who muttered against the abandonment of what they saw as Russia's holy role as the last spiritual hope of Christendom. When the czarevich fled abroad at the instigation of foreign agents, Peter sent his own agents to lure the young man back. When Alexis returned under a false promise that he would be safe, he was immediately imprisoned in the Peter and Paul Fortress, where he was brutally tortured with the knout, a traditional Russian cat-o'-nine-tails whip into which bits of metal and broken glass were worked. The details of Alexis Petrovich's final days are murky, but it is said that on the day before his death, he and his father were reconciled and embraced each other. It is also said by other sources that Peter had Alexis murdered.

SIGNIFICANCE

By the time Peter the Great died in 1725, the center of gravity of Russian politics had irrevocably shifted from Moscow to St. Petersburg. Although the traditionalists grumbled, subsequent Russian monarchs continued to hold court in that city on the verge of the Arctic Circle, where the Sun never fully sets during the height of summer.

The un-Russian characteristics of St. Petersburg had profound effects on Russian literature as it developed, for the literati of Russian society were necessarily noblemen and others who would be required to appear at court there. St. Petersburg developed a reputation as a place not quite of this Earth, where extraordinary things could happen. A significant Russian literature of the fantastic sprang up, set in this liminal city. In Alexander Pushkin's poem *Medniy vsadnik* (1837; *The Bronze Horseman*, 1899), the famous statue of Peter the Great comes to life and chases the protagonist through the streets of his city. In Nikolai Gogol's short story "Nos" (1836; "The Nose," 1946), the protagonist's nose can detach from his face and take human form, with a rank higher than that of its former owner. Even in realistic fiction such as Fyodor Dostoevski's novel *Idiot* (1868; *The Idiot*, 1887), the White Nights were a time when people could go mad and commit terrible crimes.

In 1914, St. Petersburg was renamed Petrograd, since a Russian name was considered desirable while the Russians fought the Germans. Following the 1917 October Revolution, the Bolsheviks returned the seat of government to the Kremlin in Moscow, considering it more secure than a city on the very edge of Russia's boundaries. Petrograd remained a center of Russian culture, however, even when it was renamed Leningrad in honor of Bolshevik leader Vladimir Ilich Lenin. The city withstood a terrible nine-hundred-day siege during World War II, in which people literally dropped in their tracks from starvation. After the 1991 fall of the Soviet Union, St. Petersburg reclaimed its old name.

—*Leigh Husband Kimmel*

FURTHER READING

Bushkovitch, Paul. *Peter the Great.* Lanham, Md.: Rowman & Littlefield, 2001. Less a straight biography of Peter the man than a study of the culture into which he was born and the ways in which he transformed it.

Cooper, Leonard. *Many Roads to Moscow: Three Historical Invasions.* New York: Coward-McCann, 1968. Of special interest is the section on the Battle of Poltava, which secured Russia's claim on St. Petersburg and its surroundings.

Cracraft, James. *The Revolution of Peter the Great.* Cambridge, Mass.: Harvard University Press, 2003. Study of the cultural changes brought about by Peter the Great's "revolution from above."

Lincoln, W. Bruce. *Sunlight at Midnight: St. Petersburg and the Rise of Modern Russia.* New York: Basic Books, 2000. A cultural history of the city of St. Petersburg and examination of how it transformed Russian culture, often in ways that Peter the Great never anticipated and would even have abhorred.

SEE ALSO: c. 1701-1721: Great Northern War; June 27, 1709: Battle of Poltava; 1724: Foundation of the St. Petersburg Academy of Sciences; May 15, 1738: Foundation of St. Petersburg's Imperial Ballet School; Aug. 10, 1767: Catherine the Great's Instruction; Mar. 28, 1776: Founding of Bolshoi Theatre Company; 1788-Sept., 1809: Russo-Swedish Wars.

RELATED ARTICLES in *Great Lives from History: The Eighteenth Century, 1701-1800*: Catherine the Great; Peter the Great; Peter III.

June 20, 1703
CHIKAMATSU PRODUCES *THE LOVE SUICIDES AT SONEZAKI*

Chikamatsu's The Love Suicides at Sonezaki *created a new puppet theater genre called domestic plays, which made tragic heroes of ordinary townspeople, the* chōnin, *rather than of the samurai.*

LOCALE: Dotonbori, Ōsaka, Japan
CATEGORY: Theater

KEY FIGURES
Chikamatsu Monzaemon (Sugimori Nobumori; 1653-1725), Japanese playwright
Takemoto Gidayū (1651-1714), Japanese chanter
Takeda Izumo (1691-1756), Japanese theatrical manager, designer, and inventor

SUMMARY OF EVENT

The military rulers of Tokugawa Japan (1600-1867) enforced rigid class divisions and adopted the condescending view of conservative Confucian ethics on the social status of merchants. Merchants were placed below warriors, peasants, and artisans on the social hierarchy. However, believing agriculture was the productive part of the economy, the shogunate taxed the farmers heavily while puzzling over the growing wealth of the *chōnin* (common townspeople).

Excluded from any political or administrative role by the samurai bureaucrats, the *chōnin* were irreverently ambivalent about the values of their "social betters" and found consolation in consumption, theater, and the brothels of the licensed quarters, a safety valve their authoritarian masters allowed. The Floating World District (Ukiyo), as it came to be known, became the focal point of emerging *chōnin* culture. Indulging in its delights entailed such obvious risks as neglecting one's livelihood or dissipating one's fortune, but the forbidden fruit of the pleasure quarter was not sex but romance. Such emotional attachments often disrupted marriages or other obligations, and courtesans' indentured status usually made enduring relationships impossible. Such was the stuff of Chikamatsu Monzaemon's play *Sonezaki shinjū* (1703; *The Love Suicides at Sonezaki*, 1961).

A central theme of the play was suicide, which was colored by association with samurai, who probably chose the taking of one's life as more dignified and less painful than the consequences of capture. In time, suicide was regarded as a way of redeeming one's honor in defeat or after having failed one's lord in some other way. Remarkably, suicide even was used to admonish one's lord with

utmost seriousness. By the Tokugawa period, the traditional samurai suicide by self-disembowelment, or *seppuku*, had become a highly formalized ceremony, one that was sensitive to personal dignity even though it also was the samurai mode of capital punishment. A samurai would tuck his sleeves firmly under his knees so his body would not topple forward, and a second samurai decapitated the first before agony could destroy the composure of the one being killed. The ugliest side of *seppuku* was that it reflected the demands of feudal lords for ultimate submission. Clearly, however, the association of samurai suicide with dignity and the restoration of honor touched the *chōnin*. Finally, while Stoicism and Christianity taught Westerners that suicide is sinful, it was not regarded as sinful in Japan. Indeed, widespread belief in salvation simply through faith in Amida Buddha led some samurai to regard suicide as a speedier path to paradise. This aspect of *seppuku*, too, was echoed in Chikamatsu's play.

Tokugawa popular theater consisted of Kabuki and Jōruri. As in Western opera, music and emotions were central to both. Kabuki grew out of skits by a troupe of female dancers and singers, and the boys who replaced them (female as well as young male performers were banned from the stage when their images were tainted by prostitution). When adult male actors took over the roles, drama emerged as a more serious enterprise. Jōruri (now called Bunraku) developed when puppeteers began miming the narratives of balladeers accompanied by the banjo-like *shamisen*. Through most of the seventeenth century, both theaters staged *jidaimono* (history pieces), depicting the fabulous heroics of warriors, romantic trials, and acts of loyalty.

Chikamatsu transformed Jōruri, elevating it to a form of literature and turning its attention to the *chōnin* themselves. From a cultured samurai family, and a page for an imperial prince and other court aristocrats in youth, he was drawn to Jōruri by chanter Uji Kaga-no-jō (1635-1711), for whom he wrote his first plays, including *Yotsugi Soga* (the soga successors), first performed in 1683 (pb. 1896), his earliest known play. The following year, Kaga-no-jō's pupil Takemoto Gidayū used the play to open his new theater in Osaka. In 1686, Chikamatsu wrote *Shusse Kagekiyo* (pr. 1686, pb. 1890; Kagekiyo the victorious) for Gidayū. Its intense heroine, reminiscent of Medea, marked a new epoch in Jōruri. However, between 1688 and 1703, Chikamatsu wrote mainly Kabuki plays for Kyoto actor Sakata Tōjūrō (1647-1709).

Typically involving well-born young men falling on hard times, the plays allowed Chikamatsu to explore human psychology, but none of his texts survive intact. (Because Jōruri chanting became a popular hobby, its plays were published. Kabuki plays, however, were not published widely.)

Chikamatsu happened to be in Osaka in the spring of 1703 during an incident that became the talk of the city. A shop assistant and a lower-ranked courtesan committed a love suicide (*shinjū*) in the woods by Sonezaki shrine. (The term *shinjū* was first used to describe a pledge of love such as an oath or a torn-off fingernail.) Within three weeks, *The Love Suicides at Sonezaki* was performed by chanter Gidayū, the first such Jōruri play. Less-conservative Kabuki, often termed a "living newspaper" because it would often reenact recent events, had staged a *shinjū* play in 1683. Once again, a Kabuki company rushed to the boards with the story of the Sonezaki suicides, ahead of Chikamatsu and Gidayū. Nevertheless, in 1703, their play was an immense success as well, packing the Takemoto Theater for months, making it financially secure, and shaping Chikamatsu's career. He moved to Osaka and devoted the rest of his life to Jōruri. *The Love Suicides at Sonezaki* also created a new Jōruri genre called *sewamono* (gossip piece, or, more commonly, domestic play, obscuring memories of earlier Kabuki *shinjū* dramas). The play describes the plight of Tokubei, a shop assistant in love with a courtesan, Ohatsu. Tokubei commits love-suicide (*shinjū*) with Ohatsu after he is cheated out of dowry money by a supposed friend for a marriage he refused to accept. He thus had been shamed, was unable to return the dowry, was jobless (he was fired for rejecting the proffered marriage), and had no possibility of redeeming Ohatsu's contract and freeing her from the life of a courtesan.

The play's hero seems inept and pathetic, and his lover seems emotionally fragile. Yet the purity of their love and the beauty of the poetic narrative describing their final journey (*michiyuki*)—praised as one of the most beautiful passages in Japanese literature—made the modest pair tragic heroes. The *michiyuki* expresses the couple's feeling that their love was the only fine thing in their lives. Desiring to preserve it unsullied, to be beautiful in death, they tie themselves to a tree. They ask Amida for salvation and union in the next life, a prospect affirmed by the narrator, who calls them models of true love who will attain Buddhahood. *The Love Suicides at Sonezaki* not only depicted ordinary *chōnin* with striking realism, it also elevated them, through literary brilliance, to a tragic level. While its dialogue is straightforward, the narrative passages have a poetic quality and textual density, which is amplified by *kakekotoba* (or pivot words), puns that conclude one phrase and take the next in a new direction. The passages also highlight allusion and the 7- and 5-syllable line counts traditional in Japanese poetry, which is impossible to replicate in translation and rarely equaled in any literature. Another innovation was that the puppeteer for Ohatsu performed in full view (she was elevated in one scene where Tokubei hid under her skirt). This practice would become universal, a unique feature of Jōruri. In 1705, Gidayū first positioned himself in public view, creating a similar precedent.

1700's

SIGNIFICANCE

The success of *The Love Suicides at Sonezaki* spawned a rash of *shinjū* plays, both Kabuki and Jōruri, and so many real *shinjū* that suicide became criminalized and the word banned from play titles. Chikamatsu wrote about thirty Kabuki plays and more than ninety Jōruri plays, of which twenty-four are *sewamono*. Their unity and literary excellence made them his finest works.

Praised as the "god of writers," Chikamatsu made Jōruri dominant for most of the eighteenth century and made Jōruri books popular throughout Japan. His most popular work, *Kokusenya kassen* (pr. 1715; *The Battles of Coxinga*, 1951), splendidly staged by Takeda Izumo, included *sewamono* elements and became a model for later *jidaimono*, although they became increasingly disjointed. Multiple authors wrote virtually self-contained acts designed to showcase florid new chanting styles and virtuoso puppeteers with new three-man puppets (1734) with movable fingers, eyes, eyebrows, and mouths. Eroding the quality of many later *jidaimono* was a preoccupation with spectacle, with a type of violence that Kabuki could not match, with stunning "revelations" (that turned on their heads famous episodes from medieval epics), and with emotionally stupefying acts of loyalty. However, the course Chikamatsu set with *The Love Suicides at Sonezaki*, exploring human passions (*ninjō*) and their clashes with the duties, obligations, and principles that give order to society (*giri*), and the often resulting pathos (*urei*), produced an extraordinary body of mature work (about seventy-five Jōruri plays after he was fifty years old). His *jidaimono* were invariably fables criticizing contemporary political ills (for example, the arbitrary use of power, instability, and overregulation), and, in *sewamono*, he probed with increasing subtlety the ways *ninjō* and *giri* interact.

Confucianism, samurai codes, and *jidaimono* embodied *giri*. The so-called Floating World fiction and art, however common, certainly manifested the *chōnin*'s desire to follow their passions, but it is interesting that a samurai-born playwright created the purest expression of *ninjō* in Tokugawa literature with his *Love Suicides at Sonezaki*. The play is a testament to the *chōnin*'s less-visible idealism.

—*R. Craig Philips*

FURTHER READING

Gerstle, C. Andrew, ed. *Chikamatsu: Five Late Plays*. New York: Columbia University Press, 2001. An excellent work on Chikamatsu's career and mature *jidaimono*.

Kato, Suichi. *The Years of Isolation*. Vol. 3 in *A History of Japanese Literature*. Tokyo: Kodansha, 1979. An insightful interpretation by a Japanese scholar trained in Western literary scholarship.

Keene, Donald. *World Within Walls: Japanese Literature of the Pre-Modern Era, 1600-1867*. New York: Columbia University Press, 1999. A solid and comprehensive analysis of Tokugawa literature

_____, trans. *Four Major Plays of Chikamatsu*. New York: Columbia University Press, 1998. Includes the text of *The Love Suicides at Sonezaki*, with a good introduction.

SEE ALSO: Feb. 4, 1701-Feb. 4, 1703: Revenge of the Forty-Seven Ronin; Dec., 1720: Japan Lifts Ban on Foreign Books.

RELATED ARTICLES in *Great Lives from History: The Eighteenth Century, 1701-1800*: Chikamatsu Monzaemon; Hakuin; Suzuki Harunobu; Tokugawa Yoshimune.

1704
NEWTON PUBLISHES *OPTICS*

Newton's Optics *established a new theory of light and a more quantitative and experimental style of science. Also, the term "light" provided the central metaphor for the intellectual age called the Enlightenment.*

LOCALE: London, England

CATEGORIES: Physics; science and technology; astronomy; mathematics

KEY FIGURES

Sir Isaac Newton (1642-1727), English physicist and mathematician

Johannes Kepler (1571-1630), German astronomer who founded the modern study of optics

René Descartes (1596-1650), French philosopher and mathematician

Robert Hooke (1635-1703), first curator of experiments for the Royal Society of London

Christiaan Huygens (1629-1695), Dutch mathematician and physicist

SUMMARY OF EVENT

Sir Isaac Newton once famously said that if he saw farther than others, it was because he "stood on the shoulders of giants." As a student at Cambridge University from 1661 to 1665, he studied carefully the work of Johannes Kepler, René Descartes, and other giants of the Scientific Revolution. This led him to a series of optical experiments and a 1672 paper on a new theory of color delivered to the Royal Society of London. A long series

of disputes followed, culminating with the publication of Newton's *Opticks* (1704; better known as *Optics*) by the Royal Society of London.

At Cambridge, Newton was introduced to optics by reading Kepler's *Dioptrice* (1611; ray optics), which initiated the modern study of optics. Newton also read Descartes's *Dioptrique* (1637; ray optics), which offered a mechanical theory of light as an instantaneous transmission of pressure transmitted by a luminous medium made up of moving particles. Descartes had claimed that the bending of light in refraction was caused by an increase in the speed of particles as they pass into a denser medium. He proposed that the colors produced in refraction were caused by particle rotations, faster for red and slower for blue. Thus, color was a modification of the pure homogeneous white light coming from these rotations. Newton's teacher at Cambridge, Isaac Barrow, gave lectures on optics in 1664, which also suggested that colors result from modifications of white light.

Newton became interested in colors caused by refraction in lenses when he used lenses to construct a telescope, producing images surrounded by colored fringes. He then obtained a prism to study how colors are formed from white light by refraction. He passed sunlight from a small hole in the window shades through his prism and refracted it to the opposite wall. When he saw that the resulting spectrum was much longer than its breadth, he began to develop the idea that white light is not homogeneous, but is a mixture of colors, and that the elongation of the spectrum comes from different colors refracting at different angles. In later years, Newton claimed that his theory of colors, along with his formulation of the calculus and the law of universal gravitation, were all conceived during the plague years of 1665 and 1666, when students were sent home from school for nearly two years.

After returning to Cambridge as a fellow, Newton constructed the first reflecting telescope, in 1668, to avoid the problem of image distortion due to refraction. The telescope was only six inches long, but it magnified forty times by focusing light with a concave mirror instead of a lens. An urgent request soon came from the Royal Society to examine the telescope, so Newton constructed an improved nine-inch version and sent it to London; the response was enthusiastic. The Royal Society asked for a written account of his invention, leading to Newton's reply, his first scientific paper, "New Theory About Light and Colours," published in the *Philosophical Transactions* of the Royal Society in March of 1672. Although this paper led to his election as a fellow of the Royal Society, it also gave rise to an extended controversy, including ten critical letters from half a dozen authors in the *Philosophical Transactions* and eleven replies by Newton. Robert Hooke led the opposition, which rejected the heterogeneous nature of light and preferred various forms of the wave theory that had been developed by Christiaan Huygens.

Soon Newton became impatient with the philosophical and hypothetical arguments of his critics and insisted that science should be primarily mathematical and experimental. After about four years, he "retreated" to doing research and teaching for about a decade. In 1684 he was finally persuaded by astronomer Edmond Halley to publish his laws of motion and universal gravitation, resulting in the masterpiece *Philosophiae naturalis principia mathematica* (1687; *The Mathematical Principles of Natural Philosophy*, 1729; best known as the *Principia*, 1848), which resolved the most difficult problems of the Scientific Revolution and established Newton's reputation.

After Hooke died in 1703, Newton was elected president of the Royal Society. A year later he published *Optics*, written in English for a more receptive audience, which now recognized the value of his experimental and mathematical arguments. *Optics* described his many experiments on light. His separation of white light with a prism associated quantitative angles of refraction with each of the colors, which he rather arbitrarily designated as seven: red, orange, yel-

Diagrams of optical phenomena created by Sir Isaac Newton to illustrate the first edition of his Optics. *The phenomena pictured include a rainbow and the refraction of light through Icelandic spar (a type of crystal) and through a prism.* (Library of Congress)

low, green, blue, indigo, and violet. He gave the first complete account of the rainbow and explained the color of a given object as the combination of colors it reflects after absorbing all others.

While the *Principia* had proved Newton a brilliant mathematician, the easier-to-read *Optics* revealed his skill as an experimenter. In book 1 of three books in the *Optics*, he describes his experiments with the spectrum. A crucial experiment demonstrated that each color is a pure component of white light by passing a single color in the spectrum through a hole and showing that a second prism refracted it the same amount without changing its color. Another experiment passed the dispersed rays of the spectrum from one prism through an inverted second prism that recombined these rays to form white light again.

In book 2 Newton examines the colored rings formed when a lens is pressed against a flat pane of glass, first studied by Hooke but called "Newton rings." Careful measurements showed that the gap between the lens and the glass increases uniformly with each ring so that the "interval of the fits" is related to the colors. Theorizing these "fits" was as close as he could get to a determination of the wavelength of light, but he avoided any such hypothesis.

In book 3 Newton discusses the 1665 experiments of astronomer Francesco Maria Grimaldi, which produced colored fringes when white light passed through two successive slits (diffraction). Newton attempts to explain this result in terms of attractive forces rather than waves. His preference for the particle theory of light led him to conclude that light travels faster when it passes into denser media. However, the more hypothetical issues about the nature of light were mostly relegated to the sixteen "queries" at the end of the 1704 edition of the *Optics*.

SIGNIFICANCE

Sir Isaac Newton's *Optics* established a more experimental and quantitative style in science for the eighteenth century, which contrasted with the earlier, more speculative, hypothetical approach. However, in the 1706 Latin edition of *Optics*, he added new queries that suggested the particle theory of light, and in the 1717 and 1730 English editions he ex-

panded on these queries. Newton's particle theory influenced other scientists, delaying the acceptance of the wave theory for nearly a century. In the nineteenth century the wavelengths of visible light were finally measured, and light was shown to slow down in denser media, as predicted by the wave theory. Newton's early ambivalence between particle and wave theories is reflected in modern quantum theory, which attributes both particle and wave properties to light.

The careful reasoning and experimental approach of the *Optics* became a paradigm for the eighteenth century Enlightenment, including its central metaphor of light. Newton's work was widely celebrated in literature and poetry, and he was considered a prophet for future progress. The laws of nature, both of motion and of light, soon came to be seen as a reflection of order and beauty, and the spectrum became a new symbol for the descriptive poet. Where the *Principia* had been viewed as cold philosophy, the *Optics* opened up the literary imagination to light and color, making itself felt in the works of poets over the next generations.

—*Joseph L. Spradley*

FURTHER READING

Andrade, E. N. da C. *Sir Isaac Newton: His Life and Work*. New York: Macmillan, 1954. A readable account of Newton's life, with a chapter on the *Optics*.

Cohen, I. Bernard, and George E. Smith, eds. *The Cambridge Companion to Newton*. New York: Cambridge University Press, 2002. This compilation on New-

---

NEWTON DEFINES THE UNIT OF LIGHT

Sir Isaac Newton began his Optics *with a series of definitions, setting out precisely the terms governing all that would follow. His first definition, excerpted below, was that of the smallest unit of light, which he called a "ray."*

By the Rays of Light I understand its least Parts, and those as well Successive in the same Lines. For it is manifest that light consists of Parts, both Successive and Contemporary; because in the same place you may stop that which comes one moment and let pass that which comes precisely after; and in the same time you may stop it in any one place, and let it pass in any other. For that part of Light which is stopp'd cannot be the same with that which is let pass. The least Light or part of Light, which may be stopp'd alone without the rest of the Light, or propagated alone, or do or suffer any thing alone, which the rest of the Light doth not or suffers not, I call a Ray of Light.

Source: Sir Isaac Newton, *Opticks: Or, A Treatise of the Reflections, Refractions, Inflections and Colours of Light—Based on the Fourth Edition London, 1730* (New York: Dover, 1952), pp. 1-2.

ton's work includes the chapter "Newton's Optics and Atomism" by Alan Shapiro.

Newton, Isaac. *Opticks: Or, A Treatise of the Reflexions, Refractions, Inflexions, and Colours of Light*. New York: Dover, 1952. This reprint of the 1730 edition of the *Optics* includes a foreword by Albert Einstein, a good historical introduction by Edmund Whittaker, a preface by Bernard Cohen, and an analytical table of contents by Duane H. D. Roller.

Nicolson, Marjorie Hope. *Newton Demands the Muse: Newton's "Opticks" and the Eighteenth Century Poets*. London: Archon Books, 1963. This classic book describes the influence of Newton and the *Optics* on the eighteenth century literary imagination.

Rossi, Paoli. *The Birth of Modern Science*. Translated by Cynthia De Nardi Ipsen. Malden, Mass.: Blackwell, 2001. This translation from the original Italian work includes a good discussion of Newton's optics in chapter 17.

SEE ALSO: 1779: Ingenhousz Discovers Photosynthesis; 1787: Herschel Begins Building His Reflecting Telescope.

RELATED ARTICLES in *Great Lives from History: The Eighteenth Century, 1701-1800:* Maria Gaetana Agnesi; George Berkeley; Comte de Buffon; Caroline; Henry Cavendish; Marquise du Châtelet; Johann Wolfgang von Goethe; Caroline Lucretia Herschel; William Herschel; David Hume; Joseph-Louis Lagrange; Colin Maclaurin; Gaspard Monge.

1704-1712
ASTRONOMY WARS IN ENGLAND

John Flamsteed was compelled by the queen of England and the Royal Society of London to publish the results of his decades-long observations of star locations. Flamsteed repudiated this unfinished, yet published, work and publicly burned most of the available copies. In the end, the conflict would hamper astronomical research in the first two decades of the eighteenth century, despite the catalog's early publication.

LOCALE: England
CATEGORIES: Astronomy; science and technology

KEY FIGURES
John Flamsteed (1646-1719), an English astronomer and Britain's first astronomer royal
Sir Isaac Newton (1642-1727), an English mathematician who was appointed warden of the Royal Mint in 1696
Edmond Halley (1656-1742), an English astronomer
Christopher Wren (1632-1723), an English architect who designed the Royal Observatory, Greenwich, and who served on a committee to compel Flamsteed to publish his findings
Queen Anne (1665-1714), queen of Great Britain, r. 1702-1714

SUMMARY OF EVENT
Book three of the first edition of Sir Isaac Newton's magnum opus *Philosophiae naturalis principia mathematica* (1687; *The Mathematical Principles of Natural Philoso-*

phy, 1729; best known as the *Principia*) contains a proposition that announced the most celebrated of Newton's scientific discoveries, the law of universal gravitation. One of the model systems Newton used to demonstrate the efficacy of his gravitational theory was the irregular movements of the Earth's moon, a conundrum that had perplexed astronomical observers for centuries. Even though the orbit of the Moon is largely influenced by the gravitational pull of the Earth, the gravitational attraction of the massive Sun, despite its great distance from the Moon, shifts the orbit of the Moon. This makes the lunar system so complex that even Newton, with all his analytical skills, could account only for the major perturbations in the lunar orbit.

Newton had wished to publish a second edition of the *Principia*, but he still was faced with the problem of lunar movements, a problem that required further refinement. Newton needed more extensive data of the Moon's movements, and for this he turned, as he had in the past, to the astronomer royal John Flamsteed.

Appointed astronomer royal on March 4, 1675, by King Charles II of England (r. 1660-1685) for the Royal Observatory, Greenwich (built in 1676, just outside London), Flamsteed labored for almost thirty years, exhaustively cataloging star positions. Because he was a perfectionist, Flamsteed had yet to publish his star catalogs, but by the beginning of the eighteenth century, many members of the Royal Society began to view the absence of published star data as a sign of Flamsteed's failure to provide the public service paid for by the Crown. It was believed that the astronomer royal should publish for the good name of the observatory and for other astronomers who wished to use his data. Needless to say, Flamsteed did not agree with this assessment. In his view, the Crown paid him a pittance, only £100 per year, which had to be supplemented with his own funds. He had to purchase his own instruments and pay his assistants. He believed that his star data were his alone, and that he would publish them when he was ready to do so.

Newton, elected president of the Royal Society in 1703, visited Flamsteed at Greenwich in April of 1704 to determine the publication status of his star catalog. During this meeting, Flamsteed claimed that the catalog was ready for publication, and so Newton asked him to submit a printing cost estimate to the society. Flamsteed, however, stalled and did not comply with this request until seven months later. When the catalog finally found its way to the Royal Society, the society agreed to publish it, and Prince George of Denmark (1653-1708), consort of Queen Anne, agreed to pay for the publication.

A society committee, which consisted of Newton and two of his friends, astronomer Edmond Halley and Christopher Wren, the architect of St. Paul's Cathedral, examined the manuscripts Flamsteed provided and were to determine their suitability for publication. Halley had interests in Flamsteed's data, too, because he desired positional data on the comet that would one day bear his name. Flamsteed loathed Halley, and in his letters he went out of his way to vilify him. To acquire data on the comet, Halley had to use Newton as an intermediary between himself and Flamsteed. The committee ruled that all the manuscripts provided should be published, and the society instructed Flamsteed to set his work into an appropriate format for the printer. Once again, however, Flamsteed hesitated and failed to cooperate. He sent the society a copy of his observations and the catalog of those star positions he had worked out, but at the same time he pointed out that the catalog was incomplete and should not be published. Flamsteed promised to produce a "more perfect copy" at a later date. Printing began in May, 1706, but stopped in 1708 with the death of Prince George. Flamsteed stopped sending data, and Newton retaliated by expelling Flamsteed from the Royal Society. The society, almost certainly with the prompting of Newton, decided that the completion of this project was jeopardized and that definitive action should be taken, since Flamsteed seemed not to be able to work quickly without outside pressure.

Queen Anne issued a royal warrant in 1710 to the

The frontispiece of the 1712 edition of John Flamsteed's Historia coelestis Britannica, *which was published by Edmond Halley against the wishes of Flamsteed.* (Hulton Archive/Getty Images)

president of the Royal Society to form a board of visitors, which would be given extensive powers to compel Flamsteed to deliver to the board, within six months after the end of each year, finished, printable copies of his annual observations. Thus, by order of the queen, the printing of the catalog resumed in 1711, but Flamsteed had done virtually nothing in the intervening seven years to make his catalog suitable for publication. In the end the Royal Society simply wearied of Flamsteed's dilatoriness and took decisive action. After reexamining Flamsteed's manuscript catalog, the Royal Society committee noted the incomplete nature of his work and asked Halley to complete the manuscripts as best he could. Halley supplied whole, print-worthy pages of Flamsteed's observations and edited the incomplete work, against Flamsteed's wishes, publishing *Historia coelestis Britannica* in 1712. In a letter to Flamsteed dated June 23, 1711, Halley had informed Flamsteed of his work with the catalog and the society's intent to publish it, which shows that Halley did not edit Flamsteed's manuscript without Flamsteed's knowledge.

Flamsteed was outraged that his archenemy, Halley, was allowed to fiddle with his life's work. Somehow, Flamsteed needed to publish a complete and corrected edition of his observations. With his wife, Flamsteed tried either to suppress the *Historia coelestis Britannica* or to insist that it not be used. It was not until 1715, with the appointment of a new lord chamberlain, Charles Paulet, second duke of Bolton (1661-1722), that Flamsteed was able to acquire three hundred of the four hundred total copies printed. He publicly burned the catalogs in 1716 on a high mound in Greenwich Park "as a sacrifice to heavenly truth." After this fit of passion, Flamsteed applied himself to preparing his astronomical catalog and observations in a form he believed to be accurate, but they were not published until after his death. Two former assistants of Flamsteed, Joseph Crosthwait and Abraham Sharp, edited his work. The three-volume *Historia coelestis Britannica* (1725; *British Catalogue of the Heavens*, partial translation, 1982) is a monument to Flamsteed's exacting labors and skill as an astronomer.

Halley succeeded Flamsteed as astronomer royal after Flamsteed's death in 1719. Flamsteed's widow and assistant, Margaret Flamsteed, was so bitter over Halley's appointment that she removed all astronomical instruments and other objects from the Greenwich observatory. At an age when most would have thought of retiring, Halley proved a productive astronomer royal and even followed the Moon through an entire eighteen-year nodal cycle.

SIGNIFICANCE

The astronomy wars hampered astronomical research in the first two decades of the eighteenth century, and the harrying political machinations of Sir Isaac Newton cast a shadow over his character. Little was gained by forcing the early publication of John Flamsteed's data. It is unlikely that, left to his own, Flamsteed would have completed his star catalog before his death. Using Flamsteed's lunar data, Newton only slightly improved his description of lunar motion in his second edition of the *Principia*, which he published in 1713, and had all mentions of Flamsteed expunged. A satisfactory theory of lunar motion continued to remain troublesome for centuries after Newton's death.

—*Michael A. Buratovich*

FURTHER READING

Christianson, Gale E. *In the Presence of the Creator: Isaac Newton and His Times*. New York: Free Press, 1984. A deeply detailed biography of Newton that honestly discusses his scientific genius and personal shortcomings.

Clark, David, and Stephen P. H. Clark. *Newton's Tyranny*. New York: Freeman, 2001. A somewhat useful discussion of the astronomy wars, but rather biased against Newton and Halley.

Cook, Alan. *Edmond Halley: Charting the Heavens and the Seas*. New York: Oxford University Press, 1998. A complete, scholarly biography of the life of Halley.

Flamsteed, John. *The Preface to John Flamsteed's "Historia coelestis Britannica": Or, "British Catalogue of the Heavens" (1725)*. Edited by Allan Chapman. Translated by Alison Dione Johnson. London: Trustees of the National Maritime Museum, 1982. The English translation of the preface to Flamsteed's major work. Includes an introduction by the editor, illustrations, charts, and appendices.

Forbes, Eric G., Lesley Murdin, and Frances Willmoth. *The Correspondence of John Flamsteed, First Astronomer Royal*. Vol. 2. Philadelphia: Institute of Physics, 1997. A compendium of Flamsteed's letters that provide extensive insights into the life and work of this temperamental but highly efficient astronomer.

_____. *The Correspondence of John Flamsteed, First Astronomer Royal*. Vol. 3. Philadelphia: Institute of Physics, 2001. A collection of Flamsteed's letters from the last sixteen years of his life, much of which elucidates the astronomy wars from his unique perspective.

Ronan, Colin A. *Edmond Halley: Genius in Eclipse*. Garden City, N.Y.: Doubleday, 1969. A sympathetic and insightful biography of Halley.

SEE ALSO: 1704: Newton Publishes *Optics*; 1705: Halley Predicts the Return of a Comet; 1725: Flamsteed's Star Catalog Marks the Transition to Modern Astronomy; 1729: Gray Discovers Principles of Electric Conductivity; 1787: Herschel Begins Building His Reflecting Telescope; 1796: Laplace Articulates His Nebular Hypothesis.

RELATED ARTICLES in *Great Lives from History: The Eighteenth Century, 1701-1800*: Queen Anne; Caroline Lucretia Herschel; William Herschel.

1704-1757
JAVANESE WARS OF SUCCESSION

After decades of growing Dutch influence in Java, uncertainty as to the rightful succession to the dynastic throne of Mataram resulted in a series of wars for the crown. These wars provided the Dutch East India Company with an opportunity, and it seized control of Java.

LOCALE: Java (now in Indonesia)

CATEGORIES: Wars, uprisings, and civil unrest; expansion and land acquisition; government and politics

KEY FIGURES

Amangkurat III (Sunan Mas; fl. 1703-1708), king of Mataram, r. 1703-1708

Surapati (d. 1706), Balinese former slave and ruler of Surabaya

Pangéran Puger (Pakubuwona I; 1648-1719), uncle of Amangkurat III and king of Mataram as Pakubuwono I, r. 1705-1719

Joan van Hoorn (1653-1711), governor general of the Dutch East Indies, 1704-1709

Amangkurat IV (1680-1726), king of Mataram, r. 1719-1726

Pakubuwono II (1711-1749), king of Mataram, r. 1726-1749

Pakubuwono III (1732-1788), king of Mataram, r. 1749-1788

Mangkubumi (1717-1792), sultan of Jogjakarta as Hamengkubuwono I, r. 1755-1792

Gustaaf Willem van Imhoff (1705-1750), governor general of Batavia, 1743-1750

Jacob Mossel (1704-1761), governor general of Batavia, 1750-1761

SUMMARY OF EVENT

In 1595, the first expedition of the Dutch Republic sailed around the Cape of Good Hope to Indonesia, then known as the East Indies, in order to gain some control of the trade in the region; they were after spices as well as gems and gold. When the Dutch arrived in mid-1596, their superior military capabilities inevitably interfered with the desire of the East Javanese state of Mataram to unify the islands of the archipelago. The Dutch East India Company (Verenigde Oostinidische Compagnie), formed in 1602, established the colony of Batavia (approximately coextensive with present-day Jakarta) in north-central Java. By 1619, it was the main Dutch outpost in the region. The company then sought to extend its supremacy over the islands by concluding agreements with various local leaders so that it could build factories. By 1678, Amangkurat II of Mataram, worried over the questionable loyalty of his vassal states, decided to make peace with the Dutch by ceding several territories to them. Thereafter, the Dutch continued a divide-and-rule policy.

Meanwhile, Surapati, a Balinese man whom the Dutch had enslaved to work at Batavia, had earlier escaped from Batavia, formed a band of Balinese renegades, and terrorized a part of the countryside that Amangkurat II had ceded to the Dutch. He finally formed a kingdom in territories claimed by Mataram. Surapati thus posed a threat to the Dutch, but they had other priorities and left him alone at first.

In 1703, Amangkurat II of Mataram died. He was succeeded by his son, Amangkurat III, known to the Dutch as Sunan Mas. The new ruler was determined to drive out the Dutch, so he formed an alliance with Surapati. Sunan Mas also quarreled with his uncle Pangéran Puger, who in turn fled to the north-central enclave of Semarang near Batavia and sought Dutch protection.

In 1704, Joan van Hoorn became governor general of the Dutch East Indies. On learning that Sunan Mas had allied with Surapati against the Dutch East India Company and that several Mataram chieftains favored Puger in the ongoing civil war, van Hoorn supplied a Dutch force to assist Puger, whom he recognized as the rightful ruler of Mataram, thereby beginning the First Javanese War of Succession. The Dutch were victorious, and in 1705, Puger was installed as Pakubuwono I of Mataram. Amangkurat III, still claiming the rightful kingship, was driven out of Mataram to the court of Surapati in Surabaya, at the eastern end of Java.

The Dutch exacted a price for supporting Pakubuwono I over Amangkurat III, however. In addition to requiring him to cede much of Mataram's domain, they forced Pakubuwono to sign a treaty (1705) granting the Dutch a monopoly on all trade involving Mataram and to accept a Dutch garrison in the Mataram capital of Kartasura, south of Batavia. In 1706, the Dutch decided to eliminate both Amangkurat and Surapati. They attacked Surabaya, killing Surapati, and in 1707 they routed the forces of Surapati's sons and Amangkurat; the latter was sent into exile in Ceylon the following year.

The Dutch were nearly supreme on Java by 1719, when they eliminated most of Surapati's partisans after a five-year struggle. However, Pakubuwono I died in that year, sparking the Second Javanese War of Succession. The Dutch named Pakubuwono's son king as Amangkurat IV, whereupon his brothers rose in revolt. After four years of conflict, the Dutch were able to eliminate the rebellion. The rebel leaders were sent into exile in 1723, some to Ceylon and the rest to the Dutch colony at the Cape of Good Hope. By this time, the Dutch had gained military control of most of Java, though they permitted local rulers to maintain traditional courts and the appearance of sovereignty.

In 1726, Amangkurat IV died, and Pakubuwono II acceded to the throne. He ruled peacefully for the better part of two decades, but in 1743, anti-Dutch factions within Mataram rebelled against him. The Dutch came to Pakubuwono II's defense, however, putting down the rebellion and forcing the king to sign a treaty that ceded to them the rest of Java, as well as the island of Madura. Their hold on the region was more secure than ever.

In 1749, the Third Javanese War of Succession began when Pakubuwono II agreed on his deathbed to cede his kingdom to the Dutch. His successor, Pakubuwono III, was then crowned by Dutch governor general Gustaaf Willem van Imhoff. The Mataram chiefs, infuriated that the Dutch claimed the power to crown their ruler, decided to support a rebellion to install the new king's brother, Mangkubumi, in his place. At the same time, a rebellion also broke out in Bantam, on the western end of Java. With Dutch forces thus divided by the simultaneous uprisings, Mangkubumi was able to advance until his nephew Mas Said made a bid to take over leadership.

In 1755, Dutch governor general Jacob Mossel signed a treaty accepting Pakubuwono III as the ruler of Surakarta, on the eastern part of Mataram, and conceding Jogjakarta on the west to Mangkubumi, who was given the title of Sultan Hamengkubuwono I. The Dutch were then free to concentrate their forces on Mas Said, who surrendered in the Treaty of Salatiga (1757); under its terms, Mas Said accepted the dominance of the Dutch East India Company in exchange for agreeing to be its vassal in control of a small part of Mataram, later known as the Mangku-Negorose Territory.

Officially, the Treaty of Salatiga marked the end of the Javanese Wars of Succession. A vestige of resistance to Dutch control of Java, nevertheless, remained. Balinese supporters of Surapati still controlled the easternmost part of the island until 1772, when the Dutch finally subdued them. Resistance to the Dutch was over, at least for a while.

SIGNIFICANCE

Although the Dutch were initially interested only in commercial wealth on Java and elsewhere in the Indonesian archipelago, they needed a friendly relationship with the local population to operate efficiently. By supporting one ruler over another in the first of three civil wars, they were able to make the victor dependent upon them militarily. Resistance continued in two later wars of succession, but the Dutch wiped out all opposition and thus assured themselves firm and stable control over the resources of Java. Soon, they controlled the rest of the archipelago. One benefit of establishing peaceful relations with their vassal sultans was that they began to cultivate coffee and sugar and to build roads to carry the cash crops to port.

Throughout the first half of the eighteenth century, the Dutch East India Company was able to dominate Java by force, but these military actions proved costly, and the company ended up operating at a net loss as a result. Its financial losses only grew worse as it increasingly competed with English and French colonies in the region. Holland was thus forced to subsidize the company, and in 1799 the Dutch East India Company's charter was allowed to expire, leaving the government in Holland in charge of Java and the rest of the Dutch East Indies as a colonial possession. Holland's role in the wars of succession had left the Javanese with a bitter hatred of the Dutch, however, and this hatred later spurred bloody anticolonial rebellions. Indonesia finally gained its independence in 1949.

—Michael Haas

FURTHER READING

Cribb, Robert. *Historical Atlas of Indonesia*. London: Curzon Press, 1997. More than three hundred full-color maps with detailed accompanying text.

Hall, D. G. E. *A History of South-East Asia*. 4th ed. New York: St. Martin's Press, 1981. The most comprehensive and detailed political history of Southeast Asia, covering the earliest migrations and states up to the 1950's.

Indonesian Traditional Polities. http://rulers.org/indotrad .html. Accessed October 12, 2005. Useful annotated tables of the rulers of all the various states and domains within what is now Indonesia.

Ricklefs, M. C. *A History of Modern Indonesia Since c. 1200*. Stanford, Calif.: Stanford University Press, 2001. Draws on sources in both Indonesian and Western languages.

Taylor, Jean Gelman. *Indonesia: Peoples and Histories*. New Haven, Conn.: Yale University Press, 2003. An updated history of Indonesia, offering a historical overview from the prehistoric period to the early twenty-first century.

SEE ALSO: Jan. 24, 1744-Aug. 31, 1829: Dagohoy Rebellion in the Philippines; 1752-1760: Alaungpaya Unites Burma; Sept., 1769-1778: Siamese-Vietnamese War; 1771-1802: Vietnamese Civil Wars.

RELATED ARTICLES in *Great Lives from History: The Eighteenth Century, 1701-1800*: Sir Joseph Banks; William Bligh.

August 13, 1704
BATTLE OF BLENHEIM

The Battle of Blenheim marked the greatest military triumph in the War of the Spanish Succession and the first English victory on the Continent since the Battle of Agincourt in 1315.

LOCALE: Blenheim, Bavaria (now in Germany)
CATEGORY: Wars, uprisings, and civil unrest

KEY FIGURES
First Duke of Marlborough (John Churchill; 1650-1772), commander in chief of the Grand Alliance army
Sarah Churchill (1660-1744), Marlborough's wife and the favorite of Queen Anne
Eugene of Savoy (François-Eugène de Savoie-Carignan; 1663-1736), general of the imperial forces and co-commander of the Grand Alliance army
Maximilian II Emanuel (1662-1726), elector of Bavaria, r. 1679-1726, and commander of the left flank of the Grand Alliance army
Duc de Villars (Claude-Louis-Hector de Villars; 1653-1734), French general
Comte de Tallard (Camille de Tallard; 1652-1728), marshal of France
Ferdinand de Marsin (1656-1706), marshal of France

SUMMARY OF EVENT
When Charles II of Spain died in 1700, the struggle for his throne precipitated the War of the Spanish Succession. Louis XIV of France wanted to place his grandson Philip of Anjou on the throne as part of a larger plan to place members of his family on every throne in Europe.

The obstacle thwarting Louis was the Grand Alliance of Austria, England, and the Netherlands. It had to be destroyed if he were to realize his ambition. The overwhelming strength of the combined Dutch and English fleets blocked France's power at sea. On land, however, Louis held the potential key to power—the French army. The best in Europe, it had never suffered defeat since Louis became king. Louis's goal of French hegemony depended upon the defeat of the Grand Alliance, and, he reasoned, a decisive blow against Vienna would destroy the Grand Alliance and leave Louis free to work his will in Europe.

Louis settled one army on the border of the Netherlands under the duc de Villars. The task of Villars's army was to hold at bay the Grand Alliance army, under the command of the first duke of Marlborough, while the main French force under the comte de Tallard and Ferdinand de Marsin attacked Vienna. When his capital of Vienna was attacked, the Holy Roman Emperor, Leopold I, fled to avoid capture. Prince Eugene of Savoy was hastily recalled from Italy to intercept the French armies, now strengthened by the Bavarian forces commanded by Maximilian II Emanuel, elector of Bavaria. Eugene's battle-hardened soldiers under his disciplined leadership rushed north to block the route to Vienna.

Among all the Dutch and English commanders, only Marlborough, captain-general of the armies, correctly assessed the true danger. Diplomats of both nations were shocked when Marlborough, who had been in secret contact with Eugene, left the Low Countries and marched his entire army south to join Eugene in defense of Vienna. It was a bold maneuver and daring strategy in an age in which warfare had settled into a pattern of sieges and indecisive field encounters. Marlborough's genius for war, however, matched his skill at diplomatic intrigue, a skill for which he was already famous and would be again. As Will and Ariel Durant wrote in *The Age of Louis XIV* (1992), "He was sometimes merciless and often unscrupulous," but he was "the organizer of victory."

Marlborough's march south to join Eugene was a masterful display of organized mobility. Nothing was left to chance. For six weeks, the army moved ten miles per day. Once in Bavaria, Marlborough destroyed everything of military value, and after a series of indecisive engagements, he joined forces with Eugene. The two captains, "one soul in two bodies," prepared to fight a decisive battle with the French.

Meanwhile, Tallard, Marsin, and Maximilian of Bavaria were encamped at the convergence of the Nebel and Danube Rivers. They were surprised on August 13, 1704, when they discovered the Grand Alliance army deployed before them, ready to attack. Eugene of Savoy swung into the line before the French left flank, confronting Marsin and Maximilian. Marlborough faced Tallard where the rivers joined at Blenheim.

The allies attacked vigorously and were repelled fiercely. Two more attacks were equally unsuccessful, and the battle remained undecided until late afternoon, when both armies were close to moral and physical exhaustion. All day, Marlborough had watched a flaw develop in the French center, as the line was continually depleted to send troops to defend both hard-pressed flanks. At precisely the right moment, he slashed into the weak French center with a combined infantry and cavalry assault. Tallard's cavalry broke before the charge.

Nine battalions of French recruits died where they stood, as Marlborough's cavalry rode over them and his infantry killed the survivors. His troops hardly slowed down as they began a wheeling movement to the right. Thirty French squadrons were forced into the Danube River by this maneuver. Many drowned. Tallard was captured, and the remainder of his infantry was forced to crowd into Blenheim, where it suffered heavy losses before surrendering.

Meanwhile, Eugene held Marsin and Maximilian of Bavaria in evenly matched combat all day until Tallard's army was destroyed. When Tallard's defeat exposed Marsin's flank, Marsin withdrew along with Maximilian. The battle ended shortly after 8:00 P.M.

Losses were heavy. The allies lost seven thousand men, and another seven thousand were wounded, out of approximately fifty-two thousand troops committed to the action. King Louis XIV's army of some fifty-six thousand troops lost twenty-one thousand and also had seven thousand wounded. Fourteen thousand French troops were taken prisoner.

The battle was decisive. For the English, Blenheim was their greatest victory since Agincourt, and Marlborough was its genius. The battle demonstrated the superi-

The duke of Marlborough leads his troops during the Battle of Blenheim. (Francis R. Niglutsch)

ority of concentrating power in active combat rather than engaging in extensive sieges, as offensive action won the day over defensive tactics. For the French, the defeat spelled the end of their prestige in arms, but it did not end the war. Neither side immediately realized the decisiveness of this event, and the war continued for another two years as a result.

SIGNIFICANCE

In the Battle of Blenheim, the threat to Vienna was blunted. French hegemony in the south ended, the Holy Roman Empire remained in the war, and the Grand Alliance endured. The whole course of the war was altered: Louis XIV was forced to abandon his grand plan to control Europe. From that time until the end of the war, France was on the defensive. Bavaria ceased to be of any assistance to France and came under the administrative control of Austria. Marlborough was richly rewarded. Queen Anne, who had already raised him to a duke in 1702, gave him the manor of Woodstock in Oxfordshire and had the lavish and extremely expensive Blenheim Palace built for him on the land there. Also in commemoration of the Battle of Blenheim, Joseph Addison, a foremost British poet, wrote a poem in 1704 entitled "The Campaign."

Blenheim has endured as one of the most decisive battles of all time. Marlborough had turned the tide of the war. All England supported the war and took Marlborough to its heart. He was at the height of his power and in complete control of military policy, but intrigue at home—he was forced to align himself with the Whig Party—and subsequent military reverses in France depleted his political strength. Nevertheless, Marlborough and Eugene were again able to recover the initiative for the allies with a victory at Oudenarde on July 12, 1708. They crowned this success with the most complicated military action of the century by going on to relieve Bruges and Ghent the following January.

The allied victory was then complete. French power was broken on land and sea, but in England the Whig Party was victorious over the Tories and Queen Anne. Treaty still eluded Europe, and Eugene and Marlborough attacked France at Malplaquet on September 11, 1709. This final carnage was the bloodiest the antagonists had fought and was a costly monument to the failure of either side to negotiate for peace.

Marlborough led the armies of the Grand Alliance for ten years and never suffered defeat. In 1711, Parliament did what no enemy could: It dismissed and censured him. When Sarah Churchill, Marlborough's influential wife and favorite of Queen Anne, fell from royal favor, the

Tories pressed for his downfall. He no longer controlled military policy and left England for the Continent in 1712. Parliament then withdrew the English army from combat. The French undid all Marlborough had accomplished by defeating Eugene's weakened army and in the end emerged victorious. The Grand Alliance was shattered, and each state made peace as best it could in the Treaty of Utrecht (1713). Marlborough returned to his former office in 1714 upon the death of Queen Anne.

—*Paul A. Whelan, updated by M. Casey Diana*

FURTHER READING

Chandler, David G, with Christopher L. Scott. *Blenheim Preparation: The English Army on the March to the Danube—Collected Essays.* Edited by James Falkner, foreword by the duke of Marlborough. Staplehurst, England: Spellmount, 2004. Chandler's essays provide an overview of Marlborough's military and diplomatic career, describing his role in numerous battles before, and including, the Battle of Blenheim.

Churchill, Winston S. *Marlborough: His Life and Times.* 6 vols. New York: Charles Scribner's Sons, 1933-1938. Marlborough's famous descendant provides detailed coverage of the Battle of Blenheim.

Deane, John Marshall. *A Journal of Marlborough's Campaigns During the War of the Spanish Succession, 1704-1711.* London: Society for Army Historical Research, 1984. Contains maps, including a large folded map, and illustrations.

Dickinson, W. Calvin. *The War of the Spanish Succession, 1702-1713: A Selected Bibliography.* Westport, Conn.: Greenwood Press, 1996. Contains listing of bibliographic sources on the Battle of Blenheim.

Durant, Will, and Ariel Durant. *The Age of Louis XIV.* Vol. 8 in *The Story of Civilization.* Reprint. New York: MJF Books, 1992. One of the true classic histories. Examines the art, politics, literature, military campaigns, and culture of the period from 1648 to 1715.

Falkner, James. *Blenheim, 1704: Marlborough's Greatest Victory.* Barnsley, South Yorkshire, England: Pen & Sword Military, 2004. A miliary guidebook, providing a detailed description of the course of the battle and the battlefield. Includes maps.

Frey, Linda, and Marsha Frey, eds. *The Treaties of the War of the Spanish Succession: An Historical and Critical Dictionary.* Westport, Conn.: Greenwood Press, 1995. Comprehensive dictionary of critical documents regarding the War of the Spanish Succession, 1701-1714, including the Battle of Blenheim. Contains a comprehensive bibliography.

Marlborough, John Churchill, duke of. *The Letters and Dispatches of John Churchill, First Duke of Marlborough, from 1702-1712.* Edited by Sir George Murray. New York: Greenwood Press, 1968. Part of the series of West Point Military Library. Covers the War of the Spanish Succession, including the Battle of Blenheim.

Thomson, George Malcolm. *The First Churchill: The Life of John, First Duke of Marlborough.* New York: William Morrow, 1980. A richly illustrated account of the Battle of Blenheim.

SEE ALSO: May 26, 1701-Sept. 7, 1714: War of the Spanish Succession; May 15, 1702-Apr. 11, 1713: Queen Anne's War; Mar. 23-26, 1708: Defeat of the "Old Pretender"; Sept. 11, 1709: Battle of Malplaquet; Apr. 11, 1713: Treaty of Utrecht; Mar. 7, 1714, and Sept. 7, 1714: Treaties of Rastatt and Baden.

RELATED ARTICLES in *Great Lives from History: The Eighteenth Century, 1701-1800*: Joseph Addison; Queen Anne; Charles VI; Sarah Churchill; Eugene of Savoy; First Duke of Marlborough.

1705
HALLEY PREDICTS THE RETURN OF A COMET

Halley's successful prediction of the return of the comet named for him was a stunning confirmation of the correctness of Newton's law of gravity and laws of motion. Halley's prediction also established that the comet Halley orbits the Sun, and that it therefore does not travel within interstellar space and pass close to the Sun only once.

LOCALE: Oxford and London, England

CATEGORIES: Astronomy; science and technology; mathematics; physics

KEY FIGURES

Edmond Halley (1656-1742), an English astronomer

Sir Isaac Newton (1642-1727), an English physicist and mathematician

Sir Christopher Wren (1632-1723), an English architect and astronomer

Robert Hooke (1635-1703), an English experimental physicist

Johann Georg Palitzsch (1723-1788), a German astronomer

SUMMARY OF EVENT

In January, 1684, three members of the Royal Society of London met in a coffeehouse to discuss what planetary orbits would be like if the attractive force of the Sun became weaker as the reciprocal of the square of a planet's distance from the Sun. Robert Hooke claimed that he had already worked out that the orbits would be ellipses, but he offered no proof. He claimed that he would give his proof after others worked at the problem, but he, too, found the problem extremely difficult. Sir Christopher Wren must have had his doubts, because he then offered a reward of any book costing up to forty shillings to anyone

who could come up with a proof within two months. No one did. The third member of the coffeehouse discussion was Edmond Halley, one of the great scientists of his day.

In August, Halley visited Sir Isaac Newton at Cambridge University to put to him the question about orbits. Newton immediately replied that the orbits would be ellipses; he had worked out the problem years before. Although Newton could not find his notes, he promised Halley that he would again work out the proof. When he received Newton's proof, Halley was so impressed that he urged Newton to expand his ideas into a book.

With Halley's frequent encouragement, Newton produced one of the greatest scientific books of all time, *Philosophiae naturalis principia mathematica* (1687; *The Mathematical Principles of Natural Philosophy,* 1729; best known as the *Principia,* 1848). Halley corrected and edited the *Principia,* and then paid for its printing. The masterpiece contained Newton's law of gravitation and his three laws of motion. The book was the key to understanding not only the great motions of planets in the heavens but also earthly and mundane things such as the falling of apples.

Book 3 of the *Principia* included Newton's collected observations of Halley's comet of 1680, along with a discussion that the comet might be in a parabolic orbit about the Sun. As book 3 neared publication, Hooke demanded that it include a preface acknowledging him as the first to formulate the law of gravitation. Hooke was one of several who had suggested that gravity becomes weaker with the reciprocal of the square of distance from the Sun, but he did not do anything with this idea. Newton was incensed and vowed to withhold publication of book 3, but by using great diplomacy, Halley persuaded Newton to proceed with publication.

HALLEY'S MANY ACCOMPLISHMENTS

By 1684, the young Edmond Halley had already made a name for himself as a precocious astronomer: He was the first to observe that the Sun rotated on an axis, during a trip to St. Helena in the South Seas. In 1680, on his Grand Tour of Italy and France, he had observed the comet that would bear his name. He had produced star catalogs and tidal tables, and he was trying to determine why Kepler's laws worked the way they did. Then, in April, his father's disfigured corpse was discovered near a riverbank; he had been missing for more than a month. Edmond's attention was redirected toward a bitter battle with his stepmother over the family estate. Four months later, Halley made the visit to Sir Isaac Newton that led to the writing of Newton's *Principia*, published in 1687 at Halley's expense.

In the meantime, Halley was supporting himself as a clerk at the Royal Society and working on a diverse array of projects, from determining the causes of the biblical Flood (which he unorthodoxly and dangerously placed earlier than the accepted date of 4004 B.C.E.) to making the connection between barometric pressure and altitude above sea level. He even calculated the height of the atmosphere, placing it with remarkable accuracy at forty-five miles. Motivated by his persistent lack of money, Halley also designed various nautical instruments: a prototype diving bell, a device for measuring the path of a ship, and another device for measuring the rate of evaporation of seawater. He even prepared life-expectancy tables that became the basis for modern life insurance. Between 1696 and 1698, he became the deputy comptroller of the Royal Mint at Chester, a post offered him by Newton, who was then the warden of the Mint. Administration did not prove to be one of Halley's many talents, however, and Newton found himself having to defend his friend against the Lord's Commissioners.

In 1698, Halley set out on another expedition to the South Seas to study the magnetic variations of the Earth's compass. The journey was abandoned (with the ship's first lieutenant facing a court-martial on their return), but Halley tried again a year later with more success. He also went on a secret mission in 1701, about which little is known, traveling to France for the Admiralty on the pretext of yet another scientific expedition. In 1703, Halley became a member of the Council of the Royal Society in recognition of his work, and in the same year, he was appointed to the Savilian chair of geometry at Oxford, where he conducted his study of comets.

years passed with little progress, and Newton became quite abusive toward Flamsteed. Finally, at Newton's request, Halley prepared Flamsteed's catalog for publication and had an incomplete version published in 1712 as *Historia coelestis Britannica* (complete version, in three volumes, published in 1725; partial English translation, 1982). The catalog extended the map of the northern skies from one thousand to three thousand stars. Astronomers were delighted with the work, but even though Halley had kept Flamsteed thoroughly informed and praised his work, Flamsteed was so enraged at Newton and Halley that he publicly burned all of the copies he could get his hands on. As a final twist in the affair, upon Flamsteed's death in 1719, Halley was appointed his successor as astronomer royal.

About 1695, Halley began to collect detailed information on comets, both ancient and modern. While many reports were too vague to be of great use, others linked a comet's position in a constellation with a time. Using a method outlined in the *Principia*, in which the five parameters defining an orbit could be deduced from three well-spaced observations, and after what he called "an immense labor," Halley published a list of orbital elements for twenty-four comets in 1705. It was published in Latin by Oxford University and again in the Royal Society's *Philosophical Transactions*, and published in English as *A Synopsis of the Astronomy of Comets*, also in 1705. The synopsis included bright comets sighted from 1337 to 1683. Halley pointed out that the orbits of the comets of August of 1531, October of 1607, and September of 1682 were so similar that these orbits were probably made by the same comet. Many had supposed that comets traveled in straight lines or in parabolic orbits (a parabola is a curve that does not cross itself). In either of those cases, a comet would pass close to the Sun once only and then vanish into interstellar space. According to Halley's calculations, some comet orbits were highly elongated ellipses, which meant that the

Halley's diplomacy would be required again during a conflict between Newton and another scientist, John Flamsteed, who made it his life's work to produce a new map of the starry heavens. Appointed astronomer royal in 1675, he was expected to share his findings. However, he always insisted that his measurements needed to be further refined; also, he had published little. Newton became president of the Royal Society in 1703. As such, he visited Flamsteed, who promised that his work would soon be ready, but it was only after several more years that Flamsteed gave a copy of his observations and a draft of his catalog to the Royal Society with the instruction that the catalog was not ready for publication. More

comets orbited the Sun and should again be observable as they continued to return.

Halley calculated that the comet of 1682 should again be visible near the end of 1758, and while Halley did not expect to live long enough to see the 1758 return, he hoped that if it did come back at the predicted time, the world would recall that this had first been predicted by an Englishman. As time passed, Halley tried to calculate the effects of Jupiter on the comet's orbit, and to complicate matters, there was one effect unknown to Halley: The jetting of matter from a comet's nucleus makes precise predictions of comet orbits impossible. (Modern calculations, and the effects of planets, show that the period of return for comet Halley has varied from sixty-eight to seventy-nine years over a period of three millennia.)

After a long and productive life, Halley died in 1742. Sixteen years later, in 1758, there was a flurry of astronomical activity, as astronomers and mathematicians tried to refine calculations for where and when Halley's comet would reappear. It was first seen on Christmas evening by Johann Georg Palitzsch, a young German astronomer. Believing he saw a faint bit of fuzz about where the comet was expected, he set up his telescope and confirmed that it was most likely the comet Halley. The news of Halley's successful prediction spread quickly. Within ten years the 1758 comet was known as Halley's comet (modern convention calls it Comet Halley), the first comet named for a person.

SIGNIFICANCE

Like swords hanging over the land, comets had been commonly taken to be ill omens from the gods. The first scientific explanation for comets was ventured by the great Greek philosopher-scientist Aristotle, who believed that comets were gases in the Earth's upper atmosphere that had caught fire and were therefore luminous. For nearly two millennia there were no known attempts to determine a comet's orbit, for during this time in scientific history, to do so would make no more sense than attempting to find the orbit of a particular cloud in the sky.

When the brilliant comet of 1577 blazed in the night sky for weeks, the renowned Danish astronomer Tycho Brahe carefully compared the background stars he saw near the comet with those stars seen by friends in other countries. The discovery that they were the same stars could only mean that the comet was not in Earth's atmosphere after all but instead was far beyond Earth's moon.

Believing that comets existed among the planets, it made sense for Halley to try to find their orbits, but calculating orbits required Newton's *Principia*. Without

Halley's urging, ongoing encouragement, and diplomacy, the *Principia* likely would not have been written. Once written, it would not have been published without Halley's corrections, editing, and funds. Furthermore, once published, its worldwide acceptance would have been slower without Halley's prediction and its confirmation by the spectacular return of Comet Halley. Halley's prediction (included in the second edition of the *Principia*, in 1713) stands as a remarkable prophecy of an event that would be witnessed fifty years in the future based on the mathematical analysis of a physical model.

—*Charles W. Rogers*

FURTHER READING

Cook, Alan. *Edmond Halley. Charting the Heavens and the Seas*. Oxford, England: Clarendon Press, 1998. A biography of Halley that includes a good description of astronomical instrumentation in the early eighteenth century and reasons for the insistence on accurate measurement.

Sagan, Carl, and Ann Druyan. *Comet*. New York: Random House, 1985. A well-written and extensive description of Halley and his work.

Schaaf, Fred. *Comet of the Century: From Halley to Hale-Bopp*. New York: Copernicus, 1997. Discusses comets in general, and comet Halley in particular. Examines Halley's discoveries and the appearances of Comet Halley beginning in 1404 B.C.E. to the return predicted for 2134 C.E.

Thrower, Norman J. W., ed. *Standing on the Shoulders of Giants: A Longer View of Newton and Halley*. Berkeley: University of California Press, 1990. Eighteen essays commemorate the three-hundredth anniversary of the *Principia* and the 1985-1986 return of comet Halley. Written especially for the serious student who wishes deeper analysis of Halley, Newton, and Comet Halley.

Weissman, Paul. "Cruisin' with Comet Halley." In *Our Worlds: The Magnetism and Thrill of Planetary Exploration*, edited by S. Alan Stern. New York: Cambridge University Press, 1999. A good discussion of Halley's work leading to his prediction of the comet's return. Includes a description of Comet Halley and its orbit.

SEE ALSO: 1704-1712: Astronomy Wars in England; 1714-1762: Quest for Longitude; 1725: Flamsteed's Star Catalog Marks the Transition to Modern Astronomy; 1735: Hadley Describes Atmospheric Circulation.

RELATED ARTICLE in *Great Lives from History: The Eighteenth Century, 1701-1800:* Jean-Sylvain Bailly.

1705-1712
NEWCOMEN DEVELOPS THE STEAM ENGINE

Thomas Newcomen built the first steam engine, providing the power to operate pumps, mostly those needed to remove water from the coal mines that had penetrated ever deeper into the English landscape.

LOCALE: England
CATEGORY: Science and technology

KEY FIGURES
Thomas Newcomen (1663-1729), an English blacksmith and inventor
Robert Hooke (1635-1703), an English scientist
Denis Papin (1647-c. 1712), a French physicist
Thomas Savery (c. 1650-1715), an English engineer
John Smeaton (1724-1792), an English engineer
James Watt (1736-1819), a Scottish engineer

SUMMARY OF EVENT

A precursor of the defining development of the eighteenth century was the emergence of a new source of power, one that was neither human nor animal in origin, nor involving the use of wind or water. Newcomen's steam engine, even though it was enormously costly to operate in terms of the fuel it consumed, did function as designed. It became the power source of choice as the eighteenth century progressed.

During the seventeenth century, individuals, especially in western Europe, had become increasingly observant of nature and how it determined the surrounding environment. People became devoted more and more to nature's study. What came to be called "science," that which embraced the observations of Galileo, Sir Isaac Newton, and others, was proving to have many practical applications for shaping the environment and for ensuring human survival. Scientific study had led to the founding in England of the Royal Society in the 1660's; its members, who classified themselves as scientists, met regularly to discuss the results of their investigations. A leading member of the Royal Society was Robert Hooke, who corresponded with individuals investigating the possibilities of adapting atmospheric power to human endeavors. Atmospheric power—that is, the power of a vacuum—had been conclusively demonstrated in 1654 by Otto von Guericke.

The Royal Society, and particularly Hooke, promoted experiments that used the power of a vacuum created by turning water into steam and then rapidly reducing it again to water in a closed container. A French émigré,

Denis Papin, who was a short-term employee of the society, built a rudimentary device that did just that; but he never developed it further. Yet it was on the basis of Papin's designs that Thomas Savery, who became a member of the Royal Society in 1705, designed his device "for raising water by the impellent force of fire," generally regarded as the first steam engine.

Thomas Newcomen came from the same part of England as Savery, but he lacked Savery's connections to the governing elite. Born at Dartmouth in 1663, and continuing to live there throughout much of his life, Newcomen was an ironmonger, a dealer in products made of iron, and perhaps was also a blacksmith. This familiarity with metal was essential to his work with the steam engine. However, Newcomen was also fundamentally interested in science, for he carried on a correspondence with Hooke of the Royal Society, from whom he may well have learned of the experimental work of Papin.

Newcomen appears to have been working on a steam engine at the same time as Savery, but Savery, more attuned to the corridors of power, secured a patent on his device in 1698, and its broad description gave him an effective monopoly over the steam engine and its development until the patent expired in 1733. When Newcomen learned of the Savery patent, he realized that his machine was, in fact, covered by the Savery patent, and he therefore established a cooperative arrangement with Savery, so that the Newcomen engine was treated as a modification of Savery's, although in fact it was different in fundamental ways.

Newcomen's machine consisted of a brass cylinder, 21 inches wide and 7 feet, 10 inches long. It was fitted with a brass piston that rode inside the cylinder. There was also a separate boiler, in which water was turned into steam. The steam was then fed into the cylinder, pushing up the piston. This steam was then condensed back into water by cold water being fed into the cylinder. The condensation created a vacuum underneath the piston that pulled it back down in the cylinder. The piston was attached by a chain to a beam that was pulled down by the piston, activating a pump in a separate pipe, pulling up any water around the bottom of the pipe.

This process of feeding steam into the cylinder and then condensing it was repeated ten times a minute. Its effective power was 5.5 horsepower, not much above the force a horse could exert, but its practical advantage was that it could be powered by a coal fire that could be kept

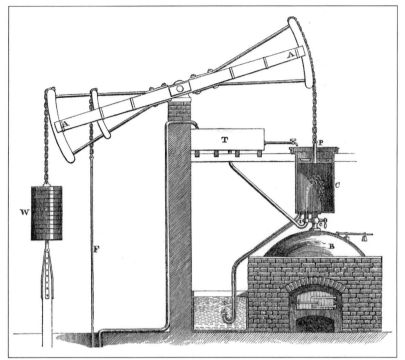

A plan depicting Thomas Newcomen's steam engine. (North Wind Picture Archives)

The first working Newcomen engine was installed in a mine near Dudley Castle in the vicinity of Wolverhampton in 1712. It worked successfully, and much is known about the engine because a drawing was made of it, published in 1719. Although technically covered by Savery's patent, the patent restriction expired in 1733 and numerous Newcomen engines (many with iron rather than brass parts) were installed in the years following. The main problem with the Newcomen engine was its enormous use of coal to fire up the boiler, but since about half the Newcomen engines were installed at coal mines to operate the pumps, this was not really a defect.

It has been estimated that at least one thousand Newcomen engines were built during the eighteenth century; many were built after parts were ordered and a local engineer built the actual pump on site. The design, by John Smeaton, of a more effective water wheel (the breast wheel) increased the power that water wheels could produce and provided some competition for the Newcomen engine, but the Newcomen engine enjoyed the enormous advantage that it could be (and was) installed anywhere, not just where there was a good stream or river.

going all day long and all night, thus easily increasing the amount of water that the attached pump could pull up out of a mine. Over the next fifty years the size of the cylinders and pistons (soon made of cast iron rather than brass) grew until they reached approximately six feet in diameter, which generated substantially more power than Newcomen's original engine. The coincidence of the development of Newcomen's engine with the adaptation of coal to the production of iron was an important synergy that helps explain the rapid spread of the Newcomen engine.

Newcomen's engine differed from Savery's design in two important ways. First, it separated the pumping action from the steam-powered action; second, it pushed the water that condensed the steam directly into the cylinder, instead of spraying the cylinder on the outside. This latter feature enabled the later engines to be substantially enlarged, while still using the vacuum pressure (the "atmospheric" pressure) to be the operative force. This was necessary because the metallurgy of the time was not able to build cylinders and pistons that could withstand pressures higher than the atmospheric pressure. It was only late in the eighteenth century, in the steam engines designed by James Watt, that this restriction was overcome.

SIGNIFICANCE

The significance of Thomas Newcomen's improved steam engine cannot be overemphasized. For the first time, mechanical power in excess of that produced by animals or humans, by wind or water, could be applied to industrial tasks, and it could be done anywhere. Without the development of steam power the Industrial Revolution would have been sharply contained and limited. Also, as the eighteenth century progressed, and new developments took place in metallurgy, far more powerful engines were built, namely the 1769 steam engine of James Watt, engines in which the power of the steam itself was used to activate the machinery. It was Newcomen's engine, however, that underlay the Industrial Revolution.

—*Nancy M. Gordon*

FURTHER READING

Briggs, Asa. *The Power of Steam: An Illustrated History of the World's Steam Age.* Chicago: University of

Chicago Press, 1982. This volume, replete with illustrations of different forms of steam engines, also explains in detail the evolution of the concept of using steam as a source of power.

Cardwell, Donald. *Wheels, Clocks, and Rockets: A History of Technology.* 1995. Rev. ed. New York: W. W. Norton, 2001. Contains an extensive description of the operating principles of Newcomen's engine.

Kanefsky, John, and John Robey. "Steam Engines in Eighteenth Century Britain: A Quantitative Assessment." *Technology and Culture* 21, no. 2 (1980): 161-186. The authors determine the approximate number of Newcomen engines that were built in the eighteenth century.

Mokyr, Joel. *The Lever of Riches: Technological Creativity and Economic Progress.* New York: Oxford University Press, 1990. This work, and others by the same author, an economic historian, assesses the role of Newcomen's engine in the economic progress of the developed world.

Petroski, Henry. "Harnessing Steam." *American Scientist* 84, no. 1 (January/February, 1996): 15. Petroski recounts how the steam engine was invented, including a description of Newcomen's engine and its application in the eighteenth century.

"Puffed Up." *Economist* 353, no. 8151 (December 31, 1999): 99. A history of the steam engine, describing Newcomen's invention and how it was used before it was redesigned by Watt. The article also analyzes the impact of the steam engine on the Industrial Revolution and on the millennium ending in 1999.

Rolt, L. T. C., and J. S. Allen. *The Steam Engine of Thomas Newcomen.* New York: Science History, 1977. The best story of both the life of Newcomen and the particular steam engine he invented. A fine introduction for amateur or engineer. Includes numerous engravings, drawings, charts, and photographs of steam power equipment as well as a list of all the known engines built by Newcomen and later builders before the Savery patent expired in 1733. Good bibliography.

Usher, Abbott Payson. *A History of Mechanical Inventions.* Cambridge, Mass.: Harvard University Press, 1954. Rev. ed. New York: Dover, 1988. Explains in detail the working of Newcomen's engine.

Wilson, C. H. "The Growth of Overseas Commerce and European Manufacture." In *The New Cambridge Modern History*, edited by J. O. Lindsay. Cambridge, England: Cambridge University Press, 1957. Sets the Newcomen engine in context.

SEE ALSO: 1723: Stahl Postulates the Phlogiston Theory; 1765-1769: Watt Develops a More Effective Steam Engine; 1767-1771: Invention of the Water Frame; Oct. 23, 1769: Cugnot Demonstrates His Steam-Powered Road Carriage; 1781-1784: Cavendish Discovers the Composition of Water; Apr., 1785: Cartwright Patents the Steam-Powered Loom.

RELATED ARTICLES in *Great Lives from History: The Eighteenth Century, 1701-1800*: Matthew Boulton; James Brindley; Henry Cavendish; Abraham Darby; John Fitch; William Murdock; Thomas Newcomen; John Roebuck; James Watt; John Wilkinson.

February, 1706-April 28, 1707
ACT OF UNION UNITES ENGLAND AND SCOTLAND

The Act of Union united England and Scotland in the nation of Great Britain, ending centuries of war and animosity between the two countries by forging a single political entity.

LOCALE: Scotland; England

CATEGORIES: Government and politics; laws, acts, and legal history

KEY FIGURES

Queen Anne (1665-1714), queen of England, Scotland, and Ireland, r. 1702-1714

Second Duke of Argyll (John Campbell; 1680-1743), Scottish nobleman and union supporter

Andrew Fletcher of Saltoun (1653?-1716), Scottish politician, writer, and union opponent

Mary II (1662-1694), queen of England, Scotland, and Ireland, r. 1689-1694

William III (1650-1702), king of England, Scotland, and Ireland, r. 1689-1702

Louis XIV (1638-1715), king of France, r. 1643-1715

James II (1633-1701), king of England, Scotland, and Ireland, r. 1685-1688

SUMMARY OF EVENT

The union of the Parliaments between Scotland and England marked the end of Scottish and, what is often not recognized, English national independence and the formal beginning of the state known as Great Britain. More significant was the subsequent evolution of new political and cultural relationships between the two states. On the European stage, the union represented one of the first instances of incorporation of two states into one by means other than conquest, by the consent of both states' representative and legislative bodies.

Since James VI of Scotland had assumed the English throne following the death of Elizabeth I in 1603, the royal crowns of the two countries had been held by one monarch in a regal union. Although James, his successors, and political observers had desired a national union to "complete" the regal union, years of war and misunderstanding prevented it. In 1688, the Roman Catholic king James II of England was forced out by a combined Protestant English and Dutch coup. The Dutch Protestant stadtholder William III of Orange and his wife, Mary, James's daughter, accepted the English parliament's invitation to rule England and Scotland jointly; the Scottish parliament had extended no such invitation.

After 1688, Scottish and English relations grew steadily worse. In the wake of the English Civil War and Oliver Cromwell's Commonwealth, religious differences between Presbyterians and Anglicans endured. Louis XIV of France openly supported James II's claim to the thrones, and James retained much support in Scotland and some in England. William's ongoing war with Louis XIV suffered declining support among the Scots, who rejected the king's policies and feared their effects on Scottish trade. William's complicity in the failure of a Scottish colonial scheme at Darien, Panama, from 1698 to 1700 further divided the English and the Scots.

In 1702, Louis XIV recognized James II's son, James Edward (the "Old Pretender"), as the rightful heir to the British thrones, and war between the countries broke out again. When William died unexpectedly that same year, his childless sister-in-law Anne assumed the crowns. The succession question arose again; by an act of succession, the English parliament would give the crowns next to the head of the House of Hanover in Germany. To the chagrin of the Scots, they were not consulted.

The years 1702 to 1703 provoked a crisis in British-Scottish affairs. Events encouraged the emergence of a body of politicians in the Scottish parliament who sought a new, vital legislative independence from English domination. They were most idealistically led by Andrew Fletcher of Saltoun, a brilliant political theorist who was also a capable legislative tactician and wholly incorruptible. The Scots had one weapon: They would refuse to

fund the war with France until they received political and economic concessions. Anne's supporters in the Scottish parliament could not win control from the various factions united by their disenchantment with the Westminster government. Frustrated with the stalemate, Anne called for negotiations in 1702 toward a union of the two states. Commissioners were chosen, but the negotiations floundered.

Pressing their advantage, the Scottish opposition was able to pass the Act of Security in 1703, which placed political and religious conditions upon Scottish financial support. Soon came an Act Anent (about) Treaty and War, asserting Scotland's right to remain neutral in any English war. New calls for union from Anne and her ministry fell on deaf ears. By February of 1705, the English retaliated against the Scottish act by passing the Alien Act, by which Scots would lose their citizenship in England. Parliament let it be known that the Alien Act would be repealed if the Scots accepted the Hanoverian succession and entered negotiations for a union. Relations were already tense, because Company of Scotland officers in August of 1704 had seized an English ship, the *Worcester*, in retaliation for a similar incident against a Scottish ship by East India Company officials. Trumped-up charges of murder were brought against the captain and three of his crew; despite the outrage of the English, the men were executed.

With the ascent of the young, arrogant, and ambitious second duke of Argyll to the head of the Crown's government in Scotland in 1705, Anne found a Scottish nobleman who could both lead and whip factions into line behind him. For the price of an English peerage and command in the English army, Argyll was willing to build support for a union in the Scottish parliament. Despite Fletcher of Saltoun's outrage, the Scottish parliament was maneuvered into allowing Anne to choose only commissioners who were in favor of a complete union. In November of 1705, the English parliament repealed the Alien Act, and the union seemed more likely than ever.

Beginning in February of 1706, thirty-one commissioners for each state met in London. By April, the fundamental tenets of the treaty of union were fixed. The two kingdoms were to be united as Great Britain with one imperial Crown, parliament, and currency system, and all would accept the Hanoverian succession. An essentially unified fiscal system meant that free trade would easily follow as well. One of the most important settlements concerned the Equivalent, or a tremendous lump sum (£398,085) given to the Scottish government to pay back salaries to public officials, offsetting Scotland's assumption of its share of the much larger English national debt (which was still growing as a result of the war). The Equivalent also compensated shareholders in the Company of Scotland for their losses in Darien.

The critical negotiations were over representation in the new British parliament. Based on taxable income, not population, a compromise was reached: Scotland would have forty-five representatives in the House of Commons and sixteen peers in the House of Lords. Considering the English representation of 513 members, this was not particularly generous. Because Scotland was so clearly the weaker of the two so-called partners, many Scots feared that their representatives would be swallowed up by England. However, steps were taken to prevent this from happening: Wisely, considering the important social and cultural differences between the two countries, a complete unification of private law, the courts, jurisdictions, and the national churches was not attempted. Scottish law and Scottish religion were to remain Scottish rather than becoming British. The final treaty was accepted by both commissions on July 22, 1706. It was then presented to the parliaments of each country.

The Scottish parliament deliberated first. The months preceding had seen supporters and opponents of the union hurl charges and counter-charges in a pamphlet war. Public outcry in Scotland against the treaty was intense; the opening of the Parliament on October 6, 1706, saw throngs of people in miserable weather cheering the opposition and threatening the unionists. Queen Anne's government distributed some £20,000 to Scottish members to help ease their decisions. Although the debates were often intense and the rhetoric frank, the opposition was fragmented, and when it finally came to a vote, the treaty would pass with little trouble. Recognizing this, by late November the Scottish opponents to union had become desperate, and antiunion riots broke out in Glasgow and Dumfries. Even a last-ditch effort by the opposition to rally popular opposition to the treaty failed, and the last article was passed January 16, 1707.

The treaty had next to be passed by the English parliament. Spurred by growing concerns about the war and the succession question, the Parliament moved with unusual dispatch. The treaty quickly passed in both the House of Commons and the House of Lords, and it received royal assent by early March. The Scots ratified the final document on March 19. Following the ratification, on April 28, 1707, the Scottish parliament was dissolved by proclamation.

SIGNIFICANCE

With the formal dissolution of the Scottish parliament in April, Scottish national independence ended. However, perhaps even more remarkable than the nearly unprecedented act of a nation's political representatives dissolving their own state is the extraordinary tenacity displayed in the following decades and centuries of authentic Scottish culture. While Great Britain became a single political entity in 1707, Scottish national identity and distinctiveness have survived, and both peoples have contributed to the history, politics, and culture of Great Britain ever since.

—Michael Kugler

FURTHER READING

Backsheider, Paula R. *Daniel Defoe: His Life*. Baltimore: Johns Hopkins University Press, 1989. The central chapters narrate Defoe's work in Scotland as an agent of Anne's government and as a pamphleteer in support of the union.

Ferguson, William. *Scotland's Relations with England: A Survey to 1707*. Edinburgh: John Donald, 1977. The last half of the work keenly narrates and analyzes the union proceedings; written from a Scottish nationalist point of view.

Levack, Brian P. *The Formation of the British State: England, Scotland, and the Union, 1603-1707*. Oxford, England: Clarendon Press, 1987. Places the union of the parliaments into a larger context of seventeenth century debates over the notion of nationhood and union.

Little, Crawford. *The Union of Crowns: The Forging of Europe's Most Independent State*. Glasgow, Scotland: Neil Wilson, 2003. The book's publisher describes it as "a warts-and-all look at the origins of the Act of Union."

Mitchison, Rosalind. *Lordship to Patronage: Scotland, 1603-1745*. London: Edward Arnold, 1983. A good history of this period, stronger in social history than political.

Rae, T. I., ed. *The Union of 1707: Its Impact on Scotland*. Glasgow, Scotland: Blackie and Son, 1974. A collection of essays by prominent Scottish historians assessing the significance of the union for later Scottish history.

Riley, P. W. J. *The Union of England and Scotland: A Study in Anglo-Scottish Politics of the Eighteenth Century*. Totowa, N.J.: Rowman & Littlefield, 1978. The fullest account of the events and negotiations leading up to the union settlement; a good complement to William Ferguson's work.

Robertson, John ed. *A Union for Empire: Political Thought and the British Union of 1707*. New York: Cambridge University Press, 1995. Collection of essays analyzing the Act of Union, including discussions of the English debate over universal monarchy, the Scottish vision of empire, and the legacy of British union in the North American colonies.

Scott, Paul H. *Andrew Fletcher and the Treaty of Union*. Edinburgh: John Donald, 1992. The most recent biography of the famous opponent of the union, it is also a good history of the union negotiations.

Whatley, Christopher H. *Bought and Sold for English Gold? The Union of 1707*. 2d ed. East Linton, East Lothian, Scotland: Tuckwell Press, 2001. The second edition of this book was published after the Scottish parliament was reestablished in 1999. Whatley views the union from both Scottish and English perspectives, and places the union within a wider European context.

SEE ALSO: May 26, 1701-Sept. 7, 1714: War of the Spanish Succession; Mar. 23-26, 1708: Defeat of the "Old Pretender"; Sept. 6, 1715-Feb. 4, 1716: Jacobite Rising in Scotland; 1721-1742: Development of Great Britain's Office of Prime Minister.

RELATED ARTICLES in *Great Lives from History: The Eighteenth Century, 1701-1800*: Queen Anne; Second Duke of Argyll; Daniel Defoe.

March 23-26, 1708

DEFEAT OF THE "OLD PRETENDER"

James Edward—the "Old Pretender" and son of James II—sailed to Scotland with an invasion force, but the French fleet assisting him was thwarted, and he returned to France, ending his bid to reclaim the English throne for the Stuarts.

LOCALE: Scotland

CATEGORIES: Wars, uprisings, and civil unrest; government and politics

KEY FIGURES

James Edward (James Francis Edward Stuart, the Old Pretender; 1688-1766), son of King James II and pretender to the British throne

Claude de Forbin (1656-1733), French commodore in command of James Edward's invasion fleet

George Byng (1663-1733), British rear admiral and later first Viscount Torrington, 1721-1733

SUMMARY OF EVENT

The short-lived Stuart Dynasty in England began in 1603, when Elizabeth I (1533-1603) died and James VI of Scotland ascended the English throne as James I (1566-1625). His son, the unfortunate Charles I (1600-1649) was beheaded in 1649 during the English Civil Wars (1642-1651), but the dynasty was restored in 1660, when Charles's son, Charles II (1630-1685), became king. Charles II arranged for his brother to succeed him as James II (1633-1701). Unlike his genial father, however, the rigid and Catholic James II oppressed English Protestants. His rule was tolerated so long is it was seen as an isolated event, but when James's son James Edward was born, Parliament feared his eventual succession and the establishment of a Catholic dynasty in England. Unwilling to allow the country to become Catholic again, Parliament arranged for James II's Protestant daughter, Mary, and her husband, William III of Orange, to assume the throne of England in the Glorious Revolution (1688-1689). When William arrived with an invasion force, James II fled London, was captured and released, and went to reside with his whole entourage at Saint-Germain, France, with the benevolent support of his cousin, Louis XIV.

Louis XIV eventually realized that he could make no peace with England and its allies without abandoning his support for the Stuarts' claim to the throne. He pledged his allegiance to Queen Anne, who had succeeded William III in 1702. Realizing their position had changed for the worse, the English court at Saint-Germain, centered around James Edward after his father's death in 1701, began to plan for an invasion of Scotland in 1708.

The French court's view of this desperate strategy is not certain, but they may have hoped for James Edward's eventual success, or they may have thought that a war in Scotland would strengthen their position in a peace settlement by forcing the English to withdraw troops from the Netherlands. Whatever the French position may have been, plans for an invasion began on February 29, 1708, when James sent a messenger to northern Scotland to alert the Jacobites to the invasion. British spies had already calculated that a large uprising in Scotland would supplement an anticipated French force of ten thousand, a large overestimate since Louis had promised but six thousand troops, of whom only a few more than five thousand actually were mustered.

Unfortunately for James, Louis had sent the duke of Berwick campaigning in Spain, thereby depriving James of the man who would have been his wisest counselor. James went ahead with his plan anyway, putting together a French invasion fleet of two transport carriers, five men-of-war, and twenty-one privateers. Twelve thousand arms were collected for the volunteers of the anticipated uprising. James assured the Scots that the Scottish parliament would be responsible for the affairs of the Kirk (church) of Scotland, and he promised back pay to all soldiers who deserted to join him. James's staff went to Dunkirk a week ahead of him, and on March 7, Louis came to Saint-Germain to give James a good-bye present, a beautiful sword with a diamond-studded hilt. That same evening, James left for the coast accompanied by several of his closest advisers—the duke of Perth, Lord Middleton, Dominic Sheldon, Lord Galmoy, Anthony

Hamilton, and Captain Gaydon. They arrived at Dunkirk on March 9.

The weather turned against James at this point. The English admiral John Leake, sailing for Spain, was blown back to Torbay by a powerful storm, and when he was then told to check on events along the French coast, he dropped anchor off Dunkirk with the result that James's ships were blockaded. James got to Dunkirk only to be frustrated by this unexpected development; moreover, he was completely exhausted and feverish, having caught the measles from his sister, Louise Marie. Commodore Claude de Forbin, commander of the French fleet, refused to challenge the harbor blockade, especially when another English squadron under Rear Admiral George Byng arrived off Gravelines. James bickered with Forbin until March 17, when the wind shifted, the English ships were blown back toward Brittany, and the French ships were able to slip away. James was ill and feverish but determined that his convoy should proceed.

Another shift in the wind delayed the French ships for several days, by which time Byng had been ordered to pursue them. In preparation for a major battle, England ordered ten battalions of exhausted troops transferred from Flanders, plus a squadron of horse grenadiers, two regiments of dragoons, several regiments of foot soldiers, and troops from the duke of Northumberland's regiment of horse. James's resources included ten battalions of troops and four hundred noncommissioned officers to lead the reinforcements they anticipated in Scotland.

The original plan was to take Edinburgh in three days, but the delays worked against James again, for when the French fleet finally arrived at the mouth of the Forth on March 23, the Scots had given them up and had left no pilots to guide the French ships. Faced with twenty-eight English ships, Forbin's vessels scattered in disarray, and although an attempt was made to reach Inverness, a strong gale convinced Forbin to head for home despite James's pleas that he be put ashore to act on his own. The only hostile action of the discouraging day was an extended exchange of

JAMES EDWARD'S FAILED INVASION OF SCOTLAND

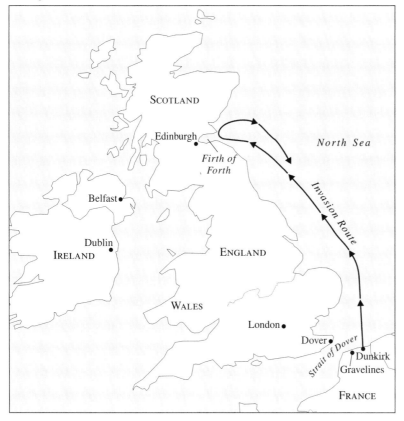

fire between the British ship *August* and Forbin's *Salisbury*, but in the next three days the *Salisbury* was captured and the surviving French ships suffered heavy damage from winds and tide as they fled the English.

SIGNIFICANCE

The humiliating defeat of his attempted invasion before he could even set foot on Scottish soil was a major event in the life of the nineteen-year-old James Edward, but it apparently strengthened his self-control. Had Forbin cooperated and put the pretender ashore, it is just possible that he could have earned the Scots' support, but Forbin was under orders from Louis not to put James's life at risk. The duke of Berwick blamed the fiasco on Louis's incompetent ministers and Forbin's timidity. Berwick agreed that had the French beached in the river, the English would have burned the ships and their supplies, but by then, he believed, the troops would have been ashore and the campaign under way. Berwick thought that James's half sister, Queen Anne, might have reconciled with him out of fear of a devastating civil war.

Brief as it was, James Edward's expedition panicked London's investors, who briefly withdrew their money from the Royal Bank. The main Jacobite leaders were arrested and imprisoned in Edinburgh but eventually released, probably in part because some of the prisoners had Whig friends whom Anne did not want to alienate before the approaching elections. James asked Spain for money to help the Scottish Catholics in the rural areas, as they had suffered the most, and he sent a secret messenger to Scotland with assurances that he could provide arms and ammunition.

James's resolve came to naught, however, when in December, 1715, a Jacobite uprising led by John Erskine, sixth earl of Mar, was foiled in deep snow and confusion. (Byng was instrumental in this defeat of James as well, for which he was created a baronet.) Finally in this uprising, twenty-seven years after the Glorious Revolution, James made it to British soil when one of his officers carried him on his back to the shore of Peterhead harbor, but this minor triumph was not to last, and James was never again to see Scotland after he left in early February, 1716. In 1745, James's son Charles (known as Bonnie Prince Charlie) led a heroic campaign that reached England but was driven back to Culloden, where in April, 1746, it was crushed, and Charles had to run for his life through the Highlands. Culloden proved the Jacobites' last gasp, as England enforced punitive measures that crippled any further aspirations by Scottish Catholics.

—Frank Day

FURTHER READING

Bevan, Bryan. *King James the Third of England: A Study of Kingship in Exile*. London: Robert Hale, 1967. A fluent survey of its topic but sketchy on the events of 1708.

Corp, Edward. *A Court in Exile: The Stuarts in France, 1689-1718*. New York: Cambridge University Press, 2004. A chapter by Edward Gregg, "France, Rome, and the Exiled Stuarts, 1689-1713," provides excellent background on the failed invasion of 1708. The chapters "The Stuarts and the Court of France" and "The Education of James III" are also informative.

Gibson, J. *Playing the Scottish Card: The Franco-Jacobite Invasion of 1708*. Edinburgh: Edinburgh University Press, 1989. The only extended account of the failed invasion.

Haile, Martin. *James Francis Edward, the Old Pretender*. London: J. M. Dent, 1907. Superseded by Miller's book but still useful.

Miller, Peggy. *James*. New York: St. Martin's Press, 1971. Superb account of James's life and aspirations. The place to begin.

Petrie, Sir Charles. *The Jacobite Movement: The First Phase, 1688-1716*. London: Eyre & Spottiswoode, 1948. Broad study by one of the leading authorities on the Jacobites.

SEE ALSO: May 26, 1701-Sept. 7, 1714: War of the Spanish Succession; Aug. 13, 1704: Battle of Blenheim; Sept. 11, 1709: Battle of Malplaquet; Sept. 6, 1715-Feb. 4, 1716: Jacobite Rising in Scotland; Aug. 19, 1745-Sept. 20, 1746: Jacobite Rebellion.

RELATED ARTICLES in *Great Lives from History: The Eighteenth Century, 1701-1800*: Queen Anne; George I; George II; George III.

1709
Darby Invents Coke-Smelting

Abraham Darby developed a coal-based process for smelting iron ore. This process facilitated a major shift in the West from manufacturing predominantly with commonly available organic materials to manufacturing finished products out of mineral components that were themselves industrially produced. Had this shift in the nature of manufacturing not occurred, the Industrial Revolution would never have come about.

Locale: Coalbrookdale, Shropshire, England

Categories: Inventions; manufacturing; science and technology

Key Figures

Abraham Darby (c. 1678-1717), English industrialist and inventor

Abraham Darby II (1711-1763), English industrialist

John Smeaton (1724-1792), English civil engineer and physicist

Abraham Darby III (1750-1789), English industrialist and engineer

John Wilkinson (1728-1808), English inventor and engineer

Summary of Event

The iron industry of the eighteenth century was based largely on methods that dated back to ancient times. Iron ore was first processed, or "smelted," in furnaces heated with charcoal made from wood. The temperature was raised to a high enough level to melt the ore by blowing air on the fire through a bellows. The pig iron thus produced was then mostly reheated to remove any remaining chemical impurities. The resulting bar iron could be worked into useful products such as nails or horseshoes, but it took eight tons of wood to produce two tons of charcoal, which in turn could smelt one ton of pig iron. With the wood supply diminishing in eighteenth century Britain, determining how to smelt with abundant coal rather than wood was increasingly necessary. Abraham Darby discovered how to do it.

Darby was born around 1678, near Dudley in Worcestershire, the son of John Darby and Ann Bayliss, both of them firmly committed Quakers. John Darby may have been a nail maker and locksmith, which activities (as was common in those days) he combined with farming. He apprenticed his son to a maker of malt mills, probably in Bristol.

When Abraham Darby had completed his apprenticeship, he set up in business in Bristol in 1699 as a malt-mill maker. By 1702, however, he had switched to the manufacture of brass castings, in cooperation with several friends. This business was incorporated in 1702 as the Bristol Brass Wire Company. In 1704, Darby journeyed to the Netherlands, reputed at the time to be the most advanced in the manufacture of brass items, and recruited a number of Dutch workmen to return to England with him. With their aid, he experimented with manufacturing in iron rather than brass, making cooking pots using sand molds. While cast-iron pots had been made before, the use of pure sand, without reinforcement with loam or clay, was new, and in 1707 Darby took out a patent on this process. Although it is not now known exactly how he managed to make the "bellied" iron pots for which his firm became famous, modern investigators speculate that he may have reinforced the molds with an outer rim, perhaps one made of wood.

Because pots made of iron were substantially cheaper than those made of brass, Darby rightly surmised that there would be a large market for them. To meet this demand, he needed larger production facilities, and these he found at Coalbrookdale, on the banks of the Severn River, in Shropshire. Mining was not new to Coalbrookdale, but Darby, who leased the property in 1709, had in mind a substantial expansion of the operation there. Luckily for him, Coalbrookdale combined three ingredients that made this expansion possible: readily available fuel in the form of coal, iron deposits near the surface, and a rapidly flowing stream that could supply water power.

Darby proposed to use the local coal, rather than charcoal made from wood, to smelt his iron ore; while previous efforts to do so with coal had been unsuccessful, Darby succeeded by "coking" the coal prior to using it in the smelting furnace. The resulting iron was not degraded by sulfur, as it would have been had raw coal been used, since smelting required loading the ore directly onto the fire. The innovation of converting to coal, of which substantial deposits existed in Britain, from charcoal made from trees in the rapidly disappearing forests of England set England on a new industrial path.

Darby died in 1717, before his operation had realized its full potential, but his widow and some of his Quaker associates carried on, incorporating the operation as the Coalbrookdale Company. In the period after his death, the company expanded, building a second furnace and adding several reverberatory furnaces, in which the pig iron they produced could be remelted and converted into bar iron, whose chemical properties differed from the pig iron produced directly in the smelting furnace. In this way, the company could supply not just the cooking pots that Darby had envisaged but also the specialty iron needed by the Birmingham and Sheffield manufacturers of many products made of malleable bar iron.

In 1730, Abraham Darby II, only six at the time of his father's death, took over operation of the company. He expanded the use of coke in the smelting of iron ore, eventually producing pig iron that had many of the qualities of the bar iron that existing manufacturers of tools and small iron products required. He also expanded the operations of the company by making many of the parts needed for the manufacture of Thomas Newcomen's steam engine, which was spreading rapidly throughout the country.

Darby's son installed the first Newcomen steam engine at the Coalbrookdale works in 1743, using it to pump water back upstream, so the water wheel that operated the bellows could be kept in continuous operation. Increasing the capacity of the bellows allowed the smelting furnace to be operated at a higher heat, leading to a more refined iron. The bellows effect was enhanced by the father of civil engineering, John Smeaton, who devised tubes that increased the airflow. The advantages of these techniques became widely known quite quickly, and they spread rapidly throughout the industry, adding to the market for steam engines and for the cast-iron parts for them made at Coalbrookdale. The production of pig iron increased dramatically in Britain in the second half of the eighteenth century. About half of this pig iron was used for castings, the remainder being further refined into bar iron.

The operations at Coalbrookdale expanded under both Abraham Darby II (who died in 1763) and his son and successor, Abraham Darby III. By the mid-1770's, the furnaces at Coalbrookdale and others owned by the Darbys were generating revenue of some £80,000 per year. The third Abraham Darby was best known, however, for his bridge over the Severn River, the first such bridge made of cast-iron parts and surviving into the twentieth century, though it had to be restricted to a footbridge as bridge traffic grew. It eventually became a museum.

Their Quaker affiliation led the Darbys to become enlightened industrialists, building houses for their workers and refusing to patent some of their innovations so as not to restrict their use. Despite this benevolent administration, however, Coalbrookdale lost the lead in innovation in the late eighteenth century. The casting of cylinders for steam engines was fundamentally altered by the development of reliable boring methods by Isaac Wilkinson and John Wilkinson. They manufactured tightly fitting parts for the steam engines of Matthew Boulton and James Watt, which began to displace Newcomen engines in the last decade of the eighteenth century.

SIGNIFICANCE

The work of the Darbys set the stage for the transformation of Britain, and subsequently the rest of the "developed" world, the world that put machines to work in place of men. The production of better-quality iron started by the Darbys was absolutely essential to the coming of this Industrial Revolution; it made possible the improvements in the steam engine that enabled later models to produce far more power than the earlier ones, which had mostly been used to power pumps. It made possible as well the development of the machine tool industry, which in turn made possible the production of ever more elaborate machines to do the work that once had been done by humans, or by low-power machines activated by wind and water. Without the achievements of the Darbys, much of the rest of the Industrial Revolution would not have been possible.

—*Nancy M. Gordon*

FURTHER READING

Ashton, T. S. *Iron and Steel in the Industrial Revolution.* Manchester, England: Manchester University Press, 1924. An old but still useful account with many details about the Darby operations.

Cardwell, Donald. *Wheels, Clocks, and Rockets: A History of Technology.* New York: W. W. Norton, 2001. Although a survey, contains a short description of the Darbys' achievements.

Fyrth, H. J., and Henry Collins. *The Foundry Workers: A Trade Union History.* Manchester, England: Amalgamated Union of Foundry Workers, 1959. Although primarily a history of the union, contains some introductory material on the Darby family.

Hyde, Charles K. *Technological Change and the British Iron Industry.* Princeton, N.J.: Princeton University Press, 1977. An absolutely essential work for an understanding of the developing iron industry. Hyde makes it clear that innovations were driven by prices.

MacLeod, Christine. *Inventing the Industrial Revolution: The English Patent System, 1660-1800.* New

York: Cambridge University Press, 1988. Although the Darby family used the patent system only once, to patent its technique of casting with sand, the author has some interesting details about the application of the system to the Darby expansion.

Raistrick, Arthur. *Quakers in Science and Industry*. New York: Augustus Kelley, 1968. A reprint of an earlier work, with added information about the Darby family and the influence of their Quaker faith on their actions.

Schubert, H. R. "Extraction and Production of Metals." In *A History of Technology*, edited by Charles Singer, E. J. Holmyard, A. R. Hall, and Trevor I. Williams. Vol. 3. Oxford, England: Oxford University Press, 1957. Describes Darby's achievements in the context of technology through the ages.

SEE ALSO: 1705-1712: Newcomen Develops the Steam Engine; 1722: Réaumur Discovers Carbon's Role in Hardening Steel; 1765-1769: Watt Develops a More Effective Steam Engine; Oct. 23, 1769: Cugnot Demonstrates His Steam-Powered Road Carriage; 1783-1784: Cort Improves Iron Processing; 1790: First Steam Rolling Mill; Dec. 20, 1790: Slater's Spinning Mill.

RELATED ARTICLES in *Great Lives from History: The Eighteenth Century, 1701-1800*: Abraham Darby; Thomas Newcomen; James Watt; John Wilkinson.

c. 1709
INVENTION OF THE PIANO

Bartolomeo Cristofori created the first pianoforte, a keyboard instrument capable of varying note volume and intensity. His invention eventually inspired contemporary instrument makers to adapt and improve his fundamental design, which became the basis for modern pianos. As the instruments became more common, composers began to write music specifically for the piano.

LOCALE: Florence (now in Italy)
CATEGORIES: Music; inventions; science and technology

KEY FIGURES
Bartolomeo Cristofori (1655-1731), Italian instrument maker
Ferdinando de' Medici (1663-1713), grand prince of Tuscany
Cosimo III de' Medici (1642-1723), grand duke of Tuscany
Francesco Scipione Maffei (1675-1755), Italian writer
Pantaleon Hebenstreit (1667-1750), German musician
Lodovico Giustini (1685-1743), Italian composer
Gottfried Silbermann (1683-1753), German instrument maker

SUMMARY OF EVENT
Prior to Bartolomeo Cristofori's invention of the piano, musicians played such predecessors as harpsichords, clavichords, virginals, and spinets. Many musicians considered those instruments unsatisfactory, and they sought keyboard instruments capable of producing stronger and more versatile sounds. During the seventeenth century, instrument makers had improved the technical design of woodwind, brass, and stringed instruments to enhance their capabilities. Thus, at the beginning of the eighteenth century, musicians playing most instruments could produce the sounds and emotional tones they desired, sounds that were compatible with the most popular and valued contemporary musical styles. The keyboard instruments seemed crude and outdated in comparison, and keyboard musicians demanded that artisans make similar improvements to their instruments so that they could play more expressively.

Aware of keyboard instruments' limitations, the mechanically gifted Cristofori contemplated how to achieve richer and more varied sounds. He initially worked as an artisan in his native Padua, where he made harpsichords and spinets, becoming well known in central Italy for his craftsmanship. By 1688, Grand Prince Ferdinando de' Medici, an art patron who enjoyed playing harpsichords, urged Cristofori to move to Florence and create and tune instruments, particularly harpsichords, for the Medici court. The previous court harpsichord maker had died, and de' Medici needed a skilled craftsman to attend to his instruments at his summer home in Pratolino in addition to the Florence court.

The musical resources of Florence enhanced Cristofori's ingenuity. He examined designs in the Medici instrument museum and heard musical performers at court and in the city. Cristofori concentrated on incorporating

Bartolomeo Cristofori perfected his piano with this 1726 model. (The Granger Collection, New York)

hammers in keyboard instruments to manipulate strings and create desired volume variations. Cristofori had access to various craftsmen and apprentices working at the court, learned about mechanisms in a variety of objects such as clocks, and evaluated available materials. He might have heard Pantaleon Hebenstreit play his stringed instrument, the pantaleon, which resembled a dulcimer and used hand-operated hammers to vibrate its strings. In the 1690's, Hebenstreit enjoyed public and royal acclaim throughout Europe, performing in courts and major cities, including Florence. Cristofori probably was aware of enthusiasm for the pantaleon, which inspired many musicians and artisans with ideas regarding the improvement of keyboards.

Wealthy Florentines and members of the artistic community encouraged Cristofori, who was particularly intrigued by timbre and volume and by the ability of hammers to influence those musical characteristics. He

adjusted harpsichord design, seeking ways to allow performers to vary volume, which harpsichords could not do. He considered the aspects of clavichords, mainly hammer construction, that made them expressive, despite producing soft sounds that were often difficult to hear. An inventory of the Medici court's instruments dated 1700 includes a piece called an *arpi cimbalo del piano e forte*, the construction of which court musical director Federigo Meccoli credited to Cristofori. A contemporary description noted that the *arpi cimbalo del piano e forte* resembled a harpsichord but manipulated its strings with wood hammers instead of quills. It also incorporated dampers and two keyboards and produced both soft (*piano*) and loud (*forte*) notes based on players' finger pressure on the keys.

By 1709, Cristofori introduced the instrument known as a *gravicembalo col piano e forte*. He utilized his harpsichord construction experience to create a case shaped like a harpsichord with a similar keyboard and equipment. Cristofori chose larger strings and strung them more tautly than those in a harpsichord. His hammers hit with more force than those in clavichords. Cristofori's early pianofortes, as contemporaries referred to them, incorporated approximately fifty-four keys on a single keyboard. Because it had one keyboard rather than two, the *gravicembalo* is a better candidate for the title of "first piano" than is the *arpi cimbalo*.

Cristofori created a unique action device for his keyboards. Piano keys, serving as levers, activated wooden hammers placed beneath strings. Each key moved a specific hammer that struck a single string or a pair of strings, according to shift controls the player operated, to produce a desired note. The shift mechanism moved the hammer slightly, causing it to hit only one string in order to produce a softer note or to hit two identically tuned strings to produce a louder and fuller note. Cristofori's main concern was ensuring that hammers resumed the ready position immediately after striking their strings, enabling musicians to play the same note several times in rapid succession if they desired. Escapements ensured that hammers rebounded from vibrating strings to avoid interference. Checks stopped hammers from bouncing. Dampers restricted string movement.

The hammers moved more swiftly than fingers could directly manipulate strings. Pianoforte performances required tactile skills. Players could play multiple notes simultaneously, using all ten fingers. Because of Cristofori's action, pianists could alter volume levels produced during performances by changing the pressure their fingers placed on piano keys to affect the amount of force with which hammers hit strings. In contrast, hammerless harpsichord volume remained constant. Cristofori's action thus provided keyboard musicians with a new dimension of performance, dynamics, through which to express their interpretations of music and develop their own styles.

In 1711, author Francesco Scipione Maffei, who traveled from Rome to meet Cristofori, penned an article about Cristofori's piano for the *Giornale dei letterati d'Italia* (journal of Italian letters), which also printed an image of Cristofori's pianoforte action. Maffei wrote that Cristofori had built a total of three pianofortes by 1711, selling two to Florentine musicians and the other to Roman cardinal Pietro Ottoboni. Cristofori had finished a fourth piano when de' Medici died two years later. Cristofori's design spread after Maffei's publication reached central Europe, especially the German states, where it was translated and published in Johann Matthe-

son's *Critica musica* in 1725, influencing instrument makers who later gained access to pianofortes exported from Italy.

After de' Medici died, his father, Cosimo III de' Medici, named Cristofori keeper of that court's instruments. Cristofori pursued pianoforte design enhancements, wrapping wooden hammers with leather to change the instrument's sound, speeding mechanical processes, and improving escapement and check functions. Cristofori crafted his final pianoforte in 1726. His apprentice, Giovanni Ferrini, also made pianofortes. Spanish Queen Maria Barbara de Braganza bought five pianofortes and studied with Domenico Scarlatti, who may have composed pianoforte music. By 1732, Florentine composer Lodovico Giustini created the first music known to have been composed for pianos, twelve sonatas entitled *Sonate da cimbalo di piano, e forte, ditto volgarmente di martelletti* (sonatas for the harpsichord of soft and loud, vulgarly known as the harpsichord of hammer blows). These sonatas included elaborate passages musicians could not play on harpsichords.

SIGNIFICANCE

Instrument makers appropriated the unique pianoforte action technology Cristofori created to build most pianos produced in the second half of the eighteenth century. Cristofori's pianoforte impacted nineteenth century music and instrument manufacturing more than it immediately influenced eighteenth century musicians, however. Some eighteenth century musicians preferred the harpsichord over the piano, because the former was both louder and simpler to play. At the time, many people considered Cristofori's pianoforte action too intricate and costly for them to invest in pianofortes.

Maffei's article expanded knowledge of Cristorfori's pianoforte and was the primary reason most eighteenth century musicians knew about his innovation. Basic information about Cristofori's invention spread throughout Western Europe and Great Britain. By the 1730's, some German instrument makers, particularly Gottfried Silbermann, who built organs for the Saxon court, incorporated aspects of Cristofori's action design in their instruments and even improved upon it. For example, although composer Johann Sebastian Bach disliked Cristofori's pianoforte, he approved and sold Silbermann's adapted design. By 1800, more composers, including Wolfgang Amadeus Mozart and Joseph Haydn, accepted the piano and wrote music specifically for that instrument. Cristofori's action became a fundamental component of all pianos.

As a middle class emerged in Europe, members of the new class bought pianos for their homes. Amateurs played for fun and self-expression. Pianos became a standard instrument for music students and fundamental to most Western musical composition and theory. Surviving Cristofori pianofortes are displayed at New York City's Metropolitan Museum of Art (1720), Rome's Museo Strumenti Musicali (1722), and Leipzig University's Musikinstrumenten-Museum (1726).

—*Elizabeth D. Schafer*

FURTHER READING

Clinkscale, Martha Novak. *Makers of the Piano, 1700-1820.* New York: Oxford University Press, 1993. Provides information about Cristofori and detailed descriptions of the three surviving Cristofori pianos and an action, noting the history of ownership of each instrument, as well as each one's unique technological features.

Crombie, David. *Piano: Evolution, Design, and Performance.* New York: Barnes & Noble Books, 1995. Includes color photographs of three Cristofori pianos and his action, showing how it worked. Illustrations of contemporary keyboard instruments, information about musicians and instrument makers, and chronologies supplement the text.

Good, Edwin M. *Giraffes, Black Dragons, and Other Pianos: A Technological History from Cristofori to the Modern Concert Grand.* 2d ed. Stanford, Calif.: Stanford University Press, 2001. Comprehensive examination of the technical aspects of Cristofori's piano action and the methods other instrument makers used to develop keyboard instruments before and after Cristofori's innovation.

Parakilas, James, ed. *Piano Roles: Three Hundred Years of Life with the Piano.* New Haven, Conn.: Yale University Press, 1999. Anthology includes an essay discussing interactions between Cristofori and Maffei and eighteenth century marketing efforts to publicize the pianoforte.

Pollens, Stewart. *The Early Pianoforte.* New York: Cambridge University Press, 1995. An outstanding history that includes extensive biographical information about Cristofori and how he invented the piano, discussing his musical patrons and peers. Appendices reproduce Maffei's Cristofori interview notes and his pianoforte article translated into several languages.

SEE ALSO: c. 1701-1750: Bach Pioneers Modern Music; Apr. 13, 1742: First Performance of Handel's *Messiah*; Jan., 1762-Nov., 1766: Mozart Tours Europe as a Child Prodigy; 1795-1797: Paganini's Early Violin Performances.

RELATED ARTICLES in *Great Lives from History: The Eighteenth Century, 1701-1800*: Johann Sebastian Bach; George Frideric Handel; Joseph Haydn; Wolfgang Amadeus Mozart; Antonio Stradivari.

1709-1747
PERSIAN-AFGHAN WARS

With the weakening of the Ṣafavid Empire during the seventeenth century, Afghan tribes under Persian occupation grew restive. Through a series of conflicts now known as the Persian-Afghan Wars, they asserted their independence and in 1722 decisively defeated the Persian army in the Battle of Gulnabad before seizing the capital city of Eṣfahān.

LOCALE: Persian Empire (now in Iran and Afghanistan)
CATEGORIES: Wars, uprisings, and civil unrest; government and politics; expansion and land acquisition

KEY FIGURES

Mir Vays Khan Hotaki (d. 1715), Afghan conqueror and founder of the Hotaki Dynasty, r. 1709-1715
Mahmud Ghilzai (d. 1725), Afghan conqueror, r. 1716-1725, and shāh of Persia, r. 1722-1725
Ḥusayn I (1668-1726), shāh of Persia, r. 1694-1722
Aḥmad Shāh Durrānī (1722?-1772), king of Afghanistan and founder of the Durrānī Dynasty, r. 1747-1772
Nādir Shāh (1688-1747), shāh of Persia and founder of the Afsharid Dynasty, r. 1736-1747
Gurgān Khan (fl. early eighteenth century), governor of Qandahār until 1709

SUMMARY OF EVENT

At the beginning of the eighteenth century, the Afghan population was wedged between two empires that had emerged in the early sixteenth century—the Ṣafavid rulers of Persia (1501-1786), and the Mughal rulers of India (1526-1858). The two powers had long fought over the Afghan region of Qandahār, and by the early eighteenth century the weakened state of the Ṣafavid Dynasty encouraged Afghan groups to rebel against their occupation. The Ṣafavid Dynasty's conversion to Shiism and its anti-Sunni policies played a further role in instigating a series of revolts by Afghan tribes in the first half of the century.

Mir Vays Khan Hotaki, a Ghilzai Pashtun and founder of the short-lived Hotaki Dynasty (1709-1738), was the first Afghan leader successfully to rebel against Persian domination. Ghilzai Afghans in Qandahār, who were effectively independent, had been kept in check by constant conflicts with another group of Afghan rebels, the Abdalis of Herat. They were also held at bay for some time by the region's Ṣafavid governor, a capable Georgian general named Gurgān Khan. Mir Vays lived as a hostage at the court of the Ṣafavid ruler in Eṣfahān while Gurgān Khan served as governor of Qandahār.

The situation changed when Mir Vays received permission to go on a pilgrimage to Mecca. There he obtained a legal decision, or fatwa, authorizing revolt against the Ṣafavids' Shia domination of western Afghanistan, which was largely Sunni. Upon his return to Qandahār, he used the fatwa to win the support of tribal chieftains, and in 1709 they staged a revolt against Gurgān Khan's troops.

The rebellion was highly effective, in large part as a result of the Ṣafavid ruler Ḥusayn I's failure to provide Gurgān Khan with adequate support. Mir Vays's revolt laid the basis for the more significant Afghan invasion of Persia a decade later. By 1720, there was political unrest at several points on the periphery of the Ṣafavid Empire, including territories in the Caucasus, Kurdistan, and Khūzestān. While the government in the capital of Eṣfahān fought off a threat from the imam of Oman on the Persian Gulf, and as danger continued to materialize in Afghan regions, the Persian chief minister Fath ʿAli Khan Dagistani and the governor Lutf ʿAli Khan were deposed by a court intrigue.

By this time, Mir Vays's son Mahmud Ghilzai was in command of Qandahār. After an initial attempt in 1719, he set out for Eṣfahān in 1721. Though he failed to take the cities of Kermān and Yazd along the way, he proceeded to march with his troops to the capital city. On March 8, 1722, he confronted the Ṣafavid army at Gulnabad, east of Eṣfahān. The Persian army was equipped with artillery and it largely outnumbered Mahmud's forces; however, it lacked a unified command. Eventually, Mahmud's army forced the Persian army to flee in the direction of Eṣfahān, and after a few days they closed in and besieged the city.

The Siege of Eṣfahān lasted for nearly seven months, causing many of the city's inhabitants to die from starvation or disease. The destruction wreaked upon the city included large-scale looting and the demolition of the state archives in Zayandeh Rud. In October of 1722, Ḥusayn I surrendered and abdicated the throne, declaring Mahmud the shāh of Persia. The Afghans captured a number of Ṣafavid princes during the Siege of Eṣfahān and imprisoned them together with the former shāh, Ḥusayn I. Later, Mahmud executed many of the princes, and in 1726 his successor ordered Ḥusayn's execution.

Though they were able conquerors, the Ghilzais were not able to command an empire. After the fall of the Ṣafavid Dynasty, no one leader or group succeeded in maintaining stability in the land for decades. Soon, a Ṣafavid prince declared himself shāh in the northern region that the Afghans had not been able to occupy. At the same time, Russian forces seized the opportunity to march into the northwest of Persia, while the Ottomans moved in on the west, occupying the region of Hamadān and Kermānshāh.

In 1725, Mahmud Ghilzai was murdered and was succeeded as shāh by his nephew Ashraf. At the time, the primary region of Persia under Afghan rule was centered in Eṣfahān. Ashraf's hold on power was precarious, and he was not able to hold on to the Ghilzai base of Qandahār, where one of Mahmud's sons was able to seize the throne. Ultimately, in 1729 Ashraf was overthrown by Nādir Shāh, and in 1730 he was assassinated. Ashraf would be the last Afghan shāh of Persia.

Upon formally taking the throne in 1736, Nādir Shāh worked to recover territories captured by the Ottomans and Russians before he marched against the Afghans in the northeast. In 1738, he reclaimed Qandahār for the Persian crown and then went on to seize Ghaznī, Kabul, and Peshawar. Nādir attempted to dissociate Twelver Shiism (*Ithnā ʿAsharīyah*) from the Persian national identity, proposing instead to integrate it into Sunni Islam in a form called the Jaʿfari faith. Some scholars have interpreted this move as an attempt to conciliate his army, which was composed largely of Sunni Afghans. The faith never took hold, however, and in the later years of his leadership, Nādir's increasingly oppressive rule began to prompt revolts. Eventually a group of Kizilbash killed him in 1747.

After Nādir Shāh was assassinated in 1747, his army disbanded and the Afghans rose up again in revolt under the leadership of one of Nādir's former Afghan lieutenants, Ahmad Shāh Durrānī. He and his troops left Persia and returned home, taking control of Qandahār and beginning a new campaign to control the territory that is now Afghanistan. Since the Persians failed to mount any significant counterattack to Aḥmad Shāh's rebellion, it marked the end of the Persian-Afghan Wars.

Although the wars with the Persian Empire were essentially over, Afghan military conflicts continued along most of the new kingdom's borders. In the period from 1747 until his death in 1773, Aḥmad Shāh Durrānī defeated the Mughals in the territory west of the Indus River and expelled the Persians from Herāt. By the time of the Afghan king's death, the Durrānī Empire extended from Central Asia to Delhi and from Kashmir to the Arabian Sea.

SIGNIFICANCE

Although Ṣafavid princes lingered on for years in Persia as political pawns, the conquest of Eṣfahān and the abdication of Ḥusayn I signaled the definitive end of the longest dynasty since the rise of Islam. Though the Afghan occupation of Eṣfahān was short-lived, Mir Vays's revolt against Persian occupation was a pivotal event in the history of the Afghan peoples. Thus, although Afghanistan was not officially recognized as a political entity until 1747, when Aḥmad Shāh Durrānī founded the Durrānī Dynasty (1747-1973), Mir Vays is typically credited with the birth of the modern Afghan state.

—*Anna Sloan*

FURTHER READING

Avery, Peter. "Nadir Shah and the Afsharid Legacy." In *From Nadir Shah to the Islamic Republic*, edited by Peter Avery, G. Hambly, and C. Melville. Vol. 7 in *The Cambridge History of Iran*. New York: Cambridge University Press, 1991. The most comprehensive source on political developments in Iran during the fall of the Ṣafavid dynasty and the reign of Nādir Shāh. Contains plates, maps, and genealogical tables.

Daniel, Elton L. *The History of Iran*. Westport, Conn.: Greenwood Press, 2001. A general survey that locates Nādir Shāh's rule in the larger scope of Persia's history. Contains maps, a glossary of terms, and a bibliographical essay.

Dickson, M. B. "The Fall of the Safavi Dynasty." *Journal of the Asiatic and Oriental Society* 82 (1962): 503-517. Comprehensive review article on the decline of the dynasty in the early eighteenth century.

Dupree, Louise. *Afghanistan*. Princeton, N.J.: Princeton University Press, 1980. General survey of the country's history, with a short introduction concerning events of the eighteenth century.

Ewans, Martin. *Afghanistan: A Short History of Its Peoples and Politics*. New York: HarperCollins, 2002. General history with opening chapters on the land's premodern and early modern history.

Lockhart, Laurence. *The Fall of the Safavi Dynasty and the Afghan Occupation of Persia*. Cambridge, England: Cambridge University Press, 1958. The study that laid out the historical framework of the late Ṣafavid period, this source still offers unsurpassed information on the end of Ṣafavid rule and the rise of Nādir Shāh. Contains illustrations, maps, a genealogical table of the Ṣafavid dynasty, and a bibliography listing primary sources, including European travelers' accounts.

_____. *Nadir Shah: A Critical Study Based Mainly upon Contemporary Sources*. London: Luzac, 1938. Bears detailed information on Nādir's relationship with Afghan forces. Contains a genealogical table, maps, and bibliography of primary sources.

Perry, John R. "The Last Safavids, 1722-1793." *Iran* 9 (1971): 59-69. Investigates the political upheaval of the early eighteenth century.

SEE ALSO: 1725-Nov., 1794: Persian Civil Wars.
RELATED ARTICLES in *Great Lives from History: The Eighteenth Century, 1701-1800*: Karīm Khān Zand; Nādir Shāh; Vaḥīd Bihbahānī.

June 27, 1709
BATTLE OF POLTAVA

Peter the Great's reformed and modernized Russian army secured a major victory over the Swedish army led by Charles XII. The victory marked the ascendancy of Russia over Sweden as a European power and secured the newly founded city of St. Petersburg as a potential capital of the Russian Empire.

LOCALE: Poltava, Ukraine, Russia (now in Ukraine)
CATEGORY: Wars, uprisings, and civil unrest

KEY FIGURES
Peter the Great (1672-1725), czar of Russia, r. 1682-1725
Charles XII (1682-1718), king of Sweden, r. 1697-1718
Ivan Stepanovich Mazepa (1639-1709), Cossack leader
Aleksandr Danilovich Menshikov (1673-1729), Russian general

SUMMARY OF EVENT
At the beginning of the eighteenth century, Sweden was a major power in northeastern Europe. Its substantial holdings in Germany were the result of Gustavus II Adolphus's victories in the Thirty Years' War (1618-1648) nearly seven decades before. In addition, Sweden held large tracts of land in eastern Europe, in what would become modern Finland, Estonia, Latvia, Lithuania, Belarus, Ukraine, and Poland.

Furthermore, Sweden was ruled by a warrior monarch. Charles XII was a sternly religious man of spartan tastes who liked nothing better than to be in the field, fighting a battle or preparing for one. After his coronation at the tender age of eighteen in 1700, Charles had left Stockholm for his first military campaign, and he never saw his country's capital again. In personal physical courage he was comparable to the great Gustavus II Adolphus, routinely entering the thick of battle without any regard for his own safety. Since he was not merely a constitutional figurehead but the actual ruler of his country, Charles's physical bravery also meant that every battle placed his country in danger of being suddenly left without a leader. He carried on his nation's civil government, such as it was, from his field headquarters wherever he might currently be campaigning and sent orders by messenger back to Stockholm.

The Great Northern War set Charles on a collision course with one of the true giants of his era, Peter the Great of Russia. Peter was not only physically huge but also possessed of a lively and inquisitive mind that sought to master pursuits far beyond the range considered usual for a reigning monarch. Determined that his nation must overcome its backwardness and imitate the culture of Western Europe or ultimately become overwhelmed by it, Peter had set Russia on a course of modernization that had attracted the wrath of his nation's traditionalists. In 1703, he had founded a new city, St. Petersburg, on land newly captured from the Swedes but not formally ceded to Russia by treaty. This city was to become Peter's window to the West, a means by which to impose upon Russia's leadership those elements of Western culture that he considered most needful.

Charles XII had handily beaten the Russians in one of the first battles of the Great Northern War. While the Swedish king was dealing with Poland-Saxony, however, Peter had used the time to rebuild his army on a modern model and had seized the Swedish territory around the area of Lake Lagoda, where he had begun to build St. Petersburg. Incensed by this affront, Charles marched his army into Russia with the intention of taking Moscow. However, the Russian forces refused to meet him in open combat, instead allowing the vast distances and substantial climatological obstacles of Russia to drain the strength of the Swedish army. At length, Charles decided to head to the warm, fertile lands of the Ukraine, where he had an ally in the Cossack leader Ivan Stepanovich Mazepa, who wanted to establish an independent Cossack state in the Ukraine.

Mazepa was a colorful figure, having studied in the West and traveled as far as the Netherlands while retaining his wild Cossack heritage. However, the story of his having been tarred, feathered, and tied to his horse as punishment for an affair with a noble lady in the court of the Polish king and subsequently found by Cossacks who made him their leader in admiration of his toughness is a fabrication. In fact, he came to the leadership of the Cossacks through a more usual route, having served under the previous leader, or hetman. Although he was elected by an assembly that had just concluded unfavorable terms with Russia, Mazepa hoped to unite all the Ukrainian Cossacks into a state that would combine Western ideas of government with traditional Cossack forms and somehow coexist peaceably with Russia.

Mazepa proved an unreliable ally to Charles, particularly after Peter's trusted military leader, Aleksandr Danilovich Menshikov, destroyed his stronghold of

Baturyn, and the harsh winter nearly broke the strength of the Swedish army. Charles refused to turn back, however, despite the recommendations of his generals after hoped-for aid from Turkey and the Crimean Tatars failed to materialize. Instead, Charles attacked the fortress of Poltava on the Vorskla River in the Ukraine, intending to use it as a jumping-off point for a drive to Moscow via Kharkhov and Kursk. His initial assault failed to attain his objective, so he settled his army in for a long and unpleasant siege.

When Peter got word that Poltava was under siege, he raised a force of more than forty-five thousand Russian troops and mounted a countersiege, surrounding the Swedish forces and trapping them so they would not be able to retreat. During the siege and countersiege, Charles was badly wounded in the foot, which incapacitated him and forced him to leave direct command of his forces to one of his field marshals. Only when the Russians had maneuvered themselves into a favorable position, on June 27, 1709, did Peter finally engage the outnumbered Swedish army in all-out battle.

A minor skirmish before the Battle of Poltava. Only after the Russian forces had maneuvered into a favorable position did the entire army engage in battle. (Francis R. Niglutsch)

Although the battle began with the better-trained Swedes pressing an advantage on the left flank, Peter used his greater weight of numbers to block their advance. Pinning the Swedes with artillery, the Russians were able to hold them until poor communication led to a collapse of the Swedish lines. The Swedes tried to flee to the Dneiper River, but after a stern pursuit from Cossacks loyal to the czar, the Russians caught up with them and forced them to surrender. Those Cossacks found among the Swedish forces were handed over to the Russians, who executed many of them on the spot as traitors to the Crown and exiled the rest to Siberia.

Charles was able to escape with a few thousand men, but he had to take refuge in Ottoman Turkey for two years before he was able to return to Sweden. Peter severely curtailed the traditional autonomy of the Don Cossacks, placing them under military rule and requiring extensive service in return for retaining a small portion of their traditional privileges. The Zaporozhian Sich, one of the oldest Cossack strongholds, was forcibly destroyed. Mazepa was vilified as a traitor, and subsequent Russian propagandists did their best to blacken his reputation, although Ukrainian nationalists stubbornly remembered him as the great patriot who built their culture.

SIGNIFICANCE

Peter the Great's victory over Charles XII marked the end of Sweden's power and the beginning of the ascendancy of Russia. By defeating the Swedish army, Peter secured his hold on the land around St. Petersburg and thus was able to declare it Russia's new capital in 1712. As a result, Peter was able to push his program of Westernization at a greater pace, forcibly removing his court from the traditional Russian environment of Moscow's Kremlin and surrounding its members with Western architecture and other elements of Western culture.

The Battle of Poltava thus secured Russia's place as a modern nation. St. Petersburg remained Russia's westward-looking capital, and in it, later Russian emperors carried on a lively correspondence with Western European monarchs and with the great thinkers of their age, although the vast mass of peasants remained largely untouched by the Petrine reforms and continued in their traditional Russian folkways. By the nineteenth century, Russia had unquestionably become one of the great powers of Europe.

—*Leigh Husband Kimmel*

FURTHER READING

Bushkovitch, Paul. *Peter the Great*. Lanham, Md.: Rowman & Littlefield, 2001. Less a straight biography of Peter than a study of the culture into which he was born and how he transformed it.

Cooper, Leonard. *Many Roads to Moscow: Three Historical Invasions*. New York: Coward-McCann, 1968. The first section deals entirely with Poltava.

Cracraft, James. *The Revolution of Peter the Great*. Cambridge, Mass.: Harvard University Press, 2003. Study of the cultural changes brought about by Peter the Great's "revolution from above."

Englund, Peter. *The Battle That Shook Europe: Poltava and the Birth of the Russian Empire*. New York: I. B.

Tauris, 2002. An in-depth study of the battle and of its consequences.

SEE ALSO: c. 1701-1721: Great Northern War; May 27, 1703: Founding of St. Petersburg; Nov. 20, 1710-July 21, 1718: Ottoman Wars with Russia, Venice, and Austria.

RELATED ARTICLES in *Great Lives from History: The Eighteenth Century, 1701-1800*: Charles XII; Peter the Great.

September 11, 1709
BATTLE OF MALPLAQUET

The bloodiest battle of the War of the Spanish Succession, the Battle of Malplaquet revealed new military tactics and attitudes whose grim toll shocked Europe.

LOCALE: Malplaquet, France
CATEGORY: Wars, uprisings, and civil unrest

KEY FIGURES

Duc de Boufflers (Louis-François de Boufflers; 1644-1711), French general

First Duke of Marlborough (John Churchill; 1650-1722), commander in chief of the English and Dutch armies

Eugene of Savoy (1663-1736), co-commander of the Grand Alliance armies

Duc de Villars (Claude-Louis-Hector de Villars; 1653-1734), French general

SUMMARY OF EVENT

The succession to the throne of Spain in the wake of the childless Charles II's death sparked controversy when none of the claimants to his throne proved acceptable to all of Europe's other great powers. Antagonized by France's growing commercial competition and territorial ambitions, England and Holland opposed the succession of King Louis XIV's eldest son, fearing a united France and Spain would be a dominating world power. On the other hand, England, Holland, and France opposed Archduke Charles of Habsburg (later Holy Roman Emperor Charles VI), who would have reunited his family's Spanish and Austrian branches to form a similarly overwhelming empire encircling France.

By the beginning of the eighteenth century, war had

changed profoundly. Maneuver, fortification, and siege craft gained new importance. Drilled intensely, soldiers were more disciplined than the marauding mercenaries of the Thirty Years' War (1618-1648) a half century earlier. Flintlock muskets tipped with socket bayonets had replaced the obsolete pike. Battalions of six hundred to eight hundred foot soldiers had become the basic units of most armies. The English and Dutch began to use platoon firing, controlled "rolling" volleys along battle lines from right to left. Cavalry was used as shock troops against enemy flanks or disordered infantry. Cumbersome artillery was dragged into battle by civilian teamsters.

In February, 1701, French occupation of fortresses between Holland and the Spanish Netherlands (present-day Belgium) led to an alliance of England, Holland, and the Holy Roman Empire. Hostilities began in Italy, where imperial general Eugene of Savoy defeated French marshals Nicolas Catinat and the duc de Villeroi. The war expanded in 1702, with England, Holland, and most German states opposing France, Spain, and Bavaria. English general John Churchill, the first duke of Marlborough, captured Huy, Limburg, and Bonn. However, the successes of the duc de Villars in Alsace enabled the French to menace Vienna in 1703. Marlborough moved his troops from the Netherlands to Bavaria, where he joined Eugene in their great victory at Blenheim on August 13, 1704. Following a year of modest successes, Eugene's victory at Turin compelled the French to evacuate northern Italy in late 1706. Similarly, Marlborough's triumph at Ramillies forced a French retreat in the Low Countries. In 1707, Marlborough made little progress in the north, and Eugene's invasion of Provence resulted in se-

The Battle of Malplaquet. (Francis R. Niglutsch)

rious losses. By the end of 1708, working together again, the two Allied generals won a resounding victory at Oudenarde, captured Lille, and drove the French inside their own borders. Efforts to negotiate peace failed. Villars's army in the north was Louis XIV's last hope of stopping an Allied invasion of France.

Assembling at Ghent, Marlborough and Eugene advanced in June, 1709. Meanwhile, though his infantry battalions were under-strength, Villars built formidable containment lines between Douai and the Upper Lys. Maneuvering as if to strike Ypres, the Allies bluffed the French marshal into moving troops from Tournai, which capitulated on September 3 after a two-month siege. Intensifying their pressure, the Allies invested Mons three days later. By September 9, Villars had moved his entire force into a defensive position in the Aulnois gap, amid

rolling fields and woods ten miles southeast of Mons. Hoping to deliver the final blow of the war, Marlborough engaged Villars near the village of Malplaquet on what is now the Belgian border.

Villars's army grouped 80,000 to 90,000 French, Bavarian, Swiss, and Irish troops in 121 infantry battalions and 260 cavalry squadrons, supported by 80 cannon. Veteran marshal the duc de Boufflers, though senior to Villars, volunteered to serve as his second in command. Eugene and Marlborough jointly led an Allied army numbering 90,000 to 110,000 Englishmen, Dutch, Austrians, Prussians, Hanoverians, Irish, Swiss, Danes, Scots, Hessians, and Saxons, formed into 128 infantry battalions and 253 cavalry squadrons with 100 cannon. Both exceptionally large for their time, the two armies camped almost within cannon shot of each other.

Eugene and the Dutch opposed Marlborough's wish for immediate battle, giving the French time to reinforce their lines. The French right stood on the edge of the Wood of Lanières, while their seasoned regiments were posted in the Wood of Taisnières on the left. Between these two wings, across 2.5 miles of open ground, earthworks entrenched the main French force, whose cavalry massed to the rear. Cannon were well placed throughout the entire line, including the two woods.

After examining the strong French position on the morning of September 11, 1709, Marlborough and Eugene decided to attack the French left flank first, using the same tactics that had brought them victory at Blenheim. Attacks on his flanks would lead Villars to draw troops from his center, which could be overwhelmed in a second attack by the Allied infantry reserve followed by a massed cavalry charge. Marlborough took command on the right, facing Boufflers, with Eugene on the left, facing Villars. At 8:30 A.M. Allied cannon fired a single volley to signal the attack. A half hour later, infantry columns led by Prussian count von Lottum and Austrian count von Schulenburg attacked French positions near the Wood of Taisnières. Farther to the Allied right, English general Withers began to move through the woods.

The Allies encountered stiffer resistance than in any of their previous battles. The first French volley mowed down hundreds of Schulenburg's men. Lottum attacked French emplacements several times without success. Marlborough sent three British battalions to cover his losses. Both Allied columns lost many officers before entering the woods. By 10:00 A.M. the Austrians had fought their way through the trees to join the Prussians, who faced deadly fire from fourteen repositioned French cannon. The well-ordered French pulled back, showing a remarkable understanding of defense in depth, an unusual tactic for the time. Years of intense drill had not solved the problems of fighting in woodlands, where obstructions would lead to disorder. The tight Allied columns deteriorated into small, disconnected mobs, and the impetus of the assault faltered.

In the Allies' center, Lord Orkney's British and Hanoverian corps and Dutch, Swiss, and Scottish battalions commanded by the prince of Orange were to wait until a decisive gain had been forced in the Taisnières. Not understanding the battle plan, the young prince of Orange assaulted Boufflers's lines early in the battle. Though Orange was defeated, his attack prevented Boufflers from going to Villars's aid. A French bayonet charge was stopped by Hessians, who moved forward to cover the Dutch, whose force was halved by casualties.

To check the Allied advance, Villars sent the Royal Irlandois, the famous Irish "Wild Geese" brigade, into the Taisnières, where, ironically, they were routed by their compatriots, the British 18th Royal Irish Regiment. The commanders on both sides personally led troops in the subsequent encounter. Though wounded, Eugene refused to quit the battle. Withers fought his way through the woods to join the fray. Along with the Irish, Villars drew his Bavarian brigade from the center to bolster his left, giving the Allies an opportunity to attack. Thirty Allied cavalry squadrons were deployed, as forty guns shelled the French center.

The resourceful Schulenburg managed to drag seven more cannon through the woods to fire on the French. Despite previous losses, Orange and Orkney attacked over open ground and captured the first line of French earthworks. Allied cavalry, infantry, and artillery combined in a great assault. Seriously wounded, Villars was carried from the field. Coming into action for the first time, Boufflers's cavalry fought hard but lacked their opponents' numbers. Now in command, Boufflers regrouped behind strongly fortified positions, but Marlborough and Eugene attacked again. An experienced old soldier, Boufflers withdrew his forces in order around 3:00 P.M., when the Allies had few intact units to pursue him.

SIGNIFICANCE

The partnership of Marlborough and Eugene was arguably the greatest team effort in military history. However, at Malplaquet, their last joint command, they showed little restraint as thousands died for no real gain in the bloodiest battle of their time. In six hours of bitter fighting, the Allies suffered twenty thousand deaths, twice that of the French. An estimated seven thousand men on both sides were killed or wounded in the Wood of Taisnières alone. The toll was to traumatize Europe, much as the horrific losses of the First Battle of the Somme (1916) would two centuries later.

The battle displayed important innovations, including defense in depth and deftly moved artillery. Though forced from the field, the French were not defeated, and a British-Imperial advance on Paris was averted. Later campaigns in Spain accomplished little. Fearing Habsburg power more than France, the English and Dutch initiated negotiations with Louis XIV, resulting in the Treaty of Utrecht in 1713. Financially troubled Holland soon lost its status as a major power. Holy Roman Emperor Charles VI fought on another year, before consenting to the Treaties of Rastatt and Baden. Efforts to balance power had replaced the assertion of dynastic rights.

Though the woods of Taisnières and Lanières have disappeared, the fields around Malplaquet remain largely untouched. A monument marks the site of the French center north of the village, and a museum at nearby Bavay commemorates the engagement.

—*Randall Fegley*

FURTHER READING

Chandler, David. *Marlborough as Military Commander.* London: Penguin, 1973. A detailed look at the English commander and warfare in his era.

Churchill, Winston S. *Marlborough: His Life and Times.* New York: Scribner, 1968. Written by Marlborough's

famous descendant and World War II prime minister, this work covers all of the English general's battles.

Weighley, Russell F. *The Age of Battles.* Bloomington: Indiana University Press, 1991. An excellent analysis of European warfare from 1631 to 1815, including Malplaquet.

SEE ALSO: May 26, 1701-Sept. 7, 1714: War of the Spanish Succession; Aug. 13, 1704: Battle of Blenheim; Apr. 11, 1713: Treaty of Utrecht; Mar. 7, 1714, and Sept. 7, 1714: Treaties of Rastatt and Baden.

RELATED ARTICLES in *Great Lives from History: The Eighteenth Century, 1701-1800*: Charles VI; Eugene of Savoy; First Duke of Marlborough.

November 20, 1710-July 21, 1718
OTTOMAN WARS WITH RUSSIA, VENICE, AND AUSTRIA

Russia invaded Ottoman territory but was humiliated at the River Pruth. The Ottomans, encouraged by their easy victory, decided to attempt to recover territory they had lost to Venice in 1699, but they were defeated when Austria intervened in the conflict.

LOCALE: The Balkans
CATEGORY: Wars, uprisings, and civil unrest

KEY FIGURES

Ahmed III (1673-1736), Ottoman sultan, r. 1703-1730
Baltacı Mehmed Paşa (1660-1712), Ottoman grand vizier, 1710-1711
Damad Ali Paşa (fl. 1713-1716), Ottoman grand vizier, 1713-1716
Peter the Great (1672-1725), czar of Russia, r. 1682-1725
Charles VI (1685-1740), Holy Roman Emperor, r. 1711-1740
Eugene of Savoy (1663-1736), Austrian commander in chief

SUMMARY OF EVENT

In 1699, the Treaty of Karlowitz ended fifteen years of unprofitable Ottoman war with the Holy League, but it left Peter the Great dissatisfied. Although Russia was a member of the Holy League, at Karlowitz it had been virtually abandoned by its allies. In July, 1696, Peter had seized Azov, at the mouth of the Don River, and he had built a fort at Taganrog, on the other side of the river, in 1699. In 1700, Russia had signed the Treaty of Constantinople with the Ottomans, which granted Russia perma-

nent diplomatic representation at Constantinople and abolished the annual tribute that Russia had long paid to the khan of the Crimea. The treaty did not satisfy Peter's long-term ambitions, however.

Sultan Ahmed III was probably aware that nothing had been permanently settled by the Treaty of Constantinople, but despite pressure from the capital's "war party," he declined to take advantage of Russia's difficulties in the Great Northern War (1701-1721) to consolidate Ottoman power. However, circumstances changed when the war came south. After Peter's victory at the Battle of Poltava (1709), the Cossack Ukraine was ravaged by Russian armies. Cossack fugitives fled into Ottoman territory, led by Hetman Ivan Stepanovich Mazepa and accompanied by the defeated Swedish king, Charles XII.

The sultan provided Charles with sanctuary at Bender, on the lower Dniester River. The Ottoman war party urged an alliance with the exiled king and the Cossacks, but the sultan positively refused. However, Baltacı Mehmed Paşa was appointed grand vizier on September 11, 1710, indicating that the war party now had the sultan's ear. On November 20, the empire declared war on Russia, and the grand vizier set out for the Pruth River in the spring of 1711. Joined by Crimean Tatars and fugitive Cossacks and Poles, his forces were said to number 120,000 men and 400 guns; their objective was to confront the approaching Russians.

It remains unclear why Peter the Great was marching toward the Pruth River, since the Great Northern War was still being fought in the Baltic region. He certainly expected active support from the Christians of Moldavia and Wallachia: Dmitri Kantemir, voyevod of Moldavia (r. 1710-1711), had entered into a secret agreement with Peter in which, in return for recognition as hereditary prince under Russian protection, he would supply the invading Russian army with provisions and forage. The voyevod of Wallachia, Constantin Brincoveanu (r. 1688-1714), made similar friendly offers.

Thus, a Russian army consisting of 40,000 infantry, 14,000 horse, and 122 guns, under the command of the aging marshal Boris Sheremetev, advanced toward Moldavia, short of supplies but anticipating Moldavian assistance. Unwisely perhaps, Peter himself, his wife Catherine, and members of his court accompanied the army. Reaching the Pruth River, they crossed into Moldavia and reached Jassy in June, 1711. Contrary to expectations, however, their reception was less than friendly and the promised supplies never materialized.

The Russians had no notion that the grand vizier's army had already reached the Pruth River, but by July 21, the Russian army was completely encircled by a far larger enemy force. Peter sued for an armistice, and legend tells that during the negotiations it was the charms of the czarina and the bribe of her jewels that led the grand vizier to grant easy terms. In reality, Baltacı Mehmed Paşa was probably astonished at his own good fortune and offered the best terms that he thought he could get. Azov was to be restored to the Ottomans and Taganrog would be demolished, as would newly built Russian forts on the Dnieper River. Permanent Russian representation at Constantinople was to end. All Ottoman prisoners were to be released, and Charles XII was to be granted safe passage. The Russian army was to be provided with provisions for its return home.

The preliminary agreement, known as the Treaty of the Pruth, was signed on July 23, 1711, amid protests from the representatives of the Swedish king and the Polish allies. The grand vizier almost certainly knew what he was doing, however. He knew his Janissary troops were growing mutinous, and he probably distrusted the machinations of the exiles at Bender. Further negotiations resulted in the Treaty of Adrianople (June 25, 1713), with assurances of twenty-five years of peace between the two powers. By then, however, the grand vizier had already been dismissed, his enemies asserting that he should have exacted harsher terms in the earlier treaty. Nevertheless, the campaign on the Pruth went some way to healing bruised Ottoman susceptibilities, which were still sore from the shame of Karlowitz.

The Treaty of Karlowitz had constituted perhaps the greatest humiliation the Ottoman Empire ever experienced at the hands of unbelievers. Some members of the Ottoman elite dreamed of revenge, and the apparent triumph at the Pruth whetted their appetites for renewed warfare. The obvious target was the Venetian Republic: At Karlowitz, Venice had aquired the Morea (Greek Peloponnese), bringing the Venetian fleet back into the Aegean. Reports from the Morea told of bitter dissatisfaction among the Greeks with their Venetian overlords. Since the fall of Baltacı Mehmed Paşa, a new belligerent grand vizier, Damad Ali Paşa, had been appointed in April, 1713. The Ottoman's excuse for going to war was aid allegedly given by the Venetians to Montenegran rebels and the refusal of the Bank of Venice to hand over the wealth of the lately executed voyevod of Wallachia. The Porte declared war on January 11, 1715.

Damad Ali Paşa led a force of more than seventy thousand troops against the undermanned Venetian garrisons. Corinth fell on July 7, followed by Argos, Nauplia, Koron, Navarino, and Modon. The conflict was over in one hundred days, with the grand vizier maintaining strict discipline among his troops, who paid for food and forage and were forbidden to plunder. Improbably, the Turks were welcomed as liberators; such was the depth of Christian sectarian bitterness. At sea, the Kapudan Paşa captured Aegina and Tenos. By July, 1716, Ottoman forces were in the Adriatic, besieging Corfu.

In Vienna, the Emperor Charles VI sought to mediate between Russia and the Ottomans, but with Ottoman forces at Corfu, the traditional enemy of the Holy Roman Empire had advanced too close for comfort. If Venice were to lose Dalmatia, then Croatia and even Styria would be threatened. The veteran president of the Imperial War Council (*Hofkriegsrat*), Eugene of Savoy, favored going to war against the Ottomans, despite opposition from the so-called Spanish Cabal at court, and on April 13, 1716, Austria joined Venice in a defensive alliance.

The Porte had not wished to provoke the emperor and had gambled on his neutrality during the reconquest of the Morea. Faced with the new threat of an Austro-Venetian alliance, however, Damad Ali Paşa led an army of 120,000 against the fortress of Peterwardein during the summer of 1716. He was defeated by Eugene and died on the battlefield on August 5, 1716. Eugene did not press his advantage. Instead, he crossed the Tisza River into the Banat and besieged Temesvar, which capitulated with honors on October 12, 1716. When the news of this disaster reached Constantinople, the Ottomans abandoned Corfu.

Eugene advanced against Belgrade, where the governor, Mustafa Paşa, commanded a garrison of thirty thousand troops. As it was imperative that Belgrade be relieved, the new grand vizier, Halil Paşa, hurried to the beleaguered city. There, he suffered an even greater defeat than the recent disaster at Peterwardein. Belgrade fell on August 18, 1717, and the Ottomans withdrew behind the line of the River Sava, although commanders in Bosnia held out with grim determination. Encouraged by Austria's victories, Venice renewed its struggle but performed indifferently in naval battles off Cape Matapan and Cerigo. This was to prove the last of many wars between the republic and the Porte.

Toward the end of 1717, the British envoy Sir Edward Wortley Montagu and the veteran Dutch diplomat Count Jacob Colyer mediated peace talks, and a treaty was signed at Passarowitz on July 21, 1718. The Porte was forced to relinquish Belgrade and Semendria, as well as much of Serbia, Oltenia ("Little Wallachia"), and the Banat of Temesvar. A supplemental commercial treaty granted Austrian subjects substantial trading privileges within Ottoman territory. Venice confirmed Ottoman possession of the Morea, Tenos, and Aegina but retained its conquests in Dalmatia, the seven Ionian islands, and four enclaves in Epirus.

SIGNIFICANCE

Notwithstanding Ottoman resilience and courage, the Treaty of Passarowitz confirmed the overwhelming superiority of European military technology, training, and organization over the Turkish war machine. Henceforward, the lands north of the Danube and Sava Rivers would be permanently lost to the Porte, although few Ottomans could reconcile themselves to the loss of Belgrade. After Passarowitz, Austria consolidated the gains won at Karlowitz and began to colonize the Banat with

German veterans. The sultan had had enough of war. In May, 1718, he appointed as grand vizier the companion of his early years, Nevshehirli Ibrahim Paşa, and between them they inaugurated the Tulip Age (*Lale devri*) of hedonism and artistic flourishing, which lasted for the next twelve years.

—*Gavin R. G. Hambly*

FURTHER READING

Hughes, Lindsey. *Russia in the Age of Peter the Great.* New Haven, Conn.: Yale University Press, 1998. Useful for the taking of Azov and the Pruth campaign.

Kurat, Akdes Nimet. "The Retreat of the Turks, 1683-1730." In *A History of the Ottoman Empire to 1730*, edited by V. J. Parry. New York: Cambridge University Press, 1976. Detailed narrative of these interlocking wars.

_____, ed. *The Despatches of Sir Robert Sutton: Ambassador in Constantinople, 1710-1714.* London: Royal Historical Society, 1953. An insider's account of the diplomatic struggle at the Porte.

McKay, Derek. *Prince Eugene of Savoy.* London: Thames & Hudson, 1977. Brief, lucid account of the campaign from Peterwardein to Belgrade.

SEE ALSO: c. 1701-1721: Great Northern War; May 26, 1701-Sept. 7, 1714: War of the Spanish Succession; June 27, 1709: Battle of Poltava; Mar. 7, 1714, and Sept. 7, 1714: Treaties of Rastatt and Baden; 1718-1730: Tulip Age; 1736-1739: Russo-Austrian War Against the Ottoman Empire; Oct., 1768-Jan. 9, 1792: Ottoman Wars with Russia.

RELATED ARTICLES in *Great Lives from History: The Eighteenth Century, 1701-1800*: Ahmed III; Charles VI; Eugene of Savoy; Peter the Great.

1710's

March 1, 1711
ADDISON AND STEELE ESTABLISH *THE SPECTATOR*

Though it lasted less than two years, Joseph Addison and Richard Steele's Whig newspaper The Spectator *set the standard for taste and prose style in early eighteenth century London.*

LOCALE: London, England
CATEGORIES: Communications; literature

KEY FIGURES
Joseph Addison (1672-1719), English journalist and
　　playwright
Richard Steele (1672-1729), English journalist and
　　playwright

SUMMARY OF EVENT

When Queen Anne came to the English throne in 1702, exactly sixty years had gone by since the Crown had any real control over the English press, and at its restoration (1660), the monarchy had ceded much of its political power to Parliament. With the decisive defeat of the French at Blenheim in 1704, the Whig Party (which generally represented the mercantile interests of the rising middle class) gained political ascendancy by identifying itself with the French war. The opposition party, the Tories (who were generally associated with the landed gentry), criticized the war and the upstart Whigs, who responded by defending their policies to the public.

The primary forum for such disputes in the seventeenth century had been the pamphlet, even though London's first newspaper, the *Weekly News*, appeared as early as 1622. By the turn of the eighteenth century, however, the newspaper had become the most efficient medium of communication, and both Whig and Tory newspapers proliferated after 1704. In addition, the Whig Party split into several factions, which delighted in denouncing each other as much as they did in attacking Tories.

It was into this world of journalistic debate that Joseph Addison and Richard Steele appeared as essayists, publishing Whiggish political opinion as well as genteel commentary on anything and everything. In 1709, when Whig leaders in Parliament overstepped their authority in what was perceived as the persecution of the Tory Henry Sacheverell, arguments on both sides became increasingly shrill. Steele, a young British-Irish journalist, captured the tone of the controversy by launching *The Tatler*, a Whig paper in which he departed from political commentary to craft witty, urbane essays on the events

and conversations of London's various coffeehouses and chocolate houses. This was not as much a departure from political journalism as it may seem today, because the coffeehouses were the centers of political discussion, as well as of literary taste. In reporting the political thoughts of London's leading citizens as they were promulgated over coffee and tobacco, Steele also described their manners, their dress, and their small talk.

Reading essays in *The Tatler* with delight, another Whig journalist, Joseph Addison, thought he detected the style of one of his public school classmates, and he was right. Addison and Steele had attended the Charterhouse school and matriculated together at Oxford, though Steele had dropped out after a year to essay a military career and the two had lost touch. Submitting entries in a similar (though more reserved) style to *The Tatler*, Addison resumed his friendship with his school chum, and their newspaper partnership began.

The first page of The Spectator *of June 7, 1711*. (Rutgers University)

ADDISON'S SPECTATOR

Joseph Addison created in the narrator of The Spectator *a noteworthy literary figure and a precursor of the modern narrator. As he describes himself in the excerpt below, the Spectator is in the world but not of the world, an observer rather than a participant. While in 1711 this remained a mere fiction of convenience, by the nineteenth century such a relationship to the world would become a problem that literature was meant to address.*

I live in the World, rather as a Spectator of Mankind, than as one of the Species; by which means I have made my self a Speculative Statesman, Soldier, Merchant, and Artizan, without ever medling with any Practical Part in Life. I am very well versed in the Theory of an Husband, or a Father, and can discern the Errors in the Oeconomy, Business, and Diversion of others, better than those who are engaged in them; as Standers-by discover Blots, which are apt to escape those who are in the Game. I never espoused any Party with Violence, and am resolved to observe an exact Neutrality between the Whigs and Tories, unless I shall be forc'd to declare myself by the Hostilities of either side. In short, I have acted in all the parts of my Life as a Looker-on, which is the Character I intend to preserve in this Paper.

Source: Joseph Addison, *The Spectator* no. 1 (March 1, 1711). Project Gutenberg. http://www.gutenberg.org/files/12030/12030.txt. Accessed November 13, 2005.

When *The Tatler* suspended publication in January of 1711, Addison and Steele regrouped, and less than two months later, beginning March 1, 1711, they launched what has since been recognized as one of the high points of English nonfiction prose style, *The Spectator*. Part of what made the new periodical successful was the "periodical essay" genre Steele had pioneered in his earlier paper. While British imitations of the essay genre invented by Michel Eyquem de Montaigne (1533-1592) in his *Essais* (1580-1588; *The Essays*, 1603) began almost immediately after their translation in 1603, it is Steele who is usually credited with adapting the essay to the British periodical. Steele's essays in *The Tatler* were every bit as personal and whimsical as Montaigne's but carried a more public tone, befitting the coffeehouse atmosphere that bred them.

The Spectator, clearly reflecting Addison's influence more than Steele's, modified the tone of the new periodical essay to make it even more genteel. The Spectator of the title was a fictional London gentleman, a looker-on who, like Steele's Tatler, frequented the gathering places of London's high society. Because he was just watching rather than "tatling," however, the essays felt like overheard conversations rather than broadcast gossip. Thus, it became easier for Tory, moderate, and nonpartisan readers to like the amiable moderator of

their news and opinion, even when a reader's opinion differed from that of the Spectator. Instead of following the actual movers and shakers of British government, the Spectator detailed the mundane adventures of fictitious but recognizable London characters, the baronet Sir Roger de Coverley, the merchant Sir Andrew Freeport, the seaman Captain Sentry, and the ladies' man Will Honeycomb.

While the Spectator and the other characters he described were invented by Addison, Steele took them over in his own contributions to the series, both rounding and deepening the characters. *The Spectator*'s increased frequency of publication made the collaboration of at least two writers necessary. While *The Tatler* had marked an increase in frequency over the typical British weekly, appearing Tuesdays, Thursdays, and Saturdays, *The Spectator* came out with a new issue every day except Sunday. Since courts, businesses, and Parliament were all silent on Sundays, no political, legal, or mercantile event in London was ever more than twenty-four hours away from being discussed in print.

Furthermore, *The Spectator*, while originating from London and covering London events, reached the whole of the British Isles. The establishment of the crown postal service, with stages leaving London every Tuesday, Thursday, and Saturday, made nationwide circulation possible: It was no accident that *The Tatler* appeared only on post days. Addison and Steele doubled production by distributing *The Spectator* daily to the coffeehouses and posting two issues at a time on post days. Readers in Liverpool might receive Monday's *Spectator* as late as Wednesday, but rarely later—extraordinary dispatch for 1711.

While Addison wrote more of *The Spectator*'s essays than Steele, any given week of the nearly two-year run of the journal boasted liberal contributions from both writers. Both writers used pseudonyms, but the convention was for modesty, not anonymity: Most Londoners knew that articles signed with the initials *C, L, I,* or *O* (for the Greek muse of history, Clio) were by Addison and that Steele's essays were those signed either *R* or *T*. Even without the signatures, moreover, the two writers' styles were immediately recognizable. Addison's contributions were essays in the fullest sense, but Steele's often took a dialectical form, as an exchange of letters, sometimes with real and sometimes with fictional correspondents. Thus the editorial positions of the paper, which were more ethical than political in nature, seemed more objective, because they were often presented in the context of opposing, or at least slightly different, points of view.

SIGNIFICANCE

Addison and Steele's *Spectator* essays became the model for English prose style for a century after their publication. Benjamin Franklin tells in his *Memoirs de la vie privée ecrits par lui-même* (1791; *The Private Life of the Late Benjamin Franklin*, 1793; *Memoirs of the Life*, 1818; best known as *Autobiography*) of developing his own prose style by a laborious process of copying and imitating his favorite *Spectator* essays. The extent to which the essays of Addison and Steele became synonymous with English prose style may be gauged by the fact that Brian McCrea's 1990 book proclaiming the demise of the traditional English literary "canon" was titled *Addison and Steele Are Dead*.

Fortunately, the obituary was premature. By writing essays on the broadest possible range of topics, Addison and Steele also succeeded in capturing the essence of their age, in all the details of dress, habit, speech, and pastime. They were indeed "spectators" of their generation's London, and through their eyes historians and sociologists can more clearly view early eighteenth century London than through any almanac or census. Finally, by loyally supporting and defending their political party, the Whigs, they produced a voice around which the rising middle class of Queen Anne's England could rally and a persona with which its members could identify in an uncertain political climate. In spite of this unquestionable party identification, *The Spectator*'s essays transcended their party and, ultimately, their time, to achieve a universal appeal.

—*John R. Holmes*

FURTHER READING

Bloom, Edward A., and Lillian D. Bloom. *Addison and Steele: The Critical Heritage*. London: Routledge and Kegan Paul, 1980. A collection of the major reviews and critiques of Addison and Steele's works from 1702 to 1979.

Bond, Richard P. *Studies in the Early English Periodical*. Chapel Hill: University of North Carolina Press, 1957. Useful background on the journalism of the era, including a detailed chapter on *The Spectator*.

Goldgar, Bertrand A. *The Curse of Party*. Lincoln: University of Nebraska Press, 1961. Background on the Whig and Tory political issues of *The Spectator*'s era, with particular focus on the reasons for Steele's break with Jonathan Swift.

Mackie, Erin, ed. *The Commerce of Everyday Life: Selections from "The Tatler" and "The Spectator."* Boston: Bedford/St. Martin's Press, 1998. Representative selections of Addison and Steele's periodical essays, with a generous introduction and headnotes, as well as select related contemporary works.

Marshall, David. "Taste and Aesthetics: Shaftesbury and Addison—Criticism and the Public Taste." In *The Eighteenth Century*. Vol. 4 in *The Cambridge History of Literary Criticism*. New York: Cambridge University Press, 1997. A chapter of a standard reference book focusing on the influence of *The Spectator* on eighteenth century taste.

SEE ALSO: Aug. 13, 1704: Battle of Blenheim; 1721-1742: Development of Great Britain's Office of Prime Minister; 1726: Swift Satirizes English Rule of Ireland in *Gulliver's Travels*; 1726-1729: Voltaire Advances Enlightenment Thought in Europe; 1736: *Gentleman's Magazine* Initiates Parliamentary Reporting; Mar. 20, 1750-Mar. 14, 1752: Johnson Issues *The Rambler*; Sept. 10, 1763: Publication of the *Freeman's Journal*; Jan. 1, 1777: France's First Daily Newspaper Appears; Jan. 4, 1792-1797: The *Northern Star* Calls for Irish Independence.

RELATED ARTICLES in *Great Lives from History: The Eighteenth Century, 1701-1800*: Joseph Addison; Queen Anne; Benjamin Franklin; Richard Steele; Jonathan Swift.

September 22, 1711-March 23, 1713
TUSCARORA WAR

Conflict over land, property, and trade led the Tuscarora Indians to declare war on European colonists in North Carolina. The Tuscaroras were decimated in the war, their society was dispersed, and the way was opened for Carolinian settlers to expand westward.

LOCALE: North Carolina (now in the United States)
CATEGORIES: Wars, uprisings, and civil unrest; diplomacy and international relations; expansion and land acquisition; colonization

KEY FIGURES
King Tom Blunt (d. 1739?) Tuscarora leader
King Tom Hancock (d. 1712), Tuscarora leader
John Barnwell (c. 1671-1724), colonial military leader
James Moore (1675/1680-1724), colonial military leader
Thomas Pollock (1654-1722), governor of North Carolina, 1712-1714, 1722

SUMMARY OF EVENT

When European settlers began arriving in North America, the Tuscarora tribe controlled nearly all the North Carolina coastal plains. The tribe's territory stretched from today's Virginia state line, south to the Cape Fear River, and inland to the Appalachians. Tribal land cut a wedge between the Algonquian tribes of the coast and the Siouan tribes of the piedmont. The Tuscaroras held a trade monopoly throughout the area.

Information about the Tuscaroras and their western holdings was limited, because the tribe denied passage through the area. Contact with settlers was infrequent as a result of the natural protection provided by swamps, sand reefs, and shallow harbors. Conflict between the tribe and the settlers began, however, when the two groups started occupying the same areas and the Indians began raids on settlers' livestock and crops. The Indians saw no problem with their actions, because there was no Tuscarora law or custom that discouraged stealing from an enemy. Settlers were helpless to prevent these attacks, because the tribe had a vicious policy of revenge. In 1705, the Tuscaroras became such a problem for the settlers that Virginia passed a law forbidding natives from hunting on patented land.

Trade agreements were established between the tribe and the settlers, but things did not go smoothly. The Tuscaroras felt the settlers were taking advantage of them and complained about being cheated. Tuscarora tribal leaders approached the Pennsylvania government in 1710. They presented eight wampum belts, signifying various grievances concerning the safety of American Indian families. No agreement was reached. Unscrupulous traders accelerated the Tuscarora discontent by describing the settlers as easy targets with no government backing or protection. Then the Tuscaroras declared war.

On September 22, 1711, approximately five hundred Tuscaroras and their allies attacked at widely scattered points along the Neuse, Trent, and Pamlico Rivers. Men, women, and children were butchered and their homes destroyed by fire. The Indians' frenzy was slowed only by fatigue and drunkenness. At the end of the two-day rampage more than 130 whites were dead and nearly 30 women and children had been captured. The frightened survivors scrambled to reach fortified garrisons.

The situation in North Carolina was desperate. Planters west of the river could not help protect those under attack without weakening their own defenses. Quaker settlers refused to fight. Governor Edward Hyde appealed to Virginia and South Carolina for help. Virginia worked to secure the loyalty and assistance of the neutral Tuscaroras who had not participated in the raids, but met with little success. South Carolina responded by sending Colonel John Barnwell and a force of five hundred native allies and thirty white men.

Barnwell's departure was delayed, and his winter march was difficult. He crossed the Neuse River in late January and marched an entire day and night to attack the Tuscarora town of Narhontes. Although the natives knew of his approach, Barnwell's raid was successful. For the next four months, Barnwell led several victorious attacks in Tuscarora territory, but he was displeased by the weak North Carolina support. In April, against orders from North Carolina, he signed a treaty with the Tuscaroras. During Barnwell's return to South Carolina, he broke the treaty by capturing native women and children to sell as slaves, thereby provoking new raids.

The summer of 1712 brought no relief. Settlers and natives were starving; no one could plant crops or hunt in safety. Residents along the Neuse and Pamlico Rivers had their homes burned, their stock stolen, and their plantations destroyed. The North Carolina Assembly held a special session in July and passed a law requiring all men between sixteen and sixty years of age to fight the natives or pay a fine. The law was widely disliked and few men obeyed it. Then a yellow fever epidemic hit the area. North Carolina's governor was one of those who died.

Thomas Pollock was chosen as the new governor until the colony could receive instructions from the Lord Proprietors. Pollock appealed to South Carolina for aid but suggested that Colonel Barnwell would not be suitable. Barnwell went before the South Carolina assembly and advised that it was necessary to prosecute the Tuscarora War to a successful conclusion. South Carolina agreed to help. A force of nine hundred Indians and approximately thirty-three soldiers was placed under the leadership of Colonel James Moore, who was experienced in fighting the American Indians.

Governor Pollock reopened negotiations with King Tom Blunt, the chief ruler of the neutral Tuscaroras in the upper towns. In September, Blunt requested peace with North Carolina. Pollock insisted Blunt's people fight on the side of the settlers and would not accept neutrality. Pollock demanded the capture of King Tom Hancock, the chief who had authorized the massacre in September, 1711. In mid-November, 1712, Hancock was delivered and executed. King Blunt then signed a treaty with North Carolina on behalf of nine Tuscarora towns.

Colonel Moore and his forces arrived in the Neuse River region in late December. Although the people were thankful for the protection, they were angered when the troops consumed all the provisions in the area. It was nearly a month before Moore's forces left for Fort Barnwell to prepare an attack on the Tuscaroras base at Fort Neoheroka.

Fort Neoheroka lay within a wide curve of Contentnea Creek and was protected on three sides by deep water and steep riverbanks. The fourth side was enclosed by an angled palisade, a fence created by pointed stakes. There were bastions, or projections, on the four main corners, and an angled passageway led from the fort to the water. The natives also had access to a network of tunnels and caves within the fort.

Moore instructed his men to create zigzag trenches to within gun range of the fort's east wall. He then built a triangular blockhouse to allow his troops to provide cross fire while men raised a battery against the fort wall. Moore also ordered a mine tunneled under the wall near the blockhouse and lined it with explosives.

Once preparations were completed, Moore placed his forces around the fort. Two captains, a battery of artillery, and more than three hundred Cherokees were assigned to the northwest area of the fort and stream to block off the most likely escape route. East of the fort and in the trenches, Moore's brother, two other captains, ten

whites, and fifty Yamasees took their positions. Colonel Moore placed himself, four other commanders, eighty whites, and four hundred members of Siouan nations in the southeast. Mulberry Battery took its place within the southern curve of the creek.

The attack began on March 20, 1713, with the blast of a trumpet. The powder in the mine failed, but the attack on the northeast quickly succeeded. Captain Maule went against the southern side of the fort instead of the southeast, as he had been ordered. This caused Maule's troops to be caught in the cross fire, and only twenty of his men escaped unhurt. Colonel Moore erected a low wall and managed to set two of the fort's blockhouses on fire. By the next morning, the fire had destroyed the structures as well as several houses within the fort. Some of the Tuscaroras hid in the caves and created problems for the attackers, but by Sunday, March 23, Moore's forces controlled the fort. Destruction of Fort Neoheroka was complete. Moore had lost fewer than sixty men and had fewer than one hundred wounded. Nearly one thousand Tuscaroras were killed or captured.

SIGNIFICANCE

As word of the destruction of Fort Neoheroka spread, other members of the Tuscarora tribe fled the region. Many headed to Virginia, where they endured great hardships and found little food. Several raiding bands continued guerrilla warfare in North Carolina, but Moore's help was no longer needed. He returned to South Carolina in September, 1713, having effectively destroyed the Tuscaroras as a military power. The colonists of North Carolina were freed to expand westward from the coast, and they eventually absorbed the Tuscaroras' lands into their territory.

—Suzanne Riffle Boyce

FURTHER READING

Graymont, Barbara, ed. *Fighting Tuscarora: The Autobiography of Chief Clinton Rickard*. Syracuse, N.Y.: Syracuse University Press, 1973. Introduction includes information about Tuscarora history. Main text chronicles the life of Chief Clinton Rickard (1882-1971) and his work for American Indian rights.

Johnson, F. Roy. *The Tuscaroras*. Vols. 1 and 2. Murfreesboro, N.C.: Johnson, 1967. Discusses history, traditions, culture, mythology, and medicine. Maps, illustrations, index, and many footnotes. Provides listings of numerous original resources.

Lee, E. Lawrence. *Indian Wars in North Carolina, 1663-1763*. Raleigh: North Carolina Department of Archives and History, Division of Archives and History,

1997. Describes the Tuscaroras and other Native Americans who lived in colonial North Carolina. Contains a separate chapter on the Tuscarora War.

Ross, Thomas E. *American Indians in North Carolina: Geographic Interpretations.* Southern Pines, N.C.: Karo Hollow Press, 1999. Chapter 2, "Indians at the Time of European Contact," contains references to the Tuscarora War. Chapter 12 describes the life and activities of the Tuscaroras today.

Snow, Dean R. *The Iroquois.* Malden, Mass.: Blackwell, 1994. Follows the development of the Iroquois Confederacy. Extensive bibliography, index.

Waldman, Carl. *Encyclopedia of Native American Tribes.* New York: Facts On File, 1988. One page summarizes events leading to Fort Neoheroka and gives some details about tribal life.

Wilson, Edmund. *Apologies to the Iroquois.* New York: Farrar, Straus & Cudahy, 1959. Contains a chapter on Tuscarora history. Also discusses land disputes at Niagara Falls in the 1960's.

SEE ALSO: May 15, 1702-Apr. 11, 1713: Queen Anne's War; Summer, 1714-1741: Fox Wars; Sept. 19, 1737: Walking Purchase; May 28, 1754-Feb. 10, 1763: French and Indian War; Oct. 5, 1759-Nov. 19, 1761: Cherokee War; May 8, 1763-July 24, 1766: Pontiac's Resistance; 1768-May 16, 1771: Carolina Regulator Movements; May 24 and June 11, 1776: Indian Delegation Meets with Congress; Oct. 22, 1784: Fort Stanwix Treaty; Oct. 18, 1790-July, 1794: Little Turtle's War; 1799: Code of Handsome Lake.
RELATED ARTICLE in *Great Lives from History: The Eighteenth Century, 1701-1800*: Daniel Boone.

1710's

December, 1711
OCCASIONAL CONFORMITY BILL

In 1711, only those who took Anglican Communion could hold public offices in Britain. The Occasional Conformity Bill stipulated that taking Communion once each year was insufficient to qualify for such offices: It was an attempt to prevent those of other faiths from feigning Anglicanism and to ensure that only authentic Anglicans could join the government.

LOCALE: London, England
CATEGORIES: Laws, acts, and legal history; government and politics; religion and theology

KEY FIGURES
Queen Anne (1665-1714), queen of England, r. 1702-1714
Second Earl of Nottingham (Daniel Finch; 1647-1730), English politician and possible originator of the Occasional Conformity Bill
William Bromley (1668-1732), English member of Parliament who introduced the bill
Henry Sacheverell (1674?-1724), Anglican clergyman
First Earl of Godolphin (Sidney Godolphin; 1645-1712), English government minister
First Duke of Marlborough (John Churchill; 1650-1722), English government minister

SUMMARY OF EVENT
The practice of "occasional conformity" originated in the response of officeholding Dissenters to two statutes

from the reign of Charles II (r. 1660-1685). The Corporation Act (1661) mandated that local officeholders take Anglican Communion; failure to do so would result in ejection from office. However, some Dissenters evaded the intent of the law by taking Communion just once a year in an Anglican church and then attending their Dissenting meetinghouse the rest of the year, a practice more prevalent among Presbyterians and Congregationalists than among Baptists and Quakers. The Test Act (1673) repeated the requirement that all civil and military officeholders take Anglican Communion, but Dissenters continued to engage in occasional conformity in order to hold office. This angered not only Anglicans but also strict Dissenters, who regarded such behavior as hypocritical.

The Toleration Act (1689), passed in the wake of the Glorious Revolution (1688-1689), accorded toleration to all Protestant Dissenters. The act may account for a decline in the late seventeenth and early eighteenth centuries in attendance at Anglican services and a drop in the amount of tithes received by the Church of England. This decline in turn caused the Tory Party to proclaim that the Church was in danger. An often cited example of occasional conformity was that of Sir Humphry Edwyne, the lord mayor of London, who in 1697 attended his Dissenting meetinghouse preceded by his two sword bearers, the symbols of his office. Not much could be done about such occasional conformity, however, because

King William III (r. 1689-1702), a Dutch Calvinist, was sympathetic to Dissenters.

It was only during the reign of Queen Anne that the Tories were able to gain numerical strength in the House of Commons and to introduce the Occasional Conformity Bill in an attempt simultaneously to strengthen the Anglican Church and to weaken Whig electoral strength because Dissenters overwhelmingly supported Whig candidates. The Whigs, more sympathetic toward Dissenters, felt that punishing occasional conformists would be tantamount to religious persecution and would divide Protestants in the face of a possible Catholic threat. The bill was first introduced in the fall of 1702 by William Bromley, a member of the House of Commons representing Oxford University. The bill may have been drafted, however, by one of the leading Tory peers, Daniel Finch, second earl of Nottingham.

The measure called for substantial fines to be levied against officeholders who attended Dissenting meetinghouses after qualifying for office by taking Anglican Communion. Anne gave her support to the bill, which passed by a wide margin in the House of Commons. The queen's husband, the Danish prince George, duke of Cumberland, voted for it in the House of Lords to support Anne, although he was an occasional conformist himself, attending private Lutheran services in addition to Anglican services. The Whigs' strength in the House of Lords enabled them to amend the bill to exempt local officeholders. Differences between the Commons' and Lords' versions could not be reconciled, so this first attempt to pass the measure failed.

On November 25, 1703, Bromley reintroduced the bill, but the queen's attitude had changed; she now viewed it as divisive, and her husband, Prince George, was not present at the vote. Aided by the absence of five Tory peers, the Whigs in the House of Lords voted down the bill by twelve votes. Fourteen bishops voted against it, and only nine voted for it.

Feelings were still running high when the bill was introduced yet again but with a new twist: Because the House of Lords could not revise a financial bill but could only accept or reject it, the Tories attempted to attach or "tack" the Occasional Conformity Bill to a land tax bill that was necessary to fund English participation in the War of the Spanish Succession. Although the Tories supported the contents of the amended bill, not all of them could bring themselves to support the controversial tactic, which was an attempt by the Commons to bypass the legitimate power of the Lords. Indeed, the first earl of Godolphin, Anne's leading minister, voted against this version of the measure for that reason. The attachment to the land tax bill therefore lost in the House of Commons by a 251 to 134 vote, and the House of Lords defeated the Occasional Conformity Bill by itself 71 to 50. The queen had attended the debates in the House of Lords to indicate her

---

PASSAGE OF THE OCCASIONAL CONFORMITY BILL

The Occasional Conformity Bill passed in late December, 1711, after a last-minute petition from the Dutch and French Protestant churches seeking exemptions for their members was rejected. The bill's passage is reported in the official proceedings of the House of Commons, published thirty years after the fact, excerpted below.

[On t]he 19th [of December, 1711], the famous Occasional Conformity-Bill with the new Title, viz. *A Bill for preserving the Protestant Religion, by better securing the Church of England as by Law established; and for confirming the Toleration granted to the Protestant Dissenters*, by an Act entitled, *An Act for exempting their Majesty's Protestant Subjects, dissenting from the Church of England, from the Penalties of certain Laws, and for the supplying the Defects thereof; and for the further securing the Protestant Succession, by requiring the Practisers of the Law in North-Britain, to take the Oaths, and subscribe the Declaration therein mentioned*, having passed the House of Lords, was sent down to the Commons, who read it immediately the first time, and gave it a second reading the next Day. On the 20th, a Petition was offered to the House on behalf of the Dutch and French Protestant Churches, praying, that they might be excepted from the Restraints laid by this Bill on English dissenting Congregations; but the Question being put, that the Petition be brought up, it passed in the Negative: After which the Commons, in a Committee of the whole House, (which that Morning was very thin) made several Amendments to the Bill. These Amendments being immediately reported and agreed to, the Bill was thereupon sent back to the House of Peers; who, the same Day, sent down a Message to the Commons to acquaint them, that they had agreed to those Amendments.

Source: "Third Parliament of Great Britain: Second Session—Begins 7/12/1711." In *1706-1713*. Vol. 4 in *The History and Proceedings of the House of Commons*, pp. 226-61. http://www.british-history.ac.uk/report.asp?compid=37679. Accessed November 13, 2005.

opposition to the bill. The "tackers" lost favor with Anne, although many of the 134 who voted for the tactic were reelected in 1705. Nevertheless, they continued to be unsuccessful in getting so-called Church-in-danger motions passed.

Successful passage of the bill finally came in December, 1711. This success resulted partly from the trial of Henry Sacheverell, a High Church clergyman (February-March, 1710). Sacheverall was prosecuted for an inflammatory sermon attacking Dissenters and toleration, and his trial alarmed those with loyalties to the High Church and the Tory Party. These factions were motivated to vote in greater numbers in the next election, and the Tories won a large electoral victory in October, 1710.

The following year, Tories used their newfound strength in Parliament to effect a bargain between Nottingham, Godolphin, and the first duke of Marlborough. Marlborough, one of England's greatest generals and the commander in chief of the combined British and Dutch armies, wished to continue the war with France. The Tories, however, were tired of the war and wished to bring it to an end. Nottingham and his followers agreed to support continuing the war in Parliament if Godolphin, Marlborough, and the Whigs would vote for the Occasional Conformity Bill in return.

The French had already supported one attempt by the Catholic James Edward, the "Old Pretender," to claim the throne of Britain, and the Whigs believed they might try again. The prospect of a Catholic revolution in Britain was deemed serious enough for the Whigs to abandon temporarily their protection of the Dissenters, and they supported the bargain between Marlborough and Nottingham. As a result, in December, 1711, the Occasional Conformity Bill easily passed both houses of Parliament. It mandated that civil and military officials who engaged in occasional conformity be heavily fined and removed from office.

SIGNIFICANCE

Although the High Church Anglicans and Tories had finally succeeded after nine years of effort in passing the Occasional Conformity Bill, the results they desired from the bill failed to materialize. Many Dissenting officeholders evaded the intent of the law by attending public Anglican services regularly and then conducting private religious services in their homes. The Tories, troubled by these developments, cast a broader net by passing the Schism Act (1714), which attacked Dissenters' schools indirectly by forbidding any attendee at a Dissenting chapel from teaching in a school. Violators

would be subject to three months' imprisonment. However, Queen Anne's death on August 1, 1714—the day the Schism Act was to go in effect—rendered it largely a dead letter, because the new monarch, George I, was a German Lutheran. As a Dissenter under English law, he was sympathetic to Dissenters and received their support in the Jacobite Rebellion of 1715-1716, which attempted to restore James Edward, realizing the Whigs' worst fears.

As a result of Dissenters' support of the Crown, the Riot Act (1715), which was passed to quell popular disturbances, included a provision making it a felony to attack a Dissenting chapel, and the government provided for compensation for the destruction of Dissenting schools and chapels. The Occasional Conformity Act and the Schism Act were both repealed by the Whig-dominated Parliament in 1719. Dissenters were now fairly well tolerated in Britain, and their academies and meetinghouses were largely undisturbed. Throughout the eighteenth century, many Dissenters became involved in reform movements, banking, and industry, and they urged the separation of church and state. It was not until 1828, however, that the Corporation Act and the Test Act were repealed.

—Mark C. Herman

FURTHER READING

Flaningam, John. "The Occasional Conformity Controversy: Ideology and Party Politics, 1697-1711." *The Journal of British Studies* 17, no. 1 (Autumn, 1977): 38-62. Analyzes the broader ideological aspects of struggle and clearly defines the differences in Tory and Whig positions.

Holmes, Geoffrey. *The Trial of Doctor Sacheverell.* London: Eyre Methuen, 1973. A detailed narrative of the event that helped the Tories gain enough power to pass the Occasional Conformity Bill.

Hoppit, Julian. *A Land of Liberty? England, 1689-1727.* New York: Oxford University Press, 2000. A solid survey that places the fight over occasional conformity within a broader religious and political context.

Snyder, Henry. "The Defeat of the Occasional Conformity Bill and the Tack." *Bulletin of the Institute of Historical Research* 41 (1968): 172-192. A detailed treatment of the political and parliamentary maneuvering that produced defeat of the bill in 1704.

Watts, Michael R. *The Dissenters.* 2 vols. Oxford, England: Clarendon Press, 1995. The most comprehensive study of the Nonconformists; places the struggle over occasional conformity and the Dissenters' attitudes within the religious history of England.

SEE ALSO: May 26, 1701-Sept. 7, 1714: War of the Spanish Succession; Mar. 23-26, 1708: Defeat of the "Old Pretender"; Apr. 11, 1713: Treaty of Utrecht; Sept. 6, 1715-Feb. 4, 1716: Jacobite Rising in Scotland.

RELATED ARTICLES in *Great Lives from History: The Eighteenth Century, 1701-1800*: Queen Anne; George I; First Duke of Marlborough.

1712
PHILIP V FOUNDS THE ROYAL LIBRARY OF SPAIN

A French aristocrat who succeeded to the Spanish throne, Philip was eager to demonstrate his support of institutions that fostered Spanish culture. By founding the Royal Library of Spain, he helped to revive the Spanish Golden Age that thrived under the Habsburgs. The Royal Library, controlled by the Crown, became the government-run National Library of Spain in 1836.

LOCALE: Madrid, Spain

CATEGORIES: Cultural and intellectual history; education; organizations and institutions

KEY FIGURES

Philip V (Philip of Anjou; 1683-1746), king of Spain, r. 1700-1746

Pierre Robinet (1652-1753), French Jesuit, confessor to Philip V, and the first head of the Royal Library

Guillaume Daubenton (1648-1723), French Jesuit, confessor to Philip V, and the second head of the Royal Library

Melchor Rafael de Macanaz (1670-1760), Spanish writer, scholar, and government minister

SUMMARY OF EVENT

During the sixteenth and seventeenth centuries the Habsburg Dynasty ruled Spain. Of Austrian origin, the dynasty's last monarch was Charles II, who died without an heir in 1700. He appointed Philip, the duke of Anjou and the grandson of King Louis XIV of France, to be his successor. A French aristocrat from the powerful Bourbon Dynasty, Philip reigned as Philip V. Threatening the balance of power in Europe, his accession prompted the start of the War of the Spanish Succession in 1701, a conflict that continued until 1714.

Because he was a foreign-born monarch, Philip V wanted to ensure support for his reign by demonstrating his solidarity with Spanish culture and character. Therefore, he encouraged the foundation of institutions of learning that were to be based on the French models that had enriched French culture. The National Library of France, one such model, began as a royal library in the fifteenth century, becoming a deposit library for newly published books in the sixteenth century. France had opened its first public library, the Mazarine Library, in 1643. The legal scholar and royal official Melchor Rafael de Macanaz, who supported the Bourbon monarchy and the assertion of royal authority, emphasized the establishment of Spanish cultural institutions to revive Spain as a nation.

Although initially designated a royal library, the institution that Philip inaugurated stipulated that its collections were to be accessible to the general public. Planned in 1711, the Biblioteca Real (the Royal Library) began operations in 1712, comprising various types of collections. The king contributed approximately six thousand books he had brought from France, and his mother, Princess Marie Anne of Bavaria, donated more than two thousand books and manuscripts, making much of the original collection, books as well as archival material, multilingual. Additionally, Philip donated a collection of medallions, coins, and other items that gave the library holdings similar to those of a museum.

To manage the library, the king appointed his Jesuit confessor, Father Pierre Robinet, a French theologian, to head the institution. (Robinet earlier had been a seminary rector and diplomatic adviser.) The library was located near the palace at Alcazar. The collections occupied a portion of that building, and the facilities for the public were installed in a historic cloister nearby. The district was actually rather raucous, an area of theaters, gaming houses, and diversion parlors. The library was open on weekdays, with hours in the morning and again in the afternoon. It had a budget based not on the king's purse but on luxury taxes. Within a few years the library's personnel included several librarians and other staff, including a guard.

Less than half the budget was allotted for acquisitions, but this did not affect the library's ability to increase its holdings. In 1716, Philip singularly enhanced the capacity of the library to grow by making it a mandatory depository library: The institution was to receive one copy not only of each commercially published book but also of government publications. Philip V also required that booksellers remit to the library their vendor lists. A tradition of Spanish national bibliography comes from these lists. The reliability with which these regulations were followed and enforced varied. The inclusion of government documents and public records, however, enhanced the archival nature of the collections. The depository policy also enhanced the Spanish-language nature of the holdings. The collections grew with additional donations from the monarch and his officials, and through confiscations. Spain's many domestic and international conflicts during the eighteenth century especially favored the latter source of collection building.

In 1715, Robinet had to leave Spain because he had to defend Macanaz against the Spanish Inquisition. Robinet later returned to France and his duties as a seminary rector, and enhanced his institution's library. His successor, both as royal confessor and as head of the royal library, was another French Jesuit, Father Guillaume Daubenton. A philosopher and seminary administrator, Daubenton took up his royal posts in 1716, returning from a trip to Rome. Daubenton divided his library duties with a Madrid parish priest, and the two augmented the library staff and carried out the king's new depository policies. Daubenton continued his library work until his death in 1723.

SIGNIFICANCE

Although not a particularly forceful or decisive ruler, King Philip V did have a significant impact on intellectual and cultural development in Spain. His idea for a royal library came with ideas for other cultural enhancements. He authorized the founding in 1713 of the Real Academia Española (the Spanish Royal Academy), which is dedicated to preserving and propagating the Spanish language. The academy's *Diccionario de la lengua España* (1714; dictionary of the Spanish language) published its twenty-second edition in 2001. In 1738, Philip authorized the establishment of the Real Academia de la Historia (the Spanish Royal Academy of History). Among this academy's principal objectives is compiling a critical dictionary of Spanish history, the *Diccionario histórico-crítico de España*, which applies an analytical perspective to past events, freeing Spain's history from myth and fable. Both of the academies developed significant libraries as well.

The Royal Library of Spain, with its original "royal" designation, should not be confused with two other "royal" libraries: the library at El Escorial and the library at Madrid's royal palace, which were private and for royal use only. El Escorial library, established by King Philip II, is among the world's most beautiful and sumptuous. Philip V's institution grew from much more modest circumstances.

The Royal Library of Spain, through its literature, ephemera, and scholarship, substantively contributed to Philip's efforts to revive the Spanish Golden Age of the seventeenth century. However, Spain's economic and political decay during the eighteenth century accelerated. Decades of destabilizing conflict followed, from the time of the Napoleonic invasion at the beginning of the nineteenth century to the Civil War (1936-1939) and to the regime of Francisco Franco (1939-1975). The library has, however, remained a keystone for Spanish culture throughout the world, having been established as a national library, La Biblioteca Nacional de España, in 1836.

—*Edward A. Riedinger*

FURTHER READING

Girón, Alicia. "The Biblioteca Nacional of Spain." *Alexandria* 6, no. 2 (1994): 91-103. Girón examines the history of the national library, describing the nature and origin of the initial holdings donated by King Philip V.

Kamen, Henry. *Golden Age Spain*. 2d ed. New York: Palgrave Macmillan, 2004. Kamen traces the rise and fall of Spanish cultural development from the late fourteenth to the mid-eighteenth century.

_____. *Philip V of Spain: The King Who Reigned Twice*. New Haven, Conn.: Yale University Press, 2001. Kamen reviews Philip V's life and reign, including the cultural objectives and policies influenced by his French background.

Laubier, Guillaume de, and Jacques Bosser. *The Most Beautiful Libraries in the World*. New York: Harry N. Abrams, 2003. An illustrated tour of the historic libraries of Europe and the United States, including El Escorial in Spain.

Lynch, John. *Bourbon Spain, 1700-1808*. New York: Basil Blackwell, 1989. Lynch, a noted specialist on Spanish history, chronicles the reigns of the Spanish Bourbons, including Philip V.

McCrank, Lawrence J. "National Library of Spain." *International Dictionary of Library Histories*. Chicago: Fitzroy Dearborn, 2001. Places the founding of the library and its early years in the context of the institution's overall history.

Mayol, Carme, and Angels Massisimo. "Libraries and

Librarianship in Spain." *IFLA Journal* 19, no. 2 (1993): 131-146. An overview of the professional development of librarianship and the general development of libraries in Spain, published in the journal of the International Federation of Library Associations and Institutions.

SEE ALSO: May 26, 1701-Sept. 7, 1714: War of the Spanish Succession; Aug. 3, 1713: Foundation of the Spanish Academy; 1785: Construction of El Prado Museum Begins.
RELATED ARTICLE in *Great Lives from History: The Eighteenth Century, 1701-1800*: Philip V.

1712
STAMP ACT

Responding to an appeal from Queen Anne to curb the licentiousness of the press, England's Parliament enacted a tax of one-half cent per sheet on periodical publications. The tax became an important source of revenue and was expanded several times during the eighteenth century. As a vehicle for censorship, it was largely ineffective.

LOCALE: London, England
CATEGORIES: Communications; government and politics

KEY FIGURES
First Viscount Bolingbroke (Henry St. John; 1678-1751), English politician and author of the stamp tax
Robert Harley (First Earl of Oxford; 1661-1724), head of the British ministry, 1710, 1711-1714
Queen Anne (1665-1714), queen of England, Scotland, and Ireland, r. 1702-1714
William Cobbett (1763-1835), radical English journalist and key opponent of taxation of newspapers
Daniel Defoe (1660-1731), English novelist and protégé of Harley

SUMMARY OF EVENT
Over the course of the tumultuous seventeenth century, English society developed an appetite for printed news. During the English Civil Wars (1642-1651), both sides produced volumes of highly polemical pamphlets and news sheets; the press was essentially free of government restraints. With the restoration of the monarchy (1660) came censorship. Under the Licensing Act of 1662, only twenty presses, all but two of them in London, were permitted to operate, and anything of a political nature required the approval of the government. Theological works came under the scrutiny of the archbishop of Canterbury. For domestic news, other than the meager offer-

ings of the quasi-official *London Gazette*, people relied on handwritten newsletters circulated through coffeehouses.

The expiration of the unpopular Licensing Act in 1693 left a vacuum in press regulation, which the publishing industry was quick to exploit. Increasing public literacy, coupled with technological innovations in printing and papermaking that lowered the cost of printed papers, created a market where none had previously existed. In the resulting explosion of periodical publications, much was created of lasting value, and many precedents were set that, over the course of half a century, determined the form that journalism was to take in a free market economy.

There was also a good deal of irresponsible journalism. Faced with restrictions on access to domestic news, some journalists resorted to inventing stories, and others mixed fact with fiction to suit partisan ends. The "licentiousness of the press" forming the subject of Queen Anne's message to Parliament in 1712 encompassed not only political and religious dissent but also libel, fraud, and pornography.

The line between religious and political dissent on one hand and outright treason on the other was by no means as well defined during the reign of Queen Anne as it was later in the century. The restoration of the monarchy under Charles II had reestablished the Anglican Church, excluding Calvinist Puritans from public life and proscribing publications espousing their unique theology as blasphemous. The Presbyterian Church remained strong in Scotland, where it became associated with nationalism and separatism. In Parliament, the moderate Whig faction espoused tolerance for these Protestant Dissenters, favoring integrating them into public life; it was unclear how far such advocacy could go before becoming a real threat to the monarchy and the established church.

By the terms of the Glorious Revolution of 1688, the

Roman Catholic James II was removed from the throne of England and replaced by his eldest daughter, Mary II, and her Protestant husband, William III. Neither they nor Anne, James's second daughter, who ascended the throne of England in 1702, had surviving heirs. According to the Royal succession as established by Parliament in 1688, Anne's successor was to be George, elector of Hanover, but substantial public sentiment supported making James II's son James Edward (the "Old Pretender") king despite his Roman Catholicism. The extreme Tory position advocating a Roman Catholic monarch backed by France (with which England was at war) was frankly treasonous. Ironically, in 1712 the supporters of James Edward included Queen Anne's principal ministers, Robert Harley and the first Viscount Bolingbroke, as well (with reservations) as Anne herself.

On February 12, 1712, Parliament agreed to take into consideration a message from Queen Anne complaining of "false and scandalous libels, such as are a reproach to any government" and calling for "a remedy equal to the mischief." The speech may have been prompted by Harley; the monarch's addresses to Parliament at the opening of the session were generally written in collaboration with the Privy Council. Harley was well aware of the power of the press and used it to his advantage. For many years he employed the celebrated writer Daniel Defoe as a progovernment apologist.

In the ensuing debate, various direct methods of controlling the press were discussed, but only a measure requiring an author's name to appear on each publication passed into law. In an era when pseudonymous authorship was the rule even in scholarly discourse, this law was never enforced.

Later in the session, a stamp tax on newspapers was inserted into a general appropriations bill. Newspapers were taxed at one-half cent per sheet, and advertisements were taxed at two shillings per insertion. This tax nearly doubled the cost of a newspaper to the consumer and caused a temporary drop in circulation. Some newspapers went out of business altogether. Others adopted a pamphlet format, evading the tax until 1725, when an act of Parliament closed this loophole. Advertising revenues and outside subsidies assumed greater importance relative to subscriptions. Single-sheet anonymous broadsides, costing a farthing and hawked by unlicensed itinerant vendors, satisfied the public's appetite for "scandalous libel." Page sizes increased while type size diminished.

As a measure to "curb the licentiousness of the press" and to stifle political and religious dissent, the Stamp Act was quite ineffective. Increasing reliance on subsidies translated into greater partisan bias. Newspapers became less discriminating in the quality of the advertising they accepted and ran more product endorsements masquerading as news stories. Because the per-copy profit to the printer declined, a periodical needed a larger minimum circulation to stay afloat, and publications such as Defoe's innovative *Review*, with a maximum circulation of about four hundred, no longer appeared.

Taxing newspapers did provide the government with a significant new source of revenue. This revenue aspect has received less attention from historians than the censorship implied in taxing the press. In an era when excise taxes provided the bulk of government revenue, periodicals represented a commodity that was easy to track and was not an absolute necessity of human existence. The tax on periodicals was raised and expanded to include more categories of publications several times over the course of the eighteenth century.

SIGNIFICANCE

The perception of the 1712 Stamp Act as a measure of censorship rather than revenue dates from the early nineteenth century, when the conditions of public life and the conduct of the press had altered considerably. Viewing taxation of the press as an oppressive measure also gains credence from the controversies surrounding the 1765 Stamp Act, which extended the provisions of various English taxes on paper documents to the American colonies. In practice, prosecutions for blasphemy, breach of privilege, and libel eclipsed taxation as a means for government control of the press in Britain in the eighteenth century.

Because any commercial enterprise will vigorously oppose a tax restricting its profits, and represent its objections as defense of the public good, newspaper editorials on the Stamp Tax need to be taken with a grain of salt. The high price of newspapers was one factor making the dissemination and consumption of news a public activity in Georgian Britain. This encouraged debate and increased the likelihood that a person of moderate means would be exposed to various shades of opinion, rather than relying on a private subscription to a single newspaper.

At the close of the century, radicals such as William Cobbett maintained that taxes on periodicals selectively stifled political messages aimed at the poor. The large circulation of some unstamped broadsides, pamphlets disguised as sermons, and the illegally distributed "twopenny trash" version of the *Political Register* would seem to bear this out. By then, improvements in press technology had made a genuinely cheap periodical possible, and increasing literacy had created a market that had not existed in 1712.

One legacy of the Stamp Tax, its enlargements, and the agitation for its repeal has been the exemption of the British and American press from government regulations affecting other types of commercial activities—from sales taxes, child labor laws, and regulations affecting street vendors, for example. Today's press was shaped by a century of regulation followed by two centuries of deregulation. Taxation was part of that process, though not, as sometimes claimed, primarily as an enforcer of political conformity.

—*Martha A. Sherwood*

FURTHER READING

Clarke, Bob. *From Grub Street to Fleet Street: An Illustrated History of English Newspapers to 1899.* London: Ashgate, 2004. Includes a clear explanation of all aspects of newspaper publishing in the early 1700's, with specific examples.

Cobbett, William, ed. *A.D. 1733-1737.* Vol. 7 in *The Parliamentary History of England: From the Earliest Period to the Year 1803.* London: T. C. Hansard, 1810. Includes Queen Anne's address to Parliament on the licentiousness of the press, and a summary of the debate.

Harris, Michael. *London Newspapers in the Age of Walpole: A Study of the Origins of the English Press.* London: Associated University Presses, 1987. Discusses the economic impact of the Stamp Act on newspaper publishers.

Hunt, F. Knight. *The Fourth Estate: Contributions Towards a History of Newspapers and of the Liberty of the Press.* London: David Bogue, 1850. Presents the case for the conventional view that the 1712 Stamp Act was mainly an attempt to limit press freedom.

Raymond, Joad, ed. *News, Newspapers, and Society in Early Modern England.* Portland, Oreg.: Frank Cass, 1999. Main emphasis is on the seventeenth century; includes information on the economic impact of the stamp tax on the publishing industry.

SEE ALSO: Mar. 1, 1711: Addison and Steele Establish *The Spectator*; 1736: *Gentleman's Magazine* Initiates Parliamentary Reporting; Mar. 20, 1750-Mar. 14, 1752: Johnson Issues *The Rambler*; Beginning Apr., 1763: The *North Briton* Controversy; Sept. 10, 1763: Publication of the *Freeman's Journal*; 1774: Hansard Begins Reporting Parliamentary Debates; Jan. 1, 1777: France's First Daily Newspaper Appears; 1792-1793: Fichte Advocates Free Speech; Jan. 4, 1792-1797: The *Northern Star* Calls for Irish Independence.

RELATED ARTICLES in *Great Lives from History: The Eighteenth Century, 1701-1800*: Queen Anne; First Viscount Bolingbroke; Daniel Defoe.

April 6, 1712
NEW YORK CITY SLAVE REVOLT

A small group of black and American Indian slaves rebelled against mistreatment and restrictive laws, leading to further legal restrictions on slaves, freed or not, including the weakening of due process rights and the prohibition against owning or inheriting property. Also, slave owners, before they could free a slave, had to pay a bond to the government as well as an annual allowance for life to each freed slave.

LOCALE: Manhattan Island (now New York City)

CATEGORIES: Wars, uprisings, and civil unrest; social issues and reform

KEY FIGURES

May Bickley (d. 1724), an attorney general who led the prosecution of those indicted in the conspiracy and revolt

Cuffee (fl. early eighteenth century) and

Dick (fl. early eighteenth century), two slaves who presumably were promised immunity to testify against others implicated in the rebellion

Robert Hunter (1666-1734), royal governor of New York, 1709-1719

Elias Neau (1662-1722), a Huguenot merchant who ministered to New York City slaves

John Sharpe (fl. early eighteenth century), an Anglican chaplain to the British garrison at Fort Anne

SUMMARY OF EVENT

The New York City slave revolt of 1712 calls attention to slavery having become more firmly established in colonial New York than in any other British province north of Chesapeake Bay. Slaves were already an integral part of the labor force when England conquered Dutch New Netherland in 1664. As European immigration lagged,

An early eighteenth century illustration of a slave market at Wall Street in New York City. (The Granger Collection, New York)

1710's

slave labor became increasingly important. Between 1703 and 1723, New York's total population almost doubled, increasing from 20,540 to 40,564; but its black population (slaves and free blacks were lumped together statistically and listed in the census as "Negroes") almost tripled, jumping from 2,253 to 6,171.

As the number of bondsmen increased, so did the anxiety level of white New Yorkers. In 1708, following the grisly murder of a Long Island planter and his family, four slaves were tried, convicted, and executed "with all the torment possible for a terror to others." Shortly thereafter, the provincial assembly passed the Act for Preventing the Conspiracy of Slaves, which defined the judicial proceedings and made death the penalty for any slave found guilty of murder or attempted murder. Fear of slave conspiracy led whites to look with ambivalence upon Anglican catechist Elias Neau's teaching among New York City blacks and American Indians.

Small-scale slave owning prevailed in New York. Few white families owned more than a slave or two, so slave husbands, wives, and children might be scattered among several households. Regulations restricting their freedom of movement were bitterly resented by slaves, because they interfered with their domestic life. Such restrictions often were more apparent than real, because slavery in New York City and surrounding villages, where slaves were most heavily concentrated, was tied to

a developing urban economy that demanded a flexible, if not free, labor supply. Slaves in New York City and Albany often hired themselves out, splitting the pay with their respective owners, but otherwise lived separately from their masters. The hustle and bustle of the urban economic scene afforded slaves considerable opportunity to meet, socialize, and discuss common grievances, despite the best efforts of whites to keep them under surveillance.

The slave uprising of April 6, 1712, apparently began as a conspiracy on March 25, the day that was formerly celebrated as New Year's Day. The ringleaders reportedly were of the Cormantine and Pawpaw peoples, Africans who had not been long in New York; a few Spanish Indian slaves; and at least one free black, a practitioner of African medicine and magic who reportedly supplied special powder to protect the rebels from the weapons of the whites. Their motivation, according to both Governor Robert Hunter and Chaplain John Sharpe, was revenge for ill treatment at the hands of their respective masters. Their goal was freedom, which, claimed Hunter and Sharpe, was to be achieved by burning New York City and killing the white people on Manhattan.

During the early morning hours of Sunday, April 6, 1712, about two dozen conspirators, armed with guns, swords, knives, and clubs, gathered in an orchard in the East Ward on the northeast edge of New York City. They

93

set fire to several outbuildings and waited in ambush for the whites who came to put out the blaze, killing nine and wounding seven. Soldiers were dispatched from the fort, but when they arrived, the rebels had dispersed, taking refuge in the woods surrounding the town. The next day, local militiamen systematically searched Manhattan Island for the rebellious blacks. Rather than surrender, six slaves killed themselves, with several cutting their own throats.

White New Yorkers were in full panic. "We have about 70 Negro's in Custody," read a dispatch from New York, dated April 14 but published in the *Boston News-Letter* on April 21, but it was "fear'd that most of the Negro's here (who are very numerous) knew of the Late Conspiracy to murder the Christians." Fear of another uprising drove the judicial proceedings. On April 9, a coroner's jury implicated thirty-eight slaves, identifying fourteen of them as murderers. In accordance with the 1708 conspiracy act, the coroner's findings were turned over to the Court of Quarter Sessions of the Peace, which convened on April 11. Attorney General May Bickley handled the prosecution, moving the trials from the Quarter Sessions to the State Supreme Court on June 3.

Forty-two slaves and one free black were indicted and tried. Crucial to both the indictments and trials was the testimony of two slaves: Cuffee, who belonged to baker Peter Vantilborough, and Dick, a boy slave owned by Harmanus Burger, a blacksmith. The coroner's jury had found Cuffee and Dick guilty of at least two murders, but Bickley apparently promised them immunity, and they became the Crown's prime witnesses. Some whites, including such substantial citizens as former mayor David Provost, coroner Henry Wileman, and lawyers Jacob Regnier and David Jamison, testified for a few of the defendants. However, the general adequacy of defense counsel may well be doubted. Many of the convictions hinged upon the dubious testimony of Cuffee and young Dick, both of whom were manipulated by Bickley, described by Governor Hunter as "a busy waspish man." Bickley also demonstrated considerable bias against certain slave defendants, depending upon who owned them. For example, Mars, belonging to Jacob Regnier, a rival attorney with whom Bickley had a private quarrel, was tried twice and acquitted before being found guilty in the third trial and sentenced to be hanged.

Most of the trials were over by early June. Twenty-three slaves were convicted of murder; fifteen slaves were acquitted, along with one free black. Two slaves were found guilty of assault with intent to kill, and two were acquitted of that charge. The twenty-five who were convicted were sentenced to death. Twenty were to be hanged; three were burned alive, one in a slow fire for eight to ten hours until consumed to ashes. Another was broken upon the wheel and left to die, and one was hung in chains and "so to continue without sustenance until death." Eleven were "executed at once," including those burned, broken at the wheel, and chained without food or water. These barbaric executions were defended by Governor Hunter as "the most exemplary that could be possibly thought of."

Yet even Hunter doubted the justice of it all. He postponed the execution of six slaves, including two Spanish American Indians taken and sold as slaves despite their claim of being free men, a pregnant slave woman, and the much tried and finally convicted Mars. At Hunter's request, Queen Anne pardoned several of them, and perhaps all of those he had reprieved (the record is rather vague), despite the efforts of Bickley in New York and of Lord Cornbury, a former governor of New York, in London to obstruct the pardons.

SIGNIFICANCE

There were other ramifications of the slave uprising. The provincial government passed laws making it impossible to free slaves without putting up a £200 bond and paying the freed slave £20 per year for life. Africans, American Indians, and mulattoes were prohibited from inheriting or otherwise owning property. Finally, due process rights were weakened for slaves accused of murder or conspiracy. In the wake of the revolt, Elias Neau, the preacher and catechist of Trinity Church, found it difficult to continue his school for blacks and American Indians. Only two of his many pupils were implicated in the conspiracy, and Chaplain John Sharpe doubted that either was involved in the violence.

After the rebellion, New Yorkers were reluctant to import slaves directly from Africa or to purchase Spanish Indians as slaves. Black slaves from the West Indies were preferred over the other two groups. Yet slavery remained a primary source of labor for both the province and city of New York, slaves constituting about 15 percent of the population. In 1730, other regulations were added to the slave code because "many Mischiefs had been Occasioned by the too great Liberty allowed to Negro and other Slaves." In 1741, white paranoia and slave discontent provoked a so-called slave conspiracy in which 150 slaves and 25 whites were jailed. Of that number, 18 slaves and 4 whites were hanged, 13 blacks were burned alive, and 70 were sold and sent to the West Indies.

—Ronald W. Howard

FURTHER READING

Goodfriend, Joyce D. *Before the Melting Pot: Society and Culture in Colonial New York City, 1664-1730*. Princeton, N.J.: Princeton University Press, 1992. Chapter 6 provides considerable insight into the life and labors of New York City slaves, both before and after the 1712 revolt.

Harris, Leslie M. *In the Shadow of Slavery: African Americans in New York City, 1626-1823*. Chicago: University of Chicago Press, 2003. Chapter 1, "Slavery in Colonial New York," includes information about the revolts of 1712 and 1741.

Hoffer, Peter Charles. *The Great New York Conspiracy of 1741: Slavery, Crime, and Colonial War*. Lawrence: University Press of Kansas, 2003. Hoffer, a legal historian, reexamines the trials of slaves who were charged with conspiring to destroy New York City in the summer of 1741. He places the litigation in a legal and historic context, and explains how the law defined and policed slavery.

Kammen, Michael. *Colonial New York: A History*. New York: Charles Scribner's Sons, 1975. Chapter 11 relates the slave revolts of 1712 and 1741 to larger social and economic problems in colonial New York society.

Lustig, Mary Lou. *Robert Hunter, 1666-1734*. Syracuse, N.Y.: Syracuse University Press, 1983. Gives a brief but pertinent summary of the slave revolts and the persons most associated with the trials.

McManus, Edgar J. *A History of Negro Slavery in New York*. Syracuse, N.Y.: Syracuse University Press, 1966. Goes into considerable detail regarding the conditions that contributed to the 1712 uprising.

Scott, Kenneth. "The Slave Insurrection in New York in 1712." *New-York Historical Society Quarterly* 45 (January, 1961): 147-165. Describes the revolt and the trials that followed, and notes the pertinent source collections.

Wood, Peter. "Slave Resistance." In *Encyclopedia of the North American Colonies*. Vol. 2. New York: Charles Scribner's Sons, 1993. Relates the 1741 New York revolt to other examples of slave resistance in North America.

SEE ALSO: 18th cent.: Expansion of the Atlantic Slave Trade; May 15, 1702-Apr. 11, 1713: Queen Anne's War; Aug., 1712: Maya Rebellion in Chiapas; 1730-1739: First Maroon War; Oct. 10, 1733-Oct. 3, 1735: War of the Polish Succession; Sept. 9, 1739: Stono Rebellion; 1760-1776: Caribbean Slave Rebellions; 1780-1781: Rebellion of Tupac Amaru II; Apr. 12, 1787: Free African Society Is Founded; Aug. 22, 1791-Jan. 1, 1804: Haitian Independence; Mar. 16, 1792: Denmark Abolishes the Slave Trade; July, 1795-Mar., 1796: Second Maroon War.

RELATED ARTICLES in *Great Lives from History: The Eighteenth Century, 1701-1800*: Benjamin Banneker; Benjamin Franklin; John Jay; Nanny; Guillaume-Thomas Raynal; Paul Revere; Benjamin Rush; Samuel Sewall; Granville Sharp; Toussaint Louverture; Phillis Wheatley.

April 13-August 11, 1712
SECOND VILLMERGEN WAR

In Switzerland's fourth and last religious war, Swiss Protestants were victorious, thus gaining constitutional equality as well as political powers commensurate with their majority status and economic wealth.

ALSO KNOWN AS: Toggenburg War
LOCALE: Northeastern Switzerland
CATEGORIES: Wars, uprisings, and civil unrest; religion and theology

KEY FIGURES

Leodegar Bürgisser (1640-1717), prince-abbot of St. Gallen
Louis XIV (1638-1715), king of France, r. 1643-1715

SUMMARY OF EVENT

The Second Villmergen War was a consequence of a Swiss religious divide that had begun in the sixteenth century. In Switzerland's Protestant-Catholic wars of 1529 and 1531, Catholic armies prevailed as a result of tactical blunders by Protestant commanders. The resulting Kappel Treaty of 1531 gave the Catholic cantons (regional states) a preponderant share of power in the federal legislature, or diet. Catholic minorities in Protestant cantons, moreover, were theoretically guaranteed religious toleration, whereas no such rights were extended to religious minorities in the Catholic cantons. Protestants were also obliged to take the federal oath, "by God and the saints," in contradiction of their beliefs.

Switzerland in the eighteenth century remained a loose confederation of thirteen cantons. The Catholic faith was established in seven of the cantons, including Schwyz, Lucerne, Uri, and Fribourg. Protestants controlled four, most notably the wealthy and powerful cantons of Zurich and Berne. Joint Catholic-Protestant administrations were set up in the cantons of Glarus and Aargau. Because Aargau was strategically located between Zurich and Berne, it was especially prone to religious conflict. In addition to the thirteen cantons, a number of neighboring city-states, most notably St. Gallen and Geneva, were tied to the Swiss confederation through alliances. Switzerland's federal diet, where unanimity or consensus was required for most important decisions, had become so weak in the previous century that it did not even hold meetings between 1663 and 1776.

Throughout the confederation, religious minorities within a given canton lived in difficult circumstances and often suffered discrimination, sometimes persecution. Social contacts between the two communities were relatively rare. Catholic cantons and cities made alliances with France and Savoy, just as Protestants sought to acquire the support of powerful states in Germany. Although Switzerland did not directly participate in the Thirty Years' War (1618-1648), Swiss mercenaries fought on both sides, and the conflict intensified religious suspicions and hatred in the country.

The first Villmergen War (1656) broke out as a result of Catholic authorities in Schwyz turning over several Protestants to the Inquisition and then forcing thirty-seven others to seek refuge in Zurich. After Schwyz refused to restore the property of the refugees, Zurich and Berne declared war on five of the Catholic cantons. Protestant leaders failed to coordinate their military operations, however, resulting in a Catholic victory in the key battle at Villmergen, which was a small village located in Aargau near the Zurich border. The war formally ended with the Treaty of Baden (1656), which preserved most of the conditions under the Kappel Treaty. Since Protestants were disproportionately prosperous and represented a growing majority of the total Swiss population, they bitterly resented their continuing second-class status within the confederation.

Religious animosities in Switzerland further increased after French king Louis XIV revoked the civil rights of Protestants in 1685. As thousands of French refugees streamed into Switzerland, the resulting dislocations and disagreements threatened to produce another civil war. The situation worsened in 1697: Another national crisis occurred in that year, when Catholics in

St. Gallen ignored an agreement and carried the cross upright in a religious procession. In large part, armed conflict was averted by Protestant fears that Louis XIV would come to the aid of Swiss Catholics should civil war occur. From 1701 to 1713, however, Louis's involvement in the War of the Spanish Succession made such an intervention very unlikely, and this situation emboldened militant Protestants to consider using military force to change the status quo.

The immediate cause of the Second Villmergen War was the building of a new road connecting the Catholic canton of Schwyz with the Austrian border by way of Wattwill, a city in the region of Toggenburg, where numerous Protestant enclaves were located. Protestants throughout northeastern Switzerland objected to the project, because they thought it could be used to oppress Protestants and because of its potential interference with Zurich's access to the Protestant portions of Glarus. The ruling Catholic abbot of St. Gallen, Leodegar Bürgisser, exercised control over a sprawling and diverse area that included Toggenburg, and he was one of the most enthusiastic supporters of the road.

Beginning in 1707, Bürgisser ordered all the men of Wattwill to work on the road. He claimed to possess the traditional right to command compulsory labor service (called the *corvée*). Wattwill's residents, however, refused, claiming that they had earlier acquired exemption from the hated *corvée*. A regional leader of Schwyz, Joseph Stadler, tried to support the Wattwill dissidents, but he was overthrown and executed in 1708. Pope Clement XI and Holy Roman Emperor Joseph I encouraged Bürgisser not to back down. Finally in early 1712, the abbot lost patience with Wattwill and dispatched troops to coerce the town's men to work.

Protestant residents of Toggenburg, led by Nabholz of Zurich, rallied to the support of Wattwill. An assembly of angry Toggenburgers declared their independence from St. Gallen. Large crowds occupied three strategically located castles and two monasteries. On April 13, two Protestant cantons, Zurich and Berne, confident that Louis XIV would remain neutral, issued a declaration of war against St. Gallen. Five of the Catholic cantons as well as the allied state of Valais responded by declaring war on the side of St. Gallen. The city-states of Geneva and Neuchâtel then came to the assistance of Berne. The rest of Switzerland remained neutral.

In contrast to the previous Villmergen war, the armies of Zurich and Berne cooperated with each other in a common strategy. In addition, the Catholic cantons, because of their limited funds, were at a disadvantage in equipment and supplies. Protestant forces captured Wyl on April 22, followed by the monastery of St. Gallen. They then prevailed in battles at Mellingen on May 22 and at Bremgarten on May 26. After Protestant soldiers captured Baden on June 1, the Catholic leaders of Lucerne and Uri signaled their desire to negotiate an end to the fighting. Representatives of the cantons began negotiations at Aarau in early July, and they reached an agreement on terms favorable to the Protestants on July 18. Hundreds of soldiers, mistakenly believing that the fighting was over, began to go home, but the governments of three cantons—Schwyz, Unterwalden, and Zug—repudiated the terms of the proposed treaty and vowed to continue fighting.

The Bernese army, led by Jean de Saconay, consisted of approximately eight thousand troops, while the Catholic army had a slight numerical advantage. The Protestant army had acquired heavy artillery and additional protective armor, however. On July 25, the two armies finally faced each other in the decisive battle of the war, which took place on a plain about a mile north of Villmergen. Catholic generals, uninformed about the enemy's artillery, ordered a frontal attack, which resulted in an overwhelming victory for the Protestants. The fighting was extremely violent. Historical records indicate that 2,000 Catholic soldiers were killed and 540 were taken prisoner, while Protestant losses totaled 206 deaths and 607 wounded. Following the battle, the Protestant army pillaged Villmergen and destroyed many of its buildings. A few days later, the three Catholic cantons signaled their willingness to accept the terms that had been negotiated at Aarau.

SIGNIFICANCE

On August 11, 1712, the Second Villmergen War formally ended with the Treaty of Aarau. As a result, Catholics of Switzerland lost their dominant position in the confederation, and they were forced to accept parity with Protestants in the jointly administered territories and in federal tribunals. Berne and Zurich expanded the areas under their control and gained a greater role in the Swiss Confederation. The peace treaty further stipulated that religious differences would henceforth be arbitrated by a special tribunal having an equal number of Catholic and Protestant judges. Somewhat later, the abbot of St. Abbot finally agreed to provide political and religious freedom to the Protestants of Toggenburg.

Some conservative Swiss Catholics hoped to reverse the terms of the Treaty of Aarau. In 1715, the Catholic cantons and France entered into a secret treaty, called the *Trucklibund* (named after the small box in which the treaty was concealed). In the treaty, France promised to provided Swiss Catholics with armed support in the event of renewed hostilities. Despite several dangerous crises, however, Swiss leaders managed to work out a number of compromises, and within a decade the *Trucklibund* was almost forgotten. The preservation of the confederation through two major eighteenth century crises, the Second Villmergen War and the *Trucklibund*, helped prepare the way for Switzerland to evolve into a unified federation during the next century.

—*Thomas Tandy Lewis*

FURTHER READING

Bonjour, Edgar, et al. *A Short History of Switzerland*. Oxford, England: Oxford University Press, 1955. Remains the most widely available general history of Switzerland in English; includes very good summaries of the Villmergen Wars.

Luck, James M. *History of Switzerland: From Before the Beginnings to the Days of the Present*. Palo Alto, Calif.: Society for Promotion of Science and Scholarship, 1986. Provides a context for understanding the complex history and political institutions of the small country.

Robertson, Ian. *Switzerland*. New York: W. W. Norton, 1992. Includes a useful historical summary that helps to understand the complexities of Swiss politics and culture.

Steinberg, Jonathan. *Why Switzerland?* New York: Cambridge University Press, 1996. A short introduction to the history, culture, and geography of the country that provides a context for the general reader.

SEE ALSO: May 26, 1701-Sept. 7, 1714: War of the Spanish Succession; July 24, 1702-Oct. 1, 1704: Camisard Risings in the Cévennes; Sept. 8, 1713: Papal Bull *Unigenitus*.

RELATED ARTICLES in *Great Lives from History: The Eighteenth Century, 1701-1800:* Jean-Paul Marat; Jacques Necker; Jean-Jacques Rousseau.

August, 1712
MAYA REBELLION IN CHIAPAS

An anticolonial, indigenous rebellion against Spanish occupation in southern Mexico, initially rooted in religious persecution but later a revolt encouraged by indigenous elites, was unprecedented in scale, longevity, and leadership structure. The rebellion led to reform of the Mexican Indian labor system by the Spanish and set in motion demands for Mexican independence from Spain.

ALSO KNOWN AS: Tzeltal Revolt

LOCALE: Chiapas, Mexico

CATEGORIES: Wars, uprisings, and civil unrest; government and politics; social issues and reform

KEY FIGURES

María López (b. c. 1699), witness to an apparition of the Virgin Mary for which she was denounced and excessively punished

Fray Simón (fl. 1712), a local parish priest who first denounced the legitimacy of the apparitional encounter and alerted the Spanish authorities

Sebastían Gómez (fl. 1712), the leader of the original cult formed in response to the apparition, who transformed the cult into a separatist religious movement

SUMMARY OF EVENT

The Maya Rebellion of 1712 was, at root, the culmination of nearly two centuries of resentment among the Tzeltal, Tzotzil, and Chol sub-Mayan Chiapas cultures, which had faced brutal enslavement and dehumanization through the Spanish *encomienda* system of forced labor. Indigenous peoples were "granted" to the conquerors along with land, and biannual tribute payments were demanded and forcefully collected by Spanish colonizers.

The Maya of mountainous Chiapas in southern Mexico were among the last Mexican Indians to be subdued by Hernán Cortés's Spanish forces, who had been sent to the area in 1522 to collect tribute after conquering the Aztec Empire in Tenochtitlán (now Mexico City). When the Chiapans resisted, more forces were dispatched to subdue the uprising. It took an additional six years, however, to completely subdue the rebellion. More than in any other part of Mexico, the Chiapas rebellion simmered, and it flared up again in 1545.

The Maya Rebellion of 1712 is unique because it was fueled, initially, by passions against religious persecution. In June of 1712, a thirteen-year-old girl, María

López, daughter of a local church overseer, willingly admitted to witnessing an apparition of the Virgin Mary, which led to the formation of a local cult and its building of an unauthorized shrine at the site of the apparition. The local parish priest, Fray Simón, alerted Church authorities of the shrine and locally denounced the miracle. He proceeded to lash both López and her father, Augustin. López, however, held to her story, and, because she was martyred after being punished, her actions strengthened the cult's resolve to resist the inevitable: a Spanish military response. Moreover, word spread about the apparition, and individuals in the region increasingly made pilgrimages to the shrine, creating a more pervasive and incendiary regional insurgence.

These events spawned a regional conspiracy originally consisting of five regional parish officeholders who, ultimately, became the rebel leaders of a burgeoning army of sorts, estimated at five thousand "soldiers of the virgin." This army had murdered numerous Catholic priests who had attempted to hold fast to institutional procedure and philosophy. More fuel was provided to the movement, along with organizational structure, after the arrival of Sebastían Gómez, a Mayan Tzotzil from nearby San Pedro Chenalo, who transformed the resistance into an actual movement by claiming authority to ordain priests and bishops. He said that heavenly conversations with San Pedro (Saint Peter) gave him the power of ordination. The insurgency thereby was converted into a local version of a "protestant" phenomenon.

The cult reformed itself as the one true church and rejected the legitimacy of the existing Roman Catholic Church, but it did not reject Christianity. In the few months that remained of 1712, rebel bands established themselves to carry the fight to the Spanish, a fight that had been funded primarily by ransacking and pillaging regional church facilities; there was an October break, however, to bring in the harvest. The riches gained by these rebel bands were substantial and widely disparate, leading to considerable dissension between bands and paralyzing to some degree the force of the resistance.

The Spanish, numbering only about two hundred, were initially unable to extinguish the revolt. They were stationed in Ciudad Real, the Spanish administrative capital in this region of Chiapas. However, an effective Spanish counteroffensive began in August with a force of about five hundred troops, assembled from various regional militias, which laid siege to Huixtan, just east of

Ciudad Real. Additional reinforcements sent from Guatemala City soon added strength to the Spanish offensive. Beginning in November of 1712, rebel bands and their leaders were beginning to face arrest, trial, and execution for what the Spanish regarded as treasonous crimes. Rebel bands were too overmatched to maintain their initial ferocity; indeed, most had been armed with wooden pikes and slingshots, clearly ineffective against superior Spanish arms. The original rebel leaders were able to continue to pester the Spanish by defying capture for another four months.

After further analysis, what seemed a popular uprising at the time appears to have been, however, the result of a local group of Mayan elites seizing the popular outrage over the treatment of María López and her father. The elites took advantage of the situation to reestablish themselves in the network among which tribute and taxes were traditionally distributed. The elites had been replaced in the network by principals in the Spanish colonial administration. The religious-based outrage provided the original fuel to the rebellion, but the longevity of the resistance among a few of the locals was attributable to those disenfranchised local elites desperately trying to regain lost wealth and power. In attempting to reassert their privileges within the militarized resistance, these elites served to dissolve ethnic solidarity. Thus, the majority of the rebels were subdued in a few months. Rebel solidarity was further fragmented by the subsequent formation of a rival cult around claims of yet another Marian apparition.

The unusual ferocity and tenacity encountered by the Spanish in this particular Mayan rebellion, nevertheless, was an eye-opening experience for the Spanish colonial administration. These factors can be attributed to the remoteness of this particular group of highland Mayan subcultures. Groups inhabiting areas nearby Ciudad Real, for example, or along connective routes with higher traffic volumes, encountered the Spanish much more frequently than did the remote highland groups participating in the 1712 rebellion. Consequently, they were more indoctrinated in accepting social relations between Spanish and the various indigenous groups, being more familiar with Spanish attitudes, behaviors, and institutions. The relatively remote highland groups benefited from a sense of unity, derived from similar lifestyles, against a common, culturally distinct, and oppressive enemy; a resistance similar to highland groups around the world.

SIGNIFICANCE

The Maya Rebellion of 1712 was unprecedented in both scale and longevity, prompting the Spanish to revise their practices concerning Mexican Indian labor. Typically, uprisings were limited to single communities reacting to threats from outsiders. The rebellions were usually short-lived and were often leaderless because of their spontaneity, making them easy to overcome. The 1712 rebellion had many unusual elements, however, including ransacking and pillaging of Mexican Indians by Mexican Indians, the formation of a cult around internal leadership, and the importation of outside leadership to further incite and organize a large army. The 1712 rebellion also was unique because of its early religious focus. Furthermore, had that initial focus not been diluted by the corrupt influence of local elites, the rebellion's impact may have been even more significant.

Also, the rebellion was a precursor to myriad small-scale rebellions of the latter half of the eighteenth century, as Mexican independence drew near. Rebels would come to articulate a vision of a new indigenous society with new leaders, institutions, rituals, and myths, powerful inspiration for later movements.

—*James Knotwell*

FURTHER READING

Gosner, Kevin, and Arij Ouweneel, eds. *Indigenous Revolts in Chiapas and the Andean Highlands.* Amsterdam: Centre for Latin American Research and Documentation, University of Amsterdam, 1996. A collection that explores the history of anticolonial uprisings and revolts in Chiapas as well as in the Andes of South America. Includes the chapter "Historical Perspectives on Maya Resistance: The Tzeltal Revolt of 1712." Illustrations and bibliography.

_____. *Soldiers of the Virgin: The Moral Economy of a Colonial Maya Rebellion.* Tucson: University of Arizona Press, 1992. A detailed presentation of the main figures, events, and historical significance of the rebellion.

Grube, Nikolai, ed. *Maya: Divine Kings of the Rain Forest.* Cologne, Germany: Kónemann, 2001. A comprehensive, 480-page examination of the Maya of Mexico. Includes the chapter "Between Conformity and Rebellion: The Maya Society in the Colonial Period (1546-1811)." Illustrations, bibliography, and index.

Macleod, Murdo J., and Robert Wasserstrom, eds. *Spaniards and Indians in Southeastern Mesoamerica: Essays on the History of Ethnic Relations.* Lincoln: University of Nebraska Press, 1983. A more general approach to understanding relations between the Spanish and the Mexican Indians.

Wasserstrom, Robert. "Ethnic Violence and Indigenous Protest: The Tzeltal (Maya) Rebellion of 1712." *Journal of Latin American Studies* 12 (1980): 1-19. Provides an additional perspective of the historical significance of the rebellion.

SEE ALSO: Apr. 6, 1712: New York City Slave Revolt; 1730-1739: First Maroon War; Sept. 9, 1739: Stono Rebellion; Jan. 24, 1744-Aug. 31, 1829: Dagohoy Rebellion in the Philippines; 1760-1776: Caribbean Slave Rebellions; May 8, 1763-July 24, 1766: Pontiac's Resistance; 1776: Foundation of the Viceroyalty of La Plata; 1780-1781: Rebellion of Tupac Amaru II; 1786: Discovery of the Mayan Ruins at Palenque; Oct. 18, 1790-July, 1794: Little Turtle's War; Aug. 22, 1791-Jan. 1, 1804: Haitian Independence; July, 1795-Mar., 1796: Second Maroon War.

RELATED ARTICLES in *Great Lives from History: The Eighteenth Century, 1701-1800*: Little Turtle; Nanny; Pontiac; Guillaume-Thomas Raynal; Toussaint Louverture; Tupac Amaru II.

1713
FOUNDING OF LOUISBOURG

Following territorial losses in Canada as a result of the Treaty of Utrecht (1713), which ended the War of the Spanish Succession, France chose to establish a new fortress at Louisbourg, on Cape Breton Island, to protect its North American interests.

LOCALE: New Breton (Nova Scotia), Canada
CATEGORIES: Colonization; expansion and land acquisition; wars, uprisings, and civil unrest

KEY FIGURES

Joseph de Monbeton de Brouillan (Saint-Ovide; 1676-1755), French officer and later governor of Isle Royale

Jean-François de Verville (c. 1680-1729), first architect of Fortress Louisbourg

Étienne Verrier (1683-1747), chief builder of Fortress Louisbourg

William Pitt the Elder (1708-1778), prime minister of Great Britain, 1757-1761, 1766-1768

SUMMARY OF EVENT

The terms of the Treaty of Utrecht (1713) required France to give up its claims to Newfoundland and Acadia (the southern part of present-day Nova Scotia) to Great Britain. The treaty further forced all French inhabitants of these areas to leave within a year. In response, the French government at Versailles began looking for a resettlement location that would not only accommodate its banished French colonists but also ensure a continued French strategic and economic presence in North American New France.

During the summer of 1713, an expeditionary force,

under the command of Joseph de Monbeton de Brouillan, known as Saint-Ovide, embarked from Placentia, Newfoundland, to Cape Breton (the northern island of present-day Nova Scotia) in search of a suitable location for the new French colony. Saint-Ovide's orders from Versailles were to find a location that would not only provide a good harbor for reestablishing the French fishing trade lost in Newfoundland but also support the building of a new fort to safeguard against further threats from England. Saint-Ovide's search led him to what was known as English Harbor, on the eastern coast of Cape Breton. The harbor had been used by French and English fishermen since the late seventeenth century; however, no major settlement had ever been erected there. With the coming of winter and the pressure to establish a new port and fortification, English Harbor became an attractive final choice for Saint-Ovide. By November of 1713, the population of the new colony numbered nearly five hundred.

In the tradition of other New Breton harbors that had been given names of saints by French fishermen, Saint-Ovide renamed English Harbor as Port Saint-Louis in honor of France's patron saint, Louis IX (1214-1270). The following year, France's King Louis XIV (1638-1715) changed the name to Louisbourg in his own honor; he also renamed Cape Breton the Isle Royale, in recognition of what the king wanted to be understood as the reestablishment of French rights to North America.

The attractiveness of Isle Royale as a new permanent settlement lay in its location. France had depended heavily on the fishing industry that the former colonies in Newfoundland had provided; Isle Royale's fishing waters offered a lucrative alternative. Another geographic

BRITISH AND FRENCH CANADIAN TERRITORIES, 1713

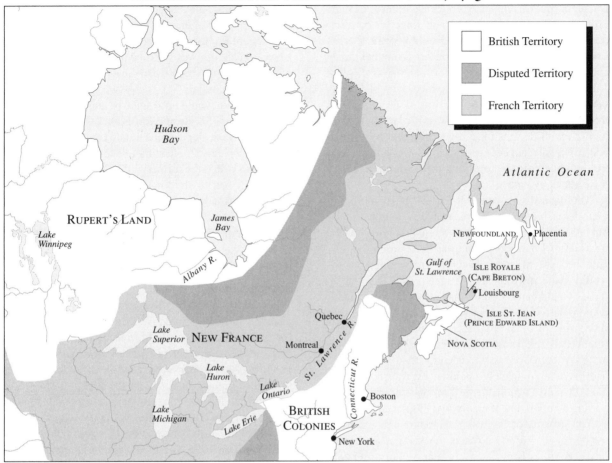

asset was the island's sailing distance from France; it offered the shortest link between the French Atlantic ports and the North American continent, which would make it quicker to supply the colony with needed materials and soldiers. Finally, Isle Royale would serve a strategic purpose: It lay at the entrance of the St. Lawrence River, the river that provided access to the French strongholds of Quebec and Montreal and other settlements in the Canadian interior.

Beyond Isle Royale's economic and strategic advantages, Saint-Ovide also saw the practical advantages of the island's location. Wildlife, forests, and mineral wealth would enable the inhabitants of the area to meet most domestic needs to sustain a port at Louisbourg. Isle Royale did not, however, provide the best advantages for farming. Scarce arable land and the short growing season would limit the island's agricultural production. Still, this limitation was mitigated by the strategic and eco-nomic advantages of the island, and Port Louisbourg and the rest of Isle Royale seemed to be the best choice for a new French colony.

Between 1715 and 1717, both French governmental and colonial officials began rethinking where to establish the administrative center of Isle Royale, debating the advantages of Port Dauphin over Port Louisbourg. While several issues surrounded the debate, the major concern was the defense of each location's harbor. Port Dauphin had more advantages as a defensible harbor than did Louisbourg. While initial debates gave the favorable nod to Port Dauphin, however, Port Louisbourg continued to expand its thriving fishing business while remaining the island's judicial center. By 1717, Louisbourg's economic success outweighed the military considerations of Port Dauphin, and the government decided to make Louisbourg the administrative center for that part of New France.

Louisbourg's harbor, though less defensible than Port Dauphin, could accommodate a greater number of ships. Moreover, the locale had sufficient stone for construction of ramparts to fortify what would become Fortress Louisbourg and its garrisons. The key figure behind the construction of Louisbourg's fortification works was Jean-François de Verville, an engineer who had been a veteran of numerous fortification siege campaigns throughout Europe since 1704. Verville began his work in 1720 with designs for a town protected by fortified walls. Verville had been instructed by Versailles to control building costs by fortifying the city only from surprise attack by land.

Verville had had plans to construct a much more elaborate defensive structure, typical of those built in Europe, but this was not to be. The view from Versailles was that invasion of Louisbourg from the shore would be difficult, because the open beaches surrounding the fort would make invaders easy targets. Thus, limited defenses would be enough to repel attackers from that direction. Verville was later replaced in 1725 by a short succession of other architects, the most notable being Étienne Verrier, whose influence would redefine the ultimate layout of Fortress Louisbourg. By 1741, the town had become completely enclosed by walls containing more than four hundred large guns and cannon and supporting a population of nearly two thousand.

The strength of Fortress Louisbourg was put to the test during the European War of the Austrian Succession (also known as King George's War by European colonists living in North America). In 1744, when word of the war reached the governor of Louisbourg, the Marquis de Duquesnel, he launched a campaign to retake the land in Acadia that had been lost to England thirty years earlier. Duquesnel's movements, although unsuccessful, alarmed the British in New England, who in turn mounted an invasion force of more than four thousand troops to take Fortress Louisbourg. The British were intent on destroying any further advances by the French in North America.

The expedition, under the command of William Pepperell of the Virginia colony, set out from Boston on March 24, 1745. Ironically, an army of British colonists from Massachusetts, New York, Pennsylvania, and New Jersey managed to sneak past Fortress Louisbourg's cannon under the dark of night and launch, the next morning, a successful surprise attack against the fort's southern battery; this was the very surprise the fort had originally been planned to deflect. Using captured French cannon, Pepperell's troops began bombarding the main fort and

town. Aided by British warships that blockaded Louisbourg's harbor, the siege of the mighty fortress lasted more than one month, with the British ultimately claiming victory. English control of the fort lasted until 1748, when Louisbourg was returned to France as a condition of the Treaty of Aix-la-Chapelle ending the War of the Austrian Succession.

Louisbourg would once again be attacked by the British in June, 1758, during the French and Indian War. Again, a British siege of one month forced the French to surrender on July 26, leaving one thousand French soldiers dead within the fortress walls. With the second seizure of the fort by the English, Louisbourg fell permanently into British hands. On directives from the British prime minister, William Pitt the Elder, orders were given to begin demolishing Louisbourg in February, 1760. On October 17, 1760, a final explosive blast brought down the fort's last remaining wall.

SIGNIFICANCE

While the loss of the French and Indian War (1754-1763) officially brought an end to French colonial ambitions in North America, the loss of Fortress Louisbourg perhaps best symbolized the end of France's New World colonial ventures. As a fortification, Louisbourg stood out as a symbol of French might across the Atlantic. Many had pronounced the fort an astonishing accomplishment. France had hoped to make the fort a counter against British power in North America, but that goal failed. Without a fortified front line to protect the entrance of the St. Lawrence River, France would give up control of the Canadian interior to Britain. That loss would bring an end to the French fur trade, which had been an important mainstay of France's colonial economy. Furthermore, having lost control of the fishing waters along Cape Breton, France would have no viable Atlantic fishing industry, and it would become more dependent upon foreign imports to feed its people.

—*Michael J. Garcia*

FURTHER READING

Chartrand, Rene. *French Fortresses in North America, 1535-1763: Quebec, Montreal, Louisbourg, and New Orleans*. Toronto, Ont.: Osprey, 2005. Provides a detailed examination of the defenses of the largest fortified French cities in Canada.

Johnston, A. J. B. *Control and Order in French Colonial Louisbourg*. East Lansing: Michigan State University Press, 2001. A good, detailed source about the founding and development of Louisbourg through its first siege in 1745.

Moore, Christopher. *Louisbourg Portraits: Five Dramatic, True Tales of People in an Eighteenth Century Garrison Town.* Toronto, Ont.: McClelland and Stewart Books, 2000. Describes living conditions of five people who lived at Louisbourg.

SEE ALSO: May 26, 1701-Sept. 7, 1714: War of the Spanish Succession; Apr. 11, 1713: Treaty of Utrecht; 1721-1742: Development of Great Britain's Office of Prime Minister; Dec. 16, 1740-Nov. 7, 1748: War of

the Austrian Succession; Oct. 18, 1748: Treaty of Aix-la-Chapelle; May 28, 1754-Feb. 10, 1763: French and Indian War; Jan., 1756-Feb. 15, 1763: Seven Years' War; June 8-July 27, 1758: Siege of Louisbourg.

RELATED ARTICLES in *Great Lives from History: The Eighteenth Century, 1701-1800*: George II; William Pitt the Elder.

April 11, 1713
TREATY OF UTRECHT

The Treaty of Utrecht was a peace agreement between Great Britain and France, concluding Britain's participation in the War of the Spanish Succession. It revised territorial boundaries in North America and Europe, settled dynastic issues, and introduced trade patterns that resulted in Britain's rise to world-power status. The war itself would not end until Austria also negotiated peace in the Treaties of Rastatt and Baden (1714).

LOCALE: Utrecht, the Netherlands
CATEGORIES: Diplomacy and international relations; expansion and land acquisition; wars, uprisings, and civil unrest

KEY FIGURES
Robert Harley (First Earl of Oxford; 1661-1724), head of the British ministry, 1710, 1711-1714
Louis XIV (1638-1715), king of France, r. 1643-1715
Marquis de Torcy (Jean-Baptiste Colbert; 1665-1746), French foreign minister
First Duke of Marlborough (John Churchill; 1650-1722), commander in chief of the British and Dutch armies
Philip V (1683-1746), king of Spain, r. 1700-January, 1724, and August 31, 1724-1746
Charles VI (1685-1740), Holy Roman Emperor, r. 1711-1740
Joseph I (1678-1711), Holy Roman Emperor, r. 1705-1711

SUMMARY OF EVENT
The Treaty of Utrecht in 1713 marked the formal termination of the War of the Spanish Succession, an international struggle that had begun in 1701. In September of that year, the naval powers England and the Netherlands

concluded the Grand Alliance with the Austrian Habsburgs. All agreed to undertake a joint military effort against King Louis XIV of France, who had recently claimed the entire dynastic inheritance of the extinct Spanish Habsburg line for his grandson Philip of Anjou, in keeping with the will of the last Habsburg king of Spain, Charles II. The extensive claims of the French Bourbons clashed directly with the equally extensive claims of the Austrian Habsburgs, represented by the Archduke Charles III, the future Emperor Charles VI.

A formal declaration of war came in May, 1702, although fighting between France and Austria had broken out in northern Italy in the previous year. Meanwhile, Louis had taken steps to secure the future accession to the French throne of Philip of Anjou, had dispatched French troops into the Spanish Netherlands, and in September had recognized James Edward, the "Old Pretender" (son of the deposed Catholic James II), as King James III of England. These attempts to increase both Bourbon and Catholic power in Europe ironically inspired the Protestant England and the Netherlands to enter into an alliance with the house of Habsburg, and through it with the Holy Roman Empire.

From September, 1701, until the negotiation of the Treaty of Utrecht in 1713, the British and the Dutch were motivated chiefly by their desire to preserve the balance of power against the establishment of a gigantic Bourbon union in both the Old World and the New. By the same token, the maritime powers refused to give unqualified support to Charles's claims to all of the Spanish inheritance, instead supporting only those claims in the Spanish Netherlands, Milan, and Sicily. The Methuen Treaty (1703) between England and Portugal brought a new partner into the Grand Alliance and changed the war's aim, which now became the enthronement of Archduke

Charles in Spain. Consequently, in the first serious, though unsuccessful, peace negotiations of the war, held in 1708, the allies demanded that Philip vacate the Spanish monarchy in favor of Charles. At this point, a new Habsburg Dynasty in Spain was at least preferable to a Bourbon one, which would have meant the combination of the Spanish world empire with that of the French.

Throughout the spring and summer in 1710, Tories replaced Whigs in government positions in England. As early as July, 1710, Robert Harley, head of the ministry,

EUROPEAN NEW WORLD POSSESSIONS AFTER THE TREATY OF UTRECHT

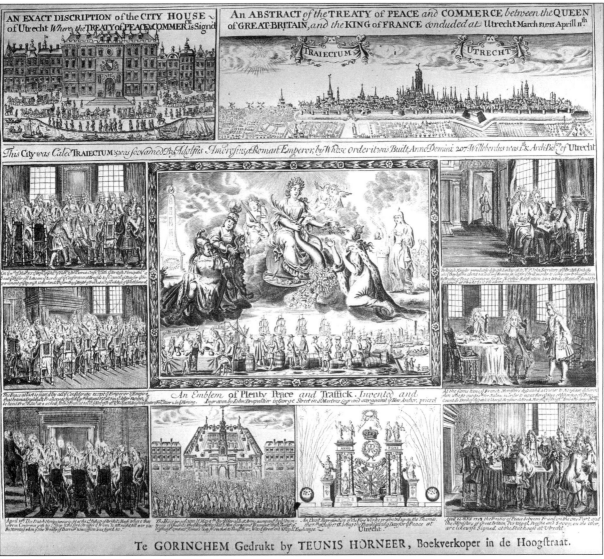

A pictorial abstract of the Treaty of Utrecht, named in this 1713 Dutch broadsheet the "Treaty of Peace and Commerce between the Queen of Great Britain and the King of France concluded at Utrecht." (Hulton Archive/Getty Images)

began secret negotiations with France through low-level intermediaries. Tremendous war expenditures and military setbacks in Spain had convinced him that peace was paramount. The Tories' determination to make peace was helped by the sudden death in April, 1711, of the Habsburg emperor, Joseph I, whose brother, the Archduke Charles, added the imperial title and those of the various Austrian lands to his claims to the Spanish inheritance. The Tory government did not wish to continue a fight which, if successful, would mean the re-creation of the empire of Charles V. By September, 1711, the English and French had concluded a set of preliminary articles which became the framework for the Treaty of Utrecht.

In December, 1711, John Churchill, first duke of Marlborough—commander of British and Dutch military forces on the Continent and a vociferous Whig opponent of peace negotiations—was relieved of his command. Hence, the peace conference finally opened at Utrecht on January 29, 1712. Robert Harley, now lord treasurer and earl of Oxford, and his French counterpart, Jean-Baptiste Colbert, marquis de Torcy, guided their diplomats through tortuous negotiations which survived a series of deaths in the French royal family that threatened to leave Philip V heir to the French throne. It was arranged for him to renounce his claims to the French throne. In May, 1712, the English government halted its military operations, and the Dutch and other allies eventually accepted the British-French arrangements that produced a settlement based upon the partition of the Spanish inheritance.

Indeed, the Treaty of Utrecht, signed on April 11, 1713, by Great Britain, France, the Netherlands, Savoy, and Prussia, was almost entirely the product of British-French diplomacy, which dealt primarily with issues relative to the Spanish succession and other matters as well. The underlying principle common to most of the major provisions of the treaty was the reaffirmation of the balance of power in Europe. According to the provisions of the treaty, France promised to recognize the Hanoverian succession in Great Britain, which in turn agreed to recognize the Bourbon accession in Spain on condition that the French and Spanish thrones never be united under the rule of one sovereign. As far as the New World was concerned, France ceded Newfoundland, Nova Scotia (Acadia), and the Hudson Bay region to Great Britain, but retained New France (Quebec).

Spain, in a separate treaty concluded on July 13, 1713, ceded to Great Britain the bastion of Gibraltar and the island of Minorca; Great Britain agreed to furnish the Spanish colonies in America with forty-eight hundred African slaves each year for thirty years. The British were permitted to send each year one vessel of five hundred tons to trade with the colonies in New Spain. Austria was assigned the Spanish territories of Milan, Sardinia, and Naples, in addition to the Spanish Netherlands (a settlement reconfirmed in the French-Austrian Treaty of Rastatt in 1714); the Habsburgs were to permit the Dutch to garrison certain fortresses along the French frontier (the so-called Barrier agreements). Savoy received the island of Sicily as a kingdom, subsequently ceded to Austria in 1720 in exchange for Sardinia, to which a royal title also applied. Finally, Prussia received international recognition for its claim to a royal title for the House of Hohenzollern. Emperor Charles VI of Austria, refusing to accept the treaty, continued the war with France until 1714, when he concluded the Treaty of Rastatt. Not until 1720, in the Treaty of the Hague, did Charles recognize the Bourbon claims to the Spanish crown.

SIGNIFICANCE

The conclusion of the Treaty of Utrecht and related treaties produced several important consequences. In general, the balance of power was restored; neither a French nor an Austrian prince succeeded in uniting his lands with those of Spain. Great Britain benefited from the war more than any other power. Receiving assurances from France concerning the impending Hanoverian succession, Great Britain emerged as the world's leading colonial and commercial power. Finally, the Treaty of Utrecht accelerated the rise of Prussia and Savoy as leading states in Germany and Italy, respectively.

—*Edward P. Keleher, updated by Mark C. Herman*

FURTHER READING

Black, Jeremy. *The Rise of the European Powers, 1679-1793*. New York: Edward Arnold, 1990. This expert on international relations provides the seventeenth and eighteenth century context for the Utrecht settlement.

_____. *A System of Ambition? British Foreign Policy, 1660-1793*. New York: Longman, 1991. The conduct of British foreign policy which produced the treaty is analyzed, and the treaty's impact on Great Britain's development as a world power is fully examined.

Davenport, Frances Gardiner, ed. *1698-1715*. Vol. 3 in *European Treaties Bearing on the United States and Its Dependencies*. Washington, D.C.: Carnegie Institution, 1934. Reprint. Gloucester, Mass.: Peter Smith, 1967. The texts of the various treaties are reproduced in the original languages and English translation with extensive notes and commentary.

Hattendorf, John B. *England in the War of the Spanish Succession: A Study of the English View and Conduct of Grand Strategy, 1702-1712*. New York: Garland, 1987. The relationship between English military undertakings and the negotiations and peace settlement are examined in this very detailed study.

Hill, Brian W. *Robert Harley: Speaker, Secretary of State, and Premier Minister*. New Haven, Conn.: Yale University Press, 1988. The role of the chief architect of the Treaty of Utrecht is examined through a perceptive analysis of Harley's domestic and foreign policy.

Trevelyan, George Macaulay. *England Under Queen Anne*. 3 vols. London: Longmans, Green, 1930-1934. Although an older publication, Trevelyan's three-volume work remains a valuable source for understanding domestic politics, military matters, and the conduct of peace negotiations. Volume 3 is particularly useful for understanding the Treaty of Utrecht.

Wolf, John B. *Louis XIV*. New York: W. W. Norton, 1968. The French perspective on the War of the Spanish Succession and the negotiations producing the Treaty of Utrecht is given in this excellent biography.

SEE ALSO: May 26, 1701-Sept. 7, 1714: War of the Spanish Succession; May 15, 1702-Apr. 11, 1713: Queen Anne's War; Aug. 13, 1704: Battle of Blenheim; Mar. 23-26, 1708: Defeat of the "Old Pre-

tender"; Sept. 11, 1709: Battle of Malplaquet; Mar. 7, 1714, and Sept. 7, 1714: Treaties of Rastatt and Baden; Sept. 6, 1715-Feb. 4, 1716: Jacobite Rising in Scotland.

RELATED ARTICLES in *Great Lives from History: The Eighteenth Century, 1701-1800*: Queen Anne; First Viscount Bolingbroke; Charles VI; First Duke of Marlborough; Philip V.

August 3, 1713
FOUNDATION OF THE SPANISH ACADEMY

The Spanish Academy was founded to regulate the use and development of the Spanish language throughout the Spanish Empire. When Spain lost that empire, the academy continued to function, in concert with the academies of the Spanish language that were established in all former Spanish colonies. These academies, taking their lead from the Spanish Academy, have served to keep the Spanish language unified into the early twenty-first century.

LOCALE: Madrid, Spain
CATEGORIES: Organizations and institutions; education

KEY FIGURES
Juan Manuel Fernández Pacheco (Marqués de Villena; 1650-1725), chief steward of Philip V
Philip V (1683-1746), king of Spain, r. 1700-January, 1724, and August 31, 1724-1746
Andrés Bello (1781-1865), Venezuelan linguist

SUMMARY OF EVENT
In 1700, Philip, duke of Anjou and grandson of King Louis XIV of France, became king of Spain. His ascension to the Spanish throne as Philip V marked the beginning of the rule of the French royal house of Bourbon in Spain. As a result of Bourbon rule, the cultivation of the Spanish language suffered, because the French language came to dominate the Spanish court and began to be spoken widely by the learned classes. Patriotic Spanish aristocrats who supported Philip V in his struggle to secure the Spanish throne in the War of the Spanish Succession believed, despite this support, that there was an urgent need to resist this trend and to promote the proper use of the Spanish language. To this end, Juan Manuel Fernández Pacheco, the Marqués de Villena and chief steward of the king, along with other learned aristocrats, proposed establishing an academy of language. The acad-

emy was established on August 3, 1713, and a royal decree issued on October 3, 1714, officially constituted it as the Royal Academy of Language.

Modeled on the Académie Française (French Academy), established in 1635, the Spanish Academy proposed to purify, standardize, and give splendor to the Spanish language. The academicians not only wanted to protect the Spanish language from the dominance of French but also sought to demonstrate that the Spanish language could be as beautiful and refined as classical Latin. Such refinement in language was a quality much esteemed by the learned classes of the time, for whom knowledge of Latin was required for advanced studies.

The academicians also wanted to prevent Spanish from suffering the corruption that befell Latin in the wake of the fall of the Roman Empire. Spanish served the needs of an empire that encompassed the world, from the North and South American continents to the Philippines and northern Africa. They wanted the Spanish language to maintain its unity while including diverse contributions from throughout Spain's worldwide empire. The preparation of a dictionary to meet all these needs was the first task assigned to the Spanish Academy by Philip V.

The earliest members of the Spanish Academy, although learned, were not trained in the science of languages or in the other skills necessary to prepare a dictionary. Nevertheless, they mastered the skills and produced a six-volume *Diccionario de autoridades* (1726-1739; dictionary of authorities). The use of "authorities" in the title was chosen as a reference to citations from classic Spanish texts written by distinguished authors from all historical periods, citations that were used to support the dictionary's definitions. Even today, scholars consult *Diccionario de autoridades* when studying Spanish texts from the eighteenth century and earlier.

The next edition of the dictionary (1780) was reduced

1710's

to one volume by eliminating the references to the authorities found in the first edition. The Spanish Academy has never given up on its desire to complete another edition of *Diccionario de autoridades*, but the magnitude of the task and the lack of resources have left its aspiration unfulfilled. It has continued, however, to revise its single-volume dictionary, with a twenty-second edition of the dictionary published in 2001.

The Spanish Academy also wanted to standardize the spelling of words. It addressed this problem to some degree in its *Diccionario de autoridades*. In its *Ortografía* (1741; orthography), it further simplified the rules for spelling. The academy revisited these rules regularly better to meet its goal of making the spelling of words correspond to their pronunciation. It issued another edition of *Ortografía* in 1763 and completed this early reform of spelling rules in its 1815 edition.

The Spanish Academy's responsibility for the regulation of the Spanish language also required the preparation of a grammar book. The first edition of *Gramática* was published in 1771. The academy also prepared critical editions of classics of Spanish literature, including *El ingenioso hidalgo don Quixote de la Mancha* (1605, 1615; *The History of the Valorous and Wittie Knight-Errant, Don Quixote of the Mancha*, 1612-1620; better known as *Don Quixote de la Mancha*) by Miguel de Cervantes in 1780.

When Spain lost its colonies in the Americas in the nineteenth century, former colonists and Spaniards alike became more aware of the importance of maintaining the unity of the Spanish language. They recalled the fate of Latin after the breakup of the Roman Empire and did not want Spanish similarly to fracture into many languages with the breakup of Spain's empire. Lovers of the Spanish language on both sides of the Atlantic sought to establish institutions to safeguard and develop it.

The Spanish Academy has recognized the academies of the Spanish language formed by Spain's former colonies. Colombia created the first such academy in 1871. It was quickly followed by Ecuador, Mexico, El Salvador, Venezuela, Chile, Peru, and Guatemala. All these countries established their academies before the close of the nineteenth century, and they had clear effects upon the original Spanish Academy back in the mother country: Echoes of Venezuelan Andrés Bello's *Gramática de la lengua castellana destinada al uso de los americanos* (1847; grammar of the Spanish language destined for the use of Americans) can be found in the 1854 edition of the Spanish Academy's *Gramática*, for example. In the 1884 edition of the Spanish Academy's dictionary appeared words contributed by the Colombian, Venezuelan, and Mexican academies. Proponents of Spanish were gratified to see that Spain and Spanish America had united to work for the good of the Spanish language.

A second wave of activity to establish language academies in the rest of Spain's former colonies began in the 1920's. Only Argentina and Uruguay do not have academies of the Spanish language formally associated with the Spanish Academy, although they work in close cooperation with the Spanish Academy and the other national academies. Puerto Rico established its academy in 1952. The last academy was incorporated in 1973 to meet the needs of the Spanish-speaking population of the United States. All these academies are members of the Association of Academies of the Spanish Language, which has developed mechanisms for the participation of all the academies in the elaboration of the Spanish Academy's dictionary and grammar in addition to its other activities designed to promote the proper use of Spanish.

SIGNIFICANCE

The Spanish Academy began regulating and developing the Spanish language at a time when vernacular languages increasingly replaced Latin as media of scholarship and great literature. The Spanish Academy produced its dictionaries and grammars to demonstrate how Spanish could rival Latin in its expression of the full range of human thought and experience. It has maintained the unity of the Spanish language while allowing for diversity in vocabulary and usage. From its inception, the Spanish Academy has been recognized as the authority on the proper and most elegant way to communicate in Spanish.

The Spanish Academy has impacted directly all Spanish speakers who have learned to read and write in Spanish since its founding. It spearheaded uniformity in spelling by publishing periodic revisions of its *Ortografía*. While English speakers must deal with variations in spelling between Great Britain and the United States, for example, for all Spanish speakers, all words are spelled the same. While English speakers struggle to spell words correctly, Spanish speakers do not have problems with spelling, because the Royal Academy revises spelling periodically to ensure that the spelling of Spanish words matches their pronunciation.

When the academy was established, Spanish society readily accepted the authority of an institution established to set the norms for correct usage of the Spanish language. It continues to enjoy great authority, although its critics claim that it is outdated and ineffective. While in the past it addressed only readers and writers, the academy's audience now includes Spanish speakers who are primarily spectators and listeners.

—Evelyn Toft

FURTHER READING

Ayala, Francisco. "The Spanish Royal Academy." In *Global Demands on Language and the Mission of the Language Academies*, edited by John Lihani. Lexington: University of Kentucky, 1988. Describes the challenges facing the Royal Academy.

Lapesa, Rafael. "La Real Academia Española: Pasado, realidad presente y futuro." *Boletín de la Real Academia Española* 67, no. 242 (1987): 329-346. Discusses precursors to the Royal Academy, its history, and its current challenges.

Salvador, Gregorio. "El español y las Academias de Lengua." *Boletín de la Real Academia Española* 72, no. 257 (1992): 411-427. Discusses the relationship between the Royal Academy and the national acade-mies that together compose the Association of Academies of the Spanish Language.

Zamora, Juan. "The Academies of the Spanish Language in the United States." In *Global Demands on Language and the Mission of the Language Academies*, edited by John Lihani. Lexington: University of Kentucky, 1988. Discusses the motives for the founding of the Royal Academy and the creation of national language academies.

Zamora Vicente, Alonso. *Real Academia Española*. Madrid: Espasa-Calpe, 1999. A detailed, richly illustrated history of the Spanish Academy. Discusses the current challenges facing the Academy and the criticisms it receives.

SEE ALSO: May 26, 1701-Sept. 7, 1714: War of the Spanish Succession; 1712: Philip V Founds the Royal Library of Spain.

RELATED ARTICLE in *Great Lives from History: The Eighteenth Century, 1701-1800*: Philip V.

September 8, 1713
PAPAL BULL *UNIGENITUS*

Clement XI issued the papal bull Unigenitus, *condemning French Jansenist teachings. The bull met stiff opposition among the French clergy, which seriously undermined papal authority.*

LOCALE: Rome, Papal States (now in Italy); France
CATEGORY: Religion and theology

KEY FIGURES

Clement XI (1649-1721), Roman Catholic pope, 1700-1721

Louis XIV (1638-1715), king of France, r. 1643-1715

Pasquier Quesnel (1634-1719), French Jansenist theologian

Louis-Antoine de Noailles (1651-1729), archbishop of Paris, 1695-1729

Duc d'Orléans (Philippe II; 1674-1723), regent of France, r. 1715-1723

SUMMARY OF EVENT

Two phenomena dominated French religious life in the early eighteenth century: Gallicanism and Jansenism. By the tenets of the first, the leaders of the Catholic Church in France retained an independence of direction from Rome that, when exercised fully, presented a challenge to papal authority and leadership of the universal Church. Jansenism, a rather strict sect of Catholicism that was heavily influenced by Calvinistic views of election and grace, had bedeviled orthodox Catholic authorities in Rome and France throughout the reign of Louis XIV.

The French cleric and theologian Pasquier Quesnel became head of the Catholic seminary in Paris in 1662 but left the post after a work of his was condemned in 1676 by the Roman Inquisition for Gallicanism. Increasingly sympathetic to Jansenism, Quesnel published an abridged and annotated version of the New Testament in French in 1671, an enlarged and more blatantly Jansenistic edition in 1678, and a yet fuller edition in 1693-1694, known by the short title *Réflexions morales* (moral reflections). Though bishop Vialart of Châlons and his successor, Louis-Antoine de Noailles, had supported the project, many French bishops condemned it in the early 1700's. On July 13, 1708, Pope Clement XI formally condemned the work at the request of the French in a brief entitled *Universi Dominici gregis*. As much as most French authorities decried Jansenism, however, the pope's threat of punishment by the Roman Inquisition rankled their Gallican sensibilities, and the document was ineffectual.

The Jansenists' activities quickened over the ensuing

CLEMENT XI ON THE LAITY'S ACCESS TO THE BIBLE

In a passage of the papal bull Unigenitus, *excerpted here, Clement XI declared that all Christians should have access to the Scriptures and that withholding the New Testament from the laity or insisting that they should access it only through readings in church was harmful.*

79. It is useful and necessary at all times, in all places, and for every kind of person, to study and to know the spirit, the piety, and the mysteries of Sacred Scripture.

80. The reading of Sacred Scripture is for all.

81. The sacred obscurity of the Word of God is no reason for the laity to dispense themselves from reading it.

82. The Lord's Day ought to be sanctified by Christians with readings of pious works and above all of the Holy Scriptures. It is harmful for a Christian to wish to withdraw from this reading.

83. It is an illusion to persuade oneself that knowledge of the mysteries of religion should not be communicated to women by the reading of Sacred Scriptures. Not from the simplicity of women, but from the proud knowledge of men has arisen the abuse of the Scriptures and have heresies been born.

84. To snatch away from the hands of Christians the New Testament, or to hold it closed against them by taking away from them the means of understanding it, is to close for them the mouth of Christ.

85. To forbid Christians to read Sacred Scripture, especially the Gospels, is to forbid the use of light to the sons of light, and to cause them to suffer a kind of excommunication.

86. To snatch from the simple people this consolation of joining their voice to the voice of the whole Church is a custom contrary to the apostolic practice and to the intention of God.

Source: Clement XI, "Condemnation of the Errors of Paschasius Quesnel." Papal Encyclicals Online. http://www.papalencyclicals.net/Clem11/c11unige.htm. Accessed November 13, 2005.

faith, hope, and charity; and finally, numbers 72-101 were matters of Church structure and authority. These last included Quesnel's teachings that only the elect constitute the true Church and that any excommunication must be supported by the entire Church. In his bull, Clement introduced the list of condemned articles with an exhortation against the fostering of "ruinous sects" and followed the catalog with a list of terms describing the Church's view of the propositions, which included false, heretical, seditious, rash, and blasphemous. The bull was entitled *Unigenitus Dei filii* (generally known simply as *Unigenitus*) and was signed by Clement on September 8, 1713.

Louis XIV received his advance copy of the bull at Fontainebleau on September 24, accepted it, and called for the French Assembly of Bishops to meet to accept it on October 16. Noailles, who was now archbishop of Paris and a cardinal, chaired the proceedings, which deliberated hotly and finally accepted the bull on January 22, 1714, by a vote of forty to nine. The Parlement of Paris registered it on February 15, and the Sorbonne did likewise on March 5. Nonetheless, Noailles, the eight dissenters, and seven other bishops—a group known later as the Appellants—openly opposed the promulgation of the bull in their dioceses, and in late February they published a widely circulated pastoral letter detailing their position.

The Appellants declared that the bull was "obscure" in its language, and they called for special declarations of clarification by the pope. Both the condemnation and the Appellants' support spurred the Jansenists in France to launch an impressive campaign against the bull. Negotiations between the king and the pope were carried out in 1715 by the Marquis de Gournay and Cardinal Fabroni, respectively. Clement could take away Noailles's status as cardinal, but he lacked the power to strip him of his French bishopic. Noailles was thus essentially protected from papal judgment by the Gallican liberties.

From the royal side, the situation was equally tricky,

months, and in 1710 Louis felt compelled to close their center at Port Royal. Louis forbade the printing of *Réflexions morales* on November 11, 1711, and once again called upon Pope Clement to issue a formal statement condemning the book. Louis insisted, however, that he and his Council preview any such document in the light of Gallican liberties. Even though this stipulation potentially undermined papal credibility even further, Clement agreed and established (February, 1712) a congregation of two cardinals, two inquisitors, and nine theologians to review the work for specific theological errors. This panel listed 101 propositions that they considered to be contrary to Church teaching, and this list went to a commission of cardinals for further review.

The contested propositions were listed in three groups: Propositions 1-43 were statements regarding grace and election; those numbered 44-71 dealt with

as it was unclear whether Louis could directly punish a bishop. Clement wrote two letters to Noailles, one threatening, the other conciliatory. He left it to Louis to decide which letter to deliver; Louis considered neither effective. For his part, Louis suggested a general council of the Church to clarify the matter, but Clement considered such a council to represent a danger to his own authority. Clearly, for some Church leaders, the pope's own declaration on a matter of faith and church order remained a matter for debate, not an infallible statement of truth. Louis died on September 1, without having arranged for a national council.

Louis XIV was succeeded by Louis XV, who was too young to yet assume the full duties of the monarchy. The regent for the young king was Philippe II, duc d'Orléans, who had no interest in religious matters. Jansenists were thus given free rein, and Noailles himself was appointed to head the Council of Conscience, which consisted largely of Jansenists and oversaw the realm's religious affairs. In 1716, emboldened faculty members at the Sorbonne moved successfully to retract the university's recognition of *Unigenitus*, as did the theology faculties at Caen, Nantes, and Rheims. Increasingly, cathedral canons and other clergy declared their opposition to the bull and their support for Quesnel; Jansenist tracts against *Unigenitus* proliferated.

Perhaps 3 percent of the French clergy, or three thousand priests, were actively opposed to the bull. Orléans feared the potential effects upon national unity and peace of the religious schism that was developing. On June 27, 1716, Clement held a consistory with thirty-eight cardinals and announced that Noailles had to accept the bull or forfeit his cardinal's status within fifty days: The Appellants had to submit to Rome's authority. Orléans blocked delivery of the letter, and the ultimatum expired without effect.

The Assembly of Bishops continued into 1717, finally adopting a list of twenty-six propositions they agreed had been improperly condemned in the bull. Subsequently, a few Appellant bishops and theology faculty wrote to the pope, demanding a general Church council, while Clement and many cardinals wrote to Noailles, begging submission to the bull. The bishops' plea was declared heretical and schismatic by the Inquisition and pope on March 8, 1718, and Clement decided to issue a bull, *Pastoralis officii*, excommunicating all who refused to accept *Unigenitus*. Noailles responded in a half-hearted if technically obedient manner in March and instructed his diocese to accept the bull in a pastoral letter of November, 1718. Other Appellants continued their opposition, especially after Clement's death in 1721, but Noailles publicly and unconditionally submitted on October 11, 1728, seven months before his own death.

SIGNIFICANCE

Opposition to *Unigenitus* was founded both in theology and in concerns about religious legal jurisdiction. Gallicanism, itself protected quite openly by French rulers, demanded the minimum interference in the French Church, even by the supreme pontiff. On the other hand, the pope's authority—which, like the king's, was divinely instituted—was to be absolute in matters of faith and morals, even if popes had bargained away other powers, such as the right to choose French bishops. The issue of Jansenism, which included huge areas of theological ambiguity, pitted these two principles against each other. Catholic monarchs throughout Europe watched as the pope's will was effectively thwarted, but by Church leaders not the secular monarch.

The Quesnel affair ended with a whimper rather than a bang, but Jansenism as a force in France was far from spent in 1728. As late as October 16, 1756, Pope Benedict XIV had to issue the bull *Ex omnibus*, which reaffirmed *Unigenitus* but allowed excommunication only against publicly notorious Jansenists. In the end, the failure of *Unigenitus* and the firestorm it ignited were signals of a truly eroded papal position, even within the Church itself.

—*Joseph P. Byrne*

FURTHER READING

Denzinger, Heinrich J. D. *The Sources of Catholic Dogma*. St. Louis, Mo.: Herder, 1957. Contains translations of the 101 condemned propositions, which are the heart of the bull. These are also available at www.papalencyclicals.net/Clem11/c11unige.htm.

Doyle, William. *Jansenism: Catholic Resistance to Authority from the Reformation to the French Revolution*. New York: St. Martin's Press, 2000. Discusses *Unigenitus* and its controversies from a position favorable to Jansenism.

McManners, John. *Church and Society in Eighteenth-Century France: The Religion of the People and the Politics of Religion*. New York: Oxford University Press, 1998. Places the bull in the context of the religious policies of Louis XIV and discusses reactions to during the early reign of Louis XV.

Pastor, Ludwig. *History of the Popes from the Close of the Middle Ages*. Vol. 33. Translated by Ernest Graff. St. Louis, Mo.: Herder, 1923-1969. Supplies a full discussion of the bull and its impact, within the biog-

1710's

raphy of Clement XI. Balanced treatment, but clearly written from the papal point of view.

SEE ALSO: July 24, 1702-Oct. 1, 1704: Camisard Risings in the Cévennes; May, 1727-1733: Jansenist "Convulsionnaires" Gather at Saint-Médard.

RELATED ARTICLES in *Great Lives from History: The Eighteenth Century, 1701-1800*: André-Hercule de Fleury; Louis XV.

1714
FAHRENHEIT DEVELOPS THE MERCURY THERMOMETER

Daniel Gabriel Fahrenheit developed sealed mercury thermometers with reliable scales that agreed with each other, revolutionizing the scientific measurement of temperature. By developing a method for calibrating different thermometers to the same scale, he made it possible for different people in different parts of the world to accurately and reliably compare temperature measurements.

LOCALE: The Netherlands; Denmark
CATEGORY: Inventions; chemistry; science and technology

KEY FIGURES

Daniel Gabriel Fahrenheit (1686-1736), German physicist
Anders Celsius (1701-1744), Swedish astronomer
Ole Rømer (1644-1710), Danish astronomer
Galileo (1564-1642); Italian mathematician, scientist, and inventor
Ferdinand II de' Medici (1610-1670), grand duke of Tuscany, r. 1621-1670, scholar, and scientist
Joseph Nicholas Delisle (1688-1768), French astronomer
René-Antoine Ferchault de Réaumur (1683-1757), French scientist
Carolus Linnaeus (1707-1778), Swedish physician and botanist
Jean Pierre Christin (1683-1755), French scientist
Baron Kelvin (William Thomson; 1824-1907), British scientist and professor at the University of Glasgow

SUMMARY OF EVENT

Temperature scales of a subjective nature were widely used by physicians in the Renaissance. Such scales could be useful for performing rough diagnoses, but they were inappropriate as instruments of scientific research and measurement. The first thermometer was constructed early in the seventeenth century by Galileo for use in his public lectures in Padua. It was a relatively crude, gas-filled, open glass vessel that enabled Galileo to demonstrate observable differences in temperature between different substances or within the same substance as it was heated or cooled. Knowledge of his device spread rapidly, and in the next century, thermometers of increasing usefulness were constructed by many different people. Ferdinand II de' Medici is credited with developing the first sealed thermometer, which prevented temperature measurements from being affected by changes in atmospheric pressure.

In 1701, a Danish astronomer named Ole Rømer made a wine-filled (alcohol) thermometer. Rømer used a scale in which the temperature of a mixture of ice and salt water was 0 degrees and that of boiling water was 60 degrees. In the same year, after the death of his parents, Daniel Gabriel Fahrenheit moved to Holland, where he began making scientific instruments. In 1708, Fahrenheit visited Rømer in Denmark and observed Rømer's methods for calibrating thermometers. Fahrenheit subsequently decided that Rømer's temperature scale was too cumbersome for common use but adopted the use of ice baths for instrument calibration.

Fahrenheit made his first alcohol thermometer in 1709. He visited Berlin in 1713 to investigate the expansion of mercury in Potsdam glass thermometers, and in 1714 he made his first reliable mercury thermometer. Fahrenheit sought to ensure that all his thermometers would produce the same measurements, and he picked three specific points on a temperature scale at which to standardize his thermometers. Like Rømer, he established 0 degrees with a mixture of ice and salt water (or ice, water, and sal ammoniac [ammonium chloride]); 32 degrees was set by a mixture of ice and pure water, and 96 degrees was set as the temperature reached when a healthy man placed a thermometer under his armpit or in his mouth.

Fahrenheit produced and calibrated thermometers using the scale he had developed, and his instruments were known to be of high quality, yielding standardized results. His thermometers were widely adopted, and his scale therefore came into wide use. Herman Boerhaave, a noted chemist, bought his thermometers from Fahrenheit and once brought to Fahrenheit's attention that his alcohol and mercury thermometers read slightly differently. Fahrenheit incorrectly attributed the differences to differences in the glass used for the thermometers' tubing, rather than to the difference between the rates of expansion of alcohol and mercury.

In 1724, Fahrenheit became a member of the English Royal Society and published the results of his investigations in its journal, *Philosophical Transactions*. His thermometers were the preferred instruments in Holland and England. After his death in 1736, scientists recalibrated Fahrenheit's thermometers, setting 212 degrees as the temperature of boiling water. Recalibration then established the normal human body temperature as 98.6 degrees, rather than the 96 degrees used by Fahrenheit.

Fahrenheit's basic design for the sealed mercury thermometer was not changed significantly after his death. The subsequent history of the instrument revolves around the development and refinement of different scales at which to calibrate it. Thermometers made for use in the late eighteenth century and throughout the nineteenth century often had two or more scales marked upon them, allowing them to be marketed to different ar-

eas where different scales were in use. The Fahrenheit thermometer scale never became popular in France, for example.

Anders Celsius, a Swedish astronomer, used René-Antoine Ferchault de Réaumur's thermometer scale, which assigned 0 degrees to the temperature of ice water and 80 degrees to the temperature of boiling water. Celsius also used a thermometer made by Joseph Nicholas Delisle, which used an inverted scale in which 0 degrees was the boiling point of water. Although not an instrument maker like Fahrenheit, Celsius did perform experiments using thermometers. Celsius suggested a new temperature scale that would place 0 degrees at water's boiling point and 100 degrees at its freezing point. Celsius worked in very cold climates in Sweden, Russia, and the North Atlantic, and using an inverted scale enabled him to avoid dealing with negative temperatures.

Celsius's inverted temperature scale was rapidly changed to a direct scale, as the boiling point of water was set at 100 degrees and its freezing point was set at 0 degrees. This change may have been suggested by Jean Pierre Christin in 1743 or 1744, although Pehr Wargentin, secretary of the Royal Swedish Academy of Sciences in 1749, mentioned an astronomer named Strømer and an instrument maker named Ekström in connection with the development of the direct temperature scale. Daniel Ekström was the manufacturer of the thermometers used by both Celsius and Carolus Linnaeus, and Linnaeus may also have been the one to invert Celsius's scale. It is certain that Linnaeus rapidly adopted the Celsius scale in his work, as did other Swedes. The Celsius scale became popular in France, although Réaumur's scale remained in use for about another century there. When metric units were introduced, the Celsius scale was referred to as the centigrade scale.

RØMER AND THE MODERN THERMOMETER

The Danish astronomer Ole Rømer played a key role in the development of the modern thermometer, paving the way for Daniel Fahrenheit's work. Rømer was particularly interested in creating a reproducible thermometer, so that experiments and observations from widely differing locales could be compared. Due to problems with hand-blowing the hollow glass tubes that were used in making thermometers, it was impossible to make them physically identical. As a result, it was necessary to find some other way to determine when they all indicated the same temperatures. Rømer's solution was to calibrate each thermometer against known reference points (such as the melting point of ice and the boiling point of water) so that it would be possible to have all the thermometers measuring temperature equally even if they were not structurally identical. It remained to assign numerical values to the various points on his scale. Rømer experimented with a number of different scales, setting various numbers for the reference points. Rømer still had not settled upon a workable scale when Daniel Fahrenheit arrived to discuss questions of measurement with him.

Historians of science would subsequently argue intensely about the extent of Rømer's role in inspiring Fahrenheit's work in thermometers and temperature scales, until the discovery of a letter in an archive in Leningrad (St. Petersburg, Russia). In the letter, Fahrenheit recounts experiments that he and Rømer performed together, which led him to an interest in improving the mechanisms of both thermometers and barometers.

SIGNIFICANCE

Throughout the English-speaking world, the Fahrenheit scale continued to be preferred until the late twentieth century, when most countries switched to the Celsius, or centigrade, scale as part of their move to the metric system. In the early twenty-first century, the Fahrenheit scale continued to be used by most people in the United States. It is still very rare to hear Celsius temperatures used in U.S. news reports or published in U.S. newspapers. In Canada, Celsius temperatures are always used in weather reports and newspapers.

In 1848, William Thomson, Baron Kelvin, devised a temperature scale that placed its 0 point at the temperature below which matter can not be cooled. This point is equal to −273.15 degrees Celsius and −459.67 degrees Fahrenheit. The Kelvin scale is used by scientists and is the international standard temperature unit. The unit of 1 degree Celsius is equal to 1 Kelvin. Therefore, the so-called triple point of water, at which temperature water vapor, ice, and liquid water can exist in equilibrium, is 273.16 Kelvin. (Kelvin temperatures omit the "degree" unit required when stating Fahrenheit and Celsius temperatures.)

—*Anita Baker-Blocker*

FURTHER READING

Halliday, David, Robert Resnick, and Jearl Walker. *Fundamentals of Physics*. 7th ed. New York: Wiley, 2004. This easy-to-understand, college-level book contains information on how thermometers are cali-

brated and the relationship between the Kelvin, Fahrenheit, and Celsius scales.

Hankins, Thomas L. *Science and the Enlightenment*. New York: Cambridge University Press, 1985. An excellent overview of eighteenth century science in the context of today's knowledge.

Middleton, W. E. Knowles. *A History of the Thermometer and Its Use in Meteorology*. Ann Arbor, Mich.: UMI Books on Demand, 1996. A comprehensive account of the development of thermometers and temperature scales from antiquity to the mid-twentieth century.

SEE ALSO: 1722: Réaumur Discovers Carbon's Role in Hardening Steel; Beginning 1735: Linnaeus Creates the Binomial System of Classification; 1742: Celsius Proposes an International Fixed Temperature Scale; Oct., 1745, and Jan., 1746: Invention of the Leyden Jar; 1748: Nollet Discovers Osmosis; 1787: Herschel Begins Building His Reflecting Telescope; 1800: Volta Invents the Battery.

RELATED ARTICLES in *Great Lives from History: The Eighteenth Century, 1701-1800*: Daniel Gabriel Fahrenheit; Carolus Linnaeus.

1714-1762
QUEST FOR LONGITUDE

John Harrison's chronometer, or timepiece, was used to make the first accurate measurement of longitude at sea, revolutionizing ocean exploration and travel. His invention opened new vistas in cartography, astronomy, world commerce, and international timekeeping, and furthered colonialism and imperialism.

LOCALE: Barrow, Lincolnshire, and London, England
CATEGORIES: Science and technology; exploration and discovery; mathematics

KEY FIGURES

John Harrison (1693-1776), inventor of the first practical chronometer
Edmond Halley (1656-1742), British royal astronomer, first expert to assist John Harrison
George Graham (1673-1751), watchmaker and patron of John Harrison
William Harrison (1728-1815), John Harrison's son and assistant

SUMMARY OF EVENT

The British parliament established the Longitude Act in 1714 to encourage a solution to a problem that had vexed mariners, merchants, and governments for hundreds of years. The problem was the inability to measure longitude accurately, especially at sea.

The concepts of latitude and longitude go back as far as the recognition of Earth's generally spherical shape. Latitude lines—the virtual, horizontal lines that parallel the equator and measure degrees north or south of the equator—had long since ceased to be a mystery. By the time of Christopher Columbus, mariners had learned that by studying the elevation of the Sun above the horizon and by observing certain "fixed" stars, they could rather easily follow an east-west path corresponding to a latitude line.

For Columbus to measure longitude—that is, distance along any latitude line he was traveling—the element of time came into play. One hour, one twenty-fourth of a day, corresponds to fifteen degrees of longitude east or west from a point of reference on an imaginary circumferential line through the poles and intersecting the equator. This reference line is called the prime meridian. It can be any longitude line; in modern times the line passing through Greenwich, England, has come to be utilized as the prime meridian. For Columbus to convert that fifteen degrees into geographical distance, he needed to know not just what time it was aboard the *Santa Maria* but what time was being registered at the same moment in some place of known longitude. Because he had no timepiece (called a chronometer beginning in the early eighteenth century) capable of this feat, he could not know the distance to India or any other landmass.

Although navigators and cartographers had most to gain from the solution of the longitude problem, and although it also attracted the attention of learned astronomers, it is not surprising, at least in retrospect, that a clock maker solved the problem. John Harrison, who was born in Yorkshire in 1693 but grew up in Barrow, Lincolnshire, made his first pendulum clock in 1713, just one year before the Longitude Act established a reward of £20,000 to the person who could devise a solution to the puzzle. Specifically, the invention had to prove accurate to within one-half of one degree of longitude on a trip from Great Britain to a port in the West Indies. The need for and the difficulty of the task are evident when one realizes that over this distance, an error of one-half degree would result in an error of several nautical miles, not a small error.

Not until 1728, however, did Harrison begin his pursuit of the great prize. In the meantime he concentrated on improving pendulum clocks. Since all metals expand in heat, metal pendulums grow longer and measure time more slowly in hot weather. Harrison overcame this problem by combining long and short strips of two different metals in one pendulum. He also invented a device that virtually eliminated friction from the escapement—that part of the clock that regulates the motion of the

---

HARRISON'S STRUGGLE FOR RECOGNITION

In 1761, sixty-eight-year-old John Harrison had succeeded in making a chronometer, which he called H-4, that met the Board of Longitude's requirements to win a £20,000 prize for a device that could determine longitude at sea. He wrote,

> I think I may make bold to say, that there is neither any other mechanical or mathematical thing in the World that is more beautiful or curious in texture than this my watch or time-keeper for the longitude.

Harrison was proud of his invention, versions of which he had been perfecting for more than three decades. In order to prove the chronometer successful, however, he needed to test it at sea. Hobbled by age, he enlisted the help of his son William to undertake the necessary ocean trials. Aboard the *Deptford* during a stormy voyage to Jamaica in the winter of 1761-1762, William succeeded in proving the chronometer prizeworthy. His father had spent the better part of his lifetime—and all of William's—perfecting the device.

However, so much time had passed since the contest had been announced that the Board of Longitude had begun to backpedal on its commitment. Several members of the Royal Society, including Astronomer Royal James Bradley and others, believed that Thomas Mayer's lunar tables would solve the longitude problem. Doubtless, issues of class were also involved: John Harrison and his son were mere clock makers.

Fearing that his success would simply be ignored, John Harrison arranged for another test, this time aboard HMS *Tartar*, bound for Barbados on March 28, 1764. Again, Harrison's son William sailed with the H-4, and again the chronometer met the board's requirements. Nevertheless, the board insisted that Harrison meet still more conditions to prove the worthiness of his chronometer. Harrison complied, creating H-5. Not until he petitioned King George III in 1773, however, did the Board of Longitude finally relent and grant the prize money. John Harrison was eighty years old. He would die three years later.

Source: Quotation of John Harrison available at MacTutor History of Mathematics Archive, School of Mathematics and Statistics, University of St. Andrews, Scotland. http://www-history.mcs.st-andrews.ac.uk/HistTopics/Longitude2.html. Accessed September, 2005.

---

wheelwork. Working with his younger brother James and with inexpensive materials (he could not afford better), he made clocks of amazing precision, accurate to within a second a month.

He entered the competition knowing that no pendulum clock would work on a sailing ship at sea, so he experimented on a mechanism that might be expected to withstand the movement caused by ocean waves. By 1730, armed with drawings of a sea clock, he went to London and called upon the great astronomer Edmond Halley. Knowing that the device of a clock maker probably would not impress a longitude board likely inclined to favor the ideas of learned astronomers and mathematicians, Halley sent Harrison to George Graham, a respected maker of watches and scientific instruments.

Encouraged by Graham, Harrison spent the next five years constructing his first sea clock. Now called H-1, it was a seventy-five-pound contraption with two large brass balances, connected by wires, taking the place of a pendulum. Tested on a sea voyage to Lisbon, it performed well enough to convince Harrison that he was on the right track.

During the next twenty-five years, Harrison strove for a smaller, lighter, and less complex chronometer, and in 1761 he completed H-4. By this time he was sixty-eight years old, but he had the assistance of his son William. William was born about the time the project began, but he grew into an able clock maker under his father's tutelage. It was William who made the sea journey to Jamaica to test his father's latest timepiece. The H-4 did not bear much resemblance to the first three versions; it looked like a somewhat oversized pocket watch, twelve centimeters (about five inches) in diameter.

William and the chronometer sailed aboard a ship called the *Deptford* in November of 1761. Checked against the local longitude, which had been determined astronomically, H-4 proved to be only five seconds slow, a deviation of only 1.25 minutes of longitude. For the total trip the error in longitude was 28.5 minutes, probably because on the return trip, completed on January 19, 1762, the *Deptford* had encountered particularly stormy seas. However, H-4 had still come within the limit of one-half of one degree.

This trip should have marked the end of the story, but the Board of Longitude insisted on further inspections and tests of the chronometer. Other claimants, including a prestigious astronomer, James Bradley, who was originally a Harrison supporter, came forward. Harrison was granted only a partial reward, and not until 1773, when he was eighty years old, did he receive the full amount of the prize.

Recognition of his feat came slowly, but eventually he was acknowledged as the true inventor of the chronometer. A modern navigator, while being honored at a dinner, proposed a toast to Harrison's memory, to the man who "started us on our trip." That navigator was American astronaut Neil Armstrong. Although the more accurate modern marine chronometer is based on principles different from Harrison's, Harrison proved that an instrument could be made to facilitate navigation into previously unknown waters.

SIGNIFICANCE

The invention of an accurate chronometer led to the expansion of knowledge of Earth's great waters. Captain James Cook, the eighteenth century maritime explorer, benefited greatly from the chronometer. In addition to increasing geographical knowledge, the chronometer enabled those aboard ship to make timed observations of heavenly bodies while at sea. These observations furthered the work of astronomers, making possible a more complete understanding of the heavens as well as the Earth.

With the problem of longitude solved, mapmakers could accurately represent the configurations and relative positions of landmasses. Being lost at sea, the universal experience of mariners up to Harrison's time, became rare. Cartographers could pinpoint small geographical hazards and thus refine nautical charts, forever changing the experience of mariners, who for centuries had been running aground with great loss of men, ships, and cargoes. Knowing distances between ports and being able to chart safe routes between them fostered maritime commerce. Of course, colonial and imperial ambitions also increased.

In the long run the mastery of longitude made possible the simplification and standardization of international timekeeping, although not until the International Meridian Conference of 1884 did the nations of the world agree to designate the longitude line passing through the old Royal Observatory in Greenwich as the prime meridian. This allowed the "opposite," 180-degree meridian in the Pacific Ocean to serve as the international date line.

—*Robert P. Ellis*

FURTHER READING

Andrewes, William J. H., ed. *The Quest for Longitude: The Proceedings of the Longitude Symposium, Harvard University.* Cambridge, Mass.: Collection of Historical Scientific Instruments, Harvard University, 1996. A lively collection of papers presented at a 1993 conference on the question of longitude that includes several chapters examining Harrison's work. Includes maps, illustrations, a bibliography, and an index.

Christianson, David. *Timepieces: Masterpieces of Chronometry.* New York: Firefly Books, 2002. Christianson provides an efficient assessment of the horological significance of Harrison's invention.

Dash, Joan. *The Longitude Prize.* New York: Farrar, Straus and Giroux, 2000. In this book written especially for young readers, Dash explores the story of

Harrison's quest to solve the longitude problem. Includes bibliographical references, an index, and illustrations.

Howse, Derek. *Greenwich Time and the Discovery of Longitude*. New York: Oxford University Press, 1980. An extensive, if highly technical, discussion of longitude and the establishment of an internationally accepted prime meridian.

Landes, Davis S. *Revolution in Time: Clocks and the Making of the Modern World*. Rev. ed. Cambridge, Mass.: Belknap Press, 2000. Contains a particularly good account of the longitude problem as faced by mariners before Harrison's contributions.

Quill, Humphrey. *John Harrison: The Man Who Found Longitude*. New York: Humanities Press, 1966. The earliest and still the most thorough book-length biography of Harrison.

Sobel, Dava. *Longitude: The True Story of a Lone Ge-*nius *Who Solved the Greatest Scientific Problem of His Time*. New York: Penguin Books, 1995. A short but engaging popular biography of John Harrison.

Wilford, John Noble. *The Mapmakers*. New York: Knopf, 1981. A history of cartography showing, in chapter 8, how Harrison's achievement furthered the arts of navigation and mapmaking.

SEE ALSO: 1735: Hadley Describes Atmospheric Circulation; 1739-1740: Hume Publishes *A Treatise of Human Nature*; 1752-Mar., 1756: Mayer's Lunar Tables Enable Mariners to Determine Longitude at Sea; Dec. 5, 1766-Mar. 16, 1769: Bougainville Circumnavigates the Globe; Aug. 25, 1768-Feb. 14, 1779: Voyages of Captain Cook.

RELATED ARTICLES in *Great Lives from History: The Eighteenth Century, 1701-1800:* Lord Anson; Louis-Antoine de Bougainville; James Cook; George Vancouver.

January 7, 1714
MILL PATENTS THE TYPEWRITER

Henry Mill created likely the first machine for printing individual letters and documents. Queen Anne, recognizing the merits of Mill's innovation, issued a patent guaranteeing his rights to manufacture and sell machines based on his design.

LOCALE: London, England

CATEGORIES: Inventions; science and technology; communications

KEY FIGURES

Henry Mill (c. 1683-1770), English engineer
Queen Anne (1665-1714), queen of England, Scotland, and Ireland, r. 1702-1714
Robert Walpole (1676-1745), English politician and later prime minister of Great Britain, 1721-1742

SUMMARY OF EVENT

During the eighteenth century, most literate people communicated by handwriting personal letters. Because printing documents with presses was costly, especially when only one or several copies were needed, businesses relied on handwritten documents to record transactions and accounts and to prepare invoices and receipts. Attorneys mostly wrote legal information in missives and ledgers. People filled out forms by hand. Such practices caused documents to be vulnerable to forgeries and mod-ifications that benefited criminals trying to deceive victims. Misunderstandings occurred when people were unable to read illegible handwriting. Handwritten documents risked damage if water distorted ink.

Henry Mill was an engineer who had gained hydraulics, engineering, and mechanics expertise while working on water supply at Norfolk's Houghton Hall. His employer, influential politician Robert Walpole, may have assisted Mill with his inventions. Mill resided in London, where he was probably aware of the vast array of scientific and technological endeavors of the early eighteenth century. Most early English patents recognized inventions related to practical uses, including tools, mill engines, and dredging machines. On April 12, 1706, Mill received a patent for a spring device that enhanced passengers' comfort on carriages.

After completing that invention, Mill contemplated a way to mechanize writing to make it more resilient and harder to tamper with. Recognizing the merits of Johann Gutenberg's printing press, Mill wanted to create a smaller device that individuals could use in their shops and homes to produce individual documents affordably. Some sources suggest sixteenth and seventeenth century inventors had devised writing machines prior to Mill's work, but most references to such devices describe types of presses; no proof exists of any direct predecessor to the typewriter as such prior to Mill's innovation.

Mill envisioned a machine that would let people create messages mechanically whenever they wanted instead of being restricted to printers' schedules. The users of such a device would not have to set type for an entire document before it was printed. Instead, they could create documents on the fly, producing each word as they thought of it, placing letters, numerals, and symbols individually and sequentially on paper until they had composed a complete message. Such a procedure would enable people to consider and change the wording of a document as they wrote. Such editing was difficult to perform with material that was already typeset for printing presses.

Sources reveal little about Mill's inventive process, but his patent provides some clues. According to the patent, Mill invested money in his writing machine project, devoting time to research. Perhaps Mill investigated printing presses and other inventors' mechanical creations to determine how his machine should operate. He might have purchased presses and equipment to experiment with possible mechanisms for his machine. Mill probably created several machines, making improvements with each successive device. His machine may have used keys and levers designated for each letter of the alphabet. Mill most likely tested his writing machine on various qualities of paper and parchment.

When he was satisfied with his results, Mill petitioned the court for a patent. On January 7, 1714, Queen Anne approved British patent number 395, recognizing Mill's invention as the first machine to place individual letters on paper. Assuring Mill commercial rights to his invention for fourteen years, the patent noted that Mill's machine produced individual letters on paper to form words and sentences. The patent mentioned that Mill's machine might be utilized to create public records and record decrees and legal decisions, because its writing was more durable than handwriting and could not be easily altered or removed by forgers. Mill probably stressed that transcribers using his writing machine could record spoken words more quickly than those who were handwriting them.

Although Mill likely demonstrated his writing machine to patent officials and possibly even to Queen Anne herself, who referred to him as a valued subject, no existing records indicate that he did so. A demonstration would have convinced officials that his machine functioned and proved that it had the potential to be socially useful. In 1714, British patents did not require inventors to submit prototypes or diagrams of their inventions to file in patent records. Inventors did not have to demonstrate that their invention worked or provide enough detail to allow others to build duplicates. As a result, historians lack models and illustrations of Mill's writing machine. Some scholars question if Mill actually completed a working writing machine. Others, based on patent information and Mill's engineering skills, believe Mill built a writing machine to submit when he sought a patent but that it did not survive for further inspection. Even though some historians of technology can hypothesize how Mill's writing machine worked, they agree that there is insufficient evidence to establish how it actually functioned.

According to most sources, Mill

An early typewriter. (Library of Congress)

probably never commercially produced either of his patented devices for distribution. Despite the benefits Mill's writing machine promised, most eighteenth century people resisted his invention, considering typed communications impersonal. Because enough printing presses were available and handwritten messages continued to appeal, the public did not have an urgent need for writing machines. Mill may well have made writing machines for his personal use and for court officials, business colleagues, and friends, but no machines are known to have existed. Limited to using supplies available at that time, Mill might have utilized leather and wooden materials that probably rotted or broke, depending on printing demands and humidity and temperature conditions where writing machines were used. As a result, no writing machines may have lasted beyond several years of use.

Starting in 1720, Mill focused on employment as the New River Company engineer and surveyor. A 1769 fire at Mill's office ruined most of his records and might have burned any writing machines then extant, as well as information concerning their invention and possible manufacture. After Mill died, his estate auctioned his surveying tools and scientific instruments, which might have included a writing machine.

SIGNIFICANCE

Most historians credit Mill as the typewriter's original inventor. Various countries claim their own inventors as the first to achieve that distinction, but no patents or proof exist to verify such assertions. Although Mill's patent is the sole evidence of his accomplishment, the lack of a model of his writing machine does not diminish his contribution to the development of typewriters. Records do not clarify how many eighteenth century inventors were aware of Mill's patent, but his concept of a mechanical device to perform writing tasks probably significantly influenced others.

Even though the public was uninterested in Mill's writing machine and it probably was not appropriated for commercial uses, his idea potentially inspired inventors to attempt to develop writing machines with keyboards to enable disabled people to communicate. By 1808, Pellegrino Turri di Castelnuovo built the first known functioning writing machine for the blind countess Carolina Fantoni da Fivizzono. Some inventors experimented with machines to write sheet music.

American John Pratt received an 1866 English patent for the pterotype writing machine. Christopher Latham Sholes, Carlos Glidden, Samuel W. Soule, and others commercialized typewriter production in the late nine-

teenth century. The typewriter was certainly well known and well-established by 1897, when it featured prominently in Bram Stoker's novel *Dracula*. Because many early typewriters were complicated, users considered them slower than handwriting. Businesses adopted typewriters, and manufacturers enhanced designs to meet specific needs. By 1905, approximately twenty-five hundred U.S. patents protected typewriter designs and supplies. Typewriters offered women new employment opportunities and some financial autonomy. They aided literacy efforts and foreshadowed the development of word processing with computers.

—Elizabeth D. Schafer

FURTHER READING

Adler, Michael H. *The Writing Machine*. London: Allen & Unwin, 1973. A chapter discusses early writing machines and various inventors' assertions that each was the first person to make a typewriter. Includes the text of Mill's writing machine patent.

Ashton, John. *Social Life in the Reign of Queen Anne: Taken from Original Sources*. New York: Charles Scribner's Sons, 1925. Reveals attitudes toward science and technology in early eighteenth century England, listing patents granted, including a description of Mill's first patent for a transportation spring.

Bliven, Bruce, Jr. *The Wonderful Writing Machine*. New York: Random House, 1954. Comments on inventors' claims to have invented the first writing machine, citing reasons to credit Mill as the actual pioneer and mentioning other eighteenth century inventors interested in similar devices.

Gregg, Edward. *Queen Anne*. 2d ed. New Haven, Conn.: Yale University Press, 2001. Emphasizes Queen Anne's role as a strong leader capable of independently making decisions, such as issuing patents and encouraging invention, contrary to many biographers' depictions.

Kishlansky, Mark. *A Monarchy Transformed: Britain, 1603-1714*. Vol. 6 in *The Penguin History of Britain*. New York: Penguin Books, 1997. Provides contextual information, particularly in a chapter focusing on Queen Anne, regarding the period of English history during which Mill engaged in his inventive activities.

Kittler, Friedrich. *Grammophone, Film, Typewriter*. Translated by Geoffrey Winthrop-Young and Michael Wutz. Stanford, Calif.: Stanford University Press, 1999. A follow-up to Kittler's earlier *Discourse Networks 1800/1900*, this cultural history continues his investigation of various mechanical devices for recording information and how each device defined and affected the culture in which it was used.

Linoff, Victor M., ed. *The Typewriter: An Illustrated History*. Mineola, N.Y.: Dover, 2000. Describes inventions inspired by Mill and early typewriter inventors, including a facsimile of the October, 1923, *Typewriter Topics*, featuring historical information and advertisements for typewriters patented from the early nineteenth through the twentieth century.

SEE ALSO: 1702 or 1706: First Arabic Printing Press; c. 1709: Invention of the Piano; Jan. 1, 1777: France's First Daily Newspaper Appears; 1798: Invention of Lithography.

RELATED ARTICLES in *Great Lives from History: The Eighteenth Century, 1701-1800*: Queen Anne; Robert Walpole.

March 7, 1714, and September 7, 1714
TREATIES OF RASTATT AND BADEN

France and the Holy Roman Empire signed the Treaties of Rastatt and Baden, officially ending the War of the Spanish Succession. The treaties supplemented the provisions of the Treaty of Utrecht (1713), which had concluded peace between all the other combatants in the war, but they failed to establish peace between the empire and Spain.

LOCALE: Rastatt, Baden-Württemberg (now in Germany); Baden, Switzerland

CATEGORIES: Diplomacy and international relations; wars, uprisings, and civil unrest

KEY FIGURES

Duc de Villars (Claude-Louis-Hector de Villars; 1653-1734), French marshal and negotiator

Eugene of Savoy (1663-1736), imperial general and negotiator

Charles VI (1685-1740), Holy Roman Emperor, r. 1711-1740

Louis XIV (1638-1715), king of France, r. 1643-1715

Philip V (1683-1746), king of Spain, r. 1700-January, 1724, and August 31, 1724-1746

Princess des Ursins (Marie-Anne de la Trémoille; 1642-1722), French princess and member of the Spanish court

SUMMARY OF EVENT

The War of the Spanish Succession (1701-1714) involved the question of who would inherit the vast Spanish empire of the last Habsburg ruler of Spain, Charles II (r. 1665-1700). The Bourbon candidate, Philip of Anjou, was designated as ruler by Charles II's will, but the other nations of Europe were unwilling to allow the Bourbons to control both Spain and France, and a major European war erupted. England, the Netherlands, and the Holy Roman Empire allied in the conflict against France and Spain, with several minor powers arrayed on either side as well.

After twelve years of global conflict, most participants in the war made peace in the Treaty of Utrecht (1713), but Austrian Emperor and Holy Roman Emperor Charles VI, who had sought recognition as king of Spain, did not join in the treaty. He chose to continue the war in the belief that Eugene of Savoy could win a decisive victory and gain advantages beyond the terms offered at Utrecht. When the French captured Landau, near Alsace, in August, 1713, and Freiburg, in southwestern Germany, in November, 1713, Charles VI finally decided to make peace and designated Eugene as plenipotentiary to negotiate terms. Louis XIV designated his commander, the duc de Villars, as the French plenipotentiary, and the two opposing generals began negotiations at Rastatt on November 26, 1713.

Villars and Eugene, who had once fought against the Turks in the campaign of 1687, were on very good terms, and both desired peace. After the formalities that opened eighteenth century diplomatic negotiations were observed, both contingents moved into separate wings of the same palace. There was a great deal of entertainment in the palace, and most evenings Villars and Eugene played cards. The Treaty of Ryswick (1697) provided the main guidelines for the deliberations at Rastatt, although portions of the Treaty of Westphalia (1648) and Treaty of Nijmegen (1679) were also consulted. The territories at issue were the border areas between France, the Holy Roman Empire, the Netherlands, and Italy.

If the provisions of the Treaty of Ryswick were followed, Kehl, Freiburg in Breisgau, and Landau would be restored to the Holy Roman Empire. Charles VI demanded the Netherlands, Naples, and Sicily, steep demands from a ruler who had refused to accept the Treaty of Utrecht and whose military campaign in 1713 was unsuccessful. Louis XIV sought to retain Landau and to be compensated for the return of Freiburg, and he demanded full restoration of his allies Max Emmanuel, elector of Bavaria, and Joseph Clemens, elector of Cologne, whose claims had been unresolved at Utrecht. France also sought a principality for the princess des Ursins.

Although he was not negotiating from a position of strength, Eugene had several advantages over Villars, whom he regarded as "timid" and not knowledgeable. Eugene had greater diplomatic experience than did Villars, and Villars believed he needed to negotiate a peace treaty successfully if he was to maintain his status at court. Eugene successfully used tactics such as threatening to break off the talks in order to win concessions, and he could count on unconditional support from Charles VI, who hinted that war might be renewed if the negotiations did not go well. By February, 1714, Eugene and Villars had produced a draft of the peace treaty; Charles VI agreed to it in principle, but Louis XIV did not accept the terms laid out in the document until Villars threatened permanently to break off the negotiations.

The Treaty of Rastatt, whose text was in French, was finalized on March 7, 1714. France retained Strasbourg and Landau and fortresses on the west side of the Rhine River, but it had to restore Alt-Breisach, Freiburg in Breisgau, and Kehl to Austria. France was to raze its fortifications on the islands in the Rhine River. The electors of Bavaria and Cologne were restored, and Louis XIV had to recognize the position of the newly created elector of Hanover. Reluctantly, Louis XIV ended his attempts to settle territory on the princess des Ursins, who had sought to gain territory in the Netherlands through the war. Instead, Charles VI gained the Spanish Netherlands—except for areas allocated to Prussia and the barrier fortresses transferred to the Dutch by the Treaty of Utrecht.

The disposition of Italian territories allotted at Utrecht was not followed by the later treaty, which allowed Charles VI to receive Naples, Milan, Mantua, Tuscan ports, and Sardinia, the latter of which would be traded for Sicily. This more rational ordering of power and territory in Italy worked to Charles's advantage. One issue remained unresolved, however: the Spanish succession. Charles VI did not recognize the new Bourbon king of Spain, Philip V, and Charles's allies in Spain, the Catalans, did not receive the right to self-government. Charles VI and Philip V would not settle their outstand-

ing problems until the Treaty of Vienna (1725). Many of the minor allies of Louis XIV and Charles VI felt ignored and betrayed by the treaty, but once Eugene and Villars had reached an accord on the main issues, they would not allow minor concerns to derail the larger settlement. Plans for a conference between France and the Holy Roman Empire at Baden in Switzerland were set in the last few articles of the treaty.

On June 5, 1714, diplomats met in Baden's town hall, and the Treaty of Baden was signed on September 7, 1714, by Eugene, Villars, and four other diplomats. This treaty was essentially a Latin version of the French text of the Treaty of Rastatt. Charles VI, who had continued the war rather than accept the Treaty of Utrecht, did gain additional benefits by this decision, and Louis XIV did finally settle matters with Charles VI and gain peace. Contemporary diplomats and subsequent historians have noted that the terms of the Utrecht, Rastatt, and Baden settlements were very similar to the terms of the Partition Treaties of 1698 and 1700. The Treaty of Vienna may be said to have finally settled the issues connected to the War of the Spanish Succession. In it, Charles VI renounced his claims to Spain and formally recognized Philip V's title as king of Spain, and Philip V relinquished claims to the Netherlands and Italian territory. Some of the Italian principalities were reordered, and Charles VI and Philip V agreed to support each other's ventures.

SIGNIFICANCE

The Treaties of Rastatt and Baden formally ended the War of the Spanish Succession for France on one side and Austria and the Holy Roman Empire on the other and brought an end to Louis XIV's bid for European hegemony. Within a year, Louis XIV would be dead and the financial effects of his many wars would begin to be felt in France. England, which had procured substantial advantages at Utrecht, emerged as the dominant power in Western Europe. The attempt by Charles VI and Eugene to gain better terms than those offered at Utrecht by continuing the war beyond April, 1713, was partially successful despite the fact that Eugene's military operations against France were hampered by lack of finances and the reappearance of the plague. Charles VI avoided having terms imposed on him at Utrecht and was in control of the Rastatt/Baden negotiations.

The border between France and the Holy Roman Empire conformed to the provisions of the Treaty of Ryswick (1697) with some modifications. One important difference between the Treaty of Westphalia (1648) and the Treaty of Ryswick (1697) was that Catholicism rather than Protestantism was to be the religion in areas restored by France, and the Rastatt and Baden agreements reflected this. Both Charles VI and Louis XIV needed peace. Cessation of the war with France enabled Charles VI and Eugene to concentrate on the Turks to the east with great success and to focus on expansion in Italy and the Mediterranean against Philip V. Austria had emerged as a major European power.

—*Mark C. Herman*

FURTHER READING

Frey, Linda, and Marsha Frey, eds. *The Treaties of the War of the Spanish Succession*. Westport, Conn.: Greenwood Press, 1995. An excellent reference source with short articles on the Treaties of Rastatt and Baden, Prince Eugene and other principals, and the territories that changed hands.

Henderson, Nicholas. *Prince Eugen of Savoy*. 1964. Reprint. London: Phoenix Press, 2002. A complete biography that emphasizes Eugene's military career and discusses his role in negotiating the treaties.

Lynn, John. *The Wars of Louis XIV*. London: Longman, 1999. Contains an extensive treatment of the War of the Spanish Succession and analysis of the terms and impact of the treaties.

McKay, Derek. *Prince Eugene of Savoy*. London: Thames and Hudson, 1977. A complete scholarly biography, it covers Eugene's military undertakings prior to the treaties and evaluates his role in negotiating them.

SEE ALSO: May 26, 1701-Sept. 7, 1714: War of the Spanish Succession; May 15, 1702-Apr. 11, 1713: Queen Anne's War; Aug. 13, 1704: Battle of Blenheim; Sept. 11, 1709: Battle of Malplaquet; Apr. 11, 1713: Treaty of Utrecht.

RELATED ARTICLES in *Great Lives from History: The Eighteenth Century, 1701-1800*: Charles VI; Eugene of Savoy; Philip V.

Summer, 1714-1741
FOX WARS

For almost three decades, the Fox Indians waged war against French settlers and against other Native American tribes, greatly destabilizing the Great Lakes region and hampering trade and diplomacy for all of that region's other inhabitants.

LOCALE: Great Lakes region, west and southwest of Lake Michigan (now in the United States)

CATEGORIES: Wars, uprisings, and civil unrest; diplomacy and international relations

KEY FIGURES

Kiala (fl. 1733-1734), Fox war chief
Mekaga (fl. 1738), minor Fox chief and negotiator
Charles de Beauharnois (1670-1749), governor general of New France, 1726-1747
Marquis de Vaudreuil (Philippe de Rigaud de Vaudreuil; 1643-1725), governor general of New France, 1703-1725

SUMMARY OF EVENT

Although the Fox people trace their own origins to the northeastern seaboard, they clearly emerged in Native American history in the late seventeenth century in the western Great Lakes region. First known under their Algonquian name, Mesquakis (People of the Red Earth),

they are referred to in the journals of early French explorers as *renards*, or foxes, a name that persists in the literature. Most of what is known about the Fox tribe and its often hostile relations with a number of its neighboring tribes comes from the eighteenth century Québécois (New France colonial) archives. Hardly a year passed between 1699 and 1742 without some reference to relations between the Foxes and representatives of Onontia, the natives' name for the French governor general of New France.

In 1699, Governor General Louis-Hector de Callières made diplomatic overtures in an attempt to make peace not only between France and the tribes of the western Great Lakes region but also among the tribes themselves. His goal was to increase profitable trade in a vast region that remained unpredictable because of recurring intertribal strife. The natives invited to Montreal were well-known tribes associated with the Iroquois Five Nations (including the Senecas) and lesser-known tribes along the western shore of Lake Michigan, including the Sacs, Winnebagos, Kickapoos, Menominees, and Foxes. In September, 1700, a peace treaty was signed by several important tribes, but many, including the Foxes, held back.

Although the Foxes and Chippewas agreed to cease fighting each other in the Wisconsin area, Fox hostilities with neighboring Sioux still raged, disrupting fur trading as far as Sioux territory in Minnesota. In their attempt to stop these conflicts, the French invited Fox chieftains Noro and Miskousouath to Montreal. There the chiefs were assured that, if they remained peaceful in their newly fortified villages at the portage point between the Fox and Wisconsin Rivers, they would have their share of French fur trade in Sioux territory.

The shortcomings of these agreements were particularly evident to Antoine de La Mothe, sieur de Cadillac, commander of the strategic post at Michilimackinac on the straits between Lakes Michigan and Huron. Cadillac's goal was to develop another, eventually much better-known, post at Detroit into a major trading center for various tribes. In 1710, he invited a number of Algonquian tribes located in the area from the Green Bay to the Wisconsin River, including Sacs, Foxes, Mascoutens, and Kickapoos, to move to eastern Michigan.

Some Foxes, together with members of other Wisconsin tribes, did go to the Detroit area, but the venture soon was reversed by Montreal's governor general, the Marquis de Vaudreuil. Not only did the Foxes expect that their cooperation with the resettlement scheme should be rewarded, but they also became entangled in skirmishes with other tribes, especially Hurons and members of the Illinois Confederacy. They even raided French colonial farms, stealing food and livestock. When the French issued orders in 1711 for them to return to Wisconsin, the Foxes became even more belligerent, proceeding to build a fort near Fort Pontchartrain on the Detroit River. It took more than a year for the French, taking advantage of alliances with Huron and Illinois Confederacy tribes, to expel the Foxes by force.

Most of the Foxes besieged in their fort on the Detroit River were massacred brutally by French-allied American Indians, despite the French commander's assurance of safe passage upon surrender. Those who escaped sought refuge among the Seneca Iroquois. These violent events on the Detroit River were bound to have repercussions among the Fox tribes that had stayed behind in Wisconsin alongside their allies, the Sacs and Winnebagos. When the defeated Foxes returned to Wisconsin, new alliances were built. In the summer of 1714, they began to attack French traders passing from Detroit to Michilimackinac. These attacks were the opening salvos of wars that were to last for twenty-seven years.

In this first stage of the Fox Wars, some Wisconsin natives hoped that the French would seek an accommodation with the Foxes. As the situation deteriorated and trade became paralyzed, many American Indians began

to call for a strong French military campaign against the Foxes. Before long, it appeared that the Foxes had long-distance ties with other allies in British territory, especially the Senecas. This complicated French strategy considerably, forcing the French to try diplomatic intervention far to the east of Wisconsin. Vaudreuil was unable to report any progress for at least three years.

Although Fox chieftains Okimaoussen and Ouchala agreed to de-escalate the conflict, warfare against the Foxes by their inveterate enemies, the Chippewas and Potawatomis, caused strife to spread into Illinois tribal areas in 1719. By 1721, the Foxes had even sealed peace with their former enemies, the Sioux, to have an ally against the Illinois. In 1725, the French reported that their own hopes to tap the Sioux fur market were seriously hampered by the Sioux-Fox alliance.

By the time of Vaudreuil's death in October, 1725, King Louis XV himself sent orders to replace the French commander at Green Bay, François Amariton, suspected of encouraging Fox raids into Illinois territory, and to step up activities against the Foxes. This task, which would lead to disastrous consequences for the Fox tribe, fell to Charles de Beauharnois, governor general of New France from 1726 to 1747.

A major campaign was set for 1728. French forces of four hundred soldiers were joined by *coureurs de bois* (freelance French fur trappers and traders) and hundreds of western natives. The French claimed success, but in reality the Foxes had withdrawn into Iowa rather than risk a battle.

The next stage of conflict came when Fox chief Kansekoe tried to force his Kickapoo allies to hand over a dozen French traders who were being held as hostages. Kickapoo refusals incited younger Fox warriors to break away from Kansekoe and attack both Kickapoo and Mascouten hunters. Both tribes soon asked for French alliance status. Then, some Winnebagos and Menominees also joined attacks against the Foxes. Declining chances for a victory again divided the Foxes. Some factions favored a peace, while more hostile tribesmen decided to leave Wisconsin and seek asylum, preferably among the Senecas. The attempted migration left them open to reprisal attacks, especially by members of the Illinois Confederacy, supported by the Foxes' former neighbors, the Potawatomis, Kickapoos, and Mascoutens. A major siege of Fox fortifications on the Illinois prairie in 1730 involved French relief forces, who joined in a general massacre of more than five hundred Foxes, including women and children.

Governor General Beauharnois reported that the remaining Foxes no longer could consider resistance. Continuing reprisals caused Foxes under Chief Kiala to try to resettle peacefully on the north bank of the Wisconsin River and to send emissaries to Montreal. Kiala's apparent failure to meet French terms tempted Beauharnois to allow Huron the Iroquois "volunteers" to pursue the refugee Foxes spread out in areas of Iowa and Illinois. Intertribal fighting continued until 1735, when two refugee groups separated, one going to the Rock River in Illinois and the other to the mouth of the Wisconsin. In 1736, White Cat, a friendly Sac chief, asked Beauharnois to grant a pardon. Beauharnois tried unsuccessfully to persuade the Sacs to gain peace by allowing the French to disperse the Foxes among other American Indian nations. Finally, in 1741, unable to hold out in the Rock River Valley against other Indians' attacks, and fearful of massive French reprisals for Fox assistance to Sioux warriors near Lake Peoria who had killed French travelers in the area, Fox chief Mekaga agreed to accept French terms of forced relocation.

SIGNIFICANCE

By the fall of 1741, the Foxes and Sacs were trekking to new settlements: Ten lodges moved to the Chicago River, three traveled to Milwaukee, and the rest made their way to their old homeland village on the Fox River in Wisconsin. The dispersal of the Foxes made them weaker, but it also made them more difficult both to protect and to control. Indeed, although the formal Fox War was over in 1741, their settlements still suffered from attacks by their Chippewa, Menominee, and Ottawa neighbors. In 1743, Beauharnois himself had to intercede to gain another joint pledge of peace.

—*Byron D. Cannon*

FURTHER READING

Edmunds, R. David, and Joseph L. Peyser. *The Fox Wars: The Mesquaki Challenge to New France.* Norman: University of Oklahoma Press, 1993. The most complete study to date of the specific events of the Fox Wars.

Hagen, William T. *The Sac and Fox Indians.* 2d ed. Norman: University of Oklahoma Press, 1980. A general history, including cultural and religious topics.

Murphy, Lucy Eldersveld. *A Gathering of Rivers: Indians, Metis, and Mining in the Western Great Lakes, 1737-1832.* Lincoln: University of Nebraska Press, 2000. A history of the Fox and other Indian communities, as well as multiracial and mining communities, in the Western Great Lakes region in the eighteenth and early nineteenth centuries. Includes information about the Fox Wars.

Parkman, Francis. *Count Frontenac and New France Under Louis XIV.* 1877. Reprint. New York: Library of America, 1983. A pioneering work providing background on French interests in the Great Lakes area just before dealings with the Foxes became focal.

White, Richard. *The Middle Ground: Indians, Empires and Republics in the Great Lakes Region, 1650-1815.* New York: Cambridge University Press, 1991. Places the Fox Wars in a wider chronological and geographical context of French, British, and American Indian relations.

SEE ALSO: Sept. 22, 1711-Mar. 23, 1713: Tuscarora War; Sept. 19, 1737: Walking Purchase; May 28, 1754-Feb. 10, 1763: French and Indian War; Oct. 5, 1759-Nov. 19, 1761: Cherokee War; May 8, 1763-July 24, 1766: Pontiac's Resistance; May 24 and June 11, 1776: Indian Delegation Meets with Congress; Oct. 22, 1784: Fort Stanwix Treaty; Oct. 18, 1790-July, 1794: Little Turtle's War; 1799: Code of Handsome Lake.

RELATED ARTICLE in *Great Lives from History: The Eighteenth Century, 1701-1800*: Thanadelthur.

1715-1737
BUILDING OF THE KARLSKIRCHE

The Karlskirche, a votive church commissioned by Emperor Charles VI, represented the supreme architectural achievement of Johann Bernhard Fischer von Erlach, who set his distinctive mark upon the Kaiserstil (the imperial style) of Baroque Vienna.

LOCALE: Vienna, Austria
CATEGORY: Architecture

KEY FIGURES
Johann Bernhard Fischer von Erlach (1656-1723),
    Austrian architect
Josef Emanuel Fischer von Erlach (1693-1742),
    Austrian architect and son of Johann Bernhard
Charles VI (1685-1740), Holy Roman Emperor,
    r. 1711-1740

SUMMARY OF EVENT
Toward the close of the seventeenth century, Vienna was a small, congested capital, huddled behind massive walls and bastions, fearful of a Turkish onslaught. When the onslaught came in 1683, however, the Ottomans were soundly defeated, and the Ottoman Empire's frontier shrank southward as a result. The emboldened Viennese expanded their city beyond its walls and into its suburbs, where the nobility initiated an extravagant building boom.

The boom, begun under Leopold I (r. 1657-1705), gathered steam under his son, Joseph I (r. 1705-1711). As an eleven-year-old, Joseph had been tutored in architecture by Johann Bernhard Fischer von Erlach, who was newly returned from Bernini's Rome with a budding reputation as a polymath in architecture and the decorative arts. When Joseph became emperor, he promoted Fischer von Erlach to superintendent of imperial buildings; the architect and his patron anticipated a long and fruitful collaboration. Soon, Fischer von Erlach was preparing designs for an extraordinary palace to outrival Versailles itself, but the scale of his plans overreached the financial resources of the monarchy, and the palace remained a pipe dream.

Joseph's premature death led to the accession of his younger brother as Charles VI. Charles was morose and taciturn, and not particularly competent as a ruler. His residence in Spain, where he had been a claimant to the throne, had led him to cultivate Spanish formality, fashion, and manners. Nevertheless, where the arts were concerned, he could be munificent and imaginative. At his accession, he had inherited Fischer von Erlach as his su-

perintendent of imperial buildings, and he was quick to appreciate the latter's immense talents, giving him some of his greatest commissions. In 1713, Vienna was devastated by plague, and Charles VI vowed to commemorate the city's recovery by building a votive church dedicated to San Carlo Borromeo, the Counter-Reformation saint after whom the emperor was named. The result was the Karlskirche, built between 1715 and 1737.

Significantly, the site chosen for the Karlskirche lay outside the ramparts of the old city, on the outskirts of the Wieden suburb, where noble families were beginning to erect summer palaces and where Fischer von Erlach would own two houses. Nearby, construction was underway on a palace for Prince Heinrich von Mansfeld-Fondi, imperial seneschal, by Johann Lucas von Hildebrandt. When the prince died in 1715, the unfinished palace was bought by Prince Adam Franz zu Schwarzenberg, who promptly replaced Hildebrandt with Fischer von Erlach. His son, Joseph Emanuel Fischer von Erlach, took over the project after his father's death, completing the Palais Schwarzenberg in 1732. Thus the Palais Schwarzenberg, not much more than a stone's throw from the Karlskirche, mirrored its architectural history.

Meanwhile, Charles VI ordered a competition among architects for his votive church. The three finalists were Ferdinando Galli da Bibiena (1657-1743), best known for his theatrical designs; Hildebrandt, Fischer von Erlach's younger rival; and Fischer von Erlach himself. Strangely, although models survive of Baroque buildings throughout Europe, none have survived in the Imperial Viennese style, including these three submissions. In any case, Charles opted for Fischer von Erlach's plan, which had aroused widespread interest.

Fischer von Erlach's friend and correspondent, the philosopher Gottfried Wilhelm Leibniz (1646-1716), who visited Vienna during 1713 and 1714, was especially interested in imperial iconography. Another friend of Fischer von Erlach, the Swedish antiquarian and numismatist Carl Gustav Heraeus, wrote in September, 1715, to Leibniz regarding the two columns in front of the church, which were the most remarkable aspect of Fischer von Erlach's design. Both men thought that these columns should illustrate the deeds of the emperor's ancestors, Charlemagne and Saint Charles, count of Flanders, symbolizing the virtues of steadfastness and fortitude. These images would eventually give way to scenes in the life of San Carlo Borromeo.

The Karlskirche, c. 1900. (Hulton Archive/Getty Images)

Fischer von Erlach seems to have taken the better part of two years to complete his design. This is confirmed by a letter from Heraeus to Leibniz on December 5, 1715, stating that the emperor had made his choice on the previous day and that Fischer von Erlach had been looking at the site outside the Carinthian Gate (Kärtnertor) and not far from the Trautson Palace, where he was already engaged on another of his indubitable masterpieces.

The Karlskirche is not a cathedral—the home church of a bishop—but a votive church, a church built as an offering; its design makes it seem more imposing than it is. Its unique—and most immediately eye-catching—features are the two immense columns on either side of its entrance portico. The columns were most likely inspired by Trajan's column in Rome, depicting Trajan's triumph over the Dacians, a monument familiar to Fischer von Erlach from his Roman years. Symbolic significance has always been attached to the Karlskirche's columns: In addition to Leibniz's and Heraeus's ideas mentioned

above, they were said to represent the two columns Boaz and Jachim in Solomon's Temple. They were also said to symbolize the Pillars of Hercules (that is, the Straits of Gibraltar), evoking the legend of Hercules' exploits in Spain and thus the Spanish monarchy, which Charles still held to be rightfully his.

Imperial commissions on the scale of the Karlskirche were, of course, invariably collaborative endeavors: Christoph Mader supervised the work on the columns, although the stone reliefs were done by Jakob Christoph Schletterer. The Italian Lorenzo Mattielli was originally commissioned to collaborate with them, but his work was deemed technically unsatisfactory (he cut too deep into the stone), and he was therefore made responsible only for the eagles and crown that topped each column's lantern.

It was characteristic of Fischer von Erlach's work that he always placed great emphasis on his buildings' facades. That of the Karlskirche was especially striking. The two great columns were flanked by elegant, three-story towers to provide proportion and harmony and to frame the columns. The towers also served a practical purpose: They allowed carriages to draw up beneath them in inclement weather, whence two side entrances and a long walkway led into the body of the church. Typical of the architect with his strict Roman training, he placed between the two columns a large Roman portico supported by six columns, on which rested a pediment with reliefs by Giovanni Stanetti illustrating the sufferings of the people of Vienna during the 1713 plague and crowned by Lorenzo Mattielli's statue of San Carlo.

Passing though this portico, a visitor would enter through a square vestibule into the body of the church, a longitudinal oval at right angles to the facade. Above this central oval was the dome drum, on which rested the great copper dome and lantern. Beyond the oval, a foreshortened choir led to the apse of the high altar, which was flanked externally by two small domed towers. On the ground floor, oval and choir opened into side chapels, while above, a broad ambulatory incorporated decorated glazed boxes, from which the scene beneath could be viewed.

The Karlskirche was not Fischer von Erlach's only commission at this time: He was also working on the Hofbibliothek (imperial library) on the Augustinerstrasse, as well as the emperor's winter riding stables. When he died in 1723, his talented son, Josef Emanuel, was left to complete them, finishing the stables in 1723 and the library in 1737, the same year he finished the church itself.

The elder Fischer von Erlach knew exactly how he wanted the finished church to look, engaging some of the greatest painters of the Austrian Baroque as his collaborators, including Martino Altomonte, Daniel Gran, and Johann Michael Rottmayr. Alberto Camesina painted San Carlo Borromeo ascending to heaven for the high altar, but the painting was overwhelmed by F. M. Prokoff's immense halo amid clouds and descending rays of sunlight. Rottmayr painted the great dome with the apotheosis of San Carlo between 1725 and 1730, while Gran and Altomonte worked on other frescoes. The final dedication of the Karlskirche took place in 1738, just two years before the emperor's death and fifteen years after the architect's.

SIGNIFICANCE

The Karlskirche, with its extraordinary combination of grandeur and grace, must be regarded as one of the most original and satisfying products of the *Kaiserstil*, the imperial Viennese Baroque style, of which Fischer von Erlach was the supreme exemplar. In the Baroque period, the florescence of artistic talent in the Holy Roman Em-

pire and the Danubian lands produced a dazzling array of artists from self-taught serfs to military engineers and aristocratic amateurs, but among them all, Fischer von Erlach was unique. Leaving an indelible stamp on the Vienna of his day, he was no mere master craftsman. With far-ranging intellectual interests and boundless curiosity regarding his art, he was that very rarest of professionals, a kind of "philosopher-architect," appropriately enough for the friend of the greatest German mind of the age. Leibniz's conception of a "Divine Mover" became for Fischer von Erlach the concept of the architect as the interpreter of a transcendent cosmos of harmony and order, grace and nature.

Not long before his death, Fischer von Erlach published a lavishly illustrated history of architectural design, *Entwurff einer historischen Architektur* (1721; *A Plan of Civil and Historical Architecture in the Representation of the Most Noted Buildings of Foreign Nations Both Ancient and Modern*, 1730), expanded from a manuscript that he had originally dedicated to Charles VI in 1712. It was translated into English in 1730 and was to be one of the most influential architectural treatises of the eighteenth century. In a sense, the Karlskirche was the embodiment of the high ideals expressed in the history over which he had ruminated for so long.

—*Gavin R. G. Hambly*

FURTHER READING

Aurenhammer, Hans. *J. B. Fischer von Erlach*. Cambridge, Mass.: Harvard University Press, 1973. The only English-language work on the architect.

Blunt, Anthony, ed. *Baroque and Rococo: Architecture and Decoration*. New York: Harper & Row, 1978. An excellent discussion of the Karlskirche.

Fergusson, Frances D. "St. Charles's Church, Vienna: The Iconography of Its Architecture." *Journal of the Society of Architectural Historians* 29 (1970): 318-326. Essential for studies of imperial iconography.

Millon, Henry A., ed. *The Triumph of the Baroque*. New York: Rizzoli, 1999. An indispensable reference to the Baroque style.

Sedlmayr, Hans. *Johann Bernard Fischer von Erlach*. Vienna, Austria: Herold, 1956. The definitive study of the architect. In German.

Wangermann, Ernst. *The Austrian Achievement, 1700-1800*. London: Thames & Hudson, 1973. Introduction to Austria's Golden Age, placing Fischer von Erlach's career in historical perspective.

SEE ALSO: Nov. 20, 1710-July 21, 1718: Ottoman Wars with Russia, Venice, and Austria; Mar. 7, 1714, and

Sept. 7, 1714: Treaties of Rastatt and Baden; 1748-1755: Construction of Istanbul's Nur-u Osmaniye Complex; 1762: *The Antiquities of Athens* Prompts Architectural Neoclassicism.

RELATED ARTICLES in *Great Lives from History: The Eighteenth Century, 1701-1800*: Charles VI; Johann Bernhard Fischer von Erlach; Johann Lucas von Hildebrandt.

September 6, 1715-February 4, 1716
JACOBITE RISING IN SCOTLAND

Supporters of the exiled Stuart Dynasty rose up in Scotland, in an attempt to overthrow the new Hanover Dynasty and place James Edward on the British throne. This Jacobite movement drew enough adherents to pose a serious threat to the Hanoverian monarchy, but it ended in failure because the Jacobites lacked good intelligence, adequate communications, and decisive military leadership.

ALSO KNOWN AS: The Fifteen Rebellion
LOCALE: Holy Island, Newcastle, and Preston, England; Braemar, Perth, and Dunblane, Scotland
CATEGORIES: Wars, uprisings, and civil unrest; government and politics

KEY FIGURES
James Edward (The "Old Pretender"; 1688-1766), Stuart pretender to the throne of Great Britain
Sixth Earl of Mar (John Erskine; 1675-1732), Scottish noble and rebel leader
Thomas Forster (c. 1675-1738), English rebel leader
Second Duke of Argyll (John Campbell; 1680-1743), Scottish noble and British military commander
George I (1660-1727), elector of Hanover, r. 1698-1727, and first Hanoverian king of Great Britain, r. 1714-1727

SUMMARY OF EVENT
The Jacobite Rising of 1715 was a rebellion against the new king of Great Britain, George I, and the Hanover Dynasty. The rebels were called Jacobites to represent their continued loyalty to the exiled James II, who had been deposed in 1688 because of his adherence to Roman Catholicism. After James II's death, his Roman Catholic son James Edward, styled James III and generally known as the "Old Pretender," became the focus of the Jacobites' hopes. In 1688, the throne had gone to James II's daughter Mary II, a Protestant, and her husband, William III; it had then passed to Mary's sister Anne. Queen Anne's successor was George I, the elector of Hanover, who was a great-grandson of James I (r. 1603-1625) and therefore had some Stuart blood. However, George I was

not only a German prince who spoke very little English, but also neither intelligent nor personally appealing. Moreover, he showed such partiality toward the Whig Party that he alienated the Tories.

The Whigs took advantage of their new ascendancy in the British government by commencing impeachment proceedings against Queen Anne's Tory leaders, causing at least two of them to flee to the Jacobite court in exile in

Jacobite leaders, who supported the exiled Stuart Dynasty, were captured by authorities of the reigning Hanover Dynasty. (Francis R. Niglutsch)

France. Now the Jacobite cause was becoming more attractive not just to its original base group of Roman Catholics and Cavaliers but also to Tories ousted from power or snubbed by the king; to opponents of the Whigs' penchant for military intervention in Europe; to High Church Anglicans, concerned that George might slight the Church of England in favor of the Nonconformists; and to those Scots who now saw the 1707 Act of Union as a grave error. Even in 1708, there had been enough opposition to the union of England and Scotland to prompt an attempt at placing young James on the Scottish throne. The attempt had failed after the invading French ships with James Edward aboard were driven off by the Royal Navy. Now, however, many more Scots believed that the union had merely given England even greater political and economic power over Scotland.

The primary force behind the rising of 1715, however, was not the claimant to the throne but a disappointed Scottish politician. After being snubbed publicly by King George I, the sixth earl of Mar decided to regain his former power by changing monarchs. In July, 1715, he began making plans for a two-front attack, one in the north and the other in the west near Newcastle. On September 6, 1715, he raised the Jacobite standard at Braemar. Soon, Mar had more than ten thousand men under his command.

Meanwhile, the Jacobites on the Continent, whom Mar had not contacted, were making preparations to land in the southwest of England. However, there were delays, which gave Hanoverian spies ample time to learn about the planned uprising. The English Jacobites were not told that the landing had been postponed, and when they gathered to welcome the invading troops, most of them were arrested. By the end of September, 1715, it was obvious that there would be no rebellion in the southwest.

Mar's attempt to seize Fort William in the western Highlands was no more successful, and instead of continuing their efforts in the west, the clansmen from that area joined the main Jacobite army. The Northumbrian campaign was no more successful. On October 10, Thomas Forster captured Holy Island but failed to reinforce it, and it was recaptured the following day. A few days later, two French ships appeared off the coast, but when they saw that the island was held by the Hanoverians, they sailed away. Shortly afterward, the

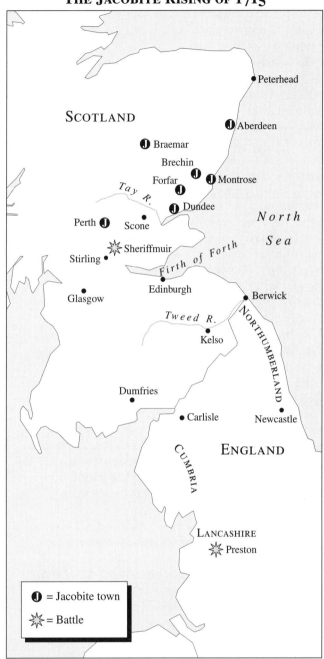

THE JACOBITE RISING OF 1715

British sent more troops to Newcastle, ending any hope that Forster could capture the city, and he rejoined Mar in Scotland. Three weeks later, however, Forster again took his troops south of the border, where he had been told there were hundreds of men eager to join him. Again, the Jacobites' intelligence was faulty. Government forces trapped the Jacobites in Preston, and over the objections of the Scots, who wanted to fight their way out, on November 14 Forster surrendered, ending the rising on the English side of the border.

In Scotland, however, the Jacobites seemed well on the way to success. Even without the "Old Pretender" present—for James Edward had not yet been able to reach England—men had flocked to join Mar's forces. John Campbell, second duke of Argyll, who was commander in chief of the Hanoverian government's forces in Scotland, had no more than four thousand men at his disposal. By now, he knew, the Jacobites outnumbered his forces by five to one. On September 14, a relatively small number of the Jacobites had taken Perth. If the larger force had immediately pressed their advantage, they could have driven south to Edinburgh and Glasgow and perhaps captured London itself. However, for a month Mar took no action. He seemed to be waiting, perhaps for James Edward to appear, perhaps for the French to arrive with reinforcements, perhaps simply for the will to commit his troops.

It was November 10 before Mar finally set forth, marching south toward Dunblane. Argyll was still outnumbered, though now only by two to one, but he had a grasp of military tactics that his opponent lacked, and he forestalled Mar by seizing the high ground of Sheriffmuir, near Dunblane. On November 13, the two forces met. Neither side won a victory, but Argyll lost the high ground during the fray and was left with only one thousand men. Again, however, Mar's timidity won the day for the Hanoverians: During the night, Mar pulled out his troops and retreated to Perth. At that point, the rising was effectively over.

James Edward finally arrived in Scotland on December 22, but the projected coronation at Scone never took place. As Argyll, now reinforced by Dutch troops, advanced toward the north, the Jacobites retreated to Perth, heartlessly burning all the villages in their path, and then scattered to their homes. James Edward, Mar, and several other leaders sneaked off to Montrose, where they caught a ship for to the Continent. Thus on February 4, 1716, the "Old Pretender" ingloriously left the country he had believed himself worthy to rule. He never returned.

SIGNIFICANCE

The rising of 1715 was the Jacobites' best chance to seize the throne of Great Britain. Never again would there be such widespread discontent in both England and Scotland; never again would the Jacobites be able to draw so many to their cause. It was not a lack of enthusiasm, but poor leadership, that caused the rising to fail. It has been said that if the same number of men had been mustered for the rising of 1745, that rebellion would have succeeded, for James Edward's son Charles Edward not only had the charm his father lacked, but he also had the capacity for courageous and decisive leadership that was so badly needed in 1715.

There were immediate consequences for the Jacobites who had participated in the rising of 1715. Some were executed, and many nobles lost their estates. Some prisoners died in jail; others chose transportation. A number escaped by bribing their captors and fled to the Continent, where they joined various foreign armies. With the Tories suspect, the Whigs could now argue that they were Britain's only defense against popery and against the hated French. However, Jacobitism was not dead. There were still some who met in secret to drink the health of the "king over the water," and long after the final rising failed, the Jacobite cause would remain the stuff of romantic legend and of popular fiction.

—*Rosemary M. Canfield Reisman*

FURTHER READING

Douglas, Hugh. *Jacobite Spy Wars: Moles, Rogues, and Treachery*. Stroud, Gloucestershire, England: Sutton, 1999. Traces the activities of Jacobite and Hanoverian agents during the period. Chronology. Illustrated.

Gooch, Leo. *The Desperate Faction? The Jacobites of Northeast England, 1688-1745*. Hull, England: University of Hull Press, 1995. Argues that Northumbrian Jacobite leaders such as Colonel Forster have been blamed unjustly for the failure of the 1715 rising.

Lenman, Bruce. *The Jacobite Risings in Britain, 1689-1746*. London: Eyre Methuen, 1980. The author disputes the view of many scholars that the Jacobite risings were clashes between Celtic tradition and Anglo-Saxon materialism. Cites evidence to prove how diverse a group the Jacobites were.

Magnusson, Magnus. *Scotland: The Story of a Nation*. New York: Atlantic Monthly Press, 2000. Contains a good description of the Battle of Sheriffmuir. Includes maps and illustrations.

Pittock, Murray. *Jacobitism*. New York: St. Martin's Press, 1998. A discussion of the political context of the rising and the reasons for its failure.

Whyte, Ian, and Kathleen Whyte. *On the Trail of the Jacobites*. New York: Routledge, 1990. Explains the widespread discontent that led to the rising of 1715, then proceeds with a detailed account of the campaigns. Maps and illustrations.

SEE ALSO: Feb., 1706-Apr. 28, 1707: Act of Union Unites England and Scotland; Mar. 23-26, 1708: Defeat of the "Old Pretender."

RELATED ARTICLES in *Great Lives from History: The Eighteenth Century, 1701-1800*: Queen Anne; Second Duke of Argyll; George I.

1718
BERNOULLI PUBLISHES HIS CALCULUS OF VARIATIONS

By the early eighteenth century, various approaches had been tried to solve several mathematical problems that had been known since antiquity. Johann I Bernoulli organized much of the earlier material and produced an account that could be followed by a wide range of mathematical readers.

LOCALE: Paris, France
CATEGORY: Mathematics

KEY FIGURES

Johann I Bernoulli (1667-1748), Swiss mathematician
Jakob I Bernoulli (1655-1705), Swiss mathematician and brother of Johann I
Sir Isaac Newton (1642-1717), English mathematician and an inventor of the calculus
Gottfried Wilhelm Leibniz (1646-1716), German philosopher and mathematician and an inventor of the calculus

SUMMARY OF EVENT

The calculus of variations was a method in applied calculus that required a full command of cutting-edge developments in mathematics in the early eighteenth century. It was therefore used as arena in which the leading mathematicians of the day could display their superior skills and knowledge. The calculus of variations was applicable to a wide range of problems, but in its earliest days there did not seem to be any common thread connecting the arguments and the solutions to these various problems. With the 1718 publication of Swiss mathematician Johann I Bernoulli's essay on the calculus in the *Histoire de l'Académie Royale des Sciences: Avec les Memoires de Mathematique et de Phisique pour la même année* (history of the royal academy of sciences: with the memoirs of mathematics and physics for the same year), the first glimmerings of a general theory emerged, a theory that was to play an important role in the natural sciences as well as in mathematics over the next two centuries.

The new field of the calculus was particularly applied to the study of the cycloid, a curve that is traced out by a point on the circumference of a circle as it rolls along a flat surface. The Dutch mathematician Christiaan Huygens had published a treatise discussing the cycloid in the previous century, *Horologium oscillatorium* (1673; English translation, 1966). Huygens was especially interested in the construction of accurate clocks, and he found that the cycloid was the curve that a pendulum should follow in order most accurately to keep time. As a result of Huygens's investigations, the mathematical community in Europe had given more attention to the cycloid than to most other geometric curves.

Before the calculus, a curve was usually expressed in the form of an explicit equation connecting two variables. After the development of the calculus by Sir Isaac Newton and Gottfried Wilhelm Leibniz in the latter half of the seventeenth century, it was recognized that curves could best be described by the variation of the points on the curve over time. Such a description of a curve took the form of a differential equation—that is, an equation specifying the derivatives of the positions of the points on the curve. Mathematicians had learned, by study of the cycloid, to recognize its unique differential equation.

Newton had posed the problem in *Philosophiae Naturalis Principia Mathematica* (1687; *The Mathematical Principles of Natural Philosophy*, 1729; best known as the *Principia*) of which physical shape would encounter the least resistance from air when rotated. To solve this problem, he made some simplifying assumptions (which were to be characteristic of the field in its later developments). His solution in the *Principia* involved geometry, but he was aware of a way to enunciate and solve the problem using the calculus.

What served as the jumping-off point for the calculus of variations was not Newton's problem, however, but a question posed by Johann I Bernoulli in a 1696 issue of *Acta Eruditorum*, a journal published in Leipzig for scholars in mathematics and other areas. Bernoulli asked what path an object traveling between two points in space should follow in order to make the journey in the least possible time. Bernoulli declared that the curve that solved the problem would be called the brachistochrone, from the Greek for "least time." The problem had originally been posed by the Italian physicist Galileo in the

131

early seventeenth century, but he had mistakenly thought that the answer was a circular arc.

Bernoulli's challenge attracted the attention of many distinguished mathematicians, including Newton, Leibniz, and Bernoulli's elder brother Jakob I Bernoulli. The results of the challenge were included in an issue of the *Acta Eruditorum* for the following year. The various contributors had taken different paths to the solution, but they all succeeded in identifying the shape of the brachistochrone as a cycloid. This came as quite a surprise to the Bernoullis, who had not thought that the curve they had learned about in Huygens's work would appear in this rather remote setting.

Newton had sent in his submission anonymously, but no one had any doubts about the origins of that solution. It was not, however, Newton's solution that was to be the most influential, but that of Jakob Bernoulli. He approached the problem by allowing a point on the curve to vary (which accounts for the name of the resulting discipline, the calculus of variations) and derived a differential equation as a result. The differential equation was that of the cycloid, and its familiarity may explain why so many solutions were forthcoming. Jakob Bernoulli's methodology, however, could be generalized to solve problems whose solutions were less familiar. Recognizing this, he pursued the method that he had developed to deal with his brother's challenge in a subsequent paper of 1701.

There were two other kinds of problems to which the calculus of variations could be applied. One was that of finding a geodesic, or the shortest path between two points on a surface. On a flat surface, or plane, it is easy to see that the geodesic is always a straight line; however, for two points located on a sphere or an ellipsoid, for example, the geodesic is less obvious. Moreover, since eighteenth century mathematicians and physicists were aware that the surface of the Earth is ellipsoid in shape, they were particularly interested in finding a method to determine the geodesic of an ellipsoid. Such an equation would have obvious benefits for navigation.

The other kind of problem that could be solved with the calculus of variations was an "isoperimetric" problem: Given a specific perimeter, what figure with that perimeter will have the greatest area? A story from classical antiquity had served as a model for the tricks that could be concealed in apparently straightforward situations, but the mathematicians of the seventeenth century were looking for a systematic way of showing, for instance, that the rectangle of given perimeter with the greatest area was always a square.

Jakob Bernoulli was able to make headway on all of these problems—brachistochrone, geodesic, and isoperimeter—with the methods he introduced in his 1701 paper, also published in the *Acta Eruditorum*. He entitled his paper "Analysis of a Great Isoperimetric Problem," and he observed that he was calling the problem great not because it was important in itself but because it led to methods that would be applicable to many other problems as well. Jakob was able to draw upon his success in solving the problem raised by his brother about the brachistochrone to attract Johann's attention to his more ambitious paper.

Despite his wealth of ideas, however, Jakob Bernoulli's exposition left a good deal to be desired. His presentation verged on the pedantic, and even those with an interest in the subject found his article difficult going. After his death in 1705, his brother Johann took up the task of providing an exposition of the bases for the calculus of variations. Johann was also trying to promote his own ideas, some of which differed significantly from those of his brother. Finally, in 1718, Johann published a paper in *Histoire de l'Académie Royale des Sciences* presenting the calculus of variations as a systematic discipline with important applications to a range of problems. Johann's 1718 paper proved to be the source from which the next generation of mathematicians was to draw in further developing and applying the calculus.

SIGNIFICANCE

Johann I Bernoulli's publication served as a guide to the mathematicians of the later eighteenth century, who gave their own formulations to some of the principles he had put forward. In particular, Bernoulli himself was the teacher of Leonhard Euler, the greatest mathematician of the rest of the century. Euler took much of his original approach to the calculus of variations from the two Bernoullis (he did not follow his own teacher, Johann, slavishly in those instances when he felt that Jakob's approach had been more fruitful). Within a few years of his study with Johann Bernoulli, Euler struck out on his own and developed the calculus of variations into a full-fledged mathematical theory. One of his great textbooks was devoted to the subject. It was in that textbook that he introduced the idea of a function, which would go well beyond the calculus of variations.

The Bernoullis were not entirely forgotten, however, even after Euler's magisterial supersession of their earlier treatment. The twentieth century mathematician Constantin Carathéodory revisited Johann Bernoulli's ideas and acknowledged their importance to his own work in the calculus of variations. The field had continued to develop in the nineteenth century, and many of the problems to which it was applied by Carathéodory and his contemporaries would have been unfamiliar to Bernoulli. Nevertheless, the idea of looking at a possible solution and trying to vary a point on it to see what sort of differential equation would result remained the source of inspiration in the calculus of variations for centuries.

—*Thomas Drucker*

FURTHER READING

Bliss, Gilbert Ames. *Calculus of Variations*. LaSalle, Ill.: Open Court, 1925. An account designed for college students that starts with several chapters on the problems that led to the Bernoullis' work.

Chabert, Jean-Luc. "The Brachistochrone Problem." In *History of Mathematics: Histories of Problems*. Paris: Ellipses, 1997. Looks at the creation of the field of calculus of variations as a response to the specific problem raised by Johann Bernoulli.

Goldstine, Herman H. *A History of the Calculus of Variations from the Seventeenth Through the Nineteenth*

Century. New York: Springer-Verlag, 1980. Supplies more contemporary mathematical reconstructions of the original arguments.

Kline, Morris. *Mathematical Thought from Ancient to Modern Times*. New York: Oxford University Press, 1972. Chapter 24 is devoted to the calculus of variations, one of the areas in which Kline himself worked.

Van Brunt, Bruce. *The Calculus of Variations*. New York: Springer, 2004. A modern treatment of the subject, starting from the work of the Bernoullis.

SEE ALSO: 1733: De Moivre Describes the Bell-Shaped Curve; 1738: Bernoulli Proposes the Kinetic Theory of Gases; 1743-1744: D'Alembert Develops His Axioms of Motion; 1748: Agnesi Publishes *Analytical Institutions*; 1748: Euler Develops the Concept of Function; 1763: Bayes Advances Probability Theory; 1784: Legendre Introduces Polynomials.

RELATED ARTICLES in *Great Lives from History: The Eighteenth Century, 1701-1800*: Jean le Rond d'Alembert; Leonhard Euler; Joseph-Louis Lagrange; Gaspard Monge.

1718
GEOFFROY ISSUES THE *TABLE OF REACTIVITIES*

Geoffroy produced the first systematic treatment of chemical reactivities. He presented a table illustrating these relationships to the French Academy of Sciences, along with a law stating that highly reactive substances will displace less reactive ones in compounds.

LOCALE: Paris, France
CATEGORIES: Chemistry; science and technology

KEY FIGURES

Étienne-François Geoffroy (Geoffroy the Elder; 1672-1731), French chemist, physician, and pharmacist
Sir Isaac Newton (1642-1727), English mathematician and physicist
Torbern Olof Bergman (1735-1784), Swedish mineralogist
Claude Louis Berthollet (1748-1822), French chemist

SUMMARY OF EVENT

Ancient Greek natural philosophers observed chemical changes and tried to explain them as functions of love or hatred between the elements. These anthropomorphic concepts satisfied alchemists for centuries, but in the Middle Ages such thinkers as Saint Albertus Magnus,

who had observed that metals reacted differently with various substances, sought to understand these phenomena in terms of an *affinitas* (affinity) or specific force holding chemical bodies together in complex substances. During the Scientific Revolution of the seventeenth century, René Descartes developed a mechanical explanation of the universe, and chemists attempted to explain their observations in terms of moving particles rather than by such "occult forces" as attraction and repulsion.

In England, Sir Isaac Newton showed that the complicated motions of the heavenly bodies could be mathematically explained in terms of a precise gravitational force, though he publicly refrained from trying to explain the nature of this force. Nevertheless, Newton was an ardent alchemist who speculated that chemical substances were composed of particles possessing short-range attractive powers that varied in strength depending on the specific chemical species. Chemical reactions were therefore caused by varying attractions between these particles.

Newton's analysis of long-range gravitational forces and short-range chemical forces fascinated Étienne-

François Geoffroy, who had traveled to England in 1698. Geoffroy was elected a fellow of the Royal Society and thereafter closely followed the work of Newton and his disciples. In France, Geoffroy pursued his teaching and research in an anti-Newtonian academic environment at the Jardin du Roi and the Collège Royal (now the Collège de France). Cartesians, the followers of Descartes's mechanical philosophy, disliked Newtonian ideas on attraction, which they saw as akin to the superstitious magical powers of ancient and medieval times. The modern mechanical worldview had no place for such forces, and the French Académie des Sciences (Academy of Sciences) went so far as to ban them from scientific discourse. Therefore, when Geoffroy began to think about ways in which he could systematize the growing experimental knowledge about chemical substances and their reactions, he expressed himself in terms of relationships (*rapports*) rather than affinities (*affinités*) or attractions.

In his research, Geoffroy performed experiments on acids, alkalis, and metals, and he also collected information on the experiments of others. Though other chemists had noticed that certain highly reactive substances could displace less reactive substances from compounds, Geoffroy was the first to organize the information on relative reactivities thus garnered into a table. In 1718, he delivered a ten-page paper, "Table des différens rapports observés en chymie entre différentes substances" ("table of the different relationships observed in chemistry between different substances") to the Académie des Sciences. The basic idea of the paper involved a compound (AB) formed from two distinct substances (A and B) and the relationship between the compound and a third substance (C). Geoffroy argued that if C is capable of forming a stronger connection to A than is B, then C will displace B and form a new compound (AC). This general proposition was combined with a table indicating which substances formed stronger connections to which other substances, the *Table of Reactivities*.

Geoffroy's general law proved less important than his sixteen-column table of specific chemical relationships, which had a great influence on eighteenth century chemists. He represented substances in his table by their alchemical symbols; for example, gold was a circle with a central dot, water was an apex-down triangle, and salt was a circle with a horizontal diameter. By populating his rows and columns with these symbols, Geoffroy made as clear as possible the relationships between various substances (the table's popularity also stimulated a revived use of these symbols among chemists).

Across the top of the table, Geoffroy placed the symbols for specific acids, alkalis, and metals, and then, in the sixteen vertical columns beneath these elements and compounds, he placed a list of substances ordered by decreasing reactivity with the substance that headed the column. For example, the second column, which was headed by the symbol for what today's chemists call hydrochloric acid, had directly beneath it the symbol for tin, which avidly reacts with this acid. Gold was at the column's bottom position, since gold does not react at all with hydrochloric acid. Similarly, under the nitric acid column, the metals were ordered from the most to the least reactive as follows: iron, copper, lead, mercury, and silver. Geoffroy also schematized reactions between acids and alkalis, which helped chemists to understand the relative strengths of these importance substances.

Although Geoffroy's table was popular and inspired other tables, it also provoked criticism on both experimental and theoretical grounds. For example, one critic pointed out that silver, which was very unreactive according to Geoffroy's table, supplanted a very reactive substance in some reactions (in today's terminology, when silver nitrate solution reacts with a solution of potassium sulfate, a precipitate of silver sulfate is formed). Some Cartesians criticized Geoffroy's table, because they interpreted what he saw as a neutral term, "relationships" (*rapports*), to be equivalent to "affinities," which they wished to exclude from their mechanical universe. Geoffroy responded that his relationships between chemical substances were due to structural features of the particles, for example, whether they were porous or pointed. Reactions could then be visualized in terms of the interlocking of these particles.

Geoffroy, like many eighteenth century chemists, exhibited both modern and old-fashioned ideas in grappling with chemical phenomena. He opposed alchemy, but his table contained a symbol for an "oily or sulfurous principle," which, in 1720, he identified with phlogiston, a principle of combustibility that later proved to be nonexistent. Geoffroy's table contained other errors, largely due to the imperfect state of chemical knowledge at the time, but it also contained important truths about reactivities and replacement reactions.

SIGNIFICANCE

Despite his table's imperfections and his limited understanding of the chemical principles behind it, Geoffroy was the first to construct an extensive arrangement of the observed reactive orders of a range of chemical reactions. At the time, chemists did not fully understand how temperature, concentration, and other factors affected reactivity. Nevertheless, what some chemists called "affinities" certainly played a role, and the increasing importance of affinity studies can be seen in the number of tables published. Between 1718 and 1750, only two tables appeared, but in the following decades the numbers accelerated: three in the 1750's, four in the 1760's, and five in the 1770's.

As the number of such tables grew, the sophistication of each new table increased as well. When Torbern Olof Bergman published his very influential table of affinities in 1775, he included fifty-nine columns for a wide variety of chemical substances. He even had one table for reactions in solutions at room temperature and another table for the fusion reactions of dry substances at high temperatures. These two tables represented Bergman's recognition that affinity relationships differed under wet and dry conditions. He also understood that to study all the possible relationships of the substances in his tables would require more than thirty thousand experiments.

By the end of the eighteenth century, chemists began to realize that tables of affinities were oversimplifications of the real complexities involved in chemical reactions. Nevertheless, great chemists such as Claude Louis Berthollet continued the tradition of chemical affinity, even though Berthollet's work actually invalidated a major presupposition behind the belief in attractive chemical forces. In his *Recherches sur les lois de l'affinité* (1801; researches on the laws of affinity) and his *Essai de statique chimique* (1803; essay on chemical statics), Berthollet demonstrated that chemical reactions were influenced by the relative amounts of starting materials. Although he continued to believe that affinity was important in chemical reactions, his work foreshadowed the laws of mass action and chemical equilibria that were discovered later in the nineteenth century. It was not until the birth of physical chemistry at the end of the nineteenth century and the application of quantum mechanics to chemistry in the twentieth century that chemists finally understood what really happens when chemical substances selectively react with one another.

—*Robert J. Paradowski*

FURTHER READING

Bensaude-Vincent, Bernadette, and Isabelle Stengers. *A History of Chemistry*. Cambridge, Mass.: Harvard University Press, 1997. Chapter 2 examines the eighteenth century and the laboratory conditions and scientific institutions that served as the background of Geoffroy's work in Paris. Index.

Brock, William H. *The Chemical Tree: A History of Chemistry*. New York: Norton, 2000. Brock discusses Geoffroy in his section on "Newton's Chemistry" in chapter 2. Bibliographical essays on each of the chapters and an index.

Leicester, Henry M. *The Historical Background of Chemistry*. New York: John Wiley & Sons, 1956. Leicester deals with Geoffroy's work on reactivities in chapter 12. References to primary and secondary sources at the ends of chapters. Name and subject indexes.

Partington, J. R. *A History of Chemistry*. Vol. 3. New York: Macmillan, 1962. Partington discusses Geoffroy's life and work in chapter 2. References to primary and secondary sources in the footnotes. Name and subject indexes.

Thackray, Arnold. *Atoms and Powers: An Essay on Newtonian Matter-Theory and the Development of Chemistry*. Cambridge, Mass.: Harvard University Press, 1970. This thematic treatment of eighteenth century chemistry emphasizes the impact of Newton's ideas on chemists. Geoffroy's table forms an important part of this analysis. Select bibliography and index.

SEE ALSO: 1722: Réaumur Discovers Carbon's Role in Hardening Steel; 1723: Stahl Postulates the Phlogiston Theory; 1738: Bernoulli Proposes the Kinetic Theory of Gases; 1740: Maclaurin's Gravitational Theory; 1745: Lomonosov Issues the First Catalog of Minerals; 1748: Nollet Discovers Osmosis; June 5, 1755: Black Identifies Carbon Dioxide; 1771: Woulfe Discovers Picric Acid; Aug. 1, 1774: Priestley Discovers Oxygen; 1781-1784: Cavendish Discovers the Composition of Water; 1786-1787: Lavoisier Devises the Modern System of Chemical Nomenclature; c. 1794-1799: Proust Establishes the Law of Definite Proportions.

RELATED ARTICLES in *Great Lives from History: The Eighteenth Century, 1701-1800*: Henry Cavendish; Antoine-Laurent Lavoisier; Nicolas Leblanc; Joseph Priestley; John Roebuck; Georg Ernst Stahl.

1710's

1718-1730
TULIP AGE

The last twelve years of the reign of Ahmed III were known to the Turks as Lale devri, *or the Tulip Age, named after the sultan's fascination with the cultivation and display of tulips. It was a period of hedonism and extravagance, artistic and literary florescence, and architectural projects, an age that was eventually extinguished by popular religious fanaticism.*

LOCALE: Constantinople (now Istanbul, Turkey)
CATEGORIES: Cultural and intellectual history; art; literature; government and politics

KEY FIGURES
Ahmed III (1673-1736), Ottoman sultan, r. 1703-1730
Nevşehirli Damat İbrahim Paşa (1660-1730), Ottoman grand vizier, 1718-1730
Ahmed Nedim (1681-1730), a Turkish poet

SUMMARY OF EVENT
In 1718, Sultan Ahmed III had ruled the Ottoman Empire for fifteen years, of which more than half had involved protracted warfare ending that year with the Treaty of Passarowitz. After the war, the sultan and his new grand vizier, Nevşehirli Damat İbrahim Paşa, were to begin dedicating themselves to peace and to the cultivation of the arts, leading to a veritable Ottoman renaissance—and to the introduction of some modest innovations from the West. In retrospect, some Turks would look back to this period as a golden age, naming it *Lale devri*, or the Tulip Age, on account of the way in which the sultan and his courtiers cultivated the tulip as the acme of beauty in life and art.

The tulip had long been familiar to the Turks, and together with other flowers it served as a trope in Persian and Turkish poetry. It was not until the reign of Ahmed III, however, that it became an obsession in Constantinople. Grown in gardens and displayed everywhere, the tulip became a motif in the decoration of rooms, in the shape of turbans, in calligraphic arabesques, in architectural ornamentation, and in the embroidery of robes, wall hangings, and rugs.

The figure most closely associated with *Lale devri* was Grand Vizier Damat. Born in Mushkara (now Nevşehir) in 1660, he entered the palace service at Edirne, where he became an intimate of the young Ahmed. When Ahmed became sultan, he promoted Damat through a series of posts at court and, in February of 1717, married him to his favorite daughter, Fatima.

Damat was appointed grand vizier in May of 1718.

Highly intelligent, inquisitive, and more open-minded than most of the Ottoman elite, a voluptuary devoted to pleasure but also to maintaining his ascendancy over his lethargic and greedy master, Damat was perhaps the first grand vizier to be interested in what the Western world could teach the Turks. Consequently, the first accredited Ottoman ambassador to Paris, Yirmisekiz Çelebi Mehmed Efendi, was instructed to observe as much as possible the ways of the French, and some of these ways were later incorporated into his widely read *Sefāretnāme* (c. 1720; book of travels). Not least among the novelties brought back from Paris were architectural drawings of Versailles, Fontainebleau, and Marly, introducing a vogue for the rococo in the palaces, pavilions, fountains, and gardens of the Ottoman capital, which soon lined both sides of the Bosporus. Damat built himself a lavish palace at Kandilli, near the so-called sweet waters of Asia. Ahmed himself built his luxurious pleasure palace of Sadabad, modeled on Marly, at Kaghitane by "the sweet waters of Europe."

These pleasure palaces were the scenes of extravagant parties, where poetry recitations, music, and dance were interspersed with sybaritic banquets and prolonged feasting (none of this likely to meet with the approval of the Muslim clergy). While these festivities continued throughout the year—Sultan Ahmed had so many children that there was always reason to celebrate a birth, a circumcision, or a marriage—the parties reached their climax when the tulips bloomed. Everywhere were flowerbeds full of tulips, tulips in glass containers in alcoves, and tulips decorating apartments, all illuminated by thousands of lamps and lamp bearers, namely, tortoises with candles on their backs ambling through gardens.

A by-product of the taste for innovation was the decision to introduce a printing press to Constantinople in 1724. Before this time, books in Greek, Armenian, and Hebrew had been printed in the capital, but never in Turkish, mainly because printing the language had been considered sacrilegious. Now, a remarkable confidant of the grand vizier, İbrahim Müteferrika, a Hungarian convert who served the empire in various administrative and diplomatic capacities, set up a printing press. He was assisted by Said Efendi, the son of the late ambassador to France, and surprisingly, he enjoyed the good will of the *şeyhülislām*. Müteferrika printed the first book in Turkish in 1727, and other books soon followed.

The sultan was a poet, painter, and calligrapher, who delighted in extending his patronage to fellow poets, artists, and musicians. The same was true of Damat, who also encouraged the translation into Turkish of works in Persian and Arabic and who forbade the export of rare manuscripts. At the Topkapi palace, the sultan established a library, appointing Nedim, the greatest poet of the Tulip Age, as librarian; Damat founded five more libraries. He reopened ceramic workshops and established tile kilns to produce ceramics of exceptional quality. Utilitarian considerations were not forgotten by Damat. He built a textile mill, markets, roads, and harbor installations, and had a plan to bring fresh water from the forest of Belgrade to Constantinople.

The essence of the Tulip Age is best expressed in the writings of Nedim, which emphasized *dolce far niente*, unrestrained passions, the pleasures of the flesh, good living, and the delights of nature. He is perhaps best remembered for expressing the very un-Islamic sentiments, "Let us laugh, let us play, let us enjoy the delights of the world to the full." His temper is well captured in the following lines:

> When the east wind leaves that curl, it carries the scent of musk and when it opens the knot of your gown, it carries the scent of roses.
> On that rose-petal lip, I would find the taste of sugar
> On that rosebud mouth, I would discover the scent of wine.

The end of the Tulip Age came swiftly and violently. Sultan Ahmed's government had provoked increasing resentment over the previous twelve years, as the sultan's extravagance had fallen heavily on all classes, but especially the poor. There was a revulsion against the libidinousness of the court. There were rumors that Damat had sought to seduce the wife of the *kadi* (the capital's principal judge) and that Damat and his friends were rowed up the Golden Horn, tossing gold coins into the bodices of their women companions.

The revolt, when it came, was predictably expressed in protest against un-Islamic behavior and disregard for the Sharia (Islamic law). The ostensible ringleader was Patrona Halil, an Albanian former Janissary and second-hand clothes dealer, who, on September 28, 1730, aroused a mob, which was soon joined by fanatical and unemployed Janissaries, to attack the Topkapi palace. The government was caught off guard. Ahmed and Damat were both in Üsküdar. Damat's sons-in-law, the governor of Constantinople and the high admiral, were

both tending their gardens by the Bosporus. Once back in the palace, the sultan, learning that the mob wanted him to hand over Damat and his infidel sons-in-law, promptly ordered their strangulation and their bodies handed to the mob. Massacre, arson, and looting were the order of the day throughout the city (Nedim was murdered trying to escape), and on October 1, the sultan abdicated and returned to the *kafes* (cage), from which he had emerged twenty-seven years before. He was succeeded by his nephew, Mahmud I (r. 1730-1754), who for months seemed a mere puppet in the hands of Patrona Halil, who strutted the streets as the city's dictator. However, Mahmud was biding his time. On November 24, 1731, Patrona Halil and his associates were invited to an audience at Topkapi. On arrival, they were promptly strangled.

SIGNIFICANCE

The twelve years of the Tulip Age made up a brilliant and creative period in Ottoman history. Neither Sultan Ahmed nor Grand Vizier Damat were reformers, but they were more open to innovation than any previous sultan or grand vizier. The winds of change were beginning to blow, and had the regime not been overthrown by popular fanaticism, Ahmed and Damat might have initiated further change.

For the twenty-first century visitor to Constantinople, the Tulip Age is exquisitely commemorated in the Sultan Ahmed fountain of 1728, situated at the gateway to Topkapi palace, on which is inscribed a long poem in praise of water by the sultan himself. Passing into the palace, one eventually reaches the sultan's dining room, appropriately decorated with panels of flower paintings and an elaborate tiled fireplace (an *ocak*). Not far away stands his library, a rectangular structure with a domed central hall, built in 1719, an example of Ottoman Baroque predating the mission to France. Sadly, nothing remains of the palace and gardens of Sadabad, however.

—*Gavin R. G. Hambly*

FURTHER READING

Andrews, Walter G., Najaat Black, and Mehmet Kalpakli, eds. *Ottoman Lyric Poetry: An Anthology.* Austin: University of Texas Press, 1977. The editors present excellent examples of Nedim's work. Includes a map and a bibliography.

Gocek, Fatma Muge. *East Encounters West: France and the Ottoman Empire in the Eighteenth Century.* New York: Oxford University Press, 1987. This work is especially useful in discussing the relationship between the Ottomans and the French.

Goodwin, Godfrey. *A History of Ottoman Architecture.* London: Thames & Hudson, 1971. An excellent resource on Tulip Age architecture and the Ottoman Baroque.

Mansel, Philip. *Constantinople: City of the World's Desire, 1453-1924.* New York: St. Martin's Press, 1996. This comprehensive book is broad in its coverage of almost half a millennium of Ottoman history.

Montagu, Lady Mary Wortley. *The Turkish Embassy Letters.* Edited by Malcolm Jack. London: Pickering & Chatto, 1993. A colorful, contemporary account of the Ottomans.

Quataert, Donald, ed. *Consumption Studies and the History of the Ottoman Empire, 1550-1922: An Introduction.* Albany: State University of New York Press, 2000. A social and economic history of consumerism and cultural consumption in the Ottoman Empire from the mid-sixteenth century to the early twentieth century. Includes the chapter "The Age of Tulips: Confluence and Conflict in Early Modern Consumer Culture (1550-1730)." Also includes bibliographical references and an index.

Shaw, Stanford J. *History of the Ottoman Empire and Modern Turkey.* New York: Cambridge University Press, 1976. The best general survey of the Ottoman Empire and of Turkey in later centuries.

Shay, M. L. *The Ottoman Empire from 1720 to 1744 as Revealed in Despatches of the Venetian Baili.* Urbana: University of Illinois Press, 1944. This early work offers indispensable contemporary observations.

Somel, Selçuk Aksin. *Historical Dictionary of the Ottoman Empire.* Lanham, Md.: Scarecrow Press, 2003. Although the entries in this excellent reference book are brief, they are detailed and include valuable cross references. An outstanding resource for all aspects of the Ottoman Empire.

SEE ALSO: 1702 or 1706: First Arabic Printing Press; Nov. 20, 1710-July 21, 1718: Ottoman Wars with Russia, Venice, and Austria.
RELATED ARTICLES in *Great Lives from History: The Eighteenth Century, 1701-1800*: Ahmed III; Levni; Mahmud I; Mustafa III.

1719-1724
STUKELEY STUDIES STONEHENGE AND AVEBURY

William Stukeley's systematic method of investigating Stonehenge, Avebury, and related prehistoric stone temple sites produced exceptional notes and drawings and became a model for archaeological fieldwork.

LOCALE: Wiltshire, England
CATEGORIES: Archaeology; science and technology; architecture

KEY FIGURES
William Stukeley (1687-1765), English antiquarian and archaeologist
John Aubrey (1626-1697), English antiquarian who discovered Avebury

SUMMARY OF EVENT
The Wiltshire prehistoric sites of Avebury and Stonehenge are significant both in their construction and in the way they are situated in the landscape. Stonehenge is the ruin of a single building. An earthen embankment surrounded by a circular excavation ditch defines the site, although additional megaliths and earthworks lie outside the circle. In contrast with the compact area of Stonehenge, Avebury is a complex that covers several square miles, with a main circular bank and ditch and lined with megaliths, delimiting the original thirty-acre site. In the eighteenth century, stones were dispersed among houses, gardens, and fields, making the layout difficult to discern. Avebury was not recognized as a human-made complex until 1649, when antiquarian John Aubrey stumbled across it during a hunting trip and discovered evidence of its intentional construction.

Although the site at Avebury had gone undetected, speculation about Stonehenge abounded for centuries. It had been noticed since medieval times, and there were conflicting theories about its origin. In the early 1600's, poet and antiquarian Edmund Bolton credited its construction to the legendary first century military and rebel leader, Queen Boudicca. English architect Inigo Jones, who made the first known architectural study of the site, believed that it was a temple built by the Romans. Later in the seventeenth century, Walter Charleton, physician to King Charles II, claimed it was built by Danes. Aubrey, after his discovery of Avebury, investigated both monuments and believed that they were of Druid origin.

William Stukeley first visited Stonehenge and Avebury (which he called, collectively, "Abury") in 1719. Although he was a trained physician, he pursued studies in theology, science, and antiquities. A member of the Society of Antiquaries and a fellow of the Royal Society, he was a colleague of the most gifted individuals of eighteenth century England. He explored the English countryside, observing and recording ancient monuments.

Stukeley was familiar with Aubrey's then-unpublished *Monumenta Britannica: Or, A Miscellany of British Antiquities* (1980-1982), which recorded Aubrey's theories along with his observations and measurements of Avebury and Stonehenge. Like Aubrey, Stukeley believed that the monuments were built in pre-Roman times. Furthermore, he felt that his theory could be proven. He speculated that compilation of data about the circles and other ancient sites could provide information not obtainable from written sources.

There are few particulars about Stukeley's visits to Avebury and Stonehenge in 1719 and 1720, but from 1721 to 1724, after he decided to develop a typology of ancient monuments, he detailed his studies. Although Aubrey's work provided an underacknowledged precedent, it was not as encompassing as the project undertaken by Stukeley, who would, each summer, conduct fieldwork and live on site. Stukeley's techniques of observation, accurate measurement, and detailed recording accompanied by carefully executed drawings have made him the foremost figure in eighteenth century English archaeology.

Close observation was a key element in developing his typological study, as evident in his *Itinerarium curiosum: Or, An Account of the Antiquitys and Remarkable Curiositys in Nature or Art* (1724). Here he noted common building characteristics, such as placement of upright stones in a circular pattern on elevated ground with a surrounding ditch, a surrounding plain, and an avenue

Stonehenge, located on the Salisbury Plain in southern England. The site is now cordoned off to protect the stone temple. (Geo. L. Shuman and Co.)

of approach. Through this typology he wanted to show that Stonehenge and Avebury had the same provenance as other stone temples in England.

Much of his work was without precedent. He developed a vocabulary to describe his findings; he coined the term "trilithon," for example, to describe two upright stones supporting a lintel. He pioneered the field of astroarchaeological studies by being the first to note that Stonehenge was astronomically aligned: The site's assumed entrance marks the point of sunrise on the summer solstice. In 1721 he was the first to discern a raised area, which he called the "avenue," extending from the entrance to Stonehenge toward the River Avon; although the lining stones were gone, he measured placement intervals after observing sockets remaining in the uncultivated ground. Also, in 1723, he discovered at Stonehenge a shallow enclosure of parallel ditches measuring 2 miles in length; he called this the "cursus," speculating that it was an ancient racetrack. At Avebury he discovered similar stone-lined constructions leading toward West Kennet and Beckhampton.

To establish his typology, Stukeley needed measurements from many ancient sites. He stressed precision, believing valid conclusions could be drawn only from accurate comparisons. In 1723 he and Lord Winchelsea took two thousand measurements at Stonehenge, attempting to detect a common, indigenous standard of measurement, which Stukeley called "Druid's cubit," to prove pre-Roman origins of megalithic sites. Through reading and correspondence he also compiled measurements of stone circles located outside the sphere of Roman occupation.

In addition to recording his observations and measurements, Stukeley developed excavation techniques, which he compared to anatomical dissection. In 1722 and 1723 he and Lord Pembroke excavated Bronze Age barrows around Stonehenge. Stukeley's careful technique surpassed anything undertaken prior to that time. He noted that stratigraphy had the potential to establish chronology. He studied construction of barrows and their funerary contents, made precise notes, and carefully drew a cross-section diagram, which was the first such visual record in British archaeology.

Drawings and diagrams played an important role in his fieldwork. From 1721 to 1723 he diagrammed the main circles within the great ditch at Avebury and also indicated the avenue of standing stones leading toward West Kennet. The avenue terminated in a double circle of standing stones called the "sanctuary" by local villagers. Stukeley then recorded what remained of the sanctu-

ary and marked discernible sites of destroyed stones.

It has been suggested that the ongoing destruction at Avebury and Stonehenge induced Stukeley to prepare records before the monuments were lost. In the Middle Ages, megaliths often were regarded as pagan relics and were buried. In the eighteenth century, the Avebury site was used as a quarry for building stone. Stukeley also noted that visitors hammered off pieces of the monuments for souvenirs. The owner of Avebury Manor destroyed part of the site's embankment to build a barn. Each year, cultivation further eliminated features of the prehistoric landscape.

After he was ordained into the Church of England in 1729, Stukeley became increasingly conjectural in interpreting the past. Responding to the perceived threat of Enlightenment secularism, he romanticized Druids and postulated that the Church of England was prefigured in their ancient religion. In three works–*Palaeographia sacra: Or, Discourses on Monuments of Antiquity That Relate to Sacred History* (1736), *Stonehenge: A Temple Restor'd to the British Druids* (1740), and *Abury: A Temple of the British Druids* (1743)—he mixed religious speculation with his scientific fieldwork.

SIGNIFICANCE

William Stukeley's writing reflected the dual nature of thought in the eighteenth century, which incorporated rational-scientific as well as religious-Romantic ideas. His linking of Avebury and Stonehenge with Druidism became an enduring fallacy that was expressed in the Romantic tradition in English literature of the late eighteenth and early nineteenth centuries. Poetry by Thomas Gray and William Collins reflected a "Druidical Revival," as did works by the artist and poet William Blake.

Because Stukeley's scientific studies were intermingled with his Druidic theories, the accuracy of his field surveys has been questioned. Subsequent studies at Stonehenge and Avebury, however, have validated his work, which has provided a valuable record of historic sites before they were subjected to additional ravages of agricultural and economic development. Early aerial photography of the 1920's corroborated Stukeley's observations of the avenue at Stonehenge. Excavations in 1930 confirmed the existence of Avebury's sanctuary, which was destroyed shortly after Stukeley's documentation. The frontispiece to *Abury* provided accurate site information that was used in Alexander Keiller's excavations of 1934 to 1938. The Beckhampton Avenue stones at Avebury no longer exist, but modern excavations substantiate Stukeley's findings.

Stukeley was a key figure in bridging antiquarianism and the emerging science of archaeology. His pioneering work, although based on Aubrey's early techniques, provided the most thorough, systematic studies of Avebury and Stonehenge attempted before the nineteenth century. His careful observations, measurements, and diagrammed descriptions were significant components in the development of the field of archaeology. He compiled enough data to recognize that these structures represented a larger group of monuments scattered across Britain. He correctly conceived of these sites as prehistoric sanctuaries. At a time when scholars still used Old Testament chronologies for establishing historical dates, he set about proving that native Britons created the monuments in pre-Roman times.

He was among the first to recognize the historic value of the sites and to express concern over their preservation. Contemporary analysis of Stukeley's detailed records reveals how much has been lost from the sites in the past two centuries, either taken or destroyed or both. Historians and archaeologists are indebted to Stukeley for charting the course and following the traces.

—*Cassandra Lee Tellier*

FURTHER READING

Chippindale, Christopher. *Stonehenge Complete*. New York: Thames and Hudson, 2004. This work examines the studies that have changed the initial interpretations of Stonehenge. Includes notes, references, photographs, drawings, and an index.

Haycock, David. *William Stukeley: Science, Religion, and Archeology in Eighteenth-Century England.* Woodbridge, England: Boydell Press, 2002. Haycock reassesses the nature of eighteenth century antiquarianism. Includes a bibliography of Stukeley's publications, extensive bibliographies of primary and secondary sources, and an index.

Piggott, Stuart. *William Stukeley: An Eighteenth-Century Antiquary.* Rev. ed. New York: Thames and Hudson, 1985. A biography of Stukeley, with many reproductions, drawings, reconstructed journal entries, reconstructed journals of fieldwork at Avebury and Stonehenge, notes and references, and an index.

Stukeley, William. *The Commentarys, Diary, and Common-Place Book and Selected Letters of William Stukeley.* London: Doppler Press, 1980. A 174-page collection of Stukeley's personal writings and letters.

_____. *Stonehenge, a Temple Restor'd to the British Druids* and *Abury, a Temple of the British Druids.* New York: Garland, 1984. Updated reprints of Stukeley's classic works on Stonehenge and Avebury. Includes an introductory essay and illustrations.

SEE ALSO: 1748: Excavation of Pompeii; 1762: *The Antiquities of Athens* Prompts Architectural Neoclassicism.

RELATED ARTICLES in *Great Lives from History: The Eighteenth Century, 1701-1800:* William Blake; Lancelot Brown; William Stukeley; Johann Joachim Winckelmann.

April 25, 1719
DEFOE PUBLISHES THE FIRST NOVEL

Robinson Crusoe, a fact-based, realistically detailed account of a shipwrecked man struggling for survival, was the first novel written in English. The genre as a whole would come to be defined in terms of several of Robinson Crusoe's *key features, especially its studied focus on character psychology, its association of detail with realism, and its alignment with middle-class values and experience.*

LOCALE: London, England
CATEGORY: Literature

KEY FIGURES

Daniel Defoe (1660-1731), English novelist
Mary Tuffley (1664-1733), Defoe's wife
First Earl of Oxford (Robert Harley; 1661-1724), disgraced former head of the ministry of England, 1710, 1711-1714, and Defoe's former patron
William III (1650-1702), king of England, r. 1689-1702

SUMMARY OF EVENT

Daniel Defoe's novel *The Life and Strange Surprizing Adventures of Robinson Crusoe, of York, Mariner, Written by Himself* (1719; commonly known as *Robinson Crusoe*) was immediately popular, going through four printings in four months and attracting a huge middle- and lower-class readership. Readers seemed to identify with the shipwrecked man's painful isolation, his search for food, water, and safety, and his ultimate mastery of his environment. Crusoe appeared to be an average Englishman, who, despite the adversity that had befallen him, was making the best of it.

A Protestant Dissenter, Defoe identified himself with the Puritans, whose rebellion against the established Church of England during the seventeenth century marked the beginning of the rise of the middle class. As a merchant, Defoe had gained a favorable business advantage through the dowry of his wife, Mary Tuffley. His fondness for trade had led to an interest in politics, specifically political writing of a sort so provocative that he was frequently imprisoned and once pilloried. He became known as the chief pamphleteer of King William III.

After Queen Anne succeeded to the throne, Defoe's political writings earned him a powerful patron in Robert Harley, who in 1710 would become the first earl of Oxford and the head of a Tory ministry. Harley secured Defoe's release in 1703 from Newgate Prison, where he had been incarcerated for seditious libel for six months (during which time his business went bankrupt). In return for his release, Defoe served Harley for years as both a writer and an intelligence agent, until the politician's fall from power led to his own imprisonment in 1715.

Defoe wrote voluminously in defense of the Dissenters, their beliefs, and their values. Through the years, Defoe had filled numerous books and pamphlets with political and economic arguments and discussions, biographies, histories, and travel adventures. His gift for lively writing included dialogue, character development, and an interest in the mundane activities of the world, all of which contributed to his role in creating a new kind of fiction.

In *Robinson Crusoe*, Defoe distilled his life experiences into an adventure story that shunned the erudite, poetic language of earlier English authors, using instead a plainspoken narrative that detailed the title character's efforts to survive on a deserted island. Defoe's realistic, precise, prose accounts of the shipwreck, Crusoe's salvaging of supplies from the ship, the building of his "fortress," and his adaptation of the island's resources to further his own existence communicated to his readers a compelling individual effort to gain control of his own environment. Defoe's audience was not the upper classes but shopkeepers, artisans, servants, and the like.

Robinson Crusoe was more than adventure story; in its preface, Defoe stated his intent to provide moral and religious instruction, in accordance with the Puritan literary tradition of his day. Because the Puritans disdained imaginative writing, specifically fiction, Defoe assured his readers that *Robinson Crusoe* was true—an illusion that was supported by his meticulous, precise details. While it was well known that a British sailor named Alexander Selkirk had in fact been marooned on an island in the Pacific Ocean for four years, Defoe's Crusoe and his adventures began essentially as a cautionary tale designed to warn readers of the evils and dangers that befell Crusoe in the story.

Early in the narrative, Crusoe disobeys his father by going to sea, a decision that results in his being shipwrecked as well as suffering guilt and remorse for his sin. The rebellion against his father, viewed by Crusoe as similar to the biblical disobedience of Adam and Eve against God (and perhaps the Puritan rebellion against the Church of England), results in his being cast off from civilization, much as Adam and Eve were

---

CRUSOE TEACHES FRIDAY ABOUT GUNS

In Daniel Defoe's Robinson Crusoe, *the title character resolves to educate his new companion, Friday. He wants to teach Friday to eat goats rather than human flesh. It is in the process of hunting, though, that Crusoe gives Friday his first lesson, showing him the power of guns for hunting.*

By-and-by I saw a great fowl, like a hawk, sitting upon a tree within shot; so, to let Friday understand a little what I would do, I called him to me again, pointed at the fowl, which was indeed a parrot, though I thought it had been a hawk; I say, pointing to the parrot, and to my gun, and to the ground under the parrot, to let him see I would make it fall, I made him understand that I would shoot and kill that bird; accordingly, I fired, and bade him look, and immediately he saw the parrot fall. He stood like one frightened again, notwithstanding all I had said to him; and I found he was the more amazed, because he did not see me put anything into the gun, but thought that there must be some wonderful fund of death and destruction in that thing, able to kill man, beast, bird, or anything near or far off; and the astonishment this created in him was such as could not wear off for a long time; and I believe, if I would have let him, he would have worshipped me and my gun. As for the gun itself, he would not so much as touch it for several days after; but he would speak to it and talk to it, as if it had answered him, when he was by himself; which, as I afterwards learned of him, was to desire it not to kill him.

Source: Daniel Defoe, *Robinson Crusoe.* Chapter 15. University of Virginia Electronic Text Center. http://etext.lib.virginia.edu/toc/modeng/public/ DefCru1.html. Accessed November 13, 2005.

The frontispiece to the first edition (1719) of Daniel Defoe's Robinson Crusoe. *(North Wind Picture Archives)*

1710's

cats he has accumulated—and records his understanding of weather patterns in order to maintain crop production.

Through the character of Crusoe and his situation, Defoe treated most economic and religious issues of his time. Crusoe's delight with fashioning a cooking pot and his surprise at new grain growing from cast-off seeds form a complex pattern with his questioning of God about the cause of his suffering and his desolation. Crusoe's need for survival in an alien and hostile place where social, religious, and economic codes no longer function forces him back on himself. However, the result of this self-reliance is that Crusoe re-creates the very social, religious, and economic codes that he supposedly left behind when he was exiled from civilization. His meticulous accounting of his wealth, which is equated with a proper religious attitude and its natural reward, demonstrates this wholesale importation of British middle-class values into a self-contained, isolated world.

Even as Defoe's own life was dependent upon social relationships, Crusoe's stark realization of his own solitude and his total remove from personal relations signals the beginning of the novel's focus on the breakdown of relationships and its primary concern with individualism. Crusoe's struggle for survival connects with his obsessive search for his own identity in a world of radical change and his establishment of a relationship with God as well as his place in the world.

SIGNIFICANCE

While many established eighteenth century writers, notably English poet Alexander Pope and Irish satirist Jonathan Swift, condemned Defoe's writing as vulgar and contemptible, numerous other authors were impressed with the number of readers Defoe attracted. Some appreciated Defoe's originality and attempted to capitalize on his success by publishing adventure stories similar in character and situation.

More modern assessments of *Robinson Crusoe* concur that it is a masterpiece. As the work generally credited with being the first novel written in English, it established a connection from the very beginning between the novel as a form and the interests and values of the emergent middle class. The novel had the ability to function as a catalog of objects and possessions, to describe in intimate detail the world of things that was the middle class's focus while simultaneously portraying the inner thoughts of a properly religious person. As a result, this new type of fiction could represent both the experience and the desires of a middle-class subject to an extent of which no previous form of literature was capable. As the develop-

expelled from the Garden of Eden. Crusoe's acknowledgment of his wretched condition and total dependence upon God marks a turning point in the novel, wherein Crusoe ceases bemoaning his miserable state and begins to work to improve his condition.

Crusoe's repentance and conversion lead directly to his desire for prosperity, the acquisition of which becomes his sole occupation. Without advantage of birth, fortune, or connections, Crusoe relies upon his own courage, ingenuity, and ambition to control nature for his own benefit and is rewarded with food, clothing, and shelter. His strong work ethic concerning the husbandry of the island provides him with everything he needs and much more. In his diary, Crusoe obsessively itemizes the materials he recovered from the shipwreck, keeps an inventory of the island—including the number of goats and

ment of the novel paralleled the rise of the middle class, it continued to produce, to mirror, and to absorb this new class's ideologies and its members' ideas about their identity and place in the world.

Using first-person narration, Defoe emphasized the character of Crusoe and his experiences by providing readers with an opportunity to observe him moving between his experiences and his thoughts. This direct portrayal of Crusoe's meditations upon his pain, his isolation, and his strategies for survival facilitated a focus upon character psychology that would become the very hallmark of the modern novel, one of the central features that would distinguish it from other forms of representation.

As Defoe's adventure story follows Crusoe's life and experiences, it assumes a linear form that lacks the symmetry of classical poetry or drama as it focuses on the randomness of experience. This randomness would ultimately shape not only the novel but drama and poetry as well, as all literary forms would be influenced by the novel once it became the dominant form of literature and narrative in the Western world. Perhaps Defoe's greatest contribution to the novel, though, is simply to be found in his creation of a fully realized character who, through circumstance, breaks with his past and begins his own search for meaning in his life.

—Mary Hurd

FURTHER READING

Backsheider, Paula R. *Daniel Defoe: Ambition and Innovation*. Lexington: University Press of Kentucky, 1986. Consideration of Defoe in relation to the literary traditions and conventions of his time.

Curtis, Laura. *The Elusive Daniel Defoe*. Lanham, Md.: Rowan and Littlefield, 1984. An argument that the ambiguities in Defoe's writings are caused by contradictory drives in his own personality.

Defoe, Daniel. *A Journal of the Plague Year*. Edited by Cynthia Wall. New York: Penguin Books, 2003. Defoe's vivid chronicle of the great plague of 1665 and its devastation of London, first published in 1723.

Novak, Maximillian E. *Daniel Defoe, Master of Fictions: His Life and Ideas*. New York: Oxford University Press, 2001. Voluminous discussion of ambiguities in Defoe's life, reputation, and writings.

Watt, Ian. *The Rise of the Novel: Studies in Defoe, Richardson, and Fielding*. 2d American ed. Berkeley: University of California Press, 2001. New edition of Watt's classic account of the social conditions, attitudes, and literary traditions of the eighteenth century, including extensive discussion of the relationship between the invention of the novel and the invention of the middle class.

West, Richard. *Daniel Defoe: The Life and Strange, Surprising Adventures*. New York: Carroll and Graf, 1998. Provides details of the seventeenth and eighteenth centuries in England, especially the political and social environment that influenced Defoe's career.

SEE ALSO: 1726: Swift Satirizes English Rule of Ireland in *Gulliver's Travels*; 1740-1741: Richardson's *Pamela* Establishes the Modern Novel; 1742: Fielding's *Joseph Andrews* Satirizes English Society.

RELATED ARTICLES in *Great Lives from History: The Eighteenth Century, 1701-1800*: Daniel Defoe; Henry Fielding; Alexander Pope; Samuel Richardson; Jonathan Swift.

1720
FINANCIAL COLLAPSE OF THE JOHN LAW SYSTEM

The fall of Scottish banker John Law's Banque Générale and the collapse of his Mississippi Company in 1720 brought down France's first national bank, ended serious attempts to modernize the state's public financing and tax systems, and indirectly contributed to the massive debts that helped precipitate the French Revolution.

LOCALE: France
CATEGORIES: Economics; organizations and institutions

KEY FIGURES
John Law (1671-1729), Scottish financier
Duc d'Orléans (Philippe II; 1674-1723), regent of France, r. 1715-1723
Louis XV (1710-1774), king of France, r. 1715-1774

SUMMARY OF EVENT

Between 1716 and 1720, Scottish financier John Law tested a radical restructuring of France's banking, tax, and colonial structure that came to be known as the Law System. In the space of less than four years, Law created a French central bank, the Banque Générale (1716), introduced true paper currency, assumed responsibility for the state debt and for tax collection (1719), and monopolized the colonial trading companies (1719). The system failed when a speculative frenzy in shares of Law's Mississippi Company led to the creation and collapse of a financial bubble in 1720. Although the system was a dismal failure in the short run, many of Law's innovations were central to modern financial institutions.

The Law System was an emergency response to decades of mounting state debt and currency manipulation in France. Under Louis XIV (r. 1643-1715), the Crown had regularly devalued the coinage in order to reduce its massive war debts. The state had also issued a wide variety of paper instruments that fulfilled some of the purposes of paper currency. Certificates and bills on the state, some of which carried interest, were tried as a fledgling form of official currency, and by 1704 the government was issuing bills unbacked by bullion. These too were repeatedly devalued by the government, however. By 1715, when the duc d'Orléans became regent for the minor King Louis XV, French finances were on the brink of collapse.

The regent, a daring if not very systematic thinker, realized that only radical reforms of the tax and financial system could break the dreary cycle of old-regime currency devaluations, bankruptcies, and show trials of financiers and tax farmers. He turned to John Law as the architect of reform. A charismatic gambler and economic theorist, Law had been trained by his father, a successful Edinburgh goldsmith and banker. Forced to flee London after killing a man in a duel, he used his mathematical skills to support himself at the gaming tables of Europe, where he met the future regent of France.

Law was not merely an adventurer: He ranks among the important preclassical economists who influenced the later eighteenth century economist Adam Smith. In his treatise *Money and Trade Considered with a Proposal for Supplying the Nation with Money* (1705), Law advanced the idea that the money supply should respond to the real needs of merchants for currency. "An addition to the Money," he explained, "adds to the National Wealth." His argument flew in the face of mercantilist theories that had been dominant in France since the time of controller general Jean-Baptiste Colbert. Mercantilists broadly viewed the wealth of the nation as being founded on a positive trade balance and on reserves of bullion. Law, much like Smith after him, was inclined to believe that wealth was founded on the prosperity and productivity of the inhabitants and that the money supply could help grease the economic wheels.

With the confidence of Orléans in his proposals, Law swiftly and audaciously constructed the system that was to bear his name. By a royal edict of 1716, Law founded the Banque Générale, which had the privilege of printing banknotes. The bank's currency could be bought with old government notes or coins and quickly became more valuable than silver, since the bank committed to never devaluing its bills. By April, 1717, the regent, impressed with the bank's success, made its notes legal tender for payment of taxes; this was the true mark of state confidence. Tax payments almost immediately improved, and bank branches flourished in Lyon, La Rochelle, Orléans, Tours, and Amiens.

Almost simultaneously, in August of 1717, Law applied to the Crown for a letter patent to take over management of Louisiana under the name of the Mississippi Company (or Company of the Occident). With exclusive trading privileges, Law proposed to exploit imaginary silver reserves on the banks of the Mississippi River. On the strength of that colonial acquisition, Law now appeared capable of a financial hat trick: creating paper

Frantic speculators trade shares in John Law's Mississippi Company. (Francis R. Niglutsch)

wealth at home, finding silver to back it abroad, and opening the road to a radically new public financing structure for the French state.

Like magnets, the bank and the trading company swiftly pulled the rest of the French financial system into their orbit. In 1718, Law's private Bank Générale became the Banque Royale, the official Crown bank. In 1719, Law was granted sole monopoly for coining money, then shortly bought out the remaining French indirect tax farms from private hands, a feat that had seemed all but impossible for generations. By year's end, Law absorbed the old Compagnie des Indes (French East India Company) into the Mississippi Company. He now enjoyed a massive monopoly over trade in China, the South Seas, and the East Indies. Flush with success, the bank assumed total responsibility for the state debt, buying out old loans and issuing new loans at 4 percent interest. By October, 1719, the last piece of the puzzle fell into place: The company took over collection of the direct

taxes, or *taille*. When Law was elevated to controller general of France in 1720, the overthrow of the old system of public finance seemed complete.

Already by 1718, however, with the creation of the Banque Royale, the seeds of disaster had been planted. The duc d'Orléans, heedless of the dangers of inflation and eager to eliminate the state debt, commanded that both banknotes of the Banque Générale and shares in the Mississippi Company be issued far in excess of what Law had projected. Law had proposed the creation of 50,000 shares in the new Compagnie Française des Indes; the regent insisted on 300,000, as a frenzied public demanded more shares. Law's private Banque Générale had issued 60 million livres in notes; in 1718, the regent ordered the printing of 1 billion livres in banknotes. France's old elites swiftly arose in protest. The Parlement of Paris, the chancellor of France, and the general tax farmers and financiers who had traditionally collected revenues and made loans to the state united in opposition.

The collapse in 1720 was swift. As share prices for the company rose into the stratosphere, more banknotes were issued to keep pace with the price. Investors suddenly realized that there was neither bullion in France nor silver in Mississippi to back the currency, and prices collapsed. Law was allowed to go into exile in December, 1720, virtually penniless. The usual suspects were put on trial, and the regent, suffering perhaps the best fate, died in the company of his mistress in 1723. Although many lost money, there were winners, especially France's small debtors, who had paid off mortgages and other debts with the inflated currency before it became worthless. By far the largest winner in the very short term was the French government, which was able to write off massive amounts of debt and to reduce interest rates during the debacle.

SIGNIFICANCE

France's lack of a national bank and of British-style public financing in the eighteenth century was a major source of political and international weakness. Throughout most of the period, the British government borrowed money at 4 percent or less, while the Dutch government could borrow at interest rates as low as 2 percent. By contrast, the French state was forced to borrow at often double those rates, topping out well beyond 7 percent. With the staggering war debts of more than 2 billion livres that France accumulated during the Seven Years' War and the American Revolutionary War, the government was forced to spend ever-larger portions of annual revenue on interest payments. By the 1780's, well over half of the state's annual revenues were going to service the national debt, leaving the government without enough cash to cover its annual operating expenses.

The spectacular failure of Law's system created such strong opposition to modern financial institutions that reforms were impossible until the French Revolution. Indeed, the French refused to use the discredited name *banque* for most financial institutions until the late twentieth century, preferring the term *crédit*. The government was forced to continue borrowing through powerful corporations, including the *parlements*, the provincial estates, and the guilds—groups that thus remained key stakeholders and opponents of any attempts at fiscal reform. Although farsighted in many of its ideas, the failure of Law's system helped lock the French state into a debt spiral that ended in insolvency. The bankruptcy of Louis XVI's government became one of the most crucial steps on the road to the French Revolution in 1789.

—*Zoë A. Schneider*

FURTHER READING

Collins, James B. *The State in Early Modern France.* New York: Cambridge University Press, 1995. Illuminates seventeenth and eighteenth century French financial institutions in the context of statebuilding.

Law, John. *Money and Trade Considered with a Pro-*

posal for Supplying the Nation with Money. London: 1705. Law's most readable treatise on the real value of money and the importance of the money supply.

Marion, Marcel. *Histoire financière de la France depuis 1715.* Paris: Rousseau et Cie, 1927. An early but authoritative source on the financial details of the Law System.

Murphy, Antoin E. *John Law: Economic Theorist and Policy Maker.* New York: Oxford University Press, 1997. The best intellectual history of Law's economic theories, placed in historical context.

Treasure, Geoffrey. *The Making of Modern Europe, 1648-1780.* London: Methuen, 1985. Considers the Law experiment in the context of European central banks, stock exchanges, and colonial enterprises.

SEE ALSO: Sept., 1720: Collapse of the South Sea Bubble; Jan., 1756-Feb. 15, 1763: Seven Years' War; Mar. 9, 1776: Adam Smith Publishes *The Wealth of Nations*; May, 1776-Sept. 3, 1783: France Supports the American Revolution; Feb. 6, 1778: Franco-American Treaties; May 5, 1789: Louis XVI Calls the Estates-General.

RELATED ARTICLES in *Great Lives from History: The Eighteenth Century, 1701-1800*: Louis XV; Adam Smith.

May, 1720-December, 1721
LAST MAJOR OUTBREAK OF PLAGUE

On May 20, 1720, a ship carrying victims of plague arrived at the French port of Marseilles. Several days later, an epidemic began in the city. By the time the disease ran its course, fifty thousand people in the city had died, as well as an equal number throughout the countryside. The epidemic represented the last major outbreak of the plague in Europe.

LOCALE: Marseilles, France
CATEGORIES: Health and medicine; natural disasters

KEY FIGURES

Jean-Baptiste Chataud (fl. early eighteenth century), captain of the *Grand St. Antoine*
Henri François Xavier de Belzunce (1671-1755), French Jesuit bishop in Marseilles
Jean Baptiste Bertrand (1670-1752), French physician

SUMMARY OF EVENT

Bubonic plague, generally referred to as plague, is the result of infection by the bacterium *Yersinia pestis*. While most wild rodents may serve as reservoirs for the agent, it is most commonly carried by rats; transmission to humans results from bites by fleas carried by these animals.

The first appearance of the bubonic plague in the Mediterranean area is suspected to have occurred as early as the third century B.C.E., according to a description later produced by Rufus of Ephesus (fl. 98-117 C.E.), a Greek physician and writer. However, the first confirmed epidemic of plague in Europe was the Plague of Justinian (542-543). While precise mortality figures are unknown, as many as ten thousand persons per day may have died in Constantinople alone. The failure of Justinian to restore Roman rule across the Mediterranean was in large part a result of the outbreak. The epidemic reached Gaul (France) through the port of Marseilles in 543.

The most devastating outbreaks of the plague in Europe occurred during the fourteenth century, when approximately one-third of the population, some 25 million persons, fell victim to a series of epidemics that came to be known collectively as the Black Death, or Great Plague. The disease appeared in Marseilles in 1346, probably carried on a ship arriving from the Middle East, where the disease had been endemic.

After the 1346 epidemic, despite occasional local outbreaks, Western Europe, particularly France, was largely spared large-scale epidemics of the plague for nearly four centuries. However, on May 25, 1720, the *Grand St. Antoine*, a ship under the command of Captain Jean-Baptiste Chataud, arrived at Marseilles. The ship's voyage had originated at Saida, Syria, in January, at a time when an outbreak of plague was occurring in that city. Seven sailors had died en route from an illness that likely had been the plague. Refused entry at several ports prior to its arrival at Marseilles, the *Grand St. Antoine* was placed in quarantine in a lazaretto near the port until the nature of the illness it carried could be determined.

The ship's cargo included textile goods, silk, wool, and cotton, which city merchants wanted for the medieval fair held at Beaucaire. As a result, the quarantine was prematurely lifted in mid-June. Among the first victims once the ship had docked were several of the porters who transported its merchandise to local warehouses. French physicians who examined the men noted the presence of "large tumors the size of hen's eggs" in the groin, the buboes typical in cases of the plague. The first cases within the general population appeared soon on the rue de l'Escale. The disease first caused the death of a young woman and, shortly afterward, her young daughter. By the end of the month, several people who had come in contact with the cloth carried on the *Grand St. Antoine* became ill with what local doctors had been calling "malignant fevers." By the end of July, the outbreak had spread beyond control.

A decree of the Parliament of Aix (August, 1720) placed the city itself under quarantine. The death penalty was threatened for anyone leaving Marseilles, and a "plague wall" was erected outside the city. Guard posts were placed at intervals behind the wall, portions of which still remain nearly three hundred years later, but by this time, thousands of people had already fled into the countryside, carrying the plague with them. The disease reached Aubagne on August 15 and Toulon the following week.

The resulting epidemic, spanning the period between 1720 and 1722, devastated southern France. Much of what is known is based upon the eyewitness accounts of Jean Baptiste Bertrand, one of the physicians who attended the victims in Marseilles. Bertrand himself contracted plague during the course of the epidemic, but he recovered. His wife and children were not as fortunate. Bertrand later recorded his observations in a lengthy treatise.

Between June, 1720, and December, 1721, nearly 95,000 persons in a provincial population of 250,000 died of plague. Of the 90,000 persons who lived in Marseilles and its surroundings, 40,000 reportedly died. Nearly every police officer succumbed, as did most other public servants (doctors, surgeons, guards). Thousands of corpses were reported in the streets, as not only the *corbeaux*, special transporters for corpses, but also beggars hired for the same purpose all died. Some idea of the devastation may be discerned from numbers reported by Bertrand: Among one hundred master hatters, fifty-three died. More than 80 percent of master joiners died in the epidemic, while 370 of 400 cobblers survived. The disease was largely spent by the end of 1721, although another, smaller outbreak of the plague came again in May, 1722. This time the epidemic lasted only until August, with mortality significantly reduced when compared with the numbers from the previous two years.

The outbreak was particularly devastating to the poor of the city, as well as to those clerics who ministered to their needs. Among the Jesuits who ministered in the province of Provence, eighteen died. Forty-three Capuchin clerics died. Numerous individuals were singled out for their service despite the devastation, particularly the local bishop, Henri François Xavier de Belzunce. Belzunce was observed providing rites of burial to those dying of the plague, ignoring the danger to himself. He also mortgaged his own property to purchase relief for victims or their survivors.

Captain Chataud was subsequently arrested for his part in docking the ship at the city. Imprisoned in the Chateau d'If, he was later brought to trial. On July 8, 1723, his case was declared *nolo contendere*, but he was spared further punishment.

The main outbreak of the plague was essentially ended by December, 1721. Reasons for its disappearance remain obscure. Certainly, a significant factor was simply the lack of potential victims, as those susceptible had either died or remained immune. The presence of other, cross-reacting bacilli in the population, which would have produced immunity against the plague bacillus, has been proposed as another possible reason for the near-disappearance of the disease. Evidence remains lacking in support of that theory, however. More likely, the stricter enforcement of quarantine measures, which prevented more plague-infested rats from entering Marseilles, accounts for the conclusion of the epidemic.

SIGNIFICANCE

Epidemics of plague in Europe had occurred periodically for much of the preceding one thousand years. However, the outbreak in Marseilles represented the last significant appearance of the disease in western Europe. Several reasons may account for this. First, the outbreak was, to an extent, self-limiting. While the role of the rat flea in spreading plague would not be determined for another hundred years, it was clear that spread of the disease was not necessarily the result of simple contagion between affected persons and the population at large. More important was the enforcement of quarantine carried out by European countries, in particular Great Britain. Quaran-

tines had previously been maintained in theory, but their actual practice was often limited. A major outbreak had occurred in 1665 throughout England; the strict enforcement of the quarantine after 1720 resulted in no further appearance of the disease.

Other factors may also have contributed to the partial disappearance of the disease, including improved sanitary procedures that reduced exposure to infected rats and better shipping practices, which prevented infected animals from being transported by sea. The memories of plague epidemics remained within the collective populations, however, as commemorative events in places such as Marseilles continued into the twentieth century.

While western Europe was relatively free of the plague after 1722, portions of eastern Europe continued to suffer the ravages of that disease. In 1770, some 300,000 persons reportedly died from the plague in portions of the Ukraine and Transylvania. The epidemic apparently died out from lack of any further susceptible population.

—*Richard Adler*

1720's

This detail from Michel Serre's 1721 painting of a plague-ravaged Marseilles shows the body of a plague victim being dragged through the streets. (The Granger Collection, New York)

FURTHER READING

Benedictow, Ole. *The Black Death, 1346-1353: The Complete History*. Rochester, N.Y.: Boydell Press, 2004. Draws upon both modern and contemporary accounts of the plague during its most devastating period, with analysis of its effects upon modern history.

Bertrand, Jean Baptiste, Jean Biraben, and Anne Plumptre. *A Historical Relation of the Plague at Marseilles in the Year 1720*. Whitby, Ont.: McGraw-Hill, 1973. In-depth observation of the origins and movement of the last major outbreak of plague in Europe.

Biraben, Jean-Noel. "Certain Demographic Characteristics of the Plague Epidemic in France, 1720-1722." *Daedalus* 97 (1968): 536-545. Statistical description of the Marseilles plague, with emphasis on demographics in the city and countryside.

McNeill, William. *Plagues and Peoples*. Garden City, N.Y.: Anchor Press, 1976. Sociological and epidemiological approach to the origin and spread of disease through human history.

Orent, Wendy. *The Mysterious Past and Terrifying Future*. Riverside, N.J.: Free Press, 2004. Historical account of the plague, with descriptions of events that could result in its reappearance.

SEE ALSO: 1753: Lind Discovers a Cure for Scurvy; Nov. 1, 1755: Great Lisbon Earthquake; 1763-1767: Famine in Southern Italy; Oct. 10-18, 1780: Great Caribbean Hurricane; 1786-1787: Tenmei Famine; 1796-1798: Jenner Develops Smallpox Vaccination.

RELATED ARTICLES in *Great Lives from History: The Eighteenth Century, 1701-1800*: Daniel Defoe; Edward Jenner; Marquis de Vauvenargues.

September, 1720
COLLAPSE OF THE SOUTH SEA BUBBLE

Fraudulent activities within the South Sea Company, political corruption, and mass mania for speculation resulted in a major stock market crash and widespread financial ruin.

LOCALE: England

CATEGORIES: Economics; trade and commerce; diplomacy and international relations; government and politics; laws, acts, and legal history

KEY FIGURES

John Blunt (1665-1733), English scrivener turned stockbroker

Robert Harley (1661-1724), first earl of Oxford, English statesman, and bibliophile

Robert Walpole (1676-1745), first earl of Oxford and English statesman

John Law (1671-1729), Scottish gambler, speculator, and financier

SUMMARY OF EVENT

The South Sea Bubble originated in 1711, when Robert Harley, the first earl of Oxford, founded the South Sea Company. Incorporated by an act of Parliament, the company was granted a monopoly of all British trade with South America and the islands of the South Sea. In exchange for this monopoly, the company assumed part of the national debt.

The War of the Spanish Succession, begun in 1701,

was draining the British government's resources and increasing its national debt. Harley carried on secret peace negotiations to end the war and secure a favorable treaty with extensive trading concessions from Spain. England hoped to prosper from the immense wealth of the Spanish colonies in South America, such as the gold and silver mines of Mexico and Peru.

Harley, who sided with the Tories, also envisioned the South Sea Company as a financial institution competing with the Bank of England, a Whig institution. Expectations of great wealth from the trade monopoly appealed to investors. Some owners of government bonds totaling £9 million traded their bonds for company stock, which the government secured at 6 percent interest. To pay this interest, the government levied permanent taxes on tobacco, goods from India, vinegar, wines, and other items. South Sea was a joint stock company, a partnership that had common capital called stock. Shares of the stock were owned by the partners, called shareholders.

In 1713, the War of the Spanish Succession ended with the Treaty of Utrecht, in which Spain granted an *asiento de negros* ("Negroes' contract") to Britain. The *asiento* was the exclusive right to supply 4,800 enslaved Africans annually to Spanish America for thirty years. The British government then sold this lucrative monopoly to the South Sea Company for £7.5 million. Imported African slave labor was essential to Spain's empire, especially for the labor-intensive mining industry. The

This political cartoon responding to the South Sea Bubble depicts gambling priests, speculators on a merry-go-round being "taken for a ride," Satan as an auctioneer, and a monument to the destruction of the city "by the South Sea." (Hulton Archive/Getty Images)

company also acquired the right to send a ship annually to trade with Peru, Chile, or Mexico. However, the first voyage of the annual vessel was delayed until 1717, and trade discontinued when England and Spain went to war again in 1718. Yet in spite of the company's lack of trade or actual commercial value, speculators continued to invest with expectations of future profit, and the South Sea Company thrived as a financial institution.

Meanwhile, in France, John Law, the innovative Scottish financier, was in exile from Scotland to avoid a death sentence for killing a man in a duel. His Mississippi Company became France's most powerful business, with authority over the French national bank (Banque Royale) and the mint. The Mississippi Company also held a monopoly on trade with France's North American colony, and it controlled the French East India and China companies. In August of 1719 this company assumed the entire national, or public, debt by substituting paper cur-

rency for gold. Increasing amounts of money were printed for loans to buy shares, as shares rose in price. Law kept driving stock prices up, and France was experiencing a speculative fever.

Inspired by Law's example and afraid of English money flowing to France, the lawyer John Blunt and the South Sea Company's directors came up with a stock-jobbing (stock-brokering) scheme similar to that of Law. In 1719 the South Sea directors proposed to assume the entire English national debt, most of which consisted of bonds and annuities, which were loans to the government in exchange for a fixed income for life. These government obligations could be exchanged at par for shares of South Sea Company stock.

In April, 1720, Parliament accepted the proposal and speculators eagerly purchased South Sea Company stocks. Blunt and the directors of the company manipulated company stocks for their own profit. Blunt drove prices higher and higher by permitting the purchase of stocks on an installment plan, issuing new loans at favorable interest rates, and then offering new subscriptions or issues of stocks to draw the money back in. As a result, the company's stock rose in price from £128.5 per share at the beginning of the year to £1,000 in July.

The success of the South Sea Company led to the appearance of hundreds of new joint-stock companies, mostly bogus imitators hoping to take advantage of the speculation mania. Threatened by this competition, the directors of the South Sea Company convinced Parliament to pass the Bubble Act of June 9, 1720, an act requiring parliamentary permission for the establishment of a company. On July 12, the lords justice in the Privy Council published an order dismissing all petitions for patents and charters and dissolving all bubble companies. Some famous, far-fetched bubbles included companies for trading in hair, for extracting silver from lead, and for building a wheel in perpetual motion.

In spite of these actions against other bubble companies, the momentum of rising prices for South Sea stock could not be sustained. In August, John Blunt sold all his South Sea stock just before prices began falling. Other insiders sold too, and soon everyone was a seller and no one was buying stocks. In September the bubble burst and there was a complete financial collapse by the end of September. The price of South Sea stock fell to £135, and other stocks lost their value. Unemployment jumped, banks failed, thousands of investors became bankrupt, and the real estate market suffered.

Furious investors demanded revenge against the South Sea Company's directors, so Parliament reconvened. An investigation of the company determined that there had been widespread fraud among company administrators and some government officials. Parliament confiscated profits made by the directors. In a settlement in August, 1721, these assets of approximately £2 million were redistributed to stockholders at £140 per share.

SIGNIFICANCE

The South Sea Bubble marked a turning point in the career of Robert Walpole, the powerful parliamentary leader who had opposed the scheme from the beginning. He successfully helped in the aftermath and made proposals to restore public confidence. As a result, he rose to power and was appointed the first lord of the treasury and chancellor of the exchequer. Walpole helped reorganize the South Sea Company, but the company ceased commercial activities with the loss of many special privileges in 1750. By 1807 it had lost all exclusive rights. Re-

maining company annuities were either converted into government stock or redeemed in 1853.

Although enormous fortunes were lost, many investors had actually made huge profits. Numerous members of the court and the Parliament took bribes from the South Sea Company and profited from secret share options. Others investors were able to sell South Sea shares when prices peaked. One notable example was Thomas Guy, who later used his stock gains to help build Guy's Hospital for the sick and poor of London.

Most significant, the collapse of the South Sea Bubble had long-term negative effects on the British economy. Sir John Barnard's act of 1734, which forbade speculative techniques such as short sale and futures and options, remained in effect until the middle of the nineteenth century. The general aversion toward speculation and the existence of joint-stock companies discouraged the entrepreneurial spirit and investment in new projects, thus delaying the Industrial Revolution for generations.

—*Alice Myers*

FURTHER READING

Balen, Malcolm. *The King, the Crook, and the Gambler: The True Story of the South Sea Bubble and the Greatest Financial Scandal in History*. New York: Fourth Estate, 2004. This complete, entertaining history includes discussion of the financial and political ramifications of the bubble. Illustrations, bibliography, and index.

Carswell, John. *The South Sea Bubble*. Dover, N.H.: Alan Sutton, 1993. Originally published in 1960, this is the classic, thorough study of the South Sea scheme. Illustrations, index, appendices, and extensive bibliography.

Chancellor, Edward. *Devil Take the Hindmost: A History of Financial Speculation*. New York: Plume, 2000. This well-researched account covers the origins of financial speculation in ancient Rome through the 1990's and has an entertaining chapter, "The Never-to-Be-Forgot or Forgiven South-Sea Scheme." Index, notes, and bibliography.

Garber, Peter M. *Famous First Bubbles*. Boston: MIT Press, 2000. The book's main premise is that major early bubbles were driven by economic and financial conditions rather than crowd irrationality. Appendices, bibliography, and index.

Kindleberger, Charles P. *Manias, Panics, and Crashes: A History of Financial Crises*. New York: Wiley Investment Classics, 2001. A well-researched examination of centuries of major financial crises, including the South Sea Bubble. Index and bibliography.

MacKay, Charles. *Extraordinary Popular Delusions and the Madness of Crowds.* New York: Three Rivers Press, 1995. This reprint of the popular, humorous classic first published in 1841 chronicles the South Sea Bubble plus other fascinating tales of mass mania, deception, and greed. Illustrations and index.

SEE ALSO: 18th cent.: Expansion of the Atlantic Slave Trade; May 26, 1701-Sept. 7, 1714: War of the Span-

ish Succession; Apr. 11, 1713: Treaty of Utrecht; 1720: Financial Collapse of the John Law System; Mar. 9, 1776: Adam Smith Publishes *The Wealth of Nations*; Jan., 1790: Hamilton's *Report on Public Credit.*

RELATED ARTICLES in *Great Lives from History: The Eighteenth Century, 1701-1800:* André-Hercule de Fleury; Robert Walpole.

December, 1720
JAPAN LIFTS BAN ON FOREIGN BOOKS

The Tokugawa shogunate lifted a nearly century-long ban on books containing minor references to Christianity. In harmony with Shogun Yoshimune's policy of promoting "practical learning," the Japanese began to import science and technology books, most of which were well illustrated and were either Chinese translations of European works or books in Dutch. Christian religious books, however, remained banned.

LOCALE: Edo (now Tokyo), Japan

CATEGORIES: Cultural and intellectual history; diplomacy and international relations; education; government and politics; science and technology

KEY FIGURES
Tokugawa Yoshimune (1684-1751), shogun, r. 1716-1745
Aoki Kon'yō (1698-1769), adviser to the shogun on Dutch scholarship
Katsuragawa Hochiku (1661-1747), expert on Dutch medicine
Noro Genjō (1694-1761), translator into Japanese of the first European pharmacology text

SUMMARY OF EVENT
A general ban on Christianity in Japan was first introduced in 1587 by Toyotomi Hideyoshi (1536-1598), the de facto military ruler of Japan. Hideyoshi, and the early Tokugawa shoguns, suspected that Portuguese traders and missionaries were using conversions to Christianity as a means to extend their sphere of influence in the country. Restrictions sporadically continued and became more severe under the Tokugawa shogunate. By 1639 the Portuguese were permanently banned from Japan. A limited number of Chinese, Korean, and Dutch traders, restricted to the Nagasaki area, were the only foreigners allowed to reside in the country.

Among the anti-Christian measures adopted was a ban on the importation or possession of any foreign books containing references to Christianity. Even nonreligious European books of all sorts were suspected by the Japanese authorities to contain peripheral references to Christianity. Such references put books on the forbidden list, no matter how unrelated they might be to the books' main contents or topics. Virtually all European books, as well as books in Chinese dealing with European subjects, were effectively banned. Foreign books were assumed to have subversive content, and their importation and possession were forbidden as a matter of course.

Tokugawa Yoshimune became shogun in 1716 and retained that position for almost three decades, until his retirement in 1745. His immediate predecessors, Tokugawa Ietsugu (r. 1713-1716), who was shogun for four years and died at the age of seven, and Tokugawa Ienobu (r. 1709-1712), shogun for only three years, were controlled by powerful advisers. Yoshimune set aside most of the people and policies that had held sway, and on his own he began carrying out institutional change, known as the reforms of the Kyoho era (1716-1736).

Yoshimune emphasized frugality in private and public life, the modernization of a moribund administrative system, and a pragmatic policy of encouraging *jitsugaku*, or useful learning, which had practical applications. In line with this policy, he concluded that the virtually total de facto ban on foreign books was restricting needed access to knowledge of new developments in science and technology overseas. Yoshimune consequently ordered restrictions lifted on foreign books containing incidental references to Christianity, while maintaining the ban on the importation of books that were primarily Christian.

Yoshimune wanted knowledge of Western science and technology to be available to merchants and artisans, as well as to privileged scholars, so foreign books began to sell and circulate quite freely in Japan. While only a limited number of Japanese specialists could read books in Dutch, many merchants and artisans were able to read a number of Chinese translations or summaries of important European books, summaries known as *kanyaku yosho*, or foreign books in Chinese translation, which also became readily available. Though Chinese rather than Dutch was often the language through which people acquired knowledge of the West, this emerging field became known as *rangaku*, Dutch studies or Dutch learning.

Because the emphasis was on the pragmatic acquisition and application of new information from Europe, and because Western religious works were still banned, relatively little attention was paid to European philosophy or political theory. However, practical applications of Western knowledge did eventually give rise to new developments in theories related to technology, science, and the arts.

A number of educated people in the urban merchant class had a special interest in mathematics because it had a direct application to business transactions. Such people were attracted to the newly available Chinese versions of European texts dealing with Western mathematics, but some of them went on to study other European innovations in science and technology. In addition, a growing interest in European styles and techniques of drawing and painting began to develop, largely because of the detailed and realistic illustrations in Dutch books. Some Japanese artists were so impressed by realistic European methods of representation that they adapted these techniques to create copperplate engravings and illustrations of their own, depicting traditional Japanese themes in a new, realistic way.

In addition to making Western books generally accessible to the reading public, Shogun Yoshimune had more personal interests in the promotion of European science and technology. He was so impressed with the Confucian scholar Aoki Kon'yō, who was studying the newly approved books in Chinese to master the basics of Western learning, that he appointed Aoki *shomotsu-kata*, the official in charge of collecting books and gathering documents for the shogunate library in Edo Castle. Aoki was instructed to collect a basic library of Chinese books on Western subjects, as well as works in Dutch. Yoshimune also had Aoki learn the Dutch language and arranged for him to have periodic conferences on Western learning with officials from the Dutch trading enclave in Nagasaki.

One of the shogun's own doctors, Katsuragawa Hochiku, used Western surgical techniques. Katsuragawa's teacher, Arashiyama Hoan (1632-1693), a doctor trained by the Dutch in Nagasaki, became a physician treating the aristocracy at the imperial court in Kyoto. In 1724, Yoshimune sent Katsuragawa to consult with Dutch physicians, also from Nagasaki, to learn more about Western medicine. Katsuragawa's heirs continued to serve as shogunate doctors, and his seventh-generation successor, Katsuragawa Hoshu (1826-1881), helped compile a Dutch-Japanese lexicon (1855-1858).

Yoshimune also had his court herbal physician, Noro Genjō, learn Dutch, so Noro could learn about pharmacology from Dutch doctors and from books in Dutch. Noro subsequently translated the *Cruydeboeck* (*A Nievve Herball*, "a new herbal," 1578), a 1554 Dutch work on botany and its pharmacological applications by the physician Rembert Dodoens (1517-1585), also known as Dodonaeus. The *Cruydeboeck* was the major work in its field at the time. While Noro's translation was imperfect, the *Cruydeboeck* was probably the first European scientific work to appear in Japanese. Noro also published Japanese digests of material gathered from Dutch books on botany, entomology, and ichthyology.

Yoshimune also applied the foreign data Noro and other shogunate scholars gathered on botany and agriculture at an experimental agricultural center he established in 1722, where foreign methods were used to grow both domestic and foreign plants and produce hardier crops. Yoshimune encouraged the widespread cultivation of new plants from overseas, such as sugarcane and sweet potato, in the hope that such new crops might help alleviate the periodic famines that afflicted Japan. Aoki Kon'yō, Yoshimune's resident Dutch studies librarian, also wrote a work on the merits of sweet potato cultivation as well as treatises on Dutch currency and the Dutch language.

SIGNIFICANCE

Under the rules of Tokugawa Yoshimune and his successor, the irresponsible Shogun Ieshige, the main focus of learning Western knowledge remained that of "useful learning" and its practical applications. The next generation contained numbers of people who were able to learn directly from books in Dutch. There was continued progress in Japanese technology, art, and education, in part because of the increasing practical application of Western learning. A famous example is a research team led by Maeno Ryotaku (1723-1803), a student of Aoki Kon'yō, and Sugita Genpaku (1733-1817), who had learned Western medicine from a shogunate physician. This team worked from a 1734 Dutch translation of *Anatomische tabellen* (1725; illustrated anatomy) by the German physician Johann Adam Kulmus (1689-1745), carrying out the first scientific dissections in Japan. The team went on to translate the Kulmus text in 1774 (*Kaitai Shinsho*), the first full-scale translation of a European scientific text into Japanese.

—*Michael McCaskey*

FURTHER READING

Boxer, Charles R. *Papers on Portuguese, Dutch, and Jesuit Influences in Sixteenth and Seventeenth Century Japan: Studies in Japanese History and Civilization.* Westport, Conn.: Greenwood Press, 1979. A detailed account, by a recognized authority, of Japan's early encounters with European cultures and religious ideologies.

Goodman, Grant Kohn. *Japan and the Dutch, 1600-1853.* Richmond, Surrey, England: Curzon, 2000. Examines 250 years of an exclusive relationship between Tokugawa Japan and the Netherlands. Extensive and detailed bibliographical references.

Johnson, Hiroko. *Western Influence on Japanese Art.* Amsterdam: Hotei/KIT, 2004. A historical study of the Akita Ranga School, an artistic by-product of *rangaku*, or Dutch studies, in eighteenth century Japan.

Kasaya, Kazuhiko, ed. *Dodonaeus in Japan: Translation and the Scientific Mind in the Tokugawa Period.* Leuven, Belgium: Leuven University Press, 2001. Explores how the European pharmacological tradition in Dodonaeus's book of herbs was adapted by Tokugawa intellectuals, and its effect on the development of modern scientific discourse in Japan.

Keene, Donald. *The Japanese Discovery of Europe, 1720-1830.* Stanford, Calif.: Stanford University Press, 1969. Keene examines the relaxation of the ban on Western books, which ultimately resulted in a nationalistic Japanese version of Western medicine.

Sansom, George Bailey. *The Western World and Japan; A Study in the Interaction of European and Asiatic Cultures.* New York: Random House, 1974. A classic history of cultural relations between Japan and the West, containing many interesting anecdotes.

SEE ALSO: June 20, 1703: Chikamatsu Produces *The Love Suicides at Sonezaki*; 1786-1787: Tenmei Famine.

RELATED ARTICLES in *Great Lives from History: The Eighteenth Century, 1701-1800*: Chikamatsu Monzaemon; Hakuin; Honda Toshiaki; Ogyū Sorai; Suzuki Harunobu; Tokugawa Yoshimune.

1720's

1721-1742
DEVELOPMENT OF GREAT BRITAIN'S OFFICE OF PRIME MINISTER

The modern concept of the prime minister functioning as the head of Britain's government evolved between 1721 and 1742, with Robert Walpole serving as the first such prime minister.

LOCALE: London, England
CATEGORY: Government and politics

KEY FIGURES

Robert Walpole (1676-1745), British prime minister, 1721-1742
George I (1660-1727), king of Great Britain, r. 1714-1727
George II (1683-1760), king of Great Britain, r. 1727-1760
Frederick Louis (1707-1751), son of George II and prince of Wales
Charles Townshend (Second Viscount Townshend; 1674-1738), British secretary of state, 1721-1730
First Duke of Newcastle (Thomas Pelham; 1693-1758), British secretary of state, 1724-1754

SUMMARY OF EVENT

Even before the eighteenth century, there were English prime ministers. Close advisers to the monarchs were occasionally called "prime ministers" in negative or derisory terms, referring to one who had excessive and unreasonable power over his colleagues in the government. However, it was Robert Walpole, the dominant figure in the British government between 1721 and 1742, who was recognized as the first prime minister in the modern sense.

In the early eighteenth century, the two major parties or factions in the British parliament were the Whigs and Tories. There was also a division between the court (the monarch and the government ministers) and the country, mostly the landed gentry, who were often suspicious of the machinations of the ministers. While never fully in ascendancy, the Tories fell from power completely when the 1715 rebellion of James Edward (the "Old Pretender") failed to overthrow King George I. Prominent

Tories who had supported James Edward were impeached or fled into exile. However, the Whigs themselves split into two factions, one led by the earls of Sunderland and Stanhope and the other led by Charles Townshend and Robert Walpole. The latter two men, who were brothers-in-law, left the government in 1717.

The royal family was also divided, with bitter quarrels between George I and Prince George, the heir to the throne. The prince set up a rival court at Leicester House in London, which became the center of political opposition to the government. Out of office, Townshend and Walpole were welcomed at Leicester House but returned to the government after a temporary reconciliation between the king and the prince.

The South Sea Company scandal brought Walpole to power. An investment scheme to assist in reducing the government debt, the South Sea Company shares peaked in the summer of 1720 and the "bubble" burst, creating a financial panic. It led to a political crisis for Sunderland and Stanhope, who had backed the scheme and had benefited personally. Back in office, Walpole, from his position in the House of Commons, protected the major figures from punishment, but he was reviled in the country as "the Skreen Master General" because he had screened or shielded the cabinet ministers from retribution.

Stanhope died in 1721, but because of his past association with Prince George, Walpole did not rank high in the king's favor. In the government that formed in April, 1721, Walpole became the first lord of the treasury as well as chancellor of the exchequer, remaining in the House of Commons, and Townshend replaced the deceased Stanhope as secretary of state in charge of foreign affairs. George intended to return Sunderland to primacy, but in the interim Walpole had proved himself the master of the House of Commons and thus indispensable to the king.

Realizing the political importance of prosperity and stability, in 1723 Walpole led in the establishment of bonded warehouses where imported tea, coffee, and cocoa beans were stored. If they were reshipped out of Britain, no tariffs were imposed on their importers, and if they were sold in the country, excise taxes would be levied when they were removed from the warehouses. The warehouses encouraged trade, discouraged illegal smuggling, increased tax receipts to the government, paid down the national debt, and allowed Walpole to reduce the land tax, which was largely paid by members of Parliament, who owned most of the land.

By 1723, the first duke of Newcastle, a master of political patronage who controlled numerous seats in the

Robert Walpole, Great Britain's first prime minister. (Library of Congress)

House of Commons, joined Walpole and Townshend, solidifying their hold on Parliament. Walpole claimed that he was no saint or reformer, and most of the members of Parliament preferred Walpole's policy of stability over dealing with controversial social issues. Believing that all men had their price, the government made extensive use of patronage, distributing offices and honors in exchange for support in Parliament. Walpole used the resources of the Crown to gather support in the country, and his support from the country strengthened his position at court. By 1725, George I had become a friend and admirer of his "prime minister."

George I died in 1727, and the new king, George II, resented Walpole for serving his father. Inasmuch as the government depended upon the support of the monarch as well as of Parliament, many predicted that Walpole's days of power were numbered. However, within a few weeks, Walpole's position of authority was assured, in part because of Queen Caroline's backing. George II shortly became and remained Walpole's strong supporter.

During the 1720's, foreign policy issues were left to Townshend. Toward the end of the decade, Britain became involved in a conflict with Spain that was due to Townshend's pro-French policies. British merchants supported an activist foreign policy against Spain for economic reasons, but Walpole opposed foreign adventures that led to war because the costs would be borne by the landed gentry, his major supporters in Parliament. In 1729, Walpole initiated the Treaty of Seville with Spain. Townshend resigned the following year. Another treaty in 1731 with Austria seemed to guarantee a permanent European peace, allowing Walpole to focus again on domestic matters.

Expanding the earlier bonded warehouse scheme, in 1733 Walpole introduced a bill treating tobacco in a similar matter, to be followed by wine. Political opposition was immediate. More excise taxes meant more tax collectors, and that meant more possibilities for patronage and corruption. Most of the opposition was motivated by political ambition rather than political philosophy: The aim was simply to bring down Walpole. Knowing when to bend, Walpole abandoned the tobacco and wine excise scheme, and he continued in power, still the master of Parliament.

Opposition to the government was building, however. The weakened Tories were no threat, but by the 1730's, disgruntled Whigs were ready to take power if Walpole faltered in Parliament or lost the support of George II. Ultimately, it was foreign policy that brought Walpole down. By the late 1730's, French prestige was on the rise, and Walpole's policy of isolation from most continental matters appeared to be unpatriotic. His majority in the House of Commons sank to about fifty. The heir apparent, Prince Frederick, after quarreling with his parents, established a rival court at Leicester House, and in 1737, Queen Caroline, always supportive of Walpole, died. When Walpole attempted to negotiate differences with Spain over trade in the New World, young patriots such as William Pitt, supported by London merchants, denounced it as a national disgrace, demanding policies to advance British glory as well as British trade. Walpole gave way, and war with Spain resulted. In 1740, the Europe-wide War of the Austrian Succession began. It was no longer Walpole's world, and in 1742 he resigned, dying in 1745.

SIGNIFICANCE

Robert Walpole became the model of the British prime minister, even though not all of his successors in the eighteenth century were willing to be known by that title. Walpole was perfectly suited to his times. More a politi-

cian than a statesman, he understood Britain's political processes and the fears and ambitions of his contemporaries, dominating them through patronage and honors, and he knew how to make himself indispensable to the monarchs. His decision to remain in the House of Commons was crucial, and most of his successors also governed from the House of Commons. He held the important financial offices of chancellor of the exchequer and first lord of the treasury. Walpole was also the first prime minister to inhabit 10 Downing Street, and he was the longest-serving prime minister, but when political opinion and passions began to flow in the direction of empire and trade, Walpole was left behind.

Despite his reputation, in several ways Walpole was not yet a modern prime minister. His success and survival depended not only upon having a majority in Parliament, particularly the House of Commons, but also upon the support of the monarch, unlike those of later prime ministers who served when the monarchy no longer had any political power. Finally, although political factions did exist, there was no defined party system in the early eighteenth century; in the 1730's, Walpole's major opponents were all Whigs. Disciplined parties would not emerge until the later nineteenth century.

—*Eugene Larson*

FURTHER READING

Black, Jeremy, ed. *Britain in the Age of Walpole.* New York: St. Martin's Press, 1984. A series of essays discussing politics and government during the era of Walpole.

Englefield, Dermon, et al. *Facts About the British Prime Ministers.* New York: H. W. Wilson, 1995. A compilation of historical material regarding the office of prime minister.

Kemp, Betty. *Sir Robert Walpole.* London: Weidenfeld and Nicolson, 1976. An excellent analysis of Walpole, including a comparison of the office of prime minister in the eighteenth century and in the twentieth century.

Marshall, Dorothy. *English People in the Eighteenth Century.* Temecula, Calif.: Textbook Publishers, 2003. Classic study of English society in the eighteenth century.

Plumb, J. H. *Sir Robert Walpole.* 2 vols. London: Cresset Press, 1956-1960. The classic biography of Walpole by one of Britain's most respected historians.

SEE ALSO: Mar. 23-26, 1708: Defeat of the "Old Pretender"; Sept. 6, 1715-Feb. 4, 1716: Jacobite Rising in Scotland; Sept., 1720: Collapse of the South Sea Bub-

1720's

ble; 1736: *Gentleman's Magazine* Initiates Parliamentary Reporting; 1739-1741: War of Jenkins's Ear; Dec. 16, 1740-Nov. 7, 1748: War of the Austrian Succession.

RELATED ARTICLES in *Great Lives from History: The Eighteenth Century, 1701-1800*: Caroline; George I; George II; George III; William Pitt the Elder; William Pitt the Younger; Robert Walpole.

1721-1750
EARLY ENLIGHTENMENT IN FRANCE

During the three decades following publication of Montesquieu's Persian Letters, *French writers produced a growing number of literary, scientific, and philosophical works advocating individual liberty, empirical investigations of all kinds, secular progress, and a skeptical attitude toward religion and tradition.*

LOCALE: France
CATEGORIES: Philosophy; literature; cultural and intellectual history; science and technology

KEY FIGURES

Pierre Bayle (1647-1706), French writer
Bernard Le Bovier de Fontenelle (1657-1757), French writer
Henri de Boulainviller (1658-1722), French historian and freethinker
Voltaire (François-Marie Arouet; 1694-1778), French poet, historian, novelist, and gadfly
Marquise du Châtelet (Gabrielle-Émilie Le Tonnelier de Breteuil; 1706-1749), French Newtonian scientist
Denis Diderot (1713-1784), French writer and encyclopedist
Jean-Jacques Rousseau (1712-1778), French philosopher
Montesquieu (Charles-Louis de Secondat; 1689-1755), French social critic and jurist
Comte de Buffon (Georges-Louis Leclerc; 1707-1788), French natural scientist
Jean le Rond d'Alembert (1717-1783), French mathematician and encyclopedist
Pierre-Louis Moreau de Maupertuis (1698-1759), French mathematician and scientist
Julien Offroy de La Mettrie (1709-1751), French radical philosopher
Étienne Bonnot de Condillac (1715-1780), French philosopher

SUMMARY OF EVENT

The metaphorical term "enlightenment" refers to the liberal intellectual movement of the eighteenth century in Western Europe and North America. It was a diverse movement with both radical and moderate wings. As for any such movement, it is impossible to provide definitive dates for its beginning and end. Because of the large numbers of outstanding French thinkers and writers, historians have often tended to identify it primarily with France, even though it was slower to gain momentum there than in England, the Netherlands, and some German states. Most likely, this was because of the absolutist character of France's government, which was committed to championing Catholic privileges and values.

Leaders of the French movement were commonly called philosophes (philosophers), even though few of them were interested in constructing a philosophical system. The philosophes defended a variety of religious ideas, including liberal Christianity, atheism, Deism (belief in a Creator who does not intervene in human affairs), and pantheism (the identification of God with nature or the universe). Despite these differences, the philosophes generally agreed in rejecting orthodox Christian creeds, and they were firmly committed to religious freedom.

In the realm of government, the majority of French Enlightenment thinkers were moderates who were sympathetic to constitutional monarchy and distrustful of republicanism and democracy. Some of them endorsed the practice of enlightened absolutism, provided that the ruler would enact reforms and respect individual liberties. Most despised slavery and were critical of rigid caste distinctions, while at the same time they generally respected the concept of private property and the right to property.

The roots of the Enlightenment can be traced to many different sources. From classical Greco-Roman civilization, the philosophes were inspired by the materialism of Lucretius, the skepticism of Pyrrhon, the secular morality of the Epicureans, and the natural law concepts of the Stoics and others. From the Renaissance, they borrowed ideas from proponents of toleration and skepticism, particularly Desiderius Erasmus and Michel Eyquem de Montaigne. Even more, the philosophes were influenced by three intellectual giants of the seventeenth century:

Sir Isaac Newton, John Locke, and Baruch Spinoza. Newton's scientific work suggested to them that the universe was a large machine, reducible to mathematical laws. Locke's attribution of the origins of ideas to sensations implied that social progress was theoretically possible. Spinoza practiced biblical criticism, defended a form of pantheism, and rejected the notion of divine providence.

At the beginning of the eighteenth century, Bernard Le Bovier de Fontenelle and Pierre Bayle were the two most prominent forerunners of the French Enlightenment. Fontenelle's forte was the interpretation of science, and he helped popularize the heliocentric astronomy of the sixteenth century cosmologist Nicolaus Copernicus. He also questioned the idea of an omnipotent God and ridiculed superstition and myths. Bayle, a French Protestant who had found refuge in the Netherlands, was author of the widely read *Dictionnaire historique et critique* (1697, 1702; *An Historical and Critical Dictionary*, 1710), which scandalized conservatives with its sympathetic discussions of Pyrrhonism and Spinoza. While acknowledging the limits of reason and professing loyalty to the Reformed Church, Bayle denounced the burning of witches and did not hesitate to question the legitimacy of religious traditions.

More than any other single occurrence, however, it was the appearance of Montesquieu's *Lettres persanes* (1721; *Persian Letters*, 1722) that marked the beginning of the French Enlightenment as a significant cultural movement. Claiming to contain the correspondence of two Persian travelers, Usbek and Rica, the imaginative novel presented a satirical attack on attitudes of intolerance and bigotry. By devoting many of the 161 letters to oppressive practices in Persian harems, Montesquieu suggested that the condition of women in a given society provided the measure of that society's level of freedom and cultural advancement. Although manifestly critical of France's government and culture, *Persian Letters* did not attract much attention from the censor. An instant best-seller, it allowed Montesquieu to sell his inherited judgeship and devote the rest of his life to literary pursuits and travel.

FRANCE THROUGH PERSIAN EYES

A founding work of the French Enlightenment was Montesquieu's Persian Letters. *Using the conceit of a series of letters written by Persian visitors to Paris freed Montesquieu to criticize aspects of French society by representing them through the eyes of strangers and portraying them as oddities. In the first excerpt here, taken from Letter 48, a Persian furnishes a self-description that is taken by scholars to refer to Montesquieu himself. In the second passage, taken from the same letter, the man asks a French friend to explain an oddity he has encountered.*

Those who take pleasure in their own instruction are never idle. Although I am not employed on any business of importance, I am yet constantly occupied. I spend my time observing, and at night I write down what I have noticed, what I have seen, what I have heard, during the day. I am interested in everything, astonished at everything; I am like a child, whose organs, still over-sensitive, are vividly impressed by the merest trifles. . . .

One day, as we were talking quietly in a large company, leaving the general conversation to the others, I said, "You will perhaps find in me more inquisitiveness than good manners; but I beg you to let me ask some questions, for I am wearied to death doing nothing, and of living with people with whom I have nothing in common. My thoughts have been busy these two days; there is not one among these men who has not put me to the torture two hundred times; in a thousand years I would never understand them; they are more invisible to me than the wives of our great king." "You have only to ask," replied he, "and I will tell you all you desire – the more willingly because I think you a discreet man, who will not abuse my confidence."

"Who is that man," said I, "who has told us so much about the banquets at which he has entertained the great, who is so familiar with your dukes, and who talks so often to your ministers, who, they tell me, are so difficult of access? He ought surely to be a man of quality; but his aspect is so mean that he is hardly an honour to the aristocracy; and, besides, I find him deficient in education. I am a stranger; but it seems to me that there is, generally speaking, a certain tone of good-breeding common to all nations, and I do not find it in him. Can it be that your upper classes are not so well trained as those of other nations?" "That man," answered he, laughing, "is a farmer-general; he is as much above others in wealth, as he is inferior to us all by birth. He might have the best people in Paris at his table, if he could make up his mind never to eat in his own house. He is very impertinent, as you see; but he excels in his cook, and is not ungrateful, for you heard how he praised him to-day."

Source: Montesquieu, "Letter XLVIII." *Persian Letters.* The Persian Letters Project, College of William and Mary. http://www.wm.edu/history/rbsche/plp/letter48.html. Accessed November 15, 2005.

1720's

By the early 1720's, France already had a number of Masonic lodges and other groups whose members were committed to unorthodox religious views. The result was a strong demand for works that had been condemned by the French censor. Henri de Boulainviller, who died in 1722, led an association of freethinkers who circulated numerous unauthorized publications and manuscripts, including the notorious *Traité des trios imposteurs* (treatise on the three impostors), which first appeared anonymously sometime before 1715. Boulainviller's admirers published posthumous editions of his Deistic interpretations of Moḥammad and Spinoza in 1730 and 1731. When the obscure parish priest Jean Meslier died in 1729, he left behind the explosive *Testament*, which denounced Christianity, private property, and inequality. Many manuscripts of the *Testament* were copied and passed around before Voltaire published an edited version later in the century.

During this period, French intellectuals often looked to England as a model for political liberties, and they also admired English accomplishments in science, philosophy, and literature. In 1733, Voltaire added to this mystique by publishing his *Letters Concerning the English Nation*, which first appeared in English and then in French as *Lettres philosophiques* the next year. Voltaire asserted that England had four virtues lacking in his own country. First, he extolled England's governmental system for limiting the powers of the king with an elected legislature, transparently implying that the French monarchy was potentially despotic. Second, he asserted that the English granted scientists and intellectuals considerable freedom and held them in high esteem. Third, he admired England's relative tolerance of a multiplicity of religions, in contrast to French laws that granted full religious freedom only to Catholicism. Finally, he asserted that the English people, including the nobility, valued commerce and entrepreneurship, whereas the French disdained trade and the merchant class.

Voltaire's *Letters Concerning the English Nation* has been called a "bomb hurled against the old order." The high court of Paris quickly condemned the book to a public burning. When Voltaire learned of an order for his imprisonment, he fled Paris, and from 1734 to 1749 he made his headquarters in the duchy of Lorraine at the château of his mistress, the marquise du Châtelet. During this period, Voltaire devoted his great energy to study and writing. In addition to books of poetry and fiction, he published a defense of worldly affluence (1736) and a popular account of Newton's scientific theories (1738).

More than simply Voltaire's mistress, du Châtelet was one of the great female intellectuals of the century. Having studied with Pierre-Louis Moreau de Maupertuis and other scientists, she had a specialized knowledge of mathematics and Newtonian physics, and she decided to write her own book about Newton with a broader scientific perspective than Voltaire's account. Her *Institutions de physique* (1740; lessons in physics) provided an excellent summary of the state of knowledge about physics at the time. Somewhat later du Châtelet would publish the standard French translation of Newton with explanatory notes.

During the 1740's, several French skeptics propagated a forbidden mechanical view of the universe. The banned writings of the marquis d'Argens, for instance, were widely available. Even more, the clandestine book *Le Philosophe* (1743; the philosopher), probably written by César du Marsais, ridiculed beliefs in Christian "fables" and described "civil society" as "the only divinity that true philosophers acknowledge." A Catholic priest, Étienne Bonnot de Condillac, helped provide an epistemological basis for a materialistic metaphysics in *Essai sur l'origine des connaissances humaines* (1746; *An Essay on the Origin of Human Knowledge*, 1756), which went beyond Locke in arguing that sensation was the only source of all knowledge.

The most infamous atheist and materialist of the century, Julien Offroy de La Mettrie, shocked pious readers with his *L'Homme machine* (1747; *Man a Machine*, 1750; also known as *L'Homme Machine: A Study in the Origins of an Idea*, 1960), which rejected the idea of an immortal soul and argued that the ability to think was simply a result of the organic construction of the brain. In his next work, *Discours sur le bonheur: Ou, L'Anti-Sénèque* (1747; *Anti-Seneca: Or, The Sovereign Good*, 1996), La Mettrie deduced moral hedonism from his materialistic premises, suggesting that people should pursue egoistic pleasure and self-aggrandizement. He acknowledged, nevertheless, society's right to repress acts that were manifestly harmful. Moderate philosophes, not wanting to be accused of encouraging immorality or social disorder, joined with conservatives in condemning La Mettrie's writings. Banished from France and Holland, he found refuge in Prussia, where he was viewed as an unbalanced extremist when he died in 1751, presumably from indigestion.

As scientists learned more about the physical universe, they increasingly tended to formulate speculative explanations without reference to God or metaphysics. In 1749, the comte de Buffon published the first volume of his monumental *Histoire naturelle, générale et*

Sir Isaac Newton's model of a universe governed by immutable physical laws was a crucial influence on Denis Diderot and Voltaire, leaders of the French Enlightenment. (Harper & Brothers)

particulière (1749-1789; *Natural History, General and Particular*, 1781-1812), which proposed a naturalistic theory of Earth's origin and speculated that the planets had most likely resulted from a collision of a large comet and the Sun. After theologians at the Sorbonne condemned parts of his work, Buffon issued a formal retraction and was much more cautious in subsequent volumes. Another noted scientist, Pierre-Louis Moreau de Maupertuis, made empirical studies of heredity in ways that foreshadowed modern theories of genetics. His book *Essai de cosmologie* (1750; essay on cosmology) contained a speculative theory of biological evolution based on the inner viability of organisms. His view of a dynamic universe in constant change stimulated the imagination of numerous philosophes.

In the area of political theory, Montesquieu's large and complex work *De l'esprit des loix* (1748; *The Spirit of the Laws*, 1750) argued that each legal system functioned according to an operating principle (or spirit). Montesquieu distinguished between three governmental forms: despotism, constitutional monarchy, and republicanism (the latter appearing in two versions, democracy and oligarchy). On the one hand, he took the relativistic position that viable political systems must be based on particular historical and geographical circumstances. On the other hand, he indicated his strong preference for a rule of established laws with "intermediary powers" dominated by hereditary noblemen. The English constitution, in his idealized interpretation, had preserved liberty through a separation into three institutions—an executive, a representative legislature, and a judiciary. *The Spirit of the Laws* was one of the seminal achievements of the moderate Enlightenment. Although it was condemned by the Vatican, the French censor allowed it to be printed and sold in Paris.

In 1750, Jean-Jacques Rousseau, the great maverick of the philosophes, burst upon the literary scene when the Dijon Academy awarded him first prize for his provocative essay *Discours sur les sciences et les arts* (1750; *A Discourse on the Arts and Sciences*, 1751), which asserted that humans once lived cooperative and nonviolent lives in a state of nature, whereas they had become greedy, violent, and alienated in modern civilizations. Although other philosophes were usually appalled by his attacks on reason and modernity, Rousseau was nevertheless affiliated with the Enlightenment by virtue of his commitment to freedom, individualism, and social criticism. *A Discourse on the Arts and Sciences* reflected his strong tendency to sympathize with outsiders and disadvantaged persons, a perspective that would become more pronounced in his later works.

Without doubt, Denis Diderot was one of the most creative and adventuresome of the major French philosophes. Like Voltaire, he was greatly influenced by the liberal British writers, and his first major publications were translations of English books. Diderot's early opposition to Catholicism soon developed into a radical Deism that tended toward atheism. His *Pensées philosophiques* (1746; English translation, 1819) was quickly condemned by the Paris Parlement (the high court). His controversial *Lettre sur les aveugles* (1749; *An Essay on Blindness*, 1750) described the universe as purposeless and without any metaphysical foundation for human morality. For this work, he was imprisoned in Vincennes for three months. He was released only after agreeing to recant the materialistic ideas of the book and to reveal the names of its publishers.

Before Diderot's imprisonment, he and Jean le Rond d'Alembert had already begun their work as joint editors of the large and comprehensive *Encyclopédie: Ou, Dictionnaire raisonné des sciences, des arts, et des métiers* (1751-1772; partial translation *Selected Essays from the Encyclopedy*, 1772; complete translation *Encyclopedia*, 1965), which would eventually become the greatest collaborative enterprise of the century. The watershed year of 1750 saw the composition of d'Alembert's *Discours préliminaire de l'Encyclopédie* (1751; *Preliminary Discourse to the Encyclopedia of Diderot*, 1963), which explained the principles to guide the multivolume compendium. In effect, d'Alembert wrote a manifesto of the Enlightenment's hopes for progress through the cultivation of reason and secular knowledge. Praising the contributions of scientists and philosophers of the past, he used the term *lumières* (lights) nineteen times and *siècle des lumières* (century of lights) twice. The following year, the first volume of the monumental *Encyclopedia* was published.

SIGNIFICANCE

Before 1721, the Enlightenment in France had been an underground movement supported only by small groups of dissident thinkers. By 1750, in contrast, the perspectives of the moderate Enlightenment were commonly accepted among the educated elite. Although radical aspects of the movement—such as atheism, democracy, and opposition to monarchy—continued to be outside the mainstream, they too had an impact on a minority of the population. By mid-century, the philosophes had laid a firm foundation for the broad diffusion of Enlightenment views that would occur during the second half of the century.

Although the influences of the Enlightenment cannot be precisely measured, there is abundant evidence of its multifaceted effects. For instance, historian Michel Vovelle has documented a decline in references to religion in the last wills and testaments written in France over the course of the eighteenth century. During the French Revolution, the ideas of the philosophes appeared to inspire both moderate reforms and radical excesses. Since then, the legacy of the Enlightenment has included a growth in scientific knowledge, secular attitudes, constitutional government, public education, the questioning of traditions, and the belief that progress is possible.

—*Thomas Tandy Lewis*

FURTHER READING

Aldridge, Alfred Owen. *Voltaire and the Century of Light.* Princeton, N.J.: Princeton University Press, 1975. Dependable account of Voltaire's life and writings.

Gay, Peter. *The Enlightenment: An Interpretation.* 2 vols. New York: Knopf, 1966, 1969. Classic work that views the Enlightenment as a single pan-European movement in which most thinkers shared compatible ideas and faced common enemies.

Goodman, Dena. *The Republic of Letters: A Cultural History of the French Enlightenment.* Ithaca, N.Y.: Cornell University Press, 1996. Focuses on the social context of salons dominated by women, where men and women cooperated and had complementary roles.

Himmelfarb, Gertrude. *The Roads to Modernity: The British, French, and American Enlightenments.* New York: Knopf, 2004. Controversial book that criticizes the French Enlightenment for glorifying abstract reason and praises English, Scottish, and American thinkers for elevating common sense and the social virtues of compassion, benevolence, and sympathy.

Israel, Jonathan. *Radical Enlightenment: Philosophy and the Making of Modernity, 1650-1750.* New York: Oxford University Press, 2001. A large and scholarly study of early antireligious proponents of extreme secularization, emphasizing the pan-European nature of the movement and the pivotal role of Spinoza.

Outran, Dorinda. *The Enlightenment.* New York: Cambridge University Press, 1995. A relatively brief summary organized by major topics, with excellent analysis of the major interpretations of the Enlightenment.

Roger, Jacques. *The Science of Life in Eighteenth-Century France.* Translated by Robert Elbrich. Stanford, Calif.: Stanford University Press, 1997. The most important treatment of Buffon and other Enlightenment scientists.

Shklar, Judith. *Montesquieu.* New York: Oxford University Press, 1987. A small book that gives an excellent introduction to Montesquieu's writings.

Spencer, Samia, ed. *French Women and the Age of Enlightenment.* Bloomington: Indiana University Press, 1984. A valuable collection of essays about the conditions and achievements of Enlightenment women, as well as the philosophes' views on women and society.

Wilson, Arthur. *Diderot.* New York: Oxford University Press, 1972. A scholarly biography that considers all aspects of Diderot's life and thought.

SEE ALSO: 1726-1729: Voltaire Advances Enlightenment Thought in Europe; 1743-1744: D'Alembert

Develops His Axioms of Motion; 1748: Montesquieu Publishes *The Spirit of the Laws*; 1749-1789: First Comprehensive Examination of the Natural World; 1751: Maupertuis Provides Evidence of "Hereditary Particles"; 1751-1772: Diderot Publishes the *Encyclopedia*; 1754: Condillac Defends Sensationalist Theory; July 27, 1758: Helvétius Publishes *De l'esprit*; Jan., 1759: Voltaire Satirizes Optimism in *Candide*; Apr., 1762: Rousseau Publishes *The Social Contract*; July, 1764: Voltaire Publishes *A Philosophical Dictionary for the Pocket*; 1770: Publication of Holbach's *The System of Nature*; 1782-1798: Publication of Rousseau's *Confessions*.

RELATED ARTICLES in *Great Lives from History: The Eighteenth Century, 1701-1800*: Jean le Rond d'Alembert; Comte de Buffon; Marquise du Châtelet; Étienne Bonnot de Condillac; Denis Diderot; Montesquieu; Jean-Jacques Rousseau; Voltaire.

1722
RÉAUMUR DISCOVERS CARBON'S ROLE IN HARDENING STEEL

René-Antoine Ferchault de Réaumur wrote a treatise on transforming iron ore into steel, revolutionizing metallurgy in France. Réaumur's recommendations and analysis not only made it possible for France to produce steel for itself rather than importing the metal but also helped pave the way for the Industrial Revolution.

LOCALE: Paris, France
CATEGORIES: Chemistry; engineering; science and technology

KEY FIGURES
René-Antoine Ferchault de Réaumur (1683-1757), French engineer and entomologist
Louis XV (1710-1774), king of France, r. 1715-1774
Jean-Baptiste Colbert (1619-1683), French statesman and controller of finances

SUMMARY OF EVENT
Modern industry began to emerge in Europe in the eighteenth century, and one of the major requirements for its full emergence was a plentiful supply of raw materials from which tools and machinery could be manufactured. Pure iron was too soft for such a purpose, but steel was ideally suited to industrial applications. Steel is composed mostly of iron, but it also contains less than 2 percent carbon, and the carbon makes it much harder and more resilient than iron alone. The French scientist and engineer René-Antoine Ferchault de Réaumur determined that carbon had this effect upon iron, making it possible to manufacture steel on a mass scale.

Réaumur came to Paris at the age of twenty. Already educated in mathematics and civil law, he continued and expanded his studies, focusing on mathematics and physics, with Pierre Varignon. Through the social contacts of a cousin, he gained the acquaintance of the president of of the Académie des Sciences, where he became a student of geometry on March 12, 1708. Only two months after being admitted, he presented his first paper in mathematics, impressing the members sufficiently that three years later he was admitted as a permanent member in mechanics.

While still a student, Réaumur was asked to produce a survey of all the arts, handicrafts, and trades of France, a project envisioned by Jean-Baptiste Colbert in the previous century but never completed. Taking up the task with the intellectual zeal of a scientist, Réaumur went far beyond cataloging the productive trades of his nation. Surveying France's goldsmiths prompted him to investigate the country's auriferous (gold-bearing) rivers; listing the artists who worked in turquoise led him to study the mineralogy and mining that supported their trade and to analyze the fossil beds of France. In addition to describing the techniques and distribution of French craftspeople, Réaumur's *Description des divers arts et métiers de France* (1710; description of the diverse arts and occupations of France) explicated the geographic and scientific factors that made their crafts possible.

In the next decade, Réaumur became obsessed with metal production, perhaps because he had inherited a steel mill on the southwest coast of France. In his survey of crafts, Réaumur had noticed that France lagged behind its neighbors in the production of steel. As a result, the French manufacturing industry depended on imported steel from Germany. Characteristically, his discussions with metalworkers led him to a scientific investigation of the principles behind their craft, in this case the chemistry of iron ore its smelted products. Iron had never before been studied chemically. Réaumur examined the different chemical compositions of iron when smelted from different types of ores and accurately surmised that the proportion of carbon in the smelted product was the primary factor determining the product's ductility or lack of ductility.

With patience and accuracy, Réaumur tested cast iron, steel, and wrought iron, and he was the first scientist to use a microscope to observe their different crystalline structures. In 1722, he published the results of twelve years of intense study in *L'Art de convertir le fer forgé* (*Memoirs on Steel and Iron*, 1956). His treatise discussed the methods for producing cast iron, wrought iron, and steel. It indicated which minerals should be added to or eliminated from steel to enhance its ductility and resistance. It introduced a method Réaumur had discovered for producing steel by adding iron oxides to melted iron, and it recommended cleaning and polishing steel stock before rolling the stock into sheets. King Louis XV was sufficiently impressed by the work that he awarded Réaumur a £12,000 pension, which Réaumur generously forwarded to the Académie des Sciences to further scientific research.

SIGNIFICANCE

While steel was already being produced when Réaumur published his treatise, the chemical principles underlying its production were unknown. Réaumur's work, by revealing those principles, revolutionized iron and steel production. His practical recommendations made it possible for the French to produce their own steel in much greater quantities, greatly reducing their dependence on foreign imports. It was his theoretical scientific analysis, however, that enabled future metallurgists and engineers to refine manufacturing techniques, ultimately superseding the methods Réaumur discovered. Thus, his work helped to establish the general usefulness of scientific analysis for developing modern industrial techniques. It

was one of many developments in the eighteenth century that made possible the Industrial Revolution.

—*Denyse Lemaire and David Kasserman*

FURTHER READING

Bunch, Bryan, with Alexander Hellemans. *The History of Science and Technology: A Browser's Guide to the Great Discoveries, Inventions, and the People Who Made Them, from the Dawn of Time to Today.* Boston: Houghton Mifflin, 2004. Provides a wealth of information, presented in lucid fashion, on the history of science and technology.

Freytag, Dean A. *The History, Making, and Modeling of Steel.* Milwaukee, Wis.: William K. Walthers, 1996. A useful overview of the changes in the processes of steel making through time.

Gribbin, John. *The Scientists: A History of Science Told Through the Lives of Its Greatest Inventors.* New York: Random House, 2002. Describes the evolution of science in the last five hundred years.

Tylecote, R. F. *A History of Metallurgy.* 2d ed. Boston: Maney, 2002. Examines the development of smelting techniques and the uses of metals from the Neolitic period until now.

SEE ALSO: 1709: Darby Invents Coke-Smelting; 1745: Lomonosov Issues the First Catalog of Minerals; 1746: Zāhir al-ʿUmar Creates a Stronghold in Galilee; 1783-1784: Cort Improves Iron Processing; 1789: Leblanc Develops Soda Production; 1790: First Steam Rolling Mill; 1797: Wollaston Begins His Work on Metallurgy.

RELATED ARTICLES in *Great Lives from History: The Eighteenth Century, 1701-1800*: Abraham Darby; Louis XV.

April 5, 1722
EUROPEAN DISCOVERY OF EASTER ISLAND

Explorer Jacob Roggeveen discovered a remote, inhabited island about 2,000 miles west of the South American continent. The hundreds of massive stone statues and absence of large trees have led to centuries of speculation about the island's history, a mystery that scientists have yet to unravel.

LOCALE: Easter Island (Rapa Nui), south Pacific Ocean
CATEGORIES: Exploration and discovery; archaeology; anthropology; environment

KEY FIGURE
Jacob Roggeveen (1659-1729), a Dutch admiral and explorer who, with his crew, discovered Easter Island

SUMMARY OF EVENT
In August of 1721, Jacob Roggeveen set sail from Holland with three small ships and 222 crew members in the service of the Dutch West India Company. The sixty-two-year-old former lawyer was setting off in search of Terra Australis Incognita (the unknown southern land, also known as Southland), the continent that explorers mistakenly believed existed in the southern Pacific Ocean.

Roggeveen's expedition was primarily a business venture, not simply a voyage of exploration. The West India Company agreed to pay Roggeveen and his heirs one-tenth of the profits for a period of ten years, if Terra Australis Incognita, or any other lands that he discovered, would generate profitable trade. There was a sense of urgency for the expedition, as other European powers were interested in finding the elusive continent as well.

Edward Davis, an English buccaneer, reportedly sighted Southland in 1687. Two descriptions of Davis's sighting were extant in 1721. Both accounts placed the broad landmass west of Chile at 27 degrees south latitude. However, the descriptions gave different longitudes. Roggeveen's strategy was to sail along the 27th parallel until he discovered the continent. From Holland, he sailed south around South America's Cape Horn and into the Pacific Ocean. He then headed north, paralleling the Chilean coast, and visited the uninhabited (but previously discovered) Juan Fernandez Islands. From there he struck a north-westerly course to the 27th parallel, and then

turned due west until he discovered an island on Easter Sunday, April 5, 1722. Roggeveen named the 66-square-mile landmass Easter Island for the occasion. Twenty-first century inhabitants of Easter Island, who number about four thousand, call their island Rapa Nui and themselves and their language Rapanui.

Easter Island was about 9 miles distant when Roggeveen's lead ship sighted it on the horizon at about 5:00 P.M. As the vessel approached the island from the east, the late afternoon tropical Sun no doubt etched a discernible silhouette of the island with its two small volcanoes at either end. "There was great joy among the people," Roggeveen wrote in his journal, "as everybody hoped that this low land [island] was the precursor of the extended coast of the unknown Southland." He dropped anchor for the night and anticipated reaching the island the next day. Unstable weather slowed his progress, however, so two days later, in the early morning of April 7,

EASTER ISLAND

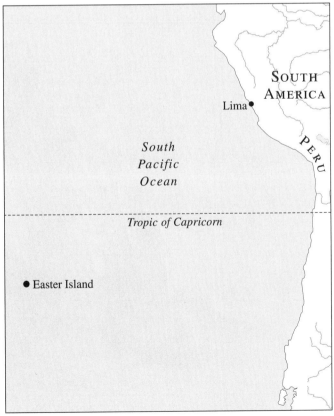

Lima

SOUTH AMERICA

PERU

South Pacific Ocean

Tropic of Capricorn

● Easter Island

Roggeveen confirmed that the island was inhabited when a lone islander paddled a flimsy canoe to the ships. By the evening of April 8, Roggeveen had spotted smoke from a fire ring on the island, moved the ships to within a quarter mile of the shore, and sent men on two sloops to examine the island, but with orders not to go ashore. The men returned to report that the islanders had waved for them to come ashore.

On the morning of April 9, islanders either paddled leaky canoes or simply swam out to the ships and were invited on board. Communication between the Dutchmen and islanders depended on expressions and signs, and soon there were misunderstandings. Roggeveen wrote that the islanders "took the hats and caps of the sailors from their heads and jumped with their plunder overboard, for they were extremely good swimmers." Roggeveen decided to use force to collect the stolen belongings. The next morning he armed 134 men with muskets, loaded them into three launches, and accompanied them to the island. He wrote in his logbook, "we marched forward a little" and "to our great astonishment and without

any expectation . . . more than thirty muskets were let off and the Indians being completely surprised and frightened by this fled, leaving behind 10 to 12 dead, besides the wounded." One of Roggeveen's men explained to him later that "some of the inhabitants . . . picked up stones and with a menacing gesture of throwing at us, by which by all appearances, the shooting from my small troop had been caused. . . ."

Fearing for their lives, the islanders quickly made amends with their visitors by giving them sixty chickens and thirty bunches of bananas. In return, the visitors "paid them the value amply with striped linen, with which they appeared to be well pleased and satisfied." The islanders then permitted Roggeveen and his men to walk about the island freely. The Dutchmen noted two prominent features about the island: a lack of large trees and hundreds of large stone sculptures resembling humans. He aptly concluded that the lack of sizable trees explained the islanders' poorly made canoes and their interest in his ships' wooden hulls.

Easter Island's mysterious stone statues (or *moai* in

An illustration of massive stone statues, called moai, *on Easter Island.* (North Wind Picture Archives)

Rapanui) impressed Roggeveen and his crew. Later visitors would count more than two hundred figures standing on massive stone platforms lining the coast. About seven hundred more were in various stages of completion and inexplicably abandoned in quarries or on ancient roads between the quarries and the coast. Scholars would later determine that the average *moai* is 13 feet tall and weighs 14 tons. In his logbook, Roggeveen wrote,

> The stone images at first caused us to be struck with astonishment, because we could not comprehend how it was possible that these people, who are devoid of heavy thick timber for making any machines, as well as strong ropes, nevertheless had been able to erect such images.

Aside from a paucity of wood, Roggeveen observed that the island was "outstandingly fruitful," with an abundance of bananas, sweet potatoes, and sugarcane, and he surmised that "although devoid of large trees and livestock, apart from fowls," the island "could be made into an earthly Paradise if it were properly cultivated and worked. . . ." He concluded that the islanders were friendly and healthy. He estimated the number of inhabitants to be in the thousands, but that the island was underpopulated given the its size and resources.

Roggeveen was the last major Dutch explorer to enter the Pacific Ocean. He sailed in the early stages of Europe's eighteenth century Age of Enlightenment. The Enlightenment was a time in which scientific observation and reason became a tool for advancing the nation-state. To "enlightened" European explorers, such as Roggeveen, it was important to spread commerce and industry to the far corners of the globe. These explorers took great pains to avoid making their stopovers vicious looting operations. They tended to romanticize the Pacific islanders, viewing them as "noble savages" who lacked the baser experiences of a worldly life. Paradoxically, notwithstanding the social liberalism of the Enlightenment, European explorers' misinterpretations, egotism, and intolerance often ignited quarrels with islanders. The interlopers seldom hesitated in brandishing or using weapons to resolve disagreements.

Roggeveen's encounter with Easter Islanders displayed the same paradox. His journal reflects an enlightened approach to exploration, as he kept a detailed record of what he observed, and even after the unfortunate killings, he sought to reestablish good relations with the islanders. Nonetheless, the Dutchman's idealism succumbed to personal hubris when he reacted to islanders' petty thievery with a show of force that had lethal conse-

quences. Sadly, quarrels and deadly encounters occurred frequently in eighteenth century Polynesia, as explorers often let arrogance and greed rather than humanistic ideals influence their decisions.

SIGNIFICANCE

Certainly, finding tiny Easter Island was a disappointment to Jacob Roggeveen, who was seeking a continent that would generate trade and make him and his heirs wealthy. The Dutchman did not know that he had discovered the easternmost island settled by Polynesian peoples—an island whose inhabitants and mysterious stone monuments would capture the world's imagination for centuries. The discovery of Southland would remain a goal of voyagers until the Englishman James Cook confirmed, during his second voyage to the Pacific Ocean (1772-1775), that no such continent existed.

Roggeveen spent only one day on Easter Island, but he took extraordinary notes for someone who had never visited such a society. His journal is an invaluable historical resource. He was unaware that Easter Island's society had been in a downturn by the time he visited. The decline remains a mystery, although scientists favor the theory that overpopulation and deforestation were causes. If these theories are correct, they would account for the end of monument building and the declining condition of Rapa Nui.

—*Richard A. Crooker*

FURTHER READING

Fischer, Steven Roger. *Island at the End of the World: The Turbulent History of Easter Island*. London: Reaktion Books, 2005. A comprehensive history of the island by a scholar of the peoples and languages of the Pacific. Fischer's examination includes discussion of how the island transformed after Roggeveen's 1722 landing, as the islanders soon faced disease and violence, but also trade relations, with the arrival of other Europeans. Illustrated.

Flenley, John, and Paul Bahn. *The Enigmas of Easter Island: Island on the Edge*. New York: Oxford University Press, 2003. Examines scientific evidence and concludes that the earliest inhabitants of Easter Island were Polynesians who deforested the island.

McCall, Grant. *Rapanui: Tradition and Survival on Easter Island*. Honolulu: University of Hawaii Press, 1994. A 205-page illustrated introduction to Easter Island, with maps and bibliographical references.

Sharp, Andrew, ed. and trans. *The Journal of Jacob Roggeveen*. Oxford, England: Clarendon Press, 1970. A translation of Roggeveen's daily logbook, originally published in 1838, with expository footnotes. Entries cover the 1721-1722 expedition. Includes maps, bibliography.

Stevenson, Christopher M., and William S. Ayres, eds. *Easter Island Archaeology: Research on Early Rapanui Culture.* Los Osos, Calif.: Bearsville Press, 2000. A work on the archaeological research of the island, including discussion of land settlement patterns and archaeological excavation. Distributed by the Easter Island Foundation. Maps, plans, and bibliography.

Van Tilburg, Jo Anne. *Easter Island Archaeology, Ecology, and Culture.* Washington, D.C.: Smithsonian Institution Press, 1994. A thorough review of what is known about the inhabitants of Easter Island before the European discovery.

SEE ALSO: Dec. 15, 1766-Mar. 16, 1769: Bougainville Circumnavigates the Globe; Aug. 25, 1768-Feb. 14, 1779: Voyages of Captain Cook.

RELATED ARTICLE in *Great Lives from History: The Eighteenth Century, 1701-1800*: James Cook.

1723
STAHL POSTULATES THE PHLOGISTON THEORY

Almost forgotten in the twenty-first century, the phlogiston theory proposed by Georg Stahl became the dominant model explaining combustion and fermentation in eighteenth century chemistry. Although the theory was later replaced after the discovery of oxygen, the phlogiston theory for a time was the basis for all serious chemical experimentation and research. It constituted the first systematic and comprehensive theory of chemistry.

LOCALE: Berlin, Prussia (now in Germany)
CATEGORIES: Chemistry; science and technology

KEY FIGURES

Georg Ernst Stahl (1660-1734), German chemist
Johann Joachim Becher (1635-1682), German scientist and Stahl's mentor
Antoine-Laurent Lavoisier (1743-1794), French chemist
Joseph Priestley (1733-1804), English chemist

SUMMARY OF EVENT

Chemistry at the beginning of the eighteenth century was still based primarily on the principles of Aristotle and the ancient idea that all matter was composed of four elements: earth, water, fire, and air. Alchemy, using a mixture of Aristotelian ideas and magical principles in its relentless search for a way to produce gold from "base" metal, dominated chemistry. Two unsolved mysteries of chemistry at the time involved the mechanisms of fermentation and combustion. A strong practical interest in metallurgy drove scientists to seek answers to the latter problem in particular.

Two phenomena associated with both combustion and fermentation had been observed: Both processes gave off heat (albeit extremely slowly in the case of fermentation), and both released some substance into the air. In the case of fermentation, the production of a colorless and odorless material was inferred from the bubbles it produced. In combustion, the release was more intense, as a great deal of heat was also produced. It was believed that combustion, like fermentation, released a colorless and odorless material in addition to the tangible smoke that it also produced. Smoke was known to contain airborne particles that later settled out of the air as soot or other substances.

A German chemist, Georg Ernst Stahl, developed a theory to account for these observations, the phlogiston theory. Although he had discussed this theory in earlier works, the publication of *Fundamenta chymiae dogmaticae et experimentalis* (1723; the fundamentals of dogmatic and experimental chemistry) represented a more complete description. As a theory of combustion, which could also be generalized to fermentation, it revolutionized chemistry in the eighteenth century. Stahl's basic proposal was that a principle he called "phlogiston" (from the Greek *phlogistos*, meaning "burnt") existed, to a greater or lesser degree, in all substances. During combustion, phlogiston was freed from the burning substance and released into the air. He considered phlogiston to be an intangible "principle," rather than an element or substance with mass.

Many of Stahl's concepts about chemistry came from his teacher Johann Joachim Becher, whose ideas combined Aristotelian philosophy and alchemy. Both Becher and Stahl were obsessed with the usual alchemical pursuit of the philosopher's stone (a mythical substance that could turn base metals into gold), and they had strong interests in metallurgy and mineralogy. They considered all substances to be mixtures of a few simple elements and a handful of "principles." Principles were indeterminate entities without apparent mass and included salt, sulfur, and mercury, as well as phlogiston. (Although the names of some of these principles, originated by Paracelsus [1493-1541], resemble the names of modern compounds or elements, they were not the same substances.)

Throughout the middle of the eighteenth century, the phlogiston theory was almost universally accepted. When applied qualitatively, it provided a plausible theory for what occurred during combustion. Substances were considered to have varying amounts of phlogiston: Flammable substances contained the most phlogiston, which was why they burned. During combustion, phlogiston was "squeezed" out into the air. The resulting substance, such as wood ash resulting from burning wood, was said to be "dephlogisticated," as all of its phlogiston had been released.

The theory also helped to explain how living organisms used air when breathing. Normal air was considered low in phlogiston. Stahl thought that a person, for example, breathed in normal air and later exhaled air with elevated levels of phlogiston. This release of phlogiston from the living system was required for survival. Once air had become saturated with phlogiston, it was no longer able to accept more, which helped to explain why air became "used up" by a mouse in a closed container and why fumes from a fire were unbreathable; in both cases, the air was fully phlogisticated. "Bad air," which was unhealthy to breathe, became equated with elevated levels of phlogiston.

Even metals contained some phlogiston, according to Stahl. When a metal, such as lead, is burned, it becomes oxidized. According to the phlogiston theory, this process, called calcination, represented loss of phlogiston. The calcinated metal was referred to as a calx and was considered to be a simpler substance than the original metal. Phlogiston could be returned to a calx by heating it with a burning material high in phlogiston, such as charcoal; this was the same process used in smelting ore.

A major problem with the phlogiston theory was that the calx weighed more than the original metal: If a calx represented a simpler substance created by taking phlogiston out of metal, one would expect the calx to weigh less, just as the ash left behind after burning a log weighs less than the original log. Stahl himself never seemed to be concerned with this problem, probably because he did not consider phlogiston to have any weight of its own. Thus, the weight gain, which had been discovered long before the birth of the phlogiston theory, was assumed

to occur by some other, unknown process. As the phlogiston theory became widely accepted, however, other chemists modified it, attributing mass to phlogiston. Once phlogiston was believed to have mass, the oxidation or calcination of metals came to represent a serious problem for the theory.

Two main theories were advanced to explain the weight gain of calx. The first was that phlogiston was so light that it had the property of "levity," which made substances less dense. Thus, as phlogiston left a metal, the metal became denser and therefore weighed more. This explanation involved a common misunderstanding about the difference between weight and density, however: An increase in density does not change the weight of a given amount of a substance. Also, the oxidized form of a metal is actually less, not more, dense than the original pure metal.

The second theory involved ascribing a negative weight to phlogiston. If phlogiston's weight were negative, then removing phlogiston from a metal would indeed increase the weight of the resulting calx. Even in the eighteenth century, however, this explanation was considered outlandish by most chemists, and it remains a source of ridicule in many modern discussions of the theory. Those who rejected both these explanations yet still chose to accept the theory typically considered the phenomenon a mystery to be solved at a later time.

Doubts about the phlogiston theory gradually became more widespread in the last few decades of the eighteenth century, dividing chemists into two opposing camps, phlogistonists and antiphlogistonists. Joseph Priestley was the most prominent of the phlogistonists, defending the theory until his death in 1804. In one of his most famous experiments, he heated some calx of lead (mercuric oxide) in a closed container and found that the air released by the calx caused a candle to burn more vigorously and that a mouse placed in the container could breathe longer than when placed in normal air. Priestley called the air inside the container "dephlogisticated air": He assumed that, by heating lead calx, he had removed phlogiston from normal air and caused it to be reabsorbed by the calx. In fact, rather than removing something from the air, Priestley had added to it when the heated mercuric oxide gave off oxygen.

Antoine-Laurent Lavoisier, the most prominent antiphlogistonist, believed that calcination produced a weight gain in metals because something in the air combined with the metal. He repeated the experiments of Priestley, interpreting the change in the lead calx as the loss of a gas into the air. This explanation solved the problem of

1720's

weight gain experienced by metals when calcinated: Lavoisier reasoned that the same gas that a calcinated metal released had bonded to it when it was originally calcinated, and the weight of the gas had been added to the weight of the pure metal at that time. Lavoisier named this new gas "oxygen." Although Lavoisier was never able to dissuade Priestley from believing in phlogiston, he did convince most other chemists of his day that the theory needed to be discarded.

By the end of the eighteenth century, most chemists had discarded the phlogiston theory in favor of Lavoisier's oxygen theory. The existence of oxygen could explain the same phenomena as phlogiston, without the latter theory's serious flaws. Weight loss during combustion was due to oxygen in the burned substance joining together with carbon to form carbon dioxide, a gas given off as a by-product. In the case of metals, for which combustion caused weight gain, oxygen joined together with the metal to form a new material, the calx form of the metal. This process of metal bonding with oxygen is now known as "oxidation." A metal calx could be converted back to its pure form by heating it with charcoal, which catalyzed the release of oxygen from the metal atoms. Even respiration was easily explained once oxygen was recognized as the component of air that gets used up in the respiration process and carbon dioxide was found to be the gas that is exhaled in that process.

SIGNIFICANCE

Some philosophers of science consider the phlogiston theory a serious setback for chemistry in the eighteenth century. Because of its roots in alchemy and its proponents' blindness to the theory's deficiencies, progress in experimental chemistry was stalled. One reason for this stalemate was that the theory was developed at a time when chemistry was primarily qualitative, so few chemists were aware that metals gained weight when calcinated, or if they were aware did not recognize the significance of the weight gain.

Throughout the eighteenth century, chemistry became progressively more quantitative, which brought the weight gain problem to the forefront of the field, encouraging chemists to look for alternative theories. Consequently, some philosophers of science consider the phlogiston theory a useful step in the development of modern chemistry that helped highlight the importance of quantitative experimentation. Moreover, the theory was in many ways the first systematic theory of modern chemistry, and, despite ultimately being discredited, it represented a transitional paradigm between those of the Mid-

dle Ages and Renaissance and those of the nineteenth and twentieth centuries.

—*Bryan D. Ness*

FURTHER READING

Conant, James Bryant. *The Overthrow of the Phlogiston Theory: The Chemical Revolution of 1775-1789*. Cambridge, Mass.: Harvard University Press, 1967. An analysis of the fall of the phlogiston theory with special emphasis on it as an example of a paradigm shift.

Djerassi, Carl, and Roald Hoffmann. *Oxygen*. Weinheim, Germany: Wiley-VCH Verlag, 2001. A play using the discovery of oxygen as its theme.

Donovan, Arthur. *Antoine Lavoisier: Science, Administration, and Revolution*. New York: Cambridge University Press, 1996. A comprehensive biography of Lavoisier with ample discussion of his debunking of the phlogiston theory.

Golinski, Jan. *Science as Public Culture: Chemistry and Enlightenment in Britain, 1760-1820*. New York: Cambridge University Press, 1992. Focuses on the history of chemistry in England during the period of the fall of the phlogiston theory.

Kuhn, Thomas S. *The Structure of Scientific Revolutions*. 3d ed. Chicago: University of Chicago Press, 1996. Kuhn's seminal text discusses the phlogiston and oxygen theories as examples of competing paradigms and explains why the latter replaced the former.

McCann, H. Gilman. *Chemistry Transformed: The Paradigmatic Shift from Phlogiston to Oxygen*. Norwood, N.J.: Ablex, 1978. Follows up on the work of Kuhn to provide in-depth analysis of the eighteenth century paradigm shift in chemistry.

Partington, James Riddick, and Douglas McKie. *Historical Studies on the Phlogiston Theory*. New York: Arno Press, 1981. A reprint of papers from the *Annals of Science* reviewing several aspects of the phlogiston theory.

Yount, Lisa. *Antoine Lavoisier: Founder of Modern Chemistry*. Berkeley Heights, N.J.: Enslow, 1997. Book about Lavoisier written for high school students.

SEE ALSO: 1714: Fahrenheit Develops the Mercury Thermometer; 1718: Geoffroy Issues the *Table of Reactivities*; 1722: Réaumur Discovers Carbon's Role in Hardening Steel; 1738: Bernoulli Proposes the Kinetic Theory of Gases; 1748: Nollet Discovers Osmosis; June 5, 1755: Black Identifies Carbon Dioxide; Aug. 1, 1774: Priestley Discovers Oxygen; 1779: Ingenhousz Discovers Photosynthesis; 1781-1784:

Cavendish Discovers the Composition of Water; 1786-1787: Lavoisier Devises the Modern System of Chemical Nomenclature; c. 1794-1799: Proust Establishes the Law of Definite Proportions.

RELATED ARTICLES in *Great Lives from History: The Eighteenth Century, 1701-1800*: Joseph Black; Henry Cavendish; Antoine-Laurent Lavoisier; Joseph Priestley; Georg Ernst Stahl.

1724
FOUNDATION OF THE ST. PETERSBURG ACADEMY OF SCIENCES

As part of his program to Westernize and modernize Russian culture, Peter the Great founded an academy of sciences on the model of the British Royal Society and the French Academy of Sciences.

LOCALE: St. Petersburg, Russia

CATEGORIES: Organizations and institutions; science and technology; education; cultural and intellectual history

KEY FIGURES

Peter the Great (1672-1725), czar of Russia, r. 1682-1725

Yury Krizhanich (1618-1683), Russian scientist and intellectual

Gottfried Wilhelm Leibniz (1646-1716), German philosopher

Henry Farquharson (1675-1739), Scottish educator and mathematician

Feofan Prokopovich (1681-1736), Danish minister and scholar

SUMMARY OF EVENT

In the early eighteenth century, Russia was significantly behind its Western counterparts in appreciating and understanding the great advances of the Scientific Revolution and the Enlightenment. Earlier in its history, Russia had been cut off from the advances of the Renaissance by a Mongol occupation. The Mongols, nomadic warriors, instituted a policy of absolute rule that was ruthlessly enforced by a brutal secret police force that forbade any contact with the West.

When the Mongols were finally driven from Russia, the anti-intellectual environment they had fostered was extended by the Russian Orthodox Church. The power of the Church rested on the belief that Moscow was the inheritor of the Christian theological purity that had been passed down from Rome and Constantinople. Moscow, as the "Third Rome," was regarded by the leaders of the Russian hierarchy as the seat of orthodoxy in the Christian world, and the Church rejected the study of any subjects that could possibly challenge their literal Christian worldview.

The Orthodox clergy, like their Mongol counterparts years earlier, blocked the dissemination of the Enlightenment ideas that both the universe and society were governed by natural laws and that it was part of God's divine plan for humankind to discover these laws through scientific research and inquiry. The writings of Francis Bacon, René Descartes, Sir Isaac Newton, and Antoni van Leeuwenhoek were unavailable to Russian scholars, and the nation's educational system and military establishment suffered from a lack of modern scientific and technological knowledge. Most important, there had developed over time a deep anti-intellectual bias within Russian culture, especially among the nobility, who completely rejected the need for formal education.

The individual who had the greatest impact on reforming the Russian educational system and creating the necessary environment for the establishment of the St. Petersburg Academy of Sciences was Czar Peter the Great. Deadly palace intrigues forced Peter as a young boy to take refuge in a suburb of Moscow that was inhabited by a large number of Europeans, especially Germans. There, in academic discussions and tutorials, the future czar was exposed to the potential intellectual power of the Enlightenment.

Peter was introduced to the writings of Yury Krizhanich, who had been an early voice in the Russian intellectual wilderness, writing a number of essays demanding a radical intellectual change in Russian civilization. He believed in absolute rule, but he also insisted it was the primary duty of the ruling family, the Romanovs, to make the necessary changes needed to bring the nation into the modern world. Most important, he believed that the Romanovs had to establish their supremacy over every aspect of Russian culture, especially the Russian Orthodox Church. If the church was not made subordinate to the state, the new advancements of the Scientific Revolution and the Enlightenment would never be allowed to flourish within Russian society. Krizhanich also emphasized the importance of social mobility, of providing the best and the brightest with the opportunity to attain positions of power and prestige based upon talent and drive, not upon their ancestry.

Another turning point in Peter's quest to establish Russia as a scientific power was his trip to Western Europe. There, he was able to experience at first hand the impact of the new scientific culture on the nations of the region. The most important person Peter met on this journey was the great Christian philosopher Gottfried Wilhelm Leibniz, whom he befriended. Their meeting would initiate a long and important correspondence that would have a profound effect on the czar's effort to establish an academy of science. Leibniz was a profoundly religious man who viewed the transformation of Russia as an important part of God's divine plan for the world. He believed God gave humankind intelligence in order to improve the human condition. He was a firm believer in the Christian and Enlightenment concept of the perfectibility of humanity.

Leibniz's view of Russia reflected the optimistic Enlightenment idea of tabula rasa popularized by John Locke. According to this belief, Russian culture was a "blank slate" (*tabula rasa*) that could be molded into a successful nation through the proper application of Enlightenment ideas. Leibniz also thought Russia occupied an important geopolitical location, connecting Western Europe and China. This was a period of widespread missionary activity in China, and the philosopher believed that the transformation of Russia would create a new Christendom that would stretch across much of the Eurasian landmass. He also viewed this as an opportunity to acquaint Western civilization with the scientific accomplishments of China.

Leibniz's plan to reform Russia was based upon the creation of a central library system, which would also house a national printing press, along with a complete overhaul of the national educational system. A nationwide system of elementary and secondary schools would focus on moral and civic education. Elementary mathematics, science, history, and literature would also be used to prepare the finest students to study at the postsecondary level. The universities would expand upon these academic disciplines and have as their main focus the training of an educated elite to run the Russian governmental bureaucracy. Finally, an academy of sciences would be established, where Russia's most prestigious scholars would carry on high-level research and make it available to the nation and the world by publishing their work in academic journals and books.

Initially both the universities and the scientific academy would be made up of mostly foreign scholars, whose goal would be to develop the first two generations of Russian academics. Leibniz emphasized that the Academy of Sciences would play the most significant part in Russian civilization. He also believed that the universities and the academy should be independent of all interference by both the government and the Church.

Peter's first step in setting this plan into motion was to acquire the services of the renowned European mathematician, Henry Farquharson. Under his leadership, a number of scientifically oriented schools, eventually including the Russian Naval Academy, were created. These educational institutions emphasized the study of Enlightenment scientific thought, and Farquharson had a number of important mathematical and scientific books translated into Russian. His standards were extremely high, and he never wavered from his educational model. His most important contribution to Russian scientific culture was the establishment of the use of Hindu-Arabic numerals. This would allow potential scholars to follow exactly the work of the great Enlightenment scientists and mathematicians.

Peter was able to challenge the reactionary Church establishment through the appointment of a Danish minister and scholar, Feofan Prokopovich, as the head of the nation's seminaries. Prokopovich was a respected academic who integrated new scientific discoveries into his theological curriculum. He forced his students to reconcile such important discoveries as Nicolaus Copernicus's heliocentric theory with their literal religious beliefs.

Resting on this solid foundation, Peter set into motion a series of decrees that led to the establishment of the St. Petersburg Academy of Sciences in 1724. Even though he died before the first set of scholars began to arrive in 1725, it was his clear vision, energy, and focus that brought the academy into existence. This reality was immortalized in a eulogy given on his behalf at the Paris Académie des Sciences praising his great work in opening Russia to the ideals of the Enlightenment.

SIGNIFICANCE

The first years of the St. Petersburg Academy of Sciences reflected the overall uncertainties of the Russian nation in the period following Peter's death. Russian society was yet unready fully to accept a rigorous scientific establishment like the St. Petersburg Academy. The culture of anti-intellectualism still dominated the Russian nobility and was in fact exacerbated by the widespread resentment of the infusion of what were perceived as German scientific ideas into Russian culture.

Over time, especially through the impact of the German-born empress Catherine the Great, the Russian intelligentsia would accept western scientific attitudes. The St. Petersburg Academy of Sciences created the foundation of the powerful Russian (and later Soviet) scientific community that at its zenith would count among its members some of the best theoretical mathematicians and physicists in the world.

—*Richard D. Fitzgerald*

FURTHER READING

Josephson, Paul. *Physics and Politics in Revolutionary Russia*. Berkeley: University of California Press, 1991. The early chapters contain an excellent overview of the impact of the legacy of the St. Petersburg Academy on the development of Russian physics. Index, charts.

Vucinich, Alexander. *Empire of Knowledge: The Academy of Sciences of the USSR*. Berkeley: University of

California Press, 1984. The first chapter has an excellent description of the legacy of both Peter I and the Enlightenment on the development of the St. Petersburg Academy. Index.

_____. *Science in Culture: A History to 1860*. Stanford, Calif.: Stanford University Press, 1963. The best single overview of early Russian science. Index.

SEE ALSO: c. 1701-1721: Great Northern War; May 27, 1703: Founding of St. Petersburg; Aug. 3, 1713: Founding of the Spanish Academy; 1721-1750: Early Enlightenment in France; May 15, 1738: Foundation of St. Petersburg's Imperial Ballet School; 1745: Lomonosov Issues the First Catalog of Minerals; Aug. 10, 1767: Catherine the Great's Instruction.

RELATED ARTICLES in *Great Lives from History: The Eighteenth Century, 1701-1800*: Catherine the Great; Peter the Great.

1725
FLAMSTEED'S STAR CATALOG MARKS THE TRANSITION TO MODERN ASTRONOMY

John Flamsteed's catalog, and later atlas, of the locations of the stars more than doubled the number of stars accurately charted and established a standard used for more than a century by navigators and theoretical cosmologists.

LOCALE: London, England
CATEGORIES: Astronomy; science and technology

KEY FIGURES

John Flamsteed (1646-1719), England's first astronomer royal
Tycho Brahe (1546-1601), a Danish astronomer
Margaret Flamsteed (1670-1730), John Flamsteed's assistant and spouse, who supervised the publication of his posthumous works
Edmond Halley (1656-1742), an English astronomer
Abraham Sharp (1651-1742) an English astronomer, who assisted Flamsteed at the Royal Observatory, Greenwich
Joseph Crosthwait (fl. 1708-1728), another of Flamsteed's assistants

SUMMARY OF EVENT

In 1725, a definitive catalog of the stars visible from Greenwich, England, appeared in three massive volumes titled *Historia coelestis Britannica* (*British Catalogue of*

the Heavens, partial translation, 1982). A fourth volume, *Atlas coelestis Britannica*, containing star charts, was published in 1729 in English. These books represented the life's work of John Flamsteed, England's first astronomer royal. Unfinished at his death in 1719, the catalog was prepared for publication by Flamsteed's assistants, Abraham Sharp and Joseph Crosthwait, and his spouse, Margaret Flamsteed, who persevered despite financial setbacks and a lack of support from Flamsteed's successor, astronomer Edmond Halley.

The first two volumes of *Historia coelestis Britannica* offered a detailed record of all of the observations made by Flamsteed at Derby and Greenwich between 1673 and 1713; the third volume was a catalog of the positions of more than three thousand stars visible from Greenwich. The star catalog represented a twofold increase in numbers beyond the catalog produced by Tycho Brahe more than a century earlier, with a corresponding increase in the precision with which the relative positions of the stars were recorded.

Flamsteed's work as astronomer royal marked the final emancipation of observational astronomy from its astrological and theological roots. Brahe's support depended on supplying horoscopes to his princely patron. The English amateur astronomer Jeremiah Horrocks, whose posthumous works Flamsteed helped edit, published landmark lunar observations in almanac form, coupling the lunar data with advice about human affairs. Flamsteed's earliest work, a lunar ephemeris, was rejected by the publisher because it lacked astrological advice and thus, the publisher reasoned, would not sell.

King Charles II established the Royal Observatory, Greenwich, in 1675 and authorized Flamsteed's salary as first astronomer royal with a quite different and wholly scientific aim: to produce an accurate chart of the heavens for navigational purposes. There was also an element of national pride involved in this first "space race." The French, under King Louis XIV, had recently established a national observatory in Paris, and the English were loath to cede preeminence in knowledge of the heavens.

In an age of rapid colonial expansion, accurate determination of longitude was becoming critical to navigators. The most promising avenues for doing so involved finding the time difference between a ship's position and some fixed point, the challenge being to determine accurately, at a remote location, what time it was in England. The position of the Moon relative to stars, and eclipses of the moons of Jupiter, potentially afforded the requisite accuracy, but existing star charts and records of the lunar orbit were clearly inadequate. To produce an adequate chart required years of observation, using instrumentation that was constantly being refined.

The key to Flamsteed's observations was a 7-foot mural arc, permanently oriented north-south along the Greenwich meridian and equipped with a telescopic sight. The size of the arc allowed for accurate calibration of angles, and the provision of a telescopic sight both increased the precision of alignment and permitted observation of stars not visible to the naked eye. Obtaining the data was a laborious process, particularly as visibility was best on clear winter nights when temperatures in the unroofed observatory room fell far below freezing. In addition to systematically cataloging stars, Flamsteed charted paths of the Moon and planets, obtained data on the precession of equinoxes, and made observations on the comets of 1680 and 1681 that enabled him to correctly deduce that the two comets were actually one celestial body orbiting around the Sun. Flamsteed's figures allowed Edmond Halley to calculate the comet's orbit and predict the periodic return of the comet that bears Halley's name.

Contemporaries questioned Flamsteed's discovery of stellar parallax, but his assertions were subsequently vindicated. Theoretical astronomers argued that if the Earth did indeed revolve around the Sun, and the stars were positioned at varying (albeit vast) distances from Earth, the brightest stars should appear to shift position relative to

the fainter and more distant ones when viewed from opposite sides of the Earth's orbit. The apparent absence of this shift led Brahe to conclude that the Earth did not revolve around the Sun, and led Sir Isaac Newton to conclude that apparent brightness of stars was not a function of distance. Flamsteed believed he had detected a shift due to parallax in the position of Sirius, and that this provided conclusive evidence that the Earth orbited the Sun. To counter critics who faulted the optics of his telescope, he made similar observations on candles shining through pinholes, showing that he could indeed measure a small parallax involving a faint light source.

Flamsteed's meticulous observations on the Moon's orbit were sought by Newton, who needed the data to check calculations based on his own gravitational theory. Newton was then working on the three-body problem, trying to characterize mathematically the complex trajectory of an object acted upon by two distinct gravitational sources. At first, Flamsteed supplied his figures freely, but he became less candid after some of them appeared in print without acknowledgment and others that were only tentative appeared prematurely. A bitter conflict, known as the astronomy wars, developed between Flamsteed, Newton, and Halley, profoundly affecting the completion and publication of Flamsteed's research.

In 1704, Flamsteed was compelled by Queen Anne and the Royal Society to produce his findings, but he did not believe that he had accumulated enough accurate measurements to produce a publishable catalog. Queen Anne's consort, Prince George of Denmark, agreed to underwrite the costs of publication. Unfortunately, the prince died before much had been accomplished, and the project fell under the direction of the Royal Society of London, of which Newton was president. Frustrated with what he saw as Flamsteed's obstructionism, Newton furnished Halley with a copy of Flamsteed's rough notes, from which Halley produced an abbreviated version of *Historia coelestis Britannica* in 1712. Flamsteed was so outraged that upon a change of government following Queen Anne's death in 1714, he obtained as many copies of the 1712 volume as he could find and burned them in public.

Flamsteed had nearly finished the first volume of the complete *Historia coelestis Britannica* at the time of his death in 1719. Upon his death, all of his papers, as well as the instruments he personally purchased or constructed for the Greenwich Observatory, passed to his wife and assistant, Margaret Flamsteed, and to his adopted niece's husband. Under Margaret's editorial direction Flamsteed's former assistants, Joseph Crosthwait and Abra-

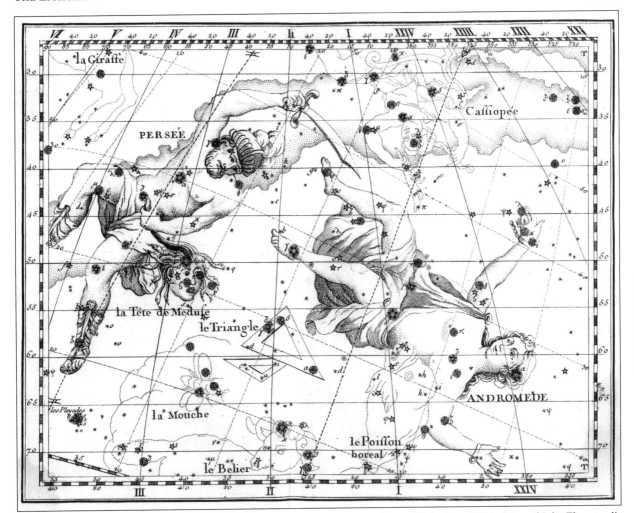

A celestial map including the constellations Andromeda, Perseus, and Triangulum, published in a 1776 edition of John Flamsteed's star catalog. (Library of Congress)

ham Sharp, completed the task of preparing a monumental body of data for publication in the form their mentor envisioned, despite lack of pay after Margaret lost most of her modest fortune after the collapse of the South Sea Bubble in 1720.

SIGNIFICANCE

John Flamsteed's star catalog set a standard for comprehensiveness and accuracy that lasted for nearly a century. A compact French edition of the atlas became the standard mariner's guide to the heavens. The catalog contained few innovations in theoretical astronomy, but it laid a foundation without which subsequent discoveries would not have been possible. It firmly established the importance of telescopic sights in mapping the heavens,

and showed what could be accomplished with the equipment available in the early eighteenth century.

An accurate star chart and detailed accounts of the lunar orbit and eclipses of the moons of Jupiter proved to be of limited practical use in determining longitude at sea, because of the difficulty of making precise observations on a moving deck, with a hand-held sextant, under less than optimal atmospheric conditions. John Harrison's invention (1735) of the chronometer—a timepiece that remained accurate on long voyages—rendered shipboard calculation of longitude from the lunar orbit unnecessary. Calculations of longitude using the stars was used, however, for determining the longitude of land-based observatories, and these, in turn, served to recalibrate chronometers during long voyages.

Thus, the Royal Observatory, Greenwich, and Flamsteed's labors failed in their original, limited aim, but while doing so opened the universe to a new generation of astronomers and established Greenwich as the zero, or prime, meridian, the center around which celestial navigation is organized.

—*Martha A. Sherwood*

FURTHER READING

Clark, David H. *Newton's Tyranny: The Suppressed Scientific Discoveries of Stephen Gray and John Flamsteed.* New York: W. H. Freeman, 2000. A thorough account of Flamsteed's discoveries and a discussion of the importance of practical astronomy.

Cook, Alan. *Edmond Halley: Charting the Heavens and the Seas.* Oxford, England: Clarendon Press, 1998. A good description of astronomical instrumentation in the early eighteenth century. Also, this work examines the reasons for the insistence on accurate measurement.

Richardson, Robert S. *The Star Lovers.* New York: Macmillan, 1967. Includes nonscholarly accounts of work of Tycho Brahe, Jeremiah Horrocks, and Edmond Halley.

Wilmoth, Frances, ed. *Flamsteed's Stars: New Perspectives on the Life and Work of the First Astronomer Royal, 1646-1719.* Suffolk, England: Boydell Press and the National Maritime Museum, 1997. A collection of conference papers, with a chapter on optics that is valuable for perspectives on the practical limitations of the equipment used in Flamsteed's time.

SEE ALSO: 1704: Newton Publishes *Optics*; 1704-1712: Astronomy Wars in England; 1705: Halley Predicts the Return of a Comet; 1714-1762: Quest for Longitude; 1729: Gray Discovers Principles of Electric Conductivity; 1748: Bradley Discovers the Nutation of Earth's Axis; 1752-Mar., 1756: Mayer's Lunar Tables Enable Mariners to Determine Longitude at Sea; 1787: Herschel Begins Building His Reflecting Telescope; 1796: Laplace Articulates His Nebular Hypothesis.

RELATED ARTICLES in *Great Lives from History: The Eighteenth Century, 1701-1800*: Queen Anne; Caroline Lucretia Herschel; William Herschel.

1725-November, 1794
PERSIAN CIVIL WARS

As the Ṣafavid Empire weakened in the seventeenth century, tribal leaders fought one another for control of Persia. Political stability was maintained intermittently under Nādir Shāh and later under the benevolent rule of Karīm Khān Zand. Periods of anarchy nevertheless marked much of the eighteenth century until the establishment of the Qājār Dynasty in 1794 finally brought a stable government to Persia.

LOCALE: Persia (now Iran)
CATEGORIES: Wars, uprisings, and civil unrest; government and politics

KEY FIGURES
Mahmud Ghilzai (d. 1725), Afghan conqueror, r. 1716-1725, and shāh of Persia, r. 1722-1725
Ṭahmāsp II (d. 1739), shāh of Persia, r. 1722-1732
Fatḥ ʿAlī Khān (d. c. 1730), Persian general and regent under Ṭahmāsp
Nādir Shāh (1688-1747), shāh of Persia, r. 1736-1747
Shāh Rukh (d. 1796), ruler of Khorasan, nominal shāh of Persia, r. 1748-1796, and grandson of Nādir Shāh
Karīm Khān Zand (c. 1705-1779), *vakil* of Persia and founder of the Zand Dynasty, r. 1751-1779

Muḥammad Ḥasan Khān (d. 1759), Qājārī military leader
Āzād Khān (fl. 1760's), Azerbaijani military leader
Zaki Khān (d. 1779), brother of Karīm Khān Zand who seized power briefly in Shīrāz, r. 1779
ʿAlī Mūrad Khān (d. 1785), member of the Hazara line of the Zand who seized Eṣfahān, r. 1782-1785
Jaʿfar Khān (d. 1789), nephew of Karīm Khān Zand who seized power in Eṣfahān, r. 1785-1789
Lotf ʿAlī Khān Zand (1769-1794), descendant of the Zand tribe who seized power in Eṣfahān, r. 1789-1794
Āghā Moḥammad Khān (1742-1797), first shāh in the Qājār Dynasty, r. 1796-1797
Fatḥ ʿAlī Shāh (1771-1834), shāh of Persia, r. 1797-1834

SUMMARY OF EVENT

After the fall of the Ṣafavid Dynasty, marked by the Afghan siege of Eṣfahān in 1722, Persia fell into a state of dissolution. Russians attacked from the north, Ottoman Turks attacked from the west, and the Afghans consolidated their positions in the south and east. Ṭahmāsp II, the third son of the Ṣafavid king Ḥusayn I, had escaped from Eṣfahān during the siege, and after the city's fall he proclaimed himself king in Qazvīn. He managed to maintain authority in the central and Caspian regions only with the aid of Qājār chief Fatḥ ʿAlī Khān.

Ṭahmāsp stayed in power for several years, largely because of a split between the Afghans in Eṣfahān and those in Qandahār caused by the assassination of Mahmud Ghilzai in 1725. Ashraf, the Afghan shāh in Eṣfahān, was left without ample troops and unable to pursue the Ṣafavid heir, and enmity between Russia and Turkey held those two forces at bay temporarily. In 1726, Nādir Khān, a member of the Afshar tribe, joined Ṭahmāsp II's army, and soon he was recruited as a protector to the king along with Fatḥ ʿAlī Khān and his troops. As Persia was in the process of being dismembered by the Ottomans and Russians, Ṭahmāsp designated Nādir Khān his military commander, and because of his military successes, Nādir was able to oust Fatḥ ʿAlī from his position at court and have him executed.

By 1736, Nādir had inflicted several defeats on the Afghans and had succeeded in driving the Turks out of northwest Iran. On the plains of Mughan, he was proclaimed shāh of Iran, ushering in a period of political stability. This stability ended after the death of Nādir Shāh in 1747, when the kingdom degenerated into anarchy. Nādir's various relatives struggled to maintain power, until his grandson Shāh Rukh sought to unite these disparate forces under his rule. However, Shāh Rukh was blinded by Mirza Sayyid Muḥammad, a distant relative of the Ṣafavids who feared that Shāh Rukh would promote his grandfather's pro-Sunni agenda. As a result, the period of turmoil was resolved in a fierce struggle between Muḥammad Ḥasan Khān, the head of the Qājār tribe in the north, and Karīm Khān Zand, leader of the Zand tribe in the south.

Karīm Khān was victorious. Taking the title of *vakil* (regent) to a child he placed on the throne as Esmāʿīl III, Karīm Khān ruled over a peaceful kingdom from his capital at Shīrāz for almost thirty years between 1751 and 1779. First, however, Karīm had to defend Eṣfahān against a series of claimants, including the Qājār Muḥammad Ḥasan Khān, the Afshar Fatḥ ʿAlī, and the Afghan Āzād Khān. During a fierce struggle for the throne, Muḥammad Ḥasan was murdered by his own tribesmen in 1759. Fatḥ ʿAlī and Āzād Khān were soon forced to join forces with Karīm in 1763 and 1765 respectively. Though he emerged as the undisputed ruler of Persia, Karīm had to defend against revolts from local rulers and tribes in Khūzestān, Kuh-i Giluya, Kermān, Fārs, and the Persian Gulf and to defeat Ḥusayn Kuli

Qājār in Astarabad and Māzandarān. Nonetheless, his rule eventually brought a period of peace to Persia.

The death of Karīm Khān Zand was followed by another fifteen years of anarchy. On Karīm's death, Āghā Moḥammad Khān escaped from imprisonment in Shīrāz and began to consolidate power in Astarabad. Because Karīm had failed to make provisions for his succession, his sons were exploited in a brutal struggle for power between Karīm's brothers and cousins. His brother Zaki Khān executed most of his rivals for the throne before Karīm Khān's funeral.

Zaki ruled in Shīrāz in the name of Karīm's son, Muḥammad ʿAlī. ʿAlī Mūrad Khān, a member of the Hazara line of the Zand tribe, seized Eṣfahān in the name of Karīm's son Abū'l Fath. Before Zaki could reach Eṣfahān to contest the seat, he was murdered by one of his own soldiers. In the meantime, another brother of Karīm, Sadik Khān, took Shīrāz in 1780, only to be killed by ʿAlī Mūrad as he claimed the city in the following year. In turn, ʿAlī Mūrad was killed on his way back to Eṣfahān after a battle with the Qājārs in the north.

From this point on, the Zands relinquished control of northern Persia to the Qājārs. Sadik's son Jaʿfar Khān was driven from Eṣfahān to Shīrāz on two accounts by Āghā Moḥammad Khān and was ultimately poisoned and beheaded in 1789. Jaʿfar's eldest son, Loṭf ʿAlī Khān Zand, sought refuge and reinforcements, and, aided by the local mayor Hājjī Ibrahim, he secured the capital. He managed to defend the city against a Qājār assault and to take back his former stronghold at Kermān.

In 1791, Loṭf ʿAlī marched on Eṣfahān; however, in the meantime, Hājjī Ibrahim had fomented a mutiny in his army and seized control of Shīrāz. In 1792, Āghā Moḥammad entered Shīrāz, and Loṭf ʿAlī was driven from his refuge in Kermān, where the Qājārs killed or blinded the entire male population in retaliation for their decision to shelter their enemy. Eventually, Loṭf ʿAlī was handed over by the governor of Bam, and Āghā Moḥammad had him tortured and executed in Tehran in November of 1794.

From this turmoil, the Qājār Dynasty emerged, ending not only the Zand line but also the rule of the Afshars in Khorāsān. In 1796, Āghā Moḥammad Khān was crowned shāh in Tehran, bringing the whole country under his authority. One year later, he was assassinated by two of his own servants; however, the accession of his nephew Fatḥ ʿAlī Shāh established the Qājār Dynasty, which would rule until 1925.

SIGNIFICANCE

Constituting decades of intermittent warfare, the Persian Civil Wars effectively ended a century of dissolute rule. Karīm Khān Zand succeeded in welding together an army from pastoral tribes and managed to form alliances among the bureaucrats and magnates of major cities such as Eṣfahān, Shīrāz, Tabrīz, and Kermān. The years preceding and following his rule, however, were rife with turmoil. His failure to designate a successor left the region open to two decades of internecine warfare and anarchy, which was subdued only with the establishment of the Qājār Dynasty. Though the reign of Āghā Moḥammad Khān was short-lived, he founded the line that would usher in Persia's modern era. From the close of the eighteenth century through the nineteenth century, Persia was unified under the Qājār Dynasty, shifting the locus of power from feuding tribal confederations to a centralized monarchy and renewing the imperial splendor last witnessed in the Ṣafavid court.

—*Anna Sloan*

FURTHER READING

Avery, Peter, Gavin Hambly, and Charles Melville, eds. *From Nadir Shah to the Islamic Republic.* Vol. 7 in *The Cambridge History of Iran.* New York: Cambridge University Press, 1991. The most comprehensive source on political developments between the fall of the Ṣafavid Dynasty and the rise of the Qājār Dynasty. Contains plates, maps, illustrations, genealogical tables, and a rich bibliography.

Daniel, Elton L. *The History of Iran.* Westport, Conn.: Greenwood Press, 2001. A general survey, which locates Karīm Khān's rule in the broader scope of Persia's history. Contains maps, a glossary of terms, and current bibliographical essay.

Perry, John R. *Karim Khan Zand: A History of Iran, 1747-1779.* Publications of the Center for Middle Eastern Studies 12. Chicago: University of Chicago Press, 1979. Among the most thorough sources on the events of the eighteenth century. Incorporates the chief Persian histories and contains a comprehensive bibliography of primary and secondary sources from both premodern and modern eras. Contains maps and illustrations.

_____. "Zand." In *The Encyclopedia of Islam*, edited by H. A. R. Gibb. Vol. 11. Rev. ed. New York: Brill, 2002. Synopsis of scholarship on the era of Karīm Khān Zand's rule and the struggles that followed his death. Includes a thorough bibliography complete with sources published in Persian.

SEE ALSO: 1709-1747: Persian-Afghan Wars.

RELATED ARTICLES in *Great Lives from History: The Eighteenth Century, 1701-1800*: Karīm Khān Zand; Nādir Shāh.

October, 1725
VICO PUBLISHES *THE NEW SCIENCE*

Vico viewed the state as emerging from primitive origins rather than reasoned philosophical argument, and his "new science" developed this thesis in analyses of both ideas and language.

LOCALE: Naples (now in Italy)
CATEGORIES: Philosophy; literature

KEY FIGURE

Giambattista Vico (1668-1744), Italian philosopher

SUMMARY OF EVENT

Giambattista Vico's *Principi di scienza nuova intorno alla natura delle nazioni per la quale si ritruovano i principi di altro sistema del diritto naturale delle genti* (1725, revised edition 1730; revised and enlarged as *Principi di scienza nuova d'intorno alla comune natura delle nazioni*, 1744; commonly known as *Scienza nuova*; *The New Science*, 1948) went through several revised editions. Collectively referred to as *The New Science*, they are sometimes now also called *The First New Science* (1725), *The Second New Science* (1730 and 1744), and *The Third New Science* (1744). By "new science," Vico refers to a form of political historiography.

Vico's *The New Science* is a study of the principles by which "the natural law of the nations" evolved via the nations' common customs from a "divine era" through a "heroic era" to a "human era." He divides this study into five major parts; book 1, justifying his form of analysis; book 2, "The Principles of This Science Concerning Ideas"; book 3, "The Principles of This Science Concerning Language"; the brief book 4, "The Ground of the Proofs That Establish This Science"; and book 5, which explains the simultaneous formation of a philosophy of history and a universal history of nations, a crucial aspect of Vico's theory.

Vico saw in history a pattern of development through

three phases common to all nations. This pattern exists, Vico asserted, because a beneficent Providence oversees humanity and fosters in people a common sense that enables them to seek justice through their free will. Vico used as one template of the universal pattern of history the evolution of ancient Egyptian society, which the Egyptians themselves understood to be divided into ages of gods, heroes, and men. Vico insisted that "the principles of this world must be discovered within the nature of our human mind and through the force of our understanding, by means of a metaphysics of the human mind"; he was convinced, moreover, that philosophical visions are always expressions of their historical context.

The first phase of the historical development of nations, according to Vico, was a primitive era marked by barbarous people whose ignorance led them to fear divine forces in the natural world. In this religious period, the first peoples "ramified" into clans tied by blood, each with its own language. The spiritual shame that men felt copulating under the open sky prompted them to drag their women into caves, leading eventually to the institution of marriage.

Vico maintains that the "unity of God" is proven by the idea of one universal God that grew over time out of the gods of the individual nations, but he is careful not to identify this universal God with Christianity, since his universal law is meant to apply to non-Christian nations as well as Christian ones. He says that "the people of God divided the world into Hebrews and gentiles," but Vico leaves the historical process vague. The third great feature of the first phase of development, along with a belief in the divine and the establishment of marriage, was burial of the dead and cultivation of the nearby fields as property to be defended against thieves.

The second, heroic phase of national development entailed a division of a region's populace into noble aristocrats (the "intelligent") and the "base" commoners (those of "feeble mind"). The aristocrats displayed the "civil arts," defined by Vico as self-consciousness, chastity in marriage, and piety toward the dead. Industrious cultivation of their fields produced the riches of the peo-

---

VICO AND ANCIENT HISTORY

Giambattista Vico begins The New Science *with a chronological table meant to illustrate the extent to which ancient history is based on myth rather than reality and to support his argument that mythology and fable are the proper objects of study for understanding the beginnings of history. In the passage excerpted here, he explains the inaccuracy of the table and the purpose of including it at the beginning of his work.*

This Chronological Table sets forth in outline the world of the ancient nations, starting from the universal flood and passing from the Hebrews through the Chaldeans, Scythians, Phoenicians, Egyptians, Greeks, and Romans down to the Second Carthaginian War. On it there appear men and deeds of the greatest renown, assigned to certain times and places by the community of scholars. These men and deeds either did not have their being at the times or in the places to which they have been commonly assigned, or never existed at all. On the other hand, from the long dark shadows where they have lain buried, notable men and most pertinent deeds emerge, through whom and by which the decisive changes in human institutions have come about. All this is set forth in these Notes, to show how uncertain, unseemly, defective, or vain are the beginnings of the humanity of the nations.

Source: Giambattista Vico, The New Science of Giambattista Vico. *3d ed. (Ithaca, N.Y.: Cornell University Press, 1984), p. 29.*

---

ple, whose strength enabled them to defend their possessions. Their generosity and sense of justice emerged in their concern for the unfortunate. In Greek fables, Vico found "ample evidence" of the origin of nobility, and Roman history provided rich materials for studying the nature of republics. The heroic law of the Romans, whose dominance lasted for 419 years, was for Vico the source of Rome's greatness, and this law in turn derived from the Laws of the Twelve Tables formed by the heroic peoples of Latium.

The final phase in the evolution of nations arose when people realized their equal right to the "utilities." This phase was marked, most notably, by the revelation of the Ten Commandments, "which contain the idea of a universal and eternal justice based upon that of human nature at its most enlightened. . . ." With the growth of popular liberty came monarchical government, "the kind of government that best conforms with the nature of [fully] developed human values."

Vico asserts that human language also evolved through three phases that paralleled the three phases of government. A language of hieroglyphics or sacred characters, "a language of the gods," was followed by a language of "symbols or emblems," evidence for which Vico finds in the heroic language of arms. The last phase was an "epistolary language" with a fixed vocabulary of words for everyday use. In the earliest phase, dominated by poetry, human qualities were attributed to inanimate nature, and "things" ultimately were treated as "intelligent substances": "This is the supreme, divine artifice of the poetic faculty, through which, in a God-like manner, from our own idea we give being to things that lack it."

In expounding his new science, Vico dismissed other philosophies that disagreed with his. Stoicism, for instance, was rejected because of the "iron severity" of its fatalism, and Epicureanism was rejected because of its vision of blind chance and its belief that the soul died with the body. Plato's fault, he said, lay in the common error of attributing to barbaric people the capacity for "exalted, divine and recondite knowledge," thereby forgetting that Providence governs the nations through humanity's common needs. Among the philosophers of his own time, Vico believed that Hugo Grotius, John Selden, and Samuel von Pufendorf failed to grasp that fear of a god originating in their own imaginations was what caused primitive peoples to evolve out of a state of nature.

SIGNIFICANCE

In the late eighteenth century, Vico's theory that human society had feral origins was sharply attacked by the Dominican G. F. Finetti on the grounds that it was a Lucretian, not Christian, theory and threatened Catholic theology. In what became a notorious controversy, Vico was defended by the Neapolitan Emanuele Duni, professor of jurisprudence at the University of Rome. By the nineteenth century, Vico's ideas were generally disseminated throughout Europe, and *The New Science* became the bible of the nationalist leaders of the Italian Risorgimento (unification). Benedetto Croce's study of Vico's thought in 1911 prompted the German philosopher Wilhelm Windelband to add a long note on Vico in his history of philosophy.

The most powerful stimulus to Vico's reputation came in 1824, when the French historian Jules Michelet read *The New Science* and was seized, as he reported, with "an incredible intoxication with his great historical principle." In 1827, Michelet published an abridged translation of *The New Science*, *Principes de la philosophie de l'histoire*, as well as a sketch of Vico's life and work in the *Biographie universelle* (universal biography). Among English intellectuals, Samuel Taylor Coleridge was Vico's most enthusiastic reader, followed by the historian Thomas Arnold and the philosopher John Stuart Mill. The Irish writer James Joyce read Vico

around 1905, and he inserted numerous whimsical allusions to him in his works, especially *Finnegans Wake* (1939). Karl Marx and Friedrich Engels probably incorporated some of Vico's thought into their own theory of historical materialism. In the introduction to their translation of Vico's *Vita di Giambattista Vico scritta da sé medesimo* (wr. 1725-1728, 1731, pb. 1818; *The Autobiography of Giambattista Vico*, 1944), Max Harold Fisch and Thomas Goddard Bergin observe that it is "no accident . . . that Vico enjoys high repute in present-day Russia as the progenitor of the theory of the class struggle."

—Frank Day

FURTHER READING

Bedani, Gino. *Vico Revisited*. New York: Oxford University Press, 1989. Discusses the sources of Vico's philosophy of jurisprudence.

Mali, Joseph. *The Rehabilitation of Myth: Vico's "New Science."* New York: Cambridge University Press, 1992. Examines the value of myth for Vico and his treatment of it in *The New Science*.

Mooney, Michael. *Vico in the Tradition of Rhetoric*. Princeton, N.J.: Princeton University Press, 1985. Influence of humanist scholars on Vico.

Pompa, Leon. *Vico: A Study of the New Science*. 2d ed. New York: Cambridge University Press, 1990. A comprehensive study by a leading Vico scholar.

Shaeffer, John D. *Sensus Communis: Vico, Rhetoric, and the Limits of Relativism*. Durham, N.C.: Duke University Press, 1990. Vico's understanding of the significance of common sense.

Stone, Harold Samuel. *Vico's Cultural History: The Production and Transmission of Ideas in Naples, 1685-1750*. New York: Brill, 1997. Vico's intellectual milieu.

Tagliacozzo, Giorgio, and Hayden White, eds. *Giambattista Vico: An International Symposium*. Baltimore: Johns Hopkins University Press, 1969. Includes Enrico De Mas's essay on "Vico's Four Authors" (Bacon, Tacitus, Plato, and Grotius).

Vico, Giambattista. *The Autobiography of Giambattista Vico*. Translated by Max Harold Frisch and Thomas Goddard Bergin. Ithaca, N.Y.: Cornell University Press, 1944. Supplements the autobiography with an informative introduction of 107 pages, including "Vico's Reputation and Influence," detailed notes, and a chronology.

_____. *The First New Science*. Edited and translated by Leon Pompa. New York: Cambridge University

Press, 2002. The first complete English translation of the 1725 text, with an introduction, chronology, bibliography, and glossary.

SEE ALSO: 1748: Montesquieu Publishes *The Spirit of the Laws*; Apr., 1762: Rousseau Publishes *The Social Contract*; Jan. 10, 1776: Paine Publishes *Common Sense*; Mar. 9, 1776: Adam Smith Publishes *The*

Wealth of Nations; 1790: Burke Lays the Foundations of Modern Conservatism; Feb. 22, 1791-Feb. 16, 1792: Thomas Paine Publishes *Rights of Man*.

RELATED ARTICLES in *Great Lives from History: The Eighteenth Century, 1701-1800*: Edmund Burke; Montesquieu; Thomas Paine; Jean-Jacques Rousseau; Adam Smith; Giambattista Vico.

1726
SWIFT SATIRIZES ENGLISH RULE OF IRELAND IN *GULLIVER'S TRAVELS*

Jonathan Swift's cutting satiric voice harshly criticized the British government and forced England to examine its treatment of its Irish colonial subjects.

LOCALE: Ireland
CATEGORY: Literature

KEY FIGURES
Jonathan Swift (1667-1745), Irish satirist
George I (1660-1727), king of Great Britain, r. 1714-1727
Queen Anne (1665-1714), queen of England, Ireland, and Scotland, r. 1702-1714

SUMMARY OF EVENT

In 1726, Jonathan Swift wrote a novel intended to criticize the government of Great Britain, specifically the treatment of the Irish by the British parliament. Indeed, with the publication of *Gulliver's Travels* (1726; originally entitled *Travels into Several Remote Nations of the World, in Four Parts, by Lemuel Gulliver, First a Surgeon, and Then a Captain of Several Ships*), Swift became the earliest British writer to use the emerging form of the novel as a vehicle for satire. Few later satires have matched the sheer savagery of Swift's critique.

By the eighteenth century, England had dominated Ireland politically for five hundred years. In addition, since breaking with the Catholic Church and becoming a Protestant nation in the sixteenth century, the English had attempted at every turn to force Ireland to do so as well. Britain's efforts to subjugate its island neighbor, however, had never been completely successful, and the Irish remained resolutely Catholic. The Irish population, moreover, remained mired in resentment of its ever-increasing poverty, while the agricultural and mineral wealth of Ireland left its shores in British ships. Swift, a lifelong Irish patriot, used his pen to further the cause of Irish nationalism. In all his literary works—whether po-

etry, fiction, or nonfiction—Swift showed such an overwhelming, passionate attachment to Ireland that he came to be called the Hibernian Patriot.

Born in Dublin, Ireland, and a prominent member of the British Tory Party from 1710 to 1714, Swift was a leading member of the English government. He was dean of St. Patrick's Cathedral in Dublin when *Gulliver's Travels* came out, and he decided to publish it anonymously, because the book severely criticized so many prominent political figures. For example, the characters of the Low-Heels and the High-Heels were meant to rep-

A drawing from an early twentieth century edition of Gulliver's Travels, *showing the "emperor" of Lilliput, George I, standing before Gulliver.* (The Granger Collection, New York)

resent Britain's principal political parties, the conservative Tories and the more liberal Whigs. The devilishly cruel, small-minded emperor of Lilliput represented King George I, while the ridiculously shrill and controlling empress of Lilliput corresponded to Queen Anne, who had been responsible for Swift's lack of advancement in the Church of England and for his lifelong banishment to Ireland.

Although he suffered great disappointment over his assignment in Ireland, Swift worked hard for his church in Dublin and fought for the cause of Irish freedom against the Whigs. The Whigs tended to treat Ireland as a subjected colony instead of as a country in its own right. *Gulliver's Travels* became one salvo in Swift's ongoing battle, as he created the character of Gulliver and the fantastic foreign lands to which he travels in order to represent satirically the principal players, situations, and events in British-Irish relations.

Part 1 of the novel is set in the land of Lilliput, where the inhabitants are merely six inches tall and Gulliver, whose name sounds like "gullible," seems to the Lilliputians to be a "Man-Mountain," representing in Swift's estimation a typically proud English middle-class man. The exceedingly prideful Gulliver becomes enmeshed in Lilliput's court politics and constantly fights with the court ministers over matters both petty and important. Of particular note is the way Lilliput treats its island neighbor Blefescu, which it threatens to enslave after it discovers the military might of their "giant weapon," Gulliver.

Part 2 takes place in Brobdingnag, a land of giants where it is Gulliver who seems six inches tall in comparison to the huge Brobdingnagians. Swift continues his commentary on English politics, but in Brobdingnag, he represents them not as they are but as they should be. The giant king is a humane and fit leader who treats his subjects well, as Swift would have the British king treat the Irish. Gulliver describes England to the Brobdingnagian king, blindly going to great lengths to explain the insidious British court policies to the monarch, unaware that his description reflects badly upon England. Indeed, Gulliver is proud and cruel, very much like a corrupt Lilliputian minister. Of particular note in the novel's second part is the poor Brobdingnagian farmer who sees in Gulliver a way to earn money. Swift portrays the effects of poverty, like those experienced by the people in rural Ireland, which force people to behave in ways they might not otherwise.

Part 3, which analyzes the scientific observations of the eighteenth

---

THE LAWS OF LILLIPUT

In the following excerpt from Gulliver's Travels, *Jonathan Swift uses his portrayal of the legal system of Lilliput to comment upon the British legal system and its deficiencies.*

They look upon Fraud as a greater Crime than Theft, and therefore seldom fail to punish it with Death; for they alledge, that Care and Vigilance, with a very common Understanding, may preserve a Man's Goods from Thieves, but Honesty has no fence against superior Cunning; and since it is necessary that there should be a perpetual Intercourse of Buying and Selling, and dealing upon Credit, where Fraud is permitted and connived at, or has no Law to punish it, the honest Dealer is always undone, and the Knave gets the advantage. I remember when I was once interceding with the King for a Criminal who had wronged his Master of a great Sum of Money, which he had received by Order, and ran away with; and happening to tell his Majesty, by way of Extenuation, that it was only a Breach of Trust; the Emperor thought it monstrous in me to offer, as a Defence, the greatest Aggravation of the Crime: and truly I had little to say in return, farther than the common Answer, that different Nations had different Customs; for, I confess, I was heartily ashamed.

Although we usually call Reward and Punishment the two Hinges upon which all Government turns, yet I could never observe this Maxim to be put in practice by any Nation except that of *Lilliput*. Whoever can there bring sufficient Proof that he has strictly observed the Laws of his Country for seventy-three Moons, has a claim to certain Privileges, according to his Quality and Condition of Life, with a proportionable Sum of Money out of a Fund appropriated for that Use: He likewise acquires the Title of *Snilpall*, or *Legal*, which is added to his Name, but does not descend to his Posterity. And these People thought it a prodigious Defect of Policy among us, when I told them that our Laws were enforced only by Penalties without any mention of Reward. It is upon this account that the Image of Justice, in their courts of Judicature, is formed with six Eyes, two before, as many behind, and on each side one, to signify Circumspection; with a Bag of Gold open in her Right Hand, and a Sword sheathed in her Left, to shew she is more disposed to Reward than to punish.

Source: Jonathan Swift, *Travels into Several Remote Nations of the World, in Four Parts: By Lemuel Gulliver, First a Surgeon, and Then a Captain of Several Ships* (London: Benjamin Motte, 1726), chapter 6. http://www.jaffebros.com/lee/gulliver/bk1/chap1-6.html. Accessed November 13, 2005.

century, takes Gulliver to Laputa, whose inhabitants—cruel dictators over their colonies in the manner of the British over Ireland—are meant to represent the British Royal Society, which Swift sees as engrossed in nonsensical speculations. The Laputans live on a floating island, dominating those who live below them. In the event of rebellion among the ground-dwellers, the dictators cause their island to hover over the offending area, so the rebels are deprived of sunlight and rain. If absolutely necessary, moreover, the island can descend to Earth, crushing all life beneath it. This vile means of control is used only as a last resort, because the Laputan king does not want to lose the income from his colonies.

The colonial capital city of Lindalino, representing Dublin, is portrayed as being in revolt during Gulliver's visit. This rebellion formed the centerpiece of Swift's allegorical account of the Irish campaign against England's attempt to introduce a debased currency into the country. The residents of Lindalino erect a tower with a large pile of "combustible fuel" to set the island afire if it attempts to descend on the city. In a manner of speaking, this was a threat against George I: Swift indicates that if England were to carry out its plan to debase Ireland's currency, a huge rebellion in Ireland would result.

In the final part of the novel, Gulliver arrives in the land of the Houyhnhnms, an ideal race of intelligent horses he comes to love. Their neighbors, the Yahoos, are this land's humans, but they run wild like beasts and sleep in kennels. Early scholars speculated that Swift referenced the Irish in his savage depiction of the Yahoos.

SIGNIFICANCE

Gulliver's Travels, with its many veiled references to English colonialism, represented an extended critique of Ireland's treatment by the British government. It arguably helped to contribute to the general tensions and dissatisfaction in Ireland that would, after similar rebellions in America and France, bring about a brief and unsuccessful Irish rebellion at the end of the eighteenth century. The novel also participated in a significant British literary phenomenon, whereby politicians who could not be attacked or even discussed directly were represented in the form of fictional characters. Indeed, when Samuel Johnson began writing reports of British parliamentary debates ten years later in *Gentleman's Magazine*, he disguised those reports as tales of the Lilliputian senate.

As well as decrying the plight of the Irish, Swift's novel may be seen as part of the larger project of criticizing British imperialism as such. *Gulliver's Travels* shed light on the corrupt nature of the British court, the nation's revolting colonial policies, and the pride of British subjects, who, Swift maintained, remained blind to the evils of colonialism. The overly proud yet nearsighted Gulliver became the vehicle through which Swift portrayed all that was wrong with the English mindset. This portrayal emphasized the contradictory nature of that mindset, as well as the extent to which British pride and arrogance caused great strife and poverty in the colonies, particularly in Ireland.

Gulliver's Travels also led the way for Swift to write *A Modest Proposal for Preventing the Children of Poor People of Ireland from Being a Burden to Their Parents or the Country, and for Making Them Beneficial to the Public* (1729), considered by many to be the best satire ever written in English. In it, a respectable Whig businessman proposes that one manner of solving Ireland's overpopulation problem and England's constant need of succulent meat would be for the Irish to fatten their children for English consumption in the form of food. Like *Gulliver's Travels*, it caused a great furor, bringing even more attention to the dire situation of the Irish.

—*M. Casey Diana*

FURTHER READING

Fauske, Christopher J. *Jonathan Swift and the Church of Ireland, 1710-1724*. Dublin: Irish Academic Press, 2002. Explores many aspects of Swift as an Irish writer and in particular how his role as a man of the cloth influenced his work.

Ferguson, Oliver Watkins. *Jonathan Swift and Ireland*. Urbana: University of Illinois Press, 1962. This scholarly book focuses primarily on Swift as both an Irishman and an Englishman, on the influence of Ireland on his political and personal life, and on the creation of his many literary works, including *Gulliver's Travels*.

King, Richard Ashe. *Swift in Ireland*. Folcroft, Pa.: Folcroft Library Editions, 1976. This concise work discusses Swift's activities in Dublin against the background of the political turmoil of the times. Addresses Ireland during the creation of *Gulliver's Travels*.

McMinn, Joseph. *Jonathan's Travels: Swift and Ireland*. Hampshire, England: Palgrave Macmillan, 1994. Fully illustrated account of Swift's travels throughout eighteenth century Ireland. The book demonstrates Swift's deep commitment to the improvement and well-being of Ireland and the Irish people, illustrating how Swift's many long solitary journeys through Ire-

1720's

land on horseback influenced the creation of his solitary hero, Lemuel Gulliver, and his love of solitary travel.

SEE ALSO: Feb., 1706-Apr. 28, 1707: Act of Union Unites England and Scotland; Mar. 1, 1711: Addison and Steele Establish *The Spectator*; Apr. 25, 1719: Defoe Publishes the First Novel; 1736: *Gentleman's*

Magazine Initiates Parliamentary Reporting; 1742: Fielding's *Joseph Andrews* Satirizes English Society; Jan., 1759: Voltaire Satirizes Optimism in *Candide*.

RELATED ARTICLES in *Great Lives from History: The Eighteenth Century, 1701-1800*: Joseph Addison; Queen Anne; Henry Fielding; George I; Samuel Johnson; Richard Steele; Jonathan Swift; Voltaire.

1726-1729
VOLTAIRE ADVANCES ENLIGHTENMENT THOUGHT IN EUROPE

After self-exile to England, Voltaire returned to France and introduced advances made by the British in the sciences and in religious tolerance, government and political theory, freethinking, and the elimination of aristocratic privilege. British thought thus became a model for the eighteenth century Enlightenment.

LOCALE: London, England
CATEGORIES: Cultural and intellectual history; philosophy; government and politics; social issues and reform; religion and theology

KEY FIGURES
Voltaire (François-Marie Arouet; 1694-1778), a French scholar
First Viscount Bolingbroke (Henry St. John; 1678-1751), a British statesman
Alexander Pope (1688-1744), a British poet
Jonathan Swift (1667-1745), an Irish writer
George Berkeley (1685-1753), an Irish philosopher and bishop
Samuel Clarke (1675-1729), an English philosopher and theologian

SUMMARY OF EVENT
In February, 1726, at a performance of the Comédie Française, Voltaire encountered the arrogant chevalier Guy Auguste de Rohan-Chabot, an insignificant descendant of an illustrious family. Rohan-Chabot publicly ridiculed Voltaire by addressing him as Monsieur de Voltaire and then asking if his name was not Monsieur Arouet instead, emphasizing Voltaire's common birth. Voltaire was given the name François-Marie Arouet at birth and was the son of a notary. In 1718, after the success of his play *Œdipe* (pb. 1719; *Oedipus*, 1761), he began to use the pseudonym Voltaire. Always quick of wit and capable of bitter sarcasm, Voltaire ignored Rohan-Chabot's question and replied that rather than dishonor-

ing his family name, he was immortalizing the name he had taken. Rohan-Chabot's first reaction was to strike Voltaire, but he resisted, for by doing so he would have provoked a duel. (Aristocrats settled disputes with each other by dueling; they did not duel with commoners because they had other ways of dealing with those they believed were their social inferiors.) Instead of dueling, Rohan-Chabot promised Voltaire a sound beating. Voltaire ignored the threat.

Three days later, Voltaire was dining at the home of a friend when a valet informed him that someone was asking to see him. At the door, Voltaire was attacked by four ruffians hired by Rohan-Chabot, who was seated in a coach nearby, watching as Voltaire was beaten. Voltaire was incensed and tried to provoke a duel. Prudently eliciting the aid of his influential family, Rohan-Chabot had Voltaire incarcerated at the Bastille. After several days of imprisonment, Voltaire was released with orders to stay fifty leagues from Paris at all times. In May, he set sail for England.

Exile from Paris would have been unbearable for any French intellectual in the eighteenth century. To be in the provinces was to be dead. Thus, Voltaire decided to visit England instead and discover this rival of France. Rivalry and open hostilities had existed between the two nations for centuries: Wars were fought to increase land holdings, and there was competition in commerce and conflict over colonial expansion. Although France remained a Catholic country with the alliance of church and state, England, primarily Protestant, had become a land of religious tolerance. Tradition and rules and government censorship still prohibited new ideas and innovation in France, while scientific investigation and philosophical speculation thrived in England.

Voltaire had long been interested in England. He had frequented the English embassy in France, and he had met and conversed with First Viscount Bolingbroke, the

Voltaire's contribution to the Enlightenment assumed legendary proportions. In this c. 1778 engraving, the world's continents—represented by Catherine the Great, Benjamin Franklin, Jean le Rond d'Alembert, and "Prince Oronoco"—attempt to pay homage at Voltaire's tomb, but they are hindered by the spirit of ignorance. (Library of Congress)

Tory Party leader who had been exiled in France. With Bolingbroke's encouragement, Voltaire already had been learning English. He was studying the works of John Locke, the seventeenth century English philosopher who had proposed that government was based on a contract and that a sovereign should obey established laws. He was corresponding with Alexander Pope, the classical English poet.

Once in England, Voltaire set about investigating all that was English. Eager to perfect his language skills, he immediately arranged for lessons in English. His teacher, a young Quaker, not only taught him English but also introduced him to the beliefs of a religion that differed greatly from the Catholicism that dominated France. Once Voltaire was fluent in English, he was able to attend theater performances, discovering William Shakespeare's work and a literature very different from the classicism of the French theater.

Voltaire was well received in England. In 1727, he was presented to King George I, frequented George's court, and participated in discussions there. In April, he attended the funeral of Sir Isaac Newton at Westminster.

The respect with which the English honored the scientist made a lasting impression on Voltaire. In addition to members of the court, Voltaire associated with members of both the Whig and Tory parties, thus gaining knowledge of English political theory; he was greatly influenced by the Deism of Bolingbroke. That same year, he was invited to the homes of Lord Peterborough, Lord Hervey, and Lady Marlborough (Sarah Churchill). He met and conversed with merchants and bankers, and published a work in English: *An Essay upon the Civil Wars of France . . . and Also upon the Epick Poetry of the European Nations from Homer Down to Milton*. In 1728, he published *La Henriade*, his epic poem on King Henry IV and the religious wars in France. It was a publication to which many members of the Whig Party subscribed.

Voltaire also made the acquaintance of Jonathan Swift, the author *Gulliver's Travels* (1726) and other social satires of the time. He spent three months in Swift's company at the home of Lord Peterborough and frequented his longtime correspondent, the poet Alexander Pope. In addition to Bolingbroke, whose theory of history also made a lasting impression on him, Voltaire spent time with Samuel Clarke, a theologian dedicated to refuting atheism, and with philosopher George Berkeley.

Before returning to France in 1729, Voltaire decided to write a book about his discoveries in England. His *Letters Concerning the English Nation* (1733; *Lettres philosophiques*, 1734; published as *Philosophical Letters*, 1961) appeared first in English and was published in London. The French version was released by Voltaire's editor at Rouen. Voltaire had been hesitant about making his text available in France, for he feared the book would bring him trouble. He had already spent time in the Bastille for his writings. In this regard, his intuition was right: The book was denounced as a scandal against religion, society, and the government. It was officially burned and an order was issued for Voltaire's arrest. He fled and went into hiding.

SIGNIFICANCE

Voltaire's *Letters Concerning the English Nation* discussed the major ideas that had occupied the French thinkers of the period, ideas shunned by the French court. The main themes of the book were religious tolerance, freedom of thought, respect for scientific investigation, constitutional government, and society. He discussed Newton's law of gravity and Locke's empiricism, and he argued that life could be improved by understanding natural law and by trusting science and the scientific method.

Voltaire also included a letter at the end of the text on the thoughts of Blaise Pascal, a seventeenth century French writer, philosopher, and scientist. In this letter, Voltaire launched his attack on the Catholic Church in France. Pascal had presented humans as victims with little or no possibility of happiness on earth. Voltaire challenged this idea. He stated that humans could find happiness through discovery and reason. With Voltaire's help, England, and English thought, became the model for social change in continental Europe.

—Shawncey Webb

FURTHER READING

Collins, J. Churton. *Voltaire, Montesquieu, and Rousseau in England*. Folcroft, Pa.: Folcroft Library Editions, 1980. An account, first published in 1908, of Voltaire's years in England. Includes discussion of his contemporaries Montesquieu and Rousseau. Includes illustrations, a bibliography, and an index.

Crocker, Lester. *An Age of Crisis: Man and World in Eighteenth Century French Thought*. Baltimore: Johns Hopkins University Press, 1959. Still one of the best presentations of the thinking of the period. A clear and concise work.

Durant, Will, and Ariel Durant. *The Age of Voltaire*. New York: Simon & Schuster, 1965. An intelligent, urbane, highly readable, and readily available account of the Enlightenment. A classic.

Gay, Peter. *The Enlightenment: An Interpretation*. 2 vols. New York: Alfred A. Knopf, 1966-1969. A lively and brilliant interpretation of the Enlightenment organized by topic. A gold mine of information.

_____. *The Party of Humanity: Essays in the French Enlightenment*. New York: W. W. Norton, 1971. A series of essays on various aspects of the Enlightenment by one of the period's most renowned historians.

Lanson, Gustave. *Voltaire*. Translated by Robert A. Wagoner. Introduction by Peter Gay. New York: John Wiley & Sons, 1966. This brief survey of Voltaire's life and work by a famous French literary historian was originally published in 1906. It is an excellent introductory volume that distinguishes between Voltaire's deeply held convictions and his more casual and whimsical arguments.

Popkin, Richard, ed. *The Columbia History of Western Philosophy*. New York: Columbia University Press, 1999. Chapter 6, useful especially to students, gives a concise overview of the Enlightenment, its origins, and its significance in the history of ideas.

Voltaire. *Letters Concerning the English Nation*. Edited by Nicholas Cronk. New York: Oxford University Press, 1999. A critical edition of Voltaire's original text, with an introduction, explanatory notes, and accounts of Voltaire by English contemporaries.

Vyverberg, Henry. *Human Nature, Cultural Diversity, and the French Enlightenment*. New York: Oxford University Press, 1989. A collection of Enlightenment thinking, with a good introduction to the period.

SEE ALSO: 1721-1750: Early Enlightenment in France; 1726: Swift Satirizes English Rule of Ireland in *Gulliver's Travels*; 1739-1740: Hume Publishes *A Treatise of Human Nature*; 1748: Montesquieu Publishes *The Spirit of the Laws*; 1749-1789: First Comprehensive Examination of the Natural World; 1751-1772: Diderot Publishes the *Encyclopedia*; 1754: Condillac Defends Sensationalist Theory; July 27, 1758: Helvétius Publishes *De l'esprit*; Jan., 1759: Voltaire Satirizes Optimism in *Candide*; Apr., 1762: Rousseau Publishes *The Social Contract*; July, 1764: Voltaire Publishes *A Philosophical Dictionary for the Pocket*; 1770: Publication of Holbach's *The System of Nature*; 1782-1798: Publication of Rousseau's *Confessions*.

RELATED ARTICLES in *Great Lives from History: The Eighteenth Century, 1701-1800*: Jean le Rond d'Alembert; George Berkeley; First Viscount Bolingbroke; James Boswell; Étienne Bonnot de Condillac; Marquis de Condorcet; Denis Diderot; Claude-Adrien Helvétius; Paul-Henri-Dietrich d'Holbach; David Hume; Madame de Pompadour; Alexander Pope; Jean-Jacques Rousseau; Jonathan Swift; Marquis de Vauvenargues; Voltaire.

May, 1727-1733
JANSENIST "CONVULSIONNAIRES" GATHER AT SAINT-MÉDARD

The convulsionnaires were a group of Jansenists who gathered at the tomb of one of their members, where miracles seemed to occur. Jansenism had been officially condemned as heretical by the Church in 1713. Thus, for miracles to occur at the tomb of one of the followers of this declared heresy represented a threat to the spiritual authority of the Church.

LOCALE: Cemetery of Saint-Médard, Paris, France
CATEGORY: Religion and theology

KEY FIGURES
François Paris (1690-1727), French Jansenist deacon
Cornelius Otto Jansen (1585-1638), founder of Jansenism
André-Hercule de Fleury (1653-1743), prime minister of France, 1726-1743
Jean Duvergier (Abbé Saint-Cyran; 1581-1643), spiritual director of Port-Royal
Louis-Basile Carré de Montgeron (1688-1754), investigator for the Paris Parlement

SUMMARY OF EVENT
Jansenism traces its origins to the writings of the Flemish theologian Cornelius Otto Jansen, who spent the greater part of his life writing a commentary on the works of Saint Augustine. In his work *Augustinus* (1640), he emphasized that humanity was in a state of total corruption and that only "grace," which could be lost at anytime, could enable human beings to overcome corruption. In spite of its pessimism, this doctrine gained considerable popularity in France. In 1636, Jansen's friend and aide Jean Duvergier, the Abbé Saint-Cyran, became the spiritual director of the Jansenist abbey of Port-Royal and introduced Jansenism (so called by enemies of the movement) into the community.

The local Jesuits opposed Jansenism. They questioned, for example, the validity of Jansen's doctrine regarding Communion, which asserted that it was sinful to take the sacrament without perfect contrition in one's heart. The Jesuits found this assertion to be in contradiction with Saint Augustine's recommendation that all believers take Communion weekly. The Jansenist leader Antoine Arnauld accused the Jesuits of moral laxity in his treatise *De la fréquente communion* (1643; on frequent Communion). This began a Jansenist-Jesuit conflict that was to last well into the eighteenth century.

The Church rejected Jansenism almost immediately. In 1653, five propositions from *Augustinus* were condemned as heretical. A papal bull of 1656 repeated the condemnation. In 1657, the French Assembly of the Clergy required all of the clergy in France to sign a formulary endorsing the condemnation. In 1713, the bull *Unigenitus*, issued by Pope Clement XI, condemned 101 propositions from *Réflexions morales* (1693-1694; moral reflections) by the Jansenist theologian Pasquier Quesnel. This act should have put an end to Jansenism; however, it did not, and the bull was not legally registered in France until 1730.

The Jansenist-Jesuit quarrel did not remain within the confines of the Church. French king Louis XIV viciously attacked the Jansenists during his reign. He feared them, just as he feared the Protestants, as a threat to his absolute power. He aligned himself with the Jesuits against Port-Royal; as a result, his opponents took up the cause of the Jansenists. Indeed, Jansenism gained most of its adherents outside the Church from among the lawyers and judges of the Palais de Justice. This group had long stood as a deterrent to abuse of royal power and opposed the theory of royal absolutism upon which Louis XIV's reign was based. Thus the Jesuit-Jansenist quarrel was closely linked to the opposition between the French courts and royal power. This situation continued during the reign of Louis XV.

In May of 1727, François Paris, a Jansenist deacon and the brother of a magistrate, died and was buried in the cemetery of Saint-Médard in Paris. Deacon Paris was very popular with the Parisian populace. He was known for his acts of charity to the poor and was considered to be a very saintly man. Therefore, many mourners visited his grave. Sometime shortly after his death, there were reports that people who went to his tomb were cured of many different types of illness. People suffering from rheumatism, cancerous tumors, blindness, deafness, and other debilitating diseases appeared at the tomb. Many left the cemetery swearing that they had been cured.

Crowds began to gather at Saint-Médard. The miraculous cures were not the only reported happenings at the tomb. There were also reports of people going into convulsions and of others speaking in tongues. Lying down on the tomb (and later just touching it) purportedly caused a believer's body to be contorted with an especially curious twisting of the limbs. These convulsions led to the pilgrims at Paris's tomb being called "convulsionnaires." As reports circulated, ever-increasing numbers of Jansenists appeared at the tomb. It had become a place of pilgrimage. The Jansenist leaders went to the tomb to offer legal assistance to anyone who had experienced a miraculous cure and was consequently being pursued by Church authorities.

The whole affair then took a sadomasochistic turn. When under the spell of the Spirit (or, according to the Jesuits, of the Devil), the convulsionnaires became rigid and were able to endure horrendous tortures. They had enormous stones dropped on their chests. One woman was supposedly able to bend backward over a sharp stick while heavy stones were dropped on her chest and yet remain unharmed. The Parlement of Paris engaged Louis-Basile Carré de Montgeron to investigate the happenings at Saint-Médard. In 1737, he published a four-volume work entitled *La Vérité des miracles* (the truth of the miracles), detailing the events at the cemetery. In addition to being a sacred place of pilgrimage for believers in Jansenism, the cemetery had become fashionable as a place of entertainment. More and more curious onlookers came to watch the spectacle that occurred day and night at the tomb.

Neither the Church nor the court found it easy to tolerate the convulsionnaires. They were a great embarrassment to the Church and a threat to its moral authority. If Jansenism was heretical, was it possible for miracles to occur on the tomb of one of its followers? How was the Church to account for the strange happenings at Saint-Médard? The Jesuits could combat the idea of divine inspiration by crediting the Devil as responsible for the contortions and convulsions of the visitors to the tomb, but the miraculous cures posed a more difficult problem. Not all of the publicity generated by the convulsionnaires and their miraculous cures was good, however. Indeed,

the happenings at Saint-Médard discredited the Jansenists in the opinion of many.

Louis XV's prime minister, Cardinal André-Hercule de Fleury, had been and was still at this time involved in a campaign to repress Jansenism and its influence. Fleury had taken over the *feuille de bénéfices* (the making of ecclesiastical appointments). Fleury excluded Jansenists from the list of priests eligible for promotion. In March of 1730, under his direction, the bull *Unigenitus*, which already governed the actions of the clergy, came to be law in the secular domain as well. When the Parlement of Paris objected, he exiled its members, many of whom were supporters of Jansenism. As part of the repression, the cemetery of Saint-Médard was closed by a royal edict issued on January 27, 1732. This eliminated the public spectacle, but the convulsionnaires continued their rituals in private homes. It was claimed that just touching the smallest amount of earth taken from the vicinity of Paris's tomb was enough to send a believer into a state of convulsion.

SIGNIFICANCE

Jansenism in its beginnings was an internal schism and problem for the Church. It dealt with questions of doctrine regarding salvation, grace, and communion. It was addressed to the clergy. The movement questioned, in particular, procedures that were being followed by the clergy in regard to Communion. It objected to the emphasis placed on good works and the lack of importance assigned to grace.

Many of the most significant followers of Jansenism within the Church came from families long associated with the legal profession. For example, Antoine Arnauld and his sister Angélique, abbess of Port-Royal, belonged to a family of lawyers. Jansenism spread rather quickly from the Church and into the secular judicial class. The members of the Parlement of Paris came from this class, and it was the Parlement of Paris that stood as a deterrent to the absolute power of the king. Thus, Jansenism became associated with the defiance of the Church and of royal authority. With the appearance of the convulsionnaires, who sought miraculous cures and divine inspiration at the tomb of a Jansenist, this defiance then manifested itself among the commoners

—*Shawncey Webb*

FURTHER READING

Bell, David A. *Lawyers and Citizens: The Making of a Political Elite in Old Régime France*. New York: Oxford University Press, 1994. Discusses Jansenism and its link to the French bar and courts; details the conflict with the king.

Ford, Franklin L. *Robe and Sword: The Regrouping of the French Aristocracy After Louis XIV*. New York: Harper and Row, 1955. Information on the differences between the nobility who had inherited their titles and the new nobility of lawyers and judges and their beliefs and life styles.

Kreiser, Robert. *Miracles, Convulsions, and Ecclesiastical Politics in Early Eighteenth Century Paris*. Princeton, N.J.: Princeton University Press, 1978. Discusses link between happenings at Saint-Médard and the politics within the Church.

McManners, John. *The Clerical Establishment and Its Ramifications*. Vol. 1 in *Church and Society in Eighteenth Century France*. London: Oxford University Press, 1999. Along with volume 2, presents every aspect of religious life in eighteenth century France.

_____. *The Religion of the People and the Politics of Religion*. Vol. 2 in *Church and Society in Eighteenth Century France*. London: Oxford University Press, 1999. Discussion of the Jesuit-Jansenist struggle.

SEE ALSO: July 24, 1702-Oct. 1, 1704: Camisard Risings in the Cévennes; Sept. 8, 1713: Papal Bull *Unigenitus*.

RELATED ARTICLES in *Great Lives from History: The Eighteenth Century, 1701-1800*: André-Hercule de Fleury; Louis XV.

October 21, 1727
TREATY OF KIAKHTA

The Treaty of Kiakhta defined trade between Russia and China for more than a century, and it freed the two empires from worrying about each other. Thus, the treaty enabled Russia to concentrate on developing its newly won position as a European power, while in China the Manchu Qing Dynasty could likewise concentrate on consolidating its control over its own far-flung and rapidly growing empire.

LOCALE: Kiakhta (Kyakhta), Transbaikalia, Russia (now in Buryatia)
CATEGORY: Diplomacy and international relations

KEY FIGURES
Catherine I (1684-1727), empress of Russia, r. 1725-1727
Tseren-van (fl. 1727), Manchu negotiator
Sava Vladislavich-Raguzinsky (c. 1670-1738), Russian ambassador
Aleksandr Danilovich Menshikov (1673-1729), key adviser to Peter the Great and Catherine I
Kangxi (K'ang-hsi; 1654-1722), emperor of China, r. 1661-1722
Peter the Great (1672-1725), czar of Russia, r. 1682-1725

SUMMARY OF EVENT
Under Genghis Khan the Mongolian people conquered China and established the Yuan Dynasty, which ruled that country from 1279 to 1368. By the end of the seventeenth century, however, the warlike spirit of the Mongols had turned inward. They became embroiled in clan rivalry while national unity disintegrated. A growing interest in Buddhist spiritual pursuits had begun to absorb them instead of military or political expansionism. Other peoples were taking their turn in the limelight of global history.

At the beginning of the eighteenth century, Romanov Russia and Manchu China pressed Mongolia from the West and East, respectively. The Treaty of Kiakhta in 1727 was an agreement between these two ascendant powers to maximize trade with each other and to minimize any threat from Mongolia. During this period, just as pioneer Americans were advised to go west to seek their fortunes, Russian explorers, adventurers, and businessmen began moving east into the vast reaches of Central Asia and Siberia for the same purpose. However, expeditions led into the Mongolian territory of the Amur River Valley by Vasily Poyarkov, Erofei Pavlovich Khabarov, and others soon ran into Chinese competition. The Russians established a permanent base of operations at Albazin and began to colonize the area, but this audacity challenged a long tradition of Chinese predominance in the region. They ejected the Russians from Albazin and marched on Nerchinsk, a base of Russian activity farther west.

Russia and China were both undergoing major transitions at this time. As only the second Romanov czar, Peter the Great was establishing Russia as a force to be reckoned with on the global stage. China was also changing dynasties. The Manchu had gained control there from the Ming in 1644, founding the Qing Dynasty, and Kangxi was also the second in his line of succession.

Both rulers had major problems elsewhere, so neither wanted a major war with the other in Central Asia. Europe was the primary focus of concern for Peter the Great. By means of a long series of confrontations with Sweden and France between 1700 and 1721 called the Great Northern War, Russia was able to extend its influence into Poland and the Baltic states. For most of his reign, Kangxi was preoccupied with eliminating the last elements of Ming resistance from central and southern China.

Russia was greatly energized by the same restless spirit of exploration, trade, and world conquest that animated the countries of Western Europe at this time, but China enjoyed many advantages in this confrontation in the Amur River Valley. This area had been part of China, or under indirect Chinese control, for several hundred years, whereas the Russians were coming from far away. Their ultimate support lay in the European part of Russia, so their supply lines extended all the way back to Moscow or St. Petersburg. The Chinese capital of Beijing was much closer. In addition, even though the Manchus were new as rulers of China, they had ancient ethnic and cultural connections with Mongolia. When finally free to focus on this northern frontier, the Manchus were able to stop the Russian advance and define the bilateral relationship on mutually beneficial terms.

The first attempt had been the Treaty of Nerchinsk in 1689, but a clearer definition of the border and terms of future trade was necessary. When both Peter the Great and Kangxi passed from the scene in the 1720's, their successors felt the need to resolve outstanding issues in this area. The widow of Peter the Great, Czarina Catherine I, and her intimate adviser, Aleksandr Danilovich Menshikov, sent Sava Vladislavich-Raguzinsky as ambassador. The Manchu delegation was headed by Tseren-van, state administrator and brother-in-law of the local khan. The negotiations opened on June 14, 1727, and the final document was signed on October 21 of that year.

The Treaty of Kiakhta consisted of eleven articles dealing with all aspects of the Russian-Chinese relationship. Eternal peace was declared between the two countries. The border between Russia and Chinese Mongolia was defined in greater detail, extending to the west. Provisions were agreed upon for each nation to return fugitives and deserters from the other nation, who might otherwise cross the border hoping to find a safe haven. Forms of diplomatic relations were outlined, as well as mechanisms for resolving future disputes. It was agreed that a Russian religious and cultural center would be opened in Beijing. Finally, institutions for future commercial relations between the two countries were established and regulations were specified.

The arrangements for trade were of special importance. Three official centers for the Russian merchants were established: Kiakhta, Nerchinsk, and Selenginsk. The number of registered Russian traders was to be limited to two hundred. Each of these traders would be allowed one trip every three years to Beijing in the company of a Chinese Mandarin host. Not counting these restrictions, trade between the countries was to be free; that is, no duties were to be charged to the buyers or sellers of merchandise.

Perhaps as important as these specific terms was another collateral agreement arrived at informally. Russians dealing with Chinese officials would not be required to kowtow. These full prostrations involved extending the body in a prone position and knocking one's head on the floor or ground. The Chinese thus recognized the Russians with a level of equality that was highly unusual, possibly even unprecedented, in the history of the empire. At the same time, however, Russians were banned completely from entering the Manchu homeland, Manchuria.

SIGNIFICANCE

The Treaty of Kiakhta marked the first successful border negotiation between China and Russia, setting the tone for the two nations' relationship for years to come. In 1768, a few supplementary provisions were agreed upon, adjusting the border in places, removing some Russian palisades, and ending the collection of questionable customs by Russian officials. Essentially, however, the Treaty of Kiakhta defined relations between Russia and China for more than one hundred years after it was signed. By the middle of the nineteenth century, the decline of the Qing Dynasty created a change in the underlying balance of power. Russia forced a renegotiation of the border, and it was redefined by the Treaty of Aigun in 1858 as the Amur River itself. The Manchurian homeland was also opened to Russian activity.

Since then, through all the massive turmoil of the Russian and Chinese revolutions in the twentieth century, the border in this area between these two major powers has remained intact. Only during the 1960's did clashes once again occur. After consolidating his revolution of 1948, Mao Zedong began to agitate politically for the return of territory from the Soviet Union that he felt had been taken unfairly. Tension built until 1969, when a series of incidents involving Damanski Island, in the Ussuri

River—an Amur tributary—took the lives of several hundred soldiers on both sides. Considering the general mayhem of the twentieth century, however, the border between China and Russia has remained amazingly quiet. The Treaty of Kiakhta must be considered an outstanding success.

Only the Mongolian people might see things in a different light. They have not enjoyed independence on a tribal or national level since the period when Kiakhta was being negotiated. All their tribes, or banners, have been subsumed into either Russia or China. The last serious resistance ended in 1757, when the Dzungar defied Chinese power and continued trying to build their own empire, including other Mongol tribes and Tibet. The rising Qing Dynasty eliminated them from the ethnic map at that time for their impertinence.

—*Steven Lehman*

FURTHER READING

Adshead, S. A. M. *China in World History*. 3d ed. New York: St. Martin's Press, 2000. A general survey of Chinese history.

Heissig, Walther. *A Lost Civilization: The Mongols Re-*

discovered. London: Thames and Hudson, 1966. Mongolian history and the history of modern scholarship on Mongolia.

Huang Pei. *Autocracy at Work: A Study of the Yung-cheng Period, 1723-1735*. Bloomington: Indiana University Press, 1974. Details of general Manchu Empire concerns while the treaty was being negotiated.

Hughes, Lindsey. *Russia in the Age of Peter the Great*. New Haven, Conn.: Yale University Press, 1998. In-depth biography of the dominant Russian personality of the time.

SEE ALSO: c. 1701-1721: Great Northern War; Nov. 20, 1710-July 21, 1718: Ottoman Wars with Russia, Venice, and Austria; 1736-1739: Russo-Austrian War Against the Ottoman Empire; 1750-1792: China Consolidates Control over Tibet; Oct., 1768-Jan. 9, 1792: Ottoman Wars with Russia; 1788-Sept., 1809: Russo-Swedish Wars.

RELATED ARTICLES in *Great Lives from History: The Eighteenth Century, 1701-1800*: Peter the Great; Yongzheng.

1720's

January 29, 1728
GAY PRODUCES THE FIRST BALLAD OPERA

With The Beggar's Opera, *John Gay established a new genre, the English ballad opera, replacing the previous British passion for Italian opera with a new appreciation of native folk songs. His work paved the way for the light operas of the nineteenth century, notably the works of Sir W. S. Gilbert and Sir Arthur Sullivan, and for the twentieth century musical.*

LOCALE: London, England
CATEGORIES: Theater; music

KEY FIGURES
John Gay (1685-1732), English poet and playwright
Jonathan Swift (1667-1745), Irish satirist and Anglican priest
Alexander Pope (1688-1744), English poet
John Rich (1692-1761), English theatrical producer
Lavinia Fenton (1710-1760), English actress

SUMMARY OF EVENT
Of all the Tory writers who organized the Scriblerus Club in 1714, only John Gay had no reliable source of income. Jonathan Swift and Thomas Parnell were clergy-

men, John Arbuthnot was a prominent physician, and the father of Alexander Pope was a prosperous merchant. By contrast, after quitting an apprenticeship to a London mercer in 1706, Gay had to seek out wealthy patrons among the nobility who would be willing to take him in or otherwise to support him until he could realize enough profits from his writing to provide for himself.

Thus, in 1712, Gay became a domestic steward in the household of the duchess of Monmouth. In 1714, he acted as secretary to Lord Clarendon on a diplomatic mission, but when Queen Anne died and the Tories were ousted from power, Gay lost that appointment. During the years that followed, he continued to cultivate connections with members of the nobility, hoping for preferment, but he was never offered a post that would pay even the expenses he incurred in the company of his potential patrons. Ironically, when he did make a considerable profit from the publication of *Poems on Several Occasions* (1720, 1731), Gay lost most of it in the collapse of the South Sea Bubble. It is probable that it was Gay whom Swift had in mind when he wrote to Pope in 1725 that among his friends were some "beggars." None of

191

THE BEGGAR'S OPERA

John Gay's The Beggar's Opera *represented a new type of musical drama, as much in its focus on tawdry, working-class life as in its formal innovations. Gay wastes no time in confronting his audience with this new subject matter, as is demonstrated by the opera's first air, sung by an old woman clothed in gray, which opens the performance.*

> THROUGH all the Employments of Life
> Each Neighbour abuses his Brother;
> Whore and Rogue they call Husband and Wife:
> All Professions be-rogue one another:
> The Priest calls the Lawyer a Cheat,
> The Lawyer be-knaves the Divine:
> And the Statesman, because he's so great,
> Thinks his Trade as honest as mine.

Source: John Gay, *The Beggar's Opera* (Eugene, Oreg.: Renascence Editions, 1995). http://darkwing.uoregon.edu/~rbear/beggar.html. Accessed November 15, 2005.

Gay's friends in the mid-1720's could have had any idea how drastically his life was about to change.

When Swift suggested in 1716 that Gay write a "Newgate pastoral," he was evidently thinking of a poem, not a dramatic production. However, several years later, Gay was inspired to write a ballad entitled "Newgate's Garland: Being a New Ballad, Shewing How Mr. *Jonathan Wild's* Throat was Cut, from Ear to Ear, with a Penknife by Mr. *Blake*, alias *Blueskin*, the Bold Highwayman, as He Stood at His Trial in the Old-Bailey" (pr. 1724). Jonathan Wild was a real person, a notorious fence, and he had evidently "peached" Blake, or turned him in for a reward.

In 1724, the ballad was included in a pantomime performed at Drury Lane Theatre. The Newgate setting, the characters, and the situation all suggest the direction in which Gay's mind was moving at that time. It is not known when he began writing *The Beggar's Opera* (pr., pb. 1728), but he reported in the fall of 1727 that it was complete. However, at that time he still had hopes of a lucrative appointment, for the former prince and princess of Wales, whom he considered his patrons, were now king and queen of England. Again, Gay was disappointed: He was offered only a minimal post as gentleman usher to the two-year-old Princess Louisa. After declining the appointment, he wrote Swift that now nothing lay in his way, and he could devote all his energies to getting *The Beggar's Opera* produced.

The first three theater managers Gay consulted turned down the work, evidently feeling that the public would not accept the odd combination of spoken words, popular music, folk tunes, and motifs from operas, of cant and high sentiments, of operatic arias sung by characters from low life. However, the duke and duchess of Queensbury, who would be lifelong friends of the playwright, evidently intervened with John Rich, the manager of the Lincoln's Inn Fields Company. They may well have served as financial guarantors for the production. In any case, the play went into rehearsal.

Lavinia Fenton, a beautiful but inexperienced young singer and actress, was cast as Polly Peachum, and after the role of Macheath was rejected by James Quin, who was the leading actor in Rich's company, Thomas Walker was given the part. The music was in good hands: The overture had been composed and the tunes arranged by a well-known musician, John Christopher Pepusch. However, when the curtain went up on Monday night, January 29, 1728, Rich remained uncertain of the work's success, and Gay's friends sitting out front were just as skeptical. It was not until the second act that the actors begin to sense approval in the audience. By the end of the performance, everyone knew that what they called "the English opera" was a hit.

Interestingly, it was a couple of weeks before anyone began seeing in *The Beggar's Opera* an attack on the Whig government of Prime Minister Robert Walpole, but spectators were delighted with the idea that the work contained references to specific politicians who might well be found sitting in the audience. There were, of course, moralists who criticized the work as encouraging depravity, and opera lovers bitterly resented what they saw as a satire of Italian opera and an attempt to replace it with an inferior sort of entertainment.

How little attention most Londoners paid to such criticisms is evident because in its opening season, *The Beggar's Opera* had an amazing run of sixty-two nights. Lavinia Fenton, as Polly, was so popular that her portrait appeared on playing cards, fans, and screens. On the final night of the run, however, another actress appeared in the part of Polly, and all of London soon discovered that Fenton had run off with the duke of Bolton, who had long been estranged from his wife. The duke and Fenton lived together happily, producing three sons. After his wife's death in 1751, the duke married his mistress, and the former Polly Peachum became the duchess of Bolton.

The production was immensely profitable for John Rich, and though John Gay did not realize as much from it, he had gained both a prestige and a financial security that he had never known before. Even the fact that the Walpole government refused to allow Gay's sequel, *Polly* (pb. 1729), to be performed in public did not result in financial losses for the writer. Gay realized a large sum from the publication of *Polly* in 1729.

The Beggar's Opera caused a rift between Gay and his longtime patron, the earl of Burlington, who blamed Gay for the decline of attendance at performances of Italian opera and the resulting demise of the Royal Academy of Music. However, when the chief composer at the Royal Academy, George Frideric Handel, abandoned the opera in favor of the oratorio, he was unknowingly establishing his future reputation: It is not for the operas he wrote but for oratorios like *Messiah* (1742) that Handel is now best known.

SIGNIFICANCE

The Beggar's Opera was performed in London at least once a year throughout the remaining years of the eighteenth century and often in the nineteenth. Renewed interest in the work was stimulated by Nigel Playfair's 1926 revival at the Lyric Theatre in London, and since that time it has frequently been performed. It has also been reworked as a contemporary satire. In 1928, with the Nazis coming into power in Germany, the writer Bertolt Brecht and the composer Kurt Weill collaborated on *Die Dreigroschenoper* (pr. 1928, pb. 1929; *The Threepenny Opera*, 1949), an adaptation of Gay's libretto. Similarly, in 1975, the Czechoslovakian writer and anti-Communist activist Václav Havel wrote *Žebrácká opera* (pr. 1975, pb. 1977; *The Beggar's Opera*, 1976), and in 1984, the British writer Alan Ayckbourn staged *A Chorus of Disapproval* (pr. 1984, pb. 1985), satirizing Margaret Thatcher's Tory government.

Although the success of *The Beggar's Opera* led immediately to the writing of inferior imitations, later in the eighteenth century the new form of ballad opera attracted respected composers like Charles Dibdin, Thomas Arne, and Stephen Storace. It also influenced the German *Singspiel*, a form that Wolfgang Amadeus Mozart utilized in 1782 for *Die Entführung aus dem Serail* (*The Abduction from the Seraglio*, 1926?). Late in the nineteenth century, W. S. Gilbert and Arthur Sullivan drew upon the ballad

opera tradition for their popular light operas, which in turn inspired the modern musical.

—Rosemary M. Canfield Reisman

FURTHER READING

Brückmann, Patricia Carr. *A Manner of Correspondence: A Study of the Scriblerus Club*. Montreal, Que.: McGill-Queen's University Press, 1997. Notes how the works of this group reflected their shared attitudes.

Dugaw, Dianne. *"Deep Play": John Gay and the Invention of Modernity*. Newark: University of Delaware Press, 2001. Focuses on Gay's use of popular forms. Includes illustrations, musical examples, and dance diagrams.

Lewis, Peter, and Nigel Wood, eds. *John Gay and the Scriblerians*. London: Vision Press, 1988. An important collection of critical essays. Chronology and index.

Nicholson, Colin. *Writing and the Rise of Finance: Capital Satires of the Early Eighteenth Century*. Reprint. New York: Cambridge University Press, 2004. Shows how writers like Gay reveal their ambivalence toward the new capitalism.

Nokes, David. *John Gay: A Profession of Friendship*. New York: Oxford University Press, 1995. A full-length biography, based on extensive research. Annotated bibliography.

Pearce, Charles E. *Polly Peachum: The Story of Lavinia Fenton and "The Beggar's Opera."* Reprint. New York: Benjamin Blom, 1968. A detailed theatrical history. Contains more than forty full-page illustrations.

Winton, Calhoun. *John Gay and the London Theatre*. Lexington: University Press of Kentucky, 1993. The standard work on Gay's theatrical career.

SEE ALSO: Sept., 1720: Collapse of the South Sea Bubble; Dec. 7, 1732: Covent Garden Theatre Opens in London; Apr. 13, 1742: First Performance of Handel's *Messiah*; Oct. 5, 1762: First Performance of Gluck's *Orfeo and Euridice*; Apr. 27, 1784: First Performance of *The Marriage of Figaro*.

RELATED ARTICLES in *Great Lives from History: The Eighteenth Century, 1701-1800*: Queen Anne; George II; George Frideric Handel; Wolfgang Amadeus Mozart; Alexander Pope; Jonathan Swift; Robert Walpole.

1720's

July, 1728-1769
RUSSIAN VOYAGES TO ALASKA

Russian explorers and scientists mounted expeditions to the northern Pacific, surveying and occupying the region. These excursions paved the way for the later Russian settlement of Alaska.

LOCALE: Northern Pacific Ocean
CATEGORIES: Exploration and discovery; colonization; expansion and land acquisition

KEY FIGURES

Vitus Jonassen Bering (1681-1741), Danish navigator employed by Peter the Great
Aleksei Ilich Chirikov (1703-1748), Russian explorer
Martin Spanberg (fl. 1725-1732), Danish explorer
Mikhail Spiridonovich Gvozdev (b. 1699?), Russian land surveyor
Ivan Fyodorov (d. 1733), Russian navigator
Pyotr Kuzmich Krenitsyn (d. 1770) Russian cartographer
Mikhail Dmitrievich Levashov (1739-1775), Russian cartographer
Grigori Ivanovich Shelikov (1747-1795), Russian merchant and fur trader
Georg Wilhelm Steller (1709-1746), German naturalist
Nikifor Trapeznikov (fl. 1743-1764), Russian merchant
Ivan Sindt (fl. 1765), German explorer

SUMMARY OF EVENT

After a Cossack discovered the Chukotski Peninsula—the easternmost "nose" of Siberia—in 1648, reports about Alaskan fur traders led people to believe that water divided North America from Asia. The German philosopher Gottfried Wilhelm Leibniz convinced Czar Peter the Great in 1716 to send an expedition eastward to confirm its existence. Peter undoubtedly was interested for scientific and imperial reasons, but also because Siberian furs were bringing less state revenue than earlier and he wished to rejuvenate this trade. In 1719, he dispatched two men to explore the Kamchatka region, located on the eastern shore of what is now the Bering Sea, across from Alaska. Although the expedition of Ivan Evreinov and Fedor Luzhin failed to show that America lay near the Kuril Islands, both were praised for locating them in relation to Japan and Kamchatka. Peter gave the next expedition more precise instructions.

The most important person associated with the early voyages to the North Pacific was Vitus Jonassen Bering. Although Danish, Bering became a captain commander of the Russian fleet, first under Peter and later under Empress Anna. From his native seaport of Horsens, Denmark, Bering had traveled to the East Indies in 1703. Recruited as a sublieutenant for the young navy of Czar Peter, Bering engaged in Russia's wars in the Baltic, Black, and Azov Seas. By 1720, he had beem promoted to captain second class. Desirous of greater rewards, he retired from service in 1724 to live on his Vyborg estate, only to be recalled by Peter later that year. Peter elevated him to captain first class and, heeding the advice of Admiral Peter Sievers, another Dane, entrusted Bering with the difficult mission to determine whether America was connected with Siberia. Days before his death on January 28, 1725, Peter gave his personal instructions for this mission, which called for Bering to sail east to America's coast and then south to the nearest European settlement.

Bering's party made the arduous Siberian journey, then built a ship, the *Saint Gabriel*, in Kamchatka. Aleksei Ilich Chirikov and Martin Spanberg, another Dane, were officers with Bering when the ship was launched in July, 1728. In August, they discovered Saint Lawrence Island, and after discussing the option of returning to Kamchatka, they proceeded northward. The ship passed through the strait that would bear Bering's name at 67°18′ north latitude. On their return, they discovered Big Diomede Island, but the fog was so heavy that Bering could not see the Alaskan shores 25 miles away. In September, Bering arrived at Kamchatka to spend the winter, only to put up sails again in June in search of land to the south and southeast. Failing that endeavor, he returned to Saint Petersburg.

When Bering arrived in the capital on March 30, 1730, his reception was warm, but he soon fell prey to petty politics at the Admiralty. He was certain that he had discovered the strait—as he had—but failed to appreciate the need for proof. As a result of indefatigable labor by the senate secretary, Ivan Kirillov, Anna was persuaded to send Bering on another, more ambitious, mission to the East. Bering was instructed by the senate to map the Siberian rivers, including the Amur, and the Pacific coast of Siberia before proceeding to America. This Great Northern Expedition (1733-1742) was to include six hundred sailors, five hundred guards, and up to two thousand laborers to haul supplies. Beginning his journey across Siberia in 1733, he found the assignments overwhelming. Forty men died before setting sail, and expenses mounted far in excess of expectations. At Okhotsk, workers constructed two ships, the *Saint Peter* and *Saint Paul*, which sailed to Kamchatka in November, 1740.

A Kolyma Cossack, Afanasy Shestakov, had organized another expedition to the East in 1726 and left for the North Pacific in 1732. Led by Ivan Fyodorov and Mikhail Gvozdev, a land surveyor and former student at the Moscow Navigation School and Naval Academy, they sailed to the Bering Strait. Parts of the Asiatic and American coastlines were charted by Gvozdev as his ship circumnavigated Big Diomede and, on August 21, sighted Alaska, thinking it another large island. Inclement weather prevented the crew from disembarking. Gvozdev's report of this discovery was ignored and not dispatched to the Admiralty until 1743. On June 4, 1741, Bering, on the *Saint Peter*, and Chirikov, commanding the *Saint Paul*, set sail to the south, with specific orders to find and claim the American coastline. Within days, fog became so heavy that the ships separated, although both had changed course to the northeast. When on July 15, Chirikov sighted land in the Alexander archipelago, fifteen of his crew went ashore, never to return. More would later die of scurvy. Before Chirikov returned to Kamchatka on October 10, he had discovered several islands, including Kayak Island.

A German naturalist, Georg Wilhelm Steller, kept a journal of the voyage of the *Saint Peter*. Catching sight of Alaskan mountains, Bering laid anchor near the Copper River, where Steller and some crewmates spent a few hours looking for ore and flora. Bering discovered Kodiak and other islands, but severe storms and a shortage of fresh water forced him to return. En route, he discovered what he called the Shumagin Islands before a storm wrecked his vessel as they anchored on November 6 at an uninhabited island. Bering died December 8 on the island that bears his name. Although thirty of his seventy-seven men died of scurvy, the survivors built another ship from the remains of the *Saint Peter*, reaching Avacha Bay on August 26, 1742.

Chirikov had gone back to sea in May in search of Bering. After reaching Attu Island, he returned to Kamchatka in July, later taking part in the charting of Russian discoveries in the Pacific Ocean, including the capes in Kyusha Island, the Anadyr Gulf, and Taui, Guba, and Atka Islands. An underwater peak in the Pacific Ocean was named after him.

After 1743, the government tired of expensive voyages and allowed merchants to organize their own expeditions. For two decades, private voyagers exploited the Aleutians rather than sailing eastward to the American mainland. Traders pooled their resources into small ven-

RUSSIAN VOYAGES TO ALASKA, 1728-1769

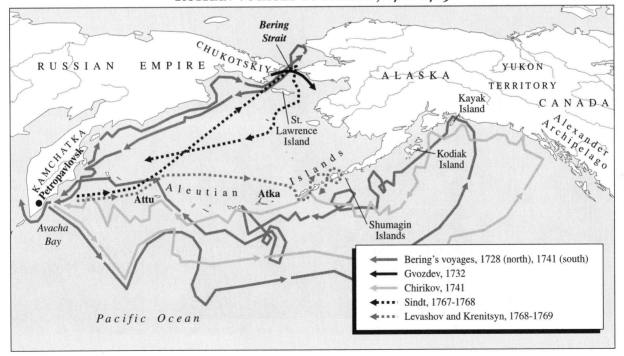

ture companies and, with permits from the state, exploited all the Aleutian Islands, sending 10 percent of their furs to the state treasury. One merchant from Irkutsk, Nikifor Trapeznikov, promoted eighteen such voyages from 1743 to 1764.

Authorities could not allow persistent reports of abuse, even slaughter, of indigenous peoples to go unheeded. Some traders seized all local women and children as hostages, and the natives supplied them with food. This concern, and the desire to map all discoveries of the merchant adventurers, led Catherine the Great to send expeditions to Alaska after 1764. One was led by a Baltic German, Ivan Sindt, who was with Bering's second expedition, but his work proved unsatisfactory, even fraudulent. Catherine then dispatched Mikhail Dmitrievich Levashov and Pyotr Kuzmich Krenitsyn eastward. Viewing their roles as cartographers, in 1764 they sailed for the Aleutians from Kamchatka and continued east to Alaska. Forced to winter on separate islands and defend against hostile native inhabitants, they returned to Kamchatka in 1769. There, Krenitsyn drowned in a river. Levashov compiled a useful ethnographic description of the natives of Unalaska and Unimak. His charts of the Aleutians proved accurate in relation to each other, but the islands were placed too close to Kamchatka.

SIGNIFICANCE

Although the expeditions never achieved all that officials had desired, the northern Pacific waters became Russian. Okhotsk became a base for the Russian navy, and Bering's settlement at Avacha Bay became the port of Petropavlovsk. The Great Northern Expedition amassed a prodigious amount of scientific data, including Steller's treatises on plants, fruits, insects, sea otters, fish, and the languages of the native peoples. More expeditions would be undertaken, but Russia's interest in Alaska was transformed in 1784 when Grigori Ivanovich Shelikov established the first Russian settlement in the Americas, on Kodiak Island.

—*John D. Windhausen*

Vitus Jonassen Bering is shipwrecked on an uninhabited island in what is now the Bering Sea. He would die there one month later. (Francis R. Niglutsch)

FURTHER READING

Barratt, Glynn. *Russia in Pacific Waters, 1715-1825.* Vancouver: University of British Columbia Press, 1981. A closely written narrative with special insights into the politics, grand and minor, of the expeditions and their participants.

Black, Lydia T. *Russians in Alaska, 1732-1867.* Fairbanks: University of Alaska Press, 2004. A history of the Russian presence in Alaska, describing the fur trade, the relationship of the Russians with the Native Americans, and other aspects of Russian frontier life. Black maintains the Russian expansion in Alaska was the culmination of centuries of social and economic change. Includes foldout maps and illustrations.

Dmytryshyn, Basil, E. A. P. Crownhart-Vaughn, and Thomas Vaughn, eds. and trans. *Russian Penetration of the North Pacific Ocean, 1700-1799.* Vol 2. Portland: Oregon Historical Society, 1988. Contains a valuable introduction to many translated documents about the explorations of Siberia and America.

Frost, O. W. *Bering: The Russian Discovery of America.* New Haven, Conn.: Yale University Press, 2003. Frost uses newly discovered materials, including personal letters and evidence derived from the discovery of Bering's grave, to examine the personality, life, and voyages of Bering and his uneasy relationship with naturalist Georg Steller.

Golder, Frank A. *Bering's Voyages.* 2 vols. New York: American Geographical Society, 1922-1925. Reprint. New York: Octagon Books, 1968. The definitive study, with documents, of the earliest expeditions to North America, viewing these voyages in the perspective of Russia's traditional eastward expansion.

Starr, S. Frederick, ed. *Russia's American Colony.* Durham, N.C.: Duke University Press, 1987. Especially valuable essays by B. P. Polevoi and James R. Gibson on differing Russian and American views of the early explorations.

Steller, Georg Wilhelm. *Journal of a Voyage with Bering, 1741-1742.* Edited and with an introduction by O. W. Frost. Translated by Margritt A. Engel and Frost. Stanford, Calif.: Stanford University Press, 1988. A beautifully written account of science, politics, and personalities, by the naturalist who accompanied Bering on his second voyage.

SEE ALSO: Oct. 21, 1727: Treaty of Kiakhta; Aug. 25, 1768-Feb. 14, 1779: Voyages of Captain Cook; July 22, 1793: Mackenzie Reaches the Arctic Ocean.

RELATED ARTICLE in *Great Lives from History: The Eighteenth Century, 1701-1800*: Vitus Jonassen Bering.

1729
GRAY DISCOVERS PRINCIPLES OF ELECTRIC CONDUCTIVITY

Stephen Gray discovered that electricity could flow from one object to another and that while some materials were conductors of electricity, other materials were insulators of electricity. His meticulous and imaginative experiments transformed the study of static electricity from a parlor amusement to a science.

LOCALE: London and Cambridge, England
CATEGORIES: Science and technology; physics

KEY FIGURES
Stephen Gray (1666-1736), amateur experimental scientist
John Flamsteed (1646-1719), England's astronomer royal and Gray's role model, who probably tutored Gray
Francis Hauksbee (1660-1713), a demonstrator of experiments for the Royal Society, who awakened Gray's interest in static electricity

Jean Théophile Desaguliers (1683-1744), a Royal Society lecturer, whom Gray assisted
Granville Wheler (1701-1770), a friend of Gray who provided him working space and help with his experiments
Charles-François de Cisternay Du Fay (1698-1739), French scientist who repeated many of Gray's experiments and continued his work

SUMMARY OF EVENT
Stephen Gray's father made a decent income dyeing cloth, and Gray carried on the family business while dabbling in science. At some time he seems to have studied with John Flamsteed, England's astronomer royal. Gray ground his own telescope lenses and measured eclipses, sunspots, and the revolutions of Jupiter's satellites. He made a microscope using as a lens a water droplet in a tiny hole made in a brass plate. It worked well enough for

him to see microscopic organisms swimming in the water, and he became widely known as a careful and talented observer. Although he was not a member, the Royal Society of London still published Gray's microscope observations in 1696.

The fellows of the Royal Society met weekly to discuss items of scientific interest, including the amber effect, in which rubbing amber enables it to attract bits of fluff, an effect that had been known since ancient times. More recently, William Gilbert showed that glass, sulfur, precious stones, resin, and sealing wax could also be "electrified," a term derived from the Greek word for amber, *elektron*. In 1706, Francis Hauksbee used a flint glass tube to demonstrate some effects of static electricity to the society, and hearing of this, Gray performed his own experiments and sent an account of them to the society in 1708. He later became friends with several society members when he became an assistant to Jean Théophile Desaguliers, who performed demonstrations for the organization.

When Gray hurt his back and could no longer work at the family trade, he applied to become a resident of Sutton's Hospital, also known as the London Charterhouse. This request was finally granted in 1719. The Charterhouse was a day school for poor boys and provided room and board for eighty male pensioners who were required to be educated enough to teach the boys. Gray continued to dabble with electrostatics but made relatively little progress. Finally, in 1729, at the age of sixty-three, he obtained a flint glass tube similar to the one used by Hauksbee. Just over 3 feet long and 1 inch in diameter, the tube acquired a static charge when rubbed with a cloth or by a dry hand. To keep dust out when the tube was not in use, Gray placed corks in the ends. He could tell when the tube had acquired "electric virtue" because it would then attract bits of feather, thread, or leaf-brass. When the tube was tested in the dark, a crackling sound and a flash of light (a spark) would sometimes occur, and Gray wondered if that light falling on a metal would convey "electric virtue" to the metal. He had previously attempted, but without success, to electrify metals by rubbing them.

Preparing for this experiment, Gray rubbed the tube, then noticing, however, that small feathers were attracted to the corks as well as to the tube. This simple observation was a breakthrough: Electric virtue could be conducted from one body to another. Flush with excitement, Gray tried every object he had at hand: An ivory ball with a hole in it was stuck on a short stick and the stick inserted in the cork; the ball suspended by wire or

3 feet of twine, silver coins, a lead ball, a fire shovel, an iron poker, metal tongs, a copper tea kettle (empty or full of hot or cold water), brick, tile, chalk, and a head of cabbage. All could be electrified when connected to the tube. Gray later found that materials such as wood or twine conduct only when the humidity is high enough.

Next, Gray wondered how far the electric virtue could be made to travel. Limited by the size of his room, he assembled 18 feet of sticks and canes and connected one end to the tube and the other to the ivory ball, which became electrified. Needing more space, during the next few months he visited his friends John Godfrey and Granville Wheler, both of whom had large homes and lands. They eventually succeeded in transmitting electric virtue down 886 feet of twine, but two more important discoveries were made along the way. Godfrey and Gray prepared a horizontal line of twine suspended by twine from nails in a ceiling beam and had absolutely no success. Gray reasoned correctly that the electric virtue flowed up the twine and was dissipated in the ceiling beam.

When Gray visited Wheler and explained the problem of suspending a horizontal line, Wheler suggested that the twine line could be suspended with silk threads; this strategy was successful. Gray supposed that the silk thread blocked the flow of electric virtue because it had a much smaller diameter than the twine. Later, however, when the silk support lines broke under the weight of long lengths of twine and they used brass wire no thicker than the silk lines to replace them, there was once again no electric flow. Gray now correctly reasoned that it was not the diameter of the support lines that was important, but that some materials allowed the flow of electric virtue into the ceiling while others blocked this flow.

As Gray continued to experiment, he wondered if people could be electrified. This led to a dramatic demonstration, called "the charity boy," which is still associated with Gray's name. The spectacle made great after-dinner entertainment for guests, and it was educational. Gray suspended two large loops of horsehair clothesline from hooks in the ceiling. He had a charity boy (a student in a private charitable school for the poor) lie horizontally, suspended in the air by one loop about his chest and the other about his legs. Then Gray used his excited glass tube to electrify the boy. Any guest who tried to touch the boy was zapped by a sharp spark, and when the boy extended his hands over insulated stands holding bits of feathers and leaf-brass, the bits jumped upward to his hands. If a guest brought a finger near the boy's nose, the finger would draw sparks from the boy's nose. The spectacle left no doubt that people could be electrified. Gray wrote a careful description of his experiments and findings, which was published by the Royal Society in 1732.

The principles of conductivity can be demonstrated in modern terms. For example, when different materials, such as a wool cloth and a glass rod, are placed into close contact and then separated (helped by rubbing), some electrons will be transferred from the glass to the wool. This leaves the glass charged positively and the wool negatively. If a small feather is brought close to the positively charged glass, it will act on the atoms of the feather to pull some electrons in each atom to the side of the atom that is closest to the glass rod. Since the average negative charge in the feather is now slightly closer than the average positive charge, the feather will be attracted to the glass. If the feather now touches the glass rod, some electrons from the feather may transfer to the rod, leaving the feather positive and the rod less positive. Both rod and feather are positively charged and the feather will now be repelled from the rod. Gray, and others, observed both the attractive and repulsive effects. In fact, one of Gray's favorite demonstrations was to repel a feather and make it float in the air by holding the tube horizontally and keeping it beneath the feather.

SIGNIFICANCE

Stephen Gray continued to experiment and publish until he became too ill. He died in 1736. He had received the Royal Society's greatest honor, the Copley Medal, in 1731, the first year it was awarded. He had received it again in 1732 and was also elected a fellow of the Royal Society. Gray's friend Desaguliers gave the modern names "conductors" and "insulators" to the two classes of materials Gray had discovered.

The French scientist Charles-François de Cisternay Du Fay visited Wheler and Gray in 1732. Inspired by their work, Du Fay came up with the two-fluid theory of electricity, which remained popular until it was super-seded by Benjamin Franklin's one-fluid theory. Since Gray was the first to send electrical signals hundreds of feet down a line, he is an ancestor of the telegraph, the telephone, and long-distance communication. Perhaps most important, just as William Gilbert made the study of magnets scientific, Gray, more than any of his predecessors, made the study of electricity scientific.

—*Charles W. Rogers*

FURTHER READING

Bodanis, David. *Electric Universe: The Shocking True Story of Electricity*. New York: Crown, 2005. A fascinating exploration of the history of electricity that looks at inventions from the lightbulb to the computer. Includes a helpful annotated bibliography.

Fara, Patricia. *An Entertainment for Angels: Electricity in the Enlightenment*. New York: Columbia University Press, 2002. Fara describes early electrical experiments and examines Gray and his work. Includes bibliographical references.

Heilbron, J. L. *Electricity in the Seventeenth and Eighteenth Centuries: A Study in Early Modern Physics*. Mineola, N.Y.: Dover, 1999. An excellent science history book that places Gray's work in context. Although there are no equations, better-prepared students will benefit most from this work. Contains an extensive bibliography.

SEE ALSO: 1733: Du Fay Discovers Two Kinds of Electric Charge; Oct., 1745, and Jan., 1746: Invention of the Leyden Jar; June, 1752: Franklin Demonstrates the Electrical Nature of Lightning; 1800: Volta Invents the Battery.

RELATED ARTICLES in *Great Lives from History: The Eighteenth Century, 1701-1800*: Henry Cavendish; Benjamin Franklin; Luigi Galvani; Joseph Priestley; Alessandro Volta.

November 9, 1729, and February, 1732
TREATY OF SEVILLE

In 1727, Spain mounted an unsuccessful attempt to recapture Gibraltar from Britain, which had held the peninsula since 1704. The Treaty of Seville ended this military conflict and contributed to the rising power of Britain and the decline of Spain in the eighteenth century.

LOCALE: Seville, Spain

CATEGORIES: Diplomacy and international relations; wars, uprisings, and civil unrest; expansion and land acquisition

KEY FIGURES

Philip V (1683-1746), king of Spain, r. 1700-1746

Isabella Farnese (1692-1766), queen consort of Spain, r. 1714-1746

Robert Walpole (1676-1745), prime minister of Britain, 1721-1742

André-Hercule de Fleury (1653-1743), prime minister of France, 1726-1743

SUMMARY OF EVENT

During the War of the Spanish Succession (1701-1714), Gibraltar was captured in August, 1704, by British-Dutch forces under the command of Admirals George Byng and George Rooke. Spain's military attempt the following year to regain the southernmost part of the Iberian Peninsula was unsuccessful. The Treaty of Utrecht, which ended the war in 1713, not only dismembered Spain's European empire but also, in Article 10, forced Spain to cede Gibraltar to the British.

Spain's King Philip V and his new Italian queen, Isabella Farnese, soon actively resisted the provisions of the treaty. They sent military expeditions in 1717 and in 1718 to attempt to regain some of their empire's former Italian territories. These Spanish incursions into Italy led to war with Britain and France from December, 1718, to 1721. Spain next attempted the diplomatic route: The Spanish negotiated with Austria to regain Gibraltar and their Italian lands, signing the First Treaty of Vienna in 1725. This treaty only provoked more alliances against Spain, however, and was ultimately unsuccessful. In all the alliances, secret pacts, and peace agreements it conducted between 1713 and 1726, Spain received promises of support for the restoration of Gibraltar. These included a famous letter of June 12, 1720, from Britain's King George I, in which he promised that he would restore the peninsula if Parliament approved. However, none of these promises was fulfilled.

By the end of 1726, Philip V decided to retake Gibraltar by force. The loss of Gibraltar had been particularly galling to the Spanish, because Spain had held Gibraltar since 1462. Moreover, the seizure of the peninsula represented the first time since Arabs invaded the country in the Middle Ages that Spain had lost part of its own soil to a foreign power. Philip effectively declared war on January 1, 1727, when he sent a letter to London stating that Article 10 of the Treaty of Utrecht was null and void as a result of British infringements of prior agreements. Spanish troops were assembled under Count de Las Torres, who decided against a direct, surprise attack on the fortress of Gibraltar. He chose, instead, the formalized and systematic operation of a siege—often the preferred mode of warfare in the first half of the eighteenth century, because it tended to be of short duration with fewer casualties than pitched battles. By early February, his forces began digging trenches and building batteries with which to initiate the attack.

On February 22, 1727, the military conflict began. The British, under the command of Lieutenant Governor Jasper Clayton, fired the first shots, seeking to halt construction of the batteries and trenches. By the end of March, 1727, despite damage to their construction efforts and weapons, Spanish batteries had launched a ten-day barrage of cannon fire. Heavy rain in April slowed the siege, as it filled the trenches and swept away batteries, but in May the Spanish launched a massive bombardment against the British that again ultimately failed.

The Spanish troops were at a disadvantage, because the British were quite secure in their elevated position at the top of the Rock of Gibraltar. British weapons and batteries, like the famous Willis's Battery, were already in place, and most of the damage to the defenders' armaments could be repaired at night. Furthermore, the fleet in the bay, under the command of Admiral Sir Charles Wager, kept the British protected and supplied with fresh provisions. The Spanish troops were also weakened by weather-related illnesses, by drunkenness, and by desertion—a common problem among mercenary troops. More than half of de Las Torres's troops were foreigners, and of the twenty-four hundred men the Spanish lost, nine hundred deserted.

With a total loss of only three hundred men, the fortified Gibraltar proved to be impregnable to a land attack by means of eighteenth century weaponry. After five months of conflict, a seven-article truce for a cease-fire was agreed to on June 24 between de Las Torres and Gibraltar's governor, David Colyear, Lord Patmore. Troops, however, remained in place on both sides until March, 1728, when Philip V ordered the cessation of the siege.

The formal resolution of the British-Spanish hostilities in 1727 was a long, drawn-out diplomatic affair. In May, 1727, even before the military action had ceased, France's new prime minister, Cardinal André-Hercule de Fleury, brokered preliminary points of agreement between Spain and Britain in line with stipulations from Britain's prime minister, Robert Walpole. On March 6, 1728, the preliminary agreements were signed at the Convention of Pardo, officially ending the siege, with further negotiations to be held in a general congress in Soissons, France, beginning June 14. Lasting for more than one year, the discussions at Soissons laid the foundation for the Treaty of Seville between Britain, Spain, and France, which was finally signed on November 9, 1729. In July, 1731, Austria agreed to accept the terms of the treaty, and the treaty's complete and final version was signed in February, 1732.

The Treaty of Seville confirmed the general terms of agreement of the Treaty of Utrecht with a few adjustments. Although Spain was allowed to take possession of fortifications in Livorno, Parma, Piacenza, and Tuscany, it had to cede Sardinia to Savoy and Sicily to Austria. Austria agreed to suspend the operation of its Ostend India Trading Company for seven years, returning the European trade balance to its status before the war.

Britain profited the most from the treaty, because the agreement dramatically strengthened Robert Walpole's ability to achieve his longstanding goals for economic expansion. Britain's commercial privileges were reinstated, particularly the Spanish *asiento de negros* ("Negroes' contract"). The *asiento* was a license from Spain to furnish slaves to its possessions in the New World that had passed from France to Britain in 1713 for a thirty-year period, but it had been superseded during the war, because Spain had embargoed British trade. Britain, through its South Sea Company, was to supply forty-eight hundred African slaves annually to Spain's overseas markets, so when the Treaty of Seville lifted the two-year embargo by Spain, Britain's resumed trade activities were quite lucrative.

The treaty, however, left untouched two areas of serious disagreement. First, demands for compensation brought by Spain and Britain against each other for longstanding trade grievances were left unresolved. Prior incidents of Spanish seizures of British ships and of illegal trading by the British remained disputes that dragged on in the courts from 1732 to 1738. Second, the ownership of Gibraltar was not explicitly discussed at the diplomatic table. The unresolved tensions over these issues would later lead to more hostilities.

SIGNIFICANCE

The Treaty of Seville essentially returned Europe to its political and economical status quo before the war. The retention of Gibraltar helped Britain remain the supreme power in the western Mediterranean and continued to give it an important base of operations for trade with the New World. With the reinstatement of the *asiento*, Britain was again poised to become the dominant commercial power in Europe and to increase its colonial power overseas. Spain, on the other hand, continued to regress militarily and economically throughout the rest of the century.

The failure of the treaty to resolve compensation issues and officially to confirm the status of Gibraltar eventually led to further conflict. Within a decade, old and new trade grievances between Spain and Britain erupted into the War of Jenkins's Ear. From 1779 to 1783, Philip V's son, Charles III, attempted one final siege against Gibraltar, which was unsuccessful, and in 1830 it became a British crown colony. The Treaty of Seville afforded only a momentary respite to the enmity between Spain and Britain on the seas and in the colonies that would continue for the rest of the eighteenth century and beyond.

—*Marsha Daigle-Williamson*

FURTHER READING

Black, Jeremy. *The British Seaborne Empire*. New Haven, Conn.: Yale University Press, 2004. Focuses on the naval component of the expansion of the British Empire, in Europe and the Americas, from its beginning to the present. Extensive notes, index.

Harvey, Maurice. *Gibraltar*. Kent, England: Spellmount, 1996. Good historical overview with helpful maps, illustrations.

Jackson, Sir William G. F. *The Rock of the Gibraltarians: A History of Gibraltar*. Cranbury, N.J.: Associated University Presses, 1987. Detailed accounts of all the sieges of Gibraltar; illustrations, photos, maps and appendices, including the text of Article 10 of the Treaty of Utrecht.

Kamen, Henry. *Philip V of Spain: The King Who Reigned Twice*. New Haven, Conn.: Yale University Press, 2001. Favorable biography of Philip; detailed account of the treaty. Glossary, index.

1720's

_____. *Spain's Road to Empire: The Making of a World Power, 1492-1763.* New York: Penguin Putnam, 2002. Account of Spain's rise and fall, militarily and economically.

Thomas, Hugh. *The Slave Trade: The Story of the Atlantic Slave Trade, 1440-1870.* New York: Simon & Schuster, 1997. Excellent in-depth discussion of the political and economic contexts for slave trade; good explanation of *asiento* and its history. Notes, bibliography, index.

SEE ALSO: May 26, 1701-Sept. 7, 1714: War of the Spanish Succession; Apr. 11, 1713: Treaty of Utrecht; 1721-1742: Development of Great Britain's Office of Prime Minister; 1739-1741: War of Jenkins's Ear; 1759: Charles III Gains the Spanish Throne; 1775: Spanish-Algerine War; June 21, 1779-Feb. 7, 1783: Siege of Gibraltar.

RELATED ARTICLES in *Great Lives from History: The Eighteenth Century, 1701-1800*: Charles III; André-Hercule de Fleury; George I; Philip V; Robert Walpole.

1730-1739
FIRST MAROON WAR

Two groups of rebellious and escaped slaves, as well as their descendants, fought British soldiers to a draw during nearly a decade of fighting in Jamaica, securing for themselves some freedoms but only at the expense of those slaves still in bondage.

LOCALE: Jamaica

CATEGORIES: Wars, uprisings, and civil unrest; social issues and reform

KEY FIGURES

Nanny (d. 1750's), leader of the Windward Maroons from 1725 to 1740

Kojo (Cudjoe; d. 1744), leader of the Leeward Maroons in the 1730's

Robert Hunter (1666-1734), a governor of Jamaica, 1728-1734, and leader of the failed attempt to take Nanny Town in 1732

Captain Stoddart (fl. 1734), leader of the successful attempt to destroy Nanny Town in 1734

SUMMARY OF EVENT

Resistance to slavery took on many forms in the American colonies. In Jamaica, Brazil, and Suriname, large numbers of enslaved Africans escaped and set up their own independent communities and kingdoms. By the eighteenth century, they were called "Maroons," derived from the Spanish word *cimarrón*, meaning wild and uncontrollable. In Jamaica, by the 1730's, there were two main groups of Maroons resisting British rule: the Windward, or eastern, society, which was led by Nanny from about 1725 to 1740, and the Leeward, or western, society, which was led by Kojo (the anglicized spelling of Cudjoe) during the First Maroon War of the 1730's.

Both groups bedeviled overly confident colonial commanders for more than a decade. Their struggle began, however, at least eighty years before the legendary contests of the 1730's. The Windward culture, in particular, prided itself on a long history of resistance to plantation slavery that stemmed from the English takeover of Jamaica from the Spanish in 1655. When Spanish settlers fled to Cuba in the wake of the British invasion, most of their enslaved Africans and a handful of their free African subjects retreated to the remote and rugged interior of eastern Jamaica, away from the coastal towns and the new slaveholders in charge. These suddenly empowered Africans became the nucleus of the Windward Maroons. At first, they tried to use Spain against Britain, hoping that division among Europeans would guarantee their liberty. In the late 1650's, Africans sided with a few Spanish holdouts, led by Don Cristóbal Arnaldo de Ysassi. Every Spanish counterattack on British settlers featured armed Africans, yet the British knew early how to play "divide and conquer" as well, offering land and the official title of magistrate to one key Maroon leader, Juan Lubolo (or Juan de Bolas). Receiving thirty acres and the legal status of a free-born Englishman for his own *palenque* (community), Lubolo defected and betrayed other Maroons by giving the British valuable intelligence about their elusive whereabouts. Even though the Spanish holdouts would give up and leave when the new "colonel of the black militia" (Lubolo) collaborated, most of the other Maroons stepped up their hit-and-run attacks, eventually ambushing Lubolo and hacking his body to pieces.

Juan de Serras, the leader of the insurgents and the avenger of Lubolo, along with his successors, limited and delayed the expansion of sugar and slavery into the interior of eastern Jamaica. Soon, however, the plantocracy was fighting a two-front war, as slave revolts on newly cleared English plantations just south of Montego Bay and Falmouth escalated into a mass escape around 1690 to the inland Cockpit Country, the genesis of the Leeward Maroons. By the 1730's, Kojo emerged as their ruler, presiding over a western African polity transplanted to the Caribbean and built on Akan, Asanti, and Fanti traditions.

This frontier kingdom drew its strength from its ethnic homogeneity and identity as a Kromanti (or Coromantine or Koromantyne) state. This identity stemmed from the original mass escape in which all of the leaders either came through or had relatives pass through the English slave factory at the Fanti town of Kromantine on the African Gold Coast. Kojo's father was one of these leaders, and thus he bestowed a historical legitimacy upon his son, who then carried on the martial and militant reputa-

tion of Kromanti and, more specifically, Akan men. A constant flow of reinforcements came as the greed of Jamaican sugar planters made them prefer physically strong bondsmen from the Gold Coast, who joined the Leeward culture even more combat-ready if they had survived the horrors of the Middle Passage and the seasoning and if they had escaped scot-free into the mountains. By the 1730's, these fighters and their families had overcome interethnic rivalries (such as the Asanti versus the Fanti) left over from the Old World to unify as Kromanti against the British colonists. A new sense of a shared ethnicity and awful experiences heartened and strengthened the cohesion of Maroon communities in the west.

In contrast, the Windward Maroons were more ethnically diverse and decentralized than their western counterparts, but they were energized and unified after 1725 by an extraordinary woman, the famous Nanny. In addi-

Sugar plantations in the West Indies, such as the one illustrated here, thrived with the labor of African slaves, who revolted against plantation owners in a decade-long conflict known as the First Maroon War. (Library of Congress)

1730's

tion to the original Spanish Maroons, the Windwards included a shipwrecked group from Madagascar and their progeny and the Kromanti survivors of a widespread slave rebellion on the Grey estate in Guanaboa Vale. Unlike Kojo's kingdom, this loosely tied confederation was more unfriendly toward new migrants, seeing them as potential spies and interlopers in their lands. Accordingly, even though they controlled more acres, they had fewer people. Yet it was the Akan and Asanti (Kromanti) belief in the power of strong women as potential political and religious leaders that paved the way for the legendary and unifying leadership of Nanny, which still inspires extant Maroon communities on the island today.

Queen Nanny, as she also was known, was born in what is now Ghana, probably in the 1680's, and emerged as a respected *obeah*, or spiritual director, by the 1720's. Imploring the help of ancestors, gods, and goddesses from all three camps of the Windwards, she became the Windwards' chief military strategist in the 1730's and reportedly trained her armies in the use of *abeng*, or cow horns, which signaled movements and feints over the valleys and hills of the east. Her armies lost once only. In 1734, British captain Stoddart used new portable artillery to destroy Nanny Town, a fortified village at the top of a steep mountain accessible only by one person at a time along a very constricted, winding trail that exposed climbers to snipers. The Windward Maroons regrouped a few miles away and then established New Nanny Town, or what became known as Moore Town, which still exists.

Land pressures forced the British to make a more concerted effort against their hard-to-pin-down foes, yet the Maroons' deployment of the *abeng*, coupled with their use of camouflage and botanical knowledge (to disguise their scent from tracking dogs), frustrated one of the greatest empires in the world. (This same difficulty with guerrilla tactics outside the standard European "rules" for warfare in the eighteenth century would doom British general Edward Braddock and his redcoats on the Pennsylvania frontier in 1755.) Tropical fevers such as malaria and yellow fever, as well as poor intelligence and impossible logistics, gave both the Leeward and Windward cultures great advantages over the British, as many soldiers fresh from Europe died before ever meeting their enemy. Ambushes made things worse for the British: Their first attempt to destroy Nanny Town in 1732 under Governor Robert Hunter failed because of repeated surprise attacks.

Eventually, though, both sides were ready for peace by 1738. Scorched-earth tactics against the insurgents wore down their ability to keep up the fight in the long term. Outside help forced the Maroons to the bargaining table. Throughout 1738 and 1739, the British hired Miskito Indian mercenaries from coastal Central America, fierce fighters who were less prone to the malaria and yellow fever that so plagued European soldiers not used to the tropics. They also uncovered the remote and hidden villages of the Maroons by using their time-honored tracking techniques. About the same time, the British invited Spanish chasseurs (bounty hunters) from Cuba and their crack bloodhounds trained in finding runaway slaves. The British also armed slaves and troops of free blacks to fight the Maroons in both the east and west.

SIGNIFICANCE

The British strategy of arming slaves and free blacks poisoned any possible united African front against slavery. Maroons in both the west and the east now felt no obligation to help the enslaved, closing their communities to any new fugitives. By the 1750's, to stave off land-hungry planters, both the Leeward and Windward Maroons eagerly became paid slave catchers, providing the isolated kingdoms with much needed revenues. This role preserved British rule at key junctures, including Tacky's Rebellion of 1760, Jamaica's largest slave rebellion on the eve of emancipation in 1832, and the largest uprising of peasants after emancipation in 1865. Maroon help was the only thing that saved the day for the outnumbered British on Jamaica.

The cornerstones of this new strange alliance were the treaties of 1739 and 1740, which gave both the Windward and Leeward Maroons limited autonomy in return for helping against future rebellions or with future runaways. Most significant, all Maroons received legal acknowledgment of their landownership and their political and judicial institutions. To the British, however, the treaties were never meant to be followed or to be permanent. For sugar estates to be profitable, they needed more acres and more people. Because Jamaica was an island, with limited acreage, Maroon lands were often chipped away and utilized by colonial planters expanding their operations. In the 1790's, in response to renewed fighting between settlers and Maroons in the west, the British deported the Windward Maroons who lived between Trelawney Town and the Cockpit Country, first to Nova Scotia and then to Sierra Leone. In 1842, eight years after slavery was abolished in Jamaica as well as the entire British Empire, the British formally annulled both treaties of 1739. The Maroons would remain semi-independent, however, as sugar monoculture declined in profit and significance. The land pressures diminished as Jamaica became an imperial backwater.

—*Charles H. Ford*

FURTHER READING

Craton, Michael. *Testing the Chains: Resistance to Slavery in the British West Indies*. Ithaca, N.Y.: Cornell University Press, 1982. This work places the Maroons of Jamaica into a comparative context with those fighting or escaping slavery on other British-controlled islands, such as Barbados and Antigua.

Gottlieb, Karla Lewis. *The Mother of Us All: A History of Queen Nanny, Leader of the Windward Jamaican Maroons*. Trenton, N.J.: Africa World Press, 2000. This popular history uncovers little-known clues about the legendary leader of the Windward Maroons.

Kopytoff, Barbara Klamon. "The Development of Jamaican Maroon Ethnicity." *Caribbean Quarterly*, nos. 2/3 (1976): 33-50. This pioneering article focuses on the ethnic identities from western Africa that were behind the resistance of the Maroons.

Robinson, Carey. *The Fighting Maroons of Jamaica*. Kingston, Jamaica: William Collins & Sangster, 1969. This work remains the most accessible chrono-

logical account of the events of the 1730's, including the treaties of 1739. Should be read with updated and specialized research.

Zips, Werner. *Black Rebels: African Caribbean Freedom Fighters in Jamaica*. Translated by Shelley L. Frisch. Princeton, N.J.: Markus Wiener, 1999. Showing both current and past Maroons as complex human beings and not just passive victims, this work synthesizes both archival and oral sources. Excellent maps, pictures, photographs, and bibliography.

SEE ALSO: 18th cent.: Expansion of the Atlantic Slave Trade; Apr. 6, 1712: New York City Slave Revolt; Aug., 1712: Maya Rebellion in Chiapas; Nov. 23, 1733: Slaves Capture St. John's Island; Sept. 9, 1739: Stono Rebellion; 1760-1776: Caribbean Slave Rebellions; 1780-1781: Rebellion of Tupac Amaru II; Aug. 22, 1791-Jan. 1, 1804: Haitian Independence; July, 1795-Mar., 1796: Second Maroon War.

RELATED ARTICLES in *Great Lives from History: The Eighteenth Century, 1701-1800*: Joseph Boulogne; Nanny; Guillaume-Thomas Raynal; Granville Sharp; Toussaint Louverture; Tupac Amaru II.

c. 1732
SOCIETY OF DILETTANTI IS ESTABLISHED

In response to a growing interest in Greek and Roman antiquities—especially among aristocratic British travelers who had seen them firsthand—the Society of Dilettanti was established in London for the study and discussion of those antiquities. The society helped fund and promote major archaeological expeditions and also contributed to the rise of neoclassicism in British art and architecture.

LOCALE: London, England
CATEGORIES: Organizations and institutions; anthropology; art; architecture

KEY FIGURES

Francis Dashwood (Fifteenth Baron Le Despencer; 1708-1781), English founder of the Society of Dilettanti and later a government minister

Charles Sackville (Earl of Middlesex; 1711-1769), English founder of the Society of Dilettanti and later second duke of Dorset, 1765-1769

George Knapton (1698-1778), English painter and later curator of the Royal Collection

SUMMARY OF EVENT

Two trends that came together in the first part of the eighteenth century made possible the foundation of the Society of Dilettanti. The first trend was the continued growth of secular clubs and societies in Britain, often building on the traditions established by the religious societies of the preceding century. That century had also seen the formation of the Royal Society, perhaps the greatest British society, under the aegis of Sir Isaac Newton. Some of the new societies—such as the Beefsteak Club or the notorious Hellfire Club—were no more than dining clubs, but others engaged in serious intellectual pursuits. For example, the Society of Antiquaries discussed the discovery, description, and explanation of various antiquarian sites, customs, and cultural expressions, particularly in Great Britain.

The second trend leading to the establishment of the Society of Dilettanti was the resumption of the Grand Tour by young British aristocrats. The tour consisted of an extended journey, often lasting several years and under the guidance of a tutor, to the centers both of contemporary culture and of ancient antiquity. Early tours focused especially on France and Italy, but as the Ottoman Empire became more receptive to European visitors, later tours also encompassed significant sites in Greece and Asia Minor (western Turkey). The English aristocrat Lord Chesterfield wrote letters to his son that stand as the epitome of fatherly guidance to a son on such a tour. These letters demonstrate that the primary purpose of the Grand Tour was to gain manners, enlarge the mind, and acquire a familiarity with the languages, customs, and traditions of other civilized nations.

The Society of Dilettanti was probably formed in either 1732 or 1733 (though some accounts put it as late as 1736) by a group of gentlemen, mainly sons of aristocrats, who had taken the Grand Tour and whose interests had been awakened to the newly discovered antiquities of Italy and Greece. The word "dilettante" means a gentleman amateur, one who will show interest in a gracious and stylish way. The society was not meant to be a study group. Rather, it was conceived as a dining club where the social interchange would be as significant as the intellectual. The society's founders sought to encourage by all means possible a greater interest in antiquities. They also aimed to develop a taste for neoclassical art and architecture at home.

The archaeology of the ancient world was still in its infancy when the Society of Dilettanti first met. The ancient site of Herculaneum was only opened for archaeological investigation in 1738, and Pompeii was excavated beginning in 1748. Thus, even the society's founding members had little idea of the scope of the antiquities awaiting discovery. Originally, the society consisted of twenty-three gentlemen and one painter, whose job became to paint each member's portrait in a somewhat parodic manner. Meetings were presided over by an archmaster, and various subcommittees were organized to facilitate society business. The balance of pleasure and profit sought by the society was greeted with contempt in some quarters. Robert Walpole, Britain's prime minister, stated that the organization was merely another excuse to get drunk.

Despite their often lavish and ostentatious lifestyles, however, the society's members really did commit themselves to its aims, and as the century progressed it became the driving force behind the development of archaeology as a science. The society encouraged the systematic description and collection of antiquities, sending out archaeological expeditions and surveys and

then publishing their findings. One of the most famous of these surveys was that conducting by James Stuart and Nicholas Revett in Athens between 1751 and 1754.

The Antiquities of Athens: Measured and Delineated by James Stuart and Nicholas Revett was published in five volumes between 1762 and 1830. Their surveys, sketches, and detailed descriptions set high standards for future archaeological surveys. To produce the work, moreover, Stuart and Revett overcame significant obstacles, including Turkish occupation of the Acropolis, plague, rivalry with the French, and loss of motivation. The Society of Dilettanti paid for the publication of the third and fourth volumes of *The Antiquities of Athens*, published in 1794 and 1816, respectively. (Volume 4, which contained details of the Parthenon marbles, was published the same year that the seventh earl of Elgin sold them to the British Museum.) The volumes made a new image of Greece available to the British public, just as the work of German archaeologist Johann Joachim Winckelmann made such an image available in Germany.

In 1766, Revett conducted an expedition to Ionia under the Society of Dilettanti's auspices together with Richard Chandler and William Pars. The first edition of the society's account of this expedition appeared in 1769 under the title *Antiquities of Ionia*. Chandler's later account appeared as *Travels in Asia Minor* (1775). A second expedition to Ionia followed in 1811, and Chandler's account of it was published beginning in 1817. Owing to the loss of plates, however, the final, fifth volume of Chandler's account was not published until 1915.

The Society of Dilettanti also found itself influential in areas other than the funding of archaeological expeditions. Its efforts to promote a neoclassical taste in architecture were especially successful. Several English aristocrats had their country mansions rebuilt in the Palladian style, for example, and the design of the British Museum, opened in 1759, constitutes a particularly visible example of the society's influence upon Enlightenment tastes in architecture. The society also helped to establish the Royal Society for Arts in 1754 and the Royal Academy of Arts in 1768.

Three original members of the Society of Dilettanti exemplify its place within eighteenth century British culture. Francis Dashwood made his first trip abroad in 1726, followed by excursions in 1729 and in 1739, when he saw the excavations just beginning at Herculaneum. He was passionate about art and antiquity. He remained an active member of the society for thirty-five years and became its archmaster in 1746. He was elected a fellow of both the Royal Society for Arts and the Royal Society. He entered Parliament as an independent, opposed to the government, but nevertheless served on various parliamentary committees. He was briefly chancellor of the exchequer (1762-1763) and then became lord lieutenant of Buckinghamshire. He served jointly as postmaster general from 1766 to the end of his life.

Charles Sackville, a politician and impresario trying to sustain an Italian opera, had made three trips to Italy as a young man before joining the society. He also entered Parliament, but his reputation for dissolution and extravagance kept him from higher office. Nevertheless, he was appointed lord lieutenant of Kent. The society's first painter, George Knapton, had spent seven years in Italy as a young man, describing the excavations at Herculaneum. He was the one society member neither highborn nor wealthy, but he was commissioned to paint each member's portrait, a tradition maintained after his death by such famous painters as Sir Joshua Reynolds. Knapton was finally appointed surveyor and keeper of the king's paintings in 1765.

SIGNIFICANCE

The membership of the Society of Dilettanti lost some of its notoriety as the century went by, though even in the very respectable next century, the society still had privately printed a monograph on the erotic paintings dedicated to Priapus at Pompeii and Herculaneum. Its sponsorship of expeditions and surveys continued, as did its more general influence on neoclassical art and architecture. However, as tastes changed with the advent of Romanticism and the Gothic style, the achievements of the society were not always fully appreciated. Romantic paintings of classical ruins displaced the dispassionate architectural surveys sponsored by the society. Only when there was a resurgence in the appreciation of objectivity and rationality in the study of antiquity have the society's contributions been appreciated.

—*David Barratt*

FURTHER READING

Constantine, David. *Early Greek Travellers and the Hellenic Ideal.* New York: Cambridge University Press, 1984. A useful account of eighteenth century aristocratic travelers.

Cust, Lionel, comp. *History of the Society of Dilettanti.*

Edited by Sidney Colvin. London: Macmillan, 1898. The most official record, with various lists of members.

Dolan, Brian. *Exploring European Frontiers: British Travellers in the Age of the Enlightenment.* London: Palgrave Macmillan, 2000. Builds on David Constantine's book, with significant references to the Dilettanti.

Harcourt-Smith, Cecil. *The Society of Dilettanti.* London: 1977. An abridged version of Lionel Cust's account together with descriptions of the society through 1932.

Kelly, Jason M. *Polite Sociability and Levantine Archaeology in the British Enlightenment: The Society of the Dilettanti, 1732-1786.* Santa Barbara: University of California, ProQuest Digital Dissertation, 2004. An examination of the Dilettanti by an American scholar.

Kemp, B. *Sir Francis Dashwood: An Eighteenth Century Independent.* New York: St. Martin's Press, 1967. A biography of the Dilettanti's archmaster.

Schnapp, Alain. *The Discovery of the Past and the Origins of Archeology.* London: British Museum Press, 1996. Chapter 4 is especially relevant to those interested in the Dilettanti.

Sloan, Kim, ed. *Discovering the World in the Eighteenth Century.* London: British Museum Press, 2003. A series of essays by leading scholars centered on the founding of the British Museum.

West, Shearer. "Libertinism and the Ideology of Male Friendship in the Portraits of the Society of the Dilettanti." *Eighteenth-Century Life* 16 (May, 1992): 76-104. A discussion of the Dilettanti portraits and their wider cultural significance.

SEE ALSO: 1719-1724: Stukeley Studies Stonehenge and Avebury; 1748: Excavation of Pompeii; 1762: *The Antiquities of Athens* Prompts Architectural Neoclassicism; Dec. 10, 1768: Britain's Royal Academy of Arts Is Founded; July 19, 1799: Discovery of the Rosetta Stone.

RELATED ARTICLES in *Great Lives from History: The Eighteenth Century, 1701-1800*: Sir Joshua Reynolds; William Stukeley; Robert Walpole; Johann Joachim Winckelmann.

1730's

June 20, 1732
SETTLEMENT OF GEORGIA

Georgia became the last of the original thirteen British colonies when it was settled in 1732 by philanthropists who hoped the new colony would relieve the plight of thousands of destitute debtors and provide a haven for persecuted Protestants from other European countries. The British Empire also saw economic and militaristic benefits from the region: It occupied the area to protect its colonies from not only the encroaching Spaniards established in Florida but also indigenous peoples, who naturally resented European settlers in their homeland.

LOCALE: Southern United States
CATEGORY: Expansion and land acquisition

KEY FIGURES

John Martin Bolzius (1703-1765), leader of the German Salzburger settlers
Mary Musgrove (c. 1700-c. 1763), an American Indian interpreter and trader who, with her husband John, assisted the Georgia settlers
James Edward Oglethorpe (1696-1785), a British parliament member who proposed the founding of Georgia and was its first civil and military leader
John Perceval (First Earl of Egmont; 1683-1748), a promoter and recorder of the Georgia venture
Tomochichi (c. 1650-1739), chief of the Yamacraw Indians who resided in the Savannah area
James Wright (1716-1785), the most successful of the royal governors

SUMMARY OF EVENT

The founding of Georgia attracted more attention in England than that of any other colony. Because the project suited both philanthropic and imperial interests, it drew support from all segments of society and government, including philanthropists, such as James Edward Oglethorpe, a member of Parliament, and Thomas Bray, founder of the Society of the Gospel in Foreign Parts. The Crown was concerned with the Span-

iards who had gradually expanded northward from their Florida settlement, establishing presidios and missions, first on the Sea Islands and then on the mainland of Georgia. In addition to protecting their frontier against the Spanish, the British government had to contend with the Yamasee Indians, who were resentful of the encroaching European settlers.

The Crown also perceived economic advantages from a new colony that could contribute raw materials for English manufacturers, provide a market for their goods, and ease the mother country's unemployment problem. Therefore, when John Perceval (later the earl of Egmont), an associate of the late Dr. Bray, acted upon the suggestion of Oglethorpe and petitioned the Crown for a tract of land south and west of Carolina between the Savannah and Altamaha Rivers, the request was approved.

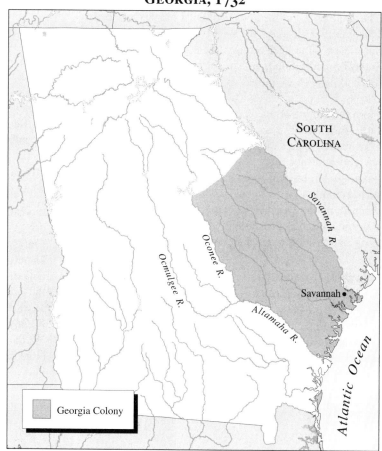

GEORGIA, 1732

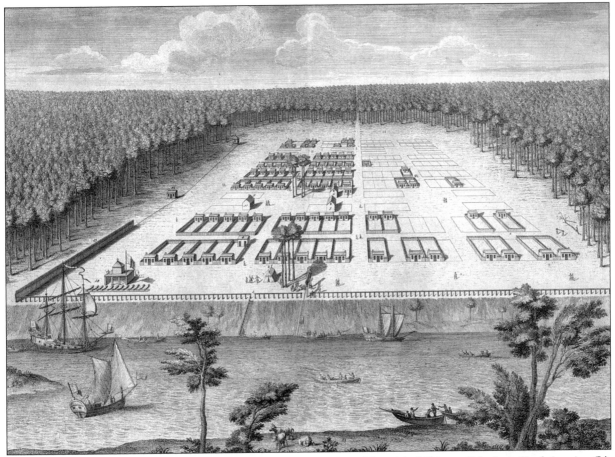

A bird's eye view of the fledgling settlement of Savannah, Georgia, the last of the original Thirteen Colonies in North America. (Library of Congress)

On June 20, 1732, the Crown conferred upon the twenty-one members of the board of trustees for Georgia a charter empowering them to found and to manage for twenty-one years the land between the Savannah and Altamaha Rivers, stretching as far westward as what had been called the South Sea (the Gulf of Mexico). Although the government took a calculated view of their enterprise, the trustees considered it the greatest philanthropic and social experiment of their age. Numerous churches, organizations, and individuals responded to their promotional campaign with contributions.

Because the settlers were to participate in a social experiment, they were individually selected from among applicants who included imprisoned debtors, the poor, and the downtrodden. Each received free passage to Georgia, tools, seeds, provisions until their first harvest, and fifty acres of land. Slaves, hard liquor, Catholics, and lawyers were prohibited in early Georgia.

In November, 1732, 114 settlers set sail on the ship *Anne*, with Oglethorpe leading the expedition to America. Disembarking in the Carolinas at Charleston in January, 1733, Oglethorpe soon chose a settlement site. With Mary Musgrove, an American Indian, serving as interpreter, Oglethorpe reached an agreement with Tomochichi, chief of the Yamacraws, a Creek group who lived in the area. On February 12, 1733 (Georgia's founder's day), the colonists arrived. With the aid of Colonel William Bull, a Carolinian, Oglethorpe laid out the city of Savannah, where settlement began. The communal arrangement provided that each family own a town lot with a garden and a piece of farmland nearby. Settlers held their land through "tail male," meaning that tenure was for life and only eldest sons could inherit land. The prohibition against the sale or rental of property eliminated the possibility of unselected immigrants becoming part of the community. Hoping once again to make silk production a profitable colonial enterprise, the Crown required each settler to clear ten acres and plant one hundred mulberry trees within ten years. Moreover, Georgia's colonial settlers were to produce wine, grow tropical plants, and provide other raw materials that would benefit the British mercantile system.

In addition to the "charity settlers," the trustees admitted approved adventurers, persons who paid their own passage to the colony. Persecuted Protestants, such as the Lutheran Salzburgers from Germany, also came. The Salzburgers, under the dynamic leadership of John Martin Bolzius, settled outside Savannah in the town of Ebenezer and quickly became the most prosperous group in early Georgia. Their church, New Jerusalem, is the oldest brick structure in the state.

Authority over Georgia's affairs was officially shared by the board of trustees and the British government, although in practice a smaller body known as the common council did most of the work. Among the most active trustees were Oglethorpe, Perceval, James Vernon, the earl of Shaftesbury (Anthony Ashley-Cooper), and Benjamin Martyn, the secretary. Although all laws passed by the trustees had to be reviewed by the king, the trustees neglected the political side of the Georgia colony. While the trustees held the philanthropic and social goals to be of primary importance, the government was concerned chiefly with the economic and defensive advantages that Georgia might contribute to the British Empire. The trustees came to distrust Sir Robert Walpole, the chancellor of the exchequer, and in order to evade the authority of the government, tried, as far as possible, to govern by regulations rather than laws. In the absence of local governmental institutions, Oglethorpe acted as Georgia's unofficial leader.

SIGNIFICANCE

Georgia's most serious problems in the early years were caused by the conflicting purposes it was expected to fulfill. Times were hard, rewards few. Inevitably, Georgia assumed a military character, and the colonists were distracted from the business of building a stable society. Oglethorpe focused much of his time on negotiating with the American Indians and leading his regiment into a series of skirmishes against the Spanish, for which he was rewarded military rank. When the fighting ended in 1743, General Oglethorpe left Georgia, never to return.

In the absence of a leader, hard times increased for the Georgia settlers; they ignored the liquor and slave prohibitions; and many resettled in other colonies. Furthermore, the trustees abandoned the colony a year before

their charter ended. Consequently, Georgia became a royal colony under the auspices of King George II, for whom the colony was named. The royal colony was under the leadership of three governors from 1754 to 1776: Captain John Reynolds, an unpopular leader who was forced back to England after serving two years; Henry Ellis, who was in poor health and did not last; and, finally, Sir James Wright, who was appointed in 1760. Under Governor Wright, colonial Georgia began to stabilize as its population grew. Among the new colonists were more than fifteen thousand African slaves who contributed much to colonial development. Wright remained governor of Georgia until the changes wrought by the American Revolution forced him from power. In 1777, under a new constitution, John Truetlen, a Salzburger, was elected the state's first governor as colonial Georgia theoretically ended.

—*Warren M. Billings, updated by Linda Rochell Lane*

FURTHER READING

Cashin, Edward J., ed. *Setting Out to Begin a New World: Colonial Georgia*. Savannah, Ga.: Beehive Press, 1995. Contains thirty primary documents from colonial Georgia, including firsthand accounts of the founding of Savannah and Frederica, descriptions of Oglethorpe's battles with mutinous soldiers, treaties with American Indians, documents regarding slavery, and information about the administration of Governor Wright.

Ettinger, Amos A. *James Edward Oglethorpe, Imperial Idealist*. Hamden, Conn.: Archon Books, 1968. A definitive biography of Georgia's founder that carefully analyzes his strengths, his weaknesses, and his life in general.

Jackson, Edwin L., Mary E. Stakes, Lawrence R. Hepburn, and Mary A. Hepburn. *The Georgia Studies Book*. Athens: University of Georgia Press, 1992. A standard textbook in many Georgia public schools. A comprehensive, illustrated work on the history of Georgia.

Jones, George Fenwick, ed. *The Salzburger Saga: Religious Exiles and Other Germans Along the Savannah*. Athens: University of Georgia Press, 1984. Commemorating the 250th anniversary of the Salzburgers' arrival in Georgia, this work overviews the Salzburgers' religious persecution in Germany, their trek to America, and their hardships and triumphs in colonial Georgia.

Lane, Mills, ed. *General Oglethorpe's Georgia*. 2 vols. Savannah, Ga.: Beehive Press, 1975. Contains colonial letters written by James Oglethorpe, colonial set- tlers, and others involved with Georgia's early settle- ment from 1733 to 1741.

McPherson, Robert G., ed. *The Journal of the Earl of Egmont: Abstract of the Trustees Proceedings for Establishing the Colony of Georgia, 1732-1738.* Athens: University of Georgia Press, 1962. A private record of the meeting of the Georgia trustees kept by Perceval in addition to the official minutes. An indispensable primary source.

Robinson, W. Stitt. *The Southern Colonial Frontier, 1607-1763.* Albuquerque: University of New Mexico Press, 1979. Places colonial Georgia in the context of other Southern colonies.

Spalding, Phinizy, and Harvey H. Jackson, eds. *Oglethorpe in Perspective: Georgia's Founder After Two*

Hundred Years. Tuscaloosa: University of Alabama Press, 1989. A collection that analyzes facets of Oglethorpe's life, his work in Parliament, and his time in Georgia as a soldier and administrator.

SEE ALSO: Sept. 22, 1711-Mar. 23, 1713: Tuscarora War; Sept. 9, 1739: Stono Rebellion; Oct. 5, 1759- Nov. 19, 1761: Cherokee War; Oct. 7, 1763: Proclamation of 1763; 1768-May 16, 1771: Carolina Regulator Movements; 1773-1788: African American Baptist Church Is Founded; 1785: First State Universities Are Established.

RELATED ARTICLES in *Great Lives from History: The Eighteenth Century, 1701-1800*: George II; Alexander McGillivray; James Edward Oglethorpe; Robert Walpole; Charles Wesley; John Wesley.

December 7, 1732
COVENT GARDEN THEATRE OPENS IN LONDON

Rivaled only by the Drury Lane Theatre and rebuilt three times after fire damage, Covent Garden Theatre was home to many of the best plays and musical productions of the eighteenth century. It has since become the foremost opera house in England.

LOCALE: London, England
CATEGORY: Theater

KEY FIGURES

John Rich (1692-1761), English founder and manager of Theater Royal, Covent Garden
Edward Shepherd (c. 1692-1747), English architect
Sir William Davenant (1606-1688) English poet and dramatist
Peg Woffington (1720?-1760), Irish actress
David Garrick (1717-1779), English actor and theatrical manager
John Philip Kemble (1757-1823), English manager of Covent Garden, 1800-1817
Sarah Siddons (1755-1831), English actress

SUMMARY OF EVENT

The first half of the eighteenth century was a time of tremendous progress in the London theater world. The number and size of theaters increased significantly, and the audiences grew to include citizens from other than the upper class. An important new stage was that of the Theatre Royal, Covent Garden, one of two theaters with

royal designation. Its founder, John Rich, began the plans for the theater in 1730. The unprecedented financial successes of his pantomimes and productions of John Gay's *The Beggar's Opera* (pr., pb. 1728) were largely responsible for his ability to embark upon the new venture. Rich, a famous actor and theater manager, had succeeded his father, Christopher Rich, in 1714 as the manager of the Lincoln's Inn Fields Theater, also located in the Covent Garden area. Rich employed the architect Edward Shepherd, who designed many other areas of Covent Garden, including the Goodman's Fields Theater, which he finished first.

Permission to build the theater was granted because Rich had been the successor to one of the letters of patent originally granted by Charles II to Sir William Davenant in 1660. The other such letter was that for the Drury Lane Theatre. The patent stated that the theaters were to produce all types of entertainment, including comic and tragic plays, opera, and other musical events. The duke of Bedford leased Rich a parcel of land 120 feet in length and 100 feet in width on Bow Street in Covent Garden, on a site originally that of a nunnery attached to Westminster Abbey. After two years of planning and recruiting subscribers, the Covent Garden Theatre celebrated its grand opening on December 7, 1732.

The elegant theater had a ceiling design showing Apollo in a group of muses along with William Shakespeare wearing a laurel wreath. It was acoustically far su-

The Covent Garden Theatre in London, in a drawing from around 1821. The theater had been rebuilt after a fire in 1806. (Library of Congress)

perior to older theaters in the area, as draperies in front and side boxes created a short reverberation time and flat ceilings helped avoid echoes. Orchestral tone was enhanced by the use of wood as the predominant building material. The theater had an orchestra pit, side boxes, a scene room, coffee room, wardrobe, and privies, the large number of which was quite a luxury for the time. Although little exact information is available as to seating capacity, financial records indicate that there were approximately thirteen hundred to fourteen hundred seats. Admission prices for the fifty-five boxes were five shillings (sixty pence) each. A seat in the pit cost one-half crown (thirty pence), and one in the gallery was one shilling (twelve pence). Seats on the stage itself, which were customary in the era, cost ten shillings. It was also a custom to allow servants to arrive on the afternoon of the performance to save places on the stage for their masters and mistresses. The revenue from opening night was £115.

The opening night production was a comedy, *The Way of the World* (pr., pb. 1700), by William Congreve, reputed to be the greatest English master of pure comedy. The theater continued to thrive with productions of both new works and older plays in new productions. *The Beggar's Opera*, Rich's earlier ticket to financial success, re-

mained a standard in the repertory. Among Rich's greatest stars were performers such as the great tragedian James Quin and the beautiful Irish actress Peg Woffington, who lived openly with the actor and manager of the Drury Lane Theatre, David Garrick, who also performed on the stage of Covent Garden. Garrick was known for the natural style of acting that he brought to eighteenth century theater, breaking the tradition of the more formal tragic style customary on the British stage.

Charles Macklin, a famous actor and playwright, also appeared at Covent Garden, often causing quarrels with the management at Drury Lane, where he had been more often employed. Known especially for such Shakespearean roles as Macbeth and Shylock, his interpretation changed the role of Shylock in *The Merchant of Venice* from a comedic role to one much more evil. In 1789, he made his last appearance at the theater as Shylock in a performance that he was unable to finish because of his aging memory. Subscriptions from two of his best-known plays supported him in his old age. They were *The Man of the World* (1781) and *Love à la Mode* (1759). Sarah Siddons was a favorite actress, most loved for her portrayal of Lady Macbeth. Actors John Henderson and Richard Wilson were often seen at Covent Garden in productions of Shakespeare's plays.

The Theatre Royal, Covent Garden, was also the scene of many musical productions, particularly the operas and oratorios of George Frideric Handel (1685-1759). Handel's operas were the first serious musical works to be performed at the theater and were a common offering from 1735 until his death. *Pastor Fido* (1712, 1734) was Handel's first opera at Covent Garden, the next one being *Ariodante* (1735). The following year both *Alcina* (1735) and *Atalanta* (1736) were added to the roster. Although productions were lavish, competition among cast members, high salary demands of the singers, and other complications caused Handel's career as an opera composer to be short lived. He soon turned to oratorios, which were more financially feasible. He wrote twenty-six English oratorios. One of the most notable was a royal performance for George II of *Messiah* in 1743, which began the tradition of oratorio performances every Lenten season at Covent Garden. Upon his death, Handel bequeathed his organ to Covent Garden Theatre.

A licensing act passed in London in 1737 made Covent Garden and Drury Lane, the two theaters with official patents, also the two officially recognized theaters in London. The act required that all productions pass a licensing committee and that the producer obtain a license from the lord chamberlain before producing a play for the public. For the next ten years, these two main theaters flourished, but otherwise the previously rapid growth of English theater was seriously hindered, as the minor houses were limited in their ability to stage productions.

SIGNIFICANCE

Modern English theater in many ways owes its traditions to the groundwork that was laid in the eighteenth century. Many new theaters were built, both large and small. New productions of old standards as well as productions of new plays were added to the repertory. A revolutionary aspect was in the casting of women in leading roles, something not before allowed by social customs. The social standing of all actors began to change, and the public treated them with a new respect. Acting techniques changed from rigid, formal styles to more natural, realistic interpretations, largely because of the influence of David Garrick and Charles Macklin. The Theatre Royal, Covent Garden, endured three fires and reconstructions, the first of which was in 1808 under John Philip Kemble's management. The new theater was designed by Sir Robert Smirke and rebuilt within a year. It suffered a fire in 1856. The present Covent Garden Theatre is the 1858 Italian Opera House built by E. M. Barry on the same site and refurbished in the 1980's. Today, as the Royal Opera House, Covent Garden remains one of the major international stages for opera and ballet.

—*Sandra C. McClain*

FURTHER READING

Borer, Mary. *Story of Covent Garden*. London: Robert Hale, 1984. Provides a good overall history of the theater with stories about actors, audiences, the surrounding neighborhood, and changes endured throughout its history. Includes illustrations of people and the theater and maps of the area.

Bucchianeri, E. A. *Handel's Path to Covent Garden: A Rocky Journey*. Bloomington, Ind.: 1st Books Library, 2002. A detailed and provocative scholarly account of Handel's place in the ever-changing London opera world of the eighteenth century. Highlights Handel's apparent need for artistic control.

Scouten, Arthur H., ed. *1729-1747*. Part 3 in *The London Stage, 1660-1800*. Carbondale: Southern Illinois University Press, 1961. A well-indexed collection of details about productions, including plays and other entertainments, casts, financial records, and commentary.

Shaw-Taylor, Desmond. *Covent Garden*. New York: Chanticleer Press, 1948. History of the three Covent Garden Theatres from 1732 to the mid-twentieth century, with emphasis on the time since the mid-nineteenth century. Colorful illustrations.

Trussler, Simon. *The Cambridge Illustrated History of the British Theatre*. New York: Cambridge University Press, 2000. Highly readable, complete history of English theater through the twentieth century. Excellent overview of actors, literature, and theaters.

Woodiwiss, Audrey. *A History of Covent Garden: Covent Garden Through the Years*. London: Conway/Covent Garden, 1982. A good place to begin research for a general overview of the history of the theater and its surroundings.

SEE ALSO: Jan. 29, 1728: Gay Produces the First Ballad Opera; Aug., 1763-Apr., 1765: David Garrick's European Tour.

RELATED ARTICLES in *Great Lives from History: The Eighteenth Century, 1701-1800*: David Garrick; George II; George Frideric Handel; Sarah Siddons; Peg Woffington.

1730's

1733
DE MOIVRE DESCRIBES THE BELL-SHAPED CURVE

Abraham de Moivre was the first person to describe the so-called normal curve, a symmetrical bell-shaped graph that symbolizes probability distribution. This graph of the average distribution of events resolved a serious issue that had been left hanging by the previous generation of mathematicians.

LOCALE: London, England
CATEGORIES: Mathematics; science and technology

KEY FIGURES
Abraham de Moivre (1667-1754), French-born English
    mathematician
Jakob I Bernoulli (1655-1705), Swiss mathematician
Nikolaus Bernoulli (1687-1759), Swiss mathematician,
    lawyer, and editor of Jakob's posthumous text

SUMMARY OF EVENT

The earliest mathematical work on probability involved problems with dice. Throws of the dice could be described by a function called the binomial distribution, which provided the probability of any given result coming up a set number of times given a set number of tosses of the dice. For example, given thirty-six tosses, 7 is most likely to come up six times; the next most likely outcomes are five times or seven times, then four times or eight times, and so on. The binomial distribution provides the exact probability of each result.

Problems relating to the binomial distribution proved difficult to answer until the mathematician Abraham de Moivre found a graphical way to approximate the function. The approximation had the shape of a bell. To continue the example of the dice, rolling six 7's would form the highest point on the bell, which would then slope downward to either side. This approximation enabled de Moivre to answer important questions about games of dice and other situations in which probability could be represented by the binomial distribution.

De Moivre was born in France to a Protestant family. He received his education in France but then left the country at the time of the revocation of the Edict of Nantes (1685) in view of the prospective danger to Protestants represented by Louis XIV's abandonment of the policy of religious tolerance protected by that edict. De Moivre's mathematical work was all done in England. Although he was a distinguished mathematician, however, he never fit into the English mathematical world.

Most of his life he had to eke out a living by tutoring students and answering questions about the applications of probability.

Nevertheless, de Moivre was highly esteemed by his contemporaries, including Sir Isaac Newton, the most eminent mathematician of the period. Newton is said to have told students with questions to ask de Moivre on the grounds that de Moivre knew the material better than did Newton. There is no evidence that Newton was being ironical in making such a strong claim, and de Moivre's name is still attached to an important theorem about powers of complex numbers.

De Moivre developed an interest in probability by reading some of the earliest treatments of the subject, which had only acquired mathematical respectability in the middle of the seventeenth century with the work of Blaise Pascal and Pierre de Fermat. He probably first read a treatise on probability by the Dutch mathematician Christiaan Huygens and shortly thereafter wrote one of the first English accounts of the subject, "De mensura sortis" (1711; on the measurement of chance), published in the *Philosophical Transactions of the Royal Society*. The progress of de Moivre's subsequent work on probability can be measured by the later editions of this text, which appeared in English as the textbook *The Doctrine of Chances: Or, A Method of Calculating the Probability of Events in Play* (1718, 1738, 1756). De Moivre also had a strong philosophical interest in the application of probability, which led him to draw philosophical conclusions from his mathematical results.

After the appearance of de Moivre's Latin text in the Royal Society's *Philosophical Transactions*, the foundations of probability theory were transformed by the posthumous appearance of Jakob I Bernoulli's *Ars conjectandi* (1713; the conjectural arts). The work was prepared for the press by Bernoulli's nephew, Nikolaus Bernoulli. Nikolaus himself had used his uncle's theories in a dissertation he submitted to the faculty of law at the University of Basel. The work was intended to illustrate the applications of probability to law, although it seems to have been of more interest to mathematicians than to lawyers.

One of the advances in Jakob I Bernoulli's treatment of probability was his formulation of the binomial distribution. The distribution was produced by looking at a sequence of identical experiments, where each had one possible target outcome (called a success) and one or more other outcomes (which would be collected together and called a failure). For example, if one throws a die a number of times, one could call a 6 a success and any other number a failure.

Bernoulli showed that the relative frequency of an event with probability p in n independent trials converges to p as n gets bigger. In other words, the odds of rolling a 6 are one in six: One could easily roll a die six times and not roll a 6; however, if one were to roll the same die one thousand times, it would be surprising if 6 did not come up about one-sixth of the time (approximately 167 times), and if one were to roll the die 1 million times, it would be extremely surprising if roughly one-sixth of the rolls did not result in 6's. The more times the die is rolled, the closer to the average or ideal theoretical results one's actual results will be. This is known as the law of large numbers, and it furnished a basis for the application of probability theory to practical situations in the physical world.

Despite demonstrating the law of large numbers theoretically, Bernoulli was unable to find a manageable way to perform the necessary arithmetic calculations to determine the probability of specific ranges of outcomes when the number of trials became large. For example, it was easy to calculate the probability of two successes in six trials, but it was much harder to perform the arithmetic in the case of two hundred successes in six hundred trials. (In both cases, the probability is close to one in three, but it is actually slightly smaller. One needs to crunch the numbers to find the exact probability.) The difficulty of performing extended arithmetic calculations made it difficult in turn to extend the general results Bernoulli had obtained to any specific situation. The algebra of dealing with the sum of many terms of a polynomial did not have an obvious solution.

De Moivre was able to see both the importance of Bernoulli's problem in this regard and the most fruitful direction to explore in order to find a solution. Earlier in his career, de Moivre had found a way to approximate factorials of large numbers. (Factorials are products of all the positive integers from 1 up to a certain number, so that 5 factorial, written 5!, is equal to $5 \times 4 \times 3 \times 2 \times 1$.) De Moivre had given credit for his method to the Scottish mathematician James Stirling, even though de Moivre had figured it out before Stirling did. The use to which de Moivre put the so-called Stirling's formula altered the course of probability theory thereafter. Indeed, de Moivre felt that the work was of such importance that he published it at his own expense.

De Moivre's application of Stirling's formula was published first in Latin as a pamphlet supplementing his *Miscellanea analytica* (1730), *Approximation ad summam terminorum binomii (a + b) in seriem expansi: Supplement to "Miscellanea Analytica"* (1733; approximation to the sum of the terms of a binomial [a + b] expanded in a series). It was later incorporated in English into subsequent editions of *The Doctrine of Chances*. What de Moivre accomplished in this pamphlet was the introduction of a curve known to mathematicians as the normal distribution and more popularly as the bell-shaped curve, or simply the bell curve. This curve would have been impossible to conceive without the calculus, but de Moivre was able to use the techniques of the calculus to make a number of statements about what the curve was like. He did not actually write down what mathematicians now regard as the strict mathematical definition of the curve, but his results indicated that he understood it well enough to use it.

The bell-shaped curve enabled de Moivre to develop a good approximation of the probability of ranges of outcomes in the binomial distribution, thereby solving the problem that had plagued Bernoulli. One of the major consequences of the curve was that it made it possible to determine the rough probability of a range of outcomes clustered around the center of the distribution for large numbers of trials. For example, if one flipped a coin 600 times, one could use de Moivre's technique to determine the likelihood of getting a number of heads between 250 and 350. Even more important, de Moivre's curve enabled the work of Bernoulli to be expressed in a more concrete, quantitative form. In evaluating the series that he obtained at values that were multiples of the square root of the number of trials, de Moivre concluded that the natural unit for measuring the deviation from the center would be that square root.

SIGNIFICANCE

The appearance of the normal distribution in the work of de Moivre permanently altered the emerging science of probability theory and its applications. One of the difficulties that Jakob Bernoulli had encountered in his work was in applying his results to statistical inference. The binomial distribution was the easiest distribution to describe mathematically, making it the best suited for creating a mathematical theory of statistical inference. De Moivre's curve was a necessary stepping stone to such a theory, which was created in the next generation by Pierre-Simon Laplace. Laplace also added a few details that de Moivre had omitted (such as a formal proof of his main result).

1730's

The bell-shaped curve has made its appearance in all sorts of investigations and has been liable to misuse as well as useful applications. The conditions underlying the proper application of the curve have been studied at length and just as studiously ignored by those who have seen it as the one necessary ingredient for a probabilistic analysis. The normal distribution has probably been cursed by students who are under the impression that it was responsible for "grading on a curve." Nevertheless, the language for measuring errors and deviations from a set standard has depended for many years on the normal distribution.

—*Thomas Drucker*

FURTHER READING

Daston, Lorraine. *Classical Probability in the Enlightenment.* Princeton, N.J.: Princeton University Press, 1988. Investigates de Moivre's use of probability (including the normal distribution) to tackle questions of religion and philosophy.

David, Florence Nightingale. *Games, Gods, and Gambling.* London: Charles Griffin, 1962. Appendix 5 offers the English version of de Moivre's presentation of the normal distribution.

Hald, Anders. *A History of Mathematical Statistics from 1750 to 1950.* New York: John Wiley and Sons, 1998. The second chapter summarizes the state of probabil-

ity in the middle of the eighteenth century after de Moivre.

_____. *A History of Probability and Statistics and Their Applications Before 1750.* New York: John Wiley, 1990. Extensive reconstruction of de Moivre's text, including what de Moivre's proof of the normal approximation might have been.

Schneider, Ivo. "Abraham de Moivre." *Statisticians of the Centuries.* New York: Springer, 2001. Schneider is the author of the definitive study of de Moivre.

Stigler, Stephen M. *The History of Statistics.* Cambridge, Mass.: Harvard University Press, 1986. Most definitive assessment of de Moivre's work for subsequent developments in probability.

SEE ALSO: 1718: Bernoulli Publishes His Calculus of Variations; 1738: Bernoulli Proposes the Kinetic Theory of Gases; 1740: Maclaurin's Gravitational Theory; 1743-1744: D'Alembert Develops His Axioms of Motion; 1748: Agnesi Publishes *Analytical Institutions*; 1748: Euler Develops the Concept of Function; 1763: Bayes Advances Probability Theory; 1784: Legendre Introduces Polynomials; 1796: Laplace Articulates His Nebular Hypothesis.

RELATED ARTICLES in *Great Lives from History: The Eighteenth Century, 1701-1800*: Comte de Buffon; Marquis de Condorcet; Joseph-Louis Lagrange.

1733
DU FAY DISCOVERS TWO KINDS OF ELECTRIC CHARGE

In extending the electrical experiments of Stephen Gray, Charles-François de Cisternay Du Fay discovered two types of electric charge, which he called vitreous and resinous electricity. He demonstrated that like charges repel and unlike charges attract, the two-fluid theory of electricity. Benjamin Franklin modified this idea with his one-fluid theory, in which an excess or deficiency of the electric fluid was designated positive or negative.

LOCALE: Paris, France
CATEGORIES: Science and technology; physics

KEY FIGURES
Charles-François de Cisternay Du Fay (1698-1739), French scientist
Francis Hauksbee (1660-1713), English instrument maker

Stephen Gray (1666-1736), English pensioner who discovered electrical conduction
Benjamin Franklin (1706-1790), American scientist, statesman, and diplomat

SUMMARY OF EVENT
The Greek natural philosopher Thales discovered the attractive effect of rubbed amber, as a result of which the Greek term *elektron* (amber) became associated with the phenomenon and eventually developed into the term "electricity." English physician William Gilbert began the modern study of electrical phenomena in the late sixteenth century when he demonstrated that about thirty materials could be electrified. During the seventeenth century, the study of electrical phenomena was often considered practice in the occult and so was often neglected. Electrical studies received impetus when the English pensioner and electrical experimenter Stephen

Gray discovered the conduction of "electric virtue" in 1729 and found a distinction between conductors and insulators. This led directly to the work of the French scientist Charles-François de Cisternay Du Fay and his two-fluid theory of electricity, in which like fluids repel and unlike fluids attract. Du Fay's work led to the experiments of Benjamin Franklin and his one-fluid theory of positive and negative electricity.

Francis Hauksbee, an uneducated instrument maker and demonstrator at the Royal Society of London, revived interest in electricity in eighteenth century England. Encouraged by Sir Isaac Newton, who was serving as the new president of the society, Hauksbee enhanced his electrical experiments in 1705 by using a long glass tube in place of amber, observing electrostatic repulsion. When he rubbed a glass tube, the tube acquired the characteristic of attracting some kinds of matter and repelling other kinds of matter.

Gray, a dyer by trade, followed up on these electrical experiments. In 1708 he transmitted to the Royal Society the results of his experiments with a glass tube, which were similarly performed by Hauksbee. Gray's first paper, which appeared in the society's *Philosophical Transactions* in 1720, described light and sparks from a glass tube when rubbed in the dark and identified several new materials that could be electrified. A second paper in 1729 described his discovery of electrical conduction. After placing corks in the ends of a glass tube to keep out dust, he found that the cork attracted and repelled a down feather. He concluded that there was an attractive "virtue" communicated to the cork by the "excited" tube.

In his 1729 paper, Gray described a series of experiments on the conduction of electric virtue. He inserted a rod into one of the corks and observed attraction to an ivory ball on the other end of the rod. He then found that metal wire from the cork in the glass tube would conduct electricity to the ivory ball. Working with friends, he was able to observe attraction by the ivory ball suspended on 34 feet of packthread from the glass tube. He then made several attempts to pass the electric virtue along a horizontal line suspended by packthread from a roof beam, but his lack of success led him to conclude that the electricity escaped through the beam (grounding). He finally succeeded by using silk thread to support his horizontal line.

Gray continued his experiments in a barn, succeeding with a packthread line up to 293 feet; when he used metal wire to support a longer line, however, the experiment failed. Using silk supports again, he succeeded in transmitting electricity up to about 650 feet. Thus, he finally recognized the basic distinction between insulators such as silk and glass and conductors such as metals and packthread. In a 1732 paper, he reported on the electrification of materials by the influence of an electrified glass tube without direct contact.

Electrical studies were soon begun in Paris at the French Academy of Sciences by Du Fay, a self-trained scientist who published papers in all the sciences recognized by the academy and became superintendent of the Royal Gardens. In 1732, Du Fay heard of Gray's experiments and reviewed the existing literature in his first memoir on electricity for the academy. In half a dozen other memoirs on electricity, Du Fay reported his experiments and discoveries. He showed that all materials could be electrified: solids by friction if properly dried and liquids by electrical influence. He repeated Gray's experiments on conduction, obtaining better results by using wet packthread supported on glass tubes up to a distance of 1,256 feet.

In 1733, Du Fay found that gold foils could be attracted to an electrified glass tube, but they would repel each other when approached or touched by the tube. This appears to be the first clear demonstration of electric repulsion. However, to his surprise, when a rod of gum resin electrified one of the gold foils, it attracted the other gold foil. This led him to recognize the existence of two kinds of electricity and to determine how they behave.

Du Fay's experiments led him to distinguish "vitreous" electricity, conducted by hard materials such as glass, rock crystal, and precious stones, and "resinous" electricity, conducted by softer materials such as amber, gum resin, and paper. He then described how electrified vitreous objects attract resinous objects, but how two vitreous objects or two resinous objects repel each other. Although Du Fay never referred to "fluids," his discovery was called the two-fluid theory of electricity, that bodies with like "electric fluids" repel and those of unlike fluids attract. Du Fay sent his results to the Royal Society, where they were translated into English and published in the *Philosophical Transactions* for 1734. Transferring electric fluid to an object came to be viewed as loading or charging the object, leading to the term "electric charge."

At Boston in 1746, Benjamin Franklin was introduced to electrostatic phenomena and began to experiment with them. In 1747 he stated his one-fluid theory of electricity, in which transferring electricity causes one object to lose electric charge, becoming negative, and the other object to gain charge, becoming positive. Later he identified positive and negative charge with Du Fay's vitreous and resinous fluids, respectively, which Franklin viewed as a surplus or deficiency of a single electric fluid. Franklin's assumption that electrification does not create or destroy charge, but only transfers it from one body to another, implies the law of conservation of electric charge.

SIGNIFICANCE

The identification of positive and negative electric charges and their properties led to the modern science of electricity. By using the mathematical terms "plus" and "minus," Benjamin Franklin suggested the possibility that electricity is quantitative and measurable. Franklin's theory led to development of the law of electric force by French engineer Charles Coulomb in 1785. The discovery of ways to maintain the flow of electric charge as an electric current opened up the field of practical electricity for heating, lighting, telegraphy, and many other applications in the nineteenth century.

Ironically, Franklin's choice of positive and negative charges turned out to be mistaken. The discovery of the electron by the English physicist J. J. Thomson at the end of the nineteenth century made it evident that vitreous materials tend to lose electrons and thus should have been called negative, while resinous materials gain electrons and should have been called positive. Electrons were therefore designated as negative and are the basic unit of negative charge. The corresponding positive unit of charge, the proton, was discovered early in the twentieth century with an equal and opposite charge, but the proton was found to have a mass nearly two thousand times larger than that of the electron.

The atomic number of an element corresponds to the number of protons in the atomic nucleus, with an equal number of electrons surrounding the nucleus. Electric current in most conductors consists of the flow of only electrons, reflecting Franklin's one-fluid theory, but both electrons and protons flow in gaseous discharges, matching Du Fay's two-fluid theory. The existence of both electrons and protons seems to favor Du Fay's theory.

—*Joseph L. Spradley*

FURTHER READING

Bodanis, David. *Electric Universe: The Shocking True Story of Electricity*. New York: Crown, 2005. A fascinating exploration of the history of electricity that looks at inventions from the light bulb to the computer. Includes a helpful annotated bibliography.

Fara, Patricia. *An Entertainment for Angels: Electricity in the Enlightenment*. New York: Columbia University Press, 2002. Fara examines early electrical experiments. Includes bibliographical references.

Heilbron, J. L. *Elements of Early Modern Physics*. Berkeley: University of California Press, 1982. The third of three chapters, "The Case of Electricity," describes eighteenth century developments, with many illustrations.

Roller, Duane, and Duane H. D. Roller. *The Development of the Concept of Electric Charge: Electricity from the Greeks to Coulomb*. Cambridge, Mass.: Harvard University Press, 1954. This classic study of early electrical studies includes extensive quotations from original sources.

Schiffer, Michael Brian. *Draw the Lightning Down: Benjamin Franklin and Electrical Technology in the Age of Enlightenment*. Berkeley: University of California Press, 2003. The first two chapters describe the electrical researches that led to Franklin's work.

Schlagel, Richard H. *From Myth to Modern Mind: A Study of the Origins and Growth of Scientific Thought*. New York: Peter Lang, 1996. Chapter 8, "The Newtonian Legacy," includes a good discussion of early electrical research.

SEE ALSO: 1729: Gray Discovers Principles of Electric Conductivity; Oct., 1745, and Jan., 1746: Invention of the Leyden Jar; June, 1752: Franklin Demonstrates the Electrical Nature of Lightning; 1800: Volta Invents the Battery.

RELATED ARTICLES in *Great Lives from History: The Eighteenth Century, 1701-1800*: Benjamin Franklin; Luigi Galvani; Joseph Priestley; Alessandro Volta.

1733
KAY INVENTS THE FLYING SHUTTLE

John Kay's flying shuttle allowed a single weaver to produce fabrics of any width, alleviating the need for two weavers to cooperate on unusually wide fabrics. The invention also lent itself in principle to mechanization, helping to begin the mechanization of the textile industry that constituted the first phase of the Industrial Revolution in England.

LOCALE: England
CATEGORIES: Inventions; manufacturing; science and technology

KEY FIGURES
John Kay (1704-c. 1780/1781), English inventor
Robert Kay (1728-1802), John Kay's son

SUMMARY OF EVENT

The eighteenth century saw the beginning of the Industrial Revolution, in which the manufacturing industries, starting with the textile industry, became mechanized. Historians have debated for many years why this revolution occurred first in England. Because a major hallmark of the Industrial Revolution was the application of mechanical power in place of human power, part of the explanation lies in the particular inventions that made this mechanization possible. John Kay's invention of the flying shuttle, for example, contributed in an important way to the process of industrial mechanization.

John Kay was born on July 16, 1704, at the Park, in Walmersley, near Bury, Lancashire, England. There is some indication that his father, who owned a woolen factory in Colchester, sent him abroad for his education. By 1730, however, he was located in Bury, making reeds and other components of woolen looms. Among his other accomplishments, Kay improved upon the reeds used to guide the thread in looms by making them of metal rather than cane, which had been used previously. These new reeds quickly came into general use among woolen weavers, because they substantially improved the quality of the fabric's texture by ensuring uniformity of the weave.

At the beginning of the 1730's, the preindustrial method of weaving was still in use. Yarn, called the weft (as opposed to the warp, the threads that were permanently strung across the loom), was wound on shuttles that were thrown from one hand to another across the loom. This use of both hands by the weaver was time-consuming. The method also restricted the width of cloth that could be woven by a single weaver to about thirty

inches, because it required a weaver to be able to reach both sides of the loom at once. If a wider fabric was desired, two weavers had to sit side by side at the loom and throw the shuttle to each other.

Kay determined to improve weaving techniques by redesigning the shuttle. He reshaped the shuttle, fitted it with tiny wheels that could track its progress across the loom, and reinforced its edges with metal to reduce wear. He also developed a "picker," a device that could start the shuttle on its path across the loom with the pull of a cord. In the existing method, the yarn that had been thrown across the loom on the shuttle was pulled tight against its predecessor with a "layer" that was activated after each pass of the shuttle. Kay created a grooved guide for the "layer," so that it always exerted the same force on the emerging cloth. These improvements meant that a weaver needed only one hand to operate the loom. The "picker" could be activated just by pulling on its cord. Kay's innovations also cut in half the amount of time required to produce a piece of cloth while simultaneously reducing the degree of skill required to do so. Weavers, members of an ancient craft who carefully guarded their status as skilled practitioners, were therefore threatened by Kay's invention.

In 1733, Kay took out a patent on his device, which he called the "fly-shuttle." The device was adopted by most of the textile producers in the north of England, who at that time produced mostly woolen cloths. Kay tried to collect royalties from the woolen manufacturers of Yorkshire, but they resisted paying. Accordingly, Kay took them to court, and although he won his lawsuits, he expended nearly all his resources on these legal battles. He appealed to Parliament, hoping to get legislative action that would restore his finances, but was unsuccessful in this effort.

Kay's invention also aroused deep hostility among the ordinary weavers of Yorkshire and Lancashire, who saw this mechanical improvement as diminishing their work opportunities. In 1753, a mob assaulted his house at Bury, destroying everything. Kay himself only barely escaped. He later moved to France, where he found occasional financial support from the French government, which commissioned him to introduce English practices to the French textile industry. He died in France, possibly in the winter of 1780-1781.

Kay appeared to have had many more ideas for inventions that would assist the textile industry. His patent for the fly-shuttle, for instance, included a device that would improve the carding of wool by aligning the fibers more uniformly. In 1746, he invented a totally automated "small ware" loom, but it appears never to have been produced. Early in life, he had invented a device for handling mohair so as to make mohair yarn more uniform. His son, Robert Kay, apparently shared his inventive talent, for in 1760 he invented a device for sorting shuttles carrying different colors of warp thread, so that they could be used uniformly to produce a pattern.

SIGNIFICANCE

Kay's invention, which continued to be used well into the nineteenth century, was the first of a long succession of labor-saving developments that characterized the Industrial Revolution. The automatic feature of the flying shuttle enabled weavers to double their productivity, and

it caused them to lose part of their status as skilled laborers. The shuttle thereby reduced labor costs dramatically, setting in motion a process that has continued into the twenty-first century. Output increased enormously, especially when devices like Kay's were employed in the manufacture of cotton textiles. Prices could be kept low, because the process was increasingly automated, and the need for workers was kept down. The product could also be sold more widely, because it cost less to produce.

Because Kay's invention reduced the need for labor in the woolen industry, he aroused substantial resentment among the workers, as a mob attack on his house illustrates. It was this same kind of reaction, early in the next century, that earned the recalcitrant workers the name Luddites, a reaction that has rarely proved able to prevent technological and industrial advances. The flying shut-

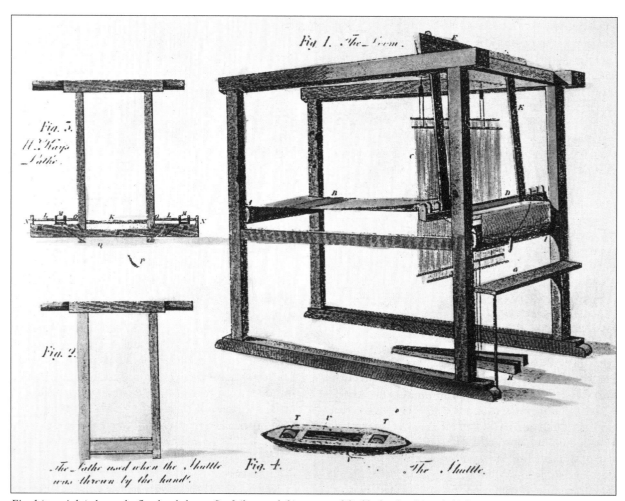

Fig. 1 (top right) shows the fly-shuttle loom, fig. 2 (bottom left) an unmodified lathe, fig. 3 (top left) depicts Kay's modified lathe, and fig. 4 (bottom right) shows Kay's shuttle of 1733. (The Granger Collection, New York)

tle, moreover, while still operated by hand, was in principle capable of being mechanized in just the way that Luddites despised, and it represented a first step toward the mechanization of textile factories in general.

By speeding up the weaving process, Kay's device stimulated efforts to improve the spinning of yarn. This stimulation of the spinning industry resulted in the inventions of the spinning jenny and the spinning mule. The increased output these inventions made possible both lowered the cost of textile production and set in motion efforts to automate weaving further. Kay's work is an outstanding example of the technical inventiveness that underlay the Industrial Revolution.

—*Nancy M. Gordon*

FURTHER READING

Cardwell, Donald. *Wheels, Clocks, and Rockets: A History of Technology.* New York: W. W. Norton, 2001. An excellent survey of important inventions; includes a simplified drawing of Kay's flying shuttle.

Landes, David S. *The Unbound Prometheus: Technological Change and Industrial Development in Western Europe from 1750 to the Present.* New York: Cambridge University Press, 1969. One of the classics on the Industrial Revolution; contains details on Kay's background.

MacLeod, Christine. *Inventing the Industrial Revolution: The English Patent System, 1660-1800.* New York: Cambridge University Press, 1988. A detailed history of the English patent system, with a number of details about Kay's attempts to enforce his patent.

Mokyr, Joel. *The Lever of Riches: Technological Creativity and Economic Progress.* New York: Oxford University Press, 1990. One of the best books on the interrelationship between technology and economics by the dean of U.S. economic historians.

Usher, Abbott Payson. *A History of Mechanical Inventions.* Rev. ed. Cambridge, Mass.: Harvard University Press, 1954. The classic book on the mechanical inventions of modern technological society, with a detailed description of Kay's flying shuttle.

SEE ALSO: 1701: Tull Invents the Seed Drill; 1705-1712: Newcomen Develops the Steam Engine; 1709: Darby Invents Coke-Smelting; 1764: Invention of the Spinning Jenny; 1765-1769: Watt Develops a More Effective Steam Engine; 1767-1771: Invention of the Water Frame; 1779: Crompton Invents the Spinning Mule; Apr., 1785: Cartwright Patents the Steam-Powered Loom; Dec. 20, 1790: Slater's Spinning Mill; 1793: Whitney Invents the Cotton Gin; 1795: Invention of the Flax Spinner.

RELATED ARTICLES in *Great Lives from History: The Eighteenth Century, 1701-1800*: James Hargreaves; John Kay.

October 10, 1733-October 3, 1735
WAR OF THE POLISH SUCCESSION

After Polish king Augustus II died in 1733, France favored the restoration of Poland's deposed former king, Stanisław I Leszczyński, while the Holy Roman Empire and its allies supported Augustus III's claim to his father's throne. The resulting War of the Polish Succession resulted in Poland becoming a pawn through which the Western European powers attempted to increase their own territory and influence.

LOCALE: Poland; Lorraine; Rhineland (now in Germany); Italy

CATEGORIES: Wars, uprisings, and civil unrest; diplomacy and international relations; expansion and land acquisition

KEY FIGURES

Louis XV (1710-1774), king of France, r. 1715-1774

André-Hercule de Fleury (1653-1743), prime minister of France, 1726-1743

Charles VI (1685-1740), Holy Roman Emperor, r. 1711-1740

Stanisław I (1677-1766), king of the Polish-Lithuanian Commonwealth, r. 1704-1709, 1733-1736, and later duke of Lorraine, r. 1738-1766

Augustus III (1696-1763), elector of Saxony, r. 1733-1763, and king of the Polish-Lithuanian Commonwealth, r. 1736-1763

Philip V (1683-1746), king of Spain, r. 1700-January, 1724, August 31, 1724-1746

Eugene of Savoy (1663-1736), French-born imperial general

Charles Fouquet de Belle-Isle (1684-1761), French
field marshal

Duke of Berwick (James Fitzjames; 1670-1734),
English soldier and illegitimate son of James II

Duc de Villars (Claude-Louis-Hector de Villars; 1653-
1734), French field marshal

Don Carlos de Bourbon (1716-1788), son of Philip V,
king of the Two Sicilies as Charles IV, r. 1734-
1759, and king of Spain as Charles III, r. 1759-1788

SUMMARY OF EVENT

The eighteenth century began in Europe with two wars,
the War of the Spanish Succession and the Great Northern
War. In 1704, during the latter conflict, King Charles XII
of Sweden invaded Poland, dethroned King Augustus II,
the elector of Saxony, and placed the Polish nobleman
Stanisław Leszczyński on the throne as King Stanisław I. When Charles was defeated in July, 1709, at the
Battle of Poltava by a coalition of Russia, Saxony, and
Denmark led by Peter the Great, Augustus II was restored to the Polish throne, while Stanisław I Leszczyński went into exile in France.

From the conclusion of the two conflicts that had
opened the century until 1733, Europe enjoyed a fragile
but generally peaceful balance of power. Agreements
concerning British, French, Spanish, and Austrian succession seemed to have been reached, and although
brief conflicts occurred during the intervening years,
none involved the whole of Europe. In 1733, however,
Augustus II died, reviving old tensions over the Polish
succession. The question of who should be the next ruler
of Poland became one of international concern.

Within two months of Augustus II's death, Louis XV
of France, who had married Stanisław I Leszczyński's
daughter Maria in 1725, sent declarations to all the courts
of Europe that he would protect free elections in Poland,
with the expectation that Stanisław would be elected.
However, Austria's Emperor Charles VI, Russia's Czarina Anna, and Prussia's Frederick William I supported
the claim of Augustus III, the new elector of Saxony, to
his father's throne. In November, 1733, Philip V, king of
Spain and uncle of the French king, agreed to support
France through the first of several "Family Compacts"
between the two Bourbon houses.

On April 27, 1733, the Polish Convocation Diet met
in twenty-seven sessions to establish guidelines and set a
date for the election of the new king. Composed of Polish
nobility and many lesser landowners and expecting support from the French, the diet declared that the election
should go to a Pole with no territory outside Poland. The

Diet of Election convened in Warsaw on August 25,
1733, and Stanisław I Leszczyński, who had arrived
from France incognito, was elected on September 10.
However, on October 5, a minority of Saxon supporters
within the Polish diet met at the Plain of Praga near
Kamien and, backed by Russian troops, elected Augustus III king of Poland and duke of Lithuania.

This second election of October 5 provoked the War
of the Polish Succession. Louis XV declared war on
Charles VI on October 10, 1733. Obliged by previous alliances to side with one or another of the warring empires, the nations of continental Europe were gradually
drawn into the war. On October 13, 1733, France's Marshal Charles Fouquet de Belle-Isle entered Lorraine unopposed and held that duchy for the duration of the war.
France launched a limited military offensive in October,
primarily on two fronts—the Rhineland and Italy—while
Austria maintained a purely defensive position, even delaying its official declaration of war until early in 1734.

On the northern front, French troops led by James
Fitzjames, the duke of Berwick, captured several fortresses in the Rhineland, including Kehl (October 29,
1733), Trarbach and the Ettlingen Lines (May, 1734),
and Philippsburg (July, 1734). The war on the southern
front, led by the duc de Villars, did not go as well for
France, because its military allies had differing motives
for their support. King Charles Emanuel of Sardinia was
satisfied with the surrender of Milan in December, 1733,
and could not be counted on for ongoing support. The
Spanish troops under Don Carlos de Bourbon, the son of
Philip V, abandoned their French allies to go to Naples in
February, 1734, where Don Carlos was welcomed as
king of Naples and, soon after, of Sicily, becoming
Charles IV of the Two Sicilies.

The fiercest battles of the war were fought in Italy in
1734: The Battle of Parma in June and the Battle of
Guastalla in September saw the heaviest losses of the
war, without resulting in lasting gains for either side.
Meanwhile, Stanisław I, who had relocated to Gdańsk at
the end of September, received little military support
from the French during the attack on that city by Russian-
Saxon forces at the beginning of 1734. When Gdańsk fell
in June after a five-month siege, Stanisław I escaped and
was harbored at Königsberg in Prussia until the armistice.

By the fall of 1734, the campaigns on both sides dwindled, and there were no serious military engagements in
1735. The war, however, cost France two of its most famous elderly and seasoned marshals, Berwick and
Villars, who died within five days of each other in June,
1734. It also saw the last appearance in the field of the

great Austrian general, Prince Eugene of Savoy.

As often happened in the eighteenth century, diplomatic efforts to reach a settlement were simultaneous with military action. Diplomacy began as early as the fall of 1734, when the British ambassador to Holland began a series of communiqués with French prime minister Cardinal André-Hercule de Fleury concerning tentative terms for a peace settlement. In the first part of 1735, negotiations by several other mediators resulted in the Preliminaries of Vienna, signed in Vienna on October 3, 1735. France and Austria officially ratified these agreements in the Third Treaty of Vienna on November 18, 1738, with the clauses concerning Spain later ratified at Versailles in April, 1739. The treaty's provisions redistributed portions of Italy to Spain and Austria and granted Stanisław I Leszczyński the title of king of Poland, in exchange for his abdication in favor of Augustus III. Stanisław received the autonomous duchy of Lorraine, while the displaced duke of Lorraine (the future Austrian emperor Francis I) inherited Tuscany.

SIGNIFICANCE

Following the War of the Spanish Succession (1702-1714) and preceding the War of the Austrian Succession (1740-1748), the War of the Polish Succession was one of the many wars in the eighteenth century over the question of dynastic succession, which was key to preserving power within a nation, as well as to maintaining a balance of power between nations. Poland's importance, however, receded after the war, as that country increasingly became a defenseless pawn in international diplomacy. Losing some of its territory in 1772 and 1793 in the first and second partitions of Poland, it ceased to exist as a nation altogether after the third partition in 1795, when the Polish king was forced to abdicate and the rest of Poland's land was parceled out to Russia, Prussia, and Austria. The question of dynastic succession in Poland thus became moot.

The War of the Polish Succession resulted in immediate as well as long-term changes to the political map of Europe. The Third Treaty of Vienna stipulated that Lorraine would return to France upon the death of Stanisław Leszczyński. This came to pass in 1766, and France no longer had a troublesome island of foreign territory within its borders. Spain regained almost all the territory it had lost to Austria and Savoy in the Treaty of Utrecht (1713) at the close of the War of the Spanish Succession, and the Spanish Bourbon Dynasty preserved its hold on the Two Sicilies until 1860. Austria regained most of its prewar Italian territory as well as Tuscany.

The aftermath of the War of the Polish Succession restored a balance of power in Europe; however, that lasted only a few years before it was again challenged.

—*Marsha Daigle-Williamson*

FURTHER READING

Campbell, Peter R. *Power and Politics in Old Regime France, 1720-1745.* New York: Routledge, 1996. Detailed discussion of French domestic and foreign policy with an emphasis on the role of Cardinal de Fleury. Copious notes, bibliography, and index.

Friedrich, Karin. *The Other Prussia: Royal Prussia, Poland, and Liberty, 1569-1772.* New York: Cambridge University Press, 2000. Focus on the political and religious self-identity of Polish Prussia, a province of the Polish-Lithuanian Commonwealth from 1466 to 1793. Extensive multilingual bibliography, index.

Kamen, Henry. *Philip V of Spain: The King Who Reigned Twice.* New Haven, Conn.: Yale University Press, 2001. Overview of Spanish diplomatic policies, military engagements, and relationship to France during Philip's reign. Diagrams, notes, brief bibliography, and index.

Lukowski, Jerzy, and Herbert Zawadzki. *A Concise History of Poland.* New York: Cambridge University Press, 2001. The first Polish history from the Middle Ages to the present day in English; a section on the War of the Polish Succession. Charts, black-and-white photos, bibliography, and index.

Sutton, John L. *The King's Honor and the King's Cardinal: The War of Polish Succession.* Lexington: University Press of Kentucky, 1980. The first full-length English book on the war; engaging account with military and diplomatic details from memoirs and letters. Bibliography and index.

SEE ALSO: c. 1701-1721: Great Northern War; May 26, 1701-Sept. 7, 1714: War of the Spanish Succession; June 27, 1709: Battle of Poltava; Apr. 11, 1713: Treaty of Utrecht; Nov. 18, 1738: Treaty of Vienna; May 31, 1740: Accession of Frederick the Great; Oct. 20, 1740: Maria Theresa Succeeds to the Austrian Throne; Dec. 16, 1740-Nov. 7, 1748: War of the Austrian Succession; Oct. 18, 1748: Treaty of Aix-la-Chapelle; Feb. 24, 1766: Lorraine Becomes Part of France.

RELATED ARTICLES in *Great Lives from History: The Eighteenth Century, 1701-1800*: Charles VI; Charles XII; Eugene of Savoy; André-Hercule de Fleury; Frederick William I; Louis XV; Peter the Great; Philip V.

1730's

November 23, 1733
SLAVES CAPTURE ST. JOHN'S ISLAND

Dozens of Amina slaves, originally from the Gold Coast of West Africa, conquered much of St. John in one of the Caribbean region's most successful slave revolts.

LOCALE: St. Jan, Danish West Indies (now St. John, U.S. Virgin Islands)

CATEGORIES: Wars, uprisings, and civil unrest; social issues and reform

KEY FIGURES

Bolombo (d. 1734), former king of the West African Adambe nation, slave overseer on St. John, and a leader of the 1733 slave rebellion

Aquashi (d. 1734), Aquambo prince and rebel leader

Kanta (d. 1734), Amina noble and rebel leader

Peter Durloo (fl. 1722-1755), Dutch settler

Philip Gardelin (d. 1740), governor of the Danish West Indies from 1733 to 1736, who issued a severe slave code in 1733, which set off the rebellion

Chevalier de Longueville (d. 1761), commander of French troops from Martinique who ultimately suppressed the St. John revolt

SUMMARY OF EVENT

During the St. John uprising of 1733-1734, a group of armed rebel slaves captured the Danish West Indian island of St. Jan (St. John) for six months. Their intention was to eliminate whites from the island, establish a traditional West African kingdom, and retain parts of the remaining population as slaves. The rebellion, punctuated by periods of stalemate, involved a slow war of attrition between the rebels and their pursuers, who included Danish and Dutch planters, West Indian slaves, free blacks, English mercenaries, and French soldiers. Ultimately, the rebels were overpowered and destroyed, in many cases by their own hand, and the plantation system on St. John was restored.

A series of natural disasters made life particularly difficult in the years and months preceding the rebellion. Unusually severe drought in 1725 and 1726 prompted many planters to divert scarce water resources to sugarcane and cotton fields at the expense of the plots on which slaves were required to produce their own food. Planters who neglected to import sufficient amounts of food forced some slaves to starve to death and others to steal for their sustenance. The threat of famine returned with another drought in the spring and summer of 1733,

followed by two hurricanes and two plagues of insects that destroyed the struggling crops.

The slave unrest generated by hunger was exacerbated by exceptionally severe slave codes. By 1733, St. John's slave population had increased by 60 percent in five years and the slave population of 1,087 greatly outnumbered the 208 whites, in spite of high levels of maroonage, or running away. Maroons might live independently in covert areas of the island or find refuge among the Spanish in Puerto Rico as converted Catholics. The desire of Danish West Indian planters and the Danish West India and Guinea Company to suppress maroonage prompted extremely harsh legislation stipulating brutal punishments for slave disobedience. Punishment included flogging, branding, burning with pincers, hanging, and the amputation of a foot, leg, hand, or ear. The articles issued by the Danish West Indian governor Philip Gardelin in September, 1733, would serve to advertise the brutal policies throughout St. John.

Another key to the 1733 uprising was the recent arrival of slaves who were members of the West African aristocracy. Cut off from their customary slave suppliers on the Gold Coast in the 1730's, Danish slavers procured captives from local elites who had taken nobles from rival nations as prisoners of war. Among the recent slave arrivals to St. John were a king, four princes, and several royal wives from three West African nations: the Amina (also known as Akan), the Aquambo (also known as Akwamu), and the Adambe. Several of the new arrivals, along with more established slaves, escaped the plantations and formed distinctive Maroon communities on St. John. The 1733 uprising was organized by these Maroon communities, who communicated with each other and plantation slaves by means of talking drums (which can sound like the intonations and rhythms of the human voice), preparing detailed plans to overtake St. John under the leadership of Adambe king Bolombo, Aquambo prince Aquashi, and Amina nobleman Kanta.

On the morning of November 23, 1733, approximately twelve slaves entered St. John's fortification at Coral Bay on the pretext of bringing bundles of wood for fuel. In those bundles were sugarcane knives. The rebel slaves killed all of the soldiers in the fort except one, who hid under a bed and ultimately escaped to St. Thomas to inform Governor Gardelin of the insurrection. The rebels then fired the garrison's cannon as a prearranged signal to the slaves throughout the island to kill their masters.

Within hours the rebels, a force of approximately one hundred, slaughtered several whites on the island. Many whites, warned by their slaves who accompanied them, escaped to St. Thomas or encamped in a plantation in the northwest of St. John that served as stronghold for the planters. The slaves who resisted the rebellion tended to be Creole (born in the West Indies) and descended from nations other than those of the rebel leaders. A white surgeon named Cornelius Bodger was spared so that he could provide medical assistance, which he did for both sides throughout the rebellion. The plantation of Peter Durloo served as a base for approximately twenty white and twenty black St. Johnians resisting the rebels. A Dutch planter from St. Thomas led a contingent of armed men, including numerous slaves, to retake the Coral Bay garrison and disperse the rebels as well as offer support and supplies to the men at Durloo's. Unable to conquer the rebel forces, the Danish looked to the English, but the armed forces of Captain Taller and, later, Captain William Maddox, were repelled by the rebel forces as well.

The standoff between the rebels and the Danish forces, a contingent that included numerous slaves from St. Thomas as well as St. Thomas's runaway-slave-tracking Free Negro Corps, led by a free black captain named Mingo Tamarin, continued for six months. Ultimately, geopolitics helped the Danes. King Louis XV of France supported his father-in-law Stanisław I in the War of the Polish Succession (1733-1738) and greatly desired Denmark's neutrality. The Danish West India and Guinea Company had purchased St. Croix from the French for a substantial fee, and the Danish crown had promised neutrality during the impending war. The French were eager to aid their new ally. From April 28 to May 25, 1734, St. John's rebels were worn down by approximately two hundred French soldiers from Martinique, including a free black corps, well trained in jungle combat and well led by Commander Chevalier de Longueville. Running low on ammunition and recognizing that they were overpowered, many of the St. John rebels chose suicide over capture. The French and Danish forces slaughtered several of the remaining rebels; others were publicly tortured and executed, including slaves who had surrendered with the promise of pardon.

About a quarter of St. John's white population and six of the slaves who defended the planters had lost their lives, and just over half of the island's ninety-two plantations had been damaged or destroyed.

SIGNIFICANCE

Almost sixty years before the Haitian revolution, the St. John slave revolt proved to be one of the most successful slave revolts in Caribbean history. It represents an important precursor to the powerful slave revolts of the late eighteenth and nineteenth centuries. The St. John rebels, prompted by hunger, an exceptionally brutal slave code, and the conventions of the West African ruling elite, tried to eliminate the planters and their families and establish a traditional West African society. The intention of the rebels was not to abolish slavery. The enslavement of prisoners of war from rival nations was an integral part of the West African social structure they intended to reinstate, and rebel leaders planned to produce sugar and cotton for exchange. While the rebel forces were able to secure some ammunition and reinforcements from neighboring islands, their supplies dwindled, and they were ultimately outnumbered and overpowered by French forces.

The Danish plantation system was quickly restored, however, and sugar production flourished in the years after the uprising. In 1746 and 1759 two incipient slave rebellions in the Danish West Indies were suppressed. In 1792, Denmark outlawed slave trading, but it would take a slave revolt in St. Croix in 1848 to bring slavery in the Danish West Indies to a definitive end.

—*Christina Proenza-Coles*

FURTHER READING

Anderson, John L. *Night of the Silent Drums*. New York: Charles Scribner's Sons, 1975. An engrossing narrative of the events of the rebellion, rigorously based on historical sources.

Dookhan, Isaac. *A History of the Virgin Islands of the United States*. Essex, England: Caribbean Universities Press, 1974. A historical overview of the islands of St. Thomas, St. John, and St. Croix, from pre-Columbian society to Danish colonization to U.S. rule after 1917.

Hall, Neville. *Slave Society in the Danish West Indies*, edited by B. W. Higman. Baltimore: Johns Hopkins University Press, 1992. A comprehensive and detailed examination of slavery in the Danish West Indies, including its legal, cultural, political, and economic aspects.

Low, Ruth, and Rafael Valls. *St. John Backtime: Eyewitness Accounts from 1718 to 1956*. St. John, U.S. Virgin Islands: Eden Hill Press, 1991. A collection of texts from primary sources, including a letter written by Commander Longueville and a court deposition from a trial of captured rebels.

1730's

Westergaard, Waldemar. *The Danish West Indies, 1671-1917.* New York: Macmillan, 1917. This work includes a definitive historical account of the rebellion based on primary documents.

SEE ALSO: 18th cent.: Expansion of the Atlantic Slave Trade; Apr. 6, 1712: New York City Slave Revolt; Aug., 1712: Maya Rebellion in Chiapas; 1730-1739: First Maroon War; Oct. 10, 1733-Oct. 3, 1735: War of the Polish Succession; Sept. 9, 1739: Stono Rebellion; 1760-1776: Caribbean Slave Rebellions; 1780-1781: Rebellion of Tupac Amaru II; Oct. 10-18, 1780: Great Caribbean Hurricane; Apr. 12, 1787: Free African Society Is Founded; Aug. 22, 1791-Jan. 1, 1804: Haitian Independence; Mar. 16, 1792: Denmark Abolishes the Slave Trade; July, 1795-Mar., 1796: Second Maroon War.

RELATED ARTICLES in *Great Lives from History: The Eighteenth Century, 1701-1800:* Louis XV; Nanny; Toussaint Louverture.

1735
HADLEY DESCRIBES ATMOSPHERIC CIRCULATION

George Hadley, an amateur scientist, described global atmospheric circulation as driven by solar heating and the rotation of the Earth. He was the first person to provide a working explanation for the atmospheric circulation patterns observed in the tropics and subtropics, including the trade winds.

LOCALE: England
CATEGORIES: Science and technology; environment; physics

KEY FIGURES
George Hadley (1685-1768), English amateur scientist and a lawyer
Gaspard-Gustave de Coriolis (1792-1843), French mathematician and physicist
Edmond Halley (1656-1742), English astronomer

SUMMARY OF EVENT
Many astute fifteenth century European navigators were familiar with the overall westerly winds of the midlatitudes, the easterly winds of the lower latitudes, and the so-called doldrums that lay in equatorial regions. It was Christopher Columbus who first demonstrated the importance of these zonal winds in transoceanic travel. Instead of sailing west from the Iberian Peninsula, Columbus first sailed the three Spanish ships under his command south to the Canary Islands before crossing the Atlantic Ocean in 1492. He used a brisk tailwind to sail from the Canary Islands to the Bahamas in thirty-six days, a southerly route that allowed Columbus to cross the Atlantic sailing within the low-latitude easterlies. Thus, he is frequently credited with having discovered the trade winds. Columbus returned to Europe sailing at a higher latitude, stopping at the Azores as he sailed in the favorable westerlies.

In the sixteenth century, the easterly trade winds in the low latitudes north and south of the equator became the preferred route between Europe and the Western Hemisphere. There was a consensus that these winds arose as the Earth rotated from west to east, but many mathematicians and astronomers argued that the Earth's rotation was insufficient to power the trade winds. British scientists, including astronomer Edmond Halley, became interested in providing a solid scientific explanation for these winds. In 1686, he published a study of the trade winds in the *Philosophical Transactions* of the Royal Society, in which he argued that solar heating caused atmospheric circulation. With the article came publication of the first weather map, which showed average winds over the oceans.

A barrister (lawyer) by training and brother of the astronomer John Hadley, George Hadley became interested in weather phenomena and wanted to provide a scientific explanation for the midlatitude westerlies and the easterly low-latitude trade winds. He realized that the trade winds could be explained only by using a rotating coordinate system under the influence of solar heating. Hadley used Halley's work on trade winds as a starting point and concluded that solar heating of the atmosphere is at its maximum at the equator, causing warm equatorial air to rise at low latitudes and move aloft toward the poles. Upward air movement occurs in the doldrums, and cooler surface air is constantly moved eastward toward the equator to be warmed. (This explanation only roughly conserves angular momentum.) Hadley envisioned this atmospheric circulation system as zonally symmetric, with the Northern and Southern Hemispheres having mirror-image latitudinal wind systems.

Hadley's explanation for the trade winds phenomenon was generally accepted when he presented his work to the Royal Society in London in 1735. Within fifty years, however, his explanation had been forgotten, and English meteorologist and physicist John Dalton and German philosopher Immanuel Kant independently proposed explanations similar to Hadley's. Eventually, meteorologists determined that Hadley's assumption of conservation of velocity instead of conservation of angular momentum was incorrect.

A century after Hadley advanced his explanation for the trade winds, Gaspard-Gustave de Coriolis explained mathematically the apparent deflection (commonly referred to as the Coriolis effect) of winds to the right in the Northern Hemisphere and to the left in the Southern Hemisphere. The amount of deflection is a function of wind speed and latitude; the Coriolis effect is zero at the equator.

SIGNIFICANCE

Sailing ships gave way to steam-powered vessels, lessening the importance of the trade winds to commerce. The study of meteorology and Earth's atmosphere remained important in other contexts, however. By the mid-1850's, two American meteorologists and a British mathematician had independently proposed a three-cell meridional circulation structure in each hemisphere. This concept maintained the low-latitude Hadley cell, with the midlatitude cell being called a Ferrel cell. The Ferrel cell was envisioned to have a rising motion at about 60 degrees latitude. The Hadley cell still was credited with supplying a westerly momentum to the midlatitudes. This structure (even when known to be scientifically inaccurate) continued to be used as a simplistic illustration of the global atmospheric circulation through most of the twentieth century.

With the proliferation of meteorological observations in the centuries following Hadley's work, atmospheric circulation was determined not to be zonally symmetric. Even though it was obvious that the trade winds were adequately described by zonal averages, observations had clearly established that large departures from zonal means were common. These departures were called eddies (as in coastal eddies) by scientists.

With the growth of observational meteorology in the late nineteenth century and with satellite meteorology beginning in the 1960's, scientific understanding of atmospheric circulation patterns grew. Satellite imagery clearly defines the region where the trade winds converge. Viewed from space over the oceans, this convergence is visible as a band of clouds caused by thunderstorm activity. This band of clouds arises in the region where Hadley concluded that warm, moist air ascends; the region is now known as the Intertropical Convergence Zone, or ITCZ. By the late twentieth century, zonally averaged atmospheric circulation was accepted as a convenient subset of the total atmospheric circulation. The term Hadley cell continues to be commonly used to refer to the zonally averaged low-latitude winds.

—*Anita Baker-Blocker*

FURTHER READING

Glickman, Todd S., ed. *Glossary of Meteorology*. 2d ed. Boston: American Meteorological Society, 2000. A definitive scientific reference for English-language meteorological terms.

Hadley, George. "Concerning the Cause of the General Trade-Winds." *Philosophical Transactions* 29 (1735): 58-62. Hadley's important paper presented to the Royal Society.

Lindzen, Richard S. *Dynamics in Atmospheric Physics*. New York: Cambridge University Press, 1990. A monograph that discusses the problems of observed atmospheric structures and atmospheric circulation. A knowledge of differential equations is needed to appreciate this book. The laminated cover shows Hadley's concept of the general circulation patterns of the atmosphere. No index.

Monmonier, Mark. *Air Apparent: How Meteorologists Learned to Map, Predict, and Dramatize Weather*. Chicago: University of Chicago Press, 2000. Written for the general reader, this book presents a nonmathematical approach to when and how scientists learned about the general circulation of the atmosphere.

Palmén, Erik, and Chester W. Newton. *Atmospheric Circulation Systems: Their Structure and Physical Interpretation*. New York: Academic Press, 1969. This college-level textbook puts the problems of angular momentum of the atmosphere into perspective. A knowledge of differential equations is helpful.

1730's

Beginning 1735
LINNAEUS CREATES THE BINOMIAL SYSTEM OF CLASSIFICATION

Carolus Linnaeus designed a hierarchical taxonomic system for naming and classifying plants and animals. His system gave each organism a two-term name that was derived from its unique defining characteristics and its position within the hierarchical system. Linnaeus's classification system brought an intellectual order to biology that persists to this day.

LOCALE: Leiden, the Netherlands
CATEGORIES: Biology; science and technology

KEY FIGURES

Carolus Linnaeus (Carl von Linné; 1707-1778),
    Swedish physician and botanist
Joseph Pitton de Tournefort (1656-1708), French
    physician and botanist
John Ray (1627-1705), English Protestant cleric and
    naturalist
Andrea Cesalpino (1525-1603),
    Italian physician, philosopher,
    and botanist
Comte de Buffon (Georges-Louis
    Leclerc; 1707-1788), naturalist
    who believed that nomenclature
    should be based on morphology

SUMMARY OF EVENT

Human dependence on plants and animals has led to classifying living entities into categories as an aid to recognizing useful types. Documents from ancient Egypt, Greece, and Rome contain catalogs of medicinally important plants. The Greek philosopher Aristotle (384-322 B.C.E.) even formulated the earliest known system of biological classification by grouping organisms according to their habitats or means of movement—air, land, or water. Classical Greek and Roman botanical works by Theophrastus (c. 372-287 B.C.E.) and Pedanius Dioscorides (c. 40-c. 90 C.E.) served as foundational references for medieval herbalists, who expanded the lists of medically useful plants but offered few systematic means to distinguish them other than descriptions or portraits of their specimens. Ordering plants according to their purported medicinal value was common; a few reference books listed animals in alphabetical order by their common names.

During the Renaissance, explorers to distant lands introduced naturalists to a flood of new plants and animals, and this new material provided the impetus for classifying plants and animals according to their relationships to one another rather than their usefulness to humans. Italian physician and botanist Andrea Cesalpino utilized the Aristotelian criteria of essential characteristics (such as reproductive organs) and accidental characteristics (such as taste, smell, and color) to specify features important to plant classification. This approach deeply influenced later naturalists. English Protestant cleric John Ray and French botanist Joseph Pitton de Tournefort helped de-

---

LINNAEUS'S SEXUAL SYSTEM

Carolus Linnaeus was interested in a wide range of topics in natural history, but his primary interest was classification. His goal was to produce a system by which one could correctly identify organisms, and his method was to use the common Aristotelian technique of downward classification.

This method involved taking a class of objects, dividing it into two groups (for example, the class of living organisms can be divided into animals and nonanimals), and continuing the process of dichotomous divisions until there was only the lowest set, the species, which could not be further divided. Such a system was highly artificial, since the basis for many of the divisions was arbitrary. However, based on his philosophical and theological commitment to the argument from the Creator's design, Linnaeus believed that if the correct characteristic was chosen as the basis of division, natural relationships would be revealed. In his typically arrogant manner, he claimed to have discovered that trait and built his system around it. He called it his "sexual system."

Linnaeus's system was more adapted to botany than to zoology. With his system, he was personally able to classify more than eighteen thousand species of plants, but his attempts to classify animals created duplications and confusion, primarily because he could not find a characteristic that would work for animals the way reproductive structures did for plants. His inclination to classify everything can also be seen in his attempts to classify diseases, humans, and even botanists.

Linnaeus should not, however, be regarded as merely a taxonomist. His essays and lectures provide evidence that he was exploring ideas that would now be considered basic to ecology and biogeography. He sought to develop, within both a theological and biological context, a concept of the harmony of nature. Finally, he tried not to allow his philosophical or theological positions to blind him to his data. As a result of his evidence, he revised his views on fixity of species to allow for a kind of evolution—formation of new species by hybridization—below the genus level.

Linnaeus Creates the Binomial System of Classification

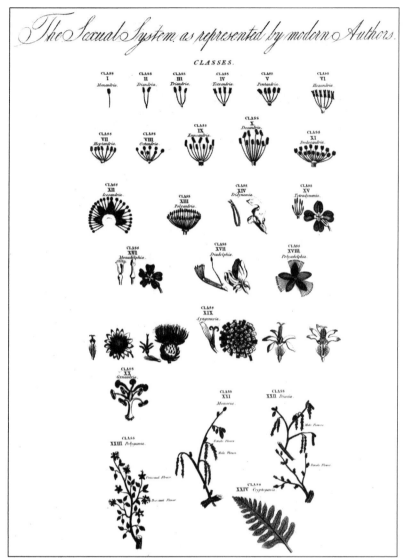

An 1810 representation of Carolus Linnaeus's sexual classification system. (Library of Congress)

fine the concept of "species" as the most fundamental unit of biological classification, and Tournefort was the first to recognize the "genus" as a basic category of classification, falling between species and families.

However, the discipline of biological classification, otherwise known as taxonomy, suffered from a lack of standardization. The names given to organisms varied from one naturalist to another. To make matters worse, the classification system of Tournefort squeezed the approximately 10,000 known species of plants into 698 genera that botanists had to memorize. Such classification systems were impractical, difficult to use, and detri-

mental to the effective analysis of the exotic material being supplied by explorers.

Though trained as a physician, Carolus Linnaeus spent the vast majority of his scientific energy on taxonomy. Linnaeus greatly simplified the conventions that governed the naming of plants and animals by using a standardized binomial nomenclature in his seminal work, *Systema naturae* (1735; *A General System of Nature: Through the Three Grand Kingdoms of Animals, Vegetables, and Minerals*, 1800-1801). Gaspard Bauhin (1560-1624) had developed binomial nomenclature almost two hundred years earlier, and Linnaeus used this naming technique to replace the cumbersome descriptions of his day with a double name in Latin called a binomen.

The first half of the binomen consisted of a capitalized genus name, designating a group composed of several species. The second part, a specific epithet, designated the species name. Linnaeus used Latin binomens to replace the long, unwieldy descriptions in Latin used by naturalists at this time. For example, the wild briar rose was known as *Rosa sylvestris inordora seu canina* (odorless woodland dog rose) or *Rosa sylvestris alba cum rubore, folio glabro* (pinkish white woodland rose with smooth leaves). Linnaeus simplified these rambling descriptions to *Rosa canina*. In the tenth edition of *A General System of Nature* (1758), Linnaeus became the first person to employ binomial nomenclature consistently and without exception to name plants and animals. Because of the simplicity of this naming system, naturalists not only could remember names but also could agree on them.

In *A General System of Nature*, Linnaeus also described a simple hierarchical system of plant classification anyone could use. He arranged plants into twenty-four "classes" according to the number and relative positions of their male reproductive organs, or stamens. He further divided these classes into sixty-five "orders," based on the number and position of the female reproductive organs, or pistils. The orders were then divided into genera, or sets of species that shared similar characteristics.

Because of the ease of using Linnaeus's taxonomic scheme, amateurs, travelers, or gardeners could employ the Linnaean system for themselves and arrive at the same conclusions. Linnaeus also demonstrated the utility of his sexual classification system in a botanical account of his 1732 expedition to Lapland, *Flora Lapponica* (1737; *The Flora of Lapland*, 1811), and in his catalog of the plants from the garden of the wealthy amateur horticulturist George Clifford, *Hortus Cliffortianus* (1738; Clifford's garden). His later work *Species plantarum* (1753; *Plant Species*, 1775) cataloged all known species of plants and expanded his taxonomic principles. These books helped his sexual classification system gain widespread acceptance and use in Europe, despite opposition from some naturalists who thought that it was too sexually explicit.

The Linnaean classification system provided a rigorous hierarchy of plant and animal categories in which small groups were nested within successively larger groups. A species, the smallest denomination into which organisms could be classified, was embedded in a larger group, the genus; one or more genera composed a family; several families were grouped into classes; and so on. Such a classification scheme easily accommodated new organisms or even new groups of organisms.

Linnaeus's nested hierarchical system received wider use and acceptance than the nonhierarchical schemes proposed by his competitors. For example Georges-Louis Leclerc, comte de Buffon, Linnaeus's principal competitor, thought that the entire morphology of the organism should be considered when deciding relatedness and not just a few "essential" structures, like the reproductive organs. To encapsulate his approach to classification, Buffon proposed a classification system that joined some organisms by means of physiology, others via anatomy, and still others by means of ecology. Buffon's system did not endear itself to others because of its almost overwhelming complexity and inability to accommodate new material without substantial changes. By 1799, fifty different classification systems existed, and of these only the taxonomic system created by Linnaeus ultimately survived.

SIGNIFICANCE

It is difficult to overestimate Carolus Linnaeus's contribution to biology, since he single-handedly made biological classification a rigorous scientific endeavor. Lin-

naeus once and for all simplified the naming system and developed a classification scheme that people with a wide range of training could successfully use. His system of taxonomy also easily accommodated the deluge of new biological material from foreign lands, and since its structure did not depend upon the criteria used to distinguish one group from another, the structure of the Linnaean classification system has survived to modern times, even though his sexual classification scheme was abandoned before the end of the eighteenth century.

Linnaeus's taxonomic scheme, which he viewed as a way of defining the initial species originally placed on Earth by God, ironically paved the way for Charles Darwin's theory of evolution, since it could also accommodate a theory of evolution by common descent. Darwin's in-depth study of barnacle classification convinced him that evolutionary relatedness was the best criterion for classifying organisms in the same group. Linnaeus's nested hierarchical taxonomic system lent itself to Darwin's theory, since grouping organisms into ever-larger categories also allowed scientists to assemble organisms according to more recently or distantly shared common ancestors.

—*Michael A. Buratovich*

FURTHER READING

Blair, Charles E. "Latin: A Living Language in the Service of the Study of Life." *Fremontia: A Journal of the California Native Plant Society* 31 (2003): 11-17. A brief discussion of the development of plant taxonomy and the role of the Latin language as a standardizing force.

Blunt, Wilfrid. *Linnaeus: The Compleat Naturalist.* Princeton, N.J.: Princeton University Press, 2001. A definitive biography on the life and work of Linnaeus by an experienced biographer.

Fara, Patricia. *Sex, Botany, and the Empire: The Story of Carl Linnaeus and Joseph Banks.* New York: Columbia University Press, 2003. An idiosyncratic but useful discussion of the work of Linnaeus and its influence on botanist Sir Joseph Banks.

Farber, Paul Lawrence. *Finding Order in Nature: The Naturalist Tradition from Linnaeus to E. O. Wilson.* Baltimore: Johns Hopkins University Press, 2000. A lively overview of the history of taxonomy from Linnaeus to modern times.

Frängsmyr, Tore, ed. *Linnaeus: The Man and His Work.* Canton, Mass.: Science History, 1994. A collection of essays on Linnaeus's work and life by Swedish Linnaeus scholars.

Gould, Stephen J. "Linnaeus's Luck?" *Natural History* 109 (2000): 48-76. An examination into why Linnaeus's classification scheme works so well and why it has accommodated and lent support to Darwin's theory of evolution.

Shanahan, Timothy. "Species." In *The Scientific Revolution: An Encyclopedia*, edited by Wilbur Applebaum. New York: Garland, 2000. A history of the species concept.

SEE ALSO: 1718: Geoffroy Issues the *Table of Reactivities*; May, 1735-1743: French Scientists Explore the Amazon River; 1742: Celsius Proposes an International Fixed Temperature Scale; 1745: Lomonosov Issues the First Catalog of Minerals; 1749-1789: First Comprehensive Examination of the Natural World; 1751: Maupertuis Provides Evidence of "Hereditary Particles"; 1757-1766: Haller Establishes Physiology as a Science; 1760's: Beginning of Selective Livestock Breeding; 1786-1787: Lavoisier Devises the Modern System of Chemical Nomenclature.

RELATED ARTICLES in *Great Lives from History: The Eighteenth Century, 1701-1800*: Sir Joseph Banks; Comte de Buffon; Carolus Linnaeus.

May, 1735-1743
FRENCH SCIENTISTS EXPLORE THE AMAZON RIVER

La Condamine and his crew rafted the 3,000-mile-long Amazon River, producing the first scientific accounts of the river and region. In addition to charting the river, he discovered the value of rubber and observed the work of Jesuit missionaries with indigenous peoples.

LOCALE: Ecuador; Brazil; French Guiana
CATEGORY: Science and technology; cartography; exploration and discovery

KEY FIGURES
Charles-Marie de La Condamine (1701-1774), French mathematician and scientist
Pedro Vicente Maldonado (1704-1748), Ecuadoran provincial official and scientist

SUMMARY OF EVENT

Although the fifteenth century saw considerable advancements in mapmaking, at the beginning of the eighteenth century maps continued to present navigational errors because of imprecision regarding the size of one degree of latitude. It was not certain whether Earth was a perfect sphere. The size of a degree of latitude would not be uniform over the globe if the sphere were not evenly curved. Moreover, Sir Isaac Newton argued that Earth was flattened at the poles and bulged at the equator. Therefore, the measure of one degree of latitude would have to be appropriately adjusted depending on one's distance from the poles.

To address this important question for the natural sciences and world navigation, the French Academy of Sciences sent an expedition to Ecuador to measure one degree of latitude at the equator. A young, wealthy, and brilliant mathematician and specialist in the emerging field of geodesy, Charles-Marie de La Condamine, was a member of the expedition. He secured his participation through the support of the noted writer Voltaire, who helped La Condamine with a considerable subsidy.

In May of 1735, a group of ten scientists and technicians set out from France for South America. Through the Caribbean, Colombia, and Panama they journeyed with their supplies and scientific equipment. By the middle of the following year they had arrived in Quito, Ecuador, and began conducting measurements in the region. The academy had selected Ecuador as the base because other locations in the world were considered too hostile or inaccessible. Ecuador, however, was Spanish territory, part of the rich mining regions that economically supported its empire.

The French scientists received permission to work in Spanish territory because the two countries shared the same ruling dynasty, the Bourbons. The scientists were accompanied by Spanish military officials throughout the expedition. In Ecuador, La Condamine met Pedro Vicente Maldonado, a young provincial official and emerging scientist with whom he formed a lasting professional partnership.

The work of measurement was a monumental task. It involved the laying of long measuring chains through the mountains, calculating and checking distances through triangulation, and displaying measurements and findings in maps and tables. The work continued throughout the rest of the decade and was successful in verifying the bulge of Earth. However, it failed to be the first to present

A lithograph depicting an eighteenth century expedition along the Amazon River. (The Granger Collection, New York)

its findings to the French Academy. Another French expedition, which had worked toward the North Pole, reported its findings to the academy in 1739.

Because of crew deaths and marriages, international conflicts, and internal strife, the Ecuador expedition began to break up at the beginning of the following decade. However, because La Condamine had associated with the Jesuits in Quito, he was able to conceive of an expedition down the Amazon River. The Jesuits maintained Indian missions throughout the region. Because the river ran through territory that both Spain and Portugal claimed, both Spanish and Portuguese Jesuits were settled in the area. A Spanish Jesuit had made the first detailed map of the 3,000-mile-long river, indicating the tributaries, missions, and tribes to be found along its course. To verify and improve upon this map, La Condamine resolved to return to Europe, accompanied by

Maldonado, by descending the Amazon, which travels in a northeasterly direction. Appreciating the value this task could have for their missionary work, the Jesuits helped the explorers acquire dugout canoes, indigenous oarsmen, and guides. The missions would serve as way stations for the expedition.

La Condamine began the journey from Ecuador in March of 1741, but he and Maldonado did not arrive at the mouth of the Amazon, in the city of Belem do Pará, until September. The two were considered no threat to Portuguese officials, since the gold and diamond mines of Brazil lay far southeast of the Amazon.

About a year after departing, in 1743, and over the course of six months, La Condamine made the first systematic and scientific observations of the river. He corrected aspects of the Jesuit map regarding the rise, flow, and tides of the river and its tributaries. He noted the varied customs and languages of indigenous groups. Ever fascinated by the plant life of the tropics, he continued the observations he began in Ecuador on quinine and the intriguing phenomenon of rubber. He believed that a canal of sorts (the Casiquiare River) connected the Amazon with the Orinoco River in Venezuela. From Brazil, La Condamine traveled to Cayenne, a French territory in Guyana, west of the Amazon. He arrived in France in 1745, after a ten-year absence.

SIGNIFICANCE

In the same year as his return, Charles-Marie de La Condamine published *Relation abrégée d'un voyage fait dans l'intérieur de l'Amérique Méridionale* (1745; *A Succinct Abridgment of a Voyage Made Within the Inland Parts of South-America*, 1747), a work in journal form about his adventures and discoveries in Brazil and Guyana. In 1751 he published a historical and technical account of his Ecuador expedition, *Journal du voyage fait par ordre du roi, à l'équateur* (journal on the voyage to the equator made by order of the king).

Of great importance for medicine and public health were his narratives relating the work of missionaries in the lower Amazon who had used an early form of inoculation since about the late 1720's to protect the indigenous population from smallpox. La Condamine would become an ardent supporter of vaccination in Europe. He also became a champion of both the utility and novelty of rubber.

La Condamine was a key patron of the campaign to standardize the system of measurement. Complicating his work in Ecuador was the multiplicity of measuring systems used by Europeans. His efforts to standardize measurement would result in the metric system, officially adopted for the first time by any country in 1795, by France.

—*Edward A. Riedinger*

FURTHER READING

Cohen, J. M. *Journeys Down the Amazon: Being the Extraordinary Adventures and Achievements of the Early Explorers*. London: C. Knight, 1975. Narrates the history of Amazon expeditions and explorers for the century prior to the time of La Condamine.

Guadalupi, Gianni, and Anthony Shugaar. *Latitude Zero: Tales of the Equator*. New York: Carroll & Graf, 2001. Relates the equatorial experiences of La Condamine and places them in the context of expeditions by others in South America, Africa, Asia, and Oceania.

Kafker, Frank A. "A List of Contributors to Diderot's *Encyclopedia*." *French Historical Studies* 3, no. 1 (Spring, 1963): 106-122. La Condamine is listed along with all other contributors the encyclopedia published between 1751 and 1772 by Denis Diderot. This article helpfully indicates the volume and page numbers of the articles.

Livingstone, David N., and Charles W. J. Withers. *Geography and Enlightenment*. Chicago: University of Chicago Press, 1999. A collection of articles that reviews the study of Earth and the development of the discipline of geography during the eighteenth century.

Smith, Anthony. *Explorers of the Amazon*. London: Viking, 1990. Includes the chapter "Charles-Marie de La Condamine: Equatorial Scientist," which provides a historical context for the voyage in relation to other European explorers from the mid-sixteenth century to the early twentieth century.

Von Hagen, Victor Wolfgang. *South America Called Them: Explorations of the Great Naturalists, La Condamine, Humboldt, Darwin, Spruce*. 3d ed. Boston: Little, Brown, 1955. Nine chapters examine the life of La Condamine, his experiences in South America from 1735 to 1743, and the significance of his work and findings.

SEE ALSO: Apr. 5, 1722: European Discovery of Easter Island; 1776: Foundation of the Viceroyalty of La Plata; July 16, 1799-July 9, 1804: Humboldt and Bonpland's Expedition.

RELATED ARTICLE in *Great Lives from History: The Eighteenth Century, 1701-1800:* George Vancouver.

August 4, 1735
TRIAL OF JOHN PETER ZENGER

Zenger published articles criticizing the governor of New York, who had him prosecuted for libel. He was acquitted based on the argument, a novel one at the time, that the truth of an utterance should be a defense in libel cases. The case became a crucial step in the evolution of the freedoms of speech and of the press in Great Britain and the United States.

LOCALE: New York City, New York (now in the United States)

CATEGORIES: Laws, acts, and legal history; government and politics; social issues and reform

KEY FIGURES

John Peter Zenger (1697-1746), German-born colonial American printer and publisher

Andrew Hamilton (1676-1741), colonial American lawyer

William Cosby (c. 1690-1736), governor of New York, 1732-1736

Richard Bradley (d. 1751), attorney general of New York, 1722-1751

Lewis Morris (1671-1746), chief justice of the New York Supreme Court, 1715-1733

James De Lancey (1703-1760), chief justice of the New York Supreme Court, 1733-1760

James Alexander (1691-1756), colonial American lawyer

SUMMARY OF EVENT

John Peter Zenger's fame rests upon his role in what is perhaps the best-known free speech case in American history. Born in Germany in 1697, Zenger emigrated to New York in 1710 and took up an apprenticeship with William Bradford, publisher of the *New York Gazette*. Bradford was then the only printer in New York and the printer for the colonial government. Zenger became a master printer whose graphic skills exceeded those of his master. He never had any formal schooling and never made any pretense of being a writer, just a printer. At age twenty-one Zenger traveled through the colonies and then settled in Maryland from 1720 to 1722. He married and served for a time as the printer for the colonial ad-

1730's

233

ministration. When his wife died, he returned to New York and entered into a partnership with Bradford.

In 1726, Zenger dissolved his partnership with Bradford to establish his own printing shop, which was patronized by a small group of New Yorkers who were leading members of the bar: Supreme Court Chief Justice Lewis Morris, Lewis Morris, Jr., James Alexander, and William Smith. He published their political broadsides and pamphlets. When Chief Justice Morris lost his office after issuing an opinion against Governor William Cosby in a dispute over the salary still owed to Cosby's immediate predecessor in office, Morris engaged Zenger to publish a pamphlet giving his side of the controversy.

Encouraged by the success of the pamphlet, Zenger's patrons persuaded him to publish an opposition newspaper for which they would anonymously write articles. Zenger was happy to oblige since a newspaper gave a printer steady work and profits. On November 5, 1733, the first issue of Zenger's *New York Weekly Journal* appeared. The *Journal* printed essays on liberty and attacks on Governor Cosby detailing his corruption and incompetence. The newspaper became an immediate success, partly because of the unpopularity of the governor and partly because of the wit and style of the articles.

Governor Cosby was not willing to tolerate the attacks and, after two months' restraint, ordered Chief Justice James De Lancey to convene a grand jury to bring Zenger to trial for libel. The first attempt in January, 1734, failed, and a second unsuccessful attempt was made in November. On October 17, 1734, a resolution was introduced into the General Assembly to have copies of Zenger's newspaper brought into the council and burned by the hands of the common hangman, to authorize the governor to offer a reward to discover the authors of the seditious libel, and

to demand the prosecution of the printer. The resolution was passed in amended form to authorize the public burning of the newspaper.

Zenger was jailed on a warrant signed by the clerk of the governor's council while another grand jury met and again refused to indict him. In January, 1735, Attorney General Richard Bradley in a bill of indictment charged Zenger with "printing and publishing several Seditious

---

FREEDOM OF THE PRESS IN A FREE SOCIETY

On November 12 and November 19, 1733, John Peter Zenger's New York Weekly Journal *published an editorial letter on the function of a free press within a free society. The second half of the letter is excerpted here.*

Inconveniences are rather to be endured than that we should suffer an entire and total destruction. Who would not lose a leg to save his neck? And who would not endanger his hand to guard his heart? The loss of liberty in general would soon follow the suppression of the liberty of the press; for as it is an essential branch of liberty, so perhaps it is the best preservation of the whole. Even a restraint of the press would have a fatal influence. No nation ancient or modern ever lost the liberty of freely speaking, writing, or publishing their sentiments but forthwith lost their liberty in general and became slaves. LIBERTY and SLAVERY! how amiable is one! how odious and abominable the other! Liberty is universal redemption, joy, and happiness; but servitude is absolute reprobation and everlasting perdition in politics.

All the venal supporters of wicked ministers are aware of the great use of the liberty of the press in a limited free monarchy: They know how vain it would be to attack it openly, and therefore endeavor to puzzle the case with words, inconsistencies, and -nonsense; but if the opinion of the most numerous, unprejudiced and impartial part of mankind is an argument of truth, the liberty of the press has that as well as reason on its side. I believe every honest Briton of whatever denomination, who loves his country, if left to his own free and unbiased judgment is a friend to the liberty of the press and an enemy to any restraint upon it. Surely all the independent Whigs, to a man, are of this opinion. By an Independent Whig, I mean one whose principles lead him to be firmly attached to the present happy establishment, both in church and state, and whose fidelity to the royal family is so staunch and riveted as not to be called in question, tho' his mind is not oversway'd, or rather necessitated, by the extraordinary weight of lucrative posts or pensions. The dread of infamy hath certainly been of great use to the cause of virtue, and is a stronger curb upon the passions and appetites of some men than any other consideration moral or religious. Whenever, therefore, the talent of satire is made use of to restrain men by the fear of' shame from immoral actions, which either do or do not fall under the cognizance of the law, it is properly, and justly, and commendably applied: On the contrary, to condemn all satire is in effect the same thing as countenancing vice by screening it from reproach and the just indignation of mankind.

Source: New York Weekly Journal, November 19, 1733. The Trial of John Peter Zenger. Famous American Trials, University of Missouri, Kansas City, School of Law. http://www.law.umkc.edu/faculty/projects/ftrials/zenger/journalissues3.html. Accessed November 13, 2005.

Libels" in two issues of his newspaper. One of these two issues, dated January 28, 1734, had asserted that the people of New York "think, as matters now stand, that their liberties and properties are precarious, and that slavery is likely to be entailed on them and their posterity." The second issue, dated April 8, 1734, contained a statement by a New York resident which declared: "We see men's deeds destroyed, judges arbitrarily displaced, new courts erected without consent of the legislature by which . . . trial by jury is taken away when a governor pleases." Because reasonable bail was denied, Zenger remained in jail nine months awaiting trial. Zenger's wife continued publication of the newspaper while he was in jail.

James Alexander, a former attorney general and author of several of the newspaper articles, and William Smith, a future attorney general and New York Supreme Court justice, defended Zenger. They argued for the removal of Chief Justice De Lancey and Justice Frederick Philipse from the case, arguing that their commissions were defective. Both were disbarred, and the court appointed John Chambers, an inexperienced lawyer and an advocate of Governor Cosby, to represent Zenger at the trial set for August 4.

After an unsuccessful attempt to pack the jury with a preselected list of the governor's supporters, the prosecution tried to equate the criticism of the governor with action against the king. Andrew Hamilton from Philadelphia had been secretly brought to New York to defend Zenger. He dramatically arose in the court to assume the defense of Zenger. He admitted the fact of publication but added that it was supported with truth. Attorney General Bradley countered that the jury must find a verdict for the king. He added that even if the charges were true, the law said that they are libel and that truth is an aggravation of the crime.

Hamilton replied that to ignore truth in matters of libel was a return to the wickedness of the Star Chamber and offered to prove the truth of the articles in the newspaper. This defense was not permitted by the court. Hamilton then argued that to determine the proper punishment for libel, the truth must be determined, since truth aggravated the libel. Again the court disallowed his argument. In summing up, Hamilton reminded the jury that an essential part of liberty was the right to oppose arbitrary power by speaking and writing the truth. The argument had an effect upon the jury. After a brief deliberation, the jury returned a verdict of not guilty. The victory was celebrated with cheers, salutes from guns aboard ships, and a dinner in honor of Hamilton. The case became widely known in the colonies and in England.

SIGNIFICANCE

Although the Zenger case did not establish a binding precedent in libel cases, it was an important step toward truth as a defense against libel. Up to that time, the role of the jury had been limited to ascertaining whether the accused had in fact published the material in question. Two important new rules were derived from Zenger's case: that juries in libel cases are competent to decide on questions of the "law" as well as those of "fact"; and that truth is a defense in a libel prosecution. These principles were not adopted into U.S. law, however, until the enactment of the Sedition Act of 1798. Zenger's trial occurred during a period of increasing demand for liberty. It proved that citizens could speak their minds, take on the authorities, and win. The trial is therefore a symbol of the fundamental freedom to criticize government and the right to publish such criticism, which is necessary to make that freedom meaningful.

—James J. Bolner, updated by Robert D. Talbott

FURTHER READING

Alexander, James. *A Brief Narrative of the Case and Trial of John Peter Zenger, Printer of the New York Weekly Journal.* Edited by Sidney N. Katz. Cambridge, Mass.: Harvard University Press, 1963. Katz states that the indirect effect of the Zenger trial was most important and that Hamilton's argument reflected the prevailing feeling about the proper relationship between government and citizens.

Burancelli, Vincent. *The Trial of Peter Zenger.* New York: New York University Press, 1957. A leading commentary on the Zenger trial emphasizing its importance in libel defense.

Emord, Jonathan W. *Freedom, Technology, and the First Amendment.* San Francisco, Calif.: Pacific Research Institute for Public Policy, 1991. Author says that Zenger's case set no legal precedent, but it did give colonial juries a means to thwart libel prosecutions.

Peck, Robert S. *The Bill of Rights and the Politics of Interpretation.* St. Paul, Minn.: West, 1992. Peck states that no precedent was established but the trial reflected a growing public sentiment for liberty.

Putnam, William Lowell. *John Peter Zenger and the Fundamental Freedom.* Jefferson, N.C.: McFarland, 1997. Comprehensive biography of Zenger. Putnam describes how Zenger's trial led to the adoption of the First Amendment in the United States and similar safeguards in Europe. The appendix includes copies of the American and English bills of rights, the Declaration of Independence, and the Declaration of the Rights of Man and of the Citizen.

Rutherford, Livingston. *John Peter Zenger: His Trial, and a Bibliography of Zenger Imprints.* New York: Dodd, Mead, 1904. A reprint of the account of the trial written by Zenger and published in his *New York Weekly Journal.*

SEE ALSO: Mar. 1, 1711: Addison and Steele Establish *The Spectator*; 1736: *Gentleman's Magazine* Initiates Parliamentary Reporting; Beginning Apr., 1763: The *North Briton* Controversy; Sept. 10, 1763: Publication of the *Freeman's Journal*; Dec. 15, 1791: U.S. Bill of Rights Is Ratified; 1792-1793: Fichte Advocates Free Speech; Jan. 4, 1792-1797: The *Northern Star* Calls for Irish Independence; June 25-July 14, 1798: Alien and Sedition Acts.

RELATED ARTICLES in *Great Lives from History: The Eighteenth Century, 1701-1800*: Gouverneur Morris; John Wilkes; John Peter Zenger.

1736
GENTLEMAN'S MAGAZINE INITIATES PARLIAMENTARY REPORTING

Between 1736 and 1746, England's first magazine established a new standard of parliamentary reporting, providing an unbiased—albeit thinly disguised— account of debates in the face of government sanctions.

LOCALE: London, England
CATEGORIES: Communications; government and politics

KEY FIGURES
Edward Cave (1691-1754), founder and managing editor of *Gentleman's Magazine*
Wiliam Guthrie (1708-1770), Scottish historian
Samuel Johnson (1709-1784), prominent British literary figure
Robert Walpole (1676-1745), prime minister of Great Britain, 1721-1742

SUMMARY OF EVENT

The ascendancy of English king Charles II (1660) heralded an era of restrictions on freedom of the press in England. The Licensing Act of 1662 limited the number of private printers in the country to twenty, all but one in London, and required review of all political publications by the secretary of state. Press reporting of debates in Parliament was out of the question. What little parliamentary reporting occurred took the form of handwritten newsletters, circulated in coffeehouses.

The expiration of the Licensing Act in 1693 opened up the field to journalism of all types; an explosion of publications ensued. This initial explosion was followed by a winnowing process, during which conflicts between the government and printers over the scope of freedom of the press, combined with the forces of the marketplace, molded Western journalism into its modern form. One of the most influential publications of early Georgian England was *Gentleman's Magazine*, founded by Edward Cave in 1731. This first "magazine," or storehouse of information, collected material from a variety of London periodicals and presented it monthly in condensed form. *Gentleman's Magazine* quickly became immensely popular, especially outside London, achieving a circulation of ten thousand by 1742. The actual readership was, of course, many times this number.

One of the many publications abstracted in *Gentleman's Magazine* was *The Political State of Great Britain*, a monthly periodical founded in 1711 that included accounts of parliamentary debates. Public access to parliamentary proceedings was far from satisfactory in 1731. A semiofficial publication, *Votes and Proceedings of Parliament*, provided no details. *The Political State of Great Britain* included more but was obliged to wait until the parliamentary session had closed before printing synopses of debates. Even then, these synopses were considered illicit and they were suppressed whenever possible. Other periodicals commented sporadically on specific issues. As a contemporary commentator observed, the clandestine nature of parliamentary reporting and occasional prosecution of printers meant that no one was willing to risk printing debates out of simple regard for the truth, and most of what appeared was partisan and inaccurate. Cave was well aware of the risks involved. In 1728, he was prosecuted and briefly imprisoned for transmitting transcripts of parliamentary debates to the *Gloucester Journal*.

Realizing that readers sought more detailed and timely reports of Parliament's debates, Cave began supplementing the material from *The Political State of Great Britain*, employing William Guthrie, who had an excellent memory, to attend the debates and sometimes attending himself. Immediately after the debate closed, Guthrie would repair to a coffeehouse and make notes from memory. After the close of Parliament, a writer combined these notes with the accounts in *The Political State of Great Britain* and materials furnished by members of Parliament to produce a narrative that ran in serial form for the remainder of the year. When *The Political State of Great Britain* ceased publication in 1736, both the *Gentleman's Magazine* and its rival, *London Magazine*, began generating their own accounts.

Unlike his contemporaries, Cave strove to provide an accurate and unbiased account of parliamentary proceedings. A moderate Whig himself—and therefore generally a supporter of Prime Minister Robert Walpole—he expected his publication to appeal to a broad spectrum of the educated public. He resisted accepting subsidies from partisan sources, a major source of financing for publications in early eighteenth century Britain. This meant that *Gentleman's Magazine* depended on copy sales and advertising for its revenue.

In April of 1738, Walpole decided to take action against an illegal practice. Complaining "I have been made to speak the very reverse of what I meant" and maintaining that partisan periodicals represented a debate with "all the learning, and the argument, thrown into one side, and on the other, nothing but what was low, mean, and ridiculous," he asked for a resolution from the House of Commons vowing to prosecute reports of debates, even when Parliament was not in session. The House complied.

The resolution left Cave in a quandary, as the debates of the 1738 session were already prepared for publication. Fortunately, he had recently engaged a youthful Samuel Johnson, later to become one of England's leading literary figures, to write up the debates. Johnson quickly penned an introduction stating that Lemuel Gulliver's grandson had returned to Lilliput and discovered that the Senate there bore a remarkable resemblance to Britain's Parliament (a reference to Jonathan Swift's 1726 satire *Gulliver's Travels*). The debates appeared, under disguised names, and Walpole was unwilling to invite ridicule by admitting that he was the original of Johnson's clever satire.

"Debates in the Senate of Lilliput" appeared from 1738 until 1746. It appeared during a time when public interest in proceedings of Parliament was at an unprecedented high because of controversies about Walpole's fiscal policies and the international crisis that had culminated in the War of the Austrian Succession (1740-1748). By 1746, interest had waned, and Cave decided

that the costs and risks associated with detailed parliamentary reporting were no longer worth their benefits.

After "Debates in the Senate of Lilliput" ceased to appear in *Gentleman's Magazine*, *London Magazine* continued its similar but less reliable feature "Proceedings of a Political Club" for several years more, ending it in 1757. In general, however, detailed accounts of parliamentary debates were unavailable to the general public between 1746 and 1771, when a series of confrontations between newspaper owners, the House of Commons, and the radical politician John Wilkes led to free reporting of debates as they occurred, although the law against such reporting was technically still in effect. Reporters were not allowed to take notes within the houses of Parliament until the end of the eighteenth century, and prosecutions for libel occurred sporadically for several more decades. The law prohibiting publication of parliamentary proceedings was finally officially rescinded in 1973.

SIGNIFICANCE

Considerable controversy exists both among historians and among literary scholars about the "Debates in the Senate of Lilliput." Based on a well-known anecdote about Samuel Johnson, in which one man at a dinner party praised the oratory of William Pitt the Elder and Johnson remarked that he had written the speech in question in a garret in Exeter Street, many historians doubt that the material published in *Gentleman's Magazine* bore much resemblance to the actual debates. William Cobbett, compiling his *Parliamentary History of England* (1806-1820), was able to compare Johnson's version of debates in the House of Lords with shorthand notes taken by a member and concluded that the speakers and their arguments were faithfully represented and that some attempt had been made to reproduce each speaker's style. Johnson's accounts, however, contain a great deal of Johnson's style as well. He could not help but turn the outline he received into beautiful English according to the literary standards of the day; indeed, he was expected to do so.

By contrast, accounts of debates in the *Morning Chronicle* after 1771 and the *London Times* after 1786 are close to being actual transcripts. They are lengthy, difficult to read, and possess literary quality only in those instances when a member of Parliament composed a speech beforehand and then memorized it. No longer constrained to wait until the close of the session to publish debates, newspapers employed relays of reporters shuttling between Parliament and the newspaper office, working directly with the compositors in an effort to get the entire text of a debate into the hands of the reading public the following morning. The news had gained in immediacy, but it had lost some of its elegance.

At the beginning of the eighteenth century, English newspapers and journals published very little domestic political news—much of it was censored at the source, and the threat of prosecution was too high. It required considerable courage and initiative to publish parliamentary debates in the 1730's. Their publication in the widely circulated *Gentleman's Magazine* was a landmark in the evolution of freedom of the press and of the right of the general public to enjoy timely access to the inner workings of government.

—*Martha A. Sherwood*

FURTHER READING

Cobbett, William, ed. *The Parliamentary History of England: From the Norman Conquest in 1066 to the Year 1803.* Vol. 10. London: T. C. Hansard, 1811. The introduction states that most of the material for 1736-1745 came from *Gentleman's Magazine* and assesses the accuracy of the magazine's reporting; the text includes a transcript of the 1738 debate on preventing reporting of Commons debates.

Hoover, Benjamin Beard. *Samuel Johnson's Parliamentary Reporting: "Debates in the Senate of Lilliput."* Berkeley: University of California Press, 1953. Includes a thorough review of parliamentary reporting from 1688 to 1750 and extensive information on Cave as editor.

Kaminski, Thomas. *The Early Career of Samuel Johnson.* New York: Oxford University Press, 1987. One chapter deals with parliamentary reports and the question of their literary versus news value.

Mathew, H. C. G., and Brian Harrison, eds. *Oxford Dictionary of National Biography: From the Earliest Times to the Year 2000.* New York: Oxford University Press, 2004. Good entry on Edward Cave. An invaluable source for biographies of obscure British historical personages.

Raymond, Joad, ed. *News, Newspapers, and Society in Early Modern England.* Portland, Oreg.: Frank Cass, 1999. Main emphasis is on the seventeenth century; provides background on parliamentary reporting and the economics of periodical publication.

SEE ALSO: Mar. 1, 1711: Addison and Steele Establish *The Spectator*; 1721-1742: Development of Great Britain's Office of Prime Minister; Dec. 16, 1740-Nov. 7, 1748: War of the Austrian Succession; Mar. 20, 1750-Mar. 14, 1752: Johnson Issues *The Rambler*; Beginning Apr., 1763: The *North Briton* Controversy; Sept. 10, 1763: Publication of the *Freeman's Journal*; 1774: Hansard Begins Reporting Parliamentary Debates; Jan. 4, 1792-1797: The *Northern Star* Calls for Irish Independence.

RELATED ARTICLES in *Great Lives from History: The Eighteenth Century, 1701-1800*: Samuel Johnson; William Pitt the Elder; Robert Walpole; John Wilkes; John Peter Zenger.

1736-1739
RUSSO-AUSTRIAN WAR AGAINST THE OTTOMAN EMPIRE

Russia, along with its ally Austria, invaded the Ottoman Empire. This ill-managed and inconclusive aggression ended in a stalemate. As a result, the Russian aggressors determined to build up their army. The Ottomans, believing that their forces were sufficient to maintain their empire, failed to augment them, setting the stage for their defeat at Russian hands later in the century.

LOCALE: Ukraine; the Balkans
CATEGORY: Wars, uprisings, and civil unrest

KEY FIGURES

Anna (Anna Ivanovna; 1693-1740), empress of Russia, r. 1730-1740

Count Andrei Ivanovich Osterman (1686-1747), first cabinet minister of Russia, 1731-1740

Burkhard Christoph von Münnich (1683-1767), German-born commander in chief of the Russian army, 1728-1740, and president of the war council, 1732-1740

Reichsgraf von Seckendorff (Friedrich Heinrich Seckendorff; 1673-1763), Austrian field marshal

Peter Lacy (1678-1751), Irish-born Russian field marshal

Claude Alexandre de Bonneval (Ahmed Pasha; 1675-1747), French soldier serving the Ottomans

Count von Niepperg (1684-1774), Austrian field marshal and negotiator

Count von Wallis (1676-1744), Irish-born Austrian field marshal and negotiator

Charles VI (1685-1740), Holy Roman Emperor, r. 1711-1740

Mahmud I (1696-1754), Ottoman sultan, r. 1730-1754

André-Hercule de Fleury (1653-1743), French prime minister, 1726-1743

Marquis de Villeneuve (Louis-Saveur Renaud; 1695-1745), French ambassador to Constantinople

SUMMARY OF EVENT

The Russian-Turkish war of 1736-1739 originated in the vanity and rapacity of Czarina Anna, in the dream of Russian hegemony over the Black Sea of her foreign minister Count Andrei Ivanovich Osterman, and in the thirst for military glory of Field Marshal Burkhard Christoph von Münnich, her commander in chief. Russia did not want to fight alone, however, so it turned to the reluctant Habsburg emperor, Charles VI, with whom it had formed a military alliance in 1726.

In 1736, the Ottoman Empire was at peace. Sultan Mahmud I was quietly pursuing the innovations initiated by his uncle, Ahmed III: The printing press set up by Ibrahim Müteferrika in 1724 was resuscitated in 1732, and several public libraries had been founded. The empire had acquired its first paper factory at Yalova. A newly completed aqueduct brought fresh water to Constantinople. Mahmud also recognized the need to modernize the army: He assigned Claude Alexandre de Bonneval—an experienced French soldier who had converted to Islam—to revive the neglected corps of bombardiers (Turkish: *humbaraci*). Bonneval submitted to the sultan a plan to modernize the army along French and Austrian lines. Predictably, Janissary opposition led to its being shelved.

Nevertheless, Bonneval was given a training ground, barracks, and workshops near Üsküdar. He engaged European officers who were Muslim converts as instructors and modernized the Ottoman cannon foundry and powder and musket factories. A new grand vizier gave Bonneval somewhat grudging support and insufficient funds but allowed him to build new facilities and schools of geometry and engineering. Despite uneven support, Bonneval persevered. His military innovations, as reported by the Russian ambassador, were impressive enough that Osterman became eager to attack the Ottomans to forestall any further military reform.

Anna declared war on the Ottoman Empire on April 12, 1736. Münnich had already launched a preemptive strike in the previous autumn against the Crimea, but with inadequate provisioning and the early onset of winter, he lost nine thousand men without ever seeing the Perekop Isthmus (the gateway to the Crimea from the Ukraine). The year 1736 saw the organization of two campaigns: Field Marshal Peter Lacy besieged Azov at the mouth of the Don River, which fell on July 1; Münnich, with a much larger force, invaded the Crimea. When the Tatars withdrew, the Russians laid waste the peninsula, but by late summer they were forced to retreat by plague, exhaustion, and lack of provisions.

Münnich had lost two thousand men in combat, as well as thirty thousand to plague, climate, and terrain. Osterman was now desperate to draw the Austrians into the conflict, but the emperor continued to delay: He had no wish to go to war, for which his forces were ill prepared, but he was determined to retain his alliance with Russia. In Vienna, the Imperial War Council (*Hofkriegsrat*) played for time. In Paris, Cardinal André-Hercule de Fleury, fearful of a shift in the European balance of power, offered French mediation on behalf of the Ottoman sultanate.

The fighting continued in 1737 but proved inconclusive. On July 13, the Russians stormed Ochakov, owing their success primarily to the explosion of the Ottoman powder magazine, but Münnich, shaken by his casualties, withdrew into the Ukraine. In Vienna, Reichsgraf von Seckendorff was appointed commander in chief in May, and on July 14, the emperor at last declared war. The Austrian plan was to attack the Ottoman border fortress of Vidin, but because of heavy flooding, Seckendorff turned south to capture Niš in Serbia, sending a small force into Bosnia and another to occupy Novi Pazar, which soon had to be abandoned. An Austrian defeat at Banja Luka drew Seckendorff himself into Bosnia, while the approach of a large Ottoman army toward Niš led to its surrender on October 16, 1737. In effect, Seckendorff was now in retreat. The *Hofkriegsrat* relieved him of his command, court-martialed him for incompetence, and imprisoned him. Meanwhile, in early winter, a large Ottoman force marched on Ochakov. Münnich was certain that the Russians could not hold the town, but surprisingly, they did.

The following year proved equally inconclusive. Austria was desperate for peace, while Russia was fearful that Fleury was organizing a hostile alliance between Sweden, anti-Russian elements in Poland, and the Ottomans. By May, the bickering allies agreed that France should broker a peace settlement. Osterman informed the marquis de Villeneuve, France's ambassador in Constantinople, that Russia was willing to restore Ochakov and Kinburn in order to retain Azov. The Austrians were willing to return to the territorial divisions that had been established by the Treaty of Passarowitz (1718). Fleury thought peace was at hand. He did not realize that the Ottomans, elated by Münnich's withdrawal from Ochakov, were in an aggressive mood and were preparing for war at the same time they urged Villeneuve to continue his mediation.

In April, 1738, the grand vizier left Constantinople for Niš. His objective was to conquer Ada Ka'le (New Orsova), an island in the Danube River that would make an impregnable base for staging raids into the Banat. Charles VI could not ignore the danger this plan represented. With his son-in-law, Francis Stephen, duke of Lorraine (the future Emperor Francis I), in nominal command of the Austrian forces, Charles appointed as effective field commander Count Königsegg, president of the *Hofkriegsrat*.

On July 4, Königsegg defeated a large Ottoman force at Cornea in the Banat, north of Ada Ka'le, but when he learned that the grand vizier was approaching with a much larger army, he retreated. Vienna was furious, but because the duke of Lorraine had fallen seriously ill, Königsegg was left in command for the remainder of the year. There were no further engagements, but a great many of the Austrian troops in the field died from disease. The news was no better from the Russian front. Münnich's goal was Bender, in lower Bessarabia, but his advance was so slow that when he reached the Dniester River in mid-August, he found sixty thousand Turkish and Tatar troops ensconced on the opposite bank, and he withdrew. Lacy ravaged the Crimea but was forced to retreat by a lack of provisions. Ochakov and Kinburn were evacuated.

By the opening of 1739, the grand vizier had taken Ada Ka'le. The *Hofkriegsrat* informed Villeneuve that it would abandon Serbia and Oltenia (Little Wallachia) to regain Ada Ka'le and Mehadiye. Belgrade would remain the linchpin of Austrian frontier defense. The grand vizier's goal was to bring his two foes to the conference table under French auspices while simultaneously investing Belgrade. On May 17, the sultan granted Villeneuve the authority to negotiate a peace settlement.

Meanwhile, with another year of war unavoidable, the *Hofkriegsrat* appointed the elderly Count von Wallis as commander in chief. In mid-July, he joined his plague-ridden army at Belgrade, where, learning that the grand vizier and his large army had reached Grocka—between Belgrade and Semendria—he advanced to meet the enemy. On July 22, 1739, the two armies engaged in a fiercely fought, daylong encounter in which the Austrians seemingly had the edge. However, when Wallis learned that another Ottoman army was threatening his communications with the north, he overruled his staff

and ordered a retreat, crossing into the Banat. He fought a successful engagement at Panchevo on July 30, after which he headed to Belgrade, only to find it already invested by Ottoman forces, including the grand vizier, Villeneuve, and a Russian representative named Cagnoni.

After Wallis's imprudent actions in the field, the *Hofkriegsrat* no longer trusted him as a negotiator. It replaced him with Count von Neipperg, who, arriving in the Ottoman camp on August 17, became a virtual hostage of the grand vizier and was forced to seek Villeneuve's protection. After grueling negotiations, Neipperg, the grand vizier, Villeneuve, and Cagnoni signed an agreement on September 18, which became the Treaty of Belgrade. Austria agreed to abandon Oltenia, Serbia, Ada Ka'le, Orsova, and Belgrade. Russia was to demolish its fortress of Azov. Neither Russian warships nor merchantmen were to enter the Black Sea, but Russian merchants could trade in Ottoman territory.

By the time the treaty was signed, ironically, Münnich had taken Khotin and on September 14 had made a triumphant entry into Jassy, but it was too late. The *Hofkriegsrat* considered disowning Neipperg, but the treaty had been guaranteed in Louis XV's name, and to disavow it was unthinkable. Russia was furious but, fearful of French and Swedish machinations with Polish dissidents, acquiesced. In December, 1739, the czarina, following the emperor and sultan, ratified the treaty. Both Wallis and Neipperg returned to Vienna to face courts-martial and imprisonment. Upon her accession, however, Empress Maria Theresa pardoned them both.

SIGNIFICANCE

The relatively ineffectual conflict between Russia, Austria, and the Ottomans had significant consequences. Despite some success, Russia paid a terrible price in human and material resources. Later in the century, Catherine the Great in her own Ottoman wars would demonstrate that she had learned well the hard-won lessons in geography and logistics of Anna's war. Austria's performance, despite some notable engagements, had left much to be desired, but the alliance with Russia was preserved. It would serve the Habsburgs well until shortly before World War I.

Fleury, by negotiating the peace, had contributed significantly to restoring France's prestige as a great power, and, for the time being, had saved the Ottoman Empire further humiliation. Once again, the sultanate had demonstrated remarkable resilience and the benefits of military reform. Having emerged virtually unscathed from the war, the empire enjoyed an unprecedented peace from 1739 to 1768. From their resilience in the face of the Russian invasion, however, the Ottoman elite drew the wrong conclusion: Deciding that their traditional military practices and technology continued to serve them well, they rejected the need for further innovation. Reform of the Ottoman army was therefore halted for three decades. When the struggle with Russia was renewed, the Russians were immeasurably stronger, and the Ottomans were weaker. Above all, the events of 1736-1739 showed that the Ottomans needed a European protector. For the present, France served that role.

—*Gavin R. G. Hambly*

FURTHER READING

Cassels, Lavender. *The Struggle for the Ottoman Empire, 1717-1740*. London: John Murray, 1966. Excellent narrative, with Villeneuve as its hero.

Roider, Karl A. *The Reluctant Ally: Austria's Policy in the Austro-Turkish War, 1737-1739*. Baton Rouge: Louisiana State University Press, 1972. Detailed monograph based on Austrian sources.

Shaw, Stanford J. *History of the Ottoman Empire and Modern Turkey*. New York: Cambridge University Press, 1976. Best account from the Ottoman viewpoint.

SEE ALSO: 1702 or 1706: First Arabic Printing Press; Nov. 20, 1710-July 21, 1718: Ottoman Wars with Russia, Venice, and Austria; Sept. 18, 1739: Treaty of Belgrade; Oct. 20, 1740: Maria Theresa Succeeds to the Austrian Throne; 1746: Zāhir al-ʿUmar Creates a Stronghold in Galilee; Oct., 1768-Jan. 9, 1792: Ottoman Wars with Russia; 1788-Sept., 1809: Russo-Swedish Wars.

RELATED ARTICLES in *Great Lives from History: The Eighteenth Century, 1701-1800*: Ahmed III; Claude Alexandre de Bonneval; Catherine the Great; Charles VI; André-Hercule de Fleury; Louis XV; Mahmud I; Maria Theresa.

1737
REVIVAL OF THE PARIS SALON

After two failed attempts to revive the official annual exhibition of art by members of the French Royal Academy earlier in the century, the salon was finally reestablished as a regular event in 1737. This institutionalization of art's public exposure created a cogent and aesthetically reactive public in Paris and a critical literature at once erudite and crudely popular that shaped both taste and art.

LOCALE: The Louvre, Paris, France
CATEGORIES: Art; organizations and institutions

KEY FIGURES

Duc d'Antin (Louis-Antoine de Pardaillan; 1665-1736), director general of the king's works to 1736
Philibert Orry (Comte de Vignory; 1689-1747), French director general of the king's works, 1737-1745, and controller general of finances, 1730-1745

SUMMARY OF EVENT

The founding of the French Académie Royale de Peinture et de Sculpture (Royal Academy of Painting and Sculpture) by Charles Le Brun in 1648 established an organization of painters and sculptors that was independent of the Parisian guild systems of the "masters." It was also independent of the market system that had been developing over much of the seventeenth century. Academicians represented a self-selecting group of the "best of the best," from among whom the king could choose his artistic servants.

Upon selection by the Royal Academy, a new member presented the group with a *morceau de réception*, an example of the artist's best work, roughly equivalent to the "masterpiece" required by the guilds for enrollment. Initially, the academy permanently displayed these pieces in its quarters in Paris, creating a gallery of masterpieces. In 1663, though, the academy agreed that each member would bring to each annual meeting in July an example of his latest work to serve as decoration for its space in the Louvre. This display in the Louvre was plagued by a rocky start, and in 1666, Jean-Baptiste Colbert, King Louis XIV's controller general of finances and patron of the academy, decided to make the display a biannual event that would be held during Holy Week (the week preceding Easter).

The 1667 exhibition, which opened on April 23, displayed representative works by most members and is considered by many critics in retrospect to have been the first *salon*, a term deriving from the room in which the works would later be displayed. From 1669, display space was provided in the Palais Royale—formerly the regent's residence in Paris—and the courtyard of the Palais Richelieu. The practice flourished until after the

The Louvre's Galérie d'Apollon was the site of an artistic competition that helped spur the revival of the Paris Salon. (Geo. L. Shuman and Co.)

1673 display, after which only weak attempts were made to remount exhibitions in 1675 and 1680.

In 1699, the academy's president, Jules Hardouin-Mansart, convinced Louis XIV to revive the exhibition and to hold it in the Louvre, in the 660-foot-long Grande Galérie. This exhibition was followed by smaller versions in 1704, on the occasion of the birth of the royal duke of Brittany, and in 1725. In the latter year, the term *salon* was first used for the rather minor ten-day public exhibition, which was held in the Louvre's huge, boxlike Salon Carré beginning on the feast day of Saint Louis (August 25). None of these three exhibitions reestablished the tradition of regular displays of the academicians' art.

In early eighteenth century Paris, an increasingly literate urban public was exposed to paintings by contemporary French and other artists in a number of venues. Painters had long displayed smaller works in prevailing styles for public consumption at the Saint-Germain Fair. In late spring of each year, Parisian Catholics celebrated the feast of Corpus Christi with plays and processions. These terminated in large and elaborate altars, which patrons, dealers, and sometimes artists decorated with paintings. Though the displays lasted only one or two

days, the altars at Pont Neuf and the Place Dauphine evolved into major venues by the mid-1730's.

A third, less accessible display was of the collection amassed by the regent and hung in the Palais Royale beginning in 1727. In the same year, the duc d'Antin, Louis-Antoine de Pardaillan, director general of the king's works (the royal buildings and all art displayed therein), established a competition among the academy's top twelve painters. Each artist's roughly six- by four-foot canvas was hung in the Louvre's Galérie d'Apollon, and the public was invited to view the collection.

In each of these four cases—the Saint-Germain Fair, the feast of Corpus Christi, the display at the Palais Royale, and the competition at the Galérie d'Apollon—the purpose of the exhibition was connected directly to the general public. Together, they signaled a shift away from the traditional stranglehold on the finest art and artists by the aristocracy and the Church. This trend culminated in the revival in 1737 of the Louvre Salon, held once more in the Salon Carré.

When the duc d'Antin died in 1736, he was replaced as director general of the king's works by Philibert Orry, comte de Vignory and controller general of finances. Orry immediately sought to revive the 1725 salon, at least in part as a way of making the work of the academicians accountable to a broader public. He announced this decision in an article in the official newspaper *Mercure de France*, adding that these artists needed to submit themselves to informed persons' judgment if they were truly to deserve their high status and recognition. It was no longer enough to be accepted by one's professional peers: Orry believed that truly great art needed to be declared so by a scrutinizing public with developed aesthetic tastes. Only in this way would the truly talented be discernible from those whose fame was falsely acquired and ill deserved.

Following precedent, the exhibition opened on August 25, Saint Louis's Day, but this time it covered every square foot of the salon's acre of display area, as well as the stairway that led to it, from eye-level up to the ceiling. Small works were ranged along the lower register, while larger and thus more visible works were hanged higher up. All the genres and styles represented in the academy appeared, from still lifes to heroic mythological and historical narratives. As in 1704 and 1725, exhibition booklets naming and describing the works were sold to many members of the huge crowds that flocked to the gallery day after day. Since admission was free, people from all social and economic classes could and did attend, as contemporary writers attest. Indeed, educating the public at large through the capital's very best art was a large part of Orry's plan in mounting the salon. It was an enormous success and the talk of the town.

SIGNIFICANCE

Repeated annually or biannually through the nineteenth century, the salon became a much anticipated event of the summer season and continued to evolve over the next 150 years. The paintings to be hanged in each salon were chosen by jury beginning in 1748. The salon came to play an enormous role in the development of an aesthetically aware general public and of a very public and widely ranging art criticism, as well as in reshaping French academic art in the latter half of the eighteenth century. In general, it made the artistic community of the Royal Academy for the first time responsible to an increasingly sophisticated public. This influence was mediated by the wide range of critics who wrote about each salon, ridiculing as readily as praising, voicing concerns that were genuinely new to Western art. In the general press and in special pamphlets and tracts, more or less knowledgeable critics shaped the opinions of the aristocrats and the shoemakers alike.

Early in the salon's revival, the painters produced art as they and their fellows within the academy saw fit, but as the century progressed, they paid ever more attention to the critical apparatus spawned by each salon, knowing that their reputation and commercial viability hanged in that new and fickle balance. To remain fashionable, patrons among the wealthy and noble also had to pay attention to the trends reflected both in the changing constellations of artistic works themselves and in the writings of various critics that, taken together, sometimes embodied popular consensus and at other times constituted a cacophony of disparate tastes and opinions.

As Orry and others recognized, this process would not automatically create a clearly identifiable public taste, such as had been found in classical Athens or early Renaissance Florence. Rather, the salons would evoke—from published criticism and other public judgments—individual aesthetic responses. Of course, from the artists' point of view this was a very risky situation: If the academy could not successfully educate and shape the public palate, popular pressure could shift or even lower the quality of artistic production. Only time would tell which of these results was most likely.

—*Joseph P. Byrne*

FURTHER READING

Crow, Thomas E. *Painters and Public Life in Eighteenth-Century Paris*. New Haven, Conn.: Yale University Press, 1985. Though a bit dated in some of its judgments, this remains the finest work in English on the salon and its role in developing an audience for and literature on painting in Paris and in affecting the stylistic trends of the mid-eighteenth century.

Fried, Michael. *Absorption and Theatricality: Painting and Beholder in the Age of Diderot*. Chicago: University of Chicago Press, 1988. Looks beyond 1737 to the evolution of the relation of viewer and painting and the changes that reflected the new and varied intimacy created by the institution of the public salon.

Levey, Michael. *Painting and Sculpture in France, 1700-1789*. New Haven, Conn.: Yale University Press, 1993. Focuses on the artists themselves rather than the salon or Royal Academy.

1730's

September 19, 1737
WALKING PURCHASE

Pennsylvania, relying on a questionable deed and practices, acquired a great deal of Lenni Lenape tribal territory. This acquisition led to a greater colonial presence, diminished the prestige of the Lenni Lenape tribe, and thereby enhanced Iroquois dominance over the other tribes of eastern Pennsylvania.

LOCALE: Bucks County, Pennsylvania (now in the
    United States)
CATEGORIES: Expansion and land acquisition;
    colonization; trade and commerce

KEY FIGURES
Thomas Penn (1702-1775), son of William Penn and
    governor of Pennsylvania
Nutimus (c. 1660-c. 1742), chief of the Lenni Lenape
James Logan (1674-1751), colonial American
    provincial official and entrepreneur

SUMMARY OF EVENT
The first half of the eighteenth century was a time of profound population growth in Pennsylvania. Europeans, especially Scotch-Irish and German settlers, came into the colony in unprecedented numbers. The steadily expanding population put considerable pressure on the provincial government to make additional acreage available for settlement. The demand for land also created potentially lucrative opportunities for aggressive speculators, particularly speculators who also served as provincial officials. Such was the case with those who initiated the 1737 Walking Purchase.

The Lenni Lenape (also known as the Delaware) were among the first Native American tribes to negotiate with William Penn. At the time that Pennsylvania was founded, the Lenni Lenapes occupied much of the land between the Delaware and Susquehanna Rivers. Penn's policies toward the Lenni Lenapes were more benevolent than were the tribal policies of most colonial administrators. Penn generally recognized native land rights and usually was tolerant of the indigenous lifestyle.

By the 1730's, Pennsylvania settlers along the Delaware River had moved well north of Philadelphia. This was Lenni Lenape territory, and the natives refused to share possession. Some provincial officials, including William Penn's son Thomas, disputed the Native American claim. The younger Penn maintained that the Lenni Lenapes had promised his father that they would surrender a portion of the land. The younger Penn no doubt also

had ulterior motives for contesting the Lenni Lenape land. While serving as the colony's governor, he was beset with ever-growing family debts. In an effort to solve his financial woes, he chose to sell some of his family's real estate. Among the most desirable and salable parts of his acreage was the Lenni Lenape land along the Delaware.

When confronted by Thomas Penn's claim to their land, the Lenni Lenapes acknowledged that the Penn family had title to a portion of the land along the Delaware. They agreed that Mechkilikishi, one of their chiefs, had granted to William Penn some acreage north of Philadelphia. According to Nutimus, a Lenni Lenape chief who was present when land was given, the Penn claim ended at the Tohickon Creek, which is about 30 miles north of Philadelphia. James Logan, an influential member of Thomas Penn's council, led several Pennsylvania officials in challenging Nutimus's assessment. He contended that Penn's land extended beyond the Forks of the Delaware, which was more than 50 miles to the north.

To resolve the dispute, Thomas Penn called Nutimus and two other Lenni Lenape chiefs to his home at Pennsbury Manor. Assisted by Logan, Penn showed the Native Americans a copy of a deed dated 1686. The agreement transferred to the Penn family a large tract of land west of the Delaware and extending "back into the woods as far as a man can walk in one day and a half."

Nutimus argued that the walk had been made and ended at the Tohickon. The creek, therefore, was the formal border between Penn land and Lenni Lenape territory. Additionally, since Nutimus's village had for several centuries occupied the Forks area, Mechkilikishi, who was chief of another Lenni Lenape village, had no authority to turn over land at the Forks to William Penn.

Nutimus's arguments were greeted with disdain by several influential Pennsylvania officials who, like Penn, had interests in the Forks area beyond providing more land for settlers. One of the most concerned Pennsylvanians was James Logan. A few years earlier, he had begun operating an iron furnace in the region and hoped to expand his facility. Two other interested parties were Andrew Hamilton and his son-in-law, William Allen. Hamilton was mayor of Philadelphia, and Allen was on his way to becoming one of the colony's most successful entrepreneurs and the chief justice of the provincial court. Allen already had begun negotiating quietly for a large tract in what is today Allentown. Once he acquired the land, he hoped to divide it into lots and sell the lots to settlers.

Although the Pennsylvanians passionately argued their claim, the 1686 deed upon which they based their arguments was suspicious in several ways. Among other shortcomings, it lacked signatures and seals. There were also blank spaces in several crucial places, including the spot where the final dimensions of the tract should have appeared. In most cases, such a document would have been voided by the British courts. When questioned about the flaws, Penn and Logan claimed that it was a copy of an original that had been lost. Nevertheless, they continued to uphold the document as valid.

In the months that followed the Pennsbury meeting, Logan quietly expanded his plan of attack. To undermine Nutimus's authority, he appealed to Iroquois representatives for support. The powerful Iroquois nation dominated most tribes throughout Pennsylvania; without their support, the Lenni Lenapes had little hope of retaining the disputed land along the Delaware. Assisted by Conrad Weiser, Logan was able to get the Iroquois to confirm the Penn claims. With Iroquois approval secured, it was just a matter of time before the Lenni Lenapes conceded to Penn's claims. On August 25, 1737, Nutimus and three other Lenni Lenape chiefs grudgingly endorsed Governor Penn's furtive 1686 treaty. A walk that would determine the extent of Penn's holdings along the Delaware was soon scheduled.

The walk began at the Wrightstown Quaker Meeting House at daybreak on September 19. Three local men known for their athletic prowess were hired by provincial authorities to make the hike. Two Native American representatives accompanied the Pennsylvanians. The Lenni Lenapes expected that the walk would conform to native customs. The walkers would walk for a while then rest, smoke a peace pipe, and share a meal before resuming their trek. The Lenni Lenapes expected that the journey would cover about 20 miles. Pennsylvania officials, however, had much different plans.

It became clear immediately that the walk would not be a leisurely stroll along the Delaware. Instead it proceeded northwest toward the Kittatiny Mountains and followed a path that had been cut through the backcountry to aid the walkers. Additionally, much of the time the walkers did not walk. They ran. The Pennsylvanians also were accompanied by supply horses carrying provisions, and boats were used to ferry the hikers across streams.

By early afternoon, the unsuspecting Lenni Lenape escorts fell far behind the Pennsylvanians. A few hours later, already well beyond the Tohickon, one Pennsylvanian dropped from exhaustion. A second walker gave up the following morning. The final Pennsylvanian persevered until noon on the second day. In all, he covered 64 miles, more than three times what the Lenni Lenapes had expected. They were forced nevertheless to cede all of this land to Pennsylvania.

SIGNIFICANCE

Even after the walk had ended, the Penns' land grab continued. Rather than draw a straight line from start to finish and then a right angle to the river, surveyors were instructed by Logan to set the borders of the walk in a zigzag course that followed the flow of the Delaware. As a result, another 750,000 acres were acquired from the Lenni Lenape.

During the months that followed, Nutimus and his tribe complained bitterly about the devious tactics employed by provincial officials. However, the Lenni Lenapes had few alternatives to accepting the results. With Walking Purchase completed, the new land was soon opened to Pennsylvania settlers and the Lenni Lenapes relegated to diminished status among Native American tribes living in the colony. The resulting power vacuum was filled, not only by the European settlers, but by the Iroquois as well. Their prestige increased as that of the Lenni Lenapes diminished, and their influence over the actions and decisions of other Native Americans also became greater. This influence of the Iroquois, as well as the resentments of lesser tribes, would affect the allegiances of Native Americans during the Revolutionary War.

—*Paul E. Doutrich*

FURTHER READING

Jennings, Francis. *The Ambiguous Iroquois Empire*. New York: W. W. Norton, 1984. Offers a detailed explanation of the duplicitous tactics used by Pennsylvania officials to acquire the Walking Purchase acreage.

Kelley, Joseph J., Jr. *Pennsylvania: The Colonial Years, 1681-1776*. Garden City, N.Y.: Doubleday, 1980. Describes the Walking Purchase and many other episodes in Pennsylvania's colonial history.

Kraft, Herbert C. *The Lenape-Delaware Indian Heritage, 10,000 B.C.-A.D. 2000*. Stanhope, N.J.: Lenape Lifeways, 2001. Kraft, an anthropologist specializing in the study of the Delaware Indians, provides a comprehensive and detailed account of the tribe's history. The concluding chapters discuss the Lenape's relations with European settlers, including land treaties and other Indian concessions to colonial settlers.

1730's

Merritt, Jane T. *At the Crossroads: Indians and Empires on a Mid-Atlantic Frontier, 1700-1763*. Chapel Hill: University of North Carolina Press, 2003. Examines the relationship between Native Americans and whites in eighteenth century Pennsylvania; includes information about the Walking Purchase. Merritt describes how the two groups were tolerant of each other until the Seven Years' War; by the 1760's, both groups were aware of racial differences and their relationship had degenerated.

Pencak, William A., and Daniel K. Richter, eds. *Friends and Enemies in Penn's Woods: Indians, Colonists, and the Racial Construction of Pennsylvania*. University Park: Pennsylvania State University Press, 2004. Collection of essays describing how and why relations between colonial settlers and Native Americans degenerated between 1682 and 1763.

Thomas, David Hurst, et al. *The Native Americans: An Illustrated History*. Atlanta, Ga.: Turner, 1993. A colorful history that includes a concise accounting of the purchase.

Tolles, Frederick B. *James Logan and the Culture of Provincial America*. Boston: Little, Brown, 1957. Details the life and career of James Logan, including his role in the Walking Purchase.

Wallace, Paul A. W. *Indians in Pennsylvania*. Harrisburg: Pennsylvania Historical and Museum Commission, 1981. Survey of Native Americans, including a general description of the Walking Purchase.

SEE ALSO: Sept. 22, 1711-Mar. 23, 1713: Tuscarora War; Summer, 1714-1741: Fox Wars; May 28, 1754-Feb. 10, 1763: French and Indian War; Oct. 5, 1759-Nov. 19, 1761: Cherokee War; May 8, 1763-July 24, 1766: Pontiac's Resistance; July 17, 1769-1824: Rise of the California Missions; May 24 and June 11, 1776: Indian Delegation Meets with Congress; Oct. 22, 1784: Fort Stanwix Treaty; Oct. 18, 1790-July, 1794: Little Turtle's War; 1799: Code of Handsome Lake.

RELATED ARTICLES in *Great Lives from History: The Eighteenth Century, 1701-1800*: Ethan Allen; John Dickinson.

1738
BERNOULLI PROPOSES THE KINETIC THEORY OF GASES

Daniel Bernoulli developed the first systematic theory to explain the behavior of gases in terms of their kinetic (or motion-related) properties. Using a mathematical approach, he established a formal relationship between, on the one hand, the many tiny collisions between individual gas molecules and the walls of a container and, on the other hand, the overall pressure exerted on the container by the gas taken as a whole.

LOCALE: St. Petersburg, Russia
CATEGORIES: Chemistry; physics; science and technology

KEY FIGURES
Daniel Bernoulli (1700-1782), Swiss mathematician and scientist
Robert Boyle (1627-1691), Irish chemist

SUMMARY OF EVENT
By the seventeenth century, scientists had noted that gases had unusual properties that they could not explain. In particular, gases were fluids in the sense that they could flow and fill a volume having an irregular shape, but they could also exert a force on the walls of a closed

container. This latter property of gases was easily demonstrated placing a gas in a container that was capped by a piston and noting that the piston was supported by the gas.

The Irish chemist Robert Boyle took the first step in developing a theory to explain some of the properties of a gas. Boyle was a careful experimentalist, and he studied the behavior of a gas held in a container topped by a piston. He kept the container and the gas at a constant temperature and measured the gas's volume and pressure, that is, the force exerted on the piston divided by the area of the piston. In 1660, Boyle published the results of a series of measurements of the pressure and volume of a gas that was held at a constant temperature. These results demonstrated that the volume of a gas is inversely proportional to the pressure it exerts, a result now known as Boyle's law.

Prior to Boyle's measurements, physicists had studied the mechanical properties of springs. It was well established that the force required to compress a spring increased linearly as the spring got shorter. Boyle suggested that the length of a spring was analogous to the volume of a gas inside a container, and the force exerted by the spring was analogous to the force exerted by the gas against the container. Thus, Boyle suggested, gases were in some sense springs that, when they were compressed or distorted, exerted a force proportional to their degree of compression. Boyle was also aware that the volume of a gas increases when the gas is heated. However, he was not able to determine a mathematical relationship between a gas's temperature and its volume, because there was no well-established temperature scale in Boyle's era. It was the development of accurate and reproducible thermometers by the German scientist Daniel Gabriel Fahrenheit, who invented the mercury thermometer in 1714, that allowed the relationship between temperature and volume to be precisely determined.

Working from Boyle's law as a starting point, the Dutch-born Swiss mathematician and physicist Daniel Bernoulli attempted to determine the physical cause of which the law was an effect. Bernoulli, who was teaching in St. Petersburg, Russia, at the time, became the first scientist to understand air pressure in terms of the behavior of the individual molecules making up the air. Unlike Boyle, who took a careful series of measurements, Bernoulli took a theoretical approach to explaining the pressure exerted by a gas. He considered a cylinder that was oriented vertically,

THE BERNOULLIS' FATHER-SON RIVALRY

In 1700, Daniel Bernoulli was born to a long line of mathematicians, physicians, and scientists. His father, Johann, was an expert in Leibnizian calculus. In 1705, Daniel's uncle Jakob died and Johann assumed his brother's vacant chair of mathematics at the University of Basel. Johann became involved in the priority disputes between Sir Isaac Newton and Gottfried Wilhelm Leibniz over the invention of calculus and demonstrated the superiority of Leibniz's notation in the solution of particular problems. After 1705, Johann worked primarily on theoretical and applied mechanics.

In the meantime, Daniel obtained his master's degree in 1716 and was taught mathematics by his father and his elder brother Nikolaus II. Attempts to place him as a commercial apprentice failed, and he studied medicine at several different universities, at last settling in Basel with a doctorate in 1721, his thesis concerning respiration. His first attempts to obtain a university post failed, but his *Exercitationes quaedam mathematicae* (1724; mathematical exercises) landed him a post at the St. Petersburg Academy. Daniel Bernoulli obtained a position in the St. Petersburg Academy in 1725 and remained there until 1733. In 1727, Leonhard Euler joined him. His most productive years were spent in St. Petersburg. He wrote an original treatise on probability, a work on oscillations, and a draft of his most famous work, *Hydrodynamica* (1738; *Hydrodynamics*, 1968), in which he expounds his kinetic theory. He returned to Basel to lecture in medicine but continued to publish in the areas that interested him most—mathematics and mechanics. His father, Johann, tried to establish priority for the founding of the field of hydrodynamics by plagiarizing his son's original work and predating the publication. This is only the worst of many examples of the antagonism that Johann felt toward his son.

In 1743, Daniel began lecturing on physiology, which was more to his liking than medicine, and he was offered the chair of physics in 1750. He lectured on physics until 1776, when he retired. His most important contributions center on his work in rational mechanics. He returned to probability theory in 1760 with his famous work on the effectiveness of the smallpox vaccine, arguing that the vaccine could extend the average lifespan by three years. He published a few more minor works on probability theory through 1776. Throughout his career, he won numerous prizes for astronomy, magnetism, navigation, and ship design. He died in Basel in 1782.

was sealed at the bottom, and had a piston at the top. The piston, which was free to move up and down but which would not allow gas to escape, had a weight on top of it. The piston and weight were supported by the pressure of the gas inside the cylinder.

Bernoulli proposed that a gas was composed of individual objects, which are now called molecules, that move very rapidly, colliding with the surface of the piston. When they hit the piston, the molecules are reflected back in the opposite direction. Each collision exerts a minute force on the piston. The macroscopic pressure exerted by the gas on the piston represents the sum of the force of all these minute collisions. Thus, the gas behaves as a fluid, expanding to occupy more volume as the pis-

ton is moved upward, increasing the available volume of the container. However, if the speed of the molecules remains constant, then as the volume of the container increases, the time required for an individual gas molecule to move across the container and strike the piston also increases. There are therefore fewer collisions in any given time interval, and the pressure exerted on the piston decreases proportionally. Bernoulli's model, published as a chapter in his *Hydrodynamica* (1738; *Hydrodynamics*, 1968), is called a "kinetic theory," because the macroscopic properties of the gas depend on molecular motion.

Bernoulli's kinetic theory was not widely accepted at the time. Most scientists believed that the molecules in a gas stayed more or less in place, repelling each other from a distance by the action of some unknown force. The British physicist Sir Isaac Newton had shown that the inverse relationship between pressure and volume of a gas could follow simply from an inverse-square law of repulsion between the gas molecules. Thus, in Bernoulli's era, the accepted model was that gas molecules were essentially fixed in position. This, too, may have been a function of the relative dearth of rigorous temperature-related experimentation, as the intimate relationship between temperature and kinetic energy was entirely unknown.

One weakness in Bernoulli's kinetic theory was that the speeds of the individual molecules in a gas could not be measured; thus, the pressure each molecule exerted on a piston could not be calculated. Bernoulli understood that it was not necessary to determine the speed of each molecule. The macroscopic pressure could be determined simply by knowing the average speed of the molecules, the mass of the molecules, and the rate of collision. Bernoulli, however, was not able to determine the relationship of the speed of a gas molecule to its temperature, which, like pressure and volume, was a measurable macroscopic property.

SIGNIFICANCE

It was not until the 1850's that the link posited by Bernoulli between the properties of the individual molecules making up a gas and the macroscopic behavior of the gas gained widespread acceptance in the scientific community. In 1859, the Scottish physicist James Clerk Maxwell attacked the problem. Maxwell adopted Bernoulli's model of gas molecules as perfectly "elastic particles" (that is, particles that obey Sir Isaac Newton's laws of motion but that lose no energy when they collide with each other or with other objects). Maxwell quickly recognized that even a small container of gas held far too many molecules to permit him to analyze this system completely using Newton's laws. However, Maxwell also realized that he simply needed to understand in principle how the microscopic picture of molecules in motion was connected with gases' macroscopic properties, which represented averages over extremely large numbers of molecules. Using a statistical approach, Maxwell was able to find the "velocity distribution function," that is, a function to determine the number of gas molecules that have a given velocity for gases at a fixed temperature.

Once Bernoulli's kinetic theory of gases gained widespread acceptance, it had a major impact on how theoretical physicists attempted to understand the large-scale

physical properties of objects. Bernoulli's work introduced several new ideas to the world of physics. In developing the first kinetic theory of gases, he proposed that the macroscopic properties of objects are due to and can be explained by the motion and behavior of the particles that make up those objects.

Thus, Bernoulli showed that by considering the behavior of the atomic and molecular constituents of matter, the large-scale physical properties of matter can be understood. This concept was important in many areas of physics: for example, the subsequent understanding of conduction of electricity, heat, and sound through matter. Bernoulli, moreover, expressed the results of his theory in terms of statistics. Statistics would arise as a science in its own right in the nineteenth century, and the use of statistical formulations in the physical sciences would become more acceptable thereafter. Statistical physics would become particularly important with the development in the twentieth century of quantum mechanics, a field of physics in which all of the properties of the particles that make up an object are expressed in probabilistic terms.

Bernoulli's work also paved the way for the modern understanding of the behavior of gases, developed by Johannes Diderik van der Waals. Van der Waals related pressure, volume, and temperature in an equation that extended the results obtained by Bernoulli to include the finite size of gas molecules and the small attractive force between the molecules, now called the van der Waals force. Van der Waals was awarded the Nobel Prize in Physics in 1910 for this work.

—George J. Flynn

FURTHER READING

Asimov, Isaac. *The History of Physics*. New York: Walker, 1966. Designed for nonspecialists; Asimov includes an excellent section, "The Kinetic Theory of Gases," which describes Bernoulli's contribution and puts that contribution in the historical context of both prior and subsequent work on the behavior of gases.

Brush, Stephen G., and Nancy S. Hall. *Kinetic Theory of Gases: An Anthology of Classic Papers with Historical Commentary*. London: Imperial College Press, 2003. This 661-page anthology contains more than two dozen papers on the kinetic theory of gases. It includes Bernoulli's "On the Properties and Motions of Elastic Fluids," excerpted from *Hydrodynamics*, as well as Boyle's concept of a "spring of the air," Newton's repulsion theory, and Maxwell's "Dynamical Theory of Gases." In addition to reprinting the classic papers, the book includes five essays providing historical commentary on the kinetic theory of gases and thermodynamics.

Ehrenfest, Paul, and Tatiana Ehrenfest. *The Conceptual Foundations of the Statistical Approach in Mechanics.* Mineola, N.Y.: Dover, 2002. Although somewhat technical, this Dover reprint of Ehrenfest's 1912 article from the *German Encyclopedia of Mathematical Sciences* describes the foundations of kinetic theory and statistical mechanics.

SEE ALSO: 1714: Fahrenheit Develops the Mercury Thermometer; 1735: Hadley Describes Atmospheric

Circulation; 1742: Celsius Proposes an International Fixed Temperature Scale; 1748: Nollet Discovers Osmosis; June 5, 1755: Black Identifies Carbon Dioxide; 1765-1769: Watt Develops a More Effective Steam Engine; Aug. 1, 1774: Priestley Discovers Oxygen; c. 1794-1799: Proust Establishes the Law of Definite Proportions.

RELATED ARTICLES in *Great Lives from History: The Eighteenth Century, 1701-1800*: Jean le Rond d'Alembert; Joseph Black; Henry Cavendish; Daniel Gabriel Fahrenheit; Colin Maclaurin; Joseph Priestley; James Watt.

May 15, 1738
FOUNDATION OF ST. PETERSBURG'S IMPERIAL BALLET SCHOOL

The St. Petersburg Imperial Ballet School's founding marked the beginning of the great tradition of Russian ballet, which was instrumental in the evolution of dance technique, choreography, and narrative ballets over the next several centuries.

LOCALE: St. Petersburg, Russia
CATEGORIES: Dance; theater; education

KEY FIGURES

Jean Baptiste Lande (d. 1748), French dancer and ballet master

Fusano (Antonio Rinaldi; fl. 1740's), Italian choreographer, dancer, and ballet master

Giulia Rinaldi (fl. 1740's), Italian ballet master and wife of Fusano

Franz Hilverding (1710-1768), Austrian choreographer

Gasparo Angiolini (1731-1803), Italian choreographer and composer

Charles le Picqué (fl. 1765-c. 1790), French dancer and ballet master

Giuseppe Canziani (fl. 1780's), Italian choreographer and ballet master

Ivan Ivanovich Valberkh (1766-1819), first native Russian ballet master and choreographer

Peter the Great (1672-1725), czar of Russia, r. 1682-1725

Anna (Anna Ivanovna; 1693-1740), empress of Russia, r. 1730-1740

Catherine the Great (1729-1796), empress of Russia, r. 1762-1796

SUMMARY OF EVENT

During his tour of Europe, Peter the Great encountered a way of life and a culture very different from those of his native Russia. He was so impressed with this lifestyle and with Western artistic activity that he decided to modernize his country. When he returned to Russia in 1698, he introduced many Western methods and traditions to his countryfolk and insisted upon changes in Russia's social, economic, and artistic life. As part of his program of Westernization, he invited many European artists and performers to Russia, including Jean Baptiste Lande, a French dancer and ballet master. Lande became the teacher of dance at the St. Petersburg Cadet Corps.

Although Lande was referred to as a ballet master, he did not teach ballet in the modern sense. The version of ballet that Peter the Great had enjoyed in Europe and that Lande taught was dance in combination with music, speech, and verse. It was a form of theatrical entertainment involving masks and costumes. The dancing included in this entertainment was often social dancing that happened to take place on stage: It was not a form of dance created solely for performance. The minuet, for example, was extremely popular in such "ballets."

After Peter the Great died in 1725, dance continued to be a part of Russian culture. In September of 1737, Lande presented a letter to Empress Anna, Peter's niece who came to the throne in 1730. In his letter, he asked her to establish a school of dance under his direction as ballet master. It is believed that in the ensuing months he presented his students from the Cadet Corps in a recital that made a very favorable impression on the empress. Thus, on May 4, 1738, Anna issued a decree acknowledging

Lande as an imperial ballet master assigned to teach various kinds of theatrical dance. However, it was not until May 15, 1738, that the decree approving Lande's salary was actually signed. Therefore, May 15, 1738, is the date usually given for the founding of the school of dance that would become the St. Petersburg Imperial Ballet School. The school's budget was to be drawn from the revenues of the royal salt tax office, which collected taxes from the salt mines.

Lande's school was intended to prepare young Russians to present theatrical dances at court. The school was housed in the Winter Palace and was composed of both girls and boys in their teens, chosen primarily from among the court servants and staff. The school taught only those subjects essential to developing dancers; no general education was provided. Thus, Lande's students, although accomplished dancers, were illiterate. The school's program comprised three years of training. At the end of the first year, students were to be ready to perform in the theater; at the end of the second year, they were to be able to execute the complete repertoire of dances; the third year was to be devoted to perfecting their talents. Upon graduation, they became members of the ballet company and were paid a salary. After ten years of service to the court, the dancers retired and received a pension.

For two years, the school thrived, but when Empress Anna died in 1740, classes were canceled for one year and Lande was sent abroad to recruit more foreign dancers. With the ascension of Empress Elizabeth Petrovna to the throne in 1741, entertainment returned to the palace. Lande was called back from Europe, and the school reopened, enjoying a period of renewed importance. The curriculum was expanded to include two different European approaches to dance. Lande taught the serious, or French, method, based on the French minuet. The comic dance, derived from the Italian commedia dell'arte, was taught by Fusano (Antonio Rinaldi) and by his wife, Giulia Rinaldi. This combination of serious and comedic dance techniques began to lay the foundation for what would become the Russian style of ballet, a melding of technical perfection and creativity. Lande died in 1748; Fusano served as ballet master until 1750, when he was replaced by a master known simply as Josette.

In the 1750's and 1760's, the school saw even greater development and perfection of both the ballet and its students. In 1758, Franz Hilverding, a Viennese choreographer, joined the dance community of St. Petersburg. He combined pantomime and dance in such a way that his choreography could be performed only by dancers who possessed the greatest level of skill in technique, movement, and mime. In 1765, one of his pupils, Gasparo Angiolini, was invited to St. Petersburg by Catherine the Great. In 1766, she established the Directorate of Imperial Theaters to administer ballet, opera, and drama, and Angiolini became ballet master at the Imperial School. In 1772, he created the first heroic Russian ballet, *Semira*. Little by little, a distinctively Russian ballet was being created as the native dancers continued to assimilate knowledge imported by foreign ballet masters.

The 1780's were a period of great advances in ballet training at the school. During this time, Giuseppe Canziani, a Venetian choreographer, and Charles le Picqué taught at St. Petersburg. Both men were disciples of Jean-Georges Noverre, a French dancer and ballet master who wrote *Lettres sur la danse et les ballets* (1760; letters on dance and ballet). This work advocated development of the *ballet d'action*, a method of choreography in which the dancers' movements were designed to reveal character and to help in creating the story line of the ballet. It was through the efforts of le Piqué that Noverre's work was translated into Russian.

Canziani took a special interest in his students, spending five to six hours a day with them. He taught the usual classes in dance movement and technique and conducted rehearsals for approaching performances. He also spent time discussing dance theory, especially that of Noverre, and talking about the most important dancers of the time. He produced outstanding dancers who brought creativity as well as technical excellence to their performance. One of his students, Ivan Ivanovich Valberkh, became the first Russian choreographer.

In 1792, although Canziani and the school's voice and acting masters strongly opposed the project, the Cazzai Plan was implemented at the Imperial Ballet School. The plan required the students to take classes in all the theatrical arts. Canziani was unable to implement this method effectively and resigned. Valberkh was appointed to his position. He was required to teach all of the students for two hours each day. Still adhering to Canziani's beliefs, he devoted additional hours to students who showed exceptional talent in dance. Despite the introduction of other dramatic arts into the curriculum, the major thrust of training at the school continued to be preparing performers to fill roles in ballets. In 1801, Charles Didelot, the father of Russian ballet, arrived in St. Petersburg. His work at the school would take Russian ballet into its Romantic period.

SIGNIFICANCE

The foundation of the St. Petersburg Imperial Ballet School ensured the continuing presence of ballet in Russia and the ongoing influence of Russia on ballet. It also provided a focal point for dancers arriving from the West. The school's connection to the Crown set a precedent for royal patronage and government funding of ballet that has been of the greatest importance to the continuing vitality and importance of the art. From these beginnings, ballet became the great Russian art form.

Throughout the nineteenth century, Russia, with its ballet theaters and schools, provided a place for ballet dancers and choreographers such as Marius Petipa to experiment and innovate. By welcoming dancers from various countries, the Russian schools brought together different styles of dance and melded them into the classical tradition. In the twentieth century, Russian dancers, choreographers, and troupes—including Vaslav Nijinsky, Georges Balanchine, and Sergei Diaghilev's Ballets Russes—brought Russian ballet to the West. This trend continued in the 1950's, when both the Bolshoi and the Kirov (St. Petersburg Ballet) companies began touring in Europe and the United States. Russian ballet became an integral part of dance in the West when Russian dancers such as Rudolf Nureyev, Natalia Markova, and Mikhail Baryshnikov opted not to return to Russia but to pursue their craft instead with American and European companies.

—*Shawncey Webb*

FURTHER READING

Cracraft, James. *The Revolution of Peter the Great.* Cambridge, Mass.: Harvard University Press, 2003. Background information on Russia at the time the Imperial Ballet School was founded.

Curtis, Mina Kirstein. *A Forgotten Empress: Anna Ivanovna and Her Era, 1730-1740.* New York: Ungar, 1974. Discusses culture at the time of the school's founding.

Lee, Carol. *Ballet in Western Culture: A History of Its Origins and Evolution.* New York: Routledge, 2002. Discusses the early origins of dance and the development of ballet in Italy, France, and Russia in the seventeenth, eighteenth, and nineteenth centuries.

Madariaga, Isabella. *Russia in the Age of Catherine the Great.* Phoenix Press, 2002. Presents the cultural atmosphere in which ballet continued to develop during the century.

Surits, Elisabeth, ed. *The Great History of the Russian Ballet: Its Art and Choreography.* Richford, Vt.: Parkstone Press, 1998. Detailed, in-depth treatment of ballet technique and performance in accordance with Russian standards.

SEE ALSO: Mar. 28, 1776: Founding of Bolshoi Theatre Company.

RELATED ARTICLES in *Great Lives from History: The Eighteenth Century, 1701-1800*: Catherine the Great; Jean Dauberval; Elizabeth Petrovna; Peter the Great.

1730's

November 18, 1738
TREATY OF VIENNA

The Treaty of Vienna was agreed to in the wake of the War of the Polish Succession. It transferred the Kingdom of the Two Sicilies from Austria to Spain and awarded the duchy of Lorraine and the county of Bar to Stanisław I Leszczyński, the deposed king of Poland.

LOCALE: Vienna, Austria
CATEGORIES: Diplomacy and international relations; expansion and land acquisition

KEY FIGURES

Stanisław I (1677-1766), king of Poland, r. 1704-1709, 1733-1736, and duke of Lorraine, r. 1738-1766

Augustus III (1696-1763), elector of Saxony and king of Poland, r. 1736-1763

Louis XV (1710-1774), king of France, r. 1715-1774

Philip V (1683-1746), king of Spain, r. 1700-January, 1724, August 31, 1724-1746

Isabella Farnese (1692-1766), queen of Spain, r. 1714-1746, and wife of king Philip V

Don Carlos de Bourbon (1716-1788), son of Philip and Isabella and king of the Two Sicilies, r. 1734-1759; later king Charles III of Spain, r. 1759-1788

Charles VI (1685-1740), Holy Roman Emperor, r. 1711-1740

Francis Stephen (1708-1765), duke of Lorraine, r. 1729-1735, and later grand duke of Tuscany, r. 1737-1765, and Holy Roman Emperor as Francis I, r. 1745-1765

Maria Theresa (1717-1780), daughter of Charles VI,

wife of Francis Stephen, and later archduchess of Austria, r. 1740-1780

André-Hercule de Fleury (1653-1743), prime minister of France, 1726-1743

SUMMARY OF EVENT

After battling for more than two years in the War of the Polish Succession, the European powers involved agreed to a cease-fire known as the Preliminary Treaty of Vienna (October 3, 1735). The War of the Polish Succession had erupted in 1733 over whether Stanisław I—supported by France, the Kingdom of Sardinia, the duchy of Savoy, and Spain—or Saxon elector Augustus III—a protégé of Russia, Prussia, and Austria—would accede to the throne of Poland. Because these great European powers were directly involved, the conflict rapidly spilled over into other festering disputes in various parts of Europe and had, by the time the Preliminary Treaty of Vienna was agreed to, developed such a degree of complexity that negotiations dragged on for three more years before the definitive Treaty of Vienna was signed on November 18, 1738.

Though the war had generally gone well for France and its main ally, Spain (apart from Stanisław I's having virtually been expelled from Poland), French prime minister André-Hercule de Fleury was somewhat anxious over the possibility that Britain and the Netherlands might be drawn in on the opposing side if the conflict persisted much longer. He had therefore thought it advantageous to negotiate while his government and its allies were still in a position of relative strength.

The question of the Polish succession itself was settled with the understanding that even though he enjoyed most of the popular support in Poland, Stanisław would renounce his claims to the throne in favor of Augustus III. However, Stanisław would be compensated with the duchy of Lorraine, the county of Bar, and the title of king for the duration of his life. The title to Lorraine and Bar was then to pass to his daughter, Maria Leszczyńska, who was the wife of King Louis XV of France—in effect, Lorraine and Bar were to come under French control. In return for what would be a considerable aggrandizement of French territory, Louis XV agreed to sign and support the Pragmatic Sanction, recognizing the succession of a woman to the throne of the Holy Roman Empire.

Habsburg emperor Charles VI of Austria had no male heir, and his eldest daughter Maria Theresa was legally prevented from succeeding under Salic law, which excluded females and reserved royal inheritance to the male line. Charles VI therefore sought to nullify the Salic law through an international agreement known as the Pragmatic Sanction. By agreeing to the sanction, the monarchs of Europe vowed to respect Maria Theresa's territorial inheritance, Salic law notwithstanding. Because France was the major continental superpower, France's support of the Pragmatic Sanction was deemed to be indispensable, and, given the long-standing enmity between the Habsburgs and the Bourbons, Louis XV's assent was a considerable breakthrough.

The hereditary duke of Lorraine, Francis III, Maria Theresa's husband, was to be compensated with the Grand Duchy of Tuscany, where the last of the Medici Dynasty of grand dukes, Gian Gastone, would die without an heir in 1737. A branch of the Habsburg Dynasty was to rule in Tuscany until 1859. In a minor border adjustment, Sardinia and Savoy received territories around Tortone and Novara, in western Lombardy, from Austria. This was a bitter disappointment for King Charles Emmanuel III of Sardinia (also duke of Savoy), who had successfully overrun and seized the duchy of Milan (Lombardy) from Austria but now had to hand back all but a sliver of land.

As an added complexity, Spain's Philip V and his influential queen, Isabella Farnese, wished to secure a kingdom for their son Don Carlos de Bourbon. Don Carlos did not seem likely to succeed to the Spanish throne, because the heir apparent was his elder half brother, Ferdinand. During the War of the Polish Succession, Don Carlos's forces had occupied the take the Two Sicilies from Austria. It was eventually agreed that Don Carlos could become ruler of the Kingdom of the Two Sicilies on the condition that it would never be united with the crown of Spain and that the same individual could not reign simultaneously over both. In addition, Don Carlos had to surrender the duchies of Parma and Piacenza, which he had inherited from his mother, to Austria. When Don Carlos eventually ascended the Spanish throne as Charles III in 1759, his third son, Ferdinand, succeeded to the throne of the Two Sicilies. The Bourbons would reign there until 1860.

SIGNIFICANCE

For Poland, the effects of the Treaty of Vienna were cataclysmic: Stanisław I was the last Polish king with a substantial following among his own people. Thereafter, the Polish crown was controlled by Russia, Prussia, and Austria, and the Polish monarchs from Augustus III governed mainly by the whim of these foreign powers, especially Russia. The treaty was thus a major step in the process leading to the three partitions of Poland and the annihilation of the Polish state by Russia, Austria, and Prussia in 1795.

France would expand and consolidate its eastern frontiers when Lorraine and Bar devolved to Louis XV through his wife Maria upon Stanisław's death in 1766. The former Polish king was very popular, and his reign, centering around his glittering court at Lunéville (which was dubbed "Little Versailles"), is considered a period of prosperity and cultural achievement in Lorraine. Charles Emmanuel III was outraged at what he perceived as Fleury's undervaluation of his contribution as an ally by conceding him a paltry strip of western Lombardy. His outrage was a factor in his decision to shift his support from France to Austria during the War of the Austrian Succession. France's adherence to the Pragmatic Sanction is considered a foundation stone of what was later termed the "Diplomatic Revolution" with Austria, whereby the former arch-enemies were to forge an alliance of mutual interests that would endure until the French Revolution.

—*Raymond Pierre Hylton*

FURTHER READING

Bernier, Olivier. *Louis the Beloved: The Life of Louis XV.* Garden City, N.Y.: Doubleday, 1984. Louis as portrayed the largely passive beneficiary of Fleury's efforts during the Vienna negotiations.

Hayes, Carlton J. H. *Modern Europe to 1870.* New York: Macmillan, 1967. Solid, succinct general history that nonetheless very effectively places the provisions of the 1738 Treaty of Vienna within the broader context.

Imbruglia, Girolamo, ed. *Naples in the Eighteenth Century: The Birth and Death of a Nation-State.* Cambridge, England: Cambridge University Press, 2000. Deals in part with the transition from Habsburg to Bourbon rule brought about by the Treaty of Vienna.

Kamen, Henry. *Philip V of Spain: The Man Who Reigned Twice.* New Haven, Conn.: Yale University Press, 2001. Concise account of the interaction between the comparatively passive Philip and his bellicose queen. Brings to light their burning resentment against France for allowing the loss of Parma to Austria.

Lynch, John. *Bourbon Spain, 1700-1808.* New York: Basil Blackwell, 1989. Good general period analysis that disappoints in that there are no details regarding the effects of the Treaty of Vienna.

Reddaway, W. F., et al. *The Cambridge History of Poland, 1697-1935.* New York: Octagon Books, 1978. Classic study (in the chapters written by William Konopcynski) presenting the Vienna agreement as a watershed event on the road to Poland's destruction in the late eighteenth century.

Wilson, Arthur McCandless. *French Foreign Policy During the Administration of Cardinal Fleury, 1726-1743: A Study in Diplomacy and Commercial Development.* Westport, Conn.: Greenwood Press, 1972. A thorough analysis of the motivations and maneuverings of the most one of the most skilled diplomatic practitioners of the era.

SEE ALSO: Oct. 10, 1733-Oct. 3, 1735: War of the Polish Succession; Feb. 24, 1766: Lorraine Becomes Part of France; Aug. 5, 1772-Oct. 24, 1795: Partitioning of Poland.

RELATED ARTICLES in *Great Lives from History: The Eighteenth Century, 1701-1800*: Charles III; Charles VI; André-Hercule de Fleury; Louis XV; Maria Theresa; Philip V.

1730's

1739-1740
HUME PUBLISHES *A TREATISE OF HUMAN NATURE*

Although not widely read or well regarded during his lifetime, Hume's first book, A Treatise of Human Nature, *has become a central work in the four-hundred-year tradition of British empiricism.*

LOCALE: Scotland; England; France
CATEGORIES: Philosophy; cultural and intellectual history

KEY FIGURES

David Hume (1711-1776), Scottish empiricist philosopher, historian, and skeptic
Francis Hutcheson (1694-1746), Scottish utilitarian philosopher and moralist
John Locke (1632-1704), English empiricist philosopher and physician
George Berkeley (1685-1753), bishop of Cloyne, British-Irish empiricist philosopher
Immanuel Kant (1724-1804), German founder of critical philosophy
Thomas Reid (1710-1796), Scottish founder of common-sense philosophy

SUMMARY OF EVENT

Before David Hume's work in philosophy, John Locke's *An Essay Concerning Human Understanding* (1690) and George Berkeley's *A Treatise Concerning the Principles of Human Knowledge* (1710) constituted the core of British empiricism. Empiricism, in general, is the argument that knowledge comes from or through sense experience, and not, as rationalism argues, solely from preexisting ideas or concepts in the mind. Hume's empiricism brought the two arguments together: Materials for thinking—perceptions—come from reflection and sensation, that is, from the intellect and sense experience.

Around 1726, at about the age of fifteen, Hume left the University of Edinburgh to teach himself law, but he soon immersed himself in philosophy and abandoned prospects of becoming a lawyer. For the next five years, Hume read philosophy on his own and became convinced that he had discovered the truth and that Locke and Berkeley had fallen short.

From 1732 to 1737, Hume wrote *A Treatise of Human Nature: Being an Attempt to Introduce the Experimental Method of Reasoning into Moral Subjects*, mostly while leading a happy-go-lucky life in Scotland and France, when he was in his early twenties. Building upon Locke, and challenging the tradition of continental rationalism,

Hume laid out in the treatise all the philosophical concepts for which he is well known. In epistemology and metaphysics he presented the contrast between impressions and ideas, the association of ideas, the rejection of traditional causality and necessary connection, the observation of constant conjunction, the rejection of persistent personal identity, and the advantages of healthy skepticism, customary belief, and habitual action. In ethics he argued for natural feeling, moral sentiment, approbation, sympathy, benevolence, utility, the rejection of natural law and natural right, and the recommendations for social justice based on self-interest tempered with the virtue of moral obligation.

The treatise first appeared anonymously in London as a cheap three-volume octavo edition in a press run of one thousand copies. It was published anonymously because doing so was common for young, unknown scholars of the time, and not because Hume had anything to hide. The first two volumes, *Of the Understanding* and *Of the Passions*, were published in January, 1739, by John Noon, and the third volume, *Of Morals*, was published in October, 1740, by Thomas Longman. The work did not sell well. In Hume's own words, it "fell dead-born from the press." Discouraged, Hume turned briefly from philosophy and moved to working in political theory, moralism, and history. It was his six-volume *History of England* (1754-1762) that made him famous during his time.

His next major philosophical work, *Philosophical Essays Concerning Human Understanding*, which appeared in 1748, went into a second edition in 1750 and was much more successful than the treatise. This was the first appearance of his masterpiece, *Enquiry Concerning Human Understanding*, which is typically known as the first *Enquiry* to distinguish it from *Enquiry Concerning the Principles of Morals* (1751; the second *Enquiry*).

The few who read *A Treatise of Human Nature* in its earliest years did not like it. The reviews were uniformly negative. Hume sent Francis Hutcheson prepublication drafts of the sections on ethics and received only a scolding in return. Hutcheson considered Hume a hedonist and a baneful influence on morality. Thomas Reid, Hutcheson's student at the University of Glasgow, did not like Hume's work either. Reid's anti-Lockeanism made him a natural opponent of Hume. The first book about Hume's philosophy, Reid's 1764 *Inquiry into the Human Mind*, was a savage attack. Reid's anti-Lockeanism showed through when he defended the everyday conceptions of what he called "the vulgar," which conflicted greatly with Lockean empiricism. For example, when Reid saw a house, he saw a house; but when Locke saw a house, he saw his idea of the house, rather than the house itself. Mainstream British empiricism, derived mostly from Locke, was too abstract and fanciful for Reid, whose commonsense epistemology would later develop into naïve realism.

Hume himself would repudiate the treatise. He considered it juvenilia, remained disappointed that it sold so few copies, and, in the 1740's, came to believe that he would have to write more carefully if he wished to gain acceptance for his philosophy. Thus, still believing entirely in the content of the treatise, he rewrote it as the *Enquiries* and as a minor work, *Dissertation on the Passions* (1757), that is, in a form calculated to be more palatable to the learned audience that he aspired to impress. This second effort succeeded.

The first *Enquiry* recasts book 1 of the treatise. The second *Enquiry* and *Dissertation on the Passions* reinvent books 2 and 3. Thematically, there is little difference between the *Enquiries* and the *Treatise of Human Nature*. The respective sections correlate well. Students can check the analogous parts against each other to aid their learning of Hume. The treatise, though, is obviously the work of an ardent young man while the *Enquiries* are more soberly constructed, more tightly argued, and subtler in their wit. Also, the treatise is much longer than both *Enquiries* together. Because the treatise takes more chances, it is more entertaining, but whether it is more intellectually satisfying than the *Enquiries* remains controversial.

SIGNIFICANCE

Immanuel Kant wrote in *Prolegomena to Any Future Metaphysics* (1783) that reflecting on David Hume's theory of causation around 1772 woke him from his "dogmatic slumber" and started him on the path toward developing the revolutionary critical philosophy that he brought to the world in 1781 with his *Critique of Pure Reason*. Kant had read the first

Enquiry, not the *Treatise of Human Nature*, which had been included in Hume's *Vermischte Schriften*, a four-volume German translation of some of his political and philosophical works prepared in the 1750's. It included in 1755 a translation of the first *Enquiry* as *Philosophische Versuche über die menschliche Erkenntniss*, but there was no translation of the *Treatise of Human Nature*.

The treatise was conspicuously absent from the first posthumous collected edition of Hume's philosophical works, published in 1777 as *Essays and Treatises on Several Subjects*. Just before he died, he wrote a famous "advertisement" for that edition, which reads, in part,

> Most of the principles, and reasonings, contained in this volume, were published in a work in three volumes, called *A Treatise of Human Nature*: A work which the Author had projected before he left College, and which he wrote and published not long after. . . . Henceforth, the Author desires, that the following Pieces may alone be regarded as containing his philosophical sentiments and principles.

1730's

HUME ON HUMAN KNOWLEDGE

Scottish philosopher David Hume argued that both sense experience and reflection were necessary for knowledge. In this excerpt from A Treatise of Human Nature, *he discusses his belief that one can know how something functions or acts in a given situation only when that "something" is placed in that situation and then observed.*

For to me it seems evident that the essence of the mind being equally unknown to us with that of external bodies, it must be equally impossible to form any notion of its powers and qualities otherwise than from careful and exact experiments, and the observation of those particular effects which result from its different circumstances and situations. And though we must endeavour to render all our principles as universal as possible, by tracing up our experiments to the utmost, and explaining all effects from the simplest and fewest causes, it is still certain we cannot go beyond experience; and any hypothesis that pretends to discover the ultimate original qualities of human nature ought at first to be rejected as presumptuous and chimerical. . . .

When I am at a loss to know the effects of one body upon another in any situation, I need only put them in that situation, and observe what results from it.

We must, therefore, glean up our experiments in this science from a cautious observation of human life, and take them as they appear in the common course of the world, by men's behaviour in company, in affairs, and in their pleasures. Where experiments of this kind are judiciously collected and compared, we may hope to establish on them a science which will not be inferior in certainty, and will be much superior in utility, to any other of human comprehension.

Source: David Hume, *A Treatise of Human Nature* (1739-1740). Excerpted in *The Enlightenment: The Culture of the Eighteenth Century*, edited by Isidor Schneider (New York: George Braziller, 1965), pp. 70, 71.

The second edition of the treatise appeared in 1817 and the third in 1874-1875. Philosophers did not begin to take the treatise seriously as a viable alternative to the *Enquiries* until the twentieth century. Norman Kemp Smith in the 1930's and 1940's was the first interpreter to examine it in depth. Thereafter, it has been a respected part of the Western philosophical canon. Despite its early neglect, the treatise has become Hume's most influential work, and many Hume scholars consider it his most significant. Their failure to accept the philosopher's posthumous wish at its word remains largely unexamined and ignored.

—Eric v.d. Luft

FURTHER READING

Baier, Annette C. *A Progress of Sentiments: Reflections of Hume's "Treatise."* Cambridge, Mass.: Harvard University Press, 1994. A key work by one of the world's foremost Hume scholars.

Capaldi, Nicholas. *David Hume: The Newtonian Philosopher.* Boston: Twayne, 1975. An accessible and authoritative biography, part of Twayne's World Leaders series.

Flew, Antony. *Hume's Philosophy of Belief.* London: Routledge and Kegan Paul, 1961. A classic examination of Hume's philosophy of religion that accepts Hume's preference for the *Enquiries* over the *Treatise of Human Nature.*

Hume, David. *An Enquiry Concerning Human Understanding: A Critical Edition.* Edited by Tom L. Beauchamp. Oxford, England: Clarendon Press, 2000. The standard edition sanctioned by the Hume Society.

_____. *An Enquiry Concerning the Principles of Morals: A Critical Edition*, edited by Tom L. Beauchamp. Oxford: Clarendon, 1998. The standard edition sanctioned by the Hume Society.

_____. *A Treatise of Human Nature.* Edited by David Fate Norton and Mary J. Norton. New York: Oxford University Press, 2000. The standard edition sanctioned by the Hume Society.

Johnson, Oliver A. *The Mind of David Hume: A Companion to Book I of "A Treatise of Human Nature."* Urbana: University of Illinois Press, 1995. A detailed analytic commentary on the treatise.

Livingston, Donald W., and James T. King. *Hume: A Re-Evaluation.* New York: Fordham University Press, 1976. Nineteen articles cover the full extent of Hume's thought, and Livingston's introduction sets the historical context.

Mossner, Ernest C. *The Life of David Hume.* 2d ed. Oxford, England: Clarendon Press, 1980. Contains the standard account of the publication history of Hume's treatise.

Norton, David Fate. *David Hume: Common-Sense Moralist, Sceptical Metaphysician.* Princeton, N.J.: Princeton University Press, 1982. A challenge to previous interpretations.

_____, ed. *The Cambridge Companion to Hume.* New York: Cambridge University Press, 1993. A broad, reliable, and accessible introduction to Hume's entire corpus.

SEE ALSO: Oct., 1725: Vico Publishes *The New Science*; 1726-1729: Voltaire Advances Enlightenment Thought in Europe; 1748: Montesquieu Publishes *The Spirit of the Laws*; 1751-1772: Diderot Publishes the *Encyclopedia*; 1754: Condillac Defends Sensationalist Theory; July 27, 1758: Helvétius Publishes *De l'esprit*; Apr., 1762: Rousseau Publishes *The Social Contract*; July, 1764: Voltaire Publishes *A Philosophical Dictionary for the Pocket*; 1770: Publication of Holbach's *The System of Nature*; 1781: Kant Publishes *Critique of Pure Reason*; 1784-1791: Herder Publishes His Philosophy of History.

RELATED ARTICLES in *Great Lives from History: The Eighteenth Century, 1701-1800*: Mary Astell; Jeremy Bentham; George Berkeley; James Boswell; Marquise du Châtelet; Étienne Bonnot de Condillac; Denis Diderot; First Baron Erskine; Adam Ferguson; Claude-Adrien Helvétius; Johann Gottfried Herder; David Hume; Immanuel Kant; William Paley; Jean-Jacques Rousseau; Adam Smith; Giambattista Vico.

1739-1741
WAR OF JENKINS'S EAR

Great Britain's launch of the War of Jenkins's Ear against Spain brought about the fall of Robert Walpole, the peaceable Whig prime minister, and committed the British government to the use of war as a tool for achieving its imperialistic goals.

LOCALE: England; the Caribbean
CATEGORIES: Wars, uprisings, and civil unrest; diplomacy and international relations

KEY FIGURES

Robert Jenkins (d. 1743), British merchant ship captain
Robert Walpole (1676-1745), prime minister of Great Britain, 1721-1742
Edward Vernon (1684-1757), commander of the British West Indian fleet
Charles Brown (1678/1679-1753), Vernon's second-in-command
Lord Anson (George Anson; 1697-1762), British admiral
Thomas Wentworth (fl 1739-1742), British general

SUMMARY OF EVENT

As the conquerors of Latin America, the Spanish claimed full sovereignty over their American colonies, allowing only Spanish merchants to trade with the colonists. In 1713, the British had forced Spain to make two exceptions: Great Britain's South Sea Company was allowed to send one merchant ship per year to Porto Bello, and, under an agreement called an *asiento de negros* ("Negroes' contract"), the British were authorized to ship five thousand slaves per year to the Spanish colonies in the Americas. Because Spain also claimed sovereignty over the seas adjacent to their colonies, they sent Spanish *guarda costas*, or coast guards, to enforce their laws. The *guarda costas* would stop British merchantmen, search them for contraband, brutally interrogate captain and crew, and often seize the ships and their cargoes.

Despite the best diplomatic efforts of Prime Minister Robert Walpole, who saw no advantage to making war, in 1738 Spain abandoned negotiations and suspended the *asiento*, prompting British merchant groups to bombard Parliament with demands for war with Spain. Britain's commercial interests were certain that with a fleet three times the size of Spain's, Great Britain would win an easy victory, leaving the way clear for British merchants to dominate trade in Latin America. Similarly motivated by self-interest were Walpole's political opponents, the

Tories. For the first time in seventeen years, they had a good chance to oust the prime minister, whom they loathed, from the office that he had effectively created. Visions of a Tory prime minister, enjoying the power and the perquisites that Walpole had monopolized since 1721, drove the opposition at least as much as any foreign policy concerns.

Thus it is clear that the mistreatment of Robert Jenkins at the hands of the Spanish was not the primary cause of the war that bears his name. In fact, the incident that supposedly motivated the war had taken place several years before it began. On April 9, 1731, the brig *Rebecca*, with Jenkins as master, was proceeding from Jamaica to London. While it was becalmed off Havana, Cuba, it was boarded by a Spanish *guarda costa* under the command of a Captain Fandino. After a search revealed no contraband, Fandino had Jenkins tortured and then, taking out his cutlass, cut off the captain's left ear. Afterward, everything of value was taken from the ship, including its navigational instruments, but Jenkins managed to get back to England, where he reported what had happened.

In September, 1731, the admiral of the West Indies included a description of the incident in a formal protest to the governor of Havana. In 1738, Jenkins is said to have appeared before a committee of the House of Commons, where he related his story and displayed his pickled ear to the committee. However, at least one scholar insists that Jenkins could not have been present in person, since he was at sea on the date in question. In any case, it is true that Jenkins's ear was mentioned in an important debate in the House of Commons, thus becoming a rallying point for those who favored war with Spain.

By the time war was declared in October, 1739, almost everyone except Walpole was enthusiastic. Even King George II and his son, the prince of Wales, who rarely agreed on anything, were certain of a great victory. Initially, all went well. In July, 1739, an able though irascible naval officer, Captain Edward Vernon, had been made vice admiral of the blue and dispatched to the West Indies. On October 23, Vernon sailed into Port Royal, Jamaica, where his five ships were joined by the *Hampton Court*, under the command of Commodore Charles Brown.

Wisely, Vice Admiral Vernon decided against a costly and uncertain land campaign against the Spanish; the best course of action, he knew, was to bombard their forts from the sea. On November 21, 1739, the *Hampton Court* led an attack against the fortified port treasure depot of Porto Bello (the present Portobelo), on the Isthmus of Panama. The Spanish surrendered the next morning. In March, 1740, the news reached England, and Vernon became a national hero. More medals were struck in his honor than for anyone else in English history, and the victory was celebrated in the popular song "Rule, Britannia," with its well-known lyric, "Britannia rules the waves."

On March 24, Vernon attempted an attack on Cartagena, on the northwest coast of present-day Colombia, but it soon became evident that the city was too well fortified to be taken except by a land assault. After capturing nearby Fort Chagre, Vernon had to wait for an expeditionary force to reach Jamaica. During the summer, troops were raised in the English colonies and in England

itself, and a great fleet was assembled. In September, Lord Anson left England with a squadron of six ships; his mission was to aid Vernon in the Isthmus of Panama and to harry Spanish shipping along the Pacific coast, perhaps even to capture the greatest prize of all, the silver-laden Spanish ship that every year made its way from Acapulco, Mexico, to Manila in the Philippines.

In January, 1741, the expeditionary force Vernon had been expecting finally arrived in Jamaica. Vernon now had thirty-three warships in his squadron, as well as a number of smaller vessels and some nine thousand troops under the command of Brigadier General Thomas Wentworth, who was inexperienced and proved to be indecisive. The two men were supposed to make their decisions jointly, but they soon began quarreling so bitterly that their mutual distrust made itself felt among the men. After making excuses for weeks, on April 9 Wentworth

British merchant-ship captain Robert Jenkins shows his severed ear to Prime Minister Robert Walpole. Jenkins's claim that his ear had been cut off by the Spanish was used by the English as a case for war. (Hulton Archive/Getty Images)

finally agreed to attack, but the assault failed, in part because of poor planning, in part because soldiers and seamen would not work together. With the rainy season upon them and large numbers of their men dying of disease, Wentworth and Vernon abandoned their campaign and returned to Jamaica. Part of the fleet returned to England immediately, and after an unsuccessful effort to capture Santiago, Cuba, Vernon followed.

Admiral Anson, too, had lost a great many men, as well as five of the six vessels under his command. However, after some raids on the coast of Chile, he set off westward in his flagship, and in 1743, he succeeded in capturing the prize he had sought and seizing the treasure it carried, which was valued at £500,000. After rounding the Cape of Good Hope, Anson evaded a French fleet and arrived safely in England on June 15, 1744. Although both Vernon and Wentworth were honored by their countrymen for their wartime leadership, it is Anson who is now best known of all those involved in the War of Jenkins's Ear.

SIGNIFICANCE

The War of Jenkins's Ear was a military and a financial failure. It is now remembered in England primarily because its sole victory inspired the composition of "Rule, Britannia" and because during the conflict Vice Admiral Vernon improved naval discipline immensely by ordering that sailors be served watered-down rum; thereafter, the drink was referred to as "grog," because Old Grog was Vernon's nickname. Vernon was also honored in the United States. While George Washington's half brother Lawrence was serving in the Caribbean with his fellow Virginians, he came to admire the vice admiral so much that after returning home, he gave a house he built the name of Mount Vernon.

Although it did not achieve its objective of opening Latin American trade to British merchants, the War of Jenkins's Ear did affect the policy decisions of the British government. With Walpole out of power, the British felt free to become involved in the War of the Austrian Succession. Moreover, after the War of Jenkins's Ear, not only national pride or territorial acquisition but also commercial interests would be considered reasonable justifications for the British to go to war. It can also be argued that by demonstrating Great Britain's military weakness,

the War of Jenkins's Ear showed the American colonists that it was possible to defeat the mother country and thus encouraged their move toward independence.

—*Rosemary M. Canfield Reisman*

FURTHER READING

Anderson, M. S. *The War of the Austrian Succession, 1740-1748.* London: Longman, 1995. Argues persuasively that the primary cause of the war was economic.

Berkeley, F. L., Jr. "The War of Jenkins' Ear." In *The Old Dominion: Essays for Thomas Perkins Abernethy*, edited by Darrett B. Rutman. Charlottesville: University Press of Virginia, 1964. Finds the war of particular interest to Americans as the only time the colonists sent troops into action abroad.

Black, Jeremy. *Walpole in Power*. Stroud, Gloucestershire: Sutton, 2001. The final chapters of this book explain how Walpole's attempts to avoid war were thwarted by his opponents.

Browning, Reed. *The War of the Austrian Succession*. New York: St. Martin's Press, 1993. Sees this period as a time when the great powers of Europe were constantly adapting their diplomatic and military strategies to fit ever-changing aims.

Williams, Glyn. *The Prize of All the Oceans: Commodore Anson's Daring Voyage and Triumphant Capture of the Spanish Treasure Galleon*. New York: Viking Penguin, 2000. A definitive study of Anson's venture. Maps, tables, and illustrations.

Woodfine, Philip. *Britannnia's Glories: The Walpole Ministry and the 1739 War with Spain*. Rochester, N.Y.: Royal Historical Society/Boydell Press, 1998. The first full-length study of the War of Jenkins's Ear. A meticulously researched, balanced account.

1730's

1739-1742
FIRST GREAT AWAKENING

The First Great Awakening, a spiritual revival in North America, gave birth to religious tolerance and inclusiveness in American society. It influenced the values that would shape the founding of the United States and the framing of the U.S. Constitution a few decades later.

LOCALE: American colonies (now in the United States)

CATEGORIES: Religion and theology; social issues and reform

KEY FIGURES

Jonathan Edwards (1703-1758), colonial American minister and theologian

George Whitefield (1714-1770), English preacher

William Tennent (1673-1745), colonial American religious leader

Gilbert Tennent (1703-1764), colonial American pastor and William's son

Samuel Buell (1716-1798), colonial American religious leader

Jonathan Dickinson (1688-1747), colonial American clergyman and educator

James Davenport (1716-1757), colonial American clergyman

Eleazar Wheelock (1711-1779), colonial American clergyman and educator

Devereux Jarratt (1733-1801), colonial American religious leader

Charles Chauncy (1705-1787), colonial American minister

Theodore J. Frelinghuysen (1691-1748), colonial American minister

Samuel Davies (1723-1761), colonial American religious leader

Shubal Stearns (1706-1771), colonial American preacher

Daniel Marshall (1706-1784), colonial American preacher

Solomon Stoddard (1643-1728/1729), colonial American religious leader

SUMMARY OF EVENT

Between 1739 and 1742, the American colonies experienced a general quickening of religious faith that became known as the Great Awakening. The young Anglican preacher George Whitefield, whose reputation as a great pulpit and open-air orator had preceded his visit, traveled through the colonies in 1739 and 1740. Everywhere, he attracted large and emotional crowds, eliciting countless conversions as well as considerable controversy. Critics condemned his enthusiasm, his censoriousness, and his extemporaneous and itinerant preaching; yet his extemporaneous preaching, his use in sermons of plain language, and his appeal to the emotions were to contribute to the emergence of the democratic and popular style of American Christianity. This manner of preaching also won for him numerous imitators, who spread the Great Awakening from New England to Georgia, among rich and poor, educated and illiterate, and in the backcountry as well as in seaboard towns and cities.

In the Middle Colonies, Gilbert Tennent was the leader of the revival among the Presbyterians. Led by Jonathan Dickinson, Presbyterians of New England background also joined in the revival. In New England, the most notorious evangelist was James Davenport, whose extravagances were even denounced by Tennent and other revivalists. Jonathan Edwards, Samuel Buell, and Eleazar Wheelock, less controversial than Davenport, were likewise instruments of the Awakening in New England. In the Southern colonies, the Great Awakening made its greatest headway on the frontier. Samuel Davies preached revivalism among the Presbyterians of Virginia and North Carolina; Shubal Stearns and Daniel Marshall drew converts to the Separate Baptist fold; and Devereux Jarratt inaugurated the Methodist phase of the Great Awakening.

The colonists were not unprepared for the Great Awakening. Prior to 1739, there had been indications of a religious quickening among several denominations. In the 1720's, the Dutch Reformed Church in New Jersey experienced a series of revivals led by Theodore J. Frelinghuysen, a native of Germany who had been influenced by the Pietistic movement within the Lutheran Church. In the mid-1730's, a "refreshing" occurred among the Presbyterians of New Jersey and Pennsylvania as a result of the preaching of a group of Scotch-Irish ministers led by Gilbert Tennent's father, William, and trained in William's Log College.

The revivals continued throughout the 1730's, coinciding with the "subscription controversy" within American Presbyterianism. New England was also the scene of religious excitement before 1739. The "harvest" of Solomon Stoddard, known as the "pope" of the Connect-

Anglican preacher George Whitefield helped inspire a religious revival in colonial America with his sermons, using plain language and an emotional style that would lead to a more democratic, popular, and decidedly American Christianity. (The Granger Collection, New York)

1730's

icut Valley, and the Northampton revival of 1734-1735, led by his grandson Jonathan Edwards, foreshadowed the later, more general, awakening. Thus, Whitefield's tour provided the catalyst, not the cause, of the Great Awakening, which represented the culmination of impulses that were already beginning to transform colonial Protestantism.

At first, the Great Awakening was celebrated as a supernatural work, the "pouring out of the grace of God upon the land." However, controversy over the origins and effects of the revival soon displaced the earlier consensus. Prorevivalists continued to defend the Great Awakening as the work of God, but opponents of the revival reacted negatively both to what they regarded as unlearned preaching and to the religious enthusiasm that it fomented. The assault by the revivalists on the orthodox clergy as "without spiritual taste and relish," an assault classically expressed in Gilbert Tennent's "The Danger of an Unconverted Ministry," could only have amplified the hostility.

The root of the disagreement between the pro- and antirevivalist parties reached to the source of religious

faith. The orthodox clergy, the most famous of whom was Charles Chauncy of Boston, tended toward a "rational" theology. It was from this group that the Unitarians later emerged. By contrast, the revivalists held that religion was a matter of the heart or the "affections," as Jonathan Edwards called them. Yet Edwards and his disciples, in what was known as the New England theology, held that both reason and the emotions were rightfully a part of religious experience. In keeping with their Puritan heritage, these Edwardseans also reaffirmed the Calvinist convictions about the depravity of human beings, the sovereignty of God, and the necessity of unmerited grace for salvation. For them, regeneration was not a matter of good conduct but the result of a "new birth" or a "change of heart" wrought by God.

In many cases, the controversy over the Great Awakening split denominations into opposing factions. The revival produced a temporary schism among the Presbyterians—between Old Sides, who opposed the Great Awakening, and New Sides, who approved it. Congregationalism was split between Old Lights and New Lights. Some prorevivalist New Lights became Separatists, withdrawing from the established Congregational churches and forming new churches of the regenerate; most of these Separate churches ultimately became Baptist, with the result that the majority of New England Baptists shifted from an Arminian to a Calvinist theology. No denomination entirely escaped the divisive effects of the Great Awakening. Divisiveness was not the decisive consequence of the Great Awakening, however.

SIGNIFICANCE

The Great Awakening contributed significantly to the unity of the diverse American colonies and ultimately to the emergence of an American national consciousness. It communicated to the colonists a common experience and a transcending conviction about America's special destiny. As for separations among the churches, these were far outweighed by a new denominational understanding of the church that the revivalists fostered. Of great significance for American religion, diverse Christian churches were coming to be regarded as but different expressions of one reality. As Gilbert Tennent remarked, all Christian societies professing the foundational principles are but diverse denominations of the "one Church of Christ."

The establishment of colleges was another institutional consequence of the revivalist impulse. As early as 1727, William Tennent established his Log College for the education of a clergy imbued with a vital inward faith. Other colleges dedicated to the education of ministerial recruits and a Christian laity were to follow. The Presbyterian Synod of New York secured a charter for the College of New Jersey (now Princeton); the Hanover Presbytery established Hampden-Sidney College; the Baptists founded the College of Rhode Island (Brown); and the Dutch Reformed opened Queens College (Rutgers). Charitable schools also were established to provide educational opportunities for the children of indentured servants, and Dartmouth College originated as a charitable school for the education of Native Americans.

Charitable schools were but one expression of the spirit of inclusiveness encouraged by the Awakening. Revivalism gave rise also to missionaries such as David Brainerd, who worked among the Delaware of eastern New Jersey, and Samuel Davies, who took his ministry to African American slaves. The first generation of revivalists paid slight attention to the institution of slavery, yet the followers of Jonathan Edwards, armed with the revivalists' conviction about the essential dignity of all created beings, spoke out against the practice of slavery. Some itinerants of the Baptist and Methodist Churches worked among black slaves, welcomed them with a surprising degree of equality into their churches, and utilized African Americans with special talents as exhorters and preachers in evangelistic endeavors. This revivalist impulse toward inclusiveness and tolerance held promise for a future pluralism that was to become a distinctive feature of religion in the United States.

—Anne C. Loveland, updated by Thomas E. Helm

FURTHER READING

Brockway, Robert W. *A Wonderful Work of God: Puritanism and the Great Awakening.* Bethlehem, Pa.: Lehigh University Press, 2003. A history of the Great Awakening, examining the movement's origins, its personalities (particularly James Davenport), and the controversies that split the movement, ministers, and congregations.

Gaustad, Edwin S. *The Great Awakening in New England.* New York: Harper & Row, 1957. A compact study of the New England awakening. Gives descriptions of the events, personages, and long-range effects of the revival.

Goen, Clarence C. *Revivalism and Separatism in New England, 1740-1800: Strict Congregationalists and Separate Baptists in the Great Awakening.* Hamden, Conn.: Archon Books, 1969. A study of the separatist movement in New England during the Great Awakening, with attention to the Congregationalists and Baptists.

Hudson, Winthrop S. "The American Context as an Area for Research in Black Church Studies." *Church History* 52, no. 2 (1983): 157-171. An account of the emerging African American church experience through the efforts of itinerant Protestant preachers during the Great Awakening.

Lambert, Frank. *Inventing the Great Awakening.* Princeton, N.J.: Princeton University Press, 1999. Lambert disagrees with some historians who claim the Great Awakening was an invention of nineteenth or twentieth century historians. He argues the awakening was created by eighteenth century evangelical preachers and examines preachers' texts to show how they constructed their own understanding of the work in which they were involved and how they developed and expanded their religious movement.

Mansfield, Stephen. *Forgotten Founding Father: The Heroic Legacy of George Whitefield.* Nashville, Tenn.: Highland Books/Cumberland House, 2001. A biography of Whitefield, describing his life, religious activities, and impact on colonial America. Examines his religion and religous activities, his friendship with Benjamin Franklin, and his support for the American Revolution.

Marsden, George M. *Jonathan Edwards: A Life.* New Haven, Conn.: Yale University Press, 2003. Comprehensive biography, using newly available sources from Yale University to examine Edwards's life within the context of the religious and cultural battles in colonial New England. Edwards is depicted as a complex thinker who struggled to reconcile his Puritan background with the secular world of the Enlightenment.

Maxson, Charles H. *The Great Awakening in the Middle Colonies.* Chicago: University of Chicago Press, 1920. A study locating the Awakening among the Dutch Reformed and Presbyterian Churches in the Middle Colonies in the context of an international evangelical revival.

Stout, Harry S. *The Divine Dramatist: George Whitefield and the Rise of Modern Evangelicalism.* Grand Rapids, Mich.: Wm. B. Eerdmans, 1991. Posits Whitefield as a hinge figure in American religious history, who transformed revivals from local to regional and national experiences.

Trinterud, Leonard J. *The Forming of an American Tradition: A Re-examination of Colonial Presbyterianism.* Philadelphia: Westminster Press, 1949. Examines the process by which an American understanding of Presbyterianism emerged out of the theological controversy and spiritual quickening of the Great Awakening.

SEE ALSO: July 17, 1769-1824: Rise of the California Missions; 1773-1788: African American Baptist Church Is Founded; Jan. 16, 1786: Virginia Statute of Religious Liberty; July 28-Oct. 16, 1789: Episcopal Church Is Established; 1790's-1830's: Second Great Awakening.

RELATED ARTICLES in *Great Lives from History: The Eighteenth Century, 1701-1800*: Francis Asbury; Jonathan Edwards; Cotton Mather; Increase Mather; Charles Wesley; John Wesley; George Whitefield.

September 9, 1739
STONO REBELLION

African slaves in South Carolina staged a rebellion that was quickly and brutally suppressed. The revolt demonstrated to white settlers, who were in the minority, the precariousness of their situation in the colonies, and it led them to pass laws designed both to increase their control over their slaves and to decrease discontent among slaves that might lead to future uprisings.

LOCALE: St. Paul's Parish, near the Stono River, South Carolina (now in the United States)

CATEGORIES: Wars, uprisings, and civil unrest; social issues and reform

KEY FIGURES

Jemmy (fl. 1739), enslaved African rebel leader

William Bull (1683-1755), lieutenant governor of South Carolina

SUMMARY OF EVENT

Conditions in South Carolina in the 1730's led to white fear of slave uprisings. The high numbers of Africans imported through Charles Town port led to legislation against Africans congregating, holding meetings, or appearing in public after nightfall. Charles Town had a watch committee to guard the port city, and the rest of the colony had a white patrol system to police Africans in militia districts. South Carolina used public punishment as a deterrent.

Contrary to their intent, these white controls increasingly led to greater resistance from newly imported Africans. Cases of verbal insolence joined arson as a recurring feature of colonial life. Whites blamed illnesses and deaths on African knowledge of plants and their poisonous powers. In the 1730's, massive importations from the Congo-Angola region meant that more than half of the colony's slaves had been there fewer than ten years. Slave unrest was blamed on outside agitators—Native Americans with assistance from both the Spanish and French. Rumors of a Spanish invasion increased after the Spanish king granted liberty to African fugitive slaves in 1733.

Tension thus was high in 1739. Then, a smallpox epidemic, coupled with the escape of slaves to Spanish Florida, led to massive loss of investments. A yellow fever epidemic hit during the summer months. In the fall, deaths decreased with the return of cool weather, but the

1730's

263

situation was ripe for insurrection. Since Sundays afforded slaves their best opportunity for meeting in communal activities, the legislature passed the Security Act in August, 1739, requiring all white men to carry firearms to churches beginning September 29 or pay a stiff fine. News of conflict between England and Spain reached Charles Town the weekend before the uprising began, explaining why the Stono Rebellion began immediately without betrayal, caught white masters in church unarmed, and had slaves marching toward Spanish St. Augustine.

The insurrection included elements typical of early rebellions in South Carolina: total surprise, brutal killings, extensive property damage, armed fighting, and extended consequences. On the morning of September 9, 1739, twenty slaves, mostly Angolans, gathered in St. Paul's Parish near Stono River, 20 miles from Charles Town. Led by a slave named Jemmy, the group broke into Hutchenson's store near the Stono Bridge to gather guns and ammunition. Storekeepers Robert Bathurst and Mr. Gibbs were beheaded. The slave band moved on to the Godfrey house, killing the family, gathering supplies, and burning the building. The slaves took the main road to Georgia, stopping at Wallace's Tavern but sparing the innkeeper, who was known to be a kind master. His white neighbor, however, lost his life, along with his wife and child.

The band continued, sacking and burning houses on Pons Pons Road and killing all the white occupants. Slave owner Thomas Rose was successfully hidden by his slaves as the band moved through. The group's numbers grew as reluctant slaves were forced to join. Increased numbers led to diminished discipline. The group took up a banner, beat on two drums, and shouted, "Liberty!" They pursued and killed any whites they encountered.

Lieutenant Governor William Bull and four other white men were traveling to Charles Town for legislative session when they encountered the rebel slaves. They escaped to warn others. By late Sunday afternoon, the band of nearly one hundred rebel slaves stopped in an open field, showing their confidence and hoping to be joined by other slaves by morning.

Nearby, white colonists had been alerted by Sunday afternoon and had organized an armed and mounted resistance of somewhere between twenty and one hundred men. Moving to the field, the white forces caught the slaves off guard, killing or wounding at least fourteen rebels. They surrounded other rebels, who were briefly questioned before being shot to death. They released the slaves who had been forced to participate. Almost one-third of the rebelling slaves escaped the fighting. Some returned to their plantations, hoping not to be missed. Upon their return, planters cut off their heads and placed them on posts to serve as a reminder for other slaves seeking freedom.

The white colony engaged in an intensive manhunt to recapture those participants who remained at large. Whites armed themselves, and guards were posted at ferry posts. By some accounts, twenty to forty rebels were captured, hanged, disemboweled, or beaten within the two following days. Another account, a month later, reported the rebels had been stopped from doing further mischief by having been "put to the most cruel Death." The Georgia general James Edward Oglethorpe called out rangers and American Indians, garrisoned soldiers at Palachicolas—a fort guarding the only point on the Savannah River where fugitives could cross—and issued a proclamation for whites to keep a watchful eye on any Africans.

Despite these acts of retribution and retaliation against both free blacks and slaves, white fears did not subside. Most whites thought persons of African descent were dangerous and possessed of a rebellious nature. By the fall of 1739, many planters near Stono had moved their wives and children in with other families for greater security. The assembly placed a special patrol along the Stono River. Outlying fugitives were still being brought in for execution by early 1740. Finally, two fugitive slaves seeking a large reward captured the last remaining leader, who had been at large for three years following the insurrection.

SIGNIFICANCE

The white minority responded to the Stono Rebellion in several ways. First, the colony tightened restrictions on all blacks, giving South Carolina the harshest penalties of any mainland colony. The colony also sought to improve conditions that provoked rebellion. Finally, the colony sought to lessen the influence of the Spanish settlement in St. Augustine as a constant source of incitement. The war against the Spanish curbed that stimulant. The white minority also tried to correct the numerical racial imbalance. A prohibitive duty on new slave imports cut the rate of importation from one thousand per year in 1730 to one hundred per year by 1740. Collected duties went to recruit white immigrants. The legislature required one white man present for every ten Africans on a plantation. Fines from this infraction went to fund additional patrols.

The government intensified efforts to control the behavior of slaves. Through the Negro Act of 1740, the legislators shaped the core of the South Carolina slave codes for more than a century. Masters who failed to retain control of slaves received fines. The right to manumit slaves was taken out of the hands of owners and turned over to the legislature. No longer could slaves have such personal liberties as freedom of movement, of education, of assembly, to raise food, and to earn money. Surveillance of African American activity increased. Slaves received rewards for informing on the actions of other slaves. The legislature discouraged the presence of free blacks in the colony.

The white minority developed several strategies of calculated benevolence. The government assessed penalties on masters known for excessive labor requirements or brutality of punishments for their slaves. A school was founded in Charles Town to train slaves to teach other slaves about selective Christian principles requiring submission and obedience.

These efforts did not lessen white dependency on African labor. Machines did not supplant their labor until after the American Revolution. White immigration did not increase substantially, despite offers of free land on the frontier. High duties reduced the importation of slaves, but the racial proportions varied slightly from those prior to insurrection.

The suppression of the Stono Rebellion was a significant turning point for the white minority. White factions had to cooperate to maintain the English colony. Techniques used to maintain white control shaped the race relations and history of South Carolina. The heightened degree of white repression and the reduction in African autonomy created a new social equilibrium in the generation before the American Revolution.

—*Dorothy C. Salem*

FURTHER READING

Aptheker, Herbert. *American Negro Slave Revolts*. Rev. ed. New York: Columbia University Press, 1969. The pioneering work on slave revolts.

Jordan, Winthrop. *White Over Black: American Attitudes Toward the Negro, 1550-1812*. Chapel Hill: University of North Carolina Press, 1968. Discusses how slave revolts influenced the status of both slaves and free blacks in the United States.

Kilson, Martin. "Toward Freedom: An Analysis of Slave Revolts in the United States." *Phylon* 25 (1964): 175-189. Analyzes the distribution of slave revolts and the environments that contributed to their occurrence.

McDougall, Walter A. *Freedom Just Around the Corner: A New American History, 1585-1828*. New York: HarperCollins, 2004. The first in a projected three-volume history of the United States by a Pulitzer Prize-winning historian. This well-researched overview of American history includes information about the Stono Rebellion in the chapter entitled "Germans, Four Sorts of Britains, and Africans."

Olwell, Robert. *Masters, Slaves, and Subjects: The Culture of Power in the South Carolina Low Country, 1740-1790*. Ithaca, N.Y.: Cornell University Press, 1998. Examines the slave society in colonial South Carolina from the end of the Stono Rebellion through the American Revolution. Describes relations among slaves and masters in a society in which both were imperial subjects of the British empire.

Thornton, John K. "African Dimensions of the Stono Rebellion." *American Historical Review* 96, no. 4 (October, 1991): 1101. Describes the causes and course of the rebellion, pointing to evidence that many of the Stono rebels were from the Kingdom of the Kongo. Provides information about related events in the eighteenth century Kongo.

Wood, Peter H. *Black Majority: Negroes in Colonial South Carolina from 1670 Through the Stono Rebellion*. New York: W. W. Norton, 1974. Examines the patterns of white control and African resistance within the socioeconomic context of colonial South Carolina. Both a narrative and an analysis of the event and its effects on the colony.

SEE ALSO: 18th cent.: Expansion of the Atlantic Slave Trade; Apr. 6, 1712: New York City Slave Revolt; 1730-1739: First Maroon War; Nov. 23, 1733: Slaves Capture St. John's Island; 1760-1776: Caribbean Slave Rebellions; Apr. 14, 1775: Pennsylvania Society for the Abolition of Slavery Is Founded; July 2, 1777-1804: Northeast States Abolish Slavery; Mar. 16, 1792: Denmark Abolishes the Slave Trade; Feb. 12, 1793: First Fugitive Slave Law; July, 1795-Mar., 1796: Second Maroon War.

RELATED ARTICLES in *Great Lives from History: The Eighteenth Century, 1701-1800*: Benjamin Banneker; Olaudah Equiano.

1730's

September 18, 1739
TREATY OF BELGRADE

The Treaty of Belgrade ended the Russo-Austrian war against the Ottoman Empire. It checked Austrian expansion into the Balkans for another century and halted Russian expansion southward for a generation.

LOCALE: Belgrade, Serbia, Ottoman Empire (now in the Federal Republic of Yugoslavia)

CATEGORIES: Diplomacy and international relations; wars, uprisings, and civil unrest

KEY FIGURES

Anna (Anna Ivanovna; 1693-1740), empress of Russia, r. 1730-1740

Mahmud I (1696-1754), Ottoman sultan, r. 1730-1754

Charles VI (1685-1740), Holy Roman Emperor, r. 1711-1740

Burkhard Christoph von Münnich (1683-1767), German-born commander in chief of the Russian army, 1728-1740, and president of the war council, 1732-1740

Count Andrei Ivanovich Osterman (1686-1747), first cabinet minister of Russia, 1731-1740

Yegen Mehmed Paşa (d. 1745), Ottoman grand vizier and leader of the war party, 1737-1739

Count von Neipperg (1684-1774), Austrian field marshal and chief negotiator

Marquis de Villeneuve (Louis-Sauveur Renaud; 1695-1745), French diplomat

Count von Wallis (1676-1744), Irish-born field marshal of the Austrian army, 1736-1739

André-Hercule de Fleury (1653-1743), prime minister of France, 1726-1743

SUMMARY OF EVENT

Russia launched a war against the Turkish empire in 1736 in part because of the misperception that the Turkish power was in rapid decline and partly because of the long-standing territorial disputes along their common frontiers with the Crimea. Since 1726, Russia had maintained ties to Austria and Spain, while keeping friendly relations with Prussia and Denmark. Austria entered the conflict more concerned about the territorial designs of its Russian ally than it was anxious to curtail Turkish might. Other European considerations made the continuation of the Russian alliance very useful for the Austrian court, and so the Habsburg Empire declared war on Turkey in the spring of the following year. The allies agreed that Russia should be given Azov and the Crimea while

Austria would acquire Bosnia and part of Albania.

Despite Russia's successful raid on the Crimean capital of Bakhchisarai (palace of the gardens), the seizure of the fortress of Kinburn on the Dnieper River, and the occupation of the port city of Azov in the East, Russian armies suffered high losses and Empress Anna was anxious to find an early end to this conflict by the end of 1736. In the following year (July-October), a conference at Nemirov failed to resolve the disagreements, and the sultan appealed to Cardinal André-Hercule de Fleury of France to mediate the conflict. By this time, Austria had entered the fray and Russian forces had seized the fortress of Ochakov (at the confluence of the Dnieper and Bug Rivers). The allied hopes were raised and so, despairing of an early end to the war, the sultan Mahmud I appointed the militant Yegen Mehmed Paşa as grand vizier. By year's end, Turkish forces had regained both Kinburn and Ochakov, and a new Russian offensive in the Crimea had failed miserably.

Austrian forces took the initiative in 1738 and advanced south of the Danube, occupying Niš, Pristina, and Novi Pazar. They also invaded Walachia and part of Moldavia north of the Danube. These successes were short-lived as the Turks rebounded next year, forced the Habsburgs to retreat from all their incursions and even surrounded Belgrade, which they had yielded to Austria in 1718.

The Russians fared better. In May of 1738, Count Andrei Ivanovich Osterman suggested to the French mediator, the marquis de Villeneuve, the desirability of opening peace discussions. When the Turks showed no interest, owing to Russia's new demands, hostilities continued. In July, Field Marshal Burkhard Christoph von Münnich, who had convinced Empress Anna that the Greeks were set to revolt against the sultan, had taken his Russian troops into Moldavia and defeated the Ottoman forces at Khotim. Two months later, after crossing the Pruth, his forces occupied Jassy.

Prior to this point, the failure of any of the combatants to gain a decisive victory enabled Cardinal Fleury of France to begin peace negotiations via his emissary, Villeneuve, in 1739. Ironically, both the Austrians in Serbia and the Russians in Walachia made significant gains in the month preceding the actual negotiations. Nevertheless, the Turks were encamped outside Belgrade and were threatening the Serbian capital. The Austrian field marshal, Count von Wallis, wrote to Vienna that Belgrade could not be defended despite the arrival of Austrian reinforcements. Four days later, on August 16, his replacement, Count von Neipperg, sent a similarly discouraging message to the Habsburg court, lamenting that there was no hope of retaining the Serbian capital. Neipperg anxiously threw himself into the negotiations with Grand Vizier Yegen Mehmed Paşa and the Russian representative, Cagnoni.

So anxious for peace was the Habsburg count that Austria agreed to cede Belgrade to the Ottomans provided that the Austrians had time to dismantle their fortifications in that Serbian city since their occupation of it in 1718. His position was undermined by the fact that the French mediator was supporting the Turkish claims in the negotiations. The Austrian court was shocked by the cession of Belgrade, as was Russia, whose field marshal recently had won a major encounter over the Turks at Khotin. Weary from the war after losing 100,000 men, however, and concerned about Swedish threats in the north, Russia accepted the treaty drawn up by the French.

The treaty that was signed on September 18, 1739, allowed the Turks to regain all of Serbia as well as Walachia. The only territory that Austria retained from the earlier Treaty at Passarowitz in 1718 was the Banat. Although victorious, Russia was compelled to withdraw from Khotin, to refrain from sailing warships and com-

mercial vessels in the Black Sea, and to abandon its plans to rebuild the naval base at Taganrog. Russia would retain Azov but without fortifications, and Russian merchants were given free access to Ottoman markets, but only via Turkish vessels. These meager results did not prevent a large celebration in St. Petersburg upon ratification of the treaty.

Despite Münnich's misgivings about Austrian concessions to the Turks while his own forces were winning on the battlefield, Empress Anna was pleased to accept the treaty, not only to end her losses of men but also because of aggressive moves by Sweden in the north. Unwilling to admit Austria's declining military might, Emperor Charles VI placed blame for the loss of Belgrade upon the inadequacies of Wallis and Neipperg, both of whom were imprisoned but released in the next reign, of Maria Theresa.

Whether Charles recognized the futility of retaining Belgrade and so looked for scapegoats to divert popular unhappiness or Wallis and Neipperg in fact gave misleading information about the weakness of military defenses at Belgrade is a question unresolved by scholars. In any case, the sultan, too, was anxious for peace after listening to the khan of the Crimea relate the difficulties of keeping his lands free from Russian incursions. Hence in April, 1739, the bellicose grand vizier was replaced

1730's

TREATY OF BELGRADE, 1739

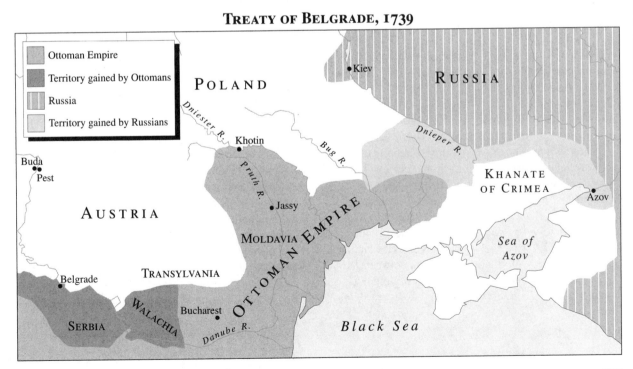

by a member of the peace faction at the Ottoman court. Cardinal Fleury was very happy with the work of Villeneuve, having kept Russia away from the Straits (Bosporus and the Dardanelles) while disguising the weakness of his Turkish ally.

SIGNIFICANCE

The Treaty of Belgrade marked the beginning of a shift in loyalties in the Balkans. The people living there came to identify less with the Habsburgs and more with their Orthodox Russian protectors. At the same time, Russia became more invested in the fate of the Balkans, and the Habsburgs began to distance themselves from the territory they had lost. This shift resulted, in part, from the absence of a coherent Habsburg policy toward the southeast, as well as from the misperception that, with little effort, the Austrians could roll back the Turks whenever they decided to do so. Whatever their perceptions, in May, 1740, the Habsburg fortress in Belgrade was razed, and Turkish control of the city resumed for the first time since 1718. The borders between Austria and the Ottoman Empire remained essentially intact for the next 140 years.

—John D. Windhausen

FURTHER READING

Cassels, Lavender. *The Struggle for the Ottoman Empire, 1717-1740*. London: Thomas Y. Crowell, 1967. The most readable work on the subject, rewarding for scholars and general readers alike. Especially strong on its treatment of diplomacy before the treaty.

Creasy, Edward S. *History of the Ottoman Turks*. Beirut, Lebanon: Khayats, 1961. This master of detailed narration provides the fullest account of the operations in the Crimea. He describes the treaty from the Turkish point of view.

Florinsky, Michael T. *Russia: A History and an Interpretation*. Vol. 1. Reprint. New York: Macmillan, 1973. Originally published in 1947, this volume is one of few scholarly surveys in English that deals with the Russian aspects of this war and treaty.

Gerolymatos, Andre. *The Balkan Wars: Conquest, Revolution, and Retribution from the Ottoman Era to the Twentieth Century and Beyond*. New York: Basic Books, 2002. Chapter 4, "Ethnicity Versus the Nation State," includes information on the war between Turkey and Russia and the resulting Treaty of Belgrade.

Goodwin, Jason. *Lords of the Horizons: A History of the Ottoman Empire*. New York: Picador, 2003. Chapter 20, "Austria and Russia," includes information on the war between the Ottoman Empire an Russia and the subsequent Treaty of Belgrade.

Jelavich, Barbara. *History of the Balkans: Eighteenth and Nineteenth Centuries*. New York: Cambridge University Press, 1983. Jelavich compares the Balkan populations under Christian and Turkish overlords. Her work contains exceptional maps of the Ottoman possessions in Europe.

Parvev, Ivan. *Hapsburgs and Ottomans: Between Vienna and Belgrade, 1683-1739*. New York: Columbia University Press, 1995. This Bulgarian historian examines Habsburg-Ottoman relations from a Balkan perspective and describes the difficulties about the conflicting ambitions of the Russian and Austrian allies.

Quataert, Donald. *The Ottoman Empire, 1700-1922*. New York: Cambridge University Press, 2000. Chapter 5, "The Ottomans and Their Wider World," includes information on Ottoman relations with Russia and Austria and the Treaty of Belgrade.

Roider, Karl A., Jr. *The Reluctant Ally: Austria's Policy in the Austrian-Turkish War, 1737-1739*. Baton Rouge: Louisiana State University Press, 1972. Probably the most important treatise covering this subject from the Austrian perspective, although not without important insights concerning Turkish and Russian involvements too.

Sugar, Peter F. *Southeastern Europe Under Ottoman Rule, 1354-1804*. Seattle: University of Washington Press, 1977. This work contains valuable appendices on rulers, geography, and treaties as well as a concentrated discussion of Turkish life in the Balkans.

SEE ALSO: Nov. 20, 1710-July 21, 1718: Ottoman Wars with Russia, Venice, and Austria; Oct. 21, 1727: Treaty of Kiakhta; 1736-1739: Russo-Austrian War Against the Ottoman Empire; Oct. 20, 1740: Maria Theresa Succeeds to the Austrian Throne; Dec. 16, 1740-Nov. 7, 1748: War of the Austrian Succession; 1746: Zāhir al-ʿUmar Creates a Stronghold in Galilee; Oct., 1768-Jan. 9, 1792: Ottoman Wars with Russia; 1788-Sept., 1809: Russo-Swedish Wars.

RELATED ARTICLES in *Great Lives from History: The Eighteenth Century, 1701-1800*: Charles VI; André-Hercule de Fleury; Mahmud I; Maria Theresa.

1740
MACLAURIN'S GRAVITATIONAL THEORY

Colin Maclaurin's prizewinning essay on tides provided an elegant mathematical proof of a key assumption of Sir Isaac Newton's gravitational theory. Maclaurin's recognition of the deflecting action of the Earth's rotation also anticipated the more fully dynamical theory of tides that Pierre-Simon Laplace later developed in the Celestial Mechanics *of 1799.*

LOCALE: Edinburgh, Scotland; Paris, France
CATEGORIES: Mathematics; physics; science and technology

KEY FIGURES

Colin Maclaurin (1698-1746), Scottish mathematician
Sir Isaac Newton (1642-1727), English mathematician and physicist
Leonhard Euler (1707-1783), Swiss mathematician and physicist
Daniel Bernoulli (1700-1782), Swiss mathematician and botanist

SUMMARY OF EVENT

In 1738, Colin Maclaurin, a professor of mathematics at the University of Edinburgh, responded to a competition to explain and predict tides sponsored by the French Académie des Sciences (Academy of Sciences). The academy's prizes brought considerable prestige to their recipients, and its annual competitions attracted submissions from Europe's best scientists. Maclaurin worked on his submission for two years, and in 1740, his paper "De Causa Physica Fluxus et Refluxus Maris" (on the physical cause of the ebb and flow of the sea) shared the prize with three other contestants—Antoine Cavalleri, a professor of mathematics at Cahors in France; Leonhard Euler, chair of mathematics at the St. Petersburg Academy of Sciences in Russia; and Daniel Bernoulli, then professor of botany at the University of Basel in Switzerland.

Observations on the frequency and magnitude of tides had long been essential to maritime navigation and coastal economies, but an adequate theoretical understanding of tides began to take shape only with the seventeenth century Scientific Revolution. Indeed, the ability to account for tides became a crucial test of the new celestial mechanics. Galileo, for example, adduced the tides as proof of the Copernican theory of the solar system, understanding them as the accelerations and decelerations that resulted from the combination of the Earth's revolution around the Sun and the Earth's rotation on its axis.

René Descartes had recognized that tides had some relationship to the Moon. He explained this relationship by hypothesizing an "ether," or intangible medium, that filled the whole of space. As celestial objects rotated, Descartes hypothesized, they created vortices in the ether. Thus, the vortex created by the Earth's rotation carried the Moon along its orbit and the tides were the consequence of the downward pressure of the Moon upon the ether and the ether upon the Earth's surface.

It was Sir Isaac Newton, however, who established the basis for a modern understanding of tides. For Newton, tides were not the result of the pressure of a hypothetical ether but of the gravitational attraction of massive objects. Newton's first theory of tides imagined the oceans on the model of a satellite making a close circular orbit of the Earth and determined the effects of gravity on this "satellite's" motion. For Newton, too, the origin of the tides lay not only in a relationship between the Earth and the Moon but also in a relationship between the Earth and the Sun.

Newton later offered a second theory of tidal activity, which Maclaurin's 1740 essay first distinguished as an "equilibrium theory" in contrast to the earlier "kinetic theory." Newton's equilibrium theory imagined the effects of the Moon's and Sun's gravity on a fluid Earth and then determined the effects of Earth's rotation. This model of tides resulting from a complex, three-body interaction among the Earth, Moon, and Sun was both more flexible and more comprehensive than Galileo's and Descartes's simple mechanical explanations. Newton's attempts to explain tides also had limitations, however. Newton's presentation was often obscure, was not always consistent, and depended at crucial points on unproven mathematical intuitions. Moreover, while Newton's account generally agreed better with existing observations than did the Galilean and Cartesian alternatives, it still required significant refinement in application.

These limitations of Newton's tidal theory, as well as the difficulty of conceiving a mechanism for instantaneous action at a distance, meant that there remained serious proponents of the Cartesian theory of vortices throughout the first half of the eighteenth century. The limitations of Newton's tidal theory also encouraged efforts to improve data on tides, in the hopes that better data would lead to a better model explaining the data. Particularly energetic in this respect was the Académie des Sciences, which issued guidelines on the measurement of tides and served as a clearinghouse for observations.

It was in order to resolve the unsettled state of tidal theory and to bring that theory more into line with empirical studies that the academy sponsored its prize competition of 1738. Of the prizewinners, the Jesuit Cavalleri had the unhappy distinction of attempting the last significant defense of Cartesian theory. Maclaurin, Euler, and Bernoulli all began from Newton's theory, and in 1742 their essays were included in the French translation by François Jacquier and Thomas LeSeur of Newton's *Philosophiae Naturalis Principia Mathematica* (1687; *The Mathematical Principles of Natural Philosophy*, 1729; best known as the *Principia*).

Maclaurin was an ideal candidate for the Académie des Sciences prize. Scottish universities had been the first in Europe to teach Newtonian science, and in 1713 the young Maclaurin was already writing a highly sophisticated master's thesis at the University of Glasgow on "Gravity and Other Forces." In 1719, Maclaurin had gone to London, where he so impressed Newton that Newton, in turn, oversaw Maclaurin's election to the Royal Society. It had been Newton, moreover, who in 1725 had recommended Maclaurin for the prestigious position of professor of mathematics at the University of Edinburgh. The previous year, Maclaurin had won his first prize from the Académie des Sciences for a study of percussion.

Throughout the 1730's, Maclaurin worked to overcome objections to the Newtonian calculus by giving it a more rigorous geometrical—in contemporary terms, "fluxional"—foundation. At the same time, Maclaurin became a prominent spokesman for the Newtonian system. His *Account of Sir Isaac Newton's Philosophical Discoveries*, posthumously published in 1748, was among the most lucid and most widely read popular expositions of the *Principia* in the eighteenth century.

Important refinements to Newtonian mechanics emerged from Maclaurin's 1740 prize essay. Newton had assumed that his two accounts of tidal action were equivalent. Maclaurin, however, demonstrated that the kinetic theory predicted tides of significantly less magnitude than those predicted by the equilibrium theory. Additionally, in the equilibrium theory, Newton had merely assumed without proof that the gravitational attraction of a single body would deform an otherwise spherical ocean of uniform depth into a prolate spheroid. In other words, the ocean would be elongated along the axis between the Earth and the attracting body and flattened at right angles to this axis.

Maclaurin used the fluxional calculus to provide an elegant proof of this assumption. Out of this proof came a correspondence with Alexis-Claude Clairaut, which led the French mathematician, in his *Théorie de la figure de la terre* (1743; theory of the shape of the Earth), to resolve another longstanding problem in Newtonian mechanics. Maclaurin, finally, was the first to consider the apparent deflection of moving bodies on rotating surfaces—what is today called the Coriolis effect after the nineteenth century French mathematician Gustave-Gaspard Coriolis.

Euler's and Bernoulli's prize essays further elaborated Newton's equilibrium theory of tidal action. Euler's paper demonstrated that it was not, as Newton believed, the vertical component but the horizontal component of gravitational attraction that played the decisive role in generating tides. Bernoulli refined Newton's theory to the point where it could be used to compile tide tables and make relatively reliable predictions.

SIGNIFICANCE

Together, Maclaurin's, Euler's, and Bernoulli's 1740 prize essays constitute the most significant contribution to the understanding of tides—and hence the practical application of gravitational theory—in the century after Newton's initial achievement. Not until the end of the eighteenth century did the French mathematician and physicist Pierre-Simon Laplace go further and undertake the daunting task of creating a fully dynamic theory of tides that would take into account, for example, the ocean's response to gravitational forces. This task was one that Maclaurin, in recognizing the deflecting action of the Earth's rotation, had anticipated but not developed.

Maclaurin's prize essay also belongs to a critical moment in the development of the calculus. In 1742, Maclaurin published *A Treatise of Fluxions*, a systematic defense of the Newtonian calculus that featured an expanded version of his 1740 prize essay. For many historians, Maclaurin's insistence on geometric techniques, for all of its evident genius, left British science ill-equipped to comprehend the remarkable achievements of continental analysis and rational mechanics. Recent scholarship, however, has been more generous. Continental analysis, this scholarship notes, was not able to replicate the rigor of Maclaurin's geometry until the 1780's; indeed, Maclaurin's results often stimulated improvements in continental analysis.

Moreover, Maclaurin's *Treatise of Fluxions* had a twofold character: If the first volume was geometric, the second volume presented the same results algebraically.

This twofold character embodied the general moderatism of the eighteenth century Scottish Enlightenment and a continuing exchange between the British and continental approaches to mathematical physics. Maclaurin's elaboration of Newton's gravitational theory founded the generalizing power of modern symbolic notation on the ancient techniques of Greek geometry. It grounded forward-looking research on applications in a conservative allegiance to rigor.

—*Charles R. Sullivan*

FURTHER READING

Cartwright, David E. *Tides: A Scientific History*. New York: Cambridge University Press, 1999. An important history of the science of tides.

Grabiner, Judith V. "Was Newton's Calculus a Dead End? The Continental Influence of Maclaurin's *Treatise of Fluxions*." *The American Mathematical Monthly* 104, no. 5 (May, 1997): 393-410. An important reconsideration of the place of *A Treatise of Fluxions* in the history of mathematics by the leading contemporary Maclaurin scholar.

Greenberg, John L. *The Problem of the Earth's Shape from Newton to Clairaut: The Rise of Mathematical Science in Eighteenth-Century Paris and the Fall of "Normal" Science*. New York: Cambridge University Press, 1995. Provides an extensive treatment of Maclaurin's contributions to Newtonian mechanics.

Guicciardini, Niccolò. *Reading the "Principia": The Debate on Newton's Mathematical Methods for Natural Philosophy, from 1687 to 1736*. New York: Cambridge University Press, 1999. A rich discussion of how Newton's masterpiece stimulated debates on the mathematization of natural philosophy.

SEE ALSO: 1704-1712: Astronomy Wars in England; 1724: Foundation of the St. Petersburg Academy of Sciences; 1738: Bernoulli Proposes the Kinetic Theory of Gases; 1743-1744: D'Alembert Develops His Axioms of Motion; 1748: Bradley Discovers the Nutation of Earth's Axis; 1748: Euler Develops the Concept of Function; 1796: Laplace Articulates His Nebular Hypothesis.

RELATED ARTICLES in *Great Lives from History: The Eighteenth Century, 1701-1800*: Leonhard Euler; Colin Maclaurin.

1740-1741
RICHARDSON'S *PAMELA* ESTABLISHES THE MODERN NOVEL

The modern English novel came into its own as a literary form with Samuel Richardson's writing of Pamela: Or, Virtue Rewarded. *With this work, the episodic method employed by the very first English novels gave way to a plot that focused on a main event, a romantic pursuit, and the realities of contemporary marriage and mores.*

LOCALE: London, England
CATEGORY: Literature

KEY FIGURES
Samuel Richardson (1689-1761), English printer and novelist
Daniel Defoe (1660-1731), English novelist
Henry Fielding (1707-1754), English novelist
Tobias Smollett (1721-1771), English novelist

SUMMARY OF EVENT
The publication of Samuel Richardson's *Pamela: Or, Virtue Rewarded* (1740-1741) in England marked the establishment of the novel as a literary form. To be sure, the roots of the novel in Western literature can be traced back to fictional narratives in ancient Greece and Rome, to the epic poem and long fictional romances, and in Eastern literature to Murasaki Shikibu's *Genji Monogatari* (c. 1001-1013; *The Tale of Genji*, 1925-1933). Later European narratives produced the romances of chivalry, and in Spain, an unknown author in 1554 wrote *Lazarillo de Tormes*, considered by some to be the first picaresque narrative. Some critics even consider *El ingenioso hidalgo don Quixote de la Mancha* (1605, 1615; *The History of the Valorous and Wittie Knight-Errant, Don Quixote of the Mancha*, 1612-1620; better known as *Don Quixote de la Mancha*) by Miguel de Cervantes to be the first novel, because his characters resembled real people who were capable of making foolish mistakes; certainly this work of fiction contributed to the development of the modern novel.

In England, there are several fictional narratives that, in retrospect, have vied for the "first novel" distinction. Among these were Daniel Defoe's *The Life and Strange Surprizing Adventures of Robinson Crusoe, of York, Mariner, Written by Himself* (1719; commonly known as *Robinson Crusoe*), which recounted the adventures of a man who was stranded on an island for twenty-four years, and *The Fortunes and Misfortunes of the Famous Moll Flanders, Written from Her Own Memorandums* (1722; commonly known as *Moll Flanders*), which followed the life of a woman who turned to thievery and prostitution but who later repented to lead an upright life. Certainly, in many ways *Robinson Crusoe* deserves the title of the first modern novel, and it is accurate to refer to Defoe as a novelist.

However, the plot of *Robinson Crusoe* relied on travel and thus separated the hero from a stable setting. While it focused on an individual, moreover, it was episodic (portraying one self-contained event after another), rather than dealing with social relationships in a coherent, unified fashion. By the same token, the plot of *Moll Flanders* lacked the sort of pattern that would emerge when a writer was skilled in using multiple angles in holding a mirror, so to speak, to reflect reality. The original sort of realism invented by the novel comes from its ability to mirror all aspects of human experience, not just those that reflect one perspective. It is the way the novel presents life, not just the kind of life it presents, that is the prime feature of novelistic realism. It is this feature that differentiates the eighteenth century novel most clearly from earlier prose fiction.

With *Pamela*, Richardson was successful in avoiding some of the major problems that Defoe had encountered. The most important problem was that of finding a plot that would fit the new form of the novel. Defoe's episodic plots were better suited to other forms, such as a heroic epic or the picaresque tale. Richardson solved this problem by avoiding the episodic methods of Defoe, basing the novel on a single action, the courtship of Pamela Andrews by Mr. B. Richardson. He used the epistolary method (that is, the novel takes the form of a series of letters), a method of which he has been acknowledged as a master.

In two volumes of fictional correspondence, Richardson posed as an anonymous editor of found letters to reveal the story of Pamela, a clever

and virtuous servant girl who works for a kind mistress, Mr. B's mother. Her mistress dies, leaving Mr. B. as her master. He then pursues her relentlessly, and, being aware of the disparity in their social classes, Pamela resists just as relentlessly. The more she resists his advances, the more desperately Mr. B. tries to trap her. At last, he consents to let her go home to her parents, but actually Mr. B. sends her to Lincolnshire to a lonely house with two overseers, Mrs. Jewkes and Colgrand. After Pamela makes an unsuccessful attempt to escape and even contemplates suicide, Mr. B. is finally convinced that she will never give in to temptation, and he offers to let her return home. Before Pamela has gone far, Mr. B. appeals to her once more. This time, however, the appeal takes the form of a proper and sincere marriage proposal. Her virtue having finally been rewarded, Pamela returns to Mr. B and gratefully accepts his proposal. The second volume recounts their married life together.

THE WARNING OF PAMELA'S FATHER

Samuel Richardson's Pamela *is an epistolary novel, consisting entirely of letters to and from the title character. Richardson wastes no time to establish the themes of his book, as the second letter of the lengthy work, excerpted here, is a warning to Pamela from her father about her new master's intentions.*

DEAR PAMELA,

Your letter was indeed a great trouble, and some comfort, to me and your poor mother. We are troubled, to be sure, for your good lady's death, who took such care of you, and gave you learning, and, for three or four years past, has always been giving you clothes and linen, and every thing that a gentlewoman need not be ashamed to appear in. But our chief trouble is, and indeed a very great one, for fear you should be brought to anything dishonest or wicked, by being set so above yourself. Every body talks how you have come on, and what a genteel girl you are; and some say you are very pretty; and, indeed, six months since, when I saw you last, I should have thought so myself, if you was not our child. But what avails all this, if you are to be ruined and undone!— Indeed, my dear Pamela, we begin to be in great fear for you; for what signify all the riches in the world, with a bad conscience, and to be dishonest! We are, 'tis true, very poor, and find it hard enough to live; though once, as you know, it was better with us. But we would sooner live upon the water, and, if possible, the clay of the ditches I contentedly dig, than live better at the price of our child's ruin.

I hope the good 'squire has no design: but when he has given you so much money, and speaks so kindly to you, and praises your coming on; and, oh, that fatal word! that he would be kind to you, if you would do as you should do, almost kills us with fears.

Source: Samuel Richardson, *Pamela: Or, Virtue Rewarded*, letter 2. Project Gutenberg. http://www.gutenberg.org/dirs/etext04/pam1w10.txt. Accessed November 13, 2005.

Unlike earlier romance writers, whose narratives were produced in the context of notions of courtly love or Catholic ideals of marriage, Richardson was able to capitalize on a relatively new marriage code: The Puritan conception of marriage had recently become accepted by Anglo-Saxon society. Thus, Richardson's novel was written to reflect what was actually going on in the society of his time and it portrayed to its readers what purported to be their own values. This portrayal took a new form, moreover, because it expanded a single intrigue, Mr. B's pursuit of Pamela, into a novel-length work. While lovers' relationships have all the qualities of romantic love, Richardson was able to incorporate basic issues of life at that time, social class conflict and conflict between the moral code and sexual instincts. This incorporation of contemporary issues and values became a hallmark of novelistic realism.

Discussions of Samuel Richardson and his novels, with relatively few exceptions, have linked him to Henry Fielding, especially in light of the fact that Fielding parodied *Pamela* in *An Apology for the Life of Mrs. Shamela Andrews* (1741) and in *The History of the Adventures of Joseph Andrews, and of His Friend Mr. Abraham Adams* (1742; commonly known as *Joseph Andrews*). These works were meant to reveal what Fielding considered to be Richardson's moral ambivalence. Both authors believed themselves to be introducing innovative forms that would reshape prose fiction, but wide differences exist between the two writers.

Fielding, well grounded in the classical literary tradition, had a more scholarly approach to fiction than did Richardson; furthermore, his awareness of historical context resulted in characters that are general types of humankind, unlike Richardson's characters, with whom a reader can identify as individuals. Fielding's picaresque type of narrative, as seen in *The History of Tom Jones, a Foundling* (1749; commonly known as *Tom Jones*), enabled him to make random observations about society, whereas Richardson's plots focused on emotional pressures in specific situations. While Fielding addressed moral issues by laughing at humanity's foibles, Richardson preferred to shock his readers into virtuous behavior.

Tobias Smollett, often categorized with Richardson and Fielding as an early English novelist, wrote loosely constructed accounts of incidents in the lives of his heroes. Comical and bitterly satiric, his novels *The Adventures of Roderick Random* (1748) and *The Expedition of Humphry Clinker* (1771), like Fielding's *Tom Jones*, return to the earlier form of the picaresque or rogue-hero type of adventure.

SIGNIFICANCE

The publication of *Pamela: Or, Virtue Rewarded* produced an extraordinary effect. It swept England with a wave of emotion. Some of the novel's success came from its appeal to female readers at a time when many British women had more leisure time than they had previously enjoyed. Richardson's expertise at analyzing the feminine mind, moreover, was unequaled. He addressed the concerns of women for security, marriage, and a proper social role.

Furthermore, Richardson was a genius of plot, and, whereas Fielding was a novelist of nature or of the outdoors, Richardson was a novelist of the interior. His was arguably the first "novel of manners," in which the action takes place largely in domestic space—in the drawing room rather than in the streets, the countryside, or the public house. His work embodied the premise that the novel reports human experience fully and authentically, providing minute details and particulars of times, places, and settings. With *Pamela*, Richardson succeeded in going beyond the episodic and the picaresque methods of his contemporaries Defoe, Fielding, and Smollett. He consolidated the form of the novel and established it as a true literary genre.

—*Victoria Price*

FURTHER READING

Beasley, Jerry C. *Novels of the 1740's.* Athens: University of Georgia Press, 1982. Examines the backgrounds, topics, and strategies used in novels of the 1740's, with particular emphasis on the novels of Richardson, Fielding, and Smollett.

Brown, Homer Obed. *Institutions of the English Novel from Defoe to Scott.* Philadelphia: Pennsylvania State University Press, 1997. Questions the premise that the novel fully attained its generic identity by 1759.

Karl, Frederick R. *A Reader's Guide to the Eighteenth-Century Novel.* New York: Noonday Press, 1974. Identifies the novel as adversarial literature and discusses the work of Defoe, Richardson, Fielding, Smollett, and Laurence Sr. 1 Discusses qualities that constitute a novel.

McKeon, Michael. *The Origins of the English Novel, 1600-1740.* Baltimore: Johns Hopkins University Press, 1987. Provides a theoretical basis for tracing the historical development of the novel genre.

Richetti, John J. *The English Novel in History, 1700-1780.* New York: Routledge, 1999. Looks at fiction and society in eighteenth century England and the roles of Defoe, Richardson, and Fielding in this regard.

1740'S

Watt, Ian. *The Rise of the Novel: Studies in Defoe, Richardson, and Fielding.* 2d American ed. Berkeley: University of California Press, 2001. A classic work that seeks to identify literary and social situations in England that could account for the emergence of three novelists—Richardson, Defoe, and Fielding—within a single generation.

SEE ALSO: Apr. 25, 1719: Defoe Publishes the First Novel; 1726: Swift Satirizes English Rule of Ireland in *Gulliver's Travels*; 1742: Fielding's *Joseph Andrews* Satirizes English Society.

RELATED ARTICLES in *Great Lives from History: The Eighteenth Century, 1701-1800*: Daniel Defoe; Henry Fielding; Samuel Richardson; Jonathan Swift.

May 31, 1740
ACCESSION OF FREDERICK THE GREAT

Frederick the Great's ascension to the Prussian throne set the kingdom on an expansionist and imperialist course. During his reign, Prussia became the dominant Germanic state, significantly changing the balance of power Europe.

LOCALE: Prussia (now in Germany)
CATEGORY: Government and politics

KEY FIGURES

Frederick the Great (1712-1786), king of Prussia, r. 1740-1786

Elizabeth Christine of Brunswick-Bevern (1715-1797), wife of Frederick the Great

Frederick William I (1688-1740), king of Prussia, r. 1713-1740, and father of Frederick the Great

Sophia Dorothea of Hanover (1687-1757), queen of Prussia, wife of Frederick William I, and mother of Frederick the Great

Frederick I (1657-1713), elector of Brandenburg as Frederick III, r. 1688-1713, and king in Prussia, r. 1701-1713

Friedrich Heinrich von Seckendorff (1673-1763), Austrian envoy to Berlin

Wilhelmina of Prussia (1709-1758), sister and confidante of Frederick the Great

Hans Hermann von Katte (1704-1730), Prussian military officer and friend of Crown Prince Frederick

Friedrich Wilhelm Grumbkow (1678-1739), Austrian agent and adviser to Frederick William I

SUMMARY OF EVENT

The rather sickly child who would become Frederick the Great was born on January 24, 1712, to Sophia Dorothea of Hanover, wife of Crown Prince Frederick William I. The aging King Frederick I responded to the birth by ordering a celebration that rivaled his own coronation as "Frederick by the Grace of God King in Prussia" in the city of Königsberg eleven years earlier. Thirteen months later, Frederick I, king in Prussia, was dead; his son Frederick William I became the first king of Prussia, gaining recognition of his royal title by France and Spain in the Treaty of Utrecht (1713). Universal recognition of the title would develop slowly, however.

The Great Elector's legacy of education, science, and the arts—in the "Athens of the North"—rapidly gave way to "Sparta" and the militarism of Frederick William I. Upon Frederick William's accession to the Prussian throne, the two main bodies of government were the General Finance Directory, responsible for the royal domains, and the General War Commissary, responsible for the army and revenue collections. Frederick William's first order of business was to balance Prussia's budget, basing financial expenditures on expected revenues. He would tolerate no burdensome national debt like that of France, Austria, and England.

By an ordinance of August 13, 1713, Frederick William declared all royal domains and property as indivisible and inalienable, lessening the influence of the nobility by filling the provincial administrators' posts with his own civil servants. He encouraged development of war materials industries, and increased the Prussian army by seven regiments. Soon, the army became a large part of the domestic consumer market and was consuming two-thirds of the state revenues. Troops were garrisoned within the recruitment districts, using peasant farmers as soldiers and the nobility as officers. Frederick William's one extravagance was the tall grenadiers who served as his personal bodyguards. Once Prince Frederick was placed in charge of his own regiment, he gained favor with the king by recruiting tall men for the army.

Crown Prince Frederick was given military responsibility at an early age, and he proved himself a capable leader, though at first he viewed the uniform as a "dead

King Frederick the Great of Prussia. (Harper & Brothers)

man's shroud." Frederick often rebelled against his father's demand for absolute obedience and suffered harsh discipline when he dared to show independence. Frederick William despised his son's intellectual pursuits, his "French" manners, and his lavish spending on extravagances such as music lessons, entertainment, and books. In one fit of temper, Frederick William destroyed an entire library of four thousand books that Frederick had secretly accumulated.

Frederick William's harsh treatment of his son worsened as the king's health failed. His mistrust of Frederick's loyalty was exacerbated by the political maneuvering of Marshal Friedrich Heinrich von Seckendorff, the Austrian envoy, and General Friedrich Wilhelm Grumbkow, Austrian adviser to Frederick William I. Fearing an alliance between Prussia and Great Britain, the Austrians successfully thwarted the efforts of Prussia's Queen Sophia Dorothea to arrange marriages for Crown Prince Frederick and Crown Princess Wilhelmina with the British ruling house of Hanover. In 1733, Prince Frederick was compelled by his father to marry Princess Elizabeth Christine of Brunswick-Bevern.

For several years prior to his marriage, Frederick was

virtually a prisoner in Prussia. With the help of Lieutenant Hans Hermann von Katte, he made plans to escape to England. The plot was betrayed, and the king had Frederick arrested and court-martialed as a military deserter. Frustrated because the court would not execute the prince, his father confined him to Küstrin and forced him to watch the execution of his friend, Lieutenant von Katte. The trauma hardened Frederick's resolve to succeed his father on the throne, and he began to concentrate his studies on economics, politics, and military science. Eventually, a formal reconciliation was effected, and, near death, Frederick William turned away from Austria, which smoothed the way for Frederick's accession to the throne.

On Tuesday, May 31, 1740, Frederick William I died. That same day in Berlin, Crown Prince Frederick was proclaimed King Frederick II of Prussia. Frederick saw no need of coronation, but he accepted homage in three places—Berlin, Königsberg, and Cleve—and encouraged the swearing of fealty to unite the country. Word of Frederick's accession was carried by envoys to foreign heads of state, who hastened to pay their respects to the new king, whose soldiers would soon acclaim him as "Frederick the Great." The old king's body lay in state in Potsdam, with the four thousand tall men of his Grenadiers in attendance. When their final salutatory volleys had been fired, Frederick II ordered the dissolution of the Potsdam Grenadiers.

One day after his accession, Frederick declared that he was "first servant of the state" and that the good of the state would have priority over his personal good. He opened the corn magazines and distributed grain to the needy. The next day he abolished the use of legal torture in criminal trials. Justice was his prime domestic policy, and he reformed the laws throughout his reign. In his political testaments of 1752 and 1768, Frederick II wrote that the duty of the sovereign was to protect the laws and legal process. Yet, no formal separation of powers existed: The courts could not limit the political power, sovereignty, and administrative authority of the absolute monarch.

SIGNIFICANCE

Frederick made few changes in his father's organization of state administration. He viewed the army as a political tool rather than a security force for Prussia's indefensible borders. Frederick II saw but two alternatives for his fragmented kingdom: He must either seek peace by compromise with all neighboring countries, or he must acquire the territories that would consolidate the scattered

1740's

275

territories. Frederick chose consolidation. As crown prince, he had discussed the ultimate necessity of linking Pomerania and East Prussia—a belief that would lead to the partition of Poland by Prussia and Russia in 1772. Word of the death of the Austrian kaiser in October, 1740, and Maria Theresa's accession to the Habsburg throne opened the door for Frederick the Great to test his military forces in a bid to take Silesia from Austria.

Frederick the Great's support of education and his intellect earned him the title of Philosopher King. He built up the German Academy of Sciences to rival that of France. He sought outstanding academicians, literary geniuses, musicians, actors, and dancers to enrich Prussian culture. Religious toleration, freedom of the press, and philanthropy, all were reforms that gained respect for Frederick II as an enlightened despot. His letters and journals reflect his understanding that he was recording his thoughts and actions for the benefit and instruction of generations to come.

By the end of the costly Silesian Wars in 1745, Frederick realized that fame and glory would neither fill an empty treasury nor keep a trained army at full strength. With most of Europe caught up in wars, Frederick faced almost constant danger from all sides. By skillful diplomacy and selective military actions, Frederick managed to ensure Prussia's survival and consolidate territories within the weakening Holy Roman Empire. As a result of his alliance with Britain in the Seven Years' War (ended 1763), Prussia emerged as a powerful force in central Europe. In the shifting balance of power in Europe, Frederick the Great guided Prussia to a position of power from which it would become a dominant force in the nineteenth century.

—Marguerite R. Plummer

FURTHER READING

Asprey, Robert B. *Frederick the Great: The Magnificent Enigma*. New York: Ticknor & Fields, 1986. A biography that reveals the personality of Frederick, as well as his view of the monarchy and the Prussian state.

Dwyer, Philip G., ed. *The Rise of Prussia: Rethinking Prussian History, 1700-1830*. New York: Longman, 2000. A collection of essays about various aspects of Prussian history, politics, and social conditions during the eighteenth and early nineteenth centuries. The essays include discussions of the reigns of Frederick William and Frederick the Great, Prussia and the Enlightenment, the development of Prussian towns, the Prussian military state, religion, and social protest.

Fischer-Fabian, S. *Prussia's Glory: The Rise of a Military State*. Translated by Lore Segal and Paul Stern. New York: Macmillan, 1981. Traces the rise of Prussia as a military power from the investiture of 1713 to Frederick the Great.

Fraser, David. *Frederick the Great: King of Prussia*. New York: A. Lane, 2000. Fraser, a general and biographer, focuses on Frederick's military career. The book contains detailed descriptions of battles and military strategy, placing these conflicts within the context of eighteenth century European diplomacy and political history.

Koch, H. W. *A History of Prussia*. New York: Longman, 1978. A comprehensive history of the Prussian state, from the Teutonic Orders to the emergence of the German state.

MacDonogh, Giles. *Frederick the Great: A Life in Deed and Letters*. New York: St. Martin's Press, 2000. Comprehensive biography, based on meticulous research into primary documents, including Frederick's correspondence. Readers already familiar with Frederick will not find new revelations, but the book is a useful introduction for students and others who want to know more about the man and his times.

Ritter, Gerhardt. *Frederick the Great: A Historical Profile*. Translated, with an introduction, by Peter Paret. Berkeley: University of California Press, 1968. An analysis of the person and monarchy of Frederick the Great.

Snyder, Louis L., ed. *Frederick the Great*. Englewood Cliffs, N.J.: Prentice-Hall, 1971. Reveals Frederick's worldview through excerpts of his writings and correspondence, and the world's view of Frederick through the eyes of selected writers.

SEE ALSO: May 26, 1701-Sept. 7, 1714: War of the Spanish Succession; Apr. 11, 1713: Treaty of Utrecht; Oct. 20, 1740: Maria Theresa Succeeds to the Austrian Throne; Dec. 16, 1740-Nov. 7, 1748: War of the Austrian Succession; June 1, 1794: Allgemeines Landrecht Recodifies Prussian Law.
RELATED ARTICLES in *Great Lives from History: The Eighteenth Century, 1701-1800*: Frederick I; Frederick the Great; Frederick William I; Maria Theresa.

October 20, 1740
MARIA THERESA SUCCEEDS TO THE AUSTRIAN THRONE

In accordance with the Pragmatic Sanction, upon the death of Charles VI Maria Theresa succeeded to the Austrian throne. Although she was one of the greatest of all Habsburg rulers, Maria Theresa's accession began an intense rivalry between Austria and Prussia that eventually led to the eclipse of Austria as a power and the creation of a German empire under Prussian leadership.

LOCALE: Vienna, Austria
CATEGORY: Government and politics

KEY FIGURES

Maria Theresa (1717-1780), archduchess of Austria, r. 1740-1780, and queen of Hungary and Bohemia, r. 1740-1780

Charles VI (1685-1740), Austrian Holy Roman Emperor, r. 1711-1740, and father of Maria Theresa

Frederick the Great (1712-1786), king of Prussia, r. 1740-1786

Francis I (1708-1765), husband of Maria Theresa, duke of Lorraine, and Holy Roman Emperor, r. 1745-1765

Charles VII (Charles Albert Wittelsbach; 1697-1745), elector of Bavaria, r. 1726-1745, and Holy Roman Emperor, r. 1742-1745

George II (1683-1760), elector of Hanover and king of Great Britain and Ireland, r. 1727-1760

André-Hercule de Fleury (1653-1743), prime minister of France, 1726-1743

Charles Fouquet de Belle-Isle (1684-1761), French marshal and diplomat

SUMMARY OF EVENT

Maria Theresa's succession to the throne of the several Austrian Habsburg lands in 1740 was by no means uncontested. Her father, Holy Roman Emperor Charles VI, had sought to ensure her peaceful accession by working diligently throughout his reign to obtain the recognition of the Austrian nobility and most of the European powers, including Prussia and France, to a series of state acts known collectively as the Pragmatic Sanction. In effect, the Pragmatic Sanction publicly proclaimed that the Austrian lands were to pass undivided, on the basis of hereditary right, to Charles's son or—in the absence of legitimate male issue—female heirs. By 1717, it was evident, for all practical purposes, that his only direct legitimate successor would be Archduchess Maria Theresa.

The remark of one contemporary observer some years later, that Charles would have secured a more effective guarantee for the Pragmatic Sanction with an army of 200,000 men rather than the promises of the great powers, was proven correct by the sudden attack of Frederick the Great of Prussia on Silesia within two months of Maria Theresa's accession. Frederick the Great had ascended the throne of Prussia early in 1740 on the death of his father, Frederick William I. The old king may have been a boor, but he was not untrustworthy. Throughout his reign of twenty-seven years, he had been a loyal prince of the Holy Roman Empire. The youthful escapades of his son and heir were well known, and thus Frederick's attack on Silesia so early in his reign both shocked and perplexed the diplomats as well as the rulers of the various European states.

The Prussian invasion of Silesia in December, 1740, marked the beginning of the War of the Austrian Succes-

Archduchess Maria Theresa of Austria. (Harper & Brothers)

sion, which was to last until 1748. Prussia's action, known specifically as the First Silesian War (1740-1742), was only the first in a series of claims advanced against various parts of the Austrian lands by European powers whose rulers found it convenient to ignore their previous acceptance of the Pragmatic Sanction. One potentially hostile state, Bavaria, had never endorsed it because the elector of Bavaria, Charles Albert of Wittelsbach, coveted not only the Austrian Alpine and Bohemian lands but also the title of Holy Roman Emperor, which he actually secured for a brief period from 1742 until his death early in 1745.

The Prussian position with respect to Maria Theresa harmonized well with the aggressive, anti-Habsburg policies of Marshal Charles Fouquet de Belle-Isle, the French general and diplomat who headed the "War Party" in France. For Belle-Isle and his confederates in the French government, the opportunity to strike a final and fatal blow against the perennial Austrian foe appeared most auspicious. Cardinal André-Hercule de Fleury, the leading minister of France from 1726 to 1743, and a staunch proponent of nonintervention in the war, was unable to dissuade Belle-Isle from his intention to form alliances with those rulers who had claims against the Habsburgs.

By pursuing a consistent policy of nonintervention and relatively peaceful coexistence with the hereditary enemies of France, Cardinal Fleury had been able to repair much of the damage done to France's financial structure by the disastrous schemes of Louis XIV. Now the ambitions of Belle-Isle and his party threatened to undo Fleury's statesmanship. During 1741, Belle-Isle made secret agreements with Prussia and Bavaria as well as Saxony, which sought to take Moravia from Austria. Even Spain, which openly coveted the Habsburg possessions in Italy, found encouragement from the wily Belle-Isle. It seemed that Maria Theresa would be allowed to retain only Hungary. If the aims of its allies were realized, France would be able at long last to dominate central Europe, thus realizing one of the consistent aims of the foreign policy of Louis XIV.

The war itself, fought on several fronts, was a complicated and involved struggle. Frederick's cooperation with his French and Bavarian allies in the expanded conflict against Maria Theresa rested solely on his desire to protect his Silesian conquest against a resurgent Austria. Accordingly, he deserted his allies on three occasions, the last time at Christmas, 1745, marking the close of the two-year Second Silesian War. Frederick's unreliability seriously impaired the joint French-Bavarian assault on western Alpine Austria and Bohemia. Maria Theresa

found additional relief in the support she received from Saxony (which had now switched sides), from the loyal Hungarian aristocracy, and from George II, elector of Hanover and king of Great Britain, who desired to restore the balance of power between Austria and France. The alliance thus formed in 1745 between Austria and Great Britain also reflected the effort of the latter to reduce French competition overseas.

By 1745, Austria's position had improved somewhat. Moreover, the death of Charles Albert in that year brought peace with Bavaria, whose new ruler agreed to cast his vote in the next imperial election for Maria Theresa's husband, Francis, duke of Lorraine, as Holy Roman Emperor. Late in the year, Austria concluded peace with Prussia. Although it was driven from the Habsburg possessions in central Europe by 1746, France had completed the conquest of the Austrian Netherlands begun the previous year. At this juncture, the threat of Russian participation on the side of Austria induced the Bourbon states of France and Spain to make peace with their Habsburg foes.

SIGNIFICANCE

Maria Theresa's succession to the throne of the Austrian lands was recognized in the Treaty of Aix-la-Chapelle (Aachen), which she signed with her adversaries in 1748. Yet these lands no longer included Silesia, which she had reluctantly conceded to Frederick the Great. Maria Theresa emerged from the conflict as the respected ruler of a resurgent Austria. She surrounded herself with men of talent and vision, such as Count Wenzel Anton von Kaunitz and Count Frederick Wilhelm von Haugwitz, and together they transformed the ramshackle Habsburg Empire into a modern state.

The struggle for Silesia, begun in the 1740's and renewed in the 1750's, marked the opening chapter in the so-called Struggle for Supremacy in central Europe between Austria and Prussia, a conflict that would last until 1866. In the war fought between them in that year, Prussia destroyed Austria's historic preeminence and substituted its own, thus laying the foundations for German unification without the inclusion of Austria.

—Edward P. Keleher,
updated by Clifton W. Potter, Jr.

FURTHER READING

Dickson, Peter G. M. *Finance and Government Under Maria Theresa, 1740-1780.* 2 vols. New York: Oxford University Press, 1987. This work is absolutely essential to an understanding of the transformation of Austria under the empress.

Dorn, Walter L. *Competition for Empire, 1740-1763*. Vol. 9 in *The Rise of Modern Europe*, edited by William L. Langer. New York: Harper & Row, 1940. Dorn presents a concise discussion of the cumbersome structure of early eighteenth century Austria in this volume, which is still valued as a standard work.

Ingrao, Charles W. *The Habsburg Monarchy, 1618-1815*. 2d ed. New York: Cambridge University Press, 2000. Describes how the Habsburg state emerged as a military and cultural power of enormous influence. Includes information on the reign of Maria Theresa.

Macartney, Carlie Aylmer. *Maria Theresa and the House of Austria*. London: English Universities Press, 1970. Written by a recognized authority on eighteenth century Austria, this work concentrates on the reforms that ensured the survival of the Empire.

McGill, William J., Jr. *Maria Theresa*. New York: Twayne, 1972. A scholarly biography free of the sentimental treatment of the empress found in many earlier works.

Pick, Robert. *Empress Maria Theresa: Her Early Years, 1717-1757*. New York: Harper & Row, 1966. Maria Theresa emerges as a skilled ruler, a wife, a mother, and a woman of extraordinary talents in this very readable biography.

Szabo, Franz A. J. *Kaunitz and Enlightened Absolutism, 1753-1780*. New York: Cambridge University Press, 1994. Biography of Count Wenzel Anton von Kaunitz, state chancellor of the Habsburg monarchy from 1753 to 1792, who helped Maria Theresa administer and modernize the Habsburg state. The book includes a great deal of information about Maria Theresa and her reign.

Thomson, M. A. "The War of the Austrian Succession." In *The New Cambridge Modern History*, edited by J. O. Lindsay. Vol. 7. Cambridge, England: Cambridge University Press, 1957. The account of the War of the Austrian Succession is particularly valuable for the nonspecialist.

SEE ALSO: Nov. 20, 1710-July 21, 1718: Ottoman Wars with Russia, Venice, and Austria; Mar. 7, 1714, and Sept. 7, 1714: Treaties of Rastatt and Baden; 1736-1739: Russo-Austrian War Against the Ottoman Empire; Nov. 18, 1738: Treaty of Vienna; May 31, 1740: Accession of Frederick the Great; Dec. 16, 1740-Nov. 7, 1748: War of the Austrian Succession; Oct. 18, 1748: Treaty of Aix-la-Chapelle; 1775-1790: Joseph II's Reforms.

RELATED ARTICLES in *Great Lives from History: The Eighteenth Century, 1701-1800*: Charles VI; André-Hercule de Fleury; Frederick the Great; George II; Wenzel Anton von Kaunitz; Maria Theresa.

December 16, 1740-November 7, 1748

WAR OF THE AUSTRIAN SUCCESSION

For eight years, the nations of Western and central Europe battered one another over dynastic, economic, and territorial concerns. Austria, Britain, and Piedmont-Sardinia led one side, while France and Spain anchored the other. In the end, the ruling families remained in power, territorial changes were paltry, and economic rivalries continued unabated.

ALSO KNOWN AS: First and Second Silesian Wars; King George's War

LOCALE: Northwestern Germany; the Netherlands; northwestern Italy; Bohemia

CATEGORIES: Wars, uprisings, and civil unrest; expansion and land acquisition

KEY FIGURES

Frederick the Great (1712-1786), king of Prussia, r. 1740-1786

Maria Theresa (1717-1780), archduchess of Austria and queen of Hungary, r. 1740-1780

Louis XV (1710-1774), king of France, r. 1715-1774

Charles VII (Charles Albert Wittelsbach; 1697-1745), elector of Bavaria, r. 1726-1745 and Holy Roman Emperor, r. 1742-1745

Charles Emmanuel III (1701-1773), king of Sardinia-Piedmont, r. 1730-1773

Charles Fouquet de Belle-Isle (1684-1761), French diplomat and general

Maurice, Comte de Saxe (1696-1750), marshal of France

1740's

SUMMARY OF EVENT

In 1740, Louis XV's France dominated Europe. Habsburg Austria sought to maintain its premier position in central Europe by curbing French influence among the German states of the Holy Roman Empire and guaranteeing Dutch autonomy. Likewise, Hanoverian Great Britain preferred a weaker France and financially subsidized the Austrians and the Dutch to further this end. Britain also vied with Bourbon Spain and France for power at sea, especially in the Caribbean, and for colonial hegemony in India and the Americas. Philip V's Spain wished to retain its Caribbean power bases and to establish one in Italy for the king's younger son, Prince Philip, whose mother hailed from the region around Parma.

Meanwhile, Frederick William I, king of Prussia, had developed the military power of his rising state to a fine edge but had refrained from using it. Britain had begun the maritime War of Jenkins's Ear with Bourbon Spain in October, 1739. In May, 1740, Frederick William died, and young Frederick the Great mounted Prussia's throne. On October 20, Holy Roman Emperor and Austrian archduke Charles VI died, after negotiating assurances from the powers of Europe that his daughter and heir, Maria Theresa, would be allowed to succeed to his throne. Maria Theresa sought the election of her husband, Grand Duke Francis Stephen of Tuscany, as the

new Holy Roman Emperor, while France sought to curb Habsburg power by supporting the election of the Wittelsbach elector of Bavaria, Charles Albert. Frederick the Great took advantage of Maria Theresa's unstable position by invading Silesia (December 16), a portion of Habsburg Bohemia. With this invasion, the War of the Austrian Succession had begun.

Austria responded to Frederick's invasion with a counterattack, but Frederick defeated this strike at the Battle of Mollwitz (April 11, 1741). Frederick also acted diplomatically: He negotiated the Treaty of Breslau (June 4) with France, gaining French acquiescence to his seizure of Silesia in return for his own promise to abandon his claims to Jülich-Berg. Both states also agreed to support the Bavarian imperial candidate.

George II of Great Britain initially supported Austria, but he withdrew his support in April after a British assault on Spanish colonial Cartegena failed. Saxony joined Prussia, France, and Bavaria against Austria in the Second Treaty of Nymphenburg (September 19). Saxon, French, and Bavarian troops poured into Bohemia and

Austrian soldiers captured at the Battle of Hohenfriedberg are marched past an army of the Quadruple Alliance. (R. S. Peale and J. A. Hill)

headed for Vienna. Prague fell on November 26. Prussia secretly withdrew from the alliance in October but rejoined in January, 1742, in order to participate in any peacemaking. By year's end, with most of Silesia, Bohemia, and Moravia overrun, Austria was on the ropes. On January 24, 1742, Charles Albert Wittelsbach of Bavaria was elected emperor as Charles VII.

Austria mounted bold counterattacks in the winter of 1742. It pushed Frederick back and took the conflict into Bavaria. Further Austrian offensives drove the French back as well and led Frederick to make peace with Maria Theresa by signing the Treaty of Berlin (July 28), which guaranteed his control of Silesia and ended the so-called First Silesian War. Saxony followed suit shortly after in the Treaty of Dresden.

Meanwhile, Spain landed an army in Italy with the intention of seizing part of Habsburg-controlled Lombardy to create a principality for Prince Philip. In February, Neighboring Piedmont-Sardinian ruler Charles Emmanuel III countered by joining Austria and Britain, whose fleet alone could stop Spanish reinforcements. An Austrian army pushed the Spaniards aside and headed for Spanish Naples, resurrecting an old dynastic claim. A second Spanish army took Piedmontese Savoy in late summer, which drew Austria's allies away from Lombardy and halted the Habsburg advance. After the failure of a relief force, the French troops trapped in Prague, led by Charles Fouquet de Belle-Isle, escaped in a daring winter breakout. By Christmas, 1742, Austria was victorious everywhere.

The year 1743 brought further Spanish defeats in Italy, particularly in the Battle of Campo Santo (February 8), and brought an allied force of British, Austrian, Hanoverian, and Hessian troops into French-dominated Bavaria. Charles VII fled Munich and settled with Austria in the Niederschönfeld Convention. The allies retreated north, narrowly avoiding destruction by the French at Dettingen (June 27). In the Treaty of Worms (September 17), Austria, Piedmont, and Britain organized their Italian and Mediterranean forces against Spain, while Spain gained France as an ally in the Treaty of Fontainebleau (October 25).

Meanwhile, in January, 1743, France completed preparations for an invasion of England, but the ships and materiel were destroyed by a powerful gale. On February 22-23, a British attack near Toulon crippled the combined Bourbon fleets, preventing France from sending any reinforcements to Italy by sea. Finally, on March 15, France declared war on Britain. Two weeks later, a French army crossed into northern Italy and advanced

into Piedmont. Despite this development, the main Austrian army in Italy broadened the conflict by unsuccessfully invading Spanish Naples in the summer. Following the Peace of Paris (June 5), which allied France and Prussia against Austria, France invaded the Austrian Netherlands. Austria countered by invading Alsace and Lorraine, and Frederick reentered the war by invading Bohemia (August 15). Frederick's gains were short-lived, and he was forced into a winter retreat, as were the French in Piedmont. Emperor Charles VII took the opportunity to regain Munich, but he died prematurely in January, 1745.

On January 8, 1745, Austria joined Saxony, Britain, and the Dutch in the Quadruple Alliance. Maria Theresa neutralized Bavaria through the Treaty of Füssen (April 22). She then turned on Frederick in Silesia but was bloodily checked at Hohenfriedberg (June 4), and Frederick proceeded into Bohemia yet again, defeating yet another Austrian army at Soor (September 30). He then overran Saxony, driving its elector into Bavaria and defeating still another Austrian force at Kesselsdorf (December 15). Austria settled this Second Silesian War in the Treaty of Dresden (December 25), and Prussia left the war.

France's Marshal Maurice, comte de Saxe, began a three-and-one-half-year campaign in the Austrian Netherlands in March. He defeated an allied army at Fontenoy (May 11) and captured Tournai on June 20. By October, he controlled half of this Austrian territory. In Italy, Bourbon armies wrested most of Lombardy away from the Austrians and split them from their Piedmontese allies. The French also froze the British by supporting Charles Edward, the Stuart Pretender, who led a Scots army to within a few days' march of London. France suffered setbacks, however, when the Canadian fortress of Louisbourg fell to the British in June, and Francis Stephen was crowned Emperor Francis I on September 13.

The campaigns of 1746 saw Saxe victorious in the Austrian Netherlands, but the Bourbon armies were flung out of Piedmont and Lombardy to seek shelter in Genoa. The Scots army was smashed at Culloden (April 27), freeing Britain once again, and Spanish monarch Philip V died, softening the Versailles-Madrid axis. Exhausted belligerents throughout Europe groped at peace, but each on his own terms. In 1747, the war in northwest Italy ground down to a stalemate, the French invasion of Dutch soil touched off a revolution that made William IV of Orange the national leader, and the British navy all but destroyed French sea power in two oceans. The Low

Countries remained a killing field, and Britain even arranged for a Russian army of thirty-seven thousand men to aid the beleaguered allies. Though 1748 opened with new commitments of troops in the Netherlands and northern Italy, the diplomats hammered out an agreement that became the Treaty of Aix-la-Chapelle. An armistice in Europe ended hostilities on June 15, and the document was signed by all belligerents between October 18 and November 7, 1748.

SIGNIFICANCE

The War of the Austrian Succession witnessed some of the largest troop concentrations and bloodiest battles in European history up to that time. By one conservative estimate, 100,000 men lost their lives on the battlefields, and scores of thousands died in sieges and brutal occupations. Though little territory was exchanged, the war did lead to major diplomatic shifts. In Germany, the dualism of Austria and Bavaria was replaced by dueling Austria and Prussia. Frederick's victories ensured Prussia's place in the European power structure, and he aligned Prussia with Britain against France, helping to curb French hegemony in Europe. At sea, the British exhibited clear dominance and set the pattern for the next two centuries. Austria sought and obtained a lasting relationship with Russia and a more surprising if shorter-lived one with France, a development sometimes called the Diplomatic Revolution. Most significant, the failure to resolve deep-rooted issues resulted in a peace that would last less than a decade.

—Joseph P. Byrne

FURTHER READING

Anderson, M. S. *War of the Austrian Succession, 1740-1748*. Boston: Pearson, 1995. Scholastic text by a renowned expert on eighteenth century war and diplomacy.

Browning, Reed. *The War of Austrian Succession*. New York: St. Martin's Press, 1995. Well-organized, detailed, and lively narrative and analytical account of the war.

Childs, John. *Armies and Warfare in Europe, 1648-1789*. New York: Holmes and Meier, 1982. Examines the history of warfare and military units in Europe.

Horn, D. B. *Great Britain and Europe in the Eighteenth Century*. New York: Oxford University Press, 1967. Close study of Britain's concerns for the European balance of power and its diplomatic and military efforts to effect it.

Wangermann, Ernst. *The Austrian Achievement, 1700-1800*. New York: Thames and Hudson, 1973. Places the war in the context of Austrian national development in the eighteenth century.

SEE ALSO: 1739-1741: War of Jenkins's Ear; May 31, 1740: Accession of Frederick the Great; Oct. 20, 1740: Maria Theresa Succeeds to the Austrian Throne; Aug. 19, 1745-Sept. 20, 1746: Jacobite Rebellion; Oct. 18, 1748: Treaty of Aix-la-Chapelle.

RELATED ARTICLES in *Great Lives from History: The Eighteenth Century, 1701-1800*: Charles VI; Frederick the Great; Frederick William I; George II; Louis XV; Maria Theresa; Philip V; Comte de Saxe.

1741
LEADHILLS READING SOCIETY PROMOTES LITERACY

As part of a wide range of reforms of the local lead-mining industry, the creation of the Leadhills Reading Society, a kind of subscription library, helped make the town's lead-mining company a model for the rest of the industrial world. Miners and their families could check out and read the library's books, and then reflect on what they read. The reading society thus promoted both literacy and critical thinking.

LOCALE: Leadhills, Scotland

CATEGORIES: Education; social issues and reform; philosophy

KEY FIGURES

James Stirling (1692-1770), Scottish mathematician

John Locke (1632-1704), English philosopher

Allan Ramsay (1684-1758), Scottish poet

SUMMARY OF EVENT

The town of Leadhills is located high in the mountains of southwestern Scotland in the middle of an area that has been mined for lead and other minerals for more than six hundred years. The village was originally called Hopetoun, which was also an appropriate name. Great hopes inspired the reforms instituted by the Scots Mines Company in the 1740's.

Lead miners in this area had been serfs until 1695. Later, some of the miners were recruited from local prisons to fill labor shortages. The work was dangerous and difficult, and most of the men were a rough-and-tumble lot. A basis for reform within the lead-mining industry in Leadhills already existed in the system of "bargaining" that had developed earlier. Work was done according to specific contracts negotiated with small groups of miners. This system put a higher premium on individual intelligence and initiative than did, for example, the larger-scale operations being run at the same time by the coal-mining companies.

The central figure behind the reforms was James Stirling, a Scotsman whose original genius was in mathematics. He attended Oxford University and became a colleague of Sir Isaac Newton. Stirling had lived in Venice, Italy, for many years and worked with mathematician Nikolaus Bernoulli at the University of Padua. He returned to London and was elected a fellow of the Royal Society of London, but his career as a mathematician was frustrated by political complications. When Stirling was only seventeen years old, his father was arrested on suspicion of involvement in the Jacobite Rebellion of 1708. Archibald Stirling was acquitted of the charges, but the association seems to have followed his son. James Stirling never received an academic appointment commensurate with his talent and accomplishments in mathematics.

He accepted his fate with good grace, however. Much to the surprise of his associates in London, he left the city in 1735 to take a position as agent for the Scots Mines Company in charge of their operations in Leadhills. He was to receive £120 per year, and he soon proved to be well worth this sum to the company and to the men working in the mines.

Stirling brought a mathematical rigor to operations in the Leadhills mines and regularly inspected the day-books or journals of the overseers. He used the increased information flow to improve safety conditions, and he limited underground shifts to six hours to help slow the potential for lead poisoning. He introduced pensions, sick days, and a charity fund for emergency relief. A physician and a schoolteacher were brought into town for the benefit of the community. Workers and their families were encouraged to build their own houses and reclaim ground in the area for the cultivation of gardens. With the cooperation of the earl of Hopetoun, they also acquired limited rights to transfer the property they developed to other employees of the company. The liquor shops in the village were closed, and drinking was tightly controlled.

Stirling's reform led directly to the founding of the Leadhills Reading Society, the first subscription library in Britain. Members paid a set fee to join and then yearly or monthly dues to remain in the club. The original Leadhills club charged five pence to join and four pence in annual dues. The library eventually developed a recreational dimension, but at first it focused on occupational and moral education. Along with the miners, the local schoolmaster and the minister were among the original twenty-three members. The society was governed by regular meetings, and the annual general meeting selected a secretary, treasurer, librarian, and three inspectors. The librarian kept records of circulation and the inspectors kept track of the condition of the books. The length of time a member was allowed to keep a book depended on the book's length.

A committee of twelve was selected to buy books. At first, the selection tended to be largely religious in nature and included Henry Scougal's *Life of God in the Soul of Man* (1677), Hugo Grotius's *The Truth of the Christian Religion* (1683), Louis Ellies Du Pin's church history (1718), Gilbert Burnet's *An Exposition of the Thirty-Nine Articles of the Church of England* (1699), and Matthew Henry's *The Communicant's Companion* (1704). Professional and technical materials were also circulated through the Reading Society. These were intended to increase understanding of the lead-mining business and improve job performance underground. Indeed, mining in Leadhills came to define the cutting edge of the technology.

The Reading Society grew and matured, leading to the acquisition of more fiction and poetry. One of the most popular writers in this vein was hometown prodigy and poet Allan Ramsay, a precursor to great Scottish poets such as Robert Ferguson and Robert Burns: *The Gentle Shepherd* (1725) is his best-known work. The son of a former Leadhills mine manager, Ramsay moved to Edinburgh at a young age and founded a circulating library there called the Easy Club around 1720. He is generally considered to have been a major inspiration to the Leadhills Reading Society, and for a time it even bore his name.

SIGNIFICANCE

The preamble to the original rules drawn up in 1743 to govern the Leadhills Reading Society begins with the following words: "We, subscribers, having agreed to form Ourselves into a SOCIETY, in order to purchase a Collection of Books, for our mutual Improvement, [do set forth] certain ARTICLES, to be observed by us, for the Establishment and Regulation of this our Society. . . ."

The key concept in the preamble was "mutual improvement," which explains the reading society's phi-

1740's

losophy. Self-improvement, even in collaboration with others, was a radical idea at the time, marking a historic shift in the ways individuals thought of themselves and their place in the world. According to traditional medieval ideology, one's place was fixed at birth. The only form of improvement possible was to accept one's position in the great chain of being that had been ordained by God. To question the social hierarchy or imagine rising within it was treasonous or, worse, blasphemous.

Perhaps the most important philosopher of the Enlightenment to articulate this change in thinking was John Locke. In *An Essay Concerning Human Understanding* (1690) he described the individual as a blank sheet of paper—a tabula rasa—upon which anything could be written. In other words, through experience and education individuals could improve themselves and grow intellectually, providing the means for contributing to society according to one's learned abilities and not merely according to one's place in the social hierarchy. The Leadhills Reading Society was an early attempt to put this fundamental Enlightenment ideal into practice.

—*Steven Lehman*

FURTHER READING

Battles, Matthew. *Library: An Unquiet History.* New York: Norton, 2003. A history of libraries as well as the forces in history that try to destroy information and communication.

Harris, Michael H. *History of Libraries in the Western World.* Metuchen, N.J.: Scarecrow Press, 1995. A general survey of library history, originally published in 1984.

Locke, John. *An Essay Concerning Human Understanding.* New York: Dover, 1959. Originally published in 1690, Locke's work sets forth a philosophical basis for educational reform.

Tweedle, Charles. *James Stirling: A Sketch of His Life and Works, Along with His Scientific Correspondence.* Oxford, England: Clarendon Press, 1922. An older, still valuable biography of Stirling, perhaps the only one of its kind.

Vincent, David. *The Rise of Mass Literacy.* Cambridge, England: Polity, 2000. Vincent examines how eighteenth century ideas about literacy and reading were practiced in the nineteenth century.

SEE ALSO: July 9, 1701: Marsh Builds Ireland's First Public Library; 1795: Murray Develops a Modern English Grammar Book.

RELATED ARTICLES in *Great Lives from History: The Eighteenth Century, 1701-1800:* Mary Astell; Johann Bernhard Basedow; John Newbery; John Witherspoon.

1742
CELSIUS PROPOSES AN INTERNATIONAL FIXED TEMPERATURE SCALE

Anders Celsius conducted a series of precise experiments that demonstrated that the melting point of snow or ice and the boiling point of water, when adjusted for atmospheric pressure, were universal constants. He used these results to establish a uniform temperature scale, which allowed the calibration of thermometers worldwide.

LOCALE: Uppsala, Sweden
CATEGORIES: Chemistry; science and technology

KEY FIGURES

Anders Celsius (1701-1744), Swedish astronomer
Daniel Gabriel Fahrenheit (1686-1736), German physicist
Carolus Linnaeus (1707-1778), Swedish physician and botanist
Jean Pierre Christin (1683-1755), French scientist

SUMMARY OF EVENT

Although it is relatively easy for humans to determine that the temperature in a room is "hot" or "cold," or to compare the temperatures of two objects by touching them, the scientific measurement of the temperature of an object developed relatively recently. Galileo, an Italian mathematician and physicist, is generally credited with inventing the thermometer in 1592. Galileo's thermometer worked on the principle that fluids and solids expand or contract as the temperature changes. Accordingly, he placed water in a glass bulb and the surface of the water moved up and down in the bulb as the temperature of the water changed.

The German physicist and inventor Daniel Gabriel Fahrenheit significantly improved on the design of the thermometer. He filled capillary tubes with alcohol, beginning in 1709, or with mercury, beginning in 1714, so the expansion of the fluid produced a significant change in its height. Fahrenheit's thermometers were capable of precise temperature measurements.

Even with Galileo's invention of the thermometer, there was no simple way to ensure that thermometers built by different people in different places around the world would read the same numerical value for the temperature of an object. Thermometers must be calibrated in order for their readings to be compared. Such calibration requires that readings be taken at two standard temperatures, which are called fixed points. The positions of these fixed points are noted and the number of divisions between the fixed points is specified, providing a numerical scale for the thermometer. Thermometers were used in meteorology, in agriculture, and sometimes indoors, so it was natural that scientists chose fixed-point temperatures within the temperature range of interest in those fields.

A major difficulty in the initial development of thermometer scales was deciding how to define the fixed points such that thermometers could be calibrated easily and reproduced all over the world. In the early years of temperature measurement, there were many different fixed points in use, but no one knew with certainty if any of these points were truly fixed. Fahrenheit constructed mercury thermometers with scales that used fixed-points at the freezing point of water, set at 32 degrees, and to human body temperature, set at 96 degrees.

It was easy to demonstrate, however, that normal body temperature varies a bit during the day, even in a single individual, and it can vary significantly in an individual who is ill. In addition, two individuals are likely to have slightly different body temperatures. Thus, human body temperature is not truly a fixed point, and two thermometers calibrated using human body temperature as a fixed point will not necessarily record exactly the same temperature for an object. A variety of other fixed points, including the melting point of butter, had been suggested by other scientists. Scientists recognized that they needed to find physical phenomena that occurred at precisely the same temperature all around the world. These phenomena could then be used as the fixed points to calibrate thermometers.

FIXED REFERENCE POINTS ON THE INTERNATIONAL TEMPERATURE SCALE		
Kelvin	*Celsius*	*Reference Point*
13.81 K	−259.34 C	Triple point of hydrogen*
17.042 K	−256.108 C	Liquid and gaseous states of hydrogen are in equilibrium at a given pressure
20.28 K	−252.87 C	Hydrogen boils
27.102 K	−246.048 C	Neon boils
54.361 K	−218.789 C	Triple point of oxygen
90.188 K	−182.962 C	Oxygen boils
273.16 K	0.01 C	Triple point of water
373.15 K	100.00 C	Water boils
692.73 K	419.58 C	Zinc freezes
1,235.08 K	961.93 C	Silver freezes
1,337.58 K	1,064.43 C	Gold freezes

*The "triple point" refers to the temperature at which a chemical element exists simultaneously (or in equilibrium) in the gaseous, liquid, and solid states.

Anders Celsius, a Swedish astronomer, became interested in problems of weights and measures, including temperature measurements, early in his career. As a student, Celsius assisted Erik Burman, a professor of astronomy at Uppsala University, in meteorological observations. At that time, there was no accepted standard for thermometers. Thus, it was impossible to compare temperature readings taken in different places, unless the same thermometer was taken from place to place or the two researchers used thermometers that had been calibrated against each other, a tedious system similar to synchronizing watches.

In 1702, Ole Rømer, a Danish astronomer, developed one of the first temperature scales. Rømer's scale was based on two physical phenomena, the boiling point of water and the temperature at which snow begins to form. Rømer had to wait until it snowed, however, to calibrate a new thermometer, and this technique would work only in parts of the world that received snow.

Since human body temperature had been shown to vary from individual to individual and from time to time in the same individual, it was important to demonstrate that any fixed points that were selected were truly universal standards. It had been established by this time, for example, that the freezing point of water varied if contaminants were dissolved in the water. For example, salt water from the ocean freezes at a significantly lower temperature than does pure water. Celsius attacked the problem of establishing a universal temperature scale by conducting a series of careful experiments. He determined

1740's

that the temperature at which pure water, in his case newly fallen snow, melts is independent of latitude and also independent of atmospheric pressure. Thus, the melting point of snow, or of pure water ice, could serve as one of the fixed points of a reliable temperature scale.

The boiling point of water posed more of a problem. Celsius showed that it did not depend on latitude, but it did vary with atmospheric pressure. Celsius measured the dependence of the boiling point of pure water on atmospheric pressure. Atmospheric pressure could be measured accurately using a barometer, which had been invented by the Italian physicist Evangelista Torricelli, one of Galileo's students, in 1643. Celsius determined that the variation of the boiling point of water relative to changes in atmospheric pressure is a constant value, and he prepared charts showing water's boiling point as different pressures. (His measurements are in good agreement with modern measurements as well.) Thus, by comparing a measurement of the boiling point of pure water with a measurement of the atmospheric pressure at which it boiled, it was possible to set the second fixed point for the calibration of a thermometer.

In 1742, Celsius published his results in the annals of the Royal Swedish Academy of Sciences in a paper titled "Observationer om twänne beständiga Grader på en Thermometer" (observations on two persistent degrees on a thermometer). In this paper, Celsius proposed a three-step procedure for calibrating a thermometer. First, the thermometer was to be placed in thawing snow or ice made from pure water and the freezing point of water was marked on the thermometer as 100 degrees. Second, the thermometer was placed in boiling water, and that point, appropriately adjusted for the measured atmospheric pressure, was marked as 0 degrees. Third, the distance between the two points was divided into one hundred equal units.

There was one major difference between the temperature scale developed by Celsius and the temperature scale used in the twenty-first century. Celsius created an inverted scale, in which higher numbers indicated increased cold rather than increased heat. Carolus Linnaeus may have been the first scientist to reverse Celsius's scale, putting the freezing point of water at 0 degrees and the boiling point at 100 degrees. However, Linnaeus's thermometers, as well as many of those used by Celsius, were built by Daniel Ekström, and it is unknown if Linneaus or Ekström actually initiated the scale reversal. A Frenchman named Jean Pierre Christin has also been suggested as the source of the inversion.

The modified temperature scale became popular in

Sweden and France in particular. It was referred to as the centigrade scale, because it was based upon one hundred equal divisions between two fixed points. It is now called the Celsius scale, honoring its inventor.

SIGNIFICANCE

From the scientific point of view, the most important contributions to the modern temperature scale were those of Celsius, because his careful experiments established two universal fixed points, which allowed thermometers built in different laboratories to be calibrated using the same temperature scale. After Celsius developed this universal temperature scale, it was possible to measure temperature very accurately, allowing comparison of results from one laboratory to another. Scientists were then able to determine how various physical properties of materials vary with temperature.

Thus, the development of a universal temperature scale was essential, for example, to the understanding of the expansion of gases as a function of their temperature and of similar changes in the volumes of liquids and solids that depend on temperature. Later, it was established that thermal and electrical conductivity also vary with temperature. The development of a universal temperature scale allowed weather records to be compared from one location to another, resulting in the eventual understanding of weather patterns and the development of weather forecasting.

—*George J. Flynn*

FURTHER READING

Asimov, Isaac. *The History of Physics*. New York: Walker, 1966. Designed for nonspecialists, this book includes an excellent chapter on temperature, including a section on temperature scales that describes Celsius's contribution and its historical context.

Chang, Hasok. *Inventing Temperature: Measurement and Scientific Progress*. New York: Oxford University Press, 2004. A 304-page account that traces the history of the development of temperature scales, including an excellent table of the various fixed points employed before Celsius established a universal standard.

Gardner, Robert, and Eric Kemer. *Science Projects About Temperature and Heat*. Berkeley Heights, N.J.: Enslow, 1994. An excellent, 128-page collection of experiments allowing students in middle school and higher to perform many of the classic experiments in the development of ideas about temperature and heat.

SEE ALSO: 1714: Fahrenheit Develops the Mercury Thermometer; 1729: Gray Discovers Principles of

Electric Conductivity; Beginning 1735: Linnaeus Creates the Binomial System of Classification; 1738: Bernoulli Proposes the Kinetic Theory of Gases; Oct., 1745, and Jan., 1746: Invention of the Leyden Jar.

RELATED ARTICLES in *Great Lives from History: The Eighteenth Century, 1701-1800*: Daniel Gabriel Fahrenheit; Carolus Linnaeus.

1742
FIELDING'S *JOSEPH ANDREWS* SATIRIZES ENGLISH SOCIETY

Originally intended as a retort to Samuel Richardson's Pamela, *a morally strident assessment of eighteenth century social relations, Fielding's* Joseph Andrews *emerged as a sweeping analysis of the foibles of eighteenth century materialism, social snobbery, and moral bankruptcy.*

LOCALE: England
CATEGORY: Literature

KEY FIGURES
Henry Fielding (1707-1754), English novelist, playwright, and political writer
Samuel Richardson (1689-1761), English author of *Pamela: Or, Virtue Rewarded*

SUMMARY OF EVENT
Henry Fielding's decision to write *The History of the Adventures of Joseph Andrews, and of His Friend Mr. Abraham Adams* (1742; commonly known as *Joseph Andrews*) grew out of his repugnance at reading Samuel Richardson's *Pamela: Or, Virtue Rewarded* (1740-1741). This story of a servant girl who successfully fends off her master's amorous advances until he agrees to marry her made Richardson, a printer-turned-author, an instant celebrity. Literary London relished the novel, a new form of writing that combined an exciting story with deep insight into its characters. Richardson found himself courted by the rich and famous, who clamored for more stories similar to this one.

Fielding was among the minority that found *Pamela* offensive and Richardson deficient in several ways. First, Fielding believed that what Richardson praised as Pamela's virtuous conduct was little more than a ploy to control her master and advance in society. He also felt that Richardson had a prurient interest in sexual matters, teasing his readers with hints of impending sexual activity. Fielding thought, too, that Richardson's attempt to present Pamela's story as if it were real was simply preposterous; the work was a fiction, and it deserved to be considered in that light.

Within months after *Pamela* made its appearance, Fielding issued *An Apology for the Life of Mrs. Shamela Andrews* (1741), a brief, anonymous riposte. Apparently not satisfied with his initial attack, he decided to write another tale, this time featuring Pamela's brother Joseph, who would serve as an example of genuine virtue. *Joseph Andrews* became, however, more than another attack on Richardson: In it, Fielding offered a satiric look at the society that applauded the conduct of Richardson's heroine.

Fielding hit upon a brilliant strategy for presenting his satire. Pamela's brother Joseph became an exemplar of chastity, while the village vicar, Parson Abraham Adams, was a model of charity. The adventures of these characters demonstrated how a society that values material possessions, promotes self-satisfaction and self-advancement, and supports long-held notions of the inherent superiority of the landed nobility continuously tramples on the key Christian virtues that Joseph and the parson were meant to represent. To make sure readers understood his position, Fielding created a narrator to tell the story and offer commentary on characters and situations. The narrator's frequent use of ironic understatement highlights the uncharitable or rapacious behavior of the people Joseph and Adams encounter.

By adopting the plot device of the journey, Fielding was able to place his principal characters in situations that exposed the evils of his society. In the novel, Joseph is a servant to Lady Booby, the aunt of the rakish villain whom Richardson calls "Squire B___" in *Pamela*. While in London, Joseph is expelled from Lady Booby's service for refusing her sexual advances. Dismayed, he travels back to the Booby estate in hopes of marrying his beloved Fanny, a servant girl. Along the way he is robbed and stripped of his clothes. Left for dead, he is ignored or reviled by a coach full of people, including a noble lady and a lawyer. Fortuitously, however, he is taken to an inn by the coach postillion.

At the inn, Joseph meets Adams, who is on his way to London to sell his sermons. When Adams learns there is

FIELDING ON THE MORAL FUNCTION OF WRITERS

Henry Fielding opens his Joseph Andrews *with a discussion of the importance of exemplary persons to guide the moral behavior of others and the calling of writers to portray such moral exemplars for the edification and betterment of society.*

It is a trite but true Observation, that Examples work more forcibly on the Mind than Precepts: And if this be just in what is odious and blameable, it is more strongly so in what is amiable and praiseworthy. Here Emulation most effectually operates upon us, and inspires our Imitation in an irresistable manner. A good Man therefore is a standing Lesson to all his Acquaintance, and of far greater use in that narrow Circle than a good Book.

But as it often happens that the best Men are but little known, and consequently cannot extend the Usefulness of their Examples a great way; the Writer may be called in aid to spread their History farther, and to present the amiable Pictures to those who have not the Happiness of knowing the Originals; and so, by communicating such valuable Patterns to the World, he may perhaps do a more extensive Service to Mankind that the Person whose Life originally afforded the Pattern.

Source: Henry Fielding, *Joseph Andrews.* In *"Joseph Andrews" and "Shamela."* (New York: Oxford University Press, 1999), p. 1.

no market for his work, the two men travel back home together, stopping at various inns and private homes where their strained financial circumstances make them dependent on strangers for sustenance. Their treatment at the hands of the various gentry, lawyers, innkeepers, and clergy they encounter provides an object lesson in how far eighteenth century society had strayed from the Christian principles to which it continued to give lip service.

As Fielding explains in the preface to the novel, his principal target is "affectation," or hypocrisy, a vice rampant at all levels of society. Nobles such as Lady Booby preach about their natural goodness, yet they are quick to use those beneath them on the social ladder to serve their own interests. It never crosses Lady Booby's mind, for example, that in trying to seduce Joseph she might be asking him to do something he abhors. She is concerned only because, in fulfilling her sexual appetite, she may be demeaning herself by pursuing a social inferior. On the other hand, the hypocrisy of people whose vanity prompts them to aspire to positions above their natural state is pilloried through the character of Lady Booby's maid, Mrs. Slipslop, a crone who fancies that she can have Joseph for herself.

Fielding's attack on the clergy is especially harsh. The contrast between the naïve but genuinely Christian Parson Adams and virtually every other clergyman in the novel exposes the hypocrisy of that profession. On sev-

eral occasions, Joseph and Adams find themselves in the presence of clergymen who refuse them alms, take from them what little they have, and complain vigorously about the demands of the poor on the Church and its ministers. Some are able to argue the most abstruse theological points but cannot find it in their hearts to act charitably toward those in need. A few even make fun of Adams for his poverty and his naïveté, expressing the belief that no respectable clergyman would allow himself to fall into such straits. Readers sensitive to the irony in the novel can see easily that Fielding has little use for ministers who willfully misunderstand their true calling.

In similar fashion, Fielding attacks the profession of law. Instead of using their knowledge to assist those in need, the lawyers and judges in *Joseph Andrews* practice their art for personal gain. Their obtuse language becomes a smoke screen behind which they can manipulate the law for the benefit of those who will provide handsome retainers or advance them in society. At one point in the novel, Adams and Joseph are condemned to prison because the person bringing charges against them is perceived to have greater influence and wealth. In Fielding's view, the perversion of law was particularly prevalent in his day, and the legal system required significant reform.

Given Fielding's attitude toward the law, it is not surprising that also scattered throughout the novel are satiric references to corrupt politicians, a group he had been criticizing for years. His authorship of a series of pamphlets and newspaper articles had made him an enemy of Prime Minister Robert Walpole's Whig administration. Fielding's attacks on the political establishment had been in part responsible for Parliament's passage of the Licensing Act to regulate the theaters in 1737, an act that Samuel Richardson supported.

Joseph Andrews also satirizes the romance, a literary genre it parallels and parodies simultaneously. Using the techniques of the burlesque and following the lead of his model, Miguel de Cervantes's *El ingenioso hidalgo don Quixote de la Mancha* (1605, 1615; *The History of the Valorous and Wittie Knight-Errant, Don Quixote of the Mancha,* 1612-1620; better known as *Don Quixote de la*

Mancha), Fielding transforms knights and ladies into footmen and serving wenches. Like Cervantes, Fielding uses the inflated language of romance to describe encounters that are little more than crude exchanges of fisticuffs. At the same time, however, he demonstrates the natural heroism and selflessness of Joseph Andrews and Parson Adams, who come to Fanny's rescue on numerous occasions when her virginity and her physical safety are threatened. Though commoners, Fielding's heroes are worthy of praise, because they struggle to uphold Christian virtues in a corrupt world.

SIGNIFICANCE

The publication of *Joseph Andrews* immediately established Fielding as Richardson's rival. Whereas Richardson treated sex and power with tragic seriousness and a Puritanical sensibility, Fielding found them subjects for comedy. Hence, *Joseph Andrews* is rightfully called the first comic novel in English. At the same time, it is the first novel directly or explicitly to promote social reform. The earlier satirical novel by Jonathan Swift, *Gulliver's Travels* (1726; originally entitled *Travels into Several Remote Nations of the World, in Four Parts, by Lemuel Gulliver, First a Surgeon, and Then a Captain of Several Ships*), had mounted an even harsher critique of British society, but it had disguised that critique behind allegory, representing England indirectly in fictional countries. Fielding attempted to hold the mirror directly up to England's social milieus, daring to show his readers his understanding of the world they shared.

Several years later, Fielding published what is generally thought his masterpiece, *The History of Tom Jones, a Foundling* (1749; commonly known as *Tom Jones*), which is longer but equally focused on social ills. His contemporaries Tobias Smollett and Laurence Sterne took up the novel form to great acclaim, and subsequent generations of writers have followed Fielding's example in linking comedy with social commentary. Most notable among Fielding's disciples is Charles Dickens (1812-1870), whose early novels seem consciously modeled on those of Fielding. The use of the intrusive narrator became a staple of the English novel, and writers such as Anthony Trollope used the technique to great advantage. In the twentieth century, the British novelist Evelyn

Waugh and the American William Faulkner were among a number of writers who produced works sharing many characteristics of *Joseph Andrews* and *Tom Jones*. Today, the tradition Fielding established remains vibrant.

—*Laurence W. Mazzeno*

FURTHER READING

Cleary, Thomas. *Henry Fielding: Political Writer.* Waterloo, Ont.: Wilfrid Laurier Press, 1984. This valuable study of the political context for all of Fielding's work includes a lengthy discussion of the political dimensions of *Joseph Andrews*.

Paulson, Ronald. *The Life of Henry Fielding.* Malden, Mass.: Blackwell, 2000. This biography by one of the most respected Fielding scholars of the twentieth century includes a chapter on *Joseph Andrews* that places the novel in the context of Fielding's life and writings.

Rivero, Albert J., ed. *Critical Essays on Henry Fielding.* New York: G. K. Hall, 1998. This collection contains three essays on *Joseph Andrews* that take advantage of "newer" critical theories to reinterpret the novel.

Rosengarten, Richard A. *Henry Fielding and the Narration of Providence.* New York: Palgrave, 2000. Rosengarten's brief monograph examines the theological and philosophical background of Fielding's novels, explaining how his view of human nature and the divine design of the world influenced the production of works such as *Joseph Andrews*.

Varey, Simon. *"Joseph Andrews": A Satire of Modern Times.* Boston: Twayne, 1990. A book-length study of the novel, Varey's work explains how Fielding uses satiric techniques to highlight the foibles of his society.

SEE ALSO: Apr. 25, 1719: Defoe Publishes the First Novel; 1721-1742: Development of Great Britain's Office of Prime Minister; 1726: Swift Satirizes English Rule of Ireland in *Gulliver's Travels*; 1740-1741: Richardson's *Pamela* Establishes the Modern Novel; Jan., 1759: Voltaire Satirizes Optimism in *Candide*.

RELATED ARTICLES in *Great Lives from History: The Eighteenth Century, 1701-1800*: Henry Fielding; Samuel Richardson; Jonathan Swift; Robert Walpole.

1740's

April 13, 1742
FIRST PERFORMANCE OF HANDEL'S *MESSIAH*

In an attempt to branch out from Italian opera, at which he was an acknowledged master, Handel composed Messiah, *an English concert oratorio that would become his most famous work. The oratorio achieved an effect for which Handel had been searching, combining artistic and popular appeal, and it has withstood both time and revision by other composers.*

LOCALE: Dublin, Ireland
CATEGORY: Music

KEY FIGURES
George Frideric Handel (1685-1759), German
    composer and musician
Charles Jennens (1700-1774), English librettist
Jonathan Swift (1667-1745), Irish satirist and dean of
    St. Patrick's Cathedral, Dublin, 1713-1745
Gottfried van Swieten (1734-1803), Austrian diplomat
    and music patron
Wolfgang Amadeus Mozart (1756-1791), Austrian
    composer

SUMMARY OF EVENT
On April 13, 1742, George Frideric Handel presented a new oratorio, *Messiah*, in Dublin, Ireland. Although German, Handel had enjoyed a successful career in London largely as a composer of Italian-style operas. However, taste in entertainment having changed, Handel turned to another large vocal form, oratorio, which appealed to a broader audience.

In fact, Handel invented the English concert version of the oratorio. By Handel's time, the oratorio was no longer intended for church performance. It had begun, like opera, in Italy, and, like opera, it was a three-part vocal work written in Italian, consisting of speechlike recitatives, melodic arias, and choruses, with instrumental accompaniment. Unlike opera, oratorio was performed without stage sets, costumes, or acting. Because of its simpler presentation and religious or devotional story line, oratorio was considered proper entertainment during the penitential season before Easter.

During the 1730's in Britain, the new ballad opera eclipsed elaborate Italian opera in popularity. Because ballad opera was lighter in style and subject matter and was performed in English rather than Italian, it appealed to the growing English middle class, attracting a wider audience. Handel began to lean toward writing oratorios

in English and successfully produced several such works. In 1739, Charles Jennens, a wealthy eccentric who had already provided Handel with libretti for several oratorios, showed him another, a compilation of biblical texts concerning the life and mission of Jesus Christ. Handel was occupied with another project and put Jennens's book aside temporarily.

By the summer of 1741, Handel was ready to consider the libretto his friend had given him. It is said that he was inspired by the text, and indeed, he might have been. In only three weeks, between August 22 and September 14, Handel finished writing the score, allegedly declaring that as he worked on the music he thought he had seen both God and Heaven.

Jennens's libretto for *Messiah* was unusual because it did not tell a story, as was customary for oratorio at that time. It consisted of three sections, but rather than dramatizing the life of Christ, it conveyed the message of Jesus's mission indirectly, through passages drawn from Old Testament prophecies of his coming, accounts in the Gospels of his birth and death, and verses from the book of Revelation declaring his redemption of humankind. Jennens conceived his text as an exercise in religious education for the audience.

Because Handel had been invited to present a series of six "musical entertainments" in Dublin, *Messiah* was first produced in that city rather than London, at Neale's new music hall in Fishamble Street. At first, Handel had trouble hiring enough singers for his chorus. The famous author Jonathan Swift, also dean of St. Patrick's Cathedral, balked at the idea of performing a sacred text in a theater and nearly refused to allow his singers to participate. He relented, but his feelings reflected a commonly held opinion and foreshadowed future problems.

Anticipation ran high. Foreseeing a large attendance, newspaper announcements requested that ladies not wear hoops under their skirts and that men leave their swords at home. The performance did not disappoint. *Messiah* was a resounding success in Dublin, drawing a huge audience and critical comments such as "sublime," "grand," and "tender" for the music and "elevated, majestic, and moving" for the text. One story about that first performance illustrates the audience's total involvement with the work: One female soloist was an acquaintance of Handel who had retired from the London stage because of well-publicized love affairs. When she finished the aria "He Was Despised," a member of the audience, the Reverend Dr. Delany, reportedly was so moved that he leaped to his feet, declaring that because of her performance her sins would be forgiven.

Encouraged by his success in Dublin, on March 23, 1743, Handel introduced *Messiah* at Covent Garden Theatre in London, where he was not so fortunate. Church officials, concerned as Swift had been in Dublin about the performance of a sacred text in a public hall, strenuously objected. The critics gave the work cool reviews. Even Jennens expressed disappointment in Handel's treatment of his libretto, declaring that the music was composed in too short a time to do justice to the text.

Handel moved on to other projects that redeemed him in the public's eye, and *Messiah* was nearly forgotten.

It was not until 1750 that Handel brought *Messiah* back. He used it to benefit London's Foundling Hospital, performing it in that institution's chapel—his only presentation of the work in a religious setting. From then on, *Messiah* was performed almost yearly at the Foundling Hospital and with increasing frequency in other locations as well, achieving great popularity by the time Handel died in 1759. In the years after Handel's death, *Messiah* continued to be a favorite. Massive performances of *Messiah*, involving hundreds, became quite popular. Its

A facsimile of the first page of George Frideric Handel's handwritten score of the Messiah. (North Wind Picture Archives)

publication in 1767 made the oratorio more widely available, and it went through several subsequent editions.

In 1789, at a concert in Vienna, *Messiah* received a performance that would change the way the work was presented for years thereafter. As a diplomat in England in the 1760's, Gottfried van Swieten had been impressed by Handel's music and had acquired a copy of the first edition of *Messiah*, which he took home to Austria. In 1789, van Swieten presented *Messiah* at several benefit concerts, having hired Wolfgang Amadeus Mozart to flesh out the accompaniment.

Although a small ensemble of strings, keyboard, and a few sparsely used winds made up *Messiah*'s original instrumentation, Handel himself augmented or diminished his forces depending on the availability of performers (and perhaps money to pay them). Mozart similarly modified the piece's ensemble: He replaced the keyboard with added strings and pairs of flutes, clarinets, oboes, bassoons, and horns, along with three trumpets and tympani. Van Swieten, meanwhile, made cuts in the text and reassigned solos. Their aim was to bring a by-then-old-fashioned masterpiece into the current style. Mozart's alterations were meant for a particular set of performances. Neither he nor van Swieten supposed that their work would become the standard for future performances of *Messiah*, but it did nonetheless. Because Mozart was an acclaimed master and because his alterations to the text and score were elegant and pleasing, his arrangement became the basis for most later revisions of the work. Only in the late twentieth century did Handel's original scoring again come to be used consistently.

One custom attached to *Messiah* has come down from its beginnings to the present. At the second London performance, King George II, who happened to be in attendance, suddenly stood up during the Hallelujah Chorus. Perhaps he was moved by the grandeur of the music. Perhaps he needed to stretch his legs (concerts at that time could last several hours). Whatever the reason, because it was against protocol to remain seated when the monarch stood, the entire audience rose to its feet, and a tradition was born that is still observed today.

SIGNIFICANCE

Handel wrote *Messiah* at a time when both composers and listeners had started to move away from the grand, complex Baroque style to lighter music that appealed to a wider audience. Handel understood this, and by writing oratorios in English that combined moving, melodic arias with stirring choruses, he became part of the transition between the Baroque and the classical styles. *Messiah* is a high point in Handel's career, and because it is unique, it remains the best-known work of a master composer and the most beloved of all oratorios.

—*JoAnne M. Rogers*

FURTHER READING

Buelow, George J. *A History of Baroque Music*. Bloomington: Indiana University Press, 2004. A good overview of Baroque music and Handel's place in that tradition.

Bullard, Roger A. *"Messiah": The Gospel According to Handel's Oratorio*. Grand Rapids, Mich.: Wm. B. Eerdmans-Lightning Source, 1993. A commentary on Jennens's libretto for *Messiah*.

Burrows, Donald. *Handel: Messiah*. New York: Cambridge University Press, 1991. This history of Handel's development of the English oratorio discusses the process of composing *Messiah*, up to its first performance.

Cottle, Andrew. "Mozart's Arrangement of *Messiah*." *Choral Journal* 31, no. 9 (April, 1991): 19-24. Mozart's changes to Handel's setting of *Messiah*.

Featherstone, J. Scott. *Hallelujah: The Story of the Coming Forth of Handel's "Messiah."* Eugene, Oreg.: ACW Press, 2001. A fictionalized account of Handel's life and the coming forth of *Messiah*.

Hogwood, Christopher. *Handel*. London: Thames & Hudson, 1984. A detailed account of Handel's life, development as a composer, and acceptance by audiences to the end of the twentieth century.

Larsen, Jens Peter. *Handel's Messiah: Origins, Composition, Sources*. New York: W. W. Norton, 1957. Examines Handel's development of English oratorio, surveys the *Messiah*, and discusses changes to text and music made by Handel to accommodate performance conditions.

Luckett, Richard, and Diane Sterling. *Handel's Messiah: A Celebration*. New York: Harvest/HBJ Books, 1995. Explores the musical and social background and performance history of the *Messiah*.

Myers, Robert Manson. *Handel's Messiah: A Touchstone of Taste*. New York: Octagon Books, 1971. A detailed account of Handel's career leading up to the *Messiah*. Includes discussion of its composition and performance history.

Robbins Landon, H. C. *Handel and His World*. Boston: Little, Brown, 1984. A compilation of earlier scholarship with corrections and commentary.

SEE ALSO: c. 1701-1750: Bach Pioneers Modern Music; Jan. 29, 1728: Gay Produces the First Ballad Opera;

Dec. 7, 1732: Covent Garden Theatre Opens in London; Jan., 1762-Nov., 1766: Mozart Tours Europe as a Child Prodigy; Oct. 5, 1762: First Performance of Gluck's *Orfeo and Euridice*; Apr. 27, 1784: First Performance of *The Marriage of Figaro*; 1795-1797:

Paganini's Early Violin Performances.

RELATED ARTICLES in *Great Lives from History: The Eighteenth Century, 1701-1800*: George II; George Frideric Handel; Wolfgang Amadeus Mozart; Jonathan Swift.

1743-1744
D'ALEMBERT DEVELOPS HIS AXIOMS OF MOTION

Drawing upon elements of Cartesian and Newtonian thought, d'Alembert formulated a set of laws describing the behavior of bodies in motion. The laws, all derived completely through mathematical calculation, combined to produce a general principle for solving problems in rational mechanics.

LOCALE: Paris, France
CATEGORIES: Physics; science and technology

KEY FIGURES
Jean le Rond d'Alembert (1717-1783), French mathematician, physicist, and *Encyclopedia* contributor
Alexis-Claude Clairaut (1713-1765), French Newtonian mathematician
Sir Isaac Newton (1642-1727), English scientist and mathematician
Daniel Bernoulli (1700-1782), Swiss physicist
René Descartes (1596-1650), French philosopher and mathematician

SUMMARY OF EVENT
Jean le Rond d'Alembert is probably best known for his collaboration with Denis Diderot on the *Encyclopédie: Ou, Dictionnaire raisonné des sciences, des arts, et des métiers* (1751-1772; partial translation *Selected Essays from the Encyclopedy*, 1772; complete translation *Encyclopedia*, 1965). His "Discours préliminaire" (preliminary discourse), which prefaced the work, was known and admired throughout Europe, and he was responsible for many of the *Encyclopedia*'s technical articles. A favorite in the salons of Paris, d'Alembert was involved in all aspects of the intellectual life of his century. Beyond these pursuits, however, d'Alembert was a mathematician and scientist of considerable expertise who made significant contributions in the field of rational mechanics. In 1741, he was admitted as a member to the French Academy of Sciences. There, he met, discoursed with, and competed with men such as Alexis-Claude Clairaut and Daniel Bernoulli.

D'Alembert received his first instruction in mathematics at the Jansenist Collège des Quatres Nations. In his classes, he was introduced to the work of Cartesian thinkers such as Pierre Varignon, Charles Reyneau, and Nicolas Malebranche. Thus, his early education in mathematics was strongly influenced by the ideas of René Descartes. This background did not, however, prevent d'Alembert from recognizing the value of Sir Isaac Newton's work. He read Newton's *Philosophiae Naturalis Principia Mathematica* (1687; *The Mathematical Principles of Natural Philosophy*, 1729; best known as the *Principia*) shortly after 1739 and Colin Maclaurin's *A Treatise of Fluxions* (1742), which gave detailed explanations of Newton's methods, before publishing his own *Traité du dynamique* (1743; treatise on dynamics) and *Traité de l'équilibre et du movement des fluides* (1744; treatise on equilibrium and on movement of fluids). D'Alembert believed that mathematics was the key to solving all problems. He rejected the use of experiments and observation. He maintained that rational mechanics was a component of mathematics along with geometry and analysis.

When d'Alembert set about writing his *Traité du dynamique*, an enormous amount of work had already been done on the laws of motion. Much of existing theory was contradictory, however, because of the problems involved in defining terms such as force, motion, and mass. D'Alembert was convinced that a logical foundation applicable to all mechanics could be found through the use of mathematics. Although d'Alembert insisted that he had rejected the theories of Descartes that he had studied in his youth, his approach to mechanics still relied heavily on Descartes's method of deduction. D'Alembert wished to discover laws of mechanics that would be as logical and self-evident as the laws of geometry. Above all, he was determined to "save" mechanics from being an experimental science.

D'Alembert, like his fellow scientists, was a great admirer of Newton, and Newton's *Principia* was for him the starting point in a study of mechanics. Thus, he developed his laws of mechanics using Newton's work as a model. In his first law, d'Alembert expressed his agreement with Newton's law of inertia, that is, that bodies do not change their state of rest or motion by themselves. They tend to remain in the same state; Newton would say, they remain in the same state until acted upon by a force. D'Alembert also was in accord with Newton's concept of hard bodies moving in a void.

D'Alembert, however, found Newton's second and third laws unacceptable, because they acknowledged force as real and relied upon experiments and observation. The logical geometric basis that he sought for the foundation of mechanics allowed no room for experiments and observations. Force was for d'Alembert a concept to be avoided because it did not lend itself to definition. He rejected not only innate force but all force. In contrast, Newton recognized force as having real existence. D'Alembert acknowledged that bodies would not move unless some external cause acted upon them but defined causes only in terms of their effects. His third law was similar to Newton's third law. Newton had stated that two bodies must act on each other equally. D'Alembert proposed the concept of equilibrium, resulting from two bodies of equal mass moving in opposite directions at equal velocities.

Because of his rejection of force as a scientific concept, d'Alembert was closer in his theories to Malebranche, who viewed the laws of motion as entirely geometrical, than he was to Newton. D'Alembert's laws of motion dealt with idealized geometrical figures rather than real objects. These figures moved through space until they impacted, causing them either to stop or to slip past one another. Change of motion was necessitated by geometry; force was an unnecessary element and only brought into play disturbing metaphysical concepts.

From the last two laws of his axioms of motion, d'Alembert derived what is now known as d'Alembert's principle: The impact of two hard bodies either is direct or is transmitted by an intermediate inflexible object or constraint. He applied his principle the next year in his *Traité de l'equilibre et du mouvements des fluides*, which was for the most part a criticism of Daniel Bernoulli's work on hydrodynamics. Although d'Alembert had used his principle successfully in his 1743 treatise, it failed to be very useful in fluid mechanics.

SIGNIFICANCE

During the eighteenth century, opinions about d'Alembert's contributions to science were many and varied. Some of his contemporaries credited him with having found a set of principles for rational mechanics; for some, his work verified Descartes's beliefs that the laws of mechanics could be deduced from matter and motion and that there was no force involved in movement. However, others criticized and rejected d'Alembert, because he refused to accept experimentation and simply eliminated concepts that he found resistant to mathematical expression. His most important contribution was d'Alembert's principle, which provided a general approach to solving mechanical problems. It was one of the first attempts to find simple and general rules for the movements of mechanical systems.

D'Alembert's laws of motion were accepted as the logical foundation of mechanics well into the nineteenth century. Ultimately, however, his refusal to discuss force proved to be a fatal flaw. Today, Newton's *Principia* is viewed as containing the basic laws of classical mechanics.

—*Shawncey Webb*

FURTHER READING

Greenberg, John L. *The Problem of the Earth's Shape from Newton to Clairaut: The Rise of Mathematical Science in Eighteenth Century Paris and the Fall of "Normal" Science*. New York: Cambridge University Press, 1995. Chronicles the spread of Newtonian physics in France and discusses d'Alembert's treatises. Readers need some scientific background.

Grimsley, Ronald. *Jean d'Alembert, 1717-1783*. Oxford, England: Clarendon Press, 1963. Considered the best biography of d'Alembert. Treats his literature and philosophy.

Hankins, Thomas L. *Jean d'Alembert: Science and the Enlightenment*. Oxford, England: Clarendon Press, 1970. Treats d'Alembert's many-faceted role in the science, culture, politics, and philosophical activities of the century. Useful for all readers.

_____. *Science and the Enlightenment*. Reprint. New York: Cambridge University Press, 1991. General history of science in the eighteenth century, placing it in the cultural context of the time and stressing the impact of science on thought of the period.

Porter, Roy, ed. *Eighteenth Century Science*. Vol. 4 in *The Cambridge History of Science*. New York: Cambridge University Press, 2003. Survey of the development of science; explores the implications of the Scientific Revolution of the seventeenth century and treats the social, political, and economic significance of science in the eighteenth century.

Shectman, Jonathan. *Groundbreaking Scientific Experiments, *Investigations, and Discoveries of the Eighteenth Century*. Westport, Conn.: Greenwood Press, 2003. Written for middle and high school students, college non-science majors, and general readers. Discusses science in the social and political climate of the period.

Yolton, John W., ed. *Philosophy, Religion, and Science in the Seventeenth and Eighteenth Centuries*. Rochester, N.Y.: University of Rochester Press, 1990. Examines the relationships of philosophy, science, and religion and their interactions in the works of René Descartes, Gottfried Wilhelm Leibniz, David Hume, and Sir Isaac Newton.

SEE ALSO: 1704: Newton Publishes *Optics*; 1718: Bernoulli Publishes His Calculus of Variations; 1723: Stahl Postulates the Phlogiston Theory; 1729: Gray

Discovers Principles of Electric Conductivity; 1733: De Moivre Describes the Bell-Shaped Curve; 1733: Du Fay Discovers Two Kinds of Electric Charge; 1738: Bernoulli Proposes the Kinetic Theory of Gases; 1740: Maclaurin's Gravitational Theory; 1748: Bradley Discovers the Nutation of Earth's Axis; 1748: Euler Develops the Concept of Function; 1759: Aepinus Publishes *Essay on the Theory of Electricity and Magnetism*; 1763: Bayes Advances Probability Theory; 1796: Laplace Articulates His Nebular Hypothesis.

RELATED ARTICLES in *Great Lives from History: The Eighteenth Century, 1701-1800*: Jean le Rond d'Alembert; Denis Diderot; Colin Maclaurin.

January 24, 1744-August 31, 1829
DAGOHOY REBELLION IN THE PHILIPPINES

The Dagohoy Rebellion was the longest-running successful revolt against Spanish colonizers in the history of the Philippine Islands. The extended conflict was representative of a lasting tradition of resistance to centralized control in the outer Philippine Islands and of the difficulties posed to any government that attempted to overcome that resistance.

LOCALE: Bohol Island, Visayas Province, Philippine Islands

CATEGORIES: Wars, uprisings, and civil unrest; government and politics; colonization

KEY FIGURES

Francisco Dagohoy (Franscico Sendrijas; d. c. 1829), Filipino rebel and military leader

Gaspar Morales (d. 1745), Spanish Jesuit curate of Inabanga

Mariano Ricafort (fl. 1825-1834), Spanish governor general of the Philippines, 1825-1830, and later governor of Cuba, 1832-1834

SUMMARY OF EVENT

The Dagohoy Rebellion was not unprecedented in the history of Spanish occupation and rule in the Philippine Islands. The Tamblot Uprising of 1621, led by a native priest, was the first such revolt to indicate the willingness of the people of Bohol Island to resist external control. The Dagohoy Rebellion, however, was, overwhelmingly, the more successful in freeing the Boholanos from

direct Spanish rule, for a variety of reasons. The terrain and remote location of the island, gradually dissipating Spanish strength in the Philippines, and the charisma and expertise of rebel leader Francisco Dagohoy all contributed to the uprising's success.

Accounts of the uprising's catalyst vary slightly, but in general, the uprising was motivated by Father Gaspar Morales's refusal to bury a constable with Christian rites. The constable had pursued and attempted to capture a lapsed Christian Filipino on Morales's orders, and the Filipino, resisting arrest, had killed him. Morales's refusal so incensed the constable's brother, one Francisco Dagohoy, that he incited local Inabangans and Talibonese to rise up against the Jesuit presence and Spanish crown in Bohol. A force of three thousand overwhelmed and killed Father Guiseppe Lamberti on January 24, 1744, before doing the same to the original perpetrator, Father Morales, a short time later. Dagohoy's initial three thousand followers soon increased to around twenty thousand, and they retreated to their strongholds in the Inabanga and Cayelanga Mountains in the interior of Bohol Island.

This Boholano force succeeded in defying repeated Spanish attempts to reassert control over the territory. Bishop Miguel Lino de Espeleta of neighboring Cebu island was the first to attempt to assuage the Dagohoy insurgents. He was unsuccessful, as were twenty attempts by Spanish governor generals to overturn the uprising by force between 1744 and 1825. General Mariano Ricafort, who became governor general of the Philippines in 1825, finally succeeded in subduing the Boholano patriots but not without a prolonged, four-year struggle. Ricafort was aided by Captain Manuel Sanz, who landed in Bohol in April, 1828, and, after a year of hard fighting, reestablished Spanish authority on August 31, 1829. Some nineteen thousand remaining insurgents were pardoned for their activities and relocated to Batuanan, Cabulao, Catigbian, and Vilar—local villages created to house these peoples.

The revolutionary exploits of Francisco Dagohoy were not limited to Bohol Island, or even to the numerous larger islands of Visayas Province. Dagohoy's success inspired numerous insurgencies throughout the colony, albeit none as successful as the Dagohoy Rebellion. The mountainous landscapes of these archipelagic islands were covered with lush, dense tropical vegetation, which provided a military advantage to the locals. Even so, the superiority of Spanish arms had quickly proved sufficient to overturn several uprisings in the outer islands both prior to and after 1744.

It was the expertise of Francisco Dagohoy in guerrilla warfare that enabled his followers to take advantage of the local terrain more effectively than other Filipino rebels. His strategic advice and training made the Dogohoy rebels difficult for the Spaniards to overcome. In addition, Dagohoy had the personal charisma and motivational skill to mobilize twenty thousand people at relatively short notice into a formidable resistance force, as well as the foresight and wherewithal to maintain his force over the long term. By 1770, he had as many as thirty thousand followers.

The longevity and effectiveness of the Dagohoy resistance was assisted by other factors as well. After the Spanish conquered Manila in 1571, they had followed their usual methods to establish a colonial presence. They had instituted centralized control of the colony, reallocated the best land among themselves, and conscripted Filipino labor through the *encomienda* system. Altogether, the Philippines experienced a typically oppressive Spanish colonial occupation. Spain's primary interests in the Philippines were as a base to serve potential expansion in East Asia, a production center for exotic spice exports, a source of new converts to Roman Catholicism, and another stage upon which to display to the world its status as a world power. The Philippines were half a world away, however, and they proved expensive to control.

The Philippine trade route actually deviated a bit from Ferdinand Magellan's original route around South America's Cape Horn. Trade ships sailed from Manila on the island of Luzon to Acapulco, Mexico. Goods moved thence overland to the Gulf of Mexico and thence to Havana, Cuba, before crossing the Atlantic to Seville, Spain. This trip made Philippine goods expensive, which, with time, diminished their value to the Spanish Empire. It also inflated the price of colonial control. By 1744, the ability of the Spanish to quell uprisings had gradually diminished, although they retained a concerted commitment to invest whatever resources were necessary to maintain control.

Spain's early attempts to subdue the Dagohoy movement netted only a few coastal garrisons but no control of the interior-based Boholanos. Moreover, the Spaniards' ability to accelerate their efforts was compromised by global events. Spain entered the Seven Years' War in 1761. A year later, the Spanish had suffered defeat in Havana, having lost some 20 percent of their navy and control of a major way station along the trade route serving the Philippines. Their Pacific influence was severely weakened.

Later in the eighteenth century, the success of both the American and French Revolutions served to inspire not only the Boholano resistance but resistance to Spain throughout their New World Empire. By the early nineteenth century, many of Spain's former colonies in the New World were nearing independence, and the cost of maintaining the empire weakened the Spanish more each year and further compromised the Manila-Acapulco-Havana trade linkage. It is a testament to the staggering amount of wealth generated through this particular colonial empire that it took so long completely to erode Spanish might, but the gradual weakening of Spain through the sum of all these activities contributed to the ability of the Dagohoy Rebellion to keep the Spanish at bay for such a long time. Eventually, however, after Dagohoy's death, the rebellion weakened. His heirs attempted to continue the resistance in his name but ultimately lacked the skills or the will to cement the permanence of the Dagohoy movement.

SIGNIFICANCE

The eighty-five years that the Dagohoy Rebellion succeeded in usurping Spanish control of this small part of the Philippines was by far the longest continuous successful rejection of Spanish authority anywhere in the New World. Although, or perhaps because, the longevity of the Dagohoy Rebellion was aided and inspired by global events, it signified the ultimate demise of Spain from the world leadership position it had enjoyed throughout the sixteenth and seventeenth centuries. Spanish insistence in devoting resources to maintain a hold on this remote, difficult to control outpost contributed to the speed with which the Spanish Empire lost its grip on European imperial supremacy.

—*James Knotwell*

FURTHER READING

Agoncillo, Teodoro A. *A History of the Filipino People.* 8th ed. Quezon City, Philippines: Garotech, 1990. Less detailed than the Zaide book, but the rebellion is discussed in the context of the larger body of Philippine history, which provides a different, useful perspective.

Zaide, Gregario. *Dagohoy: Champion of Philippine Freedom.* Manila, Philippines: Enriquez, Alduan, 1941.

Book-length accounts of this particular period in Philippine history are rare, and this is among the most useful.

SEE ALSO: May 26, 1701-Sept. 7, 1714: War of the Spanish Succession; 1704-1757: Javanese Wars of Succession; Aug., 1712: Maya Rebellion in Chiapas; Nov. 9, 1729, and Feb., 1732: Treaty of Seville; Nov. 18, 1738: Treaty of Vienna; 1750: Treaty of Madrid; 1752-1760: Alaungpaya Unites Burma; Sept., 1769-1778: Siamese-Vietnamese War; 1771-1802: Vietnamese Civil Wars; 1775: Spanish-Algerine War; 1776: Foundation of the Viceroyalty of La Plata; 1780-1781: Rebellion of Tupac Amaru II.

RELATED ARTICLES in *Great Lives from History: The Eighteenth Century, 1701-1800*: Charles III; Philip V.

1745
LOMONOSOV ISSUES THE FIRST CATALOG OF MINERALS

Soon after returning from scientific studies in Germany, Mikhail Vasilyevich Lomonosov began sorting and cataloging the mineral cabinet of the Kunstkammer *in St. Petersburg. His resulting catalog of more than thirty-five hundred mineral specimens was published in 1745.*

LOCALE: St. Petersburg, Russia
CATEGORIES: Geology; science and technology

KEY FIGURES

Mikhail Vasilyevich Lomonosov (1711-1765), Russian scientist, poet, and educator
Peter the Great (1672-1725), czar of Russia, r. 1682-1725
Elizabeth Petrovna (1709-1762), empress of Russia, r. 1741-1762
Peter Simon Pallas (1741-1811), German-born scientist and director of the St. Petersburg Mineral Cabinet, 1767

SUMMARY OF EVENT

The history of the A. E. Fersman Mineralogical Museum, one of the finest such museums in the world, begins with Czar Peter the Great's interest in science and his desire to bring science to the attention of the Russian people. By the close of the seventeenth century, Peter started collecting unusual biological and anatomical specimens, sparked by his first trip to Europe in 1679. He kept these specimens in what was then known as a *Kunstkammer*, German for "cabinet of curiosities."

In 1703, as part of Peter's desire to modernize and westernize Russia, he began construction of his new capital of St. Petersburg on the Baltic Sea. He was eager to show his *Kunstkammer* to ordinary Russians, to educate them, to stimulate their interest in Western science, and to impress them with the knowledge, resources, and wealth of their monarch. The cabinet thus began to be exhibited to visitors in Kikin's Palace, St. Petersburg, in 1714. In 1716, a collection of 1,195 mineral specimens was purchased from Dr. I. Gotvald, a physician in Gdańsk, as the base of a mineralogical collection called the Mineral Cabinet. Items of geological interest that Peter received as gifts from foreign leaders were added to the Mineral Cabinet. These included a 16-centimeter-long specimen of native silver wire known as the Silver Horn, given to him by the king of Sweden in 1718.

Peter the Great founded the St. Petersburg Academy of Sciences in 1724. Members of the academy were actively recruited from various European countries, especially Germany. The *Kunstkammer* was formally put in the control of the Academy of Sciences. Mining companies throughout Russia sent samples to the *Kunstkammer*'s Mineral Cabinet, and by the early 1740's, the collection included more than three thousand minerals, fossils, gems, and rocks. The responsibility for curating the Mineral Cabinet had fallen to Johann Gmelin, a German scientist, who had left St. Petersburg to participate in a Siberian expedition lasting from 1733-1743.

The Russian scientist Mikhail Vasilyevich Lomonosov returned to his native country in 1741. He had spent several years studying abroad and had received degrees in metallurgy at the University of Marburg and in mining engineering at the University of Freiburg, Austria. Lomonosov had returned to teach chemistry at the University of St. Petersburg, while Gmelin was still away on his Siberian expedition. Lomonosov was quickly made a member of St. Petersburg Academy of Sciences and appointed director of the Mineral Cabinet.

In 1742, Lomonosov was imprisoned for views hostile to the aristocracy and objections to certain academy policies. He continued to work while imprisoned and wrote two poems dedicated to Empress Elizabeth Petrovna, who decided to free him early in 1743. After his release from prison, Lomonosov resumed his duties as director of the Mineral Cabinet, cataloged the entire thirty-five-hundred-specimen collection, and published the results in 1745 under the auspices of the Russian academy. This was a precedent-setting accomplishment, in that it was the first research paper in mineralogy to be published by the St. Petersburg Academy of Sciences.

Lomonosov's catalog helped establish the reputation of St. Petersburg's *Kunstkammer* as one of a very few public museums in Europe. (Oxford's Ashmolean Museum was founded in 1683; the British Museum would not be founded until 1753.) The catalog played an important role in establishing the *Kunstkammer*'s reputation as more than a repository of bizarre anatomical specimens. It also demonstrated Lomonosov's credentials as a learned Russian scientist affiliated with the *Kunstkammer*.

In addition to producing the catalog of the Mineral Cabinet, Lomonosov directed construction of Russia's first chemical laboratory, where he kept records of the measure, weight, and composition of various substances. Lomonosov recognized the importance of studying pure metals and salts. He believed that minerals were mixtures of primary particles (now referred to as atoms) and that their structure, color, and weight were important. Lomonosov was the first scientist to establish that amber, peat, and coal arose from plant remains. His chemical analysis of amber showed that its specific gravity was identical to that of pine resin. He also separated water from amber, which produced an odor associated with growing plants.

Lomonosov was interested in the common genesis of related minerals, a concept now known as paragenesis. Over the next 250 years, considerable work on paragenesis would be conducted under the auspices of the academy. He was also interested in the crystallographic properties of minerals and recorded crystal interfacial angles. He wrote a paper on the geometric arrangements of ideal spheres in crystal lattices.

In 1747, a damaging fire swept through the *Kunstkammer*, and only the Mineral Cabinet's most valuable specimens (including the Silver Horn) were saved. Specimens continued to arrive, however. The first meteorite, the 687-kilogram, stony iron *Pallasovo Zheleso* (Pallas's Iron) was sent from Medvedevo (Siberia) in 1762 and arrived in St. Petersburg in 1772. This meteorite was acquired on a Siberian expedition by Peter Simon Pallas and, after its arrival at the Mineral Cabinet, was studied by academician Ernst Florens Friedrich Chladni, who realized that its unique composition of olivine and nickel iron was extraterrestrial. All meteorites of this compositional type are now referred to as pallasites.

After the Mineral Cabinet was established in its restored building, Pallas, then its director, had a new catalog of the collection prepared in 1789. The Mineral Cabinet contained about twenty thousand specimens in 1836. Early in the twentieth century, specimens in the Mineral Cabinet were divided into five collections: the Systematic Collection (more than ninety thousand specimens, showing crystallographic and mineralogical features), the Crystal Collection (more than thirty-one thousand specimens, representing mineral associations and ore types), the Location Collection, the Pseudomorph Collection (containing examples of crystallogenesis under various conditions), and the Gems and Stone Art Collection (including thirty items designed by Peter Carl Fabergé and handcrafted from semiprecious gemstones). The Meteorite Collection includes more than 447 specimens from various sites in Russia and all over the world, including a large collection of tektites, natural glass objects sometimes associated with meteorites.

SIGNIFICANCE

Mikhail Vasilyevich Lomonosov was the first Russian-born scientist to become a member of the St. Petersburg Academy of Sciences. By publishing a catalog of the Mineral Cabinet, detailing the geological contents of the *Kunstkammer*, he was able to place Russian mineralogy at the forefront of European science. As museums outside Russia were later established, mineral collections were displayed following the Mineral Cabinet's precedent. Lomonosov worked for many years at the *Kunstkammer*, and the Lomonosov Museum was founded there in 1947. This museum was dedicated to the early years of the Academy of Sciences, and it included a display re-creating Lomonosov's office and laboratory.

Over the two centuries following the fire that almost

destroyed it, the Mineral Cabinet grew steadily. Following the 1919 Russian Revolution, the Mineral Cabinet was placed under the direction of A. E. Fersman. It was at this time that the museum acquired Fabergé's collection, as well as several other private collections. The Mineral Cabinet moved from St. Petersburg to Moscow in 1934; its contents, then estimated to include eighty thousand specimens, filled thirty railroad cars. Relocation was completed to host the Seventeenth International Geological Congress in Moscow in 1937. The museum was renamed to honor Fersman, its longtime director, in 1955. The museum building was reconstructed in preparation for the Twenty-Seventh International Geological Congress, held in Moscow in 1984.

Between 1772 and 1996, one meteorite type (pallasite) and thirty-two mineral species were named in honor of staff members of the Mineral Cabinet. The minerals lomosovite and lomosovite-beta were named in honor of Lomonosov. In 2000, an oxalate mineral discovered in the Chelkar salt dome in Kazakhstan was named "novgorodovaite" after the current director, Margarita Ivanovna Novgorodova.

At the start of the twenty-first century, the A. E. Fersman Mineralogical Museum housed one of the most complete mineral collections in the world, including more than twenty-three hundred of about four thousand known mineral species. Its collection has been curated using Dana's Mineralogical Classification. About ten thousand of its specimens are viewable on the World Wide Web. Its scientists continue in Mikhail Lomonosov's tradition of mineralogical research and publication.

—Anita Baker-Blocker

FURTHER READING

Fersman, A. E. *Geochemistry for Everyone*. Moscow: Foreign Languages, 1958. A posthumously published book that provides a look at the great esteem in which Lomonosov was held by his successors and his enormous influence on the science of mineralogy. Fersman, a preeminent geochemist, discusses the importance of geology in people's everyday lives in a book written especially for high school students, which includes many references to the Mineral Cabinet and its successor, the Fersman Museum.

Generalov, Mikhail. "A. E. Fersman Mineralogical Museum: An Embassy of the Mineral Kingdom in Russia." *Rocks and Minerals* 76, no. 1 (January/February, 2001): 17-21. An examination of the Fersman Museum's collection of minerals from the vast Russian landscape.

Popova, V. I., et al. "Murzinka: Alabasha Pegmatite Field." *Mineralogical Almanac* 5 (2002). The gem-laden Alabasha pegmatite field was studied by A. E. Fersman in the early 1920's, and its history, geology, and mineralogy are discussed in a magazine format, laden with color photos of crystalline mineral specimens from the Fersman Museum.

Rundqvist, Dmitrii V. *Mineral Collections of Russia, Part II: Twelve Museum Collections*. Vol 3. in *Mineralogical Almanac*. Moscow: Ocean Pictures, 2000. This book contains a twenty-five-page essay on mineralogical collections in the Russian Empire from the eighteenth to the twentieth century.

SEE ALSO: 1718: Geoffroy Issues the *Table of Reactivities*; 1722: Réaumur Discovers Carbon's Role in Hardening Steel; 1724: Foundation of the St. Petersburg Academy of Sciences; 1785-1788: Hutton Proposes the Geological Theory of Uniformitarianism; 1797: Wollaston Begins His Work on Metallurgy.

RELATED ARTICLES in *Great Lives from History: The Eighteenth Century, 1701-1800*: Elizabeth Petrovna; Mikhail Vasilyevich Lomonosov; Peter the Great.

1740's

August 19, 1745-September 20, 1746
JACOBITE REBELLION

The attempt by Charles Edward to launch an invasion of Great Britain through the Highlands of Scotland astounded the world by coming very close to success. However, the withdrawal of the prince's army back into Scotland gave the Hanoverian monarchy the chance to regroup and eventually to crush Charles Edward's Jacobite uprising.

ALSO KNOWN AS: The Forty-Five Rebellion
LOCALE: Great Britain, as far south as Derby
CATEGORIES: Wars, uprisings, and civil unrest; government and politics

KEY FIGURES
Charles Edward (Bonnie Prince Charlie; 1720-1788), pretender to the throne of Great Britain
James Edward (The "Old Pretender"; 1688-1766), pretender to the British throne and father of Charles Edward
George II (1683-1760), elector of Hanover and king of Great Britain, r. 1727-1760
Lord George Murray (1694-1760), Scottish rebel commander
Duke of Cumberland (William Augustus; 1721-1765), son of King George II and British military commander
Sir John Cope (1690-1760), British general
Flora MacDonald (1722-1790), Scotswoman loyal to the Jacobites
George Wade (1673-1748), British commander in chief superseded by Cumberland

SUMMARY OF EVENT
From the time that the Catholic King James II had been overthrown in the Glorious Revolution (1688), his family and their supporters in Great Britain and Ireland—known as Jacobites—schemed to regain the British throne. After James's death in exile in 1701, the Jacobites' hopes rested on his son, James Edward, the "Old Pretender," who maintained a court-in-exile in France. Three attempts were made to restore the "king over the water," but James Edward proved to be a lethargic, uninspiring leader, earning the nickname of "Old Mr. Melancholy." Three attempted Jacobite insurrections in Scotland, in 1708, 1715, and 1719, obtained only limited success before evaporating in futility.

In order to perpetuate the Protestant succession to the throne, the German House of Hanover, which claimed descent from the Stuart King James I, had been installed upon the British throne by Parliament in 1714. Under its second monarch, George II, the Hanover Dynasty seemed by 1745 to be immovably secure, and Jacobite threats were generally dismissed as fantasy. However, James Edward's son Charles Edward, a dashing personality whom his admirers dubbed Bonnie Prince Charlie, planned to journey to northern Scotland, where he hoped to raise the clans in rebellion and, with French support, to depose George and become King Charles III.

Landing on July 25, 1745, at Moidart in the Scottish Highlands, the Bonnie Prince at first met with an indifferent response and only gradually attracted supporters. However, at Glenfinnan on August 19, 1745, Charles Edward took the bold step of unfurling the Stuart standard, officially proclaiming the uprising. He was initially joined by younger members of the Camerons of Lochiel, the MacDonalds, and the duke of Atholl. Quickly amassing a small force of fifteen hundred men, Charles Edward set an ambush for government forces at the Pass of Corrieyairack. The British commander in Scotland, General Sir John Cope, had already been faced with chronic desertion from his ranks. Warned of the trap set by the pretender, Cope ordered his men northeast to Aberdeen, thinking that the rebels would try to secure the surrounding region and could thus be lured into the open.

It was a serious miscalculation. In an audacious move, Charles Edward's forces marched unopposed to the southeast and directly into the Lowlands, capturing Perth on September 4, taking on new recruits at a spectacular rate, and entering the Scottish capital of Edinburgh on September 16. The outmaneuvered Cope hurriedly brought his troops by sea and landed just west of Edinburgh, deploying in a marshy area called Prestonpans. There, on September 21, the Jacobites' ablest general, Lord George Murray, discovered an unguarded path leading through the marsh that enabled him to outflank Cope's army during the early morning and launch a surprise attack. The Hanoverians were thrown into total confusion by the fierce Highlander charge, and in less than one-half hour they had fled the field, leaving Charles Edward in control of Scotland and poised to invade English soil.

Taking the initiative on November 1, 1745, Charles Edward and Murray outmaneuvered yet another British army, this one led by seventy-two-year-old Field Marshal George Wade, and entered England from the west,

SCOTLAND, C. 1745-1746

the government. In a heated war council meeting, Charles Edward advocated taking London, but in the end he reluctantly acceded to Murray's opinion, and on what Jacobites later dubbed "Black Friday" (December 5, 1745), the rebels retreated north.

The decision not to press on—one of history's possible turning points—has remained controversial, but it is certain that the rebellion lost much of its impetus and Cumberland's forces regained the initiative in the wake of the Jacobite withdrawal. French aid did not materialize, and British troops in turn entered Scotland. Murray proved that he was still a dangerous adversary, however, by defeating the Hanoverians under Lieutenant General Henry Hawley at the Battle of Falkirk (January 16, 1746). Though the Jacobites scored some minor successes in capturing Inverness and Fort Augustus, they were steadily forced northward.

On April 16, the rebels chose to stand and fight on the open ground of Drummossie Moor, near Culloden. Perhaps resentful of Murray for having browbeaten him into making the withdrawal from Derby, Charles Edward spurned the older commander's advice that it would be suicidal to face the Hanoverians across a level plain that offered no protection: He deployed his men in such a fashion that they faced a relentless artillery barrage once battle was joined. Moreover, Bonnie Prince Charlie seemed confused during the battle and exerted no decisive leadership in the field. Perhaps as a result, a wild and ill-advised Highlander onslaught was mounted against Cumberland's strong defensive positions. The onslaught broke upon the Hanover duke's defenses, and the Battle of Culloden became a rout.

From April 16 to September 20, 1746, Charles Edward was on the run. A price of £30,000 was placed on his head, and Cumberland's army scoured the Highlands for him, looting, pillaging, massacring suspected Jacobites, and launching such a protracted campaign of terror that the duke thereafter received the sobriquet of "Butcher." The flight of Bonnie Prince Charlie became an epic. Among those who sheltered and succored the "Young Pretender," the most famous was Flora Mac-Donald, who at one stage lent the prince women's clothing and passed him off as her maidservant "Betty Burke."

besieging the garrison at Carlisle. Carlisle fell on November 15, and again virtually unchallenged—Wade was unable to reach them in time—the Jacobite army marched into Manchester and then to Derby, some 130 miles north of London, on December 4, 1745. Murray had deftly given the new British commander, the duke of Cumberland, the slip. Cumberland was the favorite son of King George II and a veteran of the War of the Austrian Succession, having been wounded at the Battle of Dettingen. At Derby, Murray seems to have lost his nerve, and he began advocating a withdrawal to Scotland, rather than advancing on London to seize control of

Flora MacDonald, a Scottish Jacobite sympathizer, meeting Charles Edward. MacDonald helped the Stuart pretender hide from the Hanoverian authorities after his forces were defeated at the Battle of Culloden. (Francis R. Niglutsch)

After hairbreadth escapes from pursuing troopers and government agents, Charles Edward was at last able to board a French vessel at Loch nan Uamh, on the western coast, and sail away on September 20, 1746, his uprising long since collapsed.

SIGNIFICANCE

Charles Edward's failure to take control of Britain marked the last serious attempt at Jacobite restoration. Upon his father's death, the prince was acknowledged by his dwindling group of followers as the rightful pretender under the title of King Charles III. However, he degenerated into an embittered alcoholic, incapable of recapturing his past moments of glory. While the Jacobite Rebellion was a military fiasco, however, it left behind a glamorous and seductive legend, and the romantic vision of the dynamic and youthful Bonnie Prince Charlie and his doomed Highland followers has maintained an almost magnetic appeal for future generations. The duke of Cumberland's depredations and the subsequent suppres-

sion of the Gaelic tongue, the kilt and tartan, and other icons of Scottish identity, on the other hand, gave rise to a long-festering atmosphere of anti-English sentiment in Scotland—sentiments which, though long abated, still carry an impact to this day.

—*Raymond Pierre Hylton*

FURTHER READING

Douglas, Hugh, and Michael J. Stead. *The Flight of Bonnie Prince Charlie*. Stroud, Gloucestershire, England: Sutton, 2000. The most detailed account of one of history's most famous tales of escape.

Erickson, Carolly. *Bonnie Prince Charlie*. New York: Lillian Morrow, 1989. Scholarly appraisal of the complex personality of Charles Edward; attempts to explain both the positive elements and the character flaws that led to the 1745 rising and its eventual failure.

Lees-Milne, James. *The Last Stuarts: British Royalty in Exile*. New York: Charles Scribner's Sons, 1983. Studies the vices and virtues that made the last Stuarts a force to reckon with until at least the mid-eighteenth century.

McLeod, John. *Dynasty: The Stuarts, 1560-1807*. New York: St. Martin's Press, 1999. Analysis of the controversial royal house that adroitly balances the myth with the reality.

MacLeod, Ruairidh H. *Flora MacDonald: The Jacobite Heroine in Scotland and North America*. London: Shepheard-Walwyn, 1997. Tries to shed further light on another legendary figure and continues this unusual lady's saga into her years as a settler in North Carolina.

Speck, W. A. *The Butcher: The Duke of Cumberland and the Suppression of the Forty-Five*. New York: Basil Blackwell, 1987. Unusual study of an individual whose name has become a byword for repression and cruelty.

SEE ALSO: Mar. 23-26, 1708: Defeat of the "Old Pretender"; Sept. 6, 1715-Feb. 4, 1716: Jacobite Rising in Scotland; Dec. 16, 1740-Nov. 7, 1748: War of the Austrian Succession.

RELATED ARTICLES in *Great Lives from History: The Eighteenth Century, 1701-1800*: George II; Flora MacDonald.

October, 1745, and January, 1746
INVENTION OF THE LEYDEN JAR

Experimenting independently in different countries, Ewald Georg von Kleist and Pieter van Musschenbroek invented the Leyden jar, the first device that could accumulate and store large amounts of electric energy. Later called a condenser or capacitor, the Leyden jar could conserve an electric charge for future use or experimentation.

LOCALE: Camin, Pomerania (now in Germany); Leiden, the Netherlands

CATEGORIES: Inventions; science and technology

KEY FIGURES

Ewald Georg von Kleist (1700-1748), German scientist and cleric

Pieter van Musschenbroek (1692-1761), Dutch physicist, mathematician, and professor

Jean-Antoine Nollet (1700-1770), French abbot and physicist

William Watson (1715-1787), English physician, apothecary, and scientist

Benjamin Franklin (1706-1790), American statesman and inventor

SUMMARY OF EVENT

Significant experimentation with electricity began after 1660, when Otto von Guericke of Magdeburg, Germany, invented the first electrical machine, which generated electricity by friction. In 1675, using an improved machine with a glass globe, Sir Isaac Newton studied sparking, attraction, and repulsion. In 1729, Stephen Gray established the important principle that electricity could travel or be transmitted, and he was the first to differenti-

ate between materials that were insulators or nonconductors (such as silk filaments) and conductors (such as metal or water).

By the early 1740's, amateurs and philosophers, as well as scientists, were performing electrical experiments and demonstrations, often for entertainment. For instance, a popular pastime was igniting combustibles such as gunpowder and alcohol by sparks from an electrical friction machine. However, experimenters still needed a way to accumulate and store electricity. The solution was the Leyden jar, invented independently by Ewald Georg von Kleist in October, 1745, and by Pieter van Musschenbroek in January, 1746.

Von Kleist was a German scientist and cleric who had become interested in electricity while studying at the University of Leyden in the 1720's. Later, he learned about the experiments of University of Leipzig professor Georg Mathias Bose, who experimented with electrical flares and sparks from water in an electrified glass vessel. Von Kleist began experimenting with his own electric generator with the goal of creating stronger flares or sparks.

In October, 1745, von Kleist accidentally invented the first condenser. He had set up a medicine bottle (a nonconductor) filled with fluid (a conductor), and inserted a nail in the cork stopper. One end of a metal wire was connected to his electrical machine's prime conductor, and the other end was placed inside the jar of fluid. While holding the jar in one hand, von Kleist connected the nail to the electric generator and electrified the nail. Touching the nail with the other hand, he received a severe shock, and the charged nail also produced sparks when it touched another object. It was then obvious to von Kleist that the nail and the jar had temporarily stored electricity. In November, he wrote letters about his invention to other scientists, but none of them could successfully replicate von Kleist's experiment before the news broke about van Musschenbroek's similar experiment in January, 1746.

Van Musschenbroek was a Dutch professor, medical doctor, mathematician, and scientific instrument maker, who, in 1729, was the first person to use the term "physics" to name what had previously called natural philosophy. Independently of von Kleist, van Musschenbroek, along with Jean Allamand of the University of Leyden and an assistant, Andreas Cunaeus, conducted the same experiment as von Kleist. However, unlike von Kleist, van Musschenbroek realized that the hand holding the jar

served as a conductor and that the bottle's exterior had to be grounded (held by a person standing on the ground) when electrifying the nail or wire.

In January, 1746, van Musschenbroek announced his invention, and in April, 1746, his discovery was presented to the Académie des Sciences (Academy of Sciences) in Paris. Van Musschenbroek was able not only to develop a working model of the condenser but also to explain the device sufficiently to allow other scientists to repeat his experiement. He was therefore credited with its invention, and the device came to be known as a Leyden jar, since it was invented at the University of Leyden.

The news of the Leyden jar spread rapidly, first in Europe and then throughout the world. Electricity became

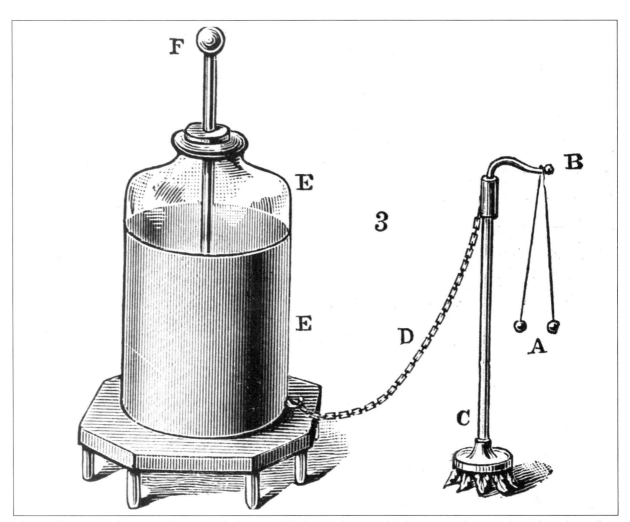

This c. 1800 drawing shows a Leyden jar attached to two pith balls, which are used to demonstrate the attractive and repulsive effects of electrical charge. (Hulton Archive/Getty Images)

more popular than ever. Even nonscientists became "electricians," performing various kinds of sensational new demonstrations. Frequently, exhibitions resulted in animals and birds being killed by electrical shock. Longer and more powerful sparks became possible with Leyden jars built into frictional static-generating machines. Some of the most elaborate and memorable demonstrations were experiments by Jean-Antoine Nollet, a French physicist, member of the Académie des Sciences, and abbot of the Grand Convent of the Carthusians in Paris. It was Nollet who coined the term "Leyden jar." Moreover, in 1745, Nollet developed a theory that electricity could travel long distances quickly, based on attraction and repulsion in a continuous flow of electrical matter between charged bodies.

Combining scientific research with spectacular effects, Nollet helped popularize electrical phenomena. At Versailles in 1746, for instance, Nollet impressed King Louis XV by sending a discharge or current from a Leyden jar through a long chain of 180 royal guards connected by pieces of wire. The discharge caused all of the soldiers to leap into the air simultaneously when the circuit was completed. Louis XV was so entertained that he requested a second demonstration be performed in Paris. Consequently, Nollet repeated the procedure with a single row of 700 monks holding hands. When the Leyden jar was discharged, all the monks jumped simultaneously into the air.

The Leyden jar also stimulated serious scientific research. Within a year of its invention, the English apothecary, scientist, and physician William Watson created an improved Leyden jar coated with metal foil on both the inside and outside. The metal foil on the outside served the purpose of the hand holding the jar in the earlier experiments. Watson attempted to devise an accurate test for measuring the velocity of electricity. In 1747, he laid out a wire circuit 12,276 feet long across the River Thames at Westminster Bridge. He then discharged an electric spark from a Leyden jar through the wire. Transmission occurred immediately, so Watson determined that the velocity of electricity was instantaneous.

In the United States, Benjamin Franklin conducted experiments using the Leyden jar. He proved that the electrical charge was stored in the glass rather than the water, as had generally been thought, and that the basis of the jar's electrostatic activity was the insulating material around the conductor. After wrapping both the inside and outside of a glass jar with lead foil and electrifying the jar, Franklin removed the wrappings and discovered that each sheet had been charged. As a result, the device was called a "condenser." In 1752, Franklin collected electrical charge in a Leyden jar during his famous experiment flying a kite in a lightning storm.

SIGNIFICANCE

With the invention of the Leyden jar, scientists finally had a device that could generate and store large quantities of electrical charge for later use. Thus, the invention was crucial for future advancements in electrical research. The Leyden jar further popularized electricity, as even nobility and royalty were drawn to the dramatic demonstrations it made possible.

The Leyden jar also marked a turning point in the field of electrotherapy, or the therapeutic use of electricity. Since about 400 B.C.E., electrical shocks from torpedo fish had been used to treat pain, gout, and other illnesses. Christian Gottlieb Kratzenstein (1723-1795) was possibly the first physician to use the Leyden jar to treat diseases. By 1752, there were forty published medical applications of electricity, and by 1789 there were seventy published uses. There were reports of successful treatment of disorders such as paralysis, epilepsy, angina pectoris, kidney stones, and sciatica. Beginning in the late 1760's, hospitals began installing electric shock machines. However, interest in electrotherapy declined toward the end of the nineteenth century.

Most significantly, the Leyden jar was the first condenser and the forerunner of modern capacitors, devices that contain two conductors separated by an insulator. In the twenty-first century, capacitors come in all sizes, including microscopic ones that are part of integrated electric circuits. The devices store electricity and are used in electric power systems, radios, televisions, computers, and various kinds of electronic equipment.

—Alice Myers

FURTHER READING

Bernal, J. D. *A History of Classical Physics from Antiquity to the Quantum.* New York: Barnes & Noble Books, 1997. Includes sections on Benjamin Franklin's Leyden jar experiments and a discussion and illustration of van Musschenbroek's experiment. Illustrations and index.

Ford, R. A. *Homemade Lightning: Creative Experiments in Electricity.* New York: McGraw-Hill, 2002. A chapter on the Leyden jar condenser describes the early jars and includes instructions for creating Leyden jars. Illustrated, with an appendix, a bibliography, and an index.

Heilbron, J. L. *Electricity in the Seventeenth and Eighteenth Centuries: A Study in Early Modern Physics.*

Mineola, N.Y.: Dover, 1999. This significant and scholarly work provides detailed chapters on the invention of the Leyden jar and Benjamin Franklin's experiments. Illustrated. Index and extensive bibliography.

Schiffer, Michael B. *Draw the Lightning Down: Benjamin Franklin and Electrical Technology in the Age of Enlightenment*. Berkeley: University of California Press, 2003. This story of Franklin and eighteenth century electrical technology discusses the Leyden jar extensively. Illustrated. Bibliography and index.

Whittaker, E. T. *A History of the Theories of Aether and Electricity*. New York: Tomash, 1987. This general history includes sections about the work of van Musschenbroek and Watson. Illustrated. Bibliography and index.

SEE ALSO: 1729: Gray Discovers Principles of Electric Conductivity; 1733: Du Fay Discovers Two Kinds of Electric Charge; 1748: Nollet Discovers Osmosis; June, 1752: Franklin Demonstrates the Electrical Nature of Lightning; 1759: Aepinus Publishes *Essay on the Theory of Electricity and Magnetism*; 1800: Volta Invents the Battery.

RELATED ARTICLES in *Great Lives from History: The Eighteenth Century, 1701-1800*: Benjamin Franklin; Louis XV.

1746
ROEBUCK DEVELOPS THE LEAD-CHAMBER PROCESS

John Roebuck found a way to produce sulfuric acid in greater quantities and at a lower price than had been possible previously. His lead-chamber process increased the British supply of sulfuric acid, making it possible to develop new applications and to export the substance for sale to foreign markets.

LOCALE: Birmingham, England
CATEGORIES: Chemistry; science and technology; manufacturing

KEY FIGURES
John Roebuck (1718-1794), English physician, chemist, and engineer
Samuel Garbett (1717-1803), English merchant
Joshua Ward (1685-1761), English physician, chemist, and manufacturer

SUMMARY OF EVENT
In the mid-eighteenth century, chemistry was beginning to make the transition from alchemical practices to the modern era. The Industrial Revolution was beginning, and manufacturing industries began to require chemicals as raw materials. Sulfuric acid, perhaps more than any other single chemical, was needed by a variety of industries, yet the supply was limited by inadequate, preindustrial methods of manufacture. Although sulfuric acid had been known for centuries, it had always been prepared in small quantities from metal sulfates. As the demand for the acid increased, it was eventually recognized that plentiful elemental sulfur was a more favorable raw material for sulfuric acid manufacture. Iron sulfide (pyrite) could also be used and was often less expensive than elemental sulfur.

Sulfur burns readily in air, releasing sulfur dioxide gas, a noxious chemical. Sulfur dioxide gas, upon further oxidation, becomes sulfur trioxide, which, when combined with water, forms sulfuric acid. Sulfuric acid itself is an oily, corrosive liquid with a high boiling point, and when pure it is nearly twice as dense as water. The conversion of sulfur dioxide to sulfur trioxide requires oxygen and a catalyst. In the eighteenth century, it was known that adding nitre (potassium nitrate) to burning sulfur could catalyze the conversion, but the details of the complex reactions involved were not then appreciated.

Joshua Ward was able to make sulfuric acid as early as 1740 by burning mixtures of sulfur and nitre and combining the resulting gases with water. His efforts were limited, however, by the relatively small and fragile glass vessels he used, and his product was expensive and available in limited quantity. At the same time, there was significant demand for the acid in the textile and metals industries. Ward patented his method in 1749 and produced the acid at Twickenham and Richmond.

Meanwhile, physician John Roebuck had become interested in chemistry during his medical education, and he decided to set up a laboratory in Birmingham with his collaborator Samuel Garbett. They attempted to improve sulfuric acid production techniques. Roebuck realized that lead was resistant to the corrosive properties of moderately concentrated sulfuric acid and designed his process so that the acid was formed in 4-by-6-by-8 foot wooden chambers lined with lead sheets. Using this method, the acid attained a concentration of about 50 percent, and it could be sold for a price about one-fourth that of Ward's product. Once this process had been demonstrated with the initial lead chambers, the scale of manufacture could be increased by building larger chambers, as well as by employing many chambers simultaneously.

Roebuck and Garbett failed to patent their process in England, and they were prevented from developing it further in Birmingham by Joshua Ward's patent. In order to continue their work, they moved to Scotland and built a manufacturing plant at Prestonpans, near Edinburgh. From Prestonpans, they had access to the sea for shipping, and they were able to begin exporting sulfuric acid to the Continent around 1750. The demand for their product led them to build 108 chambers at Prestonpans and even more at a second plant at Burntisland. The total volume of production at the two locations of almost 130,000 cubic feet of acid. In recognition of his achievements in science and technology, Roebuck was made a fellow of the Royal Society in 1764.

The manufacture and sale of the acid were very profitable, but eventually the secrets of the lead-chamber process became generally known. Lacking patent protection, Roebuck and Garbett faced widespread competition. The French soon learned how to build lead-chamber plants, and by 1786 they were operating four such installations. The first lead-chamber plant in the United States was built in 1793 near Philadelphia, and by 1804 it could produce 250 tons of acid each year. In 1917, this plant was sold to the DuPont Corporation.

SIGNIFICANCE

The sulfuric acid made available in quantity by Roebuck's lead-chamber process found many uses in the chemical industry. In the eighteenth century, for example, sulfuric acid began to be used to bleach linen and cotton. Chlorine bleaches were not yet available in quantity. After 1789, with the introduction of the Leblanc process for making sodium carbonate, that industry became a major consumer of sulfuric acid. Sodium carbonate was needed for soap and glass making and had been obtained from wood ashes or other plant sources. The Leblanc process (no longer used) enabled the manufacture of sodium carbonate from readily available salt (sodium chloride) through a series of reactions in which the salt first reacted with sulfuric acid to form sodium sulfate. British

production of sodium carbonate reached 70,000 tons per year by 1850.

The lead-chamber process was further developed and improved throughout the nineteenth century. Major improvements included the Gay-Lussac tower (named for its designer, Joseph-Louis Gay-Lussac) and the Glover tower. In the first of these towers, excess oxides of nitrogen are absorbed in sulfuric acid which trickles down over tile fragments against the gas stream. This prevents them from being emitted as pollutants. The acid from the Gay-Lussac tower is then processed in the Glover tower, where it gives up the oxides of nitrogen it has absorbed so that they can be recycled. This process also causes the acid to become more concentrated.

The lead-chamber process was gradually superseded by the contact process, invented in 1831. The contact process avoids the complex chemistry associated with nitrogen oxides altogether. Instead, it achieves the catalytic conversion of sulfur dioxide to sulfur trioxide through the use of a solid catalyst. A platinum catalyst is very effective but expensive. Modern sulfuric acid plants use a contact catalyst consisting of vanadium pentoxide. The emergence of the synthetic dye industry in the 1880's created a demand for extremely concentrated grades of acid (oleum) that were advantageously made by the contact process. The last lead-chamber installations were taken out of service in the 1970's.

After 1842, large quantities of sulfuric acid began to be used in the manufacture of phosphate fertilizers. J. B. Lawes (1814-1900) in England used the reaction of sulfuric acid with phosphate minerals, such as coprolite, to make soluble phosphates for agricultural use. By the 1860's, annual production of these fertilizers had reached 150,000 tons in Britain. Not only phosphates but also nitrogen fertilizers were in demand. Ammonia from the distillation of soft coal could be absorbed in sulfuric acid to form ammonium sulfate—a form of nitrogen fertilizer. This use of coal with sulfuric acid expanded alongside the increasing use of coal tar as a source of chemicals for the dye industry. In the twenty-first century, fertilizer manufacturing consumes more sulfuric acid than any other industry.

As the steel and petroleum industries developed, they began to use sulfuric acid as well. Steel plates could be cleaned of surface rust by acid treatment, and sulfuric acid was used in alkylation reactions that produce improved quality motor fuels. In addition, in the eighteenth and nineteenth centuries, several explosives were discovered that were made by nitrating various materials with a mixture of sulfuric and nitric acids. Explosives such as nitrocellulose, nitroglycerin, picric acid, and tri-nitrotoluene (TNT) are all made by nitration reactions that involve sulfuric acid.

The many uses of sulfuric acid and its enormous production make it arguably the single most significant heavy chemical. Annual U.S. production of the acid exceeds 40 million tons.

—*John R. Phillips*

FURTHER READING

Clow, A., and N. C. Clow. *The Chemical Revolution.* Freeport, N.Y.: Books for Libraries Press, 1970. A wide-ranging study of the beginnings of the chemical industry, devoting a chapter to vitriol (sulfuric acid) in the Industrial Revolution.

Dunn, Kevin M. *Caveman Chemistry.* Parkland, Fla.: Universal, 2003. Chapter 18 contains a simple experiment to demonstrate the lead-chamber process using a 2-liter soda bottle.

Kent, James A. *Riegel's Handbook of Industrial Chemistry.* 7th ed. New York: Van Nostrand Reinhold, 1974. A detailed description of the lead-chamber process in its twentieth century form.

Kiefer, D. M. "Sulfuric Acid: Pumping up the Volume—Today's Chemist at Work." *Chemistry Chronicles* 10, no. 9 (September, 2001). Traces the adoption of the lead-chamber process in various countries from the late eighteenth to the twentieth century.

SEE ALSO: 1722: Réaumur Discovers Carbon's Role in Hardening Steel; 1771: Woulfe Discovers Picric Acid; 1789: Leblanc Develops Soda Production; c. 1794-1799: Proust Establishes the Law of Definite Proportions.

RELATED ARTICLES in *Great Lives from History: The Eighteenth Century, 1701-1800*: Nicolas Leblanc; John Roebuck.

1746
ZĀHIR AL-ʿUMAR CREATES A STRONGHOLD IN GALILEE

Zāhir al-ʿUmar seized the Crusader city of Acre, resurrecting and fortifying it against Ottoman forces. With Ottoman leaders facing external threats from Russia, they were unable to defeat Zāhir and reconquer Acre.

LOCALE: Acre, Sidon, Syria, Ottoman Empire (now in Israel)

CATEGORIES: Expansion and land acquisition; wars, uprisings, and civil unrest; government and politics

KEY FIGURES

Zāhir al-ʿUmar (d. 1775), Galilean tax farmer and military leader

Ibrāhīm al-Ṣabbāgh (d. 1775), Melkite Christian who served as wazir to Zāhir

Süleyman Paşa (d. 1743), governor of Damascus, r. 1734-1738, 1741-1743

Esad Paşa (fl. 1743-1757), governor of Damascus, r. 1743-1757

Muḥammad Bey (d. 1775), Egyptian ruler, r. 1773-1775

SUMMARY OF EVENT

When the Ottoman Empire incorporated the area east of the Mediterranean Sea as Syria in the early sixteenth century, it had three main administrative centers. Damascus served as the primary administrative center, since the

main route for pilgrims to Mecca passed through this ancient city, which controlled all the territory east of the Rift (Jordan River) Valley, as well as southern Palestine. Tripoli, the second center, governed the northern coastal plain. The central coastal region, from just north of Haifa to Beirut, was governed by the coastal city of Sidon. This included the entire area of Galilee, from Acre east to Tiberias and Safed. Galilee was a relatively insignificant area with a few small villages and various Bedouin tribes roaming through the hills. Even the once-important Crusader port of Acre had been reduced to a small fishing village of about three hundred.

Among the various Bedouin tribes, the Zaydan clan inhabited the region between Tiberias and Safed on the eastern side of Galilee. In the seventeenth century, they began coming into prominence through their trade relations with Damascus. The Druze had served the governor of Sidon as tax farmers for Galilee, but Zāhir al-ʿUmar's grandfather and father, members of the Zaydan clan, were appointed to the roll of *multazims* (tax farmers) of Tiberias.

When Zāhir al-ʿUmar was born around 1690, he was not destined for leadership. His older brother Saʿd was expected to take over as head of the clan. However, at the death of his father in 1706, Zāhir received authority over the tax farms. This was a clever ploy on the part of his brother: It meant that Saʿd could not be held accountable to Sidon should the clan default on payments. Besides, Zāhir was still a teenager. Over the next several decades he became something of a folk hero, proving himself a strong fighter and a defender of justice.

Through his continued trade contacts, Zāhir married the daughter of a leading figure of Damascus and settled in Nazareth. There, the Saqr tribe called upon him to represent them to the Ottoman administration. The governor of Sidon himself appointed Zāhir as the tax farmer of both Tiberias and ʿArraba, a town located farther west, near Acre. He then married the daughter of the ruler of Baʿna, gaining control of the northeast portion of Galilee. With the help of the mercenary Aḥmad Āghā al-Dinkizli and more than one thousand of his troops, Zāhir next turned south to challenge the al-Jarrar clan from Janīn, who controlled access to Nābulus from the north.

The governor of Damascus, Süleyman Paşa, realized the threat of Zāhir's growing power base and attempted to take Tiberias from him in a series of attacks from 1738 to 1743, but Zāhir was able to withstand him. In 1743, Süleyman was succeeded as governor of Damascus by Esad Paşa. Esad Paşa was less aggressive than his predecessor had been, and there was peace between Damascus and Galilee for the next fourteen years.

Zāhir had already been developing a trading base in Acre for some time, especially by building relationships with the French merchants of the city. He appointed Yūsuf al-Qāssis, a Melkite Christian, as his agent in Acre. The governor of Sidon was aware of Zāhir's interests and rejected his request to obtain rights for the tax farm of Acre. Zāhir was determined, however. In 1746, he took the city by force, killed the local *multazim*, and took his place. While the French recognized him with the title of governor of Acre, he was officially only the *multazim*, living in a nearby castle at Dayr Hana.

From 1746 on, Zāhir made it a priority to raise the status of Acre. He built a wall around the city and added fortifications and other buildings. Most of all, he encouraged new residents to develop the city in order to help it regain the status it had achieved during the Crusades. Jews and Christians flocked to Zāhir's territory, where they found both religious tolerance and favorable economic conditions. Acre soon became the leading exporter of cotton to Europe.

Zāhir was successful in keeping Damascus at bay and expanding his influence to Haifa and Tantura. By 1768, the Ottomans had granted him the titles shaykh of Acre; amir of Nazareth, Tiberias, and Safed; and shaykh of all of Galilee. Istanbul was occupied at this time with a war against Russia (1768-1774) and seemed willing to let Zāhir rule as long as there was a balance of power in Syria. The Turks encouraged the new governor of Damascus, Uthman Paşa al-Kurji, to play a stronger role in the region, appointing his two sons Muḥammad and Darwish as governors of Tripoli and Sidon respectively.

Zāhir's political adviser, Ibrāhīm al-Ṣabbāgh, urged him to seek an alliance with Ali Bey al-Kabir of Egypt. In 1770, Ali Bey dispatched troops to Gaza and Jaffa. The following year, he added another thirty-five thousand troops and marched to Damascus. When Ali Bey then suddenly reversed positions, Uthman Paşa of Damascus marched against Zāhir. Once again, Zāhir prevailed in battle at the Daughters of Jacob Bridge on the upper Jordan River. He then took advantage of retreating Egyptian forces and conquered the coastal city of Jaffa. Ali Bey, in turn, was defeated by Muḥammad Bey, who took over Egyptian rule and became a new threat to Zāhir.

Uthman Paşa had become much more conciliatory toward Zāhir after his defeat at Zāhir's hands and lobbied with Istanbul for Zāhir to be named as the new governor of Sidon. Istanbul was ready to make this appointment but hesitated as it awaited payment of back taxes from Galilee. In the meantime, Zāhir restored relationships with the Druze, Metualis, and his other traditional rivals on the edge of Galilee. When Istanbul signed a peace treaty with Russia in 1774, it was able to turn its attention to the internal issues of the empire. It recalled Uthman, who had become allied to Zāhir, and appointed Muḥammad Bey as the new governor of Damascus.

Istanbul also encouraged Egypt to invade Palestine. Muḥammad Bey took Jaffa on May 20, 1775, and threatened Acre to the north. With all the inhabitants fleeing the capital city, Zāhir himself, now a man in his middle eighties, left the city on May 24. Zāhir's own son Ali, an opportunist, announced that he was taking over his father's rule, but he disappeared after one week. Muḥammad entered Acre, seeming to bring Zāhir's rule to an end.

To Zāhir's good fortune, the Egyptian ruler became ill and died in Acre within two weeks. His troops retreated to Egypt, and Zāhir returned to Acre on June 12, with al-Dinkizli mobilizing Zāhir's royal troops. Istanbul was determined not to allow Zāhir to reassert his rule, however. Hasan Kapudan Paşa, the admiral of the Ottoman navy, was dispatched to Acre with instructions to collect back taxes from Zāhir. The shayk of Galilee seemed willing to pay off his debts and to compromise with the Ottoman powers. However, the demand resulted in a power struggle between two of Zāhir's advisers, Ibrāhīm al-

1740's

Ṣabbāgh and Aḥmad Āghā al-Dinkizli. Caught in the crossfire between these two, Zāhir died violently in 1775.

SIGNIFICANCE

Galilee in the eighteenth century was a political force to be reckoned with. At other times, it may have been considered a kingdom or a province in its own right. However, as a border region, it remained a part of the province of Sidon even though it encroached upon the rule of Damascus. Eventually, Zāhir al-ʿUmar controlled most of Sidon, although he was never recognized by Ottoman authorities as its governor. Zāhir's longevity alone is impressive, as he amassed and retained power in Galilee from 1706 to 1775. His true uniqueness, though, lies in the fact that he was primarily a trader who used political skills to control and influence the region within which he sought to trade. Economic development was his first concern, and conquering Acre was merely a means to an end. So successful was Zāhir in his economic projects that Acre increased from a village of three hundred to a city of twenty-five thousand under his control.

For many of those who swelled the population of the city, Acre's attraction lay in Zāhir's moderate tax policy, his reasonable enforcement, and the tax breaks he gave to newcomers. Zāhir obtained a monopoly of the Galilee cotton trade, achieving high prices so that Acre soon became the major exporter of cotton to Europe. This brought further improvements and prosperity to Acre, and all of Galilee enjoyed economic success unparalleled in the four centuries of Ottoman rule.

Perhaps the most impressive aspect of Zāhir's accomplishments is that they were made independently of Ottoman rule. With Istanbul facing external threats from Russia, it had no choice but to allow Galilee some degree of autonomy. Following the death of Zāhir, both the thriving city of Acre and the role of Galilee in trade would continue. However, local leadership waned. In Zāhir's place, Ahmad Paṣa al-Jazzar, a trained Mamlūk, was installed at Acre to do the bidding of his Ottoman masters.

—*Fred Strickert*

FURTHER READING

Barbir, Karl. *Ottoman Rule in Damascus, 1708-1758*. Princeton, N.J.: Princeton University Press, 1980. A study of Zāhir's principal rival at the time of his ascendancy.

Joudah, Ahmad Hasan. *Revolt in Palestine in the Eighteenth Century*. Princeton, N.J.: Princeton University Press, 1987. A detailed scholarly study based on Arabic sources and unpublished archives.

Philipp, Thomas. *Acre: The Rise and Fall of a Palestinian City, 1730-1831*. New York: Columbia University Press, 2001. Study of the city that Zāhir made his capital.

Quataert, Donald. *The Ottoman Empire, 1700-1922*. New York: Cambridge University Press, 2000. Survey of the Ottoman Empire that treats social, economic, and political history.

SEE ALSO: 1718-1730: Tulip Age; 1736-1739: Russo-Austrian War Against the Ottoman Empire; 1748-1755: Construction of Istanbul's Nur-u Osmaniye Complex; Oct., 1768-Jan. 9, 1792: Ottoman Wars with Russia.

RELATED ARTICLE in *Great Lives from History: The Eighteenth Century, 1701-1800*: Mahmud I.

1746-1754
CARNATIC WARS

The Carnatic Wars established British superiority over the French in India and provided an opening for the British East India Company, allowing it gradually to extend its political control over most of the Indian subcontinent.

LOCALE: The Carnatic, southern India (now in Andhra Pradesh, Tamil Nadu, and Karnataka, India)

CATEGORIES: Wars, uprisings, and civil unrest; colonization; expansion and land acquisition

KEY FIGURES

Robert Clive (1725-1774), British soldier and colonial administrator and later First Baron Clive of Plassey, 1762-1774

Joseph-François Dupleix (1697-1763), French governor of India, 1742-1754

Stringer Lawrence (1697-1775), British major general

Comte de Lally (Thomas Arthur Lally; 1700-1766) French military commander

Āṣaf Jāh I (1671-1748), niẓām-ul-mulk of Hyderabad, r. 1724-1748

Nāṣir Jung (d. 1750), son of Āṣaf Jāh and pretender nizam of Hyderabad, r. 1748-1750

Muẓaffar Jung (d. 1751), son of Āṣaf Jāh and pretender nizam of Hyderabad, r. 1750-1751

Anwār-ud-Dīn (fl. 1744-1749), nawab of the Carnatic, r. 1744-1749

Chanda Sahib (d. c. 1751), Hindu military leader

Hyder Ali (1722-1782), ruler of Mysore, r. 1761-1782

Bertrand-François Mahé de La Bourdonnais (1699-1753), French governor of Mauritius and Réunion, 1735-1746

Marquis de Bussy-Castelnau (Charles-Joseph Pâtissier; 1718?-1785), French military commander

First Marquess Cornwallis (Charles Cornwallis; 1738-1805), British governor general of India, 1786-1793

Richard Wellesley (1760-1842), British governor general of India, r. 1797-1805

Tipu Sultan (1750-1799), sultan of Mysore, r. 1782-1799

SUMMARY OF EVENT

After Vasco da Gama of Portugal discovered a sea route to India in 1498, many of the European maritime nations, such as the British, the Danes, the Dutch, the French, and the Portuguese, tried to establish trade relationships with India and other parts of southern and eastern Asia. The British East India Company was chartered in 1600, and a French East India Company was established in 1664. Both established trading posts on the southern coast of India—the British in Madras and the French in Pondicherry.

Initially, the French company was not a significant competitor of the British. However, by 1740, the French were approaching parity with the British in trading volume. The other European companies had little mercantile importance in the region, and the British and the French vied for supremacy in India. Their rivalry on the subcontinent corresponded with ongoing British-French hostilities in Europe and North America, and it would continue until 1789, when the capture of the state of Mysore marked the establishment of full British hegemony in the south, as the French East India Company dwindled to an insignificant entity commercially and politically.

The southernmost part of India (the Deccan) had never really been under the rule of the Mughals, even at the peak of their power. The last of the great Mughal emperors, Aurangzeb, died in 1707, and by this time a number of feuding states coexisted with the nizam—theoretically a vassal of the Mughals. There were four major powers in south India at this time—the British and the French sided with the one or the other as the occasion arose.

In 1745, when four British ships appeared off the coast, Joseph-François Dupleix, the governor of French Pondicherry, appealed for help to Anwār-ud-Dīn, the nawab (ruler) of the Carnatic. Anwār-ud-Dīn agreed, and the British threat was averted. The next year, 1746, Bertrand-François Mahé de La Bourdonnais, a French admiral and governor of Mauritius and Réunion, arrived with a fleet and attacked and occupied the British East India Company's port of Madras, officially beginning the Carnatic Wars. Dupleix and La Bourdonnais had major differences of opinion in the wake of their victory, however, and the latter returned to Mauritius and then to France. Anwār-ud-Dīn then threatened the French and attacked Madras, but he was soundly defeated.

In 1748, Major General Stringer Lawrence of the British East India Company tried to attack Pondicherry, but he too was defeated. The French were now in a secure position in southern India. However, later that year in the Treaty of Aix-la-Chappelle, which ended the War of the Austrian Succession in Europe, Madras was returned to the British.

Both the French and the British conducted themselves in India largely by assuming the role of kingmaker to native regimes. The capital of the Deccan was at Hyderabad. The Muslim ruler, niẓām-ul-mulk Āṣaf Jāh I, died in 1748. His eldest son, Ghaziuddin, was poisoned by the Marāthās and the fight for the throne unfolded between his second son, Nāṣir Jung (supported by the English), and his grandson Muẓaffar Jung (supported by the French). Nāṣir Jung won but reneged on his promises to reward his British allies. He made a treaty with the French, but Dupleix attacked and killed him and put Muẓaffar Jung on the throne. The French commander, the marquis de Bussy-Castelnau, also captured the important fort of Jinjee. Muẓaffar Jung, the new nizam, rewarded the French with land and trade advantages.

Meanwhile, Sayajee was the legitimate Hindu ruler of the state of Tanjore. He had been driven out and his kingdom usurped by his brother, Pratap Sing. Sayajee appealed to the British for help. The British were able to return Sayajee to the throne of Tanjore and obtained money and land in exchange. By the same token, the Hindu ruler of Trichinopoly was killed by the Muslim Chanda Sahib. Chanda Sahib was captured and imprisoned by the Marāthās. Freed by the British, Chanda Sahib was killed and Trichinopoly occupied by the Marāthās until it was taken over by the nizam. In 1749, Mohammad Ali, a Muslim, became the ruler and renewed his state's alliance with the British. Trichinopoly was unsuccessfully besieged by the French from 1751 to 1756. Ultimately the state became British property.

The state of the Carnatic had a Muslim ruler with his capital at Arcot. It was ultimately captured by Hyder Ali, a Muslim and an ally of the French, who had defeated a Hindu ruler to acquire the state of Mysore with its capital at Seringapattam. The British would defeat Hyder Ali's son Tipu and conquer Mysore (and Carnatic) in 1783.

The final important group in eighteenth century India were the Marāthās. A loosely organized Hindu group initially formed to fight the Mughals, their centers of power were in Poona and Satara. The ruler, or *peshwa*, was Bālājī Rao, though the Marāthās often fought in the south under the leadership of a chieftain, Morārī Rao.

The early Carnatic Wars came to an end in 1754, when Dupleix was recalled to France and his conduct of hostilities against the British East India Company ended. The peace was short-lived, however, because the Seven Years' War broke out in Europe just two years later. The branch of the Seven Years' War that was fought in India is often seen as a continuation of the Carnatic Wars and is sometimes referred to as the Third Carnatic War.

An illustration of the Carnatic Wars purporting to show the death of Anwār-ud-Dīn during battle. (Hulton Archive/Getty Images)

SIGNIFICANCE

In the wake of the Carnatic Wars, and especially after 1783, the British were entrenched in southern India. The French presence in the region was gradually weakening because of discord between the local authorities (exemplified by the conflict between La Bourdonnais and Dupleix), the indecision of the French authorities in Paris, and their distrust of agents such as Dupleix. Dupleix, a consummate politician, had acquired enormous power and wealth in India but was recalled to Paris to face charges in 1754. His replacement was unable to maintain the French influence in the region, especially since the French East India Company was financially strapped. Similarly, the successful marquis de Bussy-Castelnau was recalled by the comte de Lally in 1758.

The British, by contrast, were led by extraordinarily capable men (both politically and militarily) such as Robert Clive, the First Marquess Cornwallis, and Richard Wellesley, and they were united by a vision of India as the jewel in the crown of the British Empire. The Carnatic Wars had laid the foundation for this vision to become reality. Clive captured the French settlement at Chandernagor in 1757 and then fought the Battle of Plassey (1757), in which he defeated and killed the nawab of Bengal. This battle effectively marked the beginning of the British Empire in India.

The only significant Indian challenger to the British was Tipu Sultan of Mysore. Tipu understood the threat posed by the British and sent emissaries to Turkey and France (1785-1786) asking for help against the British and facilities for trade. He even sent a message to the king of the English complaining against the depredations of the British in south India. Ultimately, none of these tactics was successful. The French expedition to Egypt in 1798 accelerated the war in India. Richard Wellesley fought a series of battles with Tipu and ultimately defeated him and captured his capital at Seringapatam in 1799. Tipu died fighting, and no significant obstacles remained to the creation of British India.

—*Ranes C. Chakravorty*

FURTHER READING

Ali, B. Sheik. "French Relations with Haider Ali and Tipu Sultan: A Record of Blunders." In *French in India and Indian Nationalism*, edited by K. S. Mathew. Vol. 1. Delhi: B. R., 1999. Explores the military and political weaknesses of the French forces in southern India.

Aniruddha, Ray. "France and Mysore: A History of Diverse French Strategies." In *State and Diplomacy Under Tipu Sultan: Documents and Essays*, edited by Irfan Habib. New Delhi: Tulika Books, 2001. Details the economic and political reasons behind the French strategies in India during the eighteenth century.

Kadam, V. S. "Franco-Marāthā Relations." In *French in India and Indian Nationalism*, edited by K. S. Mathew. Vol. 1. Delhi: B. R., 1999. Describes the important role of Marāthā forces in the shifting of political power in southern India.

Lafont, Jean-Marie. "Observations on the French Military Presence in the Indian States, 1750-1899." In *The French in India and Indian Nationalism*, edited by K. S. Mathew. Vol. 1. Delhi: B. R., 1999. Useful discussion of French military strength and strategies in India.

Ramaswami, N. S. *Political History of the Carnatic Under the Nawabs*. New Delhi: Abhinav, 1984. This 436-page overview includes plates, a bibliography, and an index.

The Rise and Growth of the British Power in India. Vol. 135 in *Encyclopedia Indica*. New Delhi: Anmol, 2004. Well-researched articles cover the period in great detail.

SEE ALSO: Dec. 16, 1740-Nov. 7, 1748: War of the Austrian Succession; Oct. 18, 1748: Treaty of Aix-la-Chapelle; May 28, 1754-Feb. 10, 1763: French and Indian War; Jan., 1756-Feb. 15, 1763: Seven Years' War; June 23, 1757: Battle of Plassey; Aug., 1767-May, 1799: Anglo-Mysore Wars; Dec., 1774-Feb. 24, 1783: First Marāthā War.

RELATED ARTICLES in *Great Lives from History: The Eighteenth Century, 1701-1800*: Robert Clive; First Marquess Cornwallis; Joseph-François Dupleix; Hyder Ali.

1746-1755
JOHNSON CREATES THE FIRST MODERN ENGLISH DICTIONARY

Samuel Johnson's Dictionary of the English Language, *the first English dictionary by a major English writer, established a new standard in comprehensiveness and sound lexical judgment.*

LOCALE: London, England
CATEGORIES: Cultural and intellectual history; education; literature

KEY FIGURES
Samuel Johnson (1709-1784), poet, biographer, essayist, and lexicographer
Lord Chesterfield (Philip Dormer Stanhope; 1694-1773), statesman and author
Robert Dodsley (1703-1764), poet, bookseller, and sponsor of Johnson's dictionary project

SUMMARY OF EVENT
The history of English dictionaries does not begin until the early seventeenth century. No English dictionary was available to William Shakespeare, and the earliest such works were concerned mainly with difficult words because it was assumed that readers needed no assistance with "easy" ones. In 1721, Nathan Bailey published his *Universal Etymological English Dictionary*, the title of which accurately depicts its main limitation, for Bailey was primarily interested in tracing the history and development of English words, and not in their definitions and usage. Both France and Italy had produced comprehensive multivolume dictionaries of French and Italian, respectively, in the preceding century, but nothing of the kind had been attempted for the English language.

Robert Dodsley, an English poet and bookseller, suggested the idea of a dictionary to Samuel Johnson, who is reported to have replied that he himself had been thinking of such an undertaking. Considering that the French Academy, consisting of forty members, had required more than a half century to produce an authoritative French dictionary, the size of the task had hitherto discouraged would-be English lexicographers, and Great Britain had no organization comparable to the French Academy.

When Johnson began to compile his *Dictionary of the English Language* in 1746, he was thirty-six years old and frustrated by the lack of a degree, which would have allowed him to practice law. He was known to his contemporaries primarily for his satiric poem *London* (1738) and a biography of a poet named Richard Savage

(1744). During the nine years of the dictionary's composition, however, Johnson rose to literary prominence as the author of works in several genres, including poetry, drama, and the essay. He was, and remains, the most accomplished man of letters ever to make an English dictionary. Indeed, his preface to the dictionary is in itself a significant English essay, and because the dictionary is laced with hundreds of quotations chosen not merely to illustrate the use of words therein but also for their aesthetic or instructive value, the dictionary is the most literary of all English lexicographic works.

Johnson worked with the assistance of only six copyists, not all of them employed simultaneously. He expected to complete the task in three years, one-third the time the dictionary actually required. There were basically three ways to gather lexical information. One way, still very important in lexicography but rarely practiced in Johnson's time, is to listen to and record the language as spoken. Another way is to begin with earlier dictionaries, though, of course, in Johnson's time, earlier dictionaries were woefully inadequate.

Johnson decided that, with few exceptions, he would confine his research to the best English writers of the preceding two hundred years, beginning with Sir Philip Sidney, whose works dated from the late 1570's. In the process of reading hundreds of works, the well-read Johnson read even more. He underlined each sentence that he intended to quote from his authors, indicating the first letter of the word he was illustrating in the margin. His copyists copied each of these sentences on a separate sheet of paper. This process of working from citation slips became the standard way of gathering information for subsequent English dictionaries and, allowing for the modifications of an electronically equipped age, remains the method still in use.

From this base of information Johnson wrote definitions for more than 40,000 words, many of which required multiple definitions. The verb "take," for example, required 134 definitions. He exemplified the word entries with approximately 114,000 quotations from writers in every field of endeavor. Because there was no single publisher willing to take complete responsibility for the project, a group of five publishers headed by Dodsley agreed to pay Johnson £1,575 in installments to support his work.

Johnson's definitions are mainly clear, objective, and enlightening, but the dictionary has become famous for a few exceptions in which Johnson expresses personal feeling or whimsicality. Thus, the word "excise" is defined as "a hateful tax levied upon commodities" and collected by "wretches," while with self-deprecating humor he defines "grubstreet" as a word deriving from the fact of a London street of that name being the home of "writers of small histories, dictionaries, and temporary poems" and thus a designation for "any mean production." Such frequently cited deviations from objective lexicography do not obscure the seriousness and competence of Johnson's work generally.

In 1747, a year after beginning work, Johnson issued *The Plan of a Dictionary of the English Language*, with a dedication to Philip Dormer Stanhope, Lord Chesterfield, a distinguished statesman who in Dodsley's opinion represented the ideal patron for the project. The busy Chesterfield contributed some advice and a small donation to Johnson, but subsequently he forgot about the dictionary. Well before the work was completed, Johnson had used up his stipend. The deteriorating health of his wife, Elizabeth, and the need to pursue other remunerative writing took time away from the immense task. After Elizabeth died in 1752, Johnson, always a melancholy man, could accomplish little work for months.

In 1753 he completed the first of the two folio volumes of the dictionary, and then, with an astonishing burst of energy, he finished the second volume in little more than a year. At this point, Dodsley had asked Chesterfield to write something in praise of the dictionary. Chesterfield, who had been ill, managed two letters of praise in a weekly newspaper, but Johnson, who had been expecting more, sent Chesterfield a bitter letter comparing the nobleman to an indifferent observer of an individual struggling in the water who then "encumbers him with help" after he has reached safety. Chesterfield did not seem to resent this largely undeserved rebuke and even expressed admiration for the power of Johnson's epistolary prose.

Although Johnson had to struggle to earn a living for several more years, the dictionary, finally completed and then published in two volumes in 1755, established his reputation as a scholar and remained unrivaled until Noah Webster's dictionaries gained popularity nearly a century later.

SIGNIFICANCE

Aside from injecting English lexicography for the first time with the linguistic and literary subtlety and judgment of a great English writer, Samuel Johnson set a high standard for all subsequent practitioners. The relatively

few eccentric examples excepted and a small number of errors aside, his definitions in *A Dictionary of the English Language* remain models of precision and clarity. His successors, including Noah Webster, who were often critical of Johnson, inevitably borrowed heavily from his definitions.

His justly famous preface to the dictionary explains the principles that guided his work and the challenges that face any lexicographer, such as, for example, the sometimes perplexing challenge of always explaining a difficult word by the use of simpler words. He also explains the secondary motives that lay behind the endeavor and what he learned in his attempt to accomplish them. The quotations with which he hoped to enlighten his readers generally, while helping to define words therein, often proved too bulky and distracting. Trimmed in number and length from his original intention, the quotations remain a notable and influential feature of the dictionary nevertheless.

Measured by modern standards, Johnson's dictionary falls short in a number of ways. Recognizing the difficulty of presenting pronunciation adequately, he restricted his coverage of the sound of English to identifying the principal accents of words. Johnson knew as much about etymology as anyone of his time, but his etymologies are not considered authoritative in the twenty-first century. He hoped to stabilize language habits that he judged elegant and correct, but as he himself recognized, language inevitably changes and grows. Even a dictionary as great as Johnson's could not answer ordinary linguistic needs two and a half centuries after its compilation.

—*Robert P. Ellis*

FURTHER READING

Johnson, Samuel. *A Dictionary of the English Language: In Which the Words Are Deduced from Their Originals, and Illustrated in Their Different Significations by Examples from the Best Writers to Which Are Prefixed, a History of the Language, and an English Grammar.* London: Times Books, 1983. A two-volume facsimile reprint of the 1755 first edition of the dictionary.

Landau, Sidney I. *The Art and Craft of Lexicography.* New York: Charles Scribner's Sons, 1984. Landau's second chapter includes a discussion of Johnson's *Plan of a Dictionary of the English Language* and of the relation of Johnson's dictionary to those of his competitors.

Lynch, Jack. *Samuel Johnson's Dictionary: Selections from the 1755 Work That Defined the English Lan-*

1740's

315

guage. New York: Walker, 2003. In addition to representing the character of the dictionary as a whole, the selections are chosen with an eye to illuminating everyday life in Johnson's time and to exhibiting Johnson's analytical mind.

McAdam, E. L., Jr., and George Milne. *Johnson's Dictionary: A Modern Selection*. New York: Random House, 1963. This long-popular book presents a substantial sampling of the most interesting of Johnson's dictionary entries in a highly readable format.

Reddick, Allen. *The Making of Johnson's Dictionary, 1746-1773*. 2d ed. New York: Cambridge University Press, 1996. A thorough treatment of the whole process of Johnson's work from its first conception through his later revision. Incorporates recent commentary and scholarship.

Romaine, Suzanne, ed. *The Cambridge History of the English Language*. Vol. 4. New York: Cambridge University Press, 1998. Chapter 6 explores concerns over English grammar and usage during the time of Johnson and his contemporaries, including Lindley Murray, who wrote and published the influential *An English Grammar* in 1795.

Sledd, James H., and Gwin J. Kolb. *Dr. Johnson's Dictionary: Essays in the Biography of a Book*. Chicago: University of Chicago Press, 1955. The best assessment of Johnson's achievement in the context of the tradition of English lexicography.

SEE ALSO: Mar. 20, 1750-Mar. 14, 1752: Johnson Issues *The Rambler*; 1751-1772: Diderot Publishes the *Encyclopedia*; July, 1764: Voltaire Publishes *A Philosophical Dictionary for the Pocket*; 1795: Murray Develops a Modern English Grammar Book.

RELATED ARTICLES in *Great Lives from History: The Eighteenth Century, 1701-1800:* James Boswell; Denis Diderot; Samuel Johnson; Voltaire.

1747
MARGGRAF EXTRACTS SUGAR FROM BEETS

At a time when Europe was dependent on expensive sugar from sugarcane grown using slave labor in the Caribbean, Andreas Marggraf discovered that sugar extracted from a European crop, the beet, was identical to that from sugarcane. His discovery eventually led to the development of a commercially successful sugar beet industry in Europe and North America.

LOCALE: Berlin, Prussia (now in Germany)
CATEGORIES: Agriculture; science and technology; manufacturing; trade and commerce

KEY FIGURES

Andreas Sigismund Marggraf (1709-1782), German chemist

Franz Karl Achard (1753-1821), German chemist and a student of Marggraf

Napoleon I (Napoleon Bonaparte; 1769-1821), military leader and emperor of France, r. 1804-1814, 1815

Benjamin Delessert (1773-1847), French industrialist

SUMMARY OF EVENT

Prior to the development of the sugar beet industry, the world's supply of refined sugar was extracted entirely from a grass called sugarcane (*Saccharum officinarum*). Sugarcane is an old crop, believed to have been harvested for the first time several thousand years ago on Pacific islands. During the Middle Ages, it was widely grown in the Mediterranean region. Nevertheless, honey long remained the major sweetener in Europe, because cane sugar was prohibitively expensive. Then, in the seventeenth and eighteenth centuries, sugarcane grown on Caribbean islands, first by the Spanish and Portuguese and later by the British and French, became the world's chief source of sugar and a major commodity in world trade.

To provide for the highly labor-intensive cultivation and processing of sugarcane, Europeans transported large numbers of slaves across the Atlantic from Africa. As larger quantities of sugar reached Europe, the price declined, and Europeans increasingly developed a "sweet tooth," though the substance remained a luxury.

In contrast to that of cane sugar, production of sugar from beets (*Beta vulgaris* in the family *Chenopodiaceae*) got off to a slow start. In the late sixteenth century, a French agronomist, Olivier de Serres, noted that beet roots that had been cooked produced a juice similar to sugar syrup. It took another 150 years, and the work of Andreas Sigismund Marggraf, to isolate and identify sugar in beet roots, and another fifty years before commercial sugar beet production got under way.

Beets come in a number of varieties, including the common garden beet, whose leaves and roots have been eaten as vegetables since ancient times. Another variety of beet has long been used as livestock fodder. The roots of sugar beets are white and sharply tapered, and commonly grow to a depth of 6 feet. Although they are biennial plants, they are commonly harvested at the end of their first growing season. All beet varieties are descendants of a wild beet plant that still grows on the European seacoast.

Marggraf, whose achievements include a number of refinements in the analytical tools of chemistry, was an expert at "wet methods," or solvent extraction, and at carefully washing and recrystallizing the end product of such extraction. In 1747, he used hot alcohol to extract the juices from several crop plants commonly grown in Europe, including the root of a beet variety used for livestock fodder. After the extraction, minute crystals appeared in the beet root's dried juice. Using a microscope, Marggraf recognized that these crystals were identical to the crystals produced by sugarcane. The sugar in both beets and cane is now known to be sucrose. Marggraf's achievement may have marked the first time a microscope was used for chemical identification.

Although Marggraf had identified beet extraction as a potential means of producing sugar in Europe, his initial extraction process was expensive—unsurprisingly, since it was invented as a method of scientific research rather than industrial production. In an effort to provide poor European farmers with a means of producing their own sugar, Marggraf later developed a less expensive method, in which beet roots were macerated to obtain the juice and a calcium hydroxide solution was used to help crystallize the sugar. His vision of a cheap, new source of sugar for the farmer did not materialize, however, and its discovery remained a mere laboratory curiosity for half a century.

The commercial potential of beet sugar was clear, though. A new source of sugar would find a ready market, because sugar was still a luxury item despite declines in price due to the burgeoning supply from the Caribbean. Furthermore, unlike sugarcane, which was a tropical crop, beets were adapted to temperate climates such as those in Europe, so they could be grown in the regions where large amounts of sugar were consumed. In addition, with antislavery sentiment on the rise in some quarters of European society, there was growing unhappiness with the slave-based Caribbean sugar industry.

In 1786, four years after Marggraf's death, the king of Prussia became interested in the commercial potential of beet sugar. A subsequent Prussian king granted Franz Karl Achard, a student of Marggraf, an estate in Silesia, where Achard began artificial selection of beets as a source of sugar. In addition, Achard built the first pilot beet-sugar refinery, at Cunern, Silesia (now in Poland), in 1802. This factory, however, was not profitable.

SIGNIFICANCE

Marggraf's discovery of sugar in beet roots led to the development of an industry that rivaled the sugarcane industry. More than any other crop plant, the modern sugar beet is an industrial crop plant developed by human efforts in plant breeding. It is tailored for processing in centralized factories. Beets have been bred, for example, to have sugar contents as high as 20 percent, compared with the original 2 percent.

The eventual rise of a successful sugar beet industry owes much to French emperor Napoleon I, who became interested in developing such an industry after the British navy cut off his empire's supply of cane sugar from the Caribbean. Napoleon financed beet research, cultivation, and factories, in the hope that sugar beets would provide a domestic source of sugar for his armies. Benjamin Delessert in 1812 became the first person to extract beet sugar in large quantities. Two years later, forty small factories had opened in France, Belgium, Germany, and Austria.

Many people were suspicious of beet sugar, however, and after Napoleon's empire fell in 1814, the French sugar beet industry collapsed, as the country eagerly returned to importing cane sugar. Even so, the French achievements in sugar beet technology were not forgotten, since sugar beets offered a source of sugar that could be cultivated domestically in quantities large enough to preclude the need for costly imports from across the Atlantic. Production subsequently increased rapidly throughout Europe. At the end of the nineteenth century, sugar beets were also being grown in North America, and beets surpassed sugarcane as a source of world sugar.

A major factor in the commercial success of sugar beets is their adaptation to temperate and cold climates. With advances in beet breeding and technology, sugar beets became an attractive crop for Europeans to grow. The success of the crop contributed significantly to the decline of the slave-based system of cane sugar production in the Caribbean, which had fueled much of Western commerce in the seventeenth and eighteenth centuries.

Sugar beets, which are by far the most important commercially grown beets, have become an important crop in many parts of the United States and southern Canada, and they are even more important in other parts of the world. The major sugar-beet growing areas are countries of the former Soviet Union as well as France, Germany,

1740's

317

the United States, Poland, and Turkey. In the United States, the states of California, Minnesota, Idaho, North Dakota, and Michigan are major growers of the sugar beet. As of the early twenty-first century, sugar beets provided close to 40 percent of the world's supply of sugar.

—*Jane F. Hill*

FURTHER READING

Hobhouse, Henry. *Seeds of Change: Five Plants That Transformed Mankind*. New York: Harper & Row, 1986. Interprets the post-Renaissance world based on plant history. Chapter 2, on sugar, describes the rise of the Caribbean sugar trade and its waning after the rise of beet sugar.

Marggraf, Andreas. *Expériences chymiques, faites dans le dessein de tirer un véritable sucre des diverses plantes, qui croissent dans nos contrées*. 1747. In *Histoire de l'Académie Royale des Sciences et Belles Lettres, année 1747*. Reprinted in the author's *Chymische schriften* 2 (1767). The results of Marggraf's attempts to extract sugar from beets and other plants.

Musgrave, Toby, and Will Musgrave. *An Empire of Plants: People and Plants That Changed the World*. London: Cassell, 2000. Richly illustrated exploration of plants important to European trade and power. Chapter 2 focuses on Caribbean cane sugar and its decline with the rise of commercial sugar beet production. Index, bibliography.

Vaughan, John G., and Catherine A. Geissler. *The New Oxford Book of Food Plants*. New York: Oxford University Press, 1997. Color illustrations and descriptions of crops including sugar beets and other kinds of beets. Glossary, indices, and bibliography.

SEE ALSO: 1701: Tull Invents the Seed Drill; 1753: Lind Discovers a Cure for Scurvy; 1760's: Beginning of Selective Livestock Breeding; 1779: Ingenhousz Discovers Photosynthesis; 1789: Leblanc Develops Soda Production; 1793: Whitney Invents the Cotton Gin.

RELATED ARTICLE in *Great Lives from History: The Eighteenth Century, 1701-1800*: Andreas Sigismund Marggraf.

1748
AGNESI PUBLISHES *ANALYTICAL INSTITUTIONS*

Maria Agnesi published one of the first introductory textbooks for beginning students in the new field of calculus. Her text, by defining the terms in which the new discipline was taught, shaped the understanding of a generation of mathematicians. One of the curves discussed in her text is still associated with her name.

LOCALE: Milan (now in Italy)
CATEGORY: Mathematics; science and technology

KEY FIGURES

Maria Gaetana Agnesi (1718-1799), Italian mathematician and philanthropist
Leonhard Euler (1707-1783), Swiss mathematician and physicist
Laura Bassi (1711-1778), Italian physicist

SUMMARY OF EVENT

Maria Gaetana Agnesi's *Instituzioni analitiche ad uso della gioventù italiana* (1748; *Analytical Institutions*, 1801) provided students with a guide to the basic elements of calculus as it had been developed by Sir Isaac Newton and Gottfried Wilhelm Leibniz in the late seventeenth century. The book was translated into several other European languages, bearing witness to its importance in the transmission of calculus throughout Europe. Agnesi herself was admired by the mathematical community, which was impressed by the mastery achieved by a woman in what was at the time thought of as a male domain.

Agnesi was born into a wealthy family that valued education. Her father was a professor of mathematics at the University of Bologna and provided every educational opportunity for his children. In particular, Maria was tutored by university professors after she displayed a remarkable talent for both languages and mathematics at an early age. She is said to have been fluent in Latin, Greek, and Hebrew by the age of nine, and her father arranged for her to give discourses on scholarly subjects at home while she was still a child.

It is not clear that Maria Agnesi enjoyed being thrust into the spotlight, and in addition to her scholarly attainments, she also displayed ill health throughout her life. This may have been a way of refusing to be made the center of attention. By 1738, she expressed an intention to enter a convent, but this plan was frustrated by her father. She was quite accomplished in mathematics, and one reason for her taking up that pursuit may have been her recognition that it was less likely that people would be invited into the house to hear her talk about the newly created

Maria Gaetana Agnesi. (Library of Congress)

subject of calculus than to hear about literary and philosophical subjects. Her work in mathematics was guided by Father Remiro Rampinelli, a member of the Benedictine order and professor of mathematics at Pavia. She acknowledged his guidance throughout her published work.

In her years as a teenager, Agnesi was already solving problems of some difficulty, but she was following well-trodden paths, so her work did not make many ripples in the mathematical community. The publication in 1748 of the two-volume *Analytical Institutions* attracted attention well beyond anything that she had accomplished earlier. The work was aimed at a younger readership than most earlier discussions of calculus, so it began from an elementary level. In addition, to reduce the level of difficulty for students in Italy, Agnesi wrote her text in Italian rather than Latin, which was the scholarly international language of the time. She did not write in the native dialect of Milan, which was at the time still under the control of the Holy Roman Empire. Instead, she wrote Italian prose suited for a broad readership throughout the Italian states.

Analytical Institutions proceeds from the basis of al-

gebra to the limits of the calculus that was known at the time. Agnesi was careful in her discussions to make sure that her target audience would be able to understand the process for solving problems in calculus. In fact, her presentation has been criticized by later mathematicians for concentrating too much on examples, at the expense of explicating the theory behind the practical applications she teaches. It was not until the next century, in fact, that any exposition of the field took a primarily theoretical approach. The method that Agnesi used had the merit of ensuring that students would be able to do mathematics and not just read about it.

The single mathematical object to which Agnesi's name is attached is a curve defined by an equation of the third degree. It is commonly known as the "witch" of Agnesi, but this is the result of a mistranslation of the Italian word for "turn." There is a certain irony in such a term being attached to the name of someone as pious as Agnesi. She was responsible neither for the invention of the curve nor for the name attached to it, but her name has been firmly associated with the curve by later generations.

Agnesi's book, as a introductory textbook rather than an analysis of the field, did little to advance the knowledge or level of discussion of the foundations of the calculus. She provided interesting discussions of arbitrarily small quantities that could be added to finite quantities without markedly changing their value. Her primary concern in dealing with the calculus, however, was simply to enable students to handle problems involving maxima and minima, and for such calculations the theoretical foundations of the discipline were not crucial. If her readers were able to appreciate how to solve differential equations, the most advanced topic she discussed, the treatise would have achieved its purpose.

The wealth of her family enabled Agnesi not only to have the book printed but also to send copies to eminent people outside the sphere of mathematics. For example, Austrian archduchess Maria Theresa received a copy and rewarded the author (who had dedicated the book to her) with a diamond ring. Even more to her taste, however, may have been the recognition she received from Pope Benedict XIV, who presented her with a gold medal and arranged for her appointment to a chair in mathematics at the University of Bologna. Within scientific circles, Agnesi received similar acclaim. The French Académie des Sciences (Academy of Sciences) arranged for a translation of the second, more advanced volume, and one of Newton's successors himself translated the book into English.

It is not clear that Agnesi ever took up the chair provided by the pope. She had moved in the direction of reli-

1740's

gious activity, and her later years were entirely devoted to philanthropy in the setting of the Church. When asked to comment on the work of a younger mathematician, she avowed that she had given up on mathematics herself. With the publication of her *Analytical Institutions*, she may have been saying farewell to the field she hoped to shape.

SIGNIFICANCE

It is easy to attribute to the *Analytical Institutions* a strictly mathematical importance it did not possess. The originality of exposition does not compare with that of Leonhard Euler, whose introduction to analysis came out the same year as Agnesi's book. While Euler's approach to the foundations of the calculus may not have been entirely satisfactory, he rethought the issues in a way that Agnesi did not.

Similarly, Agnesi's position as a woman in the European intellectual world may not have been quite so distinctive as historians of mathematics suggest. While she may have been the first woman to be offered a chair in mathematics at a European university, Laura Bassi had been teaching physics at the University of Bologna since 1732. Bassi encouraged Agnesi to take up the position there but failed to convince her younger colleague.

On the other hand, there is no doubt that the publication of the *Analytical Institutions* made a difference in the perception of the ability of women to do mathematics at the highest level. Women were an important part of the intellectual life of Europe in the eighteenth century, but there may have been skepticism about their interest in something so abstract as mathematics. Agnesi demonstrated that a woman could master the full extent of the mathematics of her time and give back to her students what she had learned. It is not a coincidence that the *Analytical Institutions* is the earliest mathematical treatise by a woman that survives.

—Thomas Drucker

FURTHER READING

Burton, David M. *The History of Mathematics: An Introduction*. 5th ed. New York: McGraw-Hill, 2003. Careful distillation of the prevalent scholarship in the history of mathematics.

Kennedy, Hubert. "Maria Gaetana Agnesi." In *Women of Mathematics*, edited by Louise Grinstein and Paul Campbell. New York: Greenwood Press, 1982. Provides cultural context rather than mathematical details.

Kramer, Edna E. "Maria Gaetana Agnesi." In *Dictionary of Scientific Biography*, edited by Charles C. Gillispie. Vol. 1. New York: Charles Scribner's Sons, 1970. Kramer, a historian of mathematics, pays tribute to Agnesi with some enthusiasm but also technical details.

Osen, Lynn M. *Women in Mathematics*. Cambridge, Mass.: MIT Press, 1974. Tribute to Agnesi's "vital and inspiring" memory in the fight for women in science.

Stigler, Stephen M. *Statistics on the Table*. Cambridge, Mass.: Harvard University Press, 1999. Examination of the sequence of events that led to the term "witch" being applied to the curve associated with Agnesi.

Truesdell, Clifford. "Maria Gaetana Agnesi." *Archive for History of the Exact Sciences* 40 (1989): 113-142. Demythologizing study of the historical impact of Agnesi's treatise.

SEE ALSO: 1718: Bernoulli Publishes His Calculus of Variations; 1733: De Moivre Describes the Bell-Shaped Curve; 1748: Euler Develops the Concept of Function; 1763: Bayes Advances Probability Theory; 1784: Legendre Introduces Polynomials.

RELATED ARTICLES in *Great Lives from History: The Eighteenth Century, 1701-1800*: Maria Gaetana Agnesi; Benedict XIV; Leonhard Euler; Maria Theresa.

1748
BRADLEY DISCOVERS THE NUTATION OF EARTH'S AXIS

After discovering the aberration of starlight in the late 1720's, James Bradley proceeded to catalog the positions of more than three thousand stars between 1727 and 1747. His catalog led him to discover the nutation of the Earth's axis as the Earth orbits the Sun.

LOCALE: England
CATEGORIES: Astronomy; science and technology

KEY FIGURES

James Bradley (1693-1762), English astronomer and clergyman
James Pound (1669-1724), English astronomer and clergyman
Edmond Halley (1656-1742), English astronomer
Samuel Molyneux (1684-1728), English astronomer and politician
Robert Hooke (1635-1703), English physicist
John Flamsteed (1646-1719), English astronomer and founder of the Greenwich Observatory
Jean le Rond d'Alembert (1717-1783), French mathematician

SUMMARY OF EVENT

While attending Balliol College, Oxford University, between 1711 and 1717, James Bradley spent a great deal of time with his uncle, the Reverend James Pound, who was a skilled astronomer. Under the instruction of Pound, Bradley gained expertise in using the astronomical instruments of the time and in making very precise astronomical observations. He learned how to repair, maintain, and build his own equipment. In 1721, Bradley gave up his position as vicar of Bridstow to become the Savilian professor of astronomy at Oxford. Using a telescope—more than 212 feet long so as to yield high magnifications—Bradley measured the diameter of Venus in 1722 and the transit of Mercury over the disc of the Sun in 1723. He also tracked the movement of Comet Halley during the latter part of 1723. He soon gained a reputation as a meticulous astronomer who made very careful observations. The precision of his approach may be confirmed through examination of an extant book of his data and calculations.

In 1725, Bradley began a series of observations at Kew Green, near London, in the observatory of his friend Samuel Molyneux. They hoped to measure the parallax of a star—that is, the apparent shift in the position of a star that occurs as a result of the Earth's movement from a given point in its orbit to the point at the opposite end of

that orbit. The astronomers used a vertical telescope more than 24 feet long that was carefully mounted to observe the position of a star that passed directly overhead, thus avoiding complications because of the refraction of light. The star Gamma Draconis fit the necessary criteria for their project: It passed through the zenith of London and was bright enough to be observed with instruments. A number of years earlier, Robert Hooke and John Flamsteed had independently observed the same star and recorded its apparent displacement relative to the Earth. Bradley and Molyneux hoped to improve the accuracy of those measurements.

As Bradley and Molyneux made their observations, they found that the apparent displacement of Gamma Draconis was far too great to be a parallax and was, moreover, in the opposite direction of what they had expected. During the course of one year, the changing position of the star traced out a small ellipse. Bradley concluded that some other unexplained effect was masking the parallax of the star. Intrigued by the problem, he mounted a telescope at his aunt's home in Wanstead and made continual observations.

After many months of careful observations and deep thinking, Bradley finally realized that the effect was produced by the finite velocity of light, which had been reported by Danish astronomer Ole Rømer while observing eclipses of the moons of Jupiter in 1675. As a result of the finite speed of light, light coming from a particular star would reach an observer on the orbiting Earth from a direction that was slightly different from the actual position of the star from which it came. Bradley's deduction, based on the resulting apparent displacement of the star, constituted the celebrated discovery of the aberration of starlight. It was the first observational proof to confirm the theory of Nicolaus Copernicus that the Earth revolves around the Sun.

Between 1727 and 1732, Bradley recorded the annual change in position of a number of fixed stars. When Edmond Halley, the astronomer royal at Greenwich, died in 1742, Bradley was appointed as his successor. After repairing the instruments at Greenwich, Bradley continued his observations and cataloged the positions of more than three thousand stars between July, 1742, and September, 1747. He discovered that when a given star had completed its shift due to aberration over the course of twelve months it did not return to the same position it had previously occupied. Initially, he thought this observation was due to instrument error. After correcting for instrument error and checking the positions of numerous other stars that he had observed between 1727 and 1747, Bradley found the same outcome and sought an explanation. He surmised that there must be a change in the location of the points on Earth from which the positions of a given star were measured.

Early in the history of the Earth, it had been realized that the tides were related to the motion of the Moon. Around 134 B.C.E., the Greek astronomer Hipparchus discovered the precession, or conical motion, of the Earth's axis because of the Moon's motion. A satisfactory explanation of the tides and precession was finally supplied by Sir Isaac Newton in the late 1680's. The changing gravitational pull of the Moon and the Sun on the Earth's equatorial bulge produced the tides and the conical motion, or precession, of the rotational axis of the Earth. This rotation is analogous to the precessional wobble of the axis of a top that is spinning in the Earth's gravitational field.

From his numerous detailed observations, Bradley concluded that the precessional motion of the Earth's axis was not uniform, as had previously been supposed. Instead, there was a sinusoidal motion superimposed on the regular conical motion. Bradley adduced this extra wobble, known as nutation, to the fact that the tidal forces produced by the Moon and the Sun vary over time. This variation is caused by the continual change in location of the Earth, Moon, and Sun relative to each other and to the fact that the Moon's orbit is inclined at about five degrees to the plane of the Earth's orbit around the Sun. As a result, the axis of the Moon's orbit around the Earth precesses, just as the axis of the Earth precesses in its motion around the Sun.

Through his careful observations of star positions between 1727 and 1747, Bradley observed that a star returned to the same location at which it was originally observed in about 18.6 years. That duration corresponded to the time it took for one full precessional cycle of the Moon's orbit. As was characteristic of all his scientific work, when all the facts were finally available, Bradley announced his discovery of the nutation of the Earth's axis on February 14, 1748. His discovery of the aberration of starlight—as well as the discovery of the subtle, uneven nodding, or nutation, of the Earth's axis to which it led—rank as two of the most important discoveries made by astronomers.

SIGNIFICANCE

Bradley's discovery of the nutation of the Earth's axis provided an enhanced understanding of the interacting

gravitational forces between the Earth, the Moon, and the Sun. French mathematician Jean le Rond d'Alembert provided the mathematical explanation for nutation in 1749. Contributions to the size of the Earth's nutation were divided into the component along the ecliptic plane (nutation in longitude) and the component perpendicular to the ecliptic plane (nutation in obliquity). These values are significant, because they contribute to the accuracy with which astronomers can determine positions of astronomical objects that are observed from the Earth.

Observations of nutation values, including amplitude and phase, provide information about how the Earth responds to known forces. This information can then be used to place constraints on the properties of the interior of the Earth. The core and mantle of the Earth respond differently to the gravitational forces of the Moon and the Sun, causing a differential rotation between the core and the mantle. Consequently, nutation observations have proven invaluable in determining the limits both of the possible geometrical shape of the core-mantle boundary of the Earth and of the possible dissipative effects produced by core-mantle boundary interactions. These limits help to determine more accurate values for the density contrast across the core-mantle boundary. Researchers in astrophysics also use nutation amplitudes to provide evidence for the differential rotation between the inner and outer cores of the Earth. This information then refines values of the density contrast that exists across the boundary between inner core and outer core.

—Alvin K. Benson

FURTHER READING

Bradley, James. *Miscellaneous Works: Correspondence of the Rev. James Bradley*. New York: Oxford University Press, 1992. Publication of Bradley's writings, including a biography of Bradley, how he analyzed his astronomical data, and a detailed description of the nutation of the Earth's axis.

Fix, John D. *Astronomy: Journey to the Cosmic Frontier*. New York: McGraw-Hill, 2001. Discusses one of Bradley's main contributions to astronomy, the aberration of starlight, which led to his discovery of the nutation of the Earth's axis.

Mathews, P. M. *Modeling of Nutation and Precession*. Washington, D.C.: American Geophysical Union, 2002. Contains diagrams that clearly illustrate the precession and nutation of the Earth's axis, how the motions are modeled, and implications that provide insights into the interior of the Earth.

Seeds, Michael A. *Foundations of Astronomy*. Belmont, Calif.: Brooks/Cole, 2004. Seeds reviews the history of understandings of the Moon and explains the fundamental ideas of precession and nutation in conjunction with Bradley's discoveries.

Zelik, Michael. *Astronomy: The Evolving Universe*. 9th ed. New York: Cambridge University Press, 2002. Reviews and illustrates the concepts of stellar parallax, aberration of starlight, precession, nutation, and contributions of James Bradley to astronomy.

SEE ALSO: 1704-1712: Astronomy Wars in England; 1705: Halley Predicts the Return of a Comet; 1714-1762: Quest for Longitude; 1725: Flamsteed's Star Catalog Marks the Transition to Modern Astronomy; 1740: Maclaurin's Gravitational Theory; 1743-1744: D'Alembert Develops His Axioms of Motion; 1796: Laplace Articulates His Nebular Hypothesis.

RELATED ARTICLE in *Great Lives from History: The Eighteenth Century, 1701-1800*: Jean le Rond d'Alembert.

1748
EULER DEVELOPS THE CONCEPT OF FUNCTION

The introduction of algebraic expressions for curves helped mathematicians to analyze geometrical figures. Leonhard Euler's 1748 work marked a change in perspective by putting the function first and the curve second. By inverting the order of the expression, Euler reconceived the very subject matter of mathematics.

LOCALE: Berlin, Prussia (now in Germany)
CATEGORIES: Mathematics; science and technology

KEY FIGURES

Leonhard Euler (1707-1783), Swiss mathematician and physicist
Johann I Bernoulli (1667-1748), Swiss mathematician
Gottfried Wilhelm Leibniz (1646-1716), German mathematician and philosopher
Joseph-Louis Lagrange (1736-1813), French mathematician

SUMMARY OF EVENT

The traditional objects of mathematical study have been numbers and geometrical shapes. In the seventeenth century, René Descartes juxtaposed algebra and geometry, allowing algebra to be used to study geometrical objects. In Descartes's conception, it was still the geometrical object that was primary; the algebraic expression was simply a translation of the shape into equations, a new way to represent the object. With the work of Leonhard Euler, however, a change began that led mathematicians to think of the expression representing a curve as the primary object of study. The geometrical object itself came to be seen as a mere illustration of equations, rather than the object the equations sought to describe. This shift shaped mathematical practice and attitudes for more than two centuries.

From ancient times to the seventeenth century, the objects of study of mathematics were clearly recognized as numbers and figures. In other words, mathematicians sought to understand and to identify the properties of numbers (arithmetic) and shapes (geometry). The purpose of algebra was simply to solve arithmetic problems. It was analogous to the use of illustrations to solve geometrical problems, even when it was recognized that the geometrical object itself could not be drawn on a piece of paper. Even arithmetic was sometimes considered to be a branch of geometry, as expressed in Euclid's *Elementa* (c. 300 B.C.E.; *The Elements of Geometrie of the Most Auncient Philosopher Euclide of Megara*, 1570; commonly known as *Elements*).

In the seventeenth century, René Descartes introduced an approach to geometry that was to transform the subject. A geometrical figure could be represented by an algebraic equation, and study of the algebraic equation and its properties enabled a mathematician to arrive at conclusions about the geometrical object. For example, if one had the equation for a given circle and one found that plugging the value 0 in for x produced an equation with no solutions for y, then one could conclude that the circle did not cross the y-axis. This kind of property was dependent on the coordinate representation of the circle, but others dealt with intrinsic properties of the figure.

Even after Descartes's innovation, however, the geometrical circle was taken by mathematicians to be prior to any algebraic representation of it. After all, even to write down an algebraic equation for a geometrical figure required selecting a coordinate system, and geometers should not have to resort to that choice in order to be able to make conclusions about shapes and figures. (That is, it should not be necessary to know where a shape is in order to know things about the unchanging properties of the shape.) The algebraic equation was a tool for arguing about the geometrical object but was only ancillary (and was dispensable).

With the advent of the calculus in the late seventeenth century, however, techniques were introduced that could apply directly to the equation for a geometric shape. For example, using the calculus, a mathematician could find the area of a parabola without using the geometric definition of the curve. Mathematicians like Pierre de Fermat earlier in the seventeenth century had been able to find expressions for the area of a given parabola directly by geometric means, but it was much harder to see how to extend those techniques to curves in general. The calculus offered a relatively easy way to extend results to general categories.

A function is a formula for obtaining values for one quantity from those for another quantity (for example, finding the distance traveled by an object given its duration of travel). By the seventeenth century, it was recognized that some functions (like the values of a polynomial) could be obtained by algebraic means and some (like the sine function) could not. While algebraically obtainable functions supported the view that numbers were the primary object of mathematics, the other kind of function not only resisted this view but also made it difficult to understand precisely what a given function did to an input value in order to produce the output value. Johann I Bernoulli offered a characterization of a quantity obtained "in any manner" from another quantity as the basis for his idea of function, which was a term subsequently employed by Gottfried Wilhelm Leibniz.

It was Euler's *Introductio in analysin infinitorum* (1748; *Introduction to Analysis of the Infinite*, 1988-1990) that put the issue of the definition of functions squarely before the mathematical audience at large. Euler had already attained quite a reputation for his mathematical ingenuity in solving problems. Benefiting, moreover, from the standing of Johann I Bernoulli, his mathematical guide at the University of Basel, he had rapidly become part of the research community. Euler was to become the most prolific mathematician of all time, as measured by published papers, and he moved back and forth between positions in St. Petersburg and Berlin. His influence on mathematical ideas and even notation was unmatched.

In the opening chapter of his *Introduction to Analysis of the Infinite*, Euler analyzes functions of various kinds. He defines a function generally as an "analytic expression," which puts an emphasis on its ability to produce a

resulting quantity by plugging an original quantity into an equational expression. There is no need to represent the quantity to be obtained as a variable on one side of the equation, so he allows for functions that are defined implicitly.

Euler then defines algebraic and transcendental functions, the latter being the kind that cannot be expressed algebraically (in which term he includes polynomials and ratios of polynomials). The discussion even takes on the difference between singly valued functions and multiply valued functions. The latter category encompasses functions in which, for example, the variable to be obtained only appears as a square, in which case one input can produce two separate outputs, one positive and one negative.

Over the course of his work, Euler tackles all sorts of interesting problems about infinite series, infinite products, and continued fractions. Many of those results were put to use by Euler himself, as well as his successors. His treatment of the idea of function at the beginning of his text, however, has perhaps been Euler's most important mathematical legacy. The algebraic expression has become the central subject for mathematical investigation, and the geometrical object that it describes has been demoted to second place.

SIGNIFICANCE

Euler's characterization of a function as an "analytic expression" was one that even he found restrictive in the course of his later mathematical career. By the end of the eighteenth century, the mathematician Joseph-Louis Lagrange had characterized a function as a combination of operations. This more inclusive idea of a function could apply to situations beyond those in which numbers were understood as quantities known in advance. In addition, one could take other sorts of mathematical objects (permutations, for example) and regard those as the ingredients to be plugged into the recipe to which the function corresponded.

The drive toward abstraction that characterized mathematics through most of the twentieth century can be seen as an outcome of Euler's treatment of function as the central idea of mathematics. The branch of mathematics called "category theory" starts with the idea of a function as primary and is not so concerned with the sort of object on which the function acts. Even the philosophy of mathematics has been influenced by the view that the nature of mathematical objects is not so important as the kind of functions that act on them.

Geometrical objects have not been entirely neglected

over the centuries since Euler wrote. It remains the case, however, that students asked to demonstrate something about geometrical objects will almost always turn to the algebraic representation. In the nineteenth century, the characterization of branches of geometry was according to the kind of function that left the geometric objects unchanged. The heritage of the idea of function has cut across all branches of mathematics and continues to affect our views of its subject matter.

—*Thomas Drucker*

FURTHER READING

Bottazzini, Umberto. *The Higher Calculus: A History of Real and Complex Analysis from Euler to Weierstrass*. New York: Springer-Verlag, 1986. Starts with a chapter on Euler's role in the formulation of functions.

Dunham, William. *Euler: The Master of Us All*. Washington, D.C.: Mathematical Association of America, 1999. The discussion of logarithms looks at the distinctive nature of transcendental functions before and after Euler.

James, Ioan. *Remarkable Mathematicians: From Euler to von Neumann*. New York: Cambridge University Press, 2002. Some biographical background with more attention on Euler's other work.

Kline, Morris. *Mathematical Thought from Ancient to Modern Times*. New York: Oxford University Press, 1972. Appeared at a time when discussion of the concept of function was a lively pedagogical issue and pursues the subject in detail through the period before Euler.

Lützen, Jesper. "Euler's Vision of a General Partial Differential Calculus for a Generalized Kind of Function." In *Sherlock Holmes in Babylon*, edited by Marlow Anderson, Victor Katz, and Robin Wilson. Washington, D.C.: Mathematical Association of America, 2004. Indicates the slow rate at which changes in the concept of function crept through the mathematical community.

SEE ALSO: 1718: Bernoulli Publishes His Calculus of Variations; 1733: De Moivre Describes the Bell-Shaped Curve; 1748: Agnesi Publishes *Analytical Institutions*; 1763: Bayes Advances Probability Theory; 1784: Legendre Introduces Polynomials.

RELATED ARTICLES in *Great Lives from History: The Eighteenth Century, 1701-1800*: Maria Gaetana Agnesi; Leonhard Euler; Joseph-Louis Lagrange.

1748
EXCAVATION OF POMPEII

The excavation of the intact ancient Roman city of Pompeii, which had been buried under layers of volcanic ash for more than sixteen centuries, caused a sensation among intellectuals and amateurs alike and brought about a revival of interest in the values and styles of the Roman world.

LOCALE: Pompeii (now in Italy)

CATEGORIES: Anthropology; architecture; cultural and intellectual history; natural disasters

KEY FIGURES

Prince d'Elbeuf (Emmanuel-Maurice de Lorraine; 1677-1763), Austrian occupier of Italy

Charles IV (1716-1788), king of the Two Sicilies, r. 1734-1759, and later king of Spain as Charles III, r. 1759-1788

Roque Joachim de Alcubierre (fl. mid-eighteenth century), Spanish excavator in charge of uncovering Herculaneum and Pompeii

Carl Jacob Weber (1712-1764), Swiss architect and engineer

Johann Joachim Winckelmann (1717-1768), German art historian and archaeologist

SUMMARY OF EVENT

For millennia, the rich volcanic soil of Mount Vesuvius produced abundant crops for the ancient peoples living in the area of the Bay of Naples. In an ironic twist of fate, that same Mount Vesuvius, which had long been inactive, reawakened on the morning of August 24, 79 C.E., burying the region and its inhabitants under thick layers of volcanic ash and lava. The thriving towns of Pompeii, Herculaneum, and Stabiae were suddenly and completely engulfed in the volcano's eruption.

The eruption of Mount Vesuvius changed the courses of rivers and altered entire coastlines, filling in areas of the bay with volcanic rock and ash. When the upheaval finally ceased, residents of Pompeii who returned in hopes of gathering their belongings had difficulty locating their city: Not only was it buried deep under meters of volcanic ash, but it was also no longer on the coast. After a short period of vain attempts to rescue what they could, the inhabitants of the former city moved away, and Pompeii was almost entirely forgotten. The area above the former city came to be known as Civitas, or the City, even though no city was ever again built on the site. Ancient Herculaneum, which now rested below meters of hardened mud, was later built over with a new city, Resina-Ercolano.

It was not until the late sixteenth century that either ancient city came to light again. Even then, the importance of the discovery went unrecognized: In the 1590's, several ancient remains were exposed during construction projects, but the artifacts were ignored. Nearly a century later, in 1689, engineers found a stone inscribed "Decurio Pompeiis." Thinking it was a reference to Pompey the Great, a statesman from the era of Republican Rome, the engineers ignored it as well.

Then, in 1709, while digging a well in Resina-Ercolano, workers brought up pieces of marble statuary. The prince d'Elbeuf, a member of the Austrian court that occupied Italy at the time, ordered the excavations to be extended, and he used the recovered treasures to decorate his nearby villa. By 1738, the excavations at Herculaneum drew the attention of Charles IV, the Austrian Bourbon king of the Two Sicilies (Naples and Sicily), who appointed Roque Joachim de Alcubierre director of excavations. Alcubierre was charged with tunneling through the ancient city to find additional treasures. The resulting destruction was enormous. No records were kept of where items were found. Tunnels were drilled and then refilled as soon as all valuable items were removed in order to prevent houses from collapsing in the city above. All items of value that Alcubierre discovered were taken to the king's palace in Naples (now the Museo Archeologico Nazionale di Napoli).

By 1748, Herculaneum appeared to have given up most of its valuable artworks, and the king ordered excavation to begin at Civitas, which, at that time, was thought to be the site of ancient Stabiae. Herculaneum had been buried under meters of rock-hard volcanic material that required arduous tunneling, but at Civitas, Pompeii was buried under layers of much lighter volcanic ash. For Alcubierre, this meant that work could go even more quickly.

Fortunately, the Swiss architect and engineer Carl Jacob Weber joined the team of excavators in 1750. Weber introduced new archaeological methodologies, including recording the locations of finds, saving "insignificant" objects such as ordinary household items, and publishing finds for review by the academic community. Weber's time-consuming and laborious techniques infu-

riated the impatient Alcubierre, and for the remainder of their time together, Alcubierre and Weber quarreled over how to run the excavations.

In 1762, when the famed art historian Johann Joachim Wincklemann visited the site, he was so appalled at Alcubierre's ramrod approach to excavation that Wincklemann wrote an open letter to all European scholars attacking Alcubierre and his mismanagement of the ancient sites. Wincklemann's letter served to awaken international interest in the excavations.

In 1763, excavators found an inscription verifying that Civitas was, in fact, the ancient city of Pompeii. For the first time, an entire ancient Roman city had been found intact. Unlike the remains of other ancient cities, such as the Rome itself, which had been exposed to the elements for centuries, Pompeii was completely preserved under layers of ash that protected it from the ravages of time. Pompeii retained the vivid, bright colors of its wall paintings and the minute details of daily life, such as foodstuffs and clothing. Even the exact locations and positions of the citizens who succumbed to the toxic fumes and extreme heat of the volcanic eruption could be recovered by filling the voids where the bodies had decomposed with plaster of Paris. Through this process, it was estimated that two thousand citizens of Pompeii perished during the eruption of Vesuvius.

The excavations at Pompeii revealed a town of about twenty thousand inhabitants as it appeared on that fateful day in August of 79 C.E. Its straight streets were lined with raised sidewalks, along which were located shops, bakeries, small restaurants, taverns, bathhouses, public latrines, laundries, apartments, and houses. At the center of town was a forum, along with temples and a large food market. The town had a covered theater and an open-air amphitheater with seating for twenty thousand people. On the outskirts of town were the lavish villas of Roman aristocrats who preferred to escape the heat and crowds of the city of Rome for the fresh air of Pompeii's seaside location. Protected for centuries by volcanic ash, the excavations revealed intact wall paintings, furniture, and mosaics, as well as perfectly preserved bronze and marble statuary.

As news about the finds at Pompeii and Herculaneum traveled across Europe, interested scholars and tourists flocked to Pompeii on their Grand Tours to experience firsthand the feeling of walking through an ancient Roman city. Block by block, the excavations continued across Pompeii, until it was realized that the exposed excavated areas were succumbing to the elements and to poorly administered tourism and even looting. It was not until the mid-nineteenth century that any truly scientific or systematic excavations were carried out at the sites. The excavations then continued with greater supervision, and archeological methods continuously improved. Today, one-third of the city of Pompeii and two-thirds of the city of Herculaneum remain unexcavated, reserved for future generations and more advanced archaeological methods.

SIGNIFICANCE

The excavation of Pompeii opened the ancient Roman world to greater scrutiny than ever before. This glimpse into another world fired the imaginations of many Europeans and American colonists who were chaffing under the excesses and despotism of despised monarchies. Scholars and statesmen began looking to the ancient

world for solutions to their own contemporary problems, finding in ancient Rome an ideal of republican values, patriotism, and reason. The desire to overthrow tyrannical monarchies and to reestablish Roman republican forms of government served as a stimulus for the revolutions in both America (1776) and France (1789).

The excavations at Pompeii also had great cultural influences in both Europe and America. The discoveries of entire ancient buildings, complete with rooms, furniture, and artifacts from everyday life, helped to initiate the neoclassical movement in art and architecture and inspired the Empire style in dress and furniture. The revival of classical aesthetics served as a statement of protest against the extravagances of the ornately decorative Baroque and rococo styles popular with the monarchs of

Pompeii, Italy, was buried under tons of volcanic ash and debris after the eruption of Mount Vesuvius in 79 C.E. Archaeologists began excavating the mostly intact ancient Roman city's ruins in 1748, sparking renewed interest in Roman art and culture. (Premier Publishing)

Europe. Neoclassical artists, such as Jacques-Louis David, painted moralizing works depicting noble Romans making personal sacrifices for the good of the state. Architects, such as Robert Adam and James Adam, designed rooms inspired by Roman originals, complete with historically accurate bright colors, such as "Pompeii red." The writer Madame de Staël wrote the novel *Corrine: Ou, L'Italie* (1807; *Corrine: Or, Italy*, 1807) based on Pompeii and the composer Giovanni Pacini wrote the opera *L'Ultimo giorno di Pompei* (pr. 1825, pb. c. 1826; the last days of Pompeii), complete with an erupting Mount Vesuvius at the ending.

The discovery of Pompeii also brought to the public's attention the importance of accurately recording and preserving evidence of the past. The excavations were initiated in a random treasure hunt to fill the palaces of Europe with precious artworks, but through time they evolved into a precise scientific endeavor to recapture and preserve not only the artworks but also the details of the everyday lives of those who lived long ago.

—*Sonia Sorrell*

FURTHER READING

Amery, Colin, and Brian Curran, Jr. *The Lost World of Pompeii.* Los Angeles: J. Paul Getty Museum, 2002. Discusses Pompeii's history, destruction, rediscovery, and preservation today, including photographs of the site.

Cassanelli, Roberto, et al. *Houses and Monuments of Pompeii: The Works of Fausto and Felice Niccolini.* Los Angeles: J. Paul Getty Museum, 2002. Collection of essays relating to the excavations of Pompeii and their influence on Western culture.

Guzzo, Pier Giovanni, et al. *Pompeii.* Los Angeles: J. Paul Getty Trust, 2000. Comprehensive guide that traces the history of Pompeii, describes the archaeological site, and includes photographs of Pompeii's buildings, paintings, and artifacts.

Parslow, Christopher Charles. *Rediscovering Antiquity: Karl Weber and the Excavation of Herculaneum, Pompeii, and Stabiae.* New York: Cambridge University Press, 1998. Excellent recounting of Weber's discoveries and his contributions to the then-fledgling field of archaeology.

Radice, Betty, trans. *The Letters of the Younger Pliny.* New York: Penguin Classics, 1976. An eyewitness account of the 79 C.E. eruption of Mount Vesuvius.

SEE ALSO: 1719-1724: Stukeley Studies Stonehenge and Avebury; 1762: *The Antiquities of Athens* Prompts Architectural Neoclassicism; 1786: Discovery of the Mayan Ruins at Palenque; July 19, 1799: Discovery of the Rosetta Stone.

RELATED ARTICLES in *Great Lives from History: The Eighteenth Century, 1701-1800*: Charles III; Madame de Staël; Johann Joachim Winckelmann.

1748
MONTESQUIEU PUBLISHES *THE SPIRIT OF THE LAWS*

The Spirit of the Laws set a standard for comparative political, cultural, and legal thought in Europe. It laid the foundation for the institution of the social sciences as disciplines more rigorous and distinct from those of the humanities.

LOCALE: France

CATEGORIES: Philosophy; literature; government and politics

KEY FIGURE

Montesquieu (Charles-Louis de Secondat; 1689-1755), French philosopher and political theorist

SUMMARY OF EVENT

Montesquieu's *De l'esprit des loix* (1748; *The Spirit of the Laws*, 1750) was one of the first attempts to provide an interpretive structure to the history of human legislation. A provincial magistrate and Bordeaux aristocrat, Montesquieu also participated in his local provincial scientific academy, had interests in scientific agriculture, and authored the influential epistolary novel *Lettres persanes* (1721; *Persian Letters*, 1722). Montesquieu's professional interest in the law was coupled by his personal interest in the explanatory power of the scientific method.

Preceded by the natural law tradition, in which the comparative history of legislation was linked to Cartesian clear and distinct moral ideas, *The Spirit of the Laws* owed its content to some of the most significant intellectual traditions of the eighteenth century. Balanced against Montesquieu's philosophical interests was his attempt to explain the English government to his French audience, both as exposition of a free government and as criticism of the French monarchy. Montesquieu joined his voice to those in French society who saw the legacy of Louis XIV's rule representing the end of French liberty. A major theme of the work concerns the threat of despotism, or the sovereign's institutionalized capricious will. Montesquieu investigated politics to reveal the principles of order—the spirit—of each government. Policy based on such principles would prevent despotism, for disordered caprice in government could be fought with adherence to the ordering principle that each government naturally exemplifies.

Montesquieu's goal was to resolve the tension between the universal and immutable laws of nature and the varied, relative laws of human society as they differed from nation to nation. Montesquieu resolved them with an account of the generation of particular positive laws by the peculiar climates and geographical circumstances of each nation. He was convinced that a nation's laws could be demonstrated to be consistent with their soil and climate; thus the civil law of Italy, a country situated in a warm climate, would differ dramatically from that of England in the colder north. Further, such laws conformed to the psychology of each nation. The southern areas were blessed with comfortable weather year round and good soil; its inhabitants had their needs met more easily. In the harsher north, survival was more painstaking, with less variety for life's amenities. The people of the north could endure more hardship and worked harder to satisfy their needs. Most important was the northern European development of an intense love of their liberty and independence. Found earliest among the Germanic tribes, this love of liberty developed in Britain, France, and most of the European north as the Germans invaded those areas.

Even this circumscribed relativity of human experience was undergirded, however, by Montesquieu's dependence upon the principles of natural jurisprudence. He was convinced of the rational status of the basic moral laws of human life. Morality is necessarily social and rational; he lauded the Stoics for their achievements in moral philosophy. Self-preservation, liberty, equality, sanctity of private property, and the father's responsibility to his children were among the most important natural laws. Montesquieu discussed these prin-

---

MONTESQUIEU ON LIBERTY

In Book 11 of The Spirit of the Laws, *Montesquieu analyzes the relationship between liberty and a state's constitution. He puts forward his own definition of liberty, which, like many other Enlightenment definitions, emphasizes the lack of contradiction between free will and moral constraints. For Montesquieu, as for Immanuel Kant and others, doing what one should do is acting freely; to act otherwise is to relinquish rather than to embrace freedom.*

It is true that in democracies the people seem to do what they want, but political liberty in no way consists in doing what one wants. In a state, that is, in a society where there are laws, liberty can consist only in having the power to do what one should want to do and in no way being constrained to do what one should not want to do.

One must put oneself in mind of what independence is and what liberty is. Liberty is the right to do everything the laws permit; and if one citizen could do what they forbid, he would no longer have liberty because the others would likewise have this same power.

Source: Montesquieu, *The Spirit of the Laws*, edited by Anne M. Cohler, Basia C. Miller, and Harold S. Stone (New York: Cambridge University Press, 1989), p. 155.

---

ciples throughout the book as the final points of appeal in almost every debate concerning justice in civil, political, and religious legislation. Perhaps more significant for Montesquieu was the republican maxim that political virtue differs from moral virtue. He recognized that what can be condemned according to Christian ethics—the passion for war, love of honor and glory—can in particular circumstances be advantageous to the public good.

An important section of the book concerned the distinctions between types of governments. Like other laws, the peculiar system of government of a people was the product of their climate and geographical context. Although he specifically discussed three types—republicanism, monarchy, and despotism—aristocracy, while technically a republican polity, occurred often in discussions of both republics and monarchy and seemed at times to function as a fourth type. A philosophical principle distinguished each form of government from the other: virtue in republics, honor in monarchies, moderation in aristocracies, and fear in despotisms.

Montesquieu traced the institutions, manners, and laws of each regime back to the condition of each of these principles. A citizen of a republic where virtue was nurtured would seek the glory of the state and the good of the public before luxury and individual honor; this was his motive for action, and the wise legislator would frame laws to guide and influence him. In the monarchy, honor

1740's

is the "spring" of that government; such envy of each citizen toward another for the nation's honors and status drove them to be good subjects, although morally less virtuous than members of a republic. At the lowest end of the political scale, the despot ruled by caprice and with no regard for laws; his subjects were little more than slaves.

What republics offered in fulfillment of humanity's natural liberty and independence they lacked in practicality. They required a community of goods; they were a polity best fitted for small nations; foreign commerce and the subsequent increased wealth of their citizens could destroy their national virtue. Their virtue was supported by military exercises, but their success at war, the result of these republican warrior virtues, could lead to the passion for empire and their eventual decline into despotism as in ancient Rome. Monarchies had achieved the greatest successes in the field of war, and the greatest empires. A government of one man, however, was always in danger of becoming the tool of his passions and whims. The most natural channel for the king to carry out his policies was the nobility; they, however, were often contemptuous of civil government. Needless wars could become the goal of nobles bent on battlefield glory; the common people often suffered greatly in a monarchy. Finally, each government could be corrupted, its principle reversed. Republics declined as they grew successful; aristocracies became hereditary and arbitrary; the long abuse of power or conquest could overcome climate and drive monarchies into despotism.

England was Montesquieu's example of the freest nation in history, as well as the nation that had used commerce and trade to the best advantage of its people. Just as moderation was the dominant and desired human virtue in society, so was balance the key principle of government. Montesquieu saw England's three branches of government as executing the perfect balance among equal powers. The ease with which power could be abused by one man or a group of men meant that the executive, legislature, and judiciary must be separated to prevent the decline of political liberty. Citizen armies and the nurture of their martial spirit functioned as another hedge against the executive. Because their climate was so harsh, the English found no satisfaction in anything, and thus Montesquieu decided that tyranny could not be easily foisted on them.

Finally, Montesquieu's thoughts on government and society were colored by his belief that disorder constantly threatened society, whether by a mob in a republic or by a despot in a monarchy. Only the utmost care and watchfulness could prevent governments from unleashing the destructiveness of human passions. England, the freest government in history, survived on its fear of despotism and its division of governmental power into a balanced polity.

SIGNIFICANCE

Many of Montesquieu's contemporaries read *The Spirit of the Laws* and complimented him on his erudition and his original perspective on political theory. Yet while some saw him as their tutor in political thought, others, such as Voltaire, also commented that *The Spirit of the Laws* was a confusing, disordered, often aphoristic book. Still, the influence of this work went far beyond Montesquieu's native France. It had a major impact on the social theories of Scottish philosophers such as David Hume, Adam Smith, and Adam Ferguson. The debates of American revolutionary theorists and, later, constitutional debates were deeply indebted to Montesquieu's ideas of the balance of powers. The initial stages of the French Revolution also owed a great deal to Montesquieu's trenchant critique of monarchic despotism.

—*Michael Kugler*

FURTHER READING

Berlin, Isaiah. "Montesquieu." In *Against the Current: Essays in the History of Ideas*, edited and with a bibliography by Henry Hardy. Princeton, N.J.: Princeton University Press, 2001. Collection of essays by the late Berlin, a noted twentieth century philosopher. The essays explore the historical importance of dissenters, such as Montesquieu, whose ideas challenged conventional wisdom.

Carrithers, David W., Michael A. Mosher, and Paul A. Rahe, eds. *Montesquieu's Science of Politics: Essays on "The Spirit of the Laws."* Lanham, Md.: Rowman & Littlefield, 2001. Collection of essays analyzing Montesquieu's best-known work and his contributions to the field of political science.

Cohler, Anne. *Montesquieu's Comparative Politics and the Spirit of American Constitutionalism.* Lawrence: University Press of Kansas, 1988. Good introduction to Montesquieu's influence on eighteenth century American political thought.

Hampson, Norman. *The Enlightenment.* New York: Penguin Books, 1990. A readable introduction to the writers and debates of the European Enlightenment.

_____. *Will and Circumstance: Montesquieu, Rousseau, and the French Revolution.* Norman: University of Oklahoma Press, 1983. Traces Montesquieu's influence on the writers, reformers, and activists of the French Revolution.

Hulling, Mark. *Montesquieu and the Old Regime*. Berkeley: University of California Press, 1976. Argues that Montesquieu was a serious and relentless critic of French monarchic culture.

Keohane, Nannerl. *Philosophy and the State in France: The Renaissance to the Enlightenment*. Princeton, N.J.: Princeton University Press, 1980. Montesquieu emerges in the larger context of French political and constitutional debates.

Montesquieu. *The Spirit of the Laws*. Translated and edited by Anne M. Cohler, Basia Carolyn Miller, and Harold Samuel Stone. New York: Cambridge University Press, 1989. The best translation of the work; also has a fine introductory essay.

Shackleton, Robert. *Montesquieu: A Critical Biography*.

New York: Oxford University Press, 1961. Good biography and dependable exposition of Montesquieu's work.

Shklar, Judith. *Montesquieu*. New York: Oxford University Press, 1987. A short, well-written introduction to Montesquieu and his work.

SEE ALSO: 1721-1750: Early Enlightenment in France; Oct., 1725: Vico Publishes *The New Science*; July 27, 1758: Helvétius Publishes *De l'esprit*; Apr., 1762: Rousseau Publishes *The Social Contract*; 1784-1791: Herder Publishes His Philosophy of History; Feb. 22, 1791-Feb. 16, 1792: Thomas Paine Publishes *Rights of Man*; 1792: Wollstonecraft Publishes *A Vindication of the Rights of Woman*.

RELATED ARTICLES in *Great Lives from History: The Eighteenth Century, 1701-1800*: Montesquieu; Jean-Jacques Rousseau; Giambattista Vico.

1748
NOLLET DISCOVERS OSMOSIS

Jean-Antoine Nollet discovered that membranes could be selectively permeable and analyzed the process by which a solvent concentrated on one side of such a membrane would pass through it until an equilibrium on either side of the membrane had been reached. Henri Dutrochet later related this process specifically to biological systems and gave it the name "osmosis."

LOCALE: Paris, France
CATEGORIES: Chemistry; science and technology

KEY FIGURES

Jean-Antoine Nollet (1700-1770), French abbot and physicist
Benjamin Franklin (1706-1790), American statesman and naturalist
Henri Dutrochet (1776-1847), French physician and naturalist
Wilhelm Pfeffer (1845-1920), German botanist
Jacobus Henricus van't Hoff (1852-1911), Dutch chemist

SUMMARY OF EVENT

It is a well-known principle that nature abhors a vacuum. A gaseous or liquid substance concentrated in one portion of a space will tend to spread out until it is evenly distributed, thereby filling "vacuums," or areas that had

been devoid of the substance. This process is known as diffusion. Osmosis is a particular kind of diffusion.

The process of osmosis involves a semipermeable membrane, that is, a barrier that can be penetrated by some substances but not by others. Osmosis occurs when a solvent diffuses across such a membrane. So, for example, if pure water is placed on one side of a semipermeable membrane and salt water is placed on the other side, the pure water will flow through the membrane, diluting the salt water. On the other hand, if there are equal concentrations of salt in the water on either side of the membrane, the equilibrium of the two solutions will prevent the water from diffusing through the membrane. Osmosis is a crucial process in biological cells and complex organisms. It is one of the means through which plants and animals regulate their internal chemistry, and it drives other processes necessary to the health of those organisms. The first examples of osmosis to be observed in a laboratory were observed by Jean-Antoine Nollet.

Nollet was born into a peasant family on November 19, 1700, in Pimpré, Oise, France. After training for the priesthood, Nollet was appointed to a deaconship (1728) and eventually served as *abbé* (abbot) of the Grand Convent of the Carthusians in Paris. Though trained primarily in theology and maintaining a strong religious conviction throughout his life, Abbé Nollet is better known for his work in experimental physics. He was a member of both the Royal Society of London, to which he was admitted in 1735, and the French Académie des Sciences (Academy of Sciences), of which he first became an associate member in 1742. He was appointed professor of experimental physics at the University of Paris. Nollet was also sought after by royalty: He provided scientific services to the duke of Savoy in Turin, Italy, and he served as physics teacher to the royal children at the court of France's Louis XV.

Much of Nollet's work centered on the question of the nature of electricity. Nollet viewed electricity as a flow of matter taking place between charged bodies. In 1748, he invented the electrometer, an instrument capable of detecting and measuring electric charges. Nollet also demonstrated the flow of electricity in a form of parlor trick: He caused an electric charge to pass through a row of men, making them all jump simultaneously.

Nollet adapted his interest in electrical flow to crude experimentation in biological systems. He was aware of German experiments observing the effects of electricity on the flow of water. Water in a thin capillary tube would simply drip from the open end. However, if electricity was applied to the tube, the water would flow in a constant stream. Nollet began a series of experiments in which he measured the rate of water transpiration in plants and animals as a function of the presence or absence of electricity. He noted an increase in the transpiration rate when the organism was electrified.

Nollet's religious views, as well as the questions dealing with the nature of electricity, later became the basis for conflict with the American statesman and naturalist Benjamin Franklin. During the 1740's, Franklin began a series of experiments addressing the question of the nature of electricity, culminating with recognition of what became the concept of conservation of charge. During the summer of 1752, Franklin carried out his famous kite experiment, demonstrating that lightning was a form of electricity. The immediate application of this work was his invention of the lightning rod, a device to protect buildings from fire resulting from lightning strikes.

Nollet, likely jealous of an "amateur's" discovery or possibly as a result of the zealotry of his religious views, argued that the lightning rod was an "offense to God." Nollet's argument was based on the idea that lightning originated from the heavens, and that by interfering with an instrument of God, one was in effect carrying out an offense against him. Though the lightning rod was quickly adopted through both Europe and the rest of the

Western world, the controversy did result in harsh words between Nollet and Franklin. Ironically, it was Nollet's observations that led to lightning rods being given their modern form: presence points on the ends of electrical conductors.

In 1748, Nollet carried out the experiments in which he discovered what is now known as the principle of osmosis. Nollet prepared a vessel containing alcohol ("spirits of wine") and enclosed the vessel within a piece of pig's bladder. After placing the covered vessel into a larger container filled with water, Nollet observed that, while the water traversed the bladder wall, the alcohol would remain trapped within the bladder. In some experiments, the bladder would expand until it burst. In addition to the principle of osmosis itself, Nollet had demonstrated the semipermeability of the bladder wall, although that term would not be invented for 150 years.

Nollet's work was carried out against the background of the Enlightenment. Prior to this period, science remained dominated by the classical views that had been held since antiquity; in no small part, this was the result of the continued influence of the Church. In the eighteenth century, however, the beliefs of antiquity came to be questioned as argument from authority was replaced by scientific methodologies, experimentation, and the use of evidence to prove one's beliefs, in philosophy no less than in physics. It was the age of Voltaire as much as that of Thomas Jefferson. The evolution of scientific experimentation represented merely one portion of the changes occurring throughout Europe.

SIGNIFICANCE

In the early decades of the nineteenth century, Nollet's countryman Henri Dutrochet became aware of Nollet's work and attempted to apply the same principle to the movement of fluids across cell membranes. While studying both plant and animal cells with a microscope, Dutrochet observed the movement of water as a solvent through the cell membrane, a process he termed osmosis. Dutrochet further observed that the direction of a solvent's flow was determined by the nature of the solvent rather than by the nature of the membrane. The solvent would always flow from a weaker, or less concentrated, solution into a stronger, or more concentrated, solution of a given solute.

Dutrochet tested his ideas by building an osmometer, an instrument capable of measuring the movement of water across an artificial barrier. Dutrochet referred to the movement of water across the barrier as "endosmosis," while the reverse movement was termed "exosmosis." The idea of the cell membrane as a barrier capable of regulating osmosis was then inimical to cell theory; it was certainly beyond Nollet's ability to apply to biology in any meaningful way. Nevertheless, Nollet's discovery represented one of the first in the developing area of experimental physics, and it would become crucial to correcting and refining cell theory.

Once a similar process was found to occur in conjunction with biological membranes, moreover, applications in several scientific fields quickly developed. German botanist Wilhelm Pfeffer, for example, explained a role for osmotic pressure in the action of fluids within plant vessels. The mathematics of osmosis and chemical equilibrium were worked out by Dutch chemist Jacobus Henricus van't Hoff. As a result, he was awarded the first Nobel Prize in Chemistry in 1901. It was van't Hoff who coined the term "semipermeable" to describe the selective penetrability of cellular membranes.

—*Richard Adler*

FURTHER READING

Franklin, Benjamin. *Autobiography of Benjamin Franklin*. New York: Buccaneer Books, 1984. Franklin discusses the controversy that arose between him and Nollet on the subject of electricity.

Gay, Peter. *The Enlightenment: The Science of Freedom*. New York: W. W. Norton, 1996. The development of what became known as science against the background of the Enlightenment. Nollet only has a brief mention, but the context of his work is apparent.

Isaacson, Walter. *Benjamin Franklin: An American Life*. New York: Simon & Schuster, 2003. Biography of Franklin that includes information about the controversy between his work on electricity and Nollet's religious views.

Kirkham, M. B. *Principles of Soil and Plant Water Relations*. St. Louis, Mo.: Elsevier, 2005. Principles of water movement in plants, the result of osmotic pressure originally described by Nollet.

Mason, E.A. "From Pig Bladders and Cracked Jars to Polysulfones: An Historical Perspective on Membrane Transport." *Journal of Membrane Science* 60 (1991): 125-145. A history of the science of membrane transport, beginning with Nollet's observations with a pig bladder.

Tompkins, Peter, and Christopher Bird. *The Secret Life of Plants*. New York: Harper & Row, 1973. This classic provides a rather anthropomorphic view of plants as "beings." Included is some background behind Nollet's initial work on the movement of water in the presence of an electric field, as well as the influence of electricity on seed germination.

SEE ALSO: 1718: Geoffroy Issues the *Table of Reactivities*; 1723: Stahl Postulates the Phlogiston Theory; 1729: Gray Discovers Principles of Electric Conductivity; 1733: Du Fay Discovers Two Kinds of Electric Charge; 1738: Bernoulli Proposes the Kinetic Theory of Gases; Oct., 1745, and Jan., 1746: Invention of the Leyden Jar; June, 1752: Franklin Demonstrates the Electrical Nature of Lightning; Aug. 1, 1774: Priestley Discovers Oxygen; 1781-1784: Cavendish Discovers the Composition of Water; c. 1794-1799: Proust Establishes the Law of Definite Proportions.

RELATED ARTICLES in *Great Lives from History: The Eighteenth Century, 1701-1800*: Benjamin Franklin; Thomas Jefferson; Louis XV; Voltaire.

1740's

1748-1755
CONSTRUCTION OF ISTANBUL'S NUR-U OSMANIYE COMPLEX

The last great work of Ottoman religious architecture, the Nur-u Osmaniye mosque complex assimilated European stylistic influences into the classical Ottoman style. Combining a mosque, school, and library, the complex has functioned since its completion as an important repository and purveyor of Islamic knowledge and faith.

LOCALE: Constantinople, Ottoman Empire (now Istanbul, Turkey)

CATEGORIES: Architecture; religion and theology

KEY FIGURES

Simeon Kalfa (fl. mid-eighteenth century), Ottoman architect of the Nur-u Osmaniye complex

Ahmed Efendi (fl. eighteenth century), Ottoman construction manager of the Nur-u Osmaniye complex

Mahmud I (1696-1754), Ottoman sultan, r. 1730-1754

Osman III (1739-1757), Ottoman sultan, r. 1754-1757, and brother of Mahmud I

Yedikuleli Seyyid Abdullah Efendi (1679-1731), Ottoman calligrapher and poet

Mehmed Rasim (1687-1755), Ottoman calligrapher

Yahya Fahreddin (d. 1756), Ottoman calligrapher

Kātipzāde Mehmed Refi Efendi (1682?-1769), Ottoman calligrapher

SUMMARY OF EVENT

Construction of the Nur-u Osmaniye complex began in 1748, during the rule of Ottoman sultan Mahmud I, and was completed under the auspices of his brother and successor Osman III in 1755. Built to replace the mosque of Fatma Hatun, which was destroyed in a fire, the complex was located to the east of Constantinople's covered bazaar. Its name, meaning "light of Osman," is thought to refer to Osman III and to a verse from the Qūʾran's Light Chapter, which is also inscribed inside the building's dome: "God is the light of the heavens and the earth." Though in keeping with the massing of Ottoman mosques and mosque complexes, or *kulliye*, the structure also exemplifies the Baroque style of the eighteenth century and the Westernizing vision of Mahmud I.

The basic form of the classical Ottoman mosque was developed as early as the fourteenth century, from the simple cubic masses of cut stone that defined small structures such as the Haji Ozbek mosque at Iznik (1333). The prototypical plan consisted of a portico and domed

prayer hall, and the interior functions of the mosque were visible from outside the structure. In keeping with such models, the mosque at the Nur-u Osmaniye complex consists of a single domed prayer hall, preceded by a courtyard of comparable size on the northwest. A main portal on the northwest opens onto the courtyard, the unique shape of which is composed of wedge-shaped segments set between nine domed bays. Light is drawn into the space by windows placed at two levels, each of which allows views outside the structure. A five-bay portico completes the courtyard and leads into the prayer hall through an axial portal.

The mosque's prayer hall is square in shape, with a semicircular *mihrab* niche, which offers the direction of prayer. The interior space is capped by a dome that measures twenty-five meters in diameter and reaches a height of more than forty-three meters. The grand crowning element is set on four monumental arches surrounded by wide galleries on three sides. Below the galleries sits an exterior arcade accessed through two side doors with steps. In three places, balconies project into the prayer hall on columns. The one to the east, which served as a space for the sultan, has gilded latticework between its columns and was accessible on horseback by way of a ramp outside the mosque. Windows at the base of the dome and sixteen windows in each of the tympana of the grand arches bring light into the domed space, where they add to the illumination provided by numerous casement windows at the ground and gallery levels.

In keeping with the classical function of the Ottoman *kulliye*, the site consists of a mosque, *medrese* (theological college), soup kitchen, tomb, library, and water fountain. At the Nur-u Osmaniye complex, these functional units are contained within a walled precinct of irregular shape, while stores were built outside in close proximity to the complex. The *medrese*, built on a traditional arcaded plan, consists of twenty domed rooms and a large classroom surrounding a courtyard. The soup kitchen adjoins the *medrese* to the west and is entered through a domed structure to the north. The complex's single-story library is set on a high platform accessed by two sets of stairs to the west. An Arabic inscription above the dual entrance hints at the structure's function: "Demand science, from the cradle to the grave." Its space consists of a domed elliptical reading room with rounded corners, surrounded by an arcade of fourteen columns.

The decoration of the complex deviates significantly

from earlier examples of Ottoman architecture, incorporating Baroque ornamentation derivative of Western European styles. The interior of the mosque is covered with gray marble panels and a thick structural cornice, and below the gallery level, calligraphic medallions crown each casement window. Baroque influences are seen in the extensive use of decorative sculptural elements such as pilasters and cornices, and in the addition of contemporary Western motifs such as garlands, finials, and scallops. On the structure's exterior, as well, the domed silhouette of the Ottoman mosque is defined with the curved outlines of Baroque buttresses anchoring the dome at its corners. The site's unique synthesis of classical Ottoman and contemporary Western styles is witnessed most clearly in the scalloped stalactite domes that crown the mosque's portals and bronze window grilles. Originally gilded, the intertwining grille patterns are particularly elaborate—a trend that would continue in Ottoman architecture in the second half of the eighteenth century.

By the mid-fifteenth century, Ottoman architects had begun to gain recognition, as individual builders developed new ideas that exceeded the well-established formulas that had previously guided stone masons. Little is known about the architect of the Nur-u Osmaniye, who has been identified as Simeon Kalfa. The likelihood of significant contributions by a European are evident in the building's Westernized forms, and such contributions would befit the eighteenth century, when Ottoman envoys were sent to European courts and returned with descriptions of Western arts. The eighteenth century was also the beginning of a period in which non-Muslims were commissioned to build important royal structures, including mosques, and artists and architects were invited to the Ottoman court from Europe.

Despite the paucity of evidence about the architect's life, the construction itself was documented in detail by the construction manager, Ahmed Efendi, in a book titled *Tarih-i Cami-i Serif-i Nur-i Osmani* (mid-eighteenth century). Moreover, a considerable amount is known about the calligraphers responsible for inscriptions on the Nur-u Osmaniye. Mehmed Rasim, the outstanding Ottoman calligrapher of the first half of the eighteenth century, penned the Qūʾranic verse on the mosque's middle gate, facing out, and devised the chronogram for its construction, which read, "May this new congregational mosque of Sultan Osman be blessed!" The calligrapher Yahya Fahreddin composed the verses inside the mosque's two side gates, and Ḥākim Efendi composed the chronogram of the *medrese:* "Ḥākim composed a chronogram in the form of a prayer; May the gate of the *medrese* be the door to knowledge." Finally, two of the most accomplished calligraphers of the eighteenth century, Yedikuleli Seyyid Abdullah Efendi and Kātipzāde Mehmed Refı Efendi, contributed verses to the structure.

SIGNIFICANCE

The inherently rich detail of Islamic architectural traditions was well suited to the Baroque influences that came into the Ottoman Empire in the early eighteenth century. The last great work of Ottoman religious architecture, the Nur-u Osmaniye mosque, assimilated these contemporary European stylistic flourishes, while maintaining the traditional features and floor plan of classical Ottoman mosques. The site preserves the legacies of sultans Mahmud I and Osman III. A tomb at the site, originally intended for Mahmud, houses the remains of Sehsuvar Valide Sultan, mother of Osman III, and the Nur-u Osmaniye library, opened in 1755, still functions as a repository for the personal manuscript collections of both rulers, a repository with more than five thousand volumes.

—*Anna Sloan*

FURTHER READING

Blair, Sheila S., and Jonathan Bloom. *The Art and Architecture of Islam, 1250-1800.* New Haven, Conn.: Yale University Press, 1994.

Bloom, Jonathan, and Sheila Blair. *Islamic Arts.* London: Phaidon Press, 1997. Two important works by leading scholars of Islamic art and architecture.

Crane, Howard. *The Garden of the Mosques: Hafiz Huseyin al-Ayvansarayi's Guide to the Muslim Monuments of Ottoman Istanbul.* New York: Brill, 2000. Translation of a rare contemporary source on Ottoman architecture. Annotated with a glossary and bibliography.

Goodwin, Godfrey. *A History of Ottoman Architecture.* London, 1971. A concise survey of architecture's development and form under the Ottoman sultans.

Kuran, Aptullah. *The Mosque in Early Ottoman Architecture.* Chicago: University of Chicago Press, 1968. Provides a background to later developments in Ottoman building, with illustrations and plans.

Necipoglu, Gulru. "Anatolia and the Ottoman Legacy." In *The Mosque: History, Architectural Development, and Regional Diversity*, edited by Martin Frishman and Hasan-Uddin Khan. New York: Thames and Hudson, 1994. Concise chapter, assimilating updated research on the development of Islamic architecture in Anatolia. Illustrated.

Unsal, Behcet. *Turkish-Islamic Architecture in Seljuk and Ottoman Times, 1071-1923.* New York: St. Mar-

1740's

tin's Press, 1973. A fine survey of Turkish building types, beginning with early Islamic buildings. Contains plates, illustrations, and maps.

SEE ALSO: 1702 or 1706: First Arabic Printing Press; 1715-1737: Building of the Karlskirche; 1718-1730:

Tulip Age; 1785: Construction of El Prado Museum Begins.

RELATED ARTICLE in *Great Lives from History: The Eighteenth Century, 1701-1800*: Mahmud I.

October 18, 1748
TREATY OF AIX-LA-CHAPELLE

The Treaty of Aix-la-Chapelle temporarily ended the set of wars known collectively as the War of the Austrian Succession. Although it merely created a pause in the conflicts between France and England that lasted throughout the eighteenth century, the treaty is noteworthy as a signal of the waning power of the Holy Roman Empire.

LOCALE: Aix-la-Chapelle (now Aachen, Germany)
CATEGORIES: Diplomacy and international relations; wars, uprisings, and civil unrest

KEY FIGURES
Maria Theresa (1717-1780), Austrian archduchess, r. 1740-1780
Frederick the Great (1712-1786), king of Prussia, r. 1740-1786
Henry Pelham (1694-1754), British prime minister, 1743-1754
Louis XV (1710-1774), king of France, r. 1715-1774

SUMMARY OF EVENT
The Treaty of Aix-la-Chapelle brought to an end almost a decade of warfare between the major European nations. Battles in these wars were fought not only in Europe but also overseas in the Caribbean, North America, and India. Generally known as the War of the Austrian Succession, in reality the conflict began in the Caribbean with the War of Jenkins's Ear, fought between the Spanish and the British over trading privileges. French ambitions contributed to the dispute, and the British-Spanish war, which broke out in 1739, was complicated the following year by the death of Holy Roman Emperor Charles VI.

Having no male heirs, Charles had attempted before his death to ensure the peaceful succession of his daughter, Maria Theresa, through the Pragmatic Sanction, a diplomatic agreement to which many of the German states, including Prussia, were partners. However, Frederick the Great, who ascended the Prussian throne also in 1740 and believed a woman ruler was by definition a

weak ruler, seized the opportunity to invade Austrian Silesia. The lure of Silesia's coal resources and cloth trade were enough to make Frederick ignore Prussia's commitment to the Pragmatic Sanction.

The subsequent conflict went through several stages in the years that followed. Maria Theresa was only twenty-three in 1740 and had no experience in the power politics of the era. Prussia's territories were diverse, and its army was among Europe's best despite Prussia's small population. Initially, the French government of Louis XV gave diplomatic support to the Austrians, fearful of the ambitions of Frederick. Soon, however, France's policy shifted against Austria, its traditional nemesis, and it formed a military alliance with Prussia. In 1742, Prussia itself switched sides: Maneuvering for diplomatic advantage, Frederick deserted France and signed a treaty with Austria, technically ending the War of the Austrian Succession with Frederick in possession of Silesia.

While Maria Theresa approved ceding Silesia to the Prussians, she demanded territorial compensation for its loss. When Prussia refused to give up any of its own territory in exchange for Silesia, the war continued. England then entered the war on Austria's side, drawn in by its desire to oppose France. Indeed, British prime minister Henry Pelham halfheartedly but consistently pursued a policy of military intervention on the Continent in order to foil French political and territorial aspirations.

Frederick was adamantly opposed to Austrian compensation in Germany, and he was suspicious of the alliance between Britain and Austria. Frederick's Prussian army thus invaded Bohemia in mid-1744, but the expected French support for the invasion did not materialize, and the Prussians were forced to retreat. Prussia itself was threatened with dismemberment in 1745, when Saxony joined Britain and Austria, and it seemed possible that Russia would join the alliance against Frederick as well. Prussia was victorious in a series of key battles, however, and in the 1745 Treaty of Dresden, Austria again conceded Silesia to Prussia. Despite these victories, though, Prussia's economy was in shambles, and Frederick left the war, again deserting his French ally.

War persisted in Italy, where Austria confronted the Bourbon armies of France and Spain. To the north, in Flanders, France focused its energies against England, its traditional enemy. By 1747, almost all of the Austrian Netherlands was under French control, and French armies threatened the neighboring United Provinces. Dutch resistance was compromised by a lack of significant military resources, as well as the provinces' desire to stay aloof from continental wars in order to maintain their commercial position as a leader in international trade. Fortunately for the Dutch, the French economy was also suffering from France's widespread military commitments.

In addition to its Italian and Dutch campaigns, France had commitments in locales far from the battlefields of Europe, notably in Canada and India. On the high seas, the British navy was more than a match for the French, who resorted to using privateers but still had little success in reducing British trade. Conversely, the French West Indies sugar colonies were near collapse because the war prevented the colonies from importing sufficient new slaves and food supplies from across the Atlantic. By 1748, all parties in the conflict had finally had enough, and an agreement was made to terminate hostilities in all theaters of the war and make peace.

The Treaty of Aix-la-Chapelle ending the War of the Austrian Succession was the result of extensive negotiations between France and Britain. Ironically, Austria, the "victim" of the Prussian invasion of Silesia that had supposedly caused the war, was effectively excluded from the treaty process and deserted by its British ally. After years of conflict, France was no longer primarily concerned with opposing Austria on the Continent and gaining territory at the latter's expense. Instead, the French simply wished to regain the territories they had lost to Britain overseas and end the British naval blockade that was damaging their colonies. To contain the threat posed to their position in Europe by an Austro-British alliance, the French cleverly made a separate peace with England, thereby effectively severing the alliance.

The treaty restored the world to a state quite close to the one it had been in before the conflict broke out in 1739 and 1740. Most of the territories conquered during the war were returned to their original holders. Madras in India was returned to Britain and Louisbourg in Canada was given back to France. The Austrian Netherlands, seized by France, were returned to Austria—an unpopular decision in France. Spain, France's Bourbon ally, reaffirmed British slave-trading rights in the West Indies, the so-called *asiento de negros* ("Negroes' contract"), which had been awarded to Britain in the Treaty of Utrecht in 1713. France also formally recognized Britain's Protestant Hanover Dynasty, finally rejecting the claims of the exiled Catholic Stuarts, who had been harbored in France since they were driven from England in the Glorious Revolution of 1688-1689.

Austria was the chief loser in the war. Although protesting that the treaty had been agreed to without its participation, Austria reluctantly accepted the Treaty of Aix-la-Chapelle. In it, Maria Theresa was forced to surrender the Italian duchies of Guastalla, Parma, and Piacenza to Bourbon Spain and, most significant, to once more cede Silesia to Prussia. Frederick left the conflict in 1745 because of Prussia's economic exhaustion and was not a party to the treaty, but Prussia proved to be the victor in the peace. In gaining Silesia with its cloth and iron resources, Prussia achieved what has been called the most significant permanent conquest of territory in Western Europe since the Renaissance, ensuring the rise of Prussia to great power status.

Without Silesia, Austria's claim to hegemony in the Holy Roman Empire was finished, and the Habsburg concerns shifted from the Rhine River to the east, where the Austrian Empire would become the major power in east-central and south-central Europe. The worldwide struggle between France and Britain over empire and commerce was not resolved, however. During the war, the British government had focused upon maintaining a continental strategy against France by allying with Austria and the Dutch republic. The Dutch proved a weak partner, and the Austrians were little better. Britain's William Pitt the Elder and others had urged a "blue water" strategy, but it took another war for that recommendation to be implemented and for France to be forced to abandon much of its non-European empire.

SIGNIFICANCE

Although it was Napoleon I who officially abolished the Holy Roman Empire in 1803, it was Frederick the Great who truly destroyed the empire, treating the emperors as the equals of kings, rather than their superiors. With the destruction of the hierarchy of deference to its traditional Habsburg rulers, Germany became merely several hundred largely independent entities. Later, Voltaire, the French philosophe, was to make the now-famous comment that the Holy Roman Empire had become neither holy nor Roman nor an empire.

The 1748 Treaty of Aix-la-Chapelle proved to be only a brief pause in a longer conflict. The French diplomat, the comte de St. Severin, implied that the treaty did end the conflict, a belief echoed by the Austrian chancellor, Count Wenzel Anton von Kaunitz. In 1756, however, war broke out again, accompanied by a diplomatic revolution that brought Habsburg Austria into league with Bourbon France and czarist Russia, while Britain joined Prussia. This revolution was engineered by Austria's Kaunitz, whose goal was to reclaim Silesia, destroy Prussia, and restore Austria to its rightful place as the leader of the German states. In that he failed, for Frederick the Great held on to Silesia, but in the ensuing Seven Years' War, the conflict between Britain and France led to French defeat in Canada and India and the establishment of the first British Empire.

—*Eugene Larson*

FURTHER READING

Browning, Reed S. *The War of the Austrian Succession.* London: Macmillan, 1995. An excellent narrative, including a discussion of the Treaty of Aix-la-Chapelle.

Dorn, Walter L. *Competition for Empire, 1740-1763.* New York: Harper & Row, 1940. A volume in the Rise of Modern Europe series, this remains a classic account of the mid-eighteenth century conflicts.

Showalter, Dennis. *The Wars of Frederick the Great.* New York: Longman, 1996. A comprehensive analysis of Frederick's military and diplomatic policies.

Thackeray, Frank W., and John E. Finding, eds. *Events that Changed the World in the Eighteenth Century.* Westport, Conn.: Greenwood Press, 1998. Includes a chapter on the wars and diplomacy of the mid-century, including the War of the Austrian Succession.

SEE ALSO: May 26, 1701-Sept. 7, 1714: War of the Spanish Succession; 1713: Founding of Louisbourg; Apr. 11, 1713: Treaty of Utrecht; 1739-1741: War of Jenkins's Ear; May 31, 1740: Accession of Frederick the Great; Oct. 20, 1740: Maria Theresa Succeeds to the Austrian Throne; Dec. 16, 1740-Nov. 7, 1748: War of the Austrian Succession; Aug. 19, 1745-Sept. 20, 1746: Jacobite Rebellion; 1746-1754: Carnatic Wars; May 28, 1754-Feb. 10, 1763: French and Indian War; Jan., 1756-Feb. 15, 1763: Seven Years' War.

RELATED ARTICLES in *Great Lives from History: The Eighteenth Century, 1701-1800*: Charles VI; Frederick the Great; Wenzel Anton von Kaunitz; Louis XV; Maria Theresa; Henry Pelham; William Pitt the Elder; Voltaire.

1749-1789
FIRST COMPREHENSIVE EXAMINATION OF THE NATURAL WORLD

Buffon's thirty-six-volume Natural History *represents the first comprehensive and systematic exploration of the natural world. Though Buffon based his conjectures on physical evidence, he was frequently proven wrong by fellow scientists. Despite the work's flaws, Buffon inspired immense respect because of the nature of the undertaking, his systematic approach to his subjects, and the high quality of his prose style.*

LOCALE: Paris, France
CATEGORIES: Science and technology; biology; geology; anthropology

KEY FIGURES

Comte de Buffon (Georges-Louis Leclerc; 1707-1788), French naturalist and superintendent of the King's Gardens
Sir Isaac Newton (1642-1727), English scientist and mathematician
Étienne Bonnot de Condillac (1715-1780), French philosopher

William Smellie (1740-1795), Scottish bookseller and translator of the *Natural History*
Thomas Jefferson (1743-1826), U.S. ambassador to Paris and later president of the United States, 1801-1809

SUMMARY OF EVENT

Georges-Louis Leclerc, who became the comte de Buffon in 1773, was made superintendent of the Jardin du Roi (King's Gardens) in 1739. As superintendent, he was responsible for maintaining and studying a host of plants and animals. Buffon began to write a detailed catalog of the garden, and it was this catalog that would eventually become *Histoire naturelle, générale et particulière* (1749-1789; *Natural History, General and Particular,* 1781-1812). By the time of his death in 1788, he had completed and published thirty-five volumes devoted to animals, birds, and geology, as well as general theories about such subjects as the qualities of people and the age of the Earth. When he assumed the position of superintendent, Buffon was already a member of the botanical section of the French Academy of Sciences, and at first he continued the efforts of his predecessor as superintendent, organizing public programs, collecting specimens, and conducting correspondence with an international cadre of scientists.

Buffon, whose intellectual hero was Sir Isaac Newton, hoped that he would be able to complete the work begun by the British scientists. If he could do that, he thought, he would be seen as Newton's equal. Using an inductive scientific method and relying on materials in the King's Gardens and those collected by others, Buffon wrote a paper putting forward a "theory of the Earth" in 1744. Here, he responded to the efforts of at least four late seventeenth century earth scientists who variously supported sacred theories of Earth's origin.

Buffon aroused the ire of the Catholic Church with his writings. He argued that the Earth was shaped by water, attempted to ascertain the precise date of Earth's creation, and posited a fiery and magnetically charged Earth's core. This consistent pursuit of material rather than divine causes for the creation of the world at best threatened and at worst directly contradicted Church doctrine.

During a period of thirty-five years, Buffon continued to advance various theories of the natural world. He discussed the effect of different climates on animals and reproduction, naturally occurring electricity in the core of the Earth, the roles of the seas in shaping the land, and human and animal migration. He believed in a molecular theory of biology, laid the foundations for anthropology, and demonstrated a rudimentary grasp of evolution when he argued that species disappeared over time. Drawn neither to travel for specimen collection nor to the laboratory for experimentation, Buffon aimed to show the scientific community he could draw more thorough and elegantly expressed arguments from extant scientific literature than from original research.

More important than any single theory put forward by Buffon was the conception and scope of his overall project. Envisioned as a fifty-volume set (the work was still incomplete at the time of his death), *Natural History* approached the entirety of the natural world as a rational, encompassable whole. The utter comprehensiveness of the massive project Buffon envisioned followed from his dedication to Newton, who put forward a model of nature as wholly ordered by rational, immutable laws. A nature governed by such laws must, Buffon thought, be wholly comprehensible if only one could produce an exhaustive accounting of the laws and understand the relationships between them.

As part of his post as superintendent, Buffon also managed the Cabinet du Roi, a natural history museum maintained for the king's pleasure. When his books were first published, Buffon enjoyed the endorsement of the king, and criticism of his work was therefore carefully presented, though scientists did not fear pointing out the problems they saw with Buffon's arguments and some of his conclusions. For example, Denis Diderot, whose monumental *Encyclopédie: Ou, Dictionnaire raisonné des sciences, des arts, et des métiers* (1751-1772; *Encyclopedia*, 1965) Buffon also hoped to displace as a key work in French culture, published his *Pensées sur l'interprétation de la nature* (1754) when the fourth volume of Buffon's *Natural History* was published. Buffon argued that naturally occurring organic molecules had genus-specific traits (or prototypes) that reappeared across mammalian species, while Diderot held to a theory of evolution called transformism, which cast doubt on Buffon's idea of degeneration or trait loss as the reason for species decline over time.

The title page of the first volume of the comte de Buffon's Natural History, *1749. (Library of Congress)*

Another theorist, Étienne Bonnot de Condillac, tested Buffon's theories of the origin and characteristics of primordial humans in his *Traité des sensations* (1754; *Condillac's Treatise on the Sensations*, 1930) and his *Traités des animaux* (1755; treatise on animals). In the 1760's and 1770's, Buffon's onetime collaborator, John Tuberville Needham, suffered the wrath of Voltaire, the leading French philosopher and author, who was angered by Buffon in 1749, when Buffon attacked Voltaire's connection of the age of the Earth with the age of fossils. Needham, who had conducted experiments for Buffon on the reproductive systems of dogs, criticized Voltaire's treatise on miracles, which in turn led Voltaire to question Buffon's theories of humanity.

Finally, and notably, Thomas Jefferson, while American ambassador to Paris, questioned Buffon's theories in ways that explicitly addressed his methods, his conclusions, and his ability to maintain a logical argument. Jefferson owned a copy of the *Natural History* in its original French. First, in his *Notes on the State of Virginia* (1781-1782), Jefferson challenged Buffon's insistence that the large Ice Age mammoth and the elephant were the same animal. He then examined two other key ideas from the *Natural History*, that ancient animals were larger than present-day animals and that domestic animals in America were in a state of devolution or degeneration. Buffon also maintained that the cooler climates of America meant that there were fewer species of animal, a claim Jefferson also felt compelled to challenge.

Another idea of Buffon's that plagued Jefferson was contained in the former's description of the peoples of the Americas. Knowing that Buffon had never traveled to America, namely North America, Jefferson took issue with Buffon's characterization of American Indians in a letter written in June, 1785. He told his correspondent, François-Jean de Chastellux, that while Buffon might be right about South American indigenous peoples, he was not right about those of North America.

On January 26, 1785, Jefferson wrote to Archibald Stuart that he had met Buffon. Jefferson then asked Stuart to arrange to send Buffon the carcass of a North American elk for his studies. The carcass of the elk, along with that of a deer, a moose, and a caribou elk, were delivered to Buffon in October, 1787, as Jefferson had planned. Jefferson's letters indicate that he met with Buffon occasionally for a little more than a year. Writing to James Madison in July, 1787, Jefferson noted that he took exception to Buffon's characterization of chemistry as similar to cooking with a recipe. He wrote, "I think it . . . among the most useful of sciences, and big with fu-

ture discoveries for the utility and safety of the human race." He later commented to several correspondents on Buffon's death, even sharing some gossip about the strained relations between Buffon's son and his wife.

In 1781, William Smellie began translating the *Natural History* into English, a project he would not live to complete. Smellie was the first to point out Buffon's contributions as a systematic thinker, appreciating the scope of the work and shaping English-speaking readers' attitudes toward the work for years to come.

SIGNIFICANCE

Buffon undertook an ambitious and controversial project when he set out to write a history of the world based on limited resources and a good deal of cribbing of the ideas of others. He seems to have provided the basis for an early amortization table as he tried to determine how many generations would be alive at any one time and how they would affect the resources of the world. He is noteworthy for his ideas on the dating and the age of the Earth, on the role of heat and cold in animal sustainability, on the sizes and distributions of animals around the world, and on the racial characteristics of peoples of the world.

His positions also sparked heated debate. He posited that Europe was superior to America, and (perhaps most criticized today) he depended more on scientific literature than he did on scientific experimentation as the source of knowledge.

Nevertheless, Buffon was a man of the Enlightenment, raising questions about people and the world and attempting to answer them outside a theological context. He tackled complex problems and provided simple and logical answers, writing for general readers. He synthesized and ordered complex forms of knowledge, and he showed both the limits and the possibilities of one bold mind at work.

Though he was controversial and has been discredited by a number of modern scientists, Buffon remains admired for his contributions to evolutionary theory, biochemistry, genetics, anthropology, natural philosophy, and literature.

—*Beverly Schneller*

FURTHER READING

Buffon, Georges-Louis Leclerc. *Natural History: General and Particular*. Translated by William Smellie. 1781. Reprint. Bristol, Avon, England: Thoemmes Press, 2000. The English translation of Buffon's work. A crucial document for eighteenth century histories of science.

Fellows, Otis E., and Stephen F. Milliken. *Buffon*. New York: Twayne, 1972. Comprehensive analysis of Buffon's life and the main ideas of the *Natural History*.

Glass, Bentley, et al. *Forerunners of Darwin, 1745-1839.* Baltimore: Johns Hopkins University Press, 1959. Discusses Buffon's place in evolutionary theory.

Jefferson, Thomas. *Writings.* New York: Library Classics, 1984. Includes "Notes on the State of Virginia" and selections from Jefferson's correspondence about Buffon.

Roger, Jacques. *Buffon: A Life in Natural History.* Translated by Sarah L. Bonnefoi. Ithaca, N.Y.: Cornell University Press, 1997. Translation of the definitive modern life of Buffon, first published in French in 1989.

SEE ALSO: Beginning 1735: Linnaeus Creates the Binomial System of Classification; 1743-1744: D'Alembert Develops His Axioms of Motion; 1747: Marggraf Extracts Sugar from Beets; 1751: Maupertuis Provides Evidence of "Hereditary Particles"; 1757: Monro Distinguishes Between Lymphatic and Blood Systems; 1757-1766: Haller Establishes Physiology as a Science; 1760's: Beginning of Selective Livestock Breeding; 1767-1768: Spallanzani Disproves Spontaneous Generation; 1779: Ingenhousz Discovers Photosynthesis.

RELATED ARTICLES in *Great Lives from History: The Eighteenth Century, 1701-1800*: Comte de Buffon; Étienne Bonnot de Condillac; Thomas Jefferson; Voltaire.

June 10, 1749
SAʿĪD BECOMES RULER OF OMAN

Ahmad ibn Saʿīd helped bring an end to the Yaʿrubi Dynasty in Oman. Establishing himself as imam of the country, he founded his own dynastic house, the House of Āl Bū Saʿīd, which continues to rule in the twenty-first century.

LOCALE: Oman

CATEGORIES: Government and politics; wars, uprisings, and civil unrest

KEY FIGURES

Ahmad ibn Saʿīd (1710-1783), imam of Oman and Zanzibar and founder of the Āl Bū Saʿīd Dynasty, r. 1749-1783

Nādir Shāh (1688-1747), shāh of Persia, r. 1736-1747

Saif II ibn Sulṭān (d. 1743), imam of Oman, r. 1719-1724, 1728-1743

Balʿarab ibn Himyar ibn Sulṭān (d. 1748), dissident imam of Oman, r. 1732-1738, 1744-1748

Taqī Khān (fl. 1737-1750), Persian military commander

SUMMARY OF EVENT

Oman was ruled for many hundreds of years by a theocracy, which meant that secular and religious authority were invested in the same institution, the imamate. The ruler, or imam, was the head of the Ibadi branch of Islam, which grew out of the same reform movement that had led to the creation of Shia Islam in the seventh century. When Ahmad ibn Saʿīd became the ruler of Oman in 1749, he founded a new dynasty called the Āl Bū Saʿīd Dynasty that fundamentally changed the nature of the imamate.

Saʿīd's accession to the imamate signaled the end of the Yaʿrubi Dynasty, which had controlled the imamate of Oman since 1650. The Yaʿariba (plural) in turn had ended 150 years of colonial rule by the Portuguese Empire and established an Omani foreign empire of their own, primarily in East Africa. Problems began, however, with the election of Sulṭān II ibn Saif as Imam in 1711. He ruled only for eight years but seriously depleted the treasury and needlessly provoked the Persians by harassing their ships.

The successor of Sulṭān II ibn Saif, Saif II ibn Sulṭān, had not yet reached puberty when he was made imam, and his accession failed to improve the situation. Although he developed into a wily political survivor, Saif was never able to control the centrifugal forces and rival factions contending for influence. A long drought and widespread hunger in the interior of Oman also put pressure on the Yaʿrubi Dynasty. The situation continued to degenerate through the 1720's and 1730's.

Because of his reputation for having a self-indulgent, decadent lifestyle, Saif II ibn Sulṭān lost support among the Ibadi fundamentalist tribes of the interior. Balʿarab ibn Himyar was put forward as a rival imam by a faction of tribal leaders in 1732. By 1737, Saif was losing support rapidly and found himself confined to the coastal city of Muscat. In desperation, he appealed to the Persian Empire for help. In response, an expeditionary force led by Latif Khan landed at Gambroon in March of that year.

The combined forces of Latif and Saif marched inland and won a decisive victory at the oasis town of Buraimi, but soon after, the two argued over the chain of command. Saif left along with his troops, and Latif was replaced by Taqī Khān as the Persian commander. Taqī, though, had trouble dealing with the forces under his command, who were almost all Huwala Arabs, and the campaign stalled. Nādir Shāh, the ruler of Persia, sent orders to press ahead, and Taqī began seizing English and Dutch ships in the area to use in his offensive. The British East India Company paid a large bribe to be left alone, but some individual English seamen were induced to join the Iranians.

In the meantime, Saif had decided that he needed the help of Iran after all, and he formed another alliance, this time with Taqī Khān. They won two more battles in the interior and took control of the towns of Bahla and Nizwa. They then took Muscat without difficulty, but even after a five-week siege, they failed to gain control of the nearby ports of Jalali and Marani, which were tactically more important. Saif again fell out with the Persians and withdrew to Barka. There, he negotiated an agreement with the rival imam, Balʿarab ibn Himyar, who renounced his claim to the throne.

Disappointed with Balʿarab's capitulation, another faction of leaders from the interior elected a new rival imam in 1743, a cousin of Saif named Sultān ibn Murshīd. He went to the assistance of Aḥmad ibn Saʿīd, the governor of Sohar, which had also come under siege by Iranian forces. Sultān was killed in action in Sohar. His death so shocked Saif II ibn Sultān that he gave up all worldly pursuits and retreated to his ancestral home in the mountains. He died there later that year.

Aḥmad ibn Saʿīd held out against the Persians for eight months, inflicting three thousand casualties upon them, but he was eventually forced to surrender. Using deft diplomacy, however, Aḥmad managed to arrange a deal with Taqī Khān whereby he was made governor of both Sohar and Barka. In partnership with the Persians, then, Aḥmad ibn Saʿīd had taken control of the rich coast of Oman, but he still faced opposition from the interior. Tribal chiefs again put forward Balʿarab ibn Himyar as rival imam.

Fortunately for Aḥmad ibn Saʿīd, war broke out between Persia and the Ottoman Empire in 1743, and the priorities of Nādir Shāh changed dramatically. Persia ceased adequately to support its forces in Oman. Aḥmad understood the situation and also withdrew his support. He stopped paying the agreed tribute to the local Persian authorities. They were thus unable to pay their troops, and the Huwala Arabs began deserting. Aḥmad invited a number of Persian officers to Barka to negotiate a solution to the problem. In the middle of the feast where dis-

cussions were being held, Aḥmad's agents entered and killed most of the Persians. His control of the coast was thereby solidified. Nādir Shāh was assassinated by his own officers in 1747, which plunged Persia into chaos and ended any threat to Aḥmad from that nation.

Aḥmad ibn Saʿīd was now free to focus on opposition in the interior. He had been born in the frontier mountain village of Adam and understood the traditional tribal mentality. With this understanding and his Hinawi tribal connections, Aḥmad was able to gain support and prevail over Balʿarab, whom he eventually killed.

Just as the Yaʿrubi had come to power in 1650 by ending the Portuguese colonial occupation, the Āl Bū Saʿīd Dynasty was founded one hundred years later by expelling the Iranians. Ironically, the dynasty has maintained and strengthened its hold on power since then by developing a close working relationship with another foreign power, Britain.

SIGNIFICANCE

Āl Bū Saʿīd's cooperation with the British began as early as 1775 under Aḥmad ibn Saʿīd himself, when both nations supported the Ottoman Empire against Persia in a struggle for control of Basra. Deeper involvement, however, developed after the decline of Āl Bū Saʿīd fortunes following the death of Saʿīd ibn Sultān (r. 1806-1856) in 1856. His domain was divided between his two sons: Thuwayn inherited control of Oman itself, while Majīd got control of most of the East African empire, particularly Zanzibar. Britain eventually became so involved in the administration of affairs that the Āl Bū Saʿīd empire became a British protectorate in all but name.

The balance of power in Oman has traditionally been contested between the maritime interests of port cities like Muscat and the Ibadi tribes inland. The Āl Bū Saʿīd Dynasty shifted the center of control decisively to the coast, away from the fundamentalist interior. Aḥmad ibn Saʿīd did not come from one of the traditional ruling families, and he used primarily military means to secure power, instead of the traditional process of vetting and selecting candidates through tribal chiefs. Therefore, he and his successors have been regarded with suspicion. Gradually, however, during the Āl Bū Saʿīd Dynasty, the traditional theocracy ceased to exist, and the ruler of Oman has come to be known as the sultan, instead of the imam.

—*Steven Lehman*

FURTHER READING

Badger, G. P., ed. *The History of the Imams and Sayyids of Oman, by Salil bin Razik.* London: Darf, 1986. First published in 1871, this is a primary source for subsequent writing on the subject.

Risso, Patricia. *Oman and Muscat*. London: Croom Helm, 1986. History of Oman from the Yaʿrubi Dynasty to the late nineteenth century, focusing on the heyday of the empire, 1775-1856.

Smith, Rex. *Studies in the Medieval History of Yemen and South Arabia*. Brookfield, Vt.: Ashgate, 1997. A collection of essays on the historical background of Oman and other countries in the region.

Vine, Peter. *The Heritage of Oman*. London: Immel, 1995. A beautifully illustrated introduction to the country, culture, and history.

Vine, Peter, and Paula Casey-Vine, eds. *Oman in History*. London: Immel, 1995. Selected papers presented at a conference at Sultan Qaboos University in 1994, covering all aspects of the history, culture, economics, and politics of Oman.

Wilkinson, John C. *The Imamate Tradition of Oman*. New York: Cambridge University Press, 1987. The most detailed account of the entire history of the Omani political system.

SEE ALSO: c. 1701: Oman Captures Zanzibar; 1709-1747: Persian-Afghan Wars; 1725-Nov., 1794: Persian Civil Wars; 1746: Zāhir al-ʿUmar Creates a Stronghold in Galilee.

RELATED ARTICLE in *Great Lives from History: The Eighteenth Century, 1701-1800*: Nādir Shāh.

1750
TREATY OF MADRID

The Treaty of Madrid altered the boundary between Portuguese and Spanish South America, formally recognizing that some lands on the western, Spanish side of the original boundary had already become de facto possessions of Portugal. Subsequent treaties reversed and modified the Madrid agreements.

LOCALE: Madrid, Spain

CATEGORIES: Diplomacy and international relations; expansion and land acquisition

KEY FIGURES

José de Carvajal y Lancáster (Joseph Lencastre; 1698-1754), Spanish chief minister and head of the Council of the Indies

Ferdinand VI (1713-1759), king of Spain, r. 1746-1759

Alexandre de Gusmão (1695-1753), Brazilian-born secretary and diplomatic adviser to the Portuguese king

John V (1689-1750), king of Portugal, r. 1706-1750

Joseph I (1714-1777), king of Portugal, r. 1750-1777

Sebastião José de Carvalho e Mello (1699-1782), Spanish foreign minister, 1750-1755, prime minister, 1755-1777, and later the marquês de Pombal, 1769-1782

SUMMARY OF EVENT

In 1494, Pope Alexander VI authorized a division of all territories yet to be discovered in the New World between Spain and Portugal. In the Treaty of Tordesillas, a line of demarcation along a north-south axis was drawn that, in South America, allotted territory east of the mouth of the Amazon River to Portugal and west of the river's mouth to Spain. Over the course of the following centuries, the Brazilian frontier advanced steadily westward, following the course of the continent's rivers and terrain, which roll steadily down to the Amazon and Plata river systems. Portuguese settlement thereby penetrated beyond the Tordesillas boundary. This settlement accelerated in the eighteenth century after gold was discovered in the interior of Brazil. Spain and Portugal were thus prompted to negotiate their boundaries in South America more definitively.

Portugal wished to consolidate its hold over the entirety of the Amazon River Basin, which extended across northern Brazil. Beyond the southern edge of Brazil, Portugal held a trading and military outpost, Colônia do Sacramento, on the left bank of the Plata River, that it was willing to cede to Spain. By giving up their claims to the Plata, the Portuguese believed they would free themselves to concentrate on the Amazon. Spain, for its part, wished to acquire Colônia do Sacramento in order to consolidate its hold over the Plata system and to suppress the smuggling of Spanish silver from Bolivia that was conducted through the port. However, to ensure that southern Brazil was protected from future Spanish incursions, Portugal sought possession of the territory of seven Spanish Jesuit missionary villages that bordered the region. These villages, populated by South American Indians and Jesuit priests, lay on the left bank of the Uru-

1750's

343

guay River, and Portugal wanted them vacated and transferred to the right bank.

On January 13, 1750, Portugal and Spain signed the Treaty of Madrid, a document with significant historical and legal consequences. Negotiating for Spain was José de Carvajal y Lancáster, chief royal minister and head of the Council of the Indies. For Portugal, Alexandre de Gusmão, the Brazilian-born secretary and adviser to King John V, conducted negotiations. Encouraging them were King Ferdinand VI of Spain and his Portuguese wife, Queen Barbara.

The Madrid document began by abrogating the Treaty of Tordesillas, which had divided the Americas in a straight line along an arbitrarily chosen line of longitude. With that boundary abolished, the new boundaries of Spanish and Portuguese America could be determined based on natural geographical contours, as well as on the current occupation of territory by the colonists of the two nations. The major part of the Amazon valley was occupied, albeit sparsely, by the Portuguese. The Plata was primarily Spanish. Thus, it made sense for the Portuguese to lay claim to the valley, which was already their territory de facto, and to abandon their outpost at Colônia do Sacramento, since it stood in de facto Spanish territory. To protect southern Brazil, the Seven Missions complex would be dismantled and their occupants moved beyond the Uruguay River. Both parties agreed to this arrangement and the treaty was signed.

No sooner had the treaty been completed, however, than conditions arose that mitigated its execution. John V died, and Joseph I ascended the Portuguese throne. The new king's foreign minister, Sebastião José de Carvalho e Mello, was in charge of executing the terms of the Treaty of Madrid, but he was opposed to the treaty. Carvalho e Mello, deeply suspicious of the Jesuits, did not believe the Spanish would abandon the Seven Missions region. He therefore delayed ordering the Portuguese evacuation of Colônia do Sacramento. This inaction aroused Spanish suspicions. Moreover, Carvalho e Mello believed in strict adherence to *uti possidetis*, the principle that occupied territory should belong to the power that occupied it. He favored continued Portuguese expansion into any territory it could occupy and opposed ceding any territories the nation had already acquired. He therefore found surrender of the settled territories of Colônia do Sacramento and the Seven Missions to a contradiction of the treaty's guiding principle.

Spanish and Portuguese surveyors and cartographers had been dispatched to determine the new colonial borders. The southern contingent was met, however, with

Indian resistance near the Seven Missions territory. The Amazon contingent never departed. Amid mutual suspicion, delays, and conflicts, Carvalho e Mello engineered a new agreement. The Treaty of El Pardo was signed on February 12, 1761, annulling the Madrid document.

Not until Carvalho e Mello's exit from office were the continuing territorial conflicts in the Plata region resolved. By the Treaty of San Ildefonso, signed on October 1, 1777, Portuguese territory was recognized as extending to Rio Grande (today the southern tip of Brazil). Spanish territory included both the Seven Missions and Colônia do Sacramento. Nonetheless, during the beginning of the following century, Portugal reclaimed both territories—it would only be able to hold the Seven Mission region permanently, however.

SIGNIFICANCE

Despite the subsequent abrogation of the Treaty of Madrid, its historic application of the international legal principle of *uti possidetis* became the basis for resolving territorial disputes between Brazil and the many Spanish American countries that it bordered. The natural contours of Brazil's terrain and rivers determined the flow of its people into the interior. For this reason, by the end of the seventeenth century, Brazilians had already occupied much of the territory of present-day Brazil, whose borders are based largely on natural geographical limits. However, only by the end of eighteenth century was there legal recognition of these limits, demarcated in final detail in treaties signed at the beginning of the twentieth century.

With Brazil's southern tip now lying as far as Rio Grande, the country extended into the northern edge of the *pampas* (savannah) of what would become Argentina and the cattle-raising culture of the gaucho cowboys (*gaúcho* in Portuguese) who lived there. The southern border of Brazil became one of the most fortified regions in the country, and it would be the one area of Brazil that witnessed significant warfare with its neighbors.

Nonetheless, neither Brazil nor Argentina would dominate the east bank of the Uruguay River. Rather, this region became the country of Uruguay, essentially a buffer state between giant neighbors. However, insofar as Brazil extended southward to the Uruguay River and controlled the headwaters of the Paraná and Paraguay Rivers, it significantly influenced the Plata system. Brazil did not, nonetheless, dominate that complex as overwhelmingly as it did the Amazon. Brazil, therefore, came to occupy a powerful geopolitical position with regard to the two major river systems of South America. Although Buenos Aires, the capital of Argentina, became the principal entrepôt of the Plata basin, it had to share this role with Montevideo, Uruguay's capital, on the northern edge of the river.

—*Edward A. Riedinger*

FURTHER READING

Alden, Dauril. *Royal Government in Brazil, with Special Reference to the Administration of the Marquis of Lavradio, Viceroy, 1769-1779.* Berkeley: University of California Press, 1968. Based on detailed research in primary sources, this book traces the political and diplomatic developments leading to the signing of the Treaty of Madrid together with subsequent modifications.

Bethell, Leslie, ed. *Colonial Brazil.* Cambridge, England: Cambridge University Press, 1986. Compilation of articles by leading specialists on early Brazilian history; places the Treaty of Madrid within its eighteenth century historical context.

Boxer, Charles. *The Golden Age of Brazil, 1695-1750: Growing Pains of a Colonial Society.* Berkeley: University of California Press, 1962. Reviews economic, demographic, and political developments in early eighteenth century Brazil that prompted initiatives for the Treaty of Madrid.

Davidson, David Michael. *Rivers and Empire: The Madeira Route and the Incorporation of the Brazilian Far West, 1737-1808.* Unpublished doctoral dissertation. Yale University, 1970. Focusing on the valley of the Madeira River, a major tributary of the Amazon, this work details Brazilian Portuguese frontier settlement dynamics that required treaty negotiations to recognize occupied territory that in legal theory was within the Spanish domain.

Fausto, Boris. *A Concise History of Brazil.* New York: Cambridge University Press, 1999. This translation of a history of Brazil by a leading Brazilian scholar places the events of the eighteenth century within the wider scope of the country's development.

Maxwell, Kenneth. *Pombal: Paradox of the Enlightenment.* New York: Cambridge University Press, 1995. Examines the life of the influential Portuguese minister who opposed the Treaty of Madrid; written by a leading scholar of Portuguese history.

Scobie, James R. *Argentina: A City and a Nation.* 2d ed. New York: Oxford University Press, 1971. Standard history of Argentina in English that places the events of the eighteenth century in the larger context of the country's development.

Whigan, Thomas. *The Politics of River Trade: Tradition and Development in the Upper Plata, 1780-1870.* Albuquerque: University of New Mexico Press, 1991. Analyzes international political and commercial issues in the Plata River system subsequent to the Treaty of Madrid and the Treaty of San Ildefonso.

SEE ALSO: c. 1701: Oman Captures Zanzibar; Aug., 1712: Maya Rebellion in Chiapas; Nov. 9, 1729, and Feb., 1732: Treaty of Seville; May, 1735-1743: French Scientists Explore the Amazon River; Nov. 18, 1738: Treaty of Vienna; 1769: Pombal Reforms the Inquisition; 1776: Foundation of the Viceroyalty of La Plata; 1780-1781: Rebellion of Tupac Amaru II; 1786: Discovery of the Mayan Ruins at Palenque; July 16, 1799-July 9, 1804: Humboldt and Bonpland's Expedition.

RELATED ARTICLE in *Great Lives from History: The Eighteenth Century, 1701-1800*: Marquês de Pombal.

1750-1792
CHINA CONSOLIDATES CONTROL OVER TIBET

Following the murder of Tibet's last king by his Chinese advisers, China consolidated its indirect rule over Tibet in 1751 and further strengthened its control over the small country after defeating a Gurkha invasion of the region.

LOCALE: Tibet (now in China)

CATEGORIES: Wars, uprisings, and civil unrest; expansion and land acquisition

KEY FIGURES

Gyurme Namgyal (d. 1750), last king of Tibet, r. 1747-1750

Qianlong (Ch'ien-lung; 1711-1799), emperor of China, r. 1735-1799

Yongzheng (Yung-cheng; 1678-1735), emperor of China, r. 1723-1735

Fu Qing (d. 1750), Chinese general and *amban*, or imperial representative in Lhasa

Labdon (d. 1750), Chinese *amban*

Lobsang Tashi (d. 1751), Tibetan rebel

Bandi (d. 1755), Chinese *amban*

Fu Kangan (d. 1796), Chinese commander who defeated the Gurkhas

SUMMARY OF EVENT

By the late seventeenth century, the emperors of China, ever concerned about invasions from the north and west, were seeking to gain control over their frontiers. This desire for security brought China into conflict with the Mongol tribe of the Zunghars on its northwestern border. Because of their shared Gelugpa Buddhist faith, the Zunghars looked to the Tibetans for aid against China. This turn of affairs intensified Chinese attention on Tibet.

In 1642, the Mongols had donated conquered Tibet to the Dalai Lama to rule. As a living bodhisattva, the Dalai Lama was not meant to rule by force. Thus the fifth Dalai Lama set up a system in which Tibet relied on a foreign force for military protection. At first, this protection was provided by a Mongol khan. The khans could not protect Tibet from China, however, and China's Zunghar wars led to the annexation of eastern Tibetan lands. In 1694, the Xining Valley was annexed. In 1696, a second annexation pushed China's border west toward the upper Yangtze River.

Tibet became a Chinese protectorate in 1710. When the Zunghars invaded Tibet in 1717, China came to the aid of the exiled seventh Dalai Lama and restored him to rule in 1720. In return for their help, China was permitted to garrison troops at Lhasa. A Chinese imperial representative, called an *amban* by the Tibetans, advised the Tibetan government. The Chinese emperor Yongzheng withdrew the garrison from 1723 until the outbreak of a Tibetan civil war in 1727. After the Chinese helped end the civil war, the garrison returned. Two Chinese *ambans* became advisers to the Tibetan government. In 1740, the Tibetan councilor Polhanas made himself king of Tibet. His son Gyurme Namgyal succeeded him in 1747.

At first, the Chinese trusted Gyurme Namgyal. In 1748, Emperor Qianlong granted his request to withdraw four hundred of the five hundred Chinese soldiers in Lhasa. In 1749, Gyurme Namgyal petitioned the emperor to send Tibetan lamas into Chinese-annexed Tibetan lands. Alarmed at the prospect of the spread of the Tibetan religion in nominally Chinese territory, the emperor refused and sent a new *amban*, Chi Shan. After his arrival, Chi Shan sent a devastating report to Qianlong. Gyurme Namgyal, the *amban* wrote, was hated by the Tibetans and was oppressive, proud, and uncooperative. The seventh Dalai Lama loathed the king. Qianlong reserved judgment and sent Fu Qing to Lhasa as a second *amban*.

Late in 1749, Gyurme Namgyal acted against his older brother. He accused him of rebellion and wrote to the emperor for help. Qianlong worried that this was a pretext to increase Gyurme Namgyal's power. He replied that the king should let the emperor decide the issue. On October 15, 1749, Gyurme Namgyal visited Chi Shan with gifts. Qianlong became angered by the poor quality of Chi Shan's reports and replaced him with a new *amban* named Labdon. While the Chinese deliberated, Gyurme Namgyal reported that his older brother had died on January 25, 1750. Publicly, he claimed his brother had died of an illness, but Gyurme Namgyal had actually sent soldiers to stab him to death.

In Beijing, a report from Yue Zhongqi, commander in Sichuan, arrived. The commander asked for permission to enter Lhasa with three thousand soldiers and seize and execute the Tibetan king. Qianlong refused, refusing as well to increase the Lhasa garrison. In Tibet, Fu Qing and Labdon realized that Gyurme Namgyal desired to remove all Chinese supervision. He replaced his dead brother's officials with his own and planned to bring soldiers into Lhasa. Unbeknownst to the Chinese, the king had contacted the Zunghars and invited them to come into Tibet after the expulsion of the Chinese.

CHINESE EXPANSION IN THE EIGHTEENTH CENTURY

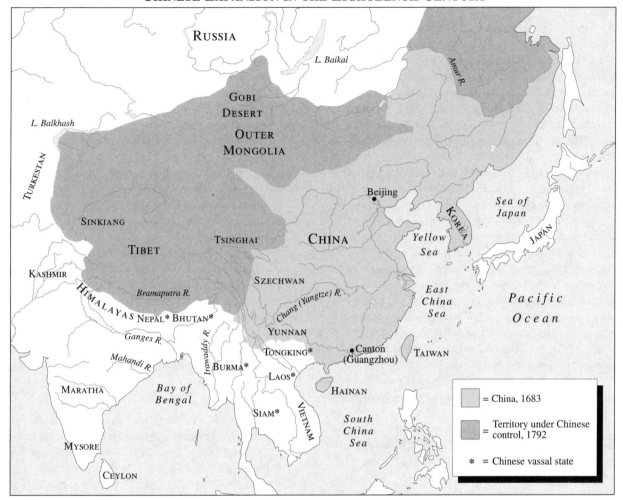

On October 8, 1750, Qianlong learned that his *ambans* planned to kill the Tibetan king. Qianlong was unhappy and advised caution, while authorizing the *ambans* to act as necessary. On November 11, 1750, the *ambans* ordered Gyurme Namgyal to their residence. In their bedroom, Fu Qing accused the king of treason. He either grabbed him so that Labdon could kill him or used his own sword. All but one of the waiting Tibetan soldiers were killed, the last one escaping through a window. After the assassination of the king, Fu Qing and Labdon ordered the Tibetan duke Pandita to form a provisional government.

The surviving Tibetan guard, Lobsang Tashi, incited a revolt. About one thousand men attacked the Chinese residence, refusing appeals of the Dalai Lama to disperse. Fu Qing killed some attackers but was wounded

three times. To avoid capture, he committed suicide. Labdon died fighting. The mob also killed Chinese soldiers and civilians. The next day, Lobsang Tashi realized that his riot had not led to the widespread anti-Chinese uprising for which he had hoped. He fled toward the Zunghars. One day later, the Dalai Lama appointed Duke Pandita as provisional king and sheltered the surviving Chinese. By November 21, Lobsang Tashi and many of his men were captured, and order was restored.

Emperor Qianlong realized that Lobsang Tashi's rebellion offered China a chance to consolidate its control over Tibet. Bandi, the new *amban* in Lhasa, pronounced judgment over twenty-seven captured rebel leaders. On January 23, Lobsang Tashi and six ringleaders were sliced to death. More than ten others were beheaded and another group strangled. All bones in the corpses were

1750's

347

crushed, and their heads were displayed on poles in Lhasa.

The new government of Tibet was inaugurated on February 26, 1751. There would be no more Tibetan king. While the Dalai Lama was the spiritual ruler, the government was carried out by a council of four Tibetan ministers and two Chinese *ambans*. The Chinese forbade contact between the Zunghars and Tibet and directly governed Tibet's foreign relations with Nepal, Bhutan, and Sikkim. The role of the Chinese *ambans* was strengthened. They commanded the Chinese garrison at Lhasa of fifteen hundred men, ran the postal communication system between Lhasa and Beijing, and supervised the Tibetan councilors.

Gyurme Namgyal's wife and son were executed for the acts of the king on March 25, 1751. Moreover, Qianlong sought to escape the judgment of history by blaming a scapegoat for allowing the crisis to get so far out of hand: The former *amban* Chi Shan was sentenced to death and allowed to commit suicide in Beijing on April 23, 1751. (The gambit was ultimately unsuccessful, as modern historians blame Qianlong for the extent of the rebellion.) Temples honoring Fu Qing and Labdon were erected in Lhasa and Beijing.

The next challenge to Chinese control over Tibet did not come from within: In 1790, Gurkhas from Nepal crossed into southern Tibet and raided its monasteries. The Chinese persuaded the raiders to return to Nepal, but in 1791, plundering Gurkhas returned. Enraged, Emperor Qianlong dispatched an army under the command of Fu Kangan to fight the Gurkhas. Early in 1792, on the frozen plateaus of the Himalayas, overshadowed by Mount Everest (Qomolangma Feng), Fu Kangan met the invading Gurkhas. Amazingly, the Chinese decisively defeated the invaders. Fu Kangan pursued the fleeing Gurkhas through the passes of the Himalayas into Nepal, almost to the gates of Kathmandu. There, the Gurkhas sued for peace, which was granted to them on the condition that they pay tribute to the emperor every five years.

After defeating the Gurkhas, the Chinese strengthened their control over Tibet. From 1792 on, the *ambans* were given even more powers. A second Chinese garrison was established at the town of Xigaze (Shigatse) to protect the Tashi Lama. With the increased Chinese military presence came an increase in overall power and influence and a corresponding decline in the power of native Tibetan institutions. From this point forward, if there was uncertainty as to who was the next incarnation of the Dalai Lama, the issue would be decided by lot, not by Tibetan council.

SIGNIFICANCE

The murder of the last Tibetan king became a welcome opportunity for the Chinese to consolidate their control over Tibet. There was almost no Tibetan opposition to the abolishment of the monarchy, which had been in existence only briefly, from 1740 to 1750. Chinese control was apparently accepted, as long as the spiritual authority of the Dalai Lama was not threatened and the Chinese did not overstress their power.

Defeat of the Gurkhas further consolidated Chinese control. By protecting the Tibetan monasteries, the Chinese demonstrated that their presence in Tibet was not without its benefits. Ironically, the defeat of the Gurkhas drove them into an alliance with the British East India Company. Nepal continued to send tribute to China every five years until 1908.

The system of Chinese rule in Tibet, modified by Qianlong in 1751 and 1792, lasted until the Chinese revolution in 1912, when the last *ambans* left Lhasa. The Dalai Lama continued to rule Tibet from 1912 until Chinese occupation in 1950 and the annexation of Tibet to the People's Republic of China in 1951. In 1959, the Dalai Lama and his council of ministers, who had ruled Tibet for 317 years since 1642, left the country for exile.

—*R. C. Lutz*

FURTHER READING

Hsu, Immanuel C. Y. *The Rise of Modern China*. 6th ed. New York: Oxford University Press, 2000. Places the events in the context of Qing Dynasty foreign policy (uses Wade-Giles). Notes, bibliography, index.

Norbu, Dawa. *China's Tibet Policy*. Richmond, England: Curzon, 2001. Good discussion of the events that are analyzed as roots of the conflict in the twentieth century (uses Pinyin). Index, bibliography.

Petech, Luciano. *China and Tibet in the Early Eighteenth Century*. Rev. ed. Leiden, the Netherlands: Brill, 1972. Still most comprehensive, detailed and scholarly account of the events. Uses Wade-Giles for Chinese, and linguistic transliteration for Tibetan names. Notes, chronology, index.

Spence, Jonathan. *The Search for Modern China*. 2d ed. New York: Norton, 1999. Most widely available book on modern Chinese history in English. The chapter "Conquest and Consolidation" discusses the events in Tibet. Maps, illustrations, notes, bibliography, index. Uses Pinyin.

SEE ALSO: Oct. 21, 1727: Treaty of Kiakhta.
RELATED ARTICLES in *Great Lives from History: The Eighteenth Century, 1701-1800*: Qianlong; Yongzheng.

March 20, 1750-March 14, 1752
JOHNSON ISSUES *THE RAMBLER*

Writing almost all the 208 essays in the semiweekly periodical The Rambler, *Samuel Johnson established himself as a prominent literary figure in eighteenth century Britain and, through his rigorous examination of literature and human affairs in general, tried to move his readers toward sound judgment and moral wisdom.*

LOCALE: London, England
CATEGORIES: Literature; philosophy

KEY FIGURES

Samuel Johnson (1709-1784), English writer and lexicographer
Edward Cave (1691-1754), English publisher and printer
John Payne (d. 1787), English publisher and bookseller
Elizabeth Carter (1717-1806), English translator and writer
Samuel Richardson (1689-1761), English novelist
Catherine Talbot (1721-1770), English writer
Lord Chesterfield (Philip Dormer Stanhope; 1694-1773), English literary patron, writer, and statesman

SUMMARY OF EVENT

The 208 essays in *The Rambler* were neither the first distinguished essays in English nor the first published periodically. Francis Bacon's essays were published in 1597, 1612, and 1625, and in 1709, Richard Steele began the series called *The Tatler*, to which Joseph Addison contributed. In 1711, shortly after the end of *The Tatler*, Steele and Addison began *The Spectator*, which ran until near the end of 1712 and was revived for about six months in 1714. Those earlier essays, especially the ones by Bacon and Addison, influenced Johnson in the mid-eighteenth century when he began *The Rambler*.

By March, 1750, the forty-year-old Johnson had struggled in London for thirteen years but was only beginning to acquire fame as a man of letters. He had written, among other works, essays for Edward Cave's *Gentleman's Magazine*, a biography of his late friend the poet Richard Savage, *Irene: A Tragedy* (pr. 1749), and the poems *London: A Poem in Imitation of the Third Satire of Juvenal* (1738) and *The Vanity of Human Wishes: The Tenth Satire of Juvenal Imitated* (1749). Furthermore, during the two years through which the *Rambler* essays appeared, Johnson, with only a few assistants,

was working on what became his magnificent *A Dictionary of the English Language: To Which Are Prefixed, a History of the Language, and an English Grammar* (1755; 2 volumes) and, in his preparatory reading, had found Bacon an especially important writer.

Nobody knows whether Johnson himself initiated the plan for a series of periodical essays or the plan came from other persons, such as the publishers Edward Cave and John Payne. Whatever the case, in the absence of the money Johnson solicited from the literary patron Lord Chesterfield for the work on the dictionary, Johnson needed the two guineas he would receive for each issue of *The Rambler* to subsist. He also needed occasional creative respites from lexicography. He took his new task seriously, as he implied by praying before the first issue that the Holy Spirit would come into him so that he could glorify God through his essays and bring himself and his readers to salvation. In light of that seriousness, the title of Johnson's periodical later seemed inappropriate to James Boswell, Johnson's famous biographer. Whether or not it was appropriate, the idea for the title probably came from Richard Savage's poem *The Wanderer* (1729).

All the *Rambler* essays were anonymous, although Johnson's close friends, knowing his style and ideas, soon realized who the main author was. Johnson wrote 201 issues in their entirety. Of the remainder, Catherine Talbot wrote one, the novelist Samuel Richardson wrote another, and the translator and poet Elizabeth Carter wrote two. Parts of three other issues were probably by authors other than Johnson. Nevertheless, he became identified with his persona Mr. Rambler—an elderly, scholarly, relentlessly honest thinker who sought less to entertain his readers than to improve them. Besides the essays he wrote as *The Rambler*, however, Johnson wrote many ostensible letters to Mr. Rambler, using various pseudonyms, to present events that the main persona would not directly know about and to draw lessons from those events.

Each issue of *The Rambler* began with a Latin or Greek motto. The number of errors in those quotations has led later scholars to surmise that Johnson quoted them from his prodigious but slightly imperfect memory. Originally, no one translated the mottoes into English; Johnson apparently assumed that educated readers knew the Western classical languages well enough to provide their own translations. Eventually, however, publishers

1750's

349

SEEING ONESELF IN ART

In The Rambler, *Samuel Johnson engaged in a distinctive blend of philosophy, social criticism, and literary criticism. In the passage excerpted here, he simultaneously discusses human nature and readership, using as examples Spanish writer Miguel de Cervantes's character Don Quixote de La Mancha and a reader's reactions to him.*

There would, however, be few enterprises of great labour or hazard undertaken, if we had not the power of magnifying the advantages which we persuade ourselves to expect from them. When the knight of La Mancha gravely recounts to his companion the adventures by which he is to signalize himself in such a mauner that he shall be summoned to the support of empires, solicited to accept the heiress of the crown which he has preserved, have honors and riches to scatter about him, and an island to bestow on his worthy squire, very few readers, amidst their mirth or pity, can deny that they have admitted visions of the same kind; though they have not, perhaps, expected events equally strange, or by means equally inadequate. When we pity him, we reflect on our own disappointments; and when we laugh, our hearts inform us that he is not more ridiculous than ourselves, except that he tells what we have only thought.

Source: Samuel Johnson, *The Rambler* no. 2 (March 24, 1750). Reprinted in *The Rambler: In Four Volumes*, vol. 1, p. 55. Rutgers Spectator Text Project, Rutgers University. http://tabula.rutgers.edu/spectator/johnson/rambler/. Accessed November 14, 2005.

furnished translations, some by Johnson himself. Of the mottoes, more came from Horace, a poet of the Augustan Age of Roman literature, than from any other author—a sign of the impression Horace had made on Johnson through the latter's years of study.

After giving the motto for an essay, Johnson pursued truth, going wherever truth took him as a Christian moralist. In the second issue, for example, writing as *The Rambler*, he followed a pertinent quotation from the ancient Roman poet Statius with a reference to the frequency with which the human tendency to neglect the present by looking to the future has met with ridicule. Johnson continued, however, by writing that, while critics of this tendency may feel superior, human beings must nevertheless look to the future if they are ever to do anything that does not provide an immediate reward. Some hopes, however, are unrealistic, and many writers, according to Johnson, go beyond reason in their expectation of fame.

Johnson's style in *The Rambler* was distinctive enough that it has given rise to the eponymous adjective "Johnsonian." Retiring as the Rambler, Johnson in his last issue wrote of his effort to purify English and to contribute to "the elegance of its construction" and "the harmony of its cadence." He defended his diction, often

Latinate, by writing that he had "familiarized the terms of philosophy by applying them to popular ideas" when he found "common words" unsuitable. His sentences throughout *The Rambler*, while varying in length and construction, often seem long and ornate to readers more than two and a half centuries later, who may fail to appreciate the careful parallelism and choices of words that helped Johnson achieve precise meanings at the time.

The Rambler ranges widely in topic, although, as Johnson also commented in the last issue, he avoided fleeting topics of popular discussion, because he was not trying to satisfy mere "temporary curiosity." Although writing in England in the mid-eighteenth century, Johnson often composed timeless essays of worldwide importance, cautioning against vain wishes, for instance, as in his story in Issues 204 and 205 about Seged, the Ethiopian king who, despite elaborate efforts, cannot find perfect happiness even for a day. In his literary criticism, Johnson wrote as a moralist, as in Issue 4, in which, after a motto from Horace, Johnson treated an increasingly popular genre by warning against those novels in which the author so mixes virtues with vices in a character that impressionable readers learn a dangerously false lesson.

SIGNIFICANCE

After two years of the pressure of writing an essay to be published almost every Tuesday and Saturday, Johnson ended *The Rambler* with the issue dated March 14, 1752, three days before his invalid wife died. Although his essays generally were more solemn than those of Addison in *The Spectator* and no more than five hundred copies of any individual issue were sold, *The Rambler* was nevertheless popular. Without permission or payment, newspapers outside London printed various essays from the series, and, less than half a year after the publication of the first issue, a collected edition of the essays began appearing.

Before Johnson died on December 13, 1784, there had been ten printings of the entire *Rambler* series, his authorship was widely known, and, through those essays and other works, he had become a literary giant. More printings followed in the remainder of the eighteenth century, and there were even more in the nineteenth. Although it would be hard to determine the extent to which Johnson succeeded in his effort "to inculcate wisdom or piety" through each issue, the collection surely affected its readers positively. In addition, it marked a step toward open professionalism in English literature. Believing that his supposed literary patron, Lord Chesterfield, had failed in his duty to support the work on the dictionary, Johnson wrote *The Rambler* to earn a living, thus showing the way for generations of writers to come.

—*Victor Lindsey*

FURTHER READING

Bate, W. Jackson. *Samuel Johnson*. New York: Harcourt Brace Jovanovich, 1977. Psychological biography with a chapter linking *The Rambler* to *The Vanity of Human Wishes*.

Boswell, James. *Life of Johnson*. 1791. Edited by R. W. Chapman. New edition, corrected by J. D. Fleeman. London: Oxford University Press, 1970. Monumental biography with an account of Johnson's work on *The Rambler*.

DeMaria, Robert, Jr. *The Life of Samuel Johnson: A Critical Biography*. Malden, Mass.: Blackwell, 1993. Johnson's career is seen as a compromise between the necessity of professional writing in English and the longing to be a European humanist scholar writing in Latin.

Johnson, Samuel. *The Rambler*. Edited by W. J. Bate and Albrecht B. Strauss. Vols. 3-5 in *The Yale Edition of the Works of Samuel Johnson*. New Haven, Conn.: Yale University Press, 1969. Standard scholarly edition with textual notes.

Kernan, Alvin. *Samuel Johnson and the Impact of Print.* Princeton, N.J.: Princeton University Press, 1989. Johnson is protrayed as England's first great author to work proudly as a professional writer in an age of print.

Korshin, Paul J. "Johnson, the Essay, and *The Rambler*." In *The Cambridge Companion to Samuel Johnson*, edited by Greg Clingham. New York: Cambridge University Press, 1997. Scholarly overview.

Lipking, Lawrence. *Samuel Johnson: The Life of an Author*. Cambridge, Mass.: Harvard University Press, 1998. Biography that discusses only those parts of Johnson's life reflected in the writing and that includes a chapter on *The Rambler*.

Lynn, Steven. *Samuel Johnson After Deconstruction: Rhetoric and "The Rambler."* Carbondale: Southern Illinois University Press, 1992. Rhetorical analysis using ideas from Harold Bloom and Jacques Derrida.

Rogers, Pat. *The Samuel Johnson Encyclopedia*. Westport, Conn.: Greenwood Press, 1996. Volume including a succinct article on *The Rambler*, with cross-references to other articles.

SEE ALSO: Mar. 1, 1711: Addison and Steele Establish *The Spectator*; 1736: *Gentleman's Magazine* Initiates Parliamentary Reporting; 1740-1741: Richardson's *Pamela* Establishes the Modern Novel; 1746-1755: Johnson Creates the First Modern English Dictionary; Sept. 10, 1763: Publication of the *Freeman's Journal*; 1774: Hansard Begins Reporting Parliamentary Debates; Jan. 1, 1777: France's First Daily Newspaper Appears; Oct. 27, 1787-May, 1788: Publication of *The Federalist*; Jan. 4, 1792-1797: The *Northern Star* Calls for Irish Independence.

RELATED ARTICLES in *Great Lives from History: The Eighteenth Century, 1701-1800*: Joseph Addison; Samuel Johnson; Samuel Richardson; Richard Steele.

1751
MAUPERTUIS PROVIDES EVIDENCE OF "HEREDITARY PARTICLES"

The theory of hereditary particles had been competing with other possible explanations of biological reproduction in 1751. However, with the publication of Système de la nature, *Maupertuis became the first scientist to provide statistical evidence that the existence of particles inherited from both parents could explain specific, empirically observable patterns in the inheritance of physical traits.*

LOCALE: France
CATEGORIES: Biology; science and technology; health and medicine

KEY FIGURE
Pierre-Louis Moreau de Maupertuis (1698-1759),
   French mathematician, biologist, and astronomer

SUMMARY OF EVENT

During the eighteenth century, there existed several theories of reproduction, but the most prominent theories involved either embryonic preformation or epigenesis. Preformation theories considered the embryo to have already been formed as a miniature human. Taken to its extreme, this theory held that all humankind was formed at creation as persons within persons, something like Russian nesting dolls. Therefore, the biblical Adam and Eve, called the mother and father of all humankind, were considered literally to have all humankind already preformed within them.

Preformationists were divided into ovists, who believed that the preformed offspring resided in the female's eggs, and spermists, who believed that the preformed offspring resided in the male's sperm. Some spermists even claimed the existence of a little human, called a homunculus, "crouching" within sperm. One problem with preformationism involved defining the role of the two sexes. Ovists considered the semen as simply nourishment for the embryo carried in the female. Spermists considered the female as simply the receptacle for the embryo that grew from the homunculus in the sperm. Another problem involved the apparent waste. What happened to eggs in the female that never received nourishment? After biologists discovered the vast numbers of sperm in semen, the apparent waste was even more troublesome. Would God design a system, it was wondered, in which so many preformed offspring were simply lost?

Preformation was problematic on a more practical level as well. If Eve or Adam contained all humankind within them when they were created, how could all the billions of future humans be contained in such a small space? Those who believed in the infinite divisibility of matter saw no difficulty; the embryos would just be smaller and smaller to infinity. As the structure of matter became better understood, however, it became clear that such a large number of ever-smaller humans could not possibly fit within Adam or Eve, because that would require the embryos to be smaller than the ultimate minimum size of matter.

Once embryo development had been observed microscopically, it became apparent that early embryos did not resemble miniature adults. Embryos started as clumps of cells that increased in size and gradually developed arms, legs, and other human features. These observations led to the gradual acceptance of the theory of epigenesis, that is, the gradual development of the human form. The latter theory also supplanted that of preformation, because it allowed for simultaneous roles for both the egg and the sperm in reproduction.

Because children appeared to possess some combination of characteristics from both parents, it was reasoned that these traits must be inherited via both the sperm and the egg. This realization led to a blending theory of inheritance: The sperm and egg were considered to be an aggregation of cells that migrated from all over the body. When the sperm and egg joined together in the uterus, the resulting embryo was therefore composed of cells derived from both parents. Children resembled both parents because their cells were literally derived directly from collections of cells derived from each parent.

Pierre-Louis Moreau de Maupertuis considered epigenesis to be the correct explanation for reproduction, but he differed somewhat in certain details. He did not believe that the sperm or egg had anything directly to do with reproduction; both simply provided nourishment of some sort for the collections of particles provided by each of the parents. He believed that particles migrated from various parts of the male body and congregated in the seminal fluid. When this seminal fluid was deposited into the woman's reproductive tract, particles from her body migrated to the uterus and, together with the particles from the male, they formed the embryo. The cells possessed some sort of memory about their position in the parent's body that allowed them to migrate to the proper positions in the developing embryo. The balance of the number of cells from each parent determined the characteristics of the developing child. The parent that contributed the greater number of particles expressing a specific anatomical characteristic was dominant over the other parent, and the former parent's trait would be expressed rather than the latter's.

Maupertuis's interest in mutants, especially the two distinctive human mutations of albinism and polydactyly (possession of extra fingers or toes), led him to apply statistics to the problem of inheritance. In 1744, an albino boy, born to a pair of African slaves in South America, was brought to Paris to be displayed to the members of the French Academy of Sciences, of which Maupertuis was a member. As a vehicle to discuss his theories on reproduction and inheritance, Maupertuis wrote about this African albino in the anonymously authored book *Dissertation physique à l'occasion du negre blanc* (1744; physical dissertation occasioned by the albino negro). He chose to present his ideas about the "corpuscles," or particles, involved in reproduction in this anonymous manner, because he feared that presenting such a provocative theory to the Academy of Sciences could affect his scientific reputation. He later expanded the book to include discussion of other traits, most notably polydactyly, under the name *Venus physique* (1745; *The Earthly Venus*, 1966).

With the publication of *Système de la nature* (1751; system of nature), again anonymously, Maupertuis gave his most complete exposition on inheritance. He included an extensive pedigree of the family of the Berlin surgeon Jacob Ruhe, in which polydactyly appeared in a number of individuals. Using this pedigree, he was able to show that polydactyly could be passed from an affected person to that person's offspring, whether the person was male or female. This supported Maupertuis's contention that particles were passed to children from both of their parents.

Maupertuis also applied statistical reasoning to the occurrence of polydactyly, comparing its incidence in the Ruhe family with its occurrence in the general population. Based on his estimate that the occurrence of polydactyly in the general population was approximately 5 in 100,000, he calculated the probability of a parent with polydactyly having a child with the trait solely by chance to be 1 in 20,000. Therefore, he reasoned, the occurrence of this condition throughout the Ruhe family line must be accounted for by inheritance and not by chance. He further concluded that because of its high occurrence in the Ruhe family, polydactyly must be a "dominant" trait.

SIGNIFICANCE

In many ways, Maupertuis's theories on inheritance, as outlined in *Système de la nature*, were revolutionary. Recognition that inheritance somehow involved particles that came together to form the embryo enabled Maupertuis to develop a theory of inheritance that was consistent with scientific observations. His use of statistics in researching biological inheritance was a first, and it was not until more than one hundred years later that Gregor Mendel would put statistics to a similar use.

Some historians of science have tried to credit Maupertuis with the first correct model of inheritance, allowing him to supplant Mendel as the father of genetics. Although *Système de la nature* represented a step forward, however, Maupertuis's theory of inheritance was lacking on two counts. First, Maupertuis saw no role for the gametes (eggs and sperm) and considered the particles that made up the embryo to be corpuscles contained in the female's reproductive tract and in the male's semen. Therefore, the particles of inheritance described by Maupertuis were different than those described by Mendel, who believed they were contained in the gametes.

Second, Maupertuis's use of the term "dominance" was different from that of Mendel. In Maupertuis's theory, dominant particles were simply more active and therefore often outcompeted "normal" particles. In other words, Maupertuis envisioned multiple hereditary particles competing for spaces in the developing embryo and defined dominant particles as those that were more likely, but not guaranteed, to win the "competition." He did not believe that the "winner" was predictable in a given case. Mendel, on the other hand, thought that each gamete contained one particle corresponding to each trait: When brought together in the embryo, dominant particles always masked the effects of "recessive" particles. Therefore, although Maupertuis's ideas were revolutionary, they lacked certain details that would emerge later in Mendel's more accurate theory of particulate inheritance in the nineteenth century.

—*Bryan D. Ness*

FURTHER READING

Emery, Alan E. H. "Pierre Louis Moreau de Maupertuis, 1698-1759." *Journal of Medical Genetics* 25 (1988): 561-564. A brief biographical sketch focusing on Maupertuis's impact on science in his time, especially his refutation of preformationist theories of reproduction.

Lancaster, H. O. "Mathematicians in Medicine and Biology—Genetics Before Mendel: Maupertuis and Réaumur." *Journal of Medical Biography* 3 (1995): 84-89.

Shows how mathematics began to be applied to biological problems.

Sandler, Iris. "Pierre Louis Moreau de Maupertuis: A Precursor to Mendel?" *Journal of the History of Biology* 16 (1983): 101-136. Argues that Maupertuis, although revolutionary, was not Mendel's precursor. Examines the differences in philosophy and understanding of biology between Maupertuis and Mendel.

Terrall, Mary. *The Man Who Flattened the Earth: Maupertuis and the Sciences in the Enlightenment.* Chicago: University of Chicago Press, 2002. A well-researched biography of Maupertuis, focusing especially on his relationship to the Enlightenment and his ability to mingle in all types of society.

SEE ALSO: 1722: Réaumur Discovers Carbon's Role in Hardening Steel; Beginning 1735: Linnaeus Creates the Binomial System of Classification; 1748: Nollet Discovers Osmosis; 1749-1789: First Comprehensive Examination of the Natural World; 1757: Monro Distinguishes Between Lymphatic and Blood Systems; 1757-1766: Haller Establishes Physiology as a Science; 1760's: Beginning of Selective Livestock Breeding; 1767-1768: Spallanzani Disproves Spontaneous Generation; 1779: Ingenhousz Discovers Photosynthesis.

RELATED ARTICLES in *Great Lives from History: The Eighteenth Century, 1701-1800*: Comte de Buffon; Carolus Linnaeus; Lazzaro Spallanzani.

1751-1772
DIDEROT PUBLISHES THE *ENCYCLOPEDIA*

The publication of Diderot's Encyclopedia *was one of the great events of the French Enlightenment. A massive work of scholarship designed to assist the triumph of reason, progress, and tolerance, the* Encyclopedia *shaped French intellectual life for several decades.*

LOCALE: Paris, France
CATEGORY: Philosophy; literature

KEY FIGURES
Denis Diderot (1713-1784), French philosopher and coeditor of the *Encyclopedia*
Jean le Rond d'Alembert (1717-1783), French mathematician and coeditor of the *Encyclopedia*
André Le Breton (1708-1779), French publisher of the *Encyclopedia*
Jean-Jacques Rousseau (1712-1778), French political philosopher
Sophie Volland (1716-1784), French correspondent and confidant of Diderot

SUMMARY OF EVENT
Denis Diderot, who was to become editor of the *Encyclopédie: Ou, Dictionnaire raisonné des sciences, des arts, et des métiers* (1751-1772; partial translation *Selected Essays from the Encyclopedy,* 1772; complete translation *Encyclopedia,* 1965)*,* was born in Langres, France, on October 5, 1713. Educated by the Jesuits, he then left for Paris to complete his studies, where he showed a marked aptitude for languages, mathematics,

and philosophy. After receiving a master of arts degree from the University of Paris in 1732, he led a rather aimless life for an extended period, characterized chiefly by a severe shortage of funds. Yet already he was becoming known for his wit, clever conversation, pleasant personality, and imaginative and powerful intellect.

Diderot's marriage to Anne-Toinette Champion was largely unhappy, but he was devoted to his daughter Angélique and took personal charge of her education. To compensate for his marriage, he found himself attracted to women of influence and intelligence, such as Sophie Volland, with whom he had an intense friendship spanning two decades. Among Diderot's closest male friends were Paul-Henri-Dietrich d'Holbach, Friedrich Melchior von Grimm, and the political philosopher Jean-Jacques Rousseau, until an unpleasant falling out between Rousseau and Diderot occurred in 1758.

Historians have subsequently labeled the eighteenth century the Enlightenment, or the Age of Reason. It produced a number of remarkable intellects, collectively known in France as the philosophes, of whom Diderot is a prime example. They were interested not simply in philosophy, but in politics, religion, science, education, and economics as well. Relying upon sensory experience and skepticism, the philosophes tended to deny the existence of a personal god, being either Deists (that is, subscribing to the notion of God as creator but as otherwise inactive) or, in the case of Diderot, atheists. They vigorously attacked the failings of society and in turn worked to ensure the triumph of reason, progress, science, and human happiness. The printed word was one of their most effective weapons.

In 1745, the publisher André Le Breton expressed a desire to print a French translation of Ephraim Chambers's *Cyclopedia* (1728). Although this project never materialized, he conceived a more ambitious one, hiring a noted mathematician, Jean le Rond d'Alembert, to serve as editor, and soon Diderot was invited to be coeditor, an understandable choice given Diderot's translation abilities and wide range of intellectual interests. By 1747, Diderot became in effect the editor in chief, with d'Alembert confining himself largely to the mathematical articles.

Diderot expanded the scope of the project and dramatically changed its purpose. This work was not intended to be simply a compilation of existing knowledge presented in an objective manner. Rather, its purpose was to change the way people thought and inspire them to action. The

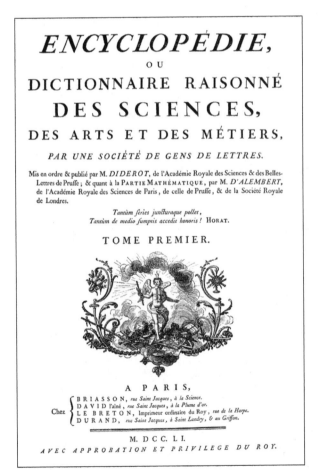

A facsimile of the cover page of the first volume of Denis Diderot's Encyclopédie, *1751.*

Encyclopedia: Or, Classified Dictionary of Sciences, Arts, and Trades (to translate its full French title) challenged tradition and authority, particularly the Church and the monarchy, attacking corruption, despotism, superstition, ignorance, and poverty. It sought to advance the frontiers of knowledge, and for this reason heavy emphasis was placed upon articles giving the most current information on the mechanical arts and industrial processes. The *Encyclopedia* was to be a tool whereby the Old Regime was discredited and weakened, to be replaced by a society that embraced reason, tolerance, and progress. Its audacity, originality, and unity of purpose differentiated it from other previous works.

The *Encyclopedia* consumed twenty-five years of Diderot's life. Published between 1751 and 1772, it eventually totaled seventeen volumes of text and eleven volumes of plates. After Diderot completed his work, another seven volumes were added, including a two-volume index. There were more than sixty thousand entries, written by approximately 150 authors. The contributors, known as encyclopedists, varied widely in background, talent, and opinions. One encyclopedist, the chevalier de Jaucourt, wrote an astounding seventeen thousand articles, or more than one-fourth of all the entries. Among some of the more famous contributors were Voltaire, Jean-Jacques Rousseau, Montesquieu, Anne-Robert-Jacques Turgot, and the marquis de Condorcet.

Diderot was deeply involved in all aspects of the enterprise, lining up contributors, editing manuscripts, proofreading, and attending to business details. In addition, he wrote about six thousand entries himself, particularly on philosophy and the industrial arts. In order to become acquainted with a topic, he would spend months in a workshop talking with artisans and craftspeople in order to better understand a technical or industrial process.

The threat of censorship continuously dogged the *Encyclopedia*. In 1752, the government suspended publication for a year, and in 1759, Pope Clement XIII condemned the work and the royal license to publish was withdrawn. Yet the work continued to be published in a clandestine fashion for several reasons. Most important, the encyclopedists practiced self-censorship, cleverly using subtlety, nuance, and irony to avoid the authorities' wrath. Contributors also made full use of their powerful friends in the king's court. Madame de Pompadour, Louis XV's mistress, used her influence as a protector, as did Chrétien-Guillaume de Malesherbes, the government censor, who was actually an enlightened individual supportive of the project.

One of the more clever subterfuges employed by Diderot was to allow a conservative author to write an article but then to cross-reference this article to a more radical entry that in effect refuted the arguments advanced in the original one. Perhaps the unhappiest moment in Diderot's life occurred in 1764, when he discovered that Le Breton had surreptitiously edited more than three hundred pages of Diderot's manuscripts in an attempt to make them more acceptable to the censors. Nevertheless, most scholars believe the changes did not detract from the overall impact of the final product.

Diderot's fame did not rest exclusively upon his editorship of the *Encyclopedia*. He was an extraordinarily prolific writer who could effortlessly write a five-thousand-word letter or a treatise of several hundred pages. He wrote novels, essays, art reviews, theatrical plays, and philosophic dissertations. Almost invariably, his themes dealt with first principles and weighty philosophic questions. Much of what he wrote, however, was either circulated in very narrow circles or remained unpublished because of its controversial content. Among some of his noteworthy books, published posthumously, were *La Religieuse* (1796; *The Nun*, 1797), *Jacques le fataliste et son maître* (wr. c. 1771, pb. 1796; *Jacques the Fatalist and His Master*, 1797), *Le Neveu de Rameau* (1821, 1891; *Rameau's Nephew* 1897), and *Le Rêve de d'Alembert* (wr. 1769, pb. 1830; *D'Alembert's Dream*, 1927). Some of the greatest minds in modern history acknowledged their intellectual debt to Diderot or admired his works; these thinkers include Karl Marx, Sigmund Freud, Auguste Comte, Arthur Schopenhauer, Honoré de Balzac, Georg Wilhelm Friedrich Hegel, Charles Baudelaire, and Johann Wolfgang von Goethe. Nevertheless, Diderot's death on July 31, 1784, did not evoke the same widespread public response as did those of Voltaire, Montesquieu, and Rousseau.

SIGNIFICANCE

The reputation of the *Encyclopedia*, unlike that of Diderot, has had a mixed history. Even by the end of the eighteenth century, its glory had faded, since much of the information it contained had become outdated and the radicalism of the French Revolution, which broke out in 1789, far exceeded the more modest reforms called for in the *Encyclopedia*. It remains of interest as a historical document, however. At the time of its publication, it had tremendous impact: It attracted more than four thousand subscribers, an impressive figure given its high cost and sheer size.

The *Encyclopedia* dominated the intellectual debate of the period, generating plays, articles, books, and angry

---

"PHILOSOPHER"

The eighteenth century was a productive and controversial time for philosophy in France. The Encyclopedia *entry "Philosopher," excerpted here, set forward the now-unknown author's definition of the philosopher and explained how a philosopher differed from a "normal" person.*

Other men are determined to act without feeling, without knowing the causes that make them move, without even imagining that there are any. The *philosopher*, by contrast, brings causes to light to the degree that he is able, and often even anticipates them, and surrenders himself to them with full knowledge: he is, so to speak, a clock that sometimes winds itself. Thus he avoids those objects which could cause feelings that are suitable neither to well-being nor to a reasonable being, and seeks those which can excite in him affections suitable to the state in which he finds himself. Reason is to the *philosopher* what grace is to the Christian. Grace determines the action of the Christian; reason determines that of the *philosopher*.

Other men are carried away by their passions, without their actions being preceded by reflection: these are men who walk in the shadows; whereas the *philosopher*, even in his passions, acts only after reflection; he walks in the night, but he is preceded by a torch.

The *philosopher* forms his principles on the basis of an infinite number of discrete observations. The people adopt a principle without thinking about the observations that produced it: They believe that the maxim exists, so to speak, in itself; but the *philosopher* follows the maxim to its source; he examines its origin; he knows its true value, and only makes the use of it that is appropriate.

Truth is not for the *philosopher* a mistress who corrupts his imagination, and that he thinks he finds everywhere; he is satisfied to be able to bring it to light when he is able to perceive it. He certainly does not confuse it with probability; he takes as true that which is true, as false that which is false, as doubtful that which is doubtful, and as probable that which is only probable. He goes further—and here is a great perfection of the *philosopher*—when he has no proper motive for judging, he remains undecided.

Source: "Philosopher," translated by Dena Goodman. The Encyclopedia of Diderot and d'Alembert: Collaborative Translation Project. http://name.umdl.umich.edu/ did2222.0000.001. Accessed November 14, 2005.

debates as to its wisdom or folly. Conservatives, clerics, and courtiers denounced the work as destructive of religion and assaulting the very fabric of society. Admirers later claimed with obvious hyperbole that it was the bible of the Enlightenment and a blueprint for the French Revolution. Yet historians generally agree that the work was highly influential, it reached the cultural and political elites of Europe, it played a significant role in undermining the legitimacy of the Old Regime, and it inspired similar encyclopedic works in other countries. The *Encyclopedia* is quite rightly regarded as an important landmark in the cultural and political history of modern Europe.

—*David C. Lukowitz*

FURTHER READING

Blom, Philipp. *Enlightening the World: "Encyclopédie," the Book That Changed the Course of History*. New York: Palgrave Macmillan, 2005. Blom relates the history of the *Encyclopedia*, describing the book's conception, efforts to suppress its publication, and the authors who faced exile, jail, and censorship to complete the work.

Brewer, Daniel, and Julie Candler Hayes, eds. *Using the "Encyclopédie": Ways of Knowing, Ways of Reading*. Oxford, England: Voltaire Foundation, 2002. Collection of essays analyzing how the *Encyclopedia* compiled knowledge, then reshaped and redirected that knowledge. Some of the essays discuss translating the *Encyclopedia*, reading the book on-line, and the book's garden references and medical discourse.

Darnton, Robert. *The Business of Enlightenment: A Publishing History of the "Encyclopédie," 1775-1800*. Cambridge, Mass.: Harvard University Press, 1979. Deals with the technical and business side of publishing subsequent editions of the *Encyclopedia* after the original edition had been completed.

Donato, Clorinda, and Robert M. Maniquis, eds. *The "Encyclopédie" and the Age of Revolution*. Boston: G. K. Hall, 1992. Examines the influence of the *Encyclopedia* upon future encyclopedic works in several countries. Superb collection of plates and engravings.

Furbank, Philip Nicholas. *Diderot*. New York: Alfred A. Knopf, 1992. An entertaining, well-balanced account of Diderot's life, placing him within the political and cultural context of his times.

Gordon, Douglas H., and Norman L. Torrey. *The Censoring of Diderot's "Encyclopedia" and the Re-established Text*. New York: Columbia University Press, 1947. A short but major scholarly contribution to the subject, delineating the areas where censorship took place. Best read by advanced-level students.

Mason, John Hope. *The Irresistible Diderot*. New York: Quartet Books, 1982. Contains lengthy translated segments of Diderot's writings, accompanied by skilled commentary. Chapter 5, "Encyclopedia," includes a sample of Diderot's contributions to that work.

Wilson, Arthur M. *Diderot*. New York: Oxford University Press, 1972. This lengthy, scholarly, two-part biography is generally regarded as the finest study of Diderot, designed for specialists and general readers.

SEE ALSO: 1721-1750: Early Enlightenment in France; 1743-1744: D'Alembert Develops His Axioms of Motion; 1748: Montesquieu Publishes *The Spirit of the Laws*; Apr., 1762: Rousseau Publishes *The Social Contract*; July, 1764: Voltaire Publishes *A Philosophical Dictionary for the Pocket*; 1770: Publication of Holbach's *The System of Nature*; 1773: Goethe Inaugurates the Sturm und Drang Movement.

RELATED ARTICLES in *Great Lives from History: The Eighteenth Century, 1701-1800*: Jean le Rond d'Alembert; Marquis de Condorcet; Denis Diderot; Johann Wolfgang von Goethe; Paul-Henri-Dietrich d'Holbach; Louis XV; Montesquieu; Madame de Pompadour; Jean-Jacques Rousseau; Anne-Robert-Jacques Turgot; Voltaire.

1750's

1752-March, 1756
MAYER'S LUNAR TABLES ENABLE MARINERS TO DETERMINE LONGITUDE AT SEA

Johann Mayer compiled and disseminated tables of astronomical distances, supplemented with mathematical formulas and instructions, to guide navigators to determine longitude at sea. These lunar tables helped sea travelers avoid dangerous areas, reduced the occurrence of shipwrecks and disappearances, and enhanced trade, exploration, and military expeditions.

LOCALE: Germany; England

CATEGORIES: Science and technology; astronomy; transportation

KEY FIGURES

Johann Tobias Mayer (1723-1762), German astronomer, mathematician, and cartographer
Leonhard Euler (1707-1783), Swiss mathematician
Nevil Maskelyne (1732-1811), astronomer royal of Great Britain, 1765-1811
James Bradley (1693-1762), astronomer royal of Great Britain, 1742-1762
John Harrison (1693-1776), English clockmaker

SUMMARY OF EVENT

Eighteenth century sea travelers lacked an accurate method for measuring longitude while aboard vessels until Johann Tobias Mayer compiled astronomical information in the 1750's that enabled navigators to compute east and west locations from the prime meridian. Prior to the mid-eighteenth century, sailors had used the length of time required to pass between two landmarks to report possible longitudes. Navigators often relied on instinct to supplement meager information. Sea conditions introduced such factors as wave turbulence, which rendered mariners' calculations more complex than land-based longitudinal measurements. Without land references in the middle of oceans, crews simply had no reliable method to determine longitudes at sea. It was relatively simple, on the other hand, to determine latitude by measuring the angle of the Sun at noon. If they were to report locations and hazards to other sea travelers, though, navigators needed precise determinations of both latitude and longitude.

Renaissance scientists, including Galileo, made many suggestions that later proved relevant to Mayer's work. Astronomical and temporal information were constants in longitude investigations. In 1514, Johann Werner hy-pothesized that one could determine longitudes based on distances between the Moon and stars. By 1675, English king Charles II had established the Royal Observatory at Greenwich and the position of astronomer royal. The astronomer royal was charged with cataloging astronomical information based on Greenwich time and the prime meridian, located at the observatory, in order to achieve better navigational techniques.

Shipwrecks motivated Spanish and Dutch rulers and the British parliament to offer incentives, including financial rewards, to anyone who could develop a reliable instrument or method to determine longitudes at sea. These governments wanted naval voyages and merchant trade to proceed safely, uninterrupted by the collisions or disappearances that could result from a lack of longitudinal information. On October 22, 1707, Rear Admiral Cloudsley Shovel and his crews on four warships crashed on the rocky coast of the Scilly Islands, near southwestern England. Confused by fog and lacking longitude details, they did not realize they were close to land.

The two thousand casualties caused by that crash became a catalyst for intensified efforts to find longitude. The British parliament approved the Longitude Act of 1714, specifying a £20,000 prize overseen by a Board of Longitude for the first practicable method of finding longitude that could be successfully tested on a voyage between Great Britain and the West Indies. The winning technique had to be consistently accurate in its determinations of longitude, within one-half degree, during the entire trip.

The British Admiralty preferred what astronomers called the lunar distance method, which combined astronomical data with time and nautical measurement factors to determine longitude. Mathematical prodigy Mayer decided to work on the longitude problem, even though he had no sea navigation experience, believing the lunar distance method had the greatest potential for success. He realized that navigators using the lunar distance method to figure longitudes needed correct star locations and reliable predictions of future lunar and solar movements during specified time periods. Mayer joined the Cosmographical Society, built a telescope to observe lunar motion and eclipses of the Earth and stars, and mapped the lunar surface, hypothesizing that the Moon lacked an atmosphere.

To collect precise measurements, Mayer designed a repeating circle, because he considered John Hadley's reflecting quadrant, introduced in 1731, to be limited and inaccurate when measuring distances between stars and the Moon. Mayer's circle could measure angles greater than 90°. Mayer skillfully made and evaluated his observations and documented astronomical information, including lunar, solar, and stellar locations and motions. He used this information to project the future positions of celestial bodies. He considered how the atmosphere and temperatures affected astronomical measurements. He began corresponding with Swiss mathematician Leonhard Euler and used Euler's equations to complement his data. By 1752, the Royal Society of Göttingen printed Mayer's lunar tables in its *Transactions*. Already teaching mathematics at Georg August Academy in Göttingen, Mayer accepted directorship of the school's observatory in 1754.

In 1755, Mayer submitted a revised copy of his lunar tables to English admiral Lord Anson, first lord of the Admiralty, who gave them to the Board of Longitude in March, 1756. Astronomer royal James Bradley studied Mayer's data and declared that it was consistent with the information he had compiled at the Greenwich Observatory. From 1757 to 1759, Captain John Campbell tested Mayer's tables at sea, using Mayer's repeating circle instead of a quadrant, but the Seven Years' War hindered effective evaluation of Mayer's data.

Nevil Maskelyne next tested Mayer's tables during a 1761-1762 voyage to St. Helena and proclaimed Mayer's tables accurate. Mayer continued making observations to enhance his lunar tables. Before he died, Mayer provided more precise tables for sea tests. Mayer's widow submitted her husband's refined tables to the Board of Longitude. Maskelyne tried them on his trips to the Barbados in 1763 and 1764. He published Mayer's tables in the *British Mariner's Guide* (1763), showing sailors how to apply the tables to measure longitude from ships.

In February, 1765, Maskelyne became the fifth astronomer royal, acquiring a seat on the Board of Longitude. He supported rewarding Mayer's heirs for his lunar tables. Several British East India Company captains told the board about their successes with Mayer's tables but commented that longitude equations were difficult to calculate. Maskelyne suggested the board approve publishing an annual almanac with Mayer's final tables and simplified trigonometric information to ease computation. A parliamentary act granted money for the *Nautical Almanac*. Praising Mayer's lunar tables, the board awarded Mayer's widow £3,000 and Euler £300. Maskelyne edited Mayer's *Tabulae motuum solis et lunae novae et correctae* (1770; new and correct table of the motion of the Sun and the Moon). The commissioners of longitude issued a revised edition the next decade. Mayer's memoirs and star catalog also appeared posthumously.

SIGNIFICANCE

Mayer's astronomical measurements and lunar tables contributed to the development of dependable techniques for navigators to identify their longitude at sea. Determining one's position at sea made it possible reliably to travel to specific ports, meet other vessels, avoid known hazards, and track and confront enemy fleets. By refining information about lunar movement and positions, Mayer sped the transition from an era of navigation by instinct and educated guesses to one of navigation based on precise and reliable astronomical computations. Indeed, Mayer's tables were precise to within a half degree, because he had carefully analyzed and honed his observations of the Moon, Sun, and stars. In addition to adopting his tables, many navigators considered Mayer's repeating circle useful. Instrument makers produced and sold the circle, improving upon its initial materials and design.

At the same time that Mayer compiled his lunar tables, carpenter and clockmaker John Harrison aspired to solve the longitude problem. He devised several chronometers, which passed trials, but the Board of Longitude hesitated to award Harrison its prize because he was not an astronomer. The Longitude Act of 1765 included restrictions aimed against Harrison, but he persisted. Explorer James Cook consulted chronometers to figure longitudes during his 1769 New Zealand journey. He considered Harrison's timing device convenient to use, especially when weather interfered with lunar methods. By 1773, King George III had convinced Parliament to designate Harrison their longitude prize's winner.

In the late eighteenth century, chronometers became commercially available. Merchants mostly used the expensive devices, while many sailors continued to rely on lunar distance methods until they could afford chronometers. Navies initially retained lunar techniques for military purposes. Able to calculate accurate longitudes consistently, sailors navigated with more confidence. Because chronometer use became widespread, the Longitude Act of 1828 repealed the Board of Longitude. Inspired by eighteenth century precedents, modern navigators look skyward to satellite technology tracking exact longitudes as they travel by water, land, and air.

—Elizabeth D. Schafer

FURTHER READING

Andrewes, William J. H., ed. *The Quest for Longitude.* Cambridge, Mass.: Collection of Historical Scientific Instruments, Harvard University, 1996. Proceedings of a November 1993 longitude symposium held at Harvard University that comprehensively explored the history of longitude research and navigation strategies. Includes an illustration of Mayer's portrait.

Forbes, Eric G. *The Birth of Scientific Navigation: The Solving in the Eighteenth Century of the Problem of Finding Longitude at Sea.* London: National Maritime Museum, 1974. The editor of volumes of Mayer's writings and correspondence with Euler tells how Mayer influenced navigation and interacted with his peers, the Board of Longitude, and the British Admiralty.

Howse, Derek. *Greenwich Time and the Longitude.* London: Philip Wilson, 1997. Describes how humans have determined longitude since ancient times, emphasizing eighteenth century developments, including Mayer's innovative tables to improve navigation. Illustrations, maps, bibliography.

_____. *Nevil Maskelyne: The Seaman's Astronomer.* Foreword by Sir Francis Graham-Smith. New York: Cambridge University Press, 1989. Examines Mayer's and Maskelyne's professional relationship as they sought to achieve accurate longitude measurement methods. Glossary, appendices, illustrations.

Sobel, Dava. *Longitude: The True Story of a Lone Genius Who Solved the Greatest Scientific Problem of His Time.* New York: Walker, 1995. Focuses on John Harrison's efforts but also discusses Mayer's lunar tables and the attempts of others to win Parliament's prize.

Williams, J. E. D. *From Sails to Satellites: The Origin and Development of Navigational Science.* New York: Oxford University Press, 1992. Places Mayer's development of his repeating circle and lunar tables in context with tools and methods used by navigators prior to and after the eighteenth century.

SEE ALSO: 1704-1712: Astronomy Wars in England; 1705: Halley Predicts the Return of a Comet; 1714-1762: Quest for Longitude; 1725: Flamsteed's Star Catalog Marks the Transition to Modern Astronomy; 1748: Bradley Discovers the Nutation of Earth's Axis; 1748: Euler Develops the Concept of Function; 1754: Büsching Publishes *A New System of Geography*; Jan., 1756-Feb. 15, 1763: Seven Years' War; 1787: Herschel Begins Building His Reflecting Telescope.

RELATED ARTICLES in *Great Lives from History: The Eighteenth Century, 1701-1800*: Lord Anson; Leonhard Euler; George III.

1752-1760
ALAUNGPAYA UNITES BURMA

The creation of the Burmese Third Empire by Alaungpaya ushered in the modern era of British colonial affiliation, featuring the exploitation of the production capacities of the Irrawaddy and Salween River Valleys to provide rice exports in the global colonial trade.

LOCALE: Burma (now in Myanmar, India, China, and Thailand)

CATEGORIES: Government and politics; expansion and land acquisition; wars, uprisings, and civil unrest

KEY FIGURES

Alaungpaya (c. 1714-1760), king of Burma, r. 1752-1760

Hsinbyushin (1736-1776), son of Alaungpaya and king of Burma, r. 1763-1776

Bodawpaya (1745-1819), son of Alaungpaya and king of Burma, r. 1782-1819

SUMMARY OF EVENT

By the mid-eighteenth century, the Burmese people had been dominated by the Mons for nearly a millennium. They had begun moving into the Irrawaddy River Valley by the ninth century, but for the next nine hundred years they remained under the yoke of the Mons rulers, who were related to the people of Siam. These centuries of oppression came to an end when Alaungpaya—a local tribal headman, or *myothugyi*—overthrew the Mons, establishing Burmese dominance around the Irrawaddy River and then expanding his sphere of influence to include the upper regions of the valley and the surrounding mountains. The Konbaung Dynasty established by Alaungpaya remained politically dominant in the region for 130 years.

The domination of the Irrawaddy region by the Mons was never as complete or as hegemonic as they desired. Indeed, long periods of political fragmentation were the rule in the Irrawaddy River Valley, as various tribal powers struggled to establish themselves as the sole source of authority. More often than not, however, it was the lowland cultures living along the river that represented the political majority, while surrounding hill tribes represented a volatile minority that was difficult to subdue but had little say in Burmese decision making. The Karens—who lived in the Irrawaddy delta and the nearby hill areas to the immediate west—were probably the most significant and most affected of the minority peoples. The Mons often captured Karens and forced the captives to serve them for a while before letting them go. Chins, Naga, and Kachins were hill tribes that represented continuous thorns in the side of Burmese rulers and disrupted plans to unify the region. In between the ruling dynasties of "Old Burma," moreover, regional unity was often disrupted by foreign invasions from China, India, Mongolia, and Central Asia.

The fragmentation of the Irrawaddy region was brought to an end by Alaungpaya, not only because he was one of the shrewdest military leaders in Burmese history but also because he had the charisma and strength of character to motivate the various hill peoples and lowland peoples to accept his rule. Alaungpaya's reign, nevertheless, was dominated by constant and intense military action. Even after he died invading Siam in 1760, Alaungpaya was succeeded by two of his sons, who continued his strategy of constant warfare and violent expansionism. Alaungpaya's campaigns of conquest began in northern Burma in 1752, when he rose up against the highland Mons who had come north from the Dawna Range in the southeast. The Mons were ultimately driven back to their home region on the Malayan Peninsula.

After driving the bulk of the Mons southward, Alaungpaya returned north to deal with numerous Mon and Talaing holdouts who remained in the two central cities of the region, Syriam and Pegu. Upon reasserting his authority over these cities, Alaungpaya turned his attention farther northward and added the Shan states of the upper plateau to his domain. During the next three or four years, he fought constantly to maintain the territory he had gained: He alternated his time between putting down various Mon uprisings in the south and defeating similar periodic resistance in the central Irrawaddy River Valley around Manipur.

Finally, in 1759, he felt either secure or ambitious enough to attempt another major conquest: He turned his attention southeastward across the Dawna Range to the Siamese culture of the Chao Phraya River Valley (in present-day Thailand). It was during this Siamese campaign the following year that Alaungpaya was mortally wounded by the explosion of his own artillery.

Before his death, Alaungpaya conquered and unified several disparate Southeast Asian peoples, establishing them all as subjects of a kingdom ruled by the lowland Burmese. Much of the appeal of King Alaungpaya to the various Burmese subcultures, transcending even his military genius and charisma, emanated from his original status as *myothugyi*, or local headman, in the upper Irrawaddy city of Shwebo, about fifty miles north of the capital at Ava. As *myothugyi*, Alaungpaya was the key personality to whom the local population acknowledged direct personal allegiance. His authority, therefore, was steeped in a more direct, familiar relationship to his constituency than was that of the traditional Burmese royal figure.

As *myothugyi*, Alaungpaya had been responsible for adjudicating disputes and local military commands. He was essentially the local police chief, judge, arbiter, tax collector, army recruiter, marriage and divorce witness, promoter and arranger of festivals and celebrations, and public works engineer, as well as assigning service obligations to members of his community. He was an indispensable bridge between the arbitrary authority of the king and his subjects. He identified more with the interests of his own people than did the often predatory royal officials. It was this identification and direct contact with common tribal people and concerns that broadened Alaungpaya's appeal and united his followers as he gained in strength and prowess.

SIGNIFICANCE

Under Alaungpaya's sons, Hsinbyushin and Bodawpaya, the Burmese Empire continued to expand, reaching its greatest territorial extent in the early nineteenth century. Burmese forces invaded Siam once more, taking the territory Alaungpaya had failed to capture. They also repelled Chinese invaders from the north and added Arakan and Assam to their imperial holdings. The empire maintained its sovereignty throughout the region it had conquered, until it was conquered in turn by Britain and assimilated into the British Empire in 1885.

Alaungpaya was the first of the Burmese kings to deal with European colonists. He received "aid" from the British East India Company in his fight against the Mons, who were supported by the French. After conquering the Mons, he secured French weaponry and artillerymen to

1750's

gain a substantial advantage in his later military campaigns. Both French and English captains knelt before Alaungpaya to receive orders in respectful silence. He was probably the last Burmese ruler to withstand manipulation by these erstwhile foreign colonial powers.

The reign of Alaungpaya brought no particular cultural, religious, or administrative enrichment to Burma. Instead, the new king brought to his throne a compelling military persistence, a warlike force of character, a tradition of direct popular interaction derived from his position as *myothugyi*, and a tremendous energetic will to extend Burmese political dominance that served to unite the Burmese people for the next century.

None of the Burmese dynasties prior to Alaungpaya's Konbaung Dynasty had been able to achieve the same level of political legitimacy among the radically diverse regional subcultures. Alaungpaya was responsible for restoring Burmese morale, as well as for filling his peoples with the sense of invincibility that would ultimately prove their undoing: The decision of Bodawpaya to transgress recognized borders into British Assam led to British intervention and placed Burma in the British imperial consciousness. The Burmese, by this time, had adopted a contemptuous attitude toward foreigners, which clouded their perceptions, preventing them from recognizing the superior military strength of British India.

—*James Knotwell*

FURTHER READING

Aung-Thwin, Michael A. *Irrigation in the Heartland of Burma: Foundations of the Pre-colonial Burmese*

State. DeKalb: Northern Illinois University, Center for Southeast Asian Studies, 1990. The formation of Burmese culture is examined from a nontraditional perspective.

_____. *Mists of Ramanna: The Legend That Was Lower Burma*. Honolulu: University of Hawaii Press, 2005. A detailed account of the formation of lowland Burmese culture as distinguished from highland culture.

_____. *Myth and History in the Historiography of Early Burma: Paradigms, Primary Sources, and Prejudices*. Athens: Ohio University Center for International Studies, 1998. Provides a useful account of the beliefs and institutions of Burmese culture during and before the time of Alaungpaya.

_____. *Pagan: The Origins of Modern Burma*. Honolulu: University of Hawaii Press, 1985. Generalized, book-length account of times leading up to Alaungpaya.

Koenig, William J. *Burmese Polity, 1752-1819: A Study of Kon Baung Politics, Administration, and Social Organization*. Ann Arbor: Center for South and Southeast Asian Studies, University of Michigan, 1990. Examination of political relations within the Konbaung Dynasty.

SEE ALSO: 1704-1757: Javanese Wars of Succession; Jan. 24, 1744-Aug. 31, 1829: Dagohoy Rebellion in the Philippines; Sept., 1769-1778: Siamese-Vietnamese War; 1771-1802: Vietnamese Civil Wars.

RELATED ARTICLE in *Great Lives from History: The Eighteenth Century, 1701-1800*: Alaungpaya.

June, 1752

FRANKLIN DEMONSTRATES THE ELECTRICAL NATURE OF LIGHTNING

By drawing lightning from storm clouds, Franklin's dangerous kite experiment conclusively demonstrated that lightning was a form of electricity. The experiment also offered further proof of his single-substance theory of electricity and showed that this fluidlike static energy could be passed from one object to another.

LOCALE: Philadelphia, Pennsylvania
CATEGORIES: Science and technology; physics;

KEY FIGURES
Benjamin Franklin (1706-1790), American scientist, statesman, and philosopher

William Franklin (1730/1731-1813), Benjamin Franklin's son and last royal governor of New Jersey

SUMMARY OF EVENT

Benjamin Franklin's kite experiment started with two related questions: What is the nature of electricity? and Is lightning a form of electricity? Franklin indicated in his autobiography that prior to this particular investigation his interest in electricity had been inspired by Adam Spencer. Spencer had lectured on the subject in Boston in 1744 and then later, at Franklin's invitation, in Philadelphia. Soon after, Franklin attempted various electrical

Benjamin Franklin found that lightning was a form of electricity, leading to his invention of the lightning rod. (Library of Congress)

tests, which he frequently reported in letters to his English friend Peter Collinson. Collinson read this correspondence at meetings of the Royal Society of London and eventually assisted in the London publication of Franklin's letters in *Experiments and Observations on Electricity* (1751-1754). Translated into several languages, this three-part work established Franklin's reputation within the scientific communities of both Europe and the American colonies.

As early as 1749, Franklin had suspected that lightning was an electrical discharge from storm clouds. In a letter to Collinson, he observed that lightning and electricity shared similarities in color, crookedness of motion, and crackling sounds. If lightning is electricity, Franklin wondered, then how did the clouds obtain this electrical static? He conjectured that salt particles found in oceans rub against water to produce an electrical charge on the surface of the seas. Through evaporation, he further speculated, this charge rises to the clouds, which during certain types of encounters release this charge as lightning.

Franklin also observed that tall objects, such as steeples, trees, or ship masts, can trigger the release of electrical energy from clouds. To protect such structures from fires caused by lightning strikes, he recommended 10-foot-long "upright rods of iron made sharp as a needle" (lightning rods). Extended from the peaks of high structures, these devices would preemptively attract "electrical fire" from the clouds. Although his report on the kite experiment in the October 19, 1752, edition of *The Pennsylvania Gazette* states that a test of his lightning-rod theory succeeded in Philadelphia, it remains uncertain whether he personally ever conducted such a trial by this date.

On the other hand, it is virtually certain that with the assistance of his twenty-one-year-old son William in June, 1752, Franklin did indeed conduct a kite test of his theory of the electrical nature of lightning. In a letter to Collinson dated October 19, 1752, as well as in the *Gazette* article published that same month, Franklin reported that during a thunderstorm he flew a kite made of a silk handkerchief tied across cedarwood crosspieces. The kite had a tail, and a foot of wire extended as an an-

1750's

363

FRANKLIN ON THE PHILADELPHIA EXPERIMENTS

In his autobiography, Benjamin Franklin recalled his experiments with electricity.

In 1746, being at Boston, I met there with a Dr. Spence, who was lately arrived from Scotland, and show'd me some electric experiments. They were imperfectly perform'd, as he was not very expert; but, being on a subject quite new to me, they equally surpris'd and pleased me. Soon after my return to Philadelphia, our library company receiv'd from Mr. P. Collinson, Fellow of the Royal Society of London, a present of a glass tube, with some account of the use of it in making such experiments. I eagerly seized the opportunity of repeating what I had seen at Boston; and, by much practice, acquir'd great readiness in performing those, also, which we had an account of from England, adding a number of new ones. I say much practice, for my house was continually full, for some time, with people who came to see these new wonders. . . .

Oblig'd as we were to Mr. Collinson for his present of the tube, etc., I thought it right he should be inform'd of our success in using it, and wrote him several letters containing accounts of our experiments. He got them read in the Royal Society, where they were not at first thought worth so much notice as to be printed in their Transactions. One paper, which I wrote for Mr. Kinnersley, on the sameness of lightning with electricity, I sent to Dr. Mitchel, an acquaintance of mine, and one of the members also of that society, who wrote me word that it had been read, but was laughed at by the connoisseurs. . . .

What gave [the work] the more sudden and general celebrity, was the success of one of its proposed experiments, made by Messrs. Dalibard and De Lor at Marly, for drawing lightning from the clouds. This engag'd the public attention every where. M. de Lor, who had an apparatus for experimental philosophy, and lectur'd in that branch of science, undertook to repeat what he called the Philadelphia Experiments; and, after they were performed before the king and court, all the curious of Paris flocked to see them. I will not swell this narrative with an account of that capital experiment, nor of the infinite pleasure I receiv'd in the success of a similar one I made soon after with a kite at Philadelphia, as both are to be found in the histories of electricity.

Source: Benjamin Franklin, *The Autobiography of Benjamin Franklin: With Introduction and Notes.* Edited by Charles W. Eliot (New York: P. F. Collier & Son, 1909).

electricity comprised two separate opposing fluids, effluence and affluence. The kite experiment refuted this prominent theory by enabling Franklin to measure the charge of the lower part of storm clouds, which he found to be negative in nature. This reading supported his theory that electricity consisted of a single "electric fluid" that circulates among and through positively and negatively charged materials. Grouping different materials on the basis of their conductivity, Franklin concluded that "A body which is a good conductor of [electrical] fire readily receives it into its substance, and conducts it thro' the whole to all the parts."

The kite experiment showed, moreover, that the common substance of lightning's electric fluid can be passed from one object to another. This principle of conductivity and transference so fascinated Franklin that three months after the kite experiment he fashioned an elaborate demonstration utilizing a 9-foot lightning rod that he had attached to the chimney of his home. This rod conveyed electricity through a glass-enclosed wire running down a stairwell to a bell, which was connected by another wire to a second bell. Both bells would ring whenever the lightning rod received an electrical charge. Sometimes so much current passed between the two bells that the entire staircase in Franklin's home lit up brilliantly, as if "with sunshine, so that one might see to pick up a pin." Franklin's wife, legend holds, was not at all pleased by this noisy apparatus or by her husband's other efforts to convert their home into a laboratory for electrical research.

SIGNIFICANCE

Benjamin Franklin's dramatic kite experiment became an instant legend. A recurrent subject for paintings and print illustrations over the centuries, the kite test is now ingrained in the world's cultural memory of Franklin. As early as 1767, Joseph Priestley, in his *History and Pres-*

tenna from its top end. The lower end of the twine descending from the kite was tied with an insulating silk ribbon, from which an iron key was suspended away from his hand by a cotton string. To keep the silk ribbon and the key dry during the storm, Franklin stood inside a doorway while flying the kite. When he passed his other hand over the key, a spark leaped from the key toward his knuckle. This transfer of energy proved that lightning was electrical in nature.

Franklin's use of a pointed-tip conductor in the kite experiment also advanced the case for his single-substance (or one-fluid) theory of electricity. At the time of his kite test, the prevalent European theory held that

ent State of Electricity, described this episode as a "capital" discovery, "the greatest, perhaps, that has been made in the whole compass of philosophy, since the time of Sir Isaac Newton."

From the standpoint of the history of physics, however, the result of Franklin's kite experiment with lightning is not considered as significant as Priestley thought. Franklin did not know that in France, a month before the Philadelphia kite test, experimenter Thomas-François Dalibard had already proved the electrical nature of lightning. This French undertaking, it is important to note, was thoroughly indebted to Franklin because it was based on findings Franklin had reported in the first volume of his highly regarded *Experiments and Observations on Electricity*. Franklin may have been second in proving that lightning was electricity, but it did not matter. His demonstration in Philadelphia was wonderfully theatrical and proved so appealing to a worldwide audience that others in Europe enthusiastically repeated his experiment.

The kite experiment in Philadelphia was, finally, most significant for the evidence it provided in support of two of Franklin's major contributions to the study of physics: his single-substance theory of electricity and his related invention of the pointed-tip lightning rod, still used today. In 1754, two years after Franklin's kite project, the Royal Society of London awarded him the Copley Medal for his electrical research and soon admitted him as a fellow. In spite of initial resistance from the French scientific community, Franklin's reputation for electrical research likewise quickly spread throughout continental Europe.

In America it was the pointed-tip lightning rod on the kite, more than his single-substance theory, that elevated Franklin's fame. Franklin's lightning-rod design, which would become the worldwide standard, was indeed more effective than the European blunt-tipped model. However, its effectiveness when employed to protect buildings from electrical fires resulting from lightning strikes was not its only value for Americans. The strategic foot

of wire "made sharp as a needle" and extended skyward from the top of the kite's wooden crosspieces was the prototype for the lightning rod that would become not only a practical invention but also an "electrifying" cultural symbol for eighteenth century America. Elated because this colonial device was superior to the European version, Americans proudly celebrated the design of Franklin's lightning rod as a symbol of their new nation's ingenuity and independence.

—*William J. Scheick*

FURTHER READING

Cohen, I. Bernard. *Benjamin Franklin's Science*. Cambridge, Mass.: Harvard University Press, 1990. Cohen's work, especially sensitive to Franklin's Newtonian heritage, also discusses other kite experiments.

Hankins, Thomas L. *Science and the Enlightenment*. New York: Cambridge University Press, 1985. Chapter 3 details the eighteenth century background of Franklin's work with electricity.

Schiffer, Michael Brian. *Draw the Lightning Down: Benjamin Franklin and Electrical Technology in the Age of the Enlightenment*. Berkeley: University of California Press, 2003. Presents Franklin as a leading figure in eighteenth century electrical research and especially highlights his theory of electricity and invention of the lightning rod.

Tanford, Charles. *Franklin Stilled the Waves*. Durham, N.C.: Duke University Press, 1989. Chapters 2 and 3 feature Franklin's work on electricity in the context of his other scientific experiments.

SEE ALSO: 1729: Gray Discovers Principles of Electric Conductivity; 1733: Du Fay Discovers Two Kinds of Electric Charge; Oct., 1745, and Jan., 1746: Invention of the Leyden Jar; 1800: Volta Invents the Battery.

RELATED ARTICLES in *Great Lives from History: The Eighteenth Century, 1701-1800:* Henry Cavendish; Benjamin Franklin; Luigi Galvani; Joseph Priestley; Alessandro Volta.

1750's

1753
LIND DISCOVERS A CURE FOR SCURVY

Building upon previous medical accounts and motivated by the medical disasters of long sea voyages, James Lind proved that citrus fruits can prevent and cure scurvy. His results, published in 1753, helped to convince the British court to order the rationing of citrus juice to all sailors, thus dramatically reducing scurvy in the Royal Navy.

LOCALE: Scotland; England
CATEGORIES: Health and medicine; exploration and discovery

KEY FIGURES

James Lind (1716-1794), a Scottish naval surgeon and physician
Aleixo de Abreu (1568-1630), a Portuguese physician specializing in tropical medicine
Lord Anson (1697-1762), an English admiral
Sir Gilbert Blane (First Baronet Blane; 1749-1834), a Scottish physician
James Cook (1728-1779), an English naval officer and explorer
Sir John Pringle (First Baronet Pringle; 1707-1782), a Scottish military physician
Boudewijn Ronsse (1525-1597), a Flemish physician
Thomas Trotter (1760-1832), a Scottish naval surgeon and physician
John Woodall (1570-1643), an English surgeon, physician, and chemist

SUMMARY OF EVENT

Scurvy is a deficiency disease caused by lack of ascorbic acid (vitamin C) in the diet. The word "ascorbic," coined in 1933, derives from the Greek prefix *a*, meaning "not," and the Latin *scorbutus*, meaning "scurvy." Ascorbic acid is necessary for the body to produce collagen, an essential structural protein. Without sufficient collagen, capillaries break down, causing the typical symptoms of scurvy, such as spongy gums, anemia, general weakness, spontaneous bleeding, muscle pain, and sometimes ulcers, tooth loss, and dementia. Sudden death from hemorrhaging may occur at any time. In children the disease interferes with growth. Symptoms appear between one and three months after the last intake of ascorbic acid. Replenishing ascorbic acid to physiologically acceptable levels by consuming citrus products will usually cure scurvy, as the acid restores collagen.

Scurvy, especially common among sailors until the end of the eighteenth century, was a major problem for merchant, naval, and whaling fleets. Naval surgeon James Lind's *A Treatise of the Scurvy* (1753) demonstrated empirically that the preserved juices of citrus fruits could prevent and cure this disease, which was dreaded among sailors on long voyages. However, Lind was not solely responsible for the conquest of scurvy. The disease came to be understood over a period of about four hundred years, from the sixteenth to the twentieth century. Citrus "therapy" was known before Lind but was not widely recognized or implemented even after his book appeared. Almost half a century passed before his recommendations were put into common maritime practice.

In 1564, Flemish physician Boudewijn Ronsse explained how sailors from northern Europe would cure themselves of scurvy by eating citrus fruits as soon as they reached Spain. English physician John Woodall, in his classic 1617 work on naval hygiene and surgery, *The Surgions Mate*, specifically mentioned limes, lemons, and oranges as cures for scurvy. In 1623, Portuguese physician Aleixo de Abreu described the use of a wide variety of natural food remedies, some of which contained ascorbic acid. John Pringle laid the foundations of modern military and naval medicine and hygiene with his *Observations on the Diseases of the Army* (1752) and *A Discourse upon Some Late Improvements of the Means for Preserving the Health of Mariners* (1776).

England and Spain were enemies between 1739 and 1748, the years occupied by the War of Jenkins's Ear and the War of the Austrian Succession. In this context, Lord Anson commanded a British fleet of six ships—the *Centurion, Gloucester, Severn, Pearl, Wager,* and *Tryal*—that circumnavigated the globe and plundered more than £400,000 of Spanish treasure between 1740 and 1744. Anson returned home a hero. Both he and the treasure were paraded through the streets. However, the strategic and political success of his mission was overshadowed by the fact that only the *Centurion* and about two hundred sailors returned with him. More than 80 percent of the fleet's crew had died of scurvy, so the voyage was widely regarded as a tragedy.

Reacting to Anson's misfortune and inspired by Woodall, Lind resolved to find an answer to the scurvy problem. In 1747, he performed one of the first controlled clinical trials in the history of medicine. Aboard the *Salisbury*, where scurvy had appeared after about a month at sea, Lind chose twelve sailors suffering from early and similar stages of the disease, divided them into six pairs, and rationed each pair a different traditional remedy for scurvy. After six days of this treatment, only the pair that received two oranges and one lemon a day showed noteworthy improvement. The pair who drank apple cider improved slightly. None of the other four pairs improved at all.

Lind published the results of his clinical trial in his 1753 treatise, which he dedicated to Anson, and followed this work with *An Essay on the Most Effectual Means of Preserving the Health of Seamen in the Royal Navy* (1757) and *An Essay on Diseases Incidental to Europeans in Hot Climates with the Method of Preventing Their Fatal Consequences* (1768). He recommended preserving citrus juice in alcohol for use on long voyages. Despite the conclusiveness of Lind's reasoning and the success of the *Salisbury* experiment, few sea captains took notice. Momentum for policy change slowly gathered, however.

Using Lind's recommendations, Captain James Cook lost only one sailor to scurvy during his second exploratory voyage from 1768 to 1771. Pringle included Cook's report in his 1776 work. Gilbert Blane commented favorably on Lind's method and his own replication of citrus therapy in *Observations on the Diseases Incident to Seamen* (1785). Nevertheless, even after these events and testimonies, the highest officers of the Admiralty (Royal Navy board) remained unconvinced. On the skeptical side was naval surgeon and physician Thomas Trotter, whose *Observations on the Scurvy* (1786) proclaimed frankly that Lind's work, even the *Salisbury* experiment, had not settled the questions of what causes scurvy or what to do about it.

Blane persisted in trying to achieve official recognition of citrus therapy for scurvy in the Royal Navy. From his prestigious posts as physician to the prince of Wales, attending physician at St. Thomas's Hospital, fellow of the Royal Society, and member of the Admiralty Board for Sick and Wounded Seamen, he lobbied vigorously for reform, recalling his own experience as ship's doctor in the American Revolutionary War when a captured cargo of limes had saved the crew from scurvy. The Admiralty was finally impressed by a nineteen-week voyage from England to Madras in 1793. The crew received regular rations of lemon juice preserved in alcohol and were entirely free of scurvy. In 1795, the Admiralty issued the order that all British naval ships must issue citrus juice to every crew member every day. By 1797, scurvy had practically disappeared from the Royal Navy.

SIGNIFICANCE

Both James Lind and Gilbert Blane were largely responsible for the dominance of British naval power until the end of the age of sail. The combination of the best ships in the world plus healthier crews proved unbeatable. In the nineteenth century, British sailors and, soon, all Britons, especially Englishmen, became known as limeys because of Blane's strict regulations on diet.

The final steps in conquering scurvy occurred in the twentieth century. Hungarian-born biochemist Albert von Nagyrapolt Szent-Györgyi discovered ascorbic acid in 1927-1928, isolating it from the adrenal glands. He subsequently found the same compound in paprika after noticing that paprika is a remedy for scurvy. In 1933, Leonard Parsons reported successful treatment of infantile scurvy with ascorbic acid. Since that time scurvy has existed only in mild cases in isolated populations with poor mixes of fruits and vegetables in their diet.

—*Eric v.d. Luft*

FURTHER READING

Bown, Stephen R. *Scurvy: How a Surgeon, a Mariner, and a Gentleman Solved the Greatest Medical Mystery of the Age of Sail.* New York: Thomas Dunne Books, St. Martin's Press, 2004. Recounts the saga of Anson, Lind, Cook, and Blane, concluding that their work contributed to Admiral Horatio Nelson's victory at Trafalgar.

Carpenter, Kenneth John. *The History of Scurvy and Vitamin C.* New York: Cambridge University Press, 1986. Supersedes Alfred Hess's book as the standard history.

Cuppage, Francis E. *James Cook and the Conquest of Scurvy.* Westport, Conn.: Greenwood Press, 1994. A readable description by a pathologist of the medical aspects of Cook's voyages.

Druett, Joan. *Rough Medicine: Surgeons at Sea in the Age of Sail.* New York: Routledge, 2002. An account of naval health care from Woodall to the early nineteenth century.

Harvie, David I. *Limeys: The True Story of One Man's War Against Ignorance, the Establishment, and the Deadly Scurvy.* Stroud, England: Sutton, 2002. An investigation of why the British naval bureaucracy took forty-two years to endorse Lind's findings.

Hess, Alfred Fabian. *Scurvy Past and Present.* Philadelphia: J. B. Lippincott, 1920. The standard history in its time.

Reiss, Oscar. *Medicine and the American Revolution: How Diseases and Their Treatments Affected the Colonial Army.* Jefferson, N.C.: McFarland, 1998. Shows how nine times as many American soldiers died from disease as from battle in the revolution and how typically marine diseases such as scurvy manifested themselves on land through long periods of poor diet.

Solomon, Joan. *Discovering the Cure for Scurvy*. Hatfield, England: Association for Science Education, 1989. A brief and clear account with maps.

SEE ALSO: Aug. 25, 1768-Feb. 14, 1779: Voyages of Captain Cook; 1796-1798: Jenner Develops Smallpox Vaccination.

RELATED ARTICLES in *Great Lives from History: The Eighteenth Century, 1701-1800*: Lord Anson; James Cook; Edward Jenner.

1754
BÜSCHING PUBLISHES *A NEW SYSTEM OF GEOGRAPHY*

In 1754, Büsching began publishing a multivolume geographical work, and by 1792 he had completed ten volumes, mostly dealing with Europe. His work was an advance over previous geographies, because it emphasized measurement and statistics rather than mere description.

LOCALE: Hamburg (now in Germany)
CATEGORY: Geography; cultural and intellectual history

KEY FIGURES

Anton Friedrich Büsching (1724-1793), German geographer, professor, and clergyman
Bernardus Varenius (1622-1650), German-born Dutch geographer
Immanuel Kant (1724-1804), German philosopher
Alexander von Humboldt (1769-1859), German explorer and scientist
Carl Ritter (1779-1859), German geographer

SUMMARY OF EVENT

Early forays in geography date to the classical world: Aristotle was one of the first to argue that the Earth was a sphere rather than a flat disk; Strabo wrote an encyclopedic geography encompassing history and descriptions of people and places across the known world; Ptolemy consolidated the geographical knowledge of the Greeks and used astronomical observations to locate places on a map of the world. Ptolemy's system was used until the sixteenth century.

Through medieval times, however, geographers contributed little knowledge that would count as scientific or systematic by later standards. They provided descriptions of other lands and peoples and attempted to ascertain the shape and size of the Earth and locate its places. Although geographers speculated about the geological processes that caused natural features such as mountains and rivers, their analyses of spatial variations in physical phenomena were relatively primitive. Their reports of the human aspects of geography were also descriptive rather than quantitative.

After classical times, geography advanced little for one thousand years, partly because the Catholic Church viewed the idea that the Earth was spherical as heresy. Ptolemy's work survived among Islamic scholars, however, who added new knowledge and concepts to the body of geographical knowledge based on the wide travels of Muslim merchants. Geographic thought in Christian Europe revived with the great explorations of the fifteenth and sixteenth centuries, which established that the Earth was spherical and led to increasingly accurate maps of physical features, such as continental outlines.

In the seventeenth century, Dutch geographer Bernhardus Varenius wrote a geography textbook on a scale not previously attempted: His *Geographia generalis* (1672; *Cosmography and Geography*, 1682; also as *A Compleat System of General Geography*, 1734) became the standard for the next century. Varenius's text divided the discipline of geography into general geography, which treated the form and dimensions of the Earth as a whole, and special geography, dealing with specific regions of the Earth.

In the second half of the eighteenth century, the Enlightenment precipitated a burst of scientific inquiry in Europe. Enlightenment thought held that human beings could understand how the universe worked by reasoning and by measuring and classifying natural processes. In Germany, this belief led to an upsurge in geographical writing, as the new data on physical geography were compiled and analyzed. Information and measurements of another kind, also useful to geographers, began to be available: The Prussian government, reasoning that the wealth or power of a state could be gauged through statistics, began compiling numerical data on the populace.

Anton Friedrich Büsching believed that the writings of his immediate predecessors in geography lacked the grounding in fact demanded by Enlightenment science, and he sought to provide the discipline with a more rigorous methodology. He also wanted geographical writing to be practical, so that travelers could rely on it for information about a country's physical and natural features, history, culture, economy, and government. In 1751, Büsching began writing his major work, *Neue Erdbeschreibung* (1754-1792; new description of the Earth; first eight volumes pb. in six volumes as *A New System of Geography*, 1762).

A New System of Geography, which dealt largely with Europe, was organized into two broad categories—one concentrating on civil and political divisions and the other on natural features. Büsching critically evaluated sources of information and verified data with scientists and other experts, including Prussian authorities. He defined geography's mission precisely, stated his methodology, and provided a comprehensive list of references. In describing natural features, he delimited geographical areas exactly, using precise scales. He incorporated the kinds of data now employed in political and economic geography—for example, census data. His was the first geography to study population density. He also correlated birth and death statistics with environmental factors such as disease, crop failures, war, and migrations, and he estimated the Earth's carrying capacity at 3 billion people. The work included information on the cities and most of the towns of Europe, as well as churches, forts, seaports, produce, manufactures, and commerce. It also described religion, language, armed forces, and politics.

Büsching, to a greater degree than many of his predecessors, explained functional interconnections within physical geography. For example, in deriving climatic conditions, he considered not just geographical latitude but also topography. Thus, he took into account the fact that, because winds may be modified by features such as mountain ranges, forests, and cities, two places at the same latitude may have distinctly different climates. He also described the cycle of evaporation and precipitation and explained flow rates of streams on the basis of the slope of the terrain and characteristics of the streambed. Further, Büsching distinguished high mountain ranges from low ones and noted large-scale geographic patterns such as the restriction of volcanic activity to coastal regions and islands.

The work included maps as well as narrative. The first part was published in 1754. By 1761, he had produced eight volumes, all dealing with Europe. In 1762, these volumes were translated into English, rearranged into six volumes and illustrated with thirty-six folding maps, and published by Andrew Millar as *A New System of Geography*. The translation incorporated three additional essays, and some footnotes, by Patrick Murdoch, a Scottish scholar.

By 1792, the year before his death, Büsching had completed ten volumes and was working on an eleventh that remained unfinished when he died. In addition to Europe, his completed volumes covered parts of Asia. Over the years, he had revised his earlier volumes many times (an eighth, revised edition was published between 1787 and 1788). His work was translated into eight languages. After his death, treatments of the rest of Asia, as well as Africa and North America, were completed by other geographers. The North American volume was written by German librarian and professor Christophe Ebeling (1741-1817) and was published in 1800-1803.

SIGNIFICANCE

Although not well known today, Anton Friedrich Büsching, in the latter half of the eighteenth century, was regarded as the world's foremost geographer. Some contemporaries considered *A New System of Geography* to be the best single source of information about Europe. Until well into the nineteenth century, most European geographical writing was based, to some extent, on this work. Its numerous reprintings and new editions and the many translations reflect its importance. Büsching established that the study of the countries of the world required scholarly research and laid the foundation for modern statistical geography, which allows data to be aggregated geographically and then analyzed.

Although Büsching gave new impetus to geography as a field of study, a more conceptual advance came in the late eighteenth century, when German philosopher Immanuel Kant (1724-1804), relying in part on Büsching's data, incorporated geography into his overall philosophical system. According to Kant, geography synthesized the other sciences through the concept of area or space. Geography, then, treated phenomena that were "beside" one another in space, in contrast to history, which treated phenomena that "follow" one another in time. This concept has guided geographical thought since Kant.

In the nineteenth century, geographers began to go beyond traditional country-by-country analyses and instead defined largely homogeneous regions in terms of physical characteristics, associations of plants and animals, or economics or political organization. Increased knowledge of geology and biology led German geographer and explorer Alexander von Humboldt (1769-1859)

1750's

to conclude that a region's climate and land formations have pronounced effects on that region's plants and animals. German geographer Carl Ritter (1779-1859), also influenced by Büsching, stressed the relationship of humans to nature and founded modern human geography. Today, geographers must study and understand the principles of the biological, earth, and social sciences. Büsching helped lead geography away from its original concern with mapping and exploration of the Earth to become a modern, wide-ranging discipline.

—*Jane F. Hill*

FURTHER READING

Büsching, Anton. *A New System of Geography*. Translated by Patrick Murdoch. London: A. Millar, 1762. Murdoch's translation of the first eight volumes of Büsching's landmark work.

Büttner, Manfred, and Reinhard Jäkel. "Anton Friedrich Büsching, 1724-1793." *Geographers: Biobibliographical Studies* 6 (1982): 7-15. An account of Büsching's life and geographical writings.

De Blij, Harm J., and Peter O. Muller. *Geography: Realms, Regions, and Concepts*. 11th ed. New York: Wiley, 2003. Textbook describing the world's human and natural characteristics.

Hacking, Ian. *The Taming of Chance*. New York: Cambridge University Press, 1990. Details the development of statistical thought. Chapter 3 describes Büsching's use of state-collected statistics.

Hoffman, Peter. *Anton Friedrich Büsching, 1724-1793: Ein Leben im Zeitalter der Aufklärung*. Berlin, Germany: Berlin Verlag, Spitz, 2000. A biography exploring Büsching as educator, theologian, and historian. Includes an index and bibliographical references. In German.

Livingstone, David N., and Charles W. J. Withers. *Geography and Enlightenment*. Chicago: University of Chicago Press, 1999. A collection that reviews the study of the Earth and the development of the discipline of geography during the eighteenth century.

Sitwell, O. F. G. *Four Centuries of Special Geography: An Annotated Guide to Books That Purport to Describe All the Countries in the World Published Before 1888, with a Critical Introduction*. Vancouver: University of British Columbia Press, 1993. Includes details about the 1762 English translation of Büsching's *Neue Erdbeschreibung*.

Unwin, Tim. *The Place of Geography*. Harlow, Essex, England: Prentice Hall, 1992. An account of geography's emergence as an academic discipline. Includes a discussion of Büsching's role in the history of geographic thought.

SEE ALSO: 1714-1762: Quest for Longitude; Oct., 1725: Vico Publishes *The New Science*; 1735: Hadley Describes Atmospheric Circulation; May, 1735-1743: French Scientists Explore the Amazon River; 1748: Bradley Discovers the Nutation of Earth's Axis; 1748: Montesquieu Publishes *The Spirit of the Laws*; 1749-1789: First Comprehensive Examination of the Natural World; 1752-Mar., 1756: Mayer's Lunar Tables Enable Mariners to Determine Longitude at Sea; 1784-1791: Herder Publishes His Philosophy of History; 1785-1788: Hutton Proposes the Geological Theory of Uniformitarianism; July 22, 1793: Mackenzie Reaches the Arctic Ocean; 1798: Malthus Arouses Controversy with His Population Theory; July 16, 1799-July 9, 1804: Humboldt and Bonpland's Expedition.

RELATED ARTICLES in *Great Lives from History: The Eighteenth Century, 1701-1800*: Johann Gottfried Herder; Immanuel Kant.

1754
CONDILLAC DEFENDS SENSATIONALIST THEORY

In Treatise on the Sensations, *Condillac defended a sensationalist theory of understanding, arguing that knowledge forms and develops solely through sensory experience. Condillac's attribution of all human cognition to sensations had an enormous impact on contemporary and subsequent philosophers, especially in France and Italy.*

LOCALE: Paris, France
CATEGORY: Philosophy

KEY FIGURES
Étienne Bonnot de Condillac (1715-1780), French philosopher
John Locke (1632-1704), English philosopher
Sir Isaac Newton (1642-1727), English mathematician and physicist
René Descartes (1596-1650), French philosopher
Denis Diderot (1713-1784), French philosopher and encyclopedist
Voltaire (François-Marie Arouet; 1694-1778), French man of letters, historian, and philosopher
Antoine-Louis-Claude Destutt de Tracy (1754-1836), French philosopher
Maine de Biran (1766-1824), French philosopher and statesman
Victor Cousin (1792-1867), French philosopher and historian

SUMMARY OF EVENT
Under the influence of the English empiricist philosopher John Locke and in revolt against the deductive rationalism of the French philosopher René Descartes, Étienne Bonnot de Condillac was convinced that all knowledge came from sensations. The belief that all human cognitions can be traced to their sensory sources is known as the sensationalist theory of knowledge. It was this theory that Condillac attempted to prove in his much celebrated *Traité des sensations* (1754; *Condillac's Treatise on the Sensations*, 1930). By drawing on a marble statue as a model, Condillac provided an ingenious genetic account of how people come to acquire knowledge. He argued that knowledge starts with the sense of smell alone, that other senses add to the picture, and that only the sense of touch can create a conception of a world external to the self.

Condillac's philosophical career could be conveniently divided into two consecutive segments, one developmental and the other original. In his first phase, Condillac was mainly engaged in developing the philosophical ideas of Locke concerning human understanding within a systematic structure inspired by the works of Sir Isaac Newton. Although Locke's *An Essay Concerning Human Understanding* (1690) and Newton's *Philosophiae Naturalis Principia Mathematica* (1687; *The Mathematical Principles of Natural Philosophy*, 1729; best known as the *Principia*) were already popular in France, and the two intellectual giants were greatly admired, it was Voltaire's *Lettres philosophiques* (1734; originally published in English as *Letters Concerning the English Nation*, 1733; also as *Philosophical Letters*, 1961), extolling English civilization, especially Locke and Newton, and his *Éléments de la philosophie de Newton* (1738; *The Elements of Sir Isaac Newton's Philosophy*, 1738) that had exercised the greatest influence on Condillac's mind.

Voltaire's exegeses clarified for Condillac the British empiricist, experience-centered way of thinking that he had felt was lacking in Descartes. Locke's meticulous tracing of ideas to their origin in experience, combined with Newton's dazzling simplification of our understanding of terrestrial and celestial motion through his law of gravitation, had seized Condillac's allegiance and imagination by 1740. Consequently, in his study of the human mind, Condillac wanted to elucidate certain basic cognitive concepts such as attention, judgment, and reasoning by analyzing them in terms of one type of "primary fact." He was trying to forge a Newtonian system to underpin a Lockean account of the mind.

Condillac's *Essai sur l'origine des connaissances humaines* (1746; *An Essay on the Origin of Human Knowledge: Being a Supplement to Mr. Locke's "Essay on the Human Understanding,"* 1756) and *Traité des systèmes* (1749; *A Treatise on Systems*, 1982) were the products of this developmental stage of his life. Condillac argued that humans depend upon the body for their knowledge, specifically upon the interaction of external things with the body's sense organs. People learn all they know by way of their bodies. There are two elements to every perception: an object acting on an organ and an impression that is triggered by that action. Judgment occurs when two impressions appear together. When there is a chain of such judgments, reasoning takes place. In this account, "understanding" refers to all the operations of the mind that arise automatically from impressions.

In the wake of these publications of the 1740's, Denis Diderot, the great French Enlightenment figure and Condillac's mentor, criticized Condillac in his *Lettre sur les aveugles* (1749; *An Essay on Blindness*, 1750) for the striking similarity of Condillac's account to George Berkeley's subjective idealism. Diderot challenged Condillac to dissociate himself from Berkeley's idealism, which asserted that all experience is a modification of the mind. This challenge from his mentor compelled Condillac to seek a proof for what he had previously merely assumed alongside Locke: that there is an external, material world responsible for causing the impressions that come to the mind and that the mind does not simply generate its own impressions without any external cause.

Condillac thus embarked upon the second and original phase of his philosophical profession, which culminated in the publication of his famous *Treatise on the Sensations* in 1754. The treatise was addressed to two problems: It attempted to show how impressions received by way of the bodily senses could give rise automatically, without reference to unobservable spirits or innate ideas, to all the mental operations. At the same time, it sought to defend the existence of an external, material world. The first task was familiar, but the second required a new approach.

Condillac ingeniously hypothesized a marble statue that was internally like a living human being. This hypothetical statue had a mind that was deprived of all ideas, and all of its senses were "closed," but it was possible to open them one at a time and thereby to analyze the relationships between the various sensations. To avoid assuming the existence of an external world, Condillac chose to examine the sense of smell first, believing that odor involves no danger of being thought of as an image of an external object but is plainly a modification of the mind. Odor in Condillac's analysis illustrates the familiar rise from mere perception to attention to memory. It also involves or induces an affective reaction, agreeableness or disagreeableness. From such experiential qualities, desires arise by a process similar to the way judgment and reasoning arise, and from these momentary desires, longer passions develop.

The question remains, however: How can the modification of the mind by a sense such as smell result in a belief in an external world? To prove such a belief valid, Condillac granted the statue the sense of touch. Other senses could not accomplish the task, but tactile sensation could, as a result of kinaesthesia. That is, by acquiring the sense of touch, the statue gained the ability to move itself mechanically by the confusedly felt contraction of its muscles. Thus, the statue first experienced double contact by, for example, touching its own chest

with its hand. This sensation of double contact involved two feelings of solidity or resistance, one located in one place (the hand) and another located in another place (the chest), as well as two feelings of exclusion.

Condillac then had the statue press its hand against an object other than its own body. This object also excluded the hand from the object's place, but now there was only one feeling of exclusion or resistance. By comparing double contact with single touch, the statue came to the awareness that there was an outward world, a world not felt from the inside but felt only as an external obstacle to the body.

SIGNIFICANCE

The *Treatise on the Sensations* and Condillac's subsequent application of its methods and conclusions to such other issues as language, liberty, morality, animals, and God heavily influenced other scholars. During his lifetime and for fifty years after his death, Condillac enjoyed fame and respect throughout Europe, and by the 1770's his philosophy was being taught by all professors in Paris. He became the spokesman for his contemporaries as their professional philosopher, and eminent scientists such as Antoine-Laurent Lavoisier acknowledged their intellectual debt to Condillac's methodology.

Condillac's influence was most directly felt by the *Idéologues*, members of a movement founded by Antoine-Louis-Claude Destutt de Tracy at the end of the eighteenth century. This movement designated a "science of ideas" devoted to empirical investigation of the origins of ideas and their relations, with the practical objective of achieving institutional reforms—beginning with the sweeping reform of the schools of France. The movement was initially very influential but was subsequently suppressed by Napoleon I.

Condillac's thought was, however, subjected to an onslaught by Maine de Biran and Victor Cousin in the early decades of the nineteenth century. These philosophers accused Condillac of producing not an analysis of the way in which the human mind worked but an artificial reconstruction of how he imagined it worked. Although Condillac's reputation never completely recovered from Biran and Cousin's attack, in the latter part of the nineteenth century his thought enjoyed a new lease on life in the philosophies of Alexander Bain, John Stuart Mill, Herbert Spencer, and Hippolyte-Adolphe Taine. Also, Condillac has enjoyed continued popularity in Italy, where, from 1758 to 1767, he was tutor to the prince of Parma. His fame spread from Parma throughout most of Italy, and widespread admiration for his thought produced a steady stream of interpreters. There has been continued interest by scholars in Condillac's psychology, metaphysics, and pedagogy.

—*Majid Amini*

FURTHER READING

Aarsleff, Hans, ed. and trans. *Condillac: Essay on the Origin of Human Knowledge.* New York: Cambridge University Press, 2001. A new translation of Condillac's first work, which established him as the major empiricist thinker and advocate of sensationalism in the history of French philosophy.

Hine, Ellen McNiven. *A Critical Study of Condillac's "Traité des systèmes."* The Hague, the Netherlands: Martinus Nijhoff, 1979. A detailed examination of Condillac's *Treatise on Systems*, which laid the groundwork for the *Treatise on the Sensations*.

Knight, Isabel F. *The Geometric Spirit: The Abbé de Condillac and the French Enlightenment.* New Haven, Conn.: Yale University Press, 1968. One of the most authoritative studies of Condillac in the English language.

O'Neal, John C. *The Authority of Experience: Sensationalist Theory in the French Enlightenment.* University Park: Pennsylvania State University Press, 1996. An investigation into the main ideas of Condillac and his fellow sensationalist philosophers and the ramifications of their sensationalist theories for education, ethics, and literature.

Pastore, Nicholas. *Selective History of Theories of Visual Perception, 1650-1950.* Oxford, England: Oxford University Press, 1971. A comparative account of Condillac's sensationalist theory of vision from the scientific perspective.

Rosenfeld, Sophia. *A Revolution in Language: The Problem of Signs in Late Eighteenth-Century France.* Stanford, Calif.: Stanford University Press, 2001. Revisits Condillac's conception of language and its impact on subsequent theories of language genesis and growth.

Yolton, John W., et al., eds. *The Blackwell Companion to the Enlightenment.* Malden, Mass.: Blackwell, 1995. A scholarly collection of philosophical articles on the ideas and intellectual impacts of Enlightenment figures, including Condillac.

SEE ALSO: 1721-1750: Early Enlightenment in France; 1739-1740: Hume Publishes *A Treatise of Human Nature*; July 27, 1758: Helvétius Publishes *De l'esprit*; July, 1764: Voltaire Publishes *A Philosophical Dictionary for the Pocket*; 1770: Publication of Holbach's *The System of Nature*; 1781: Kant Publishes *Critique of Pure Reason*; 1784-1791: Herder Publishes His Philosophy of History.

RELATED ARTICLES in *Great Lives from History: The Eighteenth Century, 1701-1800*: Étienne Bonnot de Condillac; Denis Diderot; David Hume; Antoine-Laurent Lavoisier; Voltaire.

May 28, 1754-February 10, 1763
FRENCH AND INDIAN WAR

The French and Indian War was the final major European conflict for control of North America before the American Revolution. Great Britain defeated France and its Native American allies to establish the dominance of the British Empire in the American northeast, but British economic dependence on the American colonies increased in the process.

ALSO KNOWN AS: Seven Years' War (in Europe; 1756-1763)

LOCALE: North America

CATEGORIES: Wars, uprisings, and civil unrest; colonization; expansion and land acquisition

KEY FIGURES

George Washington (1732-1799), colonial American military officer, 1753-1758, member of Virginia House of Burgesses, 1759-1774, and president of the United States, 1789-1797

James Wolfe (1727-1759), British general

Louis-Joseph de Montcalm (1712-1759), French general

William Pitt the Elder (1708-1778), British prime minister, 1757-1761, 1766-1768

Pontiac (Obwandiyag; c. 1720-1769), Ottawa chief and military leader

SUMMARY OF EVENT

The French and Indian War was the North American part of a larger conflict fought between France and Great Britain for control of colonies in North America and India and for hegemony in Europe. The European phase of the conflict became known as the Seven Years' War

1750's

(1756-1763). Both Great Britain and France claimed large territories in North America. In addition to the Thirteen Colonies spread out along the Atlantic coast, the British claimed what is now northern Canada. The French claimed a huge section of the inner continent, stretching from New Orleans in the south to what is now Montana in the northwest and Quebec in the northeast. The French built a series of forts along the Mississippi River and its tributaries to defend their claims. One of these tributaries, the Ohio River, flowed southwest along the western frontiers of Pennsylvania and Virginia. Both French and British claimed this land. British colonists worried about a French invasion and resented the French presence, which limited western expansion.

In 1754, 150 soldiers from Virginia, led by the twenty-two-year-old Lieutenant Colonel George Washington, headed west to secure British claims by building a fort at the fork where the Monongahela and Allegheny Rivers meet to form the Ohio River. When they arrived, they discovered that the French had built a fort there already, Fort Duquesne. Washington entrenched his forces

at the hurriedly constructed British Fort Necessity. He then attacked a small encampment of French soldiers on May 28, 1754, beginning the war. The French of Fort Duquesne struck back, and on July 3, 1754, Washington was forced to surrender Fort Necessity. He and his men were allowed to return to Virginia in return for releasing French prisoners and promising not to return to the disputed Ohio Valley territory for one year.

As they struggled to expand their North American empires, the British and French did not consider the rights or needs of the people who had been living on the land for thousands of years before Europeans arrived. The only time Europeans took serious notice of the First Americans was when they needed allies in wartime. Both the French and the British sought and received support from some native peoples. For their part, Native Americans, by siding with one party or the other, could get access to European weapons and perhaps succeed in driving at least one group of invading Europeans from the land. Algonquians and Hurons allied themselves with the French, whom they had known mainly as fur traders over

MAJOR BATTLES IN THE FRENCH AND INDIAN WAR, 1754-1760

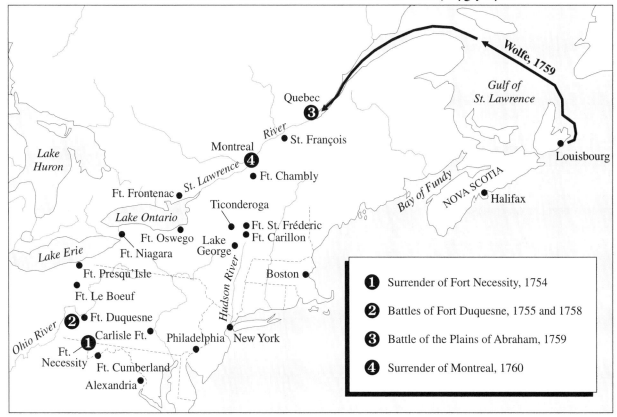

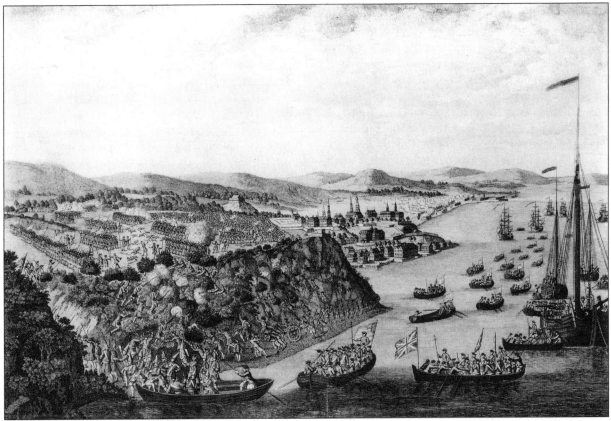

The Battle of the Plains of Abraham saw the fall of Quebec, French Canada's capital, on September 13, 1759, and its capture and control by the British. The battle effectively ended France's stronghold in North America. (Library of Congress)

the past century and a half. The French seemed less intrusive and permanent than the British, who cleared the land for farming. The Algonquians were, moreover, traditional rivals of those tribes allied with the Iroquois Confederacy. By selling goods at low prices and exploiting traditional enmities, the British also were able to find native allies, including the Mohawks, one of the most powerful Iroquois nations, who agreed to help the British against the French and Algonquians.

The war went poorly for the British at first. With thirteen separate colonial governments involved, decisions were difficult to make. Nor were British soldiers accustomed to the American landscape. In 1755, the British general Edward Braddock was badly defeated when he attacked the French at Fort Duquesne. The French and their Native American allies easily scouted out and ambushed Braddock's troops, shooting from behind trees at the British soldiers, whose red coats made good targets. The French won a series of battles until 1757, when the tide changed.

The British had had some advantages from the beginning. There were twenty times as many British in North America as French, and the British had the most powerful navy in the world. Then, in 1757, a dynamic new leader, William Pitt the Elder, took over the British government. Pitt sent Britain's best generals to lead the war against the French and motivated British colonists to support the war effort by offering high prices for supplies purchased in America.

A year later, the Lenni Lenapes (Delawares), an Algonquian people living in Pennsylvania, withdrew their support from the French, leaving Fort Duquesne vulnerable to attack. The British attacked successfully and renamed the fort to honor their new leader. The city that grew on the site of the fort, Pittsburgh, still contains William Pitt's name.

The decisive battle came in 1759, when Pitt sent General James Wolfe to attack the city of Quebec, the French capital. If the British could take this city, they would win the war. Quebec, located at the top of a high cliff that rose

1750's

375

steeply from the banks of the St. Lawrence River, was easier to defend than to attack. The French general in charge, the Louis-Joseph de Montcalm, was an experienced leader, but even he was taken by surprise when Wolfe moved four thousand troops across the St. Lawrence River in small boats, found ways to scale the cliffs, and attacked in the early hours of the morning. Both generals were killed in the battle, but news of the British victory reached Wolfe before he died. This Battle of the Plains of Abraham was the turning point for the French, effectively ending their stronghold in North America.

When the British took Montreal in 1760, fighting ended in North America. There was no formal peace treaty until the war between France and Prussia, Great Britain's ally in central Europe, finally ground to a halt three years later.

Then, in the Peace of Paris (February 10, 1763), the French ceded Canada and all French lands east of the Mississippi to Great Britain. France retained the land it claimed west of the Mississippi, including the key port of New Orleans. Spain, which had allied itself with France against Great Britain, was forced to give up Florida. The rights of the indigenous nations that had prior claim to all of this land were not considered.

SIGNIFICANCE

The French and Indian War had important consequences for the early development of American history. It increased Great Britain's needs for its North American colonies but had the opposite effect on the colonists' needs for Great Britain. With the French gone, the need for the protection of the British military began to disappear as well. To some colonists, it seemed that the redcoats were starting to get in the way. The British Proclamation of 1763 forbade colonists to settle land west of a line drawn along the Appalachian Mountains. Welcomed by the followers of the Ottawa chief Pontiac, who earlier that year had brought many American Indian nations together to defend their lands against European invasion, the proclamation disappointed those colonists who had expected to benefit from land opened up by the French defeat. In effect, the proclamation had little effect in preserving Western lands for their Indian inhabitants as colonists began to push west anyway.

The war brought the colonies closer together. There had been a first effort, called the Plan of Union, to unite the colonies under one government. Although the Plan of Union, discussed by representatives of several colonies in Albany, New York, in 1754, was unsuccessful—the individual colonial governments being hesitant to give up any

power—the fact that some sort of union was even discussed reflected a growing tendency to see the colonies as a unified entity distinct from the mother country, England.

Seven years of fighting on three continents and all the world's oceans had exhausted British resources as well. War debts forced the British government to increase tax rates drastically. These rates, however, only applied to British citizens in Great Britain. British citizens in North America continued to pay relatively low taxes. To many British, it seemed only fair that the British in the colonies pay their share for the war that had made their homes safe from invasion.

The self-confidence of the colonists had grown as they helped fight a successful war. They believed they had the same rights to representative government as British citizens in Great Britain. One of these was the right to send representatives to the body of government that levies taxes. Colonists accepted taxes levied by colonial governments, where they were represented, but rejected taxes levied by the British parliament, to which they were not allowed to send representatives. British efforts to tax the colonies, despite colonial protest, thus became one of the causes for the outbreak of the American Revolution.

—T. W. Dreier

FURTHER READING

Anderson, Fred. *Crucible of War: The Seven Years' War and the Fate of Empire in British North America, 1754-1766.* New York: Random House, 2000. Definitive, meticulously researched, 932-page account. Anderson explains the significance of the Seven Years' War in North America, concluding that Americans had to remove the French from their colonies before they could develop the concepts of democracy needed to eventually defy the British. Includes one hundred landscapes, portraits, maps, and charts.

_____. *A People's Army: Massachusetts Soldiers and Society in the Seven Years' War.* Chapel Hill: University of North Carolina Press, 1984. This illustrated regional study reveals how average colonists experienced and affected the war.

Auth, Stephen F. *The Ten Years War: Indian-White Relations in Pennsylvania, 1755-1765.* New York: Garland, 1989. Includes Native American perspectives missing in many studies. Final chapter shows the war's implications for later treatment of Native Americans.

Fowler, William M., Jr. *Empires at War: The French and Indian War and the Struggle for North America, 1754-1763.* New York: Walker, 2005. Narrative account of the war, describing its causes, the incident that touched off the conflict in 1754, and the battles. Places the war in a wider European context.

Hamilton, Edward P. *The French and Indian Wars: The Story of Battles and Forts in the Wilderness*. Garden City, N.Y.: Doubleday, 1962. The first chapters of this narrative history discuss the role played by George Washington.

Jennings, Francis. *Empire of Fortune: Crowns, Colonies, and Tribes in the Seven Years' War in America*. New York: W. W. Norton, 1988. A comprehensive study by a major scholar; offers easily accessible information on all aspects of the war. Illustrations, maps, and indices.

Marston, Daniel. *The French-Indian War, 1754-1769*. Oxford, England: Osprey, 2002. Military history, focusing on the battles in the war. Traces the development of the British army and the military reforms that ultimately led Great Britain to victory.

Schwartz, Seymoor. *The French and Indian War, 1754-1763: The Imperial Struggle for North America*. New York: Simon & Schuster, 1994. A concise and well-illustrated study that provides a thoughtful, readable overview.

SEE ALSO: May 26, 1701-Sept. 7, 1714: War of the Spanish Succession; May 15, 1702-Apr. 11, 1713: Queen Anne's War; 1746-1754: Carnatic Wars; July, 1755-Aug., 1758: Acadians Are Expelled from Canada; Jan., 1756-Feb. 15, 1763: Seven Years' War; June 23, 1757: Battle of Plassey; Nov. 5, 1757: Battle of Rossbach; June 8-July 27, 1758: Siege of Louisbourg; Oct. 5, 1759-Nov. 19, 1761: Cherokee War; Feb. 10, 1763: Peace of Paris; May 8, 1763-July 24, 1766: Pontiac's Resistance.

RELATED ARTICLES in *Great Lives from History: The Eighteenth Century, 1701-1800*: Louis-Joseph de Montcalm; William Pitt the Elder; Pontiac; George Washington; James Wolfe.

June 19-July 10, 1754
ALBANY CONGRESS

To preserve their alliance with the Iroquois and to prepare for war with the French, a congress of colonial delegates drafted a plan to unify the American colonies under a single government. The Plan of Union was rejected by the colonies, and the British government, rather than colonial officials, became responsible for conducting diplomacy with Native Americans.

LOCALE: Albany, New York (now in the United States)

CATEGORIES: Government and politics; diplomacy and international relations

KEY FIGURES

James De Lancey (1703-1760), lieutenant governor of New York

Thomas Hutchinson (1711-1780), Massachusetts delegate to the Albany Congress

Benjamin Franklin (1706-1790), Pennsylvania delegate to the Albany Congress

Hendrick (c. 1680-1755), Mohawk leader

SUMMARY OF EVENT

In June of 1753, the Mohawk leader Hendrick declared the breaking of the Covenant Chain, the symbol of the Ir-

oquois Confederacy's alliance with New York and the other colonies. Hendrick's action shocked colonial and imperial officials. From their perspective, Hendrick's timing could not have been worse. Tensions between the French and English were increasing, and British officials had based their military strategy for North America on an British-Iroquois alliance. Just when the Iroquois alliance was most needed, the Mohawks had voided the centerpiece of Britain's military strategy for North America. Something had to be done, and that something was the Albany Congress of 1754.

Hendrick's declaration represented a culmination of events dating back a decade. In 1744, the Onondaga, believing they were ceding the Shenandoah Valley to Virginia, agreed to the Treaty of Lancaster. Virginians, however, used this treaty to claim the entire Ohio region. Over the next decade, Virginian officials opened nearly 300,000 acres of land to settlement through land companies such as the Ohio Company of Virginia. King George's War (1740-1748), as the War of the Austrian Succession was known to colonial Americans, temporarily delayed settlement. Once the war ended, however, the Ohio Company renewed its efforts at settling the region. French officials responded by sending Captain de Céleron into the Ohio Valley in 1750. French soldiers

1750's

377

also began building forts in the region. One such outpost, Presque Isle, was in the heart of Iroquoia. When the Iroquois asked for assistance in removing the French from Presque Isle, Virginian officials refused to help. By the early 1750's, the Mohawks and other Indian groups felt themselves trapped between the English and French.

Following Virginia's response to the Iroquois, members of the Board of Trade recommended that King George II call a congress to address Indian complaints about colonial behavior. In September, 1753, the Board of Trade notified colonial governors that King George II wanted all colonies having a relationship with the Iroquois to attend a conference that was to resolve existing Iroquois complaints about land and trade with the colonists. The resulting Albany Congress was unlike any other British-Iroquois conference. It was the first intercolonial-Indian conference called by London officials.

The proposed conference met with the approval of Massachusetts governor William Shirley and the Pennsylvanian Benjamin Franklin. However, the lieutenant governors of New York and Virginia were less enthralled with the board's directive. New York lieutenant governor James De Lancey could not escape the conference. Robert Dinwiddie of Virginia, however, failed to send a representative to Albany. Still, when the conference began in June of 1754, representatives from nine colonies attended.

The delegates met at Albany for specific reasons. It was the historic meeting place for Iroquois-European conferences. Albany was the site of one of the two council fires the English and Iroquois maintained. As one of the anchors of the Covenant Chain, Albany was a site where official business could be conducted and ratified. It was also the closest city to the frontier that delegates could reach by boat.

When representatives met at Albany, they needed not only to address Iroquois complaints but also to prepare for war. Delegates saw the two issues as interrelated. On June 19, 1754, they created a seven-person committee to prepare James De Lancey's opening speech to the American Indians. Five days later, the representatives created a second committee to consider "some Method of affecting the Union between the Colonies." This latter delegation produced the Plan of Union associated with the Albany Congress. It did so, however, "as a Branch of Indian Affairs." Mohawk leaders such as Hendrick hoped confederation would allow the colonists to speak with a single voice. Some delegates agreed. They thought colonial confederation would alleviate the problems of which the

Iroquois complained. Therefore, the Albany Plan of Union was designed primarily as a mechanism for conducting Indian affairs.

Besides improving colonial policy toward the natives, representatives thought colonial confederation would improve their military preparedness and help them defeat New France. There were mutual security reasons for confederation. Politicians did not prepare their plan to tamper with each colony's internal autonomy.

Common wisdom maintains that Benjamin Franklin is the father of the colonial confederation. There is, however, some evidence to suggest that Thomas Hutchinson of Massachusetts wrote the plan. If Hutchinson was the author, then American Indian affairs were probably an important influence on the Plan of Union, because Hutchinson was a member of the original subcommittee appointed to study American Indian affairs. Franklin was not.

Whoever the author was, the Plan of Union contained specific proposals. It created a unicameral legislature, to be called the grand council. This council would consist of forty-eight representatives chosen from the lower houses of the colonies. Representation in the grand council would be limited to members of the lower houses of assembly in the colonies, because it was assumed that only directly elected representatives had the right to tax the colonists. Initially, representation in the grand council would be based on the population of each colony. After three years, representation would be based on the revenue a colony generated for the confederation, so as to reward participation. In both its name and the number of delegates, the Plan of Union paid homage to the Iroquois League.

The new government also would have a president general. This executive would receive his salary directly from England, so the president general would be independent of the colonial legislatures. This proposal recognized the problems confronting the relationship between governor and lower house in colonial America. The proposed confederation government had eight functions. One of the most important was the right to direct all Indian treaties for the colonies. The government also would make declarations of war and peace toward the natives, make all land purchases from the natives in the name of the king, and regulate trade with the natives. Purchased land would reside outside the existing boundaries of established colonies. The government would direct the creation of settlements in the territory, would rule them in the name of the king, and would be responsible for the defense of the frontier.

The Plan of Union also gave the proposed government the ability to tax. The grand council could enforce an excise tax on luxury goods. The government would secure additional money by regulating the Indian trade. Traders would be required to carry licenses and post bonds of good behavior before being allowed to trade with the natives. Traders were to purchase these licenses and bonds from the confederation government. Trade would be restricted to specific forts, built just for that purpose. It was hoped that by regulating trade with the Indians, many of the problems associated with the traders would be curtailed. Finally, the government would receive quitrent from colonists as they settled lands newly purchased from the Indians. Politicians thus pursued colonial confederation as a method of addressing Indian affairs.

SIGNIFICANCE

The delegates to the Albany Congress approved the Plan of Union on July 10 and adjourned to take the proposals back to their respective colonies. Not one colonial legislature accepted the plan. Legislators in seven colonies voted down the Plan of Union. The other six legislatures let the issue die away during the French and Indian War. Each colonial legislature had specific reasons for rejecting the plan. Some politicians feared that the plan gave too much power to the governor. Others feared the creation of a president general. Still others believed that the confederation government threatened the Western lands included in their original charters.

Colonial legislators were not the only ones to repudiate the Plan of Union. The Board of Trade rejected it too, believing the idea of a grand council to be cumbersome. They wanted a smaller council, with delegates chosen by the royal governors. They also thought that the Albany Plan gave too much power to colonial assemblies. From the Board of Trade's perspective, the Albany Congress was a failure.

If the Albany Congress was a failure, it was an important one. The congress showed how different England and America had grown since the Glorious Revolution in the 1680's. The Seven Years' War would strain the imperial-colonial relationship even more. The failure of delegates to the Albany Congress to address Iroquois complaints directly forced the home government to become an active participant in colonial-Indian relations. The result was the creation of an Indian superintendent system. This new system, begun in 1755, made imperial policies, not colonial desires, the primary focus of British-Iroquois dialogue in the years to come.

—*Michael J. Mullin*

FURTHER READING

Alden, John R. "The Albany Congress and the Creation of the Indian Superintendencies." *Mississippi Valley Historical Review* 27, no. 2 (September, 1940): 193-210. Describes how the Albany Congress led British officials to create the Indian superintendent system.

Fenton, William N. *The Great Law and the Longhouse: A Political History of the Iroquois Confederacy.* Norman: University of Oklahoma Press, 1998. Chapter 30, "The Albany Congress Mends the Chain," describes the congress within the context of Iroquois politics and law.

Gipson, Lawrence Henry. "The Drafting of the Albany Plan of Union: The Problem of Semantics." *Pennsylvania History* 26, no. 4 (October, 1959): 291-316. Argues that Thomas Hutchinson was responsible for writing the Albany Plan of Union.

Hopkins, Stephen. *A True Representation of the Plan Formed at Albany.* Providence, R.I.: Sidney S. Rider, 1880. Hopkins, who represented Rhode Island at the Albany Congress, details the issues that delegates discussed concerning Indian affairs.

Mullin, Michael J. "The Albany Congress and Colonial Confederation." *Mid-America* 72, no. 2 (April-July, 1990): 93-105. Discusses the role of Indian affairs at the Congress.

Newbold, Robert C. *The Albany Congress and Plan of Union of 1754.* New York: Vantage Press, 1955. A summation of the scholarship on Albany at the time.

Shannon, Timothy J. *Indians and Colonists at the Crossroads of Empire: The Albany Congress of 1754.* Ithaca, N.Y.: Cornell University Press, 2000. A major study of the Albany Congress. Shannon disagrees with other historians who maintain that the Congress and the Plan of Union were a "dress rehearsal" for the Constitutional Convention and American independence; Shannon argues that the congress and plan increased the level of British imperial power over the colonies.

1750's

June 5, 1755
BLACK IDENTIFIES CARBON DIOXIDE

Joseph Black showed that when intensely heated, magnesia alba (magnesium carbonate) and chalk (calcium carbonate) produced "fixed air," a gas later called carbon dioxide with unique physical and chemical properties.

LOCALES: Glasgow and Edinburgh, Scotland
CATEGORIES: Chemistry; science and technology; health and medicine

KEY FIGURES
Joseph Black (1728-1799), Scottish chemist, physicist, and physician
Daniel Rutherford (1749-1819), Scottish chemist and Black's student, who discovered "mephitic air," or nitrogen
William Cullen (1710-1790), University of Glasgow's first lecturer in chemistry

SUMMARY OF EVENT

For more than two thousand years alchemists considered air an element, but the Scottish chemist Joseph Black, by discovering that carbon dioxide was a different kind of "air," made an important contribution to modern chemistry. His studies at the Universities of Glasgow and Edinburgh prepared him well for this discovery. At Glasgow, where he studied medicine, the lectures of William Cullen sparked his interest in chemistry, and it was at Edinburgh, where he received his medical degree in 1754, that he wrote his doctoral dissertation, marking the beginnings of his significant work in chemistry.

This dissertation, *De humore acido a cibis orto et magnesia alba* (1754; *On Acid Humor Arising from Foods, and on White Magnesia*, 1973), had its origin in Black's desire to investigate magnesia alba's ability to dissolve gall and kidney stones, but when he found it lacked this ability, he decided to study its effect on stomach acidity. He prepared magnesia alba (magnesium carbonate) by reacting Epsom salt (magnesium sulfate) with pearl ash (potassium carbonate). Although the first part of Black's dissertation did examine the medical use of magnesia alba as an antacid, the second, more creative part of the work examined his own experiments on magnesia and some of magnesia's chemical reactions.

In the two years before completing his dissertation, Black discovered that magnesia alba, when vigorously heated, produced a previously unknown compound, "calcined magnesia" (magnesium oxide), which weighed

less than the magnesia alba with which he started. Similarly, when he heated chalk (calcium carbonate), the quicklime (calcium oxide) he produced weighed less than the chalk. He attributed the lost weight of the chalk and magnesia alba to a new "air" that was not the same as ordinary air. Since this air could be combined with (or "fixed into") quicklime to form chalk, he called the gas "fixed air." He showed that birds and small animals perished in fixed air, and that fixed air could extinguish a candle flame. Black also found that burning charcoal produced this gas, as did the respiration of humans and animals. Black even developed a specific reagent to test for fixed air. By dissolving quicklime in water, he made limewater, a reagent that turned cloudy in the presence of fixed air.

After solving the puzzle of magnesia alba's and chalk's weight loss on heating, Black investigated the other products of these reactions, quicklime and calcined magnesia, and the puzzling observation that when milk alkalis were added to these substances, they became caustic. The substances that Black called "mild alkalis" are today recognized as compounds such as potassium and sodium carbonate. For example, when Black reacted slaked lime (calcium hydroxide) with potash (potassium carbonate), he obtained chalk (calcium carbonate) and "caustic potash" (potassium hydroxide). Black was fascinated by what he called "caustication." He knew that limestone (calcium carbonate) became caustic (in the form of quicklime) when it lost its fixed air, and he was able to explain why caustic alkalis became mild after standing for some time in air. The caustic alkali reacted with the fixed air in the atmosphere to form a mild alkali. Since, in these studies, Black carefully weighed both reactants and products, he was able to detail fixed air's participation in a cycle of reactions.

Black made his first public presentation of his discoveries about fixed air on June 5, 1755, when he read his paper, "Experiments upon Magnesia Alba, Quicklime, and Some Other Alcaline Substances," before the Physical, Literary, and Philosophical Society of Edinburgh. The paper was published in 1756 in volume 2 of *Essays and Observations, Physical and Literary*. Black's principal findings were that fixed air was a unique gaseous chemical substance and that it was a measurable part of such alkaline materials as magnesia alba, limestone, potash, and soda (sodium carbonate). Black intended to follow this influential paper with further serious studies of fixed air, but his increasingly burdensome responsibilities at Glasgow and, after 1766, at Edinburgh interfered with his chemical research. Nevertheless, he turned over some of the problems raised by his fixed-air research to one of his students, Daniel Rutherford, who in 1772 discovered another new "air." When Rutherford removed from ordinary air all the gases produced by either combustion (the burning of a candle) or respiration (the breathing of a mouse), what remained was a new gas he called "mephitic air" because no animal could live in it. Mephitic air is now called nitrogen, and Rutherford is credited with its discovery.

Rutherford was not the only distinguished student of Black. In his thirty-three-year career at Edinburgh, Black taught students from all over the world, including France, Germany, the United States, and Russia. Many of his students went on to distinguished careers in medicine, chemistry, and physics. Although he was aware of the weaknesses of the phlogiston theory—which explained combustion, respiration, and other phenomena in terms of a "weightless fluid," or substance, called phlogiston—Black did try to explain his experimental results in terms of its principles. However, late in his career, Black began to teach the new chemical ideas of the French chemist Antoine-Laurent Lavoisier, who had been deeply influenced by Black's experiments on fixed air.

SIGNIFICANCE

Traditional historians of science consider Joseph Black the founder of quantitative pneumatic chemistry because he reasoned on the basis of meticulously executed experiments to conclusions based on quantitative arguments. Using refined techniques of analysis and synthesis, Black falsified the old idea of a single elemental air and showed that a new gas could be created and that it could be combined chemically with a solid to produce a new compound. Once Black had established that fixed air was a unique chemical substance, other scientists, such as the English natural philosopher Joseph Priestley, discovered many new gases, including oxygen, which in Lavoisier's hands became the central element of the chemical revolution.

Some revisionist historians of science have questioned the classic characterization of Black as the great quantifier of chemistry, claiming that he emphasized microscale attractive forces rather than macroscale weight relationships as the key to understanding chemical phenomena. Other scholars consider Black's significance to be his liberation of chemistry from traditionally allied disciplines such as medicine and metallurgy. Still other scholars see the importance of Black's studies on carbon dioxide as the beginning of the breakdown of the barrier between animate and inanimate substances, because carbon dioxide

---

THEORY AND PRACTICE IN BLACK'S CAREER

The Scottish chemist Joseph Black stood at the crossroads between the great cultural transformation that was the European Enlightenment and the great economic transformation that was the Industrial Revolution. His life work balanced a calling to make the study of chemistry "philosophical" (less subordinate to the pharmaceutical needs of medicine and more an autonomous science of its own) with a civic commitment to the "improvement" of Scotland.

In 1766, his mentor William Cullen having been appointed a professor of medicine, Black took up the chair of chemistry at Edinburgh. In his new position, Black increasingly focused on applied chemistry. Already, at Glasgow, Black had forged a close relationship with James Watt, who had been appointed instrument maker to the university. In 1769, Black loaned Watt the money needed to obtain a patent on his steam engine. As Watt himself affirmed, the methodological and theoretical foundation for his invention was laid by Black's meticulous program of experimentation and his investigation of latent and specific heats. Now, in the 1770's and 1780's, Scottish agricultural improvers like Henry Home, Lord Kames, sought Black's chemical imprimatur for their proposals, even as entrepreneurs sought Black's advice on the metallurgy of coal and iron, the bleaching of textiles, and the manufacture of glass.

Britain's preeminent professor of chemistry, Black was uniquely influential. Across his career, he introduced Scottish "philosophical chemistry" to as many as five thousand students. He shared his dedication to university and industry, "philosophy" and "improvement," with the profusion of clubs in eighteenth century Scotland. He was a member not only of the Philosophical Society (later Royal Society) of Edinburgh but also of less formal civic groups such as the Select Society and the Poker Club. Dearest to Black was the Oyster Club, weekly dinners with his closest friends—William Cullen, the geologist James Hutton, and the author of *The Wealth of Nations*, Adam Smith.

The balance that Black achieved was a model for chemistry's continuing career in Britain as a public science and marked a critical moment in European cultural history, a moment before specialization would estrange the "two cultures" of the sciences and the humanities, a moment when chemistry remained a liberal, gentlemanly vocation.

1750's

was produced both by burning inanimate charcoal and by the respiration of animate mice. Because of his phlogistic views, Black is not categorized among the modern chemists, but his chemical discoveries greatly influenced the new chemical ideas of Priestley, Henry Cavendish, and Lavoisier.

—*Robert J. Paradowski*

FURTHER READING

Black, Joseph. *On Acid Humor Arising from Foods, and on White Magnesia*. Translated by Thomas Hanson. Minneapolis, Minn.: Bell Museum of Pathobiology, 1973. The English translation of Black's medical degree dissertation of 1754. Brief, forty pages.

Brock, William H. *The Chemical Tree: A History of Chemistry*. New York: Norton, 2000. This reprint of a book in the Norton History of Science series is an updated survey of the history of chemistry. Black's work is analyzed in chapters 3 and 4. Includes excellent descriptive bibliographies for all chapters, and a good index.

Ihde, Aaron J. *The Development of Modern Chemistry*. New York: Dover, 1984. This reprint of a work first published in 1964 emphasizes the evolution of chemical disciplines from the seventeenth through the twentieth centuries. Ihde analyzes Black's work in his chapter on "pneumatic chemistry." Includes appendices, an extensive annotated bibliography, and name and subject indexes.

Jungnickel, Christa, and Russell McCormmach. *Cavendish: The Experimental Life*. Lewisburg, Pa.: Bucknell, 1999. The award-winning first edition of this biography has been extensively revised and expanded in this updated edition, in which the influence of Black's chemical and physical work on Cavendish is discussed. Illustrations, bibliography, and index.

Partington, J. R. A. *History of Chemistry*. Vol. 3. London: Macmillan, 1962. This comprehensive history of chemistry contains a detailed discussion of Black's life and contributions (chapter 4). Includes many references to primary sources in the footnotes and indexes of names and subjects.

Ramsay, William. *Life and Letters of Joseph Black, M.D.* London: Constable, 1918. This work remains the only book-length biographical study of Black, and it contains letters and other primary source materials not available elsewhere.

SEE ALSO: 1718: Geoffroy Issues the *Table of Reactivities*; 1723: Stahl Postulates the Phlogiston Theory; 1738: Bernoulli Proposes the Kinetic Theory of Gases; 1742: Celsius Proposes an International Fixed Temperature Scale; 1745: Lomonosov Issues the First Catalog of Minerals; 1757-1766: Haller Establishes Physiology as a Science; 1771: Woulfe Discovers Picric Acid; Aug. 1, 1774: Priestley Discovers Oxygen; 1781-1784: Cavendish Discovers the Composition of Water; 1786-1787: Lavoisier Devises the Modern System of Chemical Nomenclature; 1789: Leblanc Develops Soda Production; c. 1794-1799: Proust Establishes the Law of Definite Proportions.

RELATED ARTICLES in *Great Lives from History: The Eighteenth Century, 1701-1800:* Joseph Black; Henry Cavendish; Antoine-Laurent Lavoisier; Nicolas Leblanc; Joseph Priestley; Georg Ernst Stahl.

July, 1755-August, 1758
ACADIANS ARE EXPELLED FROM CANADA

The British forcibly expelled most of the French population of Nova Scotia, which had been called Acadia when it was under French control. Many French Acadians subsequently returned to Nova Scotia or found new homelands elsewhere, especially in Louisiana.

LOCALE: Nova Scotia (now in Canada); Louisiana (now in the United States)

CATEGORIES: Colonization; expansion and land acquisition; government and politics; wars, uprisings, and civil unrest

KEY FIGURES

Charles Lawrence (c. 1709-1760), British governor of Nova Scotia, 1754-1760

William Shirley (1694-1771), governor of Massachusetts, 1741-1756

Edward Braddock (1695-1755), commander in chief of British forces in North America

Robert Monckton (1726-1782),

John Winslow (1703-1774), and

John Handfield (c. 1700-c. 1763), British officers in charge of the deportation of Acadians

Joseph Broussard dit Beausoleil (1702-1765), French Acadian who led a group migrating to Louisiana

Antonio de Ulloa (1716-1795), Spanish governor of Louisiana, 1766-1768

Alejandro O'Reilly (1725-1794), Spanish governor of Louisiana, 1769

SUMMARY OF EVENT

In 1713, the Treaty of Utrecht awarded the French colony of Acadia to the British, who renamed it Nova Scotia. The Acadians were given the option of either moving to Isle Royale (Cape Breton Island) or Isle Saint Jean (Prince Edward Island), which were still French possessions, or staying in their settlements and swearing allegiance to England. The British, who saw the Acadian farmers as a source of food for their soldiers and as a buffer against local Indians, discouraged emigration by decreeing that Acadians would not be compensated for their property and forbidding them to build boats. The French for their part did not object to this treatment of their colonists, because they viewed the Acadians as strategically located allies in future wars.

The Acadians enjoyed a relatively peaceful existence, until England and France intensified their competition for Canada's maritime provinces. In 1749, the British founded Halifax as the capital of Nova Scotia to counterbalance the power of Louisbourg, on Isle Royale. In 1751 the French built Fort Beauséjour and Fort Gaspéreau in Nova Scotia and forced some Acadians to move to present-day New Brunswick to establish a claim to the territory.

In 1754, fighting broke out between French and British troops in the upper Ohio Valley, precipitating the French and Indian War, which led to the Seven Years' War in 1756. As a result, Charles Lawrence, the British governor of Nova Scotia, decided to take extreme measures to address the "Acadian problem." Acadians had steadfastly refused to take an unqualified oath of allegiance to England, insisting on maintaining their rights to emigrate, remain Catholic, and remain neutral during war. Lawrence decided forcibly to deport the Acadians if they continued to insist on these qualifications. William Shirley, the governor of Massachusetts, supported Lawrence's plan and convinced General Edward Braddock, commander in chief of British forces in North America, to send troops to attack Fort Beauséjour. When the fort fell on June 16, 1755, the last obstacle to the implementation of Lawrence's policy was removed.

In July of 1755, Lawrence ordered the arrest of two groups of Acadians who refused to take the oath and decided that all Acadians would be relocated to England's American colonies. Major John Handfield, Colonel Robert Monckton, and Lieutenant Colonel John Winslow were ordered to orchestrate the mass arrests and deportations from various parts of Nova Scotia. During the fall of 1755, more than six thousand Acadians had their property confiscated and their farms destroyed and were forcibly exiled to Massachusetts, Connecticut, New York, Pennsylvania, Maryland, North and South Carolina, and Georgia. When Virginia refused to take 1,150 exiles, those Acadians were sent to England: Many of them later emigrated to France.

The capture and deportation of Acadians continued for years. Some Acadians avoided arrest and deportation by fleeing to northern New Brunswick, Isle Saint Jean, and Quebec. However, about thrity-five hundred Acadians on Isle Saint Jean and Isle Royale were finally deported to France in August of 1758, after the fall of Louisbourg ended French control in those areas. The British broke up families, separating women and young children from men and boys, and the unsanitary and

Inhabitants of Acadia (Nova Scotia), in French Canada, were forcibly expelled from the region by the British, who were competing with the French for control of Canada's maritime provinces. (Francis R. Niglutsch)

overcrowded conditions on ships killed many of the Acadian deportees. Upon arrival in the various colonies, some exiles were forced into indentured servitude on farms or sold into slavery. Mortality rates were high for these displaced people, who were left to live on whatever stipends were provided for the poor locally. Furthermore, the exiles were hated by the colonists because of anti-Catholic bigotry and resentment over the cost of their upkeep. Although August, 1758, marked the end of the most concerted phase of mass deportations from Nova Scotia, the explusions did not end completely until 1763. By this time, three-fourths of the Acadian population, more than ten thousand people, had been deported and dispersed.

Many exiled Acadians were understandably anxious to leave New England, and they were given permission by some colonies to do so as early as 1756. At that time, the British barred Acadians from returning to Nova Scotia, but many did go back later, when the restriction was lifted. Others went to Quebec to join those who had fled

there in 1755. In 1763, when the Peace of Paris ended the Seven Years' War and gave all Acadians eighteen months to emigrate, they established settlements in numerous places, including Saint Pierre, Miquelon, Martinique, Santo Domingo, and Saint Dominique (Haiti).

In 1765, Joseph Broussard dit Beausoleil led a group of about two hundred Acadians from Saint Dominique to the Attakapas region of Louisiana (now Vermilion, Lafayette, Saint Martins, Iberia, and Saint Mary parishes) to join about twenty Acadians from New York who had traveled there the year before. When word spread that the Spanish colonial government in Louisiana welcomed Catholics in search of a homeland, many other Acadians journeyed there. The French government was anxious to reduce France's large Acadian population, and Spain agreed to provide them with free land in Louisiana. In 1785, sixteen hundred Acadians took the offer and emigrated from France. By 1788, there were about three thousand Acadians in Louisiana.

The Acadians became a political force soon after their

arrival in Louisiana. In 1766, Governor Antonio de Ulloa began forcing Acadians to locate on the boundaries between Spanish and British territory to assist with colonial defense. The Acadians, unhappy at once again being used as pawns in two colonial powers' territorial disputes, participated in a revolt in 1768 that drove Ulloa from office. His successor, Alejandro O'Reilly, allowed the disgruntled Acadians to move away from the border areas. The Acadians also advanced economically very quickly in Louisiana, significantly contributing to the colony's productivity and achieving a standard of living that was comparable to what they had had in Nova Scotia before their exile.

SIGNIFICANCE

The forcible deportation of the Acadians had an immediate and long-lasting impact on the ethnic compositions of both Nova Scotia and the exiles' areas of destination. The redistribution of the Acadian population not only vastly decreased their numbers in Nova Scotia but also established sizable Acadian enclaves throughout North America and parts of Europe. As a result, the most significant concentrations of Acadian-heritage people today are located in New England, Quebec, France, and Louisiana, with about forty thousand residing in Canada's Maritime Provinces (Nova Scotia, New Brunswick, and Prince Edward Island).

The effects of the Acadian presence have been especially pronounced in Louisiana. In 1779, Spain allied itself with the colonies in the Revolutionary War, and from 1779 to 1781, an army made up mostly of Acadians took Baton Rouge, Mobile, Pensacola, and several British forts. These victories were strategically significant, because they prevented the English from attacking the colonies via the Mississippi River or Florida, and Great Britain never regained any of its possessions in the lower Mississippi Valley.

The Acadian population that dominated southern Louisiana in the eighteenth century incorporated elements of Spanish, English, French, German, African, and American Indian cultures to develop what came to be called the Cajun culture. Cajuns are credited with establishing the rice, shrimp, and cattle industries, which are still mainstays of Louisiana's economy today. Anti-Cajun discrimination resulted in legally mandated English-only education in 1921 as part of an effort completely to eliminate the Cajun language and culture. In the late 1960's, the Louisiana state legislature created the Council for the Development of French in Louisiana to promote the restoration of Cajun culture and established Acadiana, an area made up of twenty-two French-speaking parishes in southern Louisiana. In the 1970's and 1980's, Cajun music and food gained international acclaim, and today people of Acadian descent comprise approximately one-fourth of the entire Louisiana population, forming a powerful political, economic, and cultural force in the state.

—*Jack Carter*

FURTHER READING

Brasseaux, Carl A. *The Founding of New Acadia: The Beginnings of Acadian Life in Louisiana, 1765-1803.* Baton Rouge: Louisiana State University Press, 1996. Describes the history of Acadians in Nova Scotia, their forced deportation and dispersal, the routes by which many found their way to south Louisiana, and their successful struggle to become a well-established population there.

Braud, Gerard-Marc. *From Nantes to Louisiana: The History of Acadia—The Odyssey of an Exiled People.* Translated by Julie Fontenot Landry. Lafayette, La.: La Rainette, 1999. Chronicles the history of the Acadians in Nova Scotia, the mass deportations to Europe and various colonies beginning in 1755, and the journey of large numbers of Acadians from France to Louisiana in 1785.

Doughty, Arthur G. *The Acadian Exiles: A Chronicle of the Land of Evangeline.* Toronto: Glasgow, Brook, 1916. Details the early history of Acadians, including the founding of Acadia, the appearance of the British and subsequent Acadian expulsions, and the exiles' numerous destinations in North America, Europe, and the Carribean.

Plank, Geoffrey. *An Unsettled Conquest: The British Campaign Against the Peoples of Acadia.* Philadelphia: University of Pennsylvania Press, 2003. A comprehensive history of the struggle between France and England over Nova Scotia, and the fates of the Mi'kmaq Indians and the Acadians who were caught in the middle.

SEE ALSO: 1713: Founding of Louisbourg; Apr. 11, 1713: Treaty of Utrecht; May 28, 1754-Feb. 10, 1763: French and Indian War; Jan., 1756-Feb. 15, 1763: Seven Years' War; June 8-July 27, 1758: Siege of Louisbourg; Feb. 10, 1763: Peace of Paris; 1783: Loyalists Migrate to Nova Scotia.
RELATED ARTICLES in *Great Lives from History: The Eighteenth Century, 1701-1800*: George II; Louis XV; William Pitt the Elder.

1750's

November 1, 1755
GREAT LISBON EARTHQUAKE

An earthquake of exceptional magnitude devastated the port city of Lisbon, Portugal. The massive destruction wrought by the quake resulted in the systematic rebuilding and modernization of the city, making it the most modern and architecturally advanced capital in Europe. The earthquake also occasioned a critical reexamination throughout Enlightenment Europe of the role of reason in nature and human affairs.

LOCALE: Lisbon, Portugal
CATEGORIES: Natural disasters; architecture; engineering

KEY FIGURES
Sebastião José de Carvalho e Mello (1699-1782), Joseph I's prime minister, 1755-1777, later the marquês de Pombal
Manuel de Maia (1672-1768), head of the corps of military engineers who organized the reconstruction of Lisbon
Joseph I (1714-1777), king of Portugal, r. 1750-1777

SUMMARY OF EVENT
On November 1, 1755, one of the most devastating earthquakes in modern history struck Lisbon, Portugal. Scientific measurement of earthquake magnitudes did not yet exist; however, based on historical evidence of the level of destruction, the quake's magnitude was most likely between 8.5 and 9.0 on the modern Richter scale. The population of the kingdom of Portugal was then almost 3 million, and about 10 percent of the population resided in Lisbon.

Located on the north bank of the Tagus River, the city lay where the river, flowing from the northeast, bent gradually to the west and entered the Atlantic Ocean. Shaped like an amphitheater, Lisbon was flat in its central area, which comprised the port district, the commercial district, and the seat of the royal government. Rising and arching around this center were low hills containing tens of thousands of houses and shops and many dozens of resplendent churches, monasteries, and convents. A magnet of global trade, especially because of its Brazilian gold, Lisbon housed a cosmopolitan population and was widely known for its wealth and opulence. Catholic clergy and religious orders composed an exceptionally large proportion of its inhabitants.

The earthquake began several hours after dawn on the Catholic holy day of All Saints. For about ten minutes during midmorning, the earth shook, rolled, and collapsed several times underneath the city. The epicenter of the earthquake was located many miles out to sea, and damage from shaking and tsunamis extended throughout southern Portugal and Spain and across Gibraltar into Morocco. The quake leveled numerous major buildings in the port area. The royal palace was destroyed, although the king was not in residence. Because of the holy day, churches were filled with morning worshipers, who were crushed under the weight of collapsing walls and roofs. Frequent aftershocks caused further damage.

Subsequent to the shocks, fires sprang up, and a wind from the northeast helped to blow the various blazes together into a general conflagration. Lasting for almost a week, the flames destroyed the rich contents of churches and palaces, consuming paintings, manuscripts, books, and tapestries. In a final assault, a sequence of tidal waves struck, some towering more than 20 feet. Within a few morning hours, quake, fire, and flood had destroyed one of the major ports of Europe.

In the hysteria of the immediate aftermath, the death toll was estimated to be as high as fifty thousand. Modern estimates now calculate that the number of fatalities was at most fifteen thousand. Not only death but also fear, hunger, and disease followed the destruction. Thousands fled the city, blocking roads and jamming passages. Prisoners escaped from jails, assaulting the living and the dead. Food could not enter the city, and countless of the injured languished without care.

Rebuilding Lisbon became the responsibility of Sebastião José de Carvalho e Mello, the principal minister of King Joseph I and the future marquês de Pombal. Energetically taking control of recovery efforts, the minister gave his immediate attention to public health. Bodies not burned in fires were collected on boats and sunk in the Tagus River. The army put out fires, cleared streets and passages, immediately executed thieves, and mounted field tents for shelter and feeding. Prices for food and building materials were fixed.

In planning the city's reconstruction, Carvalho e Mello paid particular attention to improving its layout. Lisbon's old, twisting, narrow streets were eliminated, especially in the flat central part of the city, which was redesigned to have wide, straight streets that crossed at right angles in a grid pattern. Near the harbor area, a spacious plaza was built. Carvalho e Mello supervised a group of skilled military engineers, headed by the veteran officer Manuel de Maia, who organized the planning and rebuilding.

To expedite construction, buildings were prefabricated, and the sizes of doors, windows, and walls were standardized. To protect against future earthquakes, building frames were made of wood that could sway under pressure without breaking. The style of these new structures, a kind of simplified or plain Baroque, came to be known as Pombaline.

SIGNIFICANCE

As a result of the earthquake, Lisbon came to be among the best-planned and best-constructed cities in eighteenth century Europe. The modernized port imported a high volume of manufactured goods, most of them from Great Britain, which had already begun to industrialize. Much of the wealth that Portugal received in the form of Brazilian gold was therefore funneled from Lisbon's docks straight into Britain's coffers, helping to capitalize the earliest stages of the Industrial Revolution.

The consequences of the earthquake, however, were not all physical or concrete: The abstract arenas of theology and philosophy were affected as well. In fact, it was in precisely these areas that the quake had its most resonant social effects. No sooner had the quake struck than the numerous clergy of Lisbon began declaring it the wrath of God striking against a sinful populace. This preaching roused many into paroxysms of fear, and such hysteria made it extremely difficult to deal with the crisis in an organized, rational manner. The civil authorities begged the clergy not to preach such fear, but their admonitions were only somewhat successful.

News of the extraordinary disaster rolled through Europe in a matter of weeks, its horrors growing with the chain of narrative. Western Europe as a whole was in the midst of an intellectual period known as the Enlightenment, the Age of Reason. Carvalho e Mello, with his rational, utilitarian views of government, was representa-

---

VOLTAIRE ON THE LISBON EARTHQUAKE

Voltaire responded to the earthquake in Lisbon with disgust, taking it as a sign that the natural laws ruling the universe—a central trope of Enlightenment thought—were neither kind nor just. The following lines are taken from a poem he wrote in the aftermath of the disaster.

Oh, unhappy mortals! Oh deplorable Earth!
O, of all mortals, you appalling assembly!
Eternal debate over useless sorrows!
Mistaken philosophers who shout "All is well,"
Run! contemplate these horrible ruins,
This debris, these shreds, these unfortunate ashes,
These women, these children piled one on the other
Under broken marbles and scattered limbs;
One hundred thousand unfortunates that the earth devours
Who, bloody, torn, and still throbbing,
Buried under their roofs, end—unaided
and in horrible torment—their lamentable days!
To the half-formed cries of their expiring voices,
To the horrific spectacle of their smoking ashes,
Will you say, "It's the effect of eternal laws
Created by a free and good God to necessitate choice"?
Will you say, seeing this pile of victims:
"God is revenged, their death is the price of their crimes"?
What crime, what fault did these children lying
Crushed and bloody in their mothers' bosoms commit?
Lisbon, which is no more, did it contain more vices
Than London or Paris, plunged in delights?
Lisbon is in ruins, and in Paris they dance.

Source: Voltaire, "Poème sur le désastre de Lisbonne: Ou, Examen de cet axiome, 'tout est bien'" (1756). http://un2sg4.unige.ch/athena/voltaire/volt_lis.html. Accessed August 1, 2005. Translated by Andy Perry.

---

tive of this movement. In the face of religious hysteria, reasonable thinkers of the Enlightenment argued that the Lisbon earthquake needed to be studied not as a supernatural event but as a natural one. The quake thus prompted a great debate between the emerging rational forces of the modern, scientific age and the declining religiosity of the medieval era.

Philosophers and other thinkers also debated about the quake's effects. Many of those who believed in a reasoned and organized world felt also that every event was for the best. Thus, they argued that while the earthquake in Lisbon was a horrible disaster, it resulted in a rebuilt and modernized city. Others replied that one could not be so sanguine and optimistic about the world. Among the leading voices of this contrary point of view was the French philosopher and poet Voltaire. In a long poem

1750's

written immediately after the earthquake and in a later famous novel, *Candide: Ou, L'Optimisme* (1759; *Candide: Or, All for the Best*, 1759; also as *Candide: Or, The Optimist*, 1762; also as *Candide: Or, Optimism*, 1947), he argued that the Lisbon tragedy proved the existence of irrational evil in the world.

Voltaire maintained that it was naive and self-serving to say that evil was always balanced by good. There were people everywhere who suffered for no reason and who would never personally benefit from their suffering. He argued that those who believed that everything that happened was for the best were those who wanted to keep things as they were, who wanted acceptance of the status quo. Such an attitude ignored those who suffered under present conditions, and it failed to respond effectively by alleviating their suffering. If ignored over a long period, such suffering could prove unbearable, rendering the sufferers violent. In relation to these arguments, it should be noted that less than half a century after the Lisbon earthquake, the suffering and outrage of the French masses burst forth against the Old Regime in the French Revolution.

The Lisbon earthquake, therefore, resounded in Europe not only as a physical event but also as a psychological and cultural one. Its force shook not only the earth but also people's minds, accelerating the process of replacing old traditions with new ones.

—*Edward A. Riedinger*

FURTHER READING

Brooks, Charles B. *Disaster at Lisbon: The Great Earthquake of 1755*. Long Beach, Calif.: Shangton Longley Press, 1994. A reassessment of the Lisbon earthquake based on modern scientific findings.

Davison, Charles. *Great Earthquakes: With 122 Illustrations*. London: Thomas Murby, 1936. Includes vivid black-and-white illustrations of the Lisbon earthquake and its aftermath.

Dynes, Russell Rowe. *The Lisbon Earthquake in 1755: Contested Meanings of the First Modern Disaster*. Newark: Disaster Research Center, University of Delaware, 1997. Analyzes the Lisbon earthquake in terms of how relief was organized, comparing such relief to modern strategies and conditions.

Kendrick, T. D. *The Lisbon Earthquake*. London: Methuen, 1956. Classic account, concisely describing the physical nature and social consequences of the quake.

Laidlar, John, comp. *Lisbon*. Oxford, England: ABC-Clio, 1997. Provides brief summaries of publications on Lisbon, with extensive entries for the earthquake of 1755.

Maxwell, Kenneth. *Pombal: Paradox of the Enlightenment*. New York: Cambridge University Press, 1995. Study by a leading scholar of Portugal places Pombal and policies regarding the Lisbon earthquake within the context of the minister's principles and objectives for government and society.

Ockman, Joan. *Out of Ground Zero: Case Studies in Urban Reinvention*. New York: Prestel, 2002. Details architectural and engineering strategies of recovery for urban disasters worldwide over the past three centuries. Chapter 1 addresses the Lisbon earthquake.

SEE ALSO: c. 1701: Oman Captures Zanzibar; 1750: Treaty of Madrid; Jan., 1759: Voltaire Satirizes Optimism in *Candide*; 1769: Pombal Reforms the Inquisition.

RELATED ARTICLES in *Great Lives from History: The Eighteenth Century, 1701-1800*: Marquês de Pombal; Voltaire.

January, 1756-February 15, 1763
SEVEN YEARS' WAR

The Seven Years's War was both the continuation of a struggle for power in Central Europe between Prussia and Austria and a chapter in the ongoing worldwide colonial rivalry between France and Britain. The war established Britain as the dominant world colonial power, and it secured Prussia's status as a major European power, building the early framework for a unified German Empire.

ALSO KNOWN AS: French and Indian War (in North America; 1754-1763)

LOCALE: Worldwide

CATEGORIES: Wars, uprisings, and civil unrest; expansion and land acquisition; diplomacy and international relations

KEY FIGURES

William Pitt the Elder (1708-1778), prime minister of Great Britain, 1757-1761, 1766-1768

Étienne François de Choiseul (1719-1785), French minister of foreign affairs, 1758-1761, and minister of war and marine, 1761-1766

Frederick the Great (1712-1786), king of Prussia, r. 1740-1786

Maria Theresa (1717-1780), archduchess of Austria and queen of Hungary and Bohemia, r. 1740-1780

Third Earl of Bute (John Stuart; 1713-1792), British secretary of state, 1761-1762, and prime minister, 1762-1763

Robert Clive (1725-1774), British soldier, colonial administrator, and member of Parliament, 1760-1774

Wenzel Anton von Kaunitz (1711-1794), state chancellor of Austria, 1753-1792

Leopold Joseph Daun (1705-1766), Austrian field marshal

Elizabeth Petrovna (1709-1762), empress of Russia, r. 1741-1762

SUMMARY OF EVENT

On the European continent, the Seven Years' War was a continuation of the struggle between Austria and Prussia over Silesia, which Frederick the Great had conquered in 1740. In North America, the Caribbean, the western coast of Africa, and India, the war was part of a long-term colonial struggle between Britain and France. Although Britain and France were not officially at war with each other until January, 1756, they started fighting the French and Indian War in North America in 1754. The ensuing continental conflict was prepared by the diplomatic activities of Wenzel Anton von Kaunitz, the chancellor of the Austrian Habsburg ruler Maria Theresa, who arranged an alliance between Austria, France, and Russia.

Maria Theresa planned to attack Prussia in the spring of 1757, but Frederick the Great struck first by invading Saxony on August 29, 1756. This attack on Saxony induced France to sign the Second Peace of Paris on May 1, 1757, in which France agreed to field an army of 129,000 men and provide generous subsidies to Austria. Russia announced that it would send 80,000 troops against Frederick, and the Diet of the Holy Roman Empire in January, 1757, voted to mobilize imperial troops against Frederick. To regain lands it had lost to Prussia in Pomerania in 1720, Sweden also joined the league against Prussia in March, 1757.

Frederick the Great's invasion of Saxony was based on his assumption that he had to fight a preventive war, which would induce the hostile coalition arrayed against him to sue for peace. In addition, Saxony's geographic location was crucial both for the protection of Frederick's base in Brandenburg and as a convenient launching area for attacks on Maria Theresa's Bohemia. Moreover, Frederick collected one-third of the entire Prussian cost of the war from Saxony.

The year 1757, however, revealed that Frederick's preventive war had turned into a war of attrition against his numerous enemies. The Austrian general Leopold Joseph Daun defeated Frederick on June 18, 1757, at the Battle of Kolin. The Russians launched their first offensive into East Prussia, defeating the Prussians at the Battle of Grossjaegersdorf on August 30, while Swedes invaded Pomerania. A combined imperial and French army in Franconia threatened Frederick's hold on Saxony. The main French army advanced into Westphalia toward Hannover, forcing the English commander to accept a truce and the Convention of Kloster Zeven in September. The Prussian capital, Berlin, was briefly occupied by Austrian troops in October.

Although Frederick the Great would have to struggle for survival against overwhelming opposition for the next four years, his victory at the Battle of Rossbach near Leipzig on November 5, 1757, over the French and German imperial forces was crucial in allowing him to continue the conflict. The victory caused the British prime minister, William Pitt the Elder, to change his policy and recommend to the British king George II that he reject

Prussian forces attack Austrians barricaded inside a church during the Battle of Leuthen. (Francis R. Niglutsch)

the Convention of Kloster Zeven and support Frederick financially and militarily against the French. With his western front thus covered, Frederick's task during much of the war was to prevent the Austrian and Russian troops from uniting against him. He confronted each power and won enough crucial battles to stave off defeat. On December 5, 1757, he defeated the Austrians at Leuthen, and he stopped the Russian advance at the Battle of Zorndorf on August 25, 1758.

The years 1759 and 1760, however, exhausted the Prussian army and its finances. Frederick's forces were defeated in several key battles in Silesia and Saxony. The Austrian and Russian troops defeated Frederick at Kunersdorf on August 12, 1759, representing the low point in the war for Frederick. In October, 1760, Berlin was occupied again by Austrian and Russian troops. Only the important battle at Torgau on November 3, 1760, brought Frederick a much-needed victory.

Frederick benefited both from a lack of coordination and growing distrust among his enemies and from the military conservatism of Field Marshall Daun. Frederick

also had the advantage of interior lines. His military ability and his unwavering commitment to the struggle were also crucial. Most important, the death of the Russian empress Elizabeth Petrovna in January, 1762, and the accession to power of Peter III caused Russia to abandon Austria and briefly join Prussia in the conflict.

The colonial conflict between Britain and France during the Seven Years' War also weakened France's support of the anti-Prussian coalition. William Pitt formed a new English government on June 29, 1757, which was committed to the defeat of the French. Pitt also sent substantial subsidies to Frederick. In contrast, the French leader, Étienne François de Choiseul, who assumed power in December, 1758, reduced subsidies to Vienna and the German states by half in order to concentrate on the colonial struggle with England. The conflict between England and France around the world was decided in England's favor by the fact that Pitt ordered the British fleet to blockade the French coast, making it difficult for the French to send replacements to the various colonies. Moreover, in the naval battle of Quiberon Bay in November, 1758, the English destroyed the French fleet.

With their victory at the Battle of the Plains of Abraham on September 13, 1759, the British captured Quebec. Pitt also sent the British fleet to the Caribbean to contain French privateers operating from Martinique and Guadeloupe, and he used the British navy to close down the French slave trade in Africa. The navy made it possible for Robert Clive, the representative of the British East India Company, to reverse French advances. The British defeated the Indian nawab at the Battle of Plassey in June, 1757, and defeated the French at Wandiwash on January 20, 1760, which led to the surrender of Pondicherry one year later. Finally, when Spain entered the war against Britain in January, 1762, the British conquered Havana in Cuba and Manila in the Philippines.

Several months after Pitt resigned in October of 1761, the new British prime minister, the third earl of Bute, stopped payments to Prussia. On December 9, 1762, Bute obtained a majority in the House of Commons in support of peace negotiations with France, which led to the Peace of Paris on February 10, 1763. Five days later, on February 15, Frederick negotiated with Maria

Theresa the Treaty of Hubertusburg, which restored the status quo of 1756.

SIGNIFICANCE

Territorially and economically, the Seven Years' War benefited Britain the most. Great Britain became the dominant world colonial power, which contributed to its rapid economic growth during the eighteenth century. The removal of the French danger from the original North American colonies, however, made it more feasible for the Americans to revolt against England after the war. Moreover, Frederick the Great, remembering how Britain had abandoned him during the last year of the war, worked hard during the American Revolutionary War to undermine British recruitment of German soldiers. The French, meanwhile, helped the American colonials with direct military aid.

The Seven Years' War dramatically changed the balance of power in Europe by establishing Prussia as a major power with a strong military tradition. Austria had to accept the loss of Silesia and the permanent rivalry of Prussia. France lost the North American colonies, its po-

PRUSSIAN CONFLICTS IN THE SEVEN YEARS' WAR

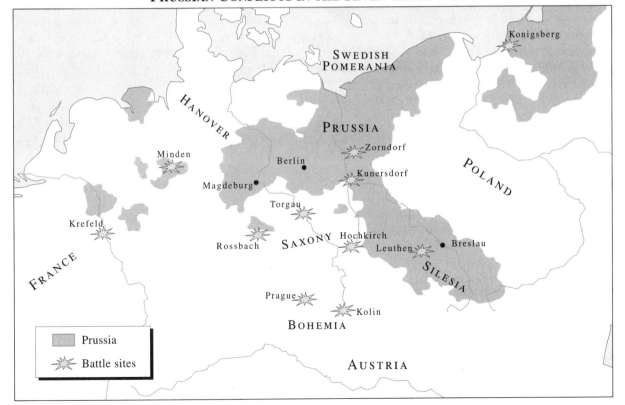

litical position in India, and its influence on the Continent for much of the rest of the century. Moreover, the huge public debt accumulated by France during the war contributed to the financial crisis that would lead to the outbreak of the French Revolution in 1789.

—*Johnpeter Horst Grill*

FURTHER READING

Dorn, Walter L. *Competition for Empire, 1740-1763.* New York: Harper and Row, 1963. Places the war in the context of European rivalries and includes chapters on both the Diplomatic Revolution and the Seven Years' War.

Hochedlinger, Michael. *Austria's Wars of Emergence: War, State, and Society in the Habsburg Monarchy, 1683-1789.* New York: Longman, 2003. Includes an excellent, concise chapter on the Seven Years' War in Central Europe.

Kennett, Lee. *The French Army in the Seven Years' War.* Durham, N.C.: Duke University Press, 1967. Organizational history of the French army arguing that the weaknesses of the French army reflected the monarchy's shortcomings and Versailles intrigues.

Lindsay, J. O., ed. *The Old Regime, 1713-1763.* Vol. 7 in *The New Cambridge Modern History.* Cambridge, England: Cambridge University Press, 1966. Informative chapters on British-French rivalries in the Caribbean, North America, and India.

Middleton, Richard. *The Bells of Victory: The Pitt-Newcastle Ministry and the Conduct of the Seven Years'*

War, 1757-1762. Reprint. New York: Cambridge University Press, 2002. Helpful for its treatment of events in the American colonies.

Schweitzer, Karl W. *War, Politics, and Diplomacy: The Anglo-Prussian Alliance, 1756-1763.* Lanham, Md.: University Press of America, 2001. A notable scholarly work on English-Prussian relations.

Showalter, Dennis. *The Wars of Frederick the Great.* New York: Longman, 1996. The best detailed history in English of the War of the Austrian Succession and the Seven Years' War by a renowned military historian.

SEE ALSO: May 31, 1740: Accession of Frederick the Great; Oct. 20, 1740: Maria Theresa Succeeds to the Austrian Throne; Dec. 16, 1740-Nov. 7, 1748: War of the Austrian Succession; May 28, 1754-Feb. 10, 1763: French and Indian War; July, 1755-Aug., 1758: Acadians Are Expelled from Canada; June 23, 1757: Battle of Plassey; Nov. 5, 1757: Battle of Rossbach; June 8-July 27, 1758: Siege of Louisbourg; Oct. 5, 1759-Nov. 19, 1761: Cherokee War; 1760-1776: Caribbean Slave Rebellions; Feb. 10, 1763: Peace of Paris; Apr. 19, 1775-Oct. 19, 1781: American Revolutionary War; July 14, 1789: Fall of the Bastille.

RELATED ARTICLES in *Great Lives from History: The Eighteenth Century, 1701-1800*: Étienne François de Choiseul; Robert Clive; Elizabeth Petrovna; Frederick the Great; George II; George III; Wenzel Anton von Kaunitz; Louis XV; Maria Theresa; Peter III; William Pitt the Elder.

1757
MONRO DISTINGUISHES BETWEEN LYMPHATIC AND BLOOD SYSTEMS

Alexander Monro observed a system of fluid absorption associated with lymphatics that appeared to possess its own valvular system. As a result, he argued the system is unique and separate from that of the circulatory system for blood.

LOCALE: Berlin, Germany
CATEGORIES: Biology; health and medicine

KEY FIGURES

Alexander Monro II (1733-1817), a Scottish physician and anatomist
William Hunter (1718-1783), a Scottish physician and surgeon
William Hewson (1739-1774), a British anatomist

Gasparo Aselli (1581-1626), an Italian anatomist who first described lymphatic vessels
Thomas Bartholin (1616-1680), a Danish physician who observed the thoracic duct in humans, and who coined the term "lymphatic"

SUMMARY OF EVENT

The existence of a system of vessels separate from the blood system was suspected for two thousand years. The first actual description of such a unique system was that by the Italian anatomist Gasparo Aselli, who in 1622 reported the release of a milky fluid from the lacteal vessels observed in the intestine of a dog. Aselli referred to these vessels as "milk veins," reflecting the prevailing (but erroneous) viewpoint that the function of these vessels was the transport of intestinal material to the liver, where it was to be used for the synthesis of blood. Aselli's illustrations were later published posthumously.

Other anatomists and physicians made similar observations of a system of vessels, including Danish physician Thomas Bartholin in his description of the human thoracic duct, now known as the vessel through which lymph is returned to the blood. In 1653, Bartholin coined the term "lymphatic" to describe the vessels of the system. Bartholin, however, did not know the function of the lymphatics.

Another physician, Alexander Monro, was one of a line of significant figures in anatomy during this era. He was the youngest son of Alexander Monro (Primus), anatomist at the University of Edinburgh. Alexander enrolled in his father's anatomy class at the age of eleven and by age twenty-one had been appointed to the position of professor of anatomy at the university (1754). In October, 1755, Monro was awarded his medical degree. His medical thesis was noteworthy in that it included original research, unusual at a time when most medical theses were basically literature reviews.

Monro's thesis described his investigations into the structure of the testis, including circulation of the blood as well as a secondary system later determined to be the lymphatics. Monro observed that if he injected mercury into the vas deferens, the resultant pressure would cause the bursting of the epididymis. The mercury, suddenly released, entered the lymphatics. The results indicated to Monro that the lymphatic vessels were not a portion of the arterial system.

Following graduation, Monro went to London, where he attended lectures delivered by William Hunter, a noted anatomist and former student of Monro's father. Hunter's research also included that of the blood and lymphatic circulations. One of Hunter's lectures, dealing with the absorbent mechanisms of the lymphatics, led Monro to believe that Hunter had read his medical thesis. There is no evidence that Hunter's observations were anything but completely independent of Monro's earlier work, however.

In 1757, Monro traveled to Berlin, where he continued his study of anatomy under Johann Friedrich Meckel (the elder), who was considered one of the outstanding physicians in that field. Monro's experimental work in Berlin was a continuation of the work in his medical thesis—the origin and function of the lymphatic system.

Monro's published work of his research in Berlin included much of what modern science would consider a literature review. He included references to previous studies and interpretations on the subject. Ironically, he did not include the work by Hunter. By injecting mercury into various tissue sites, as well as injections directly into lymphatic vessels, Monro demonstrated that there is no direct communication between the arteries and veins that carry blood and the lymphatic vessels; that is, they are separate systems. Furthermore, the movement of fluids through the lymphatics is directional—lymph flows in one direction and enters the blood stream near the heart at the subclavian vein.

Monro also observed that the swelling of lymphatic glands (buboes) occurs in the vicinity of infections; more specifically, he observed that venereal disease (sexually transmitted diseases) resulted in swellings in the region of the genitals. Infections in various places in the body would result in the movement of the (then unknown) agent through the nearest lymphatics toward the thoracic duct, from which the infection would enter the blood stream. Monro's conclusion was that the lymphatic vessels are "absorbents," draining fluid from body tissues and returning it to the bloodstream.

Monro was not the only individual to claim priority in discovering the lymphatic system. The strongest claim in the dispute was that by Hunter. Although Hunter had not published his observations of the lymphatic system earlier in his career, notes originating with Charles White, a student of Hunter, included references to the lymphatics as early as 1752. Monro eventually attacked Hunter over the issue of priority, arguing, without substantiation, that Hunter had obtained his ideas only after reading Monro's medical thesis.

Hunter was not the only one who claimed the discovery. William Hewson had studied with Hunter during the 1750's, attended medical school, and, in 1762, became Hunter's partner. In the late 1760's, Hewson published several papers in which he demonstrated a role for the lymphatic system in a number of vertebrates, including humans. As a result of this work, Hewson was elected as a fellow to the Royal Society. In his papers, Hewson stated he had observed the presence of lymphatics in organisms such as fish and turtles as early as 1762. Monro quickly disputed Hewson's claims of priority, arguing instead that he, Monro, had observed such structures in these animals some five years earlier. The issue was never completely settled during Monro's lifetime and was eventually dropped.

The matter of who should be accorded the honor for discovering the lymphatic system is one of figuring out who initially provided the information to his peers. The greater issue for the period, however, is represented by

1750's

the expansion of scientific investigation beyond the classical views of early Greek or Roman theory. Indeed, the period represented one of enlightened thought in all fields of human endeavor, including the arts and sciences as depicted in writings from persons as diverse as Voltaire, Adam Smith, and Thomas Jefferson. The Industrial Revolution would shortly supersede the agricultural economy of most of Europe.

Whereas actual applications to scientific practice were limited during this period, the introduction of the smallpox vaccine being the most notable exception, scientific theory had begun a significant period of expansion. For example, rather than relying on outmoded views of anatomy dating to Galen nearly eighteen hundred years earlier, eighteenth century anatomists carried out direct observations and experimentation. The discoveries by William Harvey of the circulation of the blood, and Monro (or Hunter) of the lymphatic system, are such examples.

SIGNIFICANCE

Issues of priority aside, the significance of the work carried out by Alexander Monro II and William Hunter lies less in proving the existence of the lymphatic system then in demonstrating it was a system separate from that of the blood. Furthermore, Monro and Hunter discovered its specific role in the body, as an absorbent that collects fluid from tissues throughout the body and then returns those fluids to the bloodstream. The existence of the lymphatic system within a wide variety of organisms was also demonstrated after later researchers combined the research carried out by the three claimants for priority; therefore, all the work of all three was important.

Monro also demonstrated that as a collecting system for fluid originating at sites of infection, the lymphatic system was capable of disseminating that infection throughout the body. Such work would later become a major factor in understanding the role of the lymphatic system in immune response.

—*Richard Adler*

FURTHER READING

Eales, Nellie. "The History of the Lymphatic System, with Special Reference to the Hunter-Monro Controversy." *Journal of the History of Medicine* (July 29, 1974): 280-294. A history of the subject, with emphasis on the arguments about who made the first discovery of the system.

Finlayson, C. P. "Alexander Monro (Secundus)." In *Dictionary of Scientific Biography*, edited by Charles Gillispie. Vol. 9. New York: Charles Scribner's Sons, 1974. A brief biography that examines Monro's major scientific achievements.

McDowell, Julie, and Michael Windelspecht. *The Lymphatic System*. Westport, Conn.: Greenwood Press, 2004. A popular account of the history and makeup of the lymphatic system.

Porter, Roy, and Maurice Kirby. *Disease, Medicine, and Society in England, 1550-1860*. New York: Cambridge University Press, 1995. A relatively brief account of the impact of disease on English society during this period, as well as the effects of medical discoveries on the evolution of public health.

SEE ALSO: 1751: Maupertuis Provides Evidence of "Hereditary Particles"; 1753: Lind Discovers a Cure for Scurvy; 1757-1766: Haller Establishes Physiology as a Science; 1796-1798: Jenner Develops Smallpox Vaccination; 1799: Discovery of the Earliest Anesthetics.

RELATED ARTICLES in *Great Lives from History: The Eighteenth Century, 1701-1800*: Daniel Gabriel Fahrenheit; Edward Jenner; Joseph Priestley; Benjamin Rush; Lazzaro Spallanzani.

1757-1766
HALLER ESTABLISHES PHYSIOLOGY AS A SCIENCE

Between 1757 and 1766, Haller published his textbook Elementa physiologiae corporis humani, *a comprehensive work that established physiology as a science independent of anatomy. Haller's discovery that contractility is a quality inherent in muscles, while sensitivity and pain perception characterize nerve function, laid the foundation of modern neurology.*

LOCALE: Lausanne and Bern, Switzerland
CATEGORIES: Biology; science and technology

KEY FIGURES

Albrecht von Haller (1708-1777), Swiss physician, anatomist, botanist, bibliographer, and poet
Herman Boerhaave (1668-1738), Dutch physician and professor of physiology, botany, and chemistry
Luigi Galvani (1737-1798), Italian physician
Alessandro Volta (1745-1827), Italian physicist

SUMMARY OF EVENT

The development of human physiology as a science required accurate anatomical understanding of the human body. Anatomical knowledge was gained through dissection of cadavers, a practice that began in Europe in the fourteenth century and gradually gained recognition in the fifteenth and especially the sixteenth century. Scientific developments of the seventeenth century led scientists to regard humans as machines, and this mechanical approach dominated research at that time. Albrecht von Haller, a former student of the Dutch mechanist Herman Boerhaave, coined the term *anatomia animata*, or living anatomy.

Boerhaave viewed the human being as a machine composed of hollow and solid elements. Influenced by the teachings of Boerhaave, Haller furthered physiologic understanding by carrying out numerous animal experiments. His areas of interest were multiple: He studied the development of chicken embryos and adopted the preformationist standpoint that the ovum contains a miniature being—a homunculus (little human)—that starts to grow once activated by semen. His work in the field of pulmonology demonstrated that lung expansion requires an airless pleural space. His research correctly ascribed digestive properties to saliva and pancreatic juices, and his understanding of the process of hearing approached that of modern science.

In his study of muscle and nerve action, Haller designed hundreds of animal experiments. Denuded anatomical areas were exposed to thermal, chemical, or mechanical injury. The different reactions of the animal to the noxious stimuli allowed Haller to differentiate between "irritable" and "sensible" tissues. Muscles exhibited "irritability," a contraction of muscle fibers upon stimulation, whereas nerves displayed "sensibility" and were responsible for pain perception. The term "irritability" had been used a century earlier by British physician Francis Glisson, who presumed that all tissues had the ability to contract. Haller, however, showed through judicious experimentation that irritablity was restricted to muscle fibers.

Having observed that compression not only of the spinal cord but also of specific brain areas interfered with the transmission of nerve impulses, Haller could only speculate on the mode of communication between nerve and muscle. He discarded the possibilities of electrical conduction and vibration, hypothesizing that "juice" flowing from the central nervous system through the peripheral nerves led to muscle contraction. The concepts of irritability and sensibility, which Haller first announced in 1739, were discussed again in his monograph *De partibus corporis humani sensibilibus et irritabilibus* (1753; *A Dissertation on the Sensible and Irritable Parts of Animals*, 1755). The full development of Haller's concept of nerve and muscle function was published in *Elementa physiologiae corporis humani* (1757-1766; elements of human physiology).

During his lifetime, Haller published three textbooks of physiology, including a heavily annotated edition of professor Boerhaave's lectures, a text entitled *Primae lineae physiologiae* (1747; *Dr. Albert Haller's Physiology*, 1754), and the multivolume set *Elementa physiologiae corporis humani*, in which he systematically presents the complete anatomic and physiologic knowledge pertaining to the human body. *Elementa physiologiae corporis humani* not only contained macro- and microanatomical information on organ systems but also encompassed their physical and chemical properties. Each organ structure and the experiments leading to the understanding of specific organ functions were discussed in minute detail. References were provided for the theories and experiments cited, and credit was given to scientists who had contributed to the data.

Haller critically analyzed the available information and avoided drawing unfounded conclusions. In addition to offering critical analysis of the existing body of knowledge about human physiology, he discussed those contexts in which insufficient or inconclusive data were available to draw firm or meaningful conclusions. His text therefore stood as a complete, well-researched scientific work of experimental physiology, detailing the entire state of the field as it then existed and emphasizing what now is the golden rule of medical science: Knowledge and understanding of the human body must be based on valid, well-conceived experiments and reflect the efforts of each contributing researcher.

Haller, who had conducted the majority of his experimental work during the seventeen years he taught as professor of anatomy, botany, and surgery at the University of Göttingen, began writing *Elementa physiologiae corporis humani* upon his return to Switzerland in 1753. The first volume, *Fibra, vasa, circuitus sanguinus* (fibers, vessels, the circulation of blood) was published in 1757, and he completed the work in 1766, when the eighth volume, *Fetus hominisque vita* (the human fetus and the life of man), came out in print. Like the first volume, the second volume, *Sanguis, ejus motus, humorum separatio* (1760; blood, its motion, and the separation of fluids), was dedicated to Frederick V of Denmark.

In the preface to volume 5, *Sensus externi interni* (1763; external and internal senses), Haller defended his theory of irritability and sensibility. The third volume (1761) treated respiratory function and voice, and volume 4, which appeared in 1762, discussed the brain, nerves, and muscles. Volume 6, *Deglutitio, ventriculus, omenta, lien, pancreas, hepar* (swallowing, stomach, omenta, spleen, pancreas, liver), and volume 7, *Intestina, chylus, urina, semen, muliebra* (intestine, chyle, urine, seminal fluid, female organs), were published in 1764 and 1765, respectively.

A complete German translation of Haller's monumental work appeared between 1759 and 1776. Portions of the work have also been translated into French and Dutch, but very little into English. In 1774, the first eight pages of *Fibra, vasa, circuitus sanguinus* were translated into English and published in *The Medical Magazine: Or, General Repository of Practical Physic and Surgery* under the title *Elements of Physiology*. Further translations were published in subsequent numbers.

Haller's support of preformationism may have delayed progress in the understanding of embryology, but his breakthrough work in neurology spurred scientists to explore how transmission of nervous impulses occurred. Luigi Galvani and Alessandro Volta, drawing inspiration from Haller, later demonstrated that muscles would contract when electrically stimulated and so paved the way for the development of electrophysiology.

SIGNIFICANCE

Albrecht von Haller's contributions to modern physiology facilitated the understanding of pathologic processes and ultimately led to progress in the treatment and prevention of disease. A mechanistic understanding of life evolved from the simplistic view of bodies as compositions of "beams and levers" and "pipes and vessels" to Haller's realization that living tissues are characterized by their specific functions: The intrinsic property of muscle is to contract and that of nerves is to feel.

The discovery that the reaction to a stimulus depended on the tissue's organizational makeup—that is, the discovery that tissue was specialized, or programmed to act a certain way—was entirely new. Haller's perception that tissues possess "vital properties" stimulated scientific thinking, leading to the concepts of an "internal milieu" and "body homeostasis." In the nineteenth century, it led to the further discovery that even nerves themselves were specialized, as the same stimulus applied to different nerves could produce sight, smell, touch, taste, or sound.

It became increasingly apparent that the harmonious functioning of living organisms required an intricate messenger system: The role of the binding of hormones to their receptors in initiating the informational cascade between different organs has been elucidated, as well as the role three-dimensional protein structures play in cellular functioning.

—*Elisabeth Faase*

FURTHER READING

Hall, Thomas. *Ideas of Life and Matters*. Vol. 1. Chicago: University of Chicago Press, 1969. Discusses the Hallerian concepts of irritability and sensibility.

Piccolino, Marco. "Biological Machines: From Mills to Molecules." *Nature Reviews: Molecular Cell Biology* 1 (2000): 149-153. Concerns the evolution of mechanistic thinking.

Porter, Roy. *Blood and Guts: A Short History of Medicine*. New York: W. W. Norton, 2002. Discusses dissection of human cadavers.

_____. *The Greatest Benefit to Mankind*. New York: W. W. Norton, 1998. Information on the different modes of scientific thought during the Enlightenment.

Roe, Shirley. *The Natural Philosophy of Albrecht von Haller*. New York: Arno Press, 1981. Includes an English summary of Haller's preface to the first volume of *Elementa physiologiae corporis humani*.

Rothschuh, Karl. *History of Physiology*. Huntington,

N.Y.: Robert E. Krieger, 1973. Contains discussion of Haller's thoughts on different organ functions.

Simmons, John. *The Scientific One Hundred: A Ranking of the Most Influential Scientists, Past and Present.* Secaucus, N.J.: Carol, 1996. A brief discussion of Haller's scientific importance.

Steinke, Hubert, and Claudia Profos. *Bibliographia Halleriana.* Basel, Switzerland: Schwabe Verlag, 2004. An extensive bibliography of Haller's works, including secondary literature.

SEE ALSO: Beginning 1735: Linnaeus Creates the Binomial System of Classification; 1748: Nollet Dis-

covers Osmosis; 1749-1789: First Comprehensive Examination of the Natural World; 1751: Maupertuis Provides Evidence of "Hereditary Particles"; 1753: Lind Discovers a Cure for Scurvy; 1757: Monro Distinguishes Between Lymphatic and Blood Systems; 1767-1768: Spallanzani Disproves Spontaneous Generation; 1796-1798: Jenner Develops Smallpox Vaccination.

RELATED ARTICLES in *Great Lives from History: The Eighteenth Century, 1701-1800*: Luigi Galvani; Alessandro Volta.

June 23, 1757
BATTLE OF PLASSEY

The British East India Company's triumph at the Battle of Plassey led first to British hegemony over Bengal and then to the establishment of the British Raj and to India taking its place as the crown jewel of the British Empire.

LOCALE: Bengal, India

CATEGORIES: Wars, uprisings, and civil unrest; colonization; expansion and land acquisition

KEY FIGURES

Robert Clive (1725-1774), British East India Company general

Alivardi Khan (1676?-1756), nawab of Bengal, 1740-1756

Sirāj al-Dawlā (d. 1757), nawab of Bengal, 1756-1757

Mir Ja'far (1691?-1765), nawab of Bengal, 1757-1760, 1763-1765

Mir Kasim (d. 1777), nawab of Bengal, 1760-1763

SUMMARY OF EVENT

The 1750's were a boom time in the riverine ports of Bengal, where the manufacturing of high-quality textiles fueled an international commerce in which European traders were involved in intense rivalries. The nawab (provincial Mughal governor) of Bengal, who also ruled Bihar and Orissa, had to keep these traders on a tight rein. In the early 1750's, that nawab was Alivardi Khan, who was very much master in his own house. Dying in 1756, he bequeathed his realm to a daughter's son, the twenty-year-old Sirāj al-Dawlā. In the British historiographical tradition, al-Dawlā was portrayed as a vicious degenerate. Some twentieth century Indian historians have

sought to rehabilitate his reputation, portraying him as a "freedom fighter." In reality, he was neither.

From the outset, Sirāj al-Dawlā was greatly incensed against the British East India Company, which had defied him by strengthening Fort William in Calcutta without his permission. He therefore made a surprise attack on the city (June 16-20, 1756). Most of its European residents fled downstream before the city fell, but those who remained were imprisoned for the night, probably unbeknown to the nawab, in a cramped, airless cell without water. About 146 prisoners were pressed into an 18-by-14-by-10-foot cell. By morning, 123 had suffocated. This cell came to be known as the Black Hole of Calcutta. Once in possession of Calcutta, Sirāj al-Dawlā did nothing to fortify Calcutta or to prepare it in any way to defend against the predictable British return. Thus, on December 14, 1756, a British force from Madras commanded by Robert Clive, the hero of the Second Carnatic War, entered the Hughli and easily retook Calcutta on January 2, 1757.

The question for Clive and the British was what to do next. The nawab had returned upriver to his capital at Murshidabad. Initially, Clive sought a negotiated settlement in the Treaty of Alingar (February 9, 1757): Peace was to be restored between the nawab and the company, and the British were to enjoy their former trading privileges. Whether Clive entered into this agreement in good faith is an open question. Shortly afterward, however, he seems to have scented treachery, partly on account of the nawab's French connections. The nawab indeed favored the French; in Europe, the Seven Years' War had set the British and French in India on a collision course, and

1750's

French reinforcements were expected daily in the Bay of Bengal. In March of 1757, Clive made a preemptive strike on French Chandernagore, in violation of the nawab's authority.

Clive now resolved to replace Sirāj al-Dawlā with someone more tractable. The nawab had no lack of enemies, including Mir Jaʿfar, brother-in-law of the former nawab, Alivardi Khan. On June 10, 1757, Mir Jaʿfar entered into a secret agreement with the British East India Company: In return for being made nawab, he agreed to confirm all the privileges granted to the company by the Treaty of Alinagar, to enter a defensive and offensive alliance with the company, to exclude the French from Bengal, and to pay £1 million to the company in compensation for the sack of Calcutta and another £500,000 to the city's European residents. Privately, moreover, Mir Jaʿfar agreed to pay very substantial sums to members of the Calcutta Council and to the British military currently in Bengal, on the assumption that, once he had become nawab, he would enjoy access to the vast treasures allegedly accumulated by Alivardi Khan.

Once this secret agreement was in place, war would decide the issue. On June 13, 1757, Clive set out for Murshidabad. His force consisted of around three thousand men. Of these, twenty-two hundred were *sepoys* (Indian troops commanded by European officers) and *topasses* (Eurasian Christian troops of partly Portuguese descent). The *sepoys* had come with Clive from the south, veterans of his Carnatic campaigns. In addition, he had eight hundred European infantry and artillerymen.

Murshidabad was just over 150 miles from Calcutta. At Plassey (Palasi), more than 90 miles upriver, Clive found the nawab and his army encamped, totaling perhaps fifty thousand men. Clive reached Plassey on the night of June 22 and prepared for battle at sunrise. The British forces were drawn up in a straight line, with their left flank protected by the Hughli River and their rear by a mango grove, which offered some protection. Immediately facing them were Sirāj al-Dawlā's best troops, a small corps of French mercenaries. Behind the French and to the east, stretching in an arc from north to southwest, were the vast majority of the nawab's troops, capa-

Bengali mobile cannon are pictured being pulled by oxen at the Battle of Plassey. (Francis R. Niglutsch)

ble of enveloping the right end of the British line, although this section consisted of the troops of the traitor Mir Ja'far.

The conflict began around 8:00 A.M. on June 23 with a vigorous exchange of cannon fire. Around noon, however, the fighting was slowed by a heavy downpour of rain, which would have been disastrous for the British, had they failed to keep their powder dry. When the rain had abated, the nawab's troops launched an unsuccessful attack, after which they fell back in disarray to their encampment, where a faction within his forces counseled the nawab's retreat. Meanwhile, Mir Ja'far had withdrawn his own forces from the fray and was awaiting the outcome of the battle.

The British then advanced against the nawab's camp, encountering little resistance. The nawab's forces were soon in full flight. The engagement had lasted less than eight hours. British casualties have been estimated at around twenty-eight killed and fifty wounded; the nawab lost perhaps five hundred men. Sirāj al-Dawlā fled toward Bihar, hoping to rally more loyal supporters, but he fell in with one of Mir Ja'far's men, who handed him over to Mir Ja'far's son, Miran. Miran ordered Mir Ja'far's execution on July 2, 1757.

Meanwhile, on June 29, 1757, Clive installed Mir Ja'far in Murshidabad as the new nawab of Bengal, Bihar, and Orissa. Clive thus initiated what has been called "the revolution in Bengal," for which he was well rewarded: He received £234,000 in a lump sum and an annual payment of £30,000. The latter sum constituted the nawab's quitrent for the districts known as the Twenty-Four Parganas, which he had ceded to the British East India Company.

In the months that followed Mir Ja'far's accession, Clive proceeded to mediate, cajole, and command: He sent his second-in-command, Colonel Francis Forde, to occupy the northern Circars, which had been assigned by the Nizam of Hyderabad to the French in 1753. Forde was then instructed to defeat the Dutch in Chinsura. Clive was eager to return to England, however, and he made the return journey in 1760, arriving on July 9. In London, he was made Baron Clive of Plassey in the peerage of Ireland, and he bought in County Clare the estate of Ballykilty, which he renamed Plassey.

Soon after Clive's departure from Bengal, the Calcutta Council decided it had had enough of Mir Ja'far. He had proved increasingly inept, and worse, the state of the Murshidabad treasury did not allow him to fulfill the reckless financial promises he had made to obtain his title. Before the year was up, he was replaced by his son-in-law, Mir Kasim, who quickly fell out in turn with the British, with whom he came to blows. After several minor skirmishes and one massacre of British prisoners in Patna (October, 1763), Mir Kasim entered Awadh and allied himself with the powerful nawab-vizier, Shuja al-Dawlā, and the Mughal emperor Shāh Alam, then a fugitive from his capital of Delhi. The alliance did him no good, however, as the forces of all three men were crushed by the company's troops under the command of Eyre Coote, at Buxar (Baksar), Bihar, on October 22, 1764. The Battle of Buxar confirmed British military dominance in India and accelerated the train of events begun at Plassey.

In London, the company's directors, appalled by news from Bengal of incompetence, corruption, and violence, sent Clive back as governor of Bengal and commander in chief. He reached India on May 3, 1765, and remained until February, 1767, vigorously cleaning the Augean stable and acquiring from Emperor Shāh Alam the *diwani* (right to collect imperial revenue) of Bengal, Bihar, and Orissa, thereby formally integrating the British East India Company into the Mughal imperial bureaucracy as an officeholder in the North Indian state system.

SIGNIFICANCE

Historians are too quick to designate past battles as decisive, meaning that they changed history, which often they did not. Plassey was no clash of titans, but it indubitably changed history. Clive's victory led to the British East India Company's takeover of Bengal, which in turn led to the spread of the British Raj over India, which lasted until the nation achieved independence in 1947. These developments had incalculable consequences for the institutional and cultural evolution of modern India.

Clive, learning from the French example, demonstrated conclusively that European-trained and -officered troops, whether themselves European or Indian, could almost invariably overcome the ill-disciplined rabbles that constituted most traditional indigenous forces in India. A brilliant leader of men, he was the first of the so-called sepoy-generals, whose later ranks included Stringer Lawrence, Sir Eyre Coote, and Arthur Wellesley (later the first duke of Wellington), and who made possible British hegemony in Asia.

The Seven Years' War has often been said to have won Great Britain the status of a world power. If so, it was the Battle of Plassey, coupled with James Wolfe's victory at Quebec and Edward Hawke's defeat of the French fleet at Quiberon Bay, that made this rise in status possible.

—*Gavin R. G. Hambly*

FURTHER READING

Davies, Marvyn A. *Clive of Plassey*. New York: Charles Scribner's Sons, 1939. A fine biography.

Didwell, Henry. *Dupleix and Clive*. London: Methuen, 1920. Detailed and very complete.

Gupta, Brijen K. *Sirajuddaullah and the East India Company*. Leiden, the Netherlands: Brill, 1966. A fine attempt to rehabilitate the nawab.

Harvey, Robert. *Clive: The Life and Death of a British Emperor*. New York: St. Martin's Press, 2000. A biography of Clive, including plates, maps, bibliography, and index.

Lawford, James, P. *Britain's Army in India, from Its Origins to the Conquest of Bengal*. London: George Allen & Unwin, 1978. Excellent on military background.

Majumdar, R. D., et al. *An Advanced History of India*. London: Macmillan, 1950. Pages 654 to 675 provide a judicious account of Indian history.

SEE ALSO: 1746-1754: Carnatic Wars; May 28, 1754-Feb. 10, 1763: French and Indian War; Jan., 1756-Feb. 15, 1763: Seven Years' War; Feb. 10, 1763: Peace of Paris; Aug., 1767-May, 1799: Anglo-Mysore Wars; Dec., 1774-Feb. 24, 1783: First Marāthā War.

RELATED ARTICLES in *Great Lives from History: The Eighteenth Century, 1701-1800*: Robert Clive; Joseph-François Dupleix; William Pitt the Elder; James Wolfe.

November 5, 1757
BATTLE OF ROSSBACH

Confronting an advancing allied army of French, German, and Austrian troops that was more than twice the size of his own, Frederick the Great wheeled his soldiers into a position from which they literally destroyed the allied forces. The defeat ended France's advance in the Seven Years' War.

LOCALE: Near Rossbach, Saxony-Anhalt (now in Germany)

CATEGORY: Wars, uprisings, and civil unrest

KEY FIGURES

Frederick the Great (1712-1786), king of Prussia, r. 1740-1786

Prince de Soubise (Charles de Rohan; 1715-1787), French field marshal

Prince von Sachsen-Hildburghausen (Joseph Friedrich Hollandinus; 1702-1787), Austrian field marshal

Friedrich Wilhelm von Seydlitz (1721-1773), Prussian cavalry commander

SUMMARY OF EVENT

On May 6, 1757, in one of the early Prussian gambits of the Seven Years' War, King Frederick the Great of Prussia routed the Austrian army at Prague and besieged the city. Austrian field marshal Leopold Joseph Daun gathered a ragtag army and went to the city's aid, defeating the Prussians at Kolin. This defeat forced Frederick to retreat from Prague and to leave Bohemia. Thanks to Frederick's impertinent invasion, moreover, he had made enemies of Austria and much of the Holy Roman Empire, as well as Sweden, Russia, and France. Each nation mobilized to march on Prussia in retaliation.

In mid-July a French army of more than 100,000 men thrust eastward against Hanover, the homeland of the kings of England and Frederick's only considerable ally. By September, this huge force had defeated the British-Hanoverian army and overrun the state. A second French army under the command of the prince de Soubise was gathered to join with the *Reichsarmee*, a coalition force of imperial infantry and cavalry from southern and central German states. Together, these forces were to march against Frederick himself, perhaps catching him in a pincer between themselves and the Austrians. In any case, they were assigned the task of driving the Prussians from Saxony and liberating that German state. The French and the *Reichsarmee*, under the high command of the Austrian prince von Sachsen-Hildburghausen, were to rendezvous at Erfurt, creating a force of perhaps forty-five thousand men.

To meet the impending threat of the invading French and imperial forces, Frederick divided his army of some sixty-five thousand men: He left forty-four thousand to the south to screen any Austrian movement against him and took the remainder, perhaps twenty-five thousand, north to confront the allied army. Frederick had command of a finely honed fighting machine whose officers knew their leader well and whose men, despite the setback in Bohemia, trusted them all. His cavalry was well drilled and equipped and could boast an especially competent commander in the young Friedrich Wilhelm von

Friedrich Wilhelm von Seydlitz leads the decisive cavalry charge at the Battle of Rossbach. (R. S. Peale and J. A. Hill)

Seydlitz. Prussian artillery had become very mobile in comparison with that of other continental powers, and thus it could be brought to bear very quickly and efficiently on the battlefield.

The forces led by Sachsen-Hildburghausen and Soubise suffered from virtually every problem that could plague a coalition army. The Austrian field marshal labeled the French commander an "ignoramus" in matters military, while the critic himself had never commanded a victorious army. The Germans in the *Reichsarmee* varied in quality from superb to dreadful and from staunchly Catholic to deeply Reformed. Many Protestant soldiers sympathized with the Lutheran Prussians and resented having to fight for the Catholic Holy Roman Empire. Pay had been low and irregular, food and other vital supplies were ill provided, and time and again troops had to be admonished against ravaging the countryside. Many of the men were raw recruits who had never fired a shot in anger. Their commanders had to count on their numerical superiority—roughly two to one—to compensate for the uneven quality and poor conditions of the allied army.

In early September, a skirmish between von Seydlitz and the Austrian cavalry announced the Prussians' arrival in the vicinity of Erfurt. The allies changed plans and used Eisenach, about thirty miles due west, as their new staging point. Frederick himself arrived in Gotha on September 15, while the allies flooded into Eisenach during the week following. Defeats in East Prussia and Pomerania forced Frederick to send vital detachments northward, leaving him with barely eleven thousand effective troops. On September 18, he heard of the Hanoverian collapse and surrender and quickly decided to abandon Gotha. Seydlitz's cavalry screened the retreat and made a mockery of the advance detachments of the allied forces who occupied the city.

A week later, Frederick moved farther eastward from Erfurt, seeking to draw the allies out, but the sluggish arrival of twelve thousand French reinforcements hampered any allied pursuit. Frederick decided that the allies were camping for the winter and led his forces out of Saxony toward Brandenburg. Sachsen-Hildburghausen recognized the opportunity to recapture Saxony for Maria Theresa and pressed forward to take Erfurt on October 17. Prussian garrisons studded Saxony, but the Austrian commander believed he could mop them up piecemeal. Leipzig proved the great obstacle, however. By October 21, Frederick had heard of the German advance, turned his reinforced army around, and came to Leipzig's defense, entering the city on October 26. Meanwhile, Soubise demanded a halt to any movement, expecting to have his army recalled to France.

Frederick used the allied indecision to his advantage, thrusting out of Leipzig toward his enemies, forcing them westward across the Saale River. Though the retreating allies burned the bridges, Frederick managed to make separate crossings at Halle, Merseburg, and Weissenfels on November 3. He quickly reconsolidated his forces near Rossbach before the allies could pounce on any of the three individual corps. Learning of his move, the allies dug in, expecting a rapid Prussian attack. This surprised Frederick, who left his men encamped along a four-mile line between the villages of Rossbach and Bedra, several miles from the new allied lines. As dawn broke on the day of battle, Soubise commanded some thirty thousand French soldiers and Sachsen-Hildburghausen close to fifteen thousand Germans and Austrians. Frederick had some twenty-two thousand Prussian troops and eighteen heavy artillery pieces to the allies' forty-five.

On November 5, the allies decided very slowly to form up in columns in order to advance on the Prussian left flank, while allied cavalry units effectively froze the Prussians' right flank. The Prussians were equally slow to recognize the movements of the swift allied cavalry screen, which preceded four huge columns of infantry. Well-placed Prussian cannon, however, opened fire on the allied squadrons, and Seydlitz quickly mobilized his own cavalry, swept around in front of the advancing allies, and charged headlong into the columns of allied horsemen. The allied cavalry was shattered, and even more important, Frederick had time to wheel his army down behind his cavalry to confront the infantry columns. He was able to create but a single line, which, with the cavalry forming his left flank, stretched for about five miles.

The allies were still crammed in column formation, offering a front of only three hundred yards. The mobile Prussian artillery quickly repositioned itself directly in front of the advancing columns at the center of the Prussian line. With no opportunity or orders to shift from column to line, the allied soldiers could do little more than march into the meat grinder that Frederick had so rapidly deployed. The result was slaughter. The Prussians poured fire into the hapless allies from three sides, while the victorious cavalry ran down fleeing men with impunity. While some allied units fought well, most broke up, and their men fled for their lives as the Prussians advanced against the disintegrating mass with guns blazing at will. Only nightfall preserved the surviving allied troops from the dragoon's sword or the sharpshooter's ball.

Frederick pursued the broken armies to Erfurt to ensure that they did not recover. The allies lost perhaps ten thousand men, including an estimated three thousand dead and wounded after the first hour and a half of fighting. Frederick counted 549 casualties, including one prisoner.

SIGNIFICANCE

The French would never march as far east again in the Seven Years' War, and they were effectively neutralized by their horrendous defeat at Rossbach. The Austrians thus lost a key ally, and they were beaten again by Frederick himself at Leuthen (December 5), where he commanded the army he had left behind three months earlier. Austria never recovered from the blows at Rossbach and Leuthen, and in the end it had to make peace with the belligerent Prussian king.

The victory at Rossbach was a key factor in Prussian success as the war dragged on. It not only made up for the earlier defeats by the Austrians but also seemed to confirm the glory of the Prussian army on the battlefield. The German allies who had been let down by the French and the Austrians would never again be as keen to join with either as allies against the Prussian masters of war. The battle may have even given impetus to German nationalistic feeling. By the same token, the military leaders of France, whose wits labeled the defeat the "amusing battle," recognized the need for serious military reform. In some ways, the reforms spurred by the Battle of Rossbach led directly to the French battlefield successes of the revolutionary and Napoleonic periods.

—*Joseph P. Byrne*

FURTHER READING

Duffy, Christopher. *The Army of Frederick the Great*. 2d ed. Chicago: Emperor's Press, 1996. A very useful study of how Frederick forged the army that performed so well at Rossbach.

_____. *Prussia's Glory: Rossbach and Leuthen, 1757.* Chicago: Emperor's Press, 2003. By far the most detailed treatment of the Battle of Rossbach in English. Well illustrated, with especially clear maps.

Kennett, L. *The French Armies in the Seven Years' War.* Durham, N.C.: Duke University Press, 1967. A significant study of the reasons behind the weaknesses of French arms.

SEE ALSO: May 31, 1740: Accession of Frederick the Great; Oct. 20, 1740: Maria Theresa Succeeds to the Austrian Throne; Dec. 16, 1740-Nov. 7, 1748: War of the Austrian Succession; May 28, 1754-Feb. 10, 1763: French and Indian War; Jan., 1756-Feb. 15, 1763: Seven Years' War; June 23, 1757: Battle of Plassey; Feb. 10, 1763: Peace of Paris; Apr. 20, 1792-Oct., 1797: Early Wars of the French Revolution; Mar., 1796-Oct. 17, 1797: Napoleon's Italian Campaigns; Apr. 12, 1798-Sept. 2, 1801: Napoleon's Egyptian Campaign.

RELATED ARTICLES in *Great Lives from History: The Eighteenth Century, 1701-1800*: Étienne François de Choiseul; Frederick the Great; Wenzel Anton von Kaunitz; Louis XV; Maria Theresa.

June 8-July 27, 1758
SIEGE OF LOUISBOURG

Nearly fifteen thousand British soldiers under Major General Jeffrey Amherst encircled and bombarded the French Canadian fortress of Louisbourg, gaining victory over the French after seven weeks. Britain's success opened up the St. Lawrence River and exposed Quebec, the center of French power in North America, to subsequent British attacks, ultimately resulting in the conquest of Canada.

LOCALE: Louisbourg, New France (now on Cape Breton Island, Nova Scotia, Canada)

CATEGORIES: Wars, uprisings, and civil unrest; expansion and land acquisition; colonization

KEY FIGURES
Lord Amherst (Jeffrey Amherst; 1717-1797), British military commander
Augustin de Boschenry de Drucour (1703-1762), French governor of Louisbourg and garrison commander
James Wolfe (1727-1759), British brigadier general
Edward Boscawen (1711-1761), British vice admiral
William Pitt the Elder (1708-1778), prime minister of Great Britain, 1757-1761, 1766-1768

SUMMARY OF EVENT
Throughout the seventeenth and eighteenth centuries, Britain and France fought a number of wars both in Europe and in their respective colonies. Canada, also known as New France, provided natural resources and a strategic location from which France could launch raids and attacks on land and sea against Britain's American colonies. In 1713, following the War of the Spanish Succession, France decided to establish an ice-free port in the entrance to the Gulf of St. Lawrence—the gateway for maritime trade with Canada. Cape Breton Island offered an ideal location, because a port there would both shield Canada and provide a base for privateers and naval squadrons. Of course, this port, named Louisbourg in honor of the king, was also likely to be a major British target.

Louisbourg was to be protected by a complex fortress featuring the "star-fort" design made famous by the French siege specialist, Sebastien Le Preste de Vauban. Vauban's fortresses depended on heavy artillery mounted atop fortified positions known as bastions. Bastions were placed so that fire from each covered the approaches to the next. Thus any attack on one bastion would be exposed to murderous cross fire from neighboring positions. In a siege on such a fortress, the role of infantry would be secondary to the fire of the artillery.

Though the French referred to the fortress as "the Gibraltar of the North," Louisbourg suffered from many weaknesses. While the deep-water port was sheltered and ice-free, the harsh climate and the long winters created a sense of isolation that corroded the garrison's morale. The construction of Louisbourg was particularly expensive. Locally quarried stone was inadequate, so proper stone was shipped in from France, but unscrupulous bureaucrats and contractors defrauded the government, substituting shoddy materials and reselling the imported stone elsewhere. The sand and seawater mix used in the mortar of the walls did not set consistently. Thus, when cannon were fired from some of the bastions, recoil

1750's

403

In a contemporary drawing, British ships enter Gabarus Bay at Louisbourg, a French stronghold, marking the first days of seven weeks of fighting. Great Britain's eventual victory and seizure of the strategic fortress marked the beginning of Britain's conquest and control of Canada. (Library of Congress)

undermined the walls below. An even more significant problem was topography. The town and fortress were too small to extend to hills that overlooked the city, so during a siege, an opponent could mount guns on these hills and fire directly into the port.

Louisbourg-based privateers posed a threat to England's colonial commerce. During King George's War, known in Europe as the War of the Austrian Succession, New England militia seized Louisbourg, but it was returned to France by the Treaty of Aix-la-Chapelle (1748), which ended that war. To challenge French shipping and protect the northern waters, the British in 1749 built a similar port on the east coast of Nova Scotia called Halifax. On the western side of Nova Scotia lived some nine thousand French settlers called Acadians. British colonial officials feared disloyalty among these Acadians, and in 1755 British troops deported the Acadians to scattered locations among the Thirteen Colonies. Many families were separated, homes and property were destroyed, and a legacy of bitterness was created. Those Acadians who avoided deportation soon began guerrilla operations against the British.

When the French and Indian War began in 1754, British strategists again planned to seize Louisbourg. The greatest strategic problem faced by the British in the operation was that they had to raise the necessary forces and supplies in Britain and the colonies and then transport them to New France. Thus, any British force would face the potential hazards of weather and French naval patrols before it could even reach Louisbourg. In 1756 and 1757, British expeditions were aborted, because large French squadrons sailed to Louisbourg before the British transports left Halifax. These French warships made impossible any British attempt to sail a large fleet of slow, vulnerable transports loaded with men, guns, and supplies. In 1758, however, an energetic new prime minister, William Pitt the Elder, sped preparations for the siege forces and ordered a more successful interdiction campaign by the Royal Navy to isolate Louisbourg. The success of the campaign was abetted by the willingness of the Royal Navy's Vice Admiral Edward Boscawen to work amicably with the operation's overall commander, Major General Lord Amherst.

In 1758, only one French squadron was able to evade

the Royal Navy and reach Louisbourg. This squadron consisted of 6 ships-of-the-line and 4 frigates, some of which had been partially stripped of guns and crews to accommodate larger cargoes. By comparison, the 127 British transports in Lord Amherst's assault sailed from Halifax under the protection of Boscawen's squadron of 23 ships-of-the-line, 18 frigates, and some lighter vessels. The French ships were too greatly outnumbered to be able to sortie against the transports. During the siege, the bulk of these crews and their cannon would be used to augment the garrison—just as Boscawen would lend some of his gun crews and heavy long-range ordnance to Amherst.

The siege lasted seven weeks and began with a British landing in Gabarus Bay on June 8, 1758. As this was the obvious place for a landing, the French had constructed obstacles and stationed troops above the shore. French fire inflicted many casualties and nearly stopped the landing, but near the west end of the bay, grenadiers and light infantry under the command of Amherst's energetic, able, and young subordinate, Brigadier General James Wolfe, managed to get ashore and outflank the defenders so that they withdrew back to the city. The hasty nature of this retreat effectively surrendered the initiative to the British.

During the following two weeks, Wolfe's aggressively led forces seized two critical positions, Lighthouse Point—which controlled access to the harbor—and Green Hill—which overlooked the city. Artillery was soon hauled to these positions, and a bombardment began. Using traditional siege techniques, the British began to dig trenches called "saps" toward the city. At intervals, these saps gave way to covered emplacements from which artillery could batter the bastions from increasingly shorter ranges. Heavy British fire soon began to destroy French guns, while the fort's structural weaknesses enhanced the effectiveness of the bombardment.

The French efforts to break the siege proved ineffective. The garrison commander, Chevalier Augustin de Boschenry de Drucour, had stationed Acadian guerrillas in the area in the hopes that they would disrupt the British camps and siege lines, but colonial rangers and British light infantry kept the Acadians at bay. French sallies, especially a poorly organized attack on the night of July 9, failed to capture or destroy British positions. The French squadron was too small to challenge Boscawen's fleet, and British guns emplaced on Lighthouse Point effectively closed the harbor. The town was too small to store extensive supplies, so by the end of July, ammunition

and food stores were low, while the British supplies afforded extensive barrages. By July 26, British fire had destroyed forty of the fortress's fifty-two guns and blasted a breach in one of the major bastions. When on July 26 British sailors launched a bold night attack that destroyed two French warships, the garrison's morale reached its nadir.

Drucour requested terms for surrender. Terms typical for the time were "the honors of war," which allowed a garrison to surrender but keep its weapons after promising to not fight again for a specified time. Such an arrangement would also allow the town's populace to remain in place. Amherst, however, demanded full surrender. On July 27, Drucour capitulated. In August, Amherst ordered that the French garrison and civilians be shipped back to France. When the war ended, British engineers blew apart the fortifications and razed the city so that Louisbourg would never again threaten Britain's American colonies.

SIGNIFICANCE

The British victory at Louisbourg was pivotal. Although the long siege made an attack on Quebec the same year impracticable, British-occupied Louisbourg both cut off French reinforcements to Canada and provided a springboard for the French and Indian War campaigns of 1759. Success at Louisbourg established Lord Amherst and his aggressive subordinate James Wolfe as the men who would lead Britain to conquer Canada. Britain's close coordination between its naval and land forces was an achievement that the French were unable to emulate, and without it, France's colonial holdings proved indefensible. Finally, Amherst's decision to deport both the garrison and the town's civilians made it clear that this was a war of conquest, not of negotiation.

—*Kevin B. Reid*

FURTHER READING

Anderson, Fred. *Crucible of War: The Seven Years' War and the Fate of the Empire in British North America, 1754-1766.* New York: Alfred A Knopf, 2001. Perhaps the best single-volume history of the French and Indian War; indispensable for understanding the strategies and the significance of the siege.

Chartrand, René. *Louisbourg, 1758: Wolfe's First Siege.* Oxford, England: Osprey, 2000. An excellent study of the siege, based on a number of firsthand accounts from the daily notes of some of the major participants. Features some fascinating photos taken from the reconstructed fortress, which is now a Canadian National Park.

1750's

Fowler, William M., Jr. *Empires at War: The French and Indian War and the Struggle for North America, 1754-1763.* New York: Walker, 2005. Narrative account of the war, describing its causes, the incident that touched off the conflict in 1754, and the battles. Places the war in a wider European context.

McLennan, John Stewart. *Louisbourg: From Its Foundation to Its Fall, 1713-1758.* 1918. Reprint. Halifax, N.S.: Book Room, 1979. This reprint of the 1918 edition provides the most comprehensive study of the construction of the fortress and the siege.

SEE ALSO: 1713: Founding of Louisbourg; Dec. 16, 1740-Nov. 7, 1748: War of the Austrian Succession; Oct. 18, 1748: Treaty of Aix-la-Chapelle; May 28, 1754-Feb. 10, 1763: French and Indian War; July, 1755-Aug., 1758: Acadians Are Expelled from Canada; Jan., 1756-Feb. 15, 1763: Seven Years' War; 1783: Loyalists Migrate to Nova Scotia; 1791: Canada's Constitutional Act.

RELATED ARTICLES in *Great Lives from History: The Eighteenth Century, 1701-1800*: Lord Amherst; William Pitt the Elder; James Wolfe.

July 27, 1758
HELVÉTIUS PUBLISHES *DE L'ESPRIT*

A major work in the field of materialist ethics and bestseller of the clandestine book trade in prerevolutionary France, De l'esprit *immediately came under attack by those in church and government who opposed Enlightenment philosophies. The book's author, Claude-Adrien Helvétius, declared self-interest to be the motivating force behind all human actions.*

LOCALE: Paris, France
CATEGORY: Philosophy

KEY FIGURES
Claude-Adrien Helvétius (1715-1771), French philosopher
Denis Diderot (1713-1784), French philosopher and encyclopedist
Chrétien-Guillaume de Lamoignon de Malesherbes (1721-1794), French minister of state and chief censor of the press, 1750-1763
Jean-Pierre Tercier (1704-1767), secretary at the French Ministry of Foreign Affairs and royal censor
Laurent Durand (c. 1712-1763), Parisian publisher of the first edition of *De l'esprit*

SUMMARY OF EVENT
In France during the Enlightenment, freedom of the press was vigorously curtailed. Authors and publishers of controversial literature worked under the constant menace of imprisonment and execution. Many of the contributing writers of Denis Diderot's *Encyclopédie: Ou, Dictionnaire raisonné des sciences, des arts, et des métiers* (1751-1772; partial translation *Selected Essays from the Encyclopedy,* 1772; complete translation *Encyclopedia,*

1965), including its editor in chief, had at some point been imprisoned, seen their books burned, or been forced into exile. In order to avoid censorship, authors published their most defiant works anonymously abroad, while publishers of condemned literature used deceptive imprints and false addresses to confound prosecutors. It therefore came as a surprise to many that Claude-Adrien Helvétius chose to publish one of the century's most controversial works of materialist philosophy in France rather than abroad.

Helvétius reportedly began work on *De l'esprit* (1758; *De l'Esprit: Or, Essays on the Mind and Its Several Faculties,* 1759) as early as 1737, but it was not until some twenty years later, probably during the spring of 1757, that a first complete draft was ready for outside appraisal. Despite the inherent difficulties and dangers of the project, friends close to Helvétius convinced him that his work should be published in France, and arrangements were made for him to discuss having it approved for publication by Jean-Pierre Tercier, an accommodating royal censor employed at the French Ministry of Foreign Affairs. Tercier, who seems to have read only portions of the text, relied mainly on the author's verbal declaration of conformity when he issued final approval on March 27, 1758.

Based on Tercier's report, a royal privilege was granted to Helvétius on March 12, 1758. By late June, the book's publisher, Laurent Durand, was about to offer it to the public when the French minister in charge of censorship, Chrétien-Guillaume de Lamoignon de Malesherbes, was alerted by a concerned inspector of the book trade and imposed a delay upon publication pending an inquest. After a second, anonymous appraisal of the work, substantive changes were required, but publication was allowed to resume.

A revised first edition of *De l'esprit* went on sale July 27, 1758, and immediately came under attack from prominent members of the Church and the government. About two weeks later, the book's royal privilege was revoked. Critics were all the more alarmed by implications that the book had received its imprimatur from duly appointed censors. They took this imprimatur as a sign that government officials had become lax or perhaps even secretly supported Enlightenment philosophers in their defiance of Church doctrine.

The author's recantations, two of which were published in September, did little to assuage his most vocal critics and in fact contributed to the public's already intense curiosity. Awash in scandal, *De l'esprit* became a bestseller. Even as religious and civil authorities hastened to proscribe its content, publishers in France, Holland, Belgium, England, and Germany brought out new editions to satisfy intense public demand. By 1760, thirteen separate editions of the work had been released in French, as well as complete translations in English and German. An Italian translation appeared only after the French Revolution, between 1797 and 1799.

De l'esprit is a work of political and moral philosophy divided into four essays and founded in radical sensationalism and utilitarian ethics. In the first essay, Helvétius summarily rejects the notion of innate ideas, defining mind as both the faculty of thought and the ability to perceive and retain physical sensations. Since knowledge is acquired through experience alone, metaphysical constructs such as matter, space, or the infinite are impossible to know. Self-love is assigned as the driving force behind all human actions, and liberty is defined as the ability to pursue one's self-interest.

In the second essay, Helvétius introduces additional philosophical concepts while exposing the inadequacies of conservative Christian asceticism and the injustices of present and past political regimes. In particular, he identifies the good of the greater number as a fundamental principle of any just society. If, as he maintains, all human actions are motivated by the pursuit of pleasure and the avoidance of pain, the legislator's principal objective must then lie in reconciling personal interests with the general interest. Helvétius asserts that, rather than combating human passion as conservative Christian moralists constantly recommend, the enlightened legislator should enact laws capable of channeling humanity's positive energies toward the good of all.

In the third essay, Helvétius proceeds to examine the faculties of the mind, the importance of human passions as a driving force behind genius, various forms of human passion and their effects on a nation's prosperity. He concludes that all individuals, given the proper circumstances and a proper education, are capable of genius. In the fourth and final essay, he discusses various attributes or qualities of the mind—imagination, wit, the ability to write with elegance, common sense, opinion, the art of good conduct—before concluding with a chapter on the importance of education as a tool of enlightenment.

In isolated comments dispersed throughout essays two, three, and four, Helvétius challenged the existence of miracles, denounced the vanity of theological disputes, and condemned an assortment of social inequities, ranging from the poverty and ignorance of the French peasantry to the evils of the slave trade. He defended his fellow Enlightenment philosophers against their enemies, inveighing against the reactionary elements in the Church and the French government who sought to silence them. He associated these reactionary elements with the superstitions of the past and of apparently exotic locales, labeling them fakirs, Brahmins, priests, magicians, and despotic viziers.

Helvétius opposed the autocratic power of monarchs; praised the stability of governments that divided power between the people, the aristocracy, and kings; and defended the freedom of speech. Like his friend Montesquieu, Helvétius recognized in civic virtue a fundamental principle of any stable democracy, yet he defined the term in a revolutionary manner. Rather than educate citizens on the "virtues" of self-sacrifice, he argued, legislators must recognize that the seeds and the strength of virtue lie in the pursuit of self-interest.

SIGNIFICANCE

De l'esprit was a profoundly revolutionary work of materialist philosophy. Those in the Church and the government who condemned the work charged that it violated divine and human laws, denied the existence of human liberty, and sought the destruction of traditional moral doctrine—in sum, that it was a dangerous and immoral book. The scandal occasioned by its officially approved publication in 1758 not only led to the book's prohibition but also provided its enemies with a convenient pretext for a vigorous public campaign against the proliferation of Enlightenment ideas in French society.

Diderot's *Encyclopedia*, temporarily banned from publication in March, 1759, was one of several works condemned by the same reactionary forces Helvétius had inadvertently unleashed. However, these partial victories obtained by the opponents of the Enlightenment were largely temporary. Work on the *Encyclopedia* was allowed to continue, and the ban placed on *De l'esprit*, although it remained in effect, failed to stem the author's popularity in a flourishing clandestine book trade. Surviving records suggest that Helvétius was one of the top ten bestselling authors of condemned literature in prerevolutionary France. His sober analysis of human conduct greatly influenced Cesare Beccaria's thoughts on the reform of criminal justice and provided a theoretical foundation for the elaboration of utilitarian ethics in the works of Jeremy Bentham and John Stuart Mill. In modern educational theory, namely in the debate over nature versus nurture, his assumption that individuals are born with equal mental abilities continues to promote lively discussion.

—Jan Pendergrass

FURTHER READING

Cumming, Ian. *Helvetius: His Life and Place in the History of Educational Thought.* New York: Routledge, 1955. A survey of Helvétius's life and works, including discussion of major philosophical precedents.

Horowitz, Iriving Louis. *Claude Helvetius: Philosopher of Democracy and Enlightenment.* New York: Pain-Whitman, 1954. A detailed examination of Helvétius in historical perspective.

Richards, Earl Jeffrey. "The Axiomatization of National Differences and National Character in the European Enlightenment: Montesquieu, Hume, d'Alembert, Helvetius, and Kant." In *Komparatistik und Europaforschung: Perspektiven vergleichender Literatur und Kulturwissenschaft,* edited by Hugo Dyserinck and Karl Ulrich Syndram. Bonn, Germany: Bouvier Verlag, 1992. Discusses Helvétius's views on the mutability of national character and climate, opposing them to those of other major Enlightenment philosophers.

Smith, David. *Bibliography of the Writings of Helvetius.* Ferney-Voltaire, France: Centre International d'Étude du XVIIIe Siècle, 2001. Includes general discussion of *De l'esprit* and descriptions of all known editions and translations from 1758 to 1999.

_____. *Helvetius: A Study in Persecution.* Oxford, England: Clarendon Press, 1965. Essential reading focused on the controversy generated by *De l'esprit.*

Wootton, David. "Helvetius: From Radical Enlightenment to Revolution." *Political Theory* 28 (2000): 307-336. Rejects the notion that Helvétius was a "disciple of Montesquieu." Sees him as a radical theorist and precursor to the French Revolution.

SEE ALSO: 1721-1750: Early Enlightenment in France; 1726-1729: Voltaire Advances Enlightenment Thought in Europe; 1748: Montesquieu Publishes *The Spirit of the Laws*; 1751-1772: Diderot Publishes the *Encyclopedia*; 1754: Condillac Defends Sensationalist Theory; Jan., 1759: Voltaire Satirizes Optimism in *Candide*; Apr., 1762: Rousseau Publishes *The Social Contract*; July, 1764: Voltaire Publishes *A Philosophical Dictionary for the Pocket*; 1770: Publication of Holbach's *The System of Nature*; 1782-1798: Publication of Rousseau's *Confessions.*

RELATED ARTICLES in *Great Lives from History: The Eighteenth Century, 1701-1800*: Cesare Beccaria; Jeremy Bentham; Étienne Bonnot de Condillac; Denis Diderot; Claude-Adrien Helvétius; Montesquieu; Voltaire.

1759
AEPINUS PUBLISHES *ESSAY ON THE THEORY OF ELECTRICITY AND MAGNETISM*

Inspired by Sir Isaac Newton's mathematical explanation of gravitational force, Aepinus's Essay on the Theory of Electricity and Magnetism *provided the first systematic, mathematical analysis of the forces of electricity and magnetism.*

LOCALE: St. Petersburg, Russia
CATEGORIES: Physics; science and technology

KEY FIGURES
Franz Maria Ulrich Theodor Hoch Aepinus (1724-1802), German natural philosopher
Sir Isaac Newton (1642-1727), English natural philosopher and mathematician
Benjamin Franklin (1706-1790), American printer, statesman, and scientist
Leonhard Euler (1707-1783), Swiss mathematician and Aepinus's patron in Berlin

SUMMARY OF EVENT
In addition to being called the "Age of Reason," the eighteenth century Enlightenment is often called the "Age of Newton" because of the immense influence Sir Isaac Newton's ideas had not only on science but also on intellectual and cultural history. Following Newton's great success in explaining the fundamental laws of the universe in his *Philosophiae naturalis principia mathematica* (1687; *The Mathematical Principles of Natural Philosophy*, 1729; best known as the *Principia*), other scientists tried to apply his synthetic, mathematical approach to chemistry and, in the case of Franz Maria Ulrich Theodor Hoch Aepinus, to electricity and magnetism.

Benjamin Franklin, who also was influenced by Newton, made experimental and theoretical contributions to the study of electricity that had a transformative effect on Aepinus. Franklin believed that he could explain electrical phenomena through the properties and actions of a subtle electrical fluid that could exist in material bodies either in surplus or in deficiency. Franklin used the mathematical terms "positive" (or "plus") for objects with more than the normal amount of this electrical fluid and "negative" (or "minus") for objects with less than the normal amount. Implied in Franklin's analysis is the idea that electricity is a measurable quantity that can be neither created nor destroyed but can be moved from object to object. This idea was later generalized as the principle of the conservation of electric charge.

Franklin described the electrical fluid as "subtle," since it could easily permeate such dense materials as metals, and he used this single fluid to explain such phenomena as electrical neutralization (that is, a parity of positive and negative electrical charge), the Leyden jar, and his lightning rod. In his explanation of the Leyden jar, a primitive device for storing electricity, Franklin used the Newtonian notion of electrification by influence (rather than by contact), and his lightning rod made use of his observation that pointed conductors were more efficient in attracting electricity than were rounded ones.

Despite Franklin's successes, his electrical ideas had some serious deficiencies. For example, his ideas failed to explain the repulsion that existed between negatively charged objects (how could a lack of fluid cause a repulsion?). Furthermore, other scientists, including Aepinus, found Franklin's notion of an "effluvia," an electrical atmosphere surrounding charged objects, unsatisfactory.

Although Aepinus was appointed as an astronomer at the Berlin Academy of Sciences in 1755, he became fascinated by electricity following Franklin's invention of the lightning rod in 1750. Aepinus lived with Swiss mathematician Leonhard Euler, who supported his research. Johann Albrecht Euler, Leonhard's son, and Johan Carl Wilcke, a Swede who was first Aepinus's student and then his collaborator, helped conduct the experiments that refuted Franklin's notion of electical effluvia. However, Aepinus's intention in these experiments was not to overthrow Franklin's single-fluid theory of electricity but to save it. Aepinus explained the troubling experimental fact that negatively charged objects repelled each other by assuming that the particles of ordinary matter possess inherent repulsive forces. Electrical fluid, Aepinus hypothesized, somehow hindered the natural repulsion of matter. When experimenters removed electrical fluid from objects, the repulsive forces between the particles of ordinary matter were unmasked, leading to the observed repulsion.

While at Berlin, Aepinus, following a suggestion by Wilcke, began research on tourmaline, a silicate crystal that had unusual thermoelectric properties. When Aepinus and Wilcke heated one face of a tourmaline crystal, it acquired an electric charge, but, to their surprise, the opposing face had the opposite charge. Aepinus became fascinated with the similarity between the positive and negative sides of this crystal, on one hand, and the north and south poles of an iron magnet, on the other. He theorized that, just as electrification was a consequence of the movement of electrical fluid, so magnetization was the result of a relocation of a subtle magnetic fluid within the iron. Aepinus pursued these ideas, without Wilcke, in St. Petersburg, Russia, where, in 1757, he became a member of the Imperial Academy of Sciences and where he tutored the son of Catherine the Great.

To solidify his prestigious position, Aepinus published, more quickly than he had originally intended, his *Tentamen theoriae electricitatis et magnetismi* (1759; *Essay on the Theory of Electricity and Magnetism*, 1979, also known as the *Tentamen*). The basic theme of the *Tentamen* is the analogy between electricity and magnetism. Like Newton, who used mathematics to explain terrestrial and celestial motions, Aepinus attempted to use mathematical methods to develop a cohesive explanation of electrical and magnetic phenomena from certain forces, without speculating about the mechanisms behind these forces.

For Aepinus, the forces guiding electrical and magnetic phenomena included attractions between the electric fluid and matter, repulsions between particles of the electric fluid, and repulsions between the particles of ordinary matter. He realized that these attractive and repulsive forces were proportional to the excess or deficiency of the electric fluid. He also analyzed induction, the phenomenon in which an object becomes electrified by a charged object that is brought near to it but prevented from making contact with it. Aepinus explained this phenomenon through his interpretation of the electrical force, which could act at a distance like gravity, and the mobility of the electric fluid in the approached object.

The *Tentamen* also contains Aepinus's theory of magnetism. He believed that the north and south poles of a magnet were locations at which the magnetic fluid either surpassed or fell short of its nonpolar amount. He attributed the permanence of polarity in iron magnets to the strong attraction between the magnetic fluid and the particles of iron. Strong similarities therefore existed between Aepinus's analysis of electricity and his treatment of magnetism.

SIGNIFICANCE

Aepinus's *Essay on the Theory of Electricity and Magnetism* is considered one of the most original and significant books in electricity. This work was important for many reasons. Using Newton's analysis of forces that act at a distance, Aepinus provided the first mathematical

treatment of electricity and magnetism. Indeed, some scholars see this application of the Newtonian concept of force as his principal contribution to the field. Although Aepinus did not discover the inverse-square law for the electrostatic force, he developed the ideas and methods that would enable later physicists to make this and other discoveries.

That it would take more than a quarter century for Charles Coulomb mathematically to describe the force between particles of the electric "fluid" shows that Aepinus was ahead of his time. Because of the highly mathematical approach of the *Tentamen*, it initially attracted few readers. René Just Haüy, a French mineralogist, aided the diffusion of Aepinus's ideas when he published an excellent summary of them in 1780. This popularization stimulated some scientists to read the *Tentamen*, where they discovered models of how to mathematize the analysis of electricity and magnetism.

Henry Cavendish became an important disciple of Aepinus's single-fluid theory of electricity and Alessandro Volta, famous for inventing the battery, had a deep respect for Aepinus's achievements, even though Volta, who did not understand advanced mathematics, took a different approach to the quantification of electricity. A major characteristic of the Enlightenment was its quantifying spirit, the quest to put ideas about nature into mathematical form in order to understand them better. Aepinus's work was very much a part of this quest, and his work continued to stimulate crucial new experiments and discoveries well into the nineteenth century.

—*Robert J. Paradowski*

FURTHER READING

Heilbron, John L. *Electricity in the Seventeenth and Eighteenth Centuries: A Study of Early Modern Physics*. New York: Dover, 1999. This reprint, with a new preface by the author, makes widely available a book originally published by the University of California Press in 1979. Aepinus's contributions to electricity are extensively and insightfully discussed. Sixty-eight-page bibliography of primary and secondary sources. Index.

Home, Roderick W. *The Effluvial Theory of Electricity*. New York: Arno Press, 1981. Home, who has published extensively on Aepinus and eighteenth century electricity, began his interests with his Indiana University dissertation (1967), which he expanded and updated in this book. Bibliography and index.

Pancaldi, Giuliano. *Volta: Science and Culture in the Age of Enlightenment*. Princeton, N.J.: Princeton University Press, 2003. Besides being an excellent scientific biography of Volta, this book contains much analysis of electrical activities in the eighteenth century, including experiments, ideas, and theories of Aepinus. Extensive notes to each of the chapters, twenty-eight-page bibliography of primary and secondary sources, and an index.

Roller, Duane, and Duane H. D. Roller. *The Development of the Concept of Electric Charge: Electricity from the Greeks to Coulomb.* Cambridge, Mass.: Harvard University Press, 1967. A succinct history of early electricity, with an analysis of the "Franklin-Aepinus one-fluid conceptual scheme." Questions for students on each of the sections, a bibliography, but no index.

Whittaker, Edmund. *A History of the Theories of Aether and Electricity.* New York: Dover, 1989. This reprint is a combination of a two-volume work originally published in 1951 and 1953. Whittaker discusses

Aepinus's contributions in chapter 2, "Electric and Magnetic Science Prior to the Introduction of Potentials." Each volume ends with indexes of subjects and of authors cited.

SEE ALSO: 1724: Foundation of the St. Petersburg Academy of Sciences; 1729: Gray Discovers Principles of Electric Conductivity; 1733: Du Fay Discovers Two Kinds of Electric Charge; 1738: Bernoulli Proposes the Kinetic Theory of Gases; 1740: Maclaurin's Gravitational Theory; 1743-1744: D'Alembert Develops His Axioms of Motion; Oct., 1745, and Jan., 1746: Invention of the Leyden Jar; June, 1752: Franklin Demonstrates the Electrical Nature of Lightning; 1800: Volta Invents the Battery.

RELATED ARTICLES in *Great Lives from History: The Eighteenth Century, 1701-1800*: Catherine the Great; Henry Cavendish; Leonhard Euler; Benjamin Franklin; Alessandro Volta.

1759
CHARLES III GAINS THE SPANISH THRONE

Under King Charles III, Spain reached the high point of its "enlightened absolutist" monarchy. Charles initiated far-reaching social, political, and economic reforms, using his nearly absolute power to improve his society and the lives of its people.

LOCALE: Spain
CATEGORIES: Government and politics; social issues and reform

KEY FIGURES
Charles III (1716-1788), king of Spain, r. 1759-1788
Count of Floridablanca (José Moñino y Redondo; 1728-1808), Spanish secretary of state for foreign affairs, 1776-1792
Pedro Rodríguez de Campomanes (1723-1802), Charles's chief economic adviser
Count of Aranda (Pedro Pablo Abarca de Bolea; 1719-1798), president of the Council of Castile
Jerónimo Grimaldi (1720-1786), Spanish secretary of state for foreign affairs, 1761-1776
Leopoldo di Gregorio Squillace (Esquilache; d.1785), Spanish minister of finance and war until 1766

SUMMARY OF EVENT
When Charles III succeeded his half brother Ferdinand VI to the throne of Spain in 1759, he inherited an empire

that had been arrested in the process of decline and was once again becoming a major power in European affairs. He was the fourth monarch of the new Bourbon Dynasty, which had succeeded to the throne after the death of the Habsburg Charles II (1700) and the resulting War of the Spanish Succession.

His father, Philip V, and his two half brothers, Louis I and Ferdinand VI, had begun and continued a policy of centralization and modernization that emulated Bourbon reforms in France. Charles inherited these reforms, but he also built upon them more effectively than any of the other Bourbons. In so doing, he had two initial advantages: His predecessors had laid the foundations for reform; and Charles also had experience in governing. Through the machinations of his mother, Isabella Farnese, he had been successively duke of Parma and Tuscany and then king of the Two Sicilies. Thus, he came to Spain prepared to rule.

Historians have portrayed Charles as Spain's enlightened despot. Certainly he aimed to establish royal absolutism and chose ministers who were familiar with the enlightened currents of the time. Yet Charles himself had little interest in intellectual matters, read almost nothing, and preferred hunting to all other activities. What distinguished him from his predecessors was a willingness to rule decisively after consultation with his ministers. Administrative centralization had been established when Charles came to the throne, but he raised it to its most efficient level. The old system of councils was replaced by well-organized ministries run by career bureaucrats, completely subservient to the king.

The first phase of Charles's reign lasted until 1766 and constituted the most radical attempt at reform. Bellicose by nature, Charles plunged Spain into the Seven Years' War in 1762, with disastrous results. Allied with his French Bourbon cousins, Charles suffered a humiliating defeat, made worse by the British capture of Havana and Manila. Although these ports were returned to Spain by the Peace of Paris, the war showed how exposed the Spanish empire was to British seapower. Imperial defenses needed expensive reforms. Meanwhile, Charles relied heavily on two Italian advisers: Jerónimo Grimaldi, who advised the king on foreign affairs, and Leopoldo di Gregorio Squillace (Hispanicized as Esquilache), who oversaw finances and the military. Along with the king's chief economic expert, Pedro Rodríguez Campomanes, they attempted to impose domestic reform on Spain. They tried to reduce aristocratic power by using commoners to staff the government and worked to increase the tax burden upon the nobility and the Catholic Church. A great problem for Spain, entailed estates and mortmain concentrated land in the hands of the aristocracy and clergy. The result was inefficient agriculture and high grain prices. In turn these caused social tension for the growing Spanish population. Campomanes, a Physiocrat who believed that a nation's wealth depended on wise use of its land, proposed reforms to redistribute land and thus create more small farmers. He also tried to deregulate the grain trade.

Such proposals heightened opposition among entrenched power groups. Resistance to the reforms, resentment of Charles's foreign advisers, and the crisis provoked by grain shortages led to a serious tumult in Madrid in March, 1766, the so-called Esquilache Revolt, which also spread to other cities. Alarmed by the violence, Charles fled Madrid, removed Squillace, but asserted royal authority in 1767 by exiling the Jesuits, reported to have helped foment the revolt. The Inquisition, that most feared of Spanish institutions, found its powers curtailed, and few cases were tried in its courts. Grimaldi retained his influence in foreign affairs, whereas domestic policy fell to the count of Aranda, president of the Council of Castile, and Campomanes, who continued to push for agrarian reform.

More than three-quarters of the arable land of Spain was held by a few families or corporations. Much of this property was still controlled by the *Mesta*, the sheepowners' guild, whose members allowed their sheep to graze on land desperately needed for agrarian production. Appointed head of the *Mesta*, Campomanes broke its hold on the land and allowed villages to enclose their lands to protect them from the sheep. He ordered the sale of uncultivated land and the division of some communal properties among the townspeople. He forced the sale of idle church lands and reduced the number of monastic establishments. He encouraged the immigration of foreign peasants to show Spaniards how to make the land produce more, and of foreign artisans to stimulate Spanish industry; he also established an agricultural school. Although many of these reforms, particularly forced sale of land, were not seen through to completion, Campomanes laid the foundation for nineteenth century reforms.

The final phase of Charles's reign lasted from 1776 to 1788. By that time, Grimaldi and Aranda had both fallen into disfavor, and the king turned administration of the government over to the count of Floridablanca. Almost immediately, Floridablanca confronted war with the British. Eager to avenge Spain's defeat during the Seven Years' War, Charles joined France in 1778 to aid the

Charles III. (North Wind Picture Archives)

North American colonists in their rebellion against George III. The successful outcome resulted in part from naval and military reforms carried out earlier by Aranda.

Floridablanca also worked to strengthen Spain's economy. Textile factories were modernized in Catalonia, thereby making the region productive again; canals and roads were constructed; tax collection was improved; and the Spanish sales tax was lowered to a reasonable level. To increase commerce with Spain's American colonies, the crown modified its mercantilist policies and decreed intra-imperial free trade in 1778. This enabled all Spanish ports to trade directly with all of Spanish America except Mexico and Venezuela, which were finally added in 1789. The upsurge in American silver production helped imperial commerce prosper. Modernization of universities and schools fostered learning, as did the establishment of economic societies that helped spread "enlightened" ideas and technology.

SIGNIFICANCE

Charles was the greatest of the eighteenth century Spanish Bourbons. He and his ministers attempted to modernize and strengthen Spain. Nevertheless, opposition from entrenched power groups such as the aristocracy and the clergy checked the reformers. Nor did the crown push through truly effective land or tax reforms. Those waited for later generations. Charles's legacy was also undermined by his incompetent son, Charles IV, who succeeded to the throne in 1788; and by the onset of the French Revolution, which not only threw Spain in turmoil but also discredited the modernizers.

—José M. Sánchez, updated by Kendall W. Brown

FURTHER READING

Herr, Richard. *The Eighteenth Century Revolution in Spain.* Princeton, N.J.: Princeton University Press, 1958. The standard intellectual history of Spain during the eighteenth century, it portrays an enlightenment imposed on the nation by the court and its ministers.

_____. *Rural Change and Royal Finances in Spain at the End of the Old Regime.* Berkeley: University of California Press, 1989. A massively detailed study of royal policy during the reigns of Charles III and Charles IV regarding agrarian reform and the partially successful attempt to invigorate agriculture by disentailing ecclesiastical and aristocratic estates.

Hull, Anthony H. *Charles III and the Revival of Spain.* Washington, D.C.: University Press of America, 1980. Provides good background on Charles's Italian career. Holds that his greatest virtue as king of Spain was his willingness to use his power pragmatically to further reform.

Kuethe, Allen J. "Towards a Periodization of the Reforms of Charles III." In *Iberian Colonies, New World Societies: Essays in Memory of Charles Gibson*, edited by Richard L. Garner and William B. Taylor. Private printing, 1985. Provides a chronological framework for understanding how reform of the Spanish empire unfolded during the reign of Charles III. Emphasizes his determination to take revenge on the British.

Lynch, John. *Bourbon Spain, 1700-1808.* Cambridge, Mass.: Basil Blackwell, 1989. The best overall treatment in English of Spain and its empire in the eighteenth century, giving Charles less credit for policy and reform initiatives than is customary.

Noel, Charles C. "Charles III of Spain." In *Enlightened Absolutism: Reform and Reformers in Later Eighteenth-Century Europe*, edited by H. M. Scott. Ann Arbor: University of Michigan Press, 1990. Portrays Charles as a leading example of a monarchy sympathetic to the intellectual currents of the eighteenth century and willing to support reforms to modernize his realms.

Stein, Stanley J., and Barbara H. Stein. *Apogee of Empire: Spain and New Spain in the Age of Charles III, 1759-1789.* Baltimore: Johns Hopkins University Press, 2003. Examines Charles's attempts to reform Spain's political, economic, and social institutions, and to modernize Spain's relationship with its colonies. The authors conclude that Charles's efforts ultimately failed, and Spain was ill prepared for future upheaval in Europe and its colonies.

1759
WEDGWOOD FOUNDS A CERAMICS FIRM

Wedgwood's ceramics company developed revolutionary new products and business techniques in response to consumer needs and the new industrial economy, producing affordable, high-quality, functional ware, as well as beautiful ornamental wares in new, refined materials. Also, he instituted new labor and management practices that increased productivity and profit.

LOCALE: Staffordshire, England
CATEGORIES: Business and labor; economics; science and technology; trade and commerce

KEY FIGURES
Josiah Wedgwood (1730-1795), a designer, manufacturer, scientist, and entrepreneur
Thomas Bentley (1730-1780), Wedgwood's principal business partner
John Flaxman (1755-1826), a Wedgwood designer who eventually directed the Wedgwood studio in Rome
Erasmus Darwin (1731-1802), a physician, inventor, and scientist who helped manage Wedgwood's company

SUMMARY OF EVENT
On July 12, 1730, Josiah Wedgwood was born into a family of potters, a tradition dating to the 1600's. After his father's death in 1739, the nine-year-old Wedgwood worked at the potter's wheel in the family business. However, at age eleven, a severe case of smallpox caused permanent damage to his right knee. No longer able to operate the potter's wheel, Wedgwood focused on researching and experimenting with glazes, colors, and pottery design. This early change of direction laid the foundation for his later success and innovations.

In 1744, Wedgwood became an apprentice under his older brother Thomas, but in 1749, Thomas rejected his brother's request for a partnership in the family business. Josiah then formed a brief partnership with another area potter, John Harrison. In 1754, Wedgwood entered a partnership with Thomas Whieldon, one of the most creative potters of the time. During the next five years, Wedgwood mastered pottery techniques, started a notebook about his experiments with glazing techniques and clay formulas, and invented a new green glaze. In 1759, he left the partnership and set up his own ceramics business at Burslem's Ivy House Works, which would become the first true ceramics factory.

Wedgwood's experimentation led to superior, longer-lasting pottery for everyday use. His factory produced a beautiful, highly durable cream-colored earthenware, which Wedgwood patented in 1763. For the first time, beautifully decorated, high-quality, and inexpensive ceramic tableware was available to those who previously could afford only pewter or wooden ware. Even the British nobility purchased Wedgwood pottery. The creamware line was so popular with Queen Charlotte, wife of King George III, that she permitted Wedgwood to call it Queen's Ware. Wedgwood used this royal approval to promote the line, which became both the standard domestic ware and a popular export.

Wedgwood also developed mass-marketing techniques for the new consumer economy. The company had expensive showrooms and exhibitions, as well as a huge sales force. International markets included North America, France, and Russia. Wedgwood saw the value of canals for the transportation of products, so in 1766 he supported the construction of the Trent & Mersey Canal, which was completed in 1777.

In 1768, Wedgwood entered a partnership with Thomas Bentley, a merchant. They had met in Liverpool in 1762 and became close friends. Bentley would be the company's sales manager, working from the London office. This remarkable alliance focused on the manufacture of unglazed decorative or ornamental stonewares mostly in the popular, neoclassical style. (Their partnership lasted until Bentley's death in 1780.) To produce this ornamental pottery, Wedgwood built a second factory, Etruria Works. Wedgwood admired the black Etruscan pottery excavated at Etruria, Italy, and duplicated it with his creation of black basalt or Egyptian ware, an unglazed, fine-grained black stoneware, which was painted or decorated. This stoneware was better than any previously produced. Black basalt products included imitation Greek red vases, life-size busts of historical figures, and candlesticks.

For the Etruria factory, Wedgwood hired capable artists, engineers, and craftspeople. He also developed innovative production techniques, including a "division of labor," which greatly increased productivity. He divided the various processes of pottery making (mixing, shaping, firing, glazing, and so forth) and assigned each component to an individual, who would specialize in that particular task. Concurrently, Wedgwood encouraged employee loyalty by providing long-term employment, an employee residential village, and improved living conditions.

His revolutionary ideas were shared by his friend, Erasmus Darwin, a physician and scientist who founded the Lunar Society, a radical social club for some of the most gifted inventors, scientists, intellectuals, and industrialists of the time. Wedgwood was a core member of this group, which met monthly and advocated the use of science to improve, among other things, manufacturing, transportation, and education. They supported capitalism, private property, and economic competition but were opposed to slavery and despotism.

By 1773, Wedgwood had transferred the production of functional ware from Burslem to Etruria. The creamware continued to be popular, and in 1774 Empress Catherine the Great of Russia ordered 952 pieces of Wedgwood's Queen's Ware. In 1775, Wedgwood experimented with a high-temperature firing of a paste containing barium sulfate that resulted in the creation of jasperware, a durable white, granularly textured, unglazed stoneware most commonly colored blue by metal oxides and ornamented with white bas-relief work in Greek classical designs or cameo portraits. Other background colors used were yellow, pink, olive, black, and sage green. The designer for the jasperware reliefs was the famous artist and sculptor John Flaxman, who became a designer at Etruria Works in 1775 and later directed Wedgwood's studio in Rome.

After Bentley's death in 1780, Darwin helped Wedgwood manage the company. In 1782 at Etruria, they installed the first steam-powered engine in a factory. In 1783, Wedgwood's invention of a pyrometer for measuring high temperatures, as in ovens for pottery firings, earned him election as a fellow of the Royal Society of London. In 1789, after three years of intense work, Wedgwood was able to make a jasper copy of the famous Portland vase, a first century glass vase that had been excavated near Rome during the time of Pope Urban VIII (1568-1644). After Margaret Bentinck, second duchess of Portland, purchased the vase in 1783, Wedgwood was determined to duplicate it. The Portland vase was made of violet-blue glass overlaid with opaque white glass containing a mythological scene in cameo relief.

On January 3, 1795, Wedgwood died, leaving a huge fortune and a flourishing business to his descendants. In 1796, Wedgwood's daughter Susannah married Erasmus's son Robert, and they were the parents of the famous English naturalist Charles Darwin, who married Emma, Wedgwood's granddaughter.

SIGNIFICANCE

Josiah Wedgwood had laid the foundation for a lasting business and enduring brand name. In response to consumer needs and social changes, Wedgwood used scientific experimentation to develop superior new ceramic ware, such as creamware, black basalt, and jasperware. Wedgwood designs in ornamental ware reflected the eighteenth century classical style of the Greek Revival. His affordable yet superior pottery appealed to the growing European bourgeois and working classes, both a part of the Industrial Revolution beginning in England in the eighteenth century.

Through revolutionary labor, management, and marketing techniques, he had created a productive and profitable company. He industrialized the making of ceramics, and his pottery works was the first modern ceramics factory, complete with specialized labor, machinery, and new inventions. His pottery was so popular that competitors had to imitate Wedgwood wares in order to survive.

The Wedgwood production facilities relocated to a newly constructed factory at Barlaston in 1940. In 1953 the company opened "Wedgwood Rooms," with bridal registries for fine china gifts, at department stores in the United States. The London Stock Exchange began offering Wedgwood shares in 1966. By the twenty-first century, Wedgwood had also established a worldwide presence with its own Web site.

—Alice Myers

FURTHER READING

Dolan, Brian. *Wedgwood: The First Tycoon*. New York: Viking, 2004. At 396 pages, this well-researched, comprehensive biography focuses on Wedgwood as a revolutionary entrepreneur and provides insights into eighteenth century British society and politics. Illustrations, bibliography, and index.

Honey, W. B. *English Pottery and Porcelain*. London: A. and C. Black, 1933. This concise history of British ceramic art contains a chapter on Wedgwood's life and career. The author defends Wedgwood as a great businessman but argues he also seemed more interested in seeking the acceptance of the wealthy than in perfecting his craft. Also discusses Wedgwood in relation to his contemporaries and his impact upon later British potters.

Koehn, Nancy. *Brand New: How Entrepreneurs Earned Consumers' Trust from Wedgwood to Dell*. Boston: Harvard Business School Press, 2001. Chapter 2 discusses Wedgwood's life and career, especially his entrepreneurial skills. There are informative sections on his partnership with Thomas Bentley, marketing, organizing the workforce, product management, finance, and capitalism. Bibliography and index.

Macht, Carol. *Classical Wedgwood Designs*. New York: Gramercy, 1957. This book examines the sources and the use of the Wedgwood designs, and jasperware's connection to the eighteenth century classical revival. Illustrations and bibliography.

Meteyard, Eliza. *The Life of Josiah Wedgwood: From His Private Correspondences and Family Papers*. 2 vols. London: Hurst and Blackett, 1865. An excellent two-volume biography that begins with England's Celtic pottery and period and continues through the Roman period and the Middle Ages. Makes for absorbing, if dated, reading.

Wedgwood, Barbara, and Hensleigh Wedgwood. *The Wedgwood Circle, 1730-1897: Four Generations of a Family and Their Friends*. Westfield, N.J.: Eastview Editions, 1980. A well-written account of four generations of the Wedgwood family, beginning with Josiah. A family history that is not as biased as readers might expect.

Wedgwood, Josiah. *The Selected Letters of Josiah Wedgwood*. Edited by Ann Finer and George Savage. London: Cory, Adams, and Mackay, 1965. A collection of letters illustrating Wedgwood's personality, accomplishments, influences, and motivations. The

introduction contains a biographical sketch. In addition, each section of the book is prefaced with a short explanation of the contents of letters to follow, with relevant biographical data about Wedgwood. An excellent source.

Williams, Peter. *Wedgwood: A Collector's Guide*. Radnor, Pa.: Wallace-Homestead, 1992. A comprehensive history of Wedgwood pottery, with detailed descriptions of the designs and processes. Color photographs and appendices.

Young, Hilary. *The Genius of Wedgwood*. London: Victoria & Albert Museum, 1995. The Victoria & Albert Museum held a special exhibition in 1995 to observe the bicentenary of Wedgwood's death. This publication provides detailed descriptions of more than five hundred exhibition pieces produced during Wedgwood's lifetime. Illustrations, with many color plates. Bibliography and index.

SEE ALSO: 1701: Plumier Publishes *L'Art de tourner*; 1762: *The Antiquities of Athens* Prompts Architectural Neoclassicism.

RELATED ARTICLES in *Great Lives from History: The Eighteenth Century, 1701-1800:* Robert and James Adam; Hester Bateman; James Brindley; Catherine the Great; Charlotte; Benjamin Franklin; Joseph Priestley; Paul Revere; Sir Joshua Reynolds; Josiah Wedgwood.

1759-1766
CONSTRUCTION OF THE BRIDGEWATER CANAL

The unique Bridgewater Canal, the first true industrial canal and the first canal to be dug from dry land and to have its own water supply, facilitated the movement of coal and other materials, aiding significantly in the development of the Industrial Revolution in Great Britain.

LOCALE: Manchester, England
CATEGORIES: Architecture; transportation; business and labor; economics; science and technology; trade and commerce

KEY FIGURES

Francis Egerton (1736-1803), a coal-mine owner, who envisioned and financed the building of the canal
John Gilbert (1724-1795), a mining engineer and canal designer
James Brindley (1716-1772), an engineer and canal designer

SUMMARY OF EVENT

Although not the first canal in Great Britain, the Bridgewater Canal is considered the most significant canal project because of its long-term impact on the British economy and on life in central Britain. During Roman times in Britain, several rivers were dammed and shaped to facilitate transport between isolated garrisons, although these garrisons were abandoned when the Roman Empire collapsed.

During the Middle Ages, canal projects reemerged in England, following the same process of pooling water in dams to improve traffic on existing rivers. The best example of this effort was the Exeter Ship Canal, constructed between 1563 and 1566. Running 5 miles from Exeter to the mouth of the River Exe, the Exeter Ship Canal boasted the first system of locks ever installed in England. An even larger project, the Mersey and Irwell

Navigation, begun in 1720 and completed in 1740, connected Liverpool to the mouth of the Severn River, permitting boats bearing up to fifty tons of cargo to reach Manchester. In 1755, the Sankey Brook Navigation (later known as the St. Helen's Canal) connected St. Helen's to the Severn. The St. Helen's was a different type of canal. Instead of merely improving an existing river course, it used only a portion of the river, and instead of building expensive locks to make the river navigable, engineers cut a new course around potential trouble spots.

These canals, however, had several problems. Because they were based upon existing rivers, they did not necessarily proceed directly to their destinations; meandering rivers added unnecessary distance to travel. They were also vulnerable to the vagaries of the weather. Spring rains flooded the rivers, summer droughts made the rivers impassable, and winter ice stopped travel altogether. What shippers needed was an independent watercourse, a canal that did not rely upon an existing river route. Engineers could build such a canal exactly where it was needed; they could regulate the water flow to make it more consistent and reliable and speed goods directly to their destination. Such a transportation system would afford tidy profits; shippers would pay a toll to use such a route.

The advantages of these new types of canals were matched only by their potential cost. The earlier canals, using existing rivers, were relatively cheap because nature had done most of the digging for them. Digging a river-independent canal would require a huge labor force on a project that might take years to complete. Another problem facing the new canal was providing a reliable water supply to keep the canal filled.

The person who overcame these limitations was Francis Egerton, the third duke of Bridgewater. Egerton had left London in 1757 to concentrate on his financial dealings in the countryside, especially his coal mines near Worsley. These mines were not profitable for two reasons. First, the mines consumed huge sums of money simply to keep from flooding, with constant pumping and tunneling to keep the mines open. Second, Egerton had to pay fees to ship coal to market in Manchester, with the coal transported by packhorse to the River Irwell, where shippers charged exorbitant prices. After observing the St. Helen's Ca-

THE BRIDGEWATER CANAL SYSTEM, 1766

nal, Egerton figured that a "purpose-dug" canal would solve both of his problems. By tunneling deep into his mines, he would make it possible for canal boats to enter the mines themselves for loading, removing the need for packhorses. The canal would also serve as a drainage system for the mines, providing a reliable source of canal water. Egerton would also avoid paying the high prices charged by the shippers on the River Irwell.

Originally, Egerton conceived a short canal that would connect his mines to the Mersey and Irwell Navigation. In 1759, he obtained permission from Parliament to begin construction. However, the managers of the Mersey and Irwell Navigation, seeing the opportunity to make a sizable profit, announced that they would charge a high toll fee for Egerton to use their canal. Unwilling to negotiate, Egerton returned to Parliament in 1760 and received permission to extend his canal to Manchester.

To help construct the new canal, Egerton employed two brilliant men who made his vision a reality. The first hired was John Gilbert, who, as land agent, would design and engineer the tunnel system that would connect the canal to the mines and transfer the water into the canal system. To lift the canal boats to different levels of the mine, Gilbert constructed incline planes powered by water machinery (equipment that was still in use a century after Gilbert installed it). Egerton also hired James Brindley, a millwright by trade who took up the task of constructing the cross-country canal. Brindley proved to be a master of organization who surveyed the canal route, acquired material, hired workers, and supervised construction. Moreover, Brindley performed his duties twice, as two construction crews, one in Worsley and one in Manchester, worked simultaneously from their respective locations until they met "half way." When completed, the canal stretched for 10 miles.

The masterpiece of Brindley's design was the Barton Aqueduct. The biggest physical obstacle to the Bridgewater Canal was the River Irwell itself, so the canal had to be designed in such a way that it could cross the river. Instead of digging into the banks of the river, Brindley convinced Egerton he could elevate the canal over the river on an aqueduct, an idea that drew derision from many quarters. Members of Parliament were unconvinced of Brindley's idea until he demonstrated for them his plan for mudding the interior of the aqueduct with clay to make it waterproof. Although critics called the aqueduct a "castle in the air," Brindley had the last laugh. With the exception of a small leak on the aqueduct's opening day, the canal remained watertight. The Barton Aqueduct, which became the symbol of the Bridgewater Canal,

turned the canal into an elevated river that is 600 feet long, 36 feet wide, and flowing 30 feet above the River Irwell.

Although intended to save money, the canal nearly drove the duke into bankruptcy. It was not until he extended the canal past Manchester (1761-1766) and connected it to existing canals that toll revenues poured in, and the duke went from nearly broke to one of England's richest men. Gilbert continued to supervise the coal mines at Worsley, but Brindley went into the canal-designing business full-time, overseeing the construction of several regional canals.

SIGNIFICANCE

When the canal opened for business in 1761, its influence was immediate. The price of coal in Manchester plunged, triggering an industrial boom that transformed the English Midlands into the center of the Industrial Revolution. The same canal that brought in coal shipped out the manufactured goods that made England the world's leading industrial power. Seeing the benefits of the Bridgewater Canal, other canal projects began in earnest throughout England, and soon a web of canals connected the growing English economy. The canal system served England well until it was supplanted by the railroad in the nineteenth century. In the early twenty-first century, many of the canals still exist, but they are used more for weekend boating excursions than the hauling of coal.

—*Steven J. Ramold*

FURTHER READING

Boughey, Joseph. *Hadfield's British Canals.* 8th ed. Stroud, England: Alan Sutton, 1994. An updated version of a book originally written by Charles Hadfield, a noted historian of the British canal system. Provides an overview of how canal engineering emerged from the Industrial Revolution of the eighteenth century through the twentieth century, including information about the Francis Egerton and James Brindley.

Freethy, Ron, and Marlene Freethy. *The Bridgewater Canal.* Bolton, England: Aurora, 1996. A study of the state of the canal in the late twentieth century, transformed from an industrial necessity to a historical and recreational entity.

Hadfield, Charles. *British Canals: An Illustrated History.* London: Newton, Abbott, and Charles, 1966. A broad history of England's canal-building boom, and the boom's influence upon the English economy.

Karwatka, Dennis. "James Brindley and Early Canal Construction." *Tech Directions* 63, no. 6 (January,

2004): 10. A tribute to Brindley and his engineering achievements.

Malet, Hugh. *The Canal Duke: A Biography of Francis, Third Duke of Bridgewater*. Manchester, England: Manchester University Press, 1977. An outstanding biography of the duke of Bridgewater, concentrating on the years when the canal was constructed, but with some discussion of his later life.

Wood, Cyril J. *The Duke's Cut: The Bridgewater Canal*. Stroud, England: Tempus, 2002. Less a discussion of

the construction of the canal than a study of its social and economic impact upon the British Midlands in the late eighteenth century.

SEE ALSO: 1759: Wedgwood Founds a Ceramics Firm; 1767-1771: Invention of the Water Frame; Nov., 1777-Jan. 1, 1781: Construction of the First Iron Bridge; 1790: First Steam Rolling Mill; 1795: Invention of the Flax Spinner.

RELATED ARTICLE in *Great Lives from History: The Eighteenth Century, 1701-1800*: James Brindley.

January, 1759
VOLTAIRE SATIRIZES OPTIMISM IN *CANDIDE*

Voltaire published his most famous philosophical tale, a global satire on human corruption that gave birth to the term "pessimism." Its impassioned advocacy of humanitarian principles, religious tolerance, social justice, and realistic confrontation with life's grimness retains its power and relevance two and a half centuries later.

LOCALE: Geneva, Switzerland; Paris, France
CATEGORIES: Literature; philosophy

KEY FIGURES

Voltaire (François-Marie Arouet; 1694-1778), French Enlightenment philosopher and writer
Gottfried Wilhelm Leibniz (1646-1716), German philosopher and scientist
Frederick the Great (Frederick II; 1712-1786), king of Prussia, r. 1740-1786
Alexander Pope (1688-1744), English satirical poet
Christian Wolff (1679-1754), Leibniz's disciple and a popularizer of his philosophy
Pierre Bayle (1647-1706), French Protestant philosophical writer
Marquise du Châtelet (Gabrielle-Émilie Le Tonnelier de Breteuil; 1706-1749), French mathematician and physicist

SUMMARY OF EVENT

The French philosopher, playwright, and author Voltaire published *Candide: Ou, L'Optimisme* (1759; *Candide: Or, All for the Best*, 1759; also as *Candide: Or, The Optimist*, 1762; also as *Candide: Or, Optimism*, 1947), his indisputable masterpiece, at the age of sixty-five. Behind the aging, ailing writer lay a series of recent disappointments that might well have contributed to the Juvenalian

"harsh indignation" expressed in his longest, best-known philosophical tale. He had lost favor at King Louis XV's court in 1747; his collaborator and mistress, the marquise du Châtelet, had died in 1749; his residency at the court of Frederick the Great of Prussia had ended in 1753, leaving him disillusioned over the rupture; and in 1755 his former relationship with the Prussian monarch rendered it impossible for Voltaire to return to his homeland. Unquestionably, however, the strongest catalyst for his panoramic exposé of his world's ills was the Great Lisbon earthquake of November 1, 1755.

Shocked at first by this natural disaster that killed possibly 100,000 people throughout Portugal and Spain and practically leveled Lisbon to the ground, Voltaire was equally shocked by religious sermons that justified the destruction as God's wrath against the wicked and endorsed the piety of burning heretics alive. He promptly wrote *Poème sur la désastre de Lisbonne* (1756; *Poem on the Lisbon Earthquake*, 1764). In 180 lines resonating with deep compassion for all the catastrophe's victims (except members of the Inquisition), Voltaire challenged the thinking that interpreted such a horror as the working of a divine Providence.

In its rejection of the notion that the disaster could have a divine purpose, the *Poem on the Lisbon Earthquake* took its place in a key theological debate initiated in 1607 by Pierre Bayle. Bayle had argued in his *Dictionnaire historique et critique* (1697, 1702; *An Historical and Critical Dictionary*, 1710) that the presence of evil in the world conflicted with belief in God's benignity, power, or wisdom, that evil predominated over good, and that Manichaeism was the soundest religious position. The most influential counterargument to Bayle had come in 1710 from the German philosopher Gottfried Wilhelm

Leibniz, whose *Essais de Théodicée sur la bonté de Dieu, la liberté de l'homme, et l'origine du mal* (1710; *Theodicy: Essays on the Goodness of God, the Freedom of Man, and the Origin of Evil*, 1951) reinstated a benevolent, omnipotent God as the designer of a harmonious world in which evil happened on the way to a greater good, or—in the words of Leibniz's disciple, Christian Wolff—for a "sufficient reason."

By the 1730's, Leibniz's ideas, systematized and popularized by Wolff, had become influential in European intellectual circles. Although a Deist and therefore a believer in a God removed from Creation, Voltaire in this decade was quite sympathetic to these optimistic ideas, which he discussed both in his correspondence with Frederick the Great of Prussia and in his daily encounters with the marquise du Châtelet, a devoted Leibnizian, at her estate in Cirey. He likewise seemed to approve a similar belief in divine Providence expressed by his English acquaintance Alexander Pope, whose *An Essay on Man* (1733-1734) proclaimed, "Whatever is, is right." Indeed, despite his early concern that optimism and providentialism denied the existence of free will, of chance, or—worst of all—of a need to improve the world, as late as 1747, Voltaire represented evil as leading to ultimate good in his first philosophical tale, *Zadig: Ou, La Destinée, Histoire orientale* (1748; originally as *Memnon: Histoire orientale*, 1747; *Zadig: Or, The Book of Fate*, 1749).

In his poem on the earthquake, however, Voltaire explicitly attacked optimism's folly and callousness, using the subtitle *An Inquiry into the Maxim, "Whatever Is, Is Right"* to impugn Pope and naming Leibniz as someone incapable of explaining humanity's endless sufferings. Bayle's name, on the other hand, he coupled with praise for a great understanding of the human condition. Three years later, adding wit, irony, and black humor, Voltaire continued his open attack on Leibniz in *Candide*, which he subtitled *Optimism* and presented as a supposed "translation from the German by Dr. Ralph."

Voltaire included a fictionalization of the earthquake itself in *Candide*'s fifth chapter, using its devastation as one of many satirical thrusts against the "best of all possible worlds" philosophy of Pangloss, his caricature of Leibniz. Later, in the tale's only other explicit reference to optimism, he had the title character define it as "the mania for insisting that all is well when one is suffering" (chapter 19). Throughout the tale, Voltaire's Manichaean philosopher Martin enunciates Baylean skepticism in opposition to Pangloss's absurdly blind optimism.

Candide's anti-German satire extended beyond

Voltaire is pictured at work in this lithograph modeled after a painting by Louis Carrogis. (Library of Congress)

Leibniz to another eminent Prussian—Frederick the Great, with whom Voltaire corresponded long after leaving his court at Potsdam. Although personally disappointed in Frederick's treatment of him, Voltaire turned to scathing public criticism only after what he considered the king's crime against humanity, undertaking the Seven Years' War (1756-1763). Raging while Voltaire composed his tale, this war—in which England allied with Prussia and Hanover against France, Russia, Austria, Sweden, and Saxony—inflicted widespread suffering and death on civilians and soldiers on both sides, in the Old World and the American colonies alike.

Voltaire opened *Candide* with a false paradise in Westphalia, the west German province where the disastrous Battle of Minden (August, 1759) was to take place. He peopled the early chapters with arrogant, brutal Prussian aristocrats and parodied Frederick's Prussian regiments in his portrayal of the sadistic Bulgar (connoting "buggers") army. As Germany's ally in the Seven Years' War, England stood equally condemned in Voltaire's eyes for brutality and injustice. He expressed this condemnation particularly in one antimilitaristic episode: In chapter 23, Voltaire had an incredulous Candide watch Admiral John Byng's execution by the English for retreating from a battle with the French—an execution that was actually carried out on March 14, 1757, despite Voltaire's petitions for clemency.

Besides delusive optimism and war—with its horrifyingly routine massacres, rapes, and disembowelments—Voltaire indicted such institutional evils as aristocratic privileges and abuses, religious (especially Catholic) persecution, monarchical tyranny, and slavery. His grief over the earthquake and other natural afflictions (plague, sexually transmitted diseases) notwithstanding, as a meliorist Voltaire focused on human-made miseries that moral progress—especially as encouraged by satire—could eradicate or ease.

For his own country, Voltaire reserved *Candide*'s longest chapter, chapter 22, but also some of his mildest criticism. His motive was not patriotic. Rather, to ensure that the French authorities would merely ban his work and not suppress it entirely, he contented himself with sniping merely at dull and malicious Paris conversations, dishonesty at cards, bad plays, and quackery—and inserting a few barbs against personal enemies who had criticized his work. Surely, however, it is no accident that Candide and Martin's ship is approaching the coast of France when Voltaire's protagonist pessimistically sums up humankind's identity as "liars, cheaters, traitors, ingrates, brigands, weaklings, deserters, cowards, enviers, gluttons, drunks, misers, profiteers, predators, slanderers, perverts, fanatics, hypocrites, and morons." Whereas the tale ends in the condensed insight that work prevents "three great evils: boredom, vice, and indigence," Candide's comprehensive list best captures the scope and bitterness of Voltaire's condemnation of the human corruption prevailing in France, Europe, the Americas, and the Middle East—everywhere, in fact, except in his mythical utopia, Eldorado.

SIGNIFICANCE

Candide's criticism of Old Regime values and institutions placed it among the Enlightenment works that paved the way for the French Revolution of 1789. Already revered near the end of his life as a defender of human rights, Voltaire later became one of the leading influences in the revolutionaries' fight for justice, liberty, and the eradication of religious superstition—three paramount concerns in *Candide*.

Beyond the effects of Voltaire's words once they were in circulation, moreover, the very publication of the tale in 1759 represented a victory for freedom of thought and of the press. Aware that his attacks on the status quo invited censorship, Voltaire not only published anonymously but also had his Swiss publishers begin covert sales in Geneva only after smuggling some of their two thousand copies and a separate manuscript copy out of the country.

Within a month, the book had set eighteenth century records as a bestseller. In February, the Paris police interrupted the printing of a sixth edition, and by March 10, 6,000 copies had been sold in Paris, as well as 200,000 copies outside France. The year of its initial publication also saw the publication of English and Italian translations, as well as sixteen more editions in French. After failing to stop circulation, officials in both Protestant Geneva and Catholic France publicly condemned the tale as indecent and scandalous. In 1762, it appeared on the Catholic Church's Index of Forbidden Books. Such official resistance doubtless only increased the book's sales and popularity: All together, more than fifty editions came out in France before Voltaire's death in 1778.

—*Margaret Bozenna Goscilo*

FURTHER READING

Gordon, Daniel. "Introduction." In *Candide*, by Voltaire. Boston: Bedford/St Martin's, 1999. Excellent assessment of the way Voltaire's paradoxical relationship to the Old Regime, his temperament, and his sexual humor shaped *Candide*.

Mason, Haydn. *Voltaire*. New York: St. Martin's Press, 1975. Examines the striking echoes between *Candide* and the preoccupations, ambivalences, and ironies evident in Voltaire's correspondence during the 1750's.

Wade, Ira O. *Voltaire and "Candide": A Study in the Fusion of History, Art, and Philosophy*. Princeton, N.J.: Princeton University Press, 1959. Authoritative study of *Candide*'s intellectual background, genesis, composition, publication, and meaning. Includes the La Vallière manuscript (original prepublication version) of the tale.

Weightman, J. G. "The Quality of Candide." In *Candide*, by Voltaire, translated and edited by Robert M. Adams. New York: W. W. Norton, 1991. Defends Voltaire against charges of shallowness, finding *Candide* effectively serious, artistic, and paradoxical.

Wootton, David. *"Candide" and Related Texts*. Indianapolis, Ind.: Hackett, 2000. A twenty-four-page introduction that offers an exceptionally clear overview of the ideological currents and crosscurrents in eighteenth century Europe that influenced Voltaire's composition of *Candide*.

1750's

SEE ALSO: 1726-1729: Voltaire Advances Enlightenment Thought in Europe; Nov. 1, 1755: Great Lisbon Earthquake; Jan., 1756-Feb. 15, 1763: Seven Years' War; July, 1764: Voltaire Publishes *A Philosophical Dictionary for the Pocket*.

RELATED ARTICLES in *Great Lives from History: The Eighteenth Century, 1701-1800*: Marquise du Châtelet; Frederick the Great; Alexander Pope; Voltaire.

January 19, 1759-August 16, 1773
SUPPRESSION OF THE JESUITS

Beginning in 1759, the governments of Portugal, France, and Spain began limiting the activities of the Society of Jesus, or Jesuits, eventually expelling the order and seizing its property. In 1773, Pope Clement XIV, under pressure from Jesuit detractors, declared the order abolished.

LOCALE: Europe and colonial territories
CATEGORIES: Religion and theology; government and politics

KEY FIGURES
Clement XIV (Giovanni Ganganelli; 1705-1774), Roman Catholic pope, 1769-1774
Sebastião José de Carvalho e Mello (1699-1782), Portuguese first minister, 1755-1777, later the marquês de Pombal
Louis XV (1710-1774), king of France, r. 1715-1774
Charles III (1716-1788), king of Spain, r. 1759-1788
Lorenzo Ricci (1703-1775), general of the Jesuit order, 1758-1773

SUMMARY OF EVENT
Ignatius of Loyola founded the Society of Jesus, or Jesuit order, of the Roman Catholic Church in the mid-sixteenth century to serve as a bulwark against the Protestant Reformation, a major force in missionary work, and an instrument of the papal will. Two centuries of success had embedded members of the order deeply into the infrastructure of the Catholic states of Europe. As preeminent educators and confessors, individual Jesuits had great influence on the royalty, bureaucrats, nobles, and wealthy burgher class of these states. Jesuits and their supporters were entrenched at the Vatican and controlled many of the mission stations in Catholic Latin America and the Caribbean.

By the mid-eighteenth century, the Jesuit order counted 22,589 members who controlled 1,180 schools, residences, and novice houses. The order had patrons and supporters at the highest levels of society, but their high profile created critics and enemies as well, from both the clerical and secular worlds. There had developed clear pro-Jesuit and anti-Jesuit camps within the Church itself and at all of Europe's Catholic courts. In Spain and Portugal, opposition to the order took the form of libelous pamphleteering, which claimed the Jesuits were profiteering in their commerce with Latin America and supporting indigenous rebellions in Paraguay.

The order gained a very influential enemy in the first minister of Portugal, the marquês de Pombal, who orchestrated anti-Jesuit sentiment in Portugal and at the Vatican. As a result, the Roman curia sent the Portuguese cardinal Francisco de Saldanha da Gama on a fact-finding mission. After Jesuits were implicated in the attempt on the Portuguese king's life on September 3, 1758, (known as the Conspiracy of the Távoras) and Saldanha submitted a scathing report stressing Jesuit impiety, Portugal's royal authorities took action. Some 180 Jesuits were arrested for *lesé majesté* (injury to the sovereign), and the order's activities in the kingdom were suspended. On January 19, 1759, King Joseph I decreed the Jesuits traitors, rebels, and enemies of himself and issued orders for their immediate expulsion from all Portuguese territories. All of their property was to revert to the Crown. The effect was the exile of 1,100 men and the imprisonment of another 250. Portuguese diplomats throughout Europe defended the actions.

The French acted next. A Jesuit named Lavallette had been trafficking in imports from the Caribbean, and his shady deals had resulted in enormous debts to creditors and banks and the bankruptcies of prominent financiers. The Parlement of Paris ruled that the order itself was liable for these debts in May, 1761. Perhaps under the influence of important Jansenists and enlightened thinkers, the Parlement then took up the much deeper issue of the very legality of the order's presence in France. The constitutions of the Society of Jesus were examined and found to be in violation of French law and custom. The Parlement found the order to be destructive, disturbing of the peace of the Church, and endangering to the faith of French subjects.

As a result of the ruling, French authorities burned the theological and philosophical works of twenty-three Jesuits. French bishops found themselves divided over the order, and King Louis XV, though personally supportive, felt great pressure to act against it. In November, 1764, he demanded that the constitutions be brought into line with French law and that the order in France become independent of the Jesuit general in Rome. Jesuit schools were closed, and all Jesuit priests were placed under the jurisdiction of French bishops pending papal cooperation. The attitude of Pope Clement XIII to these events was defiant: Let the Jesuits be as they are, he decreed, or let them not be at all. His bull *Apostolicum* of January 7, 1765, placed the order in France directly under his protection.

Like Louis XV, Spain's King Charles III felt similar pressure from anti-Jesuit bureaucrats, nobles, and intellectuals. He heard claims that Jesuits were researching his paternity; the count of Aranda blamed the order for instigating a riot in Madrid in March, 1766. The Extraordinary Council of Castile investigated the claims and found the Jesuits guilty in a secret statement of January 29, 1767. The king finally signed an order of expulsion on February 27. On the night of March 21, soldiers attacked the Jesuit houses in Madrid simultaneously, and troops carried out similar attacks throughout Spain on April 12. Some 2,267 Jesuits underwent exile from Spain's colonies. Spanish Naples purged their thirty-one houses on the night of November 3, 1767; Parma, Sicily, and Malta followed soon after.

Pope Clement XIII had resisted the Spanish expulsion order, but he died in 1769. His successor, the more pliable Clement XIV, feared the threats of the Bourbon and Braganza monarchs to nationalize the Catholic Church within their realms. France seized the papal territory of Avignon, and Naples seized that of Benevento as pressure mounted. Clerical anti-Jesuit sentiment at the Vatican, especially from Dominicans, also played its part in Clement's final decision. He tried to appease the monarchs by reducing Jesuit activities and prerogatives in Rome and abroad, and he took away from them control of the Irish and Roman Colleges in Rome. He sought aid from Archduchess Maria Theresa, a longtime supporter of the order, but even she advised in favor of papal suppression of the order, influenced by her own desire to make Bourbon marriage deals.

Finally, Clement prepared the necessary documents: The order of suppression that eliminated the Society of Jesus and the papal brief (letter) *Dominus ac Redemptor*, which introduced it, were dated July 21, 1773. The pope read these documents to the Jesuit general, Lorenzo Ricci, on August 16. The brief claimed Jesuit disobedience, arrogance, and unwillingness to reform without citing specifics. More damning, it stated that the order had become a source of dissension in the Church, threatening the Church's peace. Unordained Jesuits were freed from their vows, and Jesuit property would be sold to provide pensions. Priests could join other orders or continue under local bishops as diocesan priests, or they could be released from their vows after one year. Jesuit churches, schools, and other real property went to other orders. The Jesuit leadership was essentially imprisoned, and the Society of Jesus ceased to exist.

SIGNIFICANCE

The suppression of the Jesuits must be viewed within the context of the programmatic secularization of key national institutions—including court life, colonial exploitation, and education—by enlightened monarchs and ministers that occurred in the later eighteenth century. The Jesuits had insinuated themselves deeply into the fabric of ruling-class life, and their eradication opened the door to new and even revolutionary influences among the seats of power. Their suppression was also a very clear sign of the irrelevance of the Papacy in international affairs: Clement XIV's decision to cave in to external pressures was merely one more concession to the threat of nationalization of Catholic churches all over Europe.

In the immediate aftermath of the suppression, most Jesuits found homes as diocesan priests or within other regular orders; fifty-five became bishops. Jesuit life was maintained in western Russia by two hundred priests. It continued in Prussia until 1786, and Jesuits also found refuge within enclaves in mostly Protestant England and the Netherlands. When the Society of Jesus was reinstated in 1814, it was reintroduced to a far more conservative Europe, in which international Catholicism was both chastened and neutered but at the same time more welcome as a force for social order. As a narrow triumph of state over Church, the effect was short-lived, but never again would a single arm of Roman Catholicism hold such sway over Europe's elite.

—*Joseph P. Byrne*

FURTHER READING

Aveling, J. C. H. *The Jesuits.* Briarcliff Manor, N.Y.: Stein and Day, 1982. Presents a critical but fair description of the Jesuits, their enemies, and the major steps in the suppression.

Barthel, Manfred. *The Jesuits: History and Legend of the Society of Jesus*. Translated by Mark Howson. New York: Morrow, 1984. Narrative history of the order; see the chapter entitled "The Holy Father Disowns His Children."

Cordara, Giulio Cesare. *On the Supression of the Society of Jesus: A Contemporary Account*. Translated by John P. Murphy. Chicago: Loyola Press, 1999. Firsthand account, written in 1779 by a Jesuit in Rome, which is apologetic for both the order and the pope's actions.

Morner, M., ed. *The Expulsion of the Jesuits from Latin America*. New York: Knopf, 1965. Detailed treatment of the process and results of the suppression in South and Central America.

Wright, Jonathan. *God's Soldiers: Adventure, Politics, Intrigue, and Power—A History of the Jesuits*. New York: Doubleday, 2004. Popular treatment of Jesuit history with a balanced discussion of the suppression within the context of Enlightenment secularization.

SEE ALSO: July 24, 1702-Oct. 1, 1704: Camisard Risings in the Cévennes; Sept. 8, 1713: Papal Bull *Unigenitus*; May, 1727-1733: Jansenist "Convulsionnaires" Gather at Saint-Médard; Oct. 20, 1740: Maria Theresa Succeeds to the Austrian Throne; 1759: Charles III Gains the Spanish Throne; 1769: Pombal Reforms the Inquisition; Oct. 2, 1792-Apr. 12, 1799: Christian Missionary Societies Are Founded.

RELATED ARTICLES in *Great Lives from History: The Eighteenth Century, 1701-1800*: Charles III; Louis XV; Maria Theresa; Marquês de Pombal.

October 5, 1759-November 19, 1761
CHEROKEE WAR

The colonies of South Carolina and Virginia waged war against the Cherokee Indians, utterly destroying several Cherokee communities. The war ended in an expansion of South Carolina's territory at the Cherokees' expense, and it presaged the Cherokee alliance with the British in the Revolutionary War.

LOCALE: South Carolina (now in the United States)
CATEGORIES: Wars, uprisings, and civil unrest; colonization; expansion and land acquisition

KEY FIGURES
William Henry Lyttelton (1724-1808), governor of South Carolina, 1756-1760, and colonial military commander
Oconostota (c. 1710-1783), Cherokee military leader
Archibald Montgomery (1719-1796), colonial American military commander
James Grant (1720-1806), colonial American military commander
Attakullakulla (1714?-1781?), Cherokee diplomat
William Bull (1710-1791), governor of South Carolina, 1760-1761
Lord Amherst (Jeffrey Amherst; 1717-1797), commander of the British forces in America

SUMMARY OF EVENT

The Cherokees, a Native American people inhabiting the southern Appalachian highlands, first encountered visitors from the Old World on May 30, 1540, during the wanderings of the Spanish explorer Hernando de Soto. For more than a century after this first meeting, the Cherokees had little direct contact with European colonists. During the late seventeenth century and early eighteenth century, trade began to develop between the Cherokees and the English colonies of Virginia, North Carolina, and South Carolina. This relationship was strengthened during the Yamasee War (1715-1716), when the Cherokees were allied with the colonists against other Native American peoples. The relationship was enhanced in 1730, when Scottish aristocrat Alexander Cuming visited the Cherokees and took seven of them to England, where they met King George II and signed a trade agreement. One of the seven was the young Attakullakulla, who would turn out to be the strongest advocate for peace with the English colonists.

The 1750's saw increasing rivalry between France and England, which evolved into the Seven Years' War (1756-1763), a conflict that had already begun to manifest itself in North America as the French and Indian War (1754-1763). Because of the threat of the French and their Native American allies, the South Carolinians built Fort Prince George near the Cherokee town of Keowee in 1753 and Fort Loudoun near the town of Chota in 1756. These forts were designed to offer protection to the Cherokees in exchange for their aid to the English in the war with the French.

From 1756 to 1759, even as the forts were being built, several violent incidents between Cherokees and colonists led the way to war. The most critical of these occurred when a group of Cherokees making their way home from an abortive battle with the French-allied Shawnee through the backcountry of Virginia were attacked by settlers, who killed twenty-four of them. The settlers defended their action by accusing the Cherokees of stealing their horses and food. The governor of Virginia, Robert Dinwiddie, offered gifts and apologies to the relatives of the victims, but many Cherokees demanded retribution. Cherokee warriors killed twenty-four settlers in South Carolina in revenge.

The Cherokee War can be thought of as officially beginning on October 5, 1759, when William Henry Lyttelton, governor of South Carolina, announced his intention to lead an army into Cherokee territory. On October 20, a peace delegation led by Oconostota, the head warrior of the Cherokees, arrived in Charles Town in an attempt to prevent further hostilities. They were placed under arrest and forced to march with the troops. When Lyttelton arrived at Fort Prince George on December 10, the prisoners were held captive inside the fort. Attakullakulla, the most important negotiator for the Cherokees, arrived on December 17 and managed to secure the release of Oconostota and several other prisoners, but twenty-two remained hostages. Lyttelton refused to release them until twenty-four Cherokees were executed for the killing of the settlers. He was forced to retreat on December 28, when symptoms of smallpox, which had been raging in the town of Keowee, began to appear among his troops.

Cherokee warriors led by Oconostota surrounded the fort as soon as Lyttelton left. On February 16, 1760, the commander of the fort was lured out with the promise of negotiation and shot by concealed warriors. In retaliation, the soldiers at the fort killed the hostages. This ended any possibility of preventing a full-scale war and led to attacks on settlers.

William Bull, lieutenant governor and Lyttelton's successor, appealed to General Jeffrey Amherst, supreme commander of British forces in North America, for help. On April 1, twelve hundred soldiers commanded by Colonel Archibald Montgomery arrived in Charles Town. On June 1, they reached Keowee, which they burned to the ground. Other towns in the area, known to the colonists as the Lower Towns, were also destroyed, along with all the crops being grown there.

During these attacks, Montgomery's troops killed sixty Cherokees and took forty prisoners, while facing little opposition. Montgomery relieved the garrison at Fort Prince George and marched toward the area known as the Middle Towns. On June 27, near the town of Echoe, Cherokee warriors launched a surprise attack on the British troops, killing twenty of them and wounding seventy. Although the Cherokees withdrew, the British were forced to retreat. A month later, they left South Carolina to rejoin the war against the French in Canada.

Meanwhile, Oconostota's warriors had surrounded Fort Loudoun. Deprived of the relief given to Fort Prince George, Captain Paul Demere, commander of the fort, surrendered on August 8 rather than face starvation. The surrendering garrison was to turn over all its munitions and be escorted safely out of Cherokee territory. Because Demere attempted to conceal some of the fort's munitions, he and thirty-two of his soldiers were killed and the rest taken prisoner.

Amherst sent two thousand troops under the command of Colonel James Grant to avenge the loss of the fort. On March 20, 1761, Grant left Charles Town, arriving at Fort Prince George on May 27. There he met with Attakullakulla, but Grant refused the Cherokee's offer to intercede with the warriors. On June 7, Grant left the fort and headed for the Middle Towns. On June 10, within 2 miles of the place where Montgomery's troops were attacked, Grant fought a battle with the Cherokees, leaving ten British soldiers killed and fifty wounded. The Cherokees withdrew because of a lack of ammunition. Grant spent the next month destroying fifteen Middle Towns and fifteen hundred acres of crops. Approximately five thousand Cherokees were forced to flee into the forest to survive on whatever food they could find in the wild.

After this devastating attack, Attakullakulla and several other Cherokee leaders met with Grant at Fort Prince George to ask for peace. A treaty was prepared demanding the execution of four Cherokee leaders, the elimination of all relations between the Cherokees and the French, the sovereignty of the British courts over all offenders within Cherokee territory, and the establishment of a line 26 miles east of Keowee as the border of South Carolina. The Cherokees could not accept the demand for executions. Attakullakulla asked to speak to Bull directly. He was allowed to travel to Charles Town and was welcomed by the governor as a loyal friend of the English. The demand for executions was dropped, and the treaty was signed on September 23. A separate treaty was signed with Virginia on November 19, officially ending the Cherokee War.

1750's

SIGNIFICANCE

Ultimately, the Cherokee War represented one episode in a longer series of wars, battles, and skirmishes between the Cherokees and the Europeans. Conflicts between the Cherokees and the colonists continued until well after the end of the American Revolution (1783), during which the Cherokees were allied with the British. A series of land cessions to the newly independent United States during the late eighteenth and early nineteenth centuries left the Cherokees with only a small portion of their land. In a final attempt to survive as an independent people, the Cherokees adopted the ways of the Americans, even going so far as to set up a government modeled after that of the United States. Despite this effort, the Cherokees were finally forced to leave their native land for Oklahoma during the infamous Trail of Tears removals in the 1830's.

—Rose Secrest

FURTHER READING

Corkran, David H. *The Cherokee Frontier: Conflict and Survival, 1740-1762*. Norman: University of Oklahoma Press, 1962. A detailed account of the complex relations between the Cherokees and English colonists during the mid-1700's.

Hatley, Tom. *The Dividing Paths: Cherokees and South Carolinians Through the Era of Revolution*. New York: Oxford University Press, 1993. Focuses on the multicultural aspects of the Cherokee War, including a discussion of the roles of women and African slaves.

Mails, Thomas E. "Transformation of a Culture." In *The Cherokee People: The Story of the Cherokees from Earliest Origins to Contemporary Times*. Tulsa, Okla.: Council Oak Books, 1992. Describes the history of relations between Cherokees and Europeans up to the Trail of Tears.

Milling, Chapman J. "The Cherokee War." In *Red Caro-linians*. Chapel Hill: University of North Carolina Press, 1940. A detailed, carefully documented account of the war. An important reference despite its age.

Nelson, Paul David. *General James Grant: Scottish Soldier and Royal Governor of East Florida*. Gainesville: University Press of Florida, 1993. The only biography of Grant, who became the first royal governor of colonial Florida after he fought in the Cherokee War. Chapter 3, "Fighting in the South, 1761-1763," describes his participation in the Cherokee War.

Oliphant, John. *Peace and War on the Cherokee Frontier, 1756-1763*. Baton Rogue: Louisiana State University Press, 2001. Detailed analysis of relations between the Cherokees and the South Carolina colonists, describing the frontier conflicts that eventually led to the Cherokee War.

Woodward, Grace Steele. "'The King, Our Father.'" In *The Cherokees*. Norman: University of Oklahoma Press, 1963. A history of the Cherokee people from the start of the Yamassee War until the end of the Cherokee War.

1760's
BEGINNING OF SELECTIVE LIVESTOCK BREEDING

1760's

Robert Bakewell, one of the most prominent of the agricultural breeders of the eighteenth century, revolutionized cattle and sheep breeding by using scientific methods to develop new breeds designed to maximize meat production.

LOCALE: England

CATEGORIES: Agriculture; biology; science and technology; economics

KEY FIGURE

Robert Bakewell (1725-1795), a British tenant farmer and animal breeder

SUMMARY OF EVENT

Livestock breeding in England at the beginning of the eighteenth century was haphazard at best. In many cases breeders simply relied on chance matings among a group of animals kept in a common enclosure. Offspring with desired traits would be kept, and the others would be sold for slaughter. The predominant principle was to "outbreed." Inbreeding, or mating between those closely related, was believed to weaken the offspring and ruin the breed. Where purposeful breeding was practiced, hybridization between different lines or breeds was the rule.

The prevailing practices resulted in a confusion of breeds, many of them local, which tended to have variable characteristics. The variability was actually maintained, if not increased, by the very practices in vogue. This led to difficulty in clearly defining breeds, as such, and largely explains why few of the breeds from this era still exist.

Although there were a few other eighteenth century breeders who made impacts on livestock breeding practices, none was as prominent as Robert Bakewell. He made his mark by a combination of innate skill, careful breeding practices, and the discarding of prevailing breeding practices. Bakewell was born into a long-standing family of tenant farmers in Dishley, Leicestershire. As a young man he traveled throughout Europe observing farming practices and livestock breeding typical of each region. When he settled back at Dishley, he apprenticed under his father, eventually inheriting the farm when his father died in 1760. It was his thorough training and methodical nature that led to his eventual success, more as a breeder than as an entrepreneur.

Bakewell's greatest innovation was to breed his animals "in-and-in." This method involved not just incidental inbreeding, but carefully planned and extensive inbreeding. Bakewell traveled all over England, and even sometimes continental Europe, in search of animals with the traits he wanted to improve upon. When he obtained animals with the right combination of traits, he would have the animals mate. Their offspring would then be carefully evaluated for improvement in the chosen traits, and those with the best match would then be bred with either a sibling or a half sibling, or even back-crossed with a parent. Bakewell would have animals that were a little more distantly related mate to counteract some of the negative impacts of inbreeding. Key to his success was keeping males and females in separate enclosures, allowing only the mixing of those males and females that were to mate.

When Bakewell first began his breeding experiments, he was met with almost universal ridicule by other farmers. Predictions were that he would weaken his herds and end up with worthless animals. Although the in-and-in approach often did lead to weaker, lower-birth-weight offspring, as well as a somewhat higher rate of birth defects, his persistence paid off with improvements in the traits he sought and the development of stable, valuable breeds. His success eventually led to wide acclaim.

Bakewell developed new breeds of cattle, sheep, horses, and pigs, but his most enduring work was with cattle and, especially, sheep. His goal for cattle and sheep was to produce animals that maximized high-fat meat production in the shortest time possible. Because the common laboring class in England worked long hours at manual labor, meat high in fat, and therefore high in calories, was preferred. Rapid growth and fattening on minimal feed was also desired because it translated into cost savings for the farmer.

By twenty-first century standards, the improved longhorn, or Leicester, bull, with its high fat content, would be a disaster for consumers and farmers alike. However, Bakewell developed this breed to meet the culinary needs and preferences of his day, rather than of the modern taste for lean beef. His goal was to develop a bull with high fat content and reduced bone diameter that could fatten adequately for butchering within a few years on a minimal amount of feed. When choosing animals to begin this process, Bakewell relied not just on his eyes; he also handled the animals extensively, evaluating bone structure and fat distribution. Some of his contemporaries considered him to have an innate sense that allowed him to select just the right animals.

Choosing the animals was only the start. He also kept extensive records on each animal for each of the traits he was attempting to improve. He also carefully monitored weight gain and the amount of feed used by each animal. His observations did not stop once the animal was butchered. He would carefully study the flesh, analyzing it for fat content and texture, and would measure bone diameter. From particularly fine specimens he sometimes preserved in alcohol portions of the animal, such as a leg joint, for later study.

Although Leicester cattle have been nearly forgotten, the Dishley, or Leicester, sheep are ancestors to many successful modern-day sheep breeds found from North America and South America to Australia and New Zealand. Bakewell's goals in producing the Dishley breed of sheep were similar to those he had for longhorn cattle—rapid production of high-fat-content meat with minimal feed—but he did not completely ignore wool characteristics. Mutton, although eaten, was typically from sheep

who were past their prime for producing wool. The Dishley was the first major sheep breed designed more specifically to be meat producers.

A more technical innovation developed by Bakewell was the progeny test. Determining which bulls or rams will be the best sires can take a long time, unless they can be mated with many different females. The proof of a good sire is its consistent production of offspring with stable, superior breed traits. Although Bakewell kept a large number of his own animals, there still were not enough of them to adequately progeny-test his bulls. This led to the establishment of the Dishley Society.

The Dishley Society was composed of Bakewell and other serious animal breeders in the areas around Dishley. By banding together and sharing information, they could hasten the development of quality breeding stock. Loaning bulls and rams for breeding service was a central activity. The more offspring a given animal sired, the more data could be accumulated about their breeding po-

A Yorkshire Longhorn bull, one of many cattle breeds developed through Robert Bakewell's innovative livestock breeding methods. (Hulton Archive/Getty Images)

tential. Thus, within a few seasons, the best sires could be identified and properly exploited for maintaining the breed.

To ensure success and to prevent loss to members the Dishley Society developed an elaborate set of principles that all members had to follow. For example, principle 6 states, "No member shall let a ram to anyone who lets or sells his rams at fairs or markets." The principles, for the most part, helped establish and maintain the society as a monopoly on the members' breeds. Violating any of the principles resulted in fines, and in more serious cases, expulsion from the society.

The Dishley Society also stipulated prices to be charged for letting rams and bulls. Some of Bakewell's best sires commanded what some considered to be exorbitant letting prices, but these higher rates attest to the quality of Bakewell's breeding stock. By the latter part of the eighteenth century, most other British livestock breeders were using Bakewell's methods. With time his practices became standard procedure, being much the same into the twenty-first century in basic principle.

SIGNIFICANCE

Bakewell was applying principles consistent with a more modern genetic approach, even though the genetic discoveries of Gregor Mendel were made decades later, and their acceptance came more than a century later. Bakewell's innovation of breeding in-and-in started a revolution in livestock breeding that paralleled the Industrial Revolution and helped provide food for the newly expanded working class. His scientific methods enabled him to see beyond the unsupported beliefs of other breeders that, for example, inbreeding was detrimental.

—*Bryan D. Ness*

FURTHER READING

Francis, John. "James Cook and Robert Bakewell: Exploration and Animal Breeding in the Eighteenth Century." *Proceedings of the Royal Society Queensland* 82 (1971): v-xxvi. An overview especially of Bakewell's sheep-breeding work and its effect on sheep breeds around the world.

Pawson, Henry Cecil. *Robert Bakewell, Pioneer Livestock Breeder.* London: Crosby Lockwood & Son, 1957. A short overview of Bakewell's life and accomplishments; about half the book is devoted to copies of some of his letters.

Stanley, Pat. *Robert Bakewell and the Longhorn Breed of Cattle.* Ipswitch, England: Farming Press, 1998. Focuses specifically on Bakewell's work on cattle breeding.

Wykes, David L. "Robert Bakewell (1725-1795) of Dishley: Farmer and Livestock Improver." *Agricultural History Review* 52 (2004): 38-55. An overview focusing on Bakewell's success as both a farmer and a livestock breeder, especially of sheep.

SEE ALSO: Beginning 1735: Linnaeus Creates the Binomial System of Classification; 1742: Celsius Proposes an International Fixed Temperature Scale; 1751: Maupertuis Provides Evidence of "Hereditary Particles"; 1757: Monro Distinguishes Between Lymphatic and Blood Systems; 1767-1768: Spallanzani Disproves Spontaneous Generation.

RELATED ARTICLES in *Great Lives from History: The Eighteenth Century, 1701-1800*: Carolus Linnaeus; Jethro Tull.

1760-1776
CARIBBEAN SLAVE REBELLIONS

The ambiguous position of the Maroons—runaway slaves—continued to affect, but not stop, slave rebellions and plots in British Jamaica, as Maroons often worked in alliance with the British. This alliance made clear that the sugar plantations could not function without the help of the Maroons. Also, colonies newly acquired from the French were rocked with their own maroonage and slave revolts.

LOCALE: Jamaica; Saint Vincent; Tobago; Dominica; Grenada

CATEGORIES: Wars, uprisings, and civil unrest; social issues and reform

KEY FIGURES

Tacky (d. 1760), an Akan leader of a 1760 revolt in Jamaica

Joseph Chatoyer (d. 1795), the elected leader of the Black Carib between the 1760's and 1770's

Pontiac (fl. 1776), a Jamaican slave who claimed an alliance between Maroons and slaves in Hanover Parish

SUMMARY OF EVENT

Sugar and slavery in the West Indies generated such unprecedented profits that they continued to spread during the eighteenth century, despite not only a constant threat but also actual outbreaks of collective slave revolts. As plantations moved to newly established colonies, the pattern of resistance that had rocked the older British colonies of Barbados and Antigua was repeated in Jamaica, Dominica, Grenada, Saint Vincent, and Tobago between 1760 and 1776.

Maroons were enslaved Africans who, after escaping their slaveholders, created their own societies in the interiors of islands far away from the sugar estates. They remained a threat to the planters, especially those planters who had been on the frontiers of European settlement. In Jamaica, where groups of Maroons had earlier fought the British Empire to a draw in the 1730's, Maroons had signed treaties with the British in 1739, guaranteeing a degree of autonomy. Yet Maroons allied themselves with their former "owners" to keep their own tenuous grip on freedom. While the planters' hold on power was based upon the pragmatic rule of "divide and conquer," slaves took advantage (as they had earlier) of wars between whites to gain their liberty. As the Middle Passage pumped hundreds of thousands of slaves into the Carib-

bean, Britain and France fought each other over control in the Caribbean, sparking many slave plots and escapes.

Occurring during the Seven Years' War (1756-1763) between Britain and France, Tacky's Rebellion (1760) in Jamaica exposed the planters' dependence upon Maroon support for putting down further slave revolts. The ongoing global conflict spread British forces thin and also interfered with food and other necessities getting to the islands, which then accelerated the inherent discontent among bondsmen being worked to death. Erupting in an area known as St. Mary's Parish, which had very few resident whites, Tacky's Rebellion took advantage of the Easter holiday to catch off guard the local planters, who were worried more about a French invasion. Led by an Akan warrior named Tacky, the insurgents planned to create their own, more ambitious version of maroonage, during which they would eventually kill all whites remaining on the island, and create their own "kingdom" rather than settle for Maroon reservations deep in the forests and hills as earlier Maroon leaders, such as Kojo and Nanny, had done a generation before after the First Maroon War (1730-1739).

Tacky's Rebellion spread from St. Mary's to points throughout western Jamaica, with the majority of conflicts in Westmoreland. There, captured slaves from the French island of Guadeloupe, who were apparently seasoned in battle, confidently dispatched of the local militia; only the bravery of Maroon mercenaries and armed slaves defending their masters saved the English. Ironically, however, the same ethnic unities forged by earlier groups of Maroons who were now on the British side shaped the outlooks and strategies of this uprising. As with his predecessors, Tacky emerged as a leader whose legitimacy was built on Akan, Asanti, and Fanti traditions. Maroons, particularly in the western part of the island, drew their strength from relative ethnic homogeneity and identity as Kromanti (the anglicized Coromantine or Koromantyne) people. This identity stemmed from the fact that many of the enslaved transported to Jamaica came through or had relatives pass through the English slave factory at the Fanti town of Kromantine on the African Gold Coast. Tacky was one of many physically strong bondsmen from the Gold Coast preferred by planters, slaves who then carried on the martial and militant reputation of Kromanti and, more specifically, Akan men. Yet that common and adopted identity was not enough to prevent a Maroon lieutenant from killing Tacky, which quickly extinguished the revolt in St. Mary's and helped the British erode resistance elsewhere as well.

Britain's victory over the Bourbon Dynasty's powers in the Seven Years' War with the Peace of Paris (1763) gave Britain four more islands in the Caribbean—Dominica, Grenada, Saint Vincent, and Tobago, called the Ceded Islands—to develop as sugar and slavery moneymakers, a prospect that disrupted cultures already there and that portended revolt and resistance in every place it was carried out. In Dominica, for example, rough terrain and thick rain forests provided shelter for many escapees from the new estates. The incoming British tried to use indigenous American Indians, the Caribs, as slave catchers of a sort, giving them their own informal autonomy on the eastern side of the island in return for refusing to take in fugitives. Yet, there were so many other locations in which to hide that Maroons improvised and found their own plots of covert sugar and other fields. The French used the Maroons and the Caribs to recapture the island during the American Revolution, a temporary reoccupation that served to bolster the Maroons' confidence when they rebelled against the reimposition of British rule in the 1780's.

On Grenada, the French influence and presence were even greater, as both French settlers—whites and free blacks—and their Francophone slaves resented the British takeover and actively sabotaged the new order at every opportunity. Yet it was in Saint Vincent that a combination of French, indigenous, and African cultures most successfully resisted the British Empire during the 1760's and 1770's. The black Caribs, an alloy of shipwrecked slaves, a stray Frenchman or two, and indigenous peoples refused to allow the British to take away their lands without a fight. Fighting a successful guerrilla war at home and gaining a few parliamentary supporters in Britain, the black Caribs, led by their elected chief, Joseph Chatoyer, were able to hang on to almost the whole northern half of the island, as outlined in a 1773 treaty. In return, the black Caribs proclaimed their loyalty to English king George III, and collusion with the French was not permitted. The Caribs also were not to give asylum to fugitives from the newly established sugar estates. Planters were not satisfied with the fugitive provision, however, because they felt that the soils and topography of the northern areas were the most conducive for sugar cultivation. Consequently, they schemed with the imperial authorities in the 1790's to defeat and to deport the black Caribs once and for all.

In contrast to Grenada and Saint Vincent, Tobago had far fewer inhabitants when the British arrived there in 1763. The Caribs and the French were not factors in Tobago, but only a year after the first land grants were distributed in 1769, a major uprising was beaten back by soldiers coming from Barbados by warship. The rebels fled to the wooded highlands, where they became Maroons. Rebellions continued throughout the 1770's; a lull in collective resistance in the 1780's and 1790's in Tobago was quickly brought to an end with the elaborate Christmas plot of 1801.

While the Ceded Islands seethed with discontent and intrigue, in Jamaica, the Hanover Parish plot of July, 1776, tried to once again exploit the notion of an empire divided and stretched too thin. With the distracting backdrop of the American Revolution and the faint echoes of patriotic sentiments among the West Indian grandees, wide racial imbalances in favor of Africans, as well as newly established plantations and forbidding geography, allowed both Kromanti and, for the first time on a wide scale, Creole in a northwestern pocket of the island to plan the end of slavery, at least locally.

Before the plan could be implemented, however, one master interrogated a domestic who had been caught with the master's gun and who then told of the wider conspiracy. The parvenu sugar magnates in Hanover were extremely lucky, in part because the rebellion had apparently been scheduled for the following week. Most dangerous to colonial authorities was furtive evidence of an alliance between the slaves of Hanover Parish and the Maroons in Trelawney Town, who were the ostensible allies of the British. These allegations, made from an inside source named Pontiac, proved to be unfounded, but the very possibility of an African popular front against slavery put local planters on edge and made them more likely to embrace deportation as the final solution to the question of the Maroons and their lands in the 1790's. In the eighteenth century, despite the colonists' suspicions about the loyalty of the Maroons, the Maroons in Jamaica remained the gendarmes of the regime, coming to the aid of the colonists in the uprisings of 1831-1832 on the eve of emancipation in 1834 as well as in the Morant's Bay rebellion of 1865, after slavery in the West Indies had long ended.

SIGNIFICANCE

Tacky's Rebellion and the Caribbean rebellions of 1760-1776 marked a beginning of a new, continuing round of slave uprisings, but these rebellions also underscored the British Empire's tenuous alliance with Maroons, particularly in Jamaica, in putting down such disturbances. Imperial ambitions and rivalries, as dramatically revealed during the Seven Years' War and its aftermath, allowed slaves to resist and to flee British rule, which, in turn, led to suppression and deportation, especially where uncultivated Maroon lands were involved, such as there were in Saint Vincent. However, the slave revolts in the Caribbean in the 1760's and 1770's paralleled similar revolts in North America, prompting at least a few individuals in the Atlantic world, including an American patriot, Colonel James Otis, to finally come out against the slave trade and slavery.

—*Charles H. Ford*

FURTHER READING

Craton, Michael. *Testing the Chains: Resistance to Slavery in the British West Indies*. Ithaca, N.Y.: Cornell University Press, 1982. The definitive work on the slave rebellions in the Caribbean during the eighteenth century.

Dirks, Robert. *The Black Saturnalia: Conflict and Its Ritual Expression on British West Indian Slave Plantations*. Gainesville: University of Florida Press, 1987. This work details the religious and political strategies of slaves and rebels in the brutal systems of sugar growing and slavery.

Linebaugh, Peter, and Marcus Rediker. *The Many-Headed Hydra: Sailors, Slaves, Commoners, and the Hidden History of the Revolutionary Atlantic*. Boston: Beacon Press, 2000. The authors provide an interesting context for the slave revolts, particularly for Tacky's Rebellion of 1760.

Richardson, Ronald Kent. *Moral Imperium: Afro-Caribbeans and the Transformation of British Rule, 1776-1838*. Westport, Conn.: Greenwood Press, 1987. This work does a good job of tracing how the British Empire in the West Indies changed from the heyday of the slave trade to just after emancipation in 1834.

Rogonzinski, Jan. *A Brief History of the Caribbean: From the Arawak and the Carib to the Present*. New York: Plume, 2000. Part 3 of this survey provides the best introduction for the general reader on the colonial rivalry inherent in the plantation system in the early modern West Indies.

Ward, J. R. *British West Indian Slavery, 1750-1834: The Process of Amelioration*. Oxford, England: Clarendon Press, 1988. The first three chapters of this work do an unparalleled job of concisely describing and explaining the plantocracy of the West Indies.

SEE ALSO: 18th cent.: Expansion of the Atlantic Slave Trade; Apr. 6, 1712: New York City Slave Revolt; Aug., 1712: Maya Rebellion in Chiapas; Nov. 23, 1733: Slaves Capture St. John's Island; Sept. 9, 1739: Stono Rebellion; Jan., 1756-Feb. 15, 1763: Seven Years' War; 1780-1781: Rebellion of Tupac Amaru II; Aug. 22, 1791-Jan. 1, 1804: Haitian Independence; July, 1795-Mar., 1796: Second Maroon War.

RELATED ARTICLES in *Great Lives from History: The Eighteenth Century, 1701-1800*: Joseph Boulogne; George III; Nanny; Guillaume-Thomas Raynal; Granville Sharp; Toussaint Louverture; Tupac Amaru II.

1762
THE ANTIQUITIES OF ATHENS PROMPTS ARCHITECTURAL NEOCLASSICISM

Stuart and Revett's The Antiquities of Athens *shifted the focus of architectural inspiration from ancient Rome to classical Greece and resulted in a uniquely Greek style of neoclassicism often referred to as Greek Revival. The work is considered a landmark in the history of archaeology.*

LOCALE: Athens, Greece; London, England
CATEGORIES: Art; architecture; literature; cultural and intellectual history

KEY FIGURES

Athenian Stuart (James Stuart; 1713-1788), English architect and painter

Nicholas Revett (1721-1804), English architect
Johann Joachim Winckelmann (1717-1768), German historian
Giovanni Battista Piranesi (1720-1778), Italian artist and writer

SUMMARY OF EVENT
In the mid-eighteenth century, what the Europeans knew about the classical world they mainly knew from depictions of Roman ruins in artworks and from Roman copies of Greek original art. The discoveries of the ancient Roman cities of Herculaneum in 1738 and Pompeii in 1748 fired the public's interest in classical antiquity and initiated a new style of art and architecture now known as

neoclassicism, a new classicism based on ancient Roman art and architecture. The term "neoclassicism" was not contemporary with the movement itself; it was first coined in the late nineteenth century to describe the stylistic period from the mid-eighteenth century to the mid-nineteenth century, during which there was a revival of ancient classical motifs in literature, art, and architecture.

During this era, travel to Italy was an essential part of the Grand Tour, an obligatory journey undertaken by Europeans of wealth and social standing to study the cultures of ancient Rome and Renaissance Italy. Travel to Christian Italy was relatively easy, rather safe, and typically quite pleasant. Travel to Greece, however, was much more challenging and considerably more dangerous because of the hostile political situation under the Ottoman Turks, who were in control of Greece at the time.

Athenian Stuart and Nicholas Revett, two intrepid English architects, were among the first European scholars to brave the uncertainties of travel in Greece. Stuart and Revett had met in London in 1742 and afterward traveled together to Rome, where they studied for several years, and then on to Naples. Stuart and Revett belonged to an organization of fellow English travelers known as

the Society of Dilettanti. In 1751, Stuart and Revett convinced the society to finance their bold proposal for an expedition to Greece to document ancient Greek architectural monuments. Their groundbreaking expedition reopened the world of ancient Greece to the West.

From 1751 to 1754, Stuart and Revett worked and lived among the Muslims in Athens. Political unrest, the presence of a Turkish army post stationed atop the Acropolis, a mosque located in the interior section of the Parthenon, and an outbreak of the plague all served to hinder progress on Stuart and Revett's project. To keep attention away from themselves, Stuart and Revett wore Turkish attire as they worked to create meticulous topographical studies and to draw painstakingly measured illustrations.

Through their combined efforts, Stuart and Revett produced the first accurate survey of the buildings on the Athenian Acropolis, which was later published in four volumes and a supplement as *The Antiquities of Athens*. The process of creating and printing the numerous plates and engravings from the hand-drawn originals was arduous and expensive, making the publication process remarkably slow. Volume 1, published in 1762, contains their surveys of minor buildings. Volume 2, published in

A photograph of the ruins of the Temple of Zeus in Greece. (Library of Congress)

A photograph of an ancient Greek tomb with two female figures. (Library of Congress)

the fount of all classical ideals. For his work on *The Antiquities of Athens* and his strong pro-Greek stance, he earned the nickname "Athenian." Johann Joachim Winckelmann, a German art scholar, argued that the classical Greeks, having flourished prior to the imperial Romans, were indeed the wellspring of classicism. Winckelmann advised young artists to study the Greeks if they wanted to become great artists; for Winckelmann, the Greeks invented beauty. The Italian artist Giovanni Battista Piranesi, however, argued against the importance of the Greeks and in favor of the supremacy of ancient Roman art and architecture in both his writings and his excellent engravings of idyllic Roman landscapes. The Greco-Roman controversy polarized neoclassicism into two camps: those who were attracted to the refined simplicity of the classical Greeks and those who favored the ornate grandeur of imperial Rome.

Upon their return to England, Stuart and Revett returned to the practice of architecture, producing numerous examples of Greek Revival and neoclassical design. During this period, the developing picturesque movement emphasized decorative elements in garden landscape settings. Artistically designed and carefully situated classical "ruins" were well suited to the picturesque ideal. Stuart and Revett designed many such classically inspired ornamental buildings for English country houses. Stuart designed a small Doric temple for the garden at Hagley Park (1758), inspired by the Temple of Hephastos in Athens. Stuart's other Greek Revival designs included a garden pavilion, called the Tower of the Winds (1764-1765), based on the octagonal building of the same name in Athens, and the Monument of Lysicrates (1764-1771), inspired by the Choragic Monument of Lysicrates in Athens. At West Wycombe, Revett designed picturesque structures such as an Ionic portico based on the Temple of Bacchus at Teo, a Temple of Flora, and an Island Temple (1778-1780).

SIGNIFICANCE

The Antiquities of Athens influenced the art world in a way that cannot be overstated—the interest in Greek art and architecture that it spawned spread throughout Europe, across to the Americas, and eventually around the world with the expansion of the colonial powers. Not only were artists and architects enamored with the classical cultures of Greece and Rome, but political leaders and philosophers also looked to the ancients for inspiration and precedent. Compared to the excesses of the grand Baroque style and the highly frivolous rococo, both of which were definitively aristocratic styles associ-

1789, was devoted to the buildings on the Acropolis; this volume came out one year after Stuart's death. Volume 3 was published in 1794 with the assistance of the Society of Dilettanti, and volume 4, which contained detailed images of the Parthenon sculptures, appeared in 1816, the same year that Lord Elgin sold the Parthenon sculptures (known as the Elgin marbles) to the British Museum. A supplement was published in 1830. From the time of Stuart and Revett's original proposal to the final book in 1830, the entire project took eighty years. The lapse of time between volumes served to prolong the public's interest in classical Greece, and each new volume fed the public's enthusiasm for ancient Greek architecture, thereby sustaining the neoclassical movement.

The Antiquities of Athens initiated a scholarly debate about the relative value and importance of ancient Greece versus ancient Rome, a debate known as the Greco-Roman controversy. Prior to *The Antiquities of Athens*, nearly all that was known of antiquity was from examples of Roman art and architecture and from Roman copies of original Greek works. Stuart and Revett's work changed this limited knowledge when it opened up the ancient Greek world. Stuart ardently favored Greece as

ated with suppressive European monarchies, Greco-Roman classicism was thought to be restrained, rational, moral, and democratic. The leaders of the American Revolution cited Greco-Roman practices to underpin and justify their fight for liberty. Once established, the new nation drew from classical sources to establish its principles of government and its national architecture. French revolutionaries, too, held up antiquity as a moral and political ideal, and neoclassicism became the defining style of revolutionary France and the Napoleonic era.

Stuart and Revett were among the first archaeologists to classify art and architecture into chronological time periods and to create a systematic history of classical art and architecture. Their practice of making accurate renderings and taking careful measurements introduced a new scholarly approach to the young science of archaeology. Rather than removing items from their original locations, Stuart and Revett drew and measured ancient buildings and sculptures in situ (in place). Because of their precise methodology and their careful attention to detail, today's scholars can see through illustration the ancient Greek buildings and sculptures that have since been moved, sold, looted, or destroyed. The work of Stuart and Revett stands as a landmark in the history of archaeology.

—*Sonia Sorrell*

FURTHER READING
Bergdoll, Barry. *European Architecture, 1750-1890.* New York: Oxford University Press, 2000. A good overview of the influence of the new discoveries in Greece and Rome during the mid-eighteenth century on the neoclassical movement in Europe.

Coltman, Viccy. *Fabricating the Antique: Neoclassicism in Britain, 1760-1800.* Chicago: University of Chicago Press, 2005. An overview of the origins and beginnings of the neoclassical movement in Britain.

Soros, S., ed. *James "Athenian" Stuart.* New Haven, Conn.: Yale University Press, 2006. A collection of essays on Stuart's architecture.

Stoneman, Richard. *A Luminous Land: Artists Discover Greece.* Los Angeles: J. Paul Getty Museum, 1998. An account of how artists have viewed Greece, including the important contributions of Stuart and Revett.

Stuart, James, and Nicholas Revett. *The Antiquities of Athens.* New York: Arno Press, 1980. An affordable reprint of Stuart and Revett's original work.

SEE ALSO: 1719-1724: Stukeley Studies Stonehenge and Avebury; 1726-1729: Voltaire Advances Enlightenment Thought in Europe; c. 1732: Society of Dilettanti Is Established; 1748: Excavation of Pompeii; Aug. 3, 1778: Opening of Milan's La Scala.

RELATED ARTICLES in *Great Lives from History: The Eighteenth Century, 1701-1800:* Robert and James Adam; Johann Wolfgang von Goethe; Immanuel Kant; Angelica Kauffmann; Gotthold Ephraim Lessing; Sir Joshua Reynolds; Friedrich Schiller; William Stukeley; Johann Joachim Winckelmann.

January, 1762-November, 1766
MOZART TOURS EUROPE AS A CHILD PRODIGY

Mozart's experiences as a child prodigy on his European tours played a large part in his later achievements as a world-famous composer.

LOCALE: Central and Western Europe
CATEGORY: Music

KEY FIGURES
Wolfgang Amadeus Mozart (1756-1791), Austrian musician and composer
Leopold Mozart (1719-1787), Austrian musician and father of Wolfgang Amadeus
Friedrich Melchior von Grimm (1723-1807), Bavarian diplomat and man of letters
Johann Christian Bach (1735-1782), son of Johann Sebastian Bach and a musician and composer

SUMMARY OF EVENT
Wolfgang Amadeus Mozart, perhaps the greatest composer of the eighteenth century along with Johann Sebastian Bach, began to play the harpsichord when he was three years old and to compose music when he was four. When he was not quite six, his father, Leopold, took him from their home in Salzburg to Munich on his first concert tour. Leopold Mozart undoubtedly wanted to share his miraculous son with an enlightened world, newly interested in gifted children. He also, however, saw an opportunity to make a fortune. The concert tours, to Munich and Vienna in 1762 and throughout Europe from 1763 through 1766, in which Wolfgang's talented elder sister Nannerl also participated, were, for the most part, enormously successful.

Not much is known about Mozart's first trip to Munich in early January, 1762, but it must have gone very well, for Leopold lost little time planning a foray to the imperial court. On September 1, 1762, the family (mother, father, and the two children) left Salzburg for Vienna. The children enchanted Archduchess Maria Theresa, her genial husband, and the musical court with their playing and their charm. By no means overawed by the archduchess, Wolgang leaped into her lap and kissed her soundly. The Mozart children left Vienna with jewels, golden baubles, more than one hundred ducats, and gala clothing— one of the little archduchesses' court dresses for Nannerl and a court suit which had been made for the Archduke Maximilian for Wolfgang. They also received an invitation from the French ambassador to visit Versailles.

After having been at home in Salzburg for less than six months, the Mozart family left on a Grand Tour of Europe in early June, 1763. They did not return until November, 1766. In Munich, they gave well-received concerts before the Elector Maximilian Joseph and other members of the Bavarian nobility, but in the bourgeois cities of Augsburg and Ulm, they met with less success. They were also unlucky at Württemberg, because Duke Karl Eugen was preoccupied with leading his troops on maneuvers and paid no attention to them. In Mannheim, at the musical court of the elector of the Palatinate, Karl Theodore, however, the children enjoyed a triumph. There, too, they heard the orchestra directed by Karl Stamitz, famous for its use of woodwinds and its dramatic crescendos and diminuendos, as well as for other subtle tonal coloring. This orchestra would leave its mark on Mozart's own music.

In Frankfurt, the Mozarts gave three well-attended concerts, where the seven-year-old Wolfgang played concertos and sonatas, improvised on the harpsichord and organ, identified single notes and chords played to him, and played on the clavier with its keyboard covered by a cloth. Johann Wolfgang von Goethe, then fourteen years old, attended the first of these concerts and later remembered being impressed by the little man with his powdered wig and tiny sword. At Koblenz, the children played for the local archbishop, and at Aachen they played for the princess Amelia, sister of Frederick the Great of Prussia, who paid them with kisses instead of money. In Brussels, they fared better. Musicales in the houses of various aristocrats netted them gold snuffboxes and needle cases, as well as many coins of the realm (thalers and louis d'or).

In Paris, the children played first for Madame de Pompadour, who had Wolfgang placed on a table, the better

to scrutinize him. A concert before Louis XV and Queen Marie followed. At some time after this, the Mozarts were honored by being allowed to stand like lackeys behind the king and queen at the royal dining table, where Wolfgang was fed tidbits by the queen. The most valuable of their Parisian acquaintances, though, was the well-connected Bavarian diplomat and man of letters Friedrich Melchior von Grimm, who made the success of the Mozarts one of his chief occupations. In an article in the *Correspondance Litteraire*, Grimm introduced the phenomenally gifted Wolfgang to the enlightened intellectual public of Europe, paying tribute to him as a virtuoso performer of others' works but stressing his own inspired improvisations.

The grandeur of the rich and powerful, as well as the squalor in which many less-fortunate Parisians lived, certainly made an impression on Mozart. He was busy absorbing musical matters, too. He attended both French and Italian operas, as well as performances of the famous Concert Spirituel, where he heard keyboard music by Johann Gottfried Eckhart, an exponent of the Sturm und Drang movement in music, and Johann Schobert, who had translated the dynamics and tonal colors of the Mannheim orchestra to keyboard compositions. Schobert especially, although Leopold Mozart did not like him or his music, exerted substantial influence on Wolfgang's early concertos and sonatas.

In early April, 1763, the Mozarts moved on to England. Four days after their arrival in London, the children appeared at Buckingham Palace to play for King George III and Queen Charlotte. There they met and became good friends with Johann Christian Bach, music master to the royal couple. A composer in the so-called *galant* style, he was an important model for young Mozart, who also learned much from the music of Karl Friedrich Abel and George Frideric Handel. Mozart attended performances of the Italian opera and took singing lessons from the celebrated castrato Giovanni Manzuoli, which certainly helped him to master the vocal style of Italian opera. From this time, opera became a dominant interest for the child, and he talked about writing an opera with children in the principal roles upon his return to Salzburg.

At first, the Mozart children's public appearances in London were very well attended. Leopold contracted a serious illness in the summer of 1764, however, bringing these appearances to an abrupt end. Wolfgang, however, was not idle. Taking advantage of the enforced silence, he composed his first symphonies. By the time Leopold recovered and the concerts were resumed, they met with only occasional success, so Wolfgang was made avail-

The young Wolfgang Amadeus Mozart is introduced to Madame de Pompadour. (Francis R. Niglutsch)

able to callers at the Mozart lodgings. These callers paid five shillings each for the privilege of testing his ability to sight read, to identify notes or chords by ear, and to improvise. One of the callers was Daines Barrington, a scholar of wide interests. In a report to the Royal Society, he recorded his astonishment at the child's ability to improvise impressive operatic scenes on a given emotion, such as love or rage. He related, too, that Wolfgang had slipped down from the keyboard to play with a cat and that his father had had some difficulty in getting him to return to the examination in progress at the clavier.

In the summer of 1765, the Mozarts left England for Holland. There a serious illness, possibly typhoid fever, brought Nannerl to death's door. Just as she recovered, the same illness attacked Wolfgang and reduced him to skin and bones. Toward the end of January, 1766, the children were well enough to appear in public again. Concerts at the Hague before Princess Caroline and Prince William followed, at which Wolfgang performed keyboard variations on the Dutch national anthem, "Willem van Nassau." Some of his new orchestral music was also played. It was clear that Wolfgang was becoming a composer.

After brief visits to the salons of Paris, to the estate of the prince de Condé in Dijon, and to Lyon, Leopold decided to head home via Switzerland. In Geneva, the Mozarts met the composer André-Étienne Grétry, who was not much impressed by Wolfgang's talent, but in Lausanne, where the Mozarts traveled next, Duke Louis Eugene of Württemberg overwhelmed them with his enthusiasm for the prodigy. Together with Samuel Tissot, a physician much interested in the phenomenon of child geniuses, the duke wrote a panegyric—published in the October 11, 1766, issue of the Lausanne periodical, *Aristide ou le Citoyen*—which described Mozart as a heaven-sent immortal. In Zürich, the Mozarts were in the company of poets Solomon Gessner and Christian Fürchtegott Gellert. The family then made a detour to Donaueschingen to visit Prince Joseph Wenzel von Fürstenberg, who welcomed them warmly and rewarded them richly. Eventually, they reached Munich, where Wolfgang performed for the elector. Immediately, however, a serious illness, possibly rheumatic fever, attacked the boy and confined him to bed for a month.

Recovered and back in Salzburg in late autumn, 1766,

Wolfgang must have missed the variety, stimulation, and excitement of travel. Leopold returned to his position as vice-chapel master, his wife returned to her domestic concerns, Nannerl returned to preparation for an acceptable station in life, and Wolfgang returned to work and study which, his father hoped, would make him a highly competent and well-rewarded composer.

SIGNIFICANCE

Fame, elevated social status, and enough money to provide a comfortable bourgeois existence for his family were three of the consequences of Mozart's early tours. The fame he garnered is significant historically, in that the international fame of a musician—or of any entertainer—was still a relatively new phenomenon. As his fame spread, people wished to see at first hand Mozart demonstrate gifts that they had already heard about, and this desire to experience the presence of a famous person built upon a growing population with disposable income, as well as the increased speed and distance of communication.

Other, negative, results of the tour included Mozart's deprivation of a "normal" childhood and a strenuous schedule that caused his physical delicacy and frequent illness. The musical, social, intellectual, and spiritual benefits the child prodigy garnered from experiences on his travels were by far the most important outcomes, however: They helped to make him a composer preeminent in universality, sympathy, and the understanding of humankind.

—*Margaret Duggan*

FURTHER READING

Gutman, Robert W. *Mozart: A Cultural Biography*. New York: Harcourt Brace, 1999. Balanced account. Views Mozart in the intellectual, political, and artistic world in which he lived. Includes bibliography, notes, and index.

King, A. Hyatt, and Monica Carolan, eds. *The Letters of Mozart and His Family*. 2d ed. 2 vols. New York: St. Martin's Press, 1966. New edition of Emily Anderson's three-volume 1938 work. Chronologically arranged. Includes notes and index.

Wignall, Harrison James. *In Mozart's Footsteps*. New York: Paragon House, 1991. Popular account of Mozart's travels. Has bibliographical references.

SEE ALSO: c. 1701-1750: Bach Pioneers Modern Music; c. 1709: Invention of the Piano; Jan. 29, 1728: Gay Produces the First Ballad Opera; Apr. 13, 1742: First Performance of Handel's *Messiah*; Oct. 5, 1762: First Performance of Gluck's *Orfeo and Euridice*; 1773: Goethe Inaugurates the Sturm und Drang Movement; Apr. 27, 1784: First Performance of *The Marriage of Figaro*; 1795-1797: Paganini's Early Violin Performances.

RELATED ARTICLES in *Great Lives from History: The Eighteenth Century, 1701-1800*: Johann Sebastian Bach; Frederick the Great; George III; George Frideric Handel; Joseph Haydn; Louis XV; Maria Theresa; Wolfgang Amadeus Mozart; Madame de Pompadour.

April, 1762
ROUSSEAU PUBLISHES *THE SOCIAL CONTRACT*

In The Social Contract, *Rousseau responded to the political tyranny of his age by arguing that government derived its legitimacy and power from the free consent of the governed. The text revolutionized political philosophy, contributing to the development of a school of thought known as social contract theory that still exists two and a half centuries later.*

LOCALE: France
CATEGORY: Philosophy

KEY FIGURES

Jean-Jacques Rousseau (1712-1778), French philosopher, novelist, and reformer
Chrétien-Guillaume de Lamoignon de Malesherbes (1721-1794), French censor
John Locke (1632-1704), English philosopher
Thomas Hobbes (1588-1679), English philosopher

SUMMARY OF EVENT

Jean-Jacques Rousseau was at the height of his fame when his *Du contrat social: Ou, Principes du droit politique* (1762; *A Treatise on the Social Contract: Or, The Principles of Politic Law*, 1764; better known as *The Social Contract*) was published. His earlier writings during the 1750's had created scandal and brought him adulation as well. As a celebrity, he appeared before his adoring reading public in strange costumes and behaved with boorish manners. He espoused the unconventional view that developing civilizations had corrupted the natural goodness of people, destroying their freedom and their free will in the process. He had also produced a successful opera and a runaway best-seller, *Julie: Ou, La Nouvelle Héloïse* (1761; *Eloise: Or, A Series of Original Letters*, 1761; also as *Julie: Or, The New Eloise*, 1968; better known as *The New Héloïse*), with its themes of forbidden love thwarted by parental disapproval and corruptive city life.

Rousseau's *Social Contract*, by contrast, dealt with political philosophy, proposing how government should operate, how individual freedom could be reconciled with the dictates of society, and how the rights of citizens could be attained in a just state. Rather than focusing on practical solutions, *The Social Contract* searched for the principles of "political right," applicable only to ideal conditions. A four-part treatise, the book set forth the principles of legitimate and stable sovereignty. The opening section establishes the foundations of political authority, tracing the transition from anarchic individualism of "the noble savage" to the collective authority of society over the individual. Entering into a contract with others to create a community, the individual surrenders all rights to the state, becoming equal to all other community members.

The second section of the text continues the theory of what is right and just in the political and moral life of the community, elaborating on various legal systems, the legislative powers that belong to the people, and the limits of sovereign power. The third section weighs the merits of four forms of government: democratic government, which Rousseau distrusts; aristocratic, which Rousseau finds acceptable if an elective aristocracy exists; monarchic, which Rousseau prefers but only if the ruler is wise and just; and a government that includes a mix of the other three. The best government for any particular community, large or small, concludes Rousseau, depends on practical, moral, and theoretical factors unique to that community. The final section presents Rousseau's plan for establishing and operating an ideal government, somewhat modeled after that of the ancient Roman republic. The plan attempts to strengthen the constitution of the state and create structures to prevent government from becoming corrupt and unjust. Opponents would be censored, banished, or put to death.

Rousseau develops several key concepts in *The Social Contract*, including the social contract itself, the general will, and sovereignty. The social contract comes about when people, fearing for their own safety or promoting their own well-being, voluntarily agree to live together as a harmonious community. Natural or individual rights and independence must give way to rational desires for the general good, shared powers, responsibilities, and

moral obligations within the community. The benevolent community, in turn, expects all members to be involved equally in the law-making process. Rousseau concludes that this community of participating individuals will then freely obey the laws that they themselves have determined.

"The general will," according to Rousseau, activates the social contract so that states and institutions come into existence. The general will is not the sum of many competing wills within the community, nor merely popular opinion. Instead, the general will reflects a public spirit in which individuals, transformed as right-thinking citizens with a love of virtue and justice, always seek the common good. Through assemblies and under the direction of wise and capable leaders, the citizenry determines community interests, makes laws, and develops the general will. Rousseau recognizes that its success depends on a shared moral vision and some ability by all individuals to reason with ideas.

Sovereignty (that is, the supreme authority over a given territory or people), according to Rousseau, is the exercising of the general will by the citizens themselves. Assemblies, held at fixed and periodic intervals with all citizens participating, vote on issues, such as whether the existing form of government should be preserved, or whether the current administrators should be replaced. To aid citizens, leaders work behind the scenes to create a communal spirit and mold the consensual will of the assembled citizens. These leaders have immense power by administering and executing the laws, controlling and censoring those elements contrary to the general will. Yet they are morally bound to serve the people, not to be their master. If the governing body attempts to subvert the general will, the citizens then have the right to replace the government. For Rousseau's readers of the eighteenth century, reared on the divine right of kings and feudal privilege, this was revolutionary. *The Social Contract* boldly advocates that the people, when enlightened and responsible, have the right to determine governance.

Rousseau's views have often been compared by scholars to those of the earlier "social contract theorists" Thomas Hobbes and John Locke, for all three explored the purposes of government and why rational individuals need government. Rousseau appreciated Hobbes's methodology and precision in defining the terms of the social contract, but he disapproved of Hobbes's negative vision of humans as being solely motivated by power and greed. Rousseau also disagreed with Hobbes's theory that once the people consented to an absolute ruler or monarch, they were obliged to obey so long as the ruler protected them.

Rousseau, as did Locke before him, espoused the view that humans, in spite of their darker side, had the potential of developing goodness, morality, and a sense of justice. Rousseau and Locke believed government should be based on the consent of the people, and both championing individual rights and limited government. Rousseau, however, differed with Locke on who actually governs: Locke desired a representative government, chosen from the people at large, where majority rule prevailed—somewhat on the order of a parliament; Rousseau insisted that every citizen participate in person and vote to determine the contents of the general will. Strangely, all three "social contract theorists"—Hobbes, Locke, and Rousseau—were persecuted and exiled when their political views became known.

In the case of Rousseau, the publication of *The Social Contract* in April and *Émile: Ou, De l'éducation* (1762; *Emilius and Sophia: Or, a New System of Education*, 1762-1763) in May made him a hunted fugitive in France and Switzerland. Before publication, French censor Chrétien-Guillaume de Lamoignon de Malesherbes, anticipating serious problems, urged his friend Rousseau to remove his name from the title page of *The Social Contract*, a fashionable way of circumventing censorship problems. Rousseau refused. By June, public outrage caused authorities in Paris and Geneva to ban and then burn both books, claiming they were subversive and challenged the existing political institutions.

After warrants were issued for Rousseau's arrest in both France and Switzerland, he fled to Germany, coming under the protection of Frederick the Great of Prussia. From 1762 until his death in 1778, Rousseau lived a vagabond's life, suffering failing health and broken spirits. His fame and influence on political reform waned, with *The Social Contract* somewhat forgotten. However, when Rousseau's *Les Confessions de J.-J. Rousseau* (1782, 1789; *The Confessions of J.-J. Rousseau*, 1783-1790; better known as *Confessions*) and *Les Rêveries du promeneur solitaire* (1782; *The Reveries of the Solitary Walker*, 1783) were published posthumously, a cult arose in France devoted to restoring Rousseau's prominence, promulgating his principles, and glorifying him as a martyr.

SIGNIFICANCE

In 1789, the organizers of the French Revolution seized on Rousseau's passionate slogans, maxims, and metaphors found in *The Social Contract* to justify their revolution. They also used the book for propaganda purposes, claiming Rousseau to be the father of republican France.

The Social Contract fired the enthusiasm for revolution not only in France but also in the American colonies. The book influenced Jeffersonian democracy with its emphasis on enlightened people governing themselves and elected officials accountable to the people.

As a social contract theorist, Rousseau also influenced political philosophers such as Immanuel Kant, Georg Wilhelm Friedrich Hegel, David Hume, Friedrich Engels, and Karl Marx. Because parts of *The Social Contract* are mystical and obscure, scholars over the centuries have variously interpreted the small book as supporting totalitarianism, nationalism, collectivism, liberal individualism, and direct democracy. The debate continues.

—*Richard Whitworth*

FURTHER READING

Cranston, Maurice. *The Noble Savage: Jean-Jacques Rousseau, 1754-1762*. Chicago: University of Chicago Press, 1991. Provides biographical data on the germination of *The Social Contract*.

Cullen, Daniel. *Freedom in Rousseau's Political Philosophy*. De Kalb: Northern Illinois University Press, 1993. Examines Rousseau's concepts of natural, civil, and moral freedom.

Levine, Andrew. *The General Will: Rousseau, Marx, Communism*. New York: Cambridge University Press, 1993. Interprets Rousseau's concept of the general will; applies it to modern Marxist, socialistic, and democratic theories.

Medina, Vicente. *Social Contract Theories: Political Obligation or Anarchy?* Savage, Md.: Rowman & Littlefield, 1990. Synthesizes the research on advocates of contractarianism, such as Hobbes, Locke, Rousseau, Kant, and Hume.

Portis, Edward B. *Reconstructing the Classics: Political Theory from Plato to Marx*. Chatham, N.J.: Chatham House, 1994. Useful in comparing the early social contract theorists with those of modern times.

Qvortrup, Mads. *The Political Philosophy of Jean-Jacques Rousseau: The Impossibility of Reason*. Manchester, England: Manchester University Press, 2003. Analysis of Rousseau's political thought. Qvortrup argues that Rousseau was not a radical, revolutionary democrat, but was a conservative constitutionalist.

Riley, Patrick, ed. *The Cambridge Companion to Rousseau*. New York: Cambridge University Press, 2001. Collection of essays providing an overview of Rousseau's life and an analysis of his ideas. Includes an essay interpreting Rousseau's political philosophy.

Rousseau, Jean-Jacques. *The Collected Writings of Rousseau.* 5 vols. Edited and translated by Christopher Kelly et al. Hanover, N.H.: University Press of New England, 1990. Volume 3 contains a standard translation of *The Social Contract*, supplemented by editorial notes.

Wokler, Robert. *Rousseau: A Very Short Introduction.* New York: Oxford University Press, 2001. One in a series of books providing concise overviews of philosophers. Chapter 4 offers an analysis of Rousseau's ideas of liberty, virtue, and citizenship.

SEE ALSO: Oct., 1725: Vico Publishes *The New Science*; 1739-1740: Hume Publishes *A Treatise of Human Nature*; 1748: Montesquieu Publishes *The Spirit of the Laws*; July 27, 1758: Helvétius Publishes *De l'esprit*; July, 1764: Voltaire Publishes *A Philosophical Dictionary for the Pocket*; 1770: Publication of Holbach's *The System of Nature*; Jan. 10, 1776: Paine Publishes *Common Sense*; July 4, 1776: Declaration of Independence; 1781: Kant Publishes *Critique of Pure Reason*; 1782-1798: Publication of Rousseau's *Confessions*; July 14, 1789: Fall of the Bastille; 1790: Burke Lays the Foundations of Modern Conservatism; Feb. 22, 1791-Feb. 16, 1792: Thomas Paine Publishes *Rights of Man*.

RELATED ARTICLES in *Great Lives from History: The Eighteenth Century, 1701-1800*: Frederick the Great; David Hume; Immanuel Kant; Louis XV; Montesquieu; Jean-Jacques Rousseau.

October 5, 1762
FIRST PERFORMANCE OF GLUCK'S *ORFEO AND EURIDICE*

Composed when he was already a famous opera composer, Gluck's work with librettist Calzabigi led him to champion revolutionary reforms in opera that have made him a key figure in the transition from the Baroque to the classical and pre-Romantic styles.

LOCALE: Vienna, Austria
CATEGORIES: Theater; music

KEY FIGURES
Christoph Gluck (1714-1787), Bavarian composer
Ranieri Calzabigi (1714-1795), Italian writer and librettist
Giacomo Durazzo (1717-1794), Italian poet and impresario
Gaetano Guadagni (1729-1792), Italian alto castrato

SUMMARY OF EVENT
Largely self-taught, Christoph Gluck gained early experience in Prague, Vienna, and Milan, developing a conservative and direct style of writing. He composed his first operas in Italy (1741-1745), for Milan, Venice, Crema, and Turin. Invited to London, he produced two operas (1746) that were poorly received. His works failed to impress George Frideric Handel, but he had success as a performer on the "musical glasses." A traveling musician for six more years, he managed to fulfill opera commissions in Dresden, Vienna, Copenhagen, Prague, and Naples, while also performing in Hamburg and Munich. It was only in 1752, at the age of thirty-eight, that he decided to settle in Vienna, where he acquired a princely patron and contacts at the imperial court.

Gluck quickly found favor with the imperial family and its circle, while he became a protégé of the powerful intendant of Vienna's theaters, Count Giacomo Durazzo. The latter secured him important employments plus commissions for numerous operas offered at court. These were at first in Italian, but Gluck then followed the new taste Durazzo was promoting for stage works in French. Durazzo's influence was yet more significant, however, since he was an enthusiastic advocate for the new program of reforming opera.

Opera in the Baroque era had been highly stylized, involving distinct set pieces (mainly arias, but also duets and ensembles) spaced between long passages of declamation over keyboard chords known as *recitativo secco* ("dry" recitative). The ultimate formalization of this idiom had been made in widely utilized librettos by the famous Pietro Metastasio (1698-1782), who since 1730 had been the court poet in Vienna and was originally a moral reformer. By Gluck's day, operas were generally quite artificial entertainments, with highly contrived plots and an emphasis upon vocal display by the singers.

The artificiality and ornamentation of the prevalent operatic style provoked a new movement in opera that valued dramatic coherence, theatrical verity, and a closer linking of music to the poetic texts being set. One of the most influential of the writers and intellectuals who advocated such reforms was Francesco Algarotti (1712-

1764), whose *Saggio sopra l'opera in musica* (1755; *An Essay on the Opera*, 1767) was a widely read critique of alleged abuses in the form. Other writers added pleas of their own, while a number of composers were influenced by their ideas, notably Tommaso Traetta (1727-1779).

In 1761, the Italian businessman, poet, and intellectual Ranieri Calzabigi arrived in Vienna. An admirer and defender of Metastasio, he was otherwise a strong advocate of reform ideals and was quickly brought into the city's theatrical life by Durazzo. Durazzo drew Calzabigi into one progressive project, the mounting of a "reform" ballet-pantomime, *Don Juan: Ou, Le Festin de Pierre* (1761), composed by Gluck. The latter had long been a traditionalist: He had composed twenty-nine operas at that point, of which twenty-one had been Italian, and sixteen of those twenty-one had used texts by Metastasio. There has been much debate as to how much of Gluck's involvement in "reform opera" was self-motivated and

how much was at Calzabigi's prompting. The composer himself later admitted Calzabigi's influence. Nevertheless, Gluck was seen by Durazzo and Calzabigi as the ideal collaborator in an opera exemplifying the ideals of the reformers.

A court occasion provided the opportunity for the production of *Orfeo ed Euridice* (*Orfeo and Euridice*), which was first performed on October 5, 1762, and constituted one of the most enduring treatments of the myth of music's first hero, Orpheus. While by no means as radical or novel as the later mythology of the opera would have it, the production was a model of dramatic clarity within direct musical expressiveness. It still included set pieces, but they were integrated into a coherent and uncluttered entity. The work was enthusiastically received, not the least thanks to its star performer, the widely admired castrato Gaetano Guadagni, who created the title role. (The following year, 1763, he created the role of Oreste in Traetta's own "reform" opera, *Ifigenia in Tauride*, and he returned in another Gluck opera in 1765. In later years, Guadagni specialized entirely in the role of Orfeo in various operatic works by Gluck and others.)

Gluck does not seem to have converted entirely to the reformed, post-Baroque style of opera, for he returned to the traditional style in five more Italian stage pieces, plus one in French. Even in these six productions, however, reform influences were undeniably evident in his work. Durazzo was forced out of the Viennese court, but Calzabigi stayed on to collaborate on two more Italian operas with Gluck, *Alceste* (pr. 1767, pb. 1769) and *Paride ed Elena* (1770). These two works sealed Gluck's commitment to the new aesthetics, especially with the greater integration of the chorus's role in the first of them.

When Gluck had *Alceste* published in 1769, it appeared with a dedicatory preface over Gluck's signature but actually written by Calzabigi. Exactly whose initiatives were paramount in the composition is not clear, but the statements made in the preface seem to fuse the ideas on which

Christoph Gluck playing the clavichord, from a portrait detail by Joseph Duplessis, 1773. (Hulton Archive/Getty Images)

the two collaborators agreed, and it stands as the clearest manifesto of the so-called Viennese reform opera movement. In this manifesto, the collaborators emphasized their goals: They sought to make the music serve the poetry and not just call attention to itself; to keep the plot clear and direct, without distracting interruptions; to use vocal forms purely for dramatic expression and not cheap display; to break down the old, arbitrary division between recitative and aria; and "to avoid complexity at the expense of clarity."

The goals expressed in the preface to *Alceste* were all intended to fulfill the understanding "that simplicity, truth, and naturalness are the great principles of beauty in all manifestations of art." The latter statement was a revealing maxim, for it matched perfectly the mentality of the pioneering art historian Johann Joachim Winckelmann in his influential (if misleading) definition of "classicism" in ancient Greek terms as "noble simplicity and calm greatness." True figures of the Enlightenment, Calzabigi and Gluck were the most effective exponents of establishing the new ideals of classicism in music and theater.

SIGNIFICANCE

Most of Gluck's operas have had uneven fates and often-limited appreciation, in unfair disdain for their seeming oversimplicity. *Orfeo and Euridice*, however, has been an exception. Berlioz, who adored Gluck, revised the French version of the opera for Pauline Viardot. In the early twenty-first century, the opera has most often been performed in the original Italian but with interpolations from the Paris revision. Richard Wagner, who saw Gluck as the preeminent "reformer" of opera before himself, made a German revision of Gluck's *Iphigénie en Aulide* (1774) aimed at updating his predecessor in his own terms. It has been *Orfeo and Euridice*, however, that has kept Gluck's name alive, surviving as the earliest opera firmly established in the standard international repertoire and an endlessly beloved vehicle for singers.

Though Antonio Salieri (1750-1825) was his one disciple and stylistic heir, Gluck left behind no true "school" for his "reform opera." Such younger contemporaries as Wolfgang Amadeus Mozart were influenced by his techniques but never fully accepted his model. Nevertheless, his principles of dramatic clarity and his replacement of the old "dry" recitative with consistent orchestral writing became standard in operatic form in the early Romantic, lyric theater of the next century. Critical and public appreciation of the "noble simplicity" of Gluck's dramatic expressiveness remains backward. Nevertheless, the tra-

dition of Gluck's role in the reform and classicizing of opera, however oversimplified, has secured him an indelible place in cultural history.

—John W. Barker

FURTHER READING

Drummond, John D. *Opera in Perspective*. Minneapolis: University of Minnesota Press, 1986. Contextual survey of operas and their history; includes a section on *Orfeo and Euridice*.

Einstein, Alfred. *Gluck*. Translated by Eric Blom. London: Dent, 1936. A long-standard study of the composer's life and career.

Grout, Donald Jay. *A Short History of Opera*. 2d ed. New York: Columbia University Press, 1965. Standard overview of the art form's history.

Howard, Patricia. *Christoph Willibald Gluck: A Guide to Research*. New York: Garland, 1987. Thoroughly assembled and annotated survey of sources and studies of the composer.

_____. *Gluck and the Birth of Modern Opera*. New York: St. Martin's Press, 1964. Probing study by the leading Gluck specialist.

_____, ed. *C. W. Gluck: Orfeo*. New York: Cambridge University Press, 1981. Topical essays on the work by a group of leading scholars and musicians.

Kerman, Joseph. *Opera as Drama*. Rev. ed. Berkeley: University of California Press, 1988. Classic study, with a fine chapter on *Orfeo and Euridice*.

Newman, Ernest. *Gluck and the Opera*. London: Bertram Dobell, 1895. Reprint. London: Gollancz, 1967. Still a penetrating study.

Sadie, Stanley, ed. *New Grove Dictionary of Music and Musicians*. Vol. 10. New York: Grove, 2001.

_____. *New Grove Dictionary of Opera*. Vol. 2. New York: Grove, 1992. Multiauthor articles on Gluck and *Orfeo and Euridice*, each with an extensive bibliography.

SEE ALSO: Jan. 29, 1728: Gay Produces the First Ballad Opera; Dec. 7, 1732: Covent Garden Theatre Opens in London; Jan., 1762-Nov., 1766: Mozart Tours Europe as a Child Prodigy; Aug. 3, 1778: Opening of Milan's La Scala; Apr. 27, 1784: First Performance of *The Marriage of Figaro*.

RELATED ARTICLES in *Great Lives from History: The Eighteenth Century, 1701-1800*: Christoph Gluck; George Frideric Handel; Wolfgang Amadeus Mozart; Johann Joachim Winckelmann.

1763
BAYES ADVANCES PROBABILITY THEORY

Thomas Bayes's work on the inverse problem in probabilities, which attempted to calculate the probabilities of causes from those of events, helped to advance investigations in the foundations of probability. Bayes's theorem is a major part of subjectivist approaches to epistemology, statistics, and inductive logic.

LOCALE: London, England
CATEGORIES: Mathematics; science and technology

KEY FIGURES
Thomas Bayes (1701/1702-1761), mathematician, clergyman, and author of the first work on inverse probabilities
Richard Price (1723-1791), clergyman and editor of Bayes's essay on probabilities
Jakob I Bernoulli (1655-1705), mathematician and author of a standard text on probability

SUMMARY OF EVENT

Thomas Bayes was a clergyman known for his mathematical interests. Little else is known of his life, however, despite extensive research by scholars interested in his work. He was educated at the University of Edinburgh in Scotland, and he spent most of his life as a minister in Tunbridge Wells, a fashionable spa not far from London. He became a fellow of the Royal Society of London in 1742, and after his death in 1761, his manuscripts came to the attention of the Reverend Richard Price, who communicated Bayes's essay about probability to the Royal Society. The essay, "An Essay Toward Solving a Problem in the Doctrine of Chances," appeared in the society's journal, *Philosophical Transactions*, in 1763, and Bayes's own introduction had been replaced by one written by Price. Bayes published nothing during his lifetime in his own name.

Bayes was deeply interested in confronting some of the fundamental issues in probability. Even though some of his views have not found universal acceptance, some of the results given in his essay have proved to be both important technical tools in probability and means for understanding the foundations of the subject. The essay itself did not long retain the interests of the scientific community, but its results were brought back to the attention of those interested in probability in the nineteenth century, and his ideas have remained central in this area of mathematics.

There had been quite a tradition of probability texts by the time that Bayes began writing, the most prominent (in English) being that of Abraham de Moivre (*The Doctrine of Chances: Or, A Method of Calculating the Probability of Events in Play*, 1718). Bayes, however, preferred to go back to the older tradition of Jakob I Bernoulli for the formulation both of the basis of the subject and of the problem he was attempting to solve. Bayes, in his essay, was looking at the general problem of determining the probability of an event if what one had to go on was the number of times that event occurred out of a certain number of trials. Much effort had been devoted since the time of the original correspondence about probability between Blaise Pascal and Pierre de Fermat in the seventeenth century to calculating the probability of various outcomes if the original probability of an event were known. The problem Bayes considered is the "inverse problem" for probabilities, trying to recover the original probability from the observation of the outcomes of trials.

Bayes started off with a definition of probability that differed from that of de Moivre, to whose work he makes no explicit reference. The tradition had been to regard the probability of an event as a fraction, which worked out if the sample space (the collection of possible outcomes) was discrete. If the sample space were continuous, however, then a definition using calculus might have been expected. Bayes avoids using explicit notions from calculus by referring to geometrical areas instead. One of the few publications of Bayes that came out during his lifetime was a defense of the ideas of the calculus as laid out by Sir Isaac Newton, so it is clear that he was well acquainted with the state of the calculus. It is unclear whether his move from calculus in his presentation of his ideas about probability was motivated by the wish for a wider readership or in deference to the geometrical style in which Newton had himself written his *Philosophiae naturalis principia mathematica* (1687; *The Mathematical Principles of Natural Philosophy*, 1729; best known as the *Principia*, 1848). Bayes seems to have been determined in being excruciatingly careful in justifying his steps, and he may have felt that the geometrical arguments lent themselves to more thorough scrutiny than arguments from calculus.

The problem that Bernoulli had originally confronted had to do with statistical inference in a binomial distribution. Given a certain number of successes out of a certain number of trials, the determination of the probability of a success on a single trial presumably involved some sort of algebraic combination of the numbers. The difficulty Bernoulli faced, however, was that the values that emerged were too complicated to calculate. Bayes gave himself the advantage of dealing with a continuous distribution (represented by points in the plane), which got around the algebraic difficulties that made Bernoulli's task insurmountable.

The image given by Bayes as the starting point for his calculations in his essay was that of a table on which balls were rolled. The table was marked off in different regions, and the locations where the balls stopped were recorded. On the basis of this model, Bayes was able to calculate what the probability was that a given ball would stop at a given place. He does not provide a justification for the choice of model, and there was a good deal of criticism in subsequent centuries over whether that picture does represent the kind of probability necessary for analyzing more general situations.

In particular, Bayes seeks to justify his model by working on the assumption that if there is no information about the distribution of the results of an experiment, there should be an equal chance of its taking on any of the possible outcomes. While Bayes is fairly careful in his statement of the circumstances under which this ignorance is allowed to dictate the distribution, most subsequent readers of his text looked at it through the lens of the later "principle of insufficient reason" introduced by the French mathematician Pierre-Simon Laplace. Those who have gone back to Bayes's original text without looking through the lens of Laplace find Bayes's model persuasively defended.

Bayes also indicates in his essay how to calculate some of the areas that arise. This is a tribute to his strength as a mathematician, and the numbers serve to illustrate the reasonableness of his approach to the inverse problem. It is unclear how much editing was done by Price in sending the manuscript to the Royal Society, although he certainly replaced Bayes's original introduction with his own. Some of Bayes's points might be easier to understand if his introduction had survived.

There is a result in probability theory known as Bayes's theorem. The theorem gives a value for the probability of one event (given another) in terms of prior probabilities and the probability of the second event given the first. It is a relatively simple formula in the case of a discrete distribution and does not appear explicitly in Bayes's essay. Nevertheless, the use of his name for the theorem is perhaps justified by the care with which he examined the application of observation to the calculation of probabilities. Although Bayes himself does not refer to the probabilities of "causes," his technique has been used to examine many issues in the philosophy of science proceeding from observation.

Significance

Thomas Bayes's work did not receive much attention from nineteenth century thinkers and writers on the subject of probability. It is not clear why he received so little attention, except that his lack of status in the field of mathematics during his lifetime may have provided little impetus for the warranted attention. Also, it is not clear why Bayes failed to publish the essay during his lifetime, although it is possible that he would not want it published because he found the philosophical side of the paper unpersuasive. It might be the case that he was continuing to work on the technical aspects of calculating the values for the expressions that involved areas.

Laplace's approach to the problem of inverse probabilities was, for many years, thought to have settled the issue of the best form such a theory should take. In the twentieth century, however, many mathematicians and philosophers began to look at Laplace's arguments more carefully and to examine Bayes's approach afresh. This led to Bayesianism emerging as the dominant philosophical approach to probability, since it could fit into either the objective perspective (which takes probabilities as measurable quantities in the world) or the subjective view (which takes probabilities as reflections of beliefs and attitudes). Some philosophers of probability have even tried to go back further into the era before Bayes, but the majority of probabilists continue to find Bayes's approach, as presented in his essay, helpful and persuasive.

—*Thomas Drucker*

Further Reading

Bayes, Thomas. *Facsimiles of Two Papers by Bayes. I. "An Essay Toward Solving a Problem in the Doctrine of Chances," and II. "A Letter on Asymptotic Series from Bayes to John Canton."* New York: Hafner, 1963. A reprint of the 1940 facsimile edition of Bayes's major paper and an additional article from the same journal volume of 1763. The first article includes Richard Price's foreword and his discussion of Bayes's essay.

Dale, Andrew I. *A History of Inverse Probability.* New York: Springer-Verlag, 1991. Follows the reception of Bayes's work to the beginning of the twentieth century.

_____. *Most Honourable Remembrance: The Life and Work of Thomas Bayes.* New York: Springer, 2003. The most complete biography, which includes Bayes's essay.

Hald, Anders. *A History of Mathematical Statistics from 1750 to 1930*. New York: John Wiley and Sons, 1998. A thorough examination of the technical parts of Bayes's essay.

Lindley, D. V. "Thomas Bayes." In *Statisticians of the Centuries*. New York: Springer, 2001. Connects Bayes's work to the twentieth century.

Shafer, Glenn. "Bayes's Two Arguments for the Rule of Conditioning." *Annals of Statistics* 10 (1982): 1075-1089. A scrupulous, critical reading of Bayes's text.

Stigler, Stephen M. *The History of Statistics*. Cambridge, Mass.: Harvard University Press, 1986. Perhaps the best explanation of Bayes's essay.

Todhunter, I. *A History of the Mathematical Theory of Probability*. New York: Chelsea, 1949. Reconstructs Bayes's mathematical arguments.

SEE ALSO: 1718: Bernoulli Publishes His Calculus of Variations; 1733: De Moivre Describes the Bell-Shaped Curve; 1740: Maclaurin's Gravitational Theory; 1743-1744: D'Alembert Develops His Axioms of Motion; 1748: Agnesi Publishes *Analytical Institutions*; 1748: Euler Develops the Concept of Function; 1784: Legendre Introduces Polynomials.

RELATED ARTICLES in *Great Lives from History: The Eighteenth Century, 1701-1800:* Maria Gaetana Agnesi; Jean le Rond d'Alembert; George Berkeley; Leonhard Euler; Joseph-Louis Lagrange; Colin Maclaurin; Gaspard Monge.

1763-1767
FAMINE IN SOUTHERN ITALY

In the mid-1760's, food shortages, intensified by insufficient harvests, feudalistic practices, and flawed food distribution systems, resulted in famine conditions, which prompted rural populations to migrate to urban areas. Because charities and governments failed to provide sufficient relief, some famine victims rioted. Several hundred thousand people died either from starvation or from diseases exacerbated by unsanitary conditions.

LOCALE: Kingdom of Naples; Tuscany; Papal States; Rome

CATEGORIES: Natural disasters; agriculture; environment; economics

KEY FIGURES

Bernardo Tanucci (1698-1793), regent of Naples, r. 1759-1767, and secretary of state, 1768-1776

Ferdinand IV (1751-1825), king of Naples, r. 1759-1806, and king of the Two Sicilies as Ferdinand I, r. 1816-1825

William Hamilton (1730-1803), English ambassador to the court of Naples, 1764-1800

Antonio Genovesi (1712-1769), Italian economist

Cesare Beccaria (1738-1794), Italian author

Pietro Verri (1728-1797), Italian publisher and writer

Alessandro Verri (1741-1816), Italian writer and editor

SUMMARY OF EVENT

In 1759, the southern Italian peninsula experienced low food supplies but survived due to aid from Sicily and the Middle East. Many people living in Naples, Tuscany, and the Papal States began experiencing famine several years later, when poor harvests resulted in demand overwhelming supplies, and food storage centers (*annona*) inefficiently gathered and distributed foodstuffs.

Agricultural conditions and methods in the southern Italian kingdoms and principalities were inferior to and differed from northern practices. Much of the south practiced feudalism: The elites—the nobility and ecclesiastical leaders—owned the majority of land, which peasants farmed. That system discouraged the use of improved implements and varied plants, which could have increased yields and replenished exhausted fields. For the most part, southern landowners, both secular and religious, were apathetic about bettering farming techniques, a course many agriculturists in Europe and northern Italy were pursuing. Wealthy landowners often lived in cities and rarely involved themselves in agricultural matters. Foreign demands controlled much of the southern Italian agricultural trade: Peasants were forced to grow olives, grapes, and inedible fiber crops, rather than grain, to sell to international markets and manufacturers in exchange for luxury goods not available in southern Italy.

Extreme winter and spring weather over a period of several years proved detrimental to most harvests in the mid-1760's. Prices rose drastically, and many people could not afford to buy such basic nutritional items as bread. By 1763, southern Italy was experiencing a famine. The famine most severely impacted already impoverished people. The wealthy could purchase available food.

Ferdinand IV, the third son of Spain's Charles III, had become king of Naples in 1759, at the age of eight. The government was effectively in the control of Ferdinand's regent, Bernardo Tanucci, who had previously dealt with food shortages by seeking external aid and relying on long-established internal charities. Tanucci stated in April, 1764, that European governments lacked sufficient food reserves to feed hungry Neapolitans, noting that a weak economy had strained all of Europe. Piedmont sent some emergency aid but not enough to sustain the entire kingdom. Few Mediterranean relief shipments arrived at Naples's port.

The famine in the Kingdom of Naples was especially severe in Campania and Capitanata provinces. Because the city of Naples historically had distributed food through its *annona* and charities, many rural people swarmed that city seeking relief. The government failed to provide sufficient food, however, and most charities were unable to respond adequately to people's needs. Selfish behavior worsened relief work. The wealthy and powerful felt entitled to receive aid first and hoarded food. Some local *annona* administrators corruptly mismanaged their supplies. In contrast, St. Paul of the Cross asked monks to give half their rations to hungry people.

Although some famine victims responded to the food shortages with open aggression, few people rioted in Naples. Most people believed God had caused the famine to punish sinners. They did not perceive the government and charitable institutions as being responsible for causing, intensifying, or prolonging the famine. Despite relatively peaceful conditions in Naples, however, agitated people did revolt in other cities, including Crotone, Altamura, and Rossone. In some rural communities, lawlessness prevailed, and villagers assaulted their feudal lords, occasionally destroying castles.

People from the state around Rome began migrating into that city in 1764, seeking nourishment and assistance. The Roman troops managed the resulting crowds, preventing irate mobs from engaging in hostilities. Gathering relief food supplies in centralized locations, the Roman *annona* and Florentine *abbondanza* provided victims with more consistent sources of foodstuffs and financial aid than their counterparts in Naples. French relief arrived by ship at the ports of Livorno and Civitavecchia.

In December, 1764, English ambassador William Hamilton commented that the bitter winter weather was contributing to the suffering of famine victims. He saw approximately two thousand patients, wearing threadbare clothing, squeezed into an overwhelmed Naples hospital. Hamilton watched starving people begging be-

cause charities' bread supplies were depleted. Epidemics, including typhus, struck large populations. Disease spread as people migrated from rural to urban areas. Poor nutrition and vitamin and protein deficiencies weakened immune systems. Deprived of grain, some people ate weeds. Famine victims obtained limited food dispersed at festivals, including the 1764 *carnevale* at Naples.

The southern Italian famine lasted through 1767 in some places and accounted for at least 300,000 deaths due to starvation or disease. Children and the elderly represented many of the losses. The Kingdom of Naples suffered the most. Casualties in the city of Naples alone totaled 40,000 people, and the kingdom lost an estimated 200,000 people. Rome, the Papal States, and Tuscany suffered fewer losses. Reduced production and loss of agricultural laborers during the famine years further devastated southern Italy's economy. European nations sought alternative trading partners. Urban-rural conflicts divided much of the population and slowed efforts to restore the countryside. The famine upset social order and revealed deficiencies in government, altruistic organizations, and agricultural practices.

SIGNIFICANCE

Some intellectuals had demanded governmental and social reforms prior to the famine. The catastrophe intensified reform efforts, because people realized the shortcomings of social institutions, both governmental and charitable, to relieve misery and their inability to deal adequately with famine conditions. Landowning nobles opposed reforms, and most government officials were unwilling to admit the extent to which their policies benefiting the privileged had enabled the famine to happen. Influenced by Enlightenment ideas, intellectuals, especially Antonio Genovesi and Cesare Beccaria, debated how to revise southern Italian policies, counter traditions that stagnated southern Italian provinces, and encourage different ways to perceive social concerns.

Pietro and Alessandro Verri published *Il Café* during the famine years, urging elites to reform agriculture and commerce. Publications targeting landowners explained how to achieve better agriculture by managing land, draining excess water, terracing slopes, and utilizing technology. Low literacy rates prevented many peasants from benefiting from such advice. Reformers targeted guilds for hindering agricultural trade. They also criticized charities, confraternities, and clerics who blocked land reforms and refused to act philanthropically to the poor. Although most reforms were unfulfilled, some *annone* and local schools and organizations improved.

The famine initiated discussion of free trade of food, especially grain. Governments controlled grain distribution, and laws forbade free trade. Although Italian leaders in the north accepted free trade, officials in Tuscany delayed permitting free trade until 1775, and leaders in Naples retained tariffs and controls to protect trade until the 1780's, when some restrictions were ended. Seeking to alter unproductive landholding practices, reform-minded officials criticized feudalism and promoted land ownership among by commoners. Twenty years after the famine, the government of Naples secured jurisdiction over numerous rural villages. The famine contributed to Neapolitans' distrust of their leaders. In 1799, when France conquered the kingdom and instituted the short-lived Parthenopean Republic in its place, many peasants supported the new republic against Ferdinand.

The famine was a catalyst for some reform attempts and challenging the governmental and societal status quo, but most governments were uninterested in immediately improving land and charity policies. Italian reform efforts during the famine influenced reformers in other countries, contributing to the increased scrutiny of feudalism in Scotland and elsewhere. After the famine, some agriculturists individually initiated reforms, seeking fertile land at previously ignored higher altitudes to plant corn and other edible crops. Official reforms did not occur until later in the century. Gradually, in famine-stricken areas, leaders approved land reforms, including some field enclosures, encouragement of crop rotation, and limitations on the feudal system. Agricultural changes and political reforms spared southern Italy the subsequent severe food shortages that affected Europe, particularly the 1840's Irish famine that killed one million people.

—Elizabeth D. Schafer

FURTHER READING

Black, Christopher F. *Early Modern Italy: A Social History*. New York: Routledge, 2001. Based on primary Italian sources, this history includes contemporary details about the southern Italian famine and how it af-fected political and socioeconomic policies and attitudes regarding agriculture, land ownership, and food distribution.

Dyson, Tim, and Cormac Ó Gráda, eds. *Famine Demography: Perspectives from the Past and Present*. New York: Oxford University Press, 2002. Scholars present case studies of specific historical and modern famines, explaining common nutritional and health factors that affect victims and how starvation alters socioeconomic patterns.

Imbruglia, Girolamo, ed. *Naples in the Eighteenth Century: The Birth and Death of a Nation State*. New York: Cambridge University Press, 2000. This anthology discusses causes and results of the 1760's famine in several essays, analyzing obstacles reformers encountered.

Newman, Lucile F., ed. *Hunger in History: Food Shortage, Poverty, and Deprivation*. New York: Basil Blackwell, 1990. Participants in Brown University's World Hunger Program examine various reasons why famines occur and persist and their impact on communities, with a chapter focusing on eighteenth century European populations.

Sereni, Emilio. *History of the Italian Agricultural Landscape*. Translated with an introduction by R. Burr Litchfield. Princeton, N.J.: Princeton University Press, 1997. An overview of how people practiced agriculture in various regions of Italy and why methods and production goals differed.

SEE ALSO: 1720: Financial Collapse of the John Law System; Sept., 1720: Collapse of the South Sea Bubble; Nov. 1, 1755: Great Lisbon Earthquake; Apr. 27-May, 1775: Flour War; Oct. 10-18, 1780: Great Caribbean Hurricane; 1786-1787: Tenmei Famine; Mar., 1796-Oct. 17, 1797: Napoleon's Italian Campaigns.

RELATED ARTICLES in *Great Lives from History: The Eighteenth Century, 1701-1800*: Cesare Beccaria; Charles III.

February 10, 1763
PEACE OF PARIS

In the Peace of Paris, Great Britain, France, and Spain made peace with one another, ending their participation in the Seven Years' War and the French and Indian War. The treaty confirmed the supremacy of the British colonial empire and the virtual destruction of the French overseas empire.

LOCALE: Paris, France

CATEGORIES: Diplomacy and international relations; wars, uprisings, and civil unrest; colonization; expansion and land acquisition

KEY FIGURES

Étienne François de Choiseul (1719-1785), French foreign affairs minister and negotiator

Fourth Duke of Bedford (John Russell; 1710-1771), British ambassador and negotiator

Third Earl of Bute (John Stuart; 1713-1792), British secretary of state, 1761-1762, and prime minister, 1762-1763

George III (1738-1820), king of England, r. 1760-1820

William Pitt the Elder (1708-1778), prime minister of Great Britain, 1757-1761, 1766-1768

SUMMARY OF EVENT

In 1763, the Peace of Paris brought to a close the British-French-Spanish phases of the war known in Europe as the Seven Years' War and in North America as the French and Indian War. The European conflict involved mainly the continuing struggle for supremacy in the German states between Prussia (supported by England) and Austria (aided by France and Russia). Simultaneously, in North America, in India, in Africa, and in the West Indies, England and France were engaged in a struggle for supremacy, another phase of the Second Hundred Years' War.

While by no means ignoring central Europe, British and French statesmen alike were well aware that the major stakes of the war would be won or lost on the North American continent. From May 28, 1754, when the French and Indian War began, to mid-1757, the French dealt the British forces a number of serious defeats on many of the worldwide fronts of the conflict. Not until the appointment of William Pitt the Elder as British foreign secretary in the summer of 1757 did Great Britain begin to turn the tide. Pitt, supremely confident of his own ability and that of his country to wage war, by the end of 1759 had forged a series of spectacular English victories over France in Canada, India, and the West Indies. The British conquest of Canada in September, 1760, elevated Pitt to the zenith of his power and encouraged him to prosecute the war even more vigorously until France was completely crushed. King George III, who ascended the throne in the following month, had decidedly different views.

King George III and his advisers, above all John Stuart, third earl of Bute, disliked Pitt and his militant war policy. Their aim was to terminate as soon as possible what was becoming an expensive conflict, in order to consolidate the young monarch's authority by associating his name with peace and good economy in government. The execution of such plans ultimately presupposed the ouster of Pitt from office, but George III and Bute both realized that their Whig adversary would have to be retained until prospects for peace improved. Hence, in 1761, George responded eagerly to the proposal of the French foreign affairs minister, Étienne François de Choiseul, that peace negotiations, begun in December, 1759, at the behest of a beleaguered Prussia but subsequently broken off, be resumed.

The reopening of negotiations in March, 1761, in Augsburg, reflected a desire for peace that was strong in both countries, but not strong enough to prevent the collapse of talks by September and a consequent prolongation of the war. Pitt's unwillingness to accede to certain French demands, among them the surrender of Great Britain's Canadian fishing monopolies, and the insistence that Great Britain incorporate in any peace treaty a settlement of outstanding disagreements with Spain, hitherto neutral, prompted Choiseul to continue the war. Thus, while continuing negotiations until September, Choiseul had entered into an alliance on August 15 with Spain, a "Family Compact" of the two Bourbon powers, wherein Spain agreed to declare war on Great Britain if peace were not concluded within eight months.

Through the interception of certain diplomatic dispatches, the British government learned of the existence of this agreement. Pitt, firm in his belief that the compact involved the intention of Spain to declare war on Great Britain, sought to persuade George III to undertake a preventive war against Spain. Others in the British government shared Pitt's view that Spain probably intended to go to war against Great Britain, but their dislike for him enabled them to use his insistence on a war with Spain as the opportunity to oust him from office.

Pitt's successors, the third earl of Bute and the fourth duke of Bedford, were themselves obliged to press for such a declaration, which came on January 1, 1762, after Spain refused to deny the existence of the compact. As the year progressed, disastrous Spanish defeats at the hands of Great Britain, including the capture of Havana, coupled with abandonment of the alliance with Prussia, created an atmosphere in which Choiseul and his British counterparts felt constrained to return to serious peace negotiations.

By early November, 1762, Choiseul and Lord Russell had worked out the outline of a settlement. The peace preliminaries signed on November 5, 1762, at Fontainebleau generated great controversy in Great Britain. In the House of Commons, Pitt argued that the British should retain the islands of Martinique, St. Lucia, Miquelon, and Gorée, and gain more than Florida in exchange for Havana. Bute countered that he would demand only what was easy for Britain to obtain and for France to yield. Public opinion was of two minds: It wanted a speedy end to the war, but it condemned the terms Bute had achieved.

Bute had his way, and the Fountainebleau agreement served as the basis for the Peace of Paris, which was formally concluded at Paris between Great Britain, France, and Spain on February 10, 1763. As far as Europe was concerned, France agreed to restore the territory of all Great Britain's German allies, including Hanover, Hesse, Brunswick, and, contingent upon the approval of Austria, Prussia's Rhenish lands as well. Among the major stipulations of the Peace of Paris pertaining to colonial affairs, France ceded to England all of Canada and French territory east of the Mississippi River, Senegal in Africa, and some islands in the West Indies, but retained certain trading stations in India. Spain ceded Florida to Great Britain, which in turn guaranteed Spanish control over Cuba. To compensate Spain for the loss of Florida, France ceded to Spain the Louisiana territory west of the Mississippi.

SIGNIFICANCE

The consequences of the war and the Peace of Paris were of considerable importance. First, the intention of Great Britain and France to terminate their struggle prompted their respective allies, Prussia and Austria, to resolve their differences in the Treaty of Hubertusburg, signed five days after the Peace of Paris. Great Britain emerged from the war at the peak of its maritime power, but its position was not so secure as the stipulations of the treaty might have indicated. The removal of the French menace made the colonists of New England less dependent on the Mother Country than they had been previously. Moreover, when the American Revolution finally broke out in 1775, Great Britain found itself isolated by a bitter France, which it had defeated, and an equally bitter Prussia, which it had deserted. France, in time, gave open support to the British colonists in America, while in the German states, Prussia hindered Britain's recruitment of troops for use in America. As a direct result of the Peace of Paris, France lost considerable territory to Great Britain in the New World and was eclipsed in India. The Peace of Paris, like most peace treaties, was not conclusive; in a few years, France was to renew its traditional rivalry with Great Britain.

—Charles H. O'Brien

FURTHER READING

Black, Jeremy. *Natural and Necessary Enemies: Anglo-French Relations in the Eighteenth Century*. London: Gerald Duckworth, 1986. Black discusses British-French relations between 1713 and 1793 against their cultural background.

_____. *Pitt the Elder*. New York: Cambridge University Press, 1992. The author offers a readable, scholarly account of Pitt's life.

Hyam, Ronald. "The Treaty of Paris, 1763." In *Reappraisals in British Imperial History*, edited by Ronald Hyam and Ged Martin. New York: Macmillan, 1975. A careful historical analysis of the Bute administration's presuppositions and policies in making a relatively moderate peace with France.

Israel, Frederick L., ed. *Major Treaty Treaties of Modern History, 1648-1966*. Vol. 1. New York: Chelsea House, 1967. The text of the Peace of Paris is reproduced; editorial commentaries are set forth on related groups of treaties.

Schweizer, Karl W. *War, Politics, and Diplomacy, 1756-1763*. Reprint. Lanham, Md.: University Press of America, 2001. Originally published in 1991 under another name, Schweizer's study analyzes the financial, political, and strategic forces influencing Pitt's attitude toward the British-Prussian alliance.

Watson, J. Steven. *The Reign of George III, 1760-1815*. Vol. 12 in *The Oxford History of England*, edited by Sir George Clark. Oxford, England: Clarendon Press, 1960. This older work contains a clear, concise discussion of the negotiations for the Peace of Paris.

Williams, Basil. *The Life of William Pitt, Earl of Chatham*. Reprint. New York: Octagon Books, 1966. Originally published in 1913, this work is a classic biography of Pitt, rather indulgent of Pitt's judgment and actions and harsh toward those of his opponents.

SEE ALSO: May 26, 1701-Sept. 7, 1714: War of the Spanish Succession; May 15, 1702-Apr. 11, 1713: Queen Anne's War; 1721-1742: Development of Great Britain's Office of Prime Minister; May 28, 1754-Feb. 10, 1763: French and Indian War; July, 1755-Aug., 1758: Acadians Are Expelled from Canada; Jan., 1756-Feb. 15, 1763: Seven Years' War;

June 23, 1757: Battle of Plassey; Nov. 5, 1757: Battle of Rossbach; June 8-July 27, 1758: Siege of Louisbourg; Oct. 5, 1759-Nov. 19, 1761: Cherokee War; May 8, 1763-July 24, 1766: Pontiac's Resistance.

RELATED ARTICLES in *Great Lives from History: The Eighteenth Century, 1701-1800*: Étienne François de Choiseul; George III; Louis XV; William Pitt the Elder.

Beginning April, 1763
THE *NORTH BRITON* CONTROVERSY

The suppression of John Wilkes's periodical The North Briton *for alleged aspersions against the British throne resulted in Wilkes's arrest, conviction, and imprisonment for seditious libel, sparking a controversy with major implications for the development of a modern free press and the beginnings of modern lobbying groups.*

LOCALE: London, England

CATEGORIES: Government and politics; laws, acts, and legal history; social issues and reform; communications; organizations and institutions

KEY FIGURES

John Wilkes (1725-1797), a publisher and politician, who challenged the British political establishment

George III (1738-1820), king of Great Britain, r. 1760-1820

William Pitt the Elder (1708-1778), British prime minister

SUMMARY OF EVENT

Until 1696, printed materials in England were required to bear the stamp of the government censor's approval, although an unauthorized, underground literature had long flourished, and the control of publishing had broken down during the English Revolution. With the lapse of the Regulation of Printing Act in that year, official censorship ended, although its place was taken by laws against seditious libel that, in effect, placed the onus of censorship on authors rather than the state. Nonetheless, a vigorous press flourished, and satire in all its forms was to be a principal genre of eighteenth century literary and artistic expression.

At the same time, the political constitution had evolved. After the revolution of 1688, the balance of

power had shifted from Crown to Parliament. The king's government was dependent on shifting parliamentary majorities whose maintenance was the responsibility of a chief official whose modern title of prime minister was only gradually adopted but whose unique position—part Crown spokesman, part power broker between Crown and Parliament—embodied the new relations between executive and legislative authority. Since, however, the fiction was assiduously maintained, then and still, that the king's government was truly his own and that the policies it espoused expressed the royal will and no other, criticism of the government at least notionally reflected on the person of the monarch. This created a tension within political discourse, particularly since the king at this point still set or approved at least the broad outlines of policy.

This tension came to a head in 1763 with the suppression of *The North Briton*, an influential political periodical, and the imprisonment of its editor John Wilkes for having criticized a speech from the throne in its forty-fifth number. The immediate consequences of this event were felt for more than a decade, and its significance for the freedom of the press was permanent.

Wilkes was the son of a prosperous London distiller. Embarking on a political career as a self-described "friend of liberty," he was appointed high sheriff of Buckingham in 1754 and elected a member of Parliament for Aylesbury in 1757, where he joined supporters of Prime Minister William Pitt the Elder. Pitt's fall in 1761 dashed his hopes of political advancement, and on June 6, 1762, with Charles Churchill, he launched *The North Briton* as a riposte to *The Briton*, the government organ edited by writer Tobias Smollett.

The new government, headed by the earl of Bute, John Stuart, was in the process of negotiating an end to the Seven Years' War (1756-1763) with France on terms widely regarded as disadvantageous by London and Liverpool merchants, and bitterly opposed by Pitt. *The North Briton* not only joined in this political opposition but also ridiculed Prime Minister Stuart, whose alleged intimacy with King George III's mother, the princess dowager, was seen as the basis of his power. Pitt himself disavowed *The North Briton*, and an offended courtier, Earl Talbot, challenged Wilkes to a duel. At Stuart's resignation in favor of George Grenville on April 11, 1763, Wilkes announced that *The North Briton*, having served its purpose, would suspend publication. The king's speech to Parliament on April 19, which indicated royal approval of the preliminary articles of the Peace of Paris, called forth a new issue of the paper, however, which appeared as no. 45 on April 23. Wilkes took care to characterize George's speech as that of "the Minister" rather than his own, which avoided directly disparaging the king but at the same time reduced him to a mouthpiece. What followed gave offense not only as an unbridled attack on policy but in depicting the monarch as the hapless victim of his own government. Issue number 45 of *The North Briton* read,

> The *Minister's speech* of last Tuesday is not to be paralleled in the annals of this country. I am in doubt whether the imposition is greater on the Sovereign, or on the nation. Every friend of this country must lament that a prince of so many great and admirable qualities, whom England truly reveres, can be brought to give the sanction of his sacred name to the most odious measures and the most unjustified public declarations from a throne ever renowned for truth, honour, and an unsullied virtue.

A general warrant was issued for the arrest of Wilkes as well as his publisher, George Kearsley, and his presumed printer, Dryden Leach. Leach had earlier ceased his association with *The North Briton*, so Richard Balfe was arrested instead. Wilkes was able to remove the next issue (46) from the press and to destroy the manuscript of number 45 before being taken into custody. From his confinement in the Tower of London, he immediately described his detention as a breach of public liberty. A large crowd accompanied him to his arraignment at Westminster on May 3, chanting "Liberty! Liberty! Wilkes forever!" The chant was shortened to "Wilkes and liberty," and it became a slogan that would rally a generation.

Wilkes was released on May 6 after the justices found that his privilege as a member of Parliament had been violated by his arrest. Wilkes, Leach, and others were

awarded substantial damages upon suit. This narrow ruling did not address the legality of general warrants as such, which had been issued by successive secretaries of state to prosecute charges of seditious libel. In effect, such warrants had taken the place of the expired Licensing Act to maintain control of the press. The seizure of Wilkes brought the legality of these warrants to the fore, and it resulted in their suppression. In 1765, they were declared null and void in the case of *Entick v. Carrington*, which was heard before the same justice, Sir Charles Pratt (now Lord Camden), who had freed Wilkes. In April, 1766, a resolution by the House of Commons denounced them as illegal and obnoxious.

The Wilkes affair, however, had only begun. Wilkes himself, seeking to pay debts by capitalizing on his celebrity, reprinted the entire run of *The North Briton* as one volume in the fall of 1763, and also prepared the private publication of *An Essay on Woman*, a ribald parody by Thomas Potter of Alexander Pope's *An Essay on Man* (1733-1734), to which Wilkes had contributed some notes and commentary. While these ventures were in progress, he imprudently vacationed in France. In his absence, the government procured a proof copy of the essay and read it aloud to a properly scandalized House of Lords. The House of Commons, meanwhile, determined *The North Briton* to be "a false, scandalous, and seditious libel," voting 273 for and 111 against, and, with the concurrence of the House of Lords, ordered it burned by the common hangman. The offending journal was rescued from the flames by a tumultuous crowd on December 3.

Parliament responded to the decision of the houses by expelling Wilkes, who, facing prosecution, then fled to France. A Middlesex grand jury indicted him in January, 1764, for publishing *The North Briton* and *An Essay on Woman* and, on November 1, declared him an outlaw.

Wilkes returned home three years later, on February 6, 1767, and sought a new seat in Parliament, which would shield him from the law while he sought a pardon. Unlike his first seat, which had been obtained with the usual patronage, Wilkes now offered himself to the electors as "a private man, unconnected with the Great, and unsupported by any Party." He was returned for Middlesex amid much tumult. While Parliament waited its session, Wilkes was arrested. A crowd stormed the King's Bench prison where he was held on May 10, and eleven persons were killed in what became known as the Massacre of St. George's Fields.

Wilkes's outlawry was reversed in the Court of King's Bench on June 8, but he was fined £11,000 and sentenced to twenty-two months in prison. Returned to prison, he was showered with gifts and funds by supporters and well-wishers from as far away as the American colonies, supported by groups such as the Sons of Liberty in Boston and the House of Assembly of South Carolina. Wilkes's birthday was the occasion of both celebration

and violence; the House of Commons expelled him again on February 3, 1769, by 219 votes to 137. The Middlesex freeholders promptly returned him to Parliament, again, only two weeks later. The House of Commons expelled him once more the following day, and the process was repeated one month later. In April, he was returned to his seat for the third time, though opposed by a Court candidate, Henry Lawes Luttrell. The commons, ignoring the poll, declared Luttrell the victor. This action led to a series of petitions protesting Wilkes's exclusion, whose subscribers included fully one-quarter of the national electorate. The petitions soon moved beyond the demand for Wilkes's seating to a call for the dissolution of the Parliament that had excluded him. A number of members of Parliament supported the demand.

Wilkes was released from prison on April 17, 1770. He had been elected an alderman of London while still confined, establishing the base from which he would be elected lord mayor in 1774. Touring the country, he was widely feted and honored, and each year he ritually claimed his seat in Parliament. Gradually, however, the Wilkite movement, which had coincided with popular agitation over rising food prices, subsided. When Wilkes was returned to Parliament for Middlesex yet again in 1774, he was seated without opposition. He remained a visible figure, but increasingly an irrelevant one. In 1780 he helped quell the anti-Catholic Gordon Riots, personally killing two citizens. This event marked his political eclipse, and when he retired from Parliament in 1789 he aptly described himself as an "extinct volcano." The French Revolution, which he observed in retirement, appalled him.

A British political cartoon symbolizing the conflict between supporters of John Wilkes and his newspaper The North Briton *and members of the censorious British government. "Wilkes and liberty" became a rallying cry, or song, after Wilkes's arrest for seditious libel.* (Library of Congress)

SIGNIFICANCE

The Wilkes affair was the most important irruption of popular politics in England between the time of the

Glorious Revolution at the end of the seventeenth century and the radical agitation of the 1790's, and it has had lasting consequences. The Society for the Supporters of the Bill of Rights, launched on Wilkes's behalf, was the precursor to modern lobbying groups. Spurred by the Wilkes case, printers successfully defied the long ban on reporting parliamentary debates, thereby gaining a major victory for a free press. Wilkes himself was one of the first politicians to make specific pledges to his constituents, an innovation that greatly troubled his erstwhile supporter, Edmund Burke. With a publicist's eye to posterity, he had his gravestone inscribed "A Friend to Liberty," and so, despite his fundamental opportunism, he has been remembered. What he lacked in lasting principle, and often in prudence, he was always willing to make up in courage.

—Robert Zaller

FURTHER READING

Boulton, James T. *The Language of Politics in the Age of Wilkes and Burke.* London: Routledge and Kegan Paul. 1951. Places the Wilkes affair in the context of the development of eighteenth century political rhetoric.

Christie, Ian R. "Radicals and Reformers in the Age of Wilkes and Wyvill." In *British Politics and Society from Walpole to Pitt, 1742-1789*, edited by Jeremy Black. New York: St. Martin's Press, 1990. Examines the parliamentary reform movement that developed during the late eighteenth century and the role of Wilkes and other radicals in that movement. With Christie's earlier work, very useful for putting the role played by Wilkes and his followers into context.

_____. *Wilkes, Wyvill, and Reform: The Parliamentary Reform Movement in British Politics, 1760-1785.* London: Macmillan. 1962. A lucid study that relates the Wilkes affair to the wider quest for parliamentary reform in the early part of George III's reign.

Nobbe, George. *North Briton: A Study in Political Propaganda.* 1939. Reprint. New York: AMS Press. 1966. An older but still useful study of the development of popular political criticism in the press.

Postgate, Raymond W. *That Devil Wilkes.* New York: Vanguard Press, 1929. An engaging biography that vividly portrays Wilkes and his era.

Reich, Jerome R. *British Friends of the American Revolution.* Armonk, N.Y.: M. E. Sharpe, 1998. Chapter 4 places Wilkes in the context of those who spoke for revolution in America.

Rude, George F. E. *Wilkes and Liberty: A Social Study of 1763 to 1774.* Oxford, England: Clarendon Press, 1962. An important study by a distinguished historian of popular culture and action that relates Wilkes to the wider movement for reform in England in the years before the American Revolution.

Thomas, Peter D. G. *John Wilkes: A Friend to Liberty.* New York: Oxford University Press, 1996. A readable biography that includes chapters on the *North Briton* controversy, Wilkes as a politician, and Wilkes's reception by Americans.

SEE ALSO: Aug. 4, 1735: Trial of John Peter Zenger; 1736: *Gentleman's Magazine* Initiates Parliamentary Reporting; Jan., 1756-Feb. 15, 1763: Seven Years' War; Jan., 1759: Voltaire Satirizes Optimism in *Candide*; Feb. 10, 1763: Peace of Paris; 1774: Hansard Begins Reporting Parliamentary Debates; Apr. 19, 1775: Battle of Lexington and Concord; Jan. 1, 1777: France's First Daily Newspaper Appears; June 2-10, 1780: Gordon Riots; 1792-1793: Fichte Advocates Free Speech; June 25-July 14, 1798: Alien and Sedition Acts.

RELATED ARTICLES in *Great Lives from History: The Eighteenth Century, 1701-1800*: Edmund Burke; George III; Samuel Johnson; Lord North; William Pitt the Elder; Alexander Pope; Voltaire; William Wilberforce; John Wilkes; John Peter Zenger.

May 8, 1763-July 24, 1766
PONTIAC'S RESISTANCE

A pan-Indian uprising led by Ottawa chief Pontiac presented the greatest threat to British expansion before the American Revolution.

LOCALE: Great Lakes region (now in the United States)

CATEGORY: Wars, uprisings, and civil unrest

KEY FIGURES

Pontiac (Obwandiyag; c. 1720-1769), Ottawa war chief who organized pan-Indian resistance to the British

Lord Amherst (Jeffrey Amherst; 1717-1797), commander of British forces in America during the French and Indian War

Henry Gladwin (1729-1791), British major who resisted Pontiac's siege of Detroit

William Johnson (1715-1774), British commander who imposed a lenient peace on Pontiac's forces

Second Earl of Shelburne (William Petty-Fitzmaurice; 1737-1805), British statesman who recommended separating western lands from the colonies

SUMMARY OF EVENT

By signing the Peace of Paris on February 10, 1763, Great Britain and France concluded the French and Indian War, nearly a decade of battle for empire in North America. Victorious, Great Britain then had to decide how to organize its vast new territories, embracing Canada and the area lying between the Appalachians and the Mississippi River. At issue in these trans-Appalachian lands were the rights, vital interests, profits, and responsibilities of the remaining Frenchmen, fur traders and trappers, British governors and colonials with claims to these territories, land speculators, the British army, and, not least, American Indians. A plan to separate trans-Appalachia from eastern British colonies and keep out settlers had been recommended by the second earl of Shelburne, then president of Britain's board of trade. Shelburne had hoped that his plan would be implemented by 1767, but despite amounting political pressure for Parliament to act on imperial reorganization, nothing was done until Shelburne had left office. What determined his successor's action and his issuance of the Proclamation of 1763 was an indigenous uprising and the siege of the British fort at Detroit by a little-known Ottawa war chief, Pontiac.

A large, imposing figure, Pontiac was born in present-day northern Ohio, the son of an Ottawa father and a Chippewa (Ojibwa) mother. Although he married several times (as was customary), only one of his wives and two sons have been identified. Esteemed for his strategic skills and his intelligence, he had become a war chief by 1755, when he was in his mid-thirties. The Ottawa, like most of their neighbors, were traders who had profited from close relationships with the French and who, therefore, fought with French forces in America during the French and Indian War. Pontiac had fought with the French when they defeated British troops commanded by General Braddock at Fort Pitt in western Pennsylvania.

France's defeat, sealed by the Peace of Paris, proved disastrous to indigenous peoples of the frontier, who were constrained thereafter to deal with the British. Contrary to the intent of the Proclamation of 1763, colonial settlers poured across the Appalachians into American Indian territories. In addition, Lord Amherst, commander in chief of British forces, discontinued bestowing on the tribes gifts and supplies, the most important of which was gunpowder. During the war, Amherst had also provided alcohol to the Indians, but he refused to dispense it at war's end. Thus, genuine hardship from a lack of gunpowder, which curtailed their hunting and disrupted their fur trade; an unslaked addiction to alcohol; discomfort from the diminution of other supplies; and increasing European encroachments on their lands furnished many Great Lakes tribes with serious grievances against the British.

On April 27, 1763, Pontiac convened a general war council in order to finalize war plans that envisaged a wholesale assault on British forts along the frontier. His call to arms solicited support from Chippewas, Lenni Lenapes (Delawares), Hurons, Illinois, Kickapoos, Miamis, Mingos, Potawatomis, Senecas, and Shawnees. On May 8, 1763, he and three hundred warriors—mostly his own tribesmen, along with Chippewas and Potawatomis—entered Fort Detroit, weapons concealed and ready to strike. Previously alerted to Pontiac's intentions, however, Major Henry Gladwin foiled Pontiac's attack from within and the Indians put Gladwin's fort under what became a six-month siege. Within weeks, every British fort west of Niagara was destroyed: Forts Sandusky, St. Joseph, Miami, Quiatenon, Venango, Le Boeuf, Michilimackinac, Edward Augustus, and Presque Isle. Forts in the Monongahela Valley, such as

Fort Ligonier, were attacked. Only Fort Pitt and Fort Detroit survived. Before the winter of 1763, the British had suffered costly ambushes such as one outside Detroit at Blood Ridge and counted two thousand casualties overall.

Fearful that their entire frontier would collapse, the British counterattacked. By late fall, tribal resistance weakened, as the Indians were not used to protracted warfare and lacked the measure of aid they had expected from the French. At Fort Pitt, blankets distributed by the fort commander, Captain Simon Ecuyer, infected besieging Indians and produced a devastating smallpox epidemic, while another of Amherst's commanders tracked the Indians with English hunting dogs. In late autumn, Pontiac lifted the siege of Detroit, although elsewhere some Indian forces continued fighting throughout 1764. Other tribes, however, had concluded peace treaties with Colonel John Bradstreet at Presque Isle as early as August, 1763. By July, 1765, Pontiac had entered peace negotiations that resulted in a treaty signed with the British at Oswego on July 24, 1766, a treaty under which he was pardoned.

Following his pardon, Pontiac was received with hostility by neighbors in his Maumee River village, and he, his family, and a handful of supporters were driven out by tribe members who wanted resistance to continue. While at a trading post in Cahokia (Illinois), Pontiac was murdered in April, 1769, by Black Dog, a Peoria Indian whom the British may have paid in hopes of forestalling future rebellions.

SIGNIFICANCE

In the aftermath of Pontiac's Resistance, the British, apprehensive about a renewal of American Indian resistance, altered their Indian policy. They abandoned their Indian posts everywhere in the West, except at Detroit, Michilimackinac, and Niagara, and cross-mountain trade was placed again in colonial hands. British authorities, seeking to remove yet another cause of Indian grievances, renewed the practice of favor-

ing tribes with sumptuous gifts. Unable to stem the tide of European settlers into trans-Appalachian tribal lands, as the Proclamation of 1763 was intended to do, British representative William Johnson negotiated a new boundary with Iroquois leaders at Fort Stanwix in September, 1768. This line was drawn farther west, in hopes of lessening chances of friction between the Indians and the settlers. Britain's concerns over American Indian affairs soon gave way to coping with rising resistance among its own colonials.

In retrospect, Pontiac's pan-Indian alliance represented the greatest threat mounted by American Indians against Great Britain's New World expansion prior to the outbreak of the American Revolution. It dramatically launched American Indian resistance to white civilization, resistance that subsequently included uprisings by Little Turtle (1790-1794) and by Tecumseh (1809-1811)

PONTIAC CALLS FOR REBELLION

Pontiac held a council to convince American Indians, who had come together from several nations, to attack the British. In this excerpt from a journal thought to have been written either by a French clergyman or other captive being held at Fort Detroit in 1763 by American Indians, Pontiac calls for the warriors to "exterminate" the British from Indian lands.

When I go see the English commander and say to him that some of our comrades are dead, instead of bewailing their death, as our French brothers do, he laughs at me and at you. If I ask anything for our sick, he refuses with the reply that he has no use for us. From all this you can see that they are seeking our ruin. Therefore, my brothers, we must all swear their destruction and wait no longer. Nothing prevents us; they are few in numbers, and we can accomplish it. All the nations who are our brothers attack them,—why should we not attack? Are we not men like them? Have I not shown you the wampum belts which I received from our Great Father [King Louis XV], the Frenchman? He tells us to strike them,—why do we not listen to his words? What do we fear? It is time. Do we fear that our brothers, the French, who are here among us will prevent us? They do not know our plans, and they could not hinder anyway, if they would. You all know as well as I that when the English came upon our lands to drive out our Father, Belestre [the French commander in Detroit], they took away all the Frenchmen's guns and [you know] that they now have no arms to protect themselves with. Therefore, it is time for us to strike. . . . They will not be slow in coming, but while we wait let us strike anyway. There is no more time to lose. When the English are defeated we shall then see what there is left to do, and we shall stop up the ways hither so that they may never come again upon our lands.

Source: Journal of Pontiac's Conspiracy, 1763, edited by Mary Agnes Burton (Detroit: Clarence Monroe Burton and the Michigan Society of the Colonial Wars, 1912), pp. 38, 40. Wisconsin Historical Society, American Journeys. www.americanjourneys.org/aj-135/. Accessed August, 2005.

and, during the last three decades of the nineteenth century, drew the U.S. military into the lengthiest and most numerous succession of campaigns in its history, ending with the Battle of Wounded Knee in 1890.

—*Mary E. Virginia*

FURTHER READING

Dowd, Gregory Evans. *War Under Heaven: Pontiac, the Indian Nations, and the British Empire*. Baltimore: Johns Hopkins University Press, 2002. Dowd reinterprets the causes and consequences of Pontiac's resistance. He maintains that the issue of status was the root of the conflict: The British held American Indians in low regard, and American Indian leaders believed the British failed to treat them with appropriate respect.

Hawke, David. *The Colonial Experience*. Indianapolis, Ind.: Bobbs-Merrill, 1966. Chapter 13 brilliantly places Pontiac's resistance in the context of Great Britain's halting steps toward imperial reorganization.

Leach, Douglas E. *Arms for Empire: A Military History of the British Colonies in North America, 1607-1763*. New York: Macmillan, 1973. A formidable study that details the increasingly impossible task Great Britain faced in trying to devise an effective military defense for a vast colonial empire against France and Spain, British colonists, and American Indians. The latter chapters provide excellent background on Pontiac's resistance.

_____. "Colonial Indian Wars." In *History of Indian-White Relations*, edited by Wilcomb B. Washburn. Vol. 4 in *Handbook of North American Indians*. Washington, D.C.: Smithsonian Institution Press, 1988. More specific in its focus than Leach's earlier study, this article combines British and American Indian politics and perspectives in the context of colonial wars.

Nester, William R. *"Haughty Conquerors": Amherst and the Great Indian Uprising of 1763*. Westport, Conn.: Praeger, 2000. A history of Pontiac's resistance. Nester describes the causes and battles of the war and American Indian victory. He also explains how, within a generation after this victory, another group of settlers and another war would take away much of what the Indians had won.

Parkman, Francis. *The Conspiracy of Pontiac and the Indian War After the Conquest of Canada*. 7th ed. Boston: Little, Brown, 1874. Despite minor inaccuracies, this remains the classic study of the subject. Based on original documents and written by one of the greatest of American historians.

Peckham, Howard. *Pontiac and the Indian Uprising*. Princeton, N.J.: Princeton University Press, 1947. Corrects Parkman's inaccuracies, updates the subject, and provides fresh insights into American Indian attitudes.

SEE ALSO: May 28, 1754-Feb. 10, 1763: French and Indian War; Oct. 5, 1759-Nov. 19, 1761: Cherokee War; Feb. 10, 1763: Peace of Paris; Oct. 7, 1763: Proclamation of 1763; Apr. 27-Oct. 10, 1774: Lord Dunmore's War; May 24 and June 11, 1776: Indian Delegation Meets with Congress; Oct. 22, 1784: Fort Stanwix Treaty; Oct. 18, 1790-July, 1794: Little Turtle's War; 1799: Code of Handsome Lake.

RELATED ARTICLES in *Great Lives from History: The Eighteenth Century, 1701-1800:* Lord Amherst; Joseph Brant; Thomas Gage; George III; William Howe; Little Turtle; Alexander McGillivray; Louis-Joseph de Montcalm; Lord North; Thanadelthur; James Wolfe.

August, 1763-April, 1765
DAVID GARRICK'S EUROPEAN TOUR

David Garrick, eighteenth century England's most prominent actor and that country's premier theater representative, toured Western Europe, establishing the reputation of English theater throughout Europe. The tour proved to be one of the most significant celebrity events of the century.

LOCALE: Western Europe
CATEGORIES: Cultural and intellectual history; theater

KEY FIGURES
David Garrick (1717-1779), an English actor, playwright, and theater manager
Eva Maria Garrick (1724-1822), David's wife and a dancer, who accompanied Garrick on the tour
George Colman the Elder (1732-1794), an English playwright and theater manager

SUMMARY OF EVENT
By 1763, David Garrick, actor and manager of the Drury Lane Theatre in London, was firmly established as the greatest English actor of his day and the most important figure of English theater. His European tour spread his reputation, and the reputation of English theater, throughout Europe. Garrick was at the height of his career in 1763, but the 1762-1763 theater season had been particularly difficult. Together, the Drury Lane and Covent Garden Theatres attempted to end the long-standing but unprofitable practice of reducing ticket prices by half after the third act. An organized audience riot at Drury Lane forced Garrick, with a personal stage appearance, to acquiesce to the mob's demand. Thus, Garrick and his wife, Eva Maria, from whom he had never been apart for more than twenty-four hours, set out for Paris and the Continent for a long-deserved rest from professional duties.

Garrick's timing was fortuitous: His reputation had preceded him, and all things English were in style. During his first night in Paris he was given the freedom of the theater of the Comédie Française, where he made numerous acquaintances among the Paris theater establishment. Initially, the Garricks spent only three weeks in Paris before proceeding to Italy, passing through Lyons, over Mount Cenis to Turin, Milan, Genoa, Florence, Rome, and, ultimately, Naples, where they spent Christmas. The journey was a triumphal tour, as notables throughout Europe vied for time with the great actor. At one point, passing near Ferney, Voltaire sent Garrick an invitation that Garrick smugly rejected because of Voltaire's well-known disdain for William Shakespeare. This rejection was taken as an insult. Throughout his tour, Garrick also was searching out-of-the-way sources for rare books to add to his extensive collection and also, evidently, to sell for a profit upon his return to England.

Garrick made the most of his acting reputation during his visits. In Naples, accompanied by Lord and Lady Spencer and Lady Oxford, he was asked by the king to go to the royal theater to test the Italian acting company by developing a scenario for a plot that they were to undertake and perform within twenty-four hours. In Parma, while dining with the duke of York and the prince of Parma, Garrick performed his famous dagger scene from *Macbeth*, for which the prince gave him a snuff box; Garrick added it to his collection of snuff boxes he had received as gifts on the tour.

It was at the residence of Mlle Clairon, a leading French actor where Garrick performed the dagger scene, along with the ghost scene from *Hamlet* and the mad scene from *King Lear*. Clairon, enraptured, threw her arms around his neck and kissed him. Embarrassed, she then turned to Garrick's wife and apologized. When riding in the countryside with the French actor Pierre-Louis-Dubus Préville, Garrick had praised him on his display of acting drunk, but Garrick also showed him some problems with the routine by himself demonstrating drunkenness in return. In doing so he fell from his horse and lay on the ground, apparently unconscious. The performance was so convincing that the veteran French actor truly believed Garrick was dead, and then turned to seek help. Garrick then sat up and laughed.

The tour also saw considerable misfortune. After especially difficult travel to Naples, in which the tour's coach had broken down during severe weather, Eva Maria caught cold and developed rheumatism in one of her hips. She was forced to keep to her bed for many days, though amusingly she did attend a masquerade, in which she dressed as a lame old woman dragging her leg. Nevertheless, the illness persisted until near the end of the tour, when Garrick, too, grew severely ill with what might have been some form of typhoid fever.

In London, fears that the Drury Lane Theatre might suffer with Garrick's absence proved unwarranted. Garrick had left the theater in the hands of his partner William Lacy, who maintained operations, and with George Colman the Elder, who maintained creative in-

David Garrick is portrayed as torn between the personifications of comedy and tragedy. (Library of Congress)

terests. Colman proved to be a major figure in London theater as he later managed Covent Garden and the Haymarket Theatres successfully while composing some of the best comic drama of the period. The major acting roles were taken over by Garrick's young protégé William Powell, who developed a significant following because of Garrick's absence.

While Garrick began the lengthy preparations to return to London he began to develop concerns about his reception back home. Throughout the tour, while he had moderately kept up with Drury Lane matters, he had missed the actors and audiences very little. Concerned that his detractors might undermine his homecoming, Garrick attempted to circumvent criticism by having Colman distribute a poem broadside titled "The Sick Monkey," which was to be self-deprecating, but hu-

mourous. The effort proved unnecessary because Garrick was welcomed back to London with enthusiasm, renewed in health and spirit. While the tour had caused him briefly to consider retirement, Garrick continued an incredibly successful career on the London stage until finally retiring in 1776. He died in 1779.

SIGNIFICANCE

David Garrick's European tour was perhaps the best known celebrity tour of the eighteenth century, bringing to English theater and, indirectly, English culture, a new respect that had been missing among continental Europeans for decades. Furthermore, Garrick's absence from the English stage allowed new talent to develop from under the shadow of the great actor. Soon after his return he assisted George Colman the Elder in writing *The Clan-*

destine *Marriage* (1766), a play that still holds the stage, and the play that essentially initiated Colman's distinguished literary career. William Powell's reputation as one of the century's great actors was to increase even upon his mentor's return, and Garrick's reputation increased as well.

In the next two years, Garrick had returned to Paris, where he was once again welcomed, this time by eminent writers and thinkers. In particular, Garrick enjoyed the regular hospitality of Paul-Henri-Dietrich d'Holbach, the philosopher. Holbach's salon, along with other social functions, helped Garrick develop lifelong acquaintances with such figures as Jean-François Marmontel, Denis Diderot, Jean le Rond d'Alembert, and Friedrich Melchior von Grimm, who were all prominent writers and critics.

—Paul Varner

FURTHER READING

Barton, Margaret. *Garrick*. New York: Macmillan, 1949. An older biography but one that treats the continental tour at great length.

Benedetti, Jean. *David Garrick and the Birth of Modern Theatre*. London: Methuen, 2001. Benedetti maintains that Garrick was the father of modern theater, who reformed theater practice to become the first international superstar.

Garrick, David. *The Journal of David Garrick, Describing His Visit to France and Italy in 1763*. Edited by George Winchester Stone, Jr. 1939. Reprint. New York: Krauss, 1966. A brief, seventy-three-page journal that highlights the tour.

Little, David M., George M. Kahrl, and Phoebe de K. Wilson, eds. *The Letters of David Garrick*. 3 vols. Cambridge, Mass.: Harvard University Press, 1963. The primary source for information on the tour.

McIntyre, Ian. *Garrick*. New York: Penguin Putnam, 1999. An exhaustively detailed, well-researched recounting of Garrick's life, career, and circle of friends.

Stone, George Winchester, Jr., and George M. Kahrl. *David Garrick: A Critical Biography*. Carbondale: Southern Illinois University Press, 1979. The definitive biography of David Garrick.

SEE ALSO: Jan. 29, 1728: Gay Produces the First Ballad Opera; Dec. 7, 1732: Covent Garden Theatre Opens in London.

RELATED ARTICLES in *Great Lives from History: The Eighteenth Century, 1701-1800*: Robert and James Adam; James Boswell; Lancelot Brown; Edmund Burke; Hannah Cowley; Thomas Gainsborough; David Garrick; George III; Samuel Johnson; Hannah More; Anne Oldfield; Richard Brinsley Sheridan; Sarah Siddons; Peg Woffington.

September 10, 1763
PUBLICATION OF THE *FREEMAN'S JOURNAL*

The Freeman's Journal *was the first independent Irish newspaper to survive for more than a few issues. During its first forty years, it evolved from a journal consisting mainly of contributed editorials to a newspaper that strove to present a comprehensive, accurate picture of Irish news. Noteworthy among its offerings were the letters collectively known as* Baratariana *and its effective support of the Union Act.*

LOCALE: Dublin, Ireland

CATEGORIES: Communications; government and politics

KEY FIGURES

Charles Lucas (1713-1771), reformist member of Ireland's Parliament for Dublin and founding contributor to the *Freeman's Journal*

Henry Brooke (c. 1703-1783), Irish playwright and first editor of the *Freeman's Journal*, 1763-1778

Henry Flood (1732-1791), leader of Irish Parliamentary opposition and principal author of *Baratariana*

Francis Higgins (1746-1802), *Freeman's Journal* editor, 1782-1802

SUMMARY OF EVENT

The *Freeman's Journal* commenced publication in Dublin, Ireland, on September 10, 1763. The periodical's founders were three Dublin commercial men, John Grant, William Braddell, and Edward Tandy. Their primary motive was profit. Also involved in the production of the paper was Charles Lucas, a writer and reforming politician who had recently returned to Ireland after a decade in exile and represented Dublin in the Irish House of Commons. Lucas's influence with the paper helped set its initial reformist tone. Although Dublin already supported several newspapers, they were either mouthpieces for a small aristocratic elite or primarily vehicles for advertisements.

The *Freeman's Journal* appeared biweekly, each issue costing a penny. Circulation in 1794 (when the paper changed hands) ranged from two to three thousand, comparing favorably with London's dailies. The paper's first editor was Henry Brooke, an Irish playwright. Under Brooke's editorship, with the aid of Lucas's pen, the paper became the chief outlet for liberal opinion on the leading nationalist controversies of the day—free trade and the independence and integrity of the Irish parliament.

These contemporary issues were interrelated. Under a 1494 statute known as Poyning's Law, the Irish parliament was completely subservient to the British parliament, which had the right to approve or reject any law passed in Ireland. Consequently, any efforts by the Irish parliament to reform trade and tax laws ran aground in England, and the cry of "no taxation without representation" rang as true in Dublin as it did in Philadelphia. English patronage further compromised the independence of both houses of Ireland's Parliament. By 1790, fewer than one-quarter of the seats in the House of Commons were occupied by elected members, and a high proportion of the peers were English absentees.

The paper's editorial stance reflected the concerns of the Dublin commercial community, which in 1763 was entirely Protestant. Under the editorship of Brooke, whose fictional writings had a strong anti-Catholic slant, the otherwise liberal *Freeman's Journal* opposed concessions to Catholics and treated Catholics contemptuously in its coverage of news relating to them. Irish nationalism of the 1760's and 1770's had a decidedly Protestant slant.

The early issues of the *Freeman's Journal* consisted mainly of letters to a nonexistent Committee for the Support of a Free Press. These covered a wide range of topics but rarely focused on current events. For some months the columns of the paper were dominated by the putative medicinal benefits of Turkish baths, which were thinly veiled advertisements for a particular Dublin entrepreneur. This lack of distinction between news items and paid advertisements was characteristic of eighteenth century newspapers, including the *London Times*.

In 1770-1771, the *Freeman's Journal* published a series of satirical letters from "a native of Barataria," which were later reprinted as *Baratariana: A Select Collection of Fugitive Political Pieces, Published During the Administration of Lord Townshend in Ireland* (1772). The principal author of these letters was Henry Flood;

Charles Lucas and Henry Grattan also contributed. Utilizing bitter invective, the "native of Barataria" attacked Sir Charles Townshend, the incoming viceroy, for his determination to replace a system of local control by a few powerful British-Irish aristocratic families with more direct government by the Crown-appointed viceroy and his cabinet. In content and style, the letters resemble the more famous "Letters of Junius" attacking George III that were published in London in the *Public Advertiser* from 1769 to 1772.

The *Freeman's Journal* played a prominent part in Irish agitation for repeal of Poyning's Law and for general parliamentary reform. The former goal was achieved in 1782, when Irish nationalists were able to use their support of the British crown during the American Revolution as a lever to win concessions from the English parliament. Much of the ostensible shift toward conservatism in the *Freeman's Journal*'s politics after 1782 resulted from a split among the nationalists, many of whom felt the "revolution of 1782" was as much reform as the country could handle.

The newly independent Irish parliament proved to be a surprisingly responsible steward of Irish affairs, despite its corruption and exclusively Protestant makeup. One of its first acts was to remove the economic disabilities on Roman Catholics, which encouraged émigrés who had prospered abroad to return to their homeland. In 1793, Catholics were granted the right to vote, to practice law, and to hold commissions in the Irish militia. By the mid-1790's, Dublin had a substantial Roman Catholic commercial and professional community, and this community, for the most part, was firmly loyal to a Tory-dominated Parliament, the English viceroy, and a cabinet controlled by Englishmen.

The *Freeman's Journal* also covered the American Revolution in considerable detail, publishing long excerpts from the American press. Initially, commentary was favorable, but as the Revolutionary War progressed, sympathy for the colonists waned. This period coincided with the growing influence of Francis Higgins, who joined the staff around 1778 and became editor in 1782. It is uncertain to what extent distancing Irish nationalism from the avowed separatism and antiroyalist sentiments of the Americans represented genuine conviction and to what extent it was based in prudent self-interest. Higgins's distaste for the anti-Catholic bias of the Continental Congress, however, was probably sincere.

Francis Higgins became a controversial figure in Irish history. A man of humble origins and a convert from Catholicism, he earned the nickname "The Sham Squire" by assuming the guise of a landowner in order to court an heiress. Under his editorship, the *Freeman's Journal* started publishing more news and less philosophy. Paid government announcements became a significant source of revenue for the paper, which began to attack the former contributor Grattan, as well as others who maintained that the reforms of 1782 did not go far enough. During the Fitzwilliam episode of 1795—when William Pitt the Younger appointed the radical Whig the second earl Fitzwilliam as viceroy and recalled him abruptly after a few months—the *Freeman's Journal* remained aloof from the general recriminations against Fitzwilliam and enthusiastically supported his successor, Sir John Jeffreys, second earl of Camden.

Higgins's role in the 1798 Irish Rebellion and its aftermath is murky. He has been accused of being a spy and an informer. Certainly, under Higgins, the *Freeman's Journal* was hostile toward anything connected with the United Irishmen, and it allotted a prominent position to coverage of rebel atrocities while glossing over the excesses of the government's forces. It is unlikely that such a well-known establishment supporter would have been privy to treasonous activity; on the other hand, Higgins may have served as an intermediary for informers.

In the wake of the rebellion, Pitt's ministry in London and the First Marquess Cornwallis's administration in Ireland initiated an effort to dissolve the Irish parliament and to merge it with that of England. The *Freeman's Journal* lent its unqualified support to this measure and was prominent in convincing the Catholic Committees, which lacked representation in the Irish parliament but wielded considerable economic clout, to support union as well. The measure succeeded, in no small part because of Pitt's willingness to pay a large number of Irish members of Parliament to relinquish their seats, and the Act of Union became law on January 1, 1801.

SIGNIFICANCE

The *Freeman's Journal* continued publication until 1926. Throughout its long history, it remained the effective mouthpiece of the Dublin commercial community. Its seeming swings between separatist nationalism and collaboration with the central government in London make sense in the light of the shifting interests of the paper's middle-class readership. The *Freeman's Journal* is therefore an invaluable resource for the historian of Irish society and politics. Reading it, one encounters a reflection of one substantial segment of public opinion in Ireland, rather than an attempt by a faction to convert the public to a stance that did not necessarily have many sup-

porters. The paper did not so much shape history as correctly identify the shape that history subsequently took.

—*Martha A. Sherwood*

FURTHER READING

Killen, John, ed. *The Decade of the United Irishmen: Contemporary Accounts*. Belfast: Blackstaff Press, 1997. Includes news stories from the *Freeman's Journal* published from 1791 to 1801.

The London Times, Microfilm Edition, 1786-1801. The *Times* copied most of its Irish news from the *Freeman's Journal*, which it regarded as the most reliable of the Irish newspapers.

McDowell, Robert Brendan. *Ireland in the Age of Imperialism and Revolution, 1760-1801*. Oxford, England: Clarendon Press, 1979. A clear, well-balanced account of Irish politics in the latter part of the eighteenth century; the role of the *Freeman's Journal* is discussed.

Madden, Richard Robert. *The History of Irish Periodical Literature from the End of the Seventeenth to the Middle of the Nineteenth Century*. New York: Johnson Reprint, 1968. Contains a wealth of information but is highly biased in favor of violent separatism and is hostile to the point of libel toward the *Freeman's Journal*.

Mathew, H. C. G., and Brian Harrison, eds. *Oxford Dictionary of National Biography: From the Earliest Times to the Year 2000*. New York: Oxford University Press, 2004. This multivolume set includes detailed biographies of Lucas, Higgins, and Brooke. It is an invaluable source for biographies of obscure British historical personages.

Munter, Robert. *The History of the Irish Newspaper, 1685-1760*. Cambridge, England: Cambridge University Press, 1967. Gives a good overview of the background, and of Charles Lucas' relationship with the press; includes some information on post-1760 events.

SEE ALSO: Feb., 1706-Apr. 28, 1707: Act of Union Unites England and Scotland; Mar. 1, 1711: Addison and Steele Establish *The Spectator*; Dec., 1711: Occasional Conformity Bill; 1726: Swift Satirizes English Rule of Ireland in *Gulliver's Travels*; 1736: *Gentleman's Magazine* Initiates Parliamentary Reporting; Mar. 20, 1750-Mar. 14, 1752: Johnson Issues *The Rambler*; Beginning Apr., 1763: The *North Briton* Controversy; 1774: Hansard Begins Reporting Parliamentary Debates; June 2-10, 1780: Gordon Riots; Jan. 4, 1792-1797: The *Northern Star* Calls for Irish

Independence; May-Nov., 1798: Irish Rebellion; July 2-Aug. 1, 1800: Act of Union Forms the United Kingdom.

October 7, 1763
PROCLAMATION OF 1763

In an effort to avoid further conflict over territorial sovereignty, the British parliament issued the Proclamation of 1763, drawing a frontier line between the American colonies and Native American lands.

LOCALE: London, England
CATEGORIES: Laws, acts, and legal history; colonization; expansion and land acquisition; diplomacy and international relations

KEY FIGURES

Lord Amherst (Jeffrey Amherst; 1717-1797), British commander in chief in North America, 1759-1763, governor general of British North America, 1760-1763, and later Baron Amherst, 1776-1797

First Earl of Hillsborough (Wills Hill; 1718-1793), British president of the Board of Trade, 1763-1765, 1766, 1768-1772

Second Earl of Shelburne (William Petty-Fitzmaurice; 1737-1805), British president of the Board of Trade, 1763, secretary of state, 1766-1768, and prime minister, 1782-1783

Second Earl of Egremont (Charles Wyndham; 1710-1763), British secretary of state, 1761-1763

William Johnson (1715-1774), Irish-born colonial American superintendent of Indian affairs, 1755-1774

Thomas Gage (1721-1787), British commander in chief in North America, 1763-1773

SUMMARY OF EVENT

In 1763, in the wake of its North American victory over France in the French and Indian War, Great Britain was faced with the question of how to control the vast domain between the Appalachian Mountains and the Mississippi River. The answer to that question interested not only Native Americans, French Canadians, and British colonial administrators but also American fur traders, merchants, and land speculators. The trans-Appalachian West had increasingly occupied the attention of British and colonial officials since the Albany Congress of 1754.

During the war, the Crown had appointed superintendents to coordinate Native American affairs, but exigen-

RELATED ARTICLES in *Great Lives from History: The Eighteenth Century, 1701-1800*: First Marquess Cornwallis; William Pitt the Younger.

cies of the moment made the new arrangement inadequate. In the eyes of Whitehall officials, the old policy of leaving control of the frontier to the individual colonies had been chaotic and ruinous. The line of Euro-American agricultural settlement had steadily edged westward, with scant regard for Native American land claims or indigenous culture. Royal governors, superintendents for Native American affairs, and British military men repeatedly had complained that the colonists disregarded Native American treaties and made fraudulent land purchases, and that Euro-American traders mistreated the tribal peoples.

The necessity of reaching an accord with the Native Americans seemed even more urgent with Pontiac's Resistance, which had begun in the spring of 1763. The indigenous population, already uneasy over the defeat of their French allies, encountered repeated insults from the British commander in chief, General Jeffrey Amherst, who refused to present them with guns, ammunition, and other gifts, as had been the French custom. They responded with violence.

Striking first in the remoter sections of the West, such as at Fort Michilimackinac, and later on the Pennsylvania frontier, roving parties of Ottawas, Chippewas, Lenni Lenapes (Delawares), and Senecas overran one British-occupied post after another; by the end of June, only Forts Detroit, Pitt, and Niagara still held out against the warriors. Amherst, near recall from the home government, dispatched relief expeditions to his remaining garrisons, and several colonies raised troops to repel the indigenous combatants. The prospect of fire and sword, the diplomatic skills of William Johnson, Pontiac's calling off the sieges, and the breakup of the coalition of tribes—which never was united on ultimate objectives—explain the demise of the rebellion and restoration of peace in 1764.

Eager to bring an end to hostilities and avoid another outbreak, the British exacted little retribution from the western tribes. During the uprising, the government announced its new policy for the West, one that had evolved from British experience in the French and Indian

PROCLAMATION LINE OF 1763

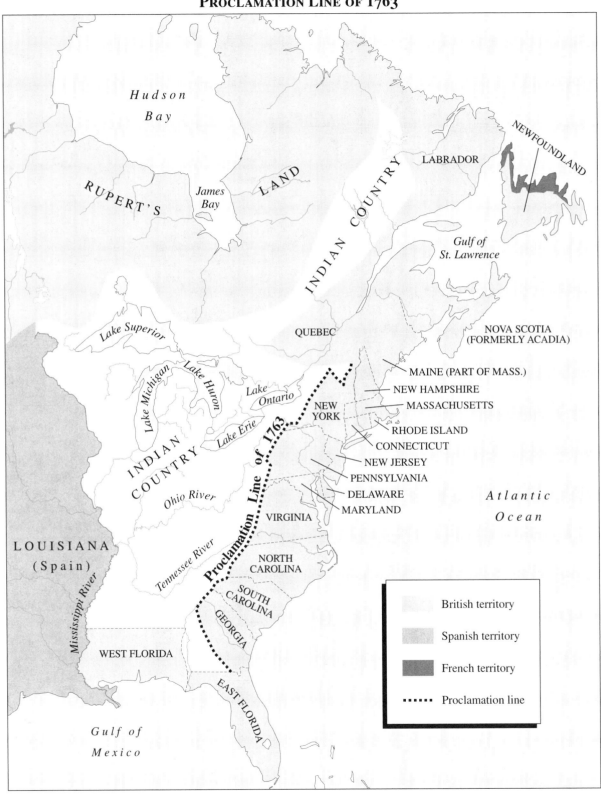

Hudson Bay

RUPERT'S LAND

James Bay

INDIAN COUNTRY

LABRADOR

NEWFOUNDLAND

Gulf of St. Lawrence

Lake Superior

QUEBEC

NOVA SCOTIA (FORMERLY ACADIA)

Lake Michigan

Lake Huron

Lake Ontario

Lake Erie

INDIAN COUNTRY

Ohio River

Proclamation Line of 1763

MAINE (PART OF MASS.)

NEW HAMPSHIRE

MASSACHUSETTS

NEW YORK

RHODE ISLAND

CONNECTICUT

NEW JERSEY

PENNSYLVANIA

DELAWARE

MARYLAND

VIRGINIA

Atlantic Ocean

LOUISIANA (Spain)

Mississippi River

Tennessee River

NORTH CAROLINA

SOUTH CAROLINA

GEORGIA

WEST FLORIDA

EAST FLORIDA

Gulf of Mexico

British territory

Spanish territory

French territory

Proclamation line

War. It was the work of no single minister or subminister, although the second earl of Egremont, the second earl of Shelburne, and the first earl of Hillsborough were keenly interested in the matter.

On October 7, 1763, King George III signed the edict now known as the Proclamation of 1763. By its terms, the recently acquired territories of Canada and East and West Florida became Crown colonies, and their inhabitants became entitled to the same rights as the English at home. The proclamation nullified all colonial claims to territories west of the crest of the Appalachians and set those lands aside for Native Americans "for the present, and until our further Pleasure be known." Wishing to monopolize the substantial and lucrative fur trade of the area, Whitehall hardly wanted colonial farmers crowding out the furbearers' habitat and local traders competing for the business. The trade with the tribal peoples would be "free and open," although traders would have to obtain a license and obey any pertinent regulations.

As the Proclamation of 1763 contained no provision for law enforcement in the area beyond provincial boundaries, an ad hoc system of confining trade to a few forts under superintendent and military supervision developed. The Crown expected that the colonials would obey the edict out of allegiance to England. Moreover, the royal government hoped that restless colonists would move northward into the thinly settled districts of Maine, Nova Scotia, and New Brunswick to offset the Catholic French Canadian population there and in Quebec, or relocate southward into Georgia to bolster that buffer province against the Spaniards.

Native Americans in the region heard about the Proclamation Line and watched some of the actual surveying with distrust and bemusement. The document promised that

the several Nations or Tribes of Indians with whom We are connected, and who live under Our Protection should not be molested or disturbed in the Possession of such Parts of our Dominions and Territories as, not having been ceded to, or purchased by Us, are reserved to them, or any of them, as their Hunting Grounds.

British general Thomas Gage rushed copies westward, because he imagined that "these Arrangements must be very satisfactory to the Indians." The tribes, however, had witnessed earlier attempts at boundary treaties, such as at Easton and Lancaster, Pennsylvania, in 1758 and 1760 respectively, and in South Carolina in 1761, crumble as squatters leapfrogged the line.

SIGNIFICANCE

In the long run, Great Britain's "western policy" failed. Land-hungry settlers spilled over into the trans-Appalachia area in defiance of the Proclamation of 1763. British troops could not guard every mountain gap, nor could they and royal superintendents force traders to patronize specific posts. Several ambitious Virginia speculators, some of whom later joined the patriot cause in the revolution, had claims across the divide. Faced with the prospect of worthless holdings, they pressed for repeal of the order. The maintenance of western garrisons was expensive, especially when American revenues for the army's upkeep failed to materialize, and when the troops did not accomplish their mission.

In 1768, the British government, beset with these problems and colonial rebelliousness in the eastern regions, adopted a policy of retrenchment in the West. Control of the trade with Native Americans reverted to the individual colonies, and British troops received orders to abandon all the interior posts except Niagara, Detroit, and Michilimackinac. Almost simultaneously, the government bowed to pressure to push the Native American boundary westward. The Treaty of Fort Stanwix (1768) with the Iroquois Confederacy and the Treaties of Hard Labor (1768) and Lochaber (1770) with the Cherokee signified this change. No longer did the trans-Appalachian West loom uppermost in British imperial policy.

—R. Don Higginbotham,
updated by Thomas L. Altherr

FURTHER READING

Anderson, Fred. *Crucible of War: The Seven Years' War and the Fate of Empire in British North America, 1754-1766.* New York: Vintage Books, 2001. This massive, meticulously detailed account of the French and Indian War includes information about the Proclamation of 1763. With illustrations from the William L. Clements Library.

Jennings, Francis. *Empire of Fortune: Crowns, Colonies, and Tribes in the Seven Years' War in America.* New York: W. W. Norton, 1988. Contains a short discussion of the Proclamation of 1763 and the Native American response.

Martin, James Kirby. *In the Course of Human Events: An Interpretive Exploration of the American Revolution.* Arlington Heights, Ill.: Harlan Davidson, 1979. Links the Proclamation of 1763 with other British decisions to control the colonies, such as stationing ships in American waters.

Nester, William R. *Haughty Conquerors: Amherst and the Great Indian Uprising of 1763*. New York: HarperCollins, 1995. This account of the Native American revolt against the British includes information about the Proclamation of 1763.

"Proclamation of 1763: Governor Henry Ellis' Plan, May 5, 1763." In *The American Revolution, 1763-1783: A Bicentennial Collection*, edited by Richard B. Morris. Columbia: University of South Carolina Press, 1970. Demonstrates the thinking by one colonial official that prompted the Proclamation of 1763.

Sosin, Jack M. *Whitehall and the Wilderness: The Middle West in British Colonial Policy, 1760-1775*. Lincoln: University of Nebraska Press, 1961. Detailed examination of royal decisions leading to the Proclamation of 1763.

Stagg, Jack. *Anglo-Indian Relations in North America to 1763 and an Analysis of the Royal Proclamation of 7 October, 1763*. Ottawa, Ont.: Research Branch, Indian and Northern Affairs Canada, 1981. Provides a detailed interpretation of the text of the Proclamation of 1763 and the Crown's motives.

Steele, Ian K. *Warpaths: Invasions of North America*. New York: Oxford University Press, 1994. Places the decisions for the Proclamation of 1763 within the context of the military actions of the recent war and earlier treaties.

SEE ALSO: May 28, 1754-Feb. 10, 1763: French and Indian War; June 19-July 10, 1754: Albany Congress; July, 1755-Aug., 1758: Acadians Are Expelled from Canada; Jan., 1756-Feb. 15, 1763: Seven Years' War; June 8-July 27, 1758: Siege of Louisbourg; Oct. 5, 1759-Nov. 19, 1761: Cherokee War; Feb. 10, 1763: Peace of Paris; May 8, 1763-July 24, 1766: Pontiac's Resistance; Dec. 14 and 27, 1763: Paxton Boys' Massacres; May 24 and June 11, 1776: Indian Delegation Meets with Congress.

RELATED ARTICLES in *Great Lives from History: The Eighteenth Century, 1701-1800*: Lord Amherst; Thomas Gage; George III.

December 14 and 27, 1763
PAXTON BOYS' MASSACRES

Growing tensions between Pennsylvania backcountry settlers and Native Americans resulted in the massacre of defenseless Susquehannocks. The massacres began a chain of events that resulted in Pennsylvania's declaration of war against several Native American tribes.

LOCALE: Lancaster, Pennsylvania, and environs (now in the United States)

CATEGORIES: Colonization; wars, uprisings, and civil unrest; diplomacy and international relations

KEY FIGURES
John Elder (1706-1792), Presbyterian minister who became a spokesman for the Paxton Boys
Benjamin Franklin (1706-1790), colonial American politician
John Penn (1729-1795), governor of Pennsylvania

SUMMARY OF EVENT

The French and Indian War was a particularly difficult time for settlers in the Pennsylvania backcountry. By the early 1750's, the harmony that had characterized the relationship between Native Americans and the colony since the time of William Penn had ended. Led by the Six Nations of the Iroquois Confederacy, various Pennsylvania tribes, encompassing numerous Native American villages throughout the region, fought to limit future European expansion onto ancestral lands. The struggle engendered much bloodshed and carnage on both sides.

During the war, the Pennsylvania Assembly, influenced by pacific Quakers, pursued a policy of negotiations rather than resorting to armed confrontation. Despite pleas from embattled backcountry residents for military assistance, provincial leaders steadfastly refused to organize or outfit an official militia. As a result, western residents were left to fend for themselves. By the 1760's, the Quaker policy had produced some minimal results. Pennsylvania authorities were able to reestablish peaceful relations with a few villages. Cooperative tribes were promised land rights, commercial opportunities, and protection from their enemies. However, many villages questioned the sincerity of the offers and remained at war. This put backcountry residents in a particularly difficult situation. It was virtually impossible for them to differentiate between peaceful and hostile natives, a distinction that could become a matter of life or death. Therefore, many homesteaders chose simply to label all of the indigenous population as hostile until all had agreed to a peace.

On the morning of December 14, 1763, the tensions generated the first of two massacres. A band of approximately four dozen angry Pennsylvania backwoodsmen attacked an unsuspecting Conestoga village situated approximately 50 miles northwest of Lancaster. The village was inhabited by fewer than two dozen Susquehannocks. A month earlier, in a petition to Governor John Penn, these same Susquehannocks had promised to maintain the peace that they claimed they had always honored. Nevertheless, the Pennsylvanians, who called themselves the Paxton Boys, complained that villagers were assisting and sheltering Native American warriors. Several of the warriors were believed to have murdered nearby settlers. In the assault, the Paxton Boys struck quickly, burning the village's huts and killing three Susquehannock men, two women, and a child.

Panicked by the raid, fourteen Susquehannock survivors fled to the safety of provincial authorities in Lancaster. Upon their arrival, the refugees were placed under protective custody and held in the town jail. It was there that the Paxton Boys found them on December 27, and it was there that the backwoodsmen committed a second massacre. Enraged that local officials would shelter the natives, a force of about one hundred well-armed Paxton Boys rode up to the jailhouse. They burst into the building, seized the keeper, and then shot and tomahawked the defenseless Susquehannocks. A few minutes later, with their task accomplished, the backwoods raiders rode off to their homes, satisfied that they had taken an important step toward easing the Native American threat within the region.

News of the two attacks created a flurry of activity in Philadelphia. Governor Penn immediately issued a proclamation instructing western magistrates to apprehend those involved in the massacres. Colonial officials, fearing additional assaults, rounded up 125 friendly Native Americans, many of whom had converted to Moravianism, and brought them to Philadelphia. Meanwhile, the colonial Assembly asked New York authorities to provide a sanctuary for the refugees. However, the New York governor denied the request. Instead, a regiment of British regulars was assigned to escort the "Moravian Indians" to a military barracks on a Delaware River island and to defend them against all potential assailants. The Assembly's precautions were not popular in the backcountry. John Elder, a Presbyterian minister and militia colonel who was alleged to be the Paxton Boys' organizer, warned that "the minds of the inhabitants are so exasperated against the Quakers" that western residents were ready to confront the Assembly and take matters into their own hands.

By late January, 1764, reports about an impending attack by the Paxton Boys swirled through Philadelphia. One letter to Governor Penn claimed that fifteen hundred well-armed backwoodsmen, a force three times larger than the British regiment guarding the Native Americans, were planning to march on the city and go door to door until they had found all the Native Americans in Philadelphia. The westerners intended to burn down the houses of those who resisted. The letter ended with a prediction that the backwoodsmen would fight to the death, if necessary.

The rumored march became a reality in early February. Although considerably smaller than most reports had forecast, a force of two hundred backwoods residents, comprising primarily Scotch-Irish Presbyterians from the lower Susquehanna River region, began a hike toward the provincial capital. Armed with muskets, tomahawks, and pistols, they announced that they were coming to Philadelphia to rectify the various abuses directed at them by the Assembly.

Intercepting the westerners at Germantown, five miles northwest of the city, Benjamin Franklin led a delegation appointed by the governor. Matthew Smith and James Gibson, two militia officers, presented Franklin with a petition that identified nine specific grievances. Surprisingly, the primary complaint had nothing to do with the colony's Native American policy. Instead, the Paxton Boys protested that the four western counties had significantly less representation in the Assembly than did the three eastern counties. If this inequity were rectified, the backwoodsmen claimed that the other eight complaints, all of which dealt with policies concerning Native Americans, would be remedied.

While Franklin conferred, other Philadelphians prepared for an attack. Some local residents insisted that the force in Germantown was simply an advance unit of Paxton Boys and that hundreds more would soon arrive. To defend the city against the "Lawless Party of Rioters," the Assembly swiftly enacted emergency legislation. Six companies, each with one hundred volunteers, were hastily organized. Cannon were pulled into defensive positions around the courthouse. Shops were closed. The roads and ferries leading into the city were blockaded. The British regiment guarding the Native American refugees was placed on alert.

Aided by the city's impressive mobilization, Franklin's deliberations proved fruitful. The westerners agreed that if their petition were promptly delivered to the governor and Assembly, they would return home. In a gesture aimed at compromise, the Philadelphia delegation announced that the Paxton Boys had been misunderstood and were, in fact, "a set of worthy men who laboured under great distress." The delegation then accompanied about thirty backwoodsmen into the city. The following day, one of the visitors was permitted to inspect several Native Americans to determine whether they had been involved in recent attacks upon settlers. They had not. Several days later, the westerners' petition was presented to the legislature.

SIGNIFICANCE

In July, 1764, the Pennsylvania Assembly responded legislatively to the Paxton Boys' demands. Pennsylvania formally declared war against the Lenni Lenapes and Shawnee tribes. A bounty for Native American scalps, another of the westerners' demands, was enacted. Money also was appropriated for the creation of an official provincial militia, something the Quaker government had steadfastly refused to do, even during the French and Indian War. The colony's search for the Paxton Boys involved in the two massacres had ended months earlier, with no arrests made.

Pennsylvania felt the impact of the Paxton Boys' activities for years to come. Most important, the crisis initiated an ongoing dispute about fair and equitable representation for western counties. It was a contest in which political power eventually shifted away from Philadelphia Quakers and toward a diverse and democratic coalition of political leadership. Ultimately, the crisis surrounding the Paxton Boys' massacres served as an initial step toward the political divisions that generated an independence movement within the colony.

—*Paul E. Doutrich*

FURTHER READING

Franz, George W. *Paxton: A Study of Community Structure and Mobility in the Colonial Pennsylvania Backcountry*. New York: Garland, 1989. Focuses on the political and socioeconomic development of the Paxton community.

Hindle, Brooke. "The March of the Paxton Boys." *William and Mary Quarterly*, 3d ser., 3 (October, 1946): 461-486. Still one of the best narrative accounts of the massacres.

Jacobs, Wilbur R. *The Paxton Riots and the Frontier Theory*. Chicago: Rand McNally, 1967. A brief booklet that includes many primary documents produced during the episode.

Kelley, Joseph J., Jr. *Pennsylvania: The Colonial Years*. Garden City, N.Y.: Doubleday, 1980. Includes a general description of the Paxton Boys episode.

Merritt, Jane T. *At the Crossroads: Indians and Empires on a Mid-Atlantic Frontier, 1700-1763*. Chapel Hill: University of North Carolina Press, 2003. An examination of the interactions between Native Americans and white settlers in eighteenth century Pennsylvania. Both groups initially were tolerant and cooperated with each other; but by the 1760's, Indians and whites were divided by racial differences, resulting in the animosity and hatred that was evident in the Paxton Boys' Massacres.

Pencak, William A., and Daniel K. Richter, eds. *Friends and Enemies in Penn's Woods: Indians, Colonists, and the Racial Construction of Pennsylvania*. University Park: Pennsylvania State University Press, 2004. Collection of essays describing how and why relations between colonial settlers and Native Americans degenerated between 1682 and the Paxton Boys' Massacres in 1763.

Schwartz, Sally. *"A Mixed Multitude": The Struggle for Toleration in Colonial Pennsylvania*. New York: New York University Press. 1987. A general history that describes the various tensions within colonial Pennsylvania and how the colony dealt with them.

1764
INVENTION OF THE SPINNING JENNY

The spinning jenny, invented by James Hargreaves in 1764, was the first in a series of inventions that adapted mechanical power to the production of textiles. It laid the foundations for the vast expansion of output achieved by the textile industry in the Industrial Revolution.

LOCALE: England
CATEGORIES: Inventions; manufacturing; science and technology

KEY FIGURES

James Hargreaves (1720-1778), English inventor of the spinning jenny
Samuel Crompton (1753-1827), English inventor of the spinning mule
John Kay (1704-c. 1780/1781), English inventor of the flying shuttle
Sir Richard Arkwright (1732-1792), English inventor of the water frame

SUMMARY OF EVENT

The decade of the 1760's was a period of great technological innovation in Britain. In particular, two devices invented during that decade transformed the production of textiles. The first of these, the spinning jenny, was the work of James Hargreaves, a weaver and carpenter whose experiences and skills gave impetus to the series of inventions that turned spinning and weaving from crafts into industries.

Although nothing is known of Hargreaves's birth and family, he appears to have been established as a handloom weaver in the town of Standhill by 1750. By that date, the flying shuttle of John Kay was beginning to transform weaving, increasing the output achieved by weavers using handlooms. This increased production capacity of handlooms, in turn, increased the demand for yarn. Yarn, however, was still produced predominantly by hand spinners working with spinning wheels in their own homes. This preindustrial arrangement was often inadequate to fulfill the demand of the growing textile industry, a demand that Hargreaves set out to satisfy.

Before cotton could be woven on a loom, it had to be carded and converted to a loose, rope-like form called a "roving." It then had to be twisted under steady pressure to form yarn, a thread strong enough to withstand the weaving process. The technical problem that Hargreaves needed to solve was how to replace the human fingers of the spinner operating a spinning wheel with mechanical devices that could simulate the twisting action of the spinner's fingers. His solution was the jenny, a device resembling the loom itself in its general design. Built on a square wooden frame, it used four spindles in place of the single spindle employed by the spinning wheel.

The jenny passed the roving through sets of rollers revolving at different speeds. This process twisted the roving while at the same time applying pressure to the strand so that the fibers were gradually stretched out to the fineness of thread. After passing through the rollers, the thread was wound under tension onto spindles on which bobbins were mounted that could then be transferred directly to the loom.

Hargreaves's machine made possible a fourfold, later an eightfold, expansion in the quantity of yarn a single spinner could produce, thereby enabling English spinners to supply the quantity of yarn required by English weavers. A further advantage of the jenny was that it required very little physical strength to operate and could therefore be "tended" by children.

At the same time that Hargreaves was developing the spinning jenny, another inventor, Sir Richard Arkwright, was creating another spinning machine called the water frame. Unlike the spinning jenny, the water frame bore little resemblance to the loom, but like the jenny, the water frame used rollers to simulate the twisting effect of human fingers. It also used multiple spindles, so that production was increased fourfold or more over that of preindustrial spinning methods.

Hargreaves began using his machine to supply the material for his own looms. Although he apparently completed the work on the jenny in 1764, he did not immediately apply for a patent for it. As word got around that such a machine existed, he sold a few copies of it to others. Then, in 1768, spinners who had learned of the jenny and feared the loss of their livelihood gathered into a mob that burst into Hargreaves's home and destroyed both the machine and the home. Hargreaves moved to Nottingham and formed a business on a small scale, producing yarn with his invention.

In 1770, Hargreaves applied for a patent on the spinning jenny. As news of the jenny spread, many manufacturers in Lancashire began using pirated versions of it. Hargreaves tried to protect his patent by suing, but in the course of legal action it was revealed that he had sold copies of the machine in the late 1760's, before he had applied for a patent, and this circumstance led to the invalidation of his patent. Hargreaves himself died in 1778, but his widow and son attempted by legal action to maintain his rights to the spinning jenny, though without success.

The pirated jennies were not the only source of Hargreaves's legal battles: The virtually contemporaneous water frame of Richard Arkwright, which also used rollers to twist the roving as it was converted into yarn, led to litigation to determine who was the actual innovator of this use of rollers. Arkwright patented his machine and thereby laid claim to the invention of the rollers, but the evidence seems to indicate that both men used rollers as an integral part of the spinning process. Their inventions were developed at the same time, so it is impossible to attribute the concept to one or the other. Hargreaves's machine, however, had the advantage that it could be operated by a single individual without the use of additional power, and this advantage led to its being adopted by a number of spinners who were operating on too small a scale to justify the application of power, whether such power was generated by a water wheel or by a steam engine.

Neither Hargreaves nor Arkwright was successful in defending his patent against those who copied their machines. Arkwright, however, built up a substantial business on the basis of his frame, which he adapted to the use of water power, whereas Hargreaves's jenny continued to be used on a small scale by individuals in small workshops. The yarn produced by Arkwright's frame could be used for the manufacture of stockings, whereas the yarn produced by Hargreaves's machine was not strong enough to be used in a variety of applications. Neither machine produced yarn of the necessary fineness, or count, to be used in the weaving of the light cotton materials that were then rapidly coming into popularity, so both machines were soon superseded by a machine that combined the features of both, the spinning mule, invented by Samuel Crompton. The mule produced yarn with counts up to three hundred, more than ten times the maximum possible on a Hargreaves machine, and as it also could be enlarged and adapted to the use of water

James Hargreaves's spinning jenny, shown in this early photograph, was used well into the nineteenth century. (Library of Congress)

power, and later, steam power, the mule became the dominant machine in the textile industry.

SIGNIFICANCE

Although Hargreaves's spinning jenny was soon superseded, his work was the first to use mechanical ingenuity to increase output on a large scale. Unlike the flying shuttle, which created the demand for more yarn, the spinning jenny was not merely a tool, helping workers to work. It was a machine that used mechanical power to amplify human labor power, greatly multiplying the productivity a spinner could achieve. This use of machines in spinning set the stage for the Industrial Revolution, in which the production of goods occurred on a mass scale in factory situations.

—*Nancy M. Gordon*

FURTHER READING

Cardwell, D. S. L. *Turning Points in Western Technology*. New York: Neale Watson Science History, 1972. Concise description of the textile inventions of the eighteenth century, along with a few diagrams.

Chapman, S. D. *The Cotton Industry in the Industrial Revolution*. London: Macmillan, 1972. Sets the inventions of the eighteenth century in the larger context of the Industrial Revolution.

Floud, Roderick, and Paul Johnson. *The Cambridge Economic History of Modern Britain*. Vol. 1. New York: Cambridge University Press, 2003. Provides the most detailed and clear explanation of the nature of the var-

ious textile inventions, complete with a number of line drawings of the different machines to facilitate understanding.

Mann, Julia de L. "The Textile Industry: Machinery for Cotton, Flax, Wool, 1760-1850." In *A History of Technology*, edited by Charles Singer. Vol. 1. New York: Oxford University Press, 1958. This chapter in the classic, multivolume history of technology explains at some length the nature of the technological innovations, complete with line drawings.

Mokyr, Joel. *The Lever of Riches: Technological Creativity and Economic Progress*. New York: Oxford University Press, 1990. Although the treatment is brief, the book contains a diagram showing how the innovation of Hargreaves was able to transform the production of yarn.

SEE ALSO: 1701: Tull Invents the Seed Drill; 1705-1712: Newcomen Develops the Steam Engine; 1709: Darby Invents Coke-Smelting; 1733: Kay Invents the Flying Shuttle; 1765-1769: Watt Develops a More Effective Steam Engine; 1767-1771: Invention of the Water Frame; 1779: Crompton Invents the Spinning Mule; Apr., 1785: Cartwright Patents the Steam-Powered Loom; Dec. 20, 1790: Slater's Spinning Mill; 1793: Whitney Invents the Cotton Gin; 1795: Invention of the Flax Spinner.

RELATED ARTICLES in *Great Lives from History: The Eighteenth Century, 1701-1800*: Sir Richard Arkwright; James Hargreaves; John Kay.

July, 1764
VOLTAIRE PUBLISHES *A PHILOSOPHICAL DICTIONARY FOR THE POCKET*

Combining satire and irony with empirical, rational, and moral arguments, Voltaire's A Philosophical Dictionary for the Pocket *attacked superstition, sectarian fanaticism, and intolerance, exposing the atrocities committed in the name of religion. Its aggressive anticlericalism and irreverent treatment of Holy Scripture shocked contemporary readers and provoked virulent public debate.*

LOCALE: Geneva, Switzerland

CATEGORIES: Philosophy; literature; religion and theology

KEY FIGURES

Voltaire (François-Marie Arouet; 1694-1778), French writer, historian, and philosopher

Jean-Jacques Rousseau (1712-1778), French writer, philosopher, and political theorist

Denis Diderot (1713-1784), French writer and encyclopedist

Pierre Bayle (1647-1706), French scholar

Frederick the Great (1712-1786), king of Prussia, r. 1740-1786

Gabriel Grasset (1725-1782), Swiss publisher

SUMMARY OF EVENT

In eighteenth century France, reference works such as Pierre Bayle's *Dictionnaire historique et critique* (1697; *An Historical and Critical Dictionary*, 1710) and Denis Diderot's monumental *Encyclopédie: Ou, Dictionnaire raisonné des sciences, des arts, et des métiers* (1751-

VOLTAIRE ON FRENCH PHILOSOPHERS

Voltaire's Philosophical Dictionary *entry, "Philosopher," excerpted here, decries the state of philosophy in his contemporary France. French philosophers themselves are not as virtuous as those of the past, he complains, and their treatment by the state is nothing short of criminal.*

One cannot read certain passages of Plato, and notably the admirable exordium of the laws of Zaleucus, without feeling in one's heart the love of honourable and generous actions. The Romans have their Cicero, who alone is worth perhaps all the philosophers of Greece. After him come men still more worthy of respect, but whom one almost despairs of imitating; Epictetus in bondage, the Antonines and the Julians on the throne.

Which is the citizen among us who would deprive himself, like Julian, Antoninus and Marcus Aurelius, of all the delicacies of our flabby and effeminate lives? who would sleep as they did on the ground? who would impose on himself their frugality? who, as they did, would march barefoot and bareheaded at the head of the armies, exposed now to the heat of the sun, now to the hoar-frost? who would command all their passions as they did? There are pious men among us; but where are the wise men? where are the resolute, just and tolerant souls?

There have been philosophers of the study in France; and all, except Montaigne, have been persecuted. It is, I think, the last degree of the malignity of our nature, to wish to oppress these very philosophers who would correct it.

I quite understand that the fanatics of one sect slaughter the enthusiasts of another sect, that the Franciscans hate the Dominicans, and that a bad artist intrigues to ruin one who surpasses him; but that the wise Charron should have been threatened with the loss of his life, that the learned and generous Ramus should have been assassinated, that Descartes should have been forced to flee to Holland to escape the fury of the ignorant, that Gassendi should have been obliged to withdraw several times to Digne, far from the calumnies of Paris; these things are a nation's eternal shame.

Source: Voltaire, "Philosopher." In *The Philosophical Dictionary*, selected and translated by H. I. Woolf (New York: Knopf, 1924). http://history.hanover.edu/texts/voltaire/volphilo.html. Accessed November 15, 2005.

1772; partial translation *Selected Essays from the Encyclopedy*, 1772; complete translation *Encyclopedia*, 1965) contributed to the dissemination of knowledge among an increasingly literate population. Specialized dictionaries and encyclopedias, including many pocket-sized editions published during the 1750's and 1760's, became tools in the hands of Enlightenment philosophers. Voltaire himself possessed more than thirty reference works in his personal library and made frequent and careful use of them in his writing. He fully understood the social and political impact such works might have.

In the early autumn of 1752, while a guest at the court of Prussia's king Frederick the Great, Voltaire set about writing his revolutionary *Dictionnaire philosophique portatif* (1764; enlarged 1769 as *La Raison par alphabet*;

also known as *Dictionnaire philosophique: A Philosophical Dictionary for the Pocket*, 1765; also as *Philosophical Dictionary*, 1945, enlarged 1962). The author's departure from Prussia the following year, however, interrupted his progress, and it was not until some eight or nine years later, in the relative calm and seclusion of his estates at Ferney and Tourney, near the Swiss border, that he resumed his efforts. In the meantime, he had written *Essai sur les mœurs et l'esprit des nations* (1756, 1763; *The General History and State of Europe*, 1754, 1759), *Poème sur la désastre de Lisbonne* (1756; *Poem on the Lisbon Earthquake*, 1764), *Candide: Ou, L'Optimisme* (1759; *Candide: Or, All for the Best*, 1759; also as *Candide: Or, The Optimist*, 1762; also as *Candide: Or, Optimism*, 1947), *L'Orphelin de la Chine* (pr., pb. 1755; *The Orphan of China*, 1756), and a number of articles for both Diderot's *Encyclopedia* and the *Dictionnaire de l'Académie française* (1762; dictionary of the French academy).

A Philosophical Dictionary for the Pocket was published anonymously by Gabriel Grasset in Geneva, Switzerland, in July, 1764. A small octavo volume of 344 pages bearing a forged London imprint, it contained seventy-three articles ranging from "Abraham" to "Vertu" (virtue)—later editions begin at "Abbé" (abbot). Conceived as an instrument for political, religious, and ethical enlightenment, its publication provoked virulent responses from critics eager to decry the danger of Voltaire's ideas to traditional religious practices. On September 10, 1764, the procurer general of Geneva prompted the city council to seize and burn all extant copies of the book, describing its content as an outrage to religion and contrary to Church dogma. By then, however, only a handful of copies could be found, the others having been quickly sold and spread throughout Europe. Other public book burnings occurred in Switzerland, Holland, and, later, France.

Anointed with scandal, Voltaire's book only increased in popularity. Before year's end, it had been reprinted in Germany, France, and England, with a new, augmented edition appearing in Amsterdam in late December, 1764. On March 19 of the following year, the Parlement of Paris ceremoniously condemned the work alongside Jean-Jacques Rousseau's *Lettres écrites de la montagne* (1764; *Letters Written from the Mountain*, 1767). Despite these and other ominous warnings to the Enlightenment philosophers, Voltaire continued his work on the dictionary, producing augmented editions in 1765 and 1767. The author's final major revision of 1769, titled *La Raison par alphabet* (reason by alphabet), encompassed 118 articles and two volumes. The accepted title for later editions became *Dictionnaire philosophique*. At the height of the work's popularity, between 1765 and 1772, conservative Protestant and Catholic writers, including Jean-Alphonse Rosset, Nicolas-Sylvestre Bergier, Charles Bonnet, Aimé-Henri Paulian, Antoine Guénée, Louis-Mayeul Chaudon, and Claude-François Nonnotte, hastened to publish refutations of the author's Deist ideas. Their sometimes indignant reactions to his philosophical dictionary serve as one measure of its initial impact.

Employing a variety of narrative strategies, Voltaire, in *A Philosophical Dictionary for the Pocket*, waged an energetic campaign against religious tyranny, bigotry, superstition, idolatry, and sectarian intolerance. As a Deist, he saw proof of a Supreme Being's existence in the evidence of cosmic design, yet he could not acknowledge the existence of a personal God willing to intervene in the course of human events. A critical reader of the Bible, Voltaire wondered at the abundance of political and moral misdeeds in Holy Scripture, making particular note of King David's thievery, Abraham's duplicity, Jephthah's cruelty, and the lack of decorum in Ezekiel. Armed with irony and skepticism, he subverted the authority of religious doctrine, calling into question the immortality of the soul, faith in miracles, and belief in resurrection.

In other entries in the dictionary, Voltaire listed crimes committed by the Papacy, from political assassination and fornication to simony and civil war. He cast doubt on the infallibility of early Christian councils that, in his view, were governed by all-too-human emotions, including hatred, ambition, jealousy, and prejudice. Tracing the sources of Christianity back to pagan culture, he reduced the major religions to the status of sects, and he uncovered in history's sundry wars and massacres a legacy of the senseless rivalry of those sects.

While the overwhelming majority of the dictionary's articles, in one way or another, concern theology, religion, and superstitious beliefs, there are noteworthy exceptions to this rule. In some cases, Voltaire addressed more specifically social inequities, human vice, good taste in literature, and the capricious nature of existing laws with little or no reference to religion. However, the number of such articles in the original work remains comparatively small. After Voltaire's death, the editors of the so-called Kehl edition of his complete works (pb. 1784-1789 in Kehl, Germany) injudiciously conflated *A Philosophical Dictionary for the Pocket* with a selection of articles taken from some of the author's other works, including *Questions sur l' "Encyclopédie"* (1770-1772; questions on the *Encyclopedia*) and articles Voltaire had written for Diderot's *Encyclopedia* and for the *Dictionnaire de l'Académie française*. The result was that, for more than a century in France, the original work's anticlerical bent had become obfuscated by the addition of materials written in a different spirit and for other purposes.

SIGNIFICANCE

A Philosophical Dictionary for the Pocket was profoundly scandalous, not because it denounced institutional abuse within the Church—something supporters of Church doctrine had been doing for centuries—but because its irreverent satire shook the very foundations of Christian society, calling into question the legitimacy and morality of organized religion. It was profoundly influential, not because it was scandalous, but because it expressed fundamental beliefs readily applicable to the human condition. It couched those beliefs in persuasive rhetoric and founded them upon empirical and historical observation, leaving readers free to reach their own conclusions. Touching a vibrant chord in his readers, Voltaire expressed many of the ideals that later inspired the French Revolution and the formation of modern democracies, including liberty of conscience and freedom of speech, separation of church and state, and a vision of greater social justice.

With its multiplicity of narrative voices and its disparate narrative styles, *A Philosophical Dictionary for the Pocket* had a liberating effect. It encouraged reader participation, promoted the abandonment of metaphysical certainties, and stimulated open debate on important social questions. After the French Revolution, Voltaire's name increasingly came to be associated with populist, republican ideals, a perception that gained currency during the highly polarized political debates of the early and mid-nineteenth century. Whether or not that perception is tenable remains a matter for historians to debate. Future generations will undoubtedly read this classic of

French literature, searching for and discovering in it some of the fundamental tenets of modern, democratic society.

—*Jan Pendergrass*

FURTHER READING

Bird, Stephen. *Reinventing Voltaire: The Politics of Commemoration in Nineteenth-Century France.* Oxford, England: Voltaire Foundation, 2000. Examines Voltaire's legacy in nineteenth century politics, art, and education.

Brown, Andrew. *Livre Dangereux: Voltaire's "Dictionnaire Philosophique": A Bibliography of the Original Editions and Catalogue of an Exhibition Held in Worcester College Library to Celebrate the Tercentenary of Voltaire's Birth.* Oxford, England: Voltaire Foundation, 1994. Includes a preface and commentary on the publishing history of Voltaire's philosophical dictionary.

Knapp, Bettina L. *Voltaire Revisited.* New York: Twayne, 2000. A survey of Voltaire's life and major works.

Kölving, Ulla, and Christiane Mervaud. *Voltaire et ses combats: Actes du congrès international, Oxford-Paris, 1994.* Vol. 1. Oxford, England: Voltaire Foundation, 1997. Includes French-language articles devoted to various aspects of Voltaire's dictionary.

Mervaud, Christiane. *Le Scandale du Dictionnaire philosophique.* La Rochelle, France: Rumeur des Ages, 1995. A look at conservative Catholic and Protestant reactions to Voltaire's philosophical dictionary. In French.

Mervaud, Christiane, et al., eds. *Dictionnaire philosophique.* Vols. 35-36 in *Les Oeuvres complètes de Voltaire.* Oxford, England: Voltaire Foundation, 1994. Mervaud's introduction covers the work's genesis, its major editions, its philosophical underpinnings, and its reception. In French.

Riley, Patrick. "The Tolerant Skepticism of Voltaire and Diderot: Against Leibnizian Optimism and 'Wise Charity.'" In *Early Modern Skepticism and the Origins of Toleration*, edited by Alan Levine. Lanham, Md.: Lexington Books, 1999. Discusses toleration in Voltaire's dictionary.

Shoaf, Richard. "Science, Sect, and Certainty in Voltaire's *Dictionnaire philosophique.*" *Journal of the History of Ideas* 46 (1985): 121-126. Discusses the limits of Voltaire's skepticism.

SEE ALSO: 1721-1750: Early Enlightenment in France; 1726-1729: Voltaire Advances Enlightenment Thought in Europe; 1748: Montesquieu Publishes *The Spirit of the Laws*; 1751-1772: Diderot Publishes the *Encyclopedia*; 1754: Condillac Defends Sensationalist Theory; July 27, 1758: Helvétius Publishes *De l'esprit*; Jan., 1759: Voltaire Satirizes Optimism in *Candide*; Apr., 1762: Rousseau Publishes *The Social Contract*; 1770: Publication of Holbach's *The System of Nature*; 1782-1798: Publication of Rousseau's *Confessions*.

RELATED ARTICLES in *Great Lives from History: The Eighteenth Century, 1701-1800:* Denis Diderot; Frederick the Great; Jean-Jacques Rousseau; Voltaire.

1765-1769
WATT DEVELOPS A MORE EFFECTIVE STEAM ENGINE

Watt's improved steam engine ushered in the low-cost, efficient use of steam power for coal mining and manufacturing and permitted the extraordinary development and diffusion of the Industrial Revolution.

LOCALE: Glasgow, Scotland
CATEGORY: Science and technology

KEY FIGURES
James Watt (1736-1819), Scottish engineer
Joseph Black (1728-1799), a professor of chemistry at the University of Glasgow
Matthew Boulton (1728-1809), owner of the Soho engineering works in Birmingham, England

Thomas Newcomen (1663-1729), inventor of an earlier steam engine called the "atmospheric engine"
John Robison (1739-1805), a lecturer and later professor of chemistry at the University of Glasgow
John Roebuck (1718-1794), owner of the Carron ironworks in Scotland

SUMMARY OF EVENT

James Watt was the son of a Scottish architect and shipbuilder. He began his career in 1757 as a maker of scientific instruments on the staff of the University of Glasgow. While there he attended the lectures of Joseph Black, who was developing his theory of latent heat, and he also became well acquainted with John Robison, a brilliant young chemist. Robison directed his attention to the problems of existing steam engines, and when Watt was asked, during the winter of 1763-1764, to repair a model of the Newcomen engine, he was led to a critical study of its workings.

The Newcomen engine, which had been in use in England since the second decade of the eighteenth century, had been designed to pump water from deep mines, but in time it came to be used in ore smelters, ironworks, and textile mills. Although the engine worked and was regarded by many as one of the marvels of the age, it had many defects, and increasing use of it emphasized its shortcomings.

The principal problem was that it operated on atmospheric pressure alone. Steam from a boiler entered a cylinder and raised a piston balanced by a counterweight; a jet of cold water forced into the cylinder then condensed the steam, and the piston returned on a downward stroke through the force of atmospheric pressure, each cycle requiring about four seconds. Newcomen's engine was highly inefficient by modern standards. It operated at atmospheric pressure or less, did not use the expansive force of steam to pull or to push anything, and wasted about 99 percent of its fuel. Critics complained that it took an iron mine to build a Newcomen engine and a coal mine to keep it going.

Watt designed improvements that were so fundamental that they constituted a series of separate inventions and rendered atmospheric engines obsolete, though many remained in use well into the nineteenth century. Watt had been interested in steam since 1761, with experiments in high-pressure steam. Watt realized that, to save fuel required for constantly reheating the cooled Newcomen cylinder, the steam should be condensed away from the cylinder, allowing it to remain hot. Black was able to help Watt apply the former's concept of latent heat to the problem of keeping the cylinder hot in the atmospheric engine. This "separate condenser," invented in 1765, was the first improvement on Newcomen's engine, and it saved three-fourths of the fuel.

Watt was a tireless, perhaps compulsive engineer. The steam engine and subsequent design improvements provoked his mind unceasingly. Over the next four years, finding time between assignments in his new career as land surveyor, Watt made two additional improvements. One was an air pump that exhausted condensed steam, and the second was enclosing the upper end of the cylinder and building a steam-tight gland around the piston. Steam, instead of air, was then used to push down the piston. Watt also designed a heat jacket for the cylinder to contain its heat.

SIGNIFICANCE

The first Watt engine, patented in 1769, was the first model in a new age of steam. It was a single-acting engine used as a pump and built at an ironworks in Scotland owned by Watt's partner, John Roebuck. The necessity of close tolerances in piston and cylinders required precision machining beyond available technology. The caster John Wilkinson was eventually able to satisfy Watt's demands for more precisely machined engine parts. Matthew Boulton, owner of the Soho engineering works in Birmingham, became Watt's partner in 1775, and he saw the possibilities for engines that would do more than pump. He persuaded Watt to develop an engine with a rotating motion through a system of intermeshed gears, and then an engine with the piston being alternately supplied on opposite sides with steam and vacuum. This engine was patented in 1782. Watt's engines did not immediately eclipse atmospheric engines, especially where cheap coal was readily at hand. Yet where coal was scarce, as in Cornwall, Watt's engines were a tremendous boon to mining, iron production, and manufacturing.

The firm of Watt and Boulton prospered for years, supplying steam engines of many types and designs for various industries. There were about five hundred Watt and Boulton engines in service by 1800. Expiration of the inventor's original patents in that year caused a rush on the part of other inventors to introduce new and improved steam engines. Watt gave up active participation in the firm in that year, having contributed more than any other individual to the age of industrial power.

—Robert F. Erickson, updated by Michael Kugler

FURTHER READING

Dickinson, H. W. *James Watt and the Steam Engine*. Oxford, England: Clarendon Press, 1927. Although dated, this work combines biography and technical explication and also helpfully relates Watt's relationship to the scientific community at the University of Glasgow.

Landes, David S. *The Unbound Prometheus: Technical Change and Industrial Development in Western Europe from 1750 to the Present*. London: Cambridge University Press, 1960. Reprinted many times, this volume is a noted treatment of technological innovation and entrepreneurship, interpreting Watt's work from a long-term, European perspective.

Marsden, Ben. *Watt's Perfect Engine: Steam and the Age of Invention*. New York: Columbia University Press, 2002. A nontechnical biography of Watt. In Marsden's opinion, Watt was less an innovator than a practical businessman with an interest in natural philosophy. Marsden describes how Watt developed the steam condenser to make Newcomen's engine more efficient.

Nahum, Andrew. *James Watt and the Power of Steam.* East Sussex, England: Wayland, 1981. A short biography that handily introduces technical aspects to the general reader.

Rolt, L. T. C. *James Watt.* New York: Arco, 1963. This fine, concise biography also puts Watt into the context of British manufacturing at the end of the eighteenth century.

Tann, Jennifer. "Introduction." In *The Engine Partnership, 1775-1825.* Vol. 1 in *The Selected Papers of Boulton and Watt.* Cambridge, Mass.: MIT Press, 1981. In addition to helping the reader discover Watt from his own words, Tann has also contributed greatly to precise knowledge of his business dealings and the diffusion of Watt engines across Europe.

Uglow, Jenny. *The Lunar Men: Five Friends Whose Curiosity Changed the World.* New York: Farrar, Straus, Giroux, 2002. Watt, his partner Matthew Boulton, and scientist Joseph Priestley were among the founders of the Lunar Society of Birmingham. Uglow's book describes how the organization invented new products, advanced science, and worked on other projects that ushered in the Industrial Revolution.

SEE ALSO: 1705-1712: Newcomen Develops the Steam Engine; 1723: Stahl Postulates the Phlogiston Theory; Oct. 23, 1769: Cugnot Demonstrates His Steam-Powered Road Carriage; 1781-1784: Cavendish Discovers the Composition of Water; Apr., 1785: Cartwright Patents the Steam-Powered Loom; 1793: Whitney Invents the Cotton Gin; 1800: Volta Invents the Battery.

RELATED ARTICLES in *Great Lives from History: The Eighteenth Century, 1701-1800*: Joseph Black; Matthew Boulton; James Brindley; Henry Cavendish; John Fitch; William Murdock; Thomas Newcomen; Joseph Priestley; John Roebuck; James Watt; Josiah Wedgwood; Eli Whitney; John Wilkinson.

March 22, 1765-March 18, 1766
STAMP ACT CRISIS

During the Stamp Act Crisis, the American colonies responded to the first direct tax levied upon the colonists with protests and boycotts. The Stamp Act was soon repealed, but the crisis became the first in a series of events that would culminate in the American Revolution.

LOCALE: Great Britain; British North America
CATEGORIES: Laws, acts, and legal history; government and politics; colonization; trade and commerce; social issues and reform

KEY FIGURES
George Grenville (1712-1770), British first lord of treasury, chancellor of exchequer, and prime minister, 1763-1765
Patrick Henry (1736-1799), member of Virginia House of Burgesses and later governor of Virginia, 1776-1779, 1784-1786
Daniel Dulany (1722-1797), colonial American lawyer and pamphleteer
Second Marquess of Rockingham (Charles Watson-Wentworth; 1730-1782), British prime minister, 1765-1766, 1782

Thomas Whatley (1726-1772), British treasury official
Benjamin Franklin (1706-1790), colonial American statesman

SUMMARY OF EVENT
In 1763, the British national debt had soared to a level double that prior to the French and Indian War. Besides finding revenues to meet the interest on this war debt, George Grenville, the prime minister, needed additional funds to administer a greatly enlarged empire. Although Parliament had never before placed direct taxes on the colonies, Grenville persuaded that body to approve the Sugar Act of 1764 and the Stamp Act of 1765. The decision to tax America was momentous in its consequences. The intensity of the colonists' opposition shocked most people in England, and on both sides of the Atlantic the crisis produced an atmosphere of tension and mistrust that influenced all subsequent British-American relations before the American Revolution.

Grenville, a narrow-minded financial expert, presented impressive statistics to show that the prosperous colonists were lightly taxed compared to the English at home. The Sugar Act grew out of Grenville's discovery that the American customs service was costing the government more to maintain than it was collecting in revenues. The colonists were evading payment of the import duties—sixpence a gallon—on foreign molasses, which was required under the Molasses Act of 1733. Grenville revamped the customs service and ordered the Royal Navy to guard against smuggling.

The Sugar Act itself cut the molasses duty to three-pence a gallon, a sum Grenville believed would be enforceable without ruining the New England rum industry. It was clear that colonial rum distillers needed more molasses than the British West Indian sugar islands could provide. The new statute placed additional duties on colonial imports, increased restrictions on colonial exports, and added to the difficulties of smugglers by strengthening the system of vice-admiralty courts. The preamble to the Sugar Act, unlike the Molasses Act, made it clear that the law of 1764 was not designed primarily to regulate trade; it stated "that a revenue be raised" in His Majesty's dominions.

Subsequently, Grenville introduced his Stamp Act, passed by Parliament and signed by the king on March 22, 1765, to become effective on November 1. Taxes fell on every kind of legal document and on playing cards, dice, and almanacs. Each item was to carry a stamp indicating payment of the tax. Offenders were to be tried in vice-admiralty courts (without trial by jury), which formerly had jurisdiction only over affairs relating to the sea and commerce. New taxes meant payments in cash, but money—always scarce in the agriculturally oriented colonies—became tighter than ever because Grenville, in 1764, had persuaded Parliament to adopt the Currency Act, which forbade the provincials from continuing to make their own paper money as legal tender.

The colonists found much to displease them in Grenville's program. Merchants thought the rum industry would not be able to stand the three-pence duty on molasses, and they found the new customs procedures complicated and difficult. The currency restrictions promised to make silver in shorter supply than ever. Colonists also thought it was unfair to try Stamp Act offenders in courts, devoid of juries, possessing authority beyond that permitted the courts in England.

Even more important to Americans, Parliament's direct taxes seemed to deprive them of their rights as British subjects to be taxed only by their elected representatives. The colonists were represented in their own assemblies but not in the House of Commons. They vigorously approved the pamphlet written by Maryland lawyer Daniel Dulany, who denied the contention of Englishman Thomas Whatley that all residents of the empire were, in effect, represented in Parliament, which allegedly looked after the interests of all, regardless of whether one had the opportunity (as many local Englishmen did not) to vote for members of the House of Commons. American writers quoted John Locke, political philosopher of England's Glorious Revolution of 1688, who said that the most esteemed right of people was the right of property, without which both life and liberty were endangered.

The Virginia House of Burgesses, prodded by young Patrick Henry, took the lead in drafting remonstrances against parliamentary taxation. Soon afterward, the Massachusetts legislature issued a call for a congress from all the colonies to meet to consider ways of securing relief.

The Pennsylvania Journal and Weekly Advertiser *published a symbolic skull and crossbones as part of the masthead of its final issue. The masthead also included "An Emblem of the Effects of the STAMP, O! the fatal Stamp" and a note reading, "The TIMES are Dreadful, Dismal, Doleful, Dolorous, and Dollar-less."* (Library of Congress)

The Stamp Act Congress, meeting October 7 to 27, 1765, in New York and attended by delegates from nine colonies, acknowledged Parliament's authority to regulate trade (to legislate) for the welfare of the whole empire, while rejecting its right to tax America. By November 1, the date the stamps were to go on sale, none were available. The Sons of Liberty had "persuaded" almost every designated stamp distributor to resign. Colonial merchants also aided the cause by curtailing imports from Britain until the oppressive Stamp Act was repealed.

In 1766, Grenville was out of office (for reasons unrelated to America), and the ministry was under the second Marquess of Rockingham. The marquess, who had opposed the Stamp Act, now listened to the outcries of British merchants suffering from the colonial economic boycott. By stressing the disruption of trade and ignoring American rioting, and by employing Benjamin Franklin's erroneous testimony that the colonists opposed only internal taxes (the Stamp Act), Rockingham secured repeal of the Stamp Act on March 18—the same day that Parliament passed the vaguely worded Declaratory Act.

The latter bill affirmed Parliament's right to "make laws and statutes . . . to bind the colonies . . . in all cases whatsoever." Americans rejoiced at the outcome without knowing the Declaratory Act's precise meaning.

SIGNIFICANCE

In the latter half of the twentieth century, many historians posited that the American Revolution was not predestined, at least not in the third quarter of the eighteenth century, especially if the mother country had displayed more enlightened leadership. Some historians placed the blame for the first imperial controversy squarely upon George Grenville. Grenville, although pretending otherwise, had made no real effort to allow the colonies to raise revenues on their own to aid in the upkeep of the empire; in fact, the prime minister discouraged Massachusetts and the agents of various colonies and London from devising means to acquire needed revenue in America.

From this viewpoint, the American colonies appear to have been less irresponsible in facing up to their imperial obligations than their traditional depictions would sug-

Patrick Henry addresses the Virginia Assembly, in a speech opposing the stamp tax. (R. S. Peale and J. A. Hill)

gest. The actual stamp tax would have been a small expense to almost all the colonists; the crux of the American opposition was therefore a philosophical rejection of taxation without representation. Later historians also part company from previous historians by demonstrating that Americans objected not only to internal taxes (the Stamp Act) but also to external taxes (the Sugar Act) in 1765-1766. During the following decade, the colonists consistently adhered to the principle that legitimate taxes could be levied only by the representatives of those taxed, while they continued to recognize the need for Parliament to legislate in the interest of harmonious trade and commerce and the welfare of all parts of the empire.

—R. Don Higginbotham,
updated by Liesel Ashley Miller

FURTHER READING

Breen, T. H. *The Marketplace of Revolution: How Consumer Politics Shaped American Independence*. New York: Oxford University Press, 2004. Breen argues that colonists' experience as consumers helped them develop new forms of social action, such as boycotts, that ultimately resulted in revolution. Includes information about the Stamp Act and the colonists' boycotts.

Bridenbaugh, Carl. *Mitre and Sceptre: Transatlantic Faiths, Ideas, Personalities, and Politics, 1689-1775*. New York: Oxford University Press, 1962. Asserts that American fears of an Anglican establishment throughout the colonies were a factor in the growth of American nationalism and a hitherto neglected cause of the American Revolution.

Gipson, Lawrence H. *The Coming of the Revolution, 1763-1775*. New York: Harper & Row, 1954. Representative of the traditional imperial school of American historiography, Gipson sees the American Revolution as an inevitable development, with growing American nationalism as the prime cause.

Johnson, Allen S. *A Prologue to Revolution: The Political Career of George Grenville, 1712-1770*. Lanham, Md.: University Press of America, 1997. Recounts the events of Grenville's ministry, including the passage of the Stamp Act and the American reaction to it.

Knollenberg, Bernhard. *Origin of the American Revolution, 1759-1766*. New York: Macmillan, 1960. Complements and amplifies the Morgans' account (see below) of the first imperial crisis. Knollenberg discovers little evidence of colonial unhappiness with the British Empire as it existed before the Seven Years' War.

Morgan, Edmund S., and Helen M. Morgan. *The Stamp Act Crisis*. Chapel Hill: University of North Carolina Press, 1995. Provides a revisionist look at the events surrounding the Stamp Act crisis and blames Grenville for the crisis. Focuses on constitutional principles and the ideas of the Revolutionists.

Raphael, Ray. *A People's History of the American Revolution: How Common People Shaped the Fight for Independence*. New York: New Press, 2001. Describes the role that farmers, laborers, women, and other "ordinary people" played in the Revolution. Includes information about the Stamp Act and the American demonstrations against the legislation.

Thomas, P. D. G. *British Politics and the Stamp Act Crisis*. Oxford, England: Clarendon Press, 1975. A study of the policies and attitudes of Great Britain toward the American colonies in the years leading up to the American Revolution.

Weslager, C. A. *The Stamp Act Congress*. Newark: University of Delaware Press, 1976. A thorough documentation of the Stamp Act Congress, wherein the principles of opposition to the Stamp Act were first formulated. Contains the first available journal of the Stamp Act Congress in its entirety.

SEE ALSO: June 29, 1767-Apr. 12, 1770: Townshend Crisis; 1768-May 16, 1771: Carolina Regulator Movements; Mar. 5, 1770: Boston Massacre; Dec. 16, 1773: Boston Tea Party; Apr. 27-Oct. 10, 1774: Lord Dunmore's War; Sept. 5-Oct. 26, 1774: First Continental Congress; Apr. 19, 1775-Oct. 19, 1781: American Revolutionary War.

RELATED ARTICLES in *Great Lives from History: The Eighteenth Century, 1701-1800*: Benjamin Franklin; George III; Patrick Henry.

February 24, 1766
LORRAINE BECOMES PART OF FRANCE

In the Treaty of Vienna (1738), which ended the War of the Polish Succession, the deposed king of Poland, Stanisław I, was installed as the sovereign duke of the independent duchy of Lorraine. The treaty stipulated that upon Stanisław's death the duchy would revert to the French crown. Thus, when he died in 1766, Lorraine lost its independence and was absorbed into France.

LOCALE: Lorraine (now in France)
CATEGORIES: Expansion and land acquisition; government and politics; diplomacy and international relations

KEY FIGURES
Louis XV (1710-1774), king of France, r. 1715-1774
Stanisław I (1677-1766), former king of Poland, r. 1704-1709, 1733-1736, and duke of Lorraine and Bar, r. 1738-1766
Marie (1703-1768), queen of France, r. 1725-1768
André-Hercule de Fleury (1653-1743), prime minister of France, 1726-1743
Germain Louis Chauvelin (1685-1762), French foreign minister, 1727-1737
Leopold Joseph (1679-1729), duke of Lorraine, r. 1697-1702, 1714-1729
Francis I (Francis Stephen; 1708-1765), duke of Lorraine, r. 1729-1735, and Holy Roman Emperor, r. 1745-1765

SUMMARY OF EVENT
Located between France and Germany, the territory of Lorraine, which gets its name from King Lothair I, was for many centuries a major source of rivalry and conflict. From the tenth century, Lorraine was a German-speaking duchy of the Holy Roman Empire. In 1648, France annexed three of the duchy's cities, Metz, Toul, and Verdun. However, with its capital in Nancy, the imperial portion of Lorraine continued to constitute a large and prosperous region. Although French troops occupied Lorraine from 1648 to 1661 and again from 1670 to 1697, it became an independent duchy connected to the empire in the Treaty of Ryswick (1697). The first duke of autonomous Lorraine, Leopold Joseph, took measures to avoid conflict with France: He disbanded the army, dismantled fortresses, welcomed French immigrants, and concentrated on developing industry and trade. Thus, during Leopold Joseph's reign, the French government

tolerated the duchy's autonomy.

When Leopold died in 1729, however, Louis XV and his officials were alarmed to observe that the new duke, Francis I, lived in Vienna and was betrothed to Maria Theresa, heiress to the Habsburg Empire. Such an enhancement of Habsburg control over Lorraine was unacceptable to the French. For two centuries, the Habsburgs had been their most dangerous enemy, and in the event of war, an imperial army could easily invade France through Lorraine. Louis XV's chief minister, André-Hercule de Fleury, although a man of patience and conciliation, was determined, at a minimum, to ensure Lorraine's neutrality. His foreign minister, Germain Louis Chauvelin, pushed for a more militaristic approach. France and the Holy Roman Empire appeared to be drifting into another armed conflict, and Lorraine was stuck right in the middle.

Rather than Lorraine, however, it was the controversy over the Polish throne that served as the cause of war between the two powers. When Poland's elective throne became vacant in 1733, the French government gave its strong support to the former king of Poland, Stanisław I, whose daughter Marie was married to Louis XV. A French squadron smuggled Stanisław into Poland, where he was elected by one faction of the Polish diet. Another faction, supported by Russia and the Holy Roman Emperor, recognized a different monarch—Augustus, elector of Saxony—as King Augustus III.

In the resulting War of the Polish Succession (1733-1735), Spain and Sardinia were allies of France, and the fighting rapidly spread to various locations in Western Europe. The three allies, despite the pleas of Stanisław I, were unwilling to commit large numbers of troops for the Polish crown, which allowed Russian and Austrian troops to prevail within the Polish theater of the war. Louis XV's government was naturally much more concerned about the future of Lorraine and its small neighbor, the duchy of Bar, both of which were occupied by French troops.

In November, 1735, the diplomatic representatives of the powers ended the fighting by agreeing to the preliminary Treaty of Vienna (ratified three years later), which included a reshuffling of several dynastic claims. Among the terms of the complex settlement, Stanisław again renounced his claims to the Polish throne while retaining his royal title. As compensation, he was awarded lifelong rule over the duchies of Lorraine and Bar, which were to revert to the French crown at his death. Francis was compensated with the duchy of Tuscany, and he signed a formal document recognizing the transfer of sovereignty over Lorraine and Bar. Emperor Charles VI agreed to accept the transfer in exchange for an endorsement of the Pragmatic Sanction, which set aside the Salic law of succession and recognized his daughter Maria Theresa as his heir.

In 1738, the sixty-year-old Stanisław was officially installed as the duke of Lorraine and Bar. In a secret compact with Louis XV, he had agreed to give Louis full authority over the financial administration of the duchy in exchange for a generous pension. The French intendant, Chaumont de La Galaizière, who represented Louis, was responsible for organizing the French system of taxation in the duchies. Because Lorraine had been a German-speaking province of the Holy Roman Empire for centuries, one of the major tasks of the new government was to make the province more culturally and linguistically French.

Duke Stanisław I's thirty-year reign was generally prosperous and peaceful. Lorraine managed to avoid serious military involvement in the War of the Austrian Succession (1741-1748) and the Seven Years' War (1756-1763). Stanisław resided in an impressive court at Lunéville, just south of Nancy, which was often called the Little Versailles. He devoted most of his time to intellectual, economic, and charitable activities. Frequently called a "beneficent philosopher," he became famous for his patronage of art, literature, and architure. He funded several free schools and established the Royal Society of Sciences and Literature. In Nancy, he is particularly remembered for the beautification of the city, where the Place Stanislas still exhibits his good taste and judgment in the choice of architects.

Stanisław, to the consternation of his pious daughter, was committed to the skeptical and liberal ideas of the Enlightenment. His court at Lunéville frequently served as a refuge for those who shared his values. In 1748-1749, Voltaire and the marquise du Châtelet took advantage of his hospitality. Even though Stanisław devoted most of his efforts to developing projects in Lorraine, he continued to take a lively interest in Polish affairs. Prominent Poles were among the members of his court. He wrote thoughtful essays in both Polish and French, and he corresponded with various intellectuals, particularly Jean-Jacques Rousseau. His most famous tract, "Glos Worlny Wolnosc Uberzpieczajacy" (1749; a free voice ensuring freedom), criticized the weakness of Polish institutions and advocated progressive changes, including greater democracy and additional liberties for the lower social classes.

Stanisław I died at the age of eighty-eight in Lunéville on February 23, 1766. On the day after the death, Louis XV's representatives informed the Estates of Lorraine and Bar that henceforth they were under the sovereignty of the French crown. The royal fleur-de-lys quickly replaced Stanisław's coat of arms. Within a few years, the two duchies were rejoined with the territories around Metz and Verdun to form the province of Lorraine.

SIGNIFICANCE

The acquisition of Lorraine represented France's largest territorial addition since Louis XIV had annexed Franche-Comté in 1674. For two centuries, French kings had tried but failed to gain sovereignty over the duchy. The accomplishment was all the more remarkable because it required so little military or financial expenditure. The addition of Lorraine, however, did not adequately compensate for the loss of France's overseas empire in the French and Indian War and the Seven Years' War.

After becoming a French province, Lorraine was allowed to keep many of its special exemptions and privileges. The preliminary treaty of 1735 had guaranteed the continuation of Lorraine's common law, its separate customs tariffs, and the traditional prerogatives of the social orders, all of which were retained until the French Revolution.

After 1766, the population of Lorraine adopted the French language and developed a strong sense of French identity, whereas the neighboring province of Alsace retained much more of its Germanic culture. With the growth of nationalism in the nineteenth century, Germans would become increasingly discontented with the status of Alsace and Lorraine, which they would conquer and annex in 1871 and again in 1940. Possession of the two provinces was not definitively settled until after World War II.

—*Thomas Tandy Lewis*

FURTHER READING

Bernier, Olivier. *Louis the Beloved: The Life of Louis XV*. New York: Doubleday, 1984. In contrast to most accounts, this well-written biography presents an extremely favorable account of the monarch and his policies.

Briggs, Robin. *Communities of Belief: Cultural and Social Tension in Early Modern France*. New York: Oxford University Press, 1989. Includes information about Lorraine under Stanisław I.

Fedorowicz, J. K., ed. *Republic of Nobles: Studies in*

Polish History to 1864. New York: Cambridge University Press, 1982. Includes scholarly essays about Stanisław I and the Polish enlightenment.

Gooch, George P. *Louis XV: The Monarchy in Decline*. Westport, Conn.: Greenwood Press, 1976. A standard and well-respected narrative that emphasizes Louis's foreign and domestic policy.

Jones, Colin. *The Great Nation: France from Louis XV to Napoleon, 1715-99*. New York: Columbia University Press, 2002. This historical survey provides a good summary of Fleury's policies in annexing Lorraine.

Putnam, Ruth. *Alsace and Lorraine: From Caesar to Kaiser, 56 B.C.-1871 A.D.* New York: G. P. Putnam's Sons. Although somewhat dated, this is one of the few English-language works devoted to the history of the two provinces. Many books and articles, of course, are available in French.

SEE ALSO: 1721-1750: Early Enlightenment in France; Oct. 10, 1733-Oct. 3, 1735: War of the Polish Succession; Nov. 18, 1738: Treaty of Vienna; Oct. 20, 1740: Maria Theresa Succeeds to the Austrian Throne; Dec. 16, 1740-Nov. 7, 1748: War of the Austrian Succession; May 28, 1754-Feb. 10, 1763: French and Indian War; Jan., 1756-Feb. 15, 1763: Seven Years' War; Feb. 10, 1763: Peace of Paris; Apr. 20, 1792-Oct., 1797: Early Wars of the French Revolution.

RELATED ARTICLES in *Great Lives from History: The Eighteenth Century, 1701-1800*: Charles VI; Marquise du Châtelet; André-Hercule de Fleury; Louis XV; Maria Theresa; Jean-Jacques Rousseau; Voltaire.

November 12, 1766
FIRST AMERICAN THEATER OPENS IN PHILADELPHIA

The Southwark Theatre opened in Philadelphia in November of 1766. For the next eight years, it was home to operas, plays, pantomimes, and other performances, including the 1767 debut of the first play by an American author. Works by Americans increased at the Southwark Theatre and at other early theaters after the Revolutionary War, and elegantly designed and better-equipped theaters appeared in greater numbers during the 1790's.

LOCALE: Philadelphia, Pennsylvania
CATEGORIES: Theater; music

KEY FIGURES

Lewis Hallam, Sr. (1714-1756), actor-manager of the most successful early acting troupe touring America

David Douglass (c. 1720-1786?), Hallam's successor, who built the Southwark Theatre

Alexander Reinagle (1756-1809), American composer and theater manager

Thomas Wignell (1753-1803), American actor and theater manager

SUMMARY OF EVENT

Except in French New Orleans, colonial American theater was dominated by British plays and actors. Williamsburg, Virginia, had the first colonial playhouse from 1716 to 1736. After Virginian interest in theater declined, probably as a result of the First Great Awakening, the building was converted into a courthouse; it was later demolished. A second structure behind the capitol was the site of a 1752 production of William Shakespeare's *The Merchant of Venice* (pr. c. 1596-1597) by Lewis Hallam, Sr.'s London Company, an itinerant troop of twelve adults and three children. Like most of the earliest "theaters," this structure was an ordinary building converted temporarily for use as a playhouse, rather than a building conceived and constructed solely as a performance space.

Charleston, South Carolina, was also an early performance site. The first American production of a ballad opera, *Flora: Or, Hob in the Wall* (pr. 1735) by English poet Colley Cibber, was given in the Dock Street (later Queen Street) Theater. A 1752 hurricane that destroyed more than five hundred buildings probably leveled this structure. Fire, a constant danger to all eighteenth century buildings, would claim Charleston's Church Street Theater (built 1773) in 1782. A better-equipped theater, built in 1793, operated until 1832, when it became part of the Medical College of South Carolina.

While drama was more readily accepted in the non-Puritan South, religious conservatives everywhere considered theater sinful. The Society of Friends (Quakers) joined Presbyterians and Baptists in denouncing drama, cockfighting, gambling, and dancing. Actors were occasionally blamed for the presence of infectious diseases, such as an epidemic of yellow fever in Philadelphia in 1793. Virginia and Maryland were the only colonies that did not legislate against drama.

Despite Quaker opposition to music and plays, Philadelphia became one of the colonies' most active performance sites. In 1724, a group of players briefly set up a "booth" on Society Hill, which was outside the city's boundaries and jurisdiction. After a hiatus of more than two decades, drama reappeared in the summer of 1749, when Walter Murray and Thomas Kean rented a warehouse from Thomas Plumsted, the lapsed Quaker mayor of Philadelphia, and presented several plays, most notably *Cato* (pr., pb. 1713), a popular tragedy by British essayist Joseph Addison.

In 1754, Hallam's London Company, which had been touring New York and Virginia, came to Philadelphia. The company renovated Plumsted's warehouse and staged plays from April 15 to June 27, despite protests by the godly. The troupe moved to Charleston and then to Jamaica, where Hallam died of yellow fever. Shortly thereafter, Mrs. Hallam, the company's leading lady, married one of the actors, David Douglass. The renamed American Company returned to the mainland in 1758 and resumed its circuit of New York, Philadelphia, Annapolis (which had a theater by 1760), Charleston, and Williamsburg. Douglass constructed a second theater on Philadelphia's Society Hill, and the company performed there from June to December, 1759, the longest American season up to that time.

Growing acceptance of drama by the more affluent citizens of Philadelphia led to increasing demand for a permanent theater, rather than the temporary and impromptu buildings that had been used thus far. This demand was first met in 1766 with the construction of the Southwark Theatre in a suburb that was technically still outside Philadelphia's boundaries. Considered the first permanent playhouse in the English colonies, the Southwark Theatre opened on November 12. It was built of brick and wood and painted red. Ninety-five by fifty feet, it was cold in winter and lit by smelly oil lamps. Pillars that held up the balcony and the roof obscured some views of the stage. The first play by an American author, the tragedy *The Prince of Parthia* (wr. 1759, pr. 1767) by Thomas Godfrey, premiered at the Southwark on April 24, 1767. Shakespeare's *Hamlet: Prince of Denmark* (pr. c. 1600-1601), *King Lear* (pr. c. 1605-1606), and *Romeo and Juliet* (pr. c. 1595-1596) were popular at the time and often adapted in productions with new songs, dialogue, and dancing—a common practice in both the eighteenth and the nineteenth centuries.

The growth of theater in New York City was similar to that in Philadelphia. In 1732, actors rented a warehouse from Governor Rip Van Dam and gave several plays, including the ever-popular Cato. In February, 1750, the Murray-Kean Company came from Philadelphia and acquired another of Van Dam's buildings in Nassau Street. Attendance was such that three years later Hallam's troupe replaced this structure with a larger one. Popular fare included Restoration dramas like John Dryden's *All for Love: Or, The World Well Lost* (pr. 1677, pb. 1678), ballad operas, and farces like David Garrick's *Miss in Her Teens: Or, The Medley of Lovers* (pr. 1747). In December, 1767, the American Company moved into a new theater on John Street; like the Southwark, it was partly wooden and painted red, but it had a larger stage than previous playhouses.

America's growing conflict with Britain did not initially discourage playgoing; indeed, Douglass's company toured successfully until October 20, 1774, when the Continental Congress passed a resolution condemning plays, gambling, and horseracing. The resolution effectively shut down the theaters. In the face of this official opposition, the actors of the American Company retreated to Jamaica, where Douglass died, probably in 1786. During the war, the Southwark Theatre was used briefly as a makeshift hospital after the Battle of Germantown (1777). Later, the John Street and Southwark Theatres were both used by occupying British troops to stage amateur productions in their time off-duty. Other would-be actors disguised their efforts as concerts, lectures on dramatic subjects, or "exhibitions," since Congress prohibited none of these. Massachusetts author Mercy Otis Warren wrote at least five pro-patriot plays between 1772 and 1779, but none was actually staged.

The antitheater resolutions passed by Congress in 1778 and later by various states became increasingly difficult to maintain once the war ended in 1783. Support by influential men such as Generals George Washington and Anthony Wayne, who made no secret of their enjoyment of plays, made these laws largely unenforceable. In May, 1785, Lewis Hallam, Jr., returned the American Company to Pennsylvania and opened the Southwark with an "exhibition." Two years later, one of the company's plays was *The Contrast* (pr. 1787) by Royall Tyler, the first comedy by an American author.

SIGNIFICANCE

The opening of the Southwark Theatre represented the beginnings of a truly American theater, as well as signaling the centrality of Philadelphia to this cultural project. As the new nation's capitol from 1781 to 1800 and a major music and publishing center, Philadelphia was the United States' premier theater site until the 1820's. For more than twenty years, America's finest playhouse was

Philadelphia's New Theater on Chesnut Street. Designed to resemble London's famous Covent Garden Theatre, it was built in 1794 by British emigrant and composer-manager Alexander Reinagle and Thomas Wignell, an actor-manager and former member of the American Company. The New Theater had excellent acoustics, an elegant gray interior with gilded decorations, and a seating capacity of around eight hundred people. In 1816, it would be the first theater to be lit by gas. Wignell and Reinagle also built and managed the Holliday Street Theater in Baltimore, which stood until 1917.

By the 1790's, American theaters, like their British counterparts, were designed to resemble classical temples, with Ionic or Corinthian columns, pediments, and statuary in homage to the ancient Greeks who invented drama. Boston's Federal Street Theater (1794), an example of this style, seated nearly one thousand people. Touring companies became larger, with as many as fifty actors or musicians. Performances usually included two plays; local talents often danced or sang between the acts. The cheapest seats were in the "pit," or the upper gallery, where African Americans sat. Since audiences could be rowdy, respectable women did not attend the theater without an escort.

The eighteenth century American theater could not have existed without an influx of British plays and the determined efforts of English traveling troupes to make a living on the stage. Despite religious conservatives' endeavors to ban plays altogether and legislation against drama during the American Revolution, the theater survived and quickly returned to major urban centers after the war. Philadelphia, New York, and Charleston led the way in building new theaters and supporting larger traveling companies. During this period, few distinctions existed between popular and cultivated entertainments; a typical performance might begin with a Shakespeare play and end with a comic afterpiece. Gradually, drama joined concerts and dancing as an acceptable pastime for the urban middle classes.

—*Dorothy T. Potter*

FURTHER READING

Brown, Jared. *The Theater in America During the Revolution*. New York: Cambridge University Press, 1995. Describes both British military theater and American dramatic efforts, by the Continental army and civilians.

Dunlap, William. *A History of the American Theater*. New York: Harper, 1832. Reprint. New York: Burt Franklin, 1963. Dunlap's experiences as an actor, playwright, and manager makes his history a valuable primary source.

Glazer, Irvin R. *Philadelphia Theaters, A-Z: A Comprehensive Descriptive Record of 813 Theaters Constructed Since 1724*. New York: Greenwood Press, 1986. Extensive description of the city's performance sites, from playhouses to movie theaters.

Ireland, Joseph N. *Records of the New York Stage from 1750 to 1860*. 2 vols. New York, 1866. Reprint. New York: Benjamin Blom, 1966. Ireland, a drama critic, used contemporary newspapers and playbills as sources.

Rankin, Hugh F. *The Theater in Colonial America*. Chapel Hill: University of North Carolina Press, 1965. Describes colonial theater from around 1700 to 1774, when the Continental Congress banned drama and other questionable amusements.

Wemyss, Francis C. *Wemyss' Chronology of the American Stage, from 1752 to 1852*. Reprint. New York: Benjamin Blom, 1968. Actor-manager Wemyss's summary of America's first theaters and lists of performers is a valuable primary source.

Wilmeth, Don B., and Christopher Bigsby, eds. *Beginnings to 1870*. Vol. 1 in *The Cambridge History of American Theater*. New York: Cambridge University Press, 1998. Includes six detailed articles on American theater history, performance sites, and popular entertainments.

Young, William C. *Documents of American Theater History: Famous American Playhouses, 1716-1899*. 2 vols. Chicago: American Library Association, 1973. Rich in detail, with excerpts from diaries, letters, and newspapers, and more than two hundred illustrations of American theaters.

SEE ALSO: Jan. 29, 1728: Gay Produces the First Ballad Opera; Dec. 7, 1732: Covent Garden Theatre Opens in London; 1739-1742: First Great Awakening; Aug., 1763-Apr., 1765: David Garrick's European Tour; Aug. 3, 1778: Opening of Milan's La Scala.

RELATED ARTICLES in *Great Lives from History: The Eighteenth Century, 1701-1800*: Joseph Addison; David Garrick; George Washington; Anthony Wayne.

December 5, 1766-March 16, 1769
BOUGAINVILLE CIRCUMNAVIGATES THE GLOBE

Bougainville organized the first successful French expedition around the world. During the voyage, in which he returned the Falkland Islands to Spanish control, he claimed many of the uncharted islands that he discovered for King Louis XV of France.

LOCALE: Worldwide

CATEGORIES: Exploration and discovery; expansion and land acquisition

KEY FIGURES

Louis-Antoine de Bougainville (1729-1811), French explorer, mathematician, scientist, writer, soldier, and statesman

Louis XV (1710-1774), king of France, r. 1715-1774

Ahutoru (c. 1745-1770), Tahitian brought back to France by Bougainville

Jean-Jacques Rousseau (1712-1778), French philosopher and writer

SUMMARY OF EVENT

Louis-Antoine de Bougainville was born on November 12, 1729, in Paris, the youngest of the three children of Pierre-Yves de Bougainville, a notary, and Marie-Françoise d'Arboulin. After his mother's death when he was five, he was raised by his aunt and his elder brother, Jean-Pierre, who encouraged him to attend the Collège des Quatre-Nations in Paris, a school founded to provide free education to sixty deserving pupils. He then studied at the University of Paris, where he realized his passion for mathematics, and later was a student of Jean le Rond d'Alembert, the famous French mathematician, philosopher, and editor of the *Encyclopédie: Ou, Dictionnaire raisonné des sciences, des arts, et des métiers* (1751-1772; partial translation *Selected Essays from the Encyclopedy*, 1772; complete translation *Encyclopedia*, 1965).

Bougainville's *Traité du calcul integral* (1752; treatise on integral calculus) established his position among French intellectuals, when he presented it to the Académie des Sciences (Academy of Sciences) in Paris in 1753. Three years later, he was elected to the Royal Society in London in January, 1756. Having joined the French army in 1750, when the French and Indian War broke out in 1754, he held several military positions, serving as aide-de-camp of Louis-Joseph, Marquis de Montcalm, during campaigns in Canada, New York, and Ohio. His fluency in English made him an especially valuable member of the staffs on which he served when negotiations with the English were required. In 1760, he returned to France, serving in Germany from 1761 until the Seven Years' War ended in 1763.

Though the war in America ended in a complete defeat for France, resulting in the territorial losses of Louisiana, Canada, the Ohio Valley, and several islands in the Caribbean, the experience was invaluable for Bougainville, whose service had allowed him to learn navigation, hone his skills at diplomacy, and cultivate a growing interest in the broader world. The need for new lands for the displaced French settlers from the lost lands in America and the desire to reestablish French pride and influence prompted Bougainville to formulate a plan to colonize the Falkland Islands, off the coast of Argentina, as a forward base from which to search for unclaimed lands in the South Pacific and ultimately circumnavigate the globe.

By the 1760's, thirteen voyages around the world had been accomplished by sailors from Spain, Portugal, Britain, and Holland, but none by the French. Thus, Bougainville hoped that his voyage not only would provide new lands for his nation but also would boost France's morale and reputation by demonstrating French navigational capabilities equal to or surpassing those of other European nations. Though his initial voyage to colonize the Falkland Islands was a success, diplomatic negotiations between France and Spain returned the islands to Spanish control. Bougainville was forced to remove his colony but not to give up his dream of French expansion into new lands in the region, nor to renounce his intention to demonstrate French skill and bravery. His voyage of circumnavigation of the globe would still be carried out.

When Bougainville's expedition left France on December 5, 1766, it carried a number of prominent scholars who would record the adventure's history and study its discoveries. Naturalist Philibert Commerson, accompanied by his valet Jeanne Baré (who was in fact a woman disguised as a man and thus became the first French woman to visit the Pacific and circumnavigate the globe), intended to catalog the plants that were discovered, hoping to find new species with medical uses. Pierre-Antoine Véron, an astronomer, made the trip in order to reach southern India, where he hoped to observe an eclipse of the Sun. Charles Routier de Romainville was the expedition's cartographer, whose vital task it was to map their discoveries, and Louis-Antoine Starot de Saint-Germain was its historian.

The trip was a perilous one, in which bad weather, treacherous currents, disease (particularly scurvy, which resulted from the lack of vitamin C in the diet of the sailors), thirst, and starvation were recurrent threats. Bougainville benefited from the use of a distillation machine to supplement his fresh water supplies, but the problems of food, weather, and disease caused considerable delays when they repeatedly forced him to divert from his course to find necessary supplies or safer conditions.

On March 21, 1768, Bougainville sighted the Tuamotu Archipelago, then Vahitahi, and, by April 7, Tahiti. During a nine-day layover on Tahiti, the French learned much about local antiscorbutic plants that could reduce the threat of scurvy among sailors. Bougainville also developed a relationship with Ereti, the chief of the district, which prompted him to evaluate the concept of the "noble savage," uncorrupted by civilization, that had recently been promulgated by Jean-Jacques Rousseau in his *Discours sur l'inégalité* (1754; *A Discourse on Inequality*, 1756). Impressed by the Tahitians, Bougainville, at Ereti's prompting, decided to transport a Tahitian (a man named Ahutoru, who may have been Ereti's brother) back to France as a confirmation of Rousseau's theory.

After leaving Tahiti, the expedition sailed west along the other Society Islands to Alofi, Samoa, Futuna, Vanuatu, and the Santa Cruz Islands. By the end of May, Bougainville discovered a new medical problem on board: Many of his crew were suffering from sexually transmitted diseases contracted during their stay on Tahiti. By the end of June, their difficulty was compounded by a critical shortage of fresh food, forcing the expedition to land on the Solomon Islands (and nearby New Ireland), where they stayed until August.

Resuming the voyage, Bougainville wisely decided against attempting to cross the Great Barrier Reef, turned north without sighting Australia, and traveled to New Britain. Passing through the Torres Strait between Australia and New Guinea, Bougainville proceeded to Ceram, Buru, and Java, where he anchored at Batavia until October, replenishing his supplies, repairing his ships, and resting his crew. Commerson, the naturalist, left the expedition at Batavia, as would the astronomer Véron when they later landed at Pondicherry in southern India. Bougainville reached Cape Town in January, 1769, approached the Azores in early March, and completed his voyage when he landed at St. Malo, France, on March 16, 1769.

Louis-Antoine de Bougainville is pictured raising the French flag on a tiny island in the Strait of Magellan. (Hulton Archive/ Getty Images)

SIGNIFICANCE

Bougainville's voyage was greeted in France as an epic adventure that demonstrated the character, skill, scientific accomplishments, and bravery of the French. Though the chronicle of the expedition would not be published for another two years, Europe was made aware by Bougainville's success that the French, recently defeated in the Seven Years' War, were resilient, competitive contributors to the intellectual, scientific, and political discourses of the eighteenth century. As important as the symbolic and psychological impact of his voyage, however, were its material results.

Bankrupted by the wars and deprived of many of its colonial holdings in America and India, France needed the new lands and new sources of income that Bougainville had discovered in Polynesia. The Society Islands that he claimed for France, including Tahiti, Wallis, and Fortuna, were a source of valuable commodities, such as spices and sugar cane, as well as an outlet for France's domestic products. In the early twenty-first century, France still controls French Polynesia, and Bougainville's accomplishments are commemorated in the names of Bougainville Island in the Solomon Archipelago, two Bougainville Straits (one between Bougainville and Choiseul Islands near New Guinea, and the other at Vanuatu), and the Bougainvillea, a beautiful, flowering, ornamental shrub.

—*Denyse Lemaire and David Kasserman*

FURTHER READING

Bergreen, Laurence. *Over the Edge of the World: Magellan's Terrifying Circumnavigation of the Globe*. New York: William Morrow, 2003. Tale of exploration in the sixteenth century. This well-written book will allow the reader to compare Magellan's journey that ended with only eighteen survivors to that of Bougainville.

Bougainville, Louis-Antoine de. *The Pacific Journal of Louis-Antoine de Bougainville, 1767-1768*. Translated and edited by John Dunmore. London: Hakluyt Society, 2002. Bougainville's journal of his voyage, detailing the discoveries, encounters, and experiences of the explorer and his crew.

Lincoln, Margarette, ed. *Science and Exploration in the Pacific: European Voyages to the Southern Oceans in the Eighteenth Century*. Rochester, N.Y.: Boydell Press, 2001. Contains essays on the exploration of the Pacific Ocean in the eighteenth century by western Europeans, including Bougainville.

Thomas, Nicholas. *The Extraordinary Voyages of Captain James Cook*. New York: Walker, 2003. The author unravels the voyage of James Cook, who, like Bougainville, went around the world searching for new lands in the Southern Hemisphere.

SEE ALSO: Apr. 5, 1722: European Discovery of Easter Island; July, 1728-1769: Russian Voyages to Alaska; May, 1735-1743: French Scientists Explore the Amazon River; 1751-1772: Diderot Publishes the *Encyclopedia*; 1753: Lind Discovers a Cure for Scurvy; May 28, 1754-Feb. 10, 1763: French and Indian War; July, 1755-Aug., 1758: Acadians Are Expelled from Canada; Jan., 1756-Feb. 15, 1763: Seven Years' War; Aug. 25, 1768-Feb. 14, 1779: Voyages of Captain Cook; July 22, 1793: Mackenzie Reaches the Arctic Ocean.

RELATED ARTICLES in *Great Lives from History: The Eighteenth Century, 1701-1800*: Jean le Rond d'Alembert; Louis-Antoine de Bougainville; James Cook; Louis XV; Jean-Jacques Rousseau.

1767-1768
SPALLANZANI DISPROVES SPONTANEOUS GENERATION

Spallanzani was among the first to show experimentally that living organisms—such as maggots in rotting meat—could not simply appear out of nowhere. Though his work was not considered conclusive on the subject, it represented the beginnings of a modern view of biology.

LOCALE: Modena and Pavia (now in Italy)
CATEGORIES: Biology; science and technology

KEY FIGURES

Lazzaro Spallanzani (1729-1799), Italian biologist
Francesco Redi (1626-1697), Italian physician
Comte de Buffon (Georges-Louis Leclerc; 1707-1788), French naturalist and author of the first comprehensive natural history
John Tuberville Needham (1713-1781), Catholic priest and collaborator with Buffon
Antoni van Leeuwenhoek (1632-1723), Dutch inventor and scientist

SUMMARY OF EVENT

Naturalists before the eighteenth century had observed many instances of what seemed to them to be the "spontaneous generation" of life. Meat left out would sprout maggots, and frogs could emerge from apparently simple mud. There was no mystery associated with these seeming miracles, however. Indeed, spontaneous generation made perfect sense to those who believed in a Creator who had the ability to produce life from abiotic matter. If life had first originated in this manner, the reasoning went, life could appear again through similar means. There also were nonreligious explanations for the phenomenon. Greek philosopher Aristotle, in the fourth century B.C.E., believed that humidity provided a form of life force to dry objects. Later naturalists argued that mud could produce frogs or eels and even had recipes for the formation of life.

The first significant experiments to address the subject of spontaneous generation were carried out by

Franceso Redi in 1668. An Italian physician and member of the Accademia del Cimento (Academy of Experiment) in Florence, Redi set up a series of experiments in which putrefying meat was placed in vessels. Some vessels were covered with gauze or were completely sealed, while others served as uncovered controls. Redi observed that only meat that was accessible to flies developed maggots. The French physicist René-Antoine Ferchault de Réaumur, more famous for developing an alcohol thermometer, would later directly observe flies depositing eggs in food.

The debate over spontaneous generation continued for more than a century, and the development of the microscope, resulting in the discovery of microscopic "animalcules" by Antoni van Leeuwenhoek, only added to the debate. Leeuwenhoek's work established that an entire world of living things existed beyond the human eye's unaided ability to see. Even if it were established that the organisms of the visible world were incapable of spontaneous generation, therefore, it might still be the case that microscopic animalcules could appear spontaneously. Support for this view could be found in experiments carried out by the British clergyman John Tuberville Needham in 1745. Since it was known by then that heat could kill microorganisms, Needham boiled chicken broth and placed it in sealed vessels. Despite this treatment, microorganisms would still appear in the broth.

Needham later went to Paris, where he met and began a collaboration with the comte de Buffon. Buffon was well noted for his contributions to the growing field of comparative anatomy in the massive work *Histoire naturelle, générale et particulière* (1749-1789; *Natural History, General and Particular*, 1781-1812). Though many of Buffon's views on the similarities of species and the age of the Earth were still controversial at the time of their publication, he was well enough respected that his support for Needham's views lent credibility to the arguments in favor of spontaneous generation.

Lazzaro Spallanzani had a differing interpretation of Needham's results, however: He believed that the broth had been contaminated before being sealed. His criticism of Needham's techniques formed the basis for a 1765 dissertation on the subject. He also, more important, devised a set of practical tests to confirm his hypothesis that Needham's samples must have been contaminated. Spallanzani's experimental procedure was relatively simple: He boiled his samples for varying periods to ensure that nothing survived and then sealed the mixture in an airtight container. Beginning with a duration of forty-

five minutes, Spallanzani tested various boiling periods, observing whether anything would still grow in the broth after each test.

Spallanzani determined that extensive boiling prevented microorganisms from growing, resulting in the medium remaining sterile. To refute the potential counterargument that boiling destroyed a "life force" that had existed in the broth and that was necessary for spontaneous generation to occur, Spallanzani sealed his vessels with semipermeable barriers. He created seals with pores of various sizes, and he observed that the number of organisms that returned to the boiled broth was a function of the pore size. The implication of this result was that contamination from air had been the source of growth in Needham's experiments.

Spallanzani also observed that there existed several classes of organisms that differed in their sensitivity to heat. One class, probably protozoa, was highly sensitive to heat, and Spallanzani labeled this class "superior animalcula." On the other hand, the class he named "lower class animalcula," probably bacteria, was less sensitive. Thus, a nonrigorous application of heat in an experiment might kill only the more sensitive microscopic organisms, leaving the less sensitive ones to "appear spontaneously" afterward.

Despite these results, Spallanzani's experiments did not resolve the issue of spontaneous generation in the minds of all scientists. The experiments' results admitted of different interpretations, especially after Joseph Priestley discovered oxygen in 1774. When it was discovered that oxygen itself was driven from Spallanzani's experimental vessels during the heating process, some scientists argued that this newly discovered gas was necessary to activate the "vital force" that caused life to appear from nothing. It would remain for Louis Pasteur in the 1860's to resolve the argument to the satisfaction of the entire scientific community. After all, spontaneous generation had been believed to exist, in one form or another, for at least two thousand years. Such an entrenched belief could not be eliminated with anything less than utterly conclusive proof.

The theory explained quite efficiently an otherwise mysterious phenomenon that, in the days before preservatives and refrigeration, was extremely common—the sudden appearance of maggots, flies, or other biological contaminants on seemingly clean foods. The advances in experimental design in the sciences during the sixteenth and seventeenth centuries allowed naturalists to test the theory. Among the first to do so was Francesco Redi. However, despite Redi's initial results, which seemed to demonstrate that infestation of maggots in meat resulted from flies, not decay, the belief in spontaneous generation continued for years. Even Redi himself was not completely convinced that spontaneous generation was impossible.

Spallanzani's work, following from Redi's, was carried out during a period in the eighteenth century in which science was undergoing significant advancement. The development of the microscope in the previous century had allowed the observation of the very small. The significance of such observations when applied to germs or contamination, however, was still misunderstood. Nevertheless, Spallanzani continued the earlier experiments of Redi on the subject by demonstrating that if water was sterilized in a sealed container, spontaneous formation of life could not occur.

Where Redi's experiments, important in their use of biological controls, had demonstrated that relatively large forms of life would not spontaneously appear, Spallanzani showed that even microscopic organisms could be eliminated through the use of heat. In the process, he brought an experimental approach to the study of such organisms, complementing the scientific approach to the macroscopic world developed by the comte de Buffon. Nicolas Appert, a French cook, several decades later would apply Spallanzani's approach in developing a method of canning as a way to preserve food.

SIGNIFICANCE

In the immediate wake of Spallanzani's experiments, however, the debate concerning spontaneous generation was not yet settled. Criticism of Spallanzani's experiments centered on the lack of a formal, scientifically rigorous understanding of the nature of life. Various vitalist arguments about a "life force" that made generation possible complicated matters tremendously: If this hypothetical force was itself intangible, it would be difficult or impossible to prove that it had not been altered by heat, the lack of air, or other effects of Spallanzani's experiments.

Moreover, because of the state of experimental design in the 1760's, Spallanzani himself never came to the conclusion that microorganisms were present in the air. The fact that there was a gas called oxygen in the air, indeed the fact that the air was composed of a mixture of different gases, was new information added to the debate in the 1770's. As a result, one could still not rule out the possibility that it was the presence of oxygen that was required for spontaneous generation to occur.

It would be nearly one hundred years before Louis Pasteur ended the debate with what became known as the "swan-neck" flask experiment. In this experiment, Pasteur placed the experimental sample in a flask that remained unsealed, but he created a curved neck for the flask that allowed air to enter normally but kept microorganisms out; the solution under such circumstances remained sterile. Still, Spallanzani's work remained an important step in the evolution of biological knowledge.

Spallanzani would continue to provide commonsense solutions to experimental problems in other areas of biology for the rest of his career. Addressing the question of how fertilization of frogs' eggs is carried out, Spallanzani dressed male frogs in "pants," noting that fertilization did not occur under such circumstances. He concluded that an external process must account for fertilization. He demonstrated the role of sperm by filtering frog semen, again noting the absence of fertilization once the semen had been filtered.

—*Richard Adler*

FURTHER READING

Brock, Thomas. *Milestones in Microbiology, 1546-1940.* Washington, D.C.: ASM Press, 1999. Compilation of original historic papers, including one by Spallanzani (1799), in various areas of microbiology. Commentary by the editor discusses the significance of each work.

Buffon, Georges-Louis Leclerc, Comte de. *Natural History: General and Particular.* Translated by William Smellie. Bristol, Avon, England: Thoemmes Press, 2001. Translation of Buffon's work on comparative anatomy and evolution, which represented an attempt to present a systematic view of nature.

Geison, Gerald. *The Private Science of Louis Pasteur.* Princeton, N.J.: Princeton University Press, 1995. Pasteur's "swan-neck flask" experiment effectively ended the debate over the validity of spontaneous generation.

Lechevalier, Hubert, and Morris Solotorovsky. *Three Centuries of Microbiology.* New York: Dover, 1974. Describes the history of the subject from Girolamo Fracastoro (sixteenth century) through geneticists of the twentieth century. Emphasis is on the leading figures during these centuries.

Lennox, J. "Teleology, Chance, and Aristotle's Theory of Spontaneous Generation." *Journal of the History of Philosophy* 19 (1981): 219-238. Summarizes Aristotle's viewpoint on the subject, significant because his was one of the earliest theories.

Strick, James. *Sparks of Life: Darwinism and the Victo-*

rian Debates over Spontaneous Generation. Cambridge, Mass.: Harvard University Press, 2000. Analysis of the scientific debates concerning spontaneous generation during the mid- to late nineteenth century.

SEE ALSO: Beginning 1735: Linnaeus Creates the Binomial System of Classification; 1747: Marggraf Extracts Sugar from Beets; 1748: Nollet Discovers Osmosis; 1749-1789: First Comprehensive Examination of the Natural World; 1751: Maupertuis Provides Evidence of "Hereditary Particles"; June 5, 1755: Black Identifies Carbon Dioxide; 1757: Monro Distinguishes Between Lymphatic and Blood Systems; 1757-1766: Haller Establishes Physiology as a Science; Aug. 1, 1774: Priestley Discovers Oxygen; 1779: Ingenhousz Discovers Photosynthesis; 1796-1798: Jenner Develops Smallpox Vaccination.

RELATED ARTICLES in *Great Lives from History: The Eighteenth Century, 1701-1800*: Comte de Buffon; Joseph Priestley; Lazzaro Spallanzani.

1767-1771
INVENTION OF THE WATER FRAME

Richard Arkwright's invention of the water frame increased the supply of high-quality yarn and significantly accelerated the development of the factory system, which was a key component of the Industrial Revolution.

LOCALE: Northern England

CATEGORIES: Inventions; science and technology; manufacturing

KEY FIGURES

Sir Richard Arkwright (1732-1792), English inventor and the father of the factory system

John Kay (1704-c. 1780/1781), English clockmaker who helped Arkwright make his first spinning frame

Thomas Highs (1718-1803), English inventor who accused Arkwright of stealing intellectual property

Jedediah Strutt (1726-1797), English inventor and stocking manufacturer who supported Arkwright

James Hargreaves (1720-1778), English inventor of the spinning jenny

Matthew Boulton (1728-1809), English industrialist

SUMMARY OF EVENT

When Sir Richard Arkwright developed his water frame, the weaving of cotton cloth was already a rapidly developing industry in England. The joint tasks of spinning cotton fiber into thread and then weaving the thread into cloth were both accomplished in private homes. Textile factories did not yet exist. Numerous entrepreneurs and inventors were searching for ways to gain a comparative advantage in order to improve their profit margins.

A number of technological improvements prepared the way for Arkwright's invention. In 1733, John Kay had patented the flying shuttle, which greatly improved the efficiency of weavers. About 1764, James Hargreaves invented the spinning jenny, a hand-powered machine that operated several spindles simultaneously. The latter machine's major limitation was that its thread was not strong enough to be used for warp (thread extending lengthwise in a loom), but could only be used for weft (the crossways yarn). Still, Hargreaves's invention was the first significant improvement upon the spinning wheel. It turned out to be impossible to keep the innovations of Kay and Hargreaves secret, and textile manufacturers throughout northern England surreptitiously used their devices without any regard to patent rights.

Arkwright began his career as an apprentice barber and paruke maker. In 1755, he set up his own shop in Deansgate. After acquiring a secret method for dyeing hair, he hired a skilled wig maker and spent much time traveling through the country to purchase human hair for the business. In his travels, Arkwright had contact with spinners and weavers. When he moved to the town of Leigh, in Lancashire, he learned that Thomas Highs, with the assistance of a clockmaker named John Kay (no relation to the inventor of the flying shuttle), had built an experimental spinning machine. The fashion of wearing wigs was on the decline, and Arkwright was looking for other means to earn his livelihood.

Arkwright had an aptitude for both technology and practical business. He was well aware that the technology of weaving cloth was more advanced than that of spinning thread, creating a bottleneck in the supply chain for the textile industry. The result was a great demand for high-quality yarn to be used as warp. Taking advantage of his knowledge of the experiments of Highs and others, Arkwright conceived the design for a more sophisticated spinning frame. Needing technical assistance to construct such a devise, he employed the clockmaker Kay and two other skilled artisans, and together they assembled a working model in 1767.

This initial model made use of four pairs of rollers that rotated at different speeds, thereby allowing the spindles to twist the yarn to the required tightness. The yarn thus produced was of a higher quality than that produced by Hargreaves's spinning jenny. Although the small prototype model was operated by hand, Arkwright envisioned that machines based on the design could be expanded in size and driven by either horses or water power. His vision for building a large-scale enterprise was probably influenced by Matthew Boulton's manufacturing plants in Birmingham.

Arkwright applied for a patent for the spinning machine in 1768, and he obtained patent number 931 on July 3, 1769. Thomas Highs would later claim that Arkwright and Kay had stolen his ideas, and a court jury would support Highs's accusation. Arkwright's method of roller spinning, moreover, was similar to a patent devised by Lewis Paul in 1738. Even though Paul's machine had been utilized only briefly, it is entirely possible that Arkwright had some knowledge of its basic principles.

In 1768, Arkwright moved to Nottingham, a center of cotton manufacturing. There, he entered into partnership with John Smalley and David Thornley, leasing some buildings in order to operate several spinning machines that were worked by horse power. The operation was moderately successful. Although Arkwright's thread was not as strong as that made by traditional spinning wheels, it was suitable for warp. At first, Arkwright's thread was used primarily for making stockings. About this time, Arkwright met Jedediah Strutt, who had previously invented a machine for manufacturing ribbed stockings. Strutt recognized the potential of Arkwright's operation and agreed to provide financial assistance.

Arkwright and his associates decided to experiment with large mills driven by water wheels. In 1771, they erected a factory on a fast-moving stream that flowed into the Derwert River in the small village of Cromford, in Derbyshire. Because the spinning machines in Cromford relied on water power, they quickly became known as water frames. Within a decade, the Cromford mill would be six stories high, and additional mills would be added as well. The operation would grow to employ eight hundred workers. In the village, Arkwright built houses for the workers, as well as a hotel, a market, and a church.

Arkwright continued to expand his business operations. He participated in the construction of several textile mills in Lancashire and Scotland. He and his employees constantly made improvement in the design of the water frame. He licensed his water frame in units of one thousand spindles, which forced the licensees to use large, centrally powered production centers. In 1775, Arkwright was granted a second patent for a carding machine, which prepared cotton, silk, and wool for spinning. By 1778, more than three hundred Arkwright-type

Sir Richard Arkwright's water frame, used in the textile industry, was a spinning machine powered by water. (Library of Congress)

factories were operating in England. Even though his patent for the water frame was revoked, he was knighted for his contributions to the cotton industry in 1786. He died a very wealthy man at Willersley Castle in Cromford.

SIGNIFICANCE

Except for James Watt's improvement of the steam engine, Sir Richard Arkwright's water frame was probably the most important industrial innovation of the eighteenth century. Because its yarn was much stronger than that of the spinning jenny, it helped make the mass production of cloth possible. Driven by water power rather than human muscle, moreover, the water frame significantly decreased the cost of yarn. Although the device initially put many traditional spinners out of work, it eventually increased employment based on growth in exports and the consumption of textile products.

Arkwright is considered to be the world's first great industrialist, and he is often called the father of modern industrial factories. Because of the water frame's size and its need for great power, it could only be operated in large buildings, not in private homes. The relatively complex machine enhanced efficiency, thus providing greater profits to investors. The invention represented a major step in the development of the factory system and industrial capitalism.

Critics of modern industrial organization correctly observe that most workers in Arkwright's mills were poorly paid and lived in squalid conditions. By bringing a large number of people into an industrialized setting, Arkwright created living conditions that were frequently worse than those in the countryside. Since water frames would later be powered by steam engines, moreover, the devices contributed to the growth of pollution from the burning of coal and other fuels.

Defenders of Arkwright, on the other hand, argue that his contribution to the process of modernization gradually helped improve the living standards for people in general. As proof, they observe that in the modern world, only a handful of people seem to want to return to the living conditions that existed before the Industrial Revolution.

—*Thomas Tandy Lewis*

FURTHER READING

Baines, Edward. *History of the Cotton Manufacture in Great Britain*. Reprint. New York: Augustus M. Kelley, 1966. A standard account of the great changes in the cotton industry during the eighteenth century.

Feldman, Anthony, and Peter Ford. *Scientists and Inventors*. New York: Facts On File, 1979. Includes essays on 155 major innovators on double-page spreads with illustrations and diagrams to explain the achievement of each.

Fitton, R. S. *Arkwrights: Spinners of Fortune*. New York: St. Martin's Press, 1989. The only scholarly biography of Arkwright, presenting him as a genius responsible for a new industrial society.

Fitton, R. S., and Wadsworth, A. P. *The Strutts and the Arkwrights*. Reprint. New York: Augustus M. Kelley, 1968. Includes a detailed account of Arkwright's life and career.

Hobsbawn, Eric. *Industry and Empire*. New York: New Press, 1999. Analysis of Britain's rise as the first industrial power, written by an outstanding left-wing historian.

Mantoux, Paul. *The Industrial Revolution in the Eighteenth Century*. Chicago: University of Chicago Press, 1983. Probably the best general history ever written about the beginning of the factory system and other aspects of the Industrial Revolution.

Pawson, Eric. *The Early Industrial Revolution: Britain in the Eighteenth Century*. New York: Harper and Row, 1979. A good general account of the technological and economic transformations of the century.

Rowland, K. T. *Eighteenth-Century Inventions*. New York: Barnes & Noble Books, 1974. Useful collection of relatively short descriptions of 130 major inventions with illustrations and suggested readings.

Usher, Abbott P. *A History of Mechanical Inventions*. Cambridge, Mass.: Harvard University Press, 1966. A standard source that includes an excellent chapter on the history of machinery in the textile industry.

Walton, Perry. *The Story of Textiles*. New York: Tudor, 1925. A well-written survey with a useful summary of Arkwright's career.

SEE ALSO: 1701: Tull Invents the Seed Drill; 1705-1712: Newcomen Develops the Steam Engine; 1709: Darby Invents Coke-Smelting; 1733: Kay Invents the Flying Shuttle; 1764: Invention of the Spinning Jenny; 1765-1769: Watt Develops a More Effective Steam Engine; 1779: Crompton Invents the Spinning Mule; Apr., 1785: Cartwright Patents the Steam-Powered Loom; Dec. 20, 1790: Slater's Spinning Mill; 1793: Whitney Invents the Cotton Gin; 1795: Invention of the Flax Spinner.

RELATED ARTICLES in *Great Lives from History: The Eighteenth Century, 1701-1800*: Sir Richard Arkwright; Matthew Boulton; James Hargreaves; John Kay.

June 29, 1767-April 12, 1770
TOWNSHEND CRISIS

Just one year after the conclusion of the Stamp Act Crisis, British laws designed to tighten the empire's economic and political controls on the colonies prompted further American resistance. The Townshend Crisis represented another step on the path to revolution.

LOCALE: Great Britain; British North America
CATEGORIES: Laws, acts, and legal history; government and politics; colonization; trade and commerce; social issues and reform

KEY FIGURES
Charles Townshend (1725-1767), British chancellor of the exchequer, 1766-1767
John Dickinson (1732-1808), colonial American lawyer
William Pitt the Elder (1708-1778), British prime minister, 1757-1761, 1766-1768
Thomas Gage (1721-1787), British commander in chief in North America, 1763-1773
Lord North (Frederick North; 1732-1792), British chancellor of the exchequer, 1767-1770, and prime minister, 1770-1782

SUMMARY OF EVENT
In 1766, after repealing the Stamp Act and imposing new domestic taxes in England, the second Marquess of Rockingham and his ministry were recalled by King George III and replaced by a coalition of diverse politicians under the ailing William Pitt the Elder. Because of his poor health, Pitt often was absent from Parliament for long periods, which enabled his ministers to pursue their own individual agendas. Pitt's most powerful minister was the chancellor of the exchequer, Charles Townshend, who inherited Great Britain's financial crisis. The problems became considerably worse after Parliament, in an attempt to appease its constituents, slashed the land tax. As a result, the British government was deprived of more than £400,000 in annual revenue. In searching for solutions to his dilemma, Townshend seized upon colonial American arguments made during the Stamp Act protest. Colonial leaders had claimed that they were opposed in principle only to internal taxes, not external taxes. Never a friend of the colonial protest, Townshend declared that if the colonists adhered to such a distinction, then they should be saddled with extensive external duties.

Despite warnings from several influential members of Parliament, Townshend steered three laws through the British government during June and July, 1767, with the first one passing on June 29. Collectively, the three acts became known as the Townshend Acts. Two of the three, the American Board of Customs Act and the New York Suspending Act, were designed to strengthen British authority within the colonies. The third, the Townshend Revenue Act of 1767, was intended to raise £40,000 by taxing glass, paint, lead, paper, and tea imported into the colonies. Because the act taxed only imported goods and therefore was an external tax, supporters of the legislation expected Americans to submit to it. Townshend planned to use the new revenues to pay for the administrative changes embodied by the first two pieces of legislation.

The colonists had grave reservations about each of the three acts. The danger in the Revenue Act of 1767 was not in the quantity of cash extracted from colonial pockets but in its potential to extend Parliament's authority over colonial American affairs. Unlike legislation prior to the Stamp Act, the new act was created to collect money, or revenue, for the British treasury exclusively from colonial America. Since the mid-seventeenth century, British trade laws had been designed to regulate commerce throughout the empire. Colonial leaders contended that, constitutionally, before Parliament could create a tax solely on the colonies, Parliament would have to include colonial representation.

Colonists also feared that if they accepted the Revenue Act, a precedent would be established and additional revenue-raising acts directed only at the colonies would soon follow. Additionally, a portion of the act's revenues was to be used to administer the colonies. This deeply troubled many Americans. During the eighteenth century, colonial legislatures had acquired significant powers to control the salaries and general remuneration of British administrators in America. By the 1760's, these powers provided a way for colonists to keep the Crown's appointed officials responsive to the will of the colonial population they served. The Revenue Act threatened to do away with those powers and, therefore, further threatened the constitutional rights of the colonists.

Adding to Parliament's perceived assault upon American rights were the American Board of Customs Act and the New York Suspending Act. The Customs Act created an American Board of Customs, with headquarters in

Boston, that reported directly to the British Treasury. The new agency, which included vice-admiralty courts in three colonial cities, had the power to administer virtually all American activities with little regard for colonial assemblies. The Board of Customs was expected to be zealous in the handling of its assignment, for a third of all fines received in the vice-admiralty courts went to the customs agents. Parliament also made British regulars stationed in the colonies available to the new Board of Customs, should the need arise.

The New York Suspending Act was an attempt to force New York to comply fully with the Quartering Act, passed in 1765, which required provincial assemblies, at their own expense, to lodge British regulars in taverns and other public houses when military barracks were not available. Firewood, candles, bedding, and other essential items also were to be provided by the province. New York, a colony frequently asked to provide such assistance, refused to comply with the law completely. In retaliation, Parliament, through the Suspending Act, sought to shut down the New York Assembly until the colony thoroughly obeyed the Quartering Act. From the colonial American perspective, this act was clearly punitive and, therefore, an abuse of constitutional authority. Colonists also considered the act an indirect tax, because it required assemblies to levy money for the upkeep of royal regiments.

The American reaction to the Townshend Acts came slowly, in part because Parliament was able to implement the acts before the colonists had time to plan their resistance. Likewise, Parliament took steps to nullify the strong-arm tactics that had been so effective during the Stamp Act protest. Nevertheless, by early 1768, colonial leaders had begun to rally their fellow Americans. Among the more influential critics was Pennsylvania lawyer John Dickinson, whose *Letters from a Farmer in Pennsylvania* became popular reading throughout America. What Dickinson lacked in originality he made up for by vigorously and clearly expressing the colonists' constitutional opposition to all forms of taxation in which the colonies were not represented.

Other writers, including Massachusetts firebrands James Otis and Samuel Adams, joined the battle, as did several colonial assemblies, with remonstrance and petitions against the unpopular actions. The Massachusetts legislature, through what it called a "circular letter," led the way with a bitter denunciation of parliamentary taxation and the scheme to pay judges and royal governors from funds other than those appropriated by the colonial assemblies. In Boston, merchants again resorted to a nonimportation agreement, as they had during the Stamp Act protest.

Aided by the reappearance of various Sons of Liberty organizations, the Boston boycott slowly spread southward during 1768 and 1769. Eventually, the tactic cut British imports to the colonies by 40 percent. In 1770, after the sudden death of Charles Townshend and William Pitt's retirement, Lord North came to power in Parliament. With the colonial boycott still in place and American resistance growing, North was able to persuade Parliament to repeal all the Townshend duties except the one on tea; the king gave his consent on April 12. The tea duty would remain as a symbol of Parliament's authority to tax.

SIGNIFICANCE

Lord North was a practical man whose way out of the crisis seemed to offer a return to more cooperative British-American relations. However, while the Townshend Acts prompted a less violent reaction in the colonies than had the Stamp Act, the new legislation represented an even greater threat to American rights. It was a threat that would not be forgotten, even after the laws were repealed. The point was made obvious when, in response to the customs collectors' appeal for protection, the first earl of Hillsborough, secretary of state for the colonies, attempted to dissolve the Massachusetts Assembly and ordered General Thomas Gage, British commander in chief in North America, to station British troops in Boston. Hillsborough's moves confirmed to many colonists that a conspiracy against American rights existed in Parliament. When the crisis ended, the belief in such a conspiracy remained, and it went a long way toward preparing the colonists psychologically for revolution.

—*Paul E. Doutrich*

FURTHER READING

Breen, T. H. *The Marketplace of Revolution: How Consumer Politics Shaped American Independence*. New York: Oxford University Press, 2004. Breen argues that colonists' experience as consumers helped them develop new forms of social action, such as boycotts, that ultimately resulted in revolution. Includes information about the Townshend Acts and the colonists' protests.

Brooke, John. *The Chatham Administration, 1766-1768*. Vol. 1 in *England in the Age of the Revolution*, edited by Louis Namier. New York: St. Martin's Press, 1956. Mirrors the approach and conclusions of the author's mentor.

Butterfield, Herbert. *George III and the Historians*. New

York: Macmillan, 1957. This historiographical monograph finds serious fault with some of the conclusions of Namier and Brooke concerning parties and principles.

Griffith, Samuel B., II. *The War for American Independence: From 1760 to the Surrender at Yorktown in 1781*. Urbana: University of Illinois Press, 2002. This history of the American Revolution, first published in 1776 under another name, describes the causes and conditions that led colonists to rebel against the British. Chapter 4 focuses on the Townshend Acts.

Jacobson, David L. *John Dickinson and the Revolution in Pennsylvania, 1764-1774*. Berkeley: University of California Press, 1965. A useful narrative of Dickinson's political ideas and activities.

Knollenberg, Bernard. *Growth of the American Revolution, 1765-1775*. New York: Free Press, 1975. Places the British policy toward colonial America in context and describes the American reaction.

Namier, Lewis B., and John Brooke. *Charles Townshend*. New York: St. Martin's Press, 1964. Depicts the charming and eloquent Townshend as also erratic, amoral, and a determined imperialist in favor of strong royal authority in the colonies. Namier maintains that the "Townshend duties" of 1767 were pushed through Parliament despite opposition from Pitt and others—they were not in fact the result of Parliament's need to prime the American pump.

Pares, Richard. *King George III and the Politicians*. Oxford, England: Oxford University Press, 1953. A brilliantly written account of the monarch's place in the political and constitutional picture, reflecting Namier's point of view.

Thomas, Peter D. G. *The Townshend Duties Crisis: The Second Phase of the Revolution, 1767-1773*. Oxford, England: Clarendon Press, 1987. A thorough assessment of how the Townshend Acts affected both England and colonial America.

Ubbelohde, Carl. *The Vice-Admiralty Courts and the American Revolution*. Chapel Hill: University of North Carolina Press, 1960. This carefully researched work asserts that "the Vice-Admiralty Courts were a minor, but persistent, cause of the American Revolution."

SEE ALSO: Mar. 22, 1765-Mar. 18, 1766: Stamp Act Crisis; 1768-May 16, 1771: Carolina Regulator Movements; Mar. 5, 1770: Boston Massacre; Dec. 16, 1773: Boston Tea Party; Apr. 27-Oct. 10, 1774: Lord Dunmore's War; Sept. 5-Oct. 26, 1774: First Continental Congress; Apr. 19, 1775-Oct. 19, 1781: American Revolutionary War.

RELATED ARTICLES in *Great Lives from History: The Eighteenth Century, 1701-1800*: John Dickinson; Thomas Gage; George III; Lord North; William Pitt the Elder.

August, 1767-May, 1799
ANGLO-MYSORE WARS

The Anglo-Mysore Wars destroyed the power of the last state in the south of India, Mysore, to oppose the British East India Company. At the end of the wars Mysore became an ally of the company as part of the subsidiary alliance system, and the city of Bangalore became an important British military base in the south of India.

ALSO KNOWN AS: Mysore Wars
LOCALE: Southern India
CATEGORIES: Wars, uprisings, and civil unrest; expansion and land acquisition; colonization

KEY FIGURES

Hyder Ali (1722-1782), ruler of Mysore, r. 1761-1782
Tipu Sultan (1750-1799), sultan of Mysore, r. 1782-1799

Warren Hastings (1732-1818), governor general of the British East India Company, 1773-1785
First Marquess Cornwallis (Charles Cornwallis; 1738-1805), governor general of the British East India Company, 1786-1793, 1805
Richard Wellesley (1760-1824), governor general of the British East India Company, 1797-1805
Sir Eyre Coote (1726-1783), Irish commander of British forces in Bengal

SUMMARY OF EVENT

The Anglo-Mysore Wars were part of the long-term expansion of the British in South Asia between 1757, when they took control of Bengal and northern India, and 1849, when they captured the Punjab. Because British power in India depended on access to the sea, the British were eager to gain control of the Mysorean coastline. British expansion in southern India was also designed to prevent any French return to India. The French had been defeated in India by 1761, but their potential return was perceived by the British as a threat to be guarded against.

The First Anglo-Mysore War (August, 1767-April, 1769) occurred when Hyder Ali, the de facto ruler of Mysore, recognized that the British represented a threat to his sovereignty since they had captured the Northern Sarkars from the French in 1758. He made a preemptive attack on the British East India Company in August of 1767. Even though Hyderabad withdrew from their alliance with Mysore, Hyder Ali pushed the British back to the city of Madras and forced the British to sign an alliance with Mysore, which they also failed to honor.

By 1780, Hyder Ali was at the height of his power, but the British had a different level of power than they had in 1769, because the Regulating Act of 1773 had unified Bengal, Bombay, and Madras under the rule of a British governor general. Three successive governors general—Warren Hastings, the First Marquess Cornwallis, and Richard Wellesley—were determined to expand British power and to destroy Mysore.

Despite, or perhaps because of, this increase in British power, in 1780, Hyder Ali invaded the Carnatic with some ninety thousand troops under his personal command, beginning the Second Anglo-Mysore War (1780-1784). Hyder Ali's lieutenants in the invasion were his son, Tipu Sultan, and a French officer named Lally, possibly related to the late comte de Lally. Tipu had been incensed by the British capture in 1779 of the French settlement at Mahe, which lay within Hyder's territory, as well as by the British betrayal of Mysore in 1771, when the Marāthās had attacked and the British had failed to honor their alliance. More recently, the British had flouted Mysorean sovereignty by marching across Mysore's territory without seeking permission.

Hyder was besieging Arcot when he learned through his military spies (*harkaras*) that the British colonel Baillie was camped at Pullalur. On September 10, 1780, Hyder and Tipu with the cavalry, and Lally with the artillery, attacked, annihilating the British. Out of a force of 3,853 men, 50 officers and 200 Europeans were captured; the rest were killed or fled for their lives. Baillie died in captivity. Hector Munro, commanding another British force at Conjeevaram, fled in panic to Madras. Arcot fell on October 31, and Hyder also captured Ambur, Sargur, and Tyagar. He celebrated his great victory with a wall-to-wall mural of the battle in his summer palace at Seringapatam, the "Baillie-Lally *Yudh*."

When news of the disaster reached Bengal, Governor General Hastings sent another army under the command of Sir Eyre Coote to Madras by sea, with support dispatched simultaneously by land. Hastings also secured alliances with the Marāthās and Hyderabad against Mysore. At battles in 1781 at Porto Novo—where Hyder lost more than ten thousand men—Wandiwash, Sholinghur, and Arni, Hyder suffered huge losses of men and equipment, but the British were unable to crush him or remove him from the Carnatic. On February 18, 1782, Tipu routed the British on the Coleroon River. Hyder retired to Arcot and died on December 7, 1782. The war continued under Tipu but concluded with the Treaty of Mangalore on March 11, 1784, which resulted in the mutual restoration of British and Mysorean territory.

The Third Anglo-Mysore War (1790-1792) began after Cornwallis engineered alliances with the nizam of Hyderabad and the Marāthās in 1788 in order to isolate Tipu, provoke him to war, and attack him on three fronts at once. Tipu, taking the bait, invaded Travancore, an ally of the British, in 1789, giving Cornwallis the excuse he sought to launch another war. In the east between May and July, 1790, the British captured frontier posts and the great fortress of Coimbatore. In the west, they occupied Satyamangalam, and in the south they captured the stronghold of Dindigul on August 22. In September, they captured the crossroads town of Palghat and were poised to march into the Mysorean heartland.

Tipu finally returned to Seringapatam and mobilized some forty thousand men. On September 9, he reached the Gajalhatti Pass, descended in a sudden, silent, and skilful attack, and left five hundred dead. The British fell back to Coimbatore, while Tipu recovered a great deal of his territory. The result was that Tipu had control of much of the territory in the east, while the British dominated the west coast. Nonetheless, the situation looked bleak for the British, causing Cornwallis to take personal command of his armies. He arrived in Madras in January, 1791, and mobilized all the British forces together.

Tipu was in Pondicherry when Cornwallis made a surprise attack into Mysore and captured the stronghold of Bangalore on March 2. Tipu was camped only nine miles away but displayed fatal indecisiveness and failed to come to the assistance of his beleaguered fort. Marching north, Cornwallis joined up with the nizam of Hyderabad's fifteen-thousand-man army. Further north, some seventeen thousand Marāthā troops, with a small contingent of British troops, captured Tipu's northern capital of Dharwad on April 4, 1791, after a siege of six months. Cornwallis and the nizam marched north on

The British assault on Seringapatam, 1799. (Hulton Archive/Getty Images)

Seringapatam, but Tipu employed a scorched-earth policy, and they began to run out of food. The monsoon rains further impeded their advance.

The two armies finally clashed on May 13 and 14, nine miles from Seringapatam. Tipu inflicted considerable damage on the British forces but then retired to the island fortress of Seringapatam. The British were out of food and draft animals, and on May 26, 1791, Cornwallis withdrew his starving army to Bangalore, reaching it on July 11. In the west, moreover, the Bombay army was routed.

On December 31, 1791, in Bangalore, Cornwallis reviewed the allied forces: His ranks consisted of twenty-two thousand British, eighteen thousand Hyderabadis, and twelve thousand Marāthās, with another twenty thousand Marāthās prepared to join up with them at Seringapatam. By February, they were camped four miles from Seringapatam. Neither the twenty thousand Marāthās nor the Bombay army had yet arrived, when Cornwallis staged a surprise night attack on Seringapatam on February 6, 1792. The attack on Tipu's 40,500 men was successful, and Tipu fell back on the fort and sued for peace. Tipu had to hand over two of his sons as

hostages to guarantee that he would pay the huge reparations demanded by the British. He lost half of his territory, including most of the western coastline and seventy fortresses, to the British and their allies.

The Fourth Anglo-Mysore War (1799) lasted only three months. After 1792, Tipu rebuilt his army. The *casus belli* for the fourth war was the Malartic Proclamation of the French governor of Mauritius, who pledged French support to Tipu. Seeing the danger of a potentially powerful French ally in the region, the new British governor general, Wellesley, determined that the power of Mysore should be destroyed once and for all, and he re-created the triple alliance of 1790. On February 11, 1799, the British army marched into Mysore. British forces numbered nearly thirty thousand, and the Marāthās and Hyderabad numbered twenty-five thousand each. On May 4, the British assaulted Seringapatam. Already wounded, Tipu was finally shot in the temple by an unknown British soldier.

SIGNIFICANCE

The Mysore Wars eradicated the power of the Muslim rulers of Mysore and established a Hindu kingdom under a raja of Mysore who was subservient to the British. The British army became established in Bangalore, which was to remain the preeminent British military base in the south until 1947. Thus, not only did Mysore cease to be a threat to British power but the British also acquired valuable territory, increasing both their hold on India and their access to resources vital to maintain that hold.

—*Roger D. Long*

FURTHER READING

Fernandes, Praxy. *The Tigers of Mysore: A Biography of Hyder Ali and Tipu Sultan*. New Delhi: Viking, 1991. This is a detailed history of the four Anglo-Mysore Wars. It is written from a nationalistic perspective and critically analyzes the accounts written by British historians and participants.

Gordon, Stewart. *The Marāthās, 1600-1818*. Part 2, vol. 4 in *The New Cambridge History of India*. New York: Cambridge University Press, 1993. An understanding of Marāthā power is essential to understand the balance of power in south India. Offers an account of Hyder Ali's military techniques in the face of superior Marāthā military power, as well as dealing with Marāthā politics at the time of the Fourth Anglo-Mysore War.

Habib, Irfan, ed. *Confronting Colonialism: Resistance and Modernization Under Haidar Ali and Tipu Sultan*. New Delhi: Tulika, 1999. This volume of twenty-five essays came out of a conference to commemorate the bicentenary of Tipu Sultan's defeat by the British at Seringapatam in 1799.

SEE ALSO: 1746-1754: Carnatic Wars; Jan., 1756-Feb. 15, 1763: Seven Years' War; June 23, 1757: Battle of Plassey; Dec., 1774-Feb. 24, 1783: First Marāthā War.

RELATED ARTICLES in *Great Lives from History: The Eighteenth Century, 1701-1800*: First Marquess Cornwallis; Hyder Ali.

August 10, 1767
CATHERINE THE GREAT'S INSTRUCTION

Catherine the Great issued her Instruction, a series of progressive principles for reforming Russian law and governance. The Instruction was one of the most modern, liberal governmental decrees of the eighteenth century, but it remained a merely theoretical decree, and the reforms Catherine intended never appeared in practice.

LOCALE: St. Petersburg, Russia
CATEGORIES: Government and politics; social issues and reform

KEY FIGURES

Catherine the Great (1729-1796), empress of Russia, r. 1762-1796

Grigori Grigoryevich Orlov (1734-1783), Catherine's paramour and political adviser

Count Nikita Ivanovich Panin (1718-1783), influential adviser to Catherine

Cesare Beccaria (1738-1794), Italian philosopher and prison reform advocate

Montesquieu (Charles-Louis de Secondat; 1689-1755), French political philosopher

Voltaire (François-Marie Arouet; 1694-1778), French philosopher, writer, and dramatist

SUMMARY OF EVENT

On August 10, 1767, Catherine the Great, empress of Russia, published her *Nakaz*, or Instruction. This lengthy document, which took two years to prepare, reflected Catherine's concern with the unsatisfactory conditions existing in Russia when she came to power in 1762. It also showed her familiarity with many advanced ideas of Western political philosophers. Dealing with almost every area of Russian life, the document was intended to be a general statement of basic philosophical principles that might affect the specific political, social, economic, and cultural life of Russia.

The document was submitted in 1767 to a legislative commission created for the purpose of transforming the Instruction into a code of laws for all Russia. Yet her advisers quickly and substantially modified the monarch's original efforts. According to Catherine herself, more than half of her proposal was eliminated or substantially modified before it reached the legislative commission. This large and cumbersome body included more than six hundred representatives of several classes and occupations such as the nobility, merchants, free peasants, and Cossacks, for example. The assembly labored for approximately two years on the project without producing a workable code for the nation. Thus the Instruction was a failure so far as its broad and substantial impact on Russian law and society are concerned.

Catherine's Instruction sought to respond to the myriad problems facing eighteenth century Russia, which had only recently entered the competitive world of European power politics. Russia's mineral and agricultural resources had to be efficiently developed, trade expanded, and revenues collected, and its army led by educated and competent officers. Its people had to be trained to serve the needs of the economy and government. Several European countries by this time had established a reasonably modern bureaucratic system staffed by members of the rising bourgeoisie and the aristocracy. Yet with most of its population imprisoned in serfdom and the remainder living provincial lives revolving about agriculture, and having little or no education, Russia scarcely had a middle class from which to recruit civil servants. The nobles were expected to serve the state, but their motivation and skills left much to be desired. The civil service Catherine inherited from her predecessors had to be made as efficient and competent as possible. Clearly, a great deal needed attention, and the German-born Catherine hoped to make substantial improvements in her adopted country.

The Instruction was intended to embody a philosophical statement of basic principles of law under which Russia could regularize the service of its nobility and develop a middle class while holding its own politically, economically, and militarily with the more advanced Western countries. Catherine's Instruction consisted of more than 650 sections dealing with social, political, economic, and cultural matters. It borrowed extensively from the ideas of the French philosopher Montesquieu and the Italian prison reformer Cesare Beccaria.

Before its publication in mid-1767, Catherine had submitted the *Nakaz* for comment and revision to several trusted advisers, notably Count Nikita Ivanovich Panin and Grigori Grigoryevich Orlov. Her close associates strongly suggested the elimination or severe qualification of many of the more liberal positions taken by the empress, and the final draft was a much revised version of the original. For instance, Catherine had sharply condemned the personal servitude of the peasant to the lord, while supporting the view that the peasant should economically support the lord so that he would be free to carry out his duties to the state; the final version said practically nothing about serfdom, although it did point to landlord greed and excessive exploitation of the peasant as a primary cause of Russia's backwardness, and it

suggested that private ownership of land by the peasant would stimulate production. While noting that Russia was primarily an agricultural country, Catherine's Instruction also emphasized the need for industrial and commercial growth.

The Instruction noted that Russia's greatest single need was for a prosperous, industrious middle class. Catherine saw this group as the basis of the prosperity and strength of the Western European countries, and she believed that Russia, itself becoming a "European" country, also needed such a class. While encouraging the growth of private industry and offering state subsidies and tariffs to aid its growth, Catherine did not favor the development of large factories. She saw these as ugly, unhealthy prisons that should not be encouraged. The desired increase in productivity could be accomplished through the expansion of cottage industry. Catherine strongly advocated the expansion of foreign commerce. The Instruction pointed out that, given the enormous size of Russia, an increase in population was vitally needed to exploit the country's natural wealth. Yet her views and intentions on the matter of population growth remained vague. The extension of Russia's frontiers in succeeding decades added substantial numbers to the empire, as one source of population growth.

Catherine believed that an economically progressive population could not exist within the existing and often capricious arbitrarily autocratic political system of Russia, however, and in the Instruction she laid down general principles for the transformation of Russia into a state which, though autocratic, would be governed by law. Catherine held the view that, because of its great size and vulnerability to attack, Russia must remain an autocracy, but one tempered with the principle of civilized government.

According to Catherine, there must be some division of authority, because of the many tasks of government, but the monarch still reigned supreme. Everyone, without exception, had to be subject to the same laws. Laws had to be applied uniformly to all social classes throughout the empire, and were not to be unevenly interpreted by judges. There must be exact descriptions of the circumstances under which a citizen could be arrested. Partial religious toleration should be introduced to remove some of the disabilities imposed on the non-Orthodox population. Within specific limits, freedom of the press should be introduced, and the general principle would hold that citizens could be punished for deeds alone and not for thoughts or intentions. Special reference was made to the notorious practice of the use of torture in legal cases, and the *Nakaz* called for its abolition. Catherine also called for substantial reductions in the use of capital punishment.

SIGNIFICANCE

The Instruction embodied Catherine's basic desire that the Russians should be citizens, not "subjects," and, as citizens, subject to the rule of law. It corresponded with her idea of the duty of both sovereign and citizens to act for mutual good under the auspices of objective laws and fundamental principles. Western intellectuals such as Voltaire praised the Russian monarch for her progressive and enlightened views. If this liberal political program had been put into effect, the history of Russia might have evolved differently. Yet operating in the realm of theory did not bring about reform to Russia, and the Instruction remained little more than a theoretical statement. Consequently, Catherine's widespread reputation as an enlightened monarch, or despot, is properly called into question.

—George F. Putnam, updated by Taylor Stults

FURTHER READING

Alexander, John T. *Catherine the Great: Life and Legend*. New York: Oxford University Press, 1989. Chapter 4 provides a very solid account of the Instruction and legislative commission, as well as Catherine's views of reform.

Beik, William. *The Modernisation of Russia, 1676-1825*. New York: Cambridge University Press, 1999. An analytical account of Russia's efforts to implement reforms and become a more modern and Westernized nation. Includes information about Catherine's *Nakaz* and her work with the legislative commission.

DeMadariaga, Isabel. *Catherine the Great: A Short History*. 2d ed. New Haven, Conn.: Yale University Press, 2002. Not a conventional biography but an examination of how Catherine governed her country. Includes information about her involvement with the legislative commission.

Dukes, Paul. *Catherine the Great and the Russian Nobility: A Study Based on the Materials of the Legislative Commission of 1767*. London: Cambridge University Press, 1967. Detailed assessment of the assembly and the problems it faced in attempting to write a new legal code.

_____. *The Making of Russian Absolutism, 1613-1801*. 2d ed. New York: Longman, 1990. This analysis interprets Catherine in the broader context of Russian autocracy.

_____, ed. *Catherine the Great's Instruction (Nakaz) to the Legislative Commission, 1767*. Vol. 2 in *Russia Under Catherine the Great*. Newtonville, Mass.: Oriental Research Partners, 1977. Provides the full text and related materials.

Thomson, G. Scott. *Catherine the Great and the Expansion of Russia*. Westport, Conn.: Greenwood Press, 1985. Reprint of a brief informative biography of Catherine that, despite its title, covers both domestic and foreign subjects.

Troyat, Henri. *Catherine the Great: A Biography*. New York: Meridian, 1994. A comprehensive account, by a prolific French author of several biographies of famous Russians.

SEE ALSO: Oct., 1768-Jan. 9, 1792: Ottoman Wars with Russia; Sept., 1773-Sept., 1774: Pugachev's Revolt; 1775-1790: Joseph II's Reforms; 1788-Sept., 1809: Russo-Swedish Wars; Nov., 1796: Catherine the Great's Art Collection Is Installed at the Hermitage.

RELATED ARTICLES in *Great Lives from History: The Eighteenth Century, 1701-1800*: Catherine the Great; Aleksey Grigoryevich Orlov; Grigori Grigoryevich Orlov; Peter the Great; Peter III.

1768-May 16, 1771
CAROLINA REGULATOR MOVEMENTS

Protesting lack of representation in the Western backcountry, the Regulators inspired vigilante insurrections. The movements highlighted the differences between settled colonies and frontier territories. and they contributed to the development of an American vigilante tradition.

LOCALE: North and South Carolina (now in the United States)

CATEGORIES: Wars, uprisings, and civil unrest; colonization; government and politics

KEY FIGURES

Herman Husband (1724-1795), North Carolina pamphleteer

William Tryon (1729-1788), British governor of North Carolina

Edmund Fanning (1739-1818), justice of the peace and recorder of deeds of Orange County, North Carolina

Samuel Johnston (1733-1816), conservative leader in the North Carolina assembly

William Bull (1710-1791), governor of South Carolina, 1760-1761

SUMMARY OF EVENT

Conflicts between the East and the West, between old established societies and new primitive settlements of the frontier, recurred throughout the history of North America. The breadth and depth of these sectional antagonisms have varied sharply according to time and place. The Regulator movements of the late 1760's and 1770's in the Carolinas illustrate the complexity of the phenomenon.

In Maryland and Virginia, the frontier folk harbored no deep-seated grievances against the East. The legislatures, although dominated by tidewater aristocrats, had established counties—with courts, justices of the peace, sheriffs, and representation in the assemblies—and had enacted statutes to build roads and bridges for facilitating trade. In North Carolina, despite the fact that the same political institutions had made their appearance in the piedmont, there was serious regional discord because of the malpractices of local officials and, to a lesser extent, because of high quitrents, inadequate arteries of transportation, and underrepresentation in the legislature.

Sheriffs, by failing to publish the tax rate, collected far more than the law permitted and lined their own pockets in the process. If a taxable person could not pay—and

cash was ever in short supply—his property was seized and sold, with the auctions rigged in favor of insiders. There was little opportunity for redress, because corrupt sheriffs acted in collusion with other county officials. These "courthouse rings" charged exorbitant fees for performing routine legal services. The symbol of the people's unhappiness was New York-born, Yale-educated Edmund Fanning, justice of the peace and recorder of deeds of Orange County.

Although violence erupted as early as 1759 in the Granville District, the initial pattern of the Regulators (a name that the aroused victims of these discriminatory practices borrowed from a simultaneous but separate reform movement in South Carolina) was to lodge formal protests with the governor and the Assembly. Humble in tone and legalistic in concept, these petitions were largely ignored or condemned on the seaboard. Only after many rebuffs did the Regulators broaden their goals to include dividing western counties and instituting secret voting so as to increase their representation in the colonial legislature. New elections in 1769 brought Herman Husband, one of their principal spokesmen, into the Assembly, along with several other Regulators and their sympathizers. James Iredell, a conservative, declared that a majority of the lower house was "of regulating principles." With their new strength, they won approval for the creation of four new counties in the backcountry.

This measure and other modest reforms concerning officers' fees and court costs in litigation lacked enforcement at the county level. Violence increased, and in September, 1770, Regulators invaded the Orange County court at Hillsborough, drove out the justices, and tried cases themselves. Fear of rebellion led the assembly to abandon its "regulating principles" by enacting the repressive Johnston Act against unlawful gatherings and by backing Governor William Tryon in sending a militia army against the Regulators. On May 16, 1771, near the banks of the Alamance Creek, 20 miles from Hillsborough, a motley throng of two thousand farmers gathered to oppose Tryon's force of fourteen hundred well-armed militias. After desultory firing and ludicrous field movements on both sides, the Regulators fled, each side sustaining nine dead. Many Regulators left the province with their families, moving across the mountains into northeastern Tennessee. The majority accepted the governor's offer of clemency.

The Regulation ended at Alamance, but in the 1770's,

justices and sheriffs in the piedmont appear to have paid stricter attention to the law in performing their duties, for patriot leaders saw the need to placate the West to achieve unity in the face of the challenge from Great Britain. There is little evidence to indicate that erstwhile Regulators supported the British cause in the American Revolution.

The backcountry of South Carolina was settled somewhat later than that of the Tarheel colony, and its chief grievance was the absence of government rather than the abuses of government that plagued frontier North Carolina. In the 1760's, newcomers flooded into the backcountry, a region suffering from the aftermath of the Cherokee War of 1759-1761. Life in the "up country" (a South Carolina expression), precarious at best, threatened a total breakdown in the face of rising lawlessness and social and economic maladjustment. The parishes of South Carolina, the local units of political and ecclesiastical authority, only theoretically extended to the backcountry. There were, it is true, justices of the peace, but their authority was limited to minor civil cases.

The absence of courts in South Carolina's backcountry meant a visit to Charleston was necessary if one desired to transact any important legal business, and such a visit entailed a week's journey on horseback or two weeks by wagon from distant stations, such as Ninety-six. In 1767, as roving bands of outlaws terrorized the region while Charleston authorities looked the other way, leading citizens, with the support of other respectable persons, formed an association for "regulating" the backcountry. Dedicated to law and order and the protection of property, the Regulators, by 1768, had dealt harshly and effectively with the criminal part of the population. Many honest men, however, felt the Regulators had gone too far by punishing immorality as well as lawlessness.

An anti-Regulator group, the Moderate movement, brought the excesses of the extremist Regulators to an end and restored control of the area to respectable property owners. A direct confrontation between the Regulators and constituted authority in Charleston never took place, partly because Lieutenant Governor William Bull and others in authority recognized the need to bring tranquillity to the interior. In addition, the Commons House of Assembly finally endeavored to solve backcountry problems, providing more legislative representation and establishing schools. These well-intentioned undertakings ran afoul of British policy and the emerging British-American conflict, but passage of the Circuit Court Act of 1769 ended a major grievance by creating four back-

country courts, with full jurisdiction in civil and criminal matters, and provisions for jury trials and the strict regulation of legal fees.

SIGNIFICANCE

Although there were obvious differences, the broad objectives of the two Regulator movements in the Carolinas were the same. Eschewing theoretical political innovations or radical social leveling, the Regulators asked principally for a redress of specific grievances, for government that was just and responsible, and for the political and legal rights to which freeborn Englishmen were everywhere entitled. Despite initial setbacks, the Regulator movements helped bring about better government in the backcountry of the Carolinas. They also gave witness to the growth of a powerful tradition of popular or vigilante justice that has come to characterize the reaction of Americans to real or perceived failures of courts and police to deal with crime.

*—R. Don Higginbotham,
updated by Charles H. O'Brien*

FURTHER READING

Brown, Richard M. *The South Carolina Regulators*. Cambridge, Mass.: Harvard University Press, 1963. A significant monograph contending that the Regulators were upstanding citizens concerned with protecting property rights and restoring order.

Cooper, William J. *The American South: A History*. 2 vols. New York: McGraw-Hill, 1990. Volume 1 offers a useful survey of conditions on the Southern frontier in the eighteenth century.

Dill, Alonzo T. *Governor Tryon and His Palace*. Chapel Hill: University of North Carolina Press, 1955. Readable, informative study of the governor who put down the North Carolina Regulators and his times.

Gipson, Lawrence H. *The Rumbling of the Coming Storm, 1766-1770: The Triumphant Empire*. Vol. 9 in *The British Empire Before the American Revolution*. New York: Alfred A. Knopf, 1965. Devotes two chapters to what the author calls "the struggle for political equality" in the Carolinas.

Johnson, George Lloyd. *The Frontier in the Colonial South: South Carolina Backcountry, 1736-1800*. Westport, Conn.: Greenwood Press, 1997. A history of frontier and pioneer life in the upper Pee Dee region of South Carolina. Chapter 5 examines "The Regulator Movement and the American Revolution."

Kars, Marjoleine. *Breaking Loose Together: The Regulator Rebellion in Pre-Revolutionary North Carolina*. Chapel Hill: University of North Carolina Press,

2002. Kars uses diaries, legal documents, personal accounts of the Regulators, and other materials to explore the rebellion. Includes information on the causes of the conflict and the rebellion's legacy in North Carolina history.

Meriwether, Robert L. *The Expansion of South Carolina, 1729-1765*. Kingsport, Tenn.: Southern, 1940. Meticulous scholarship by a leading authority on South Carolina history.

Powell, William. *North Carolina Through Four Centuries*. Chapel Hill: University of North Carolina Press, 1989. A readable yet scholarly narrative, a third of which is devoted to the colonial period.

Woodmason, Charles. *The Carolina Backcountry on the Eve of the Revolution: The Journal and Other Writings of Charles Woodmason, Anglican Itinerant.* Edited by Richard J. Hooker. Chapel Hill: University of North Carolina Press, 1953. Woodmason, an itinerant Church of England clergyman who sympathized with the Regulators, paints a vivid and sometimes amusing picture of life in their region.

SEE ALSO: Apr. 6, 1712: New York City Slave Revolt; June 20, 1732: Settlement of Georgia; Sept. 19, 1737: Walking Purchase; Sept. 9, 1739: Stono Rebellion; Oct. 5, 1759-Nov. 19, 1761: Cherokee War; Dec. 14 and 27, 1763: Paxton Boys' Massacres; July-Nov., 1794: Whiskey Rebellion.

RELATED ARTICLES in *Great Lives from History: The Eighteenth Century, 1701-1800*: Daniel Boone; James Edward Oglethorpe.

August 25, 1768-February 14, 1779
VOYAGES OF CAPTAIN COOK

Three voyages led by James Cook reliably mapped most of the Pacific Ocean, discovered new island archipelagos, led to the British settlement of Australia and New Zealand, and established Great Britain as a leading trading and maritime nation. Cook was also the first sea captain to use citrus fruits to prevent scurvy among mariners.

LOCALE: Pacific Ocean; England
CATEGORIES: Exploration and discovery; cartography; health and medicine

KEY FIGURES

James Cook (1728-1779), commander of three voyages to explore and map the Pacific
Edward Hawke (1705-1781), first lord of the Admiralty, who appointed Cook to command the *Endeavour*
George III (1738-1820), king of England, r. 1760-1820, who allocated £4,000 to support the *Endeavour*'s voyage
Joseph Banks (1743-1820), English aristocrat and naturalist, who joined the *Endeavour*'s voyage to collect and document new flora and fauna

SUMMARY OF EVENT

By the 1760's the Pacific basin, though visited by several European navigators, remained largely unexplored and unmapped. Hoping to observe an expected transit of Venus across the Sun from the Pacific, the British Royal Society pushed for a new voyage. Both the society and the Crown also wanted information about a vast, undiscovered continent called Terra Australis Incognita (unknown southern land, or Southland) rumored to exist in the southern latitudes, offering the prospect of empire and productive trade.

Lord of the Admiralty Edward Hawke wanted an experienced ship's master to lead the mission. James Cook, who had served as master of a survey ship off the Canadian east coast, was the Royal Navy's surprising choice for commander. He was given the *Endeavour*, a 106-foot, flat-bottomed coal collier rebuilt to carry a crew of ninety-six, scientific equipment, and supplies for at least a year's voyage. George III personally allocated £4,000 for the refitting and supply of the ship. His first voyage was set to begin August 25, 1768.

Cook's first voyage entailed the assignment to observe, from Tahiti, the transit of Venus, but this effort failed. In the meantime, however, Cook's party recorded much about the behaviors and way of life of the indigenous Tahitians. The islanders were more friendly than hostile, although they were inclined to filch mariners' property. Cook's secret orders were to proceed southwest from Tahiti and search for the unknown continent. Failing to find it, he continued to New Zealand, which the Dutch navigator Abel Janszoon Tasman had discovered, but not explored, a century earlier. Cook's expedition was wary of the warlike Maori inhabitants but managed to land, communicate with them, and collect food and biological samples. The *Endeavour* sailed completely around the two large islands and mapped them.

This essentially completed Cook's assigned mission. However, the lure of undiscovered territory was strong. Sailing west, the *Endeavour* landed at Botany Bay, Australia, which Cook named for the many new plant species collected there by Joseph Banks and his colleague Daniel Solander. Turning north, the ship sailed inside the Great Barrier Reef, where unpredictable coral hazards almost wrecked it. At Batavia (now Jakarta, Indonesia), they landed for major repairs. The Dutch trading station was swampy, with malaria and dysentery prevalent. Virtually the whole ship's contingent became sick, and there were several deaths. Cook sailed on across the Indian Ocean as soon as he could, arriving in Britain in July of 1771.

The voyage had achieved all its goals and gathered a huge amount of information about Pacific geography, flora and fauna, and inhabitants and cultures. In addition, Cook's diet regimen of providing sauerkraut and citrus

syrups had enabled the crew to avoid scurvy. His insistence on cleanliness minimized other diseases on board. Cook was promoted to commander and held a short audience with the king, but Banks and his exotic specimens drew the greatest public acclaim.

The Admiralty concurred with the idea of a second voyage. In 1772, Cook set out again, this time to explore the southernmost latitudes of the Pacific. An additional vessel, the *Adventure*, accompanied his ship, the *Resolution*. They sailed south after Cape Town, South Africa, still in search of the elusive unknown continent, although Cook had begun to doubt its existence. For the next four months the *Resolution* battled gales and dodged icebergs, and it lost track of the other ship. After rendezvousing in New Zealand, the expedition sailed due east for two thousand miles, surveying the last temperate stretch of ocean in fruitless search of a continent. A second venture into colder seas followed. The *Resolution* recorded whales and penguins, was trapped among ice-

British explorer and naval officer James Cook is depicted here just before his death at the hands of indigenous Hawaiians, who attacked Cook and his crew in retaliation after a local chief was shot by a crew member. (Hulton Archive/Getty Images)

bergs several times, and crossed the Antarctic circle twice. Cook guessed a large continent stretched beyond, but clearly it bore no resemblance to the fabled, lush Terra Australis Incognita. In fact, he came very close to Antarctica. Crisscrossing a wide area, the expedition then discovered some thirty new islands, including New Caledonia, before exploring the South Atlantic's colder reaches and turning homeward.

Upon his return, Cook was promoted to captain and inducted into the Royal Society. There were plans for a third voyage, this time to explore the North Pacific and look for another rumored phenomenon, the Northwest Passage. However, Cook's health and patience had been battered by the previous voyages. He was not sure he would, or could, lead a third, but when the chance arrived, the adventure proved irresistible to Cook. On July 12, 1776, a refitted *Resolution* and a second ship, the *Discovery*, set out, stopping at New Zealand, Tonga, and Tahiti before heading due north. The next landfall was the Hawaiian island of Maui, previously unknown to Europeans. After naming the islands for the earl of Sandwich, the ships sailed on to the coast of what is now Oregon, along the Pacific Northwest coast of the United States. Amid fog and storm they traveled north, exploring many inlets but finding none that cut far inland. Sailing into the Aleutians, the expedition made contact with Russian fur traders as well as hospitable Aleut Indians. Reluctant to winter in the Arctic, Cook sailed back to Hawaii and anchored there on January 17, 1779.

The landing coincided with the date when Hawaiians expected their god Lono to arrive, bringing peace and prosperity. They welcomed Cook as Lono and feted the entire crew as part of a god's retinue. On February 4, 1779, pleased with the hospitable treatment, the mariners departed. One week out, a storm broke the *Resolution*'s mainmast. There was no choice but to turn back for repairs. This time they were not welcomed. Lono's season was over; it was time for Ku, the king's ancestor god, to take over. This time, Cook was not recognized as a god, however. Hawaiians also felt they could not afford to provide more food to the visitors. The stage was set for tragic misunderstanding.

When Hawaiians stole the *Resolution*'s only large boat, Cook blockaded the harbor. A high-ranking chief, attempting to launch his canoe, was shot. Angry Hawaiians attacked the crewmen. Cook, who had gone ashore to direct a marine retreat, was killed. He had been clubbed, stoned, and stabbed to death. Four marines also were killed. Charles Clerke assumed command, ordered the new mainmast brought on board, and demanded Cook's body be returned. Rather than extract further revenge, Clerke left.

Clerke tried to carry out Cook's plan, but impassable Arctic ice defeated the search for the Northwest Passage. When the ships docked in London in October, 1780, they had been at sea for more than four years. Clerke had died of tuberculosis on the return home. The three voyages had yielded an incredible trove of knowledge and opened Earth's largest ocean to navigation and new settlement.

SIGNIFICANCE

In many ways, James Cook was the first modern explorer. His boundless curiosity, his forbearance when confronted with such extreme customs as cannibalism, and his measured responses to the filching and other minor aggravations from indigenous peoples succeeded where previous explorers' cultural prejudices led them astray. The voluminous journals of the voyages, along with artists' renderings, specimen gathering, and observations recorded by the ships' scientific teams, likewise set a high standard for future expeditions. Not only explorers but also contemporary disciplines such as anthropology have learned from his approaches and discoveries.

Naval customs and navigation practices also benefited from his innovations. The maps produced by his voyages, many of them showing hitherto unknown islands and features, were invaluable to future mariners. Although Royal Navy surgeon James Lind had suggested in 1753 that citrus fruits would prevent scurvy on long voyages, Cook was virtually the first captain to put Lind's theory into practice. His success in keeping his crews healthy proved the theory, so that future generations were spared scurvy's ravages. On his second voyage, Cook tested four chronometers for measuring longitude; one of these, designed by watchmaker Larcum Kendall, gave the first accurate measures of longitude ever taken in the Pacific.

Most significant was Cook's discovery and documentation of so many new land areas. Some, like the Hawaiian Islands and New Caledonia, had been unknown to Europeans. Others, such as Australia and New Zealand, had been sighted, but nothing was known about their size, climate, and other natural features. England was soon to lose many of its North American colonies to American independence, so the discovery of the latter two lands in the temperate zone offered welcome a substitute as places for investment and colonization. Cook is celebrated in these countries with much the same awe that Americans traditionally give to Christopher Columbus.

—Emily Alward

FURTHER READING

Allen, Oliver E. "The Great Ocean's Greatest Explorer." In *The Pacific Navigators*. Alexandria, Va.: Time-Life Books, 1980. A lavishly illustrated account with paintings by the expeditions' artists. A cutaway drawing of the *Endeavour* shows how it was able to hold so many people and supplies.

Blumberg, Rhoda. *The Remarkable Voyages of Captain Cook*. New York: Bradbury Press, 1991. A fact-filled and illuminating book written for young adults. Contains many illustrations, maps, and footnotes.

Bown, Stephen R. *Scurvy: How a Surgeon, a Mariner, and a Gentleman Solved the Greatest Medical Mystery of the Age of Sail*. New York: Thomas Dunne Books, 2004. Recounts how surgeon James Lind's theory about preventing scurvy among mariners was practiced by Cook, saving the lives of countless crew members during long voyages.

Cook, James. *The Journals*. Edited by Philip Edwards. London: Penguin Books, 2000. Captain Cook's journals, indispensable for any serious study of the voyages. This new one-volume abridgment includes helpful added material by the collection's editor.

Salmond, Anne. *The Trial of the Cannibal Dog*. New Haven, Conn.: Yale University Press, 2003. A retelling that emphasizes some of the more exotic adventures and discoveries. Also gives much eighteenth century cultural background and examines shipboard tensions.

Shute, Nancy. "Captain Cook, Anthropologist." *U.S. News and World Report* 136, no. 7 (February 23, 2004): 73. Highlights Cook's objective attitude toward indigenous cultures and questions the recent revisionist view of Cook as an agent of imperialism.

SEE ALSO: Apr. 5, 1722: European Discovery of Easter Island; July, 1728-1769: Russian Voyages to Alaska; 1735: Hadley Describes Atmospheric Circulation; 1752-Mar., 1756: Mayer's Lunar Tables Enable Mariners to Determine Longitude at Sea; Dec. 5, 1766-Mar. 16, 1769: Bougainville Circumnavigates the Globe.

RELATED ARTICLES in *Great Lives from History: The Eighteenth Century, 1701-1800:* Joseph Banks; William Bligh; Louis-Antoine de Bougainville; James Cook; George III; Richard Howe; Sir Alexander Mackenzie; Arthur Phillip; George Rodney; George Vancouver.

October, 1768-January 9, 1792
OTTOMAN WARS WITH RUSSIA

In two hard-fought wars between 1768 and 1792, the Ottoman Empire experienced defeats so decisive that it ceased to be a great power. Russia's rise to power continued, however, as vast new territories were added to its sovereign possessions.

ALSO KNOWN AS: Russo-Turkish Wars

LOCALE: Eastern Europe

CATEGORIES: Wars, uprisings, and civil unrest; expansion and land acquisition

KEY FIGURES

Mustafa III (1717-1774), Ottoman sultan, r. 1757-1774

ʿAbd al-Hamid I (1725-1789), Ottoman sultan, r. 1774-1789

Muhsinzade Mehmed Paşa (1706-1774), Ottoman grand vizier, 1765-1768, 1771-1774

Catherine the Great (1729-1796), Russian empress, r. 1762-1796

Joseph II (1741-1790), king of Germany, r. 1764-1790, and Holy Roman Emperor, r. 1765-1790

SUMMARY OF EVENT

During 1767-1768, Catherine the Great's suppression of the rebellion in Poland led Russian forces to pursue fugitives across the border into Ottoman territory. This incursion constituted a *casus belli* (cause of war). Sultan Mustafa III and his *diwan* (council of state) had long anticipated Russian aggression. Russian agents had been at work in Moldavia, Wallachia, Albania, and Montenegro. In defiance of the Treaty of Belgrade (1739), Russian border-forts were being constructed along the River Bug. The Ottoman government suspected that Russia's dismantling of the Polish-Lithuanian Commonwealth was secretly aimed at removing any buffer between Russian and Ottoman territory in order to facilitate a coming invasion. The Ottoman grand vizier Muhsinzade Mehmed Paşa opposed war on the grounds that the Ottoman forces were unprepared, but he was overruled: In October, 1768, the sultan declared war.

Catherine was eager for military glory. She quickly mobilized armies to strike into Moldavia, to cross the

Perekop Isthmus into the Crimea—whose khan was an Ottoman vassal—to descend the Don to the Sea of Azov, and to invade Mingrelia (Georgia). A new grand vizier, Mehmed Emin Paşa, led an Ottoman army into Moldavia to no purpose, falling back before the Russian advance. With extraordinary rapidity, the Russian commander, Count P. A. Rumyantsev, overran Moldavia, Wallachia, and the Danube forts and was poised to penetrate Bulgaria (1769-1770). When the Ottomans took a stand at Kagul (August 1, 1770), the grand vizier lost one-third of his men in its defense and another third streaming back across the Danube River. He was recalled to Constantinople and executed.

Posing as the protector of Orthodox Ottoman subjects, Catherine sent a fleet into the Mediterranean under the command of Count Aleksey Grigoryevich Orlov. Russian troops landed in the Morea, supposedly to collaborate with local rebels, but former Grand Vizier Muhsinzade Mehmed Paşa expelled them. However, the Russians did better at sea, sinking the Ottoman fleet in Cheshme Bay (June 25-26, 1770), although the Ottomans beat off an invasion of Lesbos.

The year 1771 proved a worse year for the Ottomans. Russian forces ravaged the Crimea from end to end and expelled the Ottoman garrisons in Mingrelia, but the Ottomans held on to Ochakov and Kinburun, at the confluence of the Dnieper and the Bug. By the end of the year, negotiations had begun, first at Fokshani and then at Bucharest. Russia demanded cession of the Crimea, and the sultan and *diwan*, with their backs to the wall, might have agreed had not the *Sheyhülislam* and the *ulema* (the religious establishment) vehemently opposed Muslims being placed under infidel rule. Fear of internal disturbances by these factions compelled the sultan to break off the talks.

Muhsinzade Mehmed Paşa, the savior of the Morea, was brought back as grand vizier in November, 1771. He worked strenuously to reform the military, but Ottoman forces suffered a massive defeat at Kozludjhi (June 20, 1771) at the hands of Aleksandr Vasilyevich Suvorov, and the grand vizier had no alternative but to come to terms. The peace conference assembled at the village of Küçük Kaynarca, Bulgaria.

The Treaty of Kuchuk Kainarji (also known as the Treaty of Küçük Kaynarca; July 21, 1774), one of the most fateful events of Ottoman history, did not involve the territorial losses of Karlowitz, for example, although it might have proved even more punitive but for the fact that Catherine too was feeling the financial drain of continuous campaigning. There was still fallout from the

first partition of Poland in 1772, and Russia was in the midst of Pugachev's Revolt.

By the terms of the treaty, the Khanate of the Crimea became free of outside interference, although the Tatars were independent only in theory, owing practical subservience to the Russian Empire. At the same time, however, the Tatars' religious allegiances continued to focus on the sultan-caliph, constituting the earliest recognition that the latter exercised extraterritorial jurisdiction over Muslims who were not his subjects.

In the Sea of Azov, Russia retained not only Azov itself but also Kerç and Yenikale, giving Russia access to the Black Sea. West of the Crimea, Russia also acquired Kinburun. Thus, the Black Sea was no longer what it had been for centuries, a Muslim lake, but was now open to Russian navigation, with Russian consulates established on its shores. There was also to be a permanent Russian ambassador in Constantinople, a source of much future mischief. Elsewhere, the Russians withdrew from the Mediterranean, Wallachia, Moldavia, Bessarabia, and Mingrelia, but in 1774, the Holy Roman Emperor Joseph II treacherously occupied upper Moldavia (the Bukovina), and the Ottomans had no choice but to confirm its loss.

As for the Christian population of the Principalities of Moldavia and Wallachia, it had given the invading Russians overt assistance, but there were to be no reprisals, and assurance was given that these non-Muslim subjects of the Porte would receive justice at the sultan's hands, with Russia reserving the right to intervene on their behalf, a sinister clause which over time would be extended to all the sultan's Orthodox subjects. Russian subjects, as Orthodox pilgrims, were to have unrestricted access to the shrines of the Holy Land.

Thus, the Treaty of Kuchuk Kainarji, while it did not dismember the Ottoman Empire per se, planted the seeds of its future disintegration in the years to come. For the moment, however, Catherine, her appetite still unsatiated, was content to pause. Mustafa III died in January, 1774, and was succeeded by his brother, 'Abd al-Hamid I, one of the least impressive members of his house.

Between 1774 and 1787, Russian interference in the Crimea led to the last khan's abdication and Russia's formal annexation of the khanate, beginning a ruthless policy of settlement and colonization, as well as Russification. Catherine's dreams of a revived Byzantine Empire, ruled by one of her descendants, were crystallizing in her mind.

Provoked by Russia's cynical disregard for its treaty obligations, the Porte went to war again in 1787. The

This 1787 cartoon portrays Catherine the Great as a "Christian Amazon" battling Sultan ʿAbd al-Hamid I, while Joseph II cowers behind her and Louis XVI and Charles III stand on the side of the sultan. (Library of Congress)

Algerine corsair, Hasan Paşa, who as Kapudan Paşa had introduced significant naval reforms, now took both military and naval forces to Ochakov, from which he planned to retake Kinburun, but his forces were defeated by Suvorov, and his fleet was destroyed (October, 1788). Ochakov was captured by the Russians with immense slaughter (December 17, 1788). Elsewhere, all was not well: Sweden had gone to war with Russia over Finland in June, 1788, and although Joseph II, Catherine's ally, had attacked the Ottomans along the Danube River, his generalship was so appalling that the Austrians were forced to retire in disarray. For a while, the Ottomans reoccupied the Banat, until Joseph abandoned his command. Marshal Loudon, a Seven Years' War veteran, regained the initiative in Bosnia and Serbia, capturing Belgrade, but Joseph died in 1790. The death of the emperor proved a windfall for the Ottomans, as his successor, Leopold II, saw no advantage to further dismembering the Ottoman Empire and made peace at Sistova (August 4, 1791) on the basis of the 1788 frontiers.

The year 1789 proved good for Russia in the field. Bender surrendered on November 3, 1789, and at the end of the following year, Suvorov took the great fortress of Ismāʿīl at the mouth of the Danube River. The road to Constantinople was now open. France, the Ottoman Empire's traditional ally, was locked in the throes of revolution, but Great Britain, hitherto unconcerned at Russia's encroachment on Ottoman territory, now sensed a danger to the balance of power, and Prime Minister William Pitt the Younger formed the Triple Alliance with Prussia and Holland to preserve it. It was partly their pressure that had brought Leopold to Sistova, but further losses were forcing the Ottomans to the negotiating table as well. By the Treaty of Jassy (January 9, 1792), the Russian frontier was extended to the Dniester River. The loss of the lands between the Bug and the Dniester Rivers was humiliating to the Ottomans, but for the time being they were spared further Russian aggression by Catherine's death on November 6, 1796.

SIGNIFICANCE

In the 1750's, the Ottoman Empire was still perceived to be a factor to be reckoned with on the European stage, despite setbacks at Karlowitz (1699), Passarowitz (1718), and Belgrade (1739). The wars with Catherine's Russia revealed, however, that despite its habitual resilience and the occasional heroism of its troops, the Ottoman Empire was a backward, disintegrating regime in need of root-and-branch reform. The fallout from the war of 1787-1792 would arouse Great Britain and, in due course, France to the need to protect the Ottomans from their northern neighbor, culminating in the Crimean War of 1854-1856. Russia may have erred in shifting its attention from the Baltic and its alliance with Prussia to the Black Sea and its Austrian alliance, but there is little doubt that for Catherine, the quintessential despot, her Ottoman triumphs were exhilarating in ways that war with Poland and Sweden were not.

—*Gavin R. G. Hambly*

FURTHER READING

Aksan, Virginia H. *An Ottoman Statesman in War and Peace: Ahmed Resmi Efendi, 1700-1783*. New York: Brill, 1995. Excellent discussion of the 1768-1774 war with Russia.

Itzkowitz, Norman, and Max Mote. *Mubadele: An Ottoman-Russian Exchange of Ambassadors*. Chicago: University of Chicago Press, 1970. A perceptive discussion of Ottoman-Russian diplomacy.

Madariaga, Isabel de. *Russia in the Age of Catherine the Great*. New Haven, Conn.: Yale University Press, 1981. Excellent account of the Russian side of the conflict.

Montefiore, S. S. *Potemkin: Catherine the Great's Imperial Partner*. New York: Vintage, 2005. A massive biography, with detailed accounts of the southern campaigns.

Shaw, Stanford J. *History of the Ottoman Empire and Modern Turkey*. Cambridge, Mass.: Cambridge University Press, 1976. An outstanding account.

SEE ALSO: 1736-1739: Russo-Austrian War Against the Ottoman Empire; Jan., 1756-Feb. 15, 1763: Seven Years' War; Aug. 5, 1772-Oct. 24, 1795: Partitioning of Poland; Sept., 1773-Sept., 1774: Pugachev's Revolt; July 21, 1774: Treaty of Kuchuk Kainarji; 1775-1790: Joseph II's Reforms; 1788-Sept., 1809: Russo-Swedish Wars.

RELATED ARTICLES in *Great Lives from History: The Eighteenth Century, 1701-1800*: Catherine the Great; Joseph II; Mustafa III; Aleksey Grigoryevich Orlov; Grigori Grigoryevich Orlov; Grigori Aleksandrovich Potemkin; Aleksandr Vasilyevich Suvorov.

October 30, 1768
METHODIST CHURCH IS ESTABLISHED IN COLONIAL AMERICA

The Methodist movement became institutionalized in colonial America with the founding of its first influential congregation and meeting house in New York City, the Wesleyan Chapel. Still standing, the chapel is now called the John Street Methodist Church.

LOCALE: New York City, New York
CATEGORIES: Organizations and institutions; religion and theology

KEY FIGURES
John Wesley (1703-1791), leader of the Methodist movement in England
George Whitefield (1714-1770), Anglican preacher whose visit to North America sparked the First Great Awakening
Philip Embury (1728-1773), director of the Methodist Society in New York City
Barbara Heck (1734-1804), Embury's cousin, who encouraged members of the Methodist Society at New York City
Thomas Webb (c. 1724-1796), military captain who joined Embury in leading the Methodist Society in New York City
Francis Asbury (1745-1816), leader of the Methodist Church in colonial America

SUMMARY OF EVENT
The founding of the first Methodist Church in America is rooted in the Methodist revival movement that spread across England after 1740. The movement was centered in the Anglican Church and focused on the notion of assurance of salvation through faith in Jesus Christ. In 1738, an Anglican priest, John Wesley, had a transforming religious experience, which he believed brought such an assurance to him personally.

Soon thereafter, an old friend from Oxford University who shared a similar belief, George Whitefield, asked Wesley to come to Bristol, England. Whitefield wanted Wesley to organize and lead those who believed they also had found this assurance during a revival that had occurred during Whitefield's preaching there. Wesley's work at Bristol initiated the Methodist movement. He organized the new believers into societies, approximately corresponding to church congregations, for teaching, spiritual growth, and religious discipline. Whitefield subsequently traveled to North America, where for several decades he experienced similar results from his preaching in the English colonies.

The Methodist movement spread rapidly from Bristol, taking Wesley to Ireland on a preaching tour during the early 1740's. By 1744, more than fifty thousand persons in Ireland had come under the influence of the Methodist movement. Among these were a group of German refugees from the Palatinate, who had settled in Limerick. One of their number was a carpenter, Philip Embury, who became a Methodist lay preacher (that is, a person authorized by Wesley to preach, but not ordained to offer any church sacraments). Unhappy with their life in Ireland, eight or ten of these refugee families departed for the English colonies in America in 1760. Among the emigrants were Embury, his cousin Barbara Heck, and her new husband, Paul Heck.

Settling in New York City, the immigrants found life difficult and fell into quiet inactivity in their religious life. According to tradition, one evening in October, 1766, Barbara Heck found her brother, her cousin Philip, and some others playing cards and gambling. This was a common amusement of the time, but to some, it was a morally questionable activity. The scene kindled Heck's religious ardor. Collecting the cards from the table into her apron, she disposed of them in the fire and warned the players to repent. She then turned her comments specifically to Philip Embury, urging him to preach "or we shall all go to hell, and God will require our blood at your hands!" At first, he objected that he had neither a place to preach nor a congregation. Soon Heck had gathered a congregation of five persons into Embury's house. These included Barbara and Paul Heck, a hired man named John Lawrence, and a black slave named Betty. Together, these individuals constituted the first Methodist Society in New York City, and apparently the second in the English colonies in America, since perhaps half a year earlier, a group had been formed in Maryland (with neither Wesley's knowledge nor his authorization).

Under Embury's preaching, the small house soon overflowed. The Methodist Society began meeting in a rented storeroom on Barrack Street, near the British military headquarters. Some musicians from the regimental bands began attending the meetings, drawn there by the different style of music they overheard during the Methodists' services. A British military captain, Thomas Webb, was drawn there too. In 1766, there had been tension in New York City over the quartering of British soldiers, resulting in clashes and violence not far from where the Methodists were meeting. When Webb entered the meeting for the first time, he stirred fears of repression similar to those which Methodists had known in England, where soldiers had tried to break up several Methodist societies. However, Webb had fallen under Wesley's influence upon hearing Wesley preach in Bristol in the late 1750's.

Webb began preaching as well, and soon he received a local preacher's license from Wesley. Having returned to America in 1766, Webb announced to the Methodist Society that he was not only a soldier of the Crown but also "a soldier of the cross and a spiritual son of John Wesley." Within a week, Webb was participating in the preaching activity and the leadership of the society. Webb's persuasiveness, and the sheer spectacle of a uniformed military officer preaching with his sword laid across the pulpit, reinforced Embury's preaching ability. Soon the storeroom became too small for the congregation.

In early 1767, the Methodist Society moved to a rigging loft on Williams Street (then called Cart and Horse Street). The new facility provided twenty-four hundred square feet of space, was lit by a large candelabra, and was heated by a corner fireplace. In this location, the congregation continued to grow. After a year, even the loft was becoming cramped, and the group prepared to build a "preaching house." A site on John Street was located, and a fund-raising effort began. Captain Webb gave £30 for the building—a third more than any other gift—and loaned an additional £300 to the effort. He also lobbied support from all parts of the city. Subscriptions to the building fund were made by Anglican clergymen, the mayor, African slaves, and some leading aristocratic families of New York City, including the Livingstons, the Stuyvesants, and the Lispenards.

A carpenter by profession, Embury designed and built the new preaching house, which was called Wesleyan Chapel. The new building, believed by many Methodist historians to be the first Methodist church building in America, was dedicated for religious services on Sunday, October 30, 1768. Because there was also a Methodist Society in Maryland, some Methodist histori-

A wood engraving of Wesley Chapel, the first Methodist church in the United States. The chapel, in New York City, was rebuilt in 1841 and still stands on John Street, its original location. (Library of Congress)

ans have suggested that a log meetinghouse there may actually have predated the building in New York City. Nevertheless, in terms of growth and development of the Methodist movement in America, if not also in physical structures, Wesleyan Chapel in New York City takes priority.

On April 11, 1768, one of the members of the Methodist Society in New York City, Thomas Taylor, wrote Wesley about the congregation's progress. Until this communication, Wesley was apparently unaware of Methodist activities in America, which were being concluded without his authorization. Taylor's goal in writing was primarily to urge Wesley to send authorized assistants to the colony to help further and direct the work there. He believed that while Embury and Webb were doing good work, they lacked the qualifications to develop the church further. Similar requests for assistants were dispatched by Captain Webb to Wesley as well. At

the 1769 Methodist conference in Leeds, Wesley responded to these requests by accepting two volunteers, Richard Boardman and Joseph Pilmoor, who were quickly sent to America. While Pilmoor worked in Philadelphia, Boardman traveled to New York City to work with the congregation meeting in Wesleyan Chapel.

Still not satisfied, Webb continued to urge Wesley to provide more assistants. At the 1771 Methodist conference in Bristol, one of the volunteers chosen to work in America was Francis Asbury. When Asbury arrived in America in late 1771, he made his way to New York City. Within a decade, Asbury had become the unquestioned leader of Methodism in America. Webb later worked in Philadelphia; Heck and her family moved to Canada, as did many other colonists during the American Revolution. Embury died in 1773. Fifty years after the Methodist Church was established in America, the number of Methodists had risen 250 percent.

SIGNIFICANCE

The Methodist Church began as the Holy Club at Oxford in England with brothers John and Charles Wesley and others, who were derisively called "methodists" by their peers because of the group's methodical devotion to worship, prayer, and study. This devotion would find its way to North America.

From his base in northeast colonial America, the church's new leader, Francis Asbury, spread the movement southward and to the frontier. New congregations multiplied yearly, until Methodist churches were to be found in virtually every city and town in the growing United States.

—*Richard A. Bennett*

FURTHER READING

Andrews, Dee E. *The Methodists and Revolutionary America, 1760-1800: The Shaping of an Evangelical Culture.* Princeton, N.J.: Princeton University Press, 2000. Comprehensive account of the origins of American Methodism. Dee places the religion's rise within the context of the American Revolution and social conditions in the Middle Atlantic states, where Methodism was first introduced. He maintains the new religion gained popularity because it was an alternative to the exclusionary politics of the period.

Bucke, Emory Stephens, ed. *The History of American Methodism.* 3 vols. New York: Abingdon Press, 1964. A voluminous scholarly work that covers virtually every aspect of the subject through the 1950's.

Luccock, Halford, and Paul Hutchinson. *The Story of Methodism.* New York: Abingdon-Cokesbury Press, 1949. A popular general survey of the growth of Methodism in both England and America, from Wesley's time to the twentieth century.

McEllhenney, John G., ed. *United Methodism in America: A Compact History.* Nashville, Tenn.: Abingdon Press, 1992. A history of the development of the Methodist Church in the United States. Includes a survey of the expansion and division of American Methodism.

Norwood, Frederick A. *The Story of American Methodism.* Nashville, Tenn.: Abingdon Press, 1974. Focuses on Methodism in the United States, with only limited information about the religion in other parts of the world. Well researched, and with useful footnotes.

Richey, Russell E. *Early American Methodism.* Bloomington: Indiana University Press, 1991. A brief history surveying the development of Methodism in the United States, primarily in the eighteenth and nineteenth centuries. Includes a bibliography.

Wigger, John H. *Taking Heaven by Storm: Methodism and the Rise of Popular Christianity in America.* New York: Oxford University Press, 1998. According to Wigger, there were 1,000 Methodists in the United States in 1770; by 1820, the number had skyrocketed to more than 250,000. The author explains the reasons for the rapid growth and describes how Methodism influenced not only other religions but also American life in general.

SEE ALSO: Aug. 4, 1735: Trial of John Peter Zenger; Dec. 16, 1773: Boston Tea Party; Sept. 17, 1787: U.S. Constitution Is Adopted; July 28-Oct. 16, 1789: Episcopal Church Is Established; 1790's-1830's: Second Great Awakening.

RELATED ARTICLES in *Great Lives from History: The Eighteenth Century, 1701-1800*: Francis Asbury; Charles Wesley; John Wesley; George Whitefield.

December, 1768-January 10, 1773
BRUCE EXPLORES ETHIOPIA

Although James Bruce was not appreciated until the end of his life, his explorations in Ethiopia led to a scientific mapping of much of the Blue Nile. Bruce's numerous naturalistic and scientific observations contributed to the growth of the natural sciences in the eighteenth century.

LOCALE: Kingdom of Ethiopia (now in Ethiopia, Sudan, and Egypt)
CATEGORIES: Exploration and discovery; science and technology

KEY FIGURE
James Bruce (1730-1794), Scottish explorer

SUMMARY OF EVENT

As a youth at the private school at Harrow, England, James Bruce demonstrated a remarkable talent for Latin and Greek. After the death of his first wife, Bruce traveled in Europe for her family's wine business and in his travels learned not only Spanish and Portuguese but also Arabic and Ge'ez, the classical language of Ethiopia, giving him the linguistic tools he needed for his future travels.

Bruce's African experience began when the second earl of Halifax appointed him British consul-general at Algiers in 1763. Bruce left this brutal posting with an assistant, Luigi Balugani, in 1765, and after exhausting explorations around North Africa, they crossed the Mediterranean Sea to Crete in January, 1767. Bruce was stricken with a fever in Crete but recovered and traveled to Beirut six months later. By the next year, he had reached Cairo and began to plan his expedition to Ethiopia.

In December, 1768, Bruce set out upon his journey. He embarked up the Nile from Cairo to the Egyptian port of Kosseir, crossed the Red Sea to the Arabian port of Jidda, and then sailed back across the Red Sea to Massawa, reaching this island gateway to Ethiopia in September, 1769. Bruce planned to make his way into central Ethiopia via the province of Tigré, but first he needed to get permission to leave Massawa from its murderous despot, known as the naybe. Bluffing with the help of letters from several authorities requesting his safe conduct, Bruce finally received the necessary permissions and departed Massawa in mid-November. His actions on the island had made him enemies, however, and he had to foil a plot to murder him by enduring a difficult journey across Mount Tarawa.

Bruce traveled on foot, leading a group of five donkeys and about twenty men, most of them porters who carried his heavy scientific equipment. The expedition's first major layover came in Adowa, the capital of Tigré, where they were hosted by a Greek named Janni, the chief administrator of Michael Suhul, the powerful *ras*, or governor, of Tigré. Bruce soon discovered that civil war was consuming much of Ethiopia, with only Tigré remaining calm, thanks to Ras Michael, who in 1767 had defeated the rebel Galla tribe. Then, in 1769, Ras Michael murdered the king and placed on the throne a decrepit prince named Hannes. Dissatisfied with his puppet, Ras Michael soon poisoned Hannes and replaced him with Hannes's son, Tecla Haimanout, a clever young man who carefully deferred to the *ras*. Made aware of these intrigues, Bruce quickly realized the challenges he faced in a country so chaotic and dangerous.

Bruce's group left Adowa on January 17 and arrived in Gondar, the Ethiopian capital, almost a month later. Of the many accounts that strained his listeners' credibility when he returned home, none were more difficult to accept than an incident he witnessed on this leg of his journey: Three herdsmen driving a cow threw the beast on her side and held her down while cutting two huge steaks from her rump. The flap over the wound was then secured by pins before being poulticed with river clay, and the movable feast was finally driven on to the next banquet site.

Bruce had earned a reputation as a doctor, and in Gondar he was summoned by a nephew of the *iteghé*, or queen, to the town of Koscam, where several of Ras Michael's relatives were ill. Two of the sufferers died before his arrival, but Bruce helped save the others. His success in curing her children won him great favor with Ras Michael's wife, Ozoro Esther, but this favor worked against him when she had the *ras* order the European healer not to leave Koscam.

Ras Michael and King Tecla Haimanout returned in March from campaigning against the Gallas, and the *ras* celebrated his victory by blinding twelve Galla prisoners and sending them off into the fields for hyenas to eat at night. The horrified Bruce saved two of the men and cared for them. Ras Michael conferred two titles on Bruce, allowed him complete freedom in his scientific studies, and overlooked an incident in which Bruce thrashed an insolent military commander. When his companion, Luigi Balugani, died of dysentery, the depressed Bruce despaired of ever being allowed to leave Gondar.

In May, 1770, however, Ras Michael left Gondar to engage a rebel army of Gallas, and Bruce followed him, arriving at the great cataract of the Blue Nile—Tisisat Falls—on May 22. Back in Gondar in June, Bruce witnessed several months of intrigues before traveling to Lake Tsana, where he confronted the Galla leader, Fasil, who assigned seven of his men to accompany him to the village of Geesh. There, on a grassy island, on November 4, 1770, Bruce gazed on the two fountains from which the Blue Nile began its way north to join the White Nile.

In December, 1771, Bruce left Gondar on his way north to Sennaar, following an inland route to Egypt, a journey made dangerous by oppressive heat and villainous chieftains. For example, Sheikh Fidele of Atbara accused Bruce of carrying gold in the chests that contained his scientific instruments, and he detained him for three weeks until a powerful Muslim Ethiopian friend of Bruce named Yasine threatened to destroy Atbara if any harm came to Bruce.

The desert crossing to Sennaar, which Bruce reached on April 29, 1772, was grueling, and temperatures in the city could reach 120 degrees Fahrenheit. Once again, Bruce was detained by a rogue ruler, this time King Ismāʿīl, who insisted he treat several of his ill wives. Virtually held captive, Bruce did not escape Sennaar until September, when he began the awful, seven-hundred-mile desert journey to Cairo. After a mid-October stopover in Shendi, Bruce pushed on to his worst ordeal yet, as sandstorms punished his group and they experienced great discomfort from the blistering days and cool nights. On November 29, twelve weeks after leaving Sennaar, the near-dead travelers collapsed in Aswan, where they drank their fill of the Nile.

On December 11, 1772, Bruce boarded a Nile riverboat, and on January 10, 1773, he disembarked in Cairo, ragged, mustachioed, and unkempt, with two English pistols stuck in one side of his girdle and a crooked knife in the other. The foul water at Sennaar had given him a guinea worm that had burrowed deep into his leg, and before this repulsive five-foot parasite could be extracted it broke off and left a virulent infection that was cured only after thirty-five agonizing days in a Marseilles hospital. Thus ended Bruce's fantastic African adventure.

SIGNIFICANCE

After such a courageous and dangerous penetration into one of the darkest areas of the globe, Bruce was embit-tered by the skepticism of such Londoners as the eminent Samuel Johnson, who had published a translation of the Jesuit missionary Jerome Lobo's account of his 1620's exploration of Ethiopia. Determined to convince his critics, Bruce began in May, 1788, to dictate his story to a secretary named Latrobe. Relying on his copious journals and essays that he had written long before, Bruce finished the job in June, 1789, and in 1790, *Travels to Discover the Source of the Nile* was published.

Travels to Discover the Source of the Nile was an uneven work—eccentrically organized, riddled with slips, stuffed with long, scholarly passages that were tedious to most readers, and embarrassingly overwritten in many places—but still a compulsively readable masterpiece of travel writing. One of Bruce's editors, C. F. Beckingham, explained that "the *Travels* really comprise three books which might well have been published separately, the story of his own travels, a history of Ethiopia from the earliest times to 1769, and a number of essays on very varied topics, such as polygamy, the origin of civilisation, the untruthfulness of Portuguese writers on Ethiopia, and the effect of the Nile on the level of the land in Ethiopia."

Bruce was not the first person to reach the source of the Blue Nile, but he brought back useful drawings of buildings, plants, animals, and birds. He collected seeds, kept meteorological and astronomical records, and purchased copies of valuable manuscripts. He provided other men a powerful stimulus to action, especially in France, where *Travels to Discover the Source of the Nile* was always taken seriously. Alan Moorehead sums up Bruce's influence by calling him the "dominant figure" who gave "direction and force" to the interest in Africa mounting in France. Bruce's death was a sad end to a life of such intense action: Hurrying to say goodbye to a visitor, he fell down the stairs of his home and died before morning. The praise on his tombstone includes these fitting remarks:

> His life was spent in performing
> Useful and splendid actions.
> He explored many distant regions,
> He discovered the source of the nile.
> He traversed the deserts of Nubia.

—Frank Day

FURTHER READING

Bruce, James. *Travels to Discover the Source of the Nile.* Edited by C. F. Beckingham. New York: Horizon

Press, 1964. The original was published in 1790 in five volumes. This is an abridgment of the second edition, Edinburgh, 1804-1805.

Moorehead, Alan. *The Blue Nile.* New York: Harper & Row, 1962. Chapters 2 and 3 summarize Bruce's travels.

Reid, J. M. *Traveller Extraordinary.* New York: W. W. Norton, 1968. Pursues the drama of Bruce's life.

Silverberg, Robert. *Bruce of the Blue Nile.* New York:

Holt, Rinehart and Winston, 1969. Popular account of Bruce's life and adventures.

SEE ALSO: c. 1701: Oman Captures Zanzibar; 1775: Spanish-Algerine War; 1779-1803: Frontier Wars in South Africa.

RELATED ARTICLES in *Great Lives from History: The Eighteenth Century, 1701-1800*: James Bruce; Samuel Johnson; Mentewab; Mungo Park.

December 10, 1768
BRITAIN'S ROYAL ACADEMY OF ARTS IS FOUNDED

Great Britain's first large-scale public display of contemporary artworks by British-born artists, including painters Thomas Gainsborough and Sir Joshua Reynolds, led to the establishment of the Royal Academy of Arts in London, Britain's first national arts academy.

LOCALE: London, England
CATEGORIES: Art; organizations and institutions

KEY FIGURES

Thomas Gainsborough (1727-1788), a major English landscape and portrait painter, who was a founding member of the Royal Academy

Sir Joshua Reynolds (1723-1792), a major English painter, who was a founder and the first president of the Royal Academy

William Hogarth (1697-1764), an English painter, editorial cartoonist, satirist, and printmaker

Francis Hayman (1707/1708-1776), an English painter and theater stage designer

George III (1738-1820), king of England, r. 1760-1820, and patron of the first national academy

SUMMARY OF EVENT

In 1648, the French monarchy had established the Academy of Painting and Sculpture, but Great Britain did not have a national arts academy for the formal or academic training of native artists. Commissions, too, would go to foreign artists. Eighteenth century Britain saw a movement calling for a national art school that would cultivate a native art tradition.

In 1755, Francis Hayman and the renowned artist Sir Joshua Reynolds formed a committee for planning a national art academy to be sponsored by the Crown. However, they were unable to obtain sponsorship by King

George II, who was indifferent to art. The artists approached the Society of Dilettanti, a group of wealthy art connoisseurs, for help with establishing the school and holding public art exhibits. However, the artists would not agree to the Society of Dilettanti's condition that it have total control of the exhibits.

Finally, in 1760, without financial support or royal

Thomas Gainsborough's Mrs. Siddons *(1785).* (Courtesy, National Gallery, London)

approval, the artists held a public exhibition at the Strand, owned by the Society of Arts. This was Britain's first large-scale public art exhibition of contemporary works by native-born artists, featuring 130 works by 69 artists. Although admission was free, 6,582 illustrated catalogs were sold at sixpence each, making a profit. However, the group quarreled and split into two factions: the Free Society of Artists, which stayed at the Strand and eventually folded in 1774, and the more prestigious Society of Artists (whose official name would eventually be the Royal Society for the Encouragement of Arts, Manufactures, and Commerce), which included Reynolds and Thomas Gainsborough.

The Society of Artists made plans to exhibit in a new

Sir Joshua Reynolds's Mrs. Siddons as the Tragic Muse *(1784).* (Courtesy, Huntington Library and Art Gallery, San Marino, California)

space in 1761, with a price of one shilling for a season's ticket. Gainsborough's work was exhibited for the first time in London at this exhibition (he provided a full-length portrait), and William Hogarth provided two engravings for the catalog. King George III, who, unlike his predecessor, was interested in art, had ascended the throne in 1760, and the society—hoping finally to win royal patronage—fired rockets in front of its quarters in honor of the new king's birthday. In 1765 the society received a royal charter and had 211 members. Entrance fees to exhibits provided significant income. However, lack of organization, internal conflicts, and disputes led to the resignations of Reynolds and many other directors in 1768.

In private meetings, William Chambers, the royal architect, and Benjamin West, an American artist living in London, helped persuade the king to support a British royal academy that would compete with its counterpart in France. In November, Reynolds invited Gainsborough to become a founding member of the Royal Academy of Arts. On December 10, 1768, King George III signed the Instrument of Foundation of the Royal Academy, in which the king declared himself the patron and protector of the academy. There would be forty elected members, called royal academicians, consisting of prominent sculptors, architects, and painters. The king would provide spaces for the academy's free art schools and annual exhibitions. Reynolds agreed to be the first president, and the academy established its first quarters at London's Pall Mall.

SIGNIFICANCE

The establishment of the Royal Academy of Arts provided for the first time a valuable place for artists to show their work to a huge audience. The academy also placed Great Britain within the international arts scene. No longer would France dominate painting in Western Europe.

FURTHER READING

Asfour, Amal, and Paul Williamson. *Gainsborough's Vision.* Liverpool, England: Liverpool University Press, 1999. This informative book discusses eighteenth century art and the artist's style and originality. Includes extensive notes, 185 illustrations, a bibliography, and an index.

Doeser, Linda. *The Life and Works of Gainsborough: A Compilation of Works from the Bridgeman Art Library.* New York: Shooting Star Press, 1995. This beautifully illustrated book includes biographical information and detailed explanatory captions with paintings.

Leonard, Jonathan Norton. *The World of Gainsborough, 1727-1788*. New York: Time-Life Books, 1969. This study provides comprehensive biographical information and analyses of Gainsborough's art. Includes illustrations, a chronology of artists, and a bibliography.

Postle, Martin. *Thomas Gainsborough*. Princeton, N.J.: Princeton University Press, 2002. This source discusses the early development of Gainsborough's art, the influence of the Royal Academy, and the artist's thoughts on landscape and portrait painting. Beautifully illustrated with color plates. Includes a chronology, a bibliography, notes, and an index.

Rosenthal, Michael, and Martin Myrone, eds. *Gainsborough: The Painter in Modern Culture*. London: Tate Gallery, 2002. At 272 pages, this catalog accompanying a Tate exhibition shows how Gainsborough's unconventional techniques, theories, and use of color have influenced modern British art. Illustrated (mostly in color).

Vaughan, William. *Gainsborough*. London: Thames & Hudson, 2002. The author uses previously unknown resources to assess Gainsborough's life and career. Includes 172 illustrations, a chronology, and a bibliography.

—*Alice Myers*

SEE ALSO: Aug. 3, 1713: Foundation of the Spanish Academy; c. 1732: Society of Dilettanti Is Established.

RELATED ARTICLES in *Great Lives from History: The Eighteenth Century, 1701-1800:* Thomas Gainsborough; George III; William Hogarth; Sir Joshua Reynolds; Benjamin West.

1769
POMBAL REFORMS THE INQUISITION

The Inquisition in Portugal was transformed from an institution of the Church to secular, state control. It continued its repressive practices, applying them to political opponents of the socioeconomic orthodoxy of the marquês de Pombal's government and its reforms.

LOCALE: Lisbon, Portugal
CATEGORIES: Government and politics; organizations and institutions; religion and theology

KEY FIGURES
Marquês de Pombal (Sebastião José de Carvalho e Mello; 1699-1782), Portuguese prime minister, 1755-1777
Paulo de Carvalho e Mendonça (1702-1770), brother of Pombal, head of the reformed Inquisition, 1769-1770, and cardinal, 1770
Clement XIV (Giovanni Ganganelli; 1705-1774), Roman Catholic pope, 1769-1774

SUMMARY OF EVENT
The Inquisition was a judicial institution of the Roman Catholic Church, established in the late Middle Ages to combat heresy, superstition, and unorthodox thought. It had the authority to jail, torture, and apply the death penalty against those it accused. It acquired a character of fanaticism not unlike modern campaigns against political and religious radicals.

Spanish monarchs obtained papal authorization for the Inquisition in their kingdom as part of their successful campaign during the fifteenth century to drive Muslims and Jews out of Spain. The Inquisition continued in that country as a means of monitoring the fidelity of those who converted from these religions rather than face exile. Observing how the Inquisition augmented Spanish royal authority, the kings of Portugal requested establishment of the religious court in their country as well. By 1547, the Portuguese Inquisition was fully installed.

In Portugal as in Spain, the Inquisition assumed authority for investigating New Christians, individuals who had converted to Catholicism from Judaism. These individuals were often also engaged in the new trades and commerce of Portugal's expanding empire. Thus, the Portuguese Inquisition came to be suspicious of elements who challenged established socioeconomic authority and of new ideas or innovative trends. It thereby became a powerful ally of the vested interests of the landed aristocracy and the traditional merchant class.

The Inquisition was headed by an inquisitor-general, a powerful religious and political office. The inquisitor-general was invariably a cardinal or bishop and on several occasions became regent of the kingdom. The Inquisition constituted a significant bureaucracy within the Portuguese state, with lawyers, prosecutors, judges, clergy, police officials, prison wardens, spies, and clerks.

In the centuries after its founding, it authorized the imprisonment and torture of thousands and the execution of hundreds of people. Executions consisted of public burnings, staged to instill maximum intimidation and loyalty to the established order.

It was not only the Inquisition that repressed Portuguese entrepreneurial initiatives. Portugal was under Spanish royal and commercial control from 1580 to 1640. Over the course of the seventeenth century, its rich, worldwide seaborne empire withered away under attack from the expanding mercantile empires of the Dutch, French, and English. Nevertheless, it held on to its colony of Brazil. During the eighteenth century, the discovery of gold and diamonds in Brazil reinstated Portugal's fortune. An extraordinary amount of this wealth, however, was traded for manufactured goods from Great Britain.

The key economic philosophy of the eighteenth century was mercantilism. One of its main principles held that the wealth of a nation was measured in the amount of gold and silver it held. Nations should be self-sufficient in terms of agriculture and manufactures, maintaining a positive and not a negative trade balance with other nations. In accord with mercantilist practice, Portugal's economy was grossly out of balance. A chief advocate of mercantilism in Portugal was the chief minister of King Joseph I, Sebastião José de Carvalho e Mello. In power for nearly a quarter century, from 1755 to 1777, he was ennobled as the Marquês de Pombal in 1769, and it is by this name that he is known to history.

Pombal understood that Portugal's economic deficiencies were linked to social and cultural inadequacies. The educational system had no curriculum to teach modern philosophy, the natural sciences, or values favoring commerce and entrepreneurship. He saw the cause of this backwardness in two sources: the Jesuit religious order, which controlled secondary and higher education, and the Inquisition, which intimidated those who would express innovative thoughts or new values.

A failed attempt to assassinate King Joseph in 1758 became the springboard whereby Carvalho e Mello addressed his criticism of both these agencies. He implicated Jesuits and reactionary aristocrats in the attempted regicide, and the king declared in 1759 that members of the order were in rebellion against the Crown. During that year and next, the Jesuits' vast properties in Brazil and Portugal were confiscated and they were expelled from Portuguese territories. Their considerable educational institutions were taken over by the royal government, and their curricula were modernized in accord with Carvalho e Mello's Enlightenment objectives.

The expulsion of the Jesuits prompted a dispute with the Papacy, and diplomatic relations between Portugal and the Vatican were suspended from 1760 to 1769. Carvalho e Mello used the decade to place the Catholic Church in Portugal under government control. Central to this objective was secularization of the Inquisition, ending its existence as an independent court system separate from the government. Already in 1768, Carvalho e Mello ended the Inquisition's police powers, incorporating them into a new office of the intendant general of police. The Inquisition's power to censor books was transferred to a Royal Censorship Board, and the distinction between Old and New Christians, which it had had the authority to determine, was abolished.

In 1769, the newly ennobled Pombal made his climactic move against the Inquisition. He ended its financial self-sufficiency, making it dependent on the state to function, by ordering it to transfer the property it confiscated to the state treasury. He abolished its authority to authorize capital punishment, ending its public burning of heretics. Finally, he appointed his brother, Paulo de Carvalho e Mendonça, archbishop of Évora, to be inquisitor general. As a measure of reconciliation between the Vatican and Portugal, Pope Clement XIV elevated Inquisitor General Carvalho e Mendonça to cardinal the following year. However, the Pombaline inquisitor held his new post and elevation only briefly, dying in 1770. The regulations for the Inquisition to follow as a royal court were completed and published by 1774. As an arm of the royal judicial system and with an extensive police, spy, and imprisonment infrastructure, the secularized Inquisition became an effective vehicle for the prosecution of Pombal's political enemies.

SIGNIFICANCE

The Marquês de Pombal's secularization of the Inquisition ended a judicial travesty that was a remnant of the late Middle Ages. Constituted in Portugal not for theological reasons but for political ones, the Inquisition became a vehicle for enforcing established sociocultural thought and practices in general. By the eighteenth century, even its rationale for censorship of books and the determination of purity of Christian descent were debilitated.

Secularization, however, did not end the Inquisition's function as an instrument of suppression; it merely shifted the paradigm of its focus. The sociocultural forces it had suppressed were the ones that Pombal promoted. Those who now opposed his "enlightened" educational program of modern philosophy, the natural sciences, and entrepreneurial values became its new enemies. The contradiction of this development is not puzzling when one considers the many wars waged by imperial powers on lesser peoples for the sake of civilization, culture, or democracy.

Pombal's secularizing reform of the Inquisition encapsulates the contradiction of "enlightened despotism." Advocating action in favor of new thought and rational ideology, it applied ancient methods of repression and violence. Ultimately, Pombal's reforms did end the Inquisition in Portugal. Less than two generations later, with the Napoleonic invasion of the country, the Inquisition was finally abolished in 1808. Who better than Napoleon I, the ultimate dictator of the Enlightenment, to give the *coup de grace* to this remnant of European theocracy?

—*Edward A. Riedinger*

FURTHER READING

Bengt, Ankarloo, and Gustav Henningsen. *Early Modern European Witchcraft: Centres and Peripheries.* Oxford, England: Clarendon Press, 1989. Includes a chapter on the administration of the Inquisition in Portugal.

Burns, E. Bradford. "The Role of Azeredo Coutinho in the Enlightenment of Brazil." *Hispanic American Historical Review* 44, no. 2 (May, 1964): 145-160. Examines the role of the inquisitor appointed by Pombal to develop clerical education in Brazil, who had a leading role in the independence movement.

Duncan, Thomas Bentley. *Pombal and the Suppression of the Portuguese Jesuits: An Inquiry into Causes and Motives.* Unpublished master's thesis. University of Chicago, 1961. Reviews scholarly literature regarding motives, methods, and consequences of Pombal's hostility to the Jesuits.

Maxwell, Kenneth. *Pombal: Paradox of the Enlightenment.* New York: Cambridge University Press, 1995. Most complete account in English of the life and work of Pombal by a noted scholar of Portuguese history. Richly illustrated.

Theileman, Werner. *Século XVIII: Século das luzes, século de Pombal.* Frankfurt, Germany: TFM, 2001. Papers from a recent European conference on Pombal and the Enlightenment.

SEE ALSO: c. 1701: Oman Captures Zanzibar; Sept. 8, 1713: Papal Bull *Unigenitus*; 1750: Treaty of Madrid; Nov. 1, 1755: Great Lisbon Earthquake; Jan. 19, 1759-Aug. 16, 1773: Suppression of the Jesuits.

RELATED ARTICLE in *Great Lives from History: The Eighteenth Century, 1701-1800:* Marquês de Pombal.

July 17, 1769-1824
RISE OF THE CALIFORNIA MISSIONS

Twenty-one Catholic missions, four military installations, and several towns established Spain's claim to Alta, or upper, California, altering the lives of thousands of American Indians.

LOCALE: Alta California (now California)

CATEGORIES: Expansion and land acquisition; colonization; religion and theology; organizations and institutions

KEY FIGURES

José de Gálvez (1720-1787), *visitador general* to New Spain, responsible for the expansion of the Spanish frontier into Alta California

Fermín de Lausen (1736-1803), Junípero Serra's successor as head of the California missions

Gaspar de Portolá (c. 1723-1784), first governor of California

Junípero Serra (1713-1784), Franciscan friar who established the first California missions

SUMMARY OF EVENT

The global Spanish Empire had gradually developed a mission system that suited imperial policy in places as distant from Spain as the Philippines, Paraguay, and Baja California. With a relatively modest investment, the Crown could extend its frontiers and establish opportunities for further expansion later.

Two or three missionaries per location could attract indigenous peoples to a different way of life. The American Indians would learn manual trades, farming, cattle-raising, smithing, tanning, weaving, and other rudimentary skills, so that they could manage the mission on their own. A few soldiers at each mission—never more than ten—enforced discipline. On occasions of serious trouble, appeal could be made to strategically placed presidios that housed sizable, highly mobile military forces capable of putting down any rebellions. When the missions developed enough, a pueblo might be established nearby, able to make use of the growing mission economy without having to follow the often austere mission routine.

The Spanish missionaries, usually members of religious orders (the regular clergy), expected to complete their work in ten years, after which the establishments were to be secularized: The administration of Church affairs would be in the hands of the secular clergy, and all the mission's properties and possessions would be dispersed. Church authorities would receive the church buildings and some surrounding land, and indigenous peoples would receive at least half of all the possessions and land.

For 160 years, missionaries in New Spain sought to evangelize the peoples of the Upper California territories, claimed for Spain by Juan Rodríguez Cabrillo in 1524 and Sebastián Vizcaíno in 1611. Without royal approval, however, ecclesiastical initiatives were not implemented in the Spanish Empire. Even many popes, as well as lowly missionaries, discovered this policy.

In 1741, Danish captain Vitus Jonassen Bering had reached Alaska and claimed much of North America's west coast. Carlos Francisco de Croix became the viceroy of New Spain in 1766. Along with José de Gálvez, *visitador general* of King Charles III, Croix laid plans for a series of missions in Alta California to blunt Russian expansionist plans. Gálvez's plans called for a mission and fort at Monterey Bay in the north. They chose San Diego in the south as the site of the first mission because it was about half the distance from the base in Loreto, Baja California. Gálvez selected Gaspar de Portolá to be governor of California and Father Junípero Serra as president of the missions.

Four foundation parties, two by land and two by sea, set out from Baja for the arduous journey. Most of the sailors died, as did many of those taking part in the overland trek. On July 17, 1769, Serra dedicated the mission of San Diego de Alcalá on a site five miles west of the present mission. Portolá pushed on to Monterey with a small party but left no permanent settlement. That came about the following year, under Serra. Between Serra and his immediate successor, Father Fermín de Lausen, eigh-

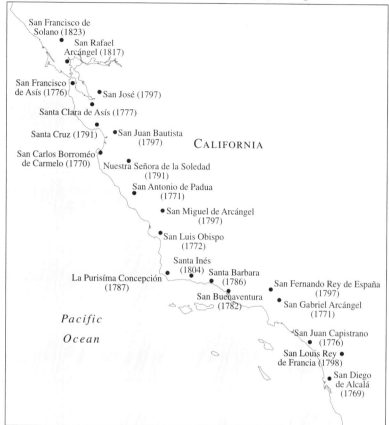

CALIFORNIA MISSIONS, 1769-1823

San Francisco de Solano (1823)
San Rafael Arcángel (1817)
San Francisco de Asís (1776)
San José (1797)
Santa Clara de Asís (1777)
Santa Cruz (1791)
San Juan Bautista (1797)
CALIFORNIA
San Carlos Borroméo de Carmelo (1770)
Nuestra Señora de la Soledad (1791)
San Antonio de Padua (1771)
San Miguel de Arcángel (1797)
San Luis Obispo (1772)
Santa Inés (1804)
Santa Barbara (1786)
La Purisíma Concepción (1787)
San Fernando Rey de España (1797)
San Buenaventura (1782)
San Gabriel Arcángel (1771)
Pacific Ocean
San Juan Capistrano (1776)
San Louis Rey de Francia (1798)
San Diego de Alcalá (1769)

teen of the twenty-one missions were built by 1798.

Economics determined the sequence of building the missions. Largely dependent on shipping for supplies in the earliest years, the missions were first clustered in three areas: south (San Diego), central (Santa Barbara Channel) and north (Monterey). Gradually, the gaps between the missions were closed to lessen their reliance on the vagaries of eighteenth century shipping. In 1776, Juan Bautista de Anza led an arduous overland expedition to San Francisco through the southern deserts, demonstrating that New Spain no longer need rely on the sea to supply California. In all, Spain founded twenty of the missions. After independence, Mexican authorities founded the last of the missions at Sonoma, San Francisco de Solano, dedicated in 1823.

In late eighteenth century California, there were about 130,000 American Indians living in many small bands. The land supported them well in a life that was not much different from the one they had lived five thousand years before. Abundant potable water, fish, and game were within easy reach. Of all the indigenous peoples of what would become the United States, they made the swiftest, most seaworthy boats, without knowing metal trades. Their loosely structured societies lacked a central organization. They had no writing system for their six languages and several dialects. There were no organized wars, although occasional raids to steal goods were not unknown. Shelter was modest, at most.

It quickly became clear to the missionaries that they needed more workers if the missions were to become self-sufficient. They stepped up recruitment of the indigenous peoples as laborers, often luring them with trinkets. The Franciscan missionary plan initially included teaching the native populations in their own languages,

A twentieth century photograph of the bell tower of Mission San Diego de Alcalá, the first of the California missions. The original building was rebuilt in 1808. (Library of Congress)

but the diversity was so extensive that that plan was abandoned, and Spanish was chosen instead to be the *lingua franca* of California.

The missions attracted people from surrounding areas with the promise of better living conditions and some amenities unavailable to those on the outside. If the indigenous converted to Christianity—a condition for remaining within the economic ambit of the mission—they were no longer at liberty to return to their previous way of life, although many did, in fact, escape. American Indians living in the mission were permitted, even encouraged, to visit their families for weeks at a time. This policy proved to be the best recruiting tool the missionaries possessed.

The workers did learn trades, and some even learned to read and write. Daily work usually finished by midmorning, and numerous feast days provided diversion from the normal regimen. By the time of secularization in 1834, approximately thirty thousand American Indians resided at the missions, with only sixty friars and three hundred soldiers along the 650 miles from San Diego to Sonoma. The missions held 230,000 cattle, 34,000 horses, and 268,000 hogs, sheep, and goats.

SIGNIFICANCE

Mission life was far removed from that visited upon the indigenous peoples' ancestors by the savage conquistadores of the sixteenth century. The process of colonization was relatively peaceful, and on balance the indigenous population fared better under the Spanish friars than people in other colonies and received better treatment than they received subsequently in Mexico or in the United States. However, because the mission system destroyed their previous tranquil existence and failed to prepare them for the promised secularization, it cannot escape historical criticism. The California Indians were introduced into an alien culture as little more than slaves; they suffered tragically from European diseases and, in the end, were ill-equipped for any other existence, either that of their own rapidly declining culture or that of the new California.

When Mexico gained independence from Spain, the new government resolved to secularize the missions. When secularization began, American Indians were either tricked into giving up their rights or their rights simply were ignored in the land grab of what had been the missions. Stranded after secularization, many of the Indians at the missions had nowhere else to go, so they stayed on, continuing menial work under new masters. Only in the twentieth century were there some modest advances in their status. The U.S. government gave most of the mission buildings back to the Catholic Church after California entered the Union. Many of the missions have been restored to a romantic, tranquil, even charming condition that belies their troubled history.

—*Daniel A. Brown*

FURTHER READING

Cook, Sherburne Friend. *The Conflict Between the California Indian and White Civilization.* 4 vols. Berkeley: University of California Press, 1943. A scholarly collection that chronicles the troubled history of American Indians during and after the mission period. Rich bibliographies.

Costo, Rupert, and Jeannette Henry Costo, eds. *The Missions of California: A Legacy of Genocide.* San Francisco, Calif.: Indian Historian Press, 1987. A collection that vigorously indicts the evils of the mission system.

Englehardt, Zephyrin. *The Missions and Missionaries of California.* 4 vols. Santa Barbara, Calif.: Mission Santa Barbara, 1929. The monumental standard reference work on the missions, giving an overall positive evaluation of the system.

Font Obrador, Bartolome. *Fr. Junipero Serra: Mallorca, Mexico, Sierra Gorda, Californias.* Palma, Mallorca, Spain: Comissio de Cultura, 1992. A biography of Serra that depends on, but summarizes well, the work of many earlier authors.

Geiger, Maynard J. *The Life and Times of Fray Junipero Serra, OFM.* 2 vols. Washington, D.C.: Academy of American Franciscan History, 1959. A large, sympathetic biography that relies heavily on original sources.

Johnson, Paul C., et al., eds. *The California Missions: A Pictorial History.* Menlo Park, Calif.: Lane, 1985. A colorful, popular, accessible, and reliable work.

Lightfoot, Kent G. *Indians, Missionaries, and Merchants: The Legacy of Colonial Encounters on the California Frontiers.* Berkeley: University of California Press, 2005. Lightfoot compares the treatment of California Indians by the Franciscan missionaries with the treatment of Russian merchants who came to the state in the eighteenth century. An anthropologist, Lightfoot bases his account on oral histories, indigenous texts, archaeological excavations, and other sources.

Sandos, James A. *Converting California: Indians and Franciscans in the Missions.* New Haven, Conn.: Yale University Press, 2004. A history of the missions from the founding of the first mission in 1769 until 1836, when the missions were turned over to the public. Sandos focuses on the religious conflicts between the missionaries and American Indians.

SEE ALSO: Jan. 19, 1759-Aug. 16, 1773: Suppression of the Jesuits; 1776: Foundation of the Viceroyalty of La Plata.

RELATED ARTICLES in *Great Lives from History: The Eighteenth Century, 1701-1800:* Vitus Jonassen Bering; José de Gálvez; Guillaume-Thomas Raynal; Junípero Serra.

September, 1769-1778
SIAMESE-VIETNAMESE WAR

Siamese and Vietnamese leaders fought for control over Cambodia, with each seeking to install their own candidate as Cambodia's new king. The two foreign powers clashed over the issue, until a rebellion in Vietnam forced the Vietnamese army home, leading to a brief peace favoring the Siamese.

LOCALE: Cambodia; southwest Vietnam

CATEGORIES: Wars, uprisings, and civil unrest; diplomacy and international relations; expansion and land acquisition

KEY FIGURES

Mac Thien Tu (d. 1780), governor of Ha Tien, r. 1735-1780

Taksin (1734-1782), king of Siam, r. 1768-1782

Nguyen Phuc Anh (1762-1820), Vietnamese nobleman and later emperor as Gia Long, r. 1802-1820

Ang Non (d. 1779), king of Cambodia, r. 1771, 1773-1779

Rama I (Thong Duang; 1737-1809), king of Siam, r. 1782-1809

SUMMARY OF EVENT

By the mid-eighteenth century, Siam and Vietnam were fiercely contesting their interests in Cambodia, the country lying between them. Siam had once been dominated by Cambodia, but it had since gained in power and now saw itself as the guardian of a dependent Cambodia. To lessen Siam's influence over them in the early seventeenth century, Cambodian kings looked toward Vietnam, which was steadily expanding southward. In 1623, the Cambodian king Chey Chetta II married Ngoc Van, a famously beautiful Vietnamese princess, and invited Vietnamese settlers into southeast Cambodia.

Soon, internal dissent among Cambodia's royal elite allowed Siam and Vietnam to deepen their influence within the country and to gain Cambodian territories in return for siding with rival Cambodian claimants to the throne. While Siam nibbled away at Cambodian lands in the west, the Vietnamese annexed much of the Mekong Delta. In 1679, the Vietnamese Nguyen lords who ruled the south welcomed an army of Chinese refugees who had opposed the new Manchu Qing Dynasty. These Chinese refugees were allowed to settle on the west coast of the new territories, facing the Gulf of Siam. Their northernmost outpost became the town of Ha Tien, right at the border to Cambodia, increasing Siamese-Vietnamese friction. A Cambodian war over royal succession led to the Siamese-Vietnamese clash of 1715, which ended with a Vietnamese victory.

In 1767, the Burmese captured and destroyed the Siamese capital of Ayutthaya, killing the king. Siam remained leaderless, until a military commander called Taksin defeated his enemies and crowned himself king in 1768. The son of a Chinese immigrant and a Siamese mother, Taksin had no noble blood, but his parents had given the boy to a Siamese aristocrat who had adopted him and raised him as a noble. Thus, when Taksin asked the new king of Cambodia, Ang Tong, for tribute, he refused, giving as his reason Taksin's common origin. Taksin sent a punitive force to Cambodia in retribution, but the Cambodians defeated Taksin's army by March of 1769.

The Cambodian king allied himself with Mac Thien Tu, the Vietnamese governor of Ha Tien and son of the late leader of the Chinese refugees who had settled there. In September, 1769, in an attempt to remove Taksin from

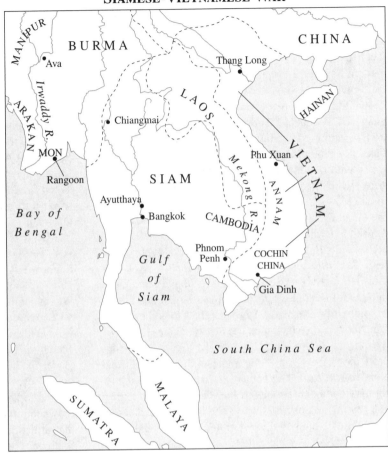

SIAMESE-VIETNAMESE WAR

power, Vietnamese troops led by Mac invaded southeast Siam. Mac attacked the Siamese towns of Trat and Chantaburi on the coast. He was victorious, until a plague broke out in his army, forcing the Vietnamese to retreat from Siam.

In 1771, Taksin launched his own invasion of Cambodia and the Vietnamese territory of Ha Tien. At the end of the autumn rainy season, Taksin sent about ten thousand Siamese soldiers to march overland into Cambodia from its western border with Siam. He embarked another force of ten thousand soldiers on warships sailing to Ha Tien. The Siamese army led by Taksin landed at Ha Tien and attacked the town. Since Vietnamese generals stationed in the Mekong Delta area refused to help Mac against the Siamese invaders, Taksin was able to conquer and destroy Ha Tien. He then moved up to meet his second army at the Cambodian capital of Phnom Penh.

At Phnom Penh, Taksin deposed Ang Tong and placed Ang Non on the Cambodian throne. A former

Cambodian prince, Ang Non had escaped a plot to kill him by fleeing to Siam. He had then been caught in the burning of Ayutthaya but managed to escape, becoming Taksin's friend in the process. Ang Tong, meanwhile, fled to the southern Vietnamese city of Gia Dinh (next to modern Saigon). He appealed for Vietnamese aid, and the Nguyen lords who ruled the south promised it to him.

In 1772, the Vietnamese counterattacked against the Siamese forces in Cambodia. Ten thousand Vietnamese troops supported by thirty galleys were sent against Taksin in Phnom Penh. Taksin burned the city and escaped with five hundred men to Ha Tien. His northern army, which had come by land, was also repulsed and forced to retreat. The Vietnamese reinstalled Ang Tong as king of Cambodia, but Ang Non fled with Taksin and refused to relinquish his claim to the throne.

In 1773, afraid for his life, Ang Tong tried to negotiate with Taksin to end Siamese support for his rival, but Taksin refused. Ang Tong retired to a small island in the middle of the Tonle Sap, Cambodia's large inland lake. In southern Vietnam, the Tay Son rebels took the city of Qui Nhon, from which many of the Vietnamese soldiers fighting the Siamese had come. As the Vietnamese withdrew their army, Ang Tong abdicated in favor of Ang Non. To save face, Ang Tong insisted he acted out of pity for his Cambodian people, to save them from prolonged war, but historians insist it was the lack of Vietnamese troops protecting him that prompted him to step down.

As Ang Non was reinstalled as king of Cambodia, Mac Thien Tu negotiated a temporary end to hostilities with Taksin. In turn, Taksin withdrew his Siamese soldiers from Ha Tien. An uneasy armistice settled over the land. During the next few years, Tay Son revolts in southern Vietnam prevented the Vietnamese from engaging the Siamese, who controlled Cambodia through Ang Non. In early 1777, only Nguyen Phuc Anh survived and escaped when the Tay Son captured Gia Dinh and killed all other members of the Nguyen lords' family. In the fall of 1777, however, Nguyen Anh recaptured Gia Dinh.

Nguyen Anh realized that internal Vietnamese stability was more important, for the moment, than control of Cambodia. Thus, to enable himself to focus his attention on the rebels threatening him, he sent a mission to Siam. In 1778, Nguyen Anh offered Siam a treaty of friendship that formally ended the war.

SIGNIFICANCE

Because of the Tay Son Rebellion, the Vietnamese temporarily abandoned their anti-Siamese Cambodian policy. They agreed to a peace that left Siam in a dominant position in Southeast Asia. The conflict, however, would continue.

With a favorable peace in Cambodia, Taksin turned to Laos. He conquered Vientiane in a military campaign from November, 1778, to April, 1779. This campaign led the Vietnamese under Nguyen Anh to send soldiers into Cambodia to depose the hated "Siamese puppet" Ang Non. In 1779, Vietnamese and Cambodian troops captured Ang Non, drowned him in the Bassac River, and killed his sons. The Vietnamese installed the boy Ang Em, son of Ang Tong, as king. In 1780, the Vietnamese formally annexed the territory of Ha Tien when Mac Thien Tu died. With this addition to its territory, Vietnam reached its present shape and capped its southward extension.

Meanwhile, in response to quarrels over a Siamese vessel at Ha Tien in early 1780, Vietnamese living in the Siamese city of Thonburi were massacred in November, 1780. Taksin sent an army into Cambodia that captured Phnom Penh, shattering the Siamese-Vietnamese peace. Vietnamese interests were saved, however, when Taksin went mad and was forced to abdicate by popular revolt in March, 1782. Learning of these events at home, the leader of the Siamese army in Cambodia concluded a quick peace with Nguyen Anh and returned to Siam. There, he had Taksin beheaded on April 7, 1782, and crowned himself King Rama I. He founded the dynasty that still ruled Siam in the early twenty-first century. Siam once again controlled Cambodia.

In 1784, Rama I lent Nguyen Anh twenty thousand Siamese soldiers and two to three hundred warships to recapture Gia Dinh from the Vietnamese rebels. Many contemporary Vietnamese historians, who favor the Tay Son for their assumed revolutionary qualities, consider this to have represented a Siamese invasion of Vietnam. Indeed, the Siamese soldiers of Nguyen Anh behaved like conquerors, looting and plundering Vietnamese towns as they advanced.

Many Vietnamese historians see their ambush on the eve of the Tet festival on January 19, 1785, as an important national victory over Siam. Only two to three thousand Siamese soldiers survived to flee home. Never again did Nguyen Anh accept Siamese troops.

The friendship of Rama I and Nguyen Anh continued, however, and it kept Vietnamese-Siamese relations cordial for the remainder of the eighteenth century. Nguyen Anh even acknowledged Rama I as a vassal and sent him symbolic gifts from 1788 until 1801. He stopped this practice when he became the emperor Gia Long after his final victory in 1802.

Early in the nineteenth century, a unified Vietnam gradually wrested Cambodia from Siamese influence. After another Cambodian war of succession, Vietnam installed its choice of king and a military garrison at Phnom Penh in 1813. Until the French made Cambodia their protectorate in 1863, Vietnam rather than Siam dominated Cambodia.

—*R. C. Lutz*

FURTHER READING

Chandler, David. *A History of Cambodia*. 2d ed. Boulder, Colo.: Westview Press, 1992. Briefly discusses the detrimental impact of the war for Cambodia in the section "Vietnamese and Thai Interference in Cambodia." Illustrated, maps, notes, bibliography, index.

Chapuis, Oscar. *A History of Vietnam*. Westport, Conn.: Greenwood Press, 1995. Briefly mentions the event in the context of Vietnamese land acquisition from Cambodia. Maps, bibliography, index.

Hall, Daniel George. *A History of Southeast Asia*. 4th ed. London: Macmillan Press, 1981. Still a standard work on the period. Chapters 24-25 and 27 cover events from Vietnamese, Cambodian, and Siamese points of view. Illustrations, maps, bibliography and index.

Terwiel, B.J. *A History of Modern Thailand, 1767-1942*. St. Lucia, N.Y.: University of Queensland Press, 1983. Strong focus on Taksin and Rama I; places the war in the context of Siamese history. Maps, notes.

Wyatt, David K., ed. *Studies in Thai History*. Reprint. Chiang Mai, Thailand: Silkworm Books, 1996. Collection of scholarly articles, some of which discuss leadership of Taksin and Rama I. Tables, footnotes.

SEE ALSO: 1704-1757: Javanese Wars of Succession; Jan. 24, 1744-Aug. 31, 1829: Dagohoy Rebellion in the Philippines; 1752-1760: Alaungpaya Unites Burma; 1771-1802: Vietnamese Civil Wars.

RELATED ARTICLES in *Great Lives from History: The Eighteenth Century, 1701-1800*: Nguyen Hue; Taksin.

October 23, 1769
CUGNOT DEMONSTRATES HIS STEAM-POWERED ROAD CARRIAGE

Cugnot invented a vehicle powered by steam called the steam dray. This three-wheeled carriage, the first of the so-called "horseless carriages," could pull up to four tons at a speed of two and one-half miles per hour.

LOCALE: Paris, France
CATEGORIES: Inventions; science and technology

KEY FIGURES
Nicolas-Joseph Cugnot (1725-1804), French inventor
Louis XV (1710-1774), king of France, r. 1715-1774

SUMMARY OF EVENT

Before the advent of mechanical means of land transportation such as automobiles, the adage that "an army moves on its stomach" was doubly true: Commanders needed to worry about feeding not only their men but their horses and pack animals as well. Nicolas-Joseph Cugnot, a child of farmers from the small village of Void, knew how much food domesticated animals could consume, and he conceived of a vehicle, powered by steam rather than animal locomotion, that could revolutionize warfare. The vehicle Cugnot conceived was a mere transport, not a tank or other mechanized weapon, but it was no less revolutionary on that account.

As a child, Cugnot attended school in Void and then in nearby Toul, where he showed great talent in mathematics and physics. This skill led him to enroll, when he was sixteen, in the École Royale du Génie, a school of military engineering about one hundred miles west of Toul. After graduating, Cugnot entered the French army as an officer in the artillery corps. Sent to Vienna when the duke of Lorraine, Francis III, was crowned Emperor Francis I of Austria, Cugnot benefited greatly by his introduction to the German-speaking world. While on post, Cugnot read *Theatrum machinarum* (1724) by German engineer Jakob Leupold, which described all the steam machines invented thus far. Introduced to the mechanical structure of steam engines, he was intrigued by the potential of such a novel source of power. Cugnot was later sent to Brussels, where he was assigned to fortification design. Wrestling with the mechanical problems involved in constructing artillery defenses and maximizing the effective use of cannon through flexible emplacement, Cugnot began to consider the possibility of using steam power to move immensely heavy weapons quickly to new positions.

In 1763, at the age of thirty-eight, Cugnot was discharged from the army. Awarded a six-hundred-franc annual pension in recognition of his invention of a new cavalry musket, he was secure from penury but certainly not wealthy. Taking advantage of his financial security, Cugnot immediately moved to Paris, where he began work on the design of a military vehicle powered by a steam machine. Needing more funds than his pension could supply, he contacted Général de Gribeauval, his superior officer in Vienna and now the inspector general of the French army. Impressed with the plans and small-scale prototype that Cugnot presented, Gribeaunal successfully guided Cugnot's project through the mazes of royal bureaucracy, gaining the support of the Marquis de Monteynard, the minister of war, and the financial support of King Louis XV.

Cugnot's first working prototype took almost six years to develop, making its debut before General Gribeaval and other high-ranking French officers in Paris on October 23, 1769. Called a *fardier à vapeur* by its inventor (and a "locomotive" by the English press that reported on it),

the machine was not a complete success. Though it moved a short distance under its own power, it needed to stop frequently to allow more steam pressure to build inside the boiler. Nevertheless, the concept had proved to be workable, and Cugnot continued development.

On April 22, 1770, the *fardier*, which had become a "steam dray" in English, was presented officially to King Louis XV and his court. The improved version was able to move at a speed of about four kilometers (two and one-half miles) per hour. It had three wheels, one in the front, which was used for steering, and two in the back. The boiler and steam engine were positioned at the front of the machine; behind the narrow driver's seat, a platform had been built on which to transport equipment. When demonstrated to the king, the smoking behemoth carried the incredible weight of four tons of equipment. Still, the problems of maintaining steam had not been satisfactorily resolved.

Nicolas-Joseph Cugnot's steam-powered carriage. (North Wind Picture Archives)

The *fardier* needed to stop every ten to twelve minutes to build up enough steam pressure to continue. Worse, it lacked any efficient way to replenish the boiler's supply of water, requiring a difficult and time-consuming process for resupply. Safety was another concern; the machine lacked both a safety valve and a pressure gauge. In fact, during a later trial, the machine malfunctioned, hit a wall, and was destroyed in the first automobile accident in recorded history.

Even with its limitations, however, the *fardier* showed considerable promise. The development of more reliable and efficient steam engines would resolve many of it's most pressing problems. Cugnot was awarded £22,000 to continue development, building a second model powered by an improved, two-cylinder steam engine. By mid-November, the new machine was ready for trial and performed admirably, pulling a two-and-one-half-ton payload from the military arsenal in the suburbs of Paris to Vincénnes at the respectable rate of two kilometers per hour. New trials were scheduled for the summer of 1771, but Cugnot's supporters fell from power, replaced by conservatives who failed to see the potential of steam power. Cugnot's invention was abandoned, his funding stopped, and his steam machine barely avoided destruction twice during the French Revolution in 1787 and 1797. Napoleon Bonaparte was apparently interested in renewing development, but Cugnot's advancing age and Bonaparte's campaign in Egypt were obstacles that could not be overcome. Although Bonaparte granted Cugnot a pension of £4,000 per year, the project was never completed. Nicolas-Joseph Cugnot died in Paris on October 2, 1804.

SIGNIFICANCE

Cugnot was among the first engineers to recognize the great potential of self-powered vehicles. While the size and weight of steam engines made them impractical for personal use, their application to military transport seemed a realistic goal. Hampered mainly by the technical limitations of steam technology at the time, Cugnot was a pragmatic engineer who persevered in developing his *fardier à vapeur* into a workable machine. Although ultimately his project was ended by superiors who lacked his vision, his mechanical accomplishment stands as the pioneering work that foreshadowed the great revolutions in power and transportation of the nineteenth century. His dream became an everyday reality in the locomotives that ran on the world's railways, the great steam tractors that transformed agriculture, and, as the twentieth century dawned, the steam-powered automobiles that competed (in many ways, successfully) with the internal combustion engine. Cugnot's second *fardier* has survived and is presently on display at the Musée des Arts et Métiers in Paris.

—*Denyse Lemaire and David Kasserman*

FURTHER READING

Burness, Tad. *Ultimate Auto Album: An Illustrated History of the Automobile*. Iola, Wis.: Krause, 2001. This is an excellent book that retraces the evolution of the automobile through time.

Eckermann, Erik, and Peter L. Albrecht. *World History of the Automobile*. Warrendale, Pa.: Society of Automotive Engineers, 2001. This book offers an extensive history the development of the automobile throughout the world.

Sutcliffe, Andrea. *Steam: The Untold Story of America's First Great Invention*. New York: Palgrave Macmillan, 2004. This book traces the development of steam power and its transformational effects in the United States.

SEE ALSO: 1705-1712: Newcomen Develops the Steam Engine; 1765-1769: Watt Develops a More Effective Steam Engine; Sept. 6-7, 1776: First Test of a Submarine in Warfare; Apr., 1785: Cartwright Patents the Steam-Powered Loom; 1790: First Steam Rolling Mill.

RELATED ARTICLES in *Great Lives from History: The Eighteenth Century, 1701-1800*: Louis XV; Maria Theresa; Thomas Newcomen; James Watt.

1770
PUBLICATION OF HOLBACH'S *THE SYSTEM OF NATURE*

Holbach's The System of Nature *argued that the source of human misery was an ignorance of nature that was both perpetrated and perpetuated by religion and its superstitious beliefs. The treatise was written to provide a framework of true understanding underpinned by the material mechanisms of nature.*

LOCALE: Paris, France
CATEGORIES: Philosophy; education

KEY FIGURES
Paul-Henri-Dietrich d'Holbach (1723-1789), German-
    born French philosopher
Denis Diderot (1713-1784), French encyclopedist
Claude-Adrien Helvétius (1715-1771), French
    philosopher
Julien Offroy de La Mettrie (1709-1751), French
    philosopher and encyclopedist

SUMMARY OF EVENT
Paul-Henri-Dietrich d'Holbach published *Système de la nature: Ou, Des lois du monde physique et du monde moral* (1770; *The System of Nature*, 1797) in 1770 under the pseudonym Mirabaud. The book turned out to be the first, and possibly the only, example of a comprehensive, unmitigated defense of atheistic materialism during the rationalist period called the Enlightenment.

The System of Nature was the culmination of a trend in contemporary ideas already expressed to varying degrees in Julien Offroy de La Mettrie's *L'Homme machine* (1747; *Man a Machine*, 1750; also known as *L'Homme Machine: A Study in the Origins of an Idea*, 1960), Denis Diderot's *Lettre sur les aveugles* (1749; *An Essay on Blindness*, 1750), and Claude-Adrien Helvétius's *De l'esprit* (1758; *De l'esprit: Or, Essays on the Mind and Its Several Faculties*, 1759). Holbach's work caused considerable consternation in France, not only in the ecclesiastical establishment but also among the French Deistic philosophes who shared many ideas and ideals with Holbach himself. *The System of Nature* was suppressed by judicial decree and brought out a torrent of denunciations, both from proponents of the Enlightenment and from those who participated in the antirationalist movement to save tradition and religion known as the Counter-Enlightenment.

The System of Nature belongs to the third and final phase of Holbach's intellectual career. The first phase began in 1749 with Holbach settling in Paris, where he associated himself with philosophes such as Étienne Bonnot de Condillac, Charles-Georges Le Roy, Jacques-André Naigeon, Jean-Jacques Rousseau, and Jean-François de Saint-Lambert. Among them, Holbach had the closest personal and philosophical ties with Diderot. The philosophes were working on the *Encyclopédie: Ou, Dictionnaire raisonné des sciences, des arts, et des métiers* (1751-1772; partial translation *Selected Essays from the Encyclopedy*, 1772; complete translation *Encyclopedia*, 1965), a project that epitomized the new rationalism of prerevolutionary France.

For more than thirty years, Holbach's *salon* was the main social center of the philosophes and a unique clearinghouse for radical ideas and an intellectual headquarters for the encyclopedists. Holbach contributed about four hundred articles dealing with chemistry, metallurgy, mineralogy, and geology to the *Encyclopedia*. His interests in those sciences inevitably informed his philosophical outlook, since his materialism dovetailed with the methodology and scope of a rigorously scientific explanation of natural phenomena. In particular, from Holbach's standpoint, geology's new evidence concerning the Earth's history undermined the doctrine of creation and also the existence of God.

Consequently, the second phase of Holbach's intellectual career was marked by an uncompromising confrontation with religion and, in particular, the Catholic Church. The works that he published between 1760 and 1770 espoused the following beliefs: The concept and cult of God stemmed from the ignorant terror of primitive humans seeking to soothe nature's destructive forces; religious beliefs have been sustained through superstition; religious history is a catalog of senseless disputes, intolerance, prejudice, persecution, and crime; the Church has exploited the gullibility of the masses for its own profit; religions have invariably supported tyrannical regimes to advance their own ambitions of domination; scriptural evidence does not withstand historical and factual objectivity tests; and theological dogmas are a maze of myths and mystifications on which no rational, just, or useful social institution can be based.

The System of Nature heralded the last phase of Holbach's intellectual progress. It indicated a more philosophical and theoretical approach to the issues with which Holbach was grappling. The treatise attempted to show that humans are entirely products of nature and subject to the laws governing the physical universe—

which itself constituted the totality of reality. The soul, or spiritual substance, was an illusion; the moral and intellectual attributes of the individual were simply the operations of his or her organic machine. Since sensibility was a primary function of the animal organism, all higher faculties were derived ultimately from the different forms that sensation took. The only means of knowing humans in nature was through the empirical and rational investigation of matter.

For Holbach, then, nature was the sum of matter and motion. All matter was actually or latently in motion, and the material universe was self-created and eternal. All change in nature represented a communication of motion, a redistribution of energy, which modified the corresponding combination or disposition of material particles, elements, or aggregates. The specific forms that nature exhibited, from terrestrial flora and fauna to heavenly bodies, were forever changing. Humanity was no exception: the ephemeral life of the species depended on the stability of its physical environment.

For Holbach, there was neither chance nor disorder in nature: all was necessity and order, an irreversible chain of causes and effects. Freedom was objectively meaningless when applied to human behavior, which, through temperament, education, and environment, manifested the universal determinism of nature. Vice and virtue did not depend on free will; the terms simply designated behaviors helping or hindering the mutual happiness of society and the individual.

Contemporaries of Holbach found these ideas quite disturbing, and there was a huge backlash against *The System of Nature*. The French Catholic Church threatened the Crown with a withdrawal of financial support unless it effectively suppressed the circulation of the book, which was condemned by the Parlement of Paris and publicly burned. Nicolas-Sylvestre Bergier, the eminent Catholic theologian of the time, wrote a critique entitled *Examen du matérialisme: Ou, Réfutation du "Système de la nature"* (1771; examination of materialism: or, refutation of *The System of Nature*), and Voltaire

---

HOLBACH ON ORDER AND NECESSITY

Arguably the single most important influence on eighteenth century philosophy was Sir Isaac Newton's description of a universe governed by rational, immutable laws of nature. Like other Enlightenment thinkers, Paul-Henri-Dietrich d'Holbach attempted in The System of Nature *to determine the relationship of human actions to those laws. In the passage here, he asserts that all human actions are determined by the same kinds of laws that determine the motion of physical objects.*

How then can it be too often repeated, that relatively to the great whole, all the motion of beings, all their modes of action, can never be but in order, that is to say, are always conformable to Nature; that in all the stages through which beings are obliged to pass, they invariably act after a mode necessarily subordinate to the universal whole? To say more, each individual being always acts in order; all its actions, the whole system of its motion, are the necessary consequence of its peculiar mode of existence; whether that be momentary or durable. Order, in political society, is the effect of a necessary series of ideas, of wills, of actions, in those who compose it; whose movements are regulated in a manner, either calculated to maintain its indivisibility, or to hasten its dissolution. Man constituted, or modified, in the manner we term virtuous, acts necessarily in that mode, from whence results the welfare of his associates: the man we stile wicked, acts necessarily in that mode, from whence springs the misery of his fellows: his Nature, being essentially different, he must necessarily act after a different mode: his individual order is at variance, but his relative order is complete: it is equally the essence of the one, to promote happiness, as it is of the other to induce misery.

Source: M. de Mirabaud [Paul-Henri-Dietrich d'Holbach], *The System of Nature: Or, The Laws of the Moral and Physical World.* Project Gutenberg. http://www.gutenberg.org/etext/8909. Accessed November 15, 2005.

---

rebuked Holbach in the article "God" in his *Dictionnaire philosophique portatif* (1764; enlarged 1769 as *La Raison par alphabet*; also known as *Dictionnaire philosophique: A Philosophical Dictionary for the Pocket*, 1765; also as *Philosophical Dictionary*, 1945, enlarged 1962). Frederick the Great of Prussia also published a refutation.

Despite certain shortcomings, however, Holbach's ideas are still of considerable interest. His critique of Christianity led toward the objective and psychological study of religion as a distinctively human invention, and *The System of Nature* remains a classic text in the development of atheistic materialism. Some see it as the philosophical expression par excellence of modern science.

SIGNIFICANCE

The System of Nature has undoubtedly immortalized Holbach. Its fame, or infamy, depending upon one's outlook, rests on the fact that for the first time in the European intellectual tradition, all the available arguments for materialism and atheism emerged from their earlier clandestine contexts and were given public exposure. Not only did the book challenge traditional religion, it also attacked the various forms of Deism or natural religion that were greatly in vogue at the time as expressions of religion in harmony with the Enlightenment. Holbach argued that both reason and experience lead to the conclusion that nature as a whole was an eternal, infinite being. It was made up of basic material elements, ceaselessly rearranged and subject in all its operations to strictly deterministic laws. Even the existence of life was merely the product of the working of mechanical natural forces. There was no such thing as free will, but scientific inquiry could discover the methods by which human beings could be "caused" to become useful and well-adjusted members of society.

The ideas of *The System of Nature* turned out to be so radical for the eighteenth century European intellectual milieu that even some of the eminent intellectual figures of the Enlightenment—such as Voltaire, Rousseau, and Frederick the Great—joined Christian thinkers and apologists in the refutation and rejection of Holbach's groundbreaking thoughts. However, Holbach's systematically secular philosophical perspective exerted enormous influence on subsequent intellectual movements, not only in Europe but also in America. Advocates and adherents of diverse and sometimes diametrically opposite schools of thought, such as secular humanism, Marxism, utilitarianism, liberalism, and behaviorism, can all legitimately claim Holbach and *The System of Nature* as powerful precursors. In the history of ideas, *The System of Nature* is one of the most prominent texts in the drive to remove the supernatural from the world and to naturalize nature.

—*Majid Amini*

FURTHER READING

Becker, Carl Lotus. *The Heavenly City of the Eighteenth Century Philosophers*. New Haven, Conn.: Yale University Press, 2003. First published in 1932, this work voices the dissenting view that though Enlightenment thinkers like Holbach managed to destroy the old St. Augustine's City of God, their new City of Man was only a reassemblage of the wreckage of the old one.

Brown, Stuart, ed. *British Empiricism and the Enlightenment*. Vol. 5 in *Routledge History of Philosophy*. New York: Routledge, 1995. A collection of philosophical articles on European Enlightenment figures, including Holbach, from the late seventeenth century to the eighteenth century.

Cragg, G. R. *The Church and the Age of Reason, 1648-1789*. New York: Atheneum, 1961. An account of the relationship between the religious establishment and the growing number of antireligious Enlightenment thinkers like Holbach.

Cushing, Max Pearson. *Baron D'Holbach: A Study of Eighteenth Century Radicalism in France*. Reprint. Whitefish, Man.: Kessinger, 2004. A detailed examination of Holbach's thoughts.

Holbach, Paul-Henri-Dietrich d'. *System of Nature*. Manchester, England: Clinamen Press, 2000. A modernized English translation of Holbach's *Système de la nature*, with a new introduction.

Kors, Alan Charles. *D'Holbach's Coterie: An Enlightenment in Paris*. Princeton, N.J.: Princeton University Press, 1976. A detailed historical account and philosophical demarcation of Holbach's intellectual circle.

Manuel, F. E. *The Eighteenth Century Confronts the Gods*. Cambridge, Mass.: Harvard University Press, 1959. A study of the rise of antitheological philosophy in the eighteenth century and Holbach's legacy of an atheistic political philosophy in the French Revolution.

Topazio, Virgil W. *D'Holbach's Moral Philosophy: Its Background and Development*. Geneva, Switzerland: Institut et Musée Voltaire, 1956. An examination of Holbach's attempt to divest ethics from religion and how to naturalize morality.

Wickwar, W. H. *Baron d'Holbach: A Prelude to the French Revolution*. Reprint. London: Allen & Unwin, 1968. Still the only full-length biography of Holbach.

SEE ALSO: 1721-1750: Early Enlightenment in France; 1726-1729: Voltaire Advances Enlightenment Thought in Europe; 1743-1744: D'Alembert Develops His Axioms of Motion; 1748: Montesquieu Publishes *The Spirit of the Laws*; 1749-1789: First Comprehensive Examination of the Natural World; 1751: Maupertuis Provides Evidence of "Hereditary Particles"; 1751-1772: Diderot Publishes the *Encyclopedia*; 1754: Condillac Defends Sensationalist Theory; July 27, 1758: Helvétius Publishes *De l'esprit*; Jan., 1759: Voltaire Satirizes Optimism in *Candide*; Apr., 1762: Rousseau Publishes *The Social Contract*; July, 1764: Voltaire Publishes *A Philosophical Dictionary for the Pocket*; 1782-1798: Publication of Rousseau's *Confessions*.

RELATED ARTICLES in *Great Lives from History: The Eighteenth Century, 1701-1800*: Étienne Bonnot de Condillac; Denis Diderot; Frederick the Great; Claude-Adrien Helvétius; Paul-Henri-Dietrich d'Holbach; Jean-Jacques Rousseau.

March 5, 1770
BOSTON MASSACRE

British soldiers in Boston fired into an unruly crowd, killing several colonists. The incident arose out of American colonists' fear and distrust of British standing armies in their midst and epitomized the growing colonial unrest of the early 1770's.

LOCALE: Boston, Massachusetts (now in the United States)

CATEGORIES: Wars, uprisings, and civil unrest; colonization

KEY FIGURES

Crispus Attucks (1723-1770),

James Caldwell (d. 1770),

Patrick Carr (d. 1770),

Samuel Gray (d. 1770), and

Samuel Maverick (c. 1753-1770), casualties of the Boston Massacre

Thomas Preston (fl. 1770), officer of the main guard at Boston

First Earl of Hillsborough (Wills Hill; 1718-1793), British secretary of state for the colonies, 1768-1772

Thomas Gage (1721-1787), British commander in chief in North America, 1763-1773

John Adams (1735-1826), colonial American lawyer and later president of the United States, 1797-1801

SUMMARY OF EVENT

On the night of March 5, 1770, a small crowd gathered around a soldier at the guard post in front of the Customs House at Boston, accusing him of striking a boy who had made disparaging remarks about a British officer. John Adams depicted the hecklers as "a motley rabble of saucy boys, negroes and mulattoes, Irish teagues and outlandish Jack tars." The sentinel's call for aid brought eight men from the Twenty-ninth Regiment and Captain Thomas Preston, officer of the day. The crowd increased, especially after someone rang the bell in the old Brick Meeting House; men and boys hurled snowballs and pieces of ice at the crimson-coated regulars and, with cries of "lobster," "bloody-back," and "coward," taunted them to retaliate.

The crowd's hostility stemmed from more than this particular incident; it rested on a series of occurrences between the Bostonians and the military during the seventeen months that the troops had been garrisoned in the city. If possible, the townspeople had expressed even more antipathy for the Customs Commissioners, who that very evening gazed uneasily from the windows of the Customs House on the scene before them in King Street. They were the real source of the trouble; their cries for protection had brought troops to Boston in the first place.

The Americans were right about the role of the commissioners, but their version of what transpired shortly after nine o'clock on the night of March 5 is highly questionable. Captain Preston probably did not order his nervous troops to fire into the angry throng, but fire they did after one of their number was clubbed on the head. Three

A Paul Revere engraving of the Boston Massacre of 1770. (R. S. Peale and J. A. Hill)

Americans died instantly, two a short time later, and six more received wounds.

"Boston Massacre" may have been a misnomer, the result of extreme harassment of the redcoats, and triggered, according to John Adams, by an unprincipled mulatto, Crispus Attucks, "to whose mad behavior, in all probability, the dreadful carnage of that night is chiefly to be ascribed." Attucks was among the casualties that night, as were James Caldwell, Patrick Carr, Samuel Gray, and Samuel Maverick.

Attucks, son of an African American father and a Massachuset Indian mother, was the first casualty of the Boston Massacre of March 5, 1770, the first death in the cause of the American Revolution. Attucks's father was a black slave in a Framington, Massachusetts, household until about 1750, when he escaped and became a sailor. Crispus's mother lived in an Indian mission at Natick. Attucks was known around Boston as one of the Sons of Liberty's most aggressive agitators. When the British claimed that he had provoked their soldiers, they may have been right. Attucks and Paul Revere were among the earliest Sons of Liberty, a clandestine society that agitated against the British by engaging in acts of propaganda and creative political mischief. The Sons of Liberty tormented Tories and their supporters, often stripping, tarring, and feathering tax collectors, then walking free at the hands of sympathetic colonial juries. They later would form the nucleus of a revolutionary armed force, but in the early years, their main business was what a later generation would call "guerrilla theater."

Americans elsewhere wondered whether their respective colonies would be the next to have a standing army in their midst, an army seemingly intent on destroying their liberties, not only by its presence but also by the use of fire and sword. At the time, however, Massachusetts had been singled out ostensibly because of the Customs Commissioners' appeal for protection. Undoubtedly, another consideration made the decision to comply an easy one for London politicians: the Massachusetts Bay Colony, with its spirited opposition to the Stamp Act (1765) and the Townshend Revenue Act (1767), had long been viewed as a hotbed of sedition.

The conduct of His Majesty's revenue collectors had incited colonial opposition. They were considered by many to be "customs racketeers," a lecherous band who played fast and loose with the complicated provisions of the Sugar Act (1764) in order to win, in vice-admiralty courts, judgments that lined their own pockets. This was substantially the opinion of New Hampshire's Governor Benning Wentworth, and the British commander in chief

in North America, General Thomas Gage, admitted almost as much to the secretary of state for the colonies, the first earl of Hillsborough. Nevertheless, Hillsborough ordered the general to dispatch regulars to the Massachusetts capital.

Gage's troops met no resistance when they landed on October 1, 1768. Despite the obvious displeasure of the populace, reflected in the town fathers' reluctance to aid in securing quarters for the soldiers (soon increased by two additional regiments), there followed months of relative calm with no mob activity against either the redcoats or the customs collectors. Lord Hillsborough, however, was determined to deal harshly with Massachusetts, and had he been able to impose his will, Parliament would have wrought changes to equal or surpass in severity the Coercive Acts of 1774.

Because of troubles in Ireland, threats from France and Spain, and the colonial boycott of British goods in protest against the Townshend duties, the government rejected Hillsborough's schemes and eventually repealed all the Townshend taxes except the one on tea.

An illustration in the Boston Gazette and Country Journal *of March 12, 1770, depicting four coffins with the initials of four of the five men killed in the Boston Massacre.* (Library of Congress)

The employment of troops against civilians was ticklish business to George III and Englishmen in general, calling forth memories of Stuart days. The logical step was to remove all the troops, but two regiments remained in Boston.

Serious tension began to build in the late summer and fall of 1769, when Bostonians believed that the redcoats were becoming permanent residents. The soldiers were subjected to every form of legal harassment by local magistrates, to say nothing of mounting acts of violence against the men in uniform. The redcoats in the ranks, like all European soldiers of their day, were hardly of the highest character, often recruited from the slums and the gin mills, and stories of theft, assault, and rape being committed by the regulars were not without considerable foundation. The culmination, foreseen by the army and townspeople alike, was the Boston Massacre.

SIGNIFICANCE

After the massacre, the last regiments of British regulars were finally pulled out of the city of Boston, leaving behind a legacy of fear and suspicion that was revived every succeeding March 5. "Massacre Day," as it was called, was commemorated by the tolling of bells and a patriot address that stressed the danger of standing armies. These armies, as the direct representatives of the power of the home country over the colonies, contributed greatly to the feelings of oppression that led to the Revolutionary War. Tension in Boston rose again in 1773, due to another act of political mischief by the Sons of Liberty, who remembered the victims of the Boston Massacre at the Boston Tea Party. In 1888, a monument to Attucks was erected at the Boston Common.

—R. Don Higginbotham,
updated by Bruce E. Johansen

FURTHER READING

Alden, John R. *General Gage in America*. Baton Rouge: Louisiana State University Press, 1948. The redcoats in Boston are treated with sympathy and fairness by Alden in his two chapters relevant to the subject.

Beer, George L. *British Colonial Policy, 1754-1765*. New York: Macmillan, 1907. Contains information about military affairs, including the once-traditional interpretation of why redcoats remained in the colonies after 1763.

Boston (Mass.) City Council. *A Memorial of Crispus Attucks, . . . from the City of Boston*. Miami, Fla:

Mnemosyne, 1969. A remembrance of the Boston Massacre lauding the sacrifices of its victims.

Dershowitz, Alan. *America on Trial: Inside the Legal Battles That Transformed Our Nation*. New York: Warner Books, 2004. Provides brief accounts of major trials during the past three hundred years, including a description of the Boston Massacre trials.

Griffith, Samuel B., II. *The War for American Independence: From 1760 to the Surrender at Yorktown in 1781*. Urbana: University of Illinois Press, 2002. This history of the American Revolution, first published in 1776 under another name, describes the causes and conditions that led colonists to rebel against the British. Chapter 5 includes a brief description of the Boston Massacre.

Hansen, Harry. *The Boston Massacre: An Episode of Dissent and Violence*. New York: Hastings House, 1970. A comprehensive account of the event and its context. One of several works on the massacre published for its bicentennial.

Miller, John C. *Sam Adams: Pioneer in Propaganda*. Boston: Little, Brown, 1936. Stresses the role of Adams as a manipulator and agitator, whose talents helped, indirectly at least, lead to the bloodshed in King Street.

Young, Alfred E. *The Shoemaker and the Tea Party: Memory and the American Revolution*. Boston: Beacon Press, 1999. Young explores how memory preserves history by examining the life of George Robert Twelves Hewes, a shoemaker who participated in the Boston Tea Party. Includes Hewes's recollections of the Boston Massacre.

Zobel, Hiller B. *The Boston Massacre*. New York: W. W. Norton, 1970. A comprehensive treatment of the event and its political and economic context.

SEE ALSO: Mar. 22, 1765-Mar. 18, 1766: Stamp Act Crisis; June 29, 1767-Apr. 12, 1770: Townshend Crisis; 1768-May 16, 1771: Carolina Regulator Movements; Dec. 16, 1773: Boston Tea Party; Apr. 27-Oct. 10, 1774: Lord Dunmore's War; Sept. 5-Oct. 26, 1774: First Continental Congress; Apr. 19, 1775-Oct. 19, 1781: American Revolutionary War.

RELATED ARTICLES in *Great Lives from History: The Eighteenth Century, 1701-1800*: John Adams; Samuel Adams; Thomas Gage; John Hancock; Paul Revere.

1770's

1771
WOULFE DISCOVERS PICRIC ACID

Peter Woulfe obtained a solution of picric acid by the action of nitric acid on indigo. The first artificial dye, the substance transformed the textile industry, but its more significant use was as an explosive, adding significant new weapons to the military arsenals of the late eighteenth century.

LOCALE: London, England

CATEGORIES: Chemistry; science and technology; manufacturing; wars, uprisings, and civil unrest

KEY FIGURES

Peter Woulfe (1727-1803), Irish alchemist
Jean-Baptiste-André Dumas (1800-1884), French chemist
Auguste Laurent (1807-1853), French chemist

SUMMARY OF EVENT

As the Industrial Revolution gained momentum, chemical experimentation began to yield discoveries that benefited industry. Peter Woulfe was an experimenter and a believer in alchemy. By modern standards, he had little fundamental understanding of his results. Nevertheless, he made a number of interesting observations and gained enough respect from the scientific community that he was made a fellow of the Royal Society in 1767.

Woulfe had become interested in nitric acid (possibly through his friendship with Joseph Priestley) and tested its effects on a number of substances, including indigo. Indigo was an important dye derived from a plant and used for centuries for its blue color. At this time, the textile industry was almost entirely dependent on natural products for dyes, including indigo, madder, cochineal, woad, and a few others. Some of the natural dyes exhibited color changes when subjected to acid treatment: Thus, Johannes Barth in 1744 treated indigo with sulfuric acid and obtained a blue dye.

Possibly these considerations inspired Woulfe to treat indigo with nitric acid. In any case, he did so and obtained a yellow solution, noting that this solution imparted a yellow color to wool or silk. This discovery is often cited as the first synthesis of an artificial dye, even though Woulfe started with a natural product, because the application of the acid changed the color of the original substance. (There is some reason to believe that potassium picrate may have been present in a potion called "tincturianitri Glauberi" made by Johannes Glauber in 1647, but details are hazy.)

Picric acid is a yellow solid, melting at 122 degrees Celsius, and is strongly acidic. Its solutions can be used to dye wool and cotton and were used for this purpose until the advances in coal tar dyes provided better yellow colors. The explosive properties of picric acid were noted by several investigators in the late eighteenth century, and it was recognized as an acid. Slowly, its relationship to other chemicals began to emerge. In addition, picric acid was found to result from the action of nitric acid on silk and other materials. It was noted that indigo was probably converted first to aniline by the nitric acid, and that the aniline was converted to picric acid in a second step. Countless chemists over the years have experienced yellow stains on their fingers after working with nitric acid. This color change has been suggested as a test for proteins and is called the xanthoproteic reaction. Probably the color is due to picric acid or related nitro compounds formed from amino acids in proteins of the skin when attacked by nitric acid.

Woulfe's discovery attracted the interest of other scientists, particularly in France, where his experiments would be repeated by (among others) the nineteenth century chemist Jean-Baptiste-André Dumas, who originated the name "picric acid," based on the Greek *pikros*, meaning bitter. Dumas also completed an elemental analysis of picric acid and determined its empirical formula. In 1841, Auguste Laurent found that picric acid could easily be made by nitration of phenol (a coal tar derivative) using nitric and sulfuric acids. This became the modern method for synthesizing the chemical.

The eighteenth century investigators noted that picric acid decomposed suddenly when heated above its melting point. The decomposition was what might today be described as a deflagration rather than an explosion, unless the heating was rapid. In 1873, Hermann Sprengel showed that picric acid in combination with other substances could be detonated by a blasting cap. By 1880, it was understood that picric acid was a powerful explosive, and moves were made to make it useful in warfare. For centuries, black powder (sulfur, charcoal, and potassium nitrate) had been the only military explosive. Picric acid was much more powerful than black powder and began to find use as a bursting charge in mines, grenades, and artillery shells. It was used in the Boer War, the Russian-Japanese War, and World War I.

Picric acid is slightly more powerful than TNT (trinitrotoluene), but it suffers from two disadvantages: As a strong acid, it is corrosive to metals, such as those forming shell casings, and its melting point is too high to enable it to be conveniently melted and poured into place as TNT is poured. Moreover, the metal picrates that are formed by corrosion of shell casings are extremely shock sensitive, leading to the strong possibility of accidental detonations. Ammonium picrate is an exception. Although a powerful explosive when detonated, it is relatively insensitive to mechanical shock and is valued as a bursting charge in armor piercing shells. These useful properties of ammonium picrate were discovered and explored at the Frankford Arsenal near Philadelphia, Pennsylvania, early in the twentieth century.

SIGNIFICANCE

The use of picric acid as a textile dye decreased after the discovery of the coal tar dyes, but its use continues in histology, where it finds application as a counter stain and fixative, and in the demonstration of hemoglobin. Misguided attempts were made to use it in beer as a substitute for hops, until it was found to be quite toxic. As a derivative of phenol, the bactericidal properties of which are well known, picric acid was also found to kill bacteria and has been used in salves for the treatment of burns. It exerts a pain-relieving effect by paralyzing the nerve endings in the skin.

Picric acid was manufactured in a number of countries as an explosive and was used by itself or in combination with various additives. In England, picric acid was mixed with petroleum jelly to make an explosive called lyddite, named for the village of Lydd in Suffolk. The French had another formulation known as mèlinite, while the Japanese called their version shimose. Picric acid was produced in large quantities in the United States during World War I by several manufacturers, including E. I. DuPont de Nemours. However, in the later stages of World War I, picric acid was beginning to be replaced by TNT. Other explosives, such as nitrocellulose ("gun cotton") and nitroglycerin, were discovered in the 1840's and became the materials of choice for commercial blasting (dynamite) and propellants for bullets (smokeless powder, cordite, and so on). Some picric acid was still being used by the Japanese in World War II.

—*John R. Phillips*

FURTHER READING

Beilsteins Handbuch Der Organischen Chemie (Beilstein's handbook of organic chemistry). 4th ed. Vol. 6. Berlin: Julius Springer, 1923. Provides a historical account of picric acid, with references to the researches of Dumas, Welter, and others.

Brown, G. I. *The Big Bang: A History of Explosives.* Stroud, Gloucestershire, England: Sutton, 1998. Contains a short account of the use of picric acid munitions in warfare from 1885 to 1918.

Meyer, R., J. Koehler, and A. Homburg. *Explosives*, 5th ed. Weinheim: Wiley-VCH, 2002. Technical details are given for the properties of many explosives, including picric acid and its derivatives.

Sprengel, H. "On a New Class of Explosives Which Are Non-Explosive During Their Manufacture, Storage, and Transport." *Journal of the Chemistry Society* 26 (1873). Picric acid is shown to detonate when set off by a cap. A fundamental discussion is given of the explosion process and its relationship to the chemical composition of the explosives.

Urbanski, T. *The Chemistry and Technology of Explosives.* Oxford, England: Pergamon, 1964. Methods of manufacture of picric acid and other explosives are discussed.

Van Gelder, A. P., and H. Schlatter. *History of the Explosives Industry in America.* New York: Arno Press, 1972. Discusses the research on picric acid derivatives for use in artillery shells, and the manufacture of picric acid in the United States.

Woulfe, Peter. "Experiments to Show the Nature of Aurum Mosaicum." *Philosophical Transactions of the Royal Society* 61 (1771): 114. The experiments with nitric acid and indigo are reported here along with many unrelated matters.

1770'S

1771-1802
VIETNAMESE CIVIL WARS

Three brothers who started the Tay Son Rebellion in the south of Vietnam ended a centuries-long system of divided feudal rule of the country, overthrew the Le Dynasty, and defeated a Chinese invasion before their forces were destroyed by a survivor of the southern lords who unified Vietnam as Emperor Gia Long.

LOCALE: Vietnam

CATEGORIES: Wars, uprisings, and civil unrest; government and politics

KEY FIGURES

Nguyen Hue (c. 1752-1792), rebel leader and self-proclaimed emperor of Vietnam as Quang Trung, r. 1788-1792

Nguyen Phuc Anh (1762-1820), Vietnamese nobleman and later emperor of Vietnam as Gia Long, r. 1802-1820

Nguyen Nhac (1743-1793), rebel leader and self-proclaimed emperor of central Vietnam as Thai Duc, r. 1778-1793

Pierre-Joseph-Georges Pigneau de Béhaine (1741-1799), bishop of Adran, 1770-1799

Nguyen Lu (1754-1788), Vietnamese rebel leader

Le Man De (d. 1793), last Le emperor of Vietnam, r. 1787-1788

SUMMARY OF EVENT

By 1771, when the Tay Son Rebellion broke out, Vietnam was divided between two ruling aristocracies, and the emperor was a mere figurehead. After fifty years of civil warfare in the seventeenth century, the Trinh lords in the north and the Nguyen lords ruling the south had observed an uneasy peace since 1673. In early 1771, however, three brothers from the central Vietnamese village of Tay Son took to the hills as outlaws and quickly gathered support from peasants, merchants, and social outcasts for what became known as the Tay Son Rebellion. On their father's side, the rebel brothers were descendants of Chinese immigrants. Their mother was Vietnamese, possibly with Cham blood. They took the last name of Nguyen, although they were not related to the ruling family.

The Tay Son Rebellion gathered strength, especially since Nguyen rule had become unpopular for its increasing taxation. In 1773, Nguyen Nhac captured the coastal town of Qui Nhon with a trick, pretending to surrender.

In the north, meanwhile, the Trinh launched an attack on the Nguyen under the pretext of fighting the Tay Son in 1774.

Early in 1775, the Trinh army conquered the Nguyen capital of Phu Xuan (modern Hue), and the Nguyen court fled to Gia Dinh (next to modern Saigon). The Tay Son found themselves caught between two feudal armies. Nguyen Nhac chose an alliance with the Trinh, while Nguyen Lu raided Gia Dinh. By March, 1776, Nguyen Nhac proclaimed himself king of Tay Son in the ruins of the old Champa capital of Vijaya, near Qui Nhon.

In 1777, the Tay Son brothers Hue and Lu attacked and conquered Gia Dinh. They killed most of the ruling family, but the dead ruler's nephew, Nguyen Phuc Anh, escaped. Close to Cambodia, Anh was rescued by Pierre-Joseph-Georges Pigneau de Béhaine, the bishop of Adran, who ran a seminary there. Pigneau developed a lifelong friendship with Anh. Thus, when the Tay Son brothers left Gia Dinh late in 1777, Nguyen Phuc Anh retook it. At Qui Nhon, meanwhile, Nguyen Nhac declared himself Emperor Thai Duc of central Vietnam.

Nguyen Phuc Anh proclaimed himself king of the south in 1780 and befriended Rama I of Siam in 1781. In the next two years, he lost and regained Gia Dinh before a strong counterattack with seaborne elephant regiments and incendiary rockets sent him fleeing to Siam in 1783. While Pigneau went to France seeking help for his friend Anh, Rama I gave Anh an army of about twenty thousand Thai soldiers and two to three hundred warships, which he landed in the Mekong Delta late in 1784. After initial victories, Anh lost control over his Thai army. On January 19, 1785, Nguyen Hue ambushed and decisively defeated it: Only two to three thousand soldiers escaped alive. Anh himself fled to Bangkok.

In 1786, famine struck the Trinh lands. Nguyen Nhac ordered Hue to take Phu Xuan, and the city fell in June. Defeated and captured, Trinh Khai committed suicide days before Nguyen Hue entered Thang Long (modern Hanoi) on July 21, 1786. Hue was made a duke and married the Le emperor's twenty-first daughter, Ngoc Han, on July 26. A few days later, the old emperor died and was succeeded by his grandson Le Man De.

In August, Nguyen Nhac arrived and ordered his brother to leave Thang Long for his new capital Phu Xuan. In early 1787, a Tay Son general accepted the abdication of a last Trinh lord, who went into a monastery. Also in 1787, the Tay Son brothers divided their territory. Nguyen Nhac ruled as central emperor, Hue held the lands north of Da Nang, and Lu ruled the south. Nguyen Phuc Anh was unwilling to let their rule go unchallenged, however. In August, 1787, he landed in southern Vietnam. In Paris on November 28, 1787, Pigneau cosigned the Treaty of Versailles between France and Cochin China. In return for aid, France was promised Vietnamese land and commercial privileges.

On September 1, 1788, Anh captured Gia Dinh, and Lu fled north, where he died. As the French government did not fulfill its obligations, the Treaty of Versailles was canceled, and Pigneau organized a private army to help Anh. In the North, Emperor Le Man De fled to China for protection. Under the influence of General Sun Shiyi, the Qianlong Emperor assembled an army of 200,000 Chinese troops. In November, 1788, General Sun's army invaded Vietnam, and the Tay Son forces melted away. On December 17, General Sun entered Thang Long. He put Le Man De back on the throne and treated him as puppet. Taking murderous revenge on court ladies and officials who had collaborated with the Tay Son, Le Man De alienated the Vietnamese. Enjoying an affair with Le Man De's mother, General Sun did not pursue the Tay Son.

Nguyen Hue turned the conflict into a war of national liberation. At a hilltop altar by his capital of Phu Xuan, he proclaimed himself Emperor Quang Trung on December 22, 1788. Four days later, he gave a nationalist speech to 100,000 of his soldiers. Quang Trung decided on a preemptive strike during the Tet holidays. He led his army north, and on January 25, 1789, overran the first Le outpost. On January 28, the first Chinese fort surrendered. A day later, Quang Trung assaulted the capital. Commanding from atop an elephant, he utterly defeated the Chinese. General Sun fled at night to China, joined by the Le emperor.

On January 30, 1789, Quang Trung entered Thang Long. He negotiated a peace with the Qianlong Emperor, who recognized his rule in return for tribute. Quang Trung returned to Phu Xuan. Yet Nguyen Phuc Anh continued his fight. On September 16, 1792, Quang Trung died. His ten-year-old son became Emperor Canh Thinh. In 1793, Nguyen Phuc Anh captured Qui Nhon. Canh Thinh's uncle retook it but refused to give it back to Nguyen Nhac, who died of rage.

Internal dissent weakened the Tay Son. In July, 1799, Nguyen Phuc Anh's forces captured Qui Nhon again, where Pigneau died on October 9. In 1800, the Tay Son sent an army and a navy to retake Qui Nhon by siege. In February, 1801, Nguyen Anh's fleet destroyed the enemy navy. On June 15, he captured Phu Xuan. Even though Qui Nhon fell to the Tay Son in September, 1801, they failed to retake Phu Xuan. Their counterattack was shattered in March, 1802, and they fled north.

On June 1, 1802, Nguyen Anh celebrated his victory at Phu Xuan. He opened the era as Emperor Gia Long, combining the names of the southern and northern capitals. Entering Thang Long on July 20, 1802, he cruelly executed captured Tay Son leaders, including Canh Thinh. Thus, the civil war of the eighteenth century ended at the beginning of the nineteenth century with a unified Vietnam. In 1803, China officially recognized Gia Long as emperor.

SIGNIFICANCE

After hundreds of years of stable—if contested—feudal divisions, Vietnam was shaken by the Tay Son Rebellion. Historians still debate the causes of this rebellion. Contemporary sources state that Nguyen Nhac was a tax collector who embezzled public funds for his gambling habit and became a rebel to avoid prosecution. Marxist Vietnamese historians see the Tay Son Rebellion as a peasant uprising and discount the latter version of events as feudalist propaganda. A third view holds that the revolt began as a local, anti-Vietnamese uprising. They state that Nguyen Nhac used ancient Cham legends, such as his early claim to have a sacred sword, and worshiped fire like the Chams. His second wife, an elephant tamer, was from the Bahnar tribe, strengthening his local ties.

Regardless of the causes, the Tay Son almost managed to conquer all of Vietnam. Nguyen Hue was a brilliant military leader who twice defeated foreign invasions, in 1784 and 1789, safeguarding Vietnam's independence. However, he could never destroy Nguyen Phuc Anh. Seeking support of the French, the Siamese, and any Vietnamese who resented the Tay Son in a struggle lasting twenty-seven years, Nguyen Phuc Anh ultimately triumphed. As Gia Long, he consolidated a unified Vietnam that would soon exert its power over Cambodia. Until the French colonial push in the later nineteenth century, Vietnam enjoyed unity, strength, and peace. The Nguyen Dynasty founded by Gia Long would be Vietnam's last, lasting to the final abdication of emperor Bao Dai in 1954.

—*R. C. Lutz*

FURTHER READING

Chapuis, Oscar. *A History of Vietnam*. Westport, Conn.: Greenwood Press, 1995. Discusses the event in great detail, especially in Chapter 6, "The Nguyen Hue Epic." Maps, bibliography, index.

1770's

Hall, Daniel George. *A History of Southeast Asia*. 4th ed. London: Macmillan Press, 1981. Still a standard work on the period. Chapter 24 thoroughly covers the war. Illustrations, maps, bibliography, and index.

Karnow, Stanley. *Vietnam: A History*. 2d ed. New York: Viking Press, 1997. Still the most widely available source in English. Chapter 3 covers the event, highlighting French involvement. Photos, chronology, index.

Li, Tana. *Nguyen Cochinchina*. Ithaca, N.Y.: Cornell University Press, 1998. Detailed study of southern

Vietnam of the period. Strongly advocates that the Tay Son Rebellion was a local rather than social uprising. The last chapter analyzes the forces behind its outbreak. Maps, notes, annexes.

SEE ALSO: 1704-1757: Javanese Wars of Succession; Jan. 24, 1744-Aug. 31, 1829: Dagohoy Rebellion in the Philippines; 1752-1760: Alaungpaya Unites Burma; Sept., 1769-1778: Siamese-Vietnamese War.

RELATED ARTICLES in *Great Lives from History: The Eighteenth Century, 1701-1800*: Nguyen Hue; Qianlong; Taksin.

August 5, 1772-October 24, 1795
PARTITIONING OF POLAND

Poland was partitioned, partly annexed, and finally completely absorbed by the more powerful states surrounding it. After the third partition, the nation of Poland no longer existed, as it had become part of the Russian, Prussian, and Austrian empires. Poland would not become a sovereign state again until the twentieth century.

LOCALE: Poland

CATEGORIES: Expansion and land acquisition; diplomacy and international relations; government and politics

KEY FIGURES

Catherine the Great (1729-1796), empress of Russia, r. 1762-1796

Frederick the Great (1712-1786), king of Prussia, r. 1740-1786

Frederick William II (1744-1797), king of Prussia, r. 1786-1797, and nephew of Frederick the Great

Maria Theresa (1717-1780), archduchess of Austria, r. 1740-1780, and mother of Joseph II

Wenzel Anton von Kaunitz (1711-1794), state chancellor of Austria, 1753-1792

Tadeusz Kościuszko (1746-1817), Polish miliary leader and engineer

Stanisław II August Poniatowski (1732-1798), king of Poland, r. 1764-1795

SUMMARY OF EVENT

By the eighteenth century, the international position of Poland had become precarious and its domestic condition unstable. Although it was one of the largest states in Europe, Poland lacked the natural frontiers that would

have enabled it to resist the expansionist policies of its three predatory neighbors: Russia, Prussia, and Austria. The threat imposed on Poland by these three countries was accentuated by the decline of Sweden and the Ottoman Empire, states which had previously kept the czars and the Habsburgs at bay. The Poles could expect no substantial help from these states, nor from France, which was preoccupied with threats from Great Britain, still another state with no real interest in Poland.

The isolation Poland encountered in the international sphere was paralleled by the instability of its domestic affairs. Ethnically, Poland was a heterogeneous state, the eastern two-thirds of which was inhabited by Lithuanians, White Russians, and Red Russians (Ukrainians). Many of these Russians embraced the Orthodox religion of neighboring Russia and were referred to by the Roman Catholic Poles as the "dissidents." Socioeconomically, the non-Polish population made up the bulk of the peasantry, who suffered under the harsh conditions of life imposed upon them by the nobility, who themselves were generally of Polish extraction. Such repression, reinforced by the religious intolerance of Polish Catholicism, caused these non-Polish peoples to look for salvation from without, especially from Russia.

Constitutionally, Poland was a weak, decentralized state presided over by a weak elective king. Participation in the national diet was restricted to the Polish nobles, any one of whom could defeat a proposition under discussion and at the same time dissolve the assembly simply by casting a veto (the so-called *liberum veto*). Such a requisite of unanimity meant that few diets lasted long enough to carry out needed reforms; hence, factions of the nobility resorted to the formation of "confederations"

PARTITIONING OF POLAND, 1772-1795

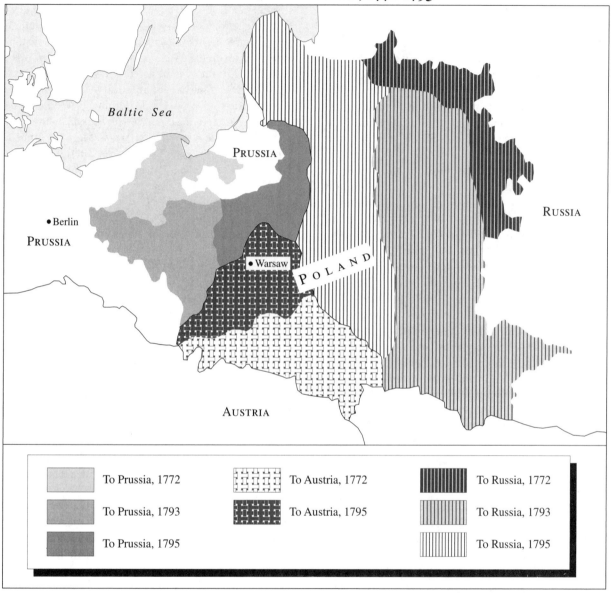

Baltic Sea

PRUSSIA

• Berlin

PRUSSIA

• Warsaw

POLAND

RUSSIA

AUSTRIA

1770's

To Prussia, 1772	To Austria, 1772	To Russia, 1772
To Prussia, 1793	To Austria, 1795	To Russia, 1793
To Prussia, 1795		To Russia, 1795

or armed leagues to secure by force what could not be accomplished by defunct institutions of government.

Seeking to make capital from these deplorable conditions, Catherine the Great of Russia and Frederick the Great of Prussia concluded an alliance in April, 1764, wherein they resolved to maintain the existing constitution of Poland. A few months later, Catherine dispatched Russian troops into Poland to secure the election of Stanisław II August Poniatowski, her former lover, as king, "because," as she put it, "he had less right than any other candidate and therefore should be all the more grateful to Russia." In her efforts to obtain Polish toleration for the "dissidents," however, Catherine touched off, in 1768, a revolt led by the antiroyalist, anti-Russian Confederation of Bar, which sought the support of France.

Although unable to provide direct aid to the Poles, France did succeed in stirring up the Turks against Russia. The Turks, however, needed little prodding, resentful as they were of the Russian advance into Poland and of Russians in general. When a Cossack band violated the Turkish frontier while pursuing some Polish rebels, the Ottoman Empire used the incident as an excuse to declare war on Russia. When Frederick and Catherine signed their alliance in 1764, they had not calculated on a Polish uprising, let alone what now seemed to be developing into an international conflict.

An alarmed Frederick now feared that Prussia would be involved not only in quelling a Polish insurrection but also in the expansionist policies of Russia, which seemed about to invade the Danubian principalities of the Ottoman Empire. This aggressive move threatened war between Russia and Austria, since Russia was encroaching on Austria's southeastern flank. Frederick's own ambitions would be thwarted if he should be caught in an Austro-Russian conflict. Thus Frederick suggested that Russia annex part of Poland instead of the Danubian principalities, and that Prussia and Austria would also take their shares of Poland to balance Russia's. This plan pleased Catherine the Great, who had long coveted parts of Poland. Maria Theresa of Austria objected to partition on both political and moral grounds, but she accepted her share of the spoils rather than see Russia and Prussia absorb all of Poland. The details were negotiated in part by Maria Theresa's state chancellor, Wenzel Anton von Kaunitz.

Under terms of the first partition, August 5, 1772, Poland lost about one-third of its territory and one-half of its inhabitants. Russia obtained the district of White Russia. Austria received Galicia and large parts of Red Russia and Podolia. Prussia's share (West Prussia) was the smallest, but it gave Prussia the vital block of territory needed for the unification of its purely German lands with outlying East Prussia. The Polish diet had no choice but to accept the partition. One contemporary observer remarked that in time Poland would be "totally swallowed up by the neighboring powers."

Total annexation occurred within twenty-five years. For a while, however, it appeared that Poland might be able to survive. Its three adversaries turned their attention from the Polish question during the 1770's and 1780's in order to fight among themselves and become involved in other ventures. Austria and Prussia resumed their struggle for supremacy in central Europe, this time over the issue of the Bavarian succession. Simultaneously, Austria allied itself with Russia against the Turks, and by 1787 another Russian-Turkish war had broken out, with the Habsburgs and Swedes taking their traditional sides. Poland, meanwhile, used this respite from outside interference to initiate needed domestic re-

forms. In May, 1791, Polish patriots enacted a new constitution abolishing elective kingship, the *liberum veto*, and the confederations. Catherine, after concluding peace with the Turks, responded to these new developments by sending Russian armies into Poland in May, 1792. The old constitution, as a result, was soon restored.

In order to forestall future efforts to strengthen the Polish state, Catherine decided during 1792 to effect a second partition of the country with Prussia, whose new sovereign, Frederick William II, was eager to compensate himself for the loss of face suffered in fighting revolutionary France. The second partition treaty of January 23, 1793, to which Austria was not a party, left Russia with most of Lithuania, the remaining parts of White Russia, most of Black Russia, and the western Ukraine. Prussia secured the area of Great Poland and the vital port of Danzig.

The second partition provoked a gallant and popular revolt, led by Tadeusz Kościuszko, who fought with distinction in the American Revolution. Kościuszko spurred a national uprising not only to secure an independent Poland but also to preserve the ideal of liberty and democracy that had been instituted in the new Polish constitution Catherine the Great had revoked. Kościuszko's revolt represented, as well, the spirit of the French Revolution, which Prussia, Russia, and Austria were determined to put down at all costs. Overwhelmed by both Russian and Prussian armies, Kościuszko was defeated, but his courageous example inspired generations of Poles, who would rebel again in 1830-1831 and in 1863, never forsaking the cause of an independent and free Poland.

After Kościuszko's defeat, Poland was partitioned a third time on October 24, 1795. Austria, invited by Catherine to participate to restrain Prussian territorial demands, received some territory north of Galicia, including Cracow. Russia acquired Courland and the remainder of Lithuania and Black Russia. Prussia obtained lands just to the south and east of East Prussia, including the Polish capital, Warsaw.

SIGNIFICANCE

The third partition of Poland in 1795 resulted in the disappearance of that state from the map of Europe until 1918. Russia was now pulled deeply into Europe, sharing long frontiers with Prussia and Austria, a fact of considerable importance when World War I broke out in 1914. Yet the powers that had participated in the division of Poland had no reason to regret the dissolution of what had really been a buffer state between them. Indeed, in modern times, Nazi Germany and Soviet Russia ignored this point in subjecting Poland to a fourth partition.

—*Edward P. Keleher, updated by Carl Rollyson*

FURTHER READING

Ascherson, Neal. *The Struggles for Poland.* New York: Random House, 1987. See especially the chapters tracing the rise and fall of independent Poland from 966 to 1900. Bibliography.

Cowie, Leonard W. *Eighteenth-Century Europe.* New York: Frederick Unger, 1963. Chapter 15 presents a concise introduction to the three partitions and the inherent weakness of eighteenth century Poland.

Davies, Norman. *Heart of Europe: The Past in Poland's Present.* New ed. New York: Oxford University Press, 2001. Works backward from the events in the early 1980's to eighteenth century Poland, emphasizing those factors that were most important in shaping the country's present. Includes maps, genealogical tables, and gazetteer.

Florinsky, Michael T. *Russia: A History and an Interpretation.* Vol. 1. Reprint. New York: Macmillan, 1973. In this work, which was first published in 1947, Florinsky provides a good discussion of the three partitions from the vantage point of the expansion of eighteenth century Russia.

Holborn, Hajo. *1648-1840.* Vol. 2 in *A History of Modern Germany.* New York: Alfred A. Knopf, 1964. Provides a brief treatment of the first partition of Poland.

Lord, Robert. *The Second Partition of Poland.* Cambridge, England: Cambridge University Press, 1915. A classic work that provides an outstanding treatment of the subject.

Lukowski, Jerzy. *The Partitions of Poland, 1772, 1793, 1795.* London: Longman, 1999. Describes the causes, course, and consequences of the three partitions and their impact on Poland and other countries in Europe. Explains the attitudes that Frederick the Great, Catherine the Great, and the Habsburgs held about Poland and the rulers' motives for the partition.

Lukowski, Jerzy, and Hubert Zawadzki. *A Concise History of Poland.* New York: Cambridge University Press, 2001. A general introduction to Polish history, divided into two parts: Poland to 1795, and Poland after 1795.

Wandycz, Piotr S. *The Lands of Partitioned Poland, 1795-1918.* Seattle: University of Washington Press, 1974. Chapters on the aftermath of the partitions, the age of insurrections, and the road to independence. Includes a bibliographical essay.

1770's

SEE ALSO: c. 1701-1721: Great Northern War; Nov. 20, 1710-July 21, 1718: Ottoman Wars with Russia, Venice, and Austria; 1736-1739: Russo-Austrian War Against the Ottoman Empire; May 31, 1740: Accession of Frederick the Great; Oct. 20, 1740: Maria Theresa Succeeds to the Austrian Throne; Dec. 16, 1740-Nov. 7, 1748: War of the Austrian Succession; Oct., 1768-Jan. 9, 1792: Ottoman Wars with Russia; 1775-1790: Joseph II's Reforms; 1788-Sept., 1809: Russo-Swedish Wars; June 1, 1794: Allgemeines Landrecht Recodifies Prussian Law.

RELATED ARTICLES in *Great Lives from History: The Eighteenth Century, 1701-1800:* Catherine the Great; Frederick the Great; Joseph II; Wenzel Anton von Kaunitz; Tadeusz Kościuszko; Maria Theresa.

1773
GOETHE INAUGURATES THE STURM UND DRANG MOVEMENT

In reaction to the dryness of Baroque and Enlightenment literature, Goethe and several of his contemporaries invented an exciting new genre of literature, Sturm und Drang, which proved immensely popular throughout Germany in the 1770's and laid the groundwork for the evolution of neoclassicism and Romanticism.

LOCALE: Germany

CATEGORIES: Literature; theater; art; music; philosophy

KEY FIGURES

Johann Wolfgang von Goethe (1749-1832), German writer and poet

Friedrich Schiller (1759-1805), German writer and poet

Friedrich Maximilian Klinger (1752-1831), German playwright

Johann Gottfried Herder (1744-1803), German philosopher and critic

Gotthold Ephraim Lessing (1729-1781), German playwright and critic

Johann Georg Hamann (1730-1788), German philosopher

Heinrich Wilhelm von Gerstenberg (1737-1823), German poet and critic

Friedrich Gottlieb Klopstock (1724-1803), German poet

Jakob Michael Reinhold Lenz (1751-1792), German playwright and poet

Karl Philipp Moritz (1756-1793), German writer

Götz von Berlichingen (1480-1562), German knight and adventurer

William Shakespeare (1564-1616), English playwright and poet

Jean-Jacques Rousseau (1712-1778), French philosopher

James Macpherson (1736-1796), Scottish folklorist and writer

SUMMARY OF EVENT

Sturm und Drang (German for "storm and stress") arguably began in the 1760's as a political rather than literary movement, but it soon became mainly literary and extended also into painting, music, and other arts. Its proponents and adherents were mainly young, disaffected men, the most famous of whom was Johann Wolfgang

von Goethe. Loosely configured and unnamed at first, the movement eventually took its name from a play by Friedrich Maximilian Klinger, *Wirrwarr: Oder, Sturm und Drang* (1776; confusion: or, storm and stress), whose title suggests raging turmoil and confusion. The Sturm und Drang movement's main intellectual antecedents were William Shakespeare, Jean-Jacques Rousseau, and Gotthold Ephraim Lessing. The high theatricality that typified not only its drama but also its novels and lyrics was chiefly due to Shakespeare's influence on Goethe. Its focus on human dignity and its advocacy of human freedom derived from Rousseau's political and social philosophy. Lessing formulated, and in the late 1760's published, what would become Sturm und Drang's principles.

Another influence on Sturm und Drang was the literary forger James Macpherson, who wrote *Fingal* (1762) and *Temora* (1763), collected as *The Works of Ossian, the Son of Fingal* (1765). These works were both supposedly written by the ancient Gaelic poet Ossian and merely translated into English by Macpherson. They were tremendously popular, and the epics were translated into German between 1764 and 1769. Macpherson fooled almost everyone except Samuel Johnson and David Hume, and the general belief that these works were artifacts of primitive culture added to their appeal and made them fountainheads of not only Sturm und Drang but also Romanticism on both sides of the English Channel. Ossian's supposed works were revealed as fakes only at the end of the nineteenth century. Among the Stürmer und Dränger, as the writers in this movement were called, the Ossian poems particularly affected Goethe and Johann Gottfried Herder. Goethe's seventy-odd Sturm und Drang poems derive mainly from Macpherson and Friedrich Gottlieb Klopstock.

Goethe's *Götz von Berlichingen mit der eisernen Hand* (pb. 1773, pr. 1774; *Götz von Berlichingen with the Iron Hand*, 1799), his first play, was the work that made him nationally famous at the age of only twenty-four. It tells the story of an idealistic military leader who rebelled against Holy Roman Emperor Maximilian I and led peasant forays against various German cities. The real Götz von Berlichingen was both an opportunistic mercenary and a popular hero like Robin Hood. Götz's own memoirs were the basis of Goethe's play, but Goethe took many liberties with this text, making Götz into more of a hero than he actually was. The iron hand of the title is a reference to the prosthesis that he wore after losing his right hand in the Siege of Landshut in 1504, as well as a metaphor for the strength of his will.

Götz von Berlichingen with the Iron Hand was not the first work of Sturm und Drang, but it was the work that brought attention to the movement and therefore can legitimately be said to have inaugurated it. Sturm und Drang was immensely popular throughout the German-speaking world for the rest of the 1770's, especially after

Goethe published the movement's most acclaimed work, the novel *Die Leiden des jungen Werthers* (1774; *The Sorrows of Young Werther*, 1779). *The Sorrows of Young Werther* was so popular that it set the fashion for young German men—blue frock coat and yellow vest—but also had dire and unforeseen social consequences, as lovesick young men committed suicide in imitation of the title character.

The span of Sturm und Drang is disputed. All scholars agree that it encompassed the period between *Götz von Berlichingen with the Iron Hand* in 1773 and Friedrich Schiller's *Die Räuber* (pb. 1781, pr. 1782; *The Robbers*, 1792), but some would see these two works as endpoints, while others would mark the beginning in the 1760's with Johann Georg Hamann's *Aesthetica in nuce* (1762; aesthetics in a nutshell), Heinrich Wilhelm von Gerstenberg's *Gedicht eines Skalden* (1766; poem of a skald), Gerstenberg's *Briefe über Merkwürdigkeiten der Literatur* (1766-1767; letters about the peculiarities of literature), or Herder's *Über die neuere deutsche Literatur: Fragmente* (1767; on recent German literature: fragments), and mark the end with Schiller's *Kabale und Liebe* (pr., pb. 1784; *Cabal and Love*, 1795) or Karl Philipp Moritz's *Anton Reiser* (1785-1794). There is universal agreement that the most important works in the movement are *Götz von Berlichingen with the Iron Hand, The Sorrows of Young Werther, The Robbers*, and the poems of Jakob Michael Reinhold Lenz.

The most prominent theme of Sturm und Drang was "the decayed world" (*die verderbte Welt*). Other typical features were emphasis on childhood and youth, exaltation of individual genius, and exploration of the themes of death, imprisonment, social disruption, religious conflict, homelessness, loss of parents, grieving, and the social position of women. Sturm und Drang gave more important roles to female characters than did previous kinds of literature. The death motif was perhaps its most poignant and included murder, suicide, patricide, fratricide, regicide, infanticide, and the deaths of heroes.

The troubles of the main characters portrayed by the movement, many of whom were outlaws as well as heroes, became metaphors for the political and social ills of the world. Sturm und Drang was strikingly nationalistic, not regarding the state, because Germany did not come into existence as a nation until 1871, but regarding the common German people and their culture. The champions of the people were often at odds with the Kingdom of Prussia, the Holy Roman Empire, the many German principalities and dukedoms, the Roman Catholic and Lutheran Churches, and other political authorities.

LIEBETRAUT'S SONG

Johann Wolfgang von Goethe's Götz von Berlichingen with the Iron Hand *is commonly thought of as the inaugural work of the Sturm und Drang movement. Reproduced here is the song sung by the character Liebetraut in act 2 of Goethe's play.*

HIS bow and dart bearing,
And torch brightly flaring,

Dan Cupid on flies;
With victory laden,
To vanquish each maiden

He roguishly tries.

Up! Up!

On! on!
His arms rattle loudly,
His wings rustle proudly,
And flames fill his eyes.

Then finds he each bosom

Defenseless and bare;
They gladly receive him

And welcome him there.
The point of his arrows

He lights in the glow;
They clasp him and kiss him

And fondle him so.
He e o! Pap!

Source: Johann Wolfgang von Goethe, *The Poems of Goethe*, translated by Edgar Alfred Bowring. 2d ed. (London: G. Bell and Sons, 1874). http://www.everypoet.com/archive/poetry/Goethe/goethe_liebetrauts_song.htm. Accessed November 15, 2005.

Almost all Sturm und Drang stories were tragedies. Oppressive social and psychological norms often overwhelmed and destroyed the hero. Sometimes, the tragedy was the main character's own fault, as in *The Sorrows of Young Werther*, but sometimes no fault of the main character at all, as in *Götz von Berlichingen with the Iron Hand*. Also, most of these works showed a curious mixture of hopefulness and defeatism. Götz's dying words were "Freedom! Freedom!," to which his faithful wife replied, "The world is a prison."

SIGNIFICANCE

The mid-eighteenth century was marked by several important, inventive, and complex turning points in German literature that constituted the beginnings of a strong German influence on world literature. From the rather stiff and mannered works of the Baroque period and the overly dry, objective, and didactic works of the Enlightenment, a new vitality broke forth in the 1760's that first became Sturm und Drang and then evolved into the clashing opposites of neoclassicism and Romanticism. Sturm und Drang was as much a product of the Enlightenment as a reaction against it. It upheld the Enlightenment belief in the value of the individual but pushed for action, extolled passion, and rejected the primacy of reason.

The movement lasted only about a decade, but the other two new developments, especially Romanticism, persisted into the nineteenth century. Romanticism, like Sturm und Drang, emphasized emotion over reason. Neoclassicism followed the Enlightenment in emphasizing reason over emotion, but, against the Enlightenment, grounded itself in ancient history and literature rather than in modern science and philosophy. In Germany, the bridge between neoclassicism and Romanticism was embodied in just one person, Goethe. His remarkable, six-decade career began with Sturm und Drang, defined all three eras, and made him the most important German writer of all time.

Sturm und Drang was a precursor of the psychological realism that became popular in the late nineteenth century. Themes of death and decay from the 1770's gave way to nineteenth century obsessions with guilt about these same themes. The idea of the decayed world was also a major aspect of the nineteenth century philosopher Georg Wilhelm Friedrich Hegel's idea of an inverted, or topsy-turvy, world, where everything is the opposite from what is expected, where common sense is no longer reliable, and where individuals think they are doing one thing but in fact are doing another.

—Eric v.d. Luft

FURTHER READING

Berlichingen, Götz von. *Autobiography*. Edited by Hannah Stephanie Marguerita Stuart. London: Duckworth, 1956. Goethe's source for his play.

Brunschwig, Henri. *Enlightenment and Romanticism in Eighteenth-Century Prussia*. Translated by Frank

The Goethe Monument, Goethe Square, Frankfurt am Main, Germany. Created by Ludwig von Schwanthaler, 1844. (Library of Congress)

Jellinek. Chicago: University of Chicago Press, 1974. A frequently cited standard work.

Duncan, Bruce. *Lovers, Parricides, and Highwaymen: Aspects of Sturm und Drang Drama*. Rochester, N.Y.: Camden House, 1999. A basic introduction.

Elliott, Rosemarie. *Wilhelm Heinse in Relation to Wieland, Winckelmann, and Goethe: Heinse's Sturm und Drang Aesthetic and New Literary Language*. Frankfurt, Germany: Peter Lang, 1996. A clear study of a minor figure in the movement.

Hill, David, ed. *Literature of the Sturm und Drang*. Rochester, N.Y.: Camden House, 2003. A collection of thirteen essays exploring the broad spectrum of the movement.

Kistler, Mark Oliver. *Drama of the Storm and Stress*. New York: Twayne, 1969. A comprehensive analysis.

Ottewell, Karen. *Lessing and the Sturm und Drang: A Reappraisal Revisited*. Frankfurt, Germany: Peter Lang, 2002. A revision of the author's doctoral thesis at the University of Cambridge, England.

Pascal, Roy. *The German Sturm und Drang*. Manchester, England: Manchester University Press, 1967. Appears in most bibliographies of eighteenth century German literature.

Runge, Edith Amelia. *Primitivism and Related Ideas in Sturm und Drang Literature*. New York: Russell & Russell, 1972. The author's doctoral thesis at Johns Hopkins University, Maryland.

Vaughan, Larry. *The Historical Constellation of the Sturm und Drang*. New York: Peter Lang, 1985. An analysis of the times out of which *Sturm und Drang* arose.

SEE ALSO: Oct. 5, 1762: First Performance of Gluck's *Orfeo and Euridice*; 1781: Kant Publishes *Critique of Pure Reason*; 1784-1791: Herder Publishes His Philosophy of History; 1792-1793: Fichte Advocates Free Speech.

RELATED ARTICLES in *Great Lives from History: The Eighteenth Century, 1701-1800*: Johann Wolfgang von Goethe; Johann Gottfried Herder; David Hume; Samuel Johnson; Friedrich Gottlieb Klopstock; Gotthold Ephraim Lessing; Jean-Jacques Rousseau; Friedrich Schiller.

1773-1788
AFRICAN AMERICAN BAPTIST CHURCH IS FOUNDED

An amalgamation of African and European forms of religious worship developed into the African American Baptist Church. The cosmologies and churches fashioned by blacks in the United States helped them survive and transcend the harsh realities of slavery in the South.

LOCALE: Savannah River Valley, Georgia
CATEGORIES: Religion and theology; organizations and institutions

KEY FIGURES
Andrew Bryan (1737-1812), a slave who was converted, purchased his freedom, and founded the Savannah Church
David George (b. 1742?) and
George Liele (1750?-1825?), slaves who became preachers and founded churches for African Americans

SUMMARY OF EVENT
The religious revivals collectively known as the First Great Awakening transformed the spiritual climate of British North America in the mid-eighteenth century. Church membership grew, and evangelical religious ideas, which emphasized a person's own relationship with God, began to acquire hegemony over the religious values propagated by the established churches. Among those people who embraced evangelical ideals were African American slaves, who found attractive the notion of a personal God, the hope for salvation, and the less-formal style of evangelical worship. This was especially true in the South, where African Americans benefited from a practice among some white evangelicals of allowing blacks to preach to other blacks and where African Americans were the targets of white missionary activity.

African Americans were particularly drawn to the Baptist faith, especially in the latter part of the eighteenth century. White Baptists, themselves often among the poorest in Southern society, actively recruited African Americans. Furthermore, Baptists did not require formal education as part of ministerial training, and what learning they did encourage centered on mastering the contents of the Bible. Even African Americans held in bondage and denied opportunities for formal education could fulfill these expectations, and more than a few became ministers. African American slaves not only joined biracial Baptist churches but also fashioned their own fellowships, where they blended the traditional folk religions they brought from Africa with the evangelical nostrums of the Europeans, thus creating a hybrid African American religion.

One area where African American Baptists flourished was the Savannah River Valley, which connected the hinterlands around Augusta, Georgia, with the port city of Savannah. Here, evangelical revivals among whites and blacks bore organizational fruit among African Americans. Indeed, African Americans formed their own Baptist church at Silver Bluff, near Augusta, in 1773, following one such revival.

About that time, a slave named George Liele heard a sermon preached by Reverend Matthew Moore, a white minister, and became convinced that he needed to respond to the gospel. "I was sure I should be found in hell, as sure as God was in heaven," Liele recalled. Baptized by Moore, Liele became a preacher and began to exhort other slaves in the vicinity of Augusta to become Christians. Liele's master, who was loyal to the British during the American Revolution, temporarily had to flee Georgia for his life and freed Liele. For the next several years, Liele and a colleague, David George, preached regularly at Silver Bluff, South Carolina, at the first black Baptist church in the Savannah River Valley region. George had been born a slave in Virginia and had run away from a cruel master before coming to the Deep South as the slave of George Galphin. Becoming convinced of his own iniquity and borrowing from whites an evangelical vocabulary and worldview, he was converted after hearing sermons in the mid-1770's by several African American preachers, including Liele.

Both George and Liele initially had become Baptists because of their own desire to go to heaven, but quickly they took it upon themselves to preach to their fellow slaves. Having found a sense of inner peace because of his religion, Liele wanted others to experience in themselves "the work which God had done for my soul." Liele and George organized other churches, including the congregation at Yama Craw, outside Savannah, in 1777.

Among those who heard Liele preach at Yama Craw was Andrew Bryan. Bryan had been born in Goose Creek, South Carolina, and was baptized by Liele in 1782. Bryan eventually purchased his freedom and devoted himself to his ministry. It was a decision not without consequences, as whites who feared an unshackled black man whipped Bryan twice and imprisoned him

once. Undeterred, he continued to preach to ever-larger congregations, which often contained both blacks and whites. In 1788, his congregation constituted itself into the Savannah Georgia First Colored Church, commonly called the Savannah Church. At the time, it boasted 575 members and would grow to more than 800 at the time of Bryan's death.

Liele, George, and Bryan stood at the forefront of an important movement among African Americans in the South. Their religious teachings fused the African concepts of a unitary universe where the sacred and profane are not segregated; the European mythologies of Heaven, Hell, and redemption; and their present reality of slavery. God would help Africans through their travail of slavery and would one day lead them out of bondage. In this melding process, certain African religious practices were proscribed. The church covenant of Liele's Yama Craw Church specifically banned the consumption of blood and strangled meat of animals offered to idols, which had been a part of some West African religious rituals. Other African practices were given an important place, such as moaning as part of religious singing. This practice originated in ecstatic African religious rituals, and moaning and wailing have been preserved in Southern gospel singing. This hybrid religious ritual did not confine itself to African American communities. The emotional shouts and ritual cadences of African worship affected the rhythms of white discourse as well, especially the sermon form, in which the preacher and congregation engage in something of a dialogue.

Liele, George, and Bryan founded churches and baptized ministers who started other churches. One man converted by George and Liele was Jesse Peter. A slave, he was allowed uncommon liberties and preached around Savannah and Augusta. He helped constitute the Springfield African Church in Augusta in 1793, which was later recognized by white Baptists for its excellent church music. Until the American Civil War, the churches started by these men existed, sometimes tenuously. Often, they had to accept direct white oversight to avoid being shut down, but they clung tenaciously to as much independence as local custom and law would allow.

SIGNIFICANCE

The careers of George Liele, David George, and Andrew Bryan also illustrate the protean political nature of evangelicalism. The formation of churches operated by African Americans reflects the capacity of blacks to avoid complete organizational enslavement as surely as the forming of a black theology kept African Americans from psychic enslavement. From these organizational and intellectual bases, African Americans could confront slavery in various ways.

Both Liele and George fled the South for the British Empire, seeking to continue their ministerial work without the specter of slavery hanging over them. Liele went to Jamaica, establishing the first Baptist churches there. George went to Canada, where he worked with both blacks and whites before organizing a back-to-Africa movement, in which one thousand Canadian blacks went with George to Sierra Leone in 1792. Bryan, however, remained in the South, calling upon African Americans to lead better lives and, sometimes stealthily, urging whites to live out the Golden Rule in dealing with blacks. At his death, he was lauded by blacks and whites alike. By establishing churches that counseled patience while teaching a theology of ultimate deliverance, African American leaders like Liele, George, and Bryan helped African Americans survive slavery by encouraging them to expect freedom soon.

—Edward R. Crowther

FURTHER READING

Bellew, Christopher Brent. *The Impact of African-American Antecedents on the Baptist Foreign Missionary Movement, 1782-1825.* Lewiston, N.Y.: Edwin Mellen Press, 2004. Describes the missionary work of Liele and George at the close of the Revolutionary War. George established missions in Nova Scotia and Sierra Leone, while Liele founded a mission in Jamaica, where he worked with Moses Baker, another black Baptist.

Fitts, LeRoy. *A History of Black Baptists.* Nashville, Tenn.: Broadman Press, 1985. A sympathetic and readable account of black Baptist leaders and churches.

Lincoln, C. Eric, and Lawrence H. Mamiya. *The Black Church in the African American Experience.* Durham, N.C.: Duke University Press, 1990. A well-written survey of African American churches since their earliest times and their meaning in the African American struggle in the United States.

Sernett, Milton C. *Afro-American Religious History: A Documentary Witness.* Durham, N.C.: Duke University Press, 1985. Contains letters from Bryan and Liele and many other representative documents of the African American religious experience.

Sobel, Mechal. *Trablin' On: The Slave Journey to an Afro-Baptist Faith.* Westport, Conn.: Greenwood Press, 1979. Emphasizes the hybrid quality of the African American Baptist Church.

Washington, James Melvin. *Frustrated Fellowship: The Black Quest for Social Power.* Mercer, Ga.: Mercer University Press, 2004. History of the African American Baptist Church originally published in 1986. Washington explains how the church enabled African Americans to achieve a "peculiar and precarious religious freedom," as well as a sense of identity, community, and social power. Paperback edition with a new preface by Quentin H. Dixie and a new foreword by Cornell West.

Wilmore, Gayraud S., ed. *African American Religious Studies: An Interdisciplinary Anthology.* Durham, N.C.: Duke University Press, 1989. A series of essays interpreting the fragmentary documentary record of early African American religious life.

SEE ALSO: June 20, 1732: Settlement of Georgia; 1739-1742: First Great Awakening; Oct. 30, 1768: Methodist Church Is Established in Colonial America; Jan. 16, 1786: Virginia Statute of Religious Liberty; July 28-Oct. 16, 1789: Episcopal Church Is Established; 1790's-1830's: Second Great Awakening.

RELATED ARTICLES in *Great Lives from History: The Eighteenth Century, 1701-1800*: Francis Asbury; Isaac Backus; Charles Carroll; Jonathan Edwards; Ann Lee; Cotton Mather; Increase Mather; Samuel Sewall; Granville Sharp; Charles Wesley; John Wesley; George Whitefield; William Wilberforce.

1770's

September, 1773-September, 1774
PUGACHEV'S REVOLT

A major rebellion in the 1770's seriously threatened the social fabric and political institutions of Russia during the rule of Empress Catherine the Great. The crisis revealed widespread discontent and anger among the population on the southeastern Russian border.

LOCALE: Russia
CATEGORIES: Wars, uprisings, and civil unrest; government and politics

KEY FIGURES

Yemelyan Ivanovich Pugachev (1742?-January 10, 1795), Cossack rebel leader
Catherine the Great (1729-1796), empress of Russia, r. 1762-1796
Voltaire (François-Marie Arouet; 1694-1778), French philosopher and literary figure

SUMMARY OF EVENT

Much of Russian history consists of the story of the expansion of the small region surrounding Moscow to its eventual size as a large empire. This expansion was achieved by wresting territory from Russia's neighbors, Sweden, Lithuania, Poland, the Ottoman Empire, and the Mongols. Russians penetrated into the regions to their southeast and east, including the Ural Mountains and two major rivers—the Don River and the Volga River—where Cossacks and other nomadic tribes lived. These groups periodically resisted the imposition of Russian control by raising the banner of rebellion. One such rebellion, conducted by Yemelyan Ivanovich Pugachev and his followers, shook the very foundations of the Russian state before the revolt collapsed.

Pugachev, born in the Cossack region near the Don River, absorbed the desire for independence from Russian authority. He had military experience as a soldier, serving in the Russian army during the Seven Years' War and the Russian-Turkish War. However, his independent ways and controversial schemes got him into periodic trouble with the authorities, and he was imprisoned on several occasions. In May, 1773, Pugachev escaped from prison in Kazan and began a new phase of his colorful and dramatic life.

Pugachev returned to Cossack territory and recruited followers who had grievances against the established order. He built on the effects of discontent in the region that the Russian military had ruthlessly suppressed

in 1771 and 1772, so his message of resistance found a receptive audience. By the peak of his revolt, it is estimated that Pugachev had as many as fifteen to twenty thousand men under his command. These included Cossacks who sought to maintain their traditional ways, army deserters, serfs who had fled their owners to escape the hardships of life as virtual slaves on landed estates, and tribal groups in the region (such as the Bashkirs and Kirgiz) who wished to maintain their nomadic way of life.

Workers in the oppressive mines and factories in the Urals also looked to Pugachev as a leader who could improve their lives. Those who opposed the prevailing dogmas of the Russian Orthodox Church, known as the Old Believers, rallied to his cause, as did tribal Muslims who resisted Christianity as the official faith of Russia. His supporters represented a wide range of social and ethnic types, but they all agreed in the desire for freedom from discrimination and oppression. They hoped this would come through a popular and sweeping revolt that would

Yemelyan Ivanovich Pugachev. (Library of Congress)

oust the government and existing authority. Pugachev issued several manifestos promising the end to serfdom, free land to everyone, ethnic rights, and religious tolerance. He also claimed to be Czar Peter III, the deposed and murdered husband of Catherine the Great, whom he declared to be a usurper of the throne. Although not true, his royal claim was believed by many who joined his movement.

The uprising began in September, 1773, when Pugachev's forces attacked government outposts at the important towns of Yaitsk and Orenburg on the Yaik River, east of the Volga River. The rebellion quickly spread, gaining support and volunteers. Although most were militarily untrained, his men obtained many weapons, including more than one hundred cannon, to use in their campaigns against government centers and Russian forces sent to crush the revolt. In a number of engagements in late 1773 and early 1774, the rebels defeated troops sent to capture them.

Widespread violence against landowners and their families became a common and tragic aspect of the rebellion, for the rebels saw them as visible and handy symbols of oppression and hardship in their daily lives. Accounts of pillage, rape, and murder created widespread panic when the rebels approached. At one point, the rebel army appeared to be heading toward Moscow. In response to this imminent threat, Catherine seriously considered leaving her capital of St. Petersburg and going to Moscow to assist in its defense.

The rebels' successful attack on the important city of Kazan in July, 1774, dealt a blow to the government, but the occupation was brief. The signing of a peace agreement with Turkey that summer ended one of the Russian-Turkish Wars (1768-1774), permitting the government to give more attention to the internal crisis. From that time, Russian forces were generally successful in their confrontations with the rebels, as they moved southward toward the Volga River region. Although Pugachev did capture Samara later in the year, he failed to take Tsaritsyn. The end of the rebellion came in mid-September, 1774, when several of Pugachev's commanders seized Pugachev and turned him over to the Russian authorities with the promise that they would be spared from punishment.

Pugachev was taken to Moscow in an iron cage and extensively questioned about the origins and purposes of the rebellion. He admitted the falsity of his claim to be Peter III. Tried secretly in December, Pugachev was sentenced to death by beheading and cutting his limbs from his body, to be displayed in Moscow as a warning to other possible dissidents. Catherine agreed to this judgment, saying that Pugachev "lived like a scoundrel and will die like a coward," but she also admitted that he was "a bold and determined man." The sentence was carried out in Moscow on January 10, 1775, before a large crowd, along with several of Pugachev's associates. After the gruesome execution and public display, the body parts were burned.

The government sought to eradicate the memory of Pugachev and the revolt. Punishments were severe, including slitting noses and cutting out tongues. Many went to Siberian exile camps for the remainder of their lives. In the spring of 1775, Catherine issued an amnesty for the lesser participants and ordered that the rebellion should never be mentioned again. Other government decrees ordered the total obliteration of his Cossack village and prohibited the use of the Pugachev name, even by members of his family, who were sent into exile. Several town and river names in areas involved in the rebellion also were changed to names still used today.

SIGNIFICANCE

Catherine the Great hoped to be recognized and remembered as an "enlightened monarch" who adopted progressive reforms for Russia. The empress worried that the Pugachev Rebellion and her response would jeopardize the positive reputation she tried to establish. She was very well read and knew the views of Western intellectuals regarding philosophical, political, legal, and social issues. In Catherine's correspondence with the noted French philosopher Voltaire and other Westerners, she sometimes admitted the need to make changes in her country. Her fame in this regard, however, generally rests more on what she said than what she did in practice. Catherine realized that talking of reform was far easier than its implementation. Philosophers could write on paper, she wrote, while her policies affected millions of people. In fact, during her long reign, the repressive laws expanding the harsh conditions of serfdom actually increased.

Serious outbreaks such as Pugachev's revolt greatly reduced Catherine's willingness to consider meaningful social and political reforms for Russia. She feared that making concessions to her opponents might create more unrest, with possible fatal consequences for the nation. Catherine's correspondence with Voltaire revealed that she would suppress any threats to her autocratic power. She realized the danger this revolt created but characterized Pugachev as little more than a common robber or thief. This attitude failed to recognize or accept that the rebellion represented far more serious social problems that had to be resolved to avoid repetition. By the time of Catherine's death in the 1790's, the violence of the French Revolution further convinced her of the need to maintain complete power over the population. The result was that any chance of reform in Russia had virtually ended.

The Pugachev rebellion illustrated the severe problems the peasantry and other lower social classes faced in Russia. Despite its suppression, the long-term impact of this violent upheaval failed to eliminate discontent among large segments of the population. Later radical leaders, such as Vladimir Ilich Lenin, asserted that the best solution to numerous problems was to eliminate the monarchy. Thus the memory of this eighteenth century crisis indirectly played a role in the final catastrophe of the early twentieth century, when the 1917 Revolution overthrew the last Russian czar, Nicholas II.

—*Taylor Stults*

FURTHER READING

Alexander, John T. *Autocratic Politics in a National Crisis: The Imperial Russian Government and Pugachev's Revolt, 1773-1775.* Bloomington: Indiana University Press, 1969. Describes the government's response to the rebel threat.

_____. *Catherine the Great: Life and Legend.* New York: Oxford University Press, 1989. Puts the rebellion in the broader context of Catherine's rule and her desire to be known as an enlightened despot.

_____. *Emperor of the Cossacks: Pugachev and the Frontier Jacquerie of 1773-1775.* Lawrence, Kans.: Coronado Press, 1973. Detailed coverage of the rebel army and military aspects of the revolt, within the broader context of European revolutions.

Avrich, Paul. *Russian Rebels, 1600-1800.* New York: Schocken, 1972. Excellent coverage of the topic in manageable length.

De Madariaga, Isabel. *Catherine the Great: A Short History.* New Haven, Conn.: Yale University Press, 2002. Solid summary of the rebellion in paperback.

Dixon, Simon. *Catherine the Great.* New York: Longman, 2001. Analysis of Catherine's governing principles, objectives, and effects.

Troyat, Henri. *Catherine the Great: A Biography.* New York: Meridian, 1994. Colorful portrayal of the monarch and her nation.

SEE ALSO: c. 1701-1721: Great Northern War; Nov. 20, 1710-July 21, 1718: Ottoman Wars with Russia, Venice, and Austria; 1726-1729: Voltaire Advances Enlightenment Thought in Europe; Oct. 21, 1727: Treaty of Kiakhta; 1736-1739: Russo-Austrian War Against the Ottoman Empire; Jan., 1756-Feb. 15, 1763: Seven Years' War; Aug. 10, 1767: Catherine the Great's Instruction; Oct., 1768-Jan. 9, 1792: Ottoman Wars with Russia; 1788-Sept., 1809: Russo-Swedish Wars.

RELATED ARTICLES in *Great Lives from History: The Eighteenth Century, 1701-1800*: Catherine the Great; Peter the Great; Peter III; Voltaire.

December 16, 1773
BOSTON TEA PARTY

A small group of protesters rallied against the British taxation of imported tea by dumping tens of thousands of pounds of tea from anchored British vessels into the Boston Harbor. The largely symbolic uprising had ushered in a series of events that led directly to war and, eventually, American independence.

LOCALE: Boston, Massachusetts

CATEGORIES: Wars, uprisings, and civil unrest; economics; government and politics

KEY FIGURES

Samuel Adams (1722-1803) and
John Hancock (1737-1793), patriots who aroused Bostonians against the continued presence of the tea ships

Thomas Hutchinson (1711-1780), governor of Massachusetts

Lord North (Frederick North; 1732-1792), prime minister of Great Britain, 1770-1782

SUMMARY OF EVENT

On the evening of December 16, 1773, three vessels lay at anchor in Boston Harbor. They carried 342 chests containing more than 90,000 pounds of dutiable tea worth about £9,000. Shortly after 6:00 p.m., between thirty and sixty men, calling themselves "Mohawks" and roughly disguised as American Indians, boarded the ships. Hundreds of silent onlookers at the wharf saw the men, organized into three groups, swiftly and systematically break open the tea chests and pour their contents into the sea.

Because the water was only two or three feet deep, the tea began to pile up, forcing the men to rake it aside to allow room for the rest. In less than three hours, they had completed their work and disappeared into the darkness; to this day, the identities of most remain unknown.

The "Destruction of the Tea," exclaimed John Adams the next day, "is so bold, so daring . . . it must have so important Consequences and so lasting, that I cannot but consider it as an Epocha [*sic*] in History." Eighteen months later, the colonists were locked in military combat with Great Britain.

The origins of the famous Tea Party are to be found in Parliament's repeal, in 1770, of all the external taxes embodied in the controversial Townshend Revenue Act, except the tax on tea, which was to remain principally as a symbol of Great Britain's right to extract cash from American purses. Although the colonists had won only a partial victory in their battle against the second British program of taxation, compared to a complete repeal of the earlier Stamp Act, the chances for an improvement in British-American relations seemed fairly bright in the years 1771-1773. The secretary of state for the colonies, Wills Hill, first earl of Hillsborough and marquis of Downshire, soothed American tempers by announcing that the British government did not intend to propose any new taxes for the colonists.

These were years of renewed commercial prosperity, during which countless Americans drank the duped brew, when all but a few ignored the frantic schemes of Samuel Adams and a radical minority to keep alive the old flames of resentment. There were, to be sure, occasional events that generated fresh ill will, such as the burning by Rhode Islanders of the royal revenue cutter *Gaspee* and the clandestine publication of Massachusetts governor Thomas Hutchinson's correspondence expressing stern criticism of the colony's patriot leaders. However, it was Parliament's Tea Act of 1773 that brought the period of quiescence to an abrupt end throughout North America. Ironically, British politicians acted not with the purpose of disciplining the Americans but with the intention of boosting the sagging fortunes of the giant British East India Company. After unsuccessful attempts to help the ailing corporation with huge investments in India, the prime minister of Great Britain, Lord North, secured passage of the Tea Act. This allowed the East India Company to sell tea directly to America for the first time, and to do so through its own agents; previously, it had sold its product to English wholesale merchants, from whom the tea passed into the hands of American wholesalers and retailers. By removing the profits formerly obtained by

Colonial American protesters, dressed as American Indians, boarded anchored British merchant ships in Boston Harbor and threw thousands of pounds of tea overboard to protest the British government's tax on imported tea. (Library of Congress)

English and American middlemen, and by the added provision eliminating English duties on tea exported to the New World possessions, the company hoped to undersell Dutch-smuggled leaves in America, even though the provincials would have to pay the remaining Townshend tax of three pence on each pound.

Everywhere in North America, Lord North's move met stiff resistance. Merchants accused the ministry of giving the East India Company and its agents a monopoly on the local tea market, which would be followed in time by other monopolies in the American trade. More frightening to Americans was the constitutional threat; they were vulnerable already since the taxed herb had been purchased in America after 1770. Now, if they consumed even more of the dutied drink, they would implicitly admit the authority of Parliament to tax them. In fact, they saw in Lord North's undertaking a cynical endeavor to get them to "barter liberty for luxury." Consignees in New York, Philadelphia, and Charleston were persuaded to resign their commissions, as the stamp tax collectors previously had been made to do. The outcome was different in Boston, where Governor Hutchinson backed the consignees and refused to let the tea ships return to England without first unloading their cargo. Moreover, in Boston Samuel Adams and John Hancock effectively increased public sentiment against the tax.

The Tea Party was a form of symbolic protest—one step beyond random violence, one step short of organized, armed rebellion. The tea dumpers chose their symbols with utmost care. As the imported tea symbolized British tyranny and taxation, so the image of the American Indian, and the Mohawk disguise, represented its antithesis: a trademark of an emerging American identity and a voice for liberty in a new land. The image of the American Indian was figured into tea-dumpers' disguises not only in Boston but also in cities all along the Atlantic seaboard. The Mohawk symbol was not picked at random: It was used as a revolutionary symbol, counterpoising the tea tax.

The image of the American Indian (particularly the Mohawk) also appeared at about the same time, in the same context, in revolutionary songs, slogans, and engravings. Paul Revere, whose midnight rides became legendary in the poetry of Henry Wadsworth Longfellow, played a crucial role in forging this sense of identity, contributing to the revolutionary cause a set of remarkable engravings that cast as America's first national symbol an American Indian woman, long before Uncle Sam came along.

Boston's patriots were not known for their civility in the face of British authority, and it was Boston's "Mohawks" who sparked physical confrontation over the tea tax. As they dumped the tea, the "Mohawks" exchanged words in a secret sign language using American Indian hand symbols, and sang,

> Rally Mohawks, and bring your axes
> And tell King George we'll pay no taxes
> on his foreign tea;
> His threats are vain, and vain to think
> To force our girls and wives to drink
> his vile Bohea!
> Then rally, boys, and hasten on
> To meet our chiefs at the Green Dragon!
> Our Warren's here, and bold Revere
> With hands to do and words to cheer,

> for liberty and laws;
> Our country's "braves" and firm defenders
> shall ne'er be left by true North Enders
> fighting freedom's cause!
> Then rally, boys, and hasten on
> To meet our chiefs at the Green Dragon.

SIGNIFICANCE

After the "Mohawks" had performed the task of unloading, Parliament's response was one of unparalleled severity. It passed the Coercive Acts in 1774 in order to bring rebellious Massachusetts to its knees, by closing the port of Boston, altering the structure of government in the colony, and allowing British officials and soldiers accused of capital offenses to be tried in England or, to avoid a hostile local jury, in a colony other than the one where the offense had occurred. The Coercive Acts also provided for the quartering of troops once more in the town of Boston, stoking the smoldering resentment of its citizens.

The Boston Tea Party is regarded by some as the first "battle" of the American Revolution, an economic one: In 1773, Britain exported 738,083 pounds of tea to the colonies. In 1774, the figure had fallen to 69,830 pounds. Imports of tea fell all along the seaboard: from 206,312 pounds to 30,161 in New England, 208,385 to 1,304 pounds in New York, and 208,191 pounds to none in Pennsylvania.

—R. Don Higginbotham,
updated by Bruce E. Johansen

FURTHER READING

Brant, Irving. *James Madison: The Virginia Revolutionist*. Indianapolis, Ind.: Bobbs-Merrill, 1941. Provides one of the best accounts of the tea crisis in Virginia.

Breen, T. H. *The Marketplace of Revolution: How Consumer Politics Shaped American Independence*. New York: Oxford University Press, 2004. Breen argues that colonists' experience as consumers helped them develop new forms of social action, such as boycotts and "tea parties," which ultimately resulted in revolution. Includes information about colonists' tea boycotts, the Tea Act, and the Boston Tea Party.

Chidsey, Donald Barr. *The Great Separation: The Story of the Boston Tea Party and the Beginning of the American Revolution*. New York: Crown, 1965. Written in a popular novelist's style, this book brings to life the issues and actions surrounding the Boston Tea Party.

Griffith, Samuel B., II. *The War for American Independence: From 1760 to the Surrender at Yorktown in*

1781. Urbana: University of Illinois Press, 2002. This history of the American Revolution, first published in 1776 under another name, describes the causes and conditions that led colonists to rebel against the British. Includes information about the Boston Tea Party.

Grinde, Donald A., Jr., and Bruce E. Johansen. "Mohawks, Axes, and Taxes." In *Exemplar of Liberty: Native America and the Evolution of Democracy*. Los Angeles: American Indian Studies Center, University of California, Los Angeles, 1991. Describes the use of American Indian images during the Boston Tea Party and in the revolutionary propaganda of the American Revolution.

Griswold, Wesley S. *The Night the Revolution Began: The Boston Tea Party, 1773*. Brattleboro, Vt.: S. Greene Press, 1972. An outline account of the Tea Party and its context, published for its bicentennial.

Labaree, Benjamin W. *The Boston Tea Party*. New York: Oxford University Press, 1964. Labaree's book remains the seminal work on the Tea Party and its political and economic context.

Raphael, Ray. *A People's History of the American Revolution: How Common People Shaped the Fight for Independence*. New York: New Press, 2001. Describes the role that farmers, laborers, women, and other "ordinary people" played in the revolution, and examines the Boston Tea Party.

Thomas, Peter David Garner. *Tea Party to Independence: The Third Phase of the American Revolution, 1773-1776*. Oxford, England: Clarendon Press, 1991. Describes events from the Tea Party to the Declaration of Independence.

Young, Alfred E. *The Shoemaker and the Tea Party: Memory and the American Revolution*. Boston: Beacon Press, 1999. Young explores how memory preserves history by examining the life of George Robert Twelves Hewes, a shoemaker who participated in the Boston Tea Party. Includes Hewes's recollections of the event and describes how he was later honored for being one the last surviving participants.

SEE ALSO: Mar. 22, 1765-Mar. 18, 1766: Stamp Act Crisis; June 29, 1767-Apr. 12, 1770: Townshend Crisis; Mar. 5, 1770: Boston Massacre; Sept. 5-Oct. 26, 1774: First Continental Congress; Apr. 19, 1775: Battle of Lexington and Concord; May 10-Aug. 2, 1775: Second Continental Congress; July 4, 1776: Declaration of Independence; Sept. 17, 1787: U.S. Constitution Is Adopted.

RELATED ARTICLES in *Great Lives from History: The Eighteenth Century, 1701-1800*: John Adams; Samuel Adams; George III; John Hancock; Patrick Henry; Thomas Hutchinson; Lord North; Paul Revere; Mercy Otis Warren.

1774
HANSARD BEGINS REPORTING PARLIAMENTARY DEBATES

In 1771, the ban upon publishing accounts of British parliamentary debates was effectively lifted. Beginning in 1774, limited accounts of Parliament's proceedings began to be published and made available to the public in an officially sanctioned format for the first time. These publications increased the freedom of the British press and helped to institute new standards for an informed British electorate.

LOCALE: London, England

CATEGORIES: Communications; government and politics

KEY FIGURES

Luke Hansard (1752-1828), English publisher
Thomas Curzon Hansard (1776-1833), English publisher
John Almon (1737-1805), English writer and publisher
William Cobbett (1763-1835), English journalist, historian, and publisher
John Wilkes (1725-1797), English politician and journalist

SUMMARY OF EVENT

Until and throughout most of the eighteenth century, the proceedings of the Parliament of Great Britain were conducted largely in secret. The official actions of Parliament were reported in the press, but publishing the remarks of individual members of either the House of Commons or the House of Lords was a breach of parliamentary privilege. Reporters and observers could attend the debates in a visitor's gallery, but each house prohibited the transcription and dissemination of speeches or debates.

Those restrictions were frequently challenged by the press, as well as by members of Parliament themselves.

Unofficial accounts of the proceedings were made in publications such as *Gentleman's Magazine* and *London Magazine*, which published accounts of parliamentary debates, thinly disguised as stories about fictitious clubs or societies.

In April of 1763, a legal battle erupted over newspapers' publication of reports of debates in the House of Commons. John Wilkes, a newspaper publisher and former member of the Commons who had been expelled, was convicted of libel for criticizing the government in his newspaper, the *North Briton*. Wilkes believed in the principle of freedom of the press, and he thought this principle extended to reporting the comments of members of Parliament. Although imprisoned for acting on this belief, Wilkes was elected an alderman of London in 1769, while still in prison, and became the city's sheriff in 1771. As sheriff, he effectively prevented the House of Commons from enforcing its decrees of breach of privilege against printers within the city, which was home to the majority of the printers in England.

Luke Hansard published the first official report of parliamentary debates in 1774. Hansard had learned the printing trade in Norwich, publishing books as well as political circulars. He left for London and joined the firm of John Hughes, then printer to the House of Commons. Hansard soon took over the business. The printer to the Commons was appointed by the speaker of the Commons and was responsible for printing parliamentary papers, including bills under consideration, statistical information, and the official reports of committees and commissions. Parliament demanded that items be transcribed, printed, and delivered quickly and efficiently, and the volume of reports grew steadily. Hansard established a reputation for being reliable, precise, and prompt. Hansard published the *Journals of the House of Commons* (1774-1828). These journals however, did not report actual debates but served as an official record of proceedings.

Hansard had competition. John Almon and, later, his partner John Debrett published the *Parliamentary Register* (1774-1780), an account that included not only official actions and motions but also speeches of members. At least some of the text was supplied by members of Parliament themselves.

SIGNIFICANCE

It was not until 1803 that the radical reformer William Cobbett (who used the pseudonym Peter Porcupine in North America) attempted to reproduce a complete and accurate record of the speeches and debates of Parliament. Cobbett edited the *Political Register*, a weekly periodical

of news and political commentary. As a supplement, Cobbett gathered information on the speeches within Parliament gleaned from newspapers and other sources. Cobbett's *Parliamentary Debates* tried to create a nonpartisan account of the discussions within Parliament. The venture proved successful, and he brought on others, including the printer Thomas Curzon Hansard, son of Luke.

Cobbett's political views, however, got him into trouble. In 1810, he was tried for sedition and libel for a pamphlet that criticized the British government over an incident in which British soldiers were flogged for mutiny by German mercenaries. Cobbett was fined and imprisoned for two years; T. C. Hansard and others received shorter terms. Eventually, Cobbett sold his interest in the publishing enterprise to Hansard. In 1813, Hansard's name joined Cobbett's on the title page.

By 1829, the record of parliamentary proceedings became *Hansard's Parliamentary Debates*. Initially, Hansard reprinted newspaper accounts of speeches (usually confirmed with the members who had given them). Eventually, Hansard had its own group of reporters in the galleries of each House to record accurately the authentic statements of members. The publication remained in the family until 1889. The family firm headed by Luke and his sons, Thomas Curzon and Luke Graves Hansard, became renowned for accuracy and neutrality in publishing official reports and accounts of debates within both houses of Parliament.

The name Hansard has since become synonymous with written coverage of parliamentary debates. Although the term was dropped from the publication's cover page when the Stationery Office of the British House of Commons took over printing the *Parliamentary Debates* in 1909, the title was reinstated in 1943 as *Hansard's Parliamentary Debates*. It was not until 1909, however, that the *Parliamentary Debates* became a (nearly) verbatim report of the speeches of Parliament. "Hansard" is also the term used for written proceedings in Australia, Canada, and New Zealand.

The release of official, authoritative reports of legislative debates has become an assumed feature of democratic governance. The secrecy of Parliament's proceedings originated in members' desire to protect themselves and their institution from the monarchy. As the power of the king declined and the power of Parliament grew, public opinion demanded more accountability. Publication of Parliament's proceedings became necessary if electors were to make informed decisions about which politicians, parties, and policies they preferred. The decades from the 1770's to the 1800's, during which these publications developed, became critical for the growth of meaningful representative government.

—*James W. Endersby*

FURTHER READING

Ford, Percy, and Grace Ford, eds. *Luke Graves Hansard, His Diary, 1814-1841: A Case Study in the Reform of Patronage*. Oxford, England: Basil Blackwell, 1962. Diary of the son of Luke and brother of Thomas Curzon, who took over the printing firm.

Hansard, John Henry. *The Hansards: Printers and Publishers*. Shannon, County Clare, Ireland: Irish University Press, 1970. A concise summary of the history of the Hansard family of publishers.

Law, William. *Our Hansard: Or, The True Mirror of Parliament*. London: Pitman, 1950. A brief history of the Hansard and its reporters.

Myers, Robin, ed. *The Auto-biography of Luke Hansard: Printer to the House, 1752-1828*. London: Printing Historical Society, 1991. Primary source material from the man who established the family business and tradition as a reliable publisher of reports for the British parliament.

Rogers, Deborah D. *Bookseller as Rogue: John Almon and the Politics of Eighteenth Century Publishing*. New York: Peter Lang, 1986. This biography of the writer and editor of the *Political Register* discusses contemporary politics and printing and the freedom of the press.

Thomas, Peter D. G. *John Wilkes: A Friend of Liberty*. New York: Clarendon, 1996. A biography of the radical politician and journalist who fought for the right of the press to criticize the government and report the deliberations of Parliament.

Trewin, J. C., and E. M. King. *Printer to the House: The Story of Hansard*. London: Methuen, 1952. Authoritative history of the Hansard family of publishers. This volume relies on the diaries and letters of the principal family members.

SEE ALSO: Mar. 1, 1711: Addison and Steele Establish *The Spectator*; 1721-1742: Development of Great Britain's Office of Prime Minister; 1736: *Gentleman's Magazine* Initiates Parliamentary Reporting; Dec. 16, 1740-Nov. 7, 1748: War of the Austrian Succession; Mar. 20, 1750-Mar. 14, 1752: Johnson Issues *The Rambler*; Beginning Apr., 1763: The *North Briton* Controversy; Sept. 10, 1763: Publication of the *Freeman's Journal*; Jan. 4, 1792-1797: The *Northern Star* Calls for Irish Independence.

RELATED ARTICLE in *Great Lives from History: The Eighteenth Century, 1701-1800*: John Wilkes.

April 27-October 10, 1774
LORD DUNMORE'S WAR

American colonists on the frontiers of Virginia and Maryland battled Shawnee Indians for control of their land. The Shawnees were defeated and relocated, as European settlers moved into Kentucky.

ALSO KNOWN AS: Dunmore's War
LOCALE: Ohio River region (now in the United States)
CATEGORIES: Wars, uprisings, and civil unrest; colonization; expansion and land acquisition

KEY FIGURES

Fourth Earl of Dunmore (John Murray; 1732-1809), governor of Virginia, 1771-1776

Cornstalk (c. 1720-1777), Shawnee leader

James Logan (Tahgahjute; c. 1725-1780), Mingo war chief

John Connolly (c. 1743-1813), Virginia's administrator for the Monongahela region

Michael Cresap (1742-1775), American colonist and land developer

SUMMARY OF EVENT

Lord Dunmore's War—named for Virginia's governor, the fourth earl of Dunmore—was a struggle between the Shawnees and Virginians in the spring and summer of 1774. It represents the culmination of events dating back to Pontiac's Resistance (1763-1766). For both the American Indians and the colonists, the war carried important ramifications. The victor would control what is now Kentucky. In order to understand how the conflict arose, one must understand the unsettled state of British-Indian relations after 1763.

Following Pontiac's Resistance, British officials had tried to create an alliance with the natives of the Ohio and Illinois region. Using the French model, Britain's Indian superintendent for the northern colonies, Sir William Johnson, tried to create a mutually intelligible world that would allow colonists and American Indians to conduct diplomatic and economic activities. Two problems undermined the superintendent's efforts. The first problem

Virginia governor John Murray, Lord Dunmore, flees the colony following violent conflicts between Shawnee Indians and the European colonists seeking control of Shawnee land on the Virginia-Maryland frontier. (Library of Congress)

confronting the relationship was the emergence of colonial communities west of the Appalachian Mountains. Colonists had settled the region in direct violation of the Proclamation of 1763.

Although British soldiers often drove them back across the mountains, the settlers often returned. Outside the range of governmental control, these settlers caused tensions with the native communities of the region. The second problem was the British government's desire to curtail expenditures relating to Indian affairs. The Crown first tried to reduce its commitment by passing some of the costs off on the colonies, but these attempts did not work. As a result, Johnson's office was unable to meet even the basic necessities for conducting Indian affairs after 1770. Taken together, colonial settlement along the frontier and reduced expenditures meant a worsening of British-Indian relations in the years preceding Lord Dunmore's War.

The Shawnees' relationship with the British reached its nadir with the completion of the Treaty of Fort Stanwix in 1768. As a result of this treaty, the Six Nations of the Iroquois ceded much of the territory south and east of the Ohio River to land speculators. The ceded land had belonged to the Shawnees, Lenni Lenapes (Delawares),

Cherokees, and Mingos, not the Six Nations. The treaty resulted in a series of confrontations between the Shawnees, who rejected the treaty, and the British. Beginning in 1769, skirmishes between the tribes and the frontier colonists became commonplace. These skirmishes continued not only because of reduced expenditures on American Indian affairs but also because of the withdrawal of British soldiers from the colonial frontier. By 1774, British soldiers were stationed at only Kaskaskia, Detroit, and Michilimackinac. Without British soldiers or Indian agents, the Ohio region became a battleground.

As tensions between the two sides escalated, Sir William Johnson worked to isolate the Shawnees from their allies. By the spring of 1774, he had isolated the Shawnees from their previous confederates, the Hurons, Miamis, and Potawatomis. His activities broke the Shawnee league. Colonists appreciated the importance of Johnson's actions when war broke out in April, 1774. For his part, British commander Thomas Gage expressed no surprise when Dunmore's War began. He had long suspected Virginia's colonial elites of supporting the frontiersmen in their move west.

The war began on April 27, 1774. On this date, Daniel

Greathouse and his followers lured an Iroquois hunting party into a trap at the mouth of the Yellow Creek. Greathouse and his men killed nine people. Those killed at Yellow Creek were followers of the Mingo war chief James Logan. Logan recruited supporters and retaliated. By July, he and his followers had claimed thirteen scalps, and Logan the Mingo proclaimed himself avenged. Because Virginians were settling on Shawnee lands. Logan focused his reprisals on Virginians in particular rather than colonists (such as Pennsylvanians) in general.

If Logan's actions had been only an isolated response to a massacre, it is doubtful that war would have erupted. However, Logan's actions were not unique. Further down the Ohio River, Michael Cresap and his associates—who were trying to develop land for future settlers—received a message from John Connolly, Virginia's resident administrator for the Monongahela region. Connolly's message implied that a colonial war with the Indians had begun. Situated hundreds of miles beyond colonial settlements, Cresap and his men acted as if war were a reality. They attacked a canoe carrying Lenni Lenape and Shawnee traders. After scalping the Indians, Cresap and his men sought protection in the community of Wheeling.

Following the Yellow Creek Massacre, and while Cresap and his men were seeking the shelter of Wheeling, Connolly participated in a condolence ceremony for the victims of Greathouse's attack. Held at Pittsburgh, the ceremony mollified the Indians' civil leadership. It did not, however, appease the warriors on either side of the cultural divide. Logan continued his attacks against squatters, and Cresap tried to raise a volunteer unit for military service against the natives. Their actions illustrated how young men on both sides of the cultural divide often dictated the actions of their elders.

As late as June, 1774, it was still possible to avert full-scale war. In July, however, Virginia's militia moved westward. Their aims were to destroy the Shawnees and open Kentucky for Virginian settlement. Virginian major Angus McDonald led four hundred Virginians across the Ohio River and destroyed five Shawnee villages, including Wakatomica, in early August. Later that month, Dunmore arrived at Pittsburgh. When Shawnee warriors refused his request to meet with him, Dunmore decided to lead an expedition against the Shawnees located along the Scioto River.

While marching to its new base of operations at Camp Charlotte, a militia detachment burned the Mingo town at the Salt Licks. In order to prevent the Virginians from invading the Scioto region, nine hundred Shawnees and their allies attacked twelve hundred Virginians at their fortifications at the mouth of the Kanawha River on October 10, 1774. This attack—the Battle of Point Pleasant—resulted in the Shawnees' defeat.

Before the Battle of Point Pleasant, the traditional leaders of the Shawnees and Lenni Lenapes had sought a negotiated settlement with Governor Dunmore. He refused to deal with the Shawnee representative, Cornstalk. Dunmore did meet with Cornstalk's Lenni Lenape counterparts, Captain Pipe and George White Eyes, who tried to mediate the problem. Their efforts resulted only in limiting the war, not preventing it. After the Battle of Point Pleasant, however, Cornstalk again tried to negotiate a settlement with Dunmore. The result was the Camp Charlotte Agreement of 1774.

Governor Dunmore dictated the terms of this agreement. He required the Shawnees to accept Virginia's interpretation of the Treaty of Fort Stanwix. He also required that the Shawnees and Mingos give him hostages as a promise of future good behavior. He demanded that the natives give up their right to hunt on the south side of the Ohio River. In exchange for their promise, Dunmore promised to prohibit Virginians from intruding on Indian lands north of the Ohio River.

While Dunmore and Cornstalk discussed peace terms, Logan refused to attend the council. He did, however, send a statement to the council through the trader John Gibson. "Logan's Lament," as it came to be known after Thomas Jefferson included it years later in his *Notes on the State of Virginia*, justified Logan's actions in the preceding months with the following words:

> Col. Cresap, the last spring, in cold blood, and unprovoked, murdered all the relations of Logan. . . . There runs not a drop of my blood in the veins of any living creature. . . . Who is there to mourn for Logan?—Not one.

In response to Logan's speech, Dunmore ordered a detachment of troops to attack the Mingos at Salt Lick Town. The attack resulted in the death of five Indians and the capture of fourteen prisoners.

SIGNIFICANCE

Following the Virginians' attack, Lord Dunmore's War became fused with the American Revolution. American patriots believed Dunmore really was not interested in claiming Kentucky for settlement; they concluded that Dunmore's real intent was the formation of an army for use against them. By 1775, colonists had turned against Governor Dunmore. As a result, the final treaty ending Lord Dunmore's War, the Treaty of Pittsburgh, was delayed until October, 1775. Following Lord Dunmore's War, Shawnee population centers in the Ohio Valley began to change. Most Shawnees left the Muskingum region and moved southwest toward the Scioto and Mad River areas.

—*Michael J. Mullin*

FURTHER READING

Clark, Jerry E. *The Shawnee.* Lexington: University Press of Kentucky, 1993. This examination of Shawnee history and culture includes information about Lord Dunmore's War.

Dowd, Gregory Evans. *A Spirited Resistance: The North American Indian Struggle for Unity, 1745-1815.* Baltimore: Johns Hopkins University Press, 1992. Chapter 3, "Revolutionary Alliances," includes information about Lord Dunmore's War.

Jacob, John J. *A Biographical Sketch of the Life of the Late Captain Michael Cresap.* Cincinnati, Ohio: J. F. Uhlhorn, 1866. John Jacob worked for Michael Cresap and later married Cresap's widow. His book challenges the notion that Cresap was responsible for the Yellow Creek Massacre.

McConnell, Michael N. *A Country Between: The Upper Ohio Valley and Its Peoples, 1724-1774.* Lincoln: University of Nebraska Press, 1992. Discusses colonial expansion from the eighteenth century Native American perspective. McConnell sees the Treaty of Fort Stanwix as a deciding factor in the coming of Lord Dunmore's War.

Mayer, Brantz. *Tah-Gah-Jute, or Logan and Cresap: An Historical Essay.* Albany, N.Y.: Munsell, 1867. The most famous study of the Cresap-Logan controversy written in the nineteenth century.

Tanner, Helen Hornbeck, ed. *Atlas of Great Lakes Indian History.* Norman: University of Oklahoma Press, 1987. This monograph traces Shawnee history through cartographic evidence. Contains a discussion of Lord Dunmore's War.

White, Richard. *The Middle Ground: Indians, Empires, and Republics in the Great Lakes Region, 1650-1815.* New York: Cambridge University Press, 1991. Discusses how both Europeans and American Indians sought accommodation and common meaning. Places Lord Dunmore's War within this context in his analysis of the event.

SEE ALSO: Sept. 22, 1711-Mar. 23, 1713: Tuscarora War; Summer, 1714-1741: Fox Wars; Sept. 19, 1737: Walking Purchase; May 28, 1754-Feb. 10, 1763: French and Indian War; Oct. 5, 1759-Nov. 19, 1761: Cherokee War; May 8, 1763-July 24, 1766: Pontiac's Resistance; May 24 and June 11, 1776: Indian Delegation Meets with Congress; Oct. 22, 1784: Fort Stanwix Treaty; Oct. 18, 1790-July, 1794: Little Turtle's War; 1799: Code of Handsome Lake.

RELATED ARTICLES in *Great Lives from History: The Eighteenth Century, 1701-1800*: Joseph Brant; Little Turtle; Pontiac.

May 20, 1774
QUEBEC ACT

With the passage of the Quebec Act, Great Britain granted limited civil rights to Canadian Catholics and extended the boundaries of Quebec province into the Ohio Valley.

LOCALE: Quebec (now in Canada)
CATEGORIES: Laws, acts, and legal history; expansion and land acquisition; religion and theology

KEY FIGURES
Sir Guy Carleton (1724-1808), governor of Quebec, 1768-1778, and later first Baron Dorchester, 1786-1808
Lord North (Frederick North; 1732-1792), British prime minister, 1770-1782

Second Earl of Dartmouth (William Legge; 1731-1801), secretary of state for the colonies, 1772-1775
James Murray (1721-1794), military governor, 1760-1763, and civil governor, 1763-1766, of Quebec and governor of Minorca, 1774-1782

SUMMARY OF EVENT
In 1774, through the efforts of Lord North, Great Britain's prime minister, the British parliament produced "An Act for Making More Effectual Provision for the Government of the Province of Quebec in North America," the first of several eighteenth and nineteenth century acts to govern the relationship between England and Canada. Among the principal provisions of the act were the assertion of trans-Allegheny power by the Crown,

rule of the province through a governor and council, and, most significant, a modicum of religious freedom for the Catholics of Quebec.

When France had ceded New France to Great Britain by the Peace of Paris in 1763, England suddenly found itself with a province of sixty-five thousand Canadian Catholics. The Articles of Capitulation (1760) provided for the continuation of the status quo with regard to religion: Catholics in the province could continue to worship in their traditional way, the French king would still appoint the bishop, and the clergy could continue to receive the tithes of the faithful. However, the treaty also included the proviso, "As far as the laws of Great Britain allow."

During the next ten years, British governors James Murray and Guy Carleton ruled the province with little clear direction from the Parliament. The few English colonists in the province were incensed that French-speaking Catholics not only had freedom to practice their religion but also could take part in civic life, even sit on juries. In no other part of the empire did such latitude prevail. Clearly, the government had to regularize this anomalous situation. Murray first and then Carleton, even more vigorously, called for a practical toleration of Catholicism in the province, although they hoped that they could attract English colonists in sufficient number so that the French-speaking colonists would leave Quebec, much as French-speaking settlers had been forced out of Acadia (Nova Scotia) a generation before.

In 1774, Parliament, under the aegis of Lord North and his secretary of state for the colonies, the second earl of Dartmouth, enacted a series of laws that Americans later called the Intolerable Acts. These laws closed the port of Boston, reorganized the administration of Massa-

QUEBEC, 1774

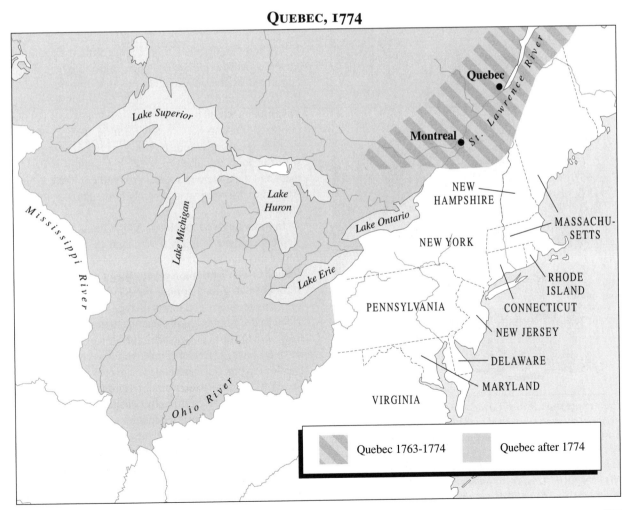

Quebec 1763-1774   Quebec after 1774

chusetts, and permitted British troops to commandeer colonists' homes. Americans judged the Quebec Act as just another of the punitive measures enacted that year.

At least three major drafts of the act circulated before May 20, 1774, when the members of Parliament agreed to the final document, largely the work of Carleton as governor of Quebec. The English-speaking colonists in the province agitated for a representative assembly in which they would hold a majority of the seats, although they constituted less than 1 percent of the population. They would have restricted even the minority seats to wealthy French-speaking rural landlords.

There were four principal concerns in the act: geography, Canadian and British law, no representative assembly, and permission for Catholics to practice their religion. First, the Parliament extended the boundaries of the

Protestants from British Canada and the American colonies despised the rights extended to Catholics through passage of the Quebec Act of 1774. The act was considered so pro-Catholic that it inspired colonists to call for revolution and American independence. This illustration, from 1776, warns of the parallels between the Quebec Act and the violent and deadly history of the hatred of Protestants worldwide. (Library of Congress)

province of Quebec down through the Ohio Valley, thus effectively keeping the American colonies east of the Alleghenies. There would be no room for the colonies to expand westward into the potentially rich fur-trading area, because this territory would now be a part of Quebec. By spelling out the boundaries of Quebec at the very beginning of the act, Parliament wanted to make it clear that none of the provisions of this act might apply to Newfoundland or any other British territory. This was an expedient for Quebec only.

Administrators in Canada, English-speaking colonists, and members of Parliament all contributed to the discussion about the forms of law to be observed in the new colony. The conclusion was a compromise to appease the non-Canadians without offending the French-speaking too much. Civil law would be governed by traditional French customs, especially regarding properties and family matters. Criminal law, however, would follow the British system of laws. British officers and courts would see to the administration of justice in these matters.

Parliament decided that a government-appointed governor would rule the province, assisted by a council appointed by the governor. In practice, this meant that the taxes would be modest, since no unrepresentative government would be able to command the respect of the populace if it imposed a heavy taxation. To appease the English-speaking colonists, however, there was provision for an eventual representative assembly if Parliament and the governor deemed it expedient in the future. Any future assembly had severely limited powers of taxation.

In order to give French-speaking Canadians freedom to practice their religion, Parliament designed an oath unlike any that could be found elsewhere in the empire. Catholics would be able to swear allegiance to the Crown without having to denounce the Papacy. This, in itself, was a major step. The terms of the Peace of Paris provided that Catholics could practice their faith in conformity with the laws of Great Britain. However, there were no such laws in England that would permit Catholics freedom to practice unimpeded. The proviso of the Quebec Act was the exercise of religion "subject to the King's supremacy." Officially, Parliament asserted the right to appoint a superintendent for Catholics, a deliberately ambiguous title. In fact, however, they settled for a bishop. Catholics could maintain their clergy through a system of tithes, as they were accustomed to doing.

To be considered along with the act itself, however, is the instruction given to the governor in administering the religious affairs of the province. Governors were encouraged to limit French culture and to curb the activity of the Catholic church at every turn by giving preeminence to the Anglican church, or Church of England. It was hoped that this province eventually would become more like Britain's other colonies and that English-speaking Anglicans or, less preferably, other Protestants would prevail.

SIGNIFICANCE

The Continental Congress, meeting in Philadelphia, immediately perceived the Quebec Act as a threat and went on record in opposition on September 17, 1774. They objected to the expansion of the provincial boundaries into the Ohio Valley, but they were especially upset about permitting Catholics to exercise their religion. Some historians consider the Quebec Act to be among the most prominent of the colonial grievances that led to war and, eventually, to independence for the American colonies.

Clearly, the Parliament sought to keep the French-speaking Canadians loyal to the Crown and to blunt the westward ambitions of the colonies to the south. They were successful in this regard. By not unduly burdening their Catholic subjects, they were able to avoid serious civil unrest that surely would have followed anything more restrictive. The Catholics of Canada accepted the provisions of the act; however, they thought that they had received in 1774 what they should have received ten years earlier in the Peace of Paris.

There is every likelihood that Great Britain would have lost Quebec had it imposed harsher terms in the act. As it was, French Canadians were quite aware of the disdain of their southern neighbors for a Catholic enclave in the empire, especially one so close. In April, 1776, an American colonial delegation from the Continental Congress, the first American diplomatic venture to a foreign country, tried to enlist Canadian support for the revolutionary cause. Samuel Chase, Benjamin Franklin, Charles Carroll, and John Carroll received a polite, but chilly, reception. England's policy worked well enough. French Canadians knew they had no other home than in the British Empire. They could not expect any help from their former French sovereign, and the American colonies objected to their very existence. Canada is today what it is, for good or ill, in no small measure as a result of the British policy of expedience in 1774.

—*Daniel A. Brown*

FURTHER READING

Burt, A. L. *The Old Province of Quebec*. Toronto: McClelland and Steward, 1968. A careful assessment of the economic implications of the enactment.

Coffin, Victor. *The Province of Quebec and the Early American Revolution*. Madison: University of Wisconsin Press, 1896. The earliest study to consider the act's implications for the liberation movement in the Thirteen Colonies.

Coupland, Reginald. *The Quebec Act: A Study in Statesmanship*. Oxford, England: Clarendon Press, 1925. An almost adulatory study of the diplomatic efforts required to secure parliamentary approval.

Lawson, Philip. *The Imperial Challenge: Quebec and Britain in the Age of American Revolution*. Montreal, Que.: McGill-Queen's University Press, 1989. Examines the effect that the conquest of Quebec had on British policies and imperial ideas, leading to the signing of the Quebec Act.

Neatby, Hilda. *The Quebec Act: Protest and Policy*. Scarborough, Ont.: Prentice Hall, 1972. Balanced narration of the events surrounding the Quebec Act and its subsequent interpretations by historians and economists.

Nelson, Paul David. *General Sir Guy Carleton, Lord Dorchester: Soldier-Statesman of Early British Canada*. Madison, N.J.: Fairleigh Dickinson University Press, 2000. Comprehensive biography of Carleton, including information about his role in designing the Quebec Act.

Thompson, Wayne. *Canada, 1995*. 12th ed. Harpers Ferry, W.Va.: Stryker-Post, 1995. A mildly anti-French account that is strong on the military dimensions of the event.

July 21, 1774
TREATY OF KUCHUK KAINARJI

While the Treaty of Kuchuk Kainarji brought only a temporary peace between Russia and the Ottoman Empire, the concessions gained by Russia were more lasting. In particular, Catherine the Great won a permanent foothold on the Black Sea for her empire.

ALSO KNOWN AS: Treaty of Küçük Kaynarca
LOCALE: Kuchuk Kainarji, Bulgaria, Ottoman Empire
(now Kaynardzha, Bulgaria)
CATEGORIES: Diplomacy and international relations; wars, uprisings, and civil unrest

KEY FIGURES

Catherine the Great (1729-1796), empress of Russia, r. 1762-1796
Mustafa III (1717-1774), sultan of the Ottoman Empire, r. 1757-1774
Aleksey Grigoryevich Orlov (1737-1808), Russian military commander
Aleksandr Vasilyevich Suvorov (1729-1800), Russian field marshal
Frederick the Great (1712-1786), king of Prussia, r. 1740-1786

SUMMARY OF EVENT

The Treaty of Kuchuk Kainarji (in Turkish, Küçük Kaynarca), signed in July, 1774, marked the ascendancy of Russia and the further weakening of the Ottoman Empire in southeastern Europe. Austria previously had broken the Turkish threat to the central Danubian Basin through the Treaty of Karlowitz in 1699. Several times throughout the eighteenth century, Russia, another adversary of the Turks, also sought to reduce Ottoman power on the European continent and, above all, to break the Turkish domination of the Black Sea. This led to numerous conflicts between the two nations, sometimes initiated by one and then the other.

The Russian-Turkish War of 1768-1774 was precipitated by Catherine's military intervention in a Polish civil war which threatened the position of the pro-Russian Polish king, Stanisłas Poniatowski. When Russian forces crossed into Turkish territory while pursuing Polish rebels opposing Poniatowski, the Ottoman sultan, Mustafa III, unwisely used the incident as an excuse to declare war on Russia. In the ensuing conflict, however, the Russians were victorious on land and sea. Russian troops overran the Danubian principalities of Wallachia and Moldavia, while the Russian Baltic fleet, under the

command of Aleksey Grigoryevich Orlov, sailed around Europe to the Aegean Sea, where it destroyed the Ottoman navy in the Battle of Chesmé on July 5-7, 1770.

Continued Russian military successes, including the conquest of the Crimea in 1771, alarmed Catherine's ally Frederick the Great, who feared that Austria, feeling threatened, would eventually launch an attack against Russia and thus precipitate a general war into which Prussia would be drawn. Consequently, Frederick urged Russia to make peace with the Turks, thereby satisfying Austria's concerns. To fulfill Russia's growing territorial ambitions, Frederick proposed that Russia join Prussia and Austria in a coordinated partition of the weakened Polish state. Catherine approved the idea of gaining territory on its western frontier, and the agreement for the first partition of Poland became a reality in August, 1772.

To the south, a Russian-Turkish armistice signed in May, 1772, began the process of peacemaking in the region. Yet stiffened Turkish resistance during 1772 and 1773, both at the negotiating table and on the battlefield, delayed a resolution of the war. Russian negotiators had expanded the list of their original demands, which the Ottoman side rejected. Not until the distinguished Russian general Aleksandr Vasilyevich Suvorov had won several resounding victories were the Turks ready to discuss peace terms seriously. After less than one week of negotiations, the Treaty of Kuchuk Kainarji was signed on July 21, 1774.

Under the terms of the treaty, the Ottoman Empire's historic control of the entire northern coast of the Black Sea was ended. Russia acquired the great estuary formed by the Dnieper and Bug rivers, where they flowed into the Black Sea. To the east, Russia acquired the entire Azov region and the Kerch straits offering access to the Black Sea. Azov, a seaport at the mouth of the Don River, had long been a Russian objective and came under its control. The Tartars of the Crimea were recognized as independent of the Turks with the right to select their own ruler.

Russia also won the important concession of free navigation for its trading vessels in Turkish waters and gained access to the historic straits dividing Europe from Asia Minor. This allowed Russian vessels to eventually reach the Mediterranean Sea, another primary goal. To the east, a portion of the Caucasus mountain region was transferred to Russian control.

The treaty included the right to construct a Russian

Catherine the Great riding at the head of her army. (Premier Publishing)

erty of Christian subjects of the Turkish ruler. In return, Russia had few obligations under the treaty other than being required to restore the Danubian Principalities of Wallachia and Moldavia to the sovereignty of the sultan.

After the treaty signing, both governments sought to strengthen their comparative position. Catherine approved it in August, 1774, while Turkish efforts to minimize Russian advantages delayed Ottoman ratification until January, 1775. Even after ratification occurred, however, both sides periodically sought to evade the spirit and several provisions of the agreement. This contained the seeds of future conflict.

SIGNIFICANCE

The provisions of the Treaty of Kuchuk Kainarji became a milestone in the history of what has been called the "Eastern Question" in its implications for the future of the Turkish state. In effect, these clauses gave Catherine and her successors the excuse to interfere in the affairs of the Ottoman Empire diplomatically and militarily. The treaty simply whetted Russia's aggressive appetite, and, by 1780, Catherine was developing her grandiose "Greek Scheme," which called for the expulsion of the Turks from southeastern Europe and the

Orthodox church in Constantinople. The sultan's government was obligated under the treaty to refer to Catherine II, its nemesis, as the "empress" of Russia. Russia was guaranteed the right to establish permanent diplomatic representation in the Turkish capital. While not appearing significant to modern observers, these provisions added to Ottoman humiliation. As further evidence of Russian dominance in the unequal treaty, the sultan's government had to pay an indemnity to Moscow as a financial penalty for declaring war on the Russians.

Finally, in the most far-reaching stipulations of the treaty, Russia secured the right to guarantee the "humane and generous government for the future" of the Danubian principalities, as well as protection of the religious lib-

restoration of the old Byzantine Empire under her grandson, Constantine. Catherine did not succeed in this goal, but she did annex the independent Crimean state in 1783, which contributed to the outbreak of a renewed Russian-Turkish war in 1787. Like the one before it, this war, concluded in 1792, served only to accentuate Russia's territorial expansion and the growing threats to peace and stability in eastern Europe. Later conflicts between these two regional powers throughout the nineteenth century led to the further weakening of the Ottoman Empire, causing its internal collapse and territorial breakup as a result of World War I in the early twentieth century.

—*Edward P. Keleher, updated by Taylor Stults*

FURTHER READING

Alexander, John T. *Catherine the Great: Life and Legend*. New York: Oxford University Press, 1989. Summarizes the Turkish war, including Catherine's opinions of Russia's struggle with its southern rival.

Anderson, M. S. *The Eastern Question, 1774-1923: A Study in International Relations*. Rev. ed. New York: St. Martin's Press, 1996. Assesses the provisions and implications of the 1774 treaty on future Russian activity in the region.

Gerolymanto, André. *The Balkan Wars: Conquest, Revolution, and Retribution from the Ottoman Era to the Twentieth Century*. New York: Basic Books, 2002. A history of the Balkans, focusing on the area's continual wars over nationalism and religion. Chapter 4 includes information about the Treaty of Kuchuk Kainarji.

Israel, Fred L., ed. *Major Treaty Treaties of Modern History, 1648-1967*. Vol. 2. New York: Chelsea House, 1967. Contains the English translation of the treaty.

Scott, H. M. *The Emergence of the Eastern Powers, 1756-1775*. New York: Cambridge University Press, 2001. Examines the rise of Russia and Prussia in the eighteenth century. Includes information about the Russian-Turkish wars and Russia's acquisition of land from the Ottoman Empire.

Stavrianos, L. S. *The Balkans Since 1453*. New York: Holt, Rinehart and Winston, 1963. Reprint. New York: New York University Press, 2000. Assesses Ottoman rule in the Balkans, and the Ottoman Empire's losing struggle with Austria and Russia to remain the dominant power in the region.

Thomson, Gladys Scott. *Catherine the Great and the Expansion of Russia*. New York: Collier Books, 1962. Useful account of Catherine's foreign policy in Europe and Asia Minor.

SEE ALSO: Nov. 20, 1710-July 21, 1718: Ottoman Wars with Russia, Venice, and Austria; Oct. 21, 1727: Treaty of Kiakhta; 1736-1739: Russo-Austrian War Against the Ottoman Empire; Oct., 1768-Jan. 9, 1792: Ottoman Wars with Russia.

RELATED ARTICLES in *Great Lives from History: The Eighteenth Century, 1701-1800*: Catherine the Great; Frederick the Great; Mustafa III; Aleksey Grigoryevich Orlov; Aleksandr Vasilyevich Suvorov.

August 1, 1774
PRIESTLEY DISCOVERS OXYGEN

By heating a brick-red compound of mercury, Joseph Priestley produced a gas whose properties of enhanced support of combustion and animal respiration led him to believe that he had discovered an amazing new substance: dephlogisticated air, or oxygen.

LOCALE: Calne, Wiltshire, England

CATEGORIES: Chemistry; science and technology; health and medicine

KEY FIGURES

Joseph Priestley (1733-1804), English natural philosopher and Unitarian minister

Carl Wilhelm Scheele (1742-1786), Swedish chemist who, independently of Priestley, discovered "fire air," or oxygen

Henry Cavendish (1731-1810), English physicist and chemist who discovered inflammable air, or hydrogen, and the composition of water

Antoine-Laurent Lavoisier (1743-1794), French chemist who made oxygen the central element of his new chemistry

Second Earl of Shelburne (William Petty-Fitzmaurice; 1737-1805), British opposition leader, 1768-1782, and later prime minister, 1782-1783

SUMMARY OF EVENT

English natural philosopher Joseph Priestley came late to the study of gases (which he called airs), approaching them as an amateur rather than a professional. After discovering that "fixed air" (carbon dioxide) formed an effervescent liquid when dissolved in water (now known as soda water), he studied "inflammable air" (hydrogen), which was discovered by English physicist and chemist Henry Cavendish. Following a suggestion by Cavendish, Priestley began collecting other airs in a pneumatic trough over mercury rather than water, and he was thus able to isolate several new gases whose solubility in water had prevented previous chemists from seeing them. One of the first such gases he found was nitrous air (nitric oxide), which he prepared by combining "spirit of nitre" (nitric acid) with various metals. This substance provided him with a method for testing the "goodness" of common air for combustion and respiration. The quantitative measure of this goodness was the volume of a brown gas (nitrogen dioxide) that formed when he reacted nitrous air with the air in question.

After discovering an "acid air" (hydrogen chloride), Priestley delivered a paper in 1772 about his observations on the different kinds of airs. These discoveries, along with his liberal social and religious views, brought him to the attention of the second earl of Shelburne (later the First Marquis of Lansdowne and England's prime minister), who offered him a position as his companion and librarian. The years Priestley spent in Shelburne's service proved to be the most productive of his life. He continued his studies of new gases at Shelburne's summer estate at Calne, near Bowood in Wiltshire. There Priestley collected over mercury an alkaline air (ammonia) that he obtained by heating a mixture of sal ammoniac (ammonium chloride) and quicklime (calcium oxide).

During this early period in Shelburne's employ Priestley made the greatest discovery of his life, although in retrospect he realized that he had actually prepared the new gas earlier, in 1771 and 1772, but had not recognized it because he then believed that nothing was purer than ordinary air. Around the same time, Carl Scheele in Sweden prepared a gas that he called "fire air" (oxygen), but his results were not published until 1777. In subsequent accounts, Priestley claimed that his discovery of "dephlogisticated air" (oxygen) was the result of chance, not planning. He had purchased a large magnifying lens and was using it to concentrate the Sun's heat on a variety of substances to see what gases were produced. A friend had given him an interesting brick-red substance, *mercurius calcinatus per se*, or red calx of mercury (mercuric oxide), and on August 1, 1774, Priestley focused sunlight on this red powder and observed that globules of liquid mercury and a colorless gas were generated. He collected this gas in an inverted vessel in a pneumatic trough filled with mercury and then studied its fascinating properties. It was not very soluble in water, but a candle flame burned faster and brighter in it than in common air. Initially, he thought that the gas might be "dephlogisticated nitrous air" (nitrous oxide), a gas he had earlier studied, but additional research showed that it behaved far differently from this other gas.

In the fall of 1774, Priestley accompanied Lord Shelburne on a trip to continental Europe, including a stay in Paris, where he met chemist Antoine-Laurent Lavoisier and told him about his experiments with the gas generated from red calx of mercury. This meeting proved to be fortuitous for Lavoisier and the future of chemistry, since Lavoisier would eventually make this elemental gas,

OXYGEN VS. PHLOGISTON

In the seventeenth and eighteenth centuries, chemistry was dominated by the idea that air was a single element, one of the four Greek elements (the others being earth, water, and fire). British chemists from Robert Boyle through Stephen Hales and Joseph Black had made "pneumatic chemistry"—manipulating and measuring "air" in its various states of purity—practically a national specialty. Chemical research was also carried on around the organizing concept of the phlogiston theory put forward by the German Georg Ernst Stahl in 1723.

Phlogiston was believed to be the element of fire, or its principle, which caused inflammability when present in a body. It was considered central to most chemical reactions. Combustion was explained as a body releasing its phlogiston. In this dual context of pneumatic chemistry and phlogiston theory, Henry Cavendish presented his study of "factitious airs," or gases contained in bodies. Most important, he isolated and identified "inflammable air," now called hydrogen. Recognizing the explosive nature of "inflammable air," Cavendish went on to identify it as phlogiston itself. He cannot be said to have discovered hydrogen, as others had separated it before him, and he did not specifically claim its discovery.

Antoine-Laurent Lavoisier's anti-phlogiston explanation was central to the revolution in chemistry that he was leading on the Continent. Lavoisier had met Joseph Priestley during his trip to Paris, and it was from Priestley that Lavoisier learned about oxygen. When Lavoisier weighed the product of calcination (oxidation in the new terminology), there was a weight gain in the calx. He offered the explanation that something was taken up in the process, rather than phlogiston being given off. This "something" he identified as oxygen—and thereby created a new chemistry. Cavendish recognized that Lavoisier's oxygen-based chemistry was essentially equivalent to a phlogiston-based chemistry, but he rejected the new ideas to the end of his life. "It seems," he wrote, "the phaenomena of nature might be explained very well on this principle, without the help of phlogiston; . . . but as the commonly received principle of phlogiston explains all phaenomena, at least as well as Mr Lavoisier's, I have adhered to that." In 1787, Lavoisier introduced his new chemistry in his *Nomenclature chimique*, and he fully elaborated it in 1789 in *Traité élémentaire de chimie*. The phlogiston theory went up in smoke.

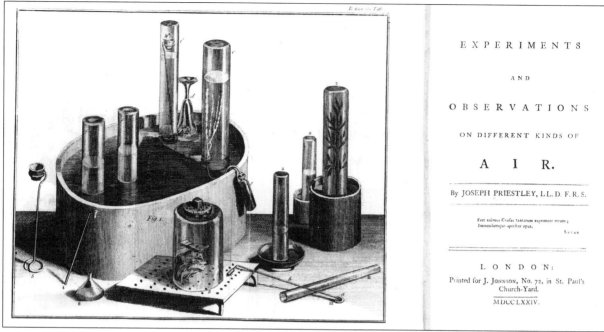

A facsimile of the frontispiece and title page of Joseph Priestley's Experiments and Observations on Different Kinds of Air *(1774-1777), which outlines his discovery of "dephlogisticated air," or oxygen.* (Library of Congress)

which he named oxygen, the centerpiece of his reform of chemistry.

Upon his return from the Continent, Priestley discovered additional wonderful properties of dephlogisticated air, and some scholars date his effective discovery of oxygen to March, 1775, because it was then that he recognized oxygen as much better than ordinary air. His test involving two mice was particularly significant. He found during the test that a mouse confined in two ounces of the "new" air lived twice as long as a mouse confined in two ounces of ordinary air. Priestley even experimented on himself, experiencing a feeling of exhilaration when he breathed in the gas. Because he was an ardent believer in the phlogiston theory, one of whose pivotal doctrines was that combustible substances contained a weightless material, called phlogiston, Priestley named his new gas dephlogisticated air, since he considered it to be common air that had been deprived of its phlogiston and thus was able to readily absorb phlogiston escaping from burning materials.

During his later career, in England and America, Priestley continued to believe in the superiority of the phlogiston theory until his death in Pennsylvania in 1804. On August 1, 1874, Priestley's great-grandson and many American chemists gathered at his grave site to commemorate the centennial of his discovery of oxygen. This meeting proved to be the beginning of what came to be called the American Chemical Society.

SIGNIFICANCE

It is a central irony of Joseph Priestley's career that the discovery he hoped would buttress the phlogiston theory ended up, in the hands of Lavoisier, totally undermining it. Besides this ironic significance, Priestley's work on oxygen and several other gases contributed to solving the chief chemical problems of the time: calcination, the role of gases in combustion, the respiration of plants and animals, and the composition of common air. Because of his discoveries some scholars have called him the father of pneumatic (gas-related) chemistry. The test that he devised for the "goodness" of air has led to his designation as the father of eudiometry, the science of measuring air's purity. Medical doctors have honored him because he was prophetic in his suggestion that oxygen be investigated as a potential healer of diseased lungs.

Priestley's being credited for the discovery of oxygen has been met with controversy: Scheele had prepared oxygen prior to Priestley (though he failed to publish his findings before Priestley), and Lavoisier, who prepared oxygen after Priestley, nevertheless understood oxygen better than anyone. Furthermore, both Priestley and

Scheele, as phlogistonists, interpreted their results in terms of a theory whose deficiencies had become obvious to Lavoisier and many others. Still, Priestley did bring reason to a new intellectual territory, that is, to the realm of different kinds of gaseous substances, and, in effect, he became the Christopher Columbus of this "new world" of chemistry.

—Robert J. Paradowski

FURTHER READING

Gibbs, F. W. *Joseph Priestley: Revolutions of the Eighteenth Century*. Garden City, N.Y.: Doubleday, 1967. In this biography for general readers, Gibbs portrays Priestley as the quintessential Enlightenment figure, whose rational approach to theology, politics, and science sheds light on various revolutionary changes during the Age of Reason. Illustrated, with a bibliography and an index.

Jaffe, Bernard. *Crucibles: The Story of Chemistry*. New York: Dover, 1998. This reprint of a classic work originally published in 1930 recounts chemistry's history through the lives and achievements of the great chemists, including Priestley. Includes a sources section and an index.

Partington, J. R. *A History of Chemistry*. Vol. 3. London: Macmillan, 1962. The seventh chapter of this comprehensive history of chemistry is devoted to the life and contributions of Priestley, with many references to primary and secondary sources in the footnotes. Includes indexes of names and subjects.

Priestley, Joseph. *A Scientific Autobiography of Joseph Priestley (1733-1804)*. Edited by Robert E. Schofield. Cambridge, Mass.: MIT Press, 1966. This collection of Priestley's scientific correspondence, with helpful commentary by the editor, makes available in a narrative format many primary materials on Priestley's ca-

reer. Includes three appendices, a general bibliography, and an index.

Schofield, Robert E. *The Enlightened Joseph Priestley: A Study of His Life and Work from 1773 to 1804*. University Park: Pennsylvania State University Press, 2004. A comprehensive two-volume biography written by a leading Priestley authority. The first volume recounts Priestley's early years in England; the second volume includes discussion of the final forty years of his life, examining his discovery of oxygen and his days in the United States.

Strathern, Paul. *Mendeleyev's Dream: The Quest for the Elements*. New York: Berkeley Books, 2000. This popular account of the history of chemistry centers on the discoveries of the elements, and Priestley's discovery of dephlogisticated air is an important part of this story. Includes a section on further reading and an index.

September 5-October 26, 1774
FIRST CONTINENTAL CONGRESS

A meeting of fifty-six delegates from the American colonies marked the beginning of an independent American government, paving the way for separation from Great Britain.

LOCALE: Philadelphia, Pennsylvania

CATEGORIES: Government and politics; organizations and institutions

KEY FIGURES

John Adams (1735-1826), author of the congressional resolution denying the right of Parliament to tax or legislate for the colonies

Samuel Adams (1722-1803), an early advocate of intercolonial assemblages

Joseph Galloway (c. 1731-1803), a conservative member of Congress and author of the Plan of Union

George Washington (1732-1799), delegate from Virginia and later president of the United States, 1789-1797

SUMMARY OF EVENT

On September 5, 1774, representatives from all the American colonies, except far-off and thinly settled Georgia, assembled at Carpenter's Hall in Philadelphia to begin the business of the First Continental Congress. The significance that Americans attached to the meeting is revealed in the quality of the men chosen to attend: Peyton Randolph, George Washington, Patrick Henry, and Richard Henry Lee of Virginia; John and Samuel Adams of Massachusetts; John and Edward Rutledge of South Carolina; Roger Sherman of Connecticut; and John Dickinson and Joseph Galloway of Pennsylvania. "There are in the congress," noted John Adams in his diary, "a collection of the greatest men upon this Continent in point of abilities, virtues, and fortune." The greatest potential, as Adams recognized, belonged not to the old and well-tried politicians but to younger men. The future lay with colonial leaders such as John Adams, George Washington, and John Jay, many of whom first became acquainted with one another during the September and October deliberations in Philadelphia.

After Parliament imposed the Coercive Acts upon Massachusetts, the cause of that colony became the cause of all American colonies. If Parliament were permitted to chastise one colony legislatively, it might choose to punish other colonies at any time. The only re-

course many colonial leaders saw was united resistance. South Carolina, among the last to hear of Massachusetts' fate, was the first outside New England to send direct aid, dispatching a shipment of rice for the beleaguered Bostonians. Other colonies soon followed South Carolina's lead. Suspicion of Parliament's motives increased after the early summer of 1774, when, with remarkably poor timing, that body passed the Quebec Act. That act gave the province of Quebec a civil government without a representative assembly. It also allowed Quebec's Catholic majority special privileges relative to their religious practices. The Quebec Act provided further evidence to colonists that a conspiracy against their rights was growing in Parliament. Thoughtful Americans concerned about the prospects of potentially violent local protest recognized the need to coordinate and control efforts to redress grievances against Parliament. With the idea of an intercolonial congress steadily gaining support, Massachusetts, in June, issued a call for a convention of deputies from each colony to be held in Philadelphia. Other colonies soon followed Massachusetts' lead, and, in September, the first congress of continental representatives became a reality.

Half the fifty-six delegates who assembled in Philadelphia were lawyers, eleven were merchants, and the rest were farmers. None of the delegates officially represented this assembly. Instead, although acknowledged leaders within their colonies, the delegates were in Philadelphia by their own choice. While the British threat to American commerce was among the delegates' chief concerns, more important was the perceived threat to individual American rights and the British constitution. A majority of the delegates, who would be labeled radicals, embraced an aggressive stance toward recent British actions. Others, identified as "reconciliators" or "conservatives," hoped to pursue a far less confrontational approach.

The intent of the Congress to stand resolutely for American rights became obvious early in the proceedings, as the delegates overwhelmingly endorsed the Suffolk Resolves. Adopted by Massachusetts' Suffolk County, these resolutions denounced the Coercive Acts as unconstitutional, urged the people to prepare militarily, and called for an immediate end to trade with the British Empire. In Philadelphia, there was informal talk about setting up a Continental army if the crisis deepened, and Charles Lee, a former British officer from Virginia, showed some of his fellow delegates a plan he had drafted for organizing colonial regiments. The Congress's adamant position on the Suffolk Resolves alarmed many of the conservative delegates. In response, Joseph Galloway proposed a far more conciliatory approach to the problems with Parliament. He called for the adoption of a Plan of Union, like the one proposed in 1754 by the Albany Congress, which would establish an American grand council. Although "an inferior and distinct branch of Parliament," the grand council would create a separate American government within the structure of the British Empire by providing colonial representation in all matters involving the American relationship with Great Britain. In a close vote, the Continental Congress rejected the idea and, in so doing, pushed the colonies toward independence from England.

The subject of commercial retaliation, which had been important in bringing about the Congress, took most of the delegates' time. On September 27, the Congress adopted a resolution banning importation from Great Britain after December 1, 1774. Three days later, the delegates voted to stop exportation to the various

parts of the empire, beginning September 10, 1775, if America's grievances were not redressed by that date. The Congress's program of economic coercion, known as the Continental Association, bound each colony to participate in the boycott and created enforcement procedures.

In addition to the formal protest of the Coercive Acts, the Continental Congress pursued a review of colonial America's relationship with Great Britain. Because Parliament had refused to recognize repeated attempts to distinguish between taxation legislation and legislation that regulated trade within the empire but did not generate revenue, many Americans concluded that Parliament had no constitutional justification to maintain authority over the colonies. Thomas Jefferson, in his pamphlet *Summary View*, expressed the thinking of many of his countryfolk. He referred to the king as the "chief magistrate" of the empire and denied the authority of Parliament to legislate for the colonies in any case. However, Jefferson went too far for some congressmen. Reluctant to repudiate Parliament completely, conservatives were

1770's

Delegates to the First Continental Congress, which marked the first independent American government and the path toward American independence. (Library of Congress)

able to secure approval of a compromise resolution, which stated that by consent, not by right, Parliament could regulate colonial American commerce in the interest of the empire as a whole.

SIGNIFICANCE

Before adjourning on October 26, the Congress scheduled another intercolonial meeting for the following spring and dispatched a series of appeals to the king, to the people of Great Britain, and to the citizens of America. The delegates called for a return to the relationship they had enjoyed with England in the years prior to 1763 and asked for a repeal or withdrawal of policies and laws, beginning with the decision to keep British regulars in colonial America and concluding with the Coercive Acts. In Great Britain, the appeals of the Congress went unheeded. As early as November 18, 1774, King George III informed his prime minister, Lord North, the earl of Guilford, that "the New England governments are in a state of rebellion [and] blows must decide whether they are to be subject to this country or independent."

With their work completed and preparations made for a second meeting of the Continental Congress, the delegates returned home. Although most recognized that they had taken important actions in addressing the British threat to American rights, few realized that they had made a significant step toward independence from England and the establishment of an autonomous American government.

—*R. Don Higginbotham,*
updated by Paul E. Doutrich

FURTHER READING

Ammerman, David. *In the Common Cause: American Response to the Coercive Acts.* Charlottesville: University Press of Virginia, 1974. Asserts that the First Continental Congress was the product of popular opposition to British legislation against the colonies.

Brown, Richard D. *Revolutionary Politics in Massachusetts: The Boston Committee of Correspondence and the Towns, 1772-1774.* Cambridge, Mass.: Harvard University Press, 1970. Examines the role that local protest organizations played immediately preceding the First Continental Congress.

Brown, Wallace. *The King's Friends: The Composition and Motives of the American Loyalist Claimants.* Providence, R.I.: Brown University Press, 1965. Examines the Loyalists, who, between 1777 and 1790, placed claims with the British government for losses suffered in America.

Burnett, Edmund C. *The Continental Congress.* New York: Macmillan, 1941. The first three chapters of this massive, detailed book are particularly relevant to the events of 1774.

Ferling, John. *A Leap in the Dark: The Struggle to Create the American Republic.* New York: Oxford University Press, 2003. A scholarly but accessible survey of the politics and politicians of the American Revolution and the early republic. Includes information on the First Continental Congress.

Jensen, Merrill. *The Founding of a Nation: A History of the American Revolution, 1763-1776.* London: Oxford University Press, 1968. In this fine narrative, the importance of the First Continental Congress is well described.

Jillson, Calvin, and Rick Wilson. *Congressional Dynamics: Structure, Coordination, and Choice in the First American Congress, 1774-1789.* Stanford, Calif.: Stanford University Press, 1994. A political analysis of the Continental Congress and the Constitutional Convention, describing how and why the delegates cast their votes.

Meigs, Cornelia L. *The Violent Men: A Study of Human Relations in the First American Congress.* New York: Macmillan, 1949. A fast-paced narrative of the years 1774 to 1776.

SEE ALSO: June 19-July 10, 1754: Albany Congress; Mar. 22, 1765-Mar. 18, 1766: Stamp Act Crisis; June 29, 1767-Apr. 12, 1770: Townshend Crisis; Mar. 5, 1770: Boston Massacre; Dec. 16, 1773: Boston Tea Party; May 20, 1774: Quebec Act; Apr. 19, 1775: Battle of Lexington and Concord; May 10-Aug. 2, 1775: Second Continental Congress; Jan. 10, 1776: Paine Publishes *Common Sense*; May, 1776-Sept. 3, 1783: France Supports the American Revolution; July 4, 1776: Declaration of Independence; Sept. 17, 1787: U.S. Constitution Is Adopted; Oct. 27, 1787-May, 1788: Publication of *The Federalist*; Apr. 30, 1789: Washington's Inauguration; Sept. 24, 1789: Judiciary Act; 1790's: First U.S. Political Parties; Dec. 15, 1791: U.S. Bill of Rights Is Ratified.

RELATED ARTICLES in *Great Lives from History: The Eighteenth Century, 1701-1800*: John Adams; Samuel Adams; John Dickinson; Benjamin Franklin; George III; Elbridge Gerry; Nathanael Greene; John Hancock; Patrick Henry; John Jay; Thomas Jefferson; Tadeusz Kościuszko; Gouverneur Morris; Lord North; Roger Sherman; George Washington.